The Handbook
of Evolutionary
Psychology

The Handbook of Evolutionary Psychology

Edited by

David M. Buss

WILEY

John Wiley & Sons, Inc.

Library of Congress Cataloging-in-Publication Data:

The handbook of evolutionary psychology / edited by David M. Buss.
    p. cm.
  Includes bibliographical references.
  ISBN-13 978-0-471-26403-3 (alk. paper)
  ISBN-10 0-471-26403-2 (alk. paper)
  1. Evolutionary psychology. 2. Human evolution. I. Buss, David M.
  BF698.95.H36   2005
  155.7—dc22

                       2004062476

Printed in the United States of America.
10 9 8 7 6 5 4 3 2 1

To Charles Darwin

Contents

Foreword   xi
   Steven Pinker

Acknowledgments   xvii

Contributors   xix

Introduction: The Emergence of Evolutionary Psychology   xxiii
   David M. Buss

PART I   FOUNDATIONS OF EVOLUTIONARY PSYCHOLOGY
   David M. Buss

1 Conceptual Foundations of Evolutionary Psychology   5
   John Tooby and Leda Cosmides
2 Life History Theory and Evolutionary Psychology   68
   Hillard S. Kaplan and Steven W. Gangestad
3 Domain Specificity and Intuitive Ontology   96
   Pascal Boyer and H. Clark Barrett
4 Methods of Evolutionary Sciences   119
   Jeffry A. Simpson and Lorne Campbell
5 Controversial Issues in Evolutionary Psychology   145
   Edward H. Hagen

PART II   SURVIVAL
   David M. Buss

6 Locating Places   177
   Irwin Silverman and Jean Choi
7 Adaptations to Predators and Prey   200
   H. Clark Barrett
8 Adaptations to Dangers from Humans   224
   Joshua D. Duntley

PART III   MATING
   David M. Buss

Adaptationism and Human Mating Psychology   255
   Donald Symons
9 Fundamentals of Human Mating Strategies   258
   David P. Schmitt
10 Physical Attractiveness in Adaptationist Perspective   292
   Lawrence S. Sugiyama

11 Adaptations to Ovulation 344
Steven W. Gangestad, Randy Thornhill, and
Christine E. Garver-Apgar

12 Female Infidelity and Sperm Competition 372
Todd K. Shackelford, Nicholas Pound, Aaron T. Goetz, and
Craig W. LaMunyon

13 Sexual Coercion 394
Neil M. Malamuth, Mark Huppin, and Bryant Paul

14 Commitment, Love, and Mate Retention 419
Lorne Campbell and Bruce J. Ellis

PART IV PARENTING AND KINSHIP
Martin Daly and Margo Wilson

15 Cooperation and Conflict among Kin 447
Jeffrey A. Kurland and Steven J. C. Gaulin

16 Evolution of Paternal Investment 483
David C. Geary

17 Parental Investment and Parent-Offspring Conflict 506
Catherine Salmon

18 Altruism and Genetic Relatedness 528
Eugene Burnstein

19 Hormones and the Human Family 552
Mark V. Flinn, Carol V. Ward, and Robert J. Noone

PART V GROUP LIVING
David M. Buss

20 Neurocognitive Adaptations Designed for Social Exchange 584
Leda Cosmides and John Tooby

21 Aggression 628
Anne Campbell

22 Managing Ingroup and Outgroup Relationships 653
Robert Kurzban and Steven Neuberg

23 Dominance, Status, and Social Hierarchies 676
Denise Cummins

24 The Evolution of Language 698
Peter F. MacNeilage and Barbara L. Davis

25 The Evolution of Cognitive Bias 724
Martie G. Haselton, Daniel Nettle, and Paul W. Andrews

26 The Evolution of Morality 747
Dennis Krebs

PART VI EVOLUTIONIZING TRADITIONAL DISCIPLINES
OF PSYCHOLOGY
David M. Buss

27 Evolutionary Cognitive Psychology 776
Peter M. Todd, Ralph Hertwig, and Ulrich Hoffrage

28 Evolutionary Social Psychology 803
Douglas T. Kenrick, Jon K. Maner, and Norman P. Li

29 Evolutionary Developmental Psychology   828
      David F. Bjorklund and Carlos Hernández Blasi
30 Evolutionary Personality Psychology   851
      Aurelio José Figueredo, Jon A. Sefcek, Geneva Vasquez,
      Barbara H. Brumbach, James E. King, and W. Jake Jacobs
31 Biological Function and Dysfunction   878
      Jerome C. Wakefield
32 Evolutionary Psychology and Mental Health   903
      Randolph M. Nesse

PART VII   APPLICATIONS OF EVOLUTIONARY PSYCHOLOGY TO
OTHER DISCIPLINES
      David M. Buss

33 Literature and Evolutionary Psychology   931
      Joseph Carroll
34 Evolutionary Psychology and the Law   953
      Owen D. Jones

Afterword   975
      Richard Dawkins

Author Index   981

Subject Index   1009

Foreword

For many years after I decided to become a psychologist I was frustrated by my chosen field, and fantasized about a day when it would satisfy the curiosity that first led me to devote my professional life to studying the mind. As with many psychology students, the frustration began with my very first class, in which the instructor performed the ritual that begins every introduction to psychology course: disabusing students of the expectation that they would learn about any of the topics that attracted them to the subject. Forget about love and hate, family dynamics, and jokes and their relation to the unconscious, they said. Psychology was a rigorous science which investigated quantifiable laboratory phenomena; it had nothing to do with self-absorption on an analyst's couch or the prurient topics of daytime talk shows. And in fact the course confined itself to "perception," which meant psychophysics, and "learning," which meant rats, and "the brain," which meant neurons, and "memory," which meant nonsense syllables, and "intelligence," which meant IQ tests, and "personality," which meant personality tests.

When I proceeded to more advanced courses, they only deepened the disappointment by revealing that the psychology canon was a laundry list of unrelated phenomena. The course on perception began with Weber's Law and Fechner's Law and proceeded to an assortment of illusions and aftereffects familiar to readers of cereal boxes. There was no there—no conception of what perception *is* or of what it is for. Cognitive psychology, too, consisted of laboratory curiosities analyzed in terms of dichotomies such as serial/parallel, discrete/analog, and top-down/bottom-up (inspiring Alan Newell's famous jeremiad, "You can't play twenty questions with nature and win"). To this day, social psychology is driven not by systematic questions about the nature of sociality in the human animal but by a collection of situations in which people behave in strange ways.

But the biggest frustration was that psychology seemed to lack any sense of *explanation*. Like the talk show guest on *Monty Python's Flying Circus* whose theory of the brontosaurus was that "the brontosaurus is skinny at one end; much, much thicker in the middle; and skinny at the other end," psychologists were content to "explain" a phenomenon by redescribing it. A student rarely enjoyed the flash of

Supported by NIH Grant HD 18381.

insight which tapped deeper principles to show why something *had* to be the way it is, as opposed to some other way it could have been.

My gold standard for a scientific explanation was set when I was a graduate student—not by anything I learned in graduate *school*, mind you, but by a plumber who came to fix the pipes in my dilapidated apartment and elucidated why they had sprung a leak. Water, he explained, obeys Newton's second law. Water is dense. Water is incompressible. When you shut off a tap, a large incompressible mass moving at high speed has to decelerate quickly. This imparts a big force to the pipes, like a car slamming into a wall, which eventually damages the threads and causes a leak. To deal with this problem, plumbers used to install a closed vertical section of pipe, a pipe riser, near each faucet. When the faucet is shut, the decelerating water compresses the column of air in the riser, which acts like a shock absorber, protecting the pipe joints. Unfortunately, this is a perfect opportunity for Henry's Law to apply, namely, that gas under pressure is absorbed by a liquid. Over time, the air in the column dissolves into the water, filling the pipe riser and rendering it useless. So every once in a while, a plumber should bleed the system and let air back into the risers, a bit of preventive maintenance the landlord had neglected. I only wished that psychology could meet that standard of explanatory elegance and show how a seemingly capricious occurrence falls out of laws of greater generality.

It's not that psychologists never tried to rationalize their findings. But when they did, they tended to recycle a handful of factors like similarity, frequency, difficulty, salience, and regularity. Each of these so-called explanations is, in the words of the philosopher Nelson Goodman, "a pretender, an impostor, a quack." Similarity (and frequency and difficulty and the rest) are in the eye of the beholder, and it is the eye of the beholder that psychologists should be trying to explain.

This dissatisfaction pushed me to the broader interdisciplinary field called cognitive science, where I found that other disciplines were stepping into the breach. From linguistics I came across Noam Chomsky's criteria for an adequate theory of language. At the lowest level was observational adequacy, the mere ability to account for linguistic behavior; this was the level at which most of psychology was stuck. Then there was descriptive adequacy, the ability to account for behavior in terms of the underlying mental representations that organize it. At the highest level was explanatory adequacy, the ability of a theory to show why *those* mental representations, and not some other ones, took root in the mind. In the case of linguistics, Chomsky continued, explanatory adequacy was rooted in the ability of a theory to solve the problem of language acquisition, explaining how children can learn an infinite language from a finite sample of sentences uttered by their parents. An explanatory theory must characterize Universal Grammar, a part of the innate structure of the mind. This faculty forces the child to analyze speech in particular ways, those consistent with the way human languages work, rather than in any of the countless logically possible ways that are consistent with the input but dead ends in terms of becoming an expressive language user (e.g., memorizing every sentence or combining nouns and verbs promiscuously). As a result, a person's knowledge of language is not just any old set of rules, but ones that conform to an algorithm powerful enough to have acquired an infinite language from a finite slice of the environment. For example, locality conditions on movement rules in syntax—the fact that you can say,

"What do you believe he saw?" but not, "What do you believe the claim that he saw?"—allow children to acquire a language from the kinds of simple sentences that are available in parental speech. In this way, a psychological phenomenon (the distribution of well-formed and malformed questions) could be explained in terms of what was necessary to solve the key problem faced by a human child in this domain.

Artificial intelligence, too, set a high standard of explanation via the work of the vision scientist David Marr. A theory of vision, he suggested, ought to characterize visual processing at three levels: the neurophysiological mechanism, the algorithm implemented by this mechanism, and, crucially, a "theory of the computation" for that domain. A theory of the computation is a formal demonstration that an algorithm can, in principle, compute the desired result, given certain assumptions about the way the world works. And the desired result, in turn, should be characterized in terms of the overall "goal" of the visual system, namely to compute a useful description of the world from the two-dimensional array of intensity and wavelength values falling on the retina. For example, the subsystem that computes the perception of shape from shading (as when we perceive the contours of a cheek or the roundness of a ping-pong ball) relies on a fact of physics that governs how the intensity of light reflecting off a surface depends on the relative angles of the illuminant, the surface, and the observer, and on the physical properties of the surface. A perceptual algorithm can exploit this bit of physics to "work backwards" from the array of light intensities, together with certain assumptions about typical illuminants and surfaces in a terrestrial environment, and compute the tangent angle of each point on a surface, yielding a representation of its shape. Many perceptual phenomena, from the way makeup changes the appearance of a face to the fact that turning a picture of craters upside down makes it look like a picture of bumps, can be explained as byproducts of this shape-from-shading mechanism. Most perception scientists quickly realized that conceiving the faculty of vision as a system of well-designed neural computers that supply the rest of the brain with an accurate description of the visible environment was a big advance over the traditional treatment of perception as a ragbag of illusions, aftereffects, and psychophysical laws.

Language and perception, alas, are just two of our many talents and faculties, and it was unsatisfying to think of the eyes and ears as pouring information into some void that constituted the rest of the brain. Might there be some comparable framework for the rest of psychology, I wondered, that addressed the engaging phenomena of mental and social life, covered its subject matter systematically rather than collecting oddities like butterflies, and explained its phenomena in terms of deeper principles? The explanations in language and vision appealed to the *function* of those faculties: in linguistics, acquiring the language of one's community; in vision, constructing an accurate description of the visible world. Both are extraordinarily difficult computational problems (as yet unsolvable by any artificial intelligence system) but ones that any child can perform with ease. And both are not esoteric hobbies but essential talents for members of our species, affording obvious advantages to their well-being. Couldn't other areas of psychology, I wondered, benefit from an understanding of the problems our mental faculties solve—in a word, what they are *for*?

When I discovered evolutionary psychology in the 1980s through the work of Donald Symons, Leda Cosmides, and John Tooby, I realized my wait was over.

Evolutionary psychology was the organizing framework—the source of "explanatory adequacy" or a "theory of the computation"—that the science of psychology
had been missing. Like vision and language, our emotions and cognitive faculties
are complex, useful, and nonrandomly organized, which means that they must be
a product of the only physical process capable of generating complex, useful, nonrandom organization, namely, natural selection. An appeal to evolution was already implicit in the metatheoretical directives of Marr and Chomsky, with their
appeal to the function of a mental faculty, and evolutionary psychology simply
shows how to apply that logic to the rest of the mind.

Just as important, the appeal to function in evolutionary psychology is itself
constrained by an external body of principles—those of the modern, replicator-
centered theory of selection from evolutionary biology—rather than being made
up on the spot. Not just any old goal can count as the function of a system shaped
by natural selection, that is, an adaptation. Evolutionary biology rules out, for example, adaptations that work toward the good of the species, the harmony of the
ecosystem, beauty for its own sake, benefits to entities other than the replicators
that create the adaptations (e.g., horses that evolve saddles), functional complexity without reproductive benefit (e.g., an adaptation to compute the digits of pi),
and anachronistic adaptations that benefit the organism in a kind of environment
other than the one in which it evolved (e.g., an innate ability to read or an innate
concept of *carburetor* or *trombone*). Natural selection also has a positive function in
psychological discovery, impelling psychologists to test new hypotheses about the
possible functionality of aspects of the mind that previously seemed functionless. For example, the social and moral emotions (sympathy, trust, guilt, anger,
gratitude) appear to be adaptations for policing reciprocity in nonzero sum
games; an eye for beauty appears to be an adaptation for detecting health and fertility in potential mates. None of this research would be possible if psychologists
had satisfied themselves with a naïve notion of function instead of the one li-
censed by modern biology.

Evolutionary psychology also provides a motivated research agenda for psychology, freeing it from its chase of laboratory curiosities. An explanatory hypothesis for some emotion or cognitive faculty must begin with a theory of how
that faculty would, on average, have enhanced the reproductive chances of the
bearer of that faculty in an ancestral environment. Crucially, the advantage must
be demonstrable by some independently motivated causal consequence of the putative adaptation. That is, laws of physics or chemistry or engineering or physiology, or some other set of laws independent of the part of our psychology being
explained must suffice to establish that the trait is useful in attaining some
reproduction-related goal. For example, using projective geometry one can show
that an algorithm can compare images from two adjacent cameras and calculate
the depth of a distant object using the disparity of the two images. If you write
out the specs for computing depth in this way—what engineers would specify if
they were building a robot that had to see in depth—you can then examine
human stereoscopic depth perception and ascertain whether humans (and other
primates) obey those specs. The closer the empirical facts about our psychology
are to the engineering specs for a well-designed system, the greater our confidence that we have explained the psychological faculty in functional terms. A
similar example comes from the wariness of snakes found in humans and many
other primates. We know from herpetology that snakes were prevalent in Africa

during the time of our evolution and that getting bitten by a snake is harmful because of the chemistry of snake venom. Crucially, these are not facts of psychology. But they help to establish that something that *is* a fact of psychology, namely the fear of snakes, is a plausible adaptation. In a similar manner, robotics can help explain motor control, game theory can explain aggression and appeasement, economics can explain punishment of free riders, and mammalian physiology (in combination of the evolutionary biology of parental investment) makes predictions about sex differences in sexuality. In each case, a "theory of the computation" is provided by an optimality analysis using a set of laws outside the part of the mind we are trying to explain. This is what entitles us to feel that we have explained the operation of that part of the mind in a noncircular way.

In contrast, it's not clear what the adaptive function of music is, or of religion. The popular hypothesis that the function of music is to keep the community together may be true, but it is not an *explanation* of why we like music, because it just begs the question of why sequences of tones in rhythmic and harmonic relations should keep the group together. Generating and sensing sequences of sounds is not an independently motivated solution to the problem of maintaining group solidarity, in the way that, say, the emotion of empathy, or a motive to punish free riders, is part of such a solution. A similar problem infects the "explanation" that people are prone to believe in incredible religious doctrines because those doctrines are comforting—in other words, that the doctrines of a benevolent shepherd, a universal plan, an afterlife, and divine retribution ease the pain of being a human. There's an element of truth to each of these suggestions, but they are not legitimate adaptationist explanations, because they beg the question of *why* the mind should find comfort in beliefs that it is capable of perceiving as false. In these and other cases, a failure to find an adaptationist explanation does not mean that no explanation is forthcoming at all. Recent books by Pascal Boyer and Scott Atran have insightfully explained the phenomenon of religious belief as a byproduct of adaptations (such as a theory of mind module and free-rider detection mechanisms) that are demonstrably useful for solving *other* adaptive problems.

Evolutionary psychology is the cure for one last problem ailing traditional psychology: its student-disillusioning avoidance of the most fascinating aspects of human mental and social life. Even if evolutionary psychology had not provided psychology with standards of explanatory adequacy, it has proved its worth by opening up research in areas of human experience that have always been fascinating to reflective people but that had been absent from the psychology curriculum for decades. It is no exaggeration to say that contemporary research on topics like sex, attraction, jealousy, love, food, disgust, status, dominance, friendship, religion, art, fiction, morality, motherhood, fatherhood, sibling rivalry, and cooperation has been opened up and guided by ideas from evolutionary psychology. Even in more traditional topics in psychology, evolutionary psychology is changing the face of theories, making them into better depictions of the real people we encounter in our lives, and making the science more consonant with common sense and the wisdom of the ages. Before the advent of evolutionary thinking in psychology, theories of memory and reasoning typically didn't distinguish thoughts about people from thoughts about rocks or houses. Theories of emotion didn't distinguish fear from anger, jealousy, or love. And theories of social relations didn't distinguish among the way people treat family, friends, lovers, enemies, and strangers.

For many reasons, then, this *Handbook* represents a remarkable milestone in the science of psychology. The theoretical rigor and empirical richness showcased in these chapters have more than fulfilled evolutionary psychology's initial promise, and they demolish lazy accusations that the field is mired in speculative story-telling or rationalizations of reactionary politics. The chapters don't, of course, summarize a firm consensus or present the final word in any of the areas they cover. (In particular, see my chapter in Christansen and Kirby's *Language Evolution* for a rather different take on the evolutionary psychology of language.) But in topics from parenting to fiction, from predation to religion, they deliver subtle and deep analyses, genuinely new ideas, and eye-opening discoveries. *The Handbook of Evolutionary Psychology* is far more than a summary of the state of the art of evolutionary psychology. It is the realization of the hope that psychology can be a systematic and explanatory science of the human condition.

STEVEN PINKER

Acknowledgments

THE CREATION OF THIS *Handbook* owes a special thanks to friends and colleagues who offered suggestions about coverage, provided reviews of individual chapters, and helped me on the long journey: Sean Conlan, Leda Cosmides, Martin Daly, Todd DeKay, Randy Diehl, Diana Fleischman, Steve Gangestad, Martie Haselton, Sarah Hill, Joonghwan Jeon, Barry X. Kuhle, Steven Pinker, David Schmitt, Todd Shackelford, Don Symons, John Tooby, Jerry Wakefield, and Margo Wilson. Josh Duntley deserves special thanks for help throughout the process, including providing excellent feedback on my general and section introductions.

An editor could not ask for a more superlative team than those at John Wiley & Sons. Jennifer Simon provided the initial inspiration by suggesting the idea of the *Handbook*. Peggy Alexander, Isabel Pratt, and Patricia Rossi at Wiley and Pam Blackmon at Publications Development Company of Texas supplied excellent help in bringing the project to fruition.

I owe a special thanks to Steven Pinker for furnishing the Foreword, Don Symons for writing a special essay for the section on mating, Martin Daly and Margo Wilson for providing an introduction to the section on parenting and kinship, and Richard Dawkins for furnishing the afterword. Most important, I thank the 60 authors who provided the 34 chapters that form the core of the *Handbook*.

Contributors

Paul W. Andrews
Virginia Institute for Psychiatric and
    Behavioral Genetics
Virginia Commonwealth University
Richmond, Virginia

H. Clark Barrett
Department of Anthropology
University of California, Los Angeles
Los Angeles, California

David F. Bjorklund
Department of Psychology
Florida Atlantic University
Boca Raton, Florida

Carlos Hernández Blasi
Departamento de Psicología
Universitat Jaume I
Castellón, Spain

Pascal Boyer
Department of Psychology
Washington University, St. Louis
St. Louis, Missouri

Barbara H. Brumbach
Department of Psychology
University of Arizona
Tucson, Arizona

Eugene Burnstein
Institute for Social Research
University of Michigan
Ann Arbor, Michigan

David M. Buss
Department of Psychology
University of Texas, Austin
Austin, Texas

Anne Campbell
Psychology Department
Durham University
Durham, England

Lorne Campbell
Department of Psychology
University of Western Ontario
Ontario, Canada

Joseph Carroll
Department of English
University of Missouri, St. Louis
St. Louis, Missouri

Jean Choi
Departmentof Psychology
University of Lethbridge
Lethbridge, Alberta, Canada

Leda Cosmides
Department of Psychology
University of California,
    Santa Barbara
Santa Barbara, California

Denise Cummins
Department of Psychology
University of California, Davis
Davis, California

Martin Daly
Department of Psychology
McMaster University
Hamilton, Ontario, Canada

Barbara L. Davis
Department of Psychology
University of Texas, Austin
Austin, Texas

Richard Dawkins
Department of Zoology
University of Oxford
Oxford, United Kingdom

Joshua D. Duntley
Department of Psychology
University of Texas, Austin
Austin, Texas

Bruce J. Ellis
Division of Family Studies and
    Human Development
University of Canterbury
Tucson, Arizona

Aurelio José Figueredo
Department of Psychology
University of Arizona
Tucson, Arizona

Mark V. Flinn
Departments of Anthropology and
    Psychological Sciences
University of Missouri
Columbia, Missouri

Steven W. Gangestad
Department of Psychology
University of New Mexico
Albuquerque, New Mexico

Christine E. Garver-Apgar
Department of Psychology
University of New Mexico
Albuquerque, New Mexico

Steven J. C. Gaulin
Department of Anthropology
University of California,
    Santa Barbara
Santa Barbara, California

David C. Geary
Department of Psychological Sciences
University of Missouri, Columbia
Columbia, Missouri

Aaron T. Goetz
Department of Psychology
Florida Atlantic University
Davie, Florida

Edward H. Hagen
Institute for Theoretical Biology
Humboldt-Universitat zu Berlin

Martie G. Haselton
Communication Studies and
    Department of Psychology
University of California,
    Los Angeles
Los Angeles, California

Ralph Hertwig
Department of Psychology
University of Basel
Basel, Switzerland

Ulrich Hoffrage
Faculty of Management and
    Business Administration
University of Lausanne
Lausanne, Switzerland

Mark Huppin
Department of Psychology
University of California,
    Los Angeles
Los Angeles, California

W. Jake Jacobs
Department of Psychology
University of Arizona
Tucson, Arizona

Owen D. Jones
Law School and Department of
    Biological Sciences
Vanderbilt University
Nashville, Tennessee

Hillard S. Kaplan
Department of Anthropology
University of New Mexico
Albuquerque, New Mexico

Douglas T. Kenrick
Department of Psychology
Arizona State University
Tempe, Arizona

James E. King
Department of Psychology
University of Arizona
Tucson, Arizona

Dennis Krebs
Department of Psychology
Simon Frazer University
Burnaby, British Columbia, Canada

Jeffrey A. Kurland
Department of Anthropology
Pennsylvania State University
University Park, Pennsylvania

Robert Kurzban
Department of Psychology
University of Pennsylvania
Philadelphia, Pennsylvania

Craig W. LaMunyon
Department of Biological Sciences
California State Polytechnic University
Pomona, California

Norman P. Li
Department of Psychology
University of Texas, Austin
Austin, Texas

Peter F. MacNeilage
Department of Psychology
University of Texas, Austin
Austin, Texas

Neil M. Malamuth
Department of Psychology
University of California,
   Los Angeles
Los Angeles, California

Jon K. Maner
Department of Psychology
Florida State University
Tallahassee, Florida

Randolph M. Nesse
Department of Psychiatry, Department
   of Psychology
Research Center for Group Dynamics
   in the Institute for Social Research
University of Michigan
Ann Arbor, Michigan

Daniel Nettle
Division of Psychology, Brain, and
   Behaviour
University of Newcastle
Newcastle, United Kingdom

Steven Neuberg
Department of Psychology
Arizona State University
Tempe, Arizona

Robert J. Noone
Family Service Center
Evanston, Illinois

Bryant Paul
Department of Telecommunications
University of Indiana
Bloomington, Indiana

Steven Pinker
Department of Psychology
Harvard University
Cambridge, Massachusetts

Nicholas Pound
Department of Psychology
Brunel University
London, United Kingdom

Catherine Salmon
Department of Psychology
University of Redlands
Redlands, California

David P. Schmitt
Department of Psychology
Bradley University
Peoria, Illinois

Jon A. Sefcek
Department of Psychology
University of Arizona
Tucson, Arizona

Todd K. Shackelford
Department of Psychology
Florida Atlantic University
Davie, Florida

Irwin Silverman
Emeritus Professor
Psychology Department
York University
Toronto, Ontario, Canada

Jeffry A. Simpson
Department of Psychology
University of Minnesota
Minneapolis, Minnesota

Lawrence S. Sugiyama
Department of Anthropology
University of Oregon
Eugene, Orgeon

Donald Symons
Emeritus Professor of Anthropology
Department of Anthropology
University of California,
 Santa Barbara
Santa Barbara, California

Randy Thornhill
Department of Biology
University of New Mexico
Albuquerque, New Mexico

Peter M. Todd
Center for Adaptive Behavior and
 Cognition
Max Planck Institute for Human
 Development
Berlin, Germany

John Tooby
Department of Anthropology
University of California, Santa Barbara
Santa Barbara, California

Geneva Vasquez
Department of Psychology
University of Arizona
Tucson, Arizona

Jerome C. Wakefield
New York University
New York, New York

Carol V. Ward
 Departments of Anthropology and
 Psychological Sciences
University of Missouri
Columbia, Missouri

Margo Wilson
Department of Psychology
McMaster University
Hamilton, Ontario, Canada

Introduction: The Emergence of Evolutionary Psychology

DAVID M. BUSS

EVOLUTIONARY PSYCHOLOGY, BROADLY conceived, dates back to Darwin. He offered this scientific vision at the end of his monumental book, *On the Origins of Species:* "In the distant future I see open fields for more important researches. Psychology will be based on a new foundation, that of the necessary acquirement of each mental power and capacity by gradation" (Darwin, 1859). This *Handbook of Evolutionary Psychology*, published 146 years after Darwin's prophetic words, symbolizes the emergence of evolutionary psychology based on his vision.

Evolutionary psychology is still a young scientific field, and there's a long and exciting road ahead. Aspects of the field's conceptual foundations remain legitimate topics of debate, such as the nature and specificity of psychological adaptations and the importance of individual differences. Many phenomena remain unexamined, awaiting new explorers of the human mind using the conceptual tools that evolutionary psychology provides. Many of the conceptual foundations are now in place, offering a solid metatheoretical framework from which to build. Hundreds of psychological and behavioral phenomena have been documented empirically, findings that would never have been discovered without the guiding framework of evolutionary psychology. Evolutionary psychology has proved its worth many times over in its theoretical and empirical harvest. If a viable *alternative* framework to evolutionary psychology exists for understanding the origins and nature of the human mind, it has not been revealed to the scientific community. This *Handbook* takes stock of where the field is today and where it needs to go.

A decade ago, a handbook of this scope would have been impossible. The empirical corpus of research testing evolutionary psychological hypotheses was too slim. Now the body of work has mushroomed at such a rapid rate that I had to make difficult decisions about what to include for this volume to keep it a reasonable length. Some important areas regrettably could not be covered. Most chapters had to be shortened, sometimes dramatically. The extensity of coverage, however, reveals that evolutionary psychology has penetrated every existing branch of psychology.

Psychologists working in some subdisciplines in times past could safely disregard evolutionary psychology. Now the robustness of evolutionary hypotheses and the rapid accumulation of empirical findings make it impossible to ignore for all but those who remain conceptually insular. Scientists working in cognitive, social, developmental, personality, neuroscience, or clinical psychology cannot afford to close their eyes to the insights offered by evolutionary psychology.

Some view evolutionary psychology as an optional perspective, an explanation of last resort, to be brought in only when all other alternatives have been exhausted. In my view, this position is naïve. Evolutionary psychology represents a true scientific revolution, a profound paradigm shift in the field of psychology. The human mind can no longer be conceived as it has been in mainstream psychology, implicitly or explicitly, as a blank slate onto which parents, teachers, and culture impose their scripts; a domain-general learning device; a set of content-free information processing mechanisms; or a content-free neural or connectionist network. Instead, the human mind comes factory-equipped with an astonishing array of dedicated psychological mechanisms, designed over deep time by natural and sexual selection, to solve the hundreds of statistically recurring adaptive problems that our ancestors confronted. Understanding these mechanisms of mind requires understanding their evolved functions—what they were designed by selection to accomplish. Just as a medical researcher's insights into the heart, liver, or kidney would be viewed as woefully incomplete without knowledge of their functions, explanations of psychological mechanisms will almost invariably be incomplete without specifying their functions. Evolutionary psychology is no longer a discretionary or elective theoretical option for psychology. It is essential and necessary.

At the current point in the history of psychology, the mainstream field is partitioned into subdisciplines—cognitive, social, personality, developmental, clinical, and hybrid areas such as cognitive neuroscience. Evolutionary psychology provides the metatheoretical foundation that unites the disparate branches of the sprawling field of psychology and suggests that the human mind cannot be logically parsed in the manner the subdisciplines imply. Consider "stranger anxiety" as a candidate psychological adaptation. Its function is to motivate the infant to recoil from potentially dangerous humans and to maintain close proximity to caregivers, thereby avoiding hazards that strangers might pose. Stranger anxiety possesses a number of well-articulated design features. It shows universality, emerging in infants in all cultures in which it has been studied. It emerges predictably during ontogeny at roughly 6 months of age, coinciding with the time when infants begin crawling away from their mothers and potentially encountering strangers. And its focus centers on strange males rather than strange females because strange males historically have been more hazardous to infants' health. Stranger anxiety shows all the characteristics of "improbable design" for achieving a specific function.

In which subdiscipline of psychology does stranger anxiety belong? It obviously involves information processing and thus could be claimed by cognitive psychology. It shows a predictable ontogenetic unfolding, so it could be claimed by developmental psychology. It is activated by interactions with others, so it belongs to social psychology. Individual infants differ in the intensity of stranger anxiety, so it falls within the province of personality psychology. The mechanism can malfunction in a minority of infants, so it's relevant to clinical psychology.

And its biological substrate must include the brain, so neuroscience can also lay claim. Obviously, stranger anxiety belongs simultaneously to all or to none.

Evolutionary psychology breaks down these traditional disciplinary boundaries and reveals them to lack logical or scientific warrant. Viewed through the theoretical lens of adaptive problems and their evolved psychological solutions, evolutionary psychology offers the only nonarbitrary means for carving the mind at its natural joints. It provides the conceptual unification of the disparate branches of psychology that currently operate in virtual isolation. And it integrates psychology theoretically with the rest of the natural sciences in a unified causal framework.

It is a great honor and privilege to serve as editor for the first reasonably comprehensive *Handbook of Evolutionary Psychology,* which contains such a high-powered assembly of scientists. The *Handbook* begins with a Foreword from Steven Pinker, who provides a powerful narrative of his intellectual journey to evolutionary psychology and describes his views about why evolutionary psychology is necessary for psychological science. The *Handbook* ends with an eloquent afterword by evolutionary biologist Richard Dawkins, whose theoretical contributions have informed much work in the discipline. Between are 34 chapters parsed into seven parts.

Part I, *Foundations of Evolutionary Psychology,* contains five chapters that outline the logic of the enterprise, the methods used, and controversial issues surrounding the field. Part II, *Survival,* contains three chapters that deal, respectively, with struggles with the physical environment, with other species (predators and prey), and with other humans. Part III, *Mating,* begins with an insightful essay by Donald Symons, in which he articulates the logic of adaptationism and offers a novel hypothesis about mate rejection anxiety. It is followed by six chapters that range in content from sexual coercion to love in long-term mating, highlighting the breadth and depth of theory and research in the domain of human mating. Part IV, *Parenting and Kinship,* contains a cogent introduction by Martin Daly and Margo Wilson and is followed by five chapters on cooperation and conflict among kin, parental investment, parent-offspring conflict, and the evolution of the human family. Part V, *Group Living,* deals with social exchange, aggression, social exclusion, status hierarchies, language, cognitive biases in mind reading, and the evolution of morality. Part VI, *Evolutionizing Traditional Disciplines of Psychology,* contains six chapters on how the conceptual foundations of the current disciplines within psychology can be informed by an evolutionary framework. Part VII, *Applications of Evolutionary Psychology to Other Disciplines,* offers two chapters, one on evolutionary psychology and literature and one on the evolutionary analysis of the law, revealing how evolutionary psychology provides insights into far-ranging and disparate disciplines. The *Handbook* ends with an Afterword by Richard Dawkins, who offers insightful reflections about the history of field.

After a long succession of conceptual advances and empirical discoveries, a robust field of evolutionary psychology has finally emerged. Darwin's prophetic vision is being realized—a psychology based on a new foundation.

PART I

FOUNDATIONS OF EVOLUTIONARY PSYCHOLOGY

DAVID M. BUSS

JOHN TOOBY AND Leda Cosmides have been true pioneers in developing the conceptual foundations of evolutionary psychology, so it is fitting that they supply the first foundational chapter. They provide a fascinating tour of the discipline's intellectual origins, showing how a series of conceptual advances, from the cognitive revolution to evolutionary game theory, led to the emergence of evolutionary psychology. Tooby and Cosmides then discuss six foundational premises on which the field rests. They explicate principles of organic design, the logic of reverse engineering, and the nature of evidence for special design and discuss how theories of good design provide powerful heuristics for psychological scientists. They describe how the framework of evolutionary psychology differs from that of traditional psychology. Finally, Tooby and Cosmides offer an intriguing novel framework for conceptualizing the functional architecture of cognition, motivation, and emotion. The original theoretical papers of Tooby and Cosmides over the past 18 years have informed virtually all work being conducted in the field of evolutionary psychology. This chapter consolidates and expands the conceptual foundations of the field.

Hillard Kaplan and Steven Gangestad argue in Chapter 2 for the integration of life history theory and evolutionary psychology, suggesting that adaptations are designed to make different budget-allocation trade-offs over the life span. They begin with a presentation of the fundamentals of life history theory. All energy budgets of an organism are finite, so trade-offs are inevitable. Kaplan and Gangestad discuss the most important trade-offs—between present and future reproduction, quality and quantity of offspring, and mating effort and parental effort. They proceed to illuminate the important effects of ecological factors such as food supply and mortality hazards on optimal life history strategies. Kaplan and Gangestad then turn to *humans* specifically, showing how life history theory informs, and can be successfully integrated with, evolutionary psychology. Most

1

intriguingly, they propose that these adaptations cannot be independent of one another in at least two ways. First, effort allocated to one (e.g., preventing cuckoldry) necessarily takes away effort allocated to others (e.g., foraging for food). Second, humans must possess *coevolved bundles* of psychological mechanisms, such as those for long-term mating linked with those for heavy-investment parenting. Kaplan and Gangestad make a persuasive argument that the integration of life history theory with evolutionary psychology provides a means for uncovering psychological adaptations designed to make important budget allocation trade-offs. It also promises to reveal how different psychological mechanisms are linked with each other, illuminated by an economic cost-benefit analysis of selection pressures.

Pascal Boyer and Clark Barrett in Chapter 3 offer an extended argument for domain specificity, using intuitive ontology—adaptations for different domains of information—as a vehicle for illuminating the tight integration of neural, developmental, and behavioral components of evolved psychological mechanisms. They document evidence from cognitive psychology and neuroscience that strongly supports a key foundational premise of evolutionary psychology, namely, that humans possess, in their words, "a federation of evolved competencies." Boyer and Barrett outline the features that specific inference systems possess, including semantic knowledge, a specialized learning logic, a dedicated set of developmental pathways, and a close correspondence with specific adaptive problems solved. They then explore several broad evolved competencies in detail, such as the ability to read the minds of others (intuitive psychology) and ability to grapple with the physical environment (intuitive physics). They argue persuasively that evolved competencies in fact are more fine grained than these ontological categories imply. Indeed, adaptations cross these ontological categories. Boyer and Barrett provide an example par excellence of how evolutionary psychology dissolves traditional disciplinary boundaries by bringing developmental, cognitive, and neuroscience evidence to bear in illuminating evolved psychological mechanisms.

Jeffrey Simpson and Lorne Campbell argue convincingly in Chapter 4 that programs of research in evolutionary psychology can and should be strengthened methodologically by using a wider array of methods and measurement techniques specifically tailored to testing "special design" predictions that follow from hypothesized psychological adaptations. They present a persuasive case for multiple research methods and multiple outcome measures, as well as increased attention to issues of the validity of these measures, in successfully illuminating the "special design" qualities of hypothesized psychological adaptations. Evolutionary psychology ultimately will convince the residue of remaining skeptics by *empirical* discoveries that cannot successfully be explained by more traditional, competing nonevolutionary explanations. This chapter provides an informative and insightful guide for anyone conducting or aspiring to conduct empirical research in evolutionary psychology.

Edward Hagen concludes the section with an insightful analysis of recurrent controversies surrounding evolutionary psychology and the misconceptions that stubbornly persist. As discussed in Chapter 5, these controversies include the conflation of levels of analysis (e.g., selfish genes versus selfish people), misunderstandings about the concept of the environment of evolutionary adaptedness (EEA), and enduring confusions about the false nature-nurture dichotomy.

Hagan clarifies the notions of modularity and specificity and refutes common criticisms of these notions. He then addresses recurrent worries about the political implications of evolutionary psychology and shows that these apprehensions are unfounded. He ends on an intriguing note, suggesting that a true science of the human mind might indeed provide tools that potentially challenge and undermine values people hold near and dear.

CHAPTER 1

Conceptual Foundations of Evolutionary Psychology

JOHN TOOBY and LEDA COSMIDES

THE EMERGENCE OF EVOLUTIONARY PSYCHOLOGY: WHAT IS AT STAKE?

THE THEORY OF evolution by natural selection has revolutionary implications for understanding the design of the human mind and brain, as Darwin himself was the first to recognize (Darwin, 1859). Indeed, a principled understanding of the network of causation that built the functional architecture of the human species offers the possibility of transforming the study of humanity into a natural science capable of precision and rapid progress. Yet, nearly a century and a half after *The Origin of Species* was published, the psychological, social, and behavioral sciences remain largely untouched by these implications, and many of these disciplines continue to be founded on assumptions evolutionarily informed researchers know to be false (Pinker, 2002; Tooby & Cosmides, 1992). Evolutionary psychology is the long-forestalled scientific attempt to assemble out of the disjointed, fragmentary, and mutually contradictory human disciplines a single, logically integrated research framework for the psychological, social, and behavioral sciences—a framework that not only incorporates the evolutionary sciences on a full and equal basis, but that systematically works out all of the revisions in existing belief and research practice that such a synthesis requires (Tooby & Cosmides, 1992).

The long-term scientific goal toward which evolutionary psychologists are working is the mapping of our universal human nature. By this, we mean the construction of a set of empirically validated, high-resolution models of the evolved mechanisms that collectively constitute universal human nature. Because the evolved function of a psychological mechanism is computational—to regulate behavior and the body adaptively in response to informational inputs—such a model consists of a description of the functional circuit logic or information

---

We dedicate this chapter to Irven DeVore, professor emeritus, Department of Anthropology, Harvard University, on the occasion of his 70th birthday.

processing architecture of a mechanism (Cosmides & Tooby, 1987; Tooby & Cosmides, 1992). Eventually, these models should include the neural, developmental, and genetic bases of these mechanisms, and encompass the designs of other species as well.

A genuine, detailed specification of the circuit logic of human nature is expected to become the theoretical centerpiece of a newly reconstituted set of social sciences, because each model of an evolved psychological mechanism makes predictions about the psychological, behavioral, and social phenomena the circuits generate or influence. (For example, the evolutionarily specialized mechanisms underlying human alliance help to explain phenomena such as racism and group dynamics; Kurzban, Tooby, & Cosmides, 2001.) A growing inventory of such models will catalyze the transformation of the social sciences from fields that are predominantly descriptive, soft, and particularistic into theoretically principled scientific disciplines with genuine predictive and explanatory power. Evolutionary psychology in the narrow sense is the scientific project of mapping our evolved psychological mechanisms; in the broad sense, it includes the project of reformulating and expanding the social sciences (and medical sciences) in light of the progressive mapping of our species' evolved architecture.

The resulting changes to the social sciences are expected to be dramatic and far-reaching because the traditional conceptual framework for the social and behavioral sciences—what we have called the *Standard Social Science Model* (SSSM)—was built from defective assumptions about the nature of the human psychological architecture (for an analysis of the SSSM, see Tooby & Cosmides, 1992). The most consequential assumption is that the human psychological architecture consists predominantly of learning and reasoning mechanisms that are general-purpose, content-independent, and equipotential (Pinker, 2002; Tooby & Cosmides, 1992). That is, the mind is blank-slate like, and lacks specialized circuits that were designed by natural selection to respond differentially to inputs by virtue of their evolved significance. This presumed psychology justifies a crucial foundational claim: Just as a blank piece of paper plays no causal role in determining the content that is inscribed on it, the blank-slate view of the mind rationalizes the belief that the evolved organization of the mind plays little causal role in generating the content of human social and mental life. The mind with its learning capacity absorbs its content and organization almost entirely from external sources. Hence, according to the standard model, the social and cultural phenomena studied by the social sciences are autonomous and disconnected from any nontrivial causal patterning originating in our evolved psychological mechanisms. Organization flows inward to the mind, but does not flow outward (Geertz, 1973; Sahlins, 1976).

Yet if—as evolutionary psychologists have been demonstrating—the blank-slate view of the mind is wrong, then the social science project of the past century is not only wrong but radically misconceived. The blank-slate assumption removes the central causal organizers of social phenomena—evolved psychological mechanisms—from the analysis of social events, rendering the social sciences powerless to understand the animating logic of the social world. Evolutionary psychology provokes so much reflexive opposition because the stakes for many social scientists, behavioral scientists, and humanists are so high: If evolutionary psychology turns out to be well-founded, then the existing superstructure of the social and behavioral sciences—the Standard Social Science Model—will have to be dismantled. Instead, a new social science framework will need to be assembled in its place that recognizes that models of psychological mechanisms are essential constituents of social theories (Boyer, 2001; Sperber, 1994, 1996; Tooby & Cosmides, 1992). Within such a framework, the circuit logic of each evolved mechanism contributes to the explanation of every social or cultural phenomenon it influences or helps to generate. For example, the nature of the social interactions between the sexes are partly rooted in the design features of evolved mechanisms for mate preference and acquisition (Buss, 1994, 2000; Daly & Wilson, 1988; Symons, 1979); the patterned incidence of violence is partly explained by our species' psychology of aggression, parenting, and sexuality (Daly & Wilson, 1988); the foundations of trade can be located in evolved cognitive specializations for social exchange (Cosmides & Tooby, 1992, this volume); both incest avoidance and love for family members are rooted in evolved mechanisms for kin recognition (Lieberman, Tooby, & Cosmides, 2003, in press-a, in press-b). Indeed, even though the field is in its infancy, evolutionary psychologists have already identified a large set of examples that touch almost every aspect of human life (see, e.g., the chapters of this volume, as well as the chapters in Barkow, Cosmides, & Tooby, 1992).

For almost a century, adherence to the Standard Social Science Model has been strongly moralized within the scholarly world, immunizing key aspects from criticism and reform (Pinker, 2002; Tooby & Cosmides, 1992). As a result, in the international scholarly community, criteria for belief fixation have often strayed disturbingly far from the scientific merits of the issues involved, whenever research trajectories produce results that threaten to undermine the credibility of the Standard Social Science Model. Nevertheless, in recent decades, the strain of ignoring, exceptionalizing, or explaining away the growing weight of evidence contradicting traditional theories has become severe. Equally, reexaminations of the arguments advanced in favor of the moral necessity of the Standard Social Science Model suggest that they—at best—result from misplaced fears (Pinker, 2002; Tooby & Cosmides, 1992). Indeed, we may all have been complicit in the perpetuation of vast tides of human suffering—suffering that might have been prevented if the scientific community had not chosen to postpone or forgo a more veridical social and behavioral science.

THE INTELLECTUAL ORIGINS OF EVOLUTIONARY PSYCHOLOGY

Despite the marginalization of Darwinism within psychology during the twentieth century, a diverse minority of thinkers tried to think through how Darwinian insights could be applied to behavior. These efforts led to many valuable approaches, including: the instinct psychology of William James and William McDougall; the ethological approach of Tinbergen, Lorenz, and von Frisch, which integrated the careful observation of animal behavior in natural contexts with investigations of its adaptive significance and physiological basis; the sociobiological approach of Richard Alexander, William Hamilton, Robert Trivers, Edward O. Wilson, and many others, which tried to explain patterns of social behavior—differences as well as universals—in humans and other species in terms of their fitness consequences; nativist approaches to language pioneered by Chomsky (1959, 1966), Lenneberg (1967), and others, which brought to wider attention the question of whether one general-purpose learning system could account for all learning; and even behaviorist psychology—quite orthodox with respect to the Standard Social Science Model—looked for phylogenetic continuities in the laws of learning that would apply across species. As valuable as each of these approaches turned out to be, conceptual handicaps internal to each program limited their scope of application and their capacity to usefully reorganize the human psychological, behavioral, and social sciences.

The way past these limitations involved isolating or deriving a core set of foundational concepts from the intersection of physics, biology, and information theory, elucidating their logical and causal interrelationships, and then building back upward from this groundwork. (A few representative concepts are *function, regulation, computational architecture, adaptation, organization, design, entropy, selection, replication, selection pressure, by-product, environment of evolutionary adaptedness,* and *task environment.*) These concepts could then be used to trace out the necessary interconnections among several previously distinct scientific programs, so that the previously independent (and inconsistent) disciplinary building blocks could be integrated into a single unified framework (Tooby & Cosmides, 1992). The building blocks from which evolutionary psychology was assembled include the modern revolution in theoretical evolutionary biology (Williams, 1966), the rise of the computational sciences (Shannon, 1948), the emergence of serious attempts to reconstruct the ancestral conditions and ways of life of humans and prehumans (e.g., Cheney et al., 1987; Lee & DeVore, 1968, 1976), and an adaptationist/computationalist resolution of the debate between environmentalists and nativists (e.g., Cosmides & Tooby, 1987; Tooby & Cosmides, 1990a, 1990b, 1992; Tooby, Cosmides, & Barrett, 2003).

The first building block of evolutionary psychology was the strain of theoretical evolutionary biology that started in the late 1950s and early 1960s, especially with the work of George Williams (Williams, 1966; Williams & Williams, 1957); William D. Hamilton (1964); and John Maynard Smith (1982). By being placed on a more rigorous, formal foundation of replicator dynamics, evolutionary biology was transformed over the ensuing decades from a vaguely conceptualized and sometimes implicitly teleological field into a principled discipline that rivals physics in its theoretical beauty and explanatory power. One face of this transformation has been the derivation of a series of elegant selectionist theories—theories of how natural selection acts on altruism, kinship, cooperation, mating, foraging, reproduction, parenting, risk taking, aggression, senescence, host-parasite interactions, intragenomic conflict, life history, communication, and many other dimensions of life. Research in biology and the human sciences informed by these theories is called sociobiology, behavioral ecology, or evolutionary ecology.

The other face of this revolution in biology is modern adaptationism—a set of deductions that are still often misunderstood, even in biology (Dawkins, 1986; Tooby & Cosmides, 1992; Tooby, Cosmides, & Barrett, 2003; Williams, 1966). Adaptationism is based on the recognition that selection is the only known natural physical process that builds highly ordered functional organization (adaptations) into the designs of species, in a world otherwise continuously assaulted by the ubiquitous entropic tendency of physical systems to become increasingly disordered with time. Thus, although not everything is functional, whenever complex functional organization is found in the architectures of species, its existence and form can be traced back to a previous history of selection. Moreover, for a given selection pressure to drive an allele systematically upward until it is incorporated into the species-typical design, the same selective cause-and-effect relationship must recur across large areas and for many generations. Complex adaptations necessarily reflect the functional demands of the cross-genera-tionally long-enduring structure of the organism's ancestral world, rather than modern, local, transient, or individual conditions. This is why evolutionary psychology as an adaptationist field concerns the functional design of mechanisms given a recurrently structured ancestral world, rather than the idea that behavior is the fitness striving of individuals tailored to unique circumstances (Symons, 1992; Tooby & Cosmides, 1990a).

Consequently, systems of complex, antientropic functional organization (adaptations) in organisms require explanation wherever they are found; their correct explanation (barring supernatural events or artificial intervention) always involves a specific history of selection in ancestral environments; and so the prediction, discovery, mapping, and understanding of the functional architecture of organisms can be greatly facilitated by analyzing the recurrent structure of a species' ancestral world, in conjunction with the selection pressures that operated ancestrally. The foundational recognition that psychological mechanisms are evolved adaptations connects evolutionary biology to psychology in the strongest possible fashion, allowing everything we know about the study of adaptations to be applied to the study of psychological mechanisms. Psychology and evolutionary biology can no longer be defensibly divorced.

George Williams's 1966 volume, *Adaptation and Natural Selection: A Critique of Some Current Evolutionary Thought* was central to both the selectionist and adaptationist revolutions. In it, Williams provided the first fully modern statement of the relationship between selection and adaptive design; clarified that selection operates at the genic level; developed strict evidentiary standards for deciding what aspects of a species' phenotype were adaptations, by-products of adaptations, or noise, and usefully distinguished the present usefulness of traits from their evolved functions (if any).[1]

The second building block of evolutionary psychology was the rise of the computational sciences and the recognition of the true character of mental phenomena. Boole (1848) and Frege (1879) formalized logic in such a way that it became possible to see how logical operations could be carried out mechanically, automatically, and hence through purely physical causation, without the need for an animate interpretive intelligence to carry out the steps. This raised the irresistible theoretical possibility that not only logic but other mental phenomena such as goals and learning also consisted of formal relationships embodied nonvitalistically in physical processes (Weiner, 1948). With the rise of information theory, the development of the first computers, and advances in neuroscience, it became widely understood that mental events consisted of transformations of

---

[1] The arguments that not every trait is an adaptation, not all beneficial effects of a trait are its functions, that phenotypes are full of by-products, and that there are constraints on developing systems were all central to Williams's 1966 critique of evolutionary biology. Thus, many of us were surprised when, 13 years later, Stephen Jay Gould and Richard Lewontin (1979) began to repeat the same critique without attribution, writing as if it were unknown to the evolutionary community they were criticizing. One striking difference between the two critiques was Williams's development of strict standards of evidence to distinguish adaptations from nonadaptations, rendering the issue a matter of empirical research rather than post hoc rhetoric.

structured informational relationships embodied as aspects of organized physical systems in the brain. This spreading appreciation constituted the cognitive revolution. The mental world was no longer a mysterious, indefinable realm, but locatable in the physical world in terms of precisely describable, highly organized causal relations.

Evolutionary psychology can therefore be seen as the inevitable intersection of the computationalism of the cognitive revolution with the adaptationism of Williams's evolutionary biology: Because mental phenomena are the expression of complex functional organization in biological systems, and complex organic functionality is the downstream consequence of natural selection, then it must be the case that the sciences of the mind and brain are adaptationist sciences, and psychological mechanisms are computational adaptations. In this way, the marriage of computationalism with adaptationism marks a major turning point in the history of ideas, dissolving the intellectual tethers that had limited fundamental progress and opening the way forward. Like Dalton's wedding of atomic theory to chemistry, computationalism and adaptationism solve each other's deepest problems, and open up new continents of scientific possibility (Cosmides & Tooby, 1987; Tooby & Cosmides, 1992; Tooby, Cosmides, & Barrett, 2003, 2005).

Sociologically speaking, the single most significant factor in triggering the renewed efforts to apply evolution to behavior was the selectionist revolution in evolutionary biology, which subsequently became known as sociobiology (Wilson, 1975). Across the world, biologists and allied researchers were electrified by the potential predictive and explanatory power of the new selectionist theories that were emerging, together with how elegantly and systematically they could be derived. Dynamic research communities formed at Oxford, Cambridge, Sussex, Michigan, Harvard, the University of California, and elsewhere. As a result of the flood of empirical and theoretical work coming out of these communities, the sociobiological revolution rapidly established itself in the biological journals as the dominant theoretical approach biologists apply to understanding the behavior of nonhumans—a position behavioral and social scientists are surprised to find that it occupies today.[2]

Under the sponsorship of Irven DeVore and E. O. Wilson, one of the most influential and dynamic of these communities gathered at Harvard. This research community fluoresced in DeVore's living room, where Harvard's Simian Seminar was held from the late 1960s through the mid-1980s. In this atmosphere of ongoing discovery, ideas and findings sparked each other in an endless chain reaction. A remarkable procession of figures in evolutionary biology, behavioral ecology, primatology, and ethology spoke at DeVore's Simian Seminar, participating in this chain reaction, and sometimes staying for protracted periods. These included George Williams, Bill Hamilton, John Maynard Smith, Ernst Mayr, Edward O.

---

[2] Intellectuals wedded to the blank slate generated an unslakable demand for seemingly authoritative dismissals of the new biology. As a result, the handful of biologists who were willing to ignore the data and supply these dismissals came to be seen as the authentic voices of scientific biology to the intellectual world at large (e.g., Gould & Lewontin, 1979). The decisive empirical success of the paradigm within biology itself—what Alcock (2001) calls "the triumph of sociobiology"—is largely unknown outside of the field, and the majority of nonbiologists labor under the misimpression that sociobiology was substantively discredited by "real" biologists.

Wilson, Richard Alexander, Richard Dawkins, Tim Clutton-Brock, Paul Harvey, Joseph Shepher, Lionel Tiger, Robin Fox, Diane Fosse, Jane Goodall, Richard Wrangham, Robert Hinde, Richard Leakey, Richard Lee, Stephen Jay Gould, Martin Daly, and Margo Wilson, and the editor of this *Handbook,* David Buss. Among the participating students who became transformed into active researchers in this environment were Bob Bailey, Peter Ellison, Steve Gaulin, Sarah Blaffer Hrdy, Melvin Konner, Jeff Kurland, Peter Rodman, Robert Sapolsky, John Seger, Barbara Smuts, Bob Trivers, and ourselves (John Tooby and Leda Cosmides).

While Wilson's contributions are deservedly famous through his books and publications, DeVore's intellectual impact is less well known because his ideas were realized through his students and colleagues. Deeply interested in human origins, DeVore pioneered three major research movements. He instigated and then championed the systematic study of primate social behavior under natural conditions (DeVore, 1965). With Chagnon, Irons, and others, he worked on applying the new selectionist biology to anthropological questions. He inaugurated the systematic, empirical investigation of living hunter-gatherers (Lee & DeVore, 1968, 1976).

DeVore and his colleague Richard Lee eschewed the "lone anthropologist" model (with its typological baggage), in which a single individual spends time documenting "the" culture of a people. In its place, they innovated a team-based approach like that found in other sciences. Their Kalahari San project brought scientists and scholars from a broad array of disciplines—anthropologists, demographers, physicians, linguists, folklorists, psychologists, ethologists, archeologists—in an attempt to document as completely as possible the behavior and lives of the !Kung San people in Botswana's Kalahari desert, before hunting and gathering as a way of life vanished forever from the planet. His goal in studying the San was to provide a detailed database that, when triangulated with other similarly detailed databases drawn from other hunter-gatherer groups, would allow new and powerful inferences to be made about the selection pressures that operated on hunter-gatherers to shape human design. Behavioral ecologists would be able to test optimal foraging models by matching foraging patterns to ecological conditions. Archaeologists could better interpret patterns found at ancestral sites by seeing patterns of campfires, animal remains, tool-making debris, and midden heaps produced by the social life of living hunter-gatherers. Physicians could gain insight into diseases of civilization by comparing diets and conditions in industrialized countries to the diets and stressors produced by a way of life that more closely resembles the conditions in which our species evolved. Developmental psychologists could gain insights into the mother-infant bond and human attachment by seeing the demands placed on infants and mothers in foraging contexts. Anthropologists could learn what social conditions foster risk pooling and food sharing; what kinds of knowledge hunter-gatherers have about animal behavior and plant life; how they use this knowledge in foraging; and how people negotiate the problems and opportunities of social life in a tiny community of interdependent, extended families (see, e.g., Lee & DeVore, 1976; Shostak, 1981). While commonplace now, these ideas were pathbreaking at the time. After all, if the human mind consists primarily of a general capacity to learn, then the particulars of the ancestral hunter-gatherer world and our prehuman history as Miocene apes left no interesting imprint on our design. In contrast, if our minds are collections of mechanisms designed to solve the adaptive problems posed by the ancestral world, then hunter-gatherer studies and primatology become indispensable sources of knowledge about modern human nature. DeVore's insistence on situating the operation of natural selection within the detailed contexts of hunter-gatherer and nonhuman primate life was a signal contribution to the application of the evolutionary sciences to humans.

Many members of the evolutionary research communities believed that the new selectionist theories straightforwardly applied to humans, although others continued to welcome the Standard Social Science Model arguments that learning had insulated human life from evolutionary patterning. Human behavior exhibited many patterns that offered ready selectionist interpretations (e.g., sex differences in the psychology of mating), but many other phenomena resisted easy interpretation and seemed to lack clear nonhuman analogues (e.g., morality, the arts, language, culture). The result was a rich and contradictory pluralism of ideas about how evolution relates to human affairs—a pluralism that is still with us.

One of the most widespread approaches to emerge is what might be called fitness teleology. Teleological explanations are found in Aristotle, and arguably constitute an evolved mode of interpretation built into the human mind. Humans find explaining things in terms of the ends they lead to intuitive and often sufficient (Baron-Cohen, 1995; Dennett, 1987; Leslie, 1987, 1994). Social science theories have regularly depended on explicitly or implicitly teleological thinking. Economics, for example, explains choice behavior not in terms of its antecedent physical or computational causes but in terms of how the behavior serves utility maximization. Of course, the scientific revolution originated in Renaissance mechanics, and seeks ultimately to explain everything (non-quantum mechanical) using forward physical causality—a very different explanatory system in which teleology is not admissible. Darwin outlined a physical process—natural selection—that produces biological outcomes that had once been attributed to natural teleological processes (Darwin, 1859). Williams (1966) mounted a systematic critique of the myriad ways teleology had nonetheless implicitly infected evolutionary biology (where it persists in Darwinian disguises). Computationalism assimilated the other notable class of apparently teleological behavior in the universe—the seeming goal directedness of living systems—to physical causation by showing how informational structures in a regulatory system can operate in a forward causal way (Weiner, 1948). The teleological end that seems to exist in the future as the point toward which things tend is in reality a regulatory process or representation in the organism in the present. The modern scientific claim would be that adaptationism and computationalism in combination can explain by forward physical causation all events that once would have been explained teleologically.

Yet, the implicit or explicit substrate underlying many attempts to apply Darwinism to human behavior was a return to the sense that human behavior was explained by the ends it serves. For a Darwinian, it was argued, choices, practices, culture, and institutions were explained to the extent that they could be interpreted as contributing to individual (or sometimes group) reproduction: That is, the explanation for human behavior is that it naturally tends toward the end of maximizing reproduction in the present and future. This theory—Darwinism transmuted into fitness teleology—parallels the economic view of individuals as selfish utility maximizers, except that Hamilton's (1964) concept of inclusive fitness is substituted for the economists' concept of utility. Both approaches assume that unbounded rationality is possible and that the mind is a general-purpose computer that can figure out, in any situation, what will maximize a given quantity over the long term (whether utility or children). Indeed, the concept of "learning" within the Standard Social Science Model itself tacitly invokes unbounded rationality, in that learning is the tendency of the general-purpose, equipotential mind to grow—by an unspecified and undiscovered computational means—whatever functional information-processing abilities it needs to serve its purposes, given time and experience in the task environment.

Evolutionary psychologists depart from fitness teleologists, traditional economists (but not neuroeconomists), and blank-slate learning theorists by arguing that neither human engineers nor evolution can build a computational device that exhibits these forms of unbounded rationality, because such architectures are impossible, even in principle (for arguments, see Cosmides & Tooby, 1987; Symons 1989, 1992; Tooby & Cosmides, 1990a, 1992). In any case, observed human behavior dramatically and systematically departs from the sociobiological predictions of generalized fitness striving (as well as the predictions of economic rationality and blank-slate learning abilities). To take one simple contrast, men will pay to have nonreproductive sex with prostitutes they believe and hope are contracepting, yet they have to be paid to contribute to sperm banks. More generally, across a range of wealthy nations, those able to afford more children choose to have fewer children—a striking disconfirmation of the prediction that humans teleologically seek to maximize reproduction or fitness (Vining, 1986). Human life is permeated with systematic deviations away from rationally maximized child-production and kin assistance.

For those eager to leap directly from theories of selection pressures to predictions of fitness maximization, there remains a missing level of causation and explanation: the informational or computational level. This level cannot be avoided if the application of Darwin's theory to humans is ever to achieve the necessary level of scientific precision. Natural selection does not operate on behavior per se; it operates on a systematically caused *relationship* between information and behavior. Running—a behavior—is neither good nor bad. Running away from a lion can promote survival and reproduction; running toward a lion will curtail both. To be adaptive, behavioral regulation needs to be functionally contingent on information; for example, *flee when you see a stalking lion.* But a systematic relationship between information and a behavioral response cannot occur unless some reliably developing piece of organic machinery causes it. These causal relations between information and behavior are created by neural circuits in the brain, which function as programs that process information. By altering the neural circuitry that develops, mutations can alter the information processing properties of these programs, creating alternative information-behavior relationships. Selection should retain or discard alternative circuit designs from a species' neural architecture on the basis of how well the information-behavior relationships they produce promote the propagation of the genetic bases of their designs. Those circuit designs that promote their own proliferation will be retained and spread, eventually becoming species-typical (or stably frequency-dependent); those that do not will eventually disappear from the population. The idea that the evolutionary causation of behavior would lead to rigid, inflexible behavior is the opposite of the truth: Evolved neural architectures are specifications of richly contingent systems for generating responses to informational inputs.

As a result of selection acting on information-behavior relationships, the human brain is predicted to be densely packed with programs that cause intricate relationships between information and behavior, including functionally specialized learning systems, domain-specialized rules of inference, default preferences that are adjusted by experience, complex decision rules, concepts that organize our experiences and databases of knowledge, and vast databases of acquired information stored in specialized memory systems—remembered episodes from our lives, encyclopedias of plant life and animal behavior, banks of information about other people's proclivities and preferences, and so on. All of these programs and the databases they create can be called on in different combinations to elicit a dazzling variety of behavioral responses. These responses are themselves information, subsequently ingested by the same evolved programs, in endless cycles that produce complex eddies, currents, and even singularities in cultural life. To get a genuine purchase on human behavior and society, researchers need to know the architecture of these evolved programs. Knowing the selection pressures will not be enough. Our behavior is not a direct response to selection pressures or to a "need" to increase our reproduction.

Hence, one of several reasons why evolutionary psychology is distinct from human sociobiology and other similar approaches lies in its rejection of fitness maximization as an explanation for behavior (Cosmides & Tooby, 1987; Daly & Wilson, 1988; Symons, 1987, 1989, 1992; Tooby & Cosmides, 1990a, 1992). The relative degree of fitness promotion under ancestral conditions is simply the design criterion by which alternative mutant designs were sorted in the evolutionary past. (The causal role fitness plays in the present is in glacially changing the relative frequencies of alternative designs with respect to future generations.) Although organisms sometimes appear to be pursuing fitness on behalf of their genes, in reality they are executing the evolved circuit logic built into their neural programs, whether this corresponds to current fitness maximization or not. Organisms are adaptation executers, not fitness pursuers. Mapping the computational architecture of the mechanisms will give a precise theory of behavior, while relying on predictions derived from fitness maximization will give a very impoverished and unreliable set of predictions about behavioral dynamics.

To summarize, evolutionary psychology's focus on psychological mechanisms as evolved programs was motivated by new developments from a series of different fields:

Advance 1: The cognitive revolution was providing, for the first time in human history, a precise language for describing mental mechanisms as programs that process information. Galileo's discovery that mathematics provided a precise language for expressing the mechanical and physical relationships enabled the birth of modern physics. Analogously, cognitive scientists' discovery that computational-informational formalisms provide a precise language for describing the design, properties, regulatory architecture, and operation of psychological mechanisms enables a modern science of mind (and its physical basis). Computational language is not just a convenience for modeling anything with complex dynamics. The brain's evolved function is computational—to use information to adaptively regulate the body and behavior—so computational and informational formalisms are by their nature the most appropriate to capture the functional design of behavior regulation.

Advance 2: Advances in paleoanthropology, hunter-gatherer studies, and primatology were providing data about the adaptive problems our ancestors had to solve to survive and reproduce and the environments in which they did so.

Advance 3: Research in animal behavior, linguistics, and neuropsychology was showing that the mind is not a blank slate, passively recording the world. Organisms come "factory-equipped" with knowledge about the world, which allows them to learn some relationships easily and others only with great effort, if at all. Skinner's hypothesis—that there is one simple learning process governed by reward and punishment—was wrong.

Advance 4: Evolutionary biology was revolutionized by being placed on a more rigorous, formal foundation of replicator dynamics, leading to the derivation of a diversity of powerful selectionist theories, and the analytic tools to recognize and differentiate adaptations, from by-products and stochastically generated evolutionary noise (Williams, 1966).

Ethology had brought together advances 2 and 3, sociobiology had connected advances 2 and 4, sometimes with 3; nativist cognitive science connected advances 1 and 3, but neglected and still shrinks from advances 2 and 4. Cognitive neuroscience partially and erratically accepts 1 and 3, but omits 2 and 4. Outside of cognitive approaches, the rest of psychology lacks much of advance 1, most of advance 3, and all of advances 2 and 4. Evolutionary anthropology appreciates advances 2 and 4, but neglects 1 and 3. Social anthropology and sociology lack all four. So it goes. If one counts the adaptationist/computationalist resolution of the nature-nurture issue as a critical advance, the situation is even bleaker.

We thought these new developments could be pieced together into an integrated framework that successfully addressed the difficulties that had plagued evolutionary and nonevolutionary approaches alike. The reason why the synthesis had not emerged earlier in the century was because the connections between the key concepts ran between fields rather than cleanly within them. Consequently, relatively few were in the fortunate position of being professionally equipped to see all the connections at once. This limited the field's initial appeal, because what seems self-evident from the synoptic vantage point seems esoteric, pedantic, or cultish from other vantage points. Nevertheless, we and those working along similar lines were confident that by bringing all four advances together, the evolutionary sciences could be united with the cognitive revolution in a way that provided a framework not only for psychology but for all of the social and behavioral sciences. To signal its distinctiveness from other approaches, the field was named *evolutionary psychology.*[3]

[3] We sometimes read that evolutionary psychology is simply sociobiology, with the name changed to avoid the bad political press that sociobiology had received. Although it is amusing (given the record) to be accused of ducking controversy, these claims are historically and substantively wrong. In the first place, evolutionary psychologists are generally admirers and defenders of sociobiology (or behavioral ecology, or evolutionary ecology). It has been the most useful and most sophisticated branch of modern evolutionary biology, and several have made contributions to this literature. Nonetheless, the lengthy and intense debates about how to apply evolution to behavior made it increasingly clear that markedly opposed views needed different labels if any theoretical and empirical project was to be clearly understood. In the 1980s, Martin Daly, Margo Wilson, Don Symons, John Tooby, Leda Cosmides, and David Buss had many discussions about what to call this new field, some at Daly and Wilson's kangaroo rat field site in Palm Desert, some in Santa Barbara,

EVOLUTIONARY PSYCHOLOGY

Like cognitive scientists, when evolutionary psychologists refer to the *mind,* they mean the set of information processing devices, embodied in neural tissue, that is responsible for all conscious and nonconscious mental activity, that generates all behavior, and that regulates the body. Like other psychologists, evolutionary psychologists test hypotheses about the design of these computational devices using methods from, for example, cognitive psychology, social psychology, developmental psychology, experimental economics, cognitive neuroscience, genetics, psysiological psychology, and cross-cultural field work.

The primary tool that allows evolutionary psychologists to go beyond traditional psychologists in studying the mind is that they take full advantage in their research of an overlooked reality: The programs comprising the human mind were designed by natural selection to solve the adaptive problems regularly faced by our hunter-gatherer ancestors—problems such as finding a mate, cooperating with others, hunting, gathering, protecting children, navigating, avoiding predators, avoiding exploitation, and so on. Knowing this allows evolutionary psychologists to approach the study of the mind like an engineer. You start by carefully specifying an adaptive information processing problem; then you do a task analysis of that problem. A task analysis consists of identifying what properties a program would have to have to solve that problem well. This approach allows you to generate hypotheses about the structure of the programs that comprise the mind, which can then be tested.

From this point of view, there are precise causal connections that link the four developments discussed earlier into a coherent framework for thinking about human nature and society (Tooby & Cosmides, 1992):

C-1: Each organ in the body evolved to serve a function: The intestines digest, the heart pumps blood, and the liver detoxifies poisons. The brain's evolved function is to extract information from the environment and use that information to generate behavior and regulate physiology. Hence, the brain is not just like a computer. It is a computer—that is, a physical system that was designed to process information (Advance 1). Its programs were designed not by an engineer, but by natural selection, a causal process that retains and discards design features based on how well they solved adaptive problems in past environments (Advance 4).

The fact that the brain processes information is not an accidental side effect of some metabolic process. The brain was designed by natural selection *to be* a computer. Therefore, if you want to describe its operation in a way that captures its evolved function, you need to think of it as composed of programs that

---

and some at the Center for Advanced Study in the Behavioral Sciences. Politics and the press did not enter these discussions, and we anticipated (correctly) that the same content-free ad hominem attacks would pursue us throughout our careers. What we *did* discuss was that this new field focused on psychology—on characterizing the adaptations comprising the psychological architecture—whereas sociobiology had not. Sociobiology had focused mostly on selectionist theories, with no consideration of the computational level and little interest in mapping psychological mechanisms. Both the subject matter of evolutionary psychology and the theoretical commitments were simply different from that of sociobiology, in the same way that sociobiology was quite different from the ethology that preceded it and cognitive psychology was different from behaviorist psychology—necessitating a new name in each case.

process information. The question then becomes: What programs are to be found in the human brain? What are the reliably developing, species-typical programs that, taken together, comprise the human mind?

C-2: Individual behavior is generated by this evolved computer, in response to information that it extracts from the internal and external environment (including the social environment, Advance 1). To understand an individual's behavior, therefore, you need to know both the information that the person registered *and* the structure of the programs that generated his or her behavior.

C-3: The programs that comprise the human brain were sculpted over evolutionary time by the ancestral environments and selection pressures experienced by the hunter-gatherers from whom we are descended (Advances 2 and 4). Each evolved program exists because it produced behavior that promoted the survival and reproduction of our ancestors better than alternative programs that arose during human evolutionary history. Evolutionary psychologists emphasize hunter-gatherer life because the evolutionary process is slow—it takes thousands of generations to build a program of any complexity. The industrial revolution—even the agricultural revolution—is too brief a period to have selected for complex new cognitive programs.[4]

C-4: Although the behavior our evolved programs generate would, on average, have been adaptive (reproduction promoting) in ancestral environments, there is no guarantee that it will be so now. Modern environments differ importantly from ancestral ones, particularly when it comes to social behavior. We no longer live in small, face-to-face societies, in seminomadic bands of 20 to 100 people, many of whom were close relatives. Yet, our cognitive programs were designed for that social world.

C-5: Perhaps most importantly, natural selection will ensure that the brain is composed of many different programs, many (or all) of which will be specialized for solving their own corresponding adaptive problems. That is, the evolutionary process will not produce a predominantly general-purpose, equipotential, domain-general architecture (Advance 3).

In fact, this is a ubiquitous engineering outcome. The existence of recurrent computational problems leads to functionally specialized application software. For example, the demand for effective word processing and good digital music playback led to different application programs because many of the design features that make a program an effective word processing program are different from those that make a program a good digital music player. Indeed, the greater the number of functionally specialized programs (or subroutines) your computer has installed, the more intelligent your computer is, and the more things it can accomplish. The same is true for organisms. Armed with this insight, we can lay to rest the myth that the more evolved organization the human mind has, the more inflexible its response. Interpreting the emotional expressions of others, seeing beauty, learning language, loving your child—all these enhancements to human mental life are made possible by specialized neural programs built by natural selection.

---

[4] Unidimensional traits, caused by quantitative genetic variation (e.g., taller, shorter), can be adjusted in less time; see Tooby & Cosmides, 1990b.

To survive and reproduce reliably as a hunter-gatherer required the solution of a large and diverse array of adaptive information-processing problems. These ranged from predator vigilance and prey stalking to plant gathering, mate selection, childbirth, parental care, coalition formation, and disease avoidance. Design features that make a program good at choosing nutritious foods, for example, are ill suited for finding a fertile mate or recognizing free riders. Some sets of problems would have required differentiated computational solutions.

The demand for diverse computational designs can be clearly seen when results from evolutionary theory (Advance 4) are combined with data about ancestral environments (Advance 2) to model different ancestral computational problems. The design features necessary for solving one problem are usually markedly different from the features required to construct programs capable of solving another adaptive problem. For example, game theoretic analyses of conditional helping show that programs designed for logical reasoning would be poorly designed for detecting cheaters in social exchange and vice versa; this incommensurability selected for programs that are functionally specialized for reasoning about reciprocity or exchange (Cosmides & Tooby, Chapter 20, this volume).

C-6: Finally, descriptions of the computational architecture of our evolved mechanisms allows a systematic understanding of cultural and social phenomena. The mind is not like a video camera, passively recording the world but imparting no content of its own. Domain-specific programs organize our experiences, create our inferences, inject certain recurrent concepts and motivations into our mental life, give us our passions, and provide cross-culturally universal frames of meaning that allow us to understand the actions and intentions of others. They invite us to think certain kinds of thoughts; they make certain ideas, feelings, and reactions seem reasonable, interesting, and memorable. Consequently, they play a key role in determining which ideas and customs will easily spread from mind to mind and which will not (Boyer, 2001; Sperber, 1994, 1996; Tooby & Cosmides, 1992). That is, they play a crucial role in shaping human culture.

Instincts are often thought of as the opposite of reasoning, decision making, and learning. But the reasoning, decision-making, and learning programs that evolutionary psychologists have been discovering (1) are complexly specialized for solving an adaptive problem, (2) reliably develop in all normal human beings, (3) develop without any conscious effort and in the absence of formal instruction, (4) are applied without any awareness of their underlying logic, and (5) are distinct from more general abilities to process information or behave intelligently. In other words, they have all the hallmarks of what we usually think of as instinct (Pinker, 1994). In fact, we can think of these specialized circuits as instincts: *reasoning instincts, decision instincts, motivational instincts, and learning instincts*. They make certain kinds of inferences and decisions just as easy, effortless, and natural to us as humans as catching flies is to a frog or burrowing is to a mole.

Consider this example from the work of Simon Baron-Cohen (1995). Like adults, normal 4-year-olds easily and automatically note eye direction in others, and use it to make inferences about the mental states of the gazer. For example, 4-year-olds, like adults, infer that when presented with an array of candy, the gazer wants the particular candy he or she is looking at. Children with autism do not make this inference. Although children with this developmental disorder can compute eye direction correctly, they cannot use that information to infer what someone wants. Normal individuals know, spontaneously and with no mental effort, that the person wants the candy he or she is looking at. This is so obvious to us that it hardly seems to require an inference at all. It is just common sense. But "common sense" is caused: It is produced by cognitive mechanisms. To infer a mental state (wanting) from information about eye direction requires a computation. There is an inference circuit—a reasoning instinct—that produces this inference. When the circuit that does this computation is broken or fails to develop, the inference cannot be made. Those with autism fail this task because they lack this reasoning instinct, even though they often acquire very sophisticated competences of other sorts. If the mind consisted of a domain-general knowledge acquisition system, narrow impairments of this kind would not be possible.

Instincts are invisible to our intuitions, even as they generate them. They are no more accessible to consciousness than our retinal cells and line detectors but are just as important in manufacturing our perceptions of the world. As a species, we have been blind to the existence of these instincts, not because we lack them but precisely because they work so well. Because they process information so effortlessly and automatically, their operation disappears unnoticed into the background. Moreover, these instincts structure our thought and experience so powerfully we mistake their products for features of the external world: Color, beauty, status, friendship, charm—all are computed by the mind and then experienced as if they were objective properties of the objects they are attributed to. These mechanisms limit our sense of behavioral possibility to choices people commonly make, shielding us from seeing how complex and regulated the mechanics of choice is. Indeed, these mechanisms make it difficult to imagine how things could be otherwise. As a result, we take normal behavior for granted: We do not realize that normal behavior needs to be explained at all.

As behavioral scientists, we need corrective lenses to overcome our instinct blindness. The brain is fantastically complex, packed with programs, most of which are currently unknown to science. Theories of adaptive function can serve as corrective lenses for psychologists, allowing us to see computational problems that are invisible to human intuition. When carefully thought out, these functional theories can lead us to look for programs in the brain that no one had previously suspected.

PRINCIPLES OF ORGANIC DESIGN

Biology is the study of organisms, and psychology is—in a fundamental sense—a branch of biology. It is the study of the evolved designs of the behavior-regulating tissues of organisms. To be effective researchers, psychologists will need to become at least minimally acquainted with the principles of organic design.

NATURAL SELECTION IS AN ENGINEER THAT DESIGNS ORGANIC MACHINES

The phenomenon that Darwin was trying to explain is the presence of functional organization in living systems—the kind of organization found in artifacts, such as clocks, spectacles, or carriages; indeed, the kind of organization that appeared to be designed by an intelligent engineer to solve a problem. Darwin realized that organisms can be thought of as *self-reproducing machines*. What distinguishes living from nonliving machines is reproduction: the presence in a machine of devices (organized components) that cause it to produce new and similarly reproducing machines. Given a population of living machines, this property—self-reproduction—drives a system of positive and negative feedback—natural selection—that can explain the remarkable fit between the design of organisms and the problems they must solve to survive and reproduce.

In contrast to human-made machines, which are designed by inventors, living machines acquire their intricate functional design over immense lengths of time, as a consequence of the fact that they reproduce themselves. Indeed, modern Darwinism has an elegant deductive structure that logically follows from Darwin's initial insight that reproduction is the defining property of life:

When an organism reproduces, genes that cause the development of its design features are introduced into its offspring. But the replication of the design of the parental machine is not always error free. As a result, randomly modified designs (i.e., mutants) are introduced into populations of reproducers. Because living machines are already exactingly organized so that they cause the otherwise improbable outcome of constructing offspring machines, random modifications will usually introduce disruptions into the complex sequence of actions necessary for self-reproduction. Consequently, most newly modified but now defective designs will remove themselves from the population: a case of negative feedback.

However, a small number of these random design modifications will, by chance, improve the system's machinery for causing its own reproduction. Such improved designs (by definition) cause their own increasing frequency in the population: a case of positive feedback.

This increase continues until (usually) such modified designs outreproduce and thereby replace the alternative designs in the population, leading to a new species-standard (or population-standard) design: a new retinal design, or blood cell, or reasoning circuit, or food preference ordering. After such an event, the population of reproducing machines is different from the ancestral population. The population has taken a step "uphill" toward a greater degree of functional organization for reproduction than it had previously. Over the long run, down chains of descent, this feedback cycle pushes designs through state-space toward increasingly well-engineered—and increasingly improbable—functional arrangements. These arrangements are *functional* in a specific sense: The elements are well organized to cause their own reproduction in the environment in which the species evolved.

For example, if a mutation appeared that caused individuals to find family members sexually repugnant, they would be less likely to conceive children incestuously. They would produce children with fewer genetic diseases, and more of these children would mature and reproduce than would the children of those who were not averse to incest. Such an incest-avoiding design would produce a larger set of healthy children every generation, down the generations. By promoting the reproduction of its bearers, the incest-avoiding circuit thereby promotes its own spread over the generations, until it eventually replaces the earlier-model sexual circuitry and becomes a universal feature of that species' design. This spontaneous feedback process—natural selection—causes functional organization to emerge naturally, without the intervention of an intelligent designer or supernatural forces.

Genes and Design   Self-reproducing systems could not exist unless there were adaptations that conserved the functional design against entropy from one generation to the next. Genes are the means by which functional design features replicate themselves from parent to offspring. They can be thought of as particles of design. These elements are transmitted from parent to offspring and together with stable features of an environment, cause the organism to develop some design features and not others. Genes have two primary ways they can propagate themselves: by increasing the probability that offspring will be produced by the organism in which they are situated or by increasing reproduction in others who are more likely than random members of the population to carry the same gene.

An individual's genetic relatives carry some of the same genes, by virtue of having received some of the same genes from a recent common ancestor. Thus, a gene in an individual that causes an increase in the reproductive rate of that individual's kin will, by so doing, tend to increase its own frequency in the population. A circuit that motivates individuals to help feed their sisters and brothers, if they are in sufficiently greater need, is an example of a program that increases kin reproduction. As Hamilton (1964) pointed out, design features that promote both direct reproduction and kin reproduction and that make efficient trade-offs between the two will replace those that do not (a process called *kin selection*).

Reproduction and Function   How well a design feature systematically promotes direct and kin reproduction is the bizarre but real engineering criterion determining whether a specific design feature will be added to or discarded from a species' design.

The concept of *adaptive behavior* can now be defined with precision. Adaptive behavior, in the evolutionary sense, is behavior that tended to promote the net lifetime reproduction of the individual or that individual's genetic relatives. By promoting the replication of the genes that built them, circuits that—systematically and over many generations—cause adaptive behavior become incorporated into a species' neural design. In contrast, behavior that undermines the reproduction of the individual or his or her genetic relatives removes the circuits causing those behaviors from the species. Such behavior is maladaptive.

Evolutionists analyze how design features are organized (in ancestral environments) to contribute to the propagation of their genetic basis because gene propagation was the final causal pathway through which a functionally improved design feature caused itself to increase in frequency until it became standard equipment in all ordinary members of the species.

Adaptive Problems Select for Adaptations   Darwin's detailed studies of plants and animals revealed complex structures composed of parts that appeared to be organized to overcome reproductive obstacles (e.g., the presence of predators) or to take advantage of reproductive opportunities (e.g., the presence of fertile mates). Enduring conditions in the world that create reproductive opportunities or obstacles constitute *adaptive problems*, such as the presence of pathogens, variance in the food supply, the vulnerability of infants, or the presence of family in an individual's social group. Adaptive problems have two defining characteristics. First, they are conditions or cause-and-effect relationships that many or most individual ancestors encountered, reappearing again and again during the evolutionary history of the species, giving natural selection enough time to design adaptations in response. Second, they are that subset of enduring relationships that could, in principle, be exploited by some property of an organism to increase its reproduction or the reproduction of its relatives. Alternative designs are retained or discarded by natural selection on the basis of how well they function as solutions to adaptive problems.

Over evolutionary time, more and more design features accumulate to form an integrated structure or device that is well engineered to solve its particular adaptive problem. Such a structure or device is called an *adaptation.* Indeed, an organism can be thought of as a collection of adaptations, together with the engineering by-products of adaptations, and evolutionary noise. The functional subcomponents of the ear, hand, intestines, uterus, or circulatory system are examples. Each of these adaptations exists in the human design now because it contributed to the process of direct and kin reproduction in the ancestral past. Adaptive problems are the only kind of problem that natural selection can design machinery for solving.

The Environment of Evolutionary Adaptedness   One key to understanding the functional architecture of the mind is to remember that its programs were not selected for because they solved the problems faced by modern humans. Instead, they were shaped by how well they solved adaptive problems among our hunter-gatherer ancestors. The second key is to understand that the developmental processes that build each program, as well as each program in its mature state, evolved to use information and conditions that were reliably present in ancestral environments. The design of each adaptation assumes the presence of certain background conditions and operates as a successful problem solver only when those conditions are met. The *environment of evolutionary adaptedness* (EEA) refers jointly to the problems hunter-gatherers had to solve and the conditions under which they solved them (including their developmental environment).

Although the hominid line is thought to have originated on edges of the African savannahs, the EEA is not a particular place or time. The EEA for a given adaptation is the statistical composite of the enduring selection pressures or cause-and-effect relationships that pushed the alleles underlying an adaptation systematically upward in frequency until they became species-typical or reached a frequency-dependent equilibrium (most adaptations are species-typical; see Hagen, Chapter 5, this volume). Because the coordinated fixation of alleles at different loci takes time, complex adaptations reflect enduring features of the ancestral world. The adaptation is the consequence of the EEA, and so the structure of the adaptation reflects the structure of the EEA. The adaptation evolved so that when it interacted with the stable features of the ancestral task environment, their interaction systematically promoted fitness (i.e., solves an adaptive problem). The concept of the EEA is essential to Darwinism, but its formalization was prompted by the evolutionary analysis of humans because human environments have changed more dramatically than the environments most other species occupy. The research problems faced by most biologists do not require them to distinguish the modern environment from a species' ancestral environment. Because adaptations evolved and assumed their modern form at different times and because different aspects of the environment were relevant to the design of each, the EEA for one adaptation may be somewhat different from the EEA for another. Conditions of terrestrial illumination, which form (part of) the EEA for the vertebrate eye, remained relatively constant for hundreds of millions of years—and can still be observed by turning off all artificial lights. In contrast, the social and foraging conditions that formed (part of) the EEA that selected for neural programs that cause human males to provision and care for their offspring (under certain conditions) is almost certainly less than two million years old.

When a program is operating outside the envelope of ancestral conditions that selected for its design, it may look like a poorly engineered problem solver. Efficient foraging, for example, requires good probability judgments, yet laboratory data suggested that people are poor intuitive statisticians, incapable of making simple inferences about conditional probabilities (Kahneman, Slovic, & Tversky, 1982). Evolutionary psychologists recognized that these findings were problematic, given that birds and insects solve similar problems with ease. The paradox evaporates when you consider the EEA for probability judgment. Behavioral ecologists presented birds and bees with information in ecologically valid formats; psychologists studying humans were not.

Being mindful of the EEA concept changes how research is designed and what is discovered. Giving people probability information in the form of absolute frequencies—an ecologically valid format for hunter-gatherers—reveals the presence of mechanisms that generate sound Bayesian inferences (Brase, Cosmides, & Tooby, 1998; Cosmides & Tooby, 1996; Gigerenzer, 1991; Gigerenzer, Todd, & the ABC Group, 1999). Indeed, EEA-minded research on judgment under uncertainty is now showing that the human mind is equipped with a toolbox of "fast-and-frugal heuristics," each designed to make well-calibrated judgments quickly on the basis of limited information (Gigerenzer & Selten, 2002; Gigerenzer, Todd, & the ABC Group, 1999; Todd, Hertwig, & Hoffrage, Chapter 27, this volume). These procedures are *ecologically rational,* providing good solutions when operating in the task environments for which they evolved (Tooby & Cosmides, in press).

Knowing the Past   It is often argued that we can know nothing about the past that is relevant to psychology because behavior doesn't fossilize. Thus, the whole field of evolutionary psychology is claimed to rest on uncertain speculation or conjecture. In reality, we know with certainty thousands of important things about our ancestors and the world they inhabited, many of which can be useful in guiding psychological research. Some of these should be obvious, although their implications may not be. For example, it is a certainty that our ancestors lived in a world in which certain principles of physics governed the motions of objects: facts that allowed Shepard (1984, 1987) to discover how the mind represents the motion of objects, both in perception and imagination. It is equally certain that hominids had eyes, looked at what interested them, and absorbed information about what they were looking at, making eye-gaze direction informative to onlookers: facts that helped Baron-Cohen (1995) to create a far-reaching research program on the cognitive basis of mind-reading, the ability to infer the mental states of others. It is certain that our ancestors, like other Old World primates, nursed; had two sexes; chose mates; had color vision calibrated to the spectral properties of sunlight; lived in a biotic environment with predatory cats, venomous snakes, and spiders; were predated on; bled when wounded; were incapacitated from injuries; were vulnerable to a large variety of parasites and pathogens; and had deleterious recessives rendering them subject to inbreeding depression if they mated with siblings. All of these conditions are known, and all pose adaptive problems. By considering these selection pressures, a careful, intelligent thinker can develop plausible, testable theories of the adaptations that arose in response to them. Selection would not plausibly have built an equipotential cognitive architecture that had to encounter the world as if it were unprepared for functionally significant sets of evolutionarily recurrent relationships. It is remarkable that such a model is so vigorously defended.

By triangulating the work of researchers in many disciplines, many other sound inferences can be made. Evolutionary psychologists, behavioral ecologists, and evolutionary biologists have already created a library of sophisticated models of the selection pressures, strategies, and trade-offs that characterize fundamental adaptive problems (Advance 4), which they use in studying processes of attention, memory, decision making, and learning in nonhuman animals. Which model is applicable for a given species depends on certain key life-history parameters. Findings from paleoanthropology, hunter-gatherer archaeology, and studies of living hunter-gatherer populations locate humans in this theoretical landscape by filling in the critical parameter values (Advance 2). Ancestral hominids were ground-living primates; omnivores,[5] exposed to a wide variety of plant toxins and meat-borne bacteria and fungi; they had a sexual division of labor involving differential rates of hunting and gathering. They were mammals with altricial young, long periods of biparental investment in offspring, enduring male-female mateships, and an extended period of physiologically obligatory female investment in pregnancy and lactation. They were a long-lived, low-fecundity species in which variance in male reproductive success was higher than variance in female reproductive success. They lived in small, nomadic, kin-based bands often of 20 to 100; they would rarely (if ever) have seen more than 1,000 people at one time; they had only modest opportunities to store provisions for the future; they engaged in cooperative hunting, defense, and aggressive coalitions; and they made tools and engaged in extensive amounts of cooperative reciprocation. When these parameters are combined with formal models from evolutionary biology and behavioral ecology, a reasonably consistent picture of ancestral life begins to appear (e.g., Tooby & DeVore, 1987). From this, researchers can refine theories of adaptive problems, develop models of their computational requirements, and test for the presence of mechanisms equipped with design features that satisfy these requirements. Most chapters in this volume provide examples of this process.

Many adaptive problems can be further illuminated by the application of evolutionary theory (see, e.g., Cosmides & Tooby, Chapter 20, this volume). For example, variance in the food supply can be buffered through food sharing, a method of pooling risk, which is stable only when the variance is primarily due to luck rather than effort. Studies of modern hunter-gatherers have allowed quantitative estimates of how much variance there is in successfully finding different kinds of foods; for example, among the Ache of Paraguay, meat and honey are high-variance foods even for skilled foragers, whereas the variance in gathering vegetable foods is low and comes from effort rather than luck. As might be pre-

---

[5] Fossil sites show extensive processing sites for animal products. Large East African woodland primates hunt and eat meat. Hunter-gatherers are observed to get a major fraction of their diet from hunting. Hunting is a dispropoportionately male activity not only in humans but in chimpanzees and baboons.

dicted from an analysis of the adaptive problems posed by variance in the food supply, Ache hunter-gatherers risk-pool with meat and honey by sharing widely at the band level, but they share gathered vegetable foods only within nuclear families (Kaplan & Hill, 1985). This analysis suggests that our minds house at least two different decision rules for sharing, each creating a different sense of what is appropriate or fair, and each triggered by a different experience of variance. This, in turn, led to the successful prediction that we have mechanisms designed to be effectively calibrated to variance and its causes (e.g., Rode, Cosmides, Hell, & Tooby, 1999; Wang, 2002).

Although behavioral scientists can be certain about a huge inventory of facts about the ancestral world that have not yet been harnessed to guide psychological research, certainty about the past is not necessary for building better hypotheses. We can derive valuable experimental hypotheses from possible rather than certain features of the ancestral world. At worst, such a hypothesis is no more likely to be falsified than the hypotheses advanced by nonevolutionary researchers, who have no principled source from which to derive their hypotheses. There are also many features of the ancestral world about which we are completely ignorant: These features simply do not form the basis for experiments.

Psychology Is Reverse Engineering

As engineers go, natural selection is superlative. It has produced exquisitely engineered biological machines—the vertebrate eye, the four-chambered heart, the liver, and the immune system—whose performance at solving problems is unrivaled by any machine yet designed by humans. (Consider the poor quality of machine vision compared to evolved vision, artificial pacemakers compared to the evolved system regulating the heart, pharmaceuticals with their negative side effects compared to the body's immune and detoxification systems.)

Psychologists—evolutionary or otherwise—are engineers working in reverse. The human neural architecture is a complex functional system, composed of programs whose design was engineered by natural selection to solve specific adaptive problems. Our job is to reverse-engineer its components: to dissect its computational architecture into functionally isolable information processing units—programs—and to determine how these units operate, both computationally and physically. To arrive at the appropriate construal, the cognitive architecture must be conceptualized as a set of parts designed to interact in such a way that they solve adaptive problems. This conceptualization requires theories of adaptive function—engineering specifications that provide analyses of what would count as good design for a particular problem. In so doing, they also provide the criteria necessary to decide whether a property of an organism is a design feature, a functionless by-product, or noise.

Many Properties of Organisms Are Not Adaptations   The cross-generationally recurrent design of an organism can be partitioned into (1) adaptations, which are present because they were selected for, (2) by-products of adaptations, which were not themselves targets of selection but are present because they are causally coupled to or produced by traits that were, and (3) noise, which was injected by the stochastic components of evolution. Consider, for example, that all brain-intact persons learn to speak (or sign) the language of their surrounding community without explicit instruction, whereas reading and writing require explicit schooling, are not mastered by every individual, and are entirely absent from some cultures. The neural programs that allow humans to acquire and use spoken language are adaptations, specialized by selection for that task (Pinker, 1994; Pinker & Bloom, 1990). But once an information processing mechanism exists, it can be deployed in activities that are unrelated to its original function. Because we have evolved learning mechanisms that cause language acquisition, we can, through laborious study and schooling, learn to write and read. But the learning mechanisms that enable these activities were not selected for *because* they caused reading and writing. The ability to read and write are by-products of adaptations for spoken language, enabled by their causal structure. Random evolutionary noise exists as well, for example, the gene variants that cause dyslexia (difficulties with learning to read).

Adaptations are present because of a prior history of selection. They are not defined as any ability or trait, however rare or modern, that is beneficial by virtue of enabling a particular individual to have more children. Suppose, for example, that a computer programmer were to become wealthy through writing code and used that wealth to have many children. This would not make computer programming, which is a very recent cultural invention, an adaptation, nor would it mean that the cognitive mechanisms that enable computer programming are adaptations designed for producing computer programs. The ability to write code is a beneficial side effect of cognitive adaptations that arose to solve entirely different problems, ones that promoted reproduction in an ancestral past.[6]

Thus, although selection creates functional organization, not all traits of organisms are functional. In fact, most "parts" of an organism are not functional for a simple reason: Most ways of conceptually dissecting a species' phenotype into parts will fail to capture functional components.[7] To see the organization that exists in a complex system, researchers need to be able to distinguish its functional components from the by-products and noise.

With a well-specified theory of an adaptive problem, researchers can identify functional and nonfunctional parts of an organism. Of the three kinds of properties, adaptations are the most important and illuminating because they explain why a system has certain parts, why these participate in certain cause-and-effect relationships with one another, and why they interact with the world in the way that they do. Adaptations are problem-solving machines and can be identified using design evidence. This entails probability judgments about the degree to

---

[6] In the case of computer programming, these adaptations might include the numerical abilities that underwrite foraging (Wynn, 1998), recursion for producing metarepresentations (Leslie, 1987), grammatical mechanisms (Pinker, 1994), certain deductive capacities (Rips, 1994), and so on. To determine which adaptations underwrite the ability to program computers would require cognitive experimentation aimed at discovering which information processing mechanisms are activated when someone is engaged in this evolutionarily novel activity. Moreover, different constellations of mechanisms might be activated when different individuals program, precisely because there has not been enough time for natural selection to produce an integrated design specifically for this purpose.

[7] Imagine you are looking inside a television and considering ways to conceptually divide its innards into parts. A random parsing is unlikely to isolate the functional units that allow a TV to transduce electromagnetic radiation into a color bitmap (its function). Indeed, most ways of dividing its insides will fail to capture *any* functional components, and any such nonfunctional "parts" will be by-products of the functional ones (Hagen, Chapter 5, this volume).

which a set of design features nonrandomly solve an independently defined ancestral adaptive problem.

Design Evidence

To determine a system's adaptive function, researchers need to produce evidence of a fit between its design and the proposed function. This requires the application of engineering standards. As an analogy, consider the relation between design and function in human-made artifacts. A ceramic mug is made of an insulating material that does not dissolve or melt when it contacts hot drinks; its shape stably contains about 8 ounces of liquid while allowing a mouth access to it; and it has a heat-dissipating handle. These properties of a mug are *design features:* properties that exist *because* they are good solutions to the problem of drinking hot beverages without burning your hands.

These properties are unlikely to occur together by chance. Moreover, other uses to which mugs are put (e.g., paperweights, pencil holders) neither predict nor explain these features (paperweights need only be heavy; pencil holders must have a containing shape, but many materials will do and no handle is needed). A mug can produce many beneficial effects, but only one of these is its function, that is, the explanation for its design. We can tell which design explanation is correct by analyzing the fit between the mug's design and a proposed function. Mugs have many interlocking properties that are good solutions to the problem of drinking hot drinks, and their properties are poorly explained by alternative theories of their function; that is how we know that they were designed for that function. The more complex the architecture, the more powerful design evidence can be. For example, there are many design features that can decide whether a toaster was intended to be a vehicle, a nutrient, a cleaner, a geological accident, or a means for toasting slices of bread.

In the same way, design evidence is criterial for claiming that a property of an organism is an adaptation, whether that property is a knee, a heart, or a neural circuit that processes information. Does the organic machinery in question have properties that cause it to solve an adaptive problem precisely, reliably, and economically? If not, then its ability to solve the problem at issue may be incidental, a side effect of a system that is well designed to perform some alternative adaptive function (Williams, 1966). For example, zoologists found that nocturnal bats have a sonar system with many of the same intricate and interlocking features of human-engineered sonar and radar systems, including features that make bat sonar a good design for finding insects and avoiding obstacles at night (e.g., higher pulse rates when hunting small moving targets than when cruising; for discussion, see Dawkins, 1986). At the same time, bat sonar is poorly suited for solving most other problems (e.g., judging the relative ripeness of fruit during the day). And there is no physical law or general metabolic process that produces bat sonar as a side effect.

Finding and pursuing small flying food items in the dark without crashing into things pose intricate computational problems, which very few arrangements of matter can solve. The bat's sonar solves these problems well. There is a tight fit between the problems' requirements and the evolved solution. It is by virtue of this excellence in design that we recognize finding insects and avoiding obstacles at night as the adaptive function of bat sonar.

Researchers can identify an aspect of an organism's physical, developmental, or psychological structure—its phenotype—as an adaptation by showing that (1) it has many design features that are improbably well suited to solving an ancestral adaptive problem, (2) these phenotypic properties are unlikely to have arisen by chance alone, and (3) they are not better explained as the by-product of mechanisms designed to solve some alternative adaptive problem or some more inclusive class of adaptive problem. Finding that a reliably developing feature of the species' architecture solves an adaptive problem with reliability, precision, efficiency, and economy is prima facie evidence that an adaptation has been located. This is like showing that an oddly shaped piece of metal easily opens the lock on your front door. It is almost certainly a key designed for your door because door locks are not easily opened by random bits of metal, by can openers or candlesticks, or even by keys designed for other doors.

To show that something is a by-product, researchers must first establish that something else is an adaptation (e.g., blood as an oxygen transport system) and then show how the feature is a side effect of the adaptation (e.g., the redness of blood is a side effect of the oxygen-carrying iron in hemoglobin). Features that are uncoordinated with functional demands are evolutionary noise (e.g., the locations of flecks of color in the eye).

THEORIES OF GOOD DESIGN ARE A HEURISTIC FOR DISCOVERY

If design evidence were important only for explaining why known properties of organisms have the form that they do (i.e., why the lens of the eye is transparent rather than opaque), its use in psychology would be limited. After all, most properties of the human mind are currently unknown. The concept of good design for solving an adaptive problem is important because it allows researchers to discover new mechanisms within the human mind. There is a systematic method for using theories of adaptive function and principles of good design for discovering new programs.

One starts with an adaptive problem encountered by human ancestors, including what information would potentially have been present in past environments for solving that problem. From the model of an adaptive problem, the researcher develops a task analysis of the kinds of computations necessary for solving that problem, concentrating on what would count as a well-designed program given the adaptive function under consideration. Based on this task analysis, hypotheses can be formulated about what kinds of programs might actually have evolved. Next, their presence can be tested for experimentally, using methods from cognitive, social, and developmental psychology, cognitive neuroscience/neuropsychology, experimental economics, cross-cultural studies—whatever methods are most appropriate for illuminating programs with the hypothesized properties. If the predicted design features are found, tests can be conducted to make sure they are not better explained by alternative hypotheses about the programs responsible. Testing includes making sure the program in question is distributed cross-culturally in the way predicted by the theory, which may predict universality, different expressions triggered by different environmental or social conditions, or local calibration by specific circumstances.

Research on the architecture of kin detection in humans provides an example of how this process of discovery can work (Lieberman et al., 2003, in press-a, in press-b, in press-c). Avoiding the deleterious effects of inbreeding was an important adaptive problem faced by our hominid ancestors. The best way to avoid the costs of inbreeding is to avoid having sex with close genetic relatives. This, in turn, requires a system for distinguishing close genetic relatives from other individuals: a kin detection system, which computes a kinship estimate for each individual with whom one lives in close association. Because genetic relatedness cannot be directly observed, it is important to consider what information relevant to estimating degrees of kinship would have been available to an ancestral hunter-gatherer. To be useful, kinship estimates would have to be based on cues that reliably predicted genetic relatedness in the social conditions under which our ancestors lived. We are looking for cues that would have been stably present across a broad variety of ancestral social conditions and habitats. For example, hunter-gatherers often live and forage in groups that fuse and fission along nuclear family lines, such that parents more frequently stay together with children, adult siblings and their families maintain association, but to a lesser degree, and so on. This would allow the cumulative duration of childhood coresidence to function as a cue to genetic relatedness. An individual who observed his or her mother caring for another infant (what we call maternal perinatal association) would be a more direct cue that the infant was a sibling. A third cue might be an olfactory signature indicating similarity of the major histocompatibility complex. Based on the stable information structure of the ancestral world, the kin detection system is expected to evolve to monitor ancestrally valid cues, and use them to compute a relatedness index for everyone in the individual's social world. This internal regulatory variable should serve as input to systems that compute the sexual value of another individual to himself or herself: All else equal, close genetic relatives should be assigned a lower sexual value than unrelated people. This sexual value estimate—another internal regulatory variable—should regulate the motivational system that generates sexual attraction. A low kinship estimate should upregulate sexual attraction whereas a high kinship estimate should downregulate sexual attraction, perhaps by activating disgust in response to the prospect of sex with that person. These and other theoretically derived predictions about the existence and architecture of the human kin detection system were empirically confirmed, along with a parallel set of predictions about kin-directed altruism. The two predicted cues—maternal perinatal association and duration of childhood coresidence—regulate sexual disgust toward genetic relatives and kin-directed altruism as well (as predicted by Hamilton, 1964). The cues used by older siblings in detecting younger ones differ from those used by younger siblings detecting older ones. The results are incompatible with a variety of alternative theories that could be put forth to explain the results (e.g., Leiberman, Tooby, & Cosmides, 2003, in press-a, in press-b). So far, the pattern found holds in a variety of different cultural settings, consistent with the hypothesis that the kin detection system develops cross-culturally as a universal mechanism of the human mind (Lieberman et al., in press-c).

Note that by starting with an adaptive problem—inbreeding avoidance—and analyzing the computational requirements of a system that solves this problem, a significant neurocomputational system was predicted, tested for, and discovered—a system that was previously unknown and uninvestigated by traditional psychologists and cognitive scientists.

It may not seem so at first glance, but notice that the kin detection system is a *learning mechanism*. Its function is to learn which individuals in a person's environment are kin and which are not, and it is designed to make this categorization on the basis of certain cues present during development, while ignoring others. For example, an individual's consciously held beliefs about who is a sibling do not predict degree of sexual aversion, once duration of childhood coresidence is controlled for (but coresidence does predict sexual aversion, controlling for beliefs about who is a sibling; Lieberman et al., 2003, in press-a). The kin detection system is not, however, a *general-purpose* learning mechanism. It is highly specialized for a narrow task and has nothing in common with mechanisms of classical and operant conditioning, the way facts are learned in school, or any other more general-purpose method of learning.[8]

NATURE AND NURTURE: AN ADAPTATIONIST PERSPECTIVE

To fully understand the concept of design evidence, we need to consider how evolutionary psychologists think about nature and nurture. Debates about the relative contribution (as it is misleadingly put) of genes and environment during development have been among the most contentious in psychology. The premises that underlie these debates are flawed, yet they are so deeply entrenched that many people, scientists and nonscientists alike, have difficulty seeing that there are better ways to think about these issues.

Rather than there being one nature-nurture issue, there are many independent issues. Unfortunately, they have become so tangled that most discussions in psychology and the social sciences are hopelessly confused. We pull the major questions apart and look at them one by one. Some of them are conceptual confusions, whereas others are genuine scientific questions whose resolution will depend on research, rather than on clear thinking alone.

Despite widespread belief to the contrary, evolutionary psychology is not another swing of the nature-nurture pendulum (Tooby & Cosmides, 1992). It shatters the traditional framework and the old categories entirely, rather than siding with any position within the old debate. Indeed, a defining characteristic of the field is the explicit rejection of the usual nature-nurture dichotomies—instinct versus reasoning, innate versus learned, biological versus cultural, nativist versus environmentalist, socially determined versus genetically determined, and so on—because they do not correspond to the actual distinctions that need to be made in the real world. Evolutionary psychologists do not see nature and nurture as in a zero-sum relationship. Nature and nurture exist in a positive sum relationship: More nature allows more nurture (Boyer, 2001; Tooby & Cosmides, 1992).

"Innate" Is Not the Opposite of "Learned"   Everyone is a nativist, whether she knows it or not. Even the most extreme advocates of the role of the environment in shaping human behavior, from Skinner to the postmodernists, make nativist claims about the "innate" structure of the evolved neural machinery that learns or responds to the environment. The only difference is whether they make the na-

---

[8] It is not known how children learn facts in school—the notion that it is via some form of general-purpose learning is an assumption, not a finding for which there is evidence. Indeed, there is starting to be evidence that school learning piggybacks off domain-specific inference mechanisms (e.g., Hirschfeld & Gelman, 1994; Sperber, 1996).

ture of their claims about this machinery explicit or allow them to remain implicit, forcing the reader to deduce them from their arguments about why people act as they do.

Imagine that you are an engineer and your project is to create a brain that can learn. To be able to learn, this brain would have to have a certain kind of structure—after all, 3-pound cauliflowers do not learn, but 3-pound brains do. To get your brain to learn, you would have to arrange the neurons in particular ways. You would have to create circuits that cause learning to occur. In short, you would have to equip your brain with programs that *cause* it to learn. The same is true when natural selection is the engineer.

Even if a program that causes a particular kind of learning was itself learned, there had to be a prior program that caused that learning to occur, and so on. Logic forces us to conclude that there had to be, at some point in the causal chain, a program that caused learning but that was itself unlearned. These unlearned programs are a part of the brain by virtue of being part of its evolved architecture. They are programs that reliably develop across the ancestrally normal range of human environments.

Both environmentalists and nativists—Pavlov, Skinner, and Chomsky alike—must agree on this point. They may disagree strongly about the computational structure of the evolved programs that cause learning but not about whether evolved learning programs exist. For example, classical and operant conditioning are widely viewed as the simplest and most general forms of learning in humans and other animals. Yet, even operant conditioning presumes the existence of evolved mechanisms that change the probability of a behavior by a certain amount, as a function of its consequences (and according to very precise equations). It also presumes that a handful of consequences—food, water, pain—are "intrinsically" reinforcing (i.e., the fact that these consequences are capable of changing the probability of a subsequent behavior is a design feature of the brain). Classical conditioning presumes the existence of a great deal of evolved equipment. In addition to the programs that compute contingencies, the animal is filled with unconditioned—that is, *unlearned*—responses, such as salivating in response to meat. Salivating in response to meat is considered to be part of the dog's evolved architecture, and what the evolved learning program does is calculate when an arbitrary stimulus, such as a bell, predicts the appearance of the meat (Gallistel & Gibbon, 2000). Thus, even in classical conditioning, the learned link between information and behavior—salivating to the sound of the bell—is caused by an evolved learning program, which takes as input both evolutionarily privileged stimulus-response pairs (meat and salivation) and information from the external environment (the contingency between the sound of the bell and the appearance of meat). The only substantive disagreement between a Skinner and a Chomsky is about the structures of the evolved programs that cause learning.

Consequently, any learned behavior is the joint product of "innate" equipment interacting with environmental inputs and, therefore, cannot be solely attributed to the action of the environment on the organism. Thus, *innate* cannot be the opposite of *learned*. It is just as mistaken to think of *evolved* as the opposite of *learned* because our evolved learning programs were organized by evolution to learn some things and not others.

To say a behavior is learned in no way undermines the claim that the behavior was organized by evolution. Behavior—if it was learned at all—was learned through the agency of evolved mechanisms. If natural selection had built a different set of learning mechanisms into an organism, that organism would learn a different set of behaviors in response to the same environment. It is these evolved mechanisms that organize the relationship between the environmental input and behavioral output and thereby pattern the behavior. For this reason, *learning is not an alternative explanation to the claim that natural selection shaped the behavior*, although many researchers assume that it is. The same goes for culture. Given that cultural ideas are absorbed via learning and inference—which is caused by evolved programs of some kind—a behavior can be, at one and the same time, *cultural, learned,* and *evolved.* (For an excellent discussion of how evolved inference mechanisms produce and structure cultural transmission, see Boyer, 2001; Sperber, 1996.)

Moreover, there does not appear to be a single program that causes learning in all domains (consider kin detection, food aversions, snake phobias, and grammar acquisition). Evidence strongly supports the view that learning is caused by a multiplicity of programs (Gallistel, 2000; Tooby & Cosmides, 1992). Without specifying which program is the cause, little is explained, if anything, by invoking learning as an explanation for a behavior. Labeling something learning does not remove the requirement to spell out the evolved machinery involved; it only makes the weak claim that interaction with the environment participated in the process (which is always the case, anyway). In short, learning is a phenomenon that requires explanation, rather than constituting an explanation itself. A coherent explanation for how people learn about a given domain must include (1) a description of what the evolved learning program looks like; (2) why it came to have that structure, both developmentally and over evolutionary time; and (3) what information is available to the organism that is executing that evolved program.

Everyone is also an environmentalist, whether he or she knows it or not. Even the most die-hard nativist understands that organisms learn—or, even more broadly, that an organism's evolved mechanisms extract information from the environment and process it to regulate behavior. Hence the environment regulates behavior, and it is the presence of evolved mechanisms that makes this possible.

Thus, evolved programs—instincts—are not the opposite of learning. They are the engines through which learning takes place. We learn only through instincts—learning and reasoning instincts. There are instincts in songbirds for learning songs, instincts in geese for learning which individual is one's mother, instincts in desert ants for learning how to return home, and instincts in humans for learning a language. The greater the number of specialized learning programs we come equipped with, the more we can learn from experience.

Specialized or General Purpose?   If the *innate versus learned* controversy is meaningless, there are genuine and illuminating questions to be answered: *What is the precise structure of these evolved learning and regulatory programs? Are there many or just a few? Which embody knowledge about enduring aspects of the world, and what knowledge do their procedures reflect? To what extent is a program—whether it governs learning or not—functionally specialized to produce the outcome that you have observed?*

What effect a given environmental factor will have on an organism depends critically on the details of the designs of its evolved cognitive programs. So the discovery of their structure is a pivotal question. Indeed, one of the few genuine nature-nurture issues concerns the extent to which each evolved program is specialized for producing a given outcome (Cosmides & Tooby, 1987; Symons, 1987; Tooby & Cosmides, 1992). Most nature-nurture issues disappear when more understanding is gained about evolution, cognitive science, and developmental biology, but this one does not.

Thus, the important question for any particular behavior is not, "Is it learned," but, "What kind of evolved programs produced it?" More specifically, "What is the nature of the universal, species-typical evolved cognitive programs through which the organism learns this particular type of behavior, acquires this kind of knowledge, or produces this form of behavior?"

For any given outcome, there are three alternative possibilities: (1) It is the product of domain-general programs, (2) it is the product of cognitive programs that are specialized for producing that outcome, or (3) it is a by-product of specialized cognitive programs that evolved to solve a different problem.

The debate about language acquisition, which began in 1959 when Noam Chomsky reviewed B. F. Skinner's book, *Verbal Behavior,* brings this issue into sharp focus, because Chomsky and Skinner disagreed about precisely these issues (Chomsky, 1959; Skinner, 1957). Both sides in the ensuing controversy admit, as coherence demands, that the human mind contains innate learning programs. But the two camps differ in their answer to the question: Does a single set of general-purpose, cognitive programs cause children to learn everything, with language as one incidental example? Or is language learning caused, in part or in whole, by programs that are specialized for performing this task—that is, by what Chomsky called a *language acquisition device?*

Questions about functional specialization cannot be answered a priori by theory or logic alone. Each hypothesis about the computational architecture of a learning mechanism—general, or specialized—must be evaluated on the basis of its coherence; explanatory economy and power; retrodictive consistency with known phenomena; and its ability to make successful, novel predictions. The theoretical tools and empirical studies necessary will differ, depending on whether the proposal is about language learning, inferring mental states, acquiring gender roles, developing friendships, eliciting jealousy, or something else. For language, 45 years of research support the hypothesis that humans have evolved programs specialized for various aspects of language acquisition, although the debate remains heated (Pinker, 1994). With the emergence of evolutionary psychology and under the weight of discoveries in many areas of biology, the debate over adaptive specializations has now widened to include all human competences.

Present at Birth?   Sometimes people think that to show that a program is part of our evolved architecture, researchers need to show that it is present from birth. Otherwise, the behavior is "learned" (by which they implicitly mean learned through general-purpose processes). But this assumes that all of the evolved programs that cause maturational development operate before birth and none after birth.

This assumption is clearly false. Teeth, breasts, and axillary hair are all standard parts of our evolved architecture, but they develop after birth, 10 or 15 years after in the case of breasts. Newborns lack teeth, but does this mean that infants and toddlers acquire their first set through learning? Does cultural pressure lead them to lose the first set in favor of the second?

Organs and design features can mature at any point of the life cycle, and this applies to the cognitive programs in our brains just as much as it does to the features of our bodies. Thus, the fact that a behavior emerges after birth tells us very little about how it was acquired or why it has a certain organization. Organs can be disassembled on schedule as well: Consider the placenta, umbilical cord, and fetal hemoglobin. Evolutionists expect—and observations confirm—that many mechanisms appear and disappear on a timetable based on when they would have been needed, under ancestral conditions, to solve the challenges of that life stage. Infants need the suckling reflex but not sexual desires; adolescents need sexual desires but not the suckling reflex.

Presence at birth is only a function of what is needed at birth, not an indicator of whether something is or is not part of our evolved architecture. Accordingly, much of what is present in adult minds may have been put there by evolution and activated through neural maturation, without depending on the accidents of personal experience. For example, infants who cannot crawl do not need a fear of heights, whereas infants who can crawl do. But experiments have demonstrated that a fear of heights is not learned by trial and error; rather, it is an evolved competence that is triggered when the baby starts to self-locomote, even if researchers contrive the situation such that the baby never experiences a fall (Campos, Bertenthal, & Kermoian, 1992).

Of course, the early presence of features is not completely irrelevant when evaluating alternative hypotheses about our evolved design. For example, the early emergence of a competence, before the social world could plausibly have acted, may falsify or undermine a particular social constructionist hypothesis. But the early *absence* of a competence does not by itself undermine the claim that it is part of our evolved design.

The Twin Fallacies of Genetic Determinism and Environmental Determinism   Traditional researchers hold a series of beliefs that are widely accepted and that sound eminently reasonable but are based on a series of fallacies about how development works. The first belief is that some behaviors are genetically determined whereas others are environmentally determined. The second is that evolutionary psychology deals only with behavior that is genetically determined, not the much larger set of behaviors that are environmentally determined. These beliefs are wrong for many reasons (Tooby & Cosmides, 1990b, 1992; Tooby, Cosmides, & Barrett, 2003), of which we mention just two (see also Hagen, Chapter 5, this volume).

First, genes are regulatory elements that use environments to construct organisms. Thus, every single component of an organism is codetermined by the interaction of genes with environments. Moreover, some of those components are computational mechanisms, designed to produce behavior on the basis of information from the environment. Seen in this way, it is senseless to ask whether kin detection or language acquisition or snake phobias are caused by the genes or the environment: These phenomena are caused by evolved mechanisms that operate on information from the environment in particular ways, and these evolved mechanisms were themselves constructed by the interaction of genes with the environment.

Second, the view that evolutionary psychology deals only with "genetic" behaviors erroneously assumes that environmental causation is nonevolutionary. In order to understand this, it is useful to distinguish "the environment" (in the sense of all properties of the universe) from a given species' developmentally relevant environment. By *developmentally relevant environment* we mean the set of properties of the world that affect the development of organisms of a given species.

Evolution acts *through* genes, but it acts on the *relationship* between the genes and the environment, choreographing their interaction to cause evolved design. Genes are the so-called units of selection, which are inherited, selected, or eliminated, so they are indeed something that evolves. But every time one gene is selected over another, one design for a developmental program is selected as well. (We all start as a single cell—brainless, limbless, gutless. Every cell and organ system subsequently develops from that cell, nonrandomly climbing toward specific organizational forms despite the onslaughts of entropy. For manifest organization to emerge, there must be naturally selected processes that cause this to happen: developmental programs.)

Developmental programs, by virtue of their design, make some parts of the world relevant to development and other parts irrelevant. Over evolutionary time, genetic variation in developmental programs (with selective retention of advantageous variants) explores the properties of the environment, discovering those that are useful sources of information in the task of regulating development and behavior; equally, selection renders those features of the environment that are unreliable or disruptive irrelevant to development. Step by step, as natural selection constructs the species' gene set (chosen from the available mutations), it selects in tandem which enduring properties of the world will be relevant to development. Thus, a species' *developmentally relevant environment*—that set of features of the world that a zygote and the subsequently developing organism depend on, interact with, or use as inputs—is just as much the creation of the evolutionary process as the genes are. Hence, natural selection can be said to store information necessary for development both in the environment and the genes.

The developmentally relevant environment can be viewed as a second system of inheritance comparable in some ways to genetic systems of inheritance. A zygote in an environment can be seen as inheriting a set of genetic determinants (including cellular machinery) and simultaneously a set of environmental determinants. The environmental determinants are transmitted or inherited in a peculiar fashion: They simply endure as physical arrangements in the world across generations over the range where the lineal series of zygotes appears. Some environmental determinants are perfectly replicated across generations (e.g., the three-dimensional nature of space, the properties of light, the properties of chemical compounds, the presence of other humans for a zygote that survives); others are replicated reliably but imperfectly (e.g., mother smiling in response to an infant's smile, the presence of fathers during childhood, a correlation between duration of childhood coresidence and genetic relatedness, cycles of drought and rain). Organismic designs successfully reproduce based on the degree to which their genetic and environmental inheritances are coordinated with each other. Change in either inheritance (either through genetic mutation or environmental change) disrupts the coordination, and the greater or more rapid the change, the greater is the disruption.

This view of development is not gene-centered or a form of "genetic determinism" if by that one means that genes by themselves determine everything, immune from environmental influence—or even that genes determine "more" than the environment does. Although not gene-centered, however, this view is very much natural selection-centered, because it is natural selection that chooses some genes rather than others and, in so doing, orchestrates the interaction between the two inheritances so that high degrees of recurrent functional order can emerge and persist, such as eyes or maternal love.

Moreover, this view explains how reliable development both can and does ordinarily occur—that is, it explains why a robust, species-typical design emerges in almost all individuals (e.g., what can be seen in *Gray's Anatomy*; Gray, 1918). The species-typical features of the genome interact with the features of evolutionarily long-enduring, species-typical environments to produce the species-typical design observable in organisms. Failures of reliable development are attributable to genetic mutation, to environmental mutation (change), or both.

The closest that the world comes to the fallacious distinction between biologically or genetically determined traits versus environmentally or socially determined traits is in the following real distinction: Some neural programs were designed by natural selection to take in substantial amounts of environmental input (e.g., the language acquisition device) whereas others were designed to take in less information (e.g., the reflex that causes the eye to blink in response to a looming figure). But in all cases, there is an underlying neural program designed by natural selection and a set of environmental regularities necessary for that program's reliable development. Indeed, as we discuss later, there is not a zero-sum relationship between nature and nurture: More nature means more nurture.

Universal Architectural Design versus Genetic Differences   How are we to reconcile the claim that there is a universal species-typical design—including a universal human nature—with the existence of individual differences, especially those caused by genetic differences between people?

At a certain level of abstraction, every species has a universal, species-typical evolved architecture. For example, we humans all have a heart, two lungs, a stomach, and so on. This is not to say there is no biochemical individuality, especially in quantitative features. Stomachs, for example, vary in size, shape, and amount of hydrochloric acid produced. Yet, all stomachs have the same basic *functional* design: They are attached at one end to an esophagus and at the other to the small intestine, they secrete the same chemicals necessary for digestion, they are made of the same cell types, and so on. Indeed, when humans are described from the point of view of their complex adaptations, differences tend to disappear, and a universal architecture emerges. This universality is not only theoretically predicted, but is empirically established (e.g., *Gray's Anatomy* describes this architecture in minute detail). This phenotypic universality is expected to be reflected at the genetic level through a largely universal and species-typical genetic architecture ("the" human genome) as well.

The logic is as follows (see Tooby, 1982; Tooby & Cosmides, 1990b, for a more complete explanation):

- Complex adaptations are intricate machines. Adaptations that consist of complexly structured functional elements require, in turn, complex specification at the genetic level. That is, they require coordinated gene expression, often involving hundreds or even thousands of genes to regulate their development.

- Like any other intricate machine, the parts of a complex adaptation must all be present and fit together precisely if the adaptation is to work properly. Parts of complex adaptations are functionally interdependent. All the genes necessary to build each component part and assemble it correctly must be reliably brought together in the same individual. Fitting together the parts specified by new genetic combinations is not a problem for organisms that reproduce by cloning but it is for sexual reproducers.

- Each new human originates sexually. A randomly selected complement of the mother's genes is recombined with a randomly selected half of the father's genes. During gamete and zygote formation, sexual reproduction automatically breaks apart existing sets of genes and randomly generates in the offspring new combinations at those loci that vary from individual to individual. This would not be a problem if the mother and father were genetically identical at all loci. But it is a problem to the extent that their genes differ at those loci underlying complex adaptations.

- Hence, the successful assembly of a complex adaptation in a new individual requires that all of the genes necessary for that adaptation be supplied by the two gametes, even though gametes are both randomly generated and consist of only half of each parent's DNA. Successful assembly would not be possible if only some individuals in the population had the complex adaptation (and the suite of genes that specified all of its necessary component parts). If in a given generation, different individuals had different complex adaptations, each of which was coded for by a different suite of genes, then during the formation of the gametes for the next generation the random sampling of subsets of the parental genes would break apart each suite. During zygote formation, these incomplete specifications of incompatible adaptations would be shuffled together. Consequently, the offspring generation would be a handicapped jumble of fragments of functionally incompatible adaptations. The simultaneous demand for functional compatibility of complex adaptations and sexual reproduction places strong constraints on the nature and distribution of functional variation.

- Specifically, the only way that each generation can be supplied with the genetic specification for complex adaptations is if the entire suite of genes necessary for coding for each complex adaptation is effectively universal and hence reliably supplied by each parent regardless of which genes are sampled. By analogy, if you attempted to build a new car engine by randomly sampling parts from two parent cars, you would fail if one parent were a Toyota and the other a Jaguar. To build a new engine whose component parts fit together, you would have to salvage parts from two parents that were of the same make and model.

- By the same token, sexually reproducing populations of organisms freely tolerate genetic variation to the extent that this variation does not impact the complex adaptive organization shared across individuals. In the car engine example, the color of the parts is functionally irrelevant to the operation of the car and thus can vary arbitrarily and superficially among cars of the same make and model. But the shapes of the parts are critical to functional performance and cannot vary if the offspring design is to function successfully.

- The constraint of functional universality applies only to adaptations whose genetic basis is complex—that is, whose genetic basis involves multiple independently segregating loci. This selection pressure starts when there are two independent loci and becomes combinatorially more powerful with each additional locus. However, if an adaptation can be coded for by a single gene in a way that is not impacted by genes at other loci, then sexual recombination does not disassemble it, and individuals may vary locally or regionally. Similarly, quantitative genetic variation (e.g., height, arm length, how easily an individual is angered) is not constrained by sexual reproduction and functional compatibility and thus may also vary locally or regionally. Quantitative genetic variation is genetic variation that shifts phenotypes dimensionally, but not outside the boundaries imposed by the demand for functional compatibility.

- Some evolved outcomes are the result of frequency-dependent selection. That is, the population stabilizes at intermediate frequencies with two or more alternative designs, such as male and female, because the relative reproductive advantage of being one over the other decreases with increasing frequency (Fisher, 1930). If the adaptation involves only a single locus, two or more alternative designs can persist indefinitely in the species.

- Finally, selection for genetic universality in complex adaptations does not rule out the possibility that some individuals express complex adaptations that others do not (as the two sexes and different life stages do). Such expression, however, must be based on a genetic architecture that is largely universal and simply activated by an environmental trigger or a simple genetic switch such as a single locus (e.g., the unrecombining regions of the Y chromosome). For example, women express a different set of complex reproductive organs than men, but not because men lack the genes necessary to code for ovaries and a uterus. If males and females were different because each lacked the complex genetic specification of the adaptations of the other sex, then when they produced offspring they would be nonreproductive individuals of intermediate sex. In other words, *functional* aspects of the architecture tend to be universal at the genetic level, even though their expression may be limited to a particular sex or age or be contingent on the presence of an eliciting cue in the environment or at a single locus.

- The living world sharply clusters into sets of organisms that share properties—species—because of the demand for functional compatibility among sexual reproducers. Indeed, it is striking the degree to which species are characterized by complex, shared, and instantly recognizable designs. Still, the degree to which functional variation can be tolerated in a species is a function of a number of variables, such as fecundity, migration rate, and population density. In species where successful parents have large numbers of offspring, reproductive rates are high, and migration rates are low between populations, populations may diverge in some complex adaptations because local mates are more likely to share functionally compatible genotypes even if there is variation elsewhere in the species. Compared with the great majority of other species, however, ancestral humans had very low fecundity, had an open breeding structure, and migrated across substantial distances. For these reasons, humans are both expected to be, and are observed to be, characterized by a greater tendency toward species typicality than many other species.

Thus, humans are free to vary genetically in their superficial, nonfunctional traits but are constrained by natural selection to share a largely universal genetic design for their complex, evolved functional architecture. Even relatively simple cognitive programs must contain a large number of interdependent processing steps, limiting the nature of the variation that can exist without violating the program's functional integrity. The psychic unity of humankind—that is, a universal and uniform human nature—is necessarily imposed to the extent and along those dimensions that our psychologies are collections of complex adaptations. In short, selection, interacting with sexual recombination, tends to impose at the genetic level near uniformity in the functional design of our complex neurocomputational machinery.

Evolutionary Psychology and Behavior Genetics Ask Different Questions   The preceding discussion provides a framework for thinking about universal design and genetic differences. Behavior geneticists, through twin studies and comparisons of kin raised together and apart, explore the extent to which *differences* between individuals are accounted for by *differences* in their genes. This difference is expressed as a heritability statistic—$h = Vg/Vg + Ve + Vge$—which tells you the proportion of variance in a population of individuals that is caused by differences in their genes (compared to all causes: variance due to differences in environment, genes, and their interaction). In contrast, evolutionary psychologists primarily explore the design of the universal, evolved psychological and neural architecture that we all share by virtue of being human.

Evolutionary psychologists are usually less interested in human characteristics that vary due to genetic differences because they recognize that these differences are unlikely to be evolved adaptations central to human nature. Of the three kinds of characteristics that are found in the design of organisms—adaptations, by-products, and noise—traits caused by genetic variants are predominantly evolutionary noise, with little adaptive significance, while complex adaptations are likely to be universal in the species.

Why is uniformity associated with functionality and variability associated with lack of function? The first reason involves the constraints on organic design imposed by sexual recombination, as explained earlier. Second, alternative genes at the same locus (the same location in the human genome) are in a zero-sum competition for relative frequency in the species: The more common one allele is, the less common the others are. Natural selection tends to eliminate genetic differences whenever two alternative alleles (genes) differ in their ability to promote reproduction (except in the case of frequency-dependent selection). Usually, the better functioning gene increases in frequency, squeezing out the less functional gene variant, until it disappears from the species. When this happens, there is no longer genetic variability at that locus: Natural selection has produced genetic uniformity instead. The more important the function, the more natural selection tends to enforce genetic uniformity. Thus, our important functional machinery tends to be universal at the genetic level, and the heritability statistic associated with this machinery will be close to zero (because there is little variation between individuals caused by genes). In contrast, whenever a mutation fails to make a functional difference, selection will not act on it, and such minor variants can build up at the locus until there is substantial genetic variability for the trait. Hence, its heritability statistic will be high (because most variation between individuals is caused by variation in genes). For this reason, genetic variability is commonly nonadaptive or maladaptive evolutionary noise: neutral variants, negative mutations on their way to being eliminated, and so on. Such variants may be, of course, of the greatest medical, personal, or practical significance, as, for example, in the search for possible genetic causes of schizophrenia, depression, and autism or the discovery that a formerly neutral variant causes differential drug metabolism. The point is, however, genetic variants causing medical vulnerabilities or personality differences are generally unlikely to be adaptations designed to cause those effects. If something is highly functional, selection usually acts to spread its genetic basis to the entire species.

There is, nonetheless, a great deal of genetic variability within species, which is in tension with the functional advantages of genetic uniformity. Aside from mutations and neutral variants, there is a third reason for this genetic diversity. Genetic variability, such as the ABO blood group system, is retained in the species because genetically based, biochemical individuality interferes with the transmission of infectious diseases from host to host (Tooby, 1982). Diseases that use or depend on a protein found in their present host are thwarted when the next individual they jump to has a different protein instead. Hence, natural selection sifts for genetic variants that supply approximately the same functional properties to the adaptations they participate in but that taste different from the point of view of disease organisms. Because we catch diseases from those we have contact with—such as our family, neighbors, and other locals—selection favors maximizing genetically based protein diversity locally, which requires pulling into every local population as many of the genetic variants found anywhere in the species as possible. Thus, this explains why individuals are so genetically different from one another, but different populations tend to be so surprisingly genetically similar.

This large collection of genetic differences introduces minor perturbations into our universal designs. The result is that each normal human expresses the universal human design, but, simultaneously, each human is slightly different from every other in personality, structure, temperament, and appearance. Macroscopically, these differences tend to be quantitative in nature—a little more of this, a little less of that—while the overall architecture remains the same.

One final category is the possibility of alternative, genetically based psychological designs that are maintained through frequency-dependent selection. The existence of male and female—two alternative designs—shows that such frequency-dependent equilibria are not only possible but also real for humans. Moreover, multiple behavioral strategies often emerge in theoretical models through frequency-dependent selection. Nevertheless, the constraints created by sexual reproduction place strong limitations on the emergence of such systems in real species (even the system of two sexes is based almost entirely on genetic uniformity). Indeed, as the case of the sexes shows, alternative phenotypic strategies can be based more easily on substantial genetic uniformity and alternative developmental pathways than on genetic differences encoding the alternative adaptations. At present in humans there are no well-established cases of frequency-dependent adaptive behavioral strategies based on alternative alleles, except for the two sexes.

The interaction of universal design with genetic variation has many implications for understanding personality variation; for discussion, see Tooby and Cosmides (1990b).

EVOLUTIONARY VERSUS TRADITIONAL APPROACHES TO PSYCHOLOGY:
HOW ARE THEY DIFFERENT?

If all psychologists are engineers working in reverse, and if the goal of all psychologists is to discover the design of the human mind, then how does evolutionary psychology differ from traditional approaches?

Traditional approaches to psychology are not guided by any specific theory of what the mind was designed to do. As animal species go, humans are startling in their capabilities—from making lemon chiffon pies to writing waka to sending probes to Titan, we are capable of solving many problems that no hunter-gatherer ever had to solve (and that no other animal does solve). It, therefore, seemed obvious to many that our minds are not designed to do anything in particular; rather, they are designed to reason and to learn, by virtue of mechanisms so general in function that they can be applied to any domain of human activity. Reasoning and learning require certain auxiliary processes: a memory to retain what is learned or inferred, perceptual systems to bring sense data to the learning and reasoning mechanisms, and attention to spotlight some aspects of perception for further analysis. But these auxiliary processes were also thought to be domain-general. Noting the disconnection between assumptions in psychology and biology, Gallistel (2000, p. 1179) made the following observation about the study of learning:

> Biological mechanisms are hierarchically nested adaptive specializations, each mechanism constituting a particular solution to a particular problem. . . . One cannot use a hemoglobin molecule as the first stage in light transduction and one cannot use a rhodopsin molecule as an oxygen carrier, any more than one can see with an ear or hear with an eye. Adaptive specialization of mechanism is so ubiquitous and so obvious in biology, at every level of analysis, and for every kind of function, that no one thinks it necessary to call attention to it as a general principle about biological mechanisms. In this light, it is odd but true that most past and contemporary theorizing about learning does not assume that learning mechanisms are adaptively specialized for the solution of particular kinds of problems. Most theorizing assumes that there is a general-purpose learning process in the brain, a process adapted only to solving the problem of learning. There is no attempt to formalize what the problem of learning is and thereby determine whether it can in fact be conceived as a single or uniform problem. From a biological perspective, this assumption is equivalent to assuming that there is a general-purpose sensory organ, which solves the problem of sensing.

The same passage could have been written about reasoning, memory, or attention. The reigning assumption has been that the function of the mind is general—to acquire information that is (roughly) true—which requires programs general enough to handle content drawn from any and all domains. Thus, the study of reasoning has concentrated on procedures that are content-free. Examples include logical procedures (which are designed to produce true conclusions from true premises, no matter what the subject matter of the premises is); mathematical procedures, such as Bayes's theorem or multiple regression (which operate over quantities of anything); and heuristics of judgment that use very general principles such as similarity (the representativeness heuristic), frequency (the availability heuristic), or what came first (anchoring and adjustment; e.g., Kahneman et al., 1982; Rips, 1994; but see Cosmides & Tooby, 1996; Gigerenzer, Todd, & the ABC Group, 1999). Memory has been conceived as a single system—after all, it had to be able to store and retrieve information from all domains of human life. When multiple memory systems are proposed, they are usually individuated by information modality or source (a storage system for perceptual representations? motor skills? general knowledge?) rather than by information content (Schacter & Tulving, 1994; but see Caramazza & Shelton, 1998; Klein, 2005; Klein, Cosmides, Tooby, & Chance, 2002; Sherry & Schacter, 1987). Attention has primarily been seen as a content-free mechanism that selects some information in an array for further processing. If true—if attention contains no domain-specialized selection procedures—it should be safe to study it using artificial stimuli that are easy to modify and manipulate in a controlled fashion (Posner, 1978; Triesman, 2005; but see Braun, 2003; Li, Van Rullen, Koch, & Perona, 2002; New, Cosmides, & Tooby, under review).

The traditional view of the mind is radically at variance with the view that emerges from evolutionary psychology. Evolutionary psychologists expect a mind packed with domain-specific, content-rich programs specialized for solving ancestral problems. For example, evolutionary psychologists would view *attention* not as a single mechanism, but as an umbrella term for a whole *suite* of mechanisms, each designed to select different information from a scene for different processing purposes. Some of these may be relatively domain-general and deployed via volitional systems to any task-relevant element in a scene—these are the attentional mechanisms that have been studied most, using artificial stimuli. The mistake is not to think these exist, but to think they are *all* that exist (Braun, 2003). For example, research with change detection and attentional blink paradigms is uncovering attentional systems that are highly domain-specific and deployed in the absence of any specific task demand. One system preferentially attends to human faces (Ro, Russell, & Lavie, 2001). A similar system snaps attention to the location at which a pair of eyes is gazing (Friesen & Kingstone, 2003). Yet another monitors animals for changes in their state and location: Changes to animals are detected more quickly and reliably than changes to buildings, plants, tools—even vehicles (New, Cosmides, & Tooby, under review). Better change detection for animals than vehicles is significant because it shows a monitoring system tuned to ancestral rather than modern priorities. Our ability to quickly detect changes in the state and location of cars on the highway has life or death consequences and is a highly trained ability in twenty-first century America, where the studies were done. Yet, we are better at detecting changes in the states and locations of animals—an ability that had foraging or sometimes predatory consequences for our hunter-gatherer ancestors but is merely a distraction in modern cities and suburbs.

The point is not just that attention will be composed of many different domain-specific mechanisms, but that each domain-specialized attentional mechanism will be part of a vertically integrated system linking the attended objects to domain-specialized inferential, learning, and memory systems. True, animals needed to be closely monitored because they presented either dangers (e.g., predators) or opportunities for hunting (prey). But once detected, other specialized processing is needed. Barrett has shown that a predator-prey inference system develops early, regardless of relevant experiences: 3- and 4-year-old children have a sophisticated understanding of predator-prey interactions, whether they grow up in urban Berlin or in a Shuar village in the jaguar- and crocodile-infested Amazon, eating animals that their fathers hunted and killed (Barrett, Chapter 7, this volume; Barrett, Tooby, & Cosmides, in press-a). Steen and Owens (2001) have shown that chase play in toddlers and preschoolers has features of special design as a system for practicing and perfecting escape from predators (see also Marks, 1987).

Learning about animals is specialized as well. Mandler and McDonough (1998) have shown that babies distinguish animals from vehicles by 7 months of age and make different inferences about the two by 11 to 14 months. A detailed knowledge of animal behavior is necessary for successful hunting (Blurton Jones & Konner, 1976; Walker, Hill, Kaplan, & McMillan, 2002), and preschoolers as well as adults are equipped with systems specialized for making inductive inferences about the properties of animals (Keil, 1994; Markman, 1989; Springer, 1992; and discussion thereof in Barrett, Cosmides, et al., in press; Boyer, 2001; Boyer & Barrett, Chapter 3, this volume). Atran and colleagues (Atran, 1998; López, Atran, Coley, Medin, & Smith, 1997) provide cross-cultural evidence for a system specialized for sorting living kinds into hierarchically organized, mutually exclusive taxonomic categories that organize inductive inferences: The closer two species are in this taxonomic structure, the more likely someone is to assume that a trait of one is present in the other. Barrett, Cosmides, et al. (in press) have found a second parallel inductive system that uses predatory role to guide inferences. This system assumes that two species are more likely to share a trait if they are both predators than if one is a predator and the other an herbivore. This system categorizes animals as predators or not on the basis of minimal dietary information scattered amid other facts about the species' natural history. That is, the category *predator* is triggered by the information "eats animals" and guides inductive learning; the effect on trait induction is strong—twice the size of the taxonomic effect (Barrett, Chapter 7, this volume; Barrett et al., in press-a). Animal-specialized memory systems appear to exist as well. For example, Caramazza provides neuropsychological evidence that information about animals is stored in a category-specific memory system, functionally and neurally separate from that which stores information about artifacts (Caramazza, 2000; Caramazza & Shelton, 1998). From a traditional psychological perspective, content effects concerning animals are no more significant than hypothetical effects about door knobs, floorings, or words that rhyme with Quetzlcoatl. From an evolutionary perspective, however, animals were a selective agent of great magnitude and duration, and it would be a surprise if our brains were not strongly shaped by their hundreds of millions of years of interaction with other species.

We are emphasizing the content-specialized nature of processing about animals to illustrate an important point. The benefit of an attentional system specialized for monitoring animals is enhanced if its output is fed into inferential systems that infer their mental states and use this information to predict their likely behavior. The inferences and predictions generated by the mental state system are more useful if they are reliably fed into decision rules that determine whether escape is necessary. The monitoring system should also feed learning mechanisms that incidentally acquire information about the animal's properties; these, in turn, should feed memory systems designed to encode, store, and retrieve information about the animals monitored, according to ecologically relevant categories such as *predator, taxonomically related,* and so on. Animal-specialized attentional, inferential, behavioral, learning, and memory systems should be *functionally integrated with one another,* forming a distinct, category-based *system.* The same should be true for other content domains. Distinct, content-based information processing systems will exist to the extent that the computational requirements for adaptive problem solving for one content area are functionally incompatible with those for another (Sherry & Shacter, 1987; Tooby & Cosmides, 1992; Tooby, Cosmides, & Barrett, 2005).

Seen from this perspective, the ordinary categories of psychology dissolve. To have a textbook chapter on *attention* and a separate one on *memory* and then *learning* and *reasoning* does not necessarily divide the mind in the most appropriate way. Evolutionary psychologists suspect that there may be a domain-specialized system for dealing with animals, with its own associated attentional, inferential, behavioral, learning, and memory circuitry that are designed to work together as an integrated system.

The organization of these specialized systems are expected to look nothing like Fodor's (1983, 2000) "pipelines" (for discussion, see Barrett, in press-b; Boyer & Barrett, Chapter 3, this volume). Some components of the system for making inferences about animals will also be activated for plants and other living things as well (e.g., taxonomic organization, Atran, 1990, or inferences that parts have functions, Keil, 1994). Other components of the animal system will be activated only in response to animals—or, more precisely, to things manifesting those psychophysical properties the system uses to detect animals, such as contingent reactivity or self-propelled motion, whether the manifesting entity is a meerkat, a robot, or a cartoon. Because many components of the animal system will be functionally specialized for solving animal-specific adaptive problems, they will be composed of representations and procedures that have little in common with those in a system for making inferences about plants, artifacts, or cooperation between people (Boyer & Barrett, Chapter 3, this volume). Nor will the boundaries between category-based systems be clean. People may be attended by the animal monitoring system but also by the system for monitoring social gestures; people may be processed as animals for inferences about growth and bodily functions, but not for inferences about social behavior. The organization of specializations will be complex and heterarchical, but with a functional logic that arose because of its excellence at solving ancestral problems of survival and reproduction.

The old categories of psychological research have not led to robust models of the human mind because they do not carve nature at the joints. Content specialization is the rule, not the exception. The easiest way to make a domain-general model of learning, reasoning, attention, or memory collapse is to introduce stimuli drawn from different adaptive domains (e.g., Anderson & Phelps, 2001; Boyer & Barrett, Chapter 3, this volume; Braun, 2003; Cosmides & Tooby, Chapter 20, this volume; Gallistel, 2000). A more reasoned research strategy is to start developing some formal (or even informal) analyses of specific adaptive problems and let these guide research. If there are general systems or principles to be found, they will eventually emerge as we gain a clear understanding of how each content-specialized system functions (for an example, see Leslie, German, & Polizzi, 2005).

Biology is not split into evolutionary biology and nonevolutionary biology: All of biology is organized by evolutionary principles. At some point, all psychology will be evolutionary psychology, simply because it will make no sense to wall off the study of humans from the rest of the natural world. When that happens, textbooks in psychology will no longer be organized according to folk psychological categories, such as *attention, memory, reasoning,* and *learning.* Their chapter headings will be more like those found in textbooks in evolutionary biology and behavioral ecology, which are organized according to adaptive problems animals must solve to survive and reproduce: foraging (hunting, gathering), kinship, predator defense, resource competition, cooperation, aggression, parental care, dominance and status, inbreeding avoidance, courtship, mateship maintenance, trade-offs between mating effort and parenting effort, mating system, sexual conflict, paternity uncertainty and sexual jealousy, signaling and communication, navigation, habitat selection, and so on (e.g., see Buss, 1999). Future psychology textbooks will surely contain some additional chapters that capture zoologically unusual aspects of human behavior, such as language acquisition, coalition formation, deep engagement friendships, counterfactual reasoning, metarepresentation, and autobiographical memory. But theories of the computational mechanisms that make these unusual abilities possible will include how they interact with and are supported by a wide variety of adaptive specializations (e.g., Boyer, 2001; Cosmides & Tooby, 2000a; Klein, German, Cosmides, & Gabriel, 2004; Leslie et al., 2005; Sperber, 1994; Sperber & Wilson, 1995; Tooby & Cosmides, 1996).

COGNITION AND MOTIVATION

In principle, modern cognitive scientists should understand that any mechanism that processes information must have a computational description. This should include psychological mechanisms that are responsible for motivation. For example, mechanisms that cause fear, romantic love, sexual jealousy, sexual attraction, the perception of beauty, or disgust should all be describable in computational or cognitive terms, which specify the relevant inputs, representations, the procedures that act on them, and regulatory outputs. Yet, most cognitive scientists would not even recognize these topics as within their domain of study.

One reason why cognitive psychologists arbitrarily limit their scope is the folk psychological distinction made between knowledge acquisition on the one hand and motivation, emotion, and preferences on the other. Those who make this distinction view cognition as the study of knowledge acquisition and leave motivation, emotion, and action to other research communities (e.g., Fodor, 2000)—a practice that presumes that knowledge and motivation are not inseparably coevolved aspects of the same unified systems of representation and action.

The Weakness of Content-Free Architectures

To some it may seem as if an evolutionary perspective supports the case that our cognitive architecture consists primarily of powerful, general-purpose problem solvers, inference engines that embody the content-free normative theories of mathematics and logic. After all, wouldn't an organism be better equipped and better adapted if it could solve a more general class of problems over a narrower class? And won't mathematical and logical inference engines produce knowledge that is true, thereby providing a sound basis for choosing the most adaptive course of action?

To be a plausible model of how the mind works, any hypothetical domain-general cognitive architecture would have had to reliably generate solutions to all of the problems that were necessary for survival and reproduction in the Pleistocene. For humans and most other species, this is a remarkably diverse, highly structured, and very complex set of problems. If it can be shown that there are essential adaptive problems that humans must have been able to solve to have propagated and that domain-general mechanisms cannot solve them, the view of the mind as consisting solely or primarily of domain-general programs fails. There appear to be a very large number of such problems—at minimum, any kind of information processing problem that involves motivation and many others as well. This leads to the inference that the human cognitive architecture contains many information processing mechanisms that are domain-specific, content-dependent, and specialized for solving particular adaptive problems (Cosmides, 1985; Cosmides & Tooby, 1987, 1994a, 1994b; Tooby & Cosmides, 1990a, 1992; Tooby, Cosmides, & Barrett, 2005).

Content-Free Is Content-Poor   Some inferences are usefully applied to some domains but not to others. For example, when predicting the behavior of people, it is useful to assume they have *beliefs* and *desires:* invisible mental states that can be inferred but never observed. When predicting the behavior of rocks rolling down a hill, computing their beliefs and desires is useless. Accordingly, the human cognitive architecture has evolved two separate inference systems for these two domains: a mind-reading system for inferring the mental states of people (which can be selectively impaired in autism; Baron-Cohen, 1995; Leslie & Thaiss, 1992) and an object mechanics system for understanding the interactions of inanimate objects (Leslie, 1994; Spelke, 1990). Each inference system is designed to be activated by cues particular to its domain of applicability (e.g., human behavior for the mind-reading system, inanimate motion for the object mechanics system). Because their domain of applicability is restricted, specialized inferences appropriate for one domain can be made without producing absurd inferences for another. This property allows domain-specific systems to include rich, contentful inferential rules. For example, in content-free logics, "If P, then Q" does not imply, "If Q, then P" because it would lead to absurd inferences ("If you saw a horse, then you saw an animal" does not imply, "If you saw an animal, then you saw a horse"). But a "logic" restricted to situations of social exchange, operating over a more content-restricted set of representations (*benefits, entitlement, obligation,* and so on), can usefully specify, "If you take the benefit, then you are obligated to satisfy the requirement" implies, "If you satisfy the requirement, then you are entitled to take the benefit"—an inference that is invalid for any content-free logic (see Cosmides & Tooby, Chapter 20, this volume). Because they can have content-restricted, specialized inference rules, domain-specific systems can arrive at correct conclusions that more general rules are necessarily barred from making. As a result, small inputs of information can generate many inductions or deductions.

Notice, however, that these powerful, content-rich inference systems are unavailable to a truly domain-general system. To maintain its domain generality, a system must be equipped with rules that generate valid inferences across all domains—people, rocks, plants, tools, nonhuman animals, and so on. It cannot take advantage of any inference rules that are useful for one domain but misleading if applied to another. It can have no mind-reading system, no object mechanics system, no predator-prey inference system, or no specializations for tool use (e.g., Defeyter & German, 2003; German & Barrett, in press). The only kinds of inference rules that are left are content-free ones, such as those found in logic and mathematics. Domain-general systems are crippled by this constraint.

Combinatorial Explosion   Combinatorial explosion paralyzes even moderately domain-general systems when encountering real-world complexity. Imagine trying to induce what caused your nausea in the absence of any privileged hypotheses. Your entire life preceded the nausea, and a truly open-minded system would have to consider every action, thought, sight, smell, taste, sound, and combination thereof as a potential cause. In deciding how to respond, every possible action would have to be considered. There would be nothing to privilege the hypothesis that the cause was a recently consumed food and nothing to privilege vomiting or future avoidance of that food as behavioral responses.

As the generality of a system is increased by adding new dimensions to a problem space or new branch points to a decision tree, the computational load increases with catastrophic rapidity. A content-free, specialization-free architecture contains no rules of relevance, procedural knowledge, or privileged hypotheses and thus could not solve any biological problem of routine complexity in the amount of time an organism has to solve it (for further discussion, see, e.g., Carruthers, in press; Gallistel, Brown, Carey, Gelman, & Keil, 1991; Gigerenzer & Selten, 2002; Keil, 1989; Markman, 1989; Tooby & Cosmides, 1992).

Acknowledging the necessity of a few "constraints" on learning will not solve this problem. As Gallistel (2000, p. 1180) notes:

> Early work focusing on the role of adaptive specialization in learning tended to formulate the problem in terms of the constraints . . . or boundaries . . . that biological considerations placed on *the* learning process. . . . [The contrasting argument] is that there is no such thing as *the* learning process; rather there are many different learning processes. While it is true that the structure of these processes constrain the outcome of learning in interesting ways, the more important point is that it is the problem-specific structure of these processes that makes learning possible.

Problem-specific learning specializations are necessary because the problem of combinatorial explosion cannot be overcome by placing a few constraints on a single, general learning process. Instead of asking, "How much specialization does a general-purpose system require?" psychologists should be asking, "How many degrees of freedom can a system *tolerate*—even a specialized, highly targeted one—and still compute decisions in useful, real-world time." Combinatorics guarantee that real systems can tolerate only a limited number. Without domain-specialized learning mechanisms, we would learn nothing at all.

Clueless Environments   Animals subsist on information. The single most limiting resource to reproduction is not food or safety or access to mates, but what makes them each possible: the information required for making adaptive behavioral choices. Many important features of the world cannot be perceived directly, however. Content-free architectures are limited to knowing what can be validly derived by general processes from perceptual information and sharply limit the range of problems they can solve. When the environment is clueless, the mechanism will be, too.

Domain-specific mechanisms are not limited in this way. When perceptual evidence is lacking or difficult to obtain, they can fill in the blanks by using cues (perceivable states or events) to infer the status of important, nonperceivable sets of conditions, provided there was a predictable probabilistic relationship between the cues and the unobservables over evolutionary time. For example, it is difficult or impossible to tell from experience that sex with siblings has a higher chance of producing defective offspring—many conceptions are lost in utereo, and whatever problems exist in children born of such matings could have been caused by any number of prior events. In contrast, a domain-specialized system can trigger disgust at the prospect of sex with a sibling, drastically reducing the probability of inbreeding. This will work, without individuals having to obtain any knowledge, conscious or otherwise, about the pitfalls of inbreeding. Incestuous sex will simply seem disgusting and wrong (Haidt, 2001; Lieberman et al., 2003). Similarly, ancestral hominids had no method by which they could directly see another person's genes to tell whether they are blood siblings or not. But a mind equipped with a domain-specific kin detection system can estimate kinship on the basis of cues, such as coresidence during childhood, that were correlated with genetic relatedness ancestrally. The person need not be aware of the cues used by this system, the computational process employed, or even the concept *genetic relative*.

What counts as adaptive behavior differs markedly from domain to domain. An architecture equipped only with content-free mechanisms must succeed at survival and reproduction by applying the same procedures to every adaptive problem. But there is no domain-general criterion of success or failure that correlates with fitness (for argument, see Cosmides & Tooby, 1987). For example, what counts as a "good" mate has little in common with a "good" lunch or a "good" brother. Designing a computational program to choose foods based on their kindness or to choose friends based on their flavor and the aggregate calories to be gained from consuming their flesh suggests the kind of functional incompatibility issues that naturally sort human activities into incommensurate motivational domains. Because what counts as the wrong thing to do differs from one class of problems to the next, there must be as many domain-specific subsystems as there are domains in which the definitions of successful behavioral outcomes are incommensurate.

A *motivational domain* is a set of represented inputs, contents, objects, outcomes, or actions that a functionally specialized set of evaluative procedures was designed by evolution to act over (e.g., representations of foods, contaminants, animate dangers, people to emulate, potential retaliations to provocations). For a given species, there is an irreducible number of these motivational domains; within each motivational domain, there is an irreducible set of domain-specific criteria or value-assigning procedures operating. For the food domain in humans, for example, criteria and value-assigning operations include salt, sweet, bitter, sour, savory, fat affordances, putrefying smell avoidance, previous history with the aversion acquisition system, temporal tracking of health consequences by the immune system, stage of pregnancy, boundaries on entities and properties considered by the system, perhaps maggot-ridden food avoidance, and scores of other factors. When the required assignments of value within a domain (e.g., food) cannot all be derived from a common neurocomputational procedure, the number of motivational elements must necessarily be multiplied to account for the data.

Thus, by evolved design, different content domains should activate different evolved criteria of value, including different trade-offs between alternative criteria. Cases of motivational incommensurability are numerous and easily identified via careful analyses of adaptive problems. Distinct and incommensurable evolved motivational principles exist for food, sexual attraction, mate acquisition, parenting, kinship, incest avoidance, coalitions, disease avoidance, friendship, predators, provocations, snakes, spiders, habitats, safety, competitors, being observed, behavior when sick, certain categories of moral transgression, and scores of other entities, conditions, acts, and relationships.

There has been little progress over the past century toward constructing an inventory of motivational domains. Without any proof or even an informal argument, psychologists have presumed that most values are derived from the environment, by computing contingencies between environmental conditions and a tiny set of reinforcers (food, water, sex, pain; Herrnstein, 1977). As a field, we have been shrugging off the issue of evolved motivations through the shell game of implying that any given motivation is secondarily acquired, without obliging ourselves to specify computationally how and from what. Yet, there are strong reasons to doubt that a system of this kind would track fitness at all (Cosmides & Tooby, 1987; Tooby, Cosmides, & Barrett, 2005).

Value and behavior cannot be induced from the environment alone. No environmental stimulus intrinsically mandates any response or any value hierarchy of responses. In the tangled bank of coevolved organisms that Darwin memorably contemplated at the end of the *Origin of Species,* naturally selected differences in the brains of different species cause them to treat the same objects in a rich and conflicting diversity of ways. The infant that is the object of caring attention by one organism is the object of predatory ambition by another, an ectoparasitic home to a third, and a barrier requiring effortful trajectory change to a fourth. It is the brains of these organisms that introduce behavior-regulatory valuation into the causal stream and natural selection that introduced into brains the neural subsystems that accomplish valuation. The same stimulus set cannot, by itself, explain differences in the preferences and actions they provoke, nor indeed, the preferences themselves.

Value is not in the world even for members of the same species. Members of the same species view the same objects differently. The very same object is one person's husband and another's father—an object of sexual preference in one case and sexual aversion in the other. Moreover, because each evolved organism is by design the center of its own unique valuer-centered web of valuations, evolved value by its nature cannot have an objective character (Cosmides & Tooby, 1981; Hamilton, 1964). Because of the structure of natural selection, social organisms are regularly in social conflict, so that the objective states of the world that are preferred by some are aversive or neutral to others (e.g., that this individual and not that should get the contested food, mating opportunity, territory, parental effort, status, grooming, and so on). This structure gives value for organisms an intrinsically indexical quality. Indeed, fitness "interests"—the causal feedback conditions of gene frequency that value computation evolved to track—cannot be properly assigned to such a high-level entity as a person but are indexical to sets of genes inside the genome defined in terms of their tendency to replicate under the same conditions (Cosmides & Tooby, 1981). Whatever else might be attainable by sense data and content-free operations, value or its regulatory equivalents must be added by our evolved architecture.

Values and Knowledge   We can now address why knowledge acquisition cannot be computationally divorced from motivation, valuation, and preferences.

To behave adaptively, some actions, entities, or states of affairs must be valued more than others, with a motivational system organized to pursue higher over lower valued options. The computations whereby value is assigned typically involve many of the same elements of conceptual structure that are the traditional objects of cognitive science (representations of persons, foods, objects, animals, actions, events). Thus, the evolution of motivational elements will mandate the evolution of an irreducible set of conceptual elements as well. Why? A valuation is not meaningful or causally efficacious for regulating behavior unless it includes some specification of *what is valued*. That is, the specification of what the value applies to generally involves conceptual structure.

For example, for natural selection to cause safe distances from snakes to be preferred to closeness to snakes, it must build the recognition of snakelike entities into our neurocomputational architecture. This system of recognition and tagging operations is, for certain purposes, equivalent to having a snake *concept,* albeit a skeletally specified one. Evidence supports the view that humans and related species do indeed have a valuation system specialized to respond to snakes (e.g., Marks, 1987; Mineka & Cook, 1993; Mineka, Davidson, Cook, & Keir, 1984; Yerkes & Yerkes, 1936). This one consideration alone forces us to add a fourth "innate idea" to Kant's space, time, and causality. Yerkes and Yerkes's finding of evolved snake fear in chimps counts as empirically based philosophical progress and as straightforward progress in the cognitive science of knowledge— derived (*pace* Fodor) from evolutionarily motivated theories of function.

This argument not only establishes the necessity of evolved motivational elements but also resurrects the argument for the necessity of "innate ideas," that is, evolved conceptual procedures within the cognitive architecture that embody knowledge about the world and are triggered by stimuli with certain features (however abstractly described). It is the specificity of the coupling to the particular valuation procedure that individuates the concept with respect to the set of motivational functions (e.g., *beloved* [your children], *suspicious* [snakes]).

Consider, for example, the series of interacting conceptual components necessary to build a snake avoidance system. The system needs a psychophysical front-end: One of its subcomponents assigns the evolved, internal tag *snake* through visual and biomechanical motion cues to a perceptual representation of some entity in the world. It has a second subcomponent that maps in a parameter, *distance,* between the *snake* and the valued entity (e.g., *self* or *child*). The distance-representing component is used by many systems. However, it also must have a component that assigns and updates different specific valuation intensities for different distances, so that farther away is better than closer for snakes (but not for food or other motivational domains). A particular bad event (e.g., an imagined snake bite) need not be specifically represented as a negative goal state in the snake avoidance system, with distance acquiring its significance through backward induction and means-ends analysis. The distance-fear relationship could fill the representation of space with a motivational manifold that itself motivates

avoidance (closeness is increasingly unpleasant). But such action-inviting affordances are not the same, computationally, as a represented goal state.

The metric of valuation against distance (and its update rules) is proprietary to
snakes, but the output value parameter it produces must be accessible to other
systems (so that distance from snakes can be ranked against other goods, like getting closer to extract your child from the python's coils). Snake, distance, person,
and the *distance* (person, snake) valuation metric all necessarily operate together
for this simple system to work. Snakes, the entity to be protected, and distance
cannot be assigned to one computational process, with valuation assigned to another. Even in this simple example, conceptual and valuation functions indivisi-
bly interpenetrate each other, with the representations necessarily coexisting
within the same structure.

Learning, another clearly cognitive topic, is implicated in snake aversion as
well, but the learning process is domain-specific. It appears that the snake avoidance system recalibrates based on individual experience, possibly slowly habituating in the absence of negative experiences or observations and increasing
sharply if snake contact leads to injury. It also narrowly accepts inputs from the
social world—a conspecific expressing fear toward a snake (but not toward other
stimuli such as rabbits or flowers)—and uses this information to recalibrate the
individual's snake valuation (Mineka & Cook, 1993, Mineka et al., 1984). Presumably, recalibration from observing conspecifics evolved because the system operates more functionally by upregulating or downregulating fear as a function of
the local distribution of fear intensities in others, which index to some degree the
local rate at which venomous snakes are encountered.

The key point is that even this apparently simple, one-function motivational
system involves a series of evolved content-specific conceptual elements, including snakes, distance, conspecifics, that fear-faces have specific referents in the
world, that snakes are one of the privileged referents of a fear-face, and the output of fear itself. Not all of these elements are unique to the snake system (although several are), but their pattern of distribution among motivational systems
is heterarchical and itself not something that could be derived by content-
independent operations acting on experience.

As this form of analysis is applied to the other tasks humans perform, we think
it will be impossible to escape the general conclusion that cognitive science intrinsically involves motivation and that the science of motivation intrinsically involves cognition. The brain evolved as a control system, designed to generate
action. From this perspective, there is not just a cognitive science of areas such as
language, intuitive physics, and number, but also a cognitive science of parenting,
eating, kinship, friendship, alliance, groups, mating, status, fighting, tools,
minds, foraging, natural history, and scores of other ancient realms of human action. Separating knowledge acquisition from motivation has placed the study of
motivation in cognitive eclipse and diverted cognitive scientists from studying
conceptual structure, motivation, and action as a single integrated system (which
they seem likely to be). It ignores the many causal pathways whereby our evolved
architecture should have been designed to manufacture, store, communicate, and
act on the basis of representations that would not qualify as a rational architecture's efficient attempt at constructing true beliefs (Gigerenzer & Murray, 1987;
Haselton & Buss, 2000; Tooby & Cosmides, in press). Evolved systems for motivational computation use conceptual structure in targeted ways, so motivational

computation and knowledge computation cannot be isolated from each other into separate systems. (For a more complete discussion, see Tooby, Cosmides, & Barrett, 2005.)

EMOTIONS AS A SOLUTION TO THE PROBLEM OF MECHANISM COORDINATION

The preceding discussion leads us to view the mind as a crowded network of evolved, domain-specific programs. Each is functionally specialized for solving a different adaptive problem that arose during hominid evolutionary history, such as face recognition, foraging, mate choice, heart rate regulation, sleep management, or predator vigilance, and each is activated by a different set of cues from the environment. But the existence of all these microprograms itself creates an adaptive problem: Programs that are individually designed to solve specific adaptive problems could, if simultaneously activated, deliver outputs that conflict with one another, interfering with or nullifying one another's functional products. For example, sleep and flight from a predator require mutually inconsistent actions, computations, and physiological states. It is difficult to sleep when your heart and mind are racing with fear, and this is no accident: Disastrous consequences would ensue if proprioceptive cues were activating sleep programs at the same time that the sight of a stalking lion was activating ones designed for predator evasion. To avoid such consequences, the mind must be equipped with superordinate programs that override some programs when others are activated (e.g., a program that deactivates sleep programs when predator evasion subroutines are activated). Furthermore, many adaptive problems are best solved by the simultaneous activation of many different *components* of the cognitive architecture, such that each component assumes one of several alternative states (e.g., predator avoidance may require simultaneous shifts in both heart rate and auditory acuity). Again, a superordinate program is needed that coordinates these components, snapping each into the right configuration at the right time.

We have proposed that emotions are such programs (Cosmides & Tooby, 2000b; Tooby, 1985; Tooby & Cosmides, 1990a). To behave functionally according to evolutionary standards, the mind's many subprograms need to be orchestrated so that their joint product at any given time is functionally coordinated, rather than cacophonous and self-defeating. This coordination is accomplished by a set of superordinate programs: the emotions. On this view, emotions are adaptations that have arisen in response to the adaptive problem of mechanism orchestration. This view implies that the exploration of the statistical structure of ancestral situations and their relationship to the mind's battery of functionally specialized programs is central to mapping the emotions because the most useful (or least harmful) deployment of programs at any given time will depend critically on the exact nature of the confronting situation.

How did emotions arise and assume their distinctive structures? Fighting, falling in love, escaping predators, confronting sexual infidelity, experiencing a failure-driven loss in status, responding to the death of a family member, and so on each involved conditions, contingencies, situations, or event types that recurred innumerable times in hominid evolutionary history. Repeated encounters with each kind of situation selected for adaptations that guided information processing, behavior, and the body adaptively through the clusters of conditions, demands, and contingencies that characterized that particular class of situation. These functions could be accomplished by engineering superordinate programs, each of which jointly mobilizes a subset of the psychological architecture's other programs in a particular configuration. Each configuration would be selected to deploy computational and physiological mechanisms in a way that, when averaged over individuals and generations, would have led to the most fitness-promoting subsequent lifetime outcome given that ancestral situation type.

This coordinated adjustment and entrainment of mechanisms is a mode of operation for the entire psychological architecture and serves as the basis for a precise computational and functional definition of each emotion state. Each emotion entrains various other adaptive programs—deactivating some, activating others, and adjusting the modifiable parameters of still others—so that the whole system operates in a particularly harmonious and efficacious way when the individual is confronting certain kinds of triggering conditions or situations. The conditions or situations relevant to the emotions are those that (1) recurred ancestrally, (2) could not be negotiated successfully unless there was a superordinate level of program coordination (i.e., circumstances in which the independent operation of programs caused no conflicts would not have selected for an emotion program and would lead to emotionally neutral states of mind), (3) had a rich and reliable repeated structure, (4) had recognizable cues signaling their presence,[9] and (5) an error would have resulted in large fitness costs. When a condition or situation of an evolutionarily recognizable kind is detected, a signal is sent out from the emotion program that activates the specific constellation of subprograms appropriate to solving the type of adaptive problems that were regularly embedded in that situation and deactivates programs whose operation might interfere with solving those types of adaptive problems. Programs directed to remain active may be cued to enter subroutines that are specific to that emotion mode and were tailored by natural selection to solve the problems inherent in the triggering situation with special efficiency.

According to this theoretical framework, an emotion is a superordinate program whose function is to direct the activities and interactions of many subprograms, including those governing perception, attention, inference, learning, memory, goal choice, motivational priorities, categorization and conceptual frameworks, physiological reactions (e.g., heart rate, endocrine function, immune function, gamete release), reflexes, behavioral decision rules, motor systems, communication processes, energy level and effort allocation, affective coloration of events and stimuli, and the recalibration of probability estimates, situation assessments, values, and regulatory variables (e.g., self-esteem, estimations of relative formidability, relative value of alternative goal states, efficacy discount rate). An emotion is not reducible to any one category of effects, such as effects on physiology, behavioral inclinations, cognitive appraisals, or feeling states, because it involves evolved instructions for all of them together, as well as other mechanisms distributed throughout the human mental and physical architecture.

All cognitive programs—including superordinate programs of this kind—are sometimes mistaken for homunculi, that is, entities endowed with free will. A homunculus scans the environment and freely chooses successful actions in a

---

[9] If there is no repeated structure or no cues to signal the presence of a repeated structure, selection cannot build an adaptation to address the situation.

way that is not systematic enough to be implemented by a program. It is the task of cognitive psychologists to replace theories that implicitly posit such an impossible entity with theories that can be implemented as fixed programs with open parameters. Emotion programs, for example, have a front-end that is designed to detect evolutionarily reliable cues that a situation exists (whether these cues reliably signal the presence of that situation in the modern world); when triggered, they entrain a specific set of subprograms: those that natural selection chose as most useful for solving the problems that situation posed in ancestral environments. Just as a computer can have a hierarchy of programs, some of which control the activation of others, the human mind can as well. Far from being internal free agents, these programs have an unchanging structure regardless of the needs of the individual or his or her circumstances because they were designed to create states that worked well in ancestral situations, regardless of their consequences in the present.

FEAR (AN EXAMPLE)

The ancestrally recurrent situation is being alone at night and a situation-detector circuit perceives cues that indicate the possible presence of a human or animal predator. The emotion mode is a fear of being stalked. (In this conceptualization of emotion, there might be several distinct emotion modes that are lumped together under the folk category *fear* but that are computationally and empirically distinguishable by the different constellation of programs each entrains.) When the situation detector signals that the individual has entered the situation "possible stalking and ambush," the following kinds of mental programs are entrained or modified:

- There are shifts in perception and attention. You may suddenly hear with far greater clarity sounds that bear on the hypothesis that you are being stalked but that ordinarily you would not perceive or attend to, such as creaks or rustling. Are the creaks footsteps? Is the rustling caused by something moving stealthily through the bushes? Signal detection thresholds shift: Less evidence is required before you respond as if there were a threat, and more true positives will be perceived at the cost of a higher rate of false alarms.
- Goals and motivational weightings change. Safety becomes a far higher priority. Other goals and the computational systems that subserve them are deactivated. You are no longer hungry; you cease to think about how to charm a potential mate; practicing a new skill no longer seems rewarding. Your planning focus narrows to the present; worries about yesterday and tomorrow temporarily vanish. Hunger, thirst, and pain are suppressed.
- Information gathering programs are redirected. Where is my baby? Where are others who can protect me? Is there somewhere I can go where I can see and hear what is going on better?
- Conceptual frames shift, with the automatic imposition of categories such as *dangerous* or *safe*. Walking a familiar and usually comfortable route may now be mentally tagged as dangerous. Odd places that you normally would not occupy—a hallway closet, the branches of a tree—suddenly may become salient as instances of the category *safe* or *hiding place*.

- Memory processes are directed to new retrieval tasks. Where was that tree I climbed before? Did my adversary and his friend look at me furtively the last time I saw them?
- Communication processes change. Depending on the circumstances, decision rules might cause you to emit an alarm cry or be paralyzed and unable to speak. Your face may automatically assume a species-typical fear expression.
- Specialized inference systems are activated. Information about a lion's trajectory or eye direction might be fed into systems for inferring whether the lion saw you. If the inference is yes, a program automatically infers that the lion knows where you are; if no, the lion does not know where you are (the "seeing-is-knowing" circuit identified by Baron-Cohen, 1995, and inactive in people with autism). This variable may automatically govern whether you freeze in terror or bolt (Barrett, Chapter 7, this volume). Are there cues in the lion's behavior that indicate whether it has eaten recently and thus is unlikely to be predatory in the near future? (Savanna ungulates, such as zebras and wildebeests, commonly make this kind of judgment; Marks, 1987.)
- Specialized learning systems are activated, as the large literature on fear conditioning indicates (e.g., LeDoux, 1995; Mineka & Cook, 1993; Pitman & Orr, 1995). If the threat is real and the ambush occurs, the victim may experience an amygdala-mediated recalibration (as in posttraumatic stress disorder) that can last for the remainder of his or her life (Pitman & Orr, 1995).
- Physiology changes. Gastric mucosa turn white as blood leaves the digestive tract (another concomitant of motivational priorities changing from feeding to safety); adrenalin spikes; heart rate may go up or down (depending on whether the situation calls for flight or immobility), blood rushes to the periphery, and so on (Cannon, 1929; Tomaka, Blascovich, Kibler, & Ernst, 1997); instructions to the musculature (face and elsewhere) are sent (Ekman, 1982). Indeed, the nature of the physiological response can depend in detailed ways on the nature of the threat and the best response option (Marks, 1987).
- Behavioral decision rules are activated. Depending on the nature of the potential threat, different courses of action will be potentiated: hiding, flight, self-defense, or even tonic immobility (the latter is a common response to actual attacks, both in other animals and in humans).[10] Some of these responses may be experienced as automatic or involuntary.

From the point of view of avoiding danger, these computational changes are crucial: They are what allowed the adaptive problem to be solved with high probability, on average over evolutionary time. In any single case they may fail because

---

[10] Marks (1987, pp. 68–69) vividly conveys how many aspects of behavior and physiology may be entrained by certain kinds of fear: "During extreme fear humans may be 'scared stiff' or 'frozen with fear.' A paralyzed conscious state with abrupt onset and termination is reported by survivors of attacks by wild animals, by shell-shocked soldiers, and by more than 50% of rape victims (Suarez & Gallup, 1979). Similarities between tonic immobility and rape-induced paralysis were listed by Suarez and Gallup (features noted by rape victims are in parentheses): (1) profound motor inhibition (inability to move); (2) Parkinsonian-like tremors (body-shaking); (3) silence (inability to call out or scream); (4) no loss of consciousness testified by retention of conditioned reactions acquired during the immobility (recall of details of the attack); (5) apparent analgesia (numbness and insensitivity to pain); (6) reduced core temperature (sensation of feeling cold); (7) abrupt onset and termination (sudden onset and remission of paralysis); (8) aggressive reactions at termination (attack of the rapist after recovery); (9) frequent inhibition of attack by a predator . . ."

they are only the evolutionarily computed best bet, based on ancestrally summed outcomes; they are not a sure bet, based on an unattainable perfect knowledge of the present.

Whether individuals report consciously experiencing fear is a separate question from whether their mechanisms assumed the characteristic configuration that, according to this theoretical approach, defines the fear emotion state. Individuals often behave as if they are in the grip of an emotion, while denying they are feeling that emotion. It is perfectly possible that individuals sometimes remain unaware of their emotion states, which is one reason subjective experience should not be considered the sine qua non of emotion. At present, both the function of conscious awareness and the principles that regulate conscious access to emotion states and other mental programs are complex and unresolved questions. Mapping the design features of emotion programs can proceed independently of their resolution, at least for the present. This computational approach also allows testing for the presence of emotion programs cross-culturally. The design features of an emotion mode should be present and ascertainable experimentally, whether the language has a word for an emotion state or not (Lutz, 1988).

THE FUNCTIONAL STRUCTURE OF AN EMOTION PROGRAM EVOLVED TO MATCH THE EVOLUTIONARILY SUMMED STRUCTURE OF ITS TARGET SITUATION

According to this framework, the sets of human emotion programs assumed their evolved designs through interacting with the statistically defined structure of human environments of evolutionary adaptedness. Each emotion program was constructed by a selective regime imposed by a particular evolutionarily recurrent situation—a cluster of repeated probabilistic relationships among events, conditions, actions, and choice consequences that endured over a sufficient stretch of evolutionary time to have had selective consequences on the design of the mind and were probabilistically associated with cues detectable by humans.

For example, the condition of having a mate plus the condition of your mate copulating with someone else constitutes a situation of sexual infidelity—a situation that has recurred over evolutionary time, even though it has not happened to every individual. Associated with this situation were cues reliable enough to allow the evolution of a "situation detector" (e.g., observing a sexual act, flirtation, or even the repeated simultaneous absence of the suspected lovers are cues that could trigger the categorization of a situation as one of infidelity). Even more importantly, there were many necessarily or probabilistically associated elements that tended to be present in the situation of infidelity as encountered among our hunter-gatherer ancestors. Additional elements include: (1) a sexual rival with a capacity for social action and violence, as well as allies of the rival; (2) a discrete probability that an individual's mate has conceived with the sexual rival; (3) changes in the net lifetime reproductive returns of investing further in the mating relationship; (4) a probable decrease in the degree to which the unfaithful mate's mechanisms value the victim of infidelity (the presence of an alternative mate lowers replacement costs); (5) a cue that the victim of the infidelity will likely have been deceived about a range of past events, leading the victim to confront the likelihood that his or her memory is permeated with false information; and (6) the victim's status and reputation for being effective at defending his or her interests in general would be likely to plummet, inviting challenges in other arenas. These are just a few of the many factors that constitute a list of elements associated in a probabilistic cluster; they constitute the evolutionary recurrent structure of a *situation* of sexual infidelity. The emotion of sexual jealousy evolved in response to these properties of the world—this situation—and there should be evidence of this in its computational design (Buss, 2000; Daly, Wilson, & Weghorst, 1982).

Emotion programs have evolved to take such elements into account, whether they can be perceived or not. Thus, not only do cues of a situation trigger an emotion mode, but also embedded in that emotion mode is a way of seeing the world and feeling about the world related to the ancestral cluster of associated elements. Depending on the intensity of the jealousy evoked, less and less evidence will be required for an individual to believe that these conditions apply to his or her situation. Individuals with morbid jealousy, for example, may hallucinate counterfactual but evolutionarily thematic contents.

To the extent that situations exhibit a structure repeated over evolutionary time, their statistical properties will be used as the basis for natural selection to build an emotion program whose detailed design features are tailored for that situation. This tailoring is accomplished by selection, acting over evolutionary time, differentially incorporating program components that dovetail with individual items on the list of properties probabilistically associated with the situation.

For example, if in ancestral situations of sexual infidelity, there was a substantially higher probability of a violent encounter than in its absence, the sexual jealousy program will have been shaped by the distillation of those encounters, and the jealousy subroutines will have been adjusted to prepare for violence in proportion to the raised probability in the ancestral world. (Natural selection acts too slowly to have updated the mind to post-hunter-gatherer conditions.) Each of these subelements and the adaptive circuits they require can be added to form a general theory of sexual jealousy.

The emotion of sexual jealousy constitutes an organized mode of operation specifically designed to deploy the programs governing each psychological mechanism so that each is poised to deal with the exposed infidelity. Physiological processes are prepared for things such as violence, sperm competition, and the withdrawal of investment; the goal of deterring, injuring, or murdering the rival emerges; the goal of punishing, deterring, or deserting the mate appears; the desire to make yourself more competitively attractive to alternative mates emerges; memory is activated to reanalyze the past; confident assessments of the past are transformed into doubts; the general estimate of the reliability and trustworthiness of the opposite sex (or indeed everyone) may decline; associated shame programs may be triggered to search for situations in which the individual can publicly demonstrate acts of violence or punishment that work to counteract an imagined or real social perception of weakness; and so on.

It is the relationship between the summed details of the ancestral condition and the detailed structure of the resulting emotion program that makes this approach so useful for emotion researchers. Each functionally distinct emotion state—fear of predators, guilt, sexual jealousy, rage, grief, and so on—corresponds to an integrated mode of operation that functions as a solution designed to take advantage of the particular structure of the recurrent situation or triggering condition to which that emotion corresponds. This approach can be used to create theories of each individual emotion, through three steps: (1) reconstructing the clusters of properties of ancestral situations, (2) constructing engineering analyses about how each of the known or suspected psychological mechanisms in the human mental architecture should be designed to deal with each ancestral condition or cluster of conditions and integrating these into a model of the emotion program, and (3) constructing or conducting experiments and other investigations to test and revise the models of emotion programs.

Evolutionarily recurrent situations can be arrayed along a spectrum in terms of how rich or skeletal is the set of probabilistically associated elements that defines the situation. A richly structured situation, such as sexual infidelity or predator ambush, will support a richly substructured emotion program in response to the many ancestrally correlated features. Many detailed adjustments will be made to many psychological mechanisms as instructions for the mode of operation. In contrast, some recurrent situations have less structure (i.e., they share fewer properties in common), so the emotion mode makes fewer highly specialized adjustments, imposes fewer specialized and compelling interpretations and behavioral inclinations, and so on. For example, surges of happiness or joy are an emotion program that evolved to respond to the recurrent situation of encountering unexpected positive events. The class of events captured by "unexpectedly positive" is extremely broad and general and has only a few additional properties in common. Emotion programs at the most general and skeletal end of this spectrum correspond to what some call "mood" (happiness, sadness, excitement, anxiety, playfulness, homesickness, and so on).

RECALIBRATIONAL EMOTIONS, EVOLVED REGULATORY VARIABLES, AND IMAGINED EXPERIENCE

Information about outcomes is not equally spread throughout all points in time and all situations. Some situations are information dense, full of ancestrally stable cues that reliably predicted the fitness consequences of certain decisions or revealed important variables (e.g., discovering who your father really is or how good a friend someone has been to you) and could, therefore, be used to alter weightings in decision rules.

Indeed, we expect that the architecture of the human mind is full of evolved variables whose function is to store summary magnitudes that are useful for regulating behavior and computation. These are not explicit concepts, representations, or goal states, but rather registers or indices that acquire their meaning by the evolved behavior-controlling and computation-controlling procedures that access them. Such regulatory variables may include measures of how valuable to the individual a mate is, a child is, your own life is, and so on; how stable or variable the food productivity of the habitat is; the distribution of condition-independent mortality in the habitat; your expected future life span or period of efficacy; how good a friend someone has been to you; the extent of your social support; your aggressive formidability; your sexual attractiveness; your status or self-esteem; the status of the coalition you belong to; present energy stores; present health; the degree to which subsistence requires collective action, and so on.

Most evolutionarily recurrent situations that select for emotion programs involve the discovery of information that allows the recomputation of one or more of these variables. Recalibration (which, when consciously accessible, appears to produce rich and distinct feeling states) is, therefore, a major functional component of most emotion programs. Jealousy, for example, involves several sets of re-calibrations (e.g., decrease in estimate of own mate value, decrease in trust). *Re-calibrational emotion programs* are emotion programs such as guilt, grief, depression, shame, and gratitude, whose primary function is to carry out such re-computations (Tooby & Cosmides, 1990a), rather than to orchestrate any short-run behavioral response. These are emotion programs that have appeared puzzling from a functional perspective because the feelings they engender inter-fere with short-term utilitarian action that an active organism might be expected to engage in.

Consider guilt. Hamilton's (1964) rule defines the selection pressures that acted to build the circuits governing how organisms are motivated to allocate benefits between self and kin. This rule says nothing, however, about the proce-dures by which a mechanism could estimate the value of, for example, a particu-lar piece of food to yourself and your kin. The fitness payoffs of such acts of assistance vary with circumstances. Consequently, each decision about where to allocate assistance depends on inferences about the relative weights of these variables. These nonconscious computations are subject to error. Imagine a mechanism that evolved to allocate food according to Hamilton's rule, situated, for example, in a hunter-gatherer woman. The mechanism in the woman has been using the best information available to her to weight the relative values of the meat to herself and her sister, perhaps reassuring her that it is safe to be away from her sister for a short time. The sudden discovery that her sister, since she was last contacted, has been starving and has become sick functions as an information-dense situation allowing the recalibration of the algorithms that weighted the relative values of the meat to self and sister. The sister's sickness functions as a cue that the previous allocation weighting was in error and that the variables need to be reweighted—including all of the weightings embedded in habitual action sequences. Guilt functions as an emotion mode specialized for recalibration of regulatory variables that control trade-offs in welfare between self and others (Tooby & Cosmides, 1990a).

One significant subcomponent of these recomputational bouts is imagined ex-perience, including both factual and counterfactual elements, to potentiate branching decision points and the variables that govern them (Cosmides & Tooby, 2000a, 2000b; Tooby & Cosmides, 2001). Previous courses of action are brought to mind ("I could have helped then; why didn't I think to?"), with the effect of re-setting choice points in decision rules. The negative valence of depression may be explained similarly: Former actions that seemed pleasurable in the past, but which ultimately turned out to lead to bad outcomes, are reexperienced in imag-ination with a new affective coloration, so that in the future entirely different weightings are called up during choices.

RECALIBRATIONAL RELEASING ENGINES

The environment of evolutionary adaptedness was full of event relationships (e.g., mother is dead) and psychophysical regularities (e.g., blood indicates injury) that cued reliable information about the functional meanings and properties of things, events, persons, and regulatory variables to the psycholog-ical architecture. For example, certain body proportions and motions indi-cated immaturity and need, activating emotion programs for nurturing in response to "cuteness" releasers (see Eibl-Eibesfeldt, 1970). Others indicated sexual attractiveness (Buss, 1994; Symons, 1979). To be moved with gratitude, to be glad to be home, to see someone desperately pleading, to hold your newborn baby in your arms for the first time, to see a family member leave on a long trip, to encounter someone desperate with hunger, to hear your baby cry with distress, to be warm while it is storming outside—these all *mean* something to us. How does this happen?

In addition to the situation-detecting algorithms associated with major emotion programs such as fear, anger, or jealousy, humans have a far larger set of evolved specializations that we call *recalibrational releasing engines* that involve situation-detecting algorithms and whose function is to trigger appropriate recalibrations, including affective recalibrations, when certain evolutionarily recognizable situations are encountered. By coordinating the mental contents of individuals in the same situation (because both intuitively know that, e.g., the loss of your mother is, as a default, experienced as a sad and painful event), these programs also facilitate communication and culture learning, both of which depend on a shared frame of reference. Although these pervasive microprograms construct a great deal of our world, investigations are only beginning into adaptations of this nature.

The Role of Imagery and Emotion in Planning   Imagery is the representation of perceptual information in a format that resembles actual perceptual input. In the evolution of animal nervous systems, simpler designs preceded more complex designs. The evolutionary designs of all modern species, including humans, use distinctive constellations of perceptual inputs as signals of states of affairs (for the rabbit, the outline of a hawk silhouette means a hawk is swooping in). Consequently, the key to unlocking and activating many complex evolved decision and evaluation programs was chained to the present—to being in an environment displaying specific perceptually detectable cues and cue constellations (sweetness, predators, running sores, emotion expressions).

A large inventory of wisdom is stored in such programs, but this information, initially, could be used only by organisms in the environment displaying the activating cues—a profound limitation. An important design advance was achieved when psychological architectures evolved in which these programs could be accessed by feeding a decoupled fictional or counterfactual set of perceptual images, or event relations, so that the response of these programs could be unleashed, experienced, and analyzed as part of planning and other motivational and recalibrational functions (Cosmides & Tooby, 2000a, 2000b; Tooby & Cosmides, 1990a, 2001). For example, the earlier design would go into a fear emotion mode and flee the predator when encountered. The new design could imagine that a planned course of action would, as a side effect, bring it into confrontation with a predator, experience (in appropriately attenuated and decoupled form) the fear program, and recognize that prospective, potential course of action as one to be avoided.

Re-creating cues through imagery in a decoupled, offline mode triggers the same emotion programs (minus their behavioral manifestations) and allows the planning function to evaluate imagined situations by using the same circuits that evaluate real situations.[11] This process would allow alternative courses of action to be evaluated in a way similar to the way in which experienced situations are evaluated. In other words, image-based representations may serve to unlock, for the purposes of planning, the same evolved mechanisms that are triggered by an actual encounter with a situation displaying the imagined perceptual and situational cues. For example, imagining the death of your child can call up the emotion state you would experience had this happened, activating previously dormant algorithms and making new information available to many different mechanisms. As many have recognized, this simulation process can help in making decisions about future plans. Even though you have never experienced the death of a child, for example, an imagined death may activate an image-based representation of extremely negative proprioceptive cues that "tell" the planning function that this is a situation to be avoided. Paradoxically, grief provoked by death may be a by-product of mechanisms designed to take imagined situations as input. It may be intense so that, if triggered by imagination in advance, it is properly deterrent. Alternatively (or additionally), grief may be intense in order to recalibrate weightings in the decision rules that governed choices prior to the death. If your child died because you made an incorrect choice (and given the absence of a controlled study with alternative realities, a bad outcome always raises the probability that you made an incorrect choice), experiencing grief will recalibrate you for subsequent choices. Death may involve guilt, grief, and depression because of the problem of recalibration of weights on courses of action. A person may be haunted by guilt, meaning that courses of action retrospectively judged to be erroneous may be replayed in imagination over and over again, until the reweighting is accomplished. (From this perspective, the fact that counterfactual reasoning in children is triggered only by negative outcomes, German, 1999, may be a design feature of a recalibrational emotion.) Similarly, joyful experiences may be savored, that is, replayed with attention to all of the details of the experience so that every step of the course of action can be colored with positive weightings as it is rehearsed, again, until the simulated experience of these pseudo-"learning trials" has sufficiently reweighted the decision rules.

CONCLUSIONS

Now that we have sketched an evolutionary perspective on cognition, motivation, and emotion and the role that imagery and decoupled cognition play in human mental life, we briefly return to an earlier question. We began our discussion of traditional versus evolutionary approaches to psychology by noting that humans are able to solve a wide array of problems that were no part of their evolutionary

---

[11] Recently, there has been a set of misguided experiments that place people under cognitive load to show that certain putatively evolved emotion programs, such as sexual jealousy, perform differently under load (DeSteno, Bartlett, Braverman, & Salovey, 2002). The idea is that evolved mechanisms must be "automatic" and, therefore, should operate uniformly regardless of cognitive load. But this last inference is incorrect. If a situation, such as sexual infidelity, must be represented vividly to activate the jealousy program, then placing someone under cognitive load will interfere with activation.

history and that this observation lent appeal to the view that the mind is a general-purpose machine. But this is to confuse the range of problems solved with the architecture that solves it. One could get breadth not only by having a general-purpose architecture (an unspecified, hypothetical, and arguably incoherent entity), but alternatively by bundling an increasing number of specializations together, each capable of solving an additional class of problems. Moreover, it leaves open the possibility of evolved architectures that include numerous specializations, plus additional components designed to exploit the specializations as a flexibly deployable array of tools to attack novel problems.

What determines whether a program can solve a problem is its causal structure, which sometimes matches an evolutionarily novel problem well enough to provide a solution. Moreover, the set of conditions that activates a domain-specific program—its actual domain of application—is necessarily larger than its proper domain of application (i.e., the set of conditions for which it evolved; Sperber, 1994). Domain-specific programs are activated by cues that were correlated ancestrally with the presence of the adaptive problem they were designed to solve. But correlation is never perfect. Contingent reactivity and self-propelled motion may reliably indicate that an object is an animal, for example, but these cues can also be present when the individual sees a child interact with a self-propelled toy, a car moving on the freeway, cartoons, or even a wind-blown branch. After all, signal detection problems are ubiquitous and will apply to situation detectors and psychophysical activating cues as well as to other problems. As humans entered the cognitive niche (Tooby & DeVore, 1985), selection may have favored the emergence of the ability to reroute inputs and outputs among cognitive specializations to allow for greater improvisation.

Last, it would be wrong to exclude the machinery of *higher cognition* from an evolutionary analysis. The evolved architecture of the mind includes specialized mechanisms that permit offline, decoupled cognition, in which metarepresentations, imagery, and a scope syntax interact with the outputs of domain-specific mechanisms to allow the counterfactual and suppositional thinking (Cosmides & Tooby, 2000a; Leslie, 1987; Sperber, 1994). Decoupled cognition may have evolved to help calibrate or recalibrate mechanisms through synthesized experience, support planning, infer other people's mental contents, or imagine solutions to social, tool use, or other ancestral problems. But it seems likely that, whether as by-products or not, decoupled cognition also permits the kind of thinking that underlies scientific discovery, religious ideas, and other uniquely human preoccupations (Boyer, 2001; Cosmides & Tooby, 2000a, 2001; Sperber, 1994; Tooby & Cosmides, 2001).

In sum, the century-long scientific program that assumed that the human psychological architecture consisted predominantly of general purpose, content-independent, equipotential mechanisms has failed to explain much of human behavior. Indeed, it has failed even to develop a set of persuasive models about what the computational architecture of putatively general purpose learning, rationality, or intelligence would look like, and cannot account for any significant kind of human activity. In contrast, evolutionary theory when joined with a computational approach to the mind leads to the conclusion that the human psychological architecture is very likely to include a large array of adaptive specializations. Evolutionary psychologists, and others, have found detailed empirical confirmation of a large series of narrow, deductive predictions derived from models of evolutionarily specialized computational adaptations.

Accordingly, we think that, over the next three or four decades, as a large-scale collaborative goal by the scientific community, it may be possible to turn human nature from a vague idea into a set of precise, high-resolution models of our evolved computational architecture—models that can be cashed out genetically, at the cellular level, developmentally, physiologically, and neurally. It will be a fundamental advance for our species to have a true, natural science of humanity.

REFERENCES

Alcock, J. (2001). *The triumph of sociobiology.* Oxford: Oxford University Press.

Anderson, A., & Phelps, E. (2001). Lesions of the human amygdala impair enhanced perception of emotionally salient events. *Nature, 411,* 305–309.

Atran, S. (1990). *Cognitive foundations of natural history.* Cambridge: Cambridge University Press.

Atran, S. (1998). Folk biology and the anthropology of science: Cognitive universals and cultural particulars. *Behavioral and Brain Sciences, 21,* 547–611.

Baron-Cohen, S. (1995). *Mindblindness: An essay on autism and theory of mind.* Cambridge, MA: MIT Press.

Barrett, H. C. (1999). *From predator-prey adaptations to a general theory of understanding behavior.* Doctoral Dissertation, Department of Anthropology, University of California, Santa Barbara.

Barrett, H. C. (in press-a). Adaptations to predators and prey. In D. M. Buss (Ed.), *Evolutionary psychology handbook.* New York: Wiley.

Barrett, H. C. (in press-b). Enzymatic computation and cognitive modularity. *Mind and Language.*

Barrett, H. C., Cosmides, L., & Tooby, J. (in press). *By descent or by design? Evidence for two modes of biological reasoning.*

Barrett, H. C., Tooby, J., & Cosmides, L. (in press). *Children's understanding of predator-prey interactions: Cultural dissociations as tests of the impact of experience on evolved inference systems.*

Blurton Jones, N. G., & Konner, M. (1976). !Kung knowledge of animal behavior (or The proper study of mankind is animals). In R. Lee & I. Devore (Eds.), *Kalahari hunter-gatherers: Studies of the !Kung San and their neighbors* (pp. 325–348). Cambridge, MA: Harvard.

Boole, G. (1848). The calculus of logic. *Cambridge and Dublin Mathematical Journal, III,* 183–198.

Boyer, P. (2001). *Religion explained: The evolutionary roots of religious thought.* New York: Basic Books.

Boyer, P., & Barrett, H. C. (in press). Domain-specificity and intuitive ontology. In D. M. Buss (Ed.), *Evolutionary psychology handbook.* New York: Wiley.

Brase, G., Cosmides, L., & Tooby, J. (1998). Individuation, counting, and statistical inference: The role of frequency and whole object representations in judgment under uncertainty. *Journal of Experimental Psychology: General, 127,* 1–19.

Braun, J. (2003). Natural scenes upset the visual applecart. *Trends in Cognitive Sciences, 7(1),* 7–9. (January).

Buss, D. M. (1994). *The evolution of desire.* New York: Basic Books.

Buss, D. M. (1999). *Evolutionary psychology: The new science of the mind.* Boston: Allyn & Bacon.

Buss, D. M. (2000). *The dangerous passion.* London: Bloomsbury Publishing.

Campos, J., Bertenthal, B., & Kermoian, R. (1992). Early experience and emotional development: The emergence of wariness of heights. *Psychological Science, 3,* 61–64.

Cannon, W. (1929). *Bodily changes in pain, hunger, fear and rage.* Researches into the function of emotional excitement. New York: Harper & Row.

Caramazza, A. (2000). The organization of conceptual knowledge in the brain. In M. S. Gazzaniga (Ed.), *The new cognitive neurosciences* (2nd ed., pp. 1037–1046). Cambridge, MA: MIT Press.

Caramazza, A., & Shelton, J. (1998). Domain-specific knowledge systems in the brain: The animate-inanimate distinction. *Journal of Cognitive Neuroscience, 10,* 1–34.

Carruthers, P. (in press). The case for massively modular models of mind. In R. Stainton (Ed.), *Contemporary debates in cognitive science.* Oxford, England: Blackwell.

Cheney, D., Seyfarth, R., Smuts, R., & Wrangham, R. (Eds.). (1987). *Primate societies* Chicago: University of Chicago Press.

Chomsky, N. (1959). A review of B. F. Skinner's verbal behavior. *Language, 35(1),* 26–58.

Chomsky, N. (1965). *Aspects of a theory of syntax.* Cambridge, MA: MIT Press.

Cosmides, L. (1985). *Deduction or Darwinian Algorithms? An explanation of the "elusive" content effect on the Wason selection task.* Doctoral dissertation, Harvard University. (UMI No. #86–02206).

Cosmides, L., & Tooby, J. (1981). Cytoplasmic inheritance and intragenomic conflict. *Journal of Theoretical Biology, 89*, 83–129.

Cosmides, L., & Tooby, J. (1987). From evolution to behavior: Evolutionary psychology as the missing link. In J. Dupre (Ed.), *The latest on the best: Essays on evolution and optimality.* Cambridge, MA: MIT Press.

Cosmides, L., & Tooby, J. (1994a). Beyond intuition and instinct blindness: The case for an evolutionarily rigorous cognitive science. *Cognition, 50*, 41–77.

Cosmides, L., & Tooby, J. (1994b). Origins of domain-specificity: The evolution of functional organization. In L. Hirschfeld & S. Gelman (Eds.), *Mapping the mind: Domain-specificity in cognition and culture.* New York: Cambridge University Press.

Cosmides, L., & Tooby, J. (1996). Are humans good intuitive statisticians after all?: Rethinking some conclusions of the literature on judgment under uncertainty. *Cognition, 58*, 1–73.

Cosmides, L., & Tooby, J. (2000a). Consider the source: The evolution of adaptations for decoupling and metarepresentation. In D. Sperber (Ed.), *Metarepresentations: A multidisciplinary perspective* (pp. 53–115). New York: Oxford University Press.

Cosmides, L., & Tooby, J. (2000b). Evolutionary psychology and the emotions. In M. Lewis & J. M. Haviland-Jones (Eds.), *Handbook of emotions* (2nd ed., pp. 91–115). New York: Guilford Press.

Cosmides, L., & Tooby, J. (2001). Unraveling the enigma of human intelligence: Evolutionary psychology and the multimodular mind. In R. J. Sternberg & J. C. Kaufman (Eds.), *The evolution of intelligence* (pp. 145–198). Hillsdale, NJ: Erlbaum.

Cosmides, L., & Tooby, J. (in press). Neurocognitive adaptations designed for social exchange. In D. M. Buss (Ed.), *Evolutionary psychology handbook.* New York: Wiley.

Daly, M., & Wilson, M. (1988). *Homicide.* New York: Aldine.

Daly, M., Wilson, M., & Weghorst, S. J. (1982). Male sexual jealousy. *Ethology and Sociobiology, 3*, 11–27.

Darwin, C. (1859). *On the origin of species.* London: John Murray.

Dawkins, R. (1986). *The blind watchmaker.* New York: Norton.

Defeyter, M. A., & German, T. (2003). Acquiring an understanding of design: Evidence from children's insight problem solving. *Cognition, 89*, 133–155.

DeSteno, D., Bartlett, M., Braverman, J., & Salovey, P. (2002). Sex differences in jealousy: Evolutionary mechanism or artifact of measurement. *Journal of Personality and Social Psychology, 83*(5): 1103–1116.

Dennett, D. (1987). *The intentional stance.* Cambridge, MA:MIT Press/Bradford.

DeVore, I. (1965) *Primate behavior: Field studies of monkeys and apes.* New York: Holt, Rinehart & Winston.

Eaton, S. B., Shostak, M., & Konner, M. (1988). *The Paleolithic prescription: A program of diet, exercise and a design for living.* New York: Harper & Row.

Eibl-Eibesfeldt, I. (1970). *Ethology: The biology of behavior.* New York: Holt, Reinhart & Winston.

Ekman, P. (Ed.). (1982). *Emotion in the human face.* (2nd ed.). Cambridge, England: Cambridge University Press.

Fisher, R. A. (1930). *The genetical theory of natural selection.* Oxford: Clarendon Press.

Fodor, J. (1983). *The modularity of mind.* Cambridge, MA: MIT Press.

Fodor, J. (2000). *The mind doesn't work that way.* Cambridge, MA: MIT Press.

Frege, G. (1879). *Begriffsschrift ('concept notation'), eine der arithmetischen nachgebildete Formelsprache des reinen denkens.* Halle A. S.

Friesen, C., & Kingstone, A. (2003). Abrupt onsets and gaze direction cues trigger independent reflexive attentional effects. *Cognition, 87*, B1–B10.

Gallistel, C. R. (2000). The replacement of general-purpose learning models with adaptively specialized learning modules. In M. S. Gazzaniga (Eds.), *The new cognitive neurosciences* (pp. 1179–1191). Cambridge, MA: MIT Press.

Gallistel, C. R., Brown, A., Carey, S., Gelman, R., & Keil, F. (1991). Lessons from animal learning for the study of cognitive development. In S. Carey & R. Gelman (Eds.), *The epigenesis of mind.* Hillsdale, NJ: Erlbaum.

Gallistel, C. R., & Gibbon, J. (2000). Time, rate and conditioning. *Psychological Review, 107*, 289–344.

Geertz, C. (1973). *The interpretation of cultures.* New York: Basic Books.

German, T. P. (1999). Children's causal reasoning: Counterfactual thinking occurs for "negative" outcomes only. *Developmental Science, 2*, 442–447.

German, T. P., & Barrett, H. C. (in press). Functional fixedness in a technologically sparse culture. *Psychological Science.*

Gigerenzer, G. (1991). How to make cognitive illusions disappear: Beyond heuristics and biases. *European Review of Social Psychology, 2,* 83–115.

Gigerenzer, G., & Murray, D. (1987). *Cognition as intuitive statistics.* Hillsdale, NJ: Erlbaum.

Gigerenzer, G., & Selten, R. (Eds.). (2002). *Bounded rationality: The adaptive toolbox.* Cambridge, MA: MIT Press.

Gigerenzer, G., Todd, P., & the ABC Research Group. (1999). *Simple heuristics that make us smart.* New York: Oxford.

Gould, S. J., & Lewontin, R. C. (1979). The spandrels of San Marco and the panglossian paradigm: A critique of the adaptationist programme. *Proceedings of the Royal Society of London. Series B, Biological Sciences, 205,* 581–598.

Gray, H. (1918). *Gray's anatomy* (20th ed.). W. Lewis (Ed.), Philadelphia: Lea & Febiger.

Haidt, J. (2001). The emotional dog and its rational tail: A social intuitionist approach to moral judgment. *Psychological Review, 108*(4), 814–834.

Hamilton, W. D. (1964). The genetical evolution of social behavior. *Journal of Theoretical Biology, 7,* 1–52.

Haselton, M. G., & Buss, D. M. (2000). Error management theory: A new perspective on biases in cross-sex mind reading. *Journal of Personality and Social Psychology, 78,* 81–91.

Herrnstein, R. J. (1977). The evolution of behaviorism. *American Psychologist, 32,* 593–603.

Hirschfeld, L. A., & Gelman, S. A. (Eds.). (1994). *Mapping the mind: Domain specificity in cognition and culture.* Cambridge, England: Cambridge University Press.

Kahneman, D., Slovic, P., & Tversky, A. (Eds.). (1982). *Judgment under uncertainty: Heuristics and biases.* Cambridge, England: Cambridge University Press.

Kaplan, H., & Hill, K. (1985). Food sharing among Ache Foragers: Tests of explanatory hypotheses. *Current Anthropology, 26*(2), 223–246.

Keil, F. (1989). *Concepts, kinds, and cognitive development.* Cambridge, MA: MIT Press.

Keil, F. C. (1994). The birth and nurturance of concepts by domains: The origins of concepts of living things. In L. A. Hirschfeld & S. A. Gelman (Eds.), *Mapping the mind: Domain specificity in cognition and culture.* Cambridge, England: Cambridge University Press.

Klein, S. (2005). The cognitive neuroscience of knowing one's self. In M. S. Gazzaniga (Ed.), *The cognitive neurosciences, III* (pp. 1077–1089). Cambridge, MA: MIT Press.

Klein, S., Cosmides, L., Tooby, J., & Chance, S. (2002). Decisions and the evolution of memory: Multiple systems, multiple functions. *Psychological Review, 109,* 306–329.

Klein, S., German, T., Cosmides, L., & Gabriel, R. (2004). A theory of autobiolographical memory: Necessary components and disorders resulting from their loss. *Social Cognition, 22*(5), 460–490.

Kurzban, R., Tooby, J., & Cosmides, L. (2001). Can race be erased? Coalitional computation and social categorization. *Proceedings of the National Academy of Sciences, 98*(26), 15387–15392.

LeDoux, J. (1995). In search of an emotional system in the brain: Leaping from fear to emotion to consciousness. In M. S. Gazzaniga (Ed.), *The cognitive neurosciences* (pp. 1049–1061). Cambridge, MA: MIT Press.

Lee, R., & DeVore, I. (Eds.). (1968). *Man the hunter.* Chicago: Aldine.

Lee, R., & DeVore, I. (Eds.). (1976). *Kalahari hunter-gatherers: Studies of the !Kung San and their neighbors.* Cambridge, MA: Harvard.

Lenneberg, E. (1967). *Biological foundations of language.* New York: John Wiley & Sons.

Leslie, A. (1987). Pretense and representation: The origins of "theory of mind." *Psychological Review, 94,* 412–426.

Leslie, A. M. (1994). ToMM, ToBy, and agency: Core architecture and domain specificity. In L. A. Hirschfeld & S. A. Gelman (Eds.), *Mapping the mind: Domain specificity in cognition and culture* (pp. 119–148). Cambridge, England: Cambridge University Press.

Leslie, A. M., German, T. P., & Polizzi, P. (2005). Belief-desire reasoning as a process of selection. *Cognitive Psychology, 50,* 45–85.

Leslie, A. M., & Thaiss, L. (1992). Domain specificity in conceptual development: Neuropsychological evidence from autism. *Cognition, 43,* 225–251.

Li, F. F., Van Rullen, R., Koch, C., & Perona, P. (2002). Rapid natural scene categorization in the near absence of attention. *Proceedings of the National Academy of Science, USA, 99,* 9596–9601.

Lieberman, D., Tooby, J., & Cosmides, L. (2003). Does morality have a biological basis? An empirical test of the factors governing moral sentiments relating to incest. *Proceedings of the Royal Society London (Biological Sciences), 270*(1517), 819–826.

Lieberman, D., Tooby, J., & Cosmides, L. (in press-a). The evolution of human incest avoidance mechanisms: An evolutionary psychological approach. In A. Wolf & J. P. Takala (Eds.),

Evolution and the moral emotions: Appreciating Edward Westermarck. Stanford, CA: Stanford University Press.

Lieberman, D., Tooby, J., & Cosmides, L. (in press-b). The architecture of the human kin detection system.

Lieberman, D., Tooby, J., & Cosmides, L. (in press-c). Kin detection and altruism in Dominica.

López, A., Atran, S., Coley, J., Medin, D., & Smith, E. (1997). The tree of life: Universals of folkbiological taxonomies and inductions. *Cognitive Psychology, 32,* 251–295.

Lutz, C. A. (1988). *Unnatural emotions: Everyday sentiments on a Micronesian Atoll and their challenge to western theory.* Chicago: University of Chicago Press.

Mandler, J., & McDonough, L. (1998). Studies in inductive inference in infancy. *Cognitive Psychology, 37*(1), 60–96.

Markman, E. (1989). *Categorization and naming in children.* Cambridge, MA: MIT Press.

Marks, I. (1987). *Fears, phobias, and rituals.* New York: Oxford.

Maynard Smith, J. (1982). *Evolution and the theory of games.* Cambridge, England: Cambridge University Press.

Mineka, S., & Cook, M. (1993). Mechanisms involved in the observational conditioning of fear. *Journal of Experimental Psychology: General, 122,* 23–38.

Mineka, S., Davidson, M., Cook, M., & Keir, R. (1984). Observational conditioning of snake fear in rhesus monkeys. *Journal of Abnormal Psychology, 93,* 355–372.

New, J., Cosmides, L., & Tooby, J. (under review). Category-specific attention to animals and people: Ancestral priorities or ontogenetic expertise?

Pinker, S. (1994). *The language instinct.* New York: Morrow.

Pinker, S. (2002). *The blank slate.* New York: Viking Press.

Pinker, S., & Bloom, P. (1990). Natural language and natural selection. *Behavioral and Brain Sciences 13*(4): 707–784.

Pitman, R., & Orr, S. (1995). Psychophysiology of emotional and memory networks in posttraumatic stress disorder. In J. McGaugh, N. Weinberger, & G. Lynch (Eds.), *Brain and memory: Modulation and mediation of neuroplasticity* (pp. 75–83). New York: Oxford.

Posner, M. (1978). *Chronometric explorations of mind.* New York: Oxford.

Rips, L. (1994). *The psychology of proof.* Cambridge, MA: MIT Press.

Ro, T., Russell, C., & Lavie, N. (2001). Changing faces: A detection advantage in the flicker paradigm. *Psychological Science, 12,* 94–99.

Rode, C., Cosmides, L., Hell, W., & Tooby, J. (1999). When and why do people avoid unknown probabilities in decisions under uncertainty? Testing some predictions from optimal foraging theory. *Cognition, 72,* 269–304.

Sahlins, M. (1976). *The use and abuse of biology: An anthropological critique of sociobiology.* Ann Arbor: University of Michigan Press.

Schacter, D., & Tulving, E. (Eds.). (1994). *Memory systems 1994.* Cambridge, MA: MIT Press.

Shannon, C. E. (1948). A mathematical theory of communication. *Bell System Technical Journal, 27* 379–423 & 623–656.

Shepard, R. N. (1984). Ecological constraints on internal representation: Resonant kinematics of perceiving, imagining, thinking, and dreaming. *Psychological Review, 91,* 417–447.

Shepard, R. N. (1987). Evolution of a mesh between principles of the mind and regularities of the world. In J. Dupre (Ed.), *The latest on the best: Essays on evolution and optimality* (pp. 251–275). Cambridge, MA: MIT Press.

Sherry, D., & Schacter, D. (1987). The evolution of multiple memory systems. *Psychological Review, 94,* 439–454.

Shostak, M. (1981). *Nisa: The life and words of a !Kung woman.* Cambridge, MA: Harvard.

Skinner, B. F. (1957). *Verbal behavior.* New York: Appleton-Century-Crofts.

Spelke, E. S. (1990). Principles of object perception. *Cognitive Science, 14,* 29–56.

Sperber, D. (1994). The modularity of thought and the epidemiology of representations. In L. A. Hirschfeld & S. A. Gelman (Eds.), *Mapping the mind: Domain specificity in cognition and culture.* Cambridge, England: Cambridge University Press.

Sperber, D. (1996). *Explaining culture: A naturalistic approach.* Oxford: Blackwell.

Sperber, D., & Wilson, D. (1995). *Relevance: Communication and cognition* (2nd ed.). Oxford, England: Blackwell.

Springer, K. (1992). Children's awareness of the implications of biological kinship. *Child Development, 63,* 950–959.

Steen, F., & Owens, S. (2001). Evolution's pedagogy: An adaptationist model of pretense and entertainment. *Journal of Cognition and Culture, 1*(4), 289–321.

Suarez, S. D., & Gallup, G. G. (1979). Tonic immobility as a response to rage in humans: A theoretical note. *Psychological Record, 29,* 315–320.

Symons, D. (1979). *The evolution of human sexuality.* New York: Oxford University Press.

Symons, D. (1987). If we're all Darwinians, what's the fuss about. In C. B. Crawford, M. F. Smith, & D. L. Krebs (Eds.), *Sociobiology and psychology* (pp. 121–146). Hillsdale, NJ: Erlbaum.

Symons, D. (1989). A critique of Darwinian anthropology. *Ethology and Sociobiology, 10,* 131–144.

Symons, D. (1992). On the use and misuse of Darwinism in the study of human behavior. In J. Barkow, L. Cosmides, & J. Tooby (Eds.), *The adapted mind: Evolutionary psychology and the generation of culture* (pp. 137–159). New York: Oxford University Press.

Tomaka, J., Blascovich, J., Kibler, J., & Ernst, J. (1997). Cognitive and physiological antecedents of threat and challenge appraisal. *Journal of Personality and Social Psychology, 73,* 63–72.

Tooby, J. (1982). Pathogens, polymorphism, and the evolution of sex. *Journal of Theoretical Biology, 97,* 557–576.

Tooby, J. (1985). The emergence of evolutionary psychology. In D. Pines (Ed.), *Emerging syntheses in science* (pp. 124–137). Santa Fe, NM: The Santa Fe Institute.

Tooby, J., & Cosmides, L. (1990a). The past explains the present: Emotional adaptations and the structure of ancestral environments. *Ethology and Sociobiology, 11,* 375–424.

Tooby, J., & Cosmides, L. (1990b). On the universality of human nature and the uniqueness of the individual: The role of genetics and adaptation. *Journal of Personality, 58,* 17–67.

Tooby, J., & Cosmides, L. (1992). The psychological foundations of culture. In J. Barkow, L. Cosmides, & J. Tooby (Eds.), *The adapted mind: Evolutionary psychology and the generation of culture* (pp. 19–136). New York: Oxford University Press.

Tooby, J., & Cosmides, L. (1996). Friendship and the banker's paradox: Other pathways to the evolution of adaptations for altruism. *Proceedings of the British Academy, 88,* 119–143.

Tooby, J., & Cosmides, L. (2001). Does beauty build adapted minds? Toward an evolutionary theory of aesthetics, fiction and the arts. *SubStance, 94/95*(1), 6–27.

Tooby, J., & Cosmides, L. (in press). Ecological rationality in a multimodular mind. In *Evolutionary psychology: Foundational papers.* Cambridge, MA: MIT Press.

Tooby, J., Cosmides, L., & Barrett, H. C. (2003). The second law of thermodynamics is the first law of psychology: Evolutionary developmental psychology and the theory of tandem, coordinated inheritances. *Psychological Bulletin, 129*(6), 858–865.

Tooby, J., Cosmides, L., & Barrett, H. C. (2005). Resolving the debate on innate ideas: Learnability constraints and the evolved interpenetration of motivational and conceptual functions. In P. Carruthers, S. Laurence, & S. Stich (Eds.), *The innate mind: Structure and content.* New York: Oxford University Press.

Tooby, J., & DeVore, I. (1987). The reconstruction of hominid behavioral evolution through strategic modeling. In W. Kinzey (Ed.), *Primate models of hominid behavior* (pp. 183–237). New York: SUNY Press.

Triesman, A. (2005). Psychological issues in selective attention. In M. S. Gazzaniga (Ed.), *The cognitive neurosciences, III* (pp. 529–544). Cambridge, MA: MIT Press.

Vining, D. R. (1986). Social versus reproductive success: The central theoretical problem of human sociobiology. *Behavioral and Brain Sciences, 9,* 167–216.

Walker, R., Hill, K., Kaplan, H., & McMillan, G. (2002). Age dependency of hunting ability among the Ache of eastern Paraguay. *Journal of Human Evolution, 42,* 639–657.

Wang, X. T. (2002). Risk as reproductive variance. *Evolution and Human Behavior, 23,* 35–57.

Weiner, N. (1948). *Cybernetics or control and communication in the animal and the machine.* Cambridge, MA: MIT Press.

Williams, G. C. (1966). *Adaptation and natural selection: A critique of some current evolutionary thought.* Princeton, NJ: Princeton University Press.

Wilson, E. O. (1975). *Sociobiology: The new synthesis.* Cambridge, MA: Belknap Press.

Wynn, K. (1998). Psychological foundations of number: Numerical competence in human infants. *Trends in Cognitive Sciences, 2,* 296–303.

Yerkes, R. M., & Yerkes, A. W. (1936). Nature and conditions of avoidance (fear) response in chimpanzee. *Journal of Comparative Psychology, 21,* 53–66.

CHAPTER 2

Life History Theory and Evolutionary Psychology

HILLARD S. KAPLAN and STEVEN W. GANGESTAD

T HE EVOLUTION OF LIFE is the result of a process in which variant forms compete to harvest energy from the environment and convert it into replicates of those forms. Individuals "capture" energy from the environment (through foraging, hunting, or cultivating) and "allocate" it to reproduction and survival-enhancing activities. Selection favors individuals who efficiently capture energy and effectively allocate it to enhance fitness within their ecological niche.

Energy does not come for free. Were individuals able to expend unlimited energy at no cost, in principle they could evolve to grow and develop so rapidly they could begin reproducing immediately after birth, massively produce offspring, and preserve themselves such that they never age. In biological reality, however, individuals must live within finite energy "budgets" (themselves earned through energy and time expenditures), never spending more than they have available. Allocation of a finite budget entails trade-offs and hence forces decisions about the relative value of possible ways to spend. Acquiring one expensive item means giving up others; consumption today may entail less tomorrow.

In the face of trade-offs, how should a budget be spent? People managing their personal expenses presumably spend it based on what they value (even if sometimes only fleetingly and later regrettably). Moreover, their decisions are often based on individual circumstances that, over time, change: Wealthy individuals can afford to spend more on luxury items than can the middle class or poor; college students often see little value in saving for retirement until, through education, they gain better employment; and people with steady, good incomes can afford to keep less as a buffer against bad times than those whose future incomes are uncertain.

Selection favors organisms' strategies for allocating energy budgets on the basis of one criterion: The strategy that leads to the allocation of energy that, on average, results in the greatest fitness is the one that wins out over others. In this sense, selection is expected to result in *fitness-maximizing* or *optimal* strategies. (Those strategies are optimal only in a restricted sense: They are optimal *under the constraints* imposed by trade-offs between allocations of energy; see Parker & Maynard Smith, 1991.)[1] Just as strategies of how to spend money depend on individual circumstances, so, too, do optimal energy allocations: Newborns optimally allocate energy differently from adults; healthy individuals optimally allocate differently from those with infectious disease. The best allocation strategy for individuals in stable circumstances differs from that of individuals whose future circumstances are unpredictable.

Fundamentally, life history theory (LHT) provides a framework that addresses how, in the face of trade-offs, organisms should allocate time and energy to tasks and traits in a way that maximizes their fitness. Optimal allocations vary across the life course, and hence LHT generally concerns the evolutionary forces that shape the timing of life events involved in development, growth, reproduction, and aging.

A major goal of evolutionary psychology is to understand the nature of psychological adaptations. Evolutionary psychology intimately connects with LHT for two reasons. First, psychological adaptations are some of what humans have been selected to invest in, at an expense; obviously, the development, maintenance, operation, and utilization of psychological adaptations require allocations of energy and time. Because their evolution has been subject to the fundamental forces of selection that LHT concerns, LHT can effectively guide inquiry into their development, nature, and operation.

Second, optimal decisions about how to invest time and energy into various life tasks themselves often require processing of specific information about the environment (current features as well as cues about what the future holds) on which allocation decisions ought to be based. Some psychological adaptations, presumably, are designed to provide and act on that information. LHT can once again guide thinking about the nature of these adaptations.

We first provide an overview of LHT. We then consider specific applications of LHT to an understanding of the human life course. Finally, we argue for ways in which LHT can and should be infused into evolutionary psychology.

LIFE HISTORY THEORY: AN OVERVIEW

In this section, we provide a broad overview of LHT.

FUNDAMENTAL TRADE-OFFS IN LIFE HISTORY THEORY

Individuals can enhance fitness in two primary ways: They can invest in traits that affect the age schedule of mortality, or they can invest in traits that affect the age schedule of fertility.[2] Ultimately, the influence of traits on inclusive fitness must be mediated through changes in mortality or fertility or both (though they

---

[1] Other constraints may also exist, for example, genetic constraints that don't allow for some phenotypes in light of an organism's developmental system. "Optimal" strategies evolve under these constraints as well (Parker & Maynard Smith, 1990). In addition, evolved strategies need not be optimal, even under constraints, in environments other than those in which they evolve.

[2] Biologists and demographers use the terms *fertility* and *fecundity* differently. For biologists, fertility refers to the ability to conceive, whereas fecundity refers to quantity of actual offspring. For demographers, fecundity (or fecundability) refers to ability to conceive, whereas fertility refers to quantity of actual offspring. We adopt the usage of demographers for this chapter.

may do so by enhancing the mortality and/or fertility of kin—for example, offspring—as well as self; Hamilton, 1964). Because of allocation trade-offs, many, if not most, traits have opposing effects on mortality and fertility, opposing effects on the same fitness component at two different points in time, or opposing effects of a fitness component of self (e.g., own fertility) and that of a related individual (e.g., offspring survival and/or fertility). Examples include: (1) A trait that increases fertility by increasing mating frequency (e.g., a mating display) may simultaneously reduce survival by compromising immune function, (2) energetic allocations to growth reduce fertility at younger ages but increase fertility at older ages, and (3) allocations to offspring viability (e.g., feeding) reduce an individual's own survival or fertility. LHT conceptualizes specific allocation trade-offs in terms of three broad, fundamental trade-offs: the present-future reproduction trade-off, the quantity-quality of offspring trade-off, and the trade-off between mating effort and parenting effort.

The Trade-Off between Present and Future Reproduction   At any point in time, an organism faces a decision. Its energy can be converted into offspring or into life-sustaining activities (e.g., additional energy harvesting, growth, predator reduction, repair) in any proportion. Allocation of energy to future reproduction entails the opportunity cost of not reproducing now. Reproducing now typically entails the cost of increasing the chance of not reproducing in the future.

Cole's paradox (Cole, 1954), an early inquiry into life history evolution, illustrates this trade-off. Imagine an asexual perennial plant that reserves energy at the end of each growing season to survive the winter and live to reproduce the next year. If it produced just one more progeny with the reserve energy and died rather than overwintered, its fitness would be unchanged, as it would have replaced itself. In principle, seeds are cheap and, if the plant could produce many with the energy it takes to overwinter, it would seem better to do so and die. In fact, however, seeds may be much less likely to survive the winter than its adult parent so that it may cost less to overwinter than to produce just one single surviving progeny (Charnov & Schaffer, 1973). The best strategy depends on which allocation results in greatest inclusive fitness.

THE PROBLEM OF SENESCENCE   In the 1950s and 1960s, the issue of current versus future reproduction was primarily applied to an understanding of why organisms senesce. Medawar (1952; see also Fisher, 1958) argued that selection is stronger on traits expressed at younger ages because a greater proportion of the population is alive to experience its effects. An organism's viability should, therefore, tend to decrease with age, as deleterious mutations whose effects are expressed only late in life should accumulate due to weaker selection against them. Williams (1957) extended this reasoning to genes that exhibit *antagonistic pleiotropy*—ones with opposing effects on fitness at two different ages (e.g., a positive effect on fertility at a younger age and a negative effect on survival at an older age). Such genes with beneficial effects early in life but deleterious effects later in life should accumulate in populations. Aging (defined as an increasing risk of mortality with age) results. Williams furthermore proposed that selection on age-specific mortality rates should be a function of *reproductive value* (RV; expected future reproduction at a given age, conditional on having reached that age), which increases until age of first reproduction and decreases thereafter. Hamilton (1966) developed a mathematical model generally supporting Williams's proposals, though it showed that selection should track expected future reproduction at a given age *not conditional* on surviving to that age. Hence, the mortality rate should be constant prior to reproduction and increase thereafter.

Life History Formulations   Williams and Hamilton assumed trade-offs but were not concerned with their cause. Gadgil and Bossert (1970) developed the first modern LHT framework—one conceptualizing trade-offs as necessarily entailed by finite energy budgets. Organisms capture energy (*resources*) from the environment. Their capture rate (or *income*) determines their energy budget. At any point in time, they can "spend" income on three different activities. Through *growth*, organisms can increase their energy capture rates in the future, thus increasing their future fertility. For this reason, organisms typically have a juvenile phase in which fertility is zero until they reach a size at which some allocation to reproduction increases fitness more than growth. Through *maintenance*, organisms repair somatic tissue, allocate energy to immune function, engage in further energy production, and so on. Through *reproduction*, organisms replicate genes. How organisms solve this energetic trade-off shapes their life histories. Because maintenance and growth affect fitness through impacts on *future* reproduction, the tripartite trade-off collapses into a *trade-off between current and future reproduction* (Bell & Koufopanou, 1986; Hill, 1993; Lessells, 1991; Roff, 1992; Stearns, 1992). The loss of future survival, energy capture, and reproduction because of energy allocation to current reproduction is referred to as the cost of reproduction (Williams, 1966).

The present-future trade-off can be analyzed by decomposing RV into two components: reproduction during the current time interval and total reproduction at all future time intervals after the current one until death (see Hill, 1993; Lessells, 1991, for reviews). In general, one of three outcomes can be expected: (1) no current reproduction, all energy allocated to the future, which occurs during the juvenile period and during unfavorable circumstances, when even a small allocation to reproduction increases fitness less than an additional allocation to growth or maintenance; (2) a mixed allocation of effort to present reproduction and to future reproduction, where, at optimum, the fitness benefits derived from an extra unit of effort to current and future reproduction are equal; or (3) full allocation to reproduction followed by death (semelparity), which occurs when even a small allocation to the future is worth less than an additional allocation to current reproduction (e.g., in spectacular fashion, salmon, whose soma decomposes as they spawn). In general, optimal life history programs maximize total allocations of energy to reproduction over the life course (Charnov, 1993).

Senescence appears to be an inevitable by-product of optimal allocation design (Kirkwood, 1990). If maintenance were perfect and, therefore, senescence did not occur, a small additional investment in further maintenance would have no effect, as the upper limit would have been reached. At this point, then, some reallocation of effort to reproduction would positively affect fitness. Hence, the disposable soma theory states, it is always optimal for organisms to allow the body to decay at a nonzero rate.

As risk of death due to difficult-to-avoid causes such as predation, accidents, and so on increases, the benefit of allocating energy and resources to the future diminishes (Kirkwood & Rose, 1991), as that energy is more likely to be "wasted." Accordingly, greater "extrinsic" mortality risks (death due to unavoidable causes) lead to faster senescence. Accordingly, much of LHT (e.g., Charnov, 1993) models life history outcomes as a function of age-specific rates of extrinsic mortality (although see later discussion on embodied capital).

The Trade-Off between Quantity and Quality of Offspring   A second major life history trade-off, first discussed by Lack (1954, 1968), concerns a division within the resources allocated to current reproduction: allocation to increase offspring *quantity* versus allocation to increase offspring *quality*. This trade-off, typically operationalized as number versus survival of offspring (e.g., Harpending, Draper, & Pennington, 1990; Lack, 1954, 1968; Lloyd, 1987; Smith & Fretwell, 1974), arises because parents have limited resources to invest in reproduction and, hence, additional offspring must reduce average investment per offspring. In a simple model, selection is expected to shape investment per offspring to maximize offspring number times rate of survival. When, as typically assumed, the benefits of investment decrease as level of investment increases (i.e., the return curve is diminishing), the optimum is reached when the proportional decrease in number of offspring produced equals the proportional increase in survival of offspring to adulthood (Harpending et al., 1990). Hence, the optimal investment is less than that required for maximal survival (as the proportional increase from investment is ~0 at maximum survival). In addition, the optimal amount of investment per offspring is independent of parental income (Smith & Fretwell, 1974), such that lifetime fertility is merely total resources divided by resources expended per offspring. More complex multigenerational models consider not only offspring survival but also the adult fitness of offspring, which can vary due to body, health, skills, and so on, accrued as a result of parental investment (Kaplan, 1996).

Sexual Reproduction, Life History Theory, and the Trade-Off between Mating and Parenting Effort   Sexual reproduction complicates the quantity-quality trade-off. Whereas offspring share roughly equal amounts of their parents' genetic material, parents may contribute unequally to their viability. Offspring are, in effect, public goods, with each parent profiting from the investments of the other parent and having an incentive to divert resources to the production of additional offspring. Conflicts of interests between the sexes result.

A near-universal outcome of sexual reproduction is the divergent evolution of the two sexes. Sex is defined by gamete size, the sex with the larger gametes being female. Larger gametes represent greater initial energetic investment in offspring. The difference in initial investment is often exaggerated with investment beyond energy in gametes, but it may also disappear or even reverse. Females provide all investment to offspring in ~95% of mammalian species, but males provide similar amounts or more total investments in most altricial birds, male brooding fish, and some insects (Clutton-Brock & Parker, 1992).

The sex difference in investment into parenting (increasing offspring quality) and mating (increasing offspring number) that typically arises should be due to a difference in the payoffs to each. When females are highly selective about mates due to greater initial investment in offspring (Trivers, 1972), those males who are eligible for mating (by virtue of female preferences, often based on genetic quality) can expect a relatively high future reproductive rate, leading them to engage in mating rather than parental effort. Males who might benefit by parenting (because of a low expected future reproductive rate derived from mating effort) don't get the chance because females don't select them (Kokko & Jennions, 2003).[3] In some circumstances—presumably ones in which the value of biparental care is substantial—females partly select males for their willingness to invest in parenting, leading to a smaller sex difference in allocation toward mating and parenting.

Competition for mates and sexual conflicts of interest lead to inefficiencies in offspring production due to what economists refer to as negative externalities. One sex (typically males) will "waste" resources on costly displays (Grafen, 1991) or fighting rather than offspring production. The sexes may furthermore interfere with each other's reproductive strategies (Rice, 1996).

ECOLOGY AND LIFE HISTORY EVOLUTION

Variations in ecological factors (e.g., food supply, mortality hazards) imply different optimal energy allocation strategies (e.g., Charnov, 1993; Kozlowski & Weigert, 1986), which lead to across- and within-species differences in life histories. Some organisms, such as bivalve mollusks, tortoises, and porcupines, apparently benefit significantly from allocations to predator defense and live long lives. Birds, bats, and primates appear to lower predation rates by spending less time in terrestrial habitats and by being able to escape to aerial strata. Primates may reduce predation through grouping and social behavior. Species that eat more variable or difficult-to-capture foods probably benefit more from investments in learning than do more simple feeders, such as grazing animals.

Species-level adaptive specializations result in bundles of life history characteristics, which can generally be arrayed on a fast-slow continuum (Promislow & Harvey, 1990). For example, mammalian species on the fast end exhibit short gestation times, early reproduction, small body size, large litters, and high mortality rates, whereas species on the slow end have the opposite features.[4]

In response to ecological variability, many, if not most, organisms are selected to be capable of slowing down or speeding up their life histories depending on conditions (e.g., food availability, density of conspecifics, mortality hazards) over several different time scales: over the short term in relation to food supply and energetic output (Hurtado & Hill, 1990; Lack, 1968), over longer time intervals through developmental effects (e.g., short adult stature in rats resulting from food shortages during youth; Shanley & Kirkwood, 2000), and through differential selection on genetic variants in different habitats (e.g., grasshoppers at different elevations; Tatar, Gray, & Carey, 1997).

Similarly, male and female parental investments vary with local ecology (Clutton-Brock & Parker, 1992). A classic example is katydids. Males provide females with "nuptial gifts" (boluses of condensed food energy) to support offspring production. Manipulations of food density, which affect the foraging time necessary for males to produce gifts, shift male and female mating effort. When food is sparse, male provisioning requires more time than female provisioning, males are in short supply, and females actively compete for males; as food density increases, this trend is reversed and males compete for females (Gwyne, 1991).

---

[3] The lack of certain paternity also leads males to devalue parental effort.

[4] A related distinction was once referred to as *r-selected* (fast) versus *K-selected* (slow) life histories (MacArthur & Wilson, 1967). The idea was that species differed in the extent to which they evolved in expanding populations or populations near carrying capacities. Because slow and fast life histories are controlled by additional factors, this particular conceptualization is now seldom used in LHT.

A mix of specialization and flexibility is fundamental to understanding human life histories and mating systems. It is generally agreed that the large human brain supports the ability to respond *flexibly* to environmental variation and to learn culturally.[5] At the same time, the commitment to a large brain, a long period of development, and sensitivity to environmental information necessary to make it fully functional require *specializations* for a specific slow life history. In fact, consideration of the learning-intensive nature of human adaptation reveals shortcomings in traditional LHT and inspires a more general approach to life history evolution, the focus of the next section.

Embodied Capital and the Brain

Growth and development can be viewed as investments in stocks of embodied capital: investments in self that can be translated into future reproduction. In a physical sense, embodied capital is organized somatic tissue (muscles, digestive organs, brains, and so on). In a functional sense, embodied capital includes strength, speed, immune function, skill, knowledge, and other abilities. Because allocations to maintenance counteract the depreciation of stocks of embodied capital with time, they, too, can be treated as investments in embodied capital. In this language, the present-future reproductive trade-off is that between investments in own embodied capital versus reproduction, and the quantity-quality trade-off is that between investments in the embodied capital of offspring versus their number.

When translated and extended into an embodied capital framework, LHT allows us to entertain possibilities not explicitly conceptualized by standard treatments. Standard models tend to treat investment in the future as physical growth. But growth is only one form of such investment, as illustrated by brain development. The brain has the capacity to transform present experiences into future performance. Brain expansion among higher primates represents an increased investment in this capacity (Armstrong & Falk, 1982; Fleagle, 1999; Parker & McKinney, 1999). But this investment is realized not only in growth of neural tissue; substantial energy and time may be allocated to encountering experiences that, through changes in neural tissue, yield benefits realized over time—investments in the future.

How selection affects these investments depends on costs and benefits realized over an organism's lifetime. Growing and maintaining neural tissue entail substantial energetic costs (e.g., Holliday, 1978) and, by curtailing "preprogrammed" behavioral routines, compromise performance early in life (e.g., consider the motoric incompetence of human infants). Hence, the *net* benefits of learning are only fully realized as the organism ages (see Figure 2.1). In a niche where there is little to learn, benefits never offset early costs and smaller brains are favored. In a more challenging niche, small brains might be better early in life but much worse later, such that large brains are favored.

Other systems may similarly become more functional through time—for example, the immune system, which requires exposure to antigens to become fully

---

[5] Naturally, learning and flexible responsiveness themselves require specialized psychological adaptations. The point here is merely that learning and flexibility entail costs in currencies of acquisition time and brain tissue.

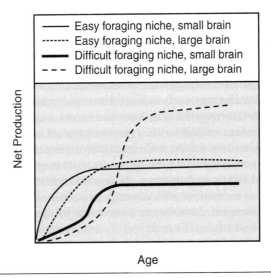

Figure 2.1   Age-Specific Effects of Brains on Net Production: Easy and Difficult Foraging Niches.

functional (presumably a reason mortality decreases from birth to the end of childhood). Embodied capital theory can address the evolution of any form of investment in a stock of capital that pays off over time.

COEVOLUTIONARY PROCESSES AND THEIR MODELING

Because the returns gained from large brains lie in the future, ecological conditions favoring them also favor greater expenditure on survival. Conversely, exogenous ecological conditions that lower mortality favor increased expenditure on survival and hence also greater investment in brain capital (Kaplan & Robson, 2002; Robson & Kaplan, 2003; cf. Carey & Judge, 2001). As expected, life span and brain size (controlling for body size) positively covary in mammals (Sacher, 1959) and primates (e.g., Allman, McLaughlin, & Hakeem, 1993; Judge & Carey, 2000; Kaplan & Robson, 2002; Kaplan et al., in press).

Standard LHT treatments are not fully adequate to model this coevolution. They assume an "extrinsic" component of mortality not subject to selection (Charnov, 1993; Kozlowski & Wiegert, 1986), which provides leverage for understanding other life history traits, such as age of first reproduction and rates of aging. But this approach is theoretically unsatisfying, as organisms exert control over virtually all causes of mortality (e.g., by altering patterns of travel to avoid predators, by investing in immune function). It is also analytically limited in that it prevents a full understanding of how mortality rates evolve. A more useful approach is to assume that what varies as a function of ecological factors are not set mortality rates, but rather *functional relationships* between mortality and efforts allocated to reducing it (see Figure 2.2 on p. 76). Exogenous variation can be thought of in terms of varying "assault" types and rates. For example, warm, humid climates favor the evolution of disease organisms and, therefore, increase the assault rate and diversity of diseases affecting organisms. These climates also entail relationships between efforts allocated to reducing them and mortality reduction.

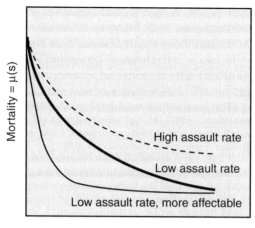

Figure 2.2   Mortality as a Function of Investments.

This alternative treatment of mortality requires dynamic programming techniques, analytical tools that are well developed in economics (e.g., formal analysis of capital investments). Robson and Kaplan (2003) used this approach to show that, indeed, allocation of effort into growing brains and reducing mortality should coevolve. (See that paper for an illustration of its analytical methods.)

COST-BENEFIT ANALYSIS AND LIFE HISTORY THEORY IN BEHAVIORAL ECOLOGY

LHT is part of a more general approach within behavioral ecology and theoretical biology: the optimality approach, which attempts to specify the strategy that would result from natural selection in the absence of genetic or developmental constraints by analyzing costs and benefits of possible strategies within a particular domain (see Parker & Maynard Smith, 1991). This approach revolutionized theoretical biology in the 1960s and 1970s (e.g., Cronin, 1991). Before then, biologists did not systematically think about selection in explicitly economic terms (maximization of benefits minus costs in the currency of fitness). Doing so led to an explosion of new theories, notably many of the "middle-level evolutionary theories" (Buss, 1995) that evolutionary psychologists rely on: for example, parental investment theory (Trivers, 1972), parent-offspring conflict (Trivers, 1974), sex allocation theory (e.g., Charnov, 1982), sperm competition theory (e.g., Parker, 1970), optimal foraging theory (Charnov, 1976), in addition to life history theory. Today, cost-benefit modeling is a core approach within evolutionary biology and the dominant one in behavioral ecology (see Grafen, 1991).

Cost-benefit analysis does not require LHT. For example, we can model foraging strategies in terms of the benefits of energy capture and the costs of expending energy, with the optimal strategy being the one that maximizes immediate net caloric intake. Such modeling is not LHT because it doesn't explicitly consider the effects of strategy choice over time. Modeling adopts a life history approach when it explicitly considers the effects of potential strategies on fitness outcomes at all subsequent ages to which the organism might live.

As originally conceived, LHT concerned the timing of life events. Increasingly, however, biologists have found that the understanding of phenomena not traditionally thought of as life history events in fact requires an explicit life history approach. Hence, LHT has increasingly subsumed costs-benefit analysis in many areas. Rather than being defined by the phenomena it explains, LHT is a general analytical approach to understanding selection.

An Example: Honest Signaling Theory   Recent developments in signaling theory illustrate this point. "Honest" signals of quality are those that individuals of higher quality ("big signalers") can afford but those of lower quality cannot. Traditionally, these signals have been thought of as *viability indicators* (Andersson, 1994)—big signalers presumably being better able to survive than others. In theory, they can "waste" more of their survival ability on a signal than others, thereby increasing fitness through fertility enhancement. A prominent instance of this model is the immunocompetence signaling model. Individuals are presumed to vary in parasite resistance (Hamilton & Zuk, 1982), and high-quality individuals signal their parasite resistance to potential mates with an immunosuppressant (e.g., testosterone-dependent signal; Folstad & Karter, 1992). Viability indicators have been contrasted with arbitrary signals (see Cronin, 1991; Fisher, 1958). The latter are presumably not honest signals of quality and hence correlated with ability to survive; rather, they presumably evolved simply because they enhanced attractiveness (e.g., by drawing attention from females due to brightness or extravagance).

Grafen (1990) first modeled selection for viability indicators. He assumed that all individuals, regardless of quality, obtain the same fitness *benefits* from a particular level of a signal (i.e., which derive from mating advantages advertised through the signal to others, who have no basis for discriminating individuals' fitness except via the signal). The signal can evolve to display quality when the fitness *costs* (in the currency of mortality) associated with developing and maintaining a particular level of the signal are less for individuals of higher quality than for those of lower quality (i.e., it evolves because of differential costs as a function of quality, not differential benefits). The signal "honestly" conveys quality because it is not in the interest of individuals of lower quality for them to "cheat" and develop a larger signal; the mortality costs they would suffer exceed the fertility benefits they could derive from the increased signal size.

Recently, limitations of Grafen's model have been noted—ones due to its not taking a life history approach (e.g., Getty, 1998, 2002). At each moment, an individual is faced with a decision of how much effort to allocate to a signal. The incremental fitness gain garnered (or loss suffered) from additional investment into the signal accrues over time, due to its effects on repeated reproductive bouts. (Indeed, a signal may be thought of as a form of embodied capital.) At the current age and all subsequent ages, fitness is the probability of living to that age times the fertility at that age. Because benefits accrue over time, the larger marginal gains from investment in a trait enjoyed by big signalers can derive from larger *benefits* (e.g., summed over several time periods) rather than lesser costs, contrary to a key assumption in Grafen's model. Although the momentary gains two individuals derive from a signal of a particular size should not vary as a function of their quality, one individual may derive greater benefit from investing in the trait than the other because of differences in expected mortality.

The implications of a life history approach are dramatic (see Getty, 2002; Kokko, Brooks, McNamara, & Houston, 2002)—indeed, LHT transforms the foundations of honest signaling theory. In a stable, honest signaling system, big signalers (i.e., those of higher quality) need not have greater survivorship than small signalers, contrary to previous thought. The relationship between age-specific mortality and signal size depends on the precise details of the signal size-fertility function and quality-dependent trade-offs between signal size and mortality. Under some conditions (e.g., when fertility gradually increases as a function of signal size; Getty, 2002), there is no reason to expect individuals of higher quality to have greater survivorship than those of lower quality. (In such cases, higher quality individuals end up signaling much more than lower quality individuals, giving them a fertility benefit but no survival advantage.) In extreme instances, individuals of higher quality may have *lower* survivorship than individuals of lower quality (Kokko et al., 2002). (Quality here cannot be defined by ability to survive per se, but rather by the ability to convert energy into replicate forms.) The same holds true of the association among immunocompetence, parasite loads, and quality: Depending on the quality-dependent marginal effects of allocating additional effort to immunocompetence, individuals of higher quality may be more or less immunocompetent than individuals of lower quality and hence have higher or lower pathogen loads (Getty, 2002; see also Kokko, Brooks, Jennions, & Morley, 2003).

In this view, the distinction between viability-indicator signal models and arbitrary signal models breaks down. *Arbitrary* signal models refer to situations in which a signal is not associated with survival but big signalers enjoy greater fertility benefits. But from a life history perspective, they may still be associated with quality. Indeed, from a life history standpoint, in all stable signaling situations in which a signal yields fitness benefits, signal size *will* relate to quality. In some situations, it will also relate to survival. In others, it will relate to fertility alone (and may even relate to survival negatively). In these latter situations, big signalers do not survive less because they *couldn't* survive more; rather, their optimal allocation strategy leads them to allocate effort into a signal at a cost to survival. Rather than define two qualitatively different signaling models, viability indicator and arbitrary models anchor two ends of a continuum of honest signaling of quality (Kokko et al., 2002). This fundamental insight was made possible when a life history approach to signaling was taken.[6]

Based on the distinction between viability-indicator models and arbitrary models of signaling, recent research has attempted to test whether facial masculinity, facial attractiveness, or symmetry are honest signals of quality by correlating them with health outcomes or longevity, with mixed results (e.g., Kalick, Zebrowitz, Langlois, & Johnson, 1998). LHT tells us that these tests cannot reveal whether these traits are honest signals of quality.

ENACTMENT OF ALLOCATION DECISIONS

We have considered the *selection pressures* that forge life histories; LHT describes these pressures. Full understanding of life histories requires analysis of all of

---

[6] These outcomes are in fact not inconsistent with Grafen's (1990) model; at the same time, however, they were not at all apparent from that model. Only a model that fully takes into account effects on fitness throughout the life course—a life history model—makes these implications clear.

Tinbergen's (1963) four questions, regarding proximate mechanisms, selective advantage, ontogeny, and phylogeny. An understanding of proximate mechanisms and their development is of particular importance. What are the mechanisms whereby life history decisions are made and executed? And how do these mechanisms develop?

LHT speaks of allocation "decisions" made by an organism, shorthand for saying that organisms differentially use energy and time for various life tasks. It does not imply a "decision maker"; LHT neither requires nor implies a "fitness maximizer" or homunculus that calculates costs and benefits. Rather, selection has presumably shaped specific psychological and physiological mechanisms to be sensitive to environmental factors that moderate optimal allocation of effort in a way that would have yielded (near-) maximal fitness (relative to alternative ways of allocating effort, given trade-offs) ancestrally under the varying circumstances and life stages it experiences.

Energy allocation decisions often require coordinated tuning of a variety of systems. Increased allocation to reproduction, for instance, should be coordinated with less allocation to growth. Increased effort to immune function in response to infection may best be synchronized with lower overall expenditure. Adaptive coordination often requires systems of communication and control distributed across a variety of somatic systems. Endocrine systems have, in part, been designed to fulfill this role.

Endocrine systems are internal communication devices. Hormones released at one site (e.g., the gonads, the adrenal cortex) are "picked up" by receptors at other sites (e.g., brain structures) and thereby affect those sites. Endocrine systems can thereby simultaneously regulate a great number of different functions and modulate allocation of energy. Naturally, the precise ways that they do so depends on the distribution of receptors and their actions in response to hormone binding. Presumably, the system has been tuned by selection (where the relevant selection pressures are, once again, described by LHT) such that endocrine action optimally modulates allocation of effort in ways.

Consider an example: reproductive hormones. During puberty, adrenarche initiates cascades of developmental changes in both sexes taking place over almost a decade. In females, mechanisms regulating energy balance lead to fat storage and regular menstrual cycling. As mediated by estrogen and other hormones, increased energy is allocated to reproductive traits and functions, including secondary sexual characteristics, while growth ultimately subsides. Males begin producing androgens in substantial quantities, which lead to greater musculature and investments in forms of mating effort, including social competition and physical performance. At the same time, some investments in immune function are withdrawn. For both sexes, modulation of psychological processes (e.g., desires, motives, situation-specific responses) is as integral to the matrix of coordinated responses as modulation of energy utilization (for an overview, see Ellison, 2001).

Reproductive hormones also regulate differential investments on shorter time scales. Pregnancy requires maternal allocation of energy to the developing fetus, which occurs through chemical communication (e.g., involving gonadotrophins) among fetal tissue, uterine tissue, the ovaries, and the brain. Indeed, fetuses that do not "reveal" their worthiness through this process may be aborted (e.g., Ellison, 2001; Haig, 1993). Male testosterone levels subside when men become fathers, facilitating reallocation of reproductive effort from mating to parenting (e.g., Gray, Kahlenberg, Barrett, Lipson, & Ellison, 2002).

A host of other endocrine and other communication systems modulate energy release, tissue-specific uptake, and psychological processes in the face of other events that signaled, ancestrally, immediate changes in optimal allocation: for example, glucocorticoid modulation of the stress response, the effects of epinephrine on energy release and utilization in fight-or-flight circumstances, and modulation of immune function and energy utilization by other tissues achieved through the action of a variety of interleukins in the face of risk of actual pathogen attack.

None of these systems demands a "central command post" directing activity of the multitude of receptor sites and, through their action, other sites are ultimately affected. Rather, the coordinated efforts are akin to that of a football team running an offensive play, where each player has a preplanned assignment, which, in concert with others' execution of their assignment, has been designed to achieve an adaptive outcome. The "design" of the "play" (assignments of individual "players") has been shaped through selection.

Reallocations of effort typically involve both physiological and psychological processes; events that initiate reallocation must be perceived and acted on for reallocation to occur. In most instances, the psychological processes involved are only vaguely understood, a theme to which we return later.

HUMAN LIFE HISTORY

We now turn to topics concerning human life histories: the evolution of large brains, development and childhood, and aging.

BRAIN AND LIFE SPAN EVOLUTION IN HUMANS

Relative to close ancestors, humans have several distinct life history features (Kaplan, Hill, Lancaster, & Hurtado, 2000): late onset of reproduction, extended period of childhood vulnerability, and long life span. In addition, we have very large brains. Even Australiopithecus had a brain only about two-thirds the size of early Homos (controlling for body size; Martin, 1981). A key question concerns the nature of the changes that caused selection to shape human life histories and forms of embodied capital to differ from our ancestors.

Differences between the diets of chimpanzees and human hunter-gatherers may be key. In one comparison, vertebrate meat contributed, on average, 60% of the calories in 10 human foraging societies (range = 30% to 80%), whereas 5 chimpanzee communities obtained about 2% of their energy from hunted foods (Kaplan et al., 2000).[7] Extracted foods (nonmobile resources embedded in a protective context such as underground, in hard shells, or bearing toxins: roots, nuts, seeds, most invertebrate products, and difficult-to-extract plant parts such as palm fiber) accounted for about 32% of the forager diet and just 3% of the chimpanzee diet. Collected resources (fruits, leaves, flowers, and other easily accessible plant parts) formed the bulk of the chimpanzee diet: 95% versus only 8% of the forager diet.

---

[7] The hunter-gatherer data come from studies on populations during periods when they were almost completely dependent on wild foods, with little modern technology (and no firearms), no significant outside interference in interpersonal violence or fertility rates, and no significant access to modern medicine.

Relative to humans, then, chimpanzees consume relatively low-quality foods easy to gather.[8] Humans generally consume nutrient-dense plant and animal resources. If chimpanzees could easily consume these foods, they would have evolved to do so because a diet of nutrient-dense foods is obviously superior to one of low-quality foods, all else equal. It makes sense to think, then, that humans possess special abilities to acquire nutrient-dense foods, including creative, skill-intensive techniques supported by a large brain. Possibly, large brains and long lives in humans are coevolved responses to an extreme commitment to learning-intensive foraging strategies and a dietary shift toward nutrient-dense but difficult-to-acquire foods, allowing them to exploit a wide variety of foods and thereby colonize all terrestrial and coastal ecosystems (Kaplan, 1997; Kaplan et al., 2000).

Age-specific acquisition rates of foods lend support to this theory. In most environments, people most easily acquire fruits. In Ache foragers, peak daily fruit production is reached by the mid- to late teens; even 2- to 3-year-olds can pick fruits from the ground at 30% the maximum adult rate. By contrast, the rate of acquiring extracted resources often increases well into adulthood. For instance, Hiwi women do not reach peak root acquisition rates until 35 to 45 (Kaplan et al., 2000); the rate of 10-year-old girls is only 15% of the adult maximum. In the Hambukushu, nut-cracking rates peak at about 35 (see also Blurton Jones, Hawkes, & Draper, 1994b). Presumably, people get better at these tasks in adulthood because they involve skills refined over time.

Human hunting may be particularly skill based. It differs qualitatively from hunting by other animals. Rather than ambush prey or use stealth and pursuit techniques, human hunters draw on and integrate a wealth of information (e.g., of ecology, seasonality, current weather, expected animal behavior, fresh animal signs) both during search and after prey are encountered (Leibenberg, 1990); tend to select prey in prime condition rather than prey made vulnerable by youth, old age, or disease (Alvard, 1995; Stiner, 1991); and regularly consider alternative courses of action in reference to spatial and temporal mental maps of resource availability, which cover areas much larger than those covered by chimpanzees (in a lifetime, perhaps, on average, 1,000 times larger; e.g., Wrangham & Smuts, 1980). Among the Hiwi, Ache, and Hadza, peak rates are reached in the mid-30s; rates of 20-year-olds are, remarkably, only 25% to 50% of the adult maximum (Kaplan et al., 2000; Marlowe, unpublished data).

Because human production heavily involves activities that require skills to perform effectively, young humans do not pay their own way. Figure 2.3 on page 82 presents net production (i.e., food acquired minus food consumed) by age for chimpanzees and human foragers (Kaplan et al., 2000). Chimpanzees have net negative production until about age 5, zero production during a period of juvenile growth, and, for females but not males, a net surplus during the reproductive phase, which is allocated to nursing. By contrast, humans produce less than they consume for about 20 years, with the trough reaching its nadir at about 14. Net production peaks much later relative to chimpanzees—but the peak is also much higher (a 1,750 versus 250 cal per day), presumably the payoff of long dependency.

---

[8] Chimpanzees consume high-density foods relative to many other primates, as they do hunt to obtain some meat and perform some extractive foraging such as termite extraction and nut cracking. Within the primate order, chimpanzees also have relatively large brains. Relative to humans, however, the quantitative difference is great.

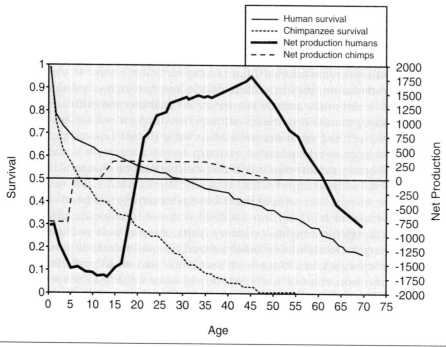

Figure 2.3 Survival and Net Food Production: Human Foragers and Chimpanzees.

Brains and skills can be thought of as forms of embodied capital. To acquire them, humans pay a substantial cost: They allocate energy and time to their acquisition and the hardware (specific brain tissue) that support their acquisition—which could have been used other ways (e.g., direct reproduction, continued foraging for fruits). These upfront costs ultimately pay off over time, as individuals put them to use to produce nutrient-dense foods not otherwise accessible. As emphasized earlier, however, investment in embodied capital can only be selected if, on average, individuals live long enough to pay off and, indeed, exceed, initial investment costs. Figure 2.3 also presents probabilities of survival by age for chimpanzees and human foragers (Kaplan et al., 2000), which reveal why the human age profile of productivity requires a long adult life span. Only about 30% of chimpanzees ever born reach 20, the age when humans finally produce as much as they consume. Less than 5% of chimpanzees reach 45, when human net production peaks. By age 15, chimpanzees have consumed 43% and produced 40% of their expected lifetime calories; by contrast, humans have consumed 22% and produced only 4% of their expected lifetime calories.

Figure 2.4 illustrates why the human age profile of production is incompatible with chimpanzee survival rates. The thin solid line plots cumulative net production by age for chimpanzees. The bold line plots expected net production for foragers (net production times the probability of being alive) at each age. The area of the deficit period, prior to age 20, approximately equals the surplus gained after 20. The dashed line shows a hypothetical expected net production profile of a human forager with a chimpanzee survival function; here, the area of the deficit is much larger than the area of the surplus because few individuals

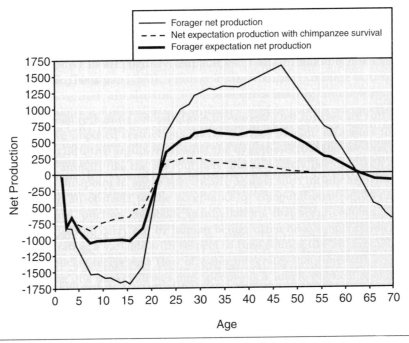

Figure 2.4 Net Production and Expected Net Production among Foragers.

survive to highly productive ages. An organism with a mortality curve like that of a chimpanzee clearly could not afford to have a production curve like that of humans; a species that has lifetime negative net production can't possibly evolve.

Quite possibly within humans, then, large brain size coevolved with a dependent juvenile period allowing skill acquisition; allocations of energy to large brain size also coevolved with allocations of energy to mortality reduction (e.g., large allocations to immune function, behavioral strategies designed to reduce mortality through predation such as formation of larger social groups and lower risk taking), resulting in long life spans.

DEVELOPMENT AND AGING

During childhood, humans allocate energy and time to growth of soma and development of embodied stocks of capital. Aging entails degradation of these stocks. Understanding the timing and rate of growth as well as degradation of different parts of the soma as well as learning requires a life history approach.

Characteristic Features of the Human Growth and Brain Development Curve Humans are generally considered extremely altricial—relatively undeveloped and nonfunctional at birth. But in some respects human babies are well developed relative to close ancestors. Compared to gorilla and chimpanzee infants, human neonates are large (3,000 grams, versus 2,327 and 1,766 for gorillas and chimpanzees, respectively; Kuzawa, 1998; Leigh & Shea, 1996). (Female adult gorillas, by contrast, weigh about 60% more than adult women.) The differences are only partly accounted for by gestation times; human fetuses gain more weight per day. Human brains are particularly large at birth—about twice the size of chimpanzee brains (indeed, the human infant brain weighs about that of an adult chimpanzee). Body composition also differs. Human neonates have 3.75 times the fat stores of infant mammals of comparable weight (Kuzawa, 1998), probably used to support rapid postnatal neural growth.

By contrast, humans grow proportionally much more slowly than chimpanzees during middle and late childhood. Ten-year-old humans are smaller than same-age chimpanzees, have low appetite, and are relatively nonproductive; indeed, parents often insist that children remain in safe places and encourage them to produce only easily and safely acquired food (Blurton Jones, Hawkes, & Draper, 1994a). In adolescence, however, humans develop a voracious appetite and experience a growth spurt not seen in chimpanzees, whose size they then surpass.

This pattern can be understood in the context of human life history outlined earlier. Infants grow fast until they comfortably support large brains. Young children do little work and do not need large bodies. Their time is dedicated to intensive learning through observation and play, as well as a large energetic allocation to the immune system (McDade, 2003; Worthman, 1999), which serves to reduce pathogen-caused mortality throughout the life span. They grow slowly. At the beginning of adolescence, when children's brains are almost ready for reproduction and higher rates of productivity, they grow and reach adult body size rapidly.

Humans stretch out intellectual development at every stage. The production of cortical neurons in mammals is limited to early fetal development within which, compared to monkeys and apes, human embryos spend an additional 25 days (Deacon, 1997; Parker & McKinney, 1999). Proliferation of neurons in early fetal development extends other phases of brain development, resulting in a larger, more complex, and more effective brain. Whereas myelination of the brain is largely complete in 3.5 years in macaques, in humans it continues to at least age 12 (Gibson, 1986). Formal abstract logical reasoning, which appears to facilitate the growth in knowledge that results in peak productivity in the mid-30s, does not emerge until age 16 to 18 (Parker & McKinney, 1999).

Timing of Developmental Achievements   A life history perspective generally expects that processes of development will be coordinated and synchronous, as whole organisms live or die. It doesn't pay to fully develop a heart without also investing in liver function and, similarly, it doesn't pay to fully invest in a brain without also investing in a body that can support it (Hill, 1993). At the same time, the relative value of some investments may shift across time, and these shifts may be key to understanding developmental sequences. Language, for instance, is arguably one of the most computationally complex and difficult cognitive processes in which humans engage, but the ability to understand and produce a near-infinite number of utterances is largely intact by the time children finish the toddler stage and before they are competent at running. Language acquisition is presumably front-loaded (by adaptations specialized for language acquisition in early childhood), even at the expense of delaying the acquisition of other capabilities, because language greatly increases the rate at which children learn about the world; the earlier its acquisition, the longer the period of its benefits. LHT offers a principled framework within which to investigate the sequencing of developmental milestones in different domains. It focuses attention on both present and future costs and benefits of different investments in specific abilities at each point in time, within the context of an overall life history strategy and a set of coadapted traits.

The Growth/Reproduction Trade-Off   A major event in the life course of an organism is its transition from a prereproductive period to a reproductive period, a transition during which, in many species, major skeletal growth ceases. In the framework of embodied capital theory, stocks of somatic capital accumulate during the prereproductive period. The enhanced future rate of reproduction that results trades off against the time not spent reproducing. The onset of reproductive capability (in human females, menarche) has been selected, in theory, to maximize the total expected reproductive output (rate at which reproduction is expected to occur times age-specific probability of survival integrated over reproductive years) under the constraints of this trade-off.

The onset of menarche may depend on individual or culturewide conditions. Draper and Harpending (1982) proposed that the trade-off between development and reproduction should depend on the expected parental effort in a population, an idea subsequently extended and revised by Belsky, Steinberg, and Draper (1990). Increased stress, this theory argues, predicts low levels of parental effort in the population when the child reaches adulthood, which favors quantity over quality and an earlier onset of reproduction. Chisholm (1999) offered an alternative life history perspective that explains the shift through the current versus future reproduction trade-off rather than a quantity-quality trade-off. He argued that the age of female menarche should be sensitive to cues that predict mortality risk: With increased risk of mortality, women should experience menarche earlier.

A variety of environmental factors do indeed influence menarche. Poor nutritional status leads to delayed menarche (e.g., Aw & Tye, 1970), presumably due to slow growth and accumulation of fat deposition, such that the benefits of continuing to grow outweigh the cost of waiting to reproduce despite the accelerated mortality schedule associated with poor diet. By contrast, earlier menarche is associated with psychosocial stressors: family conflict (Moffitt, Caspi, Belsky, & Silva, 1992), absence of positive harmonious relations with parents (particularly fathers; Ellis, McFadyen-Ketchum, Dodge, Pettit, & Bates, 1999) in middle childhood (e.g., Ellis & Garber, 2000; Graber, Brooks-Gunn, & Warren, 1995; Steinberg, 1988), and divorce and father absence (Ellis & Garber, 2000; Jones, Leeton, McLeod, & Wood, 1972; Moffitt et al., 1992; Surbey, 1990).

It is interesting that father absence and familial discord or lack of closeness appear to independently predict menarche (Ellis & Garber, 2000). Moreover, the former's relation may be driven by the presence of a stepfather or other adult male figure rather than father absence per se. Girls in stepfather-present homes reach puberty earlier than ones in single-mother homes. And the earlier a new male figure enters a girl's life, the earlier she reaches puberty (an association not accounted for by timing of divorce per se; Ellis & Garber, 2000). These findings suggest alternative life history explanations. Rather than being driven by a focus on quantity over quality or increased mortality, the effect of exposure to alternative father figures may lead to earlier onset of the reproductive period because their presence signals a conflict of interest between mothers and others over degree of investment in their offspring. (In addition, stepfathers may be a risk for sexual or physical abuse.) If daughters can expect to receive less investment, a shortened prereproductive period may optimize net benefits. In addition, it could particularly pay daughters in such situations to seek support from romantic partners. Consistent with this interpretation, Ellis and Garber (2000) report hints that the accelerating effect of a significant mother-boyfriend relationship is enhanced when characterized by dyadic conflict.

Aging and Differential Decline across Domains   As discussed earlier, trade-offs between current and future reproduction purportedly entail aging. Individuals cannot simultaneously maximize fitness and perfectly maintain somatic tissue.

Both male physical strength and fluid intelligence peak early in the reproductive period (as a life history perspective expects of investments that deteriorate through somatic decline; e.g., Kirkwood, 1990). Knowledge-based embodied capital (crystallized intelligence) and productivity, however, continue to increase through the first 4 to 5 decades of life (Horn, 1968; Kaplan et al., 2000). Mortality rates remain low and virtually constant. Offspring dependency loads on parents in foragers peak about age 40, just before grandparenthood begins. Through middle age, dependency loads diminish, as does productivity. After age 60, physical and psychological deterioration is rapid and mortality rates rise dramatically. Older adults attempt to be productive, reallocating their time to skill-intensive but less energy-intensive activities. In addition, they may effectively instruct youth, drawing on their knowledge of the habitat and sociopolitical skills. The human life course has almost certainly been positively shaped by selection through middle age but questions remain about age 60+. These years may be a nonfunctional period of collapse that takes time. Alternatively, aspects of this phase may have been shaped by important inclusive fitness benefits produced during it.

These alternatives may offer unique predictions. If old age is merely a period of collapse, near-synchronous aging of different abilities might be expected (Hill, 1993). An evolved strategy that allocates resources across different somatic components in a way that keeps decline in step is expected, for a healthy heart or brain is of little value if the liver can no longer eliminate toxins. If, however, individuals contribute to inclusive fitness in old age through knowledge transfer, we might expect that crystallized intelligence and language ability were selected to senesce at rates slower than other physiological systems.

It appears that, indeed, humans are designed to experience slow aging of the brain compared to other physiological systems. Macaques exhibit Alzheimer's-like neuropathology (senile plaques, neurocytoskeletal abnormalities) and cerebral atrophy by age 22 to 25. In contrast, humans rarely show such changes before age 60 (<1%); they are common (>30%) only in the 80s (Finch & Sapolsky, 1999). An understanding of the differential allocation to somatic repair during the human life course is only now taking shape.

PSYCHOLOGICAL ADAPTATIONS WITHIN A LIFE HISTORY FRAMEWORK

We have discussed human life history phenomena—the timing of developmental events, reproduction, and aging—within the framework of modern LHT. As noted earlier, however, LHT has come to be an approach within theoretical biology that offers insights into the selection on just about any evolved outcome. (We specifically discussed life history approaches to signaling.) We now turn to consider examples of how a life history approach can be applied to the understanding of psychological adaptations.

LIFE HISTORY PERSPECTIVES ON PSYCHOLOGICAL ADAPTATIONS

Evolutionary psychology attempts to understand psychological adaptations. The mainstream approach has several core elements (see, e.g., Buss, 1995, 2004; Tooby & Cosmides, 1992):

- Psychological adaptations are assumed to be domain-specific—information-processing specializations designed to accept specific input and act in particular ways on that input. In this sense, psychological adaptations are modular and many in number.
- Each psychological adaptation is assumed to represent a solution to an ancestral adaptive problem (e.g., detection of cheaters in reciprocal exchange, cuckoldry avoidance, kin detection, avoidance of toxic foods). Psychological adaptations tend to be special purpose and numerous because each adaptive problem demands specific mappings of information to outcomes that cannot be handled proficiently by general purpose information processing algorithms.
- Generally, human psychological adaptations are universal.

Evolutionary psychology research programs generally seek to identify specific psychological adaptations (i.e., specify ways in which information is specially processed within specific problem domains). In general, research strategies either begin with a specific adaptive problem and ask what sort of psychological adaptations would have solved it, or begin with a psychological phenomenon and ask how it might reflect a solution to an adaptive problem. As evidenced by this volume, this perspective has yielded many successes.

Psychological Adaptations and a Life History Framework   The core elements of this perspective within evolutionary psychology are perfectly compatible with LHT. Nonetheless, several additional observations about psychological adaptations follow from LHT:

- All features or activities require allocation of resources: energy, time, neural resources, and so on. Individuals should have evolved to allocate resources optimally under the constraints of trade-offs (in ancestral environments). But individuals should not have evolved *perfect* solutions to adaptive problems. As noted earlier, individuals cannot optimize fitness by perfectly repairing their soma. Repair of soma in the face of factors that damage it (e.g., free radicals) is clearly an adaptive problem. And individuals have evolved specialized adaptations to repair soma. But optimally, in the face of trade-offs, individuals will not perfectly repair it (even though, in principle, they may be able to do so) and hence will deteriorate. Similarly, trade-offs force compromises in the solutions of every life task.[9]

---

[9] The marginal value theorem implies that, at maximal fitness, the marginal value of allocation to all possible allocations is identical. The only way in which we could perfectly solve a particular problem at this optimum (i.e., the marginal gain be zero at optimum for that domain) is if the solution were cost free. But solutions are never cost free.

This need not imply that the structures of information processing algorithms themselves are compromised (though they may be). All information processing requires allocation of time and effort from limited shared resources (energy, attention, etc.), and a life history perspective implies that trade-offs in the allocation of these resources to the *utilization and operation* of specialized psychological adaptations compromise solutions in domains of adaptive problems.

For example, sexual jealousy is purportedly a specialized evolved response to threats to a romantic relationship (e.g., Buss, 2000). In both sexes, a partner suspected of having sex with another person (or suspected of being interested in sex with another person) may signal that a mate may abandon the relationship for another partner (or divert resources into another relationship). In men, a partner's infidelity may also threaten cuckoldry because men could potentially invest in offspring not their own. In men, then, sexual jealousy may be a particularly powerful motive designed to prevent cuckoldry (see Buss, 2000).

From a life history perspective, we should not expect that men will prevent cuckoldry *at all costs*. Cuckoldry prevention requires allocation of time and energy to monitoring mates and potential rivals. Furthermore, deserting a mate because cuckoldry is possible imposes costs of needing to find a new mate. Just as optimal allocation of effort cannot possibly prevent aging, despite the tremendous benefits of survival, optimal allocation cannot possibly perfectly solve the problem of cuckoldry.

• Ancestrally, conditions probably affected optimal allocation of effort into particular adaptive domains, leading selection to favor adjustments in allocations based on these conditions. To the extent that, within or across populations or at different points across the life span, individuals are exposed to different conditions, they may differentially allocate resources to solving adaptive problems. This is not to deny the universal nature of design but rather is to emphasize the conditional nature of (potentially universal) allocation rules.

For example, how much men will invest in anticuckoldry tactics should depend on cues of their marginal benefits and costs. In some cultures, some lower status men may tolerate their wives bearing other men's children early in marriage (and even care for those children) because such a strategy appears to offer their best chance to reproduce (see Marlowe, 2000). Brown and Moore (2003) reasoned that women with partners of low fitness are more likely to be unfaithful to them. Consistent with this expectation, he found that men with high fluctuating asymmetry (a marker of developmental instability and, possibly, fitness) are more jealous than men with low fluctuating asymmetry. Perhaps, even though men of low mate value may be tolerant of infidelity *ceteris paribus,* they may be at sufficiently greater risk of infidelity that the net effect is that they tend to be more jealous overall.

• Although information processing specializations themselves may be modular, allocation of resources into their development and/or utilization cannot be independent. Rather, trade-offs mean that decisions about allocation of effort into particular domains will have implications for allocation of effort into other domains.

For example, how much men allocate effort to avoiding cuckoldry should depend not only on the costs and benefits of cuckoldry avoidance but also on the costs and benefits of competing activities.

• In addressing the question of the extent to which individuals will invest in particular adaptations in the face of trade-offs, LHT considers the intertemporal implications of decisions. The fitness effects of these decisions depend on how they aggregate throughout the life course, from the time the decisions are made until death.[10] Individuals are expected to allocate effort to those adaptations that they would most benefit (through time) from doing so (in ancestral conditions).

For example, Mauck, Marschall, and Parker (1999) modeled the effect of mortality rate on male willingness to invest in an offspring not his own. Deserting a mate entails costs to reproduction, particularly if he will need to find and attract a new mate following desertion. As the mortality rate increases, search time for mates is particularly costly because it represents current allocation of effort for future benefits, which become more uncertain as the mortality rate increases. Hence, the model predicts that mortality rate decreases the net benefits of deserting a mate when paternity is uncertain, rendering investment in other males' offspring more likely. Possibly partly for this reason, rates of extra-pair paternity appear to be higher in societies living in traditional conditions and relatively high mortality rates (e.g., Cerda-Flores, Barton, Marty-Gonzalez, Rivas, & Chakraborty, 1999) than in modern societies with high-quality sanitation and low rates of pathogens (e.g., Sasse, Muller, Chakraborty, & Ott, 1994).

- LHT expects that allocations of effort to various tasks will have coevolved with one another such that, for instance, mating and parenting strategies consist of coadapted bundles of characteristics. Hence, individual adaptations cannot be considered fully separate from others not only because allocations compete with one another, but also because each will be most beneficial in the context of other characteristics, which themselves demand allocation of effort.

For example, as the benefit of paternal investment (or exposure to cues that would have signaled benefits of paternal investment ancestrally) increases, not only should paternal investment increase, but also investment in seeking multiple mates should generally decrease. As individual men see increased opportunities to have multiple mates, they may invest in offspring less (e.g., Gangestad & Simpson, 2000). Less investment in offspring may entail lower benefits from mate guarding and cuckoldry prevention. Conversely, as men pay high costs to ensure paternity (e.g., because mate guarding severely interferes with production activities such as long-term hunting forays, in light of the ecology), they may also invest less in offspring.

- The *variations* across and within populations may hold keys to understanding mating and parenting strategies and adaptations, for they reveal how individuals are designed to make trade-offs. This need not imply that the variations are of particular importance in and of themselves. Rather, the variations may be useful for addressing basic questions about the selection pressures that forged the adaptations by revealing the ecological factors that moderate investment in them.

For example, some have argued that emotional and sexual jealousy have evolved in response to different selection pressures: desertion and loss of resources versus cuckoldry (e.g., Buss, 2000). If so, then variations in them should be sensitive to different ecological factors and be parts of different bundles of allocations within broader mating and parenting strategies. Examination of variations in emotional and sexual jealousy across and within populations can provide

---

[10] Indeed, fitness effects can reverberate after the death of the actor through the reproductive success of kin.

key information about the conditional nature of allocations to them and hence the forces of selection that led to them.

HOW PSYCHOLOGICAL ADAPTATIONS SOLVE LIFE HISTORY TRADE-OFFS

Execution of the decisions regarding fundamental life history trade-offs is distributed across the soma. Hormonal systems governing the transition to reproduction, mating effort, fertility status, reproductive rate, maternal-fetal exchange of resources, parental investment, responses to stressors, and disease defenses are just a few examples. These systems do not require centralized "decision makers." Information processing is not restricted to neural tissue; information is processed throughout the somatic components involved.

This is not to say that cognitive processes are not critical to allocation decisions. The stress response, for instance, requires the perception of a stressor. Reallocation of effort to parenting with birth of a child involves responding to new circumstances. Differential effort based on health of the child or paternity certainty requires perception of relevant cues. Differential male mating effort as a function of attractiveness entails assessment of own attractiveness. Decisions about whether and how much to invest in particular social relationships depend on perceptions of that relationship and its benefits. In general, allocations of effort themselves depend on psychological adaptations.

Throughout this chapter, we have emphasized how allocation decisions should be dependent on the shape and nature of return curves. In some instances, simple cues may effectively signal changes in the return curves (e.g., detection of foreign antigens signals greater marginal gains from investment in immune defenses). In many interesting cases, however, the relevant cues will be multiple and in need of integration. Consider, for example, the trade-off between nutritional payoffs to increased food consumption with predation avoidance. At each point in time, an organism receives visual, auditory, and olfactory information about the potential presence of predators as well as its foraging success. It decides whether to continue foraging, engage in vigilance, or invoke a predator-avoidance routine. A variety of factors are important, for example, the time of last eating, the organism's reproductive state, its more general nutritional state, the density of predators, and the return rate of foraging. The impact and weighting of these factors may depend importantly on individual difference factors (e.g., the foraging of subordinate baboons, compared to dominant ones, is less deterred by lion vocalizations because they have less access to food and hence take greater mortality risks to obtain food; S. Johnson, personal communication). To make optimal decisions, the organism must assess relevant cues and integrate them.

Other examples abound. For instance, parents in traditional societies appear to make decisions about their children's activities (most notably, simple foraging with immediate benefits versus complex foraging with future benefits via training) adaptively based on returns and costs of those activities (e.g., Bock, 1995). They appear to assess, in some way, the payoffs and risks to various activities to children and make decisions about children's activities accordingly. With modernization and the importance of education to adult productivity, parents the world over reduce their number of children, enhance allocation of investment in each child, and delay their own reproduction to achieve better outcomes for their children. These phenomena raise questions of how individuals come to decide that quality is important not only after they have had children but before they have had a first child and how these assessment processes were shaped ancestrally (i.e., the nature of the evolved psychological processes involved).

Very little is now known about the precise nature of the adaptations by which organisms solve most trade-off problems. A primary task of evolutionary psychology should be to address the psychological processes involved in these solutions.

CONCLUSIONS

This chapter has developed several themes:

1. Life histories are composed of specialized, coadapted bundles of features that regulate age schedules of fertility and mortality and respond flexibly in response to local ecology.
2. LHT directs attention to three fundamental trade-offs in the allocation of time and energy: (1) present versus future reproduction; (2) quantity versus quality of offspring, and (3) mating versus parenting effort.
3. Humans exhibit a specialized life history involving learning- and brain-intensive, prolonged, costly development, and extremely productive adulthood, and a long life span.
4. LHT offers a new perspective for organizing research in developmental/life span psychology, modeling the growth and decline of abilities in terms of present and future costs and benefits and in terms of coadapted life history strategies.
5. LHT suggests new approaches to standard problems investigated by evolutionary psychologists by explicitly modeling cost-benefit trade-offs as they change over the life course and in response to individual condition.
6. Human psychology and its physical substrates can be thought of as a distributed processing system, utilizing multiple modalities, that both serves to allocate time and energy efficiently among alternative and competing functions and is itself subject to selection, based on its immediate and long-term costs and benefits.

Over the past 40 years, evolutionary biology has witnessed a tremendous explosion in understanding of adaptations, particularly as they relate to behavior. A key foundation of these developments is economic cost-benefit analysis of selection pressures. LHT is not a particular domain of cost-benefit analysis; rather, it is a broad, overarching perspective within which understanding of adaptation must ultimately be situated. The past 15 years have seen rapid and exciting developments of LHT and its applications. Its application to an understanding of human evolved psychology is in its infancy. We hope that the next 15 years will see equally exciting developments in the integration of life history theory and evolutionary psychology.

REFERENCES

Allman, J., McLaughlin, T., & Hakeem, A. (1993). Brain weight and life-span in primate species. *Proceedings of the National Academy of Sciences*, pp. 118–122.

Alvard, M. (1995). Intraspecific prey choice by Amazonian hunters. *Current Anthropology, 36,* 789–818.

Andersson, M. B. (1994). *Sexual selection.* Princeton, NJ: Princeton University Press.

Armstrong, E., & Falk, D. (Eds.). (1982). *Primate brain evolution.* New York: Plenum Press.

Aw, E., & Tye, C. Y. (1970). Age of menarche of a group of Singapore girls. *Human Biology, 42,* 329–336.

Bell, G., & Koufopanou, V. (1986). The cost of reproduction. *Oxford Surveys in Evolutionary Biology, 3,* 83–131.

Belsky, J., Steinberg, L., & Draper, P. (1991). Childhood experience, interpersonal development, and reproductive strategy: An evolutionary theory of socialization. *Child Development, 62,* 647–670.

Blurton Jones, N. G., Hawkes, K., & Draper, P. (1994a). Differences between Hadza and !Kung children's work: Original affluence or practical reason. In E. S. Burch & L. Ellana (Eds.), *Key issues in hunter gatherer research* (pp. 189–215). Oxford, England: Berg.

Blurton Jones, N. G., Hawkes, K., & Draper, P. (1994b). Foraging returns of !Kung adults and children: Why didn't !Kung children forage? *Journal of Anthropological Research, 50,* 217–248.

Bock, J. A. (1995). *The determinants of variation in children's activities in a Southern African community.* Unpublished PhD Dissertation thesis. University of New Mexico, Albuquerque.

Brown, W. M., & Moore, C. (2003). Fluctuating asymmetry and romantic jealousy. *Evolution and Human Behavior, 24,* 113–117.

Buss, D. M. (1995). Evolutionary psychology: A new paradigm for psychological science. *Psychological Inquiry, 6,* 1–30.

Buss, D. M. (2000). *The dangerous passion.* New York: Free Press.

Buss, D. M. (2004). *Evolutionary psychology: The new science of the mind.* Boston: Allyn & Bacon.

Carey, J. R., & Judge, D. S. (2001). Life span extension in humans is self-reinforcing: A general theory of longevity. *Population and Development Review, 27,* 411–436.

Cerda-Flores, R. M., Barton, S. A., Marty-Gonzalez, L. F., Rivas, F., & Chakraborty, R. (1999). Estimation of nonpaternity in the Mexican population of Nueveo Leon: A validation study with blood group markers. *American Journal of Physical Anthropology, 109,* 281–293.

Charnov, E. L. (1976). Optimal foraging: The marginal value theorem. *Theoretical Population Biology, 9,* 129–136.

Charnov, E. L. (1982). *The theory of sex allocation.* Princeton, NJ: Princeton University Press.

Charnov, E. L. (1993). *Life history invariants: Some explanations of symmetry in evolutionary ecology.* Oxford, England: Oxford University Press.

Charnov, E. L., & Schaffer, W. M. (1973). Life history consequences of natural selection: Cole's paradox revisited. *American Naturalist, 107,* 103–137.

Chisholm, J. S. (1999). *Death, hope and sex: Steps to an evolutionary ecology of mind and morality.* Cambridge, England: Cambridge University Press.

Clutton-Brock, T. H., & Parker, G. A. (1992). Potential reproductive rates and the operation of sexual selection. *Quarterly Review of Biology, 67,* 437–456.

Cole, L. C. (1954). The population consequences of life history phenomena. *Quarterly Review of Biology, 29,* 103–137.

Cronin, H. (1991). *The ant and the peacock.* Cambridge, England: Cambridge University Press.

Deacon, T. W. (1997). *The symbolic species.* New York: Norton.

Draper, P., & Harpending, H. (1982). Father absence and reproductive strategy: An evolutionary perspective. *Anthropological Research, 38,* 255–273.

Ellis, B. J., & Garber, J. (2000). Psychosocial antecedents of variation in girls' pubertal timing: Maternal depression, stepfather presence, and marital and family stress. *Child Development, 71,* 485–501.

Ellis, B. J., McFadyen-Ketchum, S., Dodge, K. A., Pettit, G. S., & Bates, G. E. (1999). Quality of early family relationships and individual differences in the timing of pubertal maturation in girls: Tests of an evolutionary model. *Journal of Personality and Social Psychology, 77,* 387–401.

Ellison, P. T. (Ed.). (2001). *Reproductive ecology and human evolution.* Hawthorne, NY: Aldine de Gruyter.

Finch, C. E., & Sapolsky, R. M. (1999). The evolution of Alzheimer disease, the reproductive schedule, and apoE isoforms. *Neurobiology and Aging, 20,* 407–428.

Fisher, R. A. (1958). *The genetical theory of natural selection.* New York: Dover.

Fleagle, J. G. (1999). *Primate adaptation and evolution.* New York: Academic Press.

Folstad, I., & Karter, A. J. (1992). Parasites, bright males, and the immunocompetence handicap. *American Naturalist, 139,* 603–622.

Gadgil, M., & Bossert, W. H. (1970). Life historical consequences of natural selection. *American Naturalist, 104,* 1–24.

Gangestad, S. W., & Simpson, J. A. (2000). The evolution of human mating: The role of trade-offs and strategic pluralism. *Behavioral and Brain Sciences, 23,* 675–687.

Getty, T. (1998). Handicap signaling: When fecundity and mortality do not add up. *Animal Behavior, 56,* 127–130.

Getty, T. (2002). Signaling health versus parasites. *American Naturalist, 159,* 363–371.

Gibson, K. R. (1986). Cognition, brain size and the extraction of embedded food resources. In J. G. Else & P. C. Lee (Eds.), *Primate ontogeny, cognition, and social behavior* (pp. 93–105). Cambridge, England: Cambridge University Press.

Graber, J. A., Brooks-Gunn, J., & Warren, M. P. (1995). The antecedents of menarcheal age: Heredity, family environment, and stressful life events. *Child Development, 66,* 346–359.

Grafen, A. (1990). Biological signals as handicaps. *Journal of Theoretical Biology, 144,* 517–546.

Grafen, A. (1991). Modeling a behavioural ecology. In J. R. Krebs & N. B. Davies (Eds.), *Behavioural ecology: An evolutionary approach* (pp. 5–31). Oxford, England: Blackwell Scientific.

Gray, P. B., Kahlenberg, S. M., Barrett, E. S., Lipson, S. F., & Ellison, P. T. (2002). Marriage and fatherhood are associated with lower testosterone in males. *Evolution and Human Behavior, 23,* 193–201.

Gwyne, D. T. (1991). Sexual competition among females: What causes courtship role reversal. *Trends in Evolution and Ecology, 6,* 118–122.

Haig, D. (1993). Genetic conflicts in human pregnancy. *Quarterly Review of Biology, 68,* 495–532.

Hamilton, W. D. (1964). The genetical evolution of social behaviour. I, II. *Journal of Theoretical Biology, 7,* 1–52.

Hamilton, W. D. (1966). The molding of senescence by natural selection. *Journal of Theoretical Biology, 12,* 12–45.

Hamilton, W. D., & Zuk, M. (1982). Heritable true fitness and bright birds: A role for parasites. *Science, 218,* 384–387.

Harpending, H. C., Draper, P., & Pennington, R. (1990). Cultural evolution, parental care, and mortality. In A. C. Swedlund & G. J. Armelagos (Eds.), *Disease in populations in transition* (pp. 251–265). New York: Gergin and Garvey.

Hill, K. (1993). Life history theory and evolutionary anthropology. *Evolutionary Anthropology, 2,* 78–88.

Holliday, M. A. (1978). Body composition and energy needs during growth. In F. Falker & J. M. Tanner (Eds.), *Human growth* (pp. 117–139). New York: Plenum Press.

Horn, J. L. (1968). Organization of abilities and the development of intelligence. *Psychological Review, 75,* 242–259.

Hurtado, A. M., & Hill, K. (1990). Seasonality in a foraging society: Variation in diet, work effort, fertility, and sexual division of labor among the Hiwi of Venezuela. *Journal of Anthropologicla Research, 46,* 293–346.

Jones, B., Leeton, J., McLeod, I., & Wood, C. (1972). Factors influencing the age of menarche in a lower socioeconomic group in Melbourne. *Medical Journal of Australia, 2,* 533–535.

Judge, D. S., & Carey, J. R. (2000). Postreproductive life predicted by primate patterns. *Journals of Gerontology Series, A, 55,* B201–B209.

Kalick, S. M., Zebrowitz, L. A., Langlois, J. H., & Johnson, R. M. (1998). Does human facial attractiveness honestly advertise health? Longitudinal data on an evolutionary question. *Psychological Science, 9,* 8–13.

Kaplan, H. S. (1996). Evolutionary and wealth flows theories of fertility: Empirical tests and new models. *Yearbook of Physical Anthropology, 39,* 91–135.

Kaplan, H. S. (1997). The evolution of the human life course. In K. Wachter & C. Finch (Eds.), *Between Zeus and Salmon: The biodemography of aging* (pp. 175–211). Washington, DC: National Academy of Sciences.

Kaplan, H. S., Gangestad, S. W., Gurven, M., Lancaster, J., Mueller, T., & Robson, A. (in press). The evolution of diet, brain, and life history among primates and humans. In W. Roebroeks (Ed.), *Brains, guts, food, and the social life of early hominins.* Cambridge, UK: Cambridge University Press.

Kaplan, H. S., Hill, K., Lancaster, J. B., & Hurtado, A. M. (2000). A theory of human life history evolution: Diet, intelligence, and longevity. *Evolutionary Anthropology, 9,* 156–185.

Kaplan, H. S., & Robson, A. (2002). The emergence of humans: The coevolution of intelligence and longevity with intergenerational transfers. *Proceedings of the National Academy of Sciences, 99,* 10221–10226.

Kirkwood, T. B. L. (1990). The disposable soma theory of aging. In D. E. Harrison (Ed.), *Genetic effects on aging, II* (pp. 9–19). Caldwell, NJ: Telford.

Kirkwood, T. B. L., & Rose, M. R. (1991). Evolution of senescence: Late survival sacrificed for reproduction. In P. H. Harvey, L. Partridge, & T. R. E. Southwood (Eds.), *The evolution of reproductive strategies* (pp. 15–24). Cambridge, England: Cambridge University Press.

Kokko, H., Brooks, R., Jennions, M. D., & Morley, J. (2003). The evolution of mate choice and mating biases. *Proceedings of the Royal Society of London. Series B, Biological Sciences, 270,* 653–664.

Kokko, H., Brooks, R., McNamara, J. M., & Houston, A. I. (2002). The sexual selection continuum. *Proceedings of the Royal Society of London. Series B, Biological Sciences, 269,* 1331–1340.

Kokko, H., Jennions, M. (2003). It takes two to tango. *Trends in Ecology and Evolution, 18,* 103–104.

Kozlowski, J., & Wiegert, R. G. (1986). Optimal allocation to growth and reproduction. *Theoretical Population, 29,* 16–37.

Kuzawa, C. W. (1998). Adipose tissue in human infancy and childhood: An evolutionary perspective. *Yearbook of Physical Anthropology, 41,* 177–209.

Lack, D. (1954). *The natural regulation of animal numbers.* Oxford, England: Oxford University Press.

Lack, D. (1968). *Ecological adaptations for breeding in birds.* London: Methuen.

Leibenberg, L. (1990). *The art of tracking: The origin of science.* Cape Town, South Africa: David Phillip.

Leigh, S. R., & Shea, B. T. (1996). Ontogeny of body size variation in African apes. *American Journal of Physical Anthropology, 99,* 43–65.

Lessells, C. M. (1991). The evolution of life histories. In J. R. Krebs & N. B. Davies (Eds.), *Behavioural ecology: An evolutionary approach* (pp. 32–65). Oxford, England: Blackwell.

Lloyd, D. G. (1987). Selection of offspring size at independence and other size-versus-number strategies. *American Naturalist, 129,* 800–817.

MacArthur, R. H., & Wilson, E. O. (1967). *The theory of island biogeography.* Princeton, NJ: Princeton University Press.

Martin, R. D. (1981). Relative brain size and basal metabolic rate in terrestrial vertebrates. *Nature, 293,* 57–60.

Marlowe, F. (2000). Good genes and paternal care in human evolution. *Behavioral and Brain Sciences, 23,* 611–612.

Mauck, R. A., Marschall, E. A., & Parker, P. G. (1999). Adult survival and imperfect assessment of parentage: Effects on male parenting decisions. *American Naturalist, 154,* 99–109.

McDade, T. W. (2003). Life history theory and the immune system: Steps toward a human ecological immunology. *Yearbook of Physical Anthropology, 46,* 100–125.

Medawar, P. B. (1952). *An unsolved problem in biology.* London: Lewis.

Moffitt, T. E., Caspi, A., Belsky, J., & Silva, P. A. (1992). Childhood experience and onset of menarche: A test of a sociobiological model. *Child Development, 63,* 47–58.

Parker, G. A. (1970). The reproductive behaviour and the nature of sexual selection in *Scarophaga stercoraria* L. (Diptera: Scatophagidae). II. The fertilization rate and the spatial and temporal relationships of each sex around the site of mating and oviposition. *Journal of Animal Ecology, 39,* 205–228.

Parker, G. A., & Maynard Smith, J. (1991). Optimality theory in evolutionary biology. *Nature, 348,* 27–33.

Parker, S. T., & McKinney, M. L. (1999). *Origins of intelligence: The evolution of cognitive development in monkeys, apes and humans.* Baltimore: Johns Hopkins Press.

Promislow, D. E. L., & Harvey, P. H. (1990). Living fast and dying young: A comparative analysis of life history variation among mammals. *Journal of Zoology, 220,* 417–437.

Rice, W. R. (1996). Sexually antagonistic male adaptation triggered by experimental arrest of female evolution. *Nature, 381,* 232–234.

Robson, A., & Kaplan, H. (2003). The evolution of human life expectancy and intelligence in hunter-gatherer economies. *American Economic Review, 93,* 150–169.

Roff, D. A. (1992). *The evolution of life histories.* London: Chapman and Hall.

Sacher, G. A. (1959). Relation of lifespan to brain weight and body weight in mammals. In G. E. W. Wolstenhome & M. O'Connor (Eds.), *CibafFoundation Colloquia on ageing* (pp. 115–133). London: Churchill.

Sasse, G., Muller, H., Chakraborty, R., & Ott, J. (1994). Estimating the frequency of nonpaternity in Switzerland. *Human Heredity, 44,* 337–343.

Shanley, D. P., & Kirkwood, T. B. L. (2000). Calorie restriction and aging: A life-history analysis. *Evolution, 54,* 740–750.

Smith, C. C., & Fretwell, S. D. (1974). The optimal balance between size and number of offspring. *American Naturalist, 108,* 499–506.

Stearns, S. C. (1992). *The evolution of life histories.* Oxford, England: Oxford University Press.

Steinberg, L. (1988). Reciprocal relation between parent-child distance and pubertal maturation. *Psychology, 24,* 122–128.

Stiner, M. (1991). An interspecific perspective on the emergence of the modern human predatory niche. In M. Stiner (Ed.), *Human predators and prey mortality* (pp. 149–185). Boulder, CO: Westview.

Surbey, M. (1990). Family composition, stress, and human menarche. In F. Bercovitch & T. Zeigler (Eds.), *The socioendocrinology of primate reproduction* (pp. 71–97). New York: Liss.

Tatar, M., Grey, D. W., & Carey, J. R. (1997). Altitudinal variation in senescence in a Melanoplus grasshopper species complex. *Oecologia, 111*, 357–364.

Tinbergen, N. (1963). On the aims and methods of ethology. *Zeitschrift für Tierpsychologie, 20,* 410–463.

Tooby, J., & Cosmides, L. (1992). The psychological foundations of culture. In J. H. Barkow, L. Cosmides, & J. Tooby (Eds.), *The adapted mind: Evolutionary psychology and the generation of culture,* pp. 19–136. Oxford, England: Oxford University Press.

Trivers, R. L. (1972). Parental investment and sexual selection. In B. Campbell (Ed.), *Sexual selection and the descent of man, 1871–1971*. Chicago: Aldine.

Trivers, R. L. (1974). Parent-offspring conflict. *American Zoologist, 14,* 264–269.

Williams, G. C. (1957). Pleitropy, natural selection and the evolution of senescence. *Evolution, 11,* 398–411.

Williams, G. C. (1966). *Adaptation and natural selection*. Princeton, NJ: Princeton University Press.

Worthman, C. M. (1999). Epidemiology of human development. In C. Panter-Brick & C. M. Worthman (Eds.), *Hormones, health and behavior: A socio-ecological and lifespan perspective* (pp. 47–105). Cambridge, England: Cambridge University Press.

Wrangham, R. W., & Smuts, B. (1980). Sex differences in behavioral ecology of chimpanzees in Gombe National Park, Tanzania. *Journal of Reproduction and Fertility (Supplement), 28,* 13–31.

CHAPTER 3

Domain Specificity and Intuitive Ontology

PASCAL BOYER and H. CLARK BARRETT

TRADITIONALLY, PSYCHOLOGISTS HAVE assumed that people come equipped only with a set of relatively domain-general faculties such as memory and reasoning, which are applied in equal fashion to diverse problems. Recent research has begun to suggest that human expertise about the natural and social environment, including what is often called *semantic knowledge,* is best construed as consisting of different *domains* of competence. Each of these corresponds to recurrent evolutionary problems, is organized along specific principles, is the outcome of a specific developmental pathway, and is based on specific neural structures. What we call a *human-evolved intuitive ontology* comprises a catalogue of broad domains of information, different sets of principles applied to these different domains as well as different learning rules to acquire more information about those objects. All this is intuitive in the sense that it is not the product of deliberate reflection on what the world is like.

This notion of an intuitive ontology as a motley of different domains informed by different principles was first popularized by developmental psychologists (R. Gelman, 1978; R. Gelman & Baillargeon, 1983) who proposed distinctions among physical-mechanical, biological, social, and numerical competencies as based on different learning principles (Hirschfeld & Gelman, 1994). In the following decades, this way of slicing up semantic knowledge received considerable support both in developmental and neuropsychology. For example, patients with focal brain damage were found to display selective impairment of one of these domains of knowledge to the exclusion of others (Caramazza, 1998). Neuroimaging and cognitive neuroscience are now adding to the picture of a federation of evolved competencies that has grown out of laboratory work with children and adults.

AN ILLUSTRATION: WHAT IS SPECIFIC ABOUT FACES

The detection and recognition of *faces* by human beings provides an excellent example of a specialized system. Humans are especially good at identifying and recognizing large numbers of different faces, automatically and effortlessly, from infancy. This has led many psychologists to argue that the standard human cognitive equipment includes a special system to handle faces.

Convergent evidence for specialization comes from many different sources. In contrast to other objects, the way facial visual information is treated is configural, taking into account the overall arrangement and relations of parts more than the parts themselves (Tanaka & Sengco, 1997; Young, Hellawell, & Hay, 1987). This is strikingly demonstrated by the finding that inverting faces makes them much more difficult to recognize, compared to objects requiring less configural processing (Farah, Wilson, Drain, & Tanaka, 1995). Developmentally, newborn infants quickly orient to faces rather than other stimuli (Morton & Johnson, 1991) and recognize different individuals early (Pascalis, de Schonen, Morton, Deruelle, & Campbell, 1995; Slater & Quinn, 2001). Neuropsychology has documented many cases of prosopagnosia or selective impairment of face recognition (Farah, 1994) where the structural processing of objects, object recognition, and even imagination for faces can be preserved while face recognition remains intact (Duchaine, 2000; Michelon & Biederman, 2003). Finally, neuroimaging studies have reliably shown a specific pattern of activation (in particular, modulation of areas of the fusiform gyrus in the temporal lobe) during identification or passive viewing of faces (Kanwisher, McDermott, & Chun, 1997). Specialized systems may handle the invariant properties of faces (that allow recognition) while other networks handle changing aspects such as gaze, smile, and emotional expression (Haxby, Hoffman, & Gobbini, 2002).

Despite this impressive evidence, some psychologists argue that the specificity of face perception is an illusion and that human beings simply become expert recognizers of faces by using unspecialized visual capacities. In this view, the newborns' skill in the face domain may be the result of a special interest in conspecifics that simply makes faces more ecologically important than other objects (Nelson, 2001). Also, we can observe the inversion effect (Diamond & Carey, 1986; Gauthier, Williams, Tarr, & Tanaka, 1998) and fusiform gyrus activation (Gauthier, Tarr, Anderson, Skudlarski, & Gore, 1999; Tarr & Gauthier, 2000) when testing trained experts in domains such as birds, automobiles, dogs, or even abstract geometrical shapes (see Kanwisher, 2000, for a detailed discussion).

This argument demonstrates the importance of gradual development and the crucial contribution of relevant experience and environmental factors. These crucial aspects of functional specialization from evolutionary origins will become clearer as we compare the face system to other kinds of specialized inferential devices typical of human intuitive ontology.

FEATURES OF DOMAIN-SPECIFIC INFERENCE SYSTEMS

The face-recognition system provides us with a good template for the features we encounter in other examples of domain-specific systems.

SEMANTIC KNOWLEDGE COMPRISES SPECIALIZED INFERENCE SYSTEMS

It is misleading to think of semantic knowledge in terms of a declarative database. Most of the knowledge that drives behavior stems from tacit inferential principles, that is, specific ways of handling information.

In the case of face recognition, configural processing seems to be a computational solution to the problem of recognizing individuals across time while tracking a surface (the face) that constantly changes in small details, with different lighting or facial expressions.

More generally, we describe intuitive ontology as a set of computational devices, each characterized by a specific input format, by specific inferential principles, and by a specific type of output (which may in turn be input to other systems). Given information that matches the input format of one particular system, activation of that system and production of the principled output are fairly automatic.

Domains Are Not Given by Reality but Are Cognitively Delimited

Faces are not a physically distinct set of objects that would be part of "the environment" of any organism. Faces are distinct objects only to an organism equipped with a special system that pays attention to the top front surface of conspecifics as a source of person-specific information.

Moreover, inferential systems are focused not necessarily on objects but on *particular aspects* of objects; thus a single physical object can trigger concurrent activation of several distinct inference systems. For instance, although faces invariably come with a particular expression, distinct systems handle the *Who is that?* and *In what mood?* questions (Haxby et al., 2002).

To coin a phrase, The human brain's intuitive ontology is *philosophically incorrect*. That is, the distinct cognitive domains—different classes of objects in our cognitive environment as distinguished by our intuitive ontology—do not always correspond to real ontological categories—different kinds of "stuff" out there. For instance, the human mind does not draw the line between living and nonliving things or between agents and objects in the same way as a scientist or a philosopher would do, as we illustrate later.

Evolutionary Design Principles Suggest the Proper Domain of a System

The domain of operation of the system is best circumscribed by evolutionary considerations. Natural selection resulted in genetic material that normally results in human brains with a specific capacity for face recognition. But why should we describe it as being about faces? It may seem more accurate to say that it is specialized in "fine-grained, intracategorical distinctions between grossly similar visual representations of middle-size objects," as some have argued. But consider this. We observe that the stimuli in question trigger specific processing only if they include a central (mouthlike) opening and two brightly contrasted (eyelike) points above that opening. We should then add these features to our description. The system would then be described as especially good at "fine-grained, intracategorical [. . .] with a central opening and [etc.]." We could add more and more features to this supposedly "neutral" description of the system.

Such semantic contortions are both redundant and misleading. Inasmuch as the only stimuli corresponding to our convoluted redescription encountered during evolution were conspecifics' faces, the redescription is redundant. But it also blurs the functional features of the system, for there are indefinitely many inferences we could extract from presentations of "fine-grained, intracategorical . . . etc."

(facelike) stimuli, only some of which are relevant to distinctions between persons.[1] A description in terms of functional design provides the best explanation for the system's choice of what is and what is not relevant in faces.

EVOLUTIONARY AND ACTUAL DOMAINS DO NOT FULLY OVERLAP

Without effortful training, the face-recognition system identifies and recognizes what it was designed to expect in its environment. As discussed earlier, the system may be retrained, with more effort, to provide identification of objects other than faces such as birds or cars. In the same way, our evolved walking, running, and jumping motor routines can be redirected to produce ballet dancing. Nevertheless, they evolved to move us closer to resources or shelter and away from predators. The fact that some cognitive system is specialized for a domain *D* does not entail that it invariably or exclusively handles *D*, nor does it mean that the specialization cannot be coopted for evolutionarily novel activities. It means that ancestors of the present organism encountered objects that belong to *D* as a stable feature of the environments where the present cognitive architecture was selected and that handling information about such objects enhanced fitness.

There may be—indeed, there very often is—a difference between the *proper* (evolutionary) and *actual* domains of a system (Sperber, 1994). On the one hand, the specialized system evolved to represent and react to a set of objects, facts, and properties (e.g., flies for the insect-detection system in the frog's visual system). On the other hand, the system reacts to a set of objects, facts, and properties (e.g., flies *as well as* any small object zooming across the visual field). Proper and actual domains are often different. Mimicry and camouflage use this noncongruence. Nonpoisonous butterflies may evolve the same bright colors as poisonous ones to avoid predation by birds. The proper (evolved) domain of the birds' bright-colored bug avoidance system is the set of poisonous insects; the actual domain is that of all insects that look like them (Sperber, 1994).

IN EVOLUTION, YOU CAN LEARN MORE ONLY IF YOU ALREADY KNOW MORE

The face recognition system does not need to store a description of each face in each possible orientation and lighting condition. It stores only particular parameters for an algorithm that connects each sighting of a face with a person's "face-entry."

Turning to other domains, we find the same use of vast information stores in the environment, together with complex processes required to find and use that information. The lexicon of a natural language (15,000 to 100,000 distinct items) is extracted through development from the utterances of other speakers. This constitutes an impressive economy for genetic transmission, as human beings can develop complete fluency without the lexicon being stored in the genome. But this external database is available only to a mind with complex phonological and syntactic predispositions (Jackendoff, 2002; Pinker & Bloom, 1990). In a similar way, the diversity and similarities between animal species are inferred from a huge

---

[1] For instance, faces vary in complexion with the varying color temperature of daylight during the day, complexion and features change with increased blood pressure when a person's head is lower than the rest of the body, overall face size is correlated with gender, complexion in women is altered by childbearing, and many others. There is no evidence that human minds register this kind of information.

variety of available natural cues (color, sound, shape, behavior, etc.), but that information is relevant only to a mind with a disposition for natural taxonomies (Atran, 1990).

In general, the more an inference system exploits external sources of information and stable aspects of the cognitive environments, the more computational power is required to home in on that information and derive inferences from it. There is in evolution a general coupling between the evolution of more sophisticated cognitive equipment and the use of more extensive information stored in environments.

EACH INFERENTIAL SYSTEM HAS A SPECIFIC LEARNING LOGIC

Infants pay attention to faces and quickly recognize familiar faces because they are biased to pay attention to small differences in this domain that they would ignore in other domains.

More generally, knowledge acquisition is informed by domain-specific learning principles (R. Gelman, 1990), which we review in the following pages. Also, different systems have different developmental schedules, including windows of development before or after which learning of a particular kind is difficult. These empirical findings have led developmental psychologists to cast doubt on the notion of a general, all-domain *learning logic* that would govern cognitive development in various domains (Hirschfeld & Gelman, 1994).

DEVELOPMENT FOLLOWS EVOLVED PATHWAYS

Consider the notion of a ballistic process. This is a process (e.g., kicking a ball) where the individual has influence over initial conditions (e.g., direction and energy of the kick), but this influence stops there and then because the motion is influenced only by external factors (e.g., friction). If brain development was one such ballistic system, the genome would assemble a brain with a particular structure and then stop working on it. From the end of organogenesis, the only functionally relevant brain changes would be brought about by interaction with external information. But that is clearly not the case. Genetic influence on many organic structures is pervasive throughout the life span, and that is true of the brain, too.

We must insist on this notion because discussions of evolved mental structures often imply that genetic influence on brain structures is indeed ballistic, so that we can draw a line between function that is specified at birth (supposedly the result of evolution) and function that emerges during development (supposedly the effect of external factors unrelated to evolution). Indeed, this seems to be the starting point of many discussions of "innateness" (Elman, Bates, Johnson, & Karmiloff-Smith, 1996) even though the assumption is biologically implausible.[2]

---

[2] Perhaps because they are mammals, many philosophers and cognitive scientists are somehow fixated on birth as the crucial cutting-off that separates evolutionary factors from environmental ones. As we said, genes influence development after birth. Conversely, note that fetuses receive a lot of external information before birth (which is why, for instance, they are prepared for the intonation contour of their mother's language).

Evolution results not just in a specific set of adult capacities but also in a specific set of developmental pathways that lead to such capacities. This result is manifest in the rather circuitous path to adult competence that children follow in many domains. For instance, young children do not build syntactic competence in a simple-to-complex manner, starting with short sentences and gradually adding elements. They start with a one-word stage, then proceed to a two-word stage, then discard that structure to adopt their language's phrase grammar. Such phenomena are present in other domains, too, as we discuss in the rest of this chapter.

Development Requires a Normal Environment

Face recognition probably would not develop in a context where people always changed faces or all looked identical. Language acquisition requires people interacting with a child in a fairly normal way. Mechanical-physical intelligence requires a world furnished with some functionally specialized man-made objects. In this sense, inference systems are similar to teeth and stomachs, which need digestible foods rather than intravenous drips for normal development, or to the visual cortex that needs retinal input for proper development.

What is "normal" about these normal features of the environment is not that they are inevitable or general (food from pills and IV drips may become common in the future, dangerous predators have vanished from most human beings' environments) but that they were generally present in the environment of evolution. Children a hundred thousand years ago were born in an environment that included natural language speakers, man-made tools, gender roles, predators, gravity, chewable food, and other stable factors that made certain mental dispositions useful adaptations to those environmental features.

Inferential Systems Orchestrate Finer Grain Neural Structures

The example of face recognition also shows how our understanding of domain specificity is crucially informed by what we know about neural structures and their functional specialization. However, the example is perhaps misleading in suggesting a straightforward mapping from functional specialization onto neural specialization.

Cognitive domains correspond to recurrent fitness-related situations or problems (e.g., predators, competitors, tools, foraging techniques, mate selection, social exchange, interactions with kin). Should we expect to find neural structures that are specifically activated by information pertaining to one of these domains?

There are empirical and theoretical reasons to expect a rather more complex picture. Neural specificity should not be confused with easily tracked anatomical localization. Local activation differences, salient though they have become because of the (literally) spectacular progress in neuroimaging techniques, are not the only index of neural specialization. A variety of crucial differences in brain function consist in time-course differences (observed in Event-related potentials, ERPs), in neurotransmitter modulation, and in spike-train patterns that are not captured by fMRI studies (Cabeza & Nyberg, 2000; Posner & Raichle, 1994).

In the current state of our knowledge of functional neuroanatomy, it would seem that most functionally separable neural systems are *more specific* than the fitness-related domains, so that high-level domain specificity requires the joint or coordinated activation of different neural systems and indeed, in many cases, consists largely of the specific coordination of distinct systems. We illustrate this point presently, when we consider the difference between living and nonliving things or the different systems involved in detecting agency.

LIVING VERSUS MAN-MADE OBJECTS: DEVELOPMENT AND IMPAIRMENT

We start with the distinction between animal and other living beings on the one hand and man-made objects on the other. It would seem that the human mind *must* include some assumptions about this difference. Indeed, developmental and cognitive evidence suggests that we can find profound differences between these two domains.

Animal species are intuitively construed in terms of species-specific "causal essences" (Atran, 1998). That is, their typical features and behavior are interpreted as consequences of possession of an undefined, yet causally relevant, quality particular to each identified species. A cat is a cat, not by virtue of having this or that external features—even though that is how we recognize it—but because it possesses some intrinsic and undefined quality that it acquires only by being born of cats. This assumption appears early in development (Keil, 1986) so that preschoolers consider the "insides" a crucial feature of identity for animals even though they use only the "outside" for identification criteria (S. A. Gelman & Wellman, 1991). Also, all animals and plants are categorized as members of a taxonomy. The specific feature here is not just that categories (e.g., snake) are embedded in other, more abstract ones (reptiles) and include more specific ones (adder) but also that the categories are mutually exclusive and jointly exhaustive, which is not the case in other domains. Although animal and plant classifications vary between human cultures, the hierarchical ranks (e.g., varietals, genus, family) are found in all ethnobiological systems and carry rank-specific expectations about body plan, physiology, and behavior (Atran, 1998).

By contrast, man-made objects are principally construed in terms of their *functions*. Although children may sometimes seem indifferent to the absence of some crucial functional features in artifacts (e.g., a central screw in a pair of scissors; Gentner & Rattermann, 1991), young children are sensitive to such functional affordances (physical features that support function) when they actually *use* tools, either familiar or novel (Kemler Nelson, 1995), and when they try to understand the use of novel objects (Richards, Goldfarb, Richards, & Hassen, 1989). Young children construe functional features in teleological terms, explaining, for instance, that scissors have sharp blades so they cut (Keil, 1986). Artifacts seem to be construed by adults in terms of their designers' intentions as well as actual use (Bloom, 1996), and preschoolers, too, consider intentions as relevant to an artifact's genuine function (S. A. Gelman & Bloom, 2000), although they are more concerned with the current user's intentions than the original creator's.

These differences between domains illustrate what we call *inferential principles.* The fact that an object is identified as either living or man-made leads to (1) paying attention to different aspects of the object, (2) producing different inferences from similar input, (3) producing categories with different internal structures (observable features index possession of an essence [animals] or presence of a human intention [artifacts]), and (4) assembling the categories themselves in different ways (there is no hierarchical, nested taxonomy for artifacts, only juxtaposed kind concepts).

Neuropsychological evidence supports this notion of distinct principles. Some types of brain damage result in impaired content or retrieval of linguistic and conceptual information in either one of the two domains. The first cases to appear in the clinical literature showed selective impairment of the living thing domain, in particular, knowledge for the names, shapes, or associative features of animals (Moss & Tyler, 2000; Sartori, Coltheart, Miozzo, & Job, 1994; Sartori, Job, Miozzo, & Zago, 1993; Sheridan & Humphreys, 1993; Warrington & McCarthy, 1983). But there is also evidence for *double dissociation,* for the symmetrical impairment in the artifact domain with preserved knowledge of living things (Sacchett & Humphreys, 1992; Warrington & McCarthy, 1987). This suggests two levels of organization of semantic information, one comprising modality-specific or modality-associated stores and the other comprising distinct category-specific stores (Caramazza & Shelton, 1998).

LIVING VERSUS MAN-MADE OBJECTS: EVOLVED AND NEURAL DOMAINS

There may be an oversimplification in any account of semantic knowledge that remains at the level of broad ontological categories such as *living* and *man-made.* For instance, it is not clear that children really develop domain-specific understandings at the level of the living thing and man-made categories. All the evidence we have concerns their inferences on medium-size animals (gradually and only partly extended to bugs, plants) and on manipulable tools with a direct, observable effect on objects (not houses or dams or lampposts).

Evolutionary consideration would suggest that specificity of semantic knowledge will be found at a more specific level, corresponding to situations that carry [specific] particular fitness consequences. In evolutionary terms, we should consider not just the categories of objects that are around an organism but also the kinds of interaction likely to impinge on the organism's fitness. From that standpoint, humans certainly do not interact with living things in general. Living things comprise plants, bacteria, and middle-size animals including human beings. Human beings interact very differently with predators, prey, potential foodstuffs, competitors, and parasites. Nor do humans handle *artifacts* in general. Man-made objects include foodstuffs, tools and weapons, buildings, shelters, visual representations, as well as paths, dams, and other modifications of the natural environment. Tools, shelters, and decorative artifacts are associated with distinct activities and circumstances. So we should expect the input format and activation cues of domain-specific inference systems to reflect this fine-grained specificity.

Indeed, this hypothesis of a set of finer grained systems receives some support from behavioral and developmental studies and, most importantly, from the available neurofunctional evidence. A host of neuroimaging studies, using both PET and fMRI scans, with either word or image recognition or generation, has showed that living things and artifacts trigger significantly different cortical activations (Gerlach, Law, Gade, & Paulson, 2000; Martin, Wiggs, Ungerleider, &

Haxby, 1996; Martin et al., 1994; Moore & Price, 1999; Perani et al., 1995; Spitzer, Kwong, Kennedy, & Rosen, 1995; Spitzer et al., 1998). However, the results are not really straightforward or even consistent.[3] Despite many difficulties, what can be observed is that (1) activation in some areas (premotor in particular) is modulated by artifacts more clearly than by other stimuli, (2) there is a more diffuse involvement of temporal areas for both categories, and (3) there are distinct activation maps rather than privileged regions.

The naming of artifacts, or even simple viewing of pictures of artifacts, seems to result in premotor activation. Viewing an artifact-like object automatically triggers the search for (and simulation of) motor plans that involve the object in question. Indeed, the areas activated (premotor cortex, anterior cingulate, orbitofrontal) are all consistent with this interpretation of a motor plan that is both activated *and* inhibited. This suggests that *man-made object* is probably not the right criterion here. Houses are man-made but do not afford motor plans that include handling. If *motor* plans are triggered, they are about *tools* rather than man-made objects in general (Moore & Price, 1999). A direct confirmation can be found in a study of *manipulable* versus *nonmanipulable* artifacts, which finds the classical left ventral frontal (premotor) activation only for the former kind of stimuli (Mecklinger, Gruenewald, Besson, Magnie, & Von Cramon, 2002).

Neuroimaging evidence for the animal domain is less straightforward. Some PET studies found specific activation of the lingual gyrus for animals, but this is also sometimes activated by artifact naming tasks (Perani et al., 1995). Some infero-temporal areas (BA20) are found to be exclusively activated by animal pictures (Perani et al., 1995), as are some occipital areas (left medial occipital; Martin et al., 1996). The latter activation would suggest only higher modulation of early visual processing for animals. This is consistent with the notion, widespread in discussions of domain-specific selective impairment, that identification of different animal species requires finer grained distinctions than that of artifacts: Animals of different species (cat, dog) often share a basic *Bauplan* (trunk, legs, head, fur) and differ in details (shape of head, limbs, etc.), while tools (e.g., screwdriver, hammer) differ in overall structure. Animal-specific activations of the posterior temporal lobe seem to vanish when the stimuli are easier to identify (Moore & Price, 1999), which would confirm this interpretation as an effect of fine-grained, relatively effortful processing.[4]

Neuroimaging findings and developmental evidence converge in supporting the evolutionarily plausible view that inference systems are not about ontological categories such as *man-made object* or *living thing* but about types of situations such as *fast identification of potential predator-prey* or *detection of possible use of tool or weapon*.

---

[3] Many early PET studies (and to some extent more recent fMRI ones) reported specific regions activated by artifacts or animals. However, many of these findings were not replicated. Also, in many of these studies the variety of activation peaks reported for either type of stimuli cannot plausibly be described as constituting a functional network. That is, there is no clear indication that joint involvement of such areas is required for the processing of such stimuli. The gross anatomy does not suggest particular and exclusive connectivity between those regions either. Finally, some of the findings may turn out to be false positives (Devlin, Russell, Davis, Price, & Moss, 2002).

[4] High interpersonal variability of activations, especially for the animal domain, is often seen as a major difficulty in such studies (Spitzer et al., 1998). It makes reports of average activations in a group of subjects especially vulnerable to statistical artifacts (Devlin et al., 2002). However, the fact that maps vary from one subject to another does not entail that there is no stable domain-based, subject-specific differentiation of activation (Spitzer et al., 1998).

ADVANTAGES OF MIND READING

A central assumption of human intuitive ontology is that some objects in the world are driven by internal states, in particular by goals and other representational states such as desires and beliefs. This has received great attention in developmental models of *theory of mind.* The term designates the various tacit assumptions that govern our intuitive interpretation of other agents' (and our own) behavior as the outcome of invisible states such as beliefs and intentions.

On the basis of tasks such as the familiar false-belief tasks, developmental psychologists suggested that the understanding of belief as representational and, therefore, possibly false did not emerge in normal children before the age of 4 (Perner, Leekam, & Wimmer, 1987) and did not develop in a normal way in autistic individuals (Baron-Cohen, Leslie, & Frith, 1985). More recently, other paradigms that avoided some difficulties of classical tasks have demonstrated a much earlier developed appreciation of false belief or mistaken perception (Leslie & Polizzi, 1998).

Having a rich explanatory psychological model of other agents' behavior is a clear example of a cognitive adaptation (Povinelli & Preuss, 1995). Indeed, above a certain degree of complexity, it is difficult to predict the behavior of complex organisms without taking the "intentional stance," that is, describing it in terms of unobservable entities such as intentions and beliefs (Dennett, 1987). The difference in predictive power is enormous even in the simplest of situations. A judgment such as "So-and-so tends to share resources" may be based on observable regularities (So-and-so sometimes leaves aside a share of her food for me to pick up). By contrast, a judgment such as "So-and-so is generous" can provide a much more reliable prediction of future behavior, by interpreting past conduct in the light of intentions and beliefs and knowing in what cases evidence counts or not toward a particular generalization (e.g., "So-and-so did not leave me a share of her food yesterday but that's because she had not seen I was there," "She is generous only with her kin," "She is generous with friends").

As in other cases where apparently broad domains are more fine-grained, we might ask whether the convenient term *theory of mind* refers to a single inference system or rather a collection of more specialized systems, whose combination produces typically human mind reading. The salience of one particular experimental paradigm (false-belief tasks) together with the existence of a specific pathology of mind reading (autism) might suggest that theory of mind is a unitary capacity, in many ways akin to a scientific account of mind and behavior (Gopnik & Wellman, 1994). This also led to speculation as to which species did or did not have theory of mind and at what point in evolution it appeared in humans (Povinelli & Preuss, 1995).

There are two distinct origin scenarios for our capacity to understand intentional agency, to create representations of other agents' behavior, beliefs, and intentions. A widely accepted *social intelligence* scenario is that higher primates evolved more and more complex intentional psychology systems to deal with social interaction. Having larger groups, more stable interaction, and more efficient coordination with other agents all bring out, given the right circumstances, significant adaptive benefits for the individual. But they all require finer and finer grained descriptions of other agents' behaviors. Social intelligence triggers an arms race resulting from higher capacity to manipulate others and a higher capacity to resist such manipulation (Whiten, 1991). It also allows the development of coalitional alliance, based on a computation of other agents' commitments to a particular purpose (hunting, warfare; Kurzban & Leary, 2001), as well as the development of friendship as an insurance policy against variance in resources (Tooby & Cosmides, 1996).

Another possible account is that (at least some aspects of) theory of mind evolved in the context of predator-prey interaction (Barrett, 1999, this volume). A heightened capacity to remain undetected by either predator or prey, as well as a better sense of how these other animals detect us, are of obvious adaptive significance for survival problems such as eating and avoiding being eaten. Indeed, some primatologists have speculated that detection of predators may have been the primary context for the evolution of agency concepts (van Schaik & Van Hooff, 1983). In the archaeological record, changes toward more flexible hunting patterns in modern humans suggest a richer, more intentional representation of the hunted animal (Mithen, 1996). Hunting and predator avoidance become much better when they are more flexible, that is, informed by contingent details about the situation at hand, so that the human does not react to all predators or prey in the same way.

These interpretations are complementary, if we remember that theory of mind is probably not a unitary capacity to produce mentalistic accounts of behavior, but a suite of distinct capacities. Humans throughout evolution did not interact with generic *intentional agents*. They interacted with predators and prey, with other animals, and with conspecifics. The latter consisted of helpful parents and siblings, potentially helpful friends, helpless offspring, dangerous rivals, and attractive mates. Also, successful interaction in such situations requires predictive models for general aspects of human behavior (a model of motivation and action, as it were) as well as particular features of each individual (a model of personality differences).

A SUITE OF AGENCY-FOCUSED INFERENCE ENGINES

These different, situation-specific models themselves orchestrate a variety of lower level neural capacities, all of which focus on particular features of animate agents and take some form of "intentional stance," that is, describe these features in terms of stipulated beliefs and intentions.

One of the crucial systems is geared at detecting *animate motion*. For some time now, cognitive psychologists have been able to describe the particular physical parameters that make motion seem animate. This system (1) takes as its input format particular patterns of motion (Michotte, 1963; Schlottman & Anderson, 1993; Tremoulet & Feldman, 2000) and (2) delivers as output an automatic interpretation of motion as animate. The system seems to develop early in infants (Baldwin, Baird, Saylor, & Clark, 2001; Rochat, Morgan, & Carpenter, 1997). These inferences are sensitive to category-specific information such as to the kind of object that is moving and the context (R. Gelman, Durgin, & Kaufman, 1995; Williams, 2000).

Animates are also detected in another way, by tracking *distant reactivity*. If a rock rolls down a hill, the only objects that will react contingently to this event at a distance—without direct contact—are the animates that turn their gaze or their head to the object, jump in surprise, run away, and so on. There is evidence that infants can detect causation at a distance (Schlottmann & Surian, 1999). This ability would provide them with a way of detecting as agents those objects that *react* to other objects' motion. In experimental settings, infants who have seen a shapeless blob reacting to their own behavior then follow that blob's orienting as if the (eyeless, faceless) blob was gazing in a particular direction (Johnson, Slaughter, & Carey, 1998). There is also evidence that detection of reactivity modulates particular neural activity, distinct from that involved in the interpretation of intentions and beliefs (Blakemore, Boyer, Pachot-Clouard, Meltzoff, & Decety, 2003).

A related capacity is *goal ascription*. Animates act in ways that are related to particular objects and states in a principled way (Blythe, Todd, & Miller, 1999). For instance, their trajectories make sense in terms of *reaching* a particular object of interest and *avoiding* nonrelevant obstacles. Infants seem to interpret the behavior of simple objects in that way. Having seen an object take a detour in its trajectory toward a goal to avoid an obstacle, they are surprised if the object maintains the same trajectory once the obstacle is removed (Csibra, Gergely, Bíró, Koós, & Brockbank, 1999), an anticipation that is also present in chimpanzees (Uller & Nichols, 2000).[5]

A very different kind of process may be required for *intention ascription*. This is the process whereby we interpret some agent's behavior as efforts toward a particular state of affairs, for example, seeing the banging of the hammer as a way of forcing the nail though the plank. There is evidence that this capacity develops early in children. For instance, young children imitate successful rather than unsuccessful gestures in the handling of tools (Want & Harris, 2001) and can use actors' apparent emotions as a clue to whether the action was successful (Phillips, Wellman, & Spelke, 2002). Young children can choose which parts of an action to imitate even if they did not observe the end result of the action (Meltzoff, 1995).[6] The capacity is particularly important for humans, given a history of tool making that required sophisticated perspective-taking abilities (Tomasello, Kruger, & Ratner, 1993).

The capacity to engage in *joint attention* is another crucial foundation for social intelligence (Baron-Cohen, 1991). Again, we find that human capacities in this respect are distinct from those of other primates and that they have a specific developmental schedule. The most salient development occurs between 9 and 12 months and follows a specific order: (1) joint engagement (playing with an object and expecting a person to cooperate), (2) communicative gestures (e.g., pointing), and (3) attention following (i.e., following people's gaze) and more complex skills such as gaze alternation (going back and forth between the object and the person; Carpenter, Nagell, & Tomasello, 1998). In normal adults, following gaze and attending to other agents' focus of attention are automatic and quasireflexive processes (Friesen & Kingstone, 1998). The comparative evidence shows that chimpanzees take gaze as a simple clue to where objects of interest may be, as opposed to taking it as indicative of the gazer's state and intentions, as all toddlers do (Povinelli & Eddy, 1996a, 1996b).

---

[5] Goal ascription, in this sense, may not require the attribution of *mental* or *representational* states to the goal-driven animate. All the system does, in view of the extant evidence, is (1) consider an object, (2) consider another object (the goal) as relevant to the first one's motion, and (3) anticipate certain trajectories in view of that goal. All this could be done by, for example, considering physical goals as endowed with some attractive force rather than considering the animate as striving to reach it.

[6] There is also evidence that even infants "parse" the flow of action into discrete segments that correspond to different goals (Baldwin et al., 2001). In adults, this segmentation is probably accomplished by distinct neural networks (Zacks et al., 2001).

A capacity for relating *facial cues to emotional states* is also early developed and seems to achieve similar adult competence in human cultures (Ekman, 1999; Keltner et al., 2003). Five-month-old infants react differently to displays of different emotions on a familiar face (D'Entremont & Muir, 1997). It seems that specific neural circuitry is involved in the detection and recognition of specific emotion types (Kesler/West et al., 2001), distinct from the general processing of facial identity. These networks partly overlap with those activated by the emotions themselves. For instance, the amygdala is activated both by the processing of frightening stimuli and frightened faces (Morris et al., 1998). The detection of emotional cues presents autistic patients with a difficult challenge (Adolphs, Sears, & Piven, 2001; Nijokiktjien et al., 2001), compounded by their difficulty in understanding the possible reasons for other people's different emotions. Williams syndrome children seem to display a dissociation between preserved processing of emotion cues and impaired understanding of goals and beliefs (theory of mind in the narrow sense), which would suggest that these are supported by distinct structures (Tager-Flusberg & Sullivan, 2000).

This survey is certainly not exhaustive but should indicate the variety of systems engaged in the smooth operation of higher theory of mind proper, that is, the process of interpreting other agents' (or one's own) behavior in terms of beliefs, intentions, memories, and inferences. Rudimentary forms of such mind-reading capacities appear very early in development (Meltzoff, 1999) and develop in fairly similar forms in normal children. Although familial circumstances can boost the development of early mind reading (Perner, Ruffman, & Leekam, 1994), this is only a subtle influence on a developmental schedule that is quite similar in many different cultures (Avis & Harris, 1991).

These various systems are activated by very different cues; they handle different input formats and produce different types of inferences. They are also, as far as we can judge given the scarce evidence, based on distinct neural systems. Early studies identified particular areas of the medial frontal lobes as specifically engaged in theory-of-mind tasks (Happé et al., 1996). There is also neuropsychological evidence that right hemisphere damage to these regions results in selective impairment of this capacity (Happé, Brownell, & Winner, 1999). Note, however, that in both cases we are considering false belief tasks, that is, the *explicit* description of another agent's *mistaken* beliefs. Actual mind reading requires other associated components, many of which are associated with distinct neural systems. The detection of gaze and attentional focus jointly engages STS and parietal areas (Allison, Puce, & McCarthy, 2000; Haxby et al., 2002). The detection of various other types of socially relevant information also activates distinct parts of STS (Allison et al., 2000). The identification of agents as reactive objects depends on selective engagement of superior parietal areas (Blakemore et al., 2003). The simple discrimination between animate and inanimate motion is probably related to joint specific activation of some MT-MST structures as well as STS (Grossman & Blake, 2001).

Different kinds of encounters with intentional agents provide contexts in which *different* cognitive adaptations result in increased fitness. Predator avoidance places a particular premium on biological motion detection and the detection of reactive objects. Social interaction requires the early development of a capacity to read emotions on faces but also the later development of a sophisticated simulation of other agents' thoughts. Dependence on hunting favors enhanced capacities for deception. The collection of neural systems that collectively support mind reading is the result of several distinct evolutionary paths.

SOLID OBJECTS AND BODIES

We argued that domain-specific inference systems are not so much focused on a specific kind of object (ontological category) as on a certain aspect of objects (cognitive domain). A good example is the set of inferential principles that helps make sense of the physical properties and behavior of solid objects—what is generally called an *intuitive physics* in the psychological literature (Kaiser, Jonides, & Alexander, 1986).

The main source of information for the contents and organization of intuitive physics comes from infant studies (Baillargeon, Kotovsky, & Needham, 1995; Spelke, 1988, 2000) that challenged the Piagetian assumption that the development of physical intuitions followed motor development (Piaget, 1930). The studies have documented the early appearance of systematic expectations about objects as units of attention (Scholl, 2001)[7] in terms of solidity (objects collide; they do not go through one another), continuity (an object has continuous, not punctuate existence in space and time), or support (unsupported objects fall; Baillargeon et al., 1995; Spelke, 1990). Also, a distinction between the roles of agent and patient in causal events seems accessible to infants (Leslie, 1984). Action at a distance is not intuitively admitted as relevant to physical events (Spelke, 1994).

However, the picture in terms of evolved systems may be slightly more complicated than that. The fact that many species manipulate the physical world in relatively agile and efficient ways does not necessarily entail that they do that on the basis of *similar* intuitive physics. In a series of ingenious experiments, Povinelli and colleagues have demonstrated systematic differences between chimpanzees and human infants (Povinelli, 2000). The chimpanzees' physical assumptions are grounded in perceptual generalizations, while those of infants seem based on assumption of underlying, invisible qualities such as force or center of mass (Povinelli, 2000). Also, human beings interact with different kinds of physical objects. In our cognitive environment, we find inert objects (like rocks), objects that we make (food, tools), and living bodies (of conspecifics or other animals). Interaction with these is likely to pose different problems and result in different kinds of principles.

The development of coherent action plans and motor behavior is crucial in terms of brain development—the infant brain undergoes massive change in that respect, and the energy expended in motor training is enormous in the first year of life—and in evolutionary terms, too. The effects of such development and the underlying systems are somewhat neglected in models of intuitive physics. This is all the more important, as neural and behavioral evidence suggests that the development of action-oriented systems and their neural implementation may be distinct from that of intuitive physics in general. That is, it may well be the case that young children and adults develop not one general intuitive physics that spans the entire ontological category of medium-size solid objects, but two quite

---

[7] This is not self-evident, especially as many classical models of attention describe surfaces, segments of the visual world, and more generally *features* rather than whole objects as the basic unit of information for attentional systems (Heslenfeld, Kenemans, Kok, & Molenaar, 1997).

distinct systems: one focused on these solid objects, their statics, and dynamics, and the other one focused on biological motion. An interesting possible consequence is that neural systems' representations of physical processes are somewhat redundant, as the same physical event is represented in two distinct ways, depending on the kind of object involved.

There is little direct evidence for dedicated neural systems handling representations of the physical behavior of solid objects. Many systems are involved, most of which are not exclusively activated by intuitive physical principles. There are few neuroimaging studies of physical or mechanical violations of the type used in developmental paradigms, but the few we have find involvement of general structures such as MT/V5 (generally involved in motion processing) and parietal attentional systems (Blakemore et al., 2001).

That biological motion is a special cognitive domain is not really controversial. In the same way as configural information is specially attended to in faces and ignored in other displays, specific processes track biological motion, that is, natural movements of animate beings (people and animals) such as walking, grasping, and so on (Ahlstrom, Blake, & Ahlstrom, 1997; Bellefeuille & Faubert, 1998; Johansson, 1973). There is now some evidence that dedicated neural structures track biological motion (see review in Decety & Grezes, 1999), with specific activation in STS, as well as medial cerebellum, on top of the regular activation of MT-MST for coherent motion (Grezes, Costes, & Decety, 1998; Grossman & Blake, 2001). These systems trigger specific inferences about the behavior of biological objects (Heptulla-Chatterjee, Freyd, & Shiffrar, 1996).

The evidence also suggests that inferences about living bodies are grounded in motor planning systems. Recent neuroimaging evidence has given extensive support to the notion that perception of other agents' motion, own motor imagery, and motor planning, as well as interpretation of goals from this motor imagery, are all tightly integrated (Blakemore & Decety, 2001). That is, perception of biological motion triggers the formation of equivalent motor plans that are subsequently blocked, probably by inhibitory influences from structures such as the orbito-frontal cortex. Now motor plans include specific expectations about the behavior of bodies and body parts. In this sense, they may be said to include a separate domain of intuitive physics.

NATURAL NUMBERS AND NATURAL OPERATIONS

Numerical cognition also illustrates how cognitive domains can diverge from ontological categories. Numerical processes could in principle consist in a single *numerosity perception* device. In fact, different processes are in charge of different aspects of number in different situations.

Numerical competence is engaged in a whole variety of distinct behaviors. Children from an early age can estimate the magnitude or continuous "numerousness" of aggregates (e.g., they prefer more sugar to less); they also estimate relative quantities of countable objects (a pile of beads is seen as bigger than another), count objects (applying a verbal counting routine, with number tags and recursive rules, to evaluate the numerosity of a set), produce numerical inferences (e.g., adding two numbers), and retrieve stored numerical facts (e.g., the fact that 2 times 6 is 12).

This variety of behaviors is reflected in a diversity of underlying processes. Against the parsimonious but misleading vision of a unitary, integrated numerical capacity, many findings in behavioral, developmental, neuropsychological, and neuroimaging studies converge to suggest a variety of representations of numbers and a variety of processes engaged in numerical inference (Dehaene, Spelke, Pinel, Stanescu, & Tsivkin, 1999). In particular, a person must distinguish between a preverbal, analogue representation of numerosities on the one hand and the verbal system of number tags and counting rules on the other (Gallistel & Gelman, 1992).[8]

This division is confirmed by neuropsychological and neuroimaging studies (Dehaene et al., 1999). One system is principally modulated by exact computation, recall of mathematical facts, and explicit application of rules, engaging activation of (mostly left hemisphere) inferior prefrontal cortex as well as areas typically activated in verbal tasks. The engagement of parietal networks in number estimation suggests a spatial representation of magnitudes, supported by the fact that magnitude estimation is impaired in subjects with spatial neglect and can be disrupted by transcranial magnetic stimulation (TMS) of the angular gyrus.[9] The analogue magnitude system encodes different numerosities as different points (or, less strictly, fuzzy locations) along a "number line," an analogical and incremental representation of magnitudes. The other network is engaged in approximation tasks and comparisons, activating bilateral inferior parietal cortex.

The distinction between systems is also relevant to development of the domain. To produce numerical inferences, children need to integrate the representations delivered by the two different systems. The first one is the representation of numerosity provided by magnitude estimation. The second one is the representation of object identity. Individuated objects allow inferences such as $(1 - 1 = 0)$ or $(2 - 1 \neq 2)$, which are observed in infants in dishabituation studies (Wynn, 1992, 2002). The acquisition process requires a systematic mapping or correspondence between two distinct representations of the objects of a collection (R. Gelman & Meck, 1992).

What can we say about the evolutionary history of these distinct capacities? We begin with magnitude estimation, the capacity to judge relative amounts or compare a set to some internal benchmark, without verbal counting. Two kinds of facts are relevant here. One is the experimental comparative evidence, showing that magnitude estimation exists in a variety of animals. Indeed, animal studies led to the best analytical model for this capacity, the notion of a counter or *accumulator* (Meck, 1997). The assumption in such models is that animals possess an event counter that can (1) trigger a specific physiological event with each occurrence of an event (not necessarily linked to event duration) and (2) store the accumulated outcome of events in some accessible register for comparisons. Such a counter would provide an analogue representation whose variance would increase with the

---

[8] Along with these two important systems, additional representational stores may be dedicated to particular numerical facts in semantic memory, to numbers represented in distinct notations, and to higher level mathematical knowledge (Campbell, 1994; Lee & Karmiloff-Smith, 1996).

[9] Magnitude estimation tasks are impaired in patients with spatial neglect (Zorzi, Priftis, & Umilta, 2002). Also, TMS results support this link between parietal spatial networks and numbers because stimulation of the angular gyrus seems to disrupt approximate magnitude estimations (Gobel, Walsh, & Rushworth, 2001).

magnitudes represented, in keeping with the available human and animal evidence (Gallistel & Gelman, 1992). There has probably been a long history of selection for magnitude estimation and comparison in humans, as this capacity is required in the sophisticated foraging practiced by human hunter-gatherers (Mithen, 1990).

Verbal counting is an entirely different affair. In the course of human history, most societies made do with rudimentary series such as "singleton—pair—triplet—a few—many" (Crump, 1990). More elaborated, recursive combinatorial systems that assign possible verbal descriptions to any numerosity are rarer in origin, though much more frequent among modern human societies. A number system is a highly "contagious" kind of cultural system, generally triggered by sustained trade. Finally, most literate societies also developed numerical notation systems, the most efficient of which are place systems where the positions of different symbols stand for the powers of a base.

These recent historical creations require cultural transmission in the form of exposure to specific behaviors (counting, noting numbers). However, "exposure" is not a causal explanation. Cultural material is transmitted inasmuch as it fits the input formats of one or several evolved inference systems. It may be relevant to see number systems, like literacy, as cultural creations that hijack prior cognitive dispositions by mimicking the input format of inference systems. This is another case where the actual and evolved domains of a system only partly overlap. Systematic verbal counting requires a sophisticated sense of *numerical individuation*, that is, an intuition that an object may be perfectly similar to another and yet be a different instance. This intuition seems to develop early in human infants (Xu & Carey, 1996).

THE EVOLVED BRAIN IS NOT PHILOSOPHICALLY CORRECT

The set of systems that we described earlier constitutes an intuitive ontology. We must keep in mind that this system is formally distinct from a catalogue of *actual* ontological categories and from *scientific* ontologies. That a cognitive ontology may depart from actual ontological categories is a familiar point in semantics (Jackendoff, 1983). As we have shown here, there are many discrepancies between the world as science or common sense see it and the kinds of objects in the world between which brain systems distinguish. The cumulative findings of neuropsychology, neuroimaging, and adult behavioral studies converge in suggesting a complex neural architecture, with many specialized systems. These systems do not correspond to the classical domains of domain specificity (e.g., intuitive psychology, intuitive physics). They are not only finer grained than broad ontological categories but also frequently cross ontological boundaries, by focusing on aspects of objects that can be found in diverse ontological categories. In other words, the evolved brain is not philosophically correct.

Although we characterized this particular combination of inference systems as specifically human, we do not mean to suggest that its emergence should be seen as the consequence of a unique hominization process. That is, the various systems probably have very different evolutionary histories. While some may well be very recent—consider, for instance, the high-level description of other agents' behaviors in terms of beliefs and intentions—some are certainly older. We alluded to this point in our description of intuitive physics, most likely an aggregate of different systems, some of which are far older than others.

CONCLUSIONS

Research in the organization of human semantic knowledge should benefit from the combination of evolutionary, neural, and developmental evidence of the kind summarized here. Research in the field has too often proceeded in the following way: (1) Identify an ontological distinction (e.g., that between living things and man-made artifacts); (2) develop specific hypotheses and gather empirical evidence for domain-specific principles and developmental patterns that differ between ontological categories; (3) try to integrate neural structures into this picture—often with much more difficulty than was expected.

We propose a slightly different agenda for the next stage of research in the field. We propose that step one should be informed by precise evolutionary considerations. This leads to a rephrasing of many classical distinctions (including that between living things and artifacts) in terms of species-specific ancestral situations, as we argued throughout this chapter. We should also rethink step two. Too often, cognitive development is viewed as a ballistic system. In that view, genes provide a newborn infant's mental dispositions, and environments provide all the subsequent changes. This, as we argued, is biologically implausible. We may anticipate great progress in our understanding of how genes drive not just the starting point but also the developmental paths themselves. This suggests a range of hypotheses about the way mental systems are primed to use specific information to create mature competencies. This change in the way we see development should lead more naturally to step three, to the formulation of conceptual specificity in terms of neural systems.

REFERENCES

Adolphs, R., Sears, L., & Piven, J. (2001). Abnormal processing of social information from faces in autism. *Journal of Cognitive Neuroscience, 13*(2), 232–240.

Ahlstrom, V., Blake, R., & Ahlstrom, U. (1997). Perception of biological motion. *Perception, 26,* 1539–1548.

Allison, T., Puce, A., & McCarthy, G. (2000). Social perception from visual cues: Role of the STS region. *Trends in Cognitive Science, 4,* 267–278.

Atran, S. A. (1990). *Cognitive foundations of natural history towards an anthropology of science.* Cambridge: Cambridge University Press.

Atran, S. A. (1998). Folk biology and the anthropology of science: Cognitive universals and cultural particulars. *Behavioral and Brain Sciences, 21*(4), 547–609.

Avis, M., & Harris, P. (1991). Belief-desire reasoning among Baka children: Evidence for a universal conception of mind. *Child Development, 62,* 460–467.

Baillargeon, R., Kotovsky, L., & Needham, A. (1995). The acquisition of physical knowledge in infancy. In D. Sperber, D. Premack, & A. James-Premack (Eds.), *Causal cognition: A multidisciplinary debate* (pp. 79–115). Oxford: Clarendon Press.

Baldwin, D. A., Baird, J. A., Saylor, M. M., & Clark, M. A. (2001). Infants parse dynamic action. *Child Development, 72*(3), 708–717.

Baron-Cohen, S. (1991). Precursors to a theory of mind: Understanding attention in others. In A. Whiten (Ed.), *Natural theories of mind.* Oxford, England: Blackwell.

Baron-Cohen, S., Leslie, A., & Frith, U. (1985). Does the autistic child have a "theory of mind"? *Cognition, 21,* 37–46.

Barrett, H. C. (1999). *Human cognitive adaptations to predators and prey.* Doctoral Dissertation, University of California, Santa Barbara.

Bellefeuille, A., & Faubert, J. (1998). Independence of contour and biological-motion cues for motion-defined animal shapes. *Perception, 27,* 225–235.

Blakemore, S.-J., Boyer, P., Pachot-Clouard, M., Meltzoff, A. N., & Decety, J. (2003). Detection of contingency and animacy in the human brain. *Cerebral Cortex, 13,* 837–844.

Blakemore, S.-J., & Decety, J. (2001). From the perception of action to the understanding of intention. *Nature Reviews Neuroscience, 2*(8), 561–567.

Blakemore, S.-J., Fonlupt, P., Pachot-Clouard, M., Darmon, C., Boyer, P., Meltzoff, A. N., et al. (2001). How the brain perceives causality: An event-related fMRI study. *Neuroreport: For Rapid Communication of Neuroscience Research, 12*(17), 3741–3746.

Bloom, P. (1996). Intention, history and artifact concepts. *Cognition, 60,* 1–29.

Blythe, P. W., Todd, P. M., & Miller, G. F. (1999). How motion reveals intention: Categorizing social interactions. In G. Gigerenzer & P. Todd (Eds.), *Simple heuristics that make us smart* (pp. 257–285). New York: Oxford University Press.

Cabeza, R., & Nyberg, L. (2000). Imaging cognition: II. An empirical review of 275 PET and fMRI studies. *Journal of Cognitive Neuroscience, 12*(1), 1–47.

Campbell, J. I. D. (1994). Architectures for numerical cognition. *Cognition, 53*(1), 1–44.

Caramazza, A. (1998). The interpretation of semantic category-specific deficits: What do they reveal about the organization of conceptual knowledge in the brain? *Neurocase: Case Studies in Neuropsychology, Neuropsychiatry, and Behavioural Neurology, 4*(4/5), 265–272.

Caramazza, A., & Shelton, J. R. (1998). Domain-specific knowledge systems in the brain: The animate-inanimate distinction. *Journal of Cognitive Neuroscience, 10*(1), 1–34.

Carpenter, M., Nagell, K., & Tomasello, M. (1998). Social cognition, joint attention, and communicative competence from 9 to 15 months of age. *Monographs of the Society for Research in Child Development, 63*(4), i-vi, 1–143.

Crump, T. (1990). *The anthropology of numbers.* Cambridge: Cambridge University Press.

Csibra, G., Gergely, G., Bíró, S., Koós, O., & Brockbank, M. (1999). Goal attribution without agency cues: The perception of "pure reason" in infancy. *Cognition, 72*(3), 237–267.

D'Entremont, B., & Muir, D. W. (1997). Five-month-olds' attention and affective responses to still-faced emotional expressions. *Infant Behavior and Development, 20*(4), 563–568.

Decety, J., & Grezes, J. (1999). Neural mechanisms subserving the perception of human actions. *Trends in Cognitive Sciences, 3,* 172–178.

Dehaene, S., Spelke, E., Pinel, P., Stanescu, R., & Tsivkin, S. (1999). Sources of mathematical thinking: Behavioral and brain-imaging evidence. *Science, 284*(5416), 970–974.

Dennett, D. C. (1987). *The intentional stance.* Cambridge, MA: MIT Press.

Devlin, J. T., Russell, R. P., Davis, M. H., Price, C. J., & Moss, K. (2002). Is there an anatomical basis for category-specificity? Semantic memory studies in P.E.T. and fMRI. *Neuropsychologia, 40*(1), 54–75.

Diamond, R., & Carey, S. (1986). Why faces are and are not special: An effect of expertise. *Journal of experimental psychology General, 115*(2), 107–117.

Duchaine, B. C. (2000). Developmental prosopagnosia with normal configural processing. *Neuroreport: For Rapid Communication of Neuroscience Research, 11*(1), 79–83.

Ekman, P. (1999). Facial expressions. In T. Dalgleish & M. J. Power (Eds.), *Handbook of cognition and emotion* (pp. 301–320). New York: Wiley.

Elman, J. L., Bates, E. A., Johnson, M. H., & Karmiloff-Smith, A. (1996). *Rethinking innateness: A connectionist perspective on development.* Cambridge, MA: MIT Press.

Farah, M. (1994). Specialization within visual object recognition: Clues from prosopagnosia and alexia. In G. R. Martha & J. Farah (Eds.), *The neuropsychology of high-level vision: Collected tutorial essays. Carnegie Mellon symposia on cognition* (pp. 133–146). Hillsdale, NJ: Erlbaum.

Farah, M., Wilson, K. D., Drain, H. M., & Tanaka, J. R. (1995). The inverted face inversion effect in prosopagnosia: Evidence for mandatory, face-specific perceptual mechanisms. *Vision Research, 35,* 2089–2093.

Friesen, C. K., & Kingstone, A. (1998). The eyes have it! Reflexive orienting is triggered by nonpredictive gaze. *Psychonomic Bulletin and Review, 5*(3), 490–495.

Gallistel, C. R., & Gelman, R. (1992). Preverbal and verbal counting and computation. *Cognition, 44*(1/2), 43–74.

Gauthier, I., Tarr, M. J., Anderson, A. W., Skudlarski, P., & Gore, J. C. (1999). Activation of the middle fusiform "face area" increases with expertise in recognizing novel objects. *Nature Neuroscience, 2*(6), 568–573.

Gauthier, I., Williams, P., Tarr, M. J., & Tanaka, J. (1998). Training "greeble" experts: A framework for studying expert object recognition processes. *Vision Research Special issue: Models of recognition, 38*(15/16), 2401–2428.

Gelman, R. (1978). Cognitive development. *Annual Review of Psychology, 29,* 297–332.

Gelman, R. (1990). First principles organize attention and learning about relevant data: Number and the animate-inanimate distinction as examples. *Cognitive Science, 14,* 79–106.

Gelman, R., & Baillargeon, R. (1983). A revision of some Piagetian concepts. In J. H. Flavell & E. M. Markman (Eds.), *Handbook of child psychology: Vol. 3. Cognitive development.* New York: Wiley.

Gelman, R., Durgin, F., & Kaufman, L. (1995). Distinguishing between animates and inanimates: Not by motion alone. In D. Sperber, D. Premack & A. Premack (Eds.), *Causal cognition: A multidisciplinary debate* (pp. 150–184). New York: Clarendon Press/Oxford University Press.

Gelman, R., & Meck, B. (1992). Early principles aid initial but not later conceptions of number. In J. Bideaud, C. Meljac & R. Gelman (Eds.), *Pathways to number: Children's developing numerical abilities* (pp. 171–189). Hillsdale, NJ: Erlbaum.

Gelman, S. A., & Bloom, P. (2000). Young children are sensitive to how an object was created when deciding what to name it. *Cognition, 76*(2), 91–103.

Gelman, S. A., & Wellman, H. M. (1991). Insides and essence: Early understandings of the nonobvious. *Cognition, 38*(3), 213–244.

Gentner, D., & Rattermann, M. J. (1991). Language and the career of similarity. In S. A. Gelman, & J. P. Byrnes (Eds.), *Perspectives on language and thought: Interrelations in development* (pp. 225–277). New York: Cambridge University Press.

Gerlach, C., Law, I., Gade, A., & Paulson, O. B. (2000). Categorization and category effects in normal object recognition: A PET study. *Neuropsychologia, 38*(13), 1693–1703.

Gobel, S., Walsh, V., & Rushworth, M. F. (2001). The mental number line and the human angular gyrus. *NeuroImage, 14*(6), 1278–1289.

Gopnik, A., & Wellman, H. (1994). The theory theory. In L. A. Hirschfeld & S. A. Gelman (Eds.), *Mapping the mind: Domain-specificity in cognition and culture.* New York: Cambridge University Press.

Grezes, J., Costes, N., & Decety, J. (1998). Top-down effect of strategy on the perception of human biological motion: A PET investigation. *Cognitive Neuropsychology, 15*(6/8), 553–582.

Grossman, E. D., & Blake, R. (2001). Brain activity evoked by inverted and imagined biological motion. *Vision Research, 41*(10/11), 1475–1482.

Happé, F., Brownell, H., & Winner, E. (1999). Acquired "theory of mind" impairments following stroke. *Cognition, 70*(3), 211–240.

Happé, F., Ehlers, S., Fletcher, P., Frith, U., Johansson, M., Gillberg, C., et al. (1996). "Theory of mind" in the brain: Evidence from a PET scan study of Asperger syndrome. *Neuroreport: An International Journal for the Rapid Communication of Research in Neuroscience, 8,* 197–201.

Haxby, J. V., Hoffman, E. A., & Gobbini, M. I. (2002). Human neural systems for face recognition and social communication. *Biological psychiatry, 51*(1), 59–67.

Heptulla-Chatterjee, S., Freyd, J. J., & Shiffrar, M. (1996). Configural processing in the perception of apparent biological motion. *Journal of Experimental Psychology: Human Perception and Performance, 22,* 916–929.

Heslenfeld, D. J., Kenemans, J. L., Kok, A., & Molenaar, P. C. M. (1997). Feature processing and attention in the human visual system: An overview. *Biological Psychology, 45*(1/3), 183–215.

Hirschfeld, L. A., & Gelman, S. A. (Eds.). (1994). *Mapping the mind: Domain-specificity in culture and cognition.* New York: Cambridge University Press.

Jackendoff, R. (1983). *Semantics and cognition.* Cambridge, MA: MIT Press.

Jackendoff, R. (2002). *Foundations of language: Brain, meaning, grammar, evolution.* Oxford, England: Oxford University Press.

Johansson, G. (1973). Visual perception of biological motion and a model for its analysis. *Perception and Psychophysics, 14*(2), 201–211.

Johnson, S., Slaughter, V., & Carey, S. (1998). Whose gaze will infants follow? The elicitation of gaze-following in 12-month-olds. *Developmental Science, 1*(2), 233–238.

Kaiser, M. K., Jonides, J., & Alexander, J. (1986). Intuitive reasoning about abstract and familiar physics problems. *Memory and Cognition, 14,* 308–312.

Kanwisher, N. (2000). Domain specificity in face perception. *Nature Neuroscience, 3*(8), 759–763.

Kanwisher, N., McDermott, J., & Chun, M. M. (1997). The fusiform face area: A module in human extrastriate cortex specialized for face perception. *Journal of Neuroscience, 17*(11), 4302–4311.

Keil, F. C. (1986). The acquisition of natural kind and artifact terms. In A. W. D. Marrar (Ed.), *Conceptual change* (pp. 73–86). Norwaood, NJ: Ablex.

Keltner, D., Ekman, P., Gonzaga, G. C., Beer, J., Scherer, K. R., Johnstone, T., et al. (2003). Part IV: Expression of emotion. In R. J. Davidson & K. R. Scherer (Eds.), *Handbook of affective sciences* (pp. 411–559). London: Oxford University Press, 2003, xvii, 1199.

Kemler Nelson, D. G. (1995). Principle-based inferences in young children's categorization: Revisiting the impact of function on the naming of artifacts. *Cognitive Development, 10,* 347–380.

Kesler/West, M. L., Andersen, A. H., Smith, C. D., Avison, M. J., Davis, C. E., Kryscio, R. J., et al. (2001). Neural substrates of facial emotion processing using fMRI. *Cognitive Brain Research, 11*(2), 213–226.

Kurzban, R., & Leary, M. R. (2001). Evolutionary origins of stigmatization: The functions of social exclusion. *Psychological Bulletin, 127*(2), 187–208.

Lee, K., & Karmiloff-Smith, A. (1996). The development of external symbol systems: The child as a notator. In R. Gelman, & T. Kit-Fong Au (Eds.), *Perceptual and cognitive development* (pp. 185–211). San Diego, CA: Academic Press.

Leslie, A. M. (1984). Spatiotemporal continuity and the perception of causality in infants. *Perception, 13*(3), 287–305.

Leslie, A. M., & Polizzi, P. (1998). Inhibitory processing in the false belief task: Two conjectures. *Developmental Science, 1*(2), 247–253.

Martin, A., Haxby, J. V., Lalonde, F. J., Wiggs, C. L., Parasuraman, R., & Ungerleider, L. G. (1994). A distributed cortical network for object knowledge. *Society for Neuroscience Abstracts, 20*(1/2), 5.

Martin, A., Wiggs, C. L., Ungerleider, L. G., & Haxby, J. V. (1996). Neural correlates of category-specific knowledge. *Nature (London), 379*(6566), 649–652.

Meck, W. H. (1997). Application of a mode-control model of temporal integration to counting and timing behaviour. In C. M. Bradshaw & E. Szabadi (Eds.), *Time and behaviour: Psychological and neurobehavioural analyses* (pp. 133–184). Amsterdam, Netherlands: North-Holland/Elsevier Science.

Mecklinger, A., Gruenewald, C., Besson, M., Magnie, M.-N., & Von Cramon, Y. (2002). Separable neuronal circuitries for manipulable and non-manipulable objects in working memory. *Cerebral Cortex, 12,* 1115–1123.

Meltzoff, A. N. (1995). Understanding the intentions of others: Re-enactment of intended acts by 18-month-old children. *Developmental Psychology, 31*(5), 838–850.

Meltzoff, A. N. (1999). Origins of theory of mind, cognition and communication. *Journal of Communication Disorders, 32*(4), 251–269.

Michelon, P., & Biederman, I. (2003). Less impairment in face imagery than face perception in early prosopagnosia. *Neuropsychologia, 41*(4), 421–441.

Michotte, A. (1963). *The perception of causality.* New York: Basic Books.

Mithen, S. J. (1990). *Thoughtful foragers: A study of prehistoric decision-making.* Cambridge: Cambridge University Press.

Mithen, S. J. (1996). *The prehistory of the mind.* London: Thames and Hudson.

Moore, C. J., & Price, C. J. (1999). A functional neuroimaging study of the variables that generate category-specific object processing differences. *Brain, 122*(5), 943–962.

Morris, J. S., Friston, K. J. B., Chel, C., Frith, C. D., Young, A. W., Calder, A. J., et al. (1998). A neuromodulatory role for the human amygdala in processing emotional facial expressions. *Brain; a journal of neurology, 121*(Pt. 1), 47–57.

Morton, J., & Johnson, M. (1991). CONSPEC and CONLERN: A two-process theory of infant face-recognition. *Psychological Review, 98,* 164–181.

Moss, H. E., & Tyler, L. K. (2000). A progressive category-specific semantic deficit for non-living things. *Neuropsychologia, 38*(1), 60–82.

Nelson, C. A. (2001). The development and neural bases of face recognition. *Infant and Child Development Special issue: Face Processing in Infancy and Early Childhood, 10*(1/2), 3–18.

Nijokiktjien, C., Verschoor, A., Sonneville, L. D., Huyser, C., Veld, V. O. H., & Toorenaar, N. (2001). Disordered recognition of facial identity and emotions in three Asperger type autists. *European Child and Adolescent Psychiatry, 10*(1), 79–90.

Pascalis, O., de Schonen, S., Morton, J., Deruelle, C., & Campbell, R. (1995). Mother's face recognition by neonates: A replication and an extension. *Infant Behavior and Development, 18*(1), 79–85.

Perani, D., Cappa, S. F., Bettinardi, V., Bressi, S., Gorno-Tempini, M., Matarrese, M., et al. (1995). Different neural systems for the recognition of animals and man-made tools. *Society for Neuroscience Abstracts, 21*(1/3), 1498.

Perner, J., Leekam, S. R., & Wimmer, H. (1987). Three year olds' difficulty with false belief. *British Journal of Developmental Psychology, 5,* 125–137.

Perner, J., Ruffman, T., & Leekam, S. R. (1994). Theory of mind is contagious: You catch it from your sibs. *Child Development, 65,* 1228–1238.

Phillips, A. T., Wellman, H. M., & Spelke, E. S. (2002). Infants' ability to connect gaze and emotional expression to intentional action. *Cognition, 85*(1), 53–78.

Piaget, J. (1930). *The child's conception of physical causality.* London: Routledge and Kegan Paul.

Pinker, S., & Bloom, P. (1990). Natural language and natural selection. *Behavioral and Brain Sciences, 13*(4), 707–784.

Posner, M. I., & Raichle, M. E. (1994). *Images of mind.* New York: Scientific American Library/Scientific American Books.

Povinelli, D. J. (2000). *Folk physics for apes: The chimpanzee's theory of how the world works.* New York: Oxford University Press.

Povinelli, D. J., & Eddy, T. J. (1996a). Chimpanzees: Joint visual attention. *Psychological Science, 7*(3), 129–135.

Povinelli, D. J., & Eddy, T. J. (1996b). What young chimpanzees know about seeing. *Monographs of the Society for Research in Child Development, 61*(3), v–vi, 1–152.

Povinelli, D. J., & Preuss, T. M. (1995). Theory of mind: Evolutionary history of a cognitive specialization. *Trends in Neurosciences, 18*(9), 418–424.

Richards, D. D., Goldfarb, J., Richards, A. L., & Hassen, P. (1989). The role of the functionality rule in the categorization of well-defined concepts. *Journal of Experimental Child Psychology, 47,* 97–115.

Rochat, P., Morgan, R., & Carpenter, M. (1997). Young infants' sensitivity to movement information specifying social causality. *Cognitive Development, 12*(4), 441–465.

Sacchett, C., & Humphreys, G. W. (1992). Calling a squirrel a squirrel but a canoe a wigwam: A category specific deficit for artefactual objects and body parts. *Cognitive Neuropsychology, 9,* 73–86.

Sartori, G., Coltheart, M., Miozzo, M., & Job, R. (1994). Category specificity and informational specificity in neuropsychological impairment of semantic memory. In C. Umilta & M. Moscovitch (Eds.), *Attention and performance 15: Conscious and nonconscious information processing* (pp. 537–550). Cambridge, MA: MIT Press.

Sartori, G., Job, R., Miozzo, M., & Zago, S. (1993). Category-specific form-knowledge deficit in a patient with herpes simplex virus encephalitis. *Journal of Clinical and Experimental Neuropsychology, 15*(2), 280–299.

Schlottman, A., & Anderson, N. H. (1993). An information integration approach to phenomenal causality. *Memory and Cognition, 21*(6), 785–801.

Schlottmann, A., & Surian, L. (1999). Do 9-month-olds perceive causation-at-a-distance? *Perception, 28*(9), 1105–1113.

Scholl, B. J. (2001). Objects and attention: The state of the art. *Cognition, 80*(1/2), 1–46.

Sheridan, J., & Humphreys, G. W. (1993). A verbal-semantic category-specific recognition impairment. *Cognitive Neuropsychology, 10*(2), 143–184.

Slater, A., & Quinn, P. C. (2001). Face recognition in the newborn infant. *Infant and Child Development Special issue: Face Processing in Infancy and Early Childhood, 10*(1/2), 21–24.

Spelke, E. S. (1988). The origins of physical knowledge. In L. Weizkrantz (Ed.), *Thought without language.* Oxford, England: Oxford University Press.

Spelke, E. S. (1990). Principles of object perception. *Cognitive Science, 14,* 29–56.

Spelke, E. S. (1994). Initial knowledge: Six suggestions. *Cognition, 50,* 431–445.

Spelke, E. S. (2000). Core knowledge. *American Psychologist, 55*(11), 1233–1243.

Sperber, D. (1994). The modularity of thought and the epidemiology of representations. In L. A. Hirschfeld & S. A. Gelman (Eds.), *Mapping the mind: Domain-specificity in cognition and culture.* New York: Cambridge University Press.

Spitzer, M., Kischka, U., Gueckel, F., Bellemann, M. E., Kammer, T., Seyyedi, S., et al. (1998). Functional magnetic resonance imaging of category-specific cortical activation: Evidence for semantic maps. *Cognitive Brain Research, 6*(4), 309–319.

Spitzer, M., Kwong, K. K., Kennedy, W., & Rosen, B. R. (1995). Category-specific brain activation in fMRI during picture naming. *Neuroreport: An International Journal for the Rapid Communication of Research in Neuroscience, 6*(16), 2109–2112.

Tager-Flusberg, H., & Sullivan, K. (2000). A componential view of theory of mind: Evidence from Williams syndrome. *Cognition, 76*(1), 59–89.

Tanaka, J. W., & Sengco, J. A. (1997). Features and their configuration in face recognition. *Memory and Cognition, 25*(5), 583–592.

Tarr, M. J., & Gauthier, I. (2000). FFA: A flexible fusiform area for subordinate-level visual processing automatized by expertise. *Nature Neuroscience, 3*(8), 764–769.

Tomasello, M., Kruger, A. C., & Ratner, H. H. (1993). Cultural learning. *Behavioral and Brain Sciences, 16,* 495–510.

Tooby, J., & Cosmides, L. (1996). Friendship and the banker's paradox: Other pathways to the evolution of adaptations for altruism. In W. G. Runciman & J. Maynard Smith (Eds.), *Evolution of social behaviour patterns in primates and man* (pp. 119–143). Oxford, England, England Oxford University Press.

Tremoulet, P. D., & Feldman, J. (2000). Perception of animacy from the motion of a single object. *Perception, 29,* 943–951.

Uller, C., & Nichols, S. (2000). Goal attribution in chimpanzees. *Cognition, 76*(2), B27–B34.

van Schaik, C. P., & Van Hooff, J. A. (1983). On the ultimate causes of primate social systems. *Behaviour, 85*(1/2), 91–117.

Want, S. C., & Harris, P. L. (2001). Learning from other people's mistakes: Causal understanding in learning to use a tool. *Child Development, 72*(2), 431–443.

Warrington, E. K., & McCarthy, R. (1983). Category-specific access dysphasia. *Brain, 106,* 859–878.

Warrington, E. K., & McCarthy, R. (1987). Categories of knowledge: Further fractionations and an attempted integration. *Brain, 110,* 1273–1296.

Whiten, A. (Ed.). (1991). *Natural theories of mind: The evolution, development and simulation of everyday mind-reading.* Oxford, England: Blackwell.

Williams, E. M. (2000). *Causal reasoning by children and adults about the trajectory, context, and animacy of a moving object.* PhD dissertation, University of California, Los Angeles.

Wynn, K. (1992). Addition and subtraction by human infants. *Nature, 358*(6389), 749–750.

Wynn, K. (2002). Do infants have numerical expectations or just perceptual preferences?: Comment. *Developmental Science, 5*(2), 207–209.

Xu, F., & Carey, S. (1996). Infants' metaphysics: The case of numerical identity. *Cognitive Psychology, 30*(2), 111–153.

Young, A. W., Hellawell, D., & Hay, D. C. (1987). Configurational information in face perception. *Perception, 16*(6), 747–759.

Zacks, J. M., Braver, T. S., Sheridan, M. A., Donaldson, D. I., Snyder, A. Z., Ollinger, J. M., et al. (2001). Human brain activity time-locked to perceptual event boundaries. *Nature neuroscience, 4*(6), 651–655.

Zorzi, M., Priftis, K., & Umilta, C. (2002). Brain damage: Neglect disrupts the mental number line. *Nature, 417*(6885), 138–139.

CHAPTER 4

Methods of Evolutionary Sciences

JEFFRY A. SIMPSON and LORNE CAMPBELL

THEORY AND RESEARCH METHODS IN THE EVOLUTIONARY SCIENCES

DARWIN (1859) BEGAN THINKING and writing about the theory of evolution by natural selection years before he published *The Origin of Species*. Although he had stumbled upon an idea that would forever change biology and the life sciences, Darwin kept his thoughts to himself for several years because he did not have sufficient evidence to support his iconoclastic views (Desmond & Moore, 1991). He needed some provisional empirical evidence for his grand theory.

Testing the theory of evolution by natural selection was no small task, so Darwin used several different methods for this purpose. For example, Darwin spoke with animal breeders to learn about artificial selection. He eventually discerned that heritable variation in domesticated traits was shaped by the preferences of breeders and likened this process to the natural selection of traits. He also surveyed the existing scientific literature on species in their natural environments, describing and cataloguing the vast amount of variation that existed within and between species. Additionally, he spent countless hours experimenting with seeds to determine whether they germinated after being exposed to various conditions. Armed with information from his observations, field studies, and experiments, Darwin was able to provide initial support for the basic premises underlying the theory of evolution by natural selection. Indeed, it was Darwin's relentless perseverance gathering data from multiple sources that permitted his theory ultimately to be embraced by the wider scientific community.

Both the theory and science of evolution have progressed tremendously since the publication of *The Origin of Species*. Darwin's belief that evolution would provide a foundation for the study of psychology is now coming to fruition as many researchers in a growing number of academic disciplines are beginning to discover the evolutionary structure and architecture of the human mind. This is a very exciting time for the evolutionary sciences. However, it is also a time for researchers to emulate the research practices of Darwin by adopting a multifaceted approach to the study of psychological adaptations. To do so, researchers must be aware of the different investigative methods that are available. To facilitate this process, we revisit some of the fundamental principles and concepts that have anchored research methods in the social and behavioral sciences for several decades. We hope to kindle (or rekindle) greater interest in methodological issues by not only showcasing the myriad research methods available to evolutionary scientists, but also by clarifying *how* different research methods and measures can be used to make clearer and stronger tests of various evolutionary-based predictions.

The chapter contains several overarching themes. One theme is that, in order to provide stronger and more definitive tests of theories, multiple research methods and outcome measures must be used to test alternate models *within* ongoing programs of evolutionary research. As we shall see, each major research method (e.g., laboratory experiments, surveys, computer simulations) and each type of outcome measure (e.g., self-reports, peer-ratings, behavioral ratings) have strengths and limitations. No single method or measure is optimal in all research contexts because the use of different methods and measures requires making trade-offs between maximizing internal validity, external validity, and the generalizability of findings across people. Both methodological triangulation within programs of research (i.e., adopting a multiple-method/multiple-measure approach when testing predicted effects) and the testing of alternative models are needed to make strong, clear inferences.

A second theme is that there has been an over-reliance on certain research methods (e.g., correlational methods) and certain measures (e.g., self-reports) in some quarters of the evolutionary sciences. In some cases, this mono-method/mono-measure predilection has impeded the rigorous testing of certain evolutionary-based phenomena; in others, it has not allowed investigators to determine whether the results predicted by evolutionary theories fit observed data better than those predicted by alternate, competing theories. This over-reliance can be remedied through greater knowledge and appreciation of the many strengths and advantages that multiple research methods and paradigms can offer.

A final organizing theme is the need to test and provide better evidence for the special design properties of purported psychological adaptations. In some cases, a multimethod/multimeasure approach should help researchers offer clearer and stronger evidence for the special design features of certain evolved traits or characteristics in humans. The telltale signs of selection and adaptation should be most evident when specific stimuli (triggering events) produce specific effects or outcomes (responses) at different levels of analysis (ranging from molecular to macro levels). Converging patterns of results from well-conducted multimethod/multimeasure studies will *increase* our confidence in the evolution of certain "specially designed" adaptations.

This chapter has four major sections: (1) we discuss how and why multimethod/multimeasure evidence for the special design of certain traits or behaviors offers more compelling evidence for their status as adaptations. We also discuss the unique inferential and methodological challenges associated with testing evolutionary theories. (2) We review classic concepts and issues surrounding *validity*. In doing so, we review the major types of validity and explain why evidence for each type is required to establish construct validity. (3) We review different types of investigative (research) methods that are organized around an adapted model proposed by Runkel and McGrath (1972). This model highlights the trade-offs entailed by the use of each research method. (4) Finally, we showcase two programs of evolutionary research that have applied multi-method/multimeasure strategies to document the special design features of certain hypothesized psychological adaptations. We conclude by proposing several ways in which current programs of evolutionary research might be strengthened and improved from a methodological standpoint.

THEORY TESTING, SPECIAL DESIGN, AND STRONG RESEARCH METHODS

Before reviewing the methodological strategies and techniques available to evolutionary researchers, it is important to understand why it is so challenging to provide compelling empirical support for evolutionary theories. Accordingly, we open this section by explaining why it is more difficult to marshal persuasive evidence for evolutionary-based theories than for theories that do not have explicit "historical origin" components. We then discuss the concept of evolved adaptations, review criticisms of the adaptationism approach, and propose how stronger and more persuasive evidence can be mounted by testing the special design properties of purported adaptations.

WHY IS IT DIFFICULT TO PROVIDE COMPELLING EVIDENCE FOR EVOLUTIONARY THEORIES?

Evolutionary scholars frequently lament that they must provide better or more empirical evidence for their articles to survive the peer-review process. This perception probably contains some truth. Evolutionary theories have a different logical structure than most other theories, especially those that make no explicit assumptions about the distal origins of human traits, attributes, or behaviors. This difference profoundly affects the way in which evolutionary theories are viewed and evaluated by scientists. Most scientists believe that a theory is more likely to be true if (1) empirical results repeatedly confirm what the theory predicts and (2) the results cannot be explained by competing theories. Methodologically strong research programs, therefore, are structured not only around testing and confirming the specific outcomes predicted by a given theory, but also around demonstrating that outcomes have sound discriminant validity properties.

When judging the truth (veracity) of a theory, scientists usually make inferential judgments at three levels (Conway & Schaller, 2002):

1. At the most basic level, they evaluate the perceived truth of a given hypothesis, which is a product of: the perceived amount of empirical support for the hypothesis, and the *inverse* of the perceived plausibility of alternate explanations.
2. At the next level, scientists make inferences about the perceived veracity of the theory from which the hypothesis is derived. This assessment hinges on: how well and clearly the hypothesis and related hypotheses are logically derived from the theory and how easily they can be derived from

alternate theories or models. Inferential evaluation usually stops here because most theories focus on contemporary psychological events and processes and make few, if any, *explicit* assumptions about their historical origins.

3. At the most abstract level, scientists judge the plausibility of the historical origins specified by a theory. This is a function of how well and clearly models of contemporary psychological events and processes have been logically derived from their historical origin theories or models, and the degree to which these theories or models cannot be deduced from alternate ones that posit different historical origins. Hence, the more temporally "removed" empirical findings are from the theoretical models from which they are derived, the more difficult it is to convince people that a theory is true.

This extra layer of inference explains why most theories that contain large historical origin components face higher hurdles in the scientific evaluation process. Because more levels of inference must be traversed, positive results from a single study are viewed as providing less support in relation to the full theory, even if they are entirely consistent with what the theory predicts. To complicate matters, the starting assumptions about the historical antecedents of a purportedly adaptive trait or psychological mechanism (e.g., assumptions about the specific environmental problems our human ancestors faced, their social and living arrangements, the most prevalent and countervailing selection pressures) are less likely to be assumed true given that the historical antecedents cannot be directly observed, manipulated, or measured.[1] Thus, the perceived likelihood that some other nonevolutionary theory might explain a hypothesized adaptation increases as scientists move from hypothetical, to psychological, to historical levels of inference.[2]

Many evolutionary theories also face stiffer evaluation hurdles because of the sheer complexity—and sometimes the imprecision—of the metatheories on which they are based. Evolutionary theories tend to be more complex than other theories, including many historical origin theories that do not have evolutionary bases (e.g., certain social structuralist theories; see Eagly, 1987). One reason for this is that inferring simple associations between distal, biologically based adaptations and the operation of current psychological processes is more complicated than inferring associations between cultural or social structural factors and current psychological processes. More complex theories typically generate a larger number of "internal" alternative explanations, making it more difficult to derive straightforward predictions about whether and how certain traits or behaviors were—or should have been—adaptive in our ancestral past (Caporael & Brewer, 2000; Dawkins, 1989).

This problem has been further compounded by the relative lack of attention devoted to (1) clarifying how different middle-level evolutionary theories should

---

[1] Some origin theorists occasionally can use fossils or other artifacts to make inferences about the historical origins of a given trait or behavior. This is less likely in the evolutionary sciences, where purported adaptations (e.g., domain-specific psychological mechanisms) leave sparse artifact trails (but see Andrews et al., 2003a; Williams, 1966, 1992).

[2] This does not mean that these perceptions are well founded. Moreover, some theories that could or should have historical origin components fail to make such assumptions explicit, rendering these models more diffuse and difficult to test.

and should not interrelate, and (2) specifying the conditions under which different theories make similar versus divergent predictions about specific outcomes (Simpson, 1999). Evolutionary theories are hierarchically organized and contain several levels of explanation, ranging from broad metatheoretical assumptions, to domain-relevant middle-level principles, to specific hypotheses, to highly specific predictions (Buss, 1995; Ketelaar & Ellis, 2000). Most middle-level evolutionary theories (e.g., parental investment, attachment, parent-offspring conflict, reciprocal altruism) extend the core assumptions of their metatheories to specific psychological domains, such as the conditions under which individuals invest in their offspring, bond with them, experience conflict with them, or assist biologically unrelated others. In some cases, middle-level theories generate competing hypotheses and predictions. Parental investment theory, for instance, makes different predictions than reciprocal altruism theory about when men should invest in young, biologically unrelated children of unattached women (see Ketelaar & Ellis, 2000). In other cases, middle-level evolutionary theories spawn hypotheses that vie with nonevolutionary theories (e.g., the debate about why homicide is so prevalent in "families"; see Daly & Wilson, 1988). Little attention is typically paid to which outcomes different competing theories or models—either evolutionary-based or otherwise—logically anticipate. Whenever possible, tests between predictions that have been logically derived from competing models should be *built into* evolutionary research programs (Holcomb, 1998).

At times, evolutionary researchers also do not fully articulate the deductive logic that connects one level of explanation (such as the basic principles of a middle-level theory) to adjacent levels (such as a specific set of concrete hypotheses). One reason for this is that evolutionary hypotheses exist along a "continuum of confidence," which ranges from: (1) clear and firm hypotheses that are unequivocally and directly derived from a middle-level theory; to (2) expectation-based hypotheses that can be logically deduced from a theory, but cannot be directly derived from it without making important auxiliary assumptions; to (3) speculative hypotheses based on casual and intuitive guesses (Ellis & Symons, 1990). If researchers are testing speculative hypotheses, rigorous deductively based predictions will be more difficult to derive from a theory.

GENERATING MORE COMPELLING EVIDENCE

How can the evolutionary sciences overcome these limitations? To begin with, researchers must develop clearer and more detailed models of the historical events that should have produced an evolved trait or attribute (Conway & Schaller, 2002). Supportive evidence must also be procured from a wider range of disciplines (e.g., anthropology, zoology, genetics, evolutionary biology) to justify the "starting assumptions" of a proposed historical theory or model and to explain why it is more probable than others. To accomplish this, evolutionary scientists must conduct more refined cost-benefit analyses relevant to the evolutionary history of each purported adaptation (Cronin, 1991). Specifically, greater attention must focus on the conceivable costs, constraints, and limitations—social, physical, behavioral, physiological, and otherwise—that might have counterweighted the conjectured benefits associated with a hypothesized adaptation. After conducting these analyses, researchers must elucidate why certain adaptations would have produced better solutions to specific evolutionarily relevant problems than other possible adaptations, and direct tests of alternative models must be performed.

The forgoing limitations might also be rectified if investigators structured more of their research around the predictions that specific evolutionary theories or models make regarding the onset, operation, and termination of specific psychological processes or mechanisms. When doing so, a clear conceptual distinction must be maintained between models of historical (evolutionary) events and the current psychological events or processes being examined. This might be achieved by organizing more research questions around Buss's (1995, pp. 5–6) incisive definition of evolved psychological mechanisms:

> An evolved psychological mechanism is a set of processes inside an organism that: (1) Exists in the form it does because it (or other mechanisms that reliably produce it) solved a specific problem of individual survival or reproduction recurrently over human evolutionary history; (2) takes only certain classes of information or input, where input (a) can be either external or internal, (b) can be actively extracted from the environment or passively received from the environment, and (c) specifies to the organism the particular adaptive problem it is facing; (3) transforms that information into output through a procedure (e.g., decision rule) in which output (a) regulates physiological activity, provides information to other psychological mechanisms, or produces manifest action and (b) solves a particular adaptive problem.

When developing and testing the deductive logic of a theory, therefore, evolutionary scientists should: (1) articulate how and why specific selection pressures should have shaped certain psychological mechanisms or processes; (2) identify the specific environmental cues that should have activated these processes in relevant ancestral environments; (3) explain how these processes should have guided thoughts, feelings, and behavior in specific social situations; and (4) specify the cues or outcomes that should have terminated these psychological processes or mechanisms. The wider adoption of this general approach could yield several benefits. First, by clarifying and more rigorously testing the deductive logic underlying an evolutionary theory or model, investigators should be in a better position to articulate how and why their theory provides a forward-thinking account of specific psychological processes or mechanisms rather than an ad hoc, backward-thinking explanation. Second, because subtle connections between different theoretical levels would be more fully explained, the theory or model being tested ought to have greater explanatory coherence. Third, sounder and more extensive deductive logic should allow researchers to derive more novel predictions. Powerful theories generate new and unforeseen predictions that cannot be easily derived from alternative theories. Many novel hypotheses are likely to involve statistical interactions in which certain psychological mechanisms are activated or terminated by very specific environmental inputs. Theories that predict specific types of context-dependent statistical interactions usually have fewer alternative explanations (Conway, Schaller, Tweed, & Hallett, 2001).

ADAPTATIONS, ADAPTATIONISM, AND STANDARDS OF EVIDENCE

At a conceptual level, most evolutionary psychologists subscribe to a general investigative orientation known as *adaptationism*. Using this approach, researchers attempt to identify the specific selection pressures that shaped the evolution of certain traits or characteristics in our ancestral past (Thornhill, 1997; Williams, 1966). This approach asks questions of the form "What is the function or purpose of this particular structure, organ, or characteristic?" Answers to such questions have produced rapid and significant advances in many areas of science. With respect to human evolution, some adaptationist research programs have used optimization modeling (e.g., testing different formal mathematical theories of possible selection pressures in the EEA; Parker & Maynard Smith, 1990) to marshal evidence for certain purported adaptations in humans. Most programs, however, have simply developed plausible, intuitive arguments regarding how a given trait or characteristic might have evolved to solve specific evolutionary problems (Williams, 1966, 1992).

The general adaptationist approach has been criticized by Gould and Lewontin (1979), who claim that most adaptationist research has used weak or inappropriate standards of evidence to identify adaptations. They argue that most adaptationist research merely demonstrates that certain outcomes are consistent with theoretical predictions without fully examining competing alternative accounts. Gould (1984) has also argued that most adaptationist research has overemphasized the importance of selection pressures and underestimated the many constraints on selection forces, leading some adaptationists to presume that adaptations exist when rigorous evidence is lacking. Gould and Lewontin (1979) maintain that many constraints—genetic, physical, and developmental—may have opposed or hindered the impact that selection pressures had on most phenotypic traits and characteristics. Thus, they claim that exaptations (i.e., preexisting traits that take on new beneficial effects without being modified by new selection pressures) are numerous, making it nearly impossible to recreate the selection history of a given trait or characteristic. Most adaptations are, in fact, probably built on earlier adaptations, exaptations, or spandrels (i.e., by-products that happen to be associated with adapted traits). The evolutionary sciences, therefore, must use methodologies that are capable of documenting specific adaptations more directly (Mayr, 1983).

What types of evidence have been gathered to test whether certain traits or psychological attributes could be adaptations? Andrews, Gangestad, and Matthews (2003a) discuss six standards of evidence: (1) *Comparative standards*, which make specific phylogenetic comparisons regarding a purportedly adaptive trait across different species; (2) *Fitness maximization standards*, which identify particular traits that should maximize fitness returns in particular environments, including current ones; (3) *Beneficial effects standards*, which focus on the fitness benefits that a presumably adaptive trait could have produced in ancestral environments; (4) *Optimal design standards*, which test formal mathematical simulations of how different selection pressures might have produced trade-offs in evolved features and how fitness could have been increased by trading off the features of one trait against others; (5) *Tight fit standards*, which examine how closely a presumably adaptive trait's features match, and should have efficiently solved, a major evolutionary problem; and (6) *Special design standards*, which identify and test the unique functional properties of a purportedly adaptive trait.[3]

---

[3] There are additional criteria and techniques that can aid in documenting adaptations (Andrews et al., 2003b). These include identifying powerful developmental biases or the maladaptive outcomes associated with certain injuries or disorders, recreating the phylogenetic history of a purported adaptation (to confirm that function emerged before structure), marshaling molecular genetic evidence for an adaptation or, in limited cases, showing evidence of possible homology with other higher primates.

The first five standards offer indirect evidence that a given trait might be an adaptation. The sixth standard—special design—provides much more rigorous evidence (Andrews et al., 2003a). *Thus, evolutionary research programs must be developed, organized, and structured around providing more firm and direct evidence for the special design properties of possible adaptations.* As more and more special design features of a hypothesized adaptation are documented, each contributing to a specific function, it becomes more plausible that the hypothesized adaptation actually evolved for that function. The best and most rigorous evolutionary research programs routinely test for special design features.

Special Design Evidence

Organisms are living historical documents (Cronin, 1991; Williams, 1992). Accordingly, adaptations should reveal remnants of the selective forces that shaped them. Before a trait can be classified as an adaptation, its primary evolutionary function or purpose must first be ascertained (Mayr, 1983; Thornhill, 1997).[4] To accomplish this, the specific selection pressures that most likely generated and shaped the functional design of the trait must be inferred. Functionally designed traits tend to perform a purpose "with sufficient precision, economy, efficiency, etc. to rule out pure chance as an adequate explanation" (Williams, 1966, pp. 10). Chance factors can include processes such as phylogenetic legacy, genetic drift, by-product effects, and mutations, any of which could be responsible for the development of a particular trait.[5]

Several additional factors also make it difficult to determine whether a particular trait is an adaptation. These include the potentially confounding effects of historically prior adaptations (e.g., those upon which more recent "secondary adaptations" might have been constructed), trade-offs between interacting adaptations (e.g., selection for camouflage from predators versus colorful ornamentation to attract mates), and counter-adaptations (e.g., countervailing mating tactics that emerge between the sexes in a species). Complicating matters, different traits may require different types of evidence to demonstrate their special design properties. For example, the special design features of many morphological traits (e.g., the human eye, body organs) have been demonstrated simply by showing that a particular trait has complex design and performs a specific function with a very high degree of precision, economy, and efficiency. Additional evidence, however, is often needed for complex behavioral and cognitive traits that are believed to be adaptations because domain-general learning processes (such as exapted learning mechanisms) can produce traits that have considerable specificity, proficiency, and complexity (see Andrews, Gangestad, & Matthews, 2003a, 2003b; Kruschke,

---

[4] The term *adaptive trait* refers to the underlying decision rules and information processing algorithms that should have been selected to guide context-specific thoughts, feelings, and behaviors. The deployment of these rules should typically have increased individuals' reproductive fitness in ancestral environments (Andrews et al., 2003a).

[5] We are not suggesting that a trait must be shaped only by natural selection forces in order to be considered an adaptation. Clearly, natural selection must operate on existing variation, most of which is generated by chance factors.

1992). For these "complex traits," further evidence for their special design properties is typically required.

Fortunately, several sources of evidence can increase our confidence about the special design of certain traits (Andrews et al., 2003a). First, "complex" trait adaptations can be documented by demonstrating that a trait is a biased outcome of a specific developmental or learning mechanism (Cummins & Cummins, 1999). These traits develop or are learned very easily, quickly, and reliably, and they tend to solve specific adaptive problems with greater proficiency than other traits that could have been produced by the same underlying mechanisms. Examples include the strong and automatic propensity to fear certain objects (e.g., snakes; Öhman & Mineka, 2001), the capacity to develop grammar and language (Pinker, 1994), the environmentally specific conditioning associated with punishment (Garcia, Hankins, & Rusiniak, 1974), and the perceptual expectations and preferences of young infants (Spelke, 1990). Second, "complex" adaptations can be demonstrated by showing that a trait's specially designed features would have solved major problems in ancestral environments, but tend to be dysfunctional or deleterious in modern-day environments. One example is the dire cravings that most people—especially young children—have for foods high in fat and sugar (Drewnowski, 1997). Third, "complex" adaptations can be documented by revealing that alternative theories or processes do not predict or cannot explain certain outcomes (e.g., the superior spatial location memory of women; Silverman & Eals, 1992; the superior cheater detection capabilities of both sexes; Cosmides, 1989). Finally, confidence in a trait's adaptive status increases when several traits all serve the same basic function (e.g., the factors that govern shifts in women's mate preferences across the reproductive cycle; Gangestad, Thornhill, & Garver-Apgar, Chapter 11, this volume).

There are some drawbacks to using special design as the sole evidentiary criteria for adaptations. For one, it might be difficult to provide unambiguous evidence for the special design features of certain adaptations. To guard against this possibility, investigators should not only test for the special design features of specific traits, but should provide some evidence for the other standards as well. Adaptations might also be difficult to identify because many "complex" traits may possess mixed design (e.g., female orgasm, the development of the neocortex; see Andrews et al., 2003a). If, for example, a trait initially evolved as an adaptation for one effect, then was exapted for a different purpose, and then became a secondary adaptation for yet another purpose, the trait could serve multiple functions that were shaped by different—and perhaps even conflicting—selection pressures. This would obscure the trait's specially designed features unless a fine-grained analysis of its design features was performed.

ISSUES OF VALIDITY

Validity is generally defined as "the best available approximation to the truth or falsity of propositions" (T. D. Cook & Campbell, 1979, pp. 37). Therefore, validity reflects the degree of truth regarding the statements, inferences, or conclusions drawn from empirical research. Since research programs have different missions, the validity of a given study must be evaluated in the context of the larger goals, purposes, and objectives of a research program.

GOALS AND OBJECTIVES OF RESEARCH

Most studies or programs of research are designed to achieve one of three general objectives: (1) to demonstrate the existence of a hypothesized effect or association, (2) to provide evidence about what causes or produces an effect, and (3) to explain the intervening psychological processes or mechanisms that mediate or moderate a causal link (Brewer, 2000). Research designed to *demonstrate* a phenomenon simply attempts to document a predicted association or effect. Demonstration research often is descriptive, such as revealing the frequency with which an event or behavior occurs or demonstrating the strength of association between two variables. Although many demonstration studies are staged in field settings, they can also be conducted in the laboratory.

A second major objective of research is to establish cause-effect relations between specific variables (e.g., if independent variable X is manipulated in a certain way, dependent variable Y should then change in predictable ways). This focus on causation reflects the "utilitarian" view of causal processes (T. D. Cook & Campbell, 1979). According to this approach, reliable causal associations between variables are confirmed, but little if any attention is devoted to explaining *how* they are generated or *why* they occur. A third fundamental objective of research—one that guides the thinking of most evolutionary scientists—is explanation (i.e., to understand intervening processes that mediate or moderate and, thus, explain how and why X causes Y). This "essentialist" view of causation (T. D. Cook & Campbell, 1979) is integral to theory testing, which usually is concerned with identifying the conditions under which causal relations do and do not exist.

A PROCESS MODEL OF VALIDITY

The procedures for establishing the validity of an operationalization or measure of a construct are similar to the procedures and rules for developing, testing, and confirming scientific theories (see Loevinger, 1957). Different types of validity offer unique sources of evidence about the general construct validity of a given scale, measure, or psychological process. Because the operations and measures used in any single study are imperfect and incomplete representations of the theoretical constructs they are designed to assess, theory testing is an ongoing, cyclical process in which constructs inform research operations, which produce revised constructs, which then suggest new and improved operations, and so on.

Two methodological traditions have influenced the way in which validity is defined and conceptualized. One tradition, grounded in experimental and quasi-experimental research, has focused primarily on the validity of independent variables, particularly their conceptualization, their operationalization, and how they are perceived by research participants (T. D. Cook & Campbell, 1979). A second tradition, emanating from nonexperimental research in personality and clinical psychology, has focused on the validity of dependent variables and psychological scales (Cronbach & Meehl, 1955; Loevinger, 1957).

Bridging these traditions, Brewer (2000) has proposed a three-stage process model that describes how hypothetical theoretical constructs are conceptually linked with three sets of measures: (1) observable stimuli (independent variables), (2) intervening physiological or cognitive processes (those that occur *within* individuals), and (3) observable responses (dependent or outcome variables). As shown

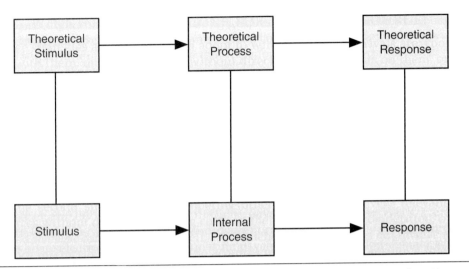

Figure 4.1   Constructs and Operationalizations. The vertical lines represent hypotheses that connect observed measures with their underlying theoretical processes/constructs. Adapted with permission from "Research Design and Issues of Validity" (pp. 3–16), by M. B. Brewer, in H. T. Reis and C. M. Judd (Eds.), 2000, *Handbook of Research Methods in Social Psychology*, New York: Cambridge University Press.

in Figure 4.1, researchers must make three *inferential connections* when planning and conducting studies. On the independent variable side, they first must make important assumptions, inferences, and decisions about how the latent causal concepts specified by their theory should be operationally defined and manifested in the independent variables. Especially if they are interested in essentialist causation, researchers must also establish solid inferential ties between the mediation processes predicted by their theory and the measures chosen as potential mediating variables. On the dependent variable side, they must derive clear inferential connections between the effects anticipated by their theory and the responses (outcomes) measured in their study. Assorted problems can undermine valid inferences from a study at any of these stages. To complicate matters, many areas of evolutionary science lack standardized measures, operations, or procedures that correspond closely with the latent theoretical constructs of interest. As a result, evolutionary scientists must frequently make large inferential leaps across each set of linkages.

These difficulties can create thorny methodological problems. For example, the validity of stimulus or response measures might be questioned if the variations (either manipulated or measured levels) in a given study do not mirror the typical levels of variation in the theoretical states that the stimuli or responses are designed to tap. It also may be difficult to predict the precise levels at which certain independent variables should (or should not) exert causal effects on specific outcome measures. And it might be challenging to anticipate the range over which certain independent variables should have their strongest effects on specific outcome measures (Rakover, 1981). Given the multitude of ways in which the validity of a study can be reduced, it is often difficult to know whether null results from a single study reflect a failure of the theory, a failure of the operationalizations at one or more of Brewer's (2000) three stages, or a failure of the measures used.

VALIDITY IN EXPERIMENTAL AND QUASI-EXPERIMENTAL RESEARCH

There are four major types of validity of primary concern in experimental and quasi-experimental research (T. D. Cook & Campbell, 1979): (1) internal validity, (2) statistical conclusion validity, (3) external validity, and (4) construct validity.

Internal validity reflects the degree to which a researcher can be confident that some manipulated variable (X) has a causal impact on an outcome measure (Y). The internal validity of a study is high when one can confidently conclude that variations in Y were produced by manipulated changes in the level or intensity of X (that is, that the independent variable had a causal impact on the dependent variable, *independent* of other possible causal factors). If third variables correlate with X, these confounds could generate spurious effects. Fortunately, true experiments control for the deleterious influence of third variables through random assignment of participants to experimental conditions and through careful operationalizations and manipulations of independent variables. Researchers must also be cognizant of the many other factors that can threaten the internal validity of a study (see T. D. Cook & Campbell, 1979).

Moderating and mediating variables can complicate causal inferences (Baron & Kenny, 1986). Moderating effects exist when there is a true causal association between an independent variable (X) and a dependent variable (Y), but this relation varies at different levels of a third variable (C). Evolutionary scientists, for instance, might posit that an experimental manipulation of high versus low impending physical threat should lead most highly threatened individuals to stand and defend themselves. However, this association could be moderated by gender, with men being more likely to adopt the "stand and defend" response under high threat than women.

Mediating effects, by comparison, occur when a third variable (C) is needed to complete the causal process (pathway) between X and Y. That is, systematic changes in an independent variable (X) predict changes in the mediator (C), which in turn predicts changes in the dependent variable (Y), statistically controlling for X. Returning to the earlier example, evolutionary scientists might also postulate that a high level of impending physical threat should lead most men to experience "challenge" physiological responses that prepare them to stand and defend. Conversely, such threats might lead most women to experience "threat" physiological responses, motivating them to engage in different tactics.

A second major type of validity, *statistical conclusion validity,* involves the degree to which a researcher can infer that two variables reliably covary, given a specified alpha level and the observed variances. Statistical conclusion validity is a special form of internal validity, one that addresses the effects of random error and the appropriate use of statistical tests rather than the effects of systematic error. This form of validity can be undermined by several factors, such as having insufficient statistical power (leading to Type II statistical errors), violating important assumptions of statistical tests (e.g., that errors are uncorrelated when they are in fact correlated), suffering from inflated experiment-wise error rates (which occur when multiple statistical tests are performed without adjusting the p values for the number of tests conducted), or when measures have low reliabilities. Statistical conclusion validity can also be threatened if treatment or condition implementations are unreliably administered, if random events occur during experiments (increasing the variance or meaning of treatments/conditions), or if respondents are heterogeneous on one or more dimensions that could affect how they interpret the meaning of treatments, independent variables, or outcome measures.

A third major form of validity, known as *external validity,* entails the degree to which a researcher can generalize from a study: (1) *to* particular target persons or settings or (2) *across* different persons, settings, and times. Researchers typically are interested in the latter form of external validity. The external validity of a study can be assessed by testing for statistical interactions, that is, whether an effect holds across different persons, settings, or times. Conducting many small, heterogeneous studies rather than a small number of large-scale ones enhances external validity. It is threatened when statistical interactions exist between selection and treatment (i.e., Do recruitment factors make it easier for certain people to enter particular treatments or conditions?), between setting and treatment (i.e., Do similar treatment or condition effects emerge across different research settings?), or between history and treatment (i.e., Do effects generalize across different time periods?).

Brewer (2000) distinguishes three forms of external validity: ecological validity, relevance, and robustness. *Ecological validity* involves the extent to which an effect occurs under conditions that are "typical" or "common" for a given population. This form of external validity is most relevant to research that has descriptive goals. *Relevance* reflects the degree to which findings are useful or applicable in solving social problems or improving the quality of life. *Robustness* has the greatest implications for evolutionary research. It reflects the degree to which a finding is replicable across different settings, people, and historical contexts.

To evaluate robustness, theorists must clearly define the populations and settings to which an effect should or should not generalize. In the evolutionary sciences, generalizability from one prototypical subject population at one time period (e.g., Westernized college students in current environments) to target populations from other time periods (e.g., typical hunters and gatherers in our ancestral past) is one of the most important external validity concerns. Although evolutionary scientists are now conducting more cross-cultural research, some areas still have fairly narrow databases from which to draw general inferences about human evolution. Similar issues plague other fields. The results of many social psychological studies, for example, must be qualified by the attributes of typical research participants (i.e., fairly intelligent, well-educated, young individuals who have fluid attitudes and self-concepts and emerging group identities; Sears, 1986). Evolutionary scientists should continue to articulate the cardinal ways in which contemporary participant populations may differ from more traditional hunter/gatherer "target" populations and how these differences might qualify how certain evolutionary studies are interpreted.

The fourth type of validity—construct validity—is the most general and encompassing form of validity. *Construct validity* reflects the degree to which operations that are intended to represent a given causal construct *or* effect construct can be explained by alternate constructs (see Cronbach & Meehl, 1955). For causal constructs, construct validity addresses the question, "Does a finding reveal a causal relation between variable X and variable Y, between variable Z and variable Y (which might also correlate with variable X), or with some other outcome variable?" For effect constructs such as outcome measures, construct validity addresses the question, "From a theoretical standpoint, does this measure/scale correlate with measures with which it should covary (convergently), and does it *not* correlate with measures with which it should not correlate (discriminantly)?"

Many independent variables are complex packages of multiple, sometimes correlated variables. When an experimenter tries to induce social isolation in participants, for example, the manipulation may generate other unanticipated states in individuals, such as heightened anxiety, depressive symptoms, or negative moods. Many of the concerns about construct validity, therefore, center on how independent variables are (or should be) operationalized in particular studies and how they are perceived by participants. An experimental manipulation might also evoke multiple hypothetical states in the same individual. If this occurs, it can be nearly impossible to identify the specific causal agent that is operative in a study. For this reason, T. D. Cook and Campbell (1979) contend that the most serious threat to the construct validity of causal constructs is a mono-operation bias— the recurrent use of a single method or paradigm to assess a theoretical construct. Conceptual replications that involve different operationalizations of the same construct are *essential* in order to demonstrate sufficient construct validity.

Multitrait-Multimethod Approaches

Gathering evidence for the construct validity of a trait or scale requires testing its convergent and discriminant validation properties. This can be accomplished with the multitrait-multimethod matrix approach (Campbell & Fiske, 1959). Measures contain three sources of variance: (1) variance that a construct was intended to assess (convergent validity components), (2) variance that a construct was *not* intended to assess (systematic error variance), and (3) random error due to unreliability of the measures. Studies can be partitioned into one of four categories: (1) monotrait-monomethod (when a single trait/scale is studied using a single research method), (2) monotrait-heteromethod (when a single trait/scale is studied using different methods), (3) heterotrait-monomethod (when different traits/scales are studied using a single method), or (4) heterotrait-heteromethod (when multiple traits/scales are studied using multiple methods). Heterotrait-heteromethod approaches are preferable because they allow investigators to test for both the convergent and the discriminant validation properties of traits/scales. Strong evidence for convergent validity emerges when a trait/scale correlates with measures that tap theoretically similar constructs, even when the trait/scale is measured with different methods (e.g., life-event data, observational data, behavioral test situation data, self-report data; Cattell, 1972). Compelling evidence for discriminant validity exists when a trait/scale does *not* correlate with measures that tap theoretically independent or unrelated constructs, even when the same methods are used.

Multitrait-multimethod techniques are not used nearly as much as they should be. One particularly pervasive problem is the over-reliance on monomethod data, especially purely self-report data. As Campbell and Fiske (1959) lament, constructs that are measured with the same method correlate more highly than when they are measured with different methods due to shared method variance. Some reported "effects" in monomethod studies, therefore, may attain conventional levels of statistical significance due to the added boost from shared method variance. Needless to say, this reduces the validity of the conclusions reached from the study.

INVESTIGATIVE METHODS

Different investigative methods (research strategies) can be classified based on the procedures and techniques that are used to describe behavior and test hypotheses. One particularly elegant classification system has been developed by Runkel and McGrath (1972; see also McGrath, 1982). They propose that there are eight higher level research strategies, each of which resides within a circumplex model (see Figure 4.2). The eight strategies fall into four quadrants, with each quadrant containing two similar strategies. The strategies are structured around two orthogonal axes: (1) the degree to which each strategy uses obtrusive versus unobtrusive procedures, and (2) the degree to which each one contains particular versus universal behavioral systems. Each strategy tends to maximize one of three mutually conflicting research goals, which are labeled A, B, and C. Ideally, researchers yearn to maximize the *generalizability* of results across populations

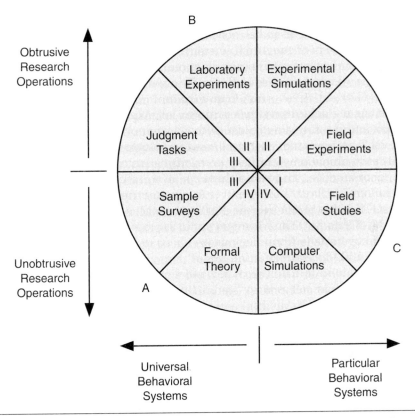

Figure 4.2   Research Strategies. A = Point of maximum concern with generality across actors; B = Point of maximum concern with precision of measurement; and C = Point of maximum concern with realism of the context. *Source:* From *Research on Human Behavior: A Systematic Guide to Method* (1972) by P. J. Runkel and J. E. McGrath (Figure 4-1, p. 85), New York: Holt, Rinehart, and Winston.

(A), the *precision* with which variables are measured (B), and the *realism* of the context in which variables are assessed (C). As shown in Figure 4.2, however, all three goals cannot be simultaneously maximized by any single research strategy. In trying to maximize one goal, the other goals are compromised. Because different research strategies come with particular advantages and liabilities, investigators must develop research programs that take advantage of the special strengths and qualities inherent in each strategy. In the following discussion, we give examples of how human mating behavior has been studied using different investigative methods.

TYPES OF STRATEGIES

The eight research strategies fall into four quadrants. The two strategies in Quadrant I involve situations that are real for research participants. Data is collected in natural settings from people who typically are not aware that they are being observed. Researchers may observe people in social contexts that are manipulated by the experimenter (in field experiments) or that naturally occur (in field studies). Field experiments, therefore, involve some form of experimental manipulation in which the researcher systematically alters the social context and then observes participants' behavior. Field studies, in contrast, do not have experimental manipulations and tend to be less obtrusive. In both cases, participants have usually chosen to be in the research setting. A major strength of these Quadrant I strategies is that they maximize mundane realism (the degree to which the research setting and operations resemble daily life events).

Clark and Hatfield (1989) provide an excellent example of a field experiment. They tested for sex differences in receptivity to sexual offers made by unknown opposite-sex individuals. More specifically, they hypothesized that men should be more willing than women to accept a sexual invitation from a total stranger. Male and female experimental accomplices of average attractiveness approached participants in a public setting and asked them one of three questions: "Would you like to go out tonight?," "Will you come over to my apartment?," or "Would you go to bed with me?." Not a single female participant accepted the offer of immediate sex; over 70% of men did. The advantages of using this methodology were that participants did not initially know they were in a study and they thought their decisions had real and immediate consequences.

Most field studies, on the other hand, exert minimal influence on participants while observing their behavior. Givens (1983) and Perper (1985), for example, have studied courtship behaviors in more naturalistic settings (e.g., bars). They have discovered five distinct phases of courting behavior: attention getting, recognition, talking, touching, and keeping time. Many of these behaviors are quite similar to courtship behaviors observed using similar unobtrusive observational methods in hunter/gatherer tribes (Eibl-Eibesfeldt, 1989). By observing people in natural settings, important patterns of behavior can be identified that might be difficult or impossible to witness in the laboratory.

There are drawbacks to field-based methods. These methods typically have less precision of measurement and control (B), and it is more difficult to generalize results across disparate populations (A). For example, because they did not randomly select participants from all possible populations, Clark and Hatfield could make inferences about only those people who entered their public setting.

Individuals who frequent public places may differ in systematic ways from those who do not, which might explain some of the variation in the huge gender differences they found.

Quadrant II strategies are defined by a high degree of experimenter control. They differ from Quadrant I strategies in that the situations to which participants are exposed are more removed from routine, everyday experiences. The main focus of Quadrant II strategies is on how different social or situational contexts systematically influence participants' thoughts, feelings, and behavior. Participants are usually randomly assigned to different experimental conditions. All procedures are identical across the experimental conditions except for the critical manipulation(s), which are introduced and tested to determine whether they have a causal impact on predicted outcomes. In a repeated measures experimental design, each participant is exposed to every experimental condition, and comparisons are then made within participants across conditions to ascertain the effect of the independent variables on the dependent measures. Experiments can also be designed to place participants in more than one context, exposing them to more than one level of a second independent variable (mixed factorial designs). Any differences that emerge either between participants placed in different experimental conditions or within participants exposed to more than one condition can be attributed to the manipulations. The high precision of measurement coupled with the ability to draw clear cause-effect conclusions is the main advantage of experimental methods. The principle difference between the two strategies in this quadrant is that experimental simulations retain some degree of mundane realism.

Evolutionary scientists are conducting more laboratory experiments to test assorted predictions. Roney (2003), for example, has recently examined on how men view and describe themselves after being exposed to highly attractive women. Men were randomly assigned to review advertisements featuring either young, attractive women or older, less attractive women. They then completed questionnaires that assessed how important having a large income and being financially successful was to them, how ambitious they felt at that moment, and which traits best described their personality. This study contained two levels (young models versus old models) of a single independent variable (model attractiveness). The men in each experimental condition received the same instructions; the only difference was the advertisements they saw. Thus, any differences in the outcome measures between the two groups must be attributed to the different advertisements. As predicted, after being exposed to young, attractive women, men rated financial concerns as more important to them, felt more ambitious, and claimed that traits related to extraversion were more descriptive of their personality—all characteristics associated with increased status, a feature that most women find appealing in prospective mates (Buss, 1989).

Although carefully conducted experiments maximize precision of measurement (B), they do not maximize generalizability across populations (A). Most experiments involve small samples of participants who are recruited from academic settings or reside in a relatively narrow geo-cultural context. As a result, it is difficult to make broad generalizations about universal psychological mechanisms from just a few experiments, even if they are well controlled. Furthermore, most experiments suffer from low mundane realism (C) because the social context is contrived. Most people rarely find themselves in many of the situations created by experimenters, and the extraneous variables that experiments try to control are often present outside the laboratory.

Quadrant III strategies are designed to minimize the influence of the social context by controlling extraneous variables (in judgment tasks) or by asking questions that are unrelated to the context in which they are assessed (in sample surveys). In judgment studies, participants' responses describe or evaluate a stimulus (instead of responding to it). In sample survey studies, participants respond to self-descriptive questions.

Singh's (1993) research on waist-to-hip ratio (WHR) is a good exemplar of an evolutionary-relevant judgment task. Singh contends that body fat distribution should be a marker of female attractiveness to the extent that body shape conveys critical information about a woman's fertility and youth. Hence, participants (judges) rated the attractiveness and health of women with different WHRs. Images near the .70 range were, in fact, rated more attractive and healthy than those that deviated from this evolutionary "ideal" value.

Buss (1989) has conducted research that exemplifies the survey methodology. He hypothesized that men and women should covet slightly different attributes in long-term mates, with men placing more emphasis on youth and beauty (cues of fertility) and women valuing status and resources (cues of provisioning ability). This hypothesis was tested in 37 cultures. Participants were asked a series of self-report questions about their personal preferences for a long-term mate. In every culture, men rated youth and beauty in long-term mates more highly than women did, whereas women rated long-term mates' status and resources more highly than men did.

One relatively new survey approach involves collecting self-report responses from participants across time (e.g., event sampling or diary studies). This approach is rapidly gaining favor among evolutionary researchers (e.g., Keller, Nesse, & Hofferth, 2001; Shackelford & Larsen, 1999). Another survey-based methodological strategy, known as meta-analysis (Cooper & Hedges, 1994), involves reviewing all empirical studies that test a similar set of hypotheses and pooling the results to calculate representative effect sizes. Valuable meta-analyses have been conducted by evolutionary scientists (e.g., Feingold, 1992; West & Sheldon, 2002). Moreover, in their classic analysis of homicide rates, Daly and Wilson (1988) have shown the usefulness of surveying public records to test evolutionary hypotheses. The study of birth order effects (Sulloway, 1996) and social prominence (Simonton, 1994) have also benefited greatly from surveying archival records. One strength of these Quadrant III strategies is that research findings are more generalizable, especially when researchers assess large samples from diverse geographical and cultural regions. Two limitations of Quadrant III strategies are their lack realism of context coupled with the fact that measurement control/precision is attenuated.

Quadrant IV strategies are theoretical rather than empirical strategies. Formal theory includes efforts to develop general theories of behavior. Computer simulations, in contrast, involve attempts to model specific behavior systems, given a particular set of theoretical constraints or parameters. Formal theory usually attempts to describe universal behavior systems and, accordingly, seeks to reach broad generalizations across different populations of people. Computer simulations are also designed to generalize across populations while manipulating different contexts, which often are prescribed by the theoretical parameters built into the models being tested.

The evolutionary sciences are rich in formal theory. Hamilton (1964), for example, introduced the concept of inclusive fitness and demonstrated how helping behaviors are governed by the degree of genetic relatedness between members of the same species. Trivers (1971) introduced the theory of reciprocal altruism to explain helping behaviors between genetically unrelated members of the same species and, in some cases, between species. Trivers (1972) also developed parental investment theory to explain certain gender differences in mating behavior. More recently, Tooby and Cosmides (1992) and Pinker (2002) have outlined the limitations of viewing the mind as a general learning device, and have proposed that the mind is equipped with domain-specific psychological mechanisms that become activated and guide thoughts, feelings, and action in circumscribed social contexts. Each of these theories posits that certain psychological processes are universal (generalizable across populations).

Kenrick and his colleagues (Kenrick, Li, & Butner, 2003; Kenrick et al., 2002) provide excellent examples of how computer simulations can be used to model and test evolutionary hypotheses. Blending dynamical systems theory with evolutionary principles, they have shown how attitudes toward restricted versus unrestricted mating orientations in women and men can be influenced by the attitudes of nearby others over time. These simulations are important because they demonstrate that different outcomes are possible when very minor changes occur in local environments.

RESEARCH PROGRAMS PROVIDING EVIDENCE FOR PSYCHOLOGICAL ADAPTATIONS

Different traits are likely to require different types of evidence to reveal their special design properties. Nevertheless, certain methodological strategies can facilitate the documentation of special design. The special design features of specific traits can be tested more rigorously by conducting research that: (1) uses multiple methods and multiple measures to assess and triangulate the major constructs, (2) tests for and systematically discounts alternative explanations for a trait's uniquely designed functional features, and (3) reveals the footprints of special design at different levels of analysis (ranging from neural mechanisms, to context-specific modes of information processing, to emotional reactions, to molar behavioral responses; see Wilson, 1998). Some research programs have begun to document the special design properties of certain hypothesized psychological adaptations. Select examples include research on the effects of father absence/involvement on daughters' pubertal development (Ellis, McFadyen-Ketchum, Dodge, Pettit, & Bates, 1999), patterns of homicide in families with biological fathers versus stepfathers (Daly & Wilson, 1988), and mother-fetus conflict during gestation (Haig, 1993). Two particularly laudatory programs of research are highlighted next.

SNAKES AND AN EVOLVED FEAR MODULE

Öhman, Mineka, and their colleagues have offered strong, programmatic, and compelling evidence that humans and closely related primates possess an evolved "fear module" for reptiles (Öhman & Mineka, 2001, 2003). What makes this program of research exemplary is the nature, quality, and type of evidence that has been gathered for the special design features of this purported adaptation. This evidence has been strengthened by the use of multiple research methods (e.g., comparative methods, interviews, field observations, experimental laboratory studies) to test carefully derived predictions, by systematically testing and ruling out alternative theories and explanations, and by documenting the unique footprints of special design at different levels of analysis (ranging from neural mechanisms to general cognitive expectations and behavioral reactions).

Several interlocking lines of evidence clearly point to an evolved fear module in higher primates (see Öhman & Mineka, 2001, for a review). Based on interviews with humans (Agras, Sylvester, & Oliveau, 1969), comparative field data on different primate species (King, 1997), and observations of primates living in captivity versus in the wild (Mineka, Keir, & Price, 1980), research has confirmed that humans and other higher primates have an acute fear of snakes that probably has distant evolutionary origins. Conducting well-designed experiments, researchers have also demonstrated that lab-raised monkeys learn to fear snakes very quickly merely by observing fearful expressions in other monkeys (M. Cook & Mineka, 1990), lab-raised monkeys show preferential conditioning to toy reptiles but not to innocuous stimuli (e.g., toy rabbits; M. Cook & Mineka, 1991), and humans who receive shocks in the presence of snakes show longer, stronger, and qualitatively different conditioning responses than do humans who are shocked in the presence of nonaversive stimuli (e.g., flowers; Öhman & Mineka, 2001). This body of evidence implies that the strong connection between snakes and aversive unconditioned stimuli most likely emanates from the evolutionary history of primates rather than from culturally mediated conditioning processes.

Further lab experiments have shown that humans readily infer illusory associations between snakes and aversive stimuli. For example, individuals are more likely to perceive that fearful stimuli (snakes) co-occur with painful experiences (shocks) than is true of other nonfearful stimuli, even when there is no covariation between pairings of shock and different stimuli (Tomarken, Sutton, & Mineka, 1995). Individuals also believe that shocks are more likely to follow exposure to dangerous stimuli (snakes and damaged electrical equipment), yet illusory correlations emerge only between snakes and shock after individuals have been exposed to a random series of stimulus/shock trials (Kennedy, Rapee, & Mazurski, 1997). Recent experiments assessing visual detection latencies have found that when people are shown large sets of stimulus pictures, snakes automatically capture their visual attention, regardless of how many distractor stimuli are present (Öhman, Flykt, & Esteves, 2001). These results suggest that humans are "prepared" to perceive associations and process visual information about snakes and aversive outcomes in systematically biased ways.

Recent experiments have also identified where in the brain the "fear circuit" might be located. Using backward masking techniques that present stimuli outside of conscious awareness, Öhman and Soares (1994, 1998) have discovered that fear responses can be learned and activated, even when backward masking prevents images of snakes from reaching higher cortical processing. This evidence indicates that these fear responses may reside in ancient neural circuits that evolved well before the neocortex.

Viewed together, this entire body of evidence strongly suggests that humans and higher primates have a fear module that evolved to reduce recurrent threats posed by dangerous and potentially lethal animals. This module is sensitive to, and is automatically activated by, a very specific class of stimuli, it operates in specific areas of the brain (the amygdala) that evolved before the neocortex, and it appears to have fairly specialized neural circuitry. This innovative program of research nicely illustrates how different research methods—lab and field experiments, field observations, comparative methods—can be used to provide compelling evidence for a specific, cross-species psychological adaptation whose footprints exist at different levels of analysis.

MATE PREFERENCES IN WOMEN ACROSS THE REPRODUCTIVE CYCLE

Gangestad, Thornhill, and their colleagues have conducted a series of well-conceptualized and carefully designed studies to test whether women have a psychological adaptation that leads them to prefer certain types of men as short-term mates during certain phases of their reproductive cycles. This line of work is elegant because the predictions are carefully derived from theoretical models (good genes sexual selection) and cross-species data, the predictions are quite specific (involving specific patterns of statistical interactions), the predictions and results are difficult to derive from competing theories or models, and logical alternative explanations have been systematically ruled out. Because Gangestad, Thornhill, and Garver-Apgar (Chapter 11, this volume) discuss this research in detail, we highlight only a few of these findings.

The Strategic Pluralism Model of mating (Gangestad & Simpson, 2000) proposes that women should have evolved to make trade-offs between two sets of attributes when evaluating men as potential mates: men's degree of general health/viability, and their degree of commitment/investment to the relationship and possible offspring. Fluctuating symmetry (FA: the extent to which individuals are bilaterally symmetrical at different locations of the body) is believed to be one possible marker of viability (see Gangestad & Simpson, 2000). If so, women should find more symmetrical men more attractive than less symmetrical men in short-term mating contexts, especially when they are ovulating (and, therefore, could conceivably transmit the "good genes" of these more viable men to their offspring). Thus, this model predicts very specific patterns of statistical interactions, predictions that cannot be easily derived *a priori* from alternative perspectives.

This hypothesis has been tested using a variety of research methods and techniques. Self-report questionnaire studies have confirmed that more symmetrical men are more likely to engage in extra-pair sex (that is, sex with another woman while being involved in an ongoing romantic relationship), and they are more prone to be selected by women as extra-pair partners (Gangestad & Thornhill, 1997). Self-report and interview studies have revealed that women are more likely to have extra-pair affairs when they are ovulating, but they are *not* more prone to have sex with their current romantic partners during ovulation (Baker & Bellis, 1990). Moreover, women report stronger sexual attraction to and fantasies about men other than their current romantic partners when they are ovulating, a pattern *not* found for current partners (Gangestad, Thornhill, & Garver, 2001).

To test predictions about olfactory markers of men's FA and women's reproductive cycle, Gangestad and Thornhill (1998) had women smell unscented T-shirts worn by men who differed in FA. If women were ovulating during the study, they rated the scents of more symmetrical men as more attractive than the scents of less symmetrical but, as predicted, this interaction effect was *not* found in nonovulating women. Providing strong discriminant validity evidence for this effect, Thornhill et al. (2001) have confirmed that, even though women prefer the scent of heterozygous major histocompatibility (MHC) alleles in men (which should be valued in primary partners because mating with an individual who has more diverse MHC alleles should limit infections within families), the preference for MHC does *not* increase when women are ovulating.

In a laboratory behavioral observation study, Simpson, Gangestad, Christensen, and Leck (1999) found that more symmetrical men displayed greater social presence and more direct intrasexually competitive tactics (rated by observers) than less symmetrical men when being interviewed by an attractive woman and competing against another man for a "lunch date." When a different group of women evaluated the videotaped interviews of these men and rated how attractive they found each man as both a short-term and a long-term mate, women who were ovulating were more attracted to men who displayed greater social presence and direct intrasexual competitiveness—the tactics displayed by more symmetrical men—in short-term but *not* in long-term mating contexts (Gangestad, Simpson, Cousins, Garver-Apgar, & Christensen, in press). Considered together, these findings confirm that women's mate preferences vary across the reproductive cycle in very specific and theoretically consistent ways.

CONCLUSIONS

The methodology of research in the evolutionary sciences can be strengthened in several ways:

- When feasible, researchers should use a wider range of research methods in their ongoing programs of work. In particular, more research programs need to be structured around experimental methods and techniques.
- A wider array of measurement and statistical techniques should be utilized.
- More solid evidence needs to be provided for the validity of major manipulations, scales, and individual-item measures before they are adopted by other researchers (e.g., experimental manipulations of "social status," self-report measures of "mate value").
- Greater attention should focus on deducing, modeling, and testing the properties of psychological mechanisms that are believed to be adaptations.
- Stronger and better evidence is needed to ascertain how well outcomes predicted by different evolutionary theories or models fit different data sets, especially in relation to competing nonevolutionary theories or models. Whenever possible, alternative constructs and explanations should be carefully derived and measured to test—and hopefully discount—competing constructs or models.
- The special design features of purported adaptations must be directly specified and tested at different levels of analysis, ranging from possible neural structures in the brain, to information processing biases or modal tendencies, to physiological responses, to covert thoughts and emotional reactions, to overt behavioral responses.

- Evidence for possible adaptations needs to be gathered for multiple evidentiary standards.
- Empirical evidence for specific hypotheses should be provided across different cultures, especially those that are more similar to the environments in which humans probably evolved.
- More effort must be devoted to deriving and testing novel predictions, particularly predictions that cannot be easily derived or explained by competing theories.

In conclusion, evolutionary scientists must emulate the methodological breadth and creativity of Darwin. This can be accomplished by using a wider assortment of research methods and statistical techniques, many of which will help investigators more clearly map out and understand the architecture of the human mind. To convince the larger scientific community of the value and the predictive, explanatory, and integrative power of evolutionary approaches, evolutionary theories and models must be developed more carefully, derived more precisely, and tested more thoroughly than most other theories. Given their tremendous explanatory and integrative power, evolutionary theories have at times proceeded ahead of solid empirical evidence, especially in the case of humans. Recent advances in research methods can close this gap. Evolutionary researchers, however, must sharpen the deductive logic underlying their theoretical models, revise and refine questionable or conflicting tenets of middle-level theories, discard or revamp problematic hypotheses, and formulate more specific and refined hypotheses that more directly test the special design properties of purported adaptations. If these goals are realized, the evolutionary sciences will experience rapid and significant theoretical and empirical advances in the coming years.

REFERENCES

Agras, S., Sylvester, D., & Oliveau, D. (1969). The epidemiology of common fears and phobias. *Comprehensive Psychiatry, 10,* 151–156.

Andrews, P. W., Gangestad, S. W., & Matthews, D. (2003a). Adaptationism: How to carry out an exaptationist program. *Behavioral and Brain Sciences, 25,* 489–504.

Andrews, P. W., Gangestad, S. W., & Matthews, D. (2003b). Adaptationism, exaptationism, and evolutionary behavioral science. *Behavioral and Brain Sciences, 25,* 534–553.

Baker, M. A., & Bellis, R. R. (1990). Do females promote sperm competition: Data for humans. *Animal Behavior, 40,* 997–999.

Baron, R. M., & Kenny, D. A. (1986). The moderator-mediator variable distinction in social psychological research: Conceptual, strategic, and statistical considerations. *Journal of Personality and Social Psychology, 51,* 1173–1182.

Brewer, M. B. (2000). Research design and issues of validity. In H. T. Reis & C. M. Judd (Eds.), *Handbook of research methods in social psychology* (pp. 3–16). New York: Cambridge University Press.

Buss, D. M. (1989). Sex differences in human mate preferences: Evolutionary hypotheses tested in 37 cultures. *Behavioral and Brain Sciences, 12,* 1–49.

Buss, D. M. (1995). Evolutionary psychology: A new paradigm for psychological science. *Psychological Inquiry, 6,* 1–30.

Campbell, D. T., & Fiske, D. W. (1959). Convergent and discriminant validation by the multitrait-multimethod matrix. *Psychological Bulletin, 56,* 81–105.

Caporael, L. R., & Brewer, M. B. (2000). Metatheories, evolution, and psychology: Once more with feeling. *Psychological Inquiry, 11,* 23–26.

Cattell, R. B. (1972). *Personality and mood by questionnaire.* San Francisco: Jossey-Bass.

Clark, R. D., & Hatfield, E. (1989). Gender differences in receptivity to sexual offers. *Journal of Psychology and Human Sexuality, 2,* 39–55.

Conway, L. G., & Schaller, M. (2002). On the verifiability of evolutionary psychological theories: An analysis of the psychology of scientific persuasion. *Personality and Social Psychology Review, 6,* 152–166.

Conway, L. G., Schaller, M., Tweed, R. G., & Hallett, D. (2001). The complexity of thinking across cultures: Interactions between culture and situational context. *Social Cognition, 19,* 228–250.

Cook, M., & Mineka, S. (1990). Selective associations in the observational conditioning of fear in rhesus monkeys. *Journal of Experimental Psychology: Animal Behavior Processes, 16,* 372–389.

Cook, M., & Mineka, S. (1991). Selective associations in the origins of phobic fears and their implications for behavior therapy. In P. Martin (Ed.), *Handbook of behavior therapy and psychological science: An integrative approach* (pp. 413–434). Oxford, England: Pergamon Press.

Cook, T. D., & Campbell, D. T. (1979). *Quasi-experimentation: Design and analysis issues for field settings.* Boston: Houghton Mifflin.

Cooper, H., & Hedges, L. V. (Eds.). (1994). *The handbook of research synthesis.* New York: Russell Sage Foundation.

Cosmides, L. (1989). The logic of social exchange: Has natural selection shaped how humans reason? *Cognition, 31,* 187–276.

Cronbach, L. J., & Meehl, P. E. (1955). Construct validity in psychological tests. *Psychological Bulletin, 52,* 281–302.

Cronin, H. (1991). *The ant and the peacock: Altruism and sexual selection from Darwin to today.* New York: Cambridge University Press.

Cummins, D. D., & Cummins, R. (1999). Biological preparedness and evolutionary explanation. *Cognition, 73,* B37-B53.

Daly, M., & Wilson, M. (1988). *Homicide.* Hawthorne, NY: Aldine de Gruyter.

Darwin, C. (1859). *On the origin of species by means of natural selection, or, preservation of favoured races in the struggle for life.* London: Murray.

Dawkins, R. (1989). *The selfish gene.* New York: Oxford University Press.

Desmond, A., & Moore, J. (1991). *The life of a tormented evolutionist.* New York: Norton.

Drewnowski, A. (1997). Taste preferences and food intake. *Annual Review of Nutrition, 17,* 237–253.

Eagly, A. H. (1987). *Sex differences in social behavior: A social-role interpretation.* Hillsdale, NJ: Erlbaum.

Eibl-Eibesfeldt, I. (1989). *Human ethology.* New York: Aldine de Gruyter.

Ellis, B. J., McFadyen-Ketchum, S., Dodge, K. A., Pettit, G., & Bates, J. (1999). Quality of early family relationships and individual differences in the timing of pubertal maturation in girls: A longitudinal test of an evolutionary model. *Journal of Personality and Social Psychology, 77,* 387–401.

Ellis, B. J., & Symons, D. (1990). Sex differences in sexual fantasy: An evolutionary psychological approach. *Journal of Sex Research, 27,* 527–555.

Feingold, A. (1992). Gender differences in mate selection preferences: A test of the parental investment model. *Psychological Bulletin, 112,* 125–139.

Gangestad, S. W., & Simpson, J. A. (2000). The evolution of human mating: Trade-offs and strategic pluralism. *Behavior and Brain Sciences, 23,* 573–587.

Gangestad, S. W., Simpson, J. A., Cousins, A. J., Garver-Apgar, C. E., & Christensen, P. N. (in press). Women's preferences for male behavioral displays change across the menstrual cycle. *Psychological Science.*

Gangestad, S. W., & Thornhill, R. (1997). The evolutionary psychology of extra-pair sex: The role of fluctuating asymmetry. *Evolution and Human Behavior, 18,* 69–88.

Gangestad, S. W., & Thornhill, R. (1998). Menstrual cycle variation in women's preferences for the scent of symmetrical men. *Proceedings of the Royal Society of London. Series B, 265,* 727–733.

Gangestad, S. W., Thornhill, R., & Garver, C. (2001). *Changes in women's sexual interests and their partners' mate retention tactics across the menstrual cycle: Evidence for shifting conflicts of interest.* Unpublished manuscript, University of New Mexico.

Garcia, J., Hankins, W. G., & Rusiniak, K. W. (1974). Behavior regulation of the milieu interne in man and rat. *Science, 185,* 824–831.

Givens, D. B. (1983). *Love signals: How to attract a mate.* New York: Crown.

Gould, S. J. (1984). Only his wings remained. *Natural History, 93,* 10–18.

Gould, S. J., & Lewontin, R. C. (1979). The spandrels of San Marco and the Panglossian paradigm: A critique of the adaptationist programme. *Proceedings of the Royal Society of London. Series B, 205,* 581–598.

Haig, D. (1993). Genetic conflicts in human pregnancy. *Quarterly Review of Biology, 68,* 495–532.

Hamilton, W. D. (1964). The genetical evolution of social behavior. *Journal of Theoretical Biology, 7,* 1–52.

Holcomb, H. R. (1998). Testing evolutionary hypotheses. In C. Crawford & D. L. Krebs (Eds.), *Handbook of evolutionary psychology* (pp. 303–336). Mahwah, NJ: Erlbaum.

Keller, M. C., Nesse, R. M., & Hofferth, S. (2001). The Trivers-Willard hypothesis of parental investment: No effect in the contemporary United States. *Evolution and Human Behavior, 22,* 343–360.

Kennedy, S. J., Rapee, R. M., & Mazurski, E. J. (1997). Covariation bias for phylogenetic versus ontogenetic fear-relevant stimuli. *Behaviour Research and Therapy, 35,* 415–422.

Kenrick, D. T., Li, N. P., & Butner, J. (2003). Dynamical evolutionary psychology: Individual decision rules and emergent social norms. *Psychological Review, 110,* 3–28.

Kenrick, D. T., Maner, J. K., Butner, J., Li, N. P., Becker, D. V., & Schaller, M. (2002). Dynamical evolutionary psychology: Mapping the domains of the new interactionist paradigm. *Personality and Social Psychology Review, 6,* 347–356.

Ketelaar, T., & Ellis, B. J. (2000). Are evolutionary explanations unfalsifiable?: Evolutionary psychology and the Lakatosian philosophy of science. *Psychological Inquiry, 11,* 1–21.

King, G. E. (1997, June). *The attentional bias for primate responses to snakes.* Paper presented at the annual meeting of the American Society of Primatologists, San Diego, CA.

Kruschke, J. K. (1992). ALCOVE: An exemplar-based connectionist model of category learning. *Psychological Review, 99,* 22–44.

Loevinger, J. (1957). Objective tests as instruments of psychological theory. *Psychological Reports, 3,* 635–694.

Mayr, E. (1983). *Toward a new philosophy of biology: Observations of an evolutionist.* Cambridge, MA: Harvard University Press.

McGrath, J. E. (1982). Dilemmatics: The study of research choices and dilemmas. In J. E. McGrath, J. Martin, & R. A. Kulka (Eds.), *Judgment calls in research* (pp. 69–102). London: Sage.

Mineka, S., Keir, R., & Price, V. (1980). Fear of snakes in wild- and laboratory-reared rhesus monkeys (Macaca mulatta). *Animal Learning and Behavior, 8,* 653–663.

Öhman, A., Flykt, A., & Esteves, F. (2001). Emotion drives attention: Detecting the snake in the grass. *Journal of Experimental Psychology: General, 131,* 466–478.

Öhman, A., & Mineka, S. (2001). Fear, phobias and preparedness: Toward an evolved module of fear and fear learning. *Psychological Review, 108,* 483–522.

Öhman, A., & Mineka, S. (2003). The malicious serpent: Snakes as a prototypical stimulus for an evolved module of fear. *Current Directions in Psychological Science, 12,* 5–9.

Öhman, A., & Soares, J. J. F. (1994). "Unconscious anxiety": Phobic responses to masked stimuli. *Journal of Abnormal Psychology, 103,* 231–240.

Öhman, A., & Soares, J. J. F. (1998). Emotional conditioning to masked stimuli: Expectancies for aversive outcomes following nonrecognized fear-irrelevant stimuli. *Journal of Experimental Psychology: General, 127,* 69–82.

Parker, G. A., & Maynard Smith, J. (1990). Optimality theory in evolutionary biology. *Nature, 348,* 27–33.

Perper, T. (1985). *Sex signals: The biology of love.* Philadelphia: ISI Press.

Pinker, S. (1994). *The language instinct.* New York: Morrow.

Pinker, S. (2002). *The blank slate: The modern denial of human nature.* New York: Viking.

Rakover, S. S. (1981). Social psychology theory and falsification. *Personality and Social Psychology Bulletin, 7,* 123–130.

Roney, J. R. (2003). Effects of visual exposure to the opposite sex: Cognitive aspects of mate attraction in human males. *Personality and Social Psychology Bulletin, 29,* 393–404.

Runkel, P. J., & McGrath, J. E. (1972). *Research on human behavior: A systematic guide to method.* New York: Holt, Rinehart and Winston.

Sears, D. O. (1986). College sophomores in the laboratory: Influence of a narrow data base on social psychology's view of human nature. *Journal of Personality and Social Psychology, 51,* 515–530.

Shackelford, T. K., & Larsen, R. (1999). Facial attractiveness and physical health. *Evolution and Human Behavior, 20,* 71–76.

Silverman, I., & Eals, M. (1992). Sex differences in spatial abilities: Evolutionary theory and data. In J. H. Barkow, L. Cosmides, & J. Tooby (Eds.), *The adapted mind: Evolutionary psychology and the generation of culture* (pp. 487–503). New York: Oxford University Press.

Simonton, D. K. (1994). *Greatness: Who makes history and why.* New York: Guilford Press.

Simpson, J. A. (1999). Attachment theory in modern evolutionary perspective. In J. Cassidy & P. R. Shaver (Eds.), *Handbook of attachment: Theory, research, and clinical applications* (pp. 115–140). New York: Guilford Press.

Simpson, J. A., Gangestad, S. W., Christensen, P. N., & Leck, K. (1999). Fluctuating asymmetry, sociosexuality, and intrasexual competitive tactics. *Journal of Personality and Social Psychology, 76,* 159–172.

Singh, D. (1993). Adaptive significance of female physical attractiveness: Role of waist-to-hip ratio. *Journal of Personality and Social Psychology, 65,* 293–307.

Spelke, E. S. (1990). Principles of object perception. *Cognitive Science, 14,* 25–56.

Sulloway, F. J. (1996). *Born to rebel: Birth order, family dynamics, and creative lives.* New York: Pantheon Books.

Thornhill, R. (1997). The concept of an evolved adaptation. In M. Daly (Ed.), *Characterizing human psychological adaptations* (pp. 4–22). London: CIBA Foundation.

Thornhill, R., Gangestad, S. W., Miller, R., Scheyd, G., Knight, J., & Franklin, M. (2001). *MHC, symmetry, and body scent attractiveness in men and women.* Unpublished manuscript, University of New Mexico.

Tomarken, A. J., Sutton, S. K., & Mineka, S. (1995). Fear-relevant illusory correlations: What types of associations promote judgmental bias? *Journal of Abnormal Psychology, 104,* 312–326.

Tooby, J., & Cosmides, L. (1992). The psychological foundations of culture. In J. H. Barkow, L. Cosmides, & J. Tooby (Eds.), *The adapted mind: Evolutionary psychology and the generation of culture* (pp. 19–136). New York: Oxford University Press.

Trivers, R. L. (1971). The evolution of reciprocal altruism. *Quarterly Review of Biology, 46,* 35–57.

Trivers, R. L. (1972). Parental investment and sexual selection. In B. Campbell (Ed.), *Sexual selection and the descent of man* (pp. 136–179). New York: Aldine de Gruyter.

West, S. A., & Sheldon, B. C. (2002). Constraints in the evolution of sex ratio adjustment. *Science, 295,* 1685–1688.

Williams, G. C. (1966). *Adaptation and natural selection.* Princeton, NJ: Princeton University Press.

Williams, G. C. (1992). *Natural selection: Domains, levels and challenges.* Oxford, England: Oxford University Press.

Wilson, E. O. (1998). *Consilence: The unity of knowledge.* New York: Knopf.

CHAPTER 5

Controversial Issues in Evolutionary Psychology

EDWARD H. HAGEN

Boy, this shit ticks me off.

—Anthropologist Jonathan Marks
commenting on evolutionary psychology[1]

ALILEO THOUGHT SUNSPOTS, recently discovered by him and others, might be clouds of some sort near the sun's surface. This clever idea was wrong, but it contained a deeper, radical truth: The physical laws governing the earth and the heavens are the same. Unifying seemingly incommensurable realms—heaven and earth, man and animal, space and time—within a single explanatory framework, as Galileo, Newton, Darwin, and Einstein did, often sparks revolutions that utterly transform science. The invention of the computer by Von Neumann, Turing, and others was such a revolution. By showing that a physical system could "think," this invention unified mind and matter, demolishing Cartesian dualism and spawning the cognitive revolution that continues to roil the human behavioral sciences.

Evolutionary psychology (EP), following Darwin, envisions a much deeper unification of mind and body, however, than that achieved by the cognitive revolution. Pervading modern computational theories of cognition is a largely unrecognized ontological dualism. Although the origins and nature of brain structures are widely assumed to be explicable by physical laws, they are implicitly assumed to have little, if any, relationship to the origins and nature of structures in the rest of the body. For example, the brain is variously viewed as hardware that runs

---

Many thanks to David Buss, Nicole Hess, Nathan Thrall, Roberto Fernández Galán, Arndt Telschow, Peter Hammerstein, and Clark Barrett for helpful comments on this chapter.
[1] Presentation at the 99th Annual Meeting of the American Anthropological Association, November 15, 2000, San Francisco. (http://www.uncc.edu/jmarks/interests/AAA00discussionevpsych .pdf).

culturally provided software, as one or more neural networks, as a Bayesian inference machine, as a semantic net, or as a hologram. Whether any of these models of the brain are correct, and many are certainly important and useful, none draw on the model that has had well over three centuries of almost unparalleled scientific success: the Western scientific model of the body as a set of tightly integrated but distinct mechanisms that function to enable and facilitate the survival and reproduction of the individual organism.

If we learned of a mysterious new structure in the body, we might reasonably assume that it, like the heart, lungs, liver, kidneys, bones, muscles, blood cells, intestines, uterus, testicles, and ovaries, performed one or more as yet unidentified functions intimately related to an individual's survival or reproduction. We would base this assumption not on evolutionary theory, but simply on the overwhelming empirical evidence that this is what all other tissues and organs do. When we then learned that this organ was responsible for a number of functions such as vision, olfaction, and motor control that had clear utility for survival and reproduction, our assumption would seem reasonable indeed. When we further learned that this organ, though constituting only 2% of the body's mass, consumed 20% of its energy and that substantial damage to this organ usually resulted in the immediate death of the organism, we would rightly conclude that the functions of this organ must be critical to the survival, and thus reproduction, of the individual. We would then seem to be on extremely solid ground if we proposed exploring the properties of this organ as a set of mechanisms designed to do just that. Indeed, given what we know about the organization of the rest of the human body and given what we already know about some of the mysterious organ's functions, we should find this proposal almost banal.

EP has proposed exactly this conclusion for our mysterious organ, the brain. Far from being met with bored nods of agreement, however, EP has been met with often scathing criticisms. This chapter revisits five of the still smoldering controversies over EP and its sister discipline sociobiology: selfish genes, the environment of evolutionary adaptedness (EEA), nature versus nurture, massive modularity, and EP's politically incorrect claims. I show that almost all scientific criticisms of these five seemingly unrelated controversies derive not from a mind-matter dualism but from a genuine mind-*body* dualism, a dualism EP rejects. EP proposes that the brain was shaped by the same process and to the same end as the rest of the body.

SELFISH GENES, SELFISH PEOPLE?

The controversies swirling around EP are often tightly bound up with Richard Dawkins's metaphor, the *selfish gene* (Dawkins, 1976). If our genes are selfish, aren't we, too, deep down, unalterably selfish? This metaphor is so powerful that it has often overshadowed what it was meant to represent: the modern synthesis of Darwin and Wallace's natural selection, Mendel's particulate inheritance, and Watson and Crick's DNA.

ORIGIN OF THE METAPHOR

The seeds of the selfish gene metaphor are present in Darwin's pregenetic formulation of natural selection. Ruffed grouse, North American game birds that live in wooded habitats, are frequently preyed on by hawks, owls, foxes, and bobcats. Ruffed grouse with camouflage feathers that better conceal the grouse will be eaten less often and thus reproduce more than grouse lacking camouflage feathers. If this trait is heritable, after many generations all ruffed grouse will have the camouflage feathers. You could say that the camouflage feathers "outcompeted" the original feathers. Because the success of the camouflage feathers came at the expense of the original feathers, you might call the camouflage feathers selfish. Note that it is the feathers that are competing and selfish, not the birds themselves. The result of competing variants of feathers with different colorations is that ruffed grouse gradually evolve better protection from predators in their woodland habitat. The metaphor of selfish heritable traits competing with each other is simply a restatement of the theory of natural selection.

We now know that gene variations (termed *alleles*) account for the heritable variation of traits such as feather coloration. What for Darwin and Wallace was the differential reproduction of organisms possessing different, heritable traits is for modern evolutionary biologists the differential reproduction of alleles for those traits. In a population of a fixed size, the increase in the frequency of an allele for superior feather coloration must correspond to a decrease in the frequencies of the alleles for inferior feather colorations. Dawkins, highlighting this ironclad logic, termed these gene variants *selfish*. Selfish genes are just a metaphor for the modern version of natural selection based on changes in the frequency of the genes that were unknown to Darwin.[2] The *selfish gene* metaphor has led to a number of very important insights in biology.

Though Dawkins's books discuss it at length, what the metaphor itself fails to convey is Darwin's original, enormously important insight: Natural selection produces well-engineered structures called *adaptations* that effectively and efficiently solve the numerous reproductive problems posed by the environment. Adaptations, not genes, are the unit of analysis in EP, an essential point that frequently confuses critics. When they do manage to focus on adaptations, critics disparage the concept: Adaptations are difficult if not impossible to identify; they are vastly outnumbered by traits that are simply incidental by-products of, for example, a large brain (therefore, EP's search for adaptations is bound to fail); or, being a product of selfish genes, adaptations must, in some sense, be inherently selfish (and because humans are not unvaryingly selfish, EP is bankrupt). It is easy to show that none of these criticisms applies to the body; therefore, if body-brain dualism is rejected, none applies to the brain.

Natural Engineering

> The careful study of [Paley's] works . . . was the only part of the Academical Course which, as I then felt and as I still believe, was of the least use to me in the education of my mind.
>
> —Charles Darwin, autobiography

---

[2] Most genes have an equal probability of transmission, but a few genes have enhanced their own transmission relative to the rest of the genome (e.g., transposable elements, B-chromosomes, and meiotic drive genes). In contrast to the definition of the term *selfish* here, which I think most closely reflects Dawkins, modern usage often restricts the term to these latter types of genes.

To claim that there is a psychological adaptation, for example, for cheater-detection (Cosmides, 1989), many critics believe that a cheater-detection gene must be found (Berwick, 1998; Orr, 2003). Absent evidence for such a gene, these critics scoff at the idea that such an adaptation might have been identified. Evolutionary psychologists rarely seek genetic data, however, a fact that critics often see as EP's fatal flaw. To see why the critics are confused, we turn first to the Christian theologian William Paley. Paley's *Natural Theology*, written at the dawn of the nineteenth century, clearly identified one of the major scientific problems that Darwin and Wallace eventually solved: the manifestation in nature of *design*. Although Paley did not conceive of the problem as a scientific problem but instead as a theological problem, his clear and incisive arguments, synthesizing a long tradition in natural theology, nonetheless form the very foundations of EP.

Paley first emphasized that, in contrast to the nonliving world, living things are characterized by mechanisms designed to accomplish specific purposes:

> CONTEMPLATING *an animal body* in its collective capacity, we cannot forget to notice, what a number of instruments are brought together, and often within how small a compass. It is a cluster of contrivances. In a canary bird, for instance, and in the single ounce of matter which composes his body (but which seems to be all employed), we have instruments for eating, for digesting, for nourishment, for breathing, for generation, for running, for flying, for seeing, for hearing, for smelling; each appropriate,—each entirely different from all the rest. (Paley, 1809, p. 185)

Paley then emphasized that organismic mechanisms are only comprehensible in relation to the environments in which they must function. Organisms are engineered for their particular environments:

> In the eel, which has to work its head through sand and gravel, the roughest and harshest substances, there is placed before the eye, and at some distance from it, a transparent, horny, convex case or covering, which, without obstructing the sight, defends the organ. To such an animal, could any thing be more wanted, or more useful?
>
> [T]he bodies of animals hold, in their constitution and properties, a close and important relation to natures altogether external to their own; to inanimate substances, and to the specific qualities of these, e.g. *they hold a strict relation to the* ELEMENTS *by which they are surrounded.*
>
> Can it be doubted, whether the *wings of birds* bear a relation to air, and the *fins of fish* to water? (Paley, p. 291)

Adaptations, the functional components of organisms, are identified not by identifying their underlying genes, but by identifying evidence of their design: the exquisite match between organism structure and environmental challenge so eloquently described by Paley. For Paley, the designer of the canary bird and every other intricate branch of the tree of life was God. For Darwin and modern science, it was natural selection.

Thousands of adaptations have been identified. Every bone, organ, tissue, cell-type, and protein is a specialized structure that evolved by natural selection and whose function has been, or will be, elucidated by analyzing the relationship between the trait's structure and its effects on the organism's survival and reproduction in a particular environment. Because almost all genes in the genome cooperate to build the organism they depend on for their mutual reproduction, scientists can, for the most part, avoid the currently intractable problem of the precise relationship between genes and complex adaptations and instead focus on the eminently tractable problem of the reproductive functions of the body, including the brain. They can confidently address the functions of hearts, lungs, blood, and uteruses using evidence of design without knowing anything about the genes that code for these organs. Similarly, we can address the functions of the brain without knowing anything about the genes that underlie these functions. Who can doubt that vision, hearing, smell, and pain—phenomena that rely critically on the brain—served crucial functions that facilitated the reproduction of the organism over evolutionary time?

If Darwin had known about genes, he would have been able to (among other things) modify the definition of adaptation to include functions that promoted the reproduction not only of the organism but also of relatives of the organism (because they are likely to share some of the organism's genes). This modification allows evolutionary researchers to analyze an extremely large set of adaptations without ever having to refer to specific genes.

Despite the tremendous success of the functional, mechanistic approach in anatomy,[3] it is sobering to recognize that almost all progress has been made with no explicit recourse to (and virtual ignorance of) evolutionary theory. The simple presumption that body structures serve survival or reproduction has provided the foundation for the stunning advances in understanding body functions over the past several centuries. Evolutionary theory would seem to be superfluous for understanding body—and therefore brain—functions. We soon see why it isn't.

SPANDRELS

Gould and Lewontin (1979) observed that because many organism "traits" are not adaptations but simply incidental by-products of other structures, by-products they termed *spandrels*,[4] organism traits might erroneously be identified as adaptations. If spandrels and adaptations were difficult or impossible to distinguish, this would undermine claims that true adaptations have been found. Gould and Lewontin were apparently unaware that George Williams (1966) had already both discussed this problem in depth and provided its solution: Adaptations will exhibit evidence of design.

Williams' criterion is critical. Without it, it is possible to assign *every* cell in the body to a spandrel. Consider this hypothetical scenario. A CAT scan produces a detailed 2D image of a cross-section of the body, like slicing open an orange and photographing the freshly revealed surface. By taking a large number of 2D scans of the body, we can build up a 3D view of the body's internal anatomy. Imagine that a team of scientists who know nothing of anatomy gets hold of a large number of CAT scans of an entire human body, revealing all its tissues in detailed cross-sectional images. Each scientist begins analyzing one of the 2D images, not realizing that the individual scans can be composited into a single, 3D model. The

---

[3] Because the word *physiology* too closely resembles the word *psychology*, I use the term *anatomy* and its derivatives to refer to all body tissues and structures excluding the nervous system.

[4] The term comes from architecture and describes the triangular space that is necessarily created when a dome is supported by arches, a space that can then be put to other uses.

scientists develop sophisticated statistical representations of the patterns in their images, scribbling down elegant equations of the images' shapes and curves. The equations are a rigorous, factual description of the entire body, but a description that is empty. The patterns of tissues revealed by the CAT scans are, if considered alone, spandrels of the true, functional organization that the team has failed to recognize. Ask the wrong questions, and virtually all normal body tissues will be seen as spandrels. Ask the right questions, and most normal body tissues will be recognized as playing a vital, functional role in the survival and reproduction of the organism.

Gould warned of the "dangers and fallacies" (Gould, 1997, p. 10750) of over-attributing adaptive functions to traits that might not be adaptations, but the real danger is to fail to consider functional hypotheses. Tonsils often become infected and, therefore, are (or were) frequently removed by surgery. Which scientific response do you prefer? (1) Mock any suggestion that tonsils might serve an important function by loudly insisting that not all traits have adaptive functions; or (2) generate and test as many functional hypotheses as you can think of to make sure that by removing the tonsils, no lasting harm is done to the patient?[5]

It seems strange that anyone could possibly fear what is in fact routine science with an outstanding record—proposing and testing functional hypotheses for organism structure. EP must recognize, however, that by rudely breaking into the cathedral of the mind and spray-painting sex, violence, and competition across what for many are the mind's beloved spandrels, it is bound to stir up some controversy. Further, many spandrels are enormously important in their own right.[6]

By failing to recognize the evolved functional organization of the brain, however, psychology and the rest of the human behavioral sciences, like our team of misguided scientists, are condemned to study nothing but spandrels.

Do Selfish Genes Create Selfish People?

EP proposes that our thoughts, feelings, and behavior are the product of psychological adaptations. EP critics fear that if psychological adaptations are a product of selfish genes, then we must all be essentially selfish. Yet, *every* adaptation in the body evolved by natural selection, that is, by selfish genes that outcompeted (replaced) alternative alleles at some point in the past. The genes coding for your hair gradually replaced less effective versions of those genes in the past and are, therefore, *selfish*. Despite this, no one is worried that selfish genes have produced selfish hair. Critics only worry when a process widely accepted to have produced the body's specialized structure is claimed to also have produced the brain's specialized structure. But describing most psychological adaptations as selfish is as nonsensical as it is for hair. The genes for vision, memory, and muscle control are all selfish, yet none of these psychological adaptations is usefully termed selfish.

There is a narrow but important set of psychological adaptations whose properties do correspond to our folk notion of selfishness. When critical resources such as food or mates are limited, genes that code for fighting abilities can increase in fre-

---

[5] Tonsils do serve an important immune function (e.g., van Kempen, Rijkers, & Van Cauwenberg, 2000), but their removal has not been demonstrated to cause significant immune deficiency (e.g., Kaygusuz et al., 2003).

[6] Women's capacity for orgasm, for example, could be a byproduct of a male adaptation for orgasm, just as male nipples are a byproduct of a female adaptation for nipples (Symons, 1979).

quency. Psychological adaptations for aggression correspond to folk notions of self-ishness, but these adaptations evolved by the same process as every other adaptation. The underlying genes are no more selfish than are the genes underlying any other adaptation. Ironically, anatomical adaptations, not psychological adaptations, provide the clearest evidence for the evolution of aggression. Large canines, antlers, and increased muscle and body mass all have evolved to injure competitors. Because these weapons would be worthless if there were not corresponding psychological adaptations enabling their effective use in combat, they constitute strong evidence that the same processes produce both anatomical and psychological adaptations, some of which are selfish in the folk sense, but most of which are not.

A final point: One of Dawkins' major arguments and one of the major achievements of sociobiology was that the modern version of natural selection predicts that the evolution of cooperation is likely to be widespread. Individuals in many species are likely to possess adaptations for both competition *and* cooperation, adaptations that are based on genes that are equally selfish. Genes for cooperation outcompeted alternative alleles. Although many challenges remain (Hammerstein, 2003), the evidence strongly bears out this prediction (e.g., Dugatkin, 1997). And despite the claims of some, cooperative adaptations based on selfish genes are not, deep down, selfish any more than your hair is, deep down, selfish.

IF MY GENES MADE ME DO IT, AM I STILL RESPONSIBLE?

Critics worry that the very idea that adaptations could produce bad behaviors will undermine law and order. But, if you tell the judge that your genes made you do it, she can tell you that her genes are making her throw you in jail. The sword cuts both ways. EP posits that each of us has an innate cognitive ability to uphold the law (e.g., Boyd & Richerson, 2001) as well as break it. This is hardly a radical idea. Laws are designed to prevent people from doing things that they might construe as being in their interest but that would impose costs on everyone else. Yet, smart people worry about EP's possible moral consequences. Despite his clever arguments to the contrary, Galileo's scientific evidence favoring the Copernican model of the solar system *was* a threat to the Church. If EP is correct, then despite its adherents' clever arguments to the contrary, it, too, might constitute a genuine threat to the contemporary moral order. EP cannot simply dismiss the critics' fears. We return to this topic later.

ARE THERE ENOUGH GENES TO BUILD PSYCHOLOGICAL ADAPTATIONS?

> Evolutionary psychology is dead but doesn't seem to know it yet.
>
> —Biologist Paul Ehrlich[7]

Some critics of EP claim that there simply aren't enough genes to code for a large number of innate cognitive adaptations (Ehrlich & Feldman, 2003). Curiously, they don't suggest that there aren't enough genes to build the thousands of anatomical adaptations that have already been discovered, they haven't suggested the theory of natural selection is wrong, nor have they called for an immediate halt to the billions of dollars of research aimed at furthering the functional

---

[7] Shwartz (2001).

understanding of cells, tissues, and organs—research that, if the critics were right, would be useless given that there aren't enough genes to build all those adaptations.

Current estimates are that humans have 20,000 to 30,000 genes. If genes and adaptations corresponded in a one-to-one fashion, then, if it took an average of 100 genes to code for an adaptation, there could be only 200 to 300 adaptations, a number we have already long surpassed in our investigation of anatomy and physiology.

Adaptations, however, are not the simple product of genes. Rather, they are the product of gene *interactions*. Although the processes by which genetic information directs the development of cells, tissues, and organs are still largely unknown, it is well known that both genes and nongene regions of DNA control the protein production of other genes and that multiple proteins combine to produce an adaptation. These simple facts fundamentally alter the math. Imagine an organism with four genes, A, B, C, and D. In the naïve view, where genes do not interact, this organism could have at most four adaptations, one coded for by each gene. But since genes do interact, this organism could have as many as 15 adaptations—not only those produced by A, B, C, and D but also those produced by all possible combinations of A, B, C, and D (AB, AC, AD, ABC, ABCD, BC, BD, etc.). For an organism with *only* 20,000 genes, the number of possible gene combinations explodes. The number of two-gene combinations, for example, is nearly 200 million. To produce an adaptation, however, often many more than two genes interact. The number of 25-gene combinations is around 10^{82} (in comparison, the universe probably contains around 10^{80} particles). An organism obviously need make use of only a minute fraction of such gene combinations to produce an incredibly rich, functionally organized phenotype with enormous numbers of adaptations.[8] Just as there are more than enough genes and gene combinations to produce thousands of anatomical and physiological adaptations, there are more than enough to produce hundreds or thousands of psychological adaptations.

THE ENVIRONMENT OF EVOLUTIONARY ADAPTEDNESS

> The pseudo-science of evolutionary psychology purports to explain human behaviors by reference to an ancestral environment. . . .
>
> —Ian Tattersall (2001, p. 657)

The EEA refers to those aspects of the ancestral environment that were relevant to the evolution, development, and functioning of an organism's adaptations—roughly, the environment in which a species evolved and to which it is adapted. The term *environment* includes the organism, its physical environment, its social environment, and other species it interacts with. Because alleles were selected and went to fixation in the past, the EEA concept, first formulated by John Bowlby of attachment theory fame (Bowlby, 1969) and incorporated into EP by Don

---

[8] Some have claimed that gene interactions are themselves an impediment to the evolution of adaptations. Although this can be true over the short term, it isn't over the long term (Hammerstein, 1996).

Symons (1979), is an essential and logically necessary aspect of the theory of natural selection.

It is the EEA concept that gives EP its power. The content of EP is almost entirely to be found in the structure of the ancestral environment, the EEA. The EEA concept has nonetheless been a lightning rod for criticism. Many critics claim we can never know anything meaningful about it (e.g., Ahouse & Berwick, 1998); others, that we often don't need to know anything about it (e.g., Smith, Borgerhoff Mulder, & Hill, 2000). What is it, do we need it, and can we know it?

REPRODUCTION AND THE CAUSAL STRUCTURE OF THE ENVIRONMENT

For a new, heritable trait to have positive reproductive consequences, it must *do* something. It must transform the organism or environment in a way that enhances the reproduction of the individuals possessing it. Reproduction is an enormously complex process in which the organism must successfully accomplish thousands of transformations of itself and its environment. Each aspect of the organism and environment that must be transformed can be transformed in countless ways, yet only a small subset of these transformations furthers the goal of reproduction, with most impeding or preventing it. Virtually all of the ways light striking the lens can be reflected and refracted, for example, will not focus the light on the retina. These transformations—these causal chains—must, therefore, be initiated by adaptations that have the special physical properties required to change things in just the right way. The shape of the lens is exactly that required to focus incident light onto the retina.

Both the things an organism must do to reproduce, as well as those things it could do to enhance reproduction, are called *selection pressures*, because they either have resulted, or could result, in selection for an adaptation. To increase in frequency, a new heritable trait must improve an organism's ability to effect a particular transformation of the environment, or it must provide an ability to effect a new transformation of the environment. In either case, it must initiate changes that propagate along causal chains—causal chains whose ultimate effects increase the number of offspring of individuals possessing the trait relative to those that do not.[9]

Crucially, these causal chains are not part of the trait itself. They constitute the essential environmental background, the EEA, of the trait. Many such causal chains propagate within the body of the organism, but many also detour far outside it. The feathers on the ruffed grouse, for example, change the spectral and intensity distributions of incident beams of light, reflecting the altered beams. These altered beams strike the retinas of predators, whose brains process the patterns of retinal activation. Depending on whether the light was reflected off uncamouflaged or camouflaged feathers, the neural computations in the predator brains will either recognize or fail to recognize the grouse, and this will either result in claws, beaks, and fangs penetrating the grouse, killing it, or the passing by of the predator, leaving the grouse unscathed.

The spread of camouflage feathers in the grouse population depends critically on the rich, preexisting causal structure of the environment inhabited by

---

[9] An adaptation can evolve if it has a positive impact on reproduction *on average*. It need not have a positive impact all the time, nor in every situation, nor even every generation.

the grouse: the colors and patterns of the forest habitat, the types of predators, the structure of their brains, and their hunting strategies. This preexisting causal structure is referred to as the EEA of the camouflage feathers. Because aspects of the causal structure of the environment that are relevant to one adaptation won't necessarily be relevant to another, the EEA is adaptation-specific. The grouse feather EEA, for example, is different from the grouse lung EEA (as shorthand, the term EEA is also used to refer to all environmental features that were relevant to an organism's reproduction). Environments change, so the causal structure of the environment an adaptation finds itself in may not correspond to the causal structure the adaptation evolved in; therefore, the adaptation may not work as designed. If the forest changes colors, for example, the camouflage feathers may no longer camouflage the grouse (but its lungs will continue to work just fine).

For humans, some aspects of the modern environment do diverge quite radically from their EEA. Automobiles kill far more people today than do spiders or snakes, for example, but people are far more averse to spiders and snakes than they are to automobiles because in the EEA, spiders and snakes were a serious threat, whereas automobiles didn't exist. We, therefore, evolved an innate aversion to spiders and snakes but not to automobiles (e.g., Öhman & Mineka, 2001).

If a species' current environment diverges too rapidly and too far from its EEA, the species will go extinct. The human species is clearly not going extinct; hence the common belief that EP claims humans currently live in an entirely novel environment is incorrect. Most aspects of the modern environment closely resemble our EEA. Hearts, lungs, eyes, language, pain, locomotion, memory, the immune system, pregnancy, and the psychologies underlying mating, parenting, friendship, and status all work as advertised—excellent evidence that the modern environment does not radically diverge from the EEA.

WHAT EVOLUTIONARY THEORY ADDS TO BRAIN RESEARCH

If the analogy between anatomical and psychological research were perfect, then, because evolutionary theory has been mostly superfluous to anatomical research, evolutionary theory would also be mostly superfluous to psychology. But, although the analogy is perfect in most respects, when it comes to actually identifying psychological adaptations, it begins to break down for technological reasons. The explosion of anatomical knowledge over the past several centuries has been based on detailed examinations, dissections, and chemical analyses of organs and tissues. Given current technology, this approach is very difficult and often impossible to apply to the human brain. Brain functions arise from structures that are generally much bigger than single neurons, but much smaller than the gross anatomical features of the brain. A cubic millimeter of human cortex, for example, contains a network of roughly 50,000 neurons and 200 million neural (synaptic) connections (Cherniak, 1990). The most sophisticated brain imaging techniques available can just barely detect whether this cubic millimeter of brain tissue is, on average, more or less active after a stimulus than before, but they are "blind" to the connections and activities of the many neural circuits contained therein. If we could "see" human neural circuits, then, as we have with the rest of

our anatomy, we could "dissect" and analyze brain functions by analyzing their structure. But, with current technology, we usually can't.[10]

In contrast to the near impossibility of examining neural circuits for most brain functions, psychologists, using a large repertoire of ingenious techniques, have amassed mountains of indirect evidence for complex brain structures. By exposing human and animal subjects to special stimuli and observing their behavioral responses, psychologists have proven that the brain is composed of large quantities of richly structured circuitry. These breakthrough findings are only now filtering out to other social sciences like economics. Yet, it cannot be overemphasized that cognitive and social psychological methods, however sophisticated, yield extremely oblique evidence of this circuitry. Subjects' immensely complex brains are constantly processing vast information flows from their senses and rich memories of past events and constantly analyzing future scenarios. Into this individually unique blizzard of cognitive activity, the psychologist injects a usually brief stimuli and records a behavioral response. Guided only by an abstract information processing model such as symbolic processing or connectionism and mostly ad hoc assumptions about cognitive domains, he or she then makes inferences about universal cognitive structure. This is like trying to infer the presence and functions of hearts, lungs, or kidneys without being able to conduct dissections and with no a priori theory of what kinds of mechanism should exist and what their functions should be. The prospects for success are grim.

Evolutionary theory can help enormously with the problem of "invisible" neural circuits and the inherent ambiguity of cognitive and social psychological evidence for them. Natural selection has mapped the structure of the environment onto the structure of organisms. Gravity, carbon fuel sources like fats and carbohydrates and their patchy distribution on the landscape, metabolic waste products, toxins, pathogens, and temperature fluctuations have all been mapped by natural selection onto the structure of the human organism in the form of our bones, muscles, tendons, blood, intestines, kidneys, liver, immune system, and sweat glands. EP proposes that, exactly like the structure of the rest of the human body, the structure of the human brain should closely reflect the structure of the human EEA. Sunlight, acoustic oscillations, volatile compounds, foraging, mates, dangerous animals, children, kin, social exchange, and group living have all been mapped by natural selection onto the structure of the human brain in the form of our visual, auditory, and olfaction abilities; our ability to navigate; our sense of taste and our preferences for foods; our sexual desires; our fears; our love of children, relatives, and friends; our aversion to incest; and our ability to detect cheaters and to form coalitions.

Because it is currently easier to study the structure of the environment than it is to map the neural circuitry of humans, EP is proposing that cognitive and social psychology and neuroscience can be fruitfully augmented with a single idea: The brain is not composed of arbitrary functions, nor simply of functions that you would expect in any information processing machine, like memory, nor of generic learning functions, but rather of a number of functions that solved specific reproductive problems in the human EEA. The a priori hypotheses about brain functions that can be generated by investigating the human EEA greatly increase the

---

[10] It is much easier to study neural circuits in animals, especially those, like lobsters, with especially simple nervous systems.

odds that the indirect methods of cognitive and social psychology will genuinely identify such functions. It is much easier to find something if you have some idea what you are looking for. If you take away only one idea from EP, take this: Though often tricky to interpret, the structure of an organism's EEA can be a masterful guide to the structure of the organism, including its brain.

IS THE ENVIRONMENT OF EVOLUTIONARY ADAPTEDNESS KNOWABLE?

No one would dispute that our lungs evolved in an oxygen atmosphere (the lung EEA) or that our immune system evolved in response to pathogens (the immune system EEA). Yet, when it comes to the selection pressures that shaped the brain, some are skeptical that the past is knowable (e.g., Ahouse & Berwick, 1998). The past, however, was much like the present. Physics was the same. Chemistry was the same. Geography, at an abstract level, was much the same—there were rivers, lakes, hills, valleys, cliffs, and caves. Ecology, at an abstract level, was also much the same—there were plants, animals, pathogens, trees, forests, predators, prey, insects, birds, spiders, and snakes. Virtually all biological facts were the same. There were two sexes, parents, children, brothers, sisters, people of all ages, and close and distant relatives. It is a common misconception that the EEA refers to aspects of the past that differ from the present, when it actually refers to the aspects of the past whether or not they correspond to aspects of the present. We know that in the EEA women got pregnant and men did not. This single fact is the basis for perhaps three-quarters or more of all EP research. The hefty array of human universals (Brown, 1991), although not as assuredly true of the past as, for example, gravity, is nonetheless another important source of hypotheses about the EEA. Adding to our already detailed scientific understanding of the past are the historians, archaeologists, and paleoanthropologists who make a living studying it.

PSYCHOLOGICAL ADAPTATIONS ARE JUST LIKE OTHER ADAPTATIONS

Despite the technological difficulty of studying neural circuitry, the equivalence of psychological adaptations and other adaptations is not mere analogy. The specialized physical/chemical configurations of adaptations give them their functional properties: the distinctive ability to effect particular environmental transformations, precipitating causal cascades that, in the EEA of the adaptation, increased reproduction. In this regard, the neural circuits constituting psychological adaptations are no different from other adaptations. Like hearts and lungs, the specialized physical/chemical configuration of a neural circuit provides a distinctive ability to effect a particular environmental transformation—usually of other neural circuits or muscles—precipitating causal cascades that, in the EEA of the adaptation, increased reproduction.

Conversely, anatomical adaptations like hearts and lungs can be thought of as information processing adaptations. Any physical system can be characterized by what is known as a state vector—the values of a large, and potentially vast, number of system parameters.[11] Adaptations are systems that change other systems.

---

[11] For example, the state vector of a volume of gas consists of the position and momentum vectors of all gas particles.

These changes can be characterized by changes in the state vector. Adaptations operate on input, the initial state vector of the target system, producing output, the transformed state vector of the target system, exactly what information processing adaptations do. In principle, the information processing model could be applied to all adaptations. There are differences in degree, however, that usefully distinguish information processing adaptations from other adaptations:

- Information processing adaptations have high information content—the system can assume a large number of distinct and detectable states. Hearts, for example, can assume only a limited number of different states (e.g., beating at different rates), whereas the retina can assume an astronomically large number of different states (e.g., all the possible combinations of activation levels of the 125 million rods and 6.5 million cones in each eye).
- State transformations in information processing adaptations require little energy. Heart muscle requires a significant amount of energy to contract compared to the activation of a cone in the retina.
- State transformations in information processing adaptations can occur very rapidly. The frequency of contractions of heart muscle is low compared to the potential frequency of state changes in cones of the retina.

Animals possess many high bandwidth sensors like eyes, ears, taste, and smell, each of which can assume a vast number of possible states in response to environmental conditions (e.g., the human hand has 17,000 sensor cells per square inch). To enable reproduction-facilitating actions by the animal, this vast quantity of information must undergo further processing by psychological adaptations.

NATURE VERSUS NURTURE

Most, if not all, controversies surrounding EP can be traced to the nature-nurture debate. The nature-nurture debate, in turn, is intimately entwined with, and perhaps identical to, body-brain dualism: Our bodies are the product of nature, and our minds, many believe, are solely the product of nurture. Rejecting brain-body dualism should, therefore, resolve the nature-nurture debate, and it does. In fact, it provides two resolutions. In the scientific study of the body, the primacy of nature—a set of inherited, panhuman functional properties—is undisputed. If brain and body organization are deeply similar, then nature should also form the foundations of brain science. The importance of nurture—learning—is, however, indisputably important to understanding the brain. The deep equivalence of brain/body organization then implies that nurture should form the foundations of anatomy. Surprisingly, these two perspectives are equivalent, as explained later. First, though, two other common solutions to the nature-nurture debate must be rejected.

GENE-ENVIRONMENT INTERACTIONS

One common attempt to resolve the nature-nurture debate is to invoke interactions of genes and environment—we are equally the product of both. This attempt fails.

Gene-environment interactions are invoked in two distinctly different contexts. The first is the development of our incredibly complex, universal phenotypes. Both genes and environment are intimately involved in virtually every step of ontogeny. This is true, but vacuous. How could genes play any role in the development of phenotypes if they did not interact with the environment (everything that isn't a gene)? Once a (nonregulatory) gene is transcribed, it's all environment from there on out. This supposed resolution to the nature-nurture debate, commonly invoked by evolutionary scholars, has no scientific content whatsoever.

The vital question of ontogeny is how genomes manage to produce nearly identical, intricately structured phenotypes. A partial answer is that, within species (and often even across closely related species), the vast majority of genes are identical in every individual. Equally importantly, the environment (everything that isn't a gene) is almost exactly the same for each individual as well. The properties of the myriad chemical compounds necessary for organism development and the principles by which they react are identical for all individuals. The proteins produced by the identical genes, which then regulate the production of other proteins, are essentially identical for all individuals. Factors that vary, such as temperature, can be dynamically maintained within a narrow range. The highly stable nature of the genome, as well as the stability of the environment in which it organizes development (but see Raser & O'Shea, 2004), explains why, when compared to the potential variability they could, in principle, express, all humans are basically identical—we resemble one another far more than we do toads, trees, or termites.[12]

The second context in which gene-environment interactions are invoked is the study of individual *differences.* Although it might seem that the study of phenotype differences is closely related to the study of phenotypes, it isn't. By definition, studying phenotype differences ignores all of the immensely complex structure those phenotypes have in common. The claim that residual differences in phenotypes could be caused by residual differences in genotypes, residual differences in environments, and/or interactions between the two is not vacuous, yet has little relevance to EP. Even though they play a hugely important role, unvarying aspects of the genome and the environment are ignored when investigating phenotypic differences. But it is the unvarying, universal portion of the genome (the vast majority of genes), as well as both unvarying and varying aspects of the environment, that EP is primarily interested in.

Conflating the vacuous claim that our universal phenotypes are the joint product of both genes and environment, with the nonvacuous but completely unrelated claim that residual differences in those phenotypes can be attributable to residual genetic differences, residual environmental differences, or their interaction, may erroneously lead to the conclusion that environmental variability is deeply implicated in the development of adaptations coded for by universal genes. Such a conclusion is very unlikely to be true. If Murphy's Law has any force, most environmental perturbations of developmental processes will disrupt the normal development of the target adaptation. I would, therefore, expect that the body is designed to ensure that developing systems "see" only the environ-

---

[12] In most species, there are gene and environment controlled "switches" that direct phenotypes to develop into one of a few discrete types, like male and female. See Hagen and Hammerstein (in press) for more detail.

mental variation they are supposed to see; much, if not most, of the time, this involves shielding developing systems from variation, not exposing them to it. We don't want the development of hearts or visual systems to be sensitive to most environmental variability. We instead want them to reliably develop despite any variability that exists.

The important exception is environmental variation that is necessary for the development and performance of the adaptation. The cardiovascular systems of people who were raised at high altitudes, for example, operate more efficiently at those altitudes than those of people who migrate to higher altitudes as adults. In these cases, specific development mechanisms have almost certainly evolved to sample *relevant* environmental variation and to then tweak the target adaptation to enhance its performance under those conditions. In some cases, the tweaking will be quite dramatic, such as acquiring a native language. In other cases, environmental cues might trigger significant shifts in developmental trajectories as part of an underlying evolved strategy—environmental sex determination in some species is a particularly dramatic example (see, e.g., Hagen & Hammerstein, 2005).

PLASTICITY

Another unsatisfying solution to the nature-nurture debate is the claim that the brain has an essential property—a secret sauce—called *plasticity*, which enables nurture (e.g., Buller & Hardcastle, 2000; Panksepp & Panksepp, 2000). Plasticity is a vague term that basically means that the brain changes in response to the environment. The real question, however, is why and how the brain can change in such useful ways. The descriptor *plastic* contributes little—if anything—to an understanding of either the why or the how of neural responses to environmental conditions. Even describing real plastics (i.e., various types of organic polymers) as plastic reveals nothing about the nature of their plasticity. The plasticity of plastic is a consequence of very specific and hierarchical microscopic properties of the polymer chains, including the types of chemical bonds found on the polymer backbone, the length of the chains, and the number and nature of links between polymer chains. Similarly, the plastic nature of the brain results from very specific and hierarchical properties of neurons and neural networks in the nervous system, and it is the latter that are of interest. At best, the term *plastic* vaguely describes a property of the nervous system (that it can change in response to environmental change); it does not explain it. See Hagen and Hammerstein (2005) for an evolutionary strategic approach to gene-environment interactions and developmental flexibility.

NURTURE IS A PRODUCT OF NATURE

One genuine solution to the nature-nurture debate requires abandoning the idea that nature and nurture are equal partners. They are not. Nurture is a product of nature. Nurture—learning in all its various forms—doesn't happen by magic. It doesn't occur simply by exposing an organism to the environment. It occurs when evolved learning adaptations are exposed to the environment. Dirt doesn't learn. Rocks don't learn. Learning is grounded in specialized adaptations that evolved just like all other adaptations (Tooby & Cosmides, 1992).

Recognizing that evolved learning mechanisms are not special to the brain deepens our understanding of nurture. Our immune system, for example, is a superb learning mechanism, one that illustrates some of the key insights that EP offers to the evolution of learning. Pathogens evolve rapidly, often within an individual organism. It would be impossible for organisms, via natural selection, to evolve defenses against a particular, rapidly changing pathogen. Natural selection, however, has discovered two things about pathogens that don't change: (1) They are made of proteins, and (2) these proteins are different from the proteins comprising the host. Natural selection's discovery of these powerful *abstractions* allowed the evolution of a specialized mechanism to fight an enormous range of different pathogens by, in simple terms, learning to recognize and eliminate foreign proteins from the body. Despite the immune system's ability to successfully combat a diverse array of pathogens, it is not a *general* learning mechanism. It doesn't learn what foods to eat or how to make different tools.

Evolved cognitive learning mechanisms can be expected to be similar to the immune system: highly specialized to acquire information about abstract domains that were relevant to reproduction in the EEA.

NATURE IS A PRODUCT OF NURTURE

EP comes down squarely in favor of the primacy of nature. It is possible, however, to view all our adaptations, including hearts, lungs, and livers, as the products of nurture. This surprising conclusion follows from the recognition that natural selection is a learning algorithm. Learning is the acquisition of useful information about the environment. Via the differential reproduction of alleles across generations, natural selection learns what kinds of transformations increase reproduction in a particular environment and stores this information in the genome. In a species, each allele that has gone to fixation by natural selection is a valuable piece of learned information about the traits that are useful for that species' reproduction in its EEA. Thus, all of the body's adaptations are, in this sense, a product of learning. Because this learning takes place across many generations, let's call it *vertical learning*.

Like all learning algorithms, natural selection can learn only stable patterns or relationships. At one level, the environment is so variable that it seems impossible that natural selection could learn anything useful. Measles differs from strep; apples differ from oranges. Higher levels of abstraction, however, can be extraordinarily stable across generations. Measles and strep are both pathogens, a large and enduring class of dangerous organisms, all of which introduce foreign proteins into the body; apples and oranges are both edible fruits, a large and enduring class of plant products that are a rich source of carbohydrates. Natural selection can learn to fight pathogens by evolving an immune system, and it can learn to identify and metabolize carbohydrate-rich fruits by evolving a suite of sensory, cognitive, and digestive systems. Natural selection tends to produce adaptations that operate, not on the variable particulars of an environment, but on abstract domains like pathogens and fruit that are highly stable across generations.

If what natural selection often tends to learn are abstractions, then, of necessity, it must also produce mechanisms that fill in the details by learning domain-specific patterns and relationships that are variable across generations (and thus cannot be directly learned by natural selection), but stable within them. Let's call these mechanisms *horizontal* learning mechanisms. Natural selection designed the immune system to detect and eliminate foreign proteins, but, in operation, the immune system must learn to detect and eliminate measles and strep. Similarly, natural selection designed our sensory systems to identify carbohydrate sources using reliable cues like color and taste, but these systems, in operation, must learn to identify particular carbohydrate sources, like apples and oranges.

These arguments suggest that learning (in the usual sense of the term) should be widespread in the body, and it is. Most body systems collect information about their environments and alter their properties in an adaptive fashion. Tanning is another example. These arguments also suggest that many organisms, including humans, will have a number of learning mechanisms specialized for particular reproductively relevant abstract domains. Learning to avoid poisonous animals is one thing; learning to locate nutritious foods, another.

The nature-nurture distinction is real and important. It is the distinction between reproductively relevant environmental patterns that are stable across many generations versus those that are stable for much shorter periods. Relatively stable environmental patterns can cause the evolution of all types of adaptations—our nature. More variable environmental patterns can cause the evolution of a narrower class of adaptations: learning adaptations—specialized aspects of our nature that enable nurture (for more on the evolution of learning and culture, see e.g., Richerson & Boyd, 2005).

Natural selection is a brilliant engineer. It is, therefore, tempting to speculate that, at least in a smart animal like humans, she could have produced a horizontal learning mechanism so powerful and effective that it obviated the need for other specialized cognitive adaptations. Could natural selection have endowed humans with a generalized über-learning mechanism that, perhaps by structuring itself during development, enables us to learn everything we need to know to survive and reproduce in almost any environment we are likely to find ourselves in, as some have argued (e.g., Buller & Hardcastle, 2000; Karmiloff-Smith, 1992)? Almost certainly not.

Reproduction is a complex business that is grounded in the complex causal structure of the environment. Natural selection learns what to do in this environment by conducting enormous numbers of experiments. Every individual in a population with genetic variation—one or more genetic mutations—is an experiment. Those mutations that have positive reproductive consequences increase their frequency in the population gene pool. Each mutation going to fixation[13] represents learned information about some aspect of the reproductively relevant causal structure of the environment. This experimental process occurs generation after generation after generation, producing a substantial body of empirically verified information about reproduction.

Contrast natural selection with a hypothetical horizontal über-mechanism in a single organism that attempts to learn the reproductive consequences of different behaviors in one lifetime. Learning requires feedback, but learning how to reproduce requires feedback from far in the future. The goal of everything organisms do is to produce offspring that themselves successfully reproduce. Information about the degree to which an individual achieves this goal, however, will not be available for an entire generation—often after the individual is dead. And even if it could change something, what should it change? Every action it has taken over its lifetime could potentially impact the reproduction of its offspring (often just

---

[13] That is, increasing its frequency to 100%. I am ignoring complications like frequency dependent selection.

by producing them in the first place). Which actions moved it closer to the goal of creating reproductive offspring, and which farther? The individual has no way of knowing. Absent a tremendous amount of prefigured knowledge about what is needed to reproduce, reproduction is unlearnable. The reproductively relevant causal structure of the environment is just too complex relative to the number of reproductive events of an individual organism. What natural selection can learn about reproduction by experimenting with thousands or millions of individuals over hundreds and thousands of generations is, to an individual organism with but one lifetime, an impenetrable fog.

MASSIVE MODULARITY

This is the Unix[14] philosophy. Write programs that do one thing and do it well.

—Doug McIlroy

The body is massively modular. It contains thousands of different parts, each with specialized functions. This means that the brain could be massively modular, but it doesn't mean that the brain *is* massively modular. It is, after all, only one organ among many. Our fingernails aren't massively modular, nor are our front teeth. It is clear, though, that living tissues are often, perhaps always, modularly organized. We can further conclude on empirical grounds alone that since natural selection designed the body, one thing natural selection does well is make modules. EP's provocative proposal that the brain consists of a large number of innate modules has come to be known as the massive modularity hypothesis (MMH).

To assess the MMH, we need to understand why our anatomy is modular. Our bodies, in a deep sense, reflect the causal structure of the world. They are modular because, crudely speaking, the world is. As a species, we interact with an extraordinarily heterogeneous physical, biological, and social world. To successfully reproduce, we must change many aspects of that world in very specific ways, and those changes can only be reliably effected by specialized structures. Our incisors have a different function than do our molars. At least to a limited degree our brains, too, are clearly modular. Vision is different from olfaction is different from motor control. Many evolutionary psychologists believe, however, that the structure of the human EEA was so rich and heterogeneous that our brain contains at least hundreds, and perhaps thousands, of modules.

Jerry Fodor, widely credited with popularizing cognitive modularity (Fodor, 1983), has, in a recent book (Fodor, 2000), criticized both the MMH and EP. If one of modularity's strongest proponents doesn't like the MMH, there must be something really wrong with it. Fodor's MMH critique is based, in part, on: (1) a narrow definition of modularity, a definition EP rejects, (2) a definition of *cognition*, which differs from EP's definition, and (3) a common misconception of domain specificity.

First, Fodor distinguishes between cognitive modularity with, and without, information encapsulation (Fodor, 2000, pp. 56–58). If, when performing the computations, modules have access only to information stored in the module itself

---

[14] Unix is the powerful computer operating system that runs most of the Internet. It is also widely used by scientists, engineers, and financial institutions requiring high levels of reliability, flexibility, and speed.

and cannot access information in other modules, the module is said to be informationally encapsulated. As a concept, information encapsulation is so unhelpful that you wonder whether its importation from computer science into cognitive science was botched. Why, except when processing speed or perhaps robustness is exceptionally important, should modules not have access to data in other modules? Most modules should communicate readily with numerous (though by no means all) other modules when performing their functions, including querying the databases of select modules.

The original computer science concept of encapsulation, in contrast, is powerful: Encapsulated modules access and modify data in numerous other modules when performing their functions, but do so only via well-defined *interfaces*. This means, roughly, that modules communicate in standardized ways and that access to a module's data and functionality is regulated by the module itself. As long as the interface between modules stays the same, programmers can tinker with modules' implementations without disrupting other modules. In computer science, it is a module's functionality that is encapsulated, not its data per se.[15]

Fodor wants to limit use of the term *module* to informationally encapsulated modules, whereas EP takes all mechanisms, with or without information encapsulation, to be modules.[16] Fodor considers this more general sense of module, which he terms "functionally individuated cognitive mechanisms" (p. 58), to be a diluted and apparently uninteresting sense of module that almost everyone already accepts. Right off the bat, Fodor and EPs are talking past each other. Let me speculate on one source of the disjunction. Cognitive scientists like Fodor want to determine what kind of machine can think like the brain. The critical concepts come from computer science: algorithms, connectionist networks, programming syntaxes, memory, object-oriented languages, and databases. Modularity is valued because it helps solve severe computational problems like combinatorial explosion. EP, in contrast, wants to determine how the brain changes the environment to facilitate and enable the reproduction of the organism. For it, a radically different set of ecological concepts is critical: finding food and mates, besting competitors, avoiding predators and toxins, and helping kin. In addition to avoiding combinatorial explosion, EP values modularity because a specialized module can most effectively cause transformations of the environment that facilitate and enable reproduction.

The second basis of Fodor's critique is an attack on Cosmides and Tooby's (1994, p. 91) argument that the brain cannot consist only of domain-general mechanisms because "there is no domain-independent criterion of [cognitive] success or failure that is correlated with fitness." Fodor justifiably counters that "there is

---

[15] The standardized way in which nerve cells communicate is a low-level example of encapsulation in the brain. Whether natural selection could have evolved this useful architecture at higher, neural network levels in the brain is an open question, but it would clearly allow individual modules to evolve without interfering with other modules.

[16] Buller and Hardcastle (2000) incorrectly claim that EP's multimodular model of the brain entails strict information encapsulation (thus, any evidence against strict information encapsulation is evidence against EP). One incorrect argument they give is that since reproductively striving men with knowledge of sperm banks don't donate all their sperm to them, EP must be assuming strict information encapsulation. The mistake with the sperm bank example is, as EPs have explained countless times, that although there is a module for having sex, there is no (and can be no) module for reproductive striving (e.g., Symons, 1987, 1989, 1990, 1992).

surely an obvious, indeed traditional, domain-general candidate for the 'success' of a cognitive system: that the beliefs that its operations arrive at should by and large be *true*" (p. 66, emphasis in the original). Unlike Fodor, however, Cosmides and Tooby aren't distinguishing between psychological mechanisms that learn about the world (cognition *sensu stricto*) and those that function to change it (what Fodor calls *conative* functions). For EP, the functions of the brain evolved because they could change the world to increase fitness over evolutionary time; learning about the world was but a means to that end.

Fodor then goes on the offensive, offering what he considers to be a two-part a priori argument against massive modularity. For it to collapse, I need to refute only one part. Fodor asks us to consider the following simple cognitive system (Figure 5.1). M1 is a cognitive module only for thinking about triangles, and M2 is a module only for thinking about squares. Because this system is based on classical computation, "M1 and M2 both respond to formal, nonsemantic properties of their input representations" (p. 72), P1 and P2, respectively. P1 must be assigned to triangles, and P2 must be assigned to squares, and this function is performed by BOX1, which receives as input representations of both triangles and squares. Fodor then asks, "Is the procedure that effects this assignment [BOX1] itself domain specific?" *Contra* Fodor, it is.

Fodor believes that because BOX1 doesn't think about just triangles or just squares, it is somehow "less modular than either M1 or M2" and that "would undermine the thesis that the mind is *massively* modular" (p. 72, emphasis in original). No, it wouldn't. The domain of BOX1 is sorting out triangles and squares. Just because BOX1 is operating on more abstract entities than M1 or M2 doesn't mean it's not domain specific, or that it isn't a module. Sorting out triangles from squares is a highly domain-specific task that requires lots of innate information about triangles and squares. Without innate information about triangles and squares, BOX1 wouldn't know whether to sort on, for example, the area of the representations, on the length of the perimeters, on those representations that had at least one right angle, or on the number of angles.

It is a very common error to believe that modules that operate on abstractions are somehow less domain specific or less modular than those that operate on more concrete representations. Computations on abstract domains require just as much specialized circuitry and innate knowledge as do computations on concrete domains. *Object*, for example, is a very abstract concept—it includes my Berlin Starbucks coffee mug, the sidewalk cobblestones, and the beautiful 400,000-year-old Schöningen spears. A specialized psychology with innate knowledge of objects is required, however, to identify instances of, and reason about, objects (e.g., Spelke, 2000). Abstract domains are just as domain-esque as concrete domains. The debate that EP is engaged in is not whether the brain is composed of a large number of modules that operate only on concrete domains versus whether a lot of those modules operate on abstract domains. The debate, rather, is whether some

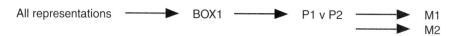

All representations ———▶ BOX1 ———▶ P1 v P2 ———▶ M1
                                                   ———▶ M2

Figure 5.1   A Simple, Multimodular Brain for Thinking about Triangles and Squares. *Source:* From *The Mind Doesn't Work That Way*, by J. Fodor, 2000, Cambridge, MA: MIT Press.

sort of relatively homogeneous computational architecture with little to no innate knowledge about the world has any chance of successfully enabling its hosting organism to reproduce. A lot of people, implicitly or explicitly, seem to think that it can. EP is a clear voice claiming that it can't. What EP is offering to cognitive science is a rich, a priori theory of what, exactly, our "functionally individuated cognitive mechanisms" should be. For example, because humans have been making stone tools for around 2 million years and picking berries from thorny vines for much longer and because stone flakes and thorns both could, for example, cause fitness-reducing injuries, it is a solid prediction of EP, untested so far as I know, that humans should have an innate concept of *sharp object.*

Turning to Fodor's critique of EP in general, it is clearly based on holding EP to standards that almost no scientific theory could meet. Irked by what he perceived to be the unduly chipper title of Steve Pinker's book on EP, *How the Mind Works,* a "jaundiced" Fodor wants to remind us that there are still *hard problems.* The foundation of EP is what Fodor calls the classical computational theory of the mind (CCTM): the idea that the brain is a computer. Despite being one of its strongest proponents, Fodor argues that the CCTM can't explain some of the brain's most interesting properties. For Fodor, these include its abductive or global cognitive processes; for others, these include the processes that produce consciousness.

Even if we grant Fodor everything here (cf. Carruthers, 2003), the CCTM underpins virtually all of cognitive science, not just EP. Fodor agrees that the CCTM is "by far the best theory of cognition that we've got" (p. 1), so he can hardly fault EP and nearly all other cognitive scientists for using it. The first three of five chapters of Fodor's book are a critique of the CCTM, not EP in particular. (Chapter 4 discusses the MMH.) Chapter 5 attempts to refute three "bad argument[s] why evolutionary psychology is a priori inevitable." Requiring EP to prove itself a priori inevitable, however, is requiring far too much. EP is not a priori inevitable. Neither were relativity or quantum mechanics. All these theories must prove themselves empirically. Philosophers like Fodor worry if they are logically forced to accept EP. Well, no. Fodor, one of EP's inventors, can refuse to accept EP, just as Einstein, one of quantum mechanic's inventors, refused to accept quantum mechanics. For EP proponents, the unification of body and brain made possible by Darwin, von Neumann, and Turing is a beautiful idea. It will be a shame if it is wrong (evolutionary psychologists are encouraged about the evidence collected to date).

POLITICAL CORRECTNESS

> To propose that [rape] serves some evolutionary function is distasteful and unnecessary.
>
> —Henry Gee, senior editor at *Nature*[17]

In 1632, Galileo's *Dialogue Concerning the Two Chief World Systems, Ptolemaic & Copernican,* was published in Florence. The *Dialogue* effectively argued that Copernican theory was the factually superior theory of cosmology. Because the major moral/political power of the day, the Catholic Church, had grounded its authority in the Ptolemaic theory, Galileo's *Dialogue* was a threat. Galileo was

---

[17] *Nature,* July 5, 2000, http://www.nature.com/NSU/000706/000706-8.html.

summoned before the Inquisition in 1633, found to be vehemently suspect of heresy, forced to formally abjure, and condemned to life imprisonment.

Like the Church, a number of contemporary thinkers have also grounded their moral and political views in scientific assumptions about the world. In the current case, these are scientific assumptions about human nature, specifically that there isn't one (Pinker, 2002). Theories calling these assumptions into question are, like Galileo's *Dialogue,* a threat. The problem is not with those who claim that there is a human nature; it is with those who have succumbed to the temptation to ground their politics in scientifically testable assumptions about humans. This is especially unwise because the science of human psychology is currently quite undeveloped. There are few solid facts and no proven theories about our behavior, thoughts, and feelings. *Any* set of assumptions will undoubtedly be challenged by future research. Yet, the inevitable research that calls into question assumptions underlying popular moral and political views will, in effect, be heresy, and heresies are, as a rule, viciously attacked. As long as important political and moral views are grounded in scientific hypotheses, a true science of human cognition and behavior will be difficult, and perhaps impossible, to achieve.

SOCIOBIOLOGY SANITIZED?

Scientific understanding of the body paralleled advancements in physics, chemistry, and technology. Until Darwin, however, no such foundations existed for understanding animal or human behavior. Even after Darwin, much animal behavior, particularly social behavior, remained mysterious. In the 1960s and 1970s, biologists developed powerful new theories that could explain animal sociality as a product of natural selection (e.g., Hamilton, 1964; Maynard Smith & Price, 1973; Trivers, 1972). Because these theories represented a biological approach to animal sociality, they became known as *sociobiology.* These theories are to the study of animal behavior what optics is to the study of vision: a set of core, abstract principles about the social world that should be reflected in the structure of animal nervous systems, much as optical principles are reflected in the structure of the eye. This was more than a small breakthrough.

Although E. O. Wilson is usually credited as the inventor of sociobiology, he had little hand in its theoretical development. His main contribution was to christen the field by publishing an outstanding book-length survey, *Sociobiology: The New Synthesis,* in 1975. And, by briefly suggesting that the theories developed to explain the social behavior of nonhuman organisms might also explain the social behavior of humans, he also ignited a firestorm of controversy that smolders to this day.

If Wilson was right, the slate is not blank. The sun of the mind does not revolve around the earth of culture, but vice versa, a heresy that many believe threatens enlightenment values of equality (Pinker, 2002). Predictably, sociobiology was attacked on extrascientific grounds. A tiny clique of Harvard faculty cast it, and proponents like Wilson, as tools of the far right. But many prominent proponents of sociobiology were leftists. Wilson himself became an ardent champion of saving the rain forests and biodiversity (Wilson, 1988), and key inventors of sociobiology such as John Maynard Smith and Robert Trivers were also left or far left (Segerstrale, 2000). The Harvard clique's stratagem prevailed nonetheless. In the war of words, sociobiology's critics, led by the brilliant essayist Stephen J. Gould, won rapid and decisive victories. Applying sociobiology to humans quickly became taboo.[18] Attempting to capitalize on these victories, critics claim that EP is only slightly sanitized sociobiology. The closer they can tie EP with sociobiology, they hope, the faster they can sink it.

Despite their dazzling rhetorical successes, sociobiology's critics have been virtual no-shows on the battlefield of science. Many readers will probably be surprised to learn that sociobiology is, as Alcock (2001) rightly claims, one of the scientific triumphs of the twentieth century. After the publication of Wilson's book, sociobiological research on nonhuman organisms exploded, generating a continuing flood of articles in top journals, including almost weekly appearances in *Nature* and *Science,* the world's premier scientific outlets. One of sociobiology's key theories, kin selection, has garnered overwhelming empirical support. Sociobiology is part of the core research and curriculum of virtually all biology departments, and it is a foundation of the work of almost all field biologists, including figures like Jane Goodall. To avoid the stigma generated by the Harvard clique, sociobiology usually isn't called that anymore—the more general term *behavioral ecology* is a common substitute.

The critics are right. EP *has* eagerly adopted sociobiology—its successes are impossible to ignore. EP is thus just as politically incorrect as sociobiology. Yet, EP is not simply sociobiology redux. First, EP, the study of animal nervous systems from an evolutionary perspective, includes numerous aspects of cognition that have nothing intrinsically to do with sociality, such as vision, navigation, and foraging. Sociobiology, in contrast, is restricted to the biology of sociality. Second, although sociobiologists usually study social *behavior,* they also study organisms like plants (Andersson, 1994), which have no nervous systems and are, therefore, outside the purview of EP. Third, EP pioneered a strong emphasis on the evolution of the neural mechanisms that generate behavior, whereas animal sociobiologists tended to emphasize the study of behavior itself. Fourth, EP emphasized that these neural mechanisms evolved in response to past selection pressures, whereas animal sociobiologists tended to investigate the fitness effects of behavior in current environments. Lately, however, animal biologists have also begun focusing on psychological mechanisms, and some of the original inventors of sociobiology were well aware of the important distinction between past and present environments (e.g., Maynard Smith, 1978).

In the final analysis, social cognition and behavior do constitute an important subset of EP, and much EP research employs theories such as kin selection, reciprocal altruism, and sexual selection that form the core of sociobiology.

Is Evolutionary Psychology Racist or Sexist?

Perhaps the most important enlightenment value, one intimately bound up with the blank slate view of human nature, is that of human equality. If EP poses a severe threat to the blank slate, and it does (Pinker, 2002), does it not also pose a severe threat to this rightly cherished value? Let me put off answering this question for a moment and first explain what EP says, scientifically, about the equality of human capabilities. The answer is simple and by now easily guessed by the

---

[18] This taboo is endorsed by many animal biologists, probably to avoid being stigmatized themselves.

reader. Across the globe, human bodies are, in their functional organization, virtually identical. People in every population have hearts, lungs, and livers, and they all work the same way. A panhuman anatomy is a solid empirical fact. EP proposes that the same evolutionary processes that lead to a panhuman anatomy also lead to a panhuman psychology (Tooby & Cosmides, 1990; see D. S. Wilson, 1994, for a partial critique). Notwithstanding the preceding, it is possible for different populations to possess minor adaptive physical differences like skin color, so it is also theoretically possible for different populations to possess minor adaptive cognitive differences, though no such differences are known to exist. Just as anatomists have prioritized a focus on panhuman anatomy, EP has prioritized a focus on panhuman psychology.

Similarly, male and female bodies are identical in most ways, but profoundly different in some. Male and female hearts are essentially identical, but testicles are very different from ovaries. EP proposes that the same is true of the brain. Male and female cognitive abilities are likely to be identical in most respects, but to differ fundamentally in domains such as mating where the sexes have recurrently faced different adaptive problems (Buss, 2004; Symons, 1979).

If you consider these implications to be racist or sexist, then EP is racist or sexist. Nothing in evolutionary theory, however, privileges one group over another or males over females. Are ovaries superior to testicles? The question is meaningless. Are male mate preferences superior to female mate preferences? The question is equally meaningless.

Is Evolutionary Psychology a Form of Genetic Determinism?

Critics often accuse evolutionary psychologists of genetic determinism, and, in one sense, they are right. It is telling evidence of a pervasive dualism, though, that anatomists escape this abuse. Although the processes whereby genetic information directs the development of bodily functions are still largely unknown, there are compelling empirical and theoretical reasons to believe that there are genes for arms, legs, and lungs. Because all humans (with rare exceptions) have arms, legs, and lungs that are built the same way, we can surmise that we all share essentially the same genes for these limbs and organs. The universal architecture of the body is genetically specified in this sense. Because psychological adaptations such as vision are no different from other adaptations in this regard, they, too, are genetically specified human universals.

This, however, is not what is usually meant by *genetically determined*. Sometimes what is meant is that behavior is genetically determined. But *genetically determined mechanisms* does not imply genetically determined behavior. Just as a genetically determined universal skeletal architecture of bones and muscles can perform a huge variety of new and different movements, so, too, can a genetically determined universal psychological architecture that evolved to be exquisitely attuned to local environmental circumstances produce countless behavioral outcomes in different individuals with different experiences and in different situations. If the brain had only 20 independent mechanisms, each of which could be in only one of two states set by local environmental conditions, the brain would have 2^{20}, or about a million, different states and, potentially, a corresponding number of different behaviors. Because the EP model of the brain posits a very large number of innately specified mechanisms (perhaps hundreds or thousands), most of which are sensitive to environmental conditions, the brain could potentially be in any one of an astronomically large number of different states with different behavior outcomes, even if many of these modules were not independent of one another. EP's model of a genetically determined, massively modular brain predicts far too much behavioral flexibility and diversity, not too little.

Is Evolutionary Psychology a Form of Social Darwinism?

Nor does an interest in genetically determined psychological mechanisms imply an interest in defending status quo social structures. According to John Horgan (1995), evolutionary psychologists are the new social Darwinists—those who supposedly want to justify current social hierarchies with Darwinian theory. Ironically, it looks like the old social Darwinists never existed. Robert Bannister, seeking the social Darwinists of the history books, "came close to concluding that someone had made the whole thing up" (Bannister, 1979; cf. Hofstadter, 1955):

> A reconsideration [of social Darwinism] alone yields two conclusions, both important although neither groundbreaking. One is that Gilded Age defenders of free market mechanisms, individualism, and laissez faire (so-called "conservatives" but in reality liberals by mid-19th century standards) rarely laced their prose with appeals to Darwinism, and virtually never in the way described in conventional accounts. Rather, they were suspicious if not downright frightened by the implications of the new theory. Such was even the case with Herbert Spencer and his American disciples—the stereotypical textbook social Darwinists—whose world view remained essentially pre-Darwinian. The second conclusion is that New Liberals, socialists, and other advocates of positive government appealed openly and with far greater regularity to Darwinism to support their causes. These appeals typically contrasted "false" readings of Darwin (i.e., of the opposition) with a "correct" one (i.e., their own). Although important in their way, these two points are essentially preliminary.
>
> To ask how the epithet social Darwinism functioned, on the other hand, is to turn the conventional account rather literally on its head. Not only was there no school (or schools) of social Darwinists: the term was a label one pinned upon anyone with whom one especially disagreed. . . . A social Darwinist, to oversimplify the case, was something nobody wanted to be. (Bannister, 1988, preface, citations omitted)

Social Darwinism is obviously still being used as an epithet. Sociobiology (and thus EP) does have an explanation for the social hierarchies that are ubiquitous in both animal and human social groups (e.g., Schjelderup-Ebbe, 1922; Wilson, 1975), but an explanation is not a justification. Neither sociobiology nor EP makes any attempt to either justify the existence of social hierarchies or any particular ranking of individuals.

Why Do People Hate Evolutionary Psychology?

Slavish support for reigning political and moral attitudes is a sure sign of scientific bankruptcy. It is reassuring, then, that EP has something to offend just about everyone. Surely you, the reader, if you are not already a jaded evolutionary psychologist, are offended by at least one of EP's speculations that there might be innate, genetically based adaptations hardwired into our brains for rape, homicide, infanticide, war, aggression, exploitation, infidelity, and deception. I know I was. If, further, you would like to see these plagues wiped from the face of the earth, you might understandably be sympathetic to critics who advance something like the following syllogism, which appears to underlie most criticisms of EP:

> I [the critic] want political change, which requires changing people. Evolutionary psychologists argue that people have innate and unchangeable natures, so they must therefore be opposed to social or political change, and are merely attempting to scientifically justify the status quo.

If EP predicted that social or political change were impossible, then it would be wrong on its face. The tremendous amount of social and political change over the course of human history is irrefutable. This is no real mystery. Consider a hypothetical population of organisms whose natures are completely genetically specified and unchangeable. Suppose, further, that these organisms have a number of identical preferences and desires, all unchangeable, but, because resources are limited, not all individuals can fulfill their desires. These creatures are, therefore, often in conflict with one another. Suppose, finally, that these organisms have the ability to negotiate. It is not difficult to see that even if individuals' natures are unchangeable, social outcomes are not. Because our hypothetical organisms are able to negotiate, they are (potentially) able to form social arrangements that are equitable, fairly dividing resources and punishing individuals who violate these agreements. When circumstances change, new agreements can be forged. Circumstances *will* change, so social change is inevitable despite the creatures' unchangeable natures. In fact, it is their genetically determined, unchangeable cognitive ability to negotiate that guarantees social change! Because humans, too, can negotiate, and can also dramatically tune their individual, innate, psychological architectures based on their experiences and current circumstances, the possibilities for social change are multiplied thousandfolds.

CONCLUSIONS

> To study metaphysics [psychology] as they have been studied appears to me like struggling at astronomy without mechanics.—Experience shows the problem of the mind cannot be solved by attacking the citadel itself.—the mind is function of the body.—we must find some stabile foundation to argue from.
>
> —Darwin, Notebook N, p. 5, quoted in Ghiselin, 1973

The bricks outside the window of my office are riddled with bullet holes, scars of the fierce house-to-house street fighting between the Red Army and the *Volkssturm*, the rag-tag defenders of the capital, in the battle for Berlin. The rear of the building remains, almost 60 years later, a bombed-out shell. The bullet holes and bomb damage are a stark reminder, if the nightly news somehow failed to be, that the world can quickly become a nightmare. Although the values and institutions that permit most of us in the West to enjoy unparalleled health, safety, and freedom were sculpted over the course of millennia, they can be almost instantly destroyed.

Galileo's unification of heaven and earth had immense scientific and social consequences, some foreseeable, most not. Galileo labored to reassure the Church that his theories and ideas were no threat to the social order it had established, but, in fact, they were. Church authorities were right to be alarmed. EP, like Galileo, has labored to reassure the intelligentsia that its unification of body and brain poses no threat to the social order, an order now based, in part, on the dualism of a blank slate ideology. But, as its critics correctly perceive, it does. If EP's modern operationalization of Darwin is correct, it will be immensely powerful. Whether the social consequences will be, at most, a minor modification of liberal democracy, as many EPs believe, or something else, is impossible to predict. (Much of the world, it is worth remembering, does not live under liberal democracy.) As some critics fear, EP might be used to justify social hierarchies and roles (e.g., Rose & Rose, 2000), but blank-slate ideologies have done the same and worse (Pinker, 2002). As some adherents hope (e.g., Singer, 2000), EP might be used to reduce the world's misery. Most likely, EP will be used for other things entirely.

Whether EP is correct or not, I hope this *Handbook* will convince you that it is not scientific window dressing for a political ideology, but rather a compelling scientific approach to human nature. This does not mean that EP is harmless. Critics, fearing EP to be a Trojan horse of the right, have raised countless objections to EP, objections that, as this chapter has shown, would border on the absurd were they raised against one of history's most successful scientific paradigms: the functional, mechanistic approach to organism anatomy. What the surprisingly myopic critics have failed to perceive is that the power of EP will not be to prevent change but to cause it.

Fully realized, EP would constitute a functional understanding of the neural circuits underlying our every thought, emotion, and action. With that understanding would come the power to mold our humanity to a disquieting degree. Perhaps it is naïve to believe that EP can keep up with the manipulative expertise of Hollywood and Madison Avenue, but serious critics of EP would do well to reread their Huxley and Orwell.

More worrisome, EP challenges the foundations of crucial enlightenment values, values we undermine at our peril. Perhaps the mix of secular and religious values on which the priceless institutions of democracy rest are like a tablecloth that can be quickly yanked out, leaving everything standing on some solid, though as yet unknown, base. But I wouldn't bet on it. We are at a crossroads. A vibrant science of human thought and behavior must always be able to question its own premises and is thus utterly unsuited to be that solid base. Yet, if we discard the secular, quasiscientific notion of the blank slate, or even subject it to genuine scientific scrutiny, we may threaten institutions far more valuable than a science of human nature. The vital question is not, as most critics seem to think, whether EP is correct, but whether any real science of the brain is prudent.

REFERENCES

Ahouse, J. C., & Berwick, R. C. (1998). Darwin on the Mind: Evolutionary psychology is in fashion— but is any of it true? A review of *How the Mind Works* by Steven Pinker. *Boston Review.* April/May issue.

Alcock, J. (2001). *The triumph of sociobiology.* Oxford, England: Oxford University Press.

Andersson, M. (1994). *Sexual selection.* Princeton, NJ: Princeton University Press.

Bannister, R. C. (1988). *Social Darwinism: Science and myth in Anglo-American social thought.* Philadelphia: Temple University Press.

Berwick, R. C. (1998, March). Steven Pinker and the limits of biology as ideology. *The Los Angeles Times Book Review, 15,* 3.

Bowlby, J. (1969). *Attachment and loss.* New York: Basic Books.

Boyd, R., & Richerson, P. J. (2001). Norms and Bounded Rationality. In G. Gigerenzer & R. Selten (Eds.), *Bounded rationality: The adaptive toolbox* (pp. 281–296). Cambridge, MA: MIT Press.

Brown, D. (1991). *Human universals.* Philadelphia: Temple University Press.

Buller, D. J., & Hardcastle, V. G. (2000). Evolutionary psychology, meet developmental neurobiology: Against promiscuous modularity. *Brain and Mind, 1,* 307–325.

Buss, D. M. (2004). *Evolutionary psychology: The new science of the mind* (2nd ed.). Boston: Allyn & Bacon.

Carruthers, P. M. (2003). On Fodor's problem. *Mind and Language, 18,* 502–523.

Cherniak, J. (1990). The bounded brain: Toward quantitative neuroanatomy. *Journal of Cognitive Neuroscience, 2,* 58–68.

Cosmides, L. (1989). The logic of social exchange: Has natural selection shaped how humans reason? Studies with the Wason selection task. *Cognition, 31,* 187–276.

Cosmides, L., & Tooby, J. (1994). Origins of domain specificity: The evolution of functional organization. In L. A. Hirschfeld & S. A. Gelman (Eds.), *Mapping the Mind: Domain Specificity in Cognition and Culture.* New York: Cambridge University Press.

Dawkins, R. (1976). *The selfish gene.* Oxford, England: Oxford University Press.

Dugatkin, L. A. (1997). *Cooperation among animals.* Oxford, England: Oxford University Press.

Ehrlich, P. R., & Feldman, M. (2003). Genes and Cultures: What Creates Our Behavioral Phenome? *Current Anthropology, 44,* 87–95.

Fodor, J. A. (1983). *The modularity of mind: An essay on faculty psychology.* Cambridge, MA: MIT Press.

Fodor, J. (2000). *The mind doesn't work that way.* Cambridge, MA: MIT Press.

Galileo, G. (1953). *Dialogue concerning the two chief world systems, Ptolemaic & Copernican.* Berkeley: University of California Press.

Ghiselin, M. T. (1973). Darwin and Evolutionary Psychology. *Science, 179,* 964–968.

Gould, S. J. (1997). The exaptive excellence of spandrels as a term and prototype. *Proceedings of the National Academy of Sciences, 94,* 10750–10755.

Gould, S. J., & Lewontin, R. C. (1979). The spandrels of San Marco and the Panglossian paradigm: A critique of the adaptationist programme. *Proceedings of the Royal Society of London. Series B, Biological Sciences, 205,* 581–598.

Hagen, E. H., & Hammerstein, P. (2005). Evolutionary biology and the strategic view of ontogeny: Genetic strategies provide robustness and flexibility in the life course. *Research in Human Development, 2,* 87–101.

Hamilton, W. D. (1964). The genetical evolution of social behaviour: I and II. *Journal of Theoretical Biology, 7,* 1–16 and 17–52.

Hammerstein, P. (1996). Darwinian adaptation, population genetics and the streetcar theory of evolution. *Journal of Mathematical Biology, 34,* 511–532.

Hammerstein, P. (Ed.). (2003). *Genetic and cultural evolution of cooperation.* Cambridge, MA: MIT Press.

Hofstadter, R. (1955). *Social Darwinism in American thought.* Boston: Beacon Press.

Horgan, J. (1995). The new social Darwinists. *Scientific American, 273,* 174–181.

Kaygusuz, I., Godekmerdan, A., Karlidag, T., Keles, E., Yalcin, S., Aral, I., et al. (2003). Early stage impacts of tonsillectomy on immune functions of children. *International Journal of Pediatric Otorhinolaryngology, 67,* 1311–1315.

Karmiloff-Smith, A. (1992). *Beyond modularity.* Cambridge, MA: MIT Press.

Maynard Smith, J. (1978). Optimization theory in evolution. *Annual Review of Ecology and Systematics, 9,* 31–56.

Maynard Smith, J., & Price, G. R. (1973). The logic of animal conflict. *Nature, 246,* 15–18.

Öhman, A., & Mineka, S. (2001). Fears, phobias, and preparedness: Toward an evolved module of fear and fear learning. *Psychological Review, 108,* 483–522.

Orr, H. A. (2003). Darwinian storytelling. *New York Review of Books, 50, February 27.*

Paley, W. (1809). *Natural theology or evidences of the existence and attributes of the deity.* London: J. Faulder.

Panksepp, J., & Panksepp, J. B. (2000). The seven sins of evolutionary psychology. *Evolution and Cognition, 6,* 108–131.

Pinker, S. (2002). *The blank slate: The modern denial of human nature.* New York: Viking.

Raser, J. M., & O'Shea, E. K. (2004). Control of stochasticity in eukaryotic gene expression. *Science,* *304,* 1811–1814.

Richerson, P. J., & Boyd, R. (2005). *Not by genes alone: How culture transformed human evolution.* Chicago: University of Chicago Press.

Rose, H., & Rose, S. (2000). *Alas poor Darwin: Arguments against evolutionary psychology.* New York: Harmony Books.

Schjelderup-Ebbe, T. (1922). Beitrage zur Sozialpsychologie des Haushuhns. *Zeitschrift fur Psychologie, 88,* 225–252.

Segerstrale, U. (2000). *Defenders of the truth: The battle for science in the sociobiology debate and beyond.* Oxford, England: Oxford University Press.

Shwartz, M. (2001). Genes don't control behavior, Ehrlich says, urging studies of cultural evolution. *Stanford Report,* April 4.

Singer, P. (2000). *A Darwinian left: Politics, evolution, and cooperation.* New Haven, CT: Yale University Press.

Smith, E. A., Borgerhoff Mulder, M., & Hill, K. (2000). Evolutionary analyses of human behaviour: A commentary on Daly & Wilson. *Animal Behaviour, 60,* F21–F26.

Spelke, E. S. (2000). Core knowledge. *American Psychologist, 55,* 1233–1243.

Symons, D. (1979). *The evolution of human sexuality.* New York: Oxford University Press.

Symons, D. (1987). Darwin and human nature. *Behavioral and Brain Sciences, 10,* 89.

Symons, D. (1989). A critique of Darwinian anthropology. *Ethology and Sociobiology, 10,* 131–144.

Symons, D. (1990). Adaptiveness and adaptation. *Ethology and Sociobiology, 1,* 427–444.

Tattersall, I. (2001). Evolution, genes, and behavior. *Zygon, 36,* 657–666.

Tooby, J., & Cosmides, L. (1990). On the universality of human nature and the uniqueness of the individual: The role of genetics and adaptation. *Journal of Personality, 58,* 17–67.

Trivers, R. (1972). The evolution of reciprocal altruism. *Quarterly Review of Biology, 46,* 35–57.

van Kempen, M. J., Rijkers, G. T., & Van Cauwenberge, P. B. (2000). The immune response in adenoids and tonsils. *International Archives of Allergy and Immunology, 122,* 8–19.

Williams, G. C. (1966). *Adaptation and natural selection: A critique of some current evolutionary thought.* Princeton, NJ: Princeton University Press.

Wilson, D. S. (1994). Adaptive genetic variation and human evolutionary psychology. *Ethology and Sociobiology, 15,* 219–235.

Wilson, E. O. (1975). *Sociobiology: The new synthesis.* Cambridge, MA: Belknap Press of Harvard University Press.

Wilson, E. O. (1988). The current state of biological diversity. In E. O. Wilson & F. M. Peter (Eds.), *Biodiversity.* Washington, DC: National Academy Press.

PART II

SURVIVAL

DAVID M. BUSS

CHARLES DARWIN COINED the apt phrase "the hostile forces of nature" to describe the elements that impede an organism's survival. He described three fundamental classes of hostile forces. The first involves *struggles with the physical environment,* such as extremes of climate and weather, falling from dangerous heights, or being swept away by landslides or tsunamis. The second involves *struggles with other species,* such as predators, parasites, and prey. The third involves *struggles with conspecifics.* To some extent, this tripartite scheme oversimplifies because adaptive problems obviously cut across classes. Finding prey for food, for example, requires navigating the physical environment, dealing with the evolved psychology of prey animals, and sometimes outcompeting conspecifics. Nonetheless, Darwin's "hostile forces of nature" provide a natural starting point for the adaptive problems of survival that humans recurrently confronted.

Irwin Silverman and Jean Choi in Chapter 6 describe theory and research on human spatial navigation and landscape preferences. These features of human evolutionary psychology are critical for a host of adaptive problems. Adaptive challenges include finding shelter that offers protection from hazardous elements, locating water sources, and finding food that can be gathered or hunted. Silverman and Choi describe important discoveries about spatial abilities, such as female superiority in spatial location memory, that were entirely missed by previous generations of psychologists who lacked the lens of evolutionary psychology.

In Chapter 7, Clark Barrett provides a groundbreaking theoretical analysis and relevant empirical studies on human interactions with two classes of species—predators and prey. He furnishes evidence for specialized psychological adaptations attuned to unique design features of predators and prey, such as self-propelled motion, morphology, contingency, and directed gaze. Although this line of research is relatively new, Barrett elucidates the exciting discoveries already made and the promise of many more to come.

Joshua Duntley devotes Chapter 8 to other humans as possibly the most important "hostile force of nature." He describes recurrent arenas of human conflict and argues that humans have adaptations both to inflict costs on other humans and to defend against having costs inflicted on them. Duntley then elucidates an exciting new coevolutionary theory of the evolutionary psychology of homicide and homicide defenses—manifestations of human conflict with the most dramatic fitness consequences.

Modern introductory textbooks in psychology are notable for their absence of attention to problems of survival. Perhaps because most view evolutionary theory as optional, they fail to offer coverage of the rich psychology of human survival adaptations. Taken together, the three chapters in this section showcase the scientific gains already made by exploring psychological adaptations to the hostile forces of nature and offer the exciting promise of many more to come.

CHAPTER 6

Locating Places

IRWIN SILVERMAN and JEAN CHOI

CONSIDERATIONS OF SPACE impact on virtually every aspect of the organism's adaptive behavior, including the search for food, water, and shelter; predator avoidance; mating strategies; social structure, and parenting. In this chapter, we focus on the evolutionary approach to two aspects of spatial behavior in humans and infrahuman animals: (1) navigation, or how the individual travels systematically from place to place, and (2) landscape preference, the kinds of places in which the individual chooses to live or visit. First, however, we introduce the reader to *domain specificity*, an integral concept of evolutionary cognitive psychology, and its relationship to spatial behavior in general.

DOMAIN SPECIFICITY OF SPATIAL BEHAVIOR

Watch a dog leap handily over a fence leaving barely enough room to clear, a child throw a ball on a near perfect arc to a target, or a honeybee return directly to its hive after a meandering search for food. Ponder the physical laws of space and motion inherent in all of these abilities. In no case are the subjects aware of these laws or capable of generalizing from them, yet the actions are performed with ease.

These examples illustrate the prevailing paradigm of evolutionary psychology, which seeks to replace the traditional social science model of mind as primarily consisting of *general purpose learning mechanisms*. The evolutionary-based perspective is that mind is composed of functionally independent or semiindependent *domain-specific mechanisms* (Cosmides & Tooby, 1992) that evolved in response to specific problems for adaptation and survival in the organism's evolutionary history.

The areas of spatial perception and behavior afford excellent examples of this model. In the preceding examples, the honeybee's navigational skills enabled it to forage over a relatively large area. The canine's ability to leap over a barrier

Preparation of this paper was supported, in part, by grants from the Social Sciences and Humanities Reseasrch Council of Canada to IS and the Natural Sciences and Engineering Research Council of Canada to JC.

facilitated both hunting and escape from predators. The human's capacity to accurately throw a projectile also aided in hunting and in agonistic encounters with other conspecifics.

Fodor (1983) presented a parallel concept to domain specificity, termed *modularity of mind.* He speculated that perceptual illusions may provide evidence for separate modules underlying perception and cognition, in that they persist even after the viewer has learned that they are inconsistent with reality. Two classic illusions by Ames (see Ittelson, 1952) aptly illustrate Fodor's point: the *rotating trapezoidal window* and the *distorted room.* Both are rooted in the phenomenon of *shape constancy,* an innately based capacity to retain the perception of bilateral symmetry of squares and rectangles, even when viewed at angles. (When a square or rectangle is viewed at an angle, the near side is larger on the retina than the far side, thus creating the retinal image of a trapezoid.)

The rotating trapezoidal window is shown in dim light to conceal depth cues and constructed so that one side always remains longer in length during rotation. In this manner, it cannot be perceived simultaneously as rotating and having the bilateral symmetry of a rectangle, because the sides of a rectangle in rotation would alternate in terms of which was longer on the retina. Viewers unconsciously resolve the conflict in favor of maintaining symmetry, by creating the illusion of oscillation at the point when the side moving toward the viewer eclipses the side moving away.

The distorted room is seen from a small opening and is constructed to resemble the way a normal room would appear on the retina from that perspective. Windows, doors, walls, and the floor and ceiling are trapezoidal, with vertical borders decreasing in size as a function of distance from the viewer. Viewers' customary perceptual adjustments to restore symmetry when entering an ordinary room are simply enhanced by these added distortions; hence, the room and all of its structures are erroneously perceived as normally shaped, though larger than they actually are.

Viewers continue to perceive the illusions even when they are made aware of the true nature of the stimuli and the bases for their misperceptions. Furthermore, when cues designed to encourage veridical perceptions are added to the scenario, they merely become integrated into the illusion. Hence, a stick hanging inside the window continues to appear to rotate when the window begins its illusory oscillation, despite the fact that it is perceived as moving through the solid surface of the window frame. People crossing the far wall of the distorted room are perceived as becoming either taller or shorter, depending on the side from which they began.

These illusions provide physical evidence for the premises underlying both modularity and domain specificity theories and, in a later section, we consider the direct relevance of perceptual constancy to human navigation. We also refer frequently to domain specificity as it applies to human and animal movement. Although, to our knowledge, this concept has not been directly applied to animal minds, it seems reasonable to assume that it has implicit relevance whenever more primitive creatures engage in what humans regard as complex cognitive tasks.

GALLISTEL'S DOMAIN GENERAL VIEW

Though the concept of domain specificity may ultimately revolutionize our views of mind, contemporary theories of cognitive psychology still remain largely domain general.

Gallistel's (1990) model, frequently cited in the spatial navigation literature, provides a case in point. Gallistel contends that the representational and computational rules presumed to underlie learning and problem solving in adult humans can be applied to all cognitive capacities of all animal species. In regard to spatial navigation, he says:

> The fact that dead reckoning computations for unrestricted courses are sufficiently complex to have imposed restrictions on the courses human navigators followed would seem an intuitive argument against the hypothesis that the nervous system of infrahuman animals like the ant routinely and accurately perform such computations. I raise this point to argue specifically against such intuitions, which I believe have been an obstacle to the acceptance of computational-representational theories of brain function. Symbolic manipulations that seem complex, hard to learn, and difficult to carry out by human beings often have simple physical realizations. Integrating a variable with respect to time sounds like an impressive operation, yet a bucket receiving a flow of water integrates that flow with respect to time. The filling of a bucket strikes most people as a simple physical operation. A symbolic (mathematical) presentation of the trigonometric and integrative operations involved in dead reckoning computations makes them sound forbidding, but the dead reckoning device on a ship is not complex. The trigonometric, decomposition operations it performs are easily simulated with plausible neural circuits. (1990, pp. 38–39)

There appears to be a semantic inconsistency, at the least, in the notion of "simple physical realizations" of representational and computational rules. The function of a rule is to unify observations within a higher order explanation in a manner that enables generalization to novel observations. If the organism is unable to understand or generalize from a rule, that is, if the individual's response is restricted to a concrete set of circumstances, as in the case of the navigational skills of an ant or a bird, then it seems confusing to identify it as a manifestation of a rule.

Differences in the approaches of evolutionary and traditional cognitive psychology extend beyond semantics, however. The domain specificity approach of evolutionary psychology is inductive in nature, focusing on species-specific ecological requirements that could account for the evolution of a given behavior. The goal is to uncover the evolved mechanisms mediating the behavior, whether these are best described in terms of cognition, conditioning, neuropsychology, olfaction, or some combination of these. In contrast, Gallistel's (1990) hypothetico-deductive approach has taken cognitive psychologists in a different research direction; that is, the search for the expression of a general set of representational and computational rules for navigational behaviors across situations and species.

Although parsimony is a basic tenet of science, the acquisition of a veridical theory of navigation across species may require a longer period of inductive inquiry than has transpired thus far. In this vein, the concept of representational/computational rules may be reminiscent of *equipotentiality*, a core principle of behaviorism that maintained that all reinforcers were equally effective for all behaviors of all species. That notion was discredited by Garcia and colleagues (Garcia, Ervin, & Koelling, 1966; Garcia & Koelling, 1966) in a series of studies on taste avoidance in rats that were seminal to the concept of domain specificity. They demonstrated that organisms were genetically programmed in an evolutionarily adaptive manner, such that particular behaviors conditioned only to particular reinforcers in particular species. Rats, scavengers by nature, could be conditioned to avoid a particular flavor solely by the negative reinforcer of induced nausea.

A hypothetico-deductive model that seeks to apply a single set of rules to navigational behavior across species will also be misled by unique, species-specific mechanisms. For example, bees and some other insects seem to navigate by using the sun as a compass, but are actually following planes of polarized light (von Frisch, 1967). Migrating locusts would appear to defy representational/computational analysis in that individuals are seen flying in different directions within the swarm, but this is the locusts' way of keeping the group on course despite wind shifts (Rainey, 1962).

Finally, it is reasonable to assume that the evolutionary development of animal and human navigational abilities began with simpler mechanisms than are described in a representational/computational analyses. This does not exclude from consideration the higher order abstractions unique to humans that have enhanced our navigational capacities to the point where we can travel to space and back, but these were derived in relatively recent evolutionary time, as a function of our emergent general analytical abilities. It does not follow that these analyses are somehow embedded in mechanisms that have worked effectively from prehistory.

The greater feasibility of a domain-specific approach to navigation is argued throughout this discussion. In this vein, we now examine the domain specificity model as it applies to *optimization*, another domain general rule that has been invoked to explain animal and human spatial movement.

OPTIMIZATION IN ANIMAL MOVEMENT

Navigation is the process by which an animal uses available cues to travel to predetermined locations. The nature and extent of travel, however, varies greatly among species. Some cover relatively short distances in their lifetimes whereas others migrate halfway around the world. Attempts to explain these differences in terms of fitness requirements have generally resided in the principle of *optimization*; that is, the presumption that evolved behavioral characteristics reflect optimal trade-offs between costs and benefits to the animal's fitness.

Alcock (1984, pp. 199–203), however, has pointed out an essential problem with optimization theory: It is usually impossible to measure evolutionary costs and benefits in the same units. For example, the benefits of migrations include greater availability of food sources and facilitation of breeding, while the costs include expenditure of energy and danger from predators along the way. Thus, the only means by which we can conclude that the positive value of the benefits exceeds the negative value of the costs is by the fact that migratory behavior has selected in for the animal—a textbook example of circular reasoning.

In fact, Alcock expresses skepticism about the cost-benefit explanations of long-range migrations (pp. 241–244) and regards the phenomenon as a continuing theoretical challenge. In general, Alcock prefers a *qualitative* approach to evolutionary analyses, whereby correspondence is established for a particular species between a particular behavioral trait and particular aspect of its adaptation. Within Cosmides and Tooby's (1992) domain specificity model, this would be phrased in terms of the correspondence of the *design features* of a specific cognitive mechanism and the *task requirements* of a specific adaptive problem.

Alcock does concede that quantitative analyses based on optimization may have utility for more circumscribed areas of behavior, where costs and benefits may be measured in the same currency; for example, calories lost and gained in foraging strategies. Janson (2000), however, has described some of the constraints of quantitatively based laboratory research on optimization of foraging behavior that limit its generalizability to behavior in vivo. He points out that laboratory experiments usually expose the animal to a single cluster of food sites that can be visited during a limited time interval; thus the only available adaptive responses for the animal are to eat at all sites and minimize travel distances between them. Janson's (1988) own studies of brown capuchin monkeys showed that the foraging behavior of these animals in their own habitat were quite different from behavior in the laboratory. Capuchins in the wild use a variety of foraging strategies, dictated by the longer term goal of consuming a fixed daily food requirement with the shortest required overall travel distance. Furthermore, they alter their strategies as distributions of food resources change, and they do not consume what cannot be digested during the course of the day. According to Janson, capuchin monkeys and many other species can find and ingest food faster than they can digest it; hence there are minimal fitness returns in increasing food intake beyond that which can be digested within a limited time period.

Janson concluded that to devise a model to predict how an animal will forage, you must first determine what the animal knows about its environment. Most researchers implicitly assume that it is very little, but some food storing birds seem to remember hundreds of seed caches (Balda & Kamil, 1988; Hilton & Krebs, 1990), and many primate species, as well, show precise recall of specific resources (Janson, 1998; Menzel, 1991). Janson also concludes that evolutionary hypotheses should be conceptualized in the context of the animal's unique attributes and requirements, an approach compatible to both Alcock's and the domain specificity perspectives.

A MAP AND A COMPASS

To navigate, you must have a map and a compass. The map, physical or mental, indicates where you are in relation to your goal. The compass refers, figuratively, to the cues you will use to get there. Generally speaking, we know more about compasses than maps; that is, there are much data about the cues animals use to reach a goal, but less about how they decide where the goal is.

Navigational cues fall into two distinct strategies, which we call *orientation versus landmark* but which have also been referred to as *Euclidean* or *geometric versus topographic, dead reckoning versus episodic,* and *allocentric versus egocentric.* The orientation strategy most effective for journeys over long distances requires the animal to maintain a sense of its own position in relation to various global markers. These include the sun, the stars, wind direction, the earth's magnetic field, and barometric changes, and usually involve the individual's proprioceptive bodily cues and biological clock. When navigating indoors by an orientation strategy, the subject uses the configuration of the structure. In contrast, the landmark strategy involves the learning and recall of visual markers and their relationships to each other along the route, including objects, turning points, and details of the terrain.

Many species possess the capacity for both strategies, but the one that is best developed and most frequently used depends on the animal's ecological requirements (Alcock, 1984; Drickamer & Vessey, 1986). Thus, migratory and homing animals primarily use an orientation strategy while animals that stay closer to home generally use a landmark strategy. Strategy is also a function of the greater availability of landmark or global cues, as illustrated in the differential navigational processes of tropical forest versus desert dwelling ants. The former use a landmark strategy for foraging, whereby the ants learn and follow the markings on the forest canopy above them. The latter use their sustained access to the sun by deriving compass information from its position. We know that these species are using these strategies by studies showing that if a forest ant is experimentally displaced to a point where it has not previously traveled, it will not be able to readily find its way back, whereas a desert ant will proceed directly on the correct path (Holldobler, 1980).

Animals that primarily use an orienting strategy often have more than one method at their disposal and use these interchangeably, in an adaptive manner. Thus, honeybees and homing pigeons orient by the sun when it is visible, but during overcast days or nights revert to methods that use the magnetic fields of the earth. Migrating birds generally use a sun-based orientation strategy for most of their journey but revert to a landmark strategy when approaching home. The orienting strategy enables them to navigate across long distances where landmarks are not available, such as over the sea, or where frequencies of landmarks along the way are too copious to recall. The landmark strategy enables them to hone in on their precise destination when approaching the completion of their journey.

Humans are, historically and prehistorically, foragers, hunters, and colonizers. Thus, we engage in short, intermediate, and long forays, and it is not surprising that we routinely use both orientation and landmark strategies.

To demonstrate this to yourself, point to some other state or country, far from your own. Now point to a place close to home, where you go on a regular basis such as a grocery or a friend's residence. You will probably use an orientation strategy for the first task, by constructing a mental image of a map that includes your own and the target's location and taking an estimate of your current compass bearing in relation to the target. You will most likely use a landmark strategy for the second task, based on the landmarks on the route you customarily take to your target (adapted from Thorndike & Hayes-Roth, 1980).

GENETIC, NEUROLOGICAL, AND DEVELOPMENTAL BASES OF NAVIGATIONAL STRATEGIES

Across studies and measures, the average heritability of spatial abilities, including those directly involved in navigation, is about .50 (Bouchard, Segal, & Lykken, 1990; Defries et al., 1976; Plomin, Pederson, Lichtenstein, & McClearn, 1994; Tambs, Sundet, & Magnus, 1984; Vandenberg, 1969).

Regarding neural mechanisms, studies with humans (e.g., Maguire, Frackowiak, & Frith, 1996; Maguire et al., 1998), monkeys (Ono & Nishijo, 1999; Rolls, Robertson, & Georges-Francois, 1997), and rats (e.g., Eichenbaum, Stewart, & Morrisa, 1990; Thinus-Blanc, Save, Pucet, & Buhot, 1991) have shown that navigational processes in general are associated with the functions of the hippocampal formation, which includes the hippocampus and the adjacent cortex in the most medial area of the temporal lobe. Other studies have shown different neurological processes within the hippocampus for tasks involving orientation and landmark strategies, which supports the notion that they evolved in a domain-specific manner. O'Keefe and Nadel (1978) first demonstrated that navigation by rats in an environment that is defined only by the shape of the enclosure, thereby requiring an orientation strategy, activates different types of neurons than those involved in landmark-based tasks. The former are called *place cells* and include neurons that encode the animal's location and specific bodily movements in relation to the geometric properties of the environment (Muller, Bostock, Taube, & Kubie, 1994; Taube, 1995, 1998; Taube, Muller, & Ranck, 1990).

Pizzamiglio, Guariglia, and Cosentino (1998) presented clinical data in humans that also demonstrated the dual neurological bases of orientation and landmark strategies. Two right hemisphere-damaged subjects were unable to orient themselves to an enclosure when its shape was the only information available, but improved considerably when a visual object was added as a cue. Two other subjects, with a different lesion site in the right hemisphere than the first two, could orient themselves using only the shape of the enclosure. Unlike right brained-intact controls, however, these subjects did not increase their performance with the addition of the cue.

Further support for domain specificity emanates from differences in the developmental stages when the two navigational strategies emerge. Children from about 2 years of age use landmark strategies, while rudimentary orientation strategies do not appear until about the age of 8 (Anooshian & Young, 1981; Blades & Medlicott, 1992; Scholnick, Fein, & Campbell, 1992). Landau and Gleitman (1985), however, performed a study with a congenitally blind girl of 31 months, in which she was led to various landmarks in a room and back again each time to the starting point. She was subsequently able to navigate from landmark to landmark, which Gallistel (1990, pp. 99–100) interpreted as evidence of orientating behavior in a very young child.

SPATIALLY RELATED SEX DIFFERENCES

Though evolutionary theorists are primarily interested in universals, group differences often provide the first clues about these. Thus, the theory of evolution by natural selection began with Darwin's observations of subgroup differences within bird and amphibian populations in the Galapagos Islands.

Generally, the focus is on interspecies differences, but any ubiquitous group difference amenable to explanation in terms of natural selection may be relevant. Thus, the pervasive bias favoring males in spatially related tasks, both in humans and infrahuman species, ultimately led to evolutionary-based theory and data on the nature of human navigational processes.

Studies of human spatial sex differences have shown a male advantage across a variety of measures, including field dependence, mental rotations, embedded figures, map reading, maze learning, and estimating the speed of a moving object. The magnitude of the sex difference varies among measures, with three-dimensional tasks showing greater differences than two-dimensional tasks and three-dimensional mental rotation tests yielding the largest and most reliable differences (Halpern, 1992; Linn & Peterson, 1985; McGee, 1979; Phillips & Silverman, 1997). Meta-analysis (Voyer, Voyer, & Bryden, 1995) has shown that the average difference between sexes for three-dimensional mental rotations, across dozens of studies, is a robust .94 by Cohen's d, indicating that the mean performance of males is nearly one standard deviation above that of females.

The male advantage in spatial tasks is highly consistent across human geographic populations and age groups. Though most studies have been conducted in North America, the sex difference across tests has been replicated in Japan (Mann, Sasanuma, Sakuma, & Masaki, 1990; Silverman, Phillips, & Silverman, 1996), England (Lynn, 1992), Scotland (Berry, 1966; Jahoda, 1980), Ghana (Jahoda, 1980), Sierra Leone (Berry, 1966), India, South Africa, and Australia (Porteus, 1965). Although the sex difference has been reported in children as young as preschoolers (McGuiness & Morley, 1991), the consensus is that it does not appear reliably across tasks until early adolescence, which is generally attributed to accelerated hormonal differentiation (Burstein, Bank, & Jarvik, 1980; Johnson & Meade, 1987). One study (Willis & Schaie, 1988) has shown that from this age, the magnitude of the difference tends to be constant throughout the life span.

The sex difference extends also across species. Studies with wild and laboratory rodents have shown that males consistently outperform females in maze learning tasks (Barrett & Ray, 1970; Binnie-Dawson & Cheung, 1982; Gaulin & Fitzgerald, 1986; Joseph, Hess, & Birecree, 1978; Williams & Meck, 1991).

Sex hormones, in terms of both organizational and activational effects, have been implicated in spatial sex differences in humans and animals (Hampson & Kimura, 1992; Kimura, 1999; Kimura & Hampson, 1993; Phillips & Silverman, 1997; Reinisch, Ziemba-Davis, & Saunders, 1991; Silverman & Phillips, 1993; Williams & Meck, 1991). Studies have shown a decrease in spatial abilities with increased estrogen levels, consistent with the direction of the sex difference. Corresponding increases in spatial performance with increased testosterone levels, however, occur reliably for females, but not males. Males have shown both direct and inverse effects in different studies (Choi & Silverman, 2002; Gouchie & Kimura, 1991; Janowsky, Oviatt, & Orwoll, 1994; Nyborg, 1983, 1984; Silverman, Kastuik, Choi, & Phillips, 1999). Nyborg (1983) has attempted to explain this paradox in terms of the fact that plasma testosterone is, under some circumstances, converted to brain estrogen, while Silverman et al. (1999) explained the differences in results in terms of the difficulty levels of the tasks used.

EVOLUTIONARY THEORIES OF SPATIAL SEX DIFFERENCES

The first systematic, evolutionary-based theory of spatial sex differences was by Gaulin and Fitzgerald (1986). The core of the theory was that spatial abilities were more strongly selected for in males than females in polygynous species, for the reason that polygynous males require navigational skills to maintain large home ranges (the area within which an animal freely travels on a regular basis), in which to seek potential mates and resources to attract mates.

The investigators tested their theory with two species of voles: one, meadow voles, which are polygynous, and the other, pine voles, which feature an open promiscuous style. Findings were consistent with predictions; sex differences both in the direction of larger home ranges and superior maze learning ability for males occurred solely for meadow voles. In a follow-up study, Jacobs, Gaulin, Sherry, and Hoffman (1990) compared sex differences in size of hippocampus (which, as described earlier, has a significant role in the mediation of spatial functions) between these species and found, again as expected, proportionally larger male hippocampi in meadow voles but no sex difference in pine voles.

Does Gaulin and Fitzgerald's mating strategy theory pertain to humans? Moderate polygyny is characteristic of our species (Symons, 1979), and a review of the cross-cultural literature on sex differences in home range size showed a near universal male bias beginning at the toddler stage (Gaulin & Hoffman, 1988). Additional support comes from Ecuyer-Dab and Robert's (2004) finding that men tended to possess larger home ranges than women, as measured by retrospective and direct accounts of their comings and goings over extended time periods. Ecuyer-Dab and Robert posited also that if there was a "functional relation" between spatial abilities and home range size in males but not females, as inferred from Gaulin and Fitzgerald's model, correlations between the two variables should be found only in the male. This was demonstrated in their study and in earlier studies of African children (Munroe & Munroe, 1971; Nerlove, Munroe, & Munroe, 1971).

Silverman and Eals (1992) questioned, however, whether the relationship between home range size and reproductive success applied to the human case. The only data that bear on the question have shown that females exhibit greater *natal dispersal* (the distance traveled by an individual from natal site to first place of breeding) than their male counterparts (Koenig, 1989), which would contradict Gaulin and Fitzgerald's theory.

Silverman and Eals (1992; Eals & Silverman, 1994) posed an alternative theory, in which the critical factor in selection for human spatial sex differences was division of labor during the Pleistocene. During that era, considered to be the most significant in human evolution, males primarily hunted while females functioned as plant food gatherers, keepers of the habitat, and caretakers of the young (Tooby & DeVore, 1987).

Silverman and Eals noted that the various spatial tests showing the strongest male bias (e.g., field independence, mental rotations, maze learning) corresponded to attributes that would enable navigation by orientation. This would be essential for successful hunting, which requires the pursuit of prey animals across unfamiliar territory and the capacity to return by a fairly direct route. They contended further that if spatial attributes associated with hunting evolved in males, it is feasible that spatial specializations that would have facilitated their own roles in the division of labor would have evolved in females.

For food gathering, success would have required finding edible plants within diverse configurations of vegetation and locating them again in ensuing growing seasons, that is, the capacity to rapidly learn and remember the contents of object arrays and the relationships of objects to one another within these arrays. Success in gathering would also be increased by peripheral perception and incidental memory for objects and their locations, inasmuch as this would allow one to assimilate such information nonpurposively, while attending to other matters. Incidental object location memory would also be useful in tending to the domicile and offspring.

There is supporting physical evidence for this analysis. Women have larger visual fields than do men; that is, they can see farther out on the periphery while fixating on a central point (Burg, 1968). They are also better than men at scanning, excelling in various tests of perceptual speed (Kimura, 1999, pp. 87–88).

Silverman and Eals (1992; Eals & Silverman, 1994) developed several methods to compare sexes on their ability to learn spatial configurations of object arrays, all of which generally supported the hypothesized female advantage. These findings have been replicated or partially replicated in various laboratories and with various research designs (e.g., Choi & Silverman, 1996; Dabbs, Chang, Strong, & Milun, 1998; Eals & Silverman, 1994; Gaulin, Silverman, Phillips, & Reiber, 1997; James & Kimura, 1997; McBurney, Gaulin, Devineni, & Adams, 1997; McGivern et al., 1997), with the most consistent differences occurring for incidental location recall.

Cherney and Ryalls (1999) claimed to have failed to replicate this sex difference, using Silverman and Eals's method whereby subjects were tested on memory for object locations in the room that they had been led to believe was a waiting room for the experiment. Whereas Silverman and Eals excluded overtly gender-related objects from the so-called waiting room, Cherney and Ryalls intentionally included these, along with neutral control objects. The interaction they anticipated between sex of subject and gender-relatedness of object was obtained and suppressed any main effects of sex, but the data for the gender-neutral controls revealed a robust difference in favor of females. Thus, the most feasible conclusions from this study were that Silverman and Eals's sex difference was replicated, but it was shown that it could be tempered by the use of gender-biased items.

In comparing the two theories of spatial sex differences, Gaulin and Fitzgerald's (1986) has the advantage in that it applies to both human and infrahuman species. Silverman and Eals's (1992), however, provides testable hypotheses about female spatial specializations. Silverman and Eals (1992) suggested that the theories may be reconciled if it is presumed that in a given species or subspecies, any difference in selection pressures between sexes related to spatial behavior may result in an evolved dimorphism. Later in this discussion, however, we describe a more precise alternative means of integrating the theories, by Ecuyer-Dab and Robert (2004).

SEXUAL DIMORPHISM IN NAVIGATIONAL STRATEGIES

Consistent with the pattern of spatial sex differences described earlier, it has been demonstrated in numerous studies that males tend to use an orientation strategy in navigational tasks, while women use a landmark strategy (e.g., Bever, 1992; Choi & Silverman, 1996, 2003; Dabbs et al., 1998 ; Galea & Kimura, 1993; Holding & Holding, 1989; Joshi, MacLean, & Carter, 1999; Lawton, 1994, 1996, 2001; Lawton & Kallai, 2002; McGuiness & Sparks, 1983; Miller & Santoni, 1986; Moffat, Hampson, & Hatzipantelis, 1998; Schmitz, 1997; Ward, Newcombe, & Overton, 1986). Specifically, males use distances and cardinal directions—that is, north, south, east, and west—while females rely more on landmarks and relative directions such as right, left, in front of, and behind.

These differences have also been demonstrated with a variety of methods, including learning routes from maps or photographs, walking through mazes, retracing computer simulated routes on virtual mazes, drawing maps, giving directions, and finding the way back after being led along an unfamiliar indoor or outdoor route.

IDENTIFYING EVOLVED MECHANISMS

Evolved mechanisms tend to remain broadly defined at this early stage of theoretical development, and more exact definitions will entail a long-term, continuing process of theoretical refinement and data gathering. Some recent research by the present authors and their colleagues, however, may provide a first approximation of an evolved mechanism for navigation by orientation.

Silverman et al. (2000) reported a study in which subjects were led, individually, on a circuitous route through a heavily wooded area. During the walk, they were stopped periodically and required to set an arrow pointing to the place from where they began. Eventually, they were asked to lead the experimenters back to the starting point by the most direct route. Men's performances surpassed women's on all of these measures, and overall performance scores were significantly related across sexes to three-dimensional mental rotations scores, but not to nonrotational spatial abilities or to general intelligence. Moreover, mental rotations scores emerged as the sole significant predictor in a multiple regression analysis that included sex as an antecedent variable, suggesting that the variance in orientation ability associated with sex appears wholly attributable to mental rotations abilities.

What do mental rotations tests measure that may function as an evolved mechanism for navigation by orientation? According to the investigators, both mental rotations and navigation by orientation require that the individual maintain the integrity of a space while exposed to it from various viewpoints. A number of studies (Cochran & Wheatley, 1989; Freedman & Rovagno, 1981; Schulz, 1991) have shown that the sole method for solving mental rotations problems with any degree of efficacy is by visualizing the rotation in three-dimensional space of one object while comparing it to another. In this manner, the subject mentally peruses the periphery of the object from various perspectives while maintaining a mental representation of its whole. Silverman et al. (2000) suggested that this is comparable, in terms of the processes involved, to walking in the woods without specific direction, as in searching for or following a prey, while maintaining a mental representation of the boundaries of the route.

Based on this explanation, Silverman et al. considered that the evolved mechanism at the core of the relationship between mental rotations and navigation by orientation appeared to be some form of perceptual constancy, whereby, "the properties of objects tend to remain constant in consciousness although our perception of the viewing conditions may change" (Coren & Ward, 1989, p. 406). Thus, we revisit the illustrations described earlier of how perceptual illusions involving shape constancy reveal its modular properties. The particular constancy that may represent the domain-specific mechanism underlying navigation by orientation, according to Silverman et al., is *space constancy,* the capacity to maintain the stability of the surrounding environment while in locomotion (Bisiach, Pattini, Rusconi, Ricci, & Bernardini, 1997; Niemann & Hoffmann, 1997; Probst, Brandt, & Degner, 1986).

Further refinements of the role of space constancy in navigation by orientation may be informed by perceptual and neuropsychological studies. A complete explanation of the evolved mechanism, however, will also require consideration of environmental interactions, inasmuch as innately based behaviors are always expressed in an environmental context. In this regard, there is evidence using the Ames illusions that exposure to lines and angles during an early critical period is salient to the development of shape constancy (Allport & Pettigrew, 1957). Similarly, the propensity of males to occupy larger home ranges from the time they are mobile suggests that this is the environmental context in which space constancy develops. Thus, the definition of the evolved mechanism underlying navigation by orientation may ultimately be extended to include the predisposition and opportunity to move within an optimally large home range during a critical period for the development of space constancy.

ONE MECHANISM OR TWO?

The question arises as to whether the diverse navigational strategies of men and women represent one mechanism or two; that is, does the females' use of a landmark strategy represent an attempt to compensate for less developed orientation abilities, or is it part of a separate evolved mechanism related to greater proficiency in recalling object locations? The latter view would apply both to the females' greater use of landmarks than distances and to their greater use of relative rather than cardinal directions. Relative directions are more efficacious for recalling and describing the locations of objects in relation to one another within a relatively small space, while cardinal directions are more suitable for processing and describing the vectors denoting longer distances.

Many investigators accept the compensation interpretation (e.g., Galea & Kimura, 1993; Lawton, 1994; Miller & Santoni, 1986; Moffat et al., 1998). Silverman and Eals's hunter-gatherer theory, however, would suggest dual mechanisms. So, also, do the prior cited neurophysiological studies demonstrating different neural processes underlying orientation and landmark strategies. As well, Gur et al. (2000) has shown differential brain site activation between men and women engaged in a spatial task.

In another approach to the question, Choi and Silverman (1996) found that in a route learning task where the sexes performed equally well, success was predicted by preferences for landmarks and relative directions for females only and preferences for distances and cardinal directions for males only. Similarly, Saucier et al. (2002) administered laboratory and field navigational tasks in which participants were required, at the direction of the experimenter, to use either an orientation or a landmark strategy. Again, sexes did not differ in performance, but males did better when using an orientation strategy while females had higher scores with a landmark strategy. In both of these studies, the observation that sexes performed equally well when using their own strategies of choice suggests that the use of landmarks is not a default strategy, but an expression of a well-developed mechanism in itself.

What would be the nature of a separate evolved mechanism mediating the unique spatial attributes of women? Silverman and Phillips (1998, p. 603) suggest that it entails "a more inclusive attentional style," while Kimura (1999, p. 15) uses the term "efficient perceptual discriminations." There is an alternative view, however, which involves imagery rather than attention or perception. Eals and Silverman (1994) found that the markedly greater abilities of females to recall object locations within arrays pertained also to unfamiliar objects, for which they did not have verbal referents. This may suggest that females have the ability to encode and recall entire scenes, in detail, by a process akin to eidetic imagery. Data purporting to show a greater "power of visualizing" for females were first reported more than a century ago by Galton (1883), and similar reports have appeared through the years (e.g., Anastasi, 1958; Sheehan, 1967).

Thus, whereby the navigational mechanism for males enables them to create mental maps of extended spaces, to which they had never been directly exposed, the corresponding mechanism for females gives them the ability to mentally construct and recreate detailed maps of smaller, previously observed spaces. This would appear to represent a highly adaptive dimorphism for the evolution of hunters and gatherers, favoring Silverman and Eals's theory, but there is a complicating factor. Rats, also, feature the sex difference in navigational strategy. When navigating in radial-arm mazes, males are capable of using distal cues such as the shape of the room, while females require landmarks (Williams, Barnett, & Meck, 1990; Williams & Meck, 1991).

As noted earlier, Ecuyer-Dab and Robert (2004) have presented a revised theory, emanating from both Gaulin and Fitzgerald's and Silverman and Eals's, that accounts for such cross-species parallels. They proposed a *twofold selection process* underlying spatial sexual dimorphisms. For males, the critical selection factor is male-male reproductive competition, which tends to be more intense in polygynous societies and would have favored the evolution of spatial abilities essential for both orientation-type navigational strategies and the effective use of projectiles. These skills would have enabled resource provision of mates and offspring by means of hunting and aided in agonistic encounters with other males, both within and between groups.

For females, the paramount selection factor for the evolution of a landmark strategy is the need for physical security for themselves and their offspring.

The greater capacity to learn and recall details of the proximate environment, which is the basis of a landmark strategy, would have facilitated navigation within a relatively narrow home range and keener attention to cues regarding the presence of predators and other dangers. Such attributes would have also aided in finding and recalling possible hiding places or escape routes from these, which would have been particularly important when pregnant or tending small children. In this model, the greater capacity for food gathering of the female is a by-product, rather than the essential selection factor, in the evolution of her spatial specializations.

Ecuyer-Dab and Robert provide examples of these sex-specific spatial strategies, which appear to operate for these purposes, in various infrahuman species. They contend further that these observations probably generalize to most mammals. Thus, they have provided a theory that can encompass the findings from both Gaulin and Fitzgerald's and Silverman and Eals's and would appear to offer the most productive venue for further research.

LANDSCAPE PREFERENCE

Having considered the mechanisms of navigation, we turn now to a related issue: the choice of where to go. Questions about landscape preference have traditionally come from the study of aesthetics, but evolutionary-based theories and data suggest that this was also a critical aspect of survival for both human and animal life.

Habitat Selection

Deermice, a common North American rodent, can be divided into two types according to whether they inhabit grasslands or forests. In a classic study, Wecker (1963) built an outdoor enclosure, half consisting of a grassland and half a forest environment. He released two samples of grassland deermice into the center of the enclosure, one a group of wild-caught mice and the other their laboratory-reared offspring, to see which environment they would prefer. Both groups showed strong affinities for the grasslands.

These findings illustrate the presumed evolutionary processes underlying landscape preferences in both humans and infrahuman animals. Landscape preferences are manifestations of habitat preferences, which, in turn, were selected for on the basis of their capacity to meet the ecological requirements of the animal. These include food, water, shelter, weather, and protection from predators.

But does a deermouse experience anything like a human when exposed to a favored landscape? Human reactions to landscapes tend to be immediate, unequivocal, and highly emotional, a response pattern that is presumed to have evolved from the needs of our forbearers to make rapid decisions regarding the benefits versus dangers of potential new habitats (Orians & Heerwagen, 1992). The capacity of landscapes to evoke positive emotions remains with our species. For example, heart rates decrease during the viewing of video clips of natural, but not urban, scenes (Laumann, Garling, & Stormark, 2003). Postoperative patients in recovery rooms with pleasant, natural views have speedier and more positive recoveries than patients without such views (Ulrich, 1984). Numerous other studies also show the psychological and physiological restorative influences of exposure to natural landscapes (see Kaplan, 1995; Parsons, Tassinary, Ulrich, Hebl, & Grossman-Alexander, 1998; Ulrich, 1983, for reviews). Thus, given that the selection pressures operating on habitat selection of the ancestral deermouse were based on the same goals of survival and reproductive success as for the proto-human, we may reasonably expect that their physiological-based emotional responses to landscapes would be functionally similar.

THE SAVANNA THEORY

Although the task of identifying the habitats and consequent landscape preferences of deermice and most other animal species seems relatively straightforward, humans have been unique in their ability to colonize a diverse range of environments. One approach to this problem, taken by Orians (1980), is to posit that human landscape preferences evolved in the habitat where the species presumably originated, the African savanna. The savanna biome features clumps of acacia trees scattered across wide grassy plains. This would have provided the human inhabitant with a readily identifiable and accessible place for the gatherer to acquire quality food—the fruits of the trees. Trees could also be used to keep watch for both prey and predators and escape from the latter. They also serve as protection from the sun. Furthermore, the plains are suitable for grazing animals, which provide opportunity for the hunter (Orians & Heerwagon, 1992).

Orians and Heerwagon (1992) had subjects in the United States, Argentina, and Australia rate the attractiveness of acacia trees, which varied in terms of trunk height, branching pattern, and canopy density and shape. Acacia trees rated most attractive by all samples were those from areas of the savanna considered to be *high quality* in their general adaptive value for humans. These were characterized by moderately dense canopies and trunks that bifurcated near the ground, which would contribute both to ease of climbing and concealment.

Orians and Heerwagon also pointed to the recurrent nature of tropical savanna themes in landscape art. They quoted Humphrey Repton (1907, p. 105), a nineteenth-century pioneer of landscape architecture, who stated: "Those pleasing combinations of trees which we admire in forest scenery will often be found to consist of forked trees, or at least trees placed so near each other that the branches intermix . . ."

Further supporting data for the savanna hypothesis, albeit equivocal, were provided by Balling and Falk (1982). They used a series of 20 slides, encompassing five biomes: savanna, desert, and deciduous, tropical rain, and coniferous forest. Subject groups ranging in age from 8 to 70 rated each for desirability, both as a place to live and to visit. Overall, the slides of the savannah were rated significantly higher on both criteria, but beginning at age 15, savanna, deciduous, and coniferous forest landscapes were all virtually tied for highest preference scores. Balling and Falk interpreted their data as supportive of an innately based preference for the savanna, but one that may be altered by experience over the life span.

HABITAT IMPRINTING THEORY

Wecker's (1963) studies contained three additional subject groups to the wild-caught grassland deermice and their laboratory-raised progeny, discussed earlier. One of these comprised deermice bred in the laboratory for 20 generations. These animals did not show preferences for either the grassland or forest environments. The other two groups consisted of offspring of the laboratory-bred mice, who were reared until weaning either in a grassland or forest enclosure. The grassland-reared group exhibited a strong later preference for grasslands, while the forest-reared group showed no preference.

Wecker's overall conclusions were that early exposure to grasslands could instill grassland preferences in grassland deermice by means of *habitat imprinting* (Thorpe, 1945), although, as demonstrated by his previously described studies of laboratory-raised progeny of wild-caught grasslands deermice, it is not a necessary prerequisite. Grassland deermice did not, however, show corresponding habitat imprinting to a forest environment when they had been reared there. Thus, habitat imprinting was regarded as a "support" for innately based preferences.

Somewhat similar findings were reported by Klopfer (1963) for chipping sparrows. Wild-caught sparrows placed in an environment containing both pine and oak branches preferred the former, as they do in their natural habitat. Sparrows who had been reared as nestlings without exposure to any kind of foliage also preferred the pine. Sparrows reared as nestlings in the presence of oak leaves, however, did not show an initial preference for either pine or oak, though they did shift gradually to pine after several months of exposure to both.

AN ALTERNATIVE VIEW

Some may question whether habitat imprinting is an appropriate term for the processes described by Wecker and Klopfer. As traditionally defined, imprinting requires both an innate predisposition to imprint and exposure to the imprinted object within an early critical period (Moltz, 1960). Wecker's deermice and Klopfer's sparrows, however, showed preferences for their species' natural habitats without benefit of early exposure, though exposure did have effects on their choices under certain conditions.

Landscape preference, as exhibited by deermice, chipping sparrows, and humans, may be more coherently described as a hardwired response in the young animal, amenable to modification in later development. Thus, as observed by Orians and Heerwagon, younger human groups showed the expected, innately based, savanna preference while adolescent and older groups, based on experiential or maturational factors or both, showed affinities of equal intensity to some forest environments. This seems analogous to human food taste preferences. Virtually all individuals show preferences from infancy to sweet substances, which is explicable from an evolutionary standpoint based on the critical role of natural sugars in the prehistoric diet (Barash, 1982). By adolescence, however, most have developed alternative food tastes as well.

This does not mitigate the role of natural selection, either in food or landscape preferences. In both, later developing, alternate preferences also reflect fitness requirements. There is evidence that children from the age of weaning tend to choose a reasonably balanced, nutritional diet when fed cafeteria style (Davis, 1928). By the same token, landscape preferences alternative to the savanna may tend also to reflect fitness requirements, as suggested by the theories described in the following sections.

PROSPECT-REFUGE THEORY

One of the more prominent contributions in this vein is Appleton's (1975). Based on his analyses of landscape paintings, Appleton concluded that landscapes with high attraction value contained a balance between *prospect* and *refuge* features. Prospect features such as elevated landforms provide an overall view of the landscape and facilitate the search for food, water, and prey. Refuge features such as groupings of trees permit the individual to see without being seen and function mainly in the interests of security. In this theory, the most important aspect of the habitat is the spatial arrangement of environmental attributes, that is, landforms, trees, open spaces, and water, inasmuch as their arrangement determines whether prospect and refuge opportunities can be effectively utilized.

Attempts to test Appleton's theory by means of comparative landscape judgments have yielded equivocal results (e.g., Clamp & Powell, 1982; Heyligers, 1981), which is likely a function of the variation of possible spatial arrangements of prospect and refuge features (Appleton, 1988). Supporting data for the theory were obtained by Mealey and Theis (1995), however, based on their contention that the relative attraction value of prospect and refuge should vary within individuals in accordance with their moods. Positive moods, they maintained, would induce a need to explore and take risks for the sake of future benefits and would thus be associated with prospect. Negative moods would give rise to a need for security and rest and would thereby be associated with refuge. As predicted, subjects reporting positive moods preferred landscapes with vast expanses and overviews, while subjects reporting mood dysphoria preferred landscapes with enclosed, protected spaces.

MYSTERY AND COMPLEXITY

Kaplan and Kaplan's (1982) analysis appears to stand in sharp contrast to the emphasis on security and simplicity in all of the theories noted earlier. In addition to *coherence,* referring to organization of the scene, and *legibility,* meaning how easily an individual can navigate within the landscape depicted, the authors included *mystery* and *complexity* as key, evolutionary-based elements of attraction in human landscape preference. Their reasoning was based on the adaptive function of curiosity for the species, particularly the predisposition to seek new information about the environment that can facilitate its mastery.

Some studies based on Kaplan and Kaplan's notions have revealed preferences for mystery, as represented by winding forest paths or obscure coves (Herzog, 1988; Kaplan, 1992). As for complexity, moderate levels appear to evoke the strongest preference levels (see Ulrich, 1983).

FUTURE DIRECTIONS

As in the case of spatial navigation, the ultimate issue for an evolutionary theory of landscape preferences is how best to conceptualize the evolved cognitive mechanisms that mediate these. All theories seem to imply a mechanism similar to the ethological construct of *innate schemata,* that is, a mental image of an ideal landscape that serves as standard for judgment. The theories differ, however, in the substance of this image. Orians maintains that it is a copy of the specific landscape in which humans evolved, while both Appleton's and Kaplan and Kaplan's theories imply that it can be any landscape type that contains features that signal fitness-related opportunities. Modern measures of brain site activation may provide a more precise methodology for the comparison of emotional responses to landscapes and thereby help to resolve this issue.

There is also a general methodological problem that needs to be addressed. Wilson, Robertson, Daly, and Wilson (1995) point to the confounds that may readily attend any attempt to compare the preference values of specific features between scenes, which has been the customary method of testing hypotheses derived from both Appleton's and Kaplan and Kaplan's theories. For example, scenes considered high in mystery by the experimenter may simply have lower and more pleasing brightness levels. Those that are judged high in refuge may be preferred by subjects simply because they are greener or more lush.

This critique may apply to studies comparing preferences for biomes in entirety, as well as to studies comparing specific features. For example, the greater preference of the savanna by preadolescents found by Balling and Falk (1982) may reflect a preference for structural simplicity in this age group.

Wilson et al. (1995) suggest a methodology whereby the same scene is manipulated so that just one feature is modified at a time, thereby allowing control of potential confounds. By this means, they were able to establish that small and subtle cues as to the water quality of seascapes have a marked effect on attraction value.

Finally, landscape preference studies that have included urban landscapes (Kaplan et al., 1972; Laumann et al., 2003; Parsons et al., 1998; Purcell, Lamb, Peron, & Falchero, 1994; Ulrich, 1981, 1983) have universally found strong preferences favoring rural scenes of any type, by both urban and rural dwellers. Ulrich (1983) concluded that the distributions of preference ratings between rural and urban scenes barely overlap, even when ordinary rural scenes are compared to urban scenes that are particularly picturesque.

This finding, in itself, provides broad support for an evolutionary perspective on landscape aesthetics in that it suggests the profound influence of prehistoric origins, even when pitted directly against life experiences. It points also to the potential adverse effects of living in the unnatural environment of high-density urban centers, particularly in light of the previously described data on the effects of landscape exposure on psychological and physical well-being.

CONCLUSIONS

The application of the evolutionary model to human navigation and landscape preference represents a relatively recent movement in the behavioral sciences, though the burgeoning theory and data reviewed in this chapter are testimony to its relevance. This review has also highlighted two major aspects of the movement: (1) the salience of an ethological approach, which has provided compelling insights about analogous processes mediating human and infrahuman adaptations in these areas, and (2) the conceptual utility of evolutionary psychology's model of mind as composed of evolved, domain-specific mechanisms.

REFERENCES

Alcock, J. A. (1984). *Animal behavior: An evolutionary approach* (3rd ed.). Sunderland, MA: Sinauer.

Allport, G. W., & Pettigrew, T. F. (1957). Cultural influence on the perception of movement: The trapezoidal illusion among Zulus. *Journal of Abnormal and Social Psychology, 55,* 104–113.

Anastasi, A. (1958). *Differential psychology* (3rd ed.). New York: Macmillan.

Annooshian, L. J., & Young, D. (1981). Developmental changes in cognitive maps of a familiar neighborhood. *Child Development, 52,* 341–348.

Appleton, J. (1975). *The experience of landscapes.* Great Britain: William Clowes and Sons.

Appleton, J. (1988). Prospects and refuges revisited. In J. L. Nasar (Ed.), *Environmental aesthetics: Theory, research and applications* (pp. 27–44). Cambridge: Cambridge University Press.

Balda, R. P., & Kamil, A. C. (1988). The spatial memory of Clark's nutcrackers: *Nucifraga Columbiana* in an analogue of the radial arm maze. *Animal Learning and Behavior, 16,* 116–122.

Balling, J. D., & Falk, J. H. (1982). Development of visual preference for natural environments. *Environment and Behaviour, 14,* 5–28.

Barash, D. P. (1982). *Sociobiology and behavior.* New York: Elsevier.

Barrett, R. J., & Ray, O. S. (1970). Behavior in the open field, Lashley III maze, shuttle box and Sidman avoidance as a function of strain, sex, and age. *Developmental Psychology, 3,* 73–77.

Berry, J. W. (1966). Temme and Eskimo perceptual skills. *International Journal of Psychology, 1,* 207–229.

Bever, T. (1992). The logical and extrinsic sources of modularity. In M. Gunnar & M. Maratsos (Eds.), *Modularity and constraints in language and cognition: Volume 25 of Minnesota symposia on child psychology* (pp. 179–212). Hillsdale: Lawrence Earlbaum.

Binnie-Dawson, J. L. M., & Cheung, Y. M. (1982). The effects of different types of neonatal feminization and environmental stimulation on changes in sex associated activity/spatial learning skills. *Biological Psychology, 15,* 109–140.

Bisiach, E., Pattini, P., Rusconi, M. L., Ricci, R., & Bernardini, B. (1997). Unilateral neglect and space constancy during passive locomotion. *Cortex, 33,* 313–322.

Blades, M., & Medlicott, L. (1992). Developmental differences in the ability to give route directions from a map. *Environmental Psychology, 12,* 175–185.

Bouchard, T. J., Jr., Segal, N. L., & Lykken, D. T. (1990). Genetic and environmental influences on special mental abilities in a sample of twins reared apart. *Acta Geneticae Medica Gemellologiae, 39,* 193–206.

Burg, A. (1968). Lateral visual field as related to age and sex. *Journal of Applied Psychology, 52,* 10–15.

Burstein, B., Bank, L., & Jarvik, L. F. (1980). Sex differences in cognitive functioning: Evidence, determinants, implications. *Human Development, 23,* 299–313.

Cherney, I. D., & Ryalls, B. O. (1999). Gender-linked differences in incidental memory of children and adults. *Journal of Experimental Child Psychology, 72,* 305–328.

Choi, J., & Silverman, I. (1996). Sexual dimorphism in spatial behaviours: Applications to route learning. *Evolution and Cognition, 2,* 165–171.

Choi, J., & Silverman, I. (2002). The relationship between testosterone and route-learning strategies in humans. *Brain and Cognition, 50,* 116–120.

Choi, J., & Silverman, I. (2003). Processes underlying sex differences in route-learning strategies in children and adolescents. *Personality and Individual Differences, 34,* 1153–1166.

Clamp, P., & Powell, M. (1982). Prospect-refuge theory under test. *Landscape Research, 7,* 7–8.

Cochran, K. F., & Wheatley, G. H. (1989). Ability and sex-related differences in cognitive strategies on spatial tasks. *Journal of General Psychology, 116,* 43–55.

Coren, S., & Ward, L. M. (1989). *Sensation and Perception* (3rd ed.). Toronto: Harcourt Brace Jovanovich.

Cosmides, L., & Tooby, J. (1992). Cognitive adaptations for social exchange. In J. H. Barkow, L. Cosmides, & L. Tooby (Eds.), *The adapted mind: Evolutionary psychology and the generation of culture* (pp. 163–228). New York: Oxford University Press.

Dabbs, J. M., Chang, E. L., Strong, R. A., & Milun, R. (1998). Spatial ability, navigation strategy, and geographic knowledge among men and women. *Evolution and Human Behavior, 19,* 89–98.

Davis, C. (1928). Self selection of diet by newly weaned infants. *American Journal of Diseases of Children, 36,* 651–679.

Defries, J. C., Ashton, G. C., Johnson, R. C., Kuse, A. R., McClearn, G. E., Mi, M. P., et al. (1976). Parent offspring resemblance for specific cognitive abilities in two ethnic groups. *Nature, 261,* 131–133.

Drickamer, L. C., & Vessey, S. H. (1986). *Animal behavior: Concepts, processes and methods.* Boston: Prindle, Weber and Schmidt.

Eals, M., & Silverman, I. (1994). The hunter-gatherer theory of spatial sex differences: Proximate factors mediating the female advantage in recall of object arrays. *Ethology and Sociobiology, 15,* 95–105.

Ecuyer-Dab, I., & Robert, M. (2004a). Spatial ability and home range size. *Journal of Comparative Psychology, 118,* 217–231.

Ecuyer-Dab, I., & Robert, M. (2004b). Have sex differences in spatial ability evolved from male competition for mating and female concern for survival? *Cognition, 91,* 221–257.

Eichenbaum, H., Stewart, C., & Morrisa, R. G. M. (1990). Hippocampal representation in place learning. *Journal of Neuroscience, 10,* 3531–3542.

Fodor, J. A. (1983). *The modularity of mind.* Cambridge, MA: MIT Press.

Freedman, R. J., & Rovagno, L. (1981). Ocular dominance, cognitive strategy, and sex differences in spatial ability. *Perceptual and Motor Skills, 52,* 651–654.

Galea, L. A. M., & Kimura, D. (1993). Sex differences in route-learning. *Personality and Individual Differences, 14,* 53–65.

Gallistel, C. R. (1990). *The organization of learning.* Cambridge, MA: MIT Press.

Galton, F. (1883). *Inquiries into human faculty and its development.* London: Macmillan.

Garcia, J., Ervin, F. R., & Koelling, R. A. (1966). Learning with prolonged delay in reinforcement. *Psychonomic Science, 5,* 121–122.

Garcia, J., & Koelling, R. A. (1966). Relation of cue to consequence in avoidance learning. *Psychonomic Science, 4,* 123–124.

Gaulin, S. J. C., & Fitzgerald, R. W. (1986). Sex differences in spatial ability: An evolutionary hypothesis and test. *The American Naturalist, 127,* 74–88.

Gaulin, S. J. C., & Hoffman, H. A. (1988). Evolution and development of sex differences in spatial ability. In L. Betzig, M. B. Mulder, & P. Turke (Eds.), *Human reproductive behavior: A Darwinian perspective* (pp. 129–152). Cambridge, MA: Cambridge University Press.

Gaulin, S. J. C., Silverman, I., Phillips, K., & Reiber, C. (1997). Activational hormone influences on abilities and attitudes: Implications for evolutionary theory. *Evolution and Cognition, 3,* 191–199.

Gouchie, C., & Kimura, D. (1991). The relationship between testosterone levels and cognitive ability patterns. *Psychoneuroendocrinology, 16,* 323–324.

Gur, R. C., Alsop, D., Giahn, D., Petty, R., Swanson, C. L., Maldjian, J. A., et al. (2000). An fMRI study of sex differences in regional activation to as verbal and a spatial task. *Brain and Language, 74,* 157–170.

Halpern, D. F. (1992). *Sex differences in cognitive abilities* (2nd ed.). Hillsdale: Erlbaum.

Hampson, E., & Kimura, D. (1992). Sex differences and hormonal influences on cognitive function in humans. In J. B. Becker, S. M. Breedlove, & D. Crews (Eds.), *Behavioural endocrinology* (pp. 357–398). Cambridge, MA: MIT Press.

Herzog, T. (1988). Danger, mystery and environmental preference. *Environment and Behavior, 20,* 320–344.

Heyligers, P. C. (1981). Prospect-refuge symbolism in dune landscapes. *Landscape Research, 6,* 7–11.

Hilton, S. C., & Krebs, J. R. (1990). Spatial memory of four species of *Parus:* Performance in an open-field analogue of a radial maze. *Quarterly Journal of Experimental Psychology, 42,* 345–368.

Holding, C. S., & Holding, D. H. (1989). Acquisition of route network knowledge by males and females. *Journal of General Psychology, 116,* 29–41.

Holldobbler, B. (1980). Canopy orientation: A new kind of orientation in ants. *Science, 210,* 86–88.

Ittleson, W. (1952). *The Ames demonstrations in perception.* Princeton, NJ: Princeton University Press.

Jacobs, L. F., Gaulin, S. J. C., Sherry, D., & Hoffman, G. E. (1990). Evolution of spatial cognition: Sex-specific patterns of spatial behavior predict hippocampal size. *Proceedings of the National Academy of Science, USA, 87,* 6349–6352.

Jahoda, G. (1980). Sex and ethnic differences on a spatial-perceptual task: Some hypotheses tested. *British Journal of Psychology, 71,* 425–431.

James, T. W., & Kimura, D. (1997). Sex differences in remembering the locations of objects in an array: Location-shift versus location-exchanges. *Evolution and Human Behavior, 18,* 155–163.

Janowsky, J. S., Oviatt, S. K., & Orwoll, E. S. (1994). Testosterone influences spatial cognition in older men. *Behavioral Neuroscience, 108,* 325–332.

Janson, C. H. (1998). Experimental evidence for spatial memory in foraging wild capuchin monkeys. *Animal Behavior, 55,* 1129–1143.

Janson, C. H. (2000). Spatial movement strategies: Theory, evidence and challenges. In S. Boinski & P. A. Garber (Eds.), *On the move: How and why animals travel in groups* (pp. 165–203). Chicago: University of Chicago Press.

Johnson, E. S., & Meade, A. C. (1987). Developmental patterns of spatial ability: An early sex difference. *Child Development, 58,* 725–740.

Joseph, R., Hess, S., & Birecree, E. (1978). Effects of hormone manipulation and exploration on sex differences in maze learning. *Behavioral Biology, 24,* 364–377.

Joshi, M. S., MacLean, M., & Carter, W. (1999). Children's journey to school: Spatial skills, knowledge and perceptions of the environment. *British Journal of Developmental Psychology, 17,* 125–139.

Kaplan, S. (1992). Environmental preference in a knowledge-seeking, knowledge-using organism. In J. H. Barkow, L. Cosmides, & J. Tooby (Eds.), *The adapted mind: Evolutionary psychology and the generation of culture* (pp. 581–598). New York: Oxford University Press.

Kaplan, S. (1995). The restorative benefits of nature: Toward an integrative framework. *Journal of Environmental Psychology, 15,* 169–182.

Kaplan, S., & Kaplan, R. (1982). *Cognition and environment: Functioning in an uncertain world.* New York: Praeger.

Kaplan, S., Kaplan, R., & Wendt, J. S. (1972). Rated preference and complexity for natural and urban visual material. *Perception and Psychophysics, 12,* 354–356.

Kimura, D. (1999). *Sex and cognition.* Cambridge, MA: MIT Press.

Kimura, D., & Hampson, E. (1993). Neural and hormonal mechanisms mediating sex differences in cognition. In P. A. Vernon (Ed.), *Biological approaches to the study of human intelligence* (pp. 375–397). Norwood, NJ: ABLEX Publishers.

Klopfer, P. H. (1963). Behavioral aspects of habitat selection: The role of early experience. *Wilson Bulletin, 75,* 15–22.

Koenig, W. D. (1989). Sex biased dispersal in the contemporary United States. *Ethology and Sociobiology, 10,* 263–278.

Landau, B., & Gleitman, L. R. (1985). *Language and experience: Evidence from the blind child.* Cambridge, MA: Harvard University Press.

Laumann, K., Garling, T., & Stormark, K. M. (2003). Selective attention and heart rate responses to natural and urban environments. *Journal of Environmental Psychology, 23,* 125–134.

Lawton, C. A. (1994). Gender differences in way-finding strategies: Relationship to spatial ability and spatial anxiety. *Sex Roles, 30,* 765–779.

Lawton, C. A. (1996). Strategies for indoor wayfinding: The role of orientation. *Journal of Environmental Psychology, 16,* 137–145.

Lawton, C. A. (2001). Gender and regional differences in spatial referents used in direction giving. *Sex Roles, 44,* 321–337.

Lawton, C. A., & Kallai, J. (2002). Gender differences in wayfinding strategies and anxiety about wayfinding: A cross-cultural comparison. *Sex Roles, 47,* 389–401.

Linn, M. C., & Peterson, A. C. (1985). Emergence and characterization of sex differences in spatial ability: A meta-analysis. *Child Development, 56*, 1479–1498.

Lynn, R. (1992). Sex differences on the differential aptitude test in British and American adolescents. *Educational Psychology, 12*, 101–106.

Maguire, E. A., Burgess, N., Donnett, J. G., Frackowiak, R. S. J., Frith, C. D., & O'Keefe, J. (1998). Knowing where and getting there: A human navigation network. *Science, 280*, 921–924.

Maguire, E. A., Frackowiak, R. S. J., & Frith, C. D. (1996). Learning to find your way: A role for the human hippocampal formation. *Proceedings of the Royal Society of London. Series B, Biological Sciences, 263*, 1745–1750.

Mann, V. A., Sasanuma, S., Sakuma, N., & Masaki, S. (1990). Sex differences in cognitive abilities: A cross-cultural perspective. *Neuropsychologia, 28*, 1063–1077.

McBurney, D. H., Gaulin, S. J. C., Devineni, T., & Adams, C. (1997). Superior spatial memory of women: Stronger evidence for the gathering hypothesis. *Evolution and Human Behavior, 18*, 165–174.

McGee, M. G. (1979). Human spatial abilities: Psychometric studies and environmental, genetic, hormonal and neurological influences. *Psychological Bulletin, 80*, 889–918.

McGivern, R. F., Huston, J. P., Byrd, D., King, T., Siegle, G. J., & Reilly, J. (1997). Sex related differences in attention in adults and children. *Brain and Cognition, 34*, 323–336.

McGuiness, D., & Morley, C. (1991). Sex differences in the development of visuo-spatial abilities in pre-school children. *Journal of Mental Imagery, 15*, 143–150.

McGuiness, D., & Sparks, J. (1983). Cognitive style and cognitive maps: Sex differences in representations of a familiar terrain. *Journal of Mental Imagery, 7*, 91–100.

Mealey, L., & Theis, P. (1995). The relationship between mood and preferences among natural landscapes: An evolutionary perspective. *Ethology and Sociobiology, 16*, 247–256.

Menzel, C. R. (1991). Cognitive aspects of foraging in Japanese monkeys. *Animal Behavior, 41*, 397–402.

Miller, L. K., & Santoni, V. (1986). Sex differences in spatial abilities: Strategic and experiential correlates. *Acta Psychologica, 62*, 225–235.

Moffat, S. D., Hampson, E., & Hatzipantelis, M. (1998). Navigation in a "virtual" maze: Sex differences and correlation with psychometric measures of spatial ability in humans. *Evolution and Human Behavior, 19*, 73–87.

Moltz, H. (1960). Imprinting: Empirical basis and theoretical significance. *Psychological Bulletin, 57*, 291–314.

Muller, R. U., Bostock, E. M., Taube, J. S., & Kubie, J. L. (1994). On the directional firing properties of hippocampal place cells. *Journal of Neuroscience, 4*, 7235–7251.

Munroe, R. L., & Munroe, R. H. (1971). Effect of environmental experience on spatial ability in an East African society. *Journal of Social Psychology, 83*, 15–22.

Nerlove, S. B., Munroe, R. H., & Munroe, R. L. (1971). Effects of environmental experience on spatial ability: A replication. *Journal of Social Psychology, 84*, 3–10.

Niemann, T., & Hoffmann, K. P. (1997). Motion processing for saccadic eye movements during the visually induced sensation of ego-motion in humans. *Vision Research, 37*, 3163–3170.

Nyborg, H. (1983). Spatial ability in men and women: Review and new theory. *Advances in Behaviour Research and Theory, 5*, 89–140.

Nyborg, H. (1984). Performances and intelligence in hormonally different groups. In G. J. DeVries, J. DeBruin, H. Uylings, & M. Cormer (Eds.), *Progress in brain research* (Vol. 61, pp. 491–508). Amsterdam: Elsevier Science.

Okeefe, J., & Nadel, L. (1978). *The Hippocampus as a cognitive map*. Oxford, England: Clarendon.

Ono, T., & Nishijo, H. (1999). Active spatial information processing in the septo-hippocampal system. *Hippocampus, 9*, 458–466.

Orians, G. H. (1980). Habitat selection: General theory and applications to human behaviour. In J. S. Lockard (Ed.), *The evolution of human social behaviour* (pp. 49–66). New York: Elsevier North Holland.

Orians, G. H., & Heerwagen, J. H. (1992). Evolved responses to landscapes. In J. H. Barkow, L. Cosmides, & J. Tooby (Ed.), *The adapted mind: Evolutionary psychology and the generation of culture* (pp. 555–579). New York: Oxford University Press.

Parsons, R., Tassinary, L. G., Ulrich, R. S., Hebl, M. R., & Grossman-Alexander, M. (1998). The view from the road: Implication for stress recovery and immunization. *Journal of Environmental Psychology, 18*, 113–139.

Phillips, K., & Silverman, I. (1997). Differences in the relationship of menstrual cycle phase to spatial performance on two- and three-dimensional tasks. *Hormones and Behavior, 32*, 167–175.

Pizzamiglio, L., Guariglia, C., & Cosentino, T. (1998). Evidence for separate allocentric and ego-centric space processing in neglect patients. *Cortex, 34,* 719–730.

Plomin, R., Pederson, N. L., Lichtenstein, P., & McClearn, G. E. (1994). Variability and stability in cognitive abilities are largely genetic later in life. *Behavior Genetics, 24,* 207–215.

Porteus, S. D. (1965). *Porteus Maze Test: Fifty years application.* Palo Alto, CA: Pacific Books.

Probst, T., Brandt, T., & Degner, D. (1986). Object motion detection affected by concurrent self-motion perception. *Behavioural and Brain Research, 22,* 1–11.

Purcell, A. T., Lamb, R. J., Peron, E. M., & Falchero, S. (1994). Preference or preferences for landscape? *Environmental Psychology, 14,* 195–209.

Rainey, R. C. (1962). The mechanisms of desert locust swarm movements and the migration of insects. *Proceedings of the XVth International Congress of Entomology, 3,* 47–49.

Reinish, J., Ziemba-Davis, M., & Saunders, S. (1991). Hormonal contributions to sexually dimorphic behavioral development in humans. *Psychoneuroendocrinology, 16,* 213–278.

Repton, H. (1907). *The art of landscape gardening.* Boston: Houghton-Mifflin.

Rolls, E. T., Robertson, R. G., & Georges-Francois, P. (1997). Spatial view cells in the primate hippocampus. *European Journal of Neuroscience, 9,* 1789–1794.

Saucier, D. M., Green, S. M., Leason, J., MacFadden, A., Bell, S., & Elias, L. J. (2002). Are sex differences in navigation caused by sexually dimorphic strategies or by differences in the ability to use the strategies? *Behavioral Neuroscience, 116,* 403–410.

Schmitz, S. (1997). Gender-related strategies in environmental development: Effects of anxiety on wayfinding in and representation of a three-dimensional maze. *Journal of Environmental Psychology, 17,* 215–228.

Scholnick, E. K., Fein, G. G., & Campbell, P. F. (1990). Changing predictors of map use in wayfinding. *Developmental Psychology, 26,* 188–193.

Schulz, K. (1991). The contribution of solution strategy to spatial performance. *Canadian Journal of Psychology, 45,* 474–491.

Sheehan, P. Q. (1967). A shortened form of Betts' questionnaire upon mental imagery. *Journal of Clinical Psychology, 23,* 386–389.

Silverman, I., Choi, J., MacKewn, A., Fisher, M., Moro, J., & Olshansky, E. (2000). Evolved mechanisms underlying wayfinding: Further studies on the hunter-gatherer theory of spatial sex differences. *Evolution and Human Behavior, 21,* 201–213.

Silverman, I., & Eals, M. (1992). Sex differences in spatial abilities: Evolutionary theory and data. In J. H. Barkow, L. Cosmides, & J. Tooby (Eds.), *The adapted mind: Evolutionary psychology and the generation of culture* (pp. 531–549). New York: Oxford Press.

Silverman, I., Kastuk, D., Choi, J., & Phillips, K. (1999). Testosterone levels and spatial ability in men. *Psychoneuroendocrinology, 24,* 813–822.

Silverman, I., & Phillips, K. (1993). Effects of estrogen changes during the menstrual cycle on spatial performance. *Ethology and Sociobiology, 14,* 250–270.

Silverman, I., & Phillips, K. (1998). The evolutionary psychology of spatial sex differences. In C. Crawford & D. L. Krebs (Eds.), *Handbook of evolutionary psychology: Ideas, issues and applications* (pp. 595–611). Mahwah, NJ: Erlbaum.

Silverman, I., Phillips, K., & Silverman, L. K. (1996). Homogeneity of effect sizes for sex across spatial tests and cultures: Implications for hormonal theories. *Brain and Cognition, 31,* 90–94.

Symons, D. (1979). *The evolution of human sexuality.* Oxford, England: Oxford University Press.

Tambs, K., Sundet, J. M., & Magnus, P. (1984). Heritability analysis of the WAIS Subtests: A study of twins. *Intelligence, 8,* 283–293.

Taube, J. S. (1995). Head direction cells recorded in the anterior thalamic nuclei in freely moving rats. *Journal of Neurosciences, 15,* 70–86.

Taube, J. S. (1998). Head directional cells and the neurophysiological basis for a sense of direction. *Progress in Neurobiology, 3,* 225–256.

Taube, J. S., Muller, R. U., & Ranck, J. B. (1990). Head direction cells recorded from the post-subiculum in freely moving rats: Description and qualitative analysis. *Journal of Neurosciences, 10,* 420–435.

Thinus-Blanc, C., Save, E., Pucet, B., & Buhot, M. C. (1991). The effects of reversible inactivations of the hippocampus on exploratory activity and spatial memory. *Hippocampus, 1,* 365–371.

Thorndike, P. W., & Hayes-Roth, B. (1980). Differences in spatial knowledge acquired from maps and navigation. Santa Monica, CA: Rand Corporation.

Thorpe, W. H. (1945). The evolutionary significance of habitat selection. *Journal of Animal Ecology, 14,* 67–70.

Tooby, J., & DeVore, I. (1987). The reconstruction of hominid behavioral evolution through strategic modeling. In W. G. Kinzey (Ed.), *The evolution of human behavior: Primate models*. New York: SUNY Press.

Ulrich, R. S. (1981). Natural vs. urban scenes: Some psychophysiological effects. *Environment and Behavior, 13,* 523–556.

Ulrich, R. S. (1983). Aesthetic and affective response to natural environment. In I. Altman & J. F. Wohlwill (Ed.), *Human behaviour and environment: Advances in theory and research* (pp. 85–125). New York: Plenum Press.

Ulrich, R. S. (1984). View through a window may influence recovery from surgery. *Science, 224,* 420–421.

Vandenburg, S. G. (1969). A twin study of spatial ability. *Multivariate Behavioral Research, 273–294.*

von Frisch, K. (1967). *The dance language and orientation of bees.* Cambridge, MA: Harvard University Press.

Voyer, D., Voyer, S., & Bryden, M. P. (1995). Magnitude of sex differences in spatial abilities: A meta-analysis and consideration of critical variables. *Psychological Bulletin, 117,* 250–270.

Ward, S. L., Newcombe, N., & Overton, W. F. (1986). Turn left at the church, or three miles north: A study of direction giving and sex differences. *Environment and Behaviour, 18,* 192–213.

Wecker, S. C. (1963). The role of early experience in habitat selection by the prairie deermouse. *Peromyscus maniculatus bairdi: Ecological Monographs, 33,* 307–325.

Williams, C. L., Barnett, A. M., & Meck, W. H. (1990). Organizational effects of early gonadal secretions on sexual differentiation of spatial memory. *Behavioral Neuroscience, 104,* 84–97.

Williams, C. L., & Meck, W. H. (1991). The organizational effects of gonadal steroids on sexually dimorphic spatial ability. *Psychoneuroendocrinology, 16,* 155–176.

Willis, S. L., & Schaie, K. W. (1988). Gender differences in spatial ability in old age: Longitudinal and intervention findings. *Sex Roles, 18,* 189–203.

Wilson, M. I., Robertson, L. D., Daly, M., & Wilson, S. A. (1995). Effects of visual cues on water assessment of water quality. *Journal of Environmental Psychology, 15,* 53–63.

CHAPTER 7

Adaptations to Predators and Prey

H. CLARK BARRETT

IMAGINE THAT YOU are a human forager, several hundred thousand years ago, moving through a complex habitat such as semiopen forest or savanna. All around you is movement: waves of breeze through the tall grass, branches, and leaves casting moving shadows across the ground and the occasional bird flitting from tree to tree. Suddenly, something moving in the grass beside the path ahead of you catches your attention. You freeze. A few moments later a dark shape becomes visible. Given its size and motion, you infer that it is an animal. But what kind of animal? Is it a predator, a game animal that you might pursue, or perhaps another human? Has it seen you? And if so, what are its intentions? Slowly, it begins to move toward you . . .

In the past, and until quite recently, a typical human would have experienced thousands of such encounters during the course of his or her life. Successfully negotiating such an encounter, be it with a predator or with a prey animal, would have required bringing to bear mechanisms and skills at all levels of cognitive architecture, from specialized detection devices in perceptual systems, to emotional responses controlling the allocation of cognitive resources, to decision-making and motor control systems. These mechanisms were shaped by millions of years of predator-prey encounters, in some cases since long before we were human. As a result, we all carry with us sophisticated perceptual and inferential machinery for dealing with predators and prey, despite the fact that most of us will rarely, if ever, use it for the purposes for which it evolved. This chapter reviews strands of research from many fields that are beginning to uncover the design features of this machinery.

PREDATORS AND PREY AS AGENTS OF SELECTION

Initially, it might seem difficult to imagine that predators and prey could have played a significant role in the evolution of the human mind, given how marginal they are in our daily lives today. From the vantage point of our offices and living rooms, we are prone to discounting the risk of injury or death by predation and

200

the skills required to capture an animal with nothing but our wits and tools of our own making. But a few moments of reflection reveal several reasons that it is likely that predators and prey were important agents of selection on ancestral humans. First, encounters with predators and prey were likely to have been much more commonplace in ancestral environments than they are today. Second, there are few interactions that have greater immediate fitness impacts on organisms than encounters with predators, with their concomitant risks of injury and possibly death, and encounters with prey, in which food acquisition is at stake. Just as there can be selection for a drowning reflex even if most people never drown—or even are at risk of drowning—so the extreme fitness consequences of even rare predator encounters can be a source of selection. Conversely, although the fitness consequences of failing to capture prey might be small over the short term, the fitness impacts over the long run, such as effects on mating success and ability to provision offspring, are likely to have been substantial. Predators and prey would have posed challenging adaptive problems for human cognitive systems, some of which would be poorly solved by preexisting mechanisms (e.g., feedback-based learning is not particularly useful when confronted by a lion for the first time). Predator and prey species are exquisitely adapted to achieve their goals of prey capture and predator evasion, and the adaptations they bring to bear in the service of these goals pose challenges to humans that would have shaped our own prey capture and predator evasion capacities in a coevolutionary arms race (Van Valen, 1973).

Dangerous animals have coexisted with our ancestors since long before we were human. The archaeological record has permitted reconstructions of the array of predators in ancestral environments at various points in space and time (e.g., Blumenschine, 1987; Rose & Marshall, 1986). This array included fast-moving mammalian predators such as felids (cats) and hyaenids (hyenas). Although some currently extant predator species from these taxa were present as far back as the Plio-Pleistocene (~5mya), there existed in the past other species of felid and hyaenid that are now extinct. The diversity of predators in past environments was even higher than today (Blumenschine, 1987; Bunn, 1994; Isaac, 1968). Human encounters with predators occurred in several contexts, including hunting of humans by predators and competitive interactions between humans and predators over kills (Brain, 1981; Brantingham, 1998; Rose & Marshall, 1996; Shipman, 1986; for recent reviews, see Stanford & Bunn, 2001). In modern environments, where the ranges of humans and predators such as large cats overlap and human activities such as hunting and foraging bring them into close proximity with predators, attacks occur regularly (Kruuk, 2002; Treves & Naughton-Treves, 1999). Together, these data suggest that cognitive mechanisms involved in predator detection and evasion would have been under selection in our lineage both before and after the origin of *Homo sapiens*.

In addition to the role of prey, humans can adopt the role of predator. Hunting is a subsistence practice in every known preagricultural society and is practiced by our closest evolutionary relatives, chimpanzees. Moreover, the archaeological record suggests that meat has been an important part of human and hominid diets for millions of years. Increased reliance on meat, a risky, high-variance food source, may have played an important role in the evolution of human sociality and social cognition (Cosmides, 1989; Stanford, 1999). Humans were certainly hunting part time by at least 1.5 million years ago and probably since long before that. For example, Shipman (1986), in a sample of animal remains from a Plio-Pleistocene site at Olduvai Gorge, found that bones processed first by humans using stone tools co-occurred with bones processed first by mammalian carnivores and later by humans, suggesting that humans were not only hunting by this time but also probably in competition with carnivores for kills. There are many other sources of archaeological evidence that humans could and did kill game animals, either with tools or by other means, and that they hunted a wide variety of prey, from large, fast ungulates to small rabbits and birds, which would have required diverse strategies and intuitive understanding of prey behavior (Bunn, 1994; Isaac, 1968; Mithen, 1996; Potts, 1989; Stanford & Bunn, 2001).

WHAT SKILLS DO PREDATORS AND PREY SELECT FOR?

To understand the kinds of cognitive capacities and mechanisms that predators and prey would have selected for, it is useful to consider the strategic problems involved in predator evasion and prey capture and to compare and contrast these with other problems that ancestral foragers would have faced. Predators are an environmental hazard that must be avoided, like cliffs or toxins. Prey animals are food items, like tubers or berries. We expect, therefore, the recruitment of some common adaptations to solve these problems, such as adaptations for hazard and risk management and adaptations for optimal foraging. The problems posed by predators and prey, however, also differ in important ways from the problems posed by cliffs, toxins, or plant foods, and thus select for some distinct skills.

The most important way in which predators and prey differ from other obstacles or problems in the environment is that predators and prey are *intentional agents:* They are animate, sentient beings that process information and behave in the service of specific goals, goals that they are well-adapted to achieve and that are in direct opposition to those of humans either as prey or as hunters. This means that predators and prey are not passive, static components of the environment that simply need to be avoided or found. The biggest problem with predators is that, unlike other dangers such as cliffs or toxins, predators come find you and are well designed to do so. The biggest problem with prey is that, unlike tubers or berries, they move, have the goal of avoiding capture, and possess adaptations such as camouflage and finely tuned sensory systems that help them achieve that goal.

These considerations suggest that predator avoidance and prey capture are likely to make use of mechanisms involved in understanding agency, from mechanisms for detecting the presence of agents in the environment to theory of mind mechanisms for reasoning about mental states. Because humans are intentional agents, too, many of the mechanisms that are brought to bear in social interaction—gaze direction detection mechanisms, for example—will also be brought to bear in predator-prey encounters. However, there are important elements of predator-prey interactions that have no analogy in human social interactions. The goals of predators and prey are distinctly asocial. Predators are things that systematically try to kill you and eat you. Prey are things you try to capture and eat and that regard you as a predator. These descriptions do not fit any human social category. Moreover, unlike human social agents, whose goals vary from situation to situation, the goals of predator and prey with respect to a human actor are relatively invariant. While individual predators might vary in current hunger levels, likelihood of attack, and specific attack strategies, the goals that they have in interacting with humans are never, for example, social exchange or mating. This makes predator-prey interactions rather unique, because the ultimate goals of the agents involved need not be monitored, and the individual's own goals remain constant through the interaction. This allows for the evolution of cognitive systems that have a highly specialized, narrow focus: killing and avoiding being killed. More broadly, the invariance of predator and prey goals is important not only for understanding them as agents but also for understanding many of the design features shared among different predators and different prey, because these goals are tied to basic evolved strategies of food acquisition and survival and, therefore, select for common adaptations, which in turn present a stable target to which our minds have adapted.

THE AGENCY SYSTEM

In this paper I focus on predator-prey adaptations that are part of the agency system, a constellation of adaptations for detecting, reasoning, and ultimately making decisions about intentional agents. Some adaptations to dangerous animals might not be part of the agency system proper, such as immediate reflexive responses to rapidly looming objects, loud noises, and striking objects such as snakes (Öhman & Mineka, 2001). These are rapid shortcuts or emergency strategies that have been selected for extreme speed and, therefore, bypass or supersede the agency system. The agency system evolved for the purposes of strategic inference about intentional agents (Byrne & Whiten, 1988; Humphrey, 1976). It is widely agreed that a major function of the agency system is *social* strategic inference. Here, I argue that there also exist components of the agency system dedicated to inference about predators and prey. According to this view, predator-prey inference is not a separate domain from intentional inference. Rather, the agency system contains some components such as eye direction detection and belief-desire reasoning mechanisms, which are used for inference about both social agents (humans) and nonsocial agents (predators and prey), as well as some components whose evolved function is specific to predator-prey inference. Because interaction with agents, broadly construed, is likely to have comprised a huge swath of the adaptive problems ancestral humans faced (including, by definition, all social interactions), many agency-related problems are not relevant to predator-prey cognition. This discussion focuses on those features of the system that are (note also that many features of the human phenotype that might have evolved partly in a predator-prey context are not discussed here, ranging from adaptations for running and throwing to life-history changes favored by increased reliance on hunting in hominid evolution; Carrier, 1984; Kaplan & Robson, 2002).

The information processing features of the agency system (see Figure 7.1 on p. 204) include (1) a perceptual triggering system designed to reliably detect agents (and to discriminate agents from nonagents), (2) perceptual mechanisms for discriminating between different kinds of agents (e.g., humans versus lions), (3) perceptual mechanisms for discriminating between possible intentions and behaviors of particular agents (e.g., attacking versus fleeing), (4) an inferential apparatus that includes, among other things, the capacity to "mind read" and to

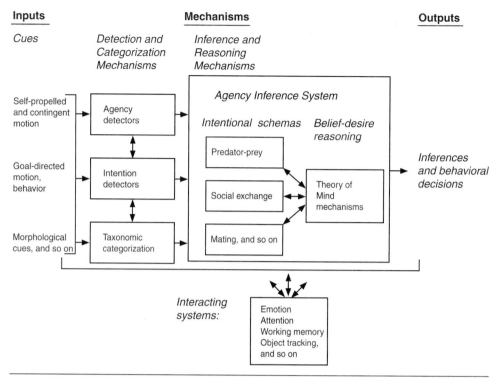

Figure 7.1 Components of the Agency System.

adopt the intentional stance with regard to agents to make inferences about their behavior, and (5) a variety of systems that modulate the agency system proper, such as emotional and executive systems, which update perceptual thresholds, direct attention, assess risk, and regulate the allocation of cognitive resources. The output of the system is in the form of inferences, judgments, and, ultimately, behavioral decisions. I review these features in turn.

AGENCY DETECTION AND DISCRIMINATION

The first problem posed by predators and prey is detecting them. In principle, we can decompose this into the problem of detecting *that* there is a living, animate thing present and the problem of determining *what* it is (predator, prey, person, or otherwise). Some cues, such as self-propelled motion, are useful for discriminating agents from nonagents, and these cues are important in triggering the agency system writ large. In addition, it is important to distinguish between different *kinds* of agent, or between agents with different goals, because different kinds of agent require different responses. This is true for all organisms. We would expect reactions to a predator to be quite different from reactions to kin or to potential mates. Many organisms also exhibit different reactions to different kinds of predators. Vervet monkeys have separate alarm calls for, and react differently to, snakes, leopards, and raptors, because different escape strategies are appropriate for each (Cheney & Seyfarth, 1990).

From a computational perspective, the problems of discriminating agents from nonagents and discriminating between different kinds of agents are enormously difficult. Consider how difficult it would be to write a computer program that could reliably pick out and identify animals from the churning confusion of in- formation that reaches our eyes and ears and that could do so across the range of environments and conditions that humans encounter. Add to this a premium on speed and the possibility of extremely impoverished information (a brief move- ment in peripheral vision, ripples in the grass, something glimpsed through a gap in the leaves), and you have a task that is both extremely difficult and of utmost importance to survival.

Because detecting predators and prey usually involves a significant amount of uncertainty and decisions must often be made quickly, the design of detection and triggering systems is expected to obey principles of signal detection theory, error management, and decision making under uncertainty (Guthrie, 1993; Haselton & Buss, 2000; Öhman & Mineka, 2001). For example, because it is more costly to fail to detect a predator when one is present than to generate a false alarm, ambiguous stimuli would be interpreted on the side of caution, with false positives being much more common than false negatives. However, there will also be strong selection for accuracy, because the costs of unnecessary vigilance and evasive procedures can be high.

SELF-PROPELLED MOTION

Behavior is movement. For this reason, motion can be used both to identify things that behave (agents) and to discriminate types of agent on the basis of how they behave. There is a substantial literature on the use of motion cues both to detect agents and to make inferences about behavior (for reviews, see Johnson, 2000; Rakison & Poulin-Dubois, 2001; Scholl & Tremoulet, 2000). Early studies by Hei- der and Simmel (1944) and Michotte (1963) suggested that there is a qualitative difference in how the cause of a particular event or action is perceived, depending on whether an object appears to be directly acted on (e.g., a collision) or not (e.g., an object that appears to follow another). A variety of studies have since con- firmed the importance of autonomous motion as an agency cue, including au- tonomous changes in trajectory while in motion (Tremoulet & Feldman, 2000).

An additional aspect of motion that may be important in the attribution of agency to objects is its goal directedness (Opfer, 2003). In a series of studies, Gergely, Csibra, and colleagues have demonstrated that motion that appears to be goal directed, for example, one object that appears to be trying to reach another object—including a fleeing object—triggers the intentional stance and specific expectations about how the objects will behave in infants as early as 9 months (Csibra, Bíró, Koós, & Gergely, 2003; Csibra, Gergely, Bíró, Koós, & Brockbank, 1999; Gergely, Nádasdy, Csibra, & Bíró, 1995). The motion signature of pursuit and evasion can not only trigger the agency system but also be used to discrimi- nate predation from other kinds of behavioral interaction and to activate infer- ence systems and procedures specific to predators and prey. Several studies have shown that people are good at discriminating pursuit and evasion from other types of motion (Abell, Happé, & Frith, 2000; Barrett, Todd, Miller, & Blythe, in press; Castelli, Happé, Frith, & Frith, 2000).

In addition to distinguishing pursuit and evasion from their motion signature, we would also expect human perceptual systems to be sensitive to objects rapidly approaching or rapidly receding from us and to use approach or flight to trigger predator and prey-specific systems. Early research on visual looming showed that a rapidly expanding circular shadow (but not a rapidly shrinking shadow) triggers defensive behaviors in rhesus monkeys, from ducking and flinching to alarm calling (Caviness, Schiff, & Gibson, 1962). These reactions have been found in a variety of species, from fishes and frogs to human infants, and specialized neural circuits have been found that compute estimated time to contact for looming visual objects (Sun & Frost, 1998). Neuhoff (2001), noting that hearing is also an important source of information about approaching predators, has found evidence for an adaptive bias in the perception of auditory looming, that is, sounds that are rapidly increasing in intensity. Neuhoff found that approaching sounds are perceived as starting and stopping closer than receding sounds the same distance away, and sounds of rising intensity are perceived as changing in loudness to a greater degree than sounds dropping in intensity by the same amount and posits an adaptive bias that provides advance warning of looming acoustic sources.

In addition to whole body motion, the visual system is sensitive to the ways that body parts of animals move and can use such cues to discriminate types of animal, types of behavior, and other qualities such as size and formidability. Several experiments have shown that people can distinguish animals from nonanimals and can even discriminate between kinds of animals (human, dog, horse, etc.) from point light displays in which illuminated points are placed on limbs or joints and the rest of the body is blacked out; this effect disappears when the displays are inverted (Bertenthal & Pinto, 1994; Johansson, 1973; Mather & West, 1993; Sumi, 1984). These results might indicate an adaptation for recognizing animals and humans at a distance and determining what they are doing and for discriminating types of animals by gait, for example, discriminating an approaching gazelle from an approaching lion.

CONTINGENCY

Another cue to agency is contingency or distant reactivity: a cause and effect relationship between the behavior of an agent and that of another or between the behavior of an agent and that of some event or condition in the environment (e.g., a loud noise; a prey's flight triggering a predator's pursuit). Johnson, Slaughter, and Carey (1998) and Johnson, Booth, and O'Hearn (2001) have shown that infants will construe even a virtually featureless blob as an agent if the object first interacts contingently with the infant, beeping in response to noises the infant makes, but not when the beeping of the object is random with respect to the infant's own vocalizations. Johnson et al. also found that having a face or facelike features was also a cue to agency. Triggering of agency construal in infants does not appear to depend on the object's being human (Johnson et al., 1998).

Interactions between predators and prey are contingent: The evasive decisions of prey depend on what a predator is doing and vice versa. Mechanisms in the visual system are sensitive to such contingent changes in behavior and can use them to discriminate even closely related goal-directed behaviors such as leading and following from pursuit and evasion (Barrett et al., in press; Csibra et al.,

2003). Moreover, the contingency of an animal's behavior on external events (noises, motion, etc.) is a powerful and important cue to the animal's attention and knowledge states. Human hunters use contingency to determine whether animals have detected them and to assess the target of an animal's attention (Barrett, 2003). Prey are likely to use contingency as well to determine whether a predator has detected them and whether it intends to attack.

MORPHOLOGY

There are many static phenotypic features, including shape, color, texture, presence of limbs, claws, teeth, eyes, and forward-facing eyes, which could in principle be used not only to discriminate agents from nonagents but also to distinguish between types of agent, for example, between different animal taxa. Possible mechanisms range from those that use some prespecified cue, such as the presence of teeth or eyes, to a perceptual template, such as a template that detects the shape of snakes or spiders, to mechanisms that link learned cues to specialized procedures, such as the activation of fear mechanisms by seeing the silhouette of an animal, such as a bear, that an individual has learned is dangerous.

Several studies have shown that infants are able to sort animals from nonanimals, for example, vehicles, on the basis of static cues such as shape (Gopnik & Meltzoff, 1987; Mandler & McDonough, 1998; Quinn & Eimas, 1996). Infants appear to be using more than just perceptual similarity to do this because the stimuli for different categories have considerable perceptual overlap. For example, even birds with outstretched wings that look very much like airplanes are grouped with perceptually dissimilar birds with wings not immediately distinguishable from the rest of the body, and planes are grouped with other dissimilar vehicles (Mandler & McDonough, 1998).

Specific perceptual templates can evolve for evolutionarily recurrent, dangerous taxa that have reliably distinguishing features, such as snakes and spiders (Öhman, 1986; Öhman & Mineka, 2001; Seligman, 1971). For example, Öhman, Flykt, and Esteves (2001) found that subjects could rapidly pick out pictures of snakes and spiders from arrays of fear-irrelevant objects (flowers and mushrooms) much faster than they could do the opposite task. Participants who had increased fear of snakes and spiders showed an additional speed advantage. Öhman et al. describe this process as parallel and preattentive. Snakes and spiders in an array are detected prior to attending to them and spontaneously "pop out." To detect flowers or mushrooms, however, subjects must attend to each object serially and make a category judgment.

Snakes and spiders, while predators, do not prey *on* humans, but rather, attack humans in self-defense (except for some large snakes such as constrictors). To date, no evidence for evolved perceptual templates for true predators on humans has been found. This might mean that the array of predators on humans over space and time was diverse enough to prevent selection for distinct templates, or it might mean that such templates have yet to be found (felids would be a likely candidate). There is evidence that such templates exist in other species and that they can persist for thousands of years even under relaxed selection (persistence of antipredator adaptations in the absence of predators is sometimes known as the "ghost of predators past" hypothesis; Byers, 1997; Peckarsky & Penton, 1988).

For example, tammar wallabies that have been isolated on a predator-free island for approximately 9,500 years exhibit an antipredator reaction to taxidermic models of several predator species including foxes and cats and to acoustic cues to predators such as howls, but do not exhibit these reactions to nonpredators (Blumstein, Daniel, Griffin, & Evans, 2000). Coss, Guse, Poran, and Smith (1993) have found similar reactions of squirrels to snakes even in populations isolated from snakes for many thousands of years. In humans, while the array of predators might have been too diverse over space and time to select for specific perceptual templates, it is possible that natural selection engineered other means for rapid learning about predators, such as social learning of the sort seen in rhesus monkeys, who can acquire fear of novel animals in a single trial if conspecifics are observed to be afraid of them (Mineka, Davidson, Cook, & Keir, 1984).

Two additional kinds of experiments have shown that there appear to be relatively low-level perceptual mechanisms dedicated to the detection of animals in the perceptual array, using static cues of some kind: experiments on peripheral detection of animals and on detection of changes in complex scenes. Thorpe, Gegenfurtner, le Fabre-Thorpe, and Bulthoff (2001) examined subjects' ability to detect animals and artifacts when presented in peripheral vision. In general, the ability to identify objects declines rapidly the more peripherally the objects are presented, and most objects in extreme peripheral vision are impossible to identify. Thorpe et al. (2001) found that this peripheral attenuation of perception was much less pronounced for pictures of animals, with above-baseline performance in areas of peripheral vision where subjects are at chance in detecting the presence of artifacts.

A second source of evidence for animal detectors comes from studies of the ability to detect changes in complex scenes. In the phenomenon known as "change blindness," subjects are frequently unaware of changes to objects in their visual field, including changes in location and identity. Using a change blindness paradigm, New, Cosmides, and Tooby (2003) found that subjects' ability to detect changes in a scene that involved animals were significantly greater than their ability to detect changes that involved nonliving objects, even when the object was much larger than an animal, such as a building. This implies the existence of perceptual mechanisms that monitor for the presence of, and changes in, agents in the environment, but that are not sensitive to changes in nonagents.

EYES

A simple cue that appears to trigger antipredator responses in other species is the presence of eyes and, more specifically, directed gaze or a contingently following gaze. Ristau (1991) found that the antipredator response of plovers—the broken wing display that draws predator attention away from offspring—was triggered specifically by approach plus gaze directed toward the nest, rather than just approach. This makes sense in that gaze direction is an important cue to what the predator is attending to. Eye stimuli exacerbate the tonic immobility response, a last-ditch emergency response to capture by a predator, in restrained chickens (Gallup, 1998). Humans are known to be exquisitely sensitive to gaze direction (Baron-Cohen, 1995), and while gaze as a triggering stimulus for antipredator mechanisms has not been specifically examined in humans, it is known to cause arousal in humans and perhaps the activation of antipredator responses (Coss &

Goldthwaite, 1995). In addition to the mere presence of eyes or directed gaze as a triggering stimulus, intentional inference systems use gaze as a source of information about an agent's specific intentions and pattern of attention (Baron-Cohen, 1995).

THE PREDATOR-PREY INFERENCE SYSTEM

In a classic paper, "The Social Function of Intellect," Humphrey (1976) observed:

> Like chess, a social interaction is typically a transaction between social partners. One animal may, for instance, wish by his own behaviour to change the behaviour of another; but since the second animal is himself reactive and intelligent the interaction soon becomes a two-way argument where each "player" must be ready to change his tactics—and maybe his goals—as the game proceeds. Thus, over and above the cognitive skills which are required merely to perceive the current state of play (and they may be considerable), the social gamesman, like the chess player, must be capable of a special sort of forward planning. Given that each move in the game may call forth several alternative responses from the other player this forward planning will take the form of a decision tree, having its root in the current situation and growing branches corresponding to the moves considered in looking ahead at different possibilities. It asks for a level of intelligence which is, I submit, unparalleled in any other sphere of living.

Humphrey intended the chess analogy to refer specifically to social interactions between members of the same species, but it applies equally well to predator-prey interactions. Predator-prey interactions are zero-sum games between reactive agents, each of which must alter his or her tactics as the interaction proceeds, depending on the moves of the other player. Like a game of chess, predator-prey interactions involve sophisticated cognitive abilities, including the ability to infer the intentions and immediate plans of the opponent and to react accordingly. In the case of humans, this is likely to involve the ability to simulate the opponent's mind, including what the opponent knows and what the opponent's immediate goals are, to predict behavior.

Predator-prey interactions, then, are likely to select for a kind of strategic intelligence that is similar in many ways to social intelligence. Social interactions and predator-prey interactions are likely to select for some common mechanisms and some mechanisms that differ between the two domains. Many mechanisms in the agency system are probably used for both types of interaction and evolved under selection to do so. However, there are several reasons that we might expect the agency system to contain a set of procedures specialized for making inferences specifically about predators and prey, that is, a *predator-prey inference system* or *predator-prey schema* (PPS) that is distinct from the system used to make social inferences (Barrett, 1999, 2004). First, predator-prey interactions are characterized by unique goals that are distinct from social goals in that one agent seeks to kill the other for the purposes of eating it. Second, the goal of predation, and the converse goal of avoiding predation, are relatively invariant during the course of a predator-prey interaction and are in fact invariant for humans with respect to entire classes of agents in the environment. Consider an approaching human: Perhaps the person wants to ask directions, to give you a message from a friend, to propose an exchange of goods, to ask you for a date, or to kill you. The parameter space of possible social goals is large and needs to be pared down before you decide what to do. For an approaching lion, there is much less ambiguity in his possible goals with respect to you and, therefore, which possible goals need attending to. All that matters from your perspective is that he might attack, and the problem is reduced to determining how likely he is to do so (based on factors such as hunger level and assessment of risk to himself in attacking you), and if so, what to do about it. For prey, a similar kind of goal invariance obtains. A partridge encountered in the woods never entertains the possibility that you might want to be its friend. Upon detecting a potential predator, it flees. The fact that it automatically assumes that you are a predator greatly constrains the space of its possible future behaviors. Because such interactions adhere so closely to a small parameter space and are a domain of inference and decision making with such clear fitness consequences, the evolution of a specialized system is plausible. Again, this system is not likely to be independent from other systems of intentional inference such as *theory of mind* mechanisms but, rather, is likely to be designed to interface with and exploit them. One possibility, as shown in Figure 7.1, is for the predator-prey inference system to be a specific content domain *within* the overarching domain of intentional reasoning; predation-specific goals could be slotted into more agency-wide mechanisms such as the theory of mind mechanism (ToMM) proper, which performs computations about epistemic mental states such as knowledge and belief (Baron-Cohen, 1995; Leslie, 1994).

The function of a predator-prey inference system would be to take perceptual cues and representations of the internal knowledge and goal states of predators and prey and use these to predict behavior and to guide behavioral decision making. Barrett (1999), building on the idea of a decision tree used to predict future moves, proposed a predator-prey inference system with the following features:

- Conceptual primitives *predator* and *prey*, defined by the goals and intentions of capturing (and killing or eating) prey and evading predator, respectively.
- Slots to represent specific internal states of predator and prey such as *prey detects predator* and for behavioral states of predator and prey such as *predator approaches prey*.
- Transition rules for going from one state to another within the inference system. For example, *predator detects prey* might generate the prediction *predator approaches prey*.
- Outputs in the form of intuitions or predictions about behavior. These will be generated in a probabilistic fashion. A variety of possibilities might be entertained simultaneously, but some will be more likely than others given the inputs available to the system, and others will be strongly counterintuitive and never entertained, for example, a prey species stalking a predator.

Barrett (1999) and Barrett, Tooby, and Cosmides (forthcoming) have tested several of the predictions of the PPS model in studies with German and Shuar children. Three-, 4-, and 5-year-old children were asked to simulate an encounter between a predator and prey using plastic models. The task included a free response portion in which children were asked to predict what would happen when the lion and zebra saw each other, for example, what the lion wants to do, what the zebra wants to do, what will happen next. Barrett et al. hypothesized that the majority of children's responses would map onto nodes in the predator-prey inference tree (e.g., "The zebra is afraid of the lion," "The lion wants to eat the zebra"), that children's responses would rarely if ever violate the inference tree (e.g., "The zebra eats the lion"), and that there would be few if any anthropomorphic or fantasy responses (e.g., "The lion and the zebra sit down to tea"). Because the PPS is hypothesized to be a universal, reliably developing part of the agency system, it was also predicted that these patterns of inference would be approximately the same in both German and Shuar children, despite large differences in culture and individual experience, including exposure to actual predators.

The majority of responses were consistent with the predator-prey inference system hypothesis (over 60% in all age groups and populations). Consistent responses included statements such as, "The lion eats the zebra" or "The zebra runs away from the lion." In contrast, very few responses were inconsistent with the PPS hypothesis, that is, "The zebra chases the lion" or "The zebra and the lion play." Out of 264 free responses (66 children on four free response questions), only 3 were violations (~1%). Anthropomorphic and fantasy answers were equally rare: Four responses, or approximately 1.5%, fell into this category. The results suggest that the predator-prey inference system is present in children in both cultures by age 3. There were no significant population differences in the proportion of correct responses produced, suggesting a similar developmental trajectory in predator-prey knowledge across populations.

While these results show that children produce surprisingly few counterintuitive predictions of predator and prey behavior on their own, using intuition-violating stimuli is a valuable means of testing for the presence of inference systems, especially in preverbal infants. For example, such intuition violation paradigms have been used to test for the presence of systems for making inferences about the properties of solid objects (Spelke, 1990). In a similar vein, a recent study by Csibra et al. (2003) suggests that at least part of the predator-prey inference system—a pursuit-evasion schema—may be present in infancy. Csibra et al. used a dishabituation paradigm to test 12-month-old infants' expectations regarding a pursuit-evasion scenario, presented using moving objects on a computer screen. In the habituation event, one object, the "chaser," was shown "pursuing" another object, the "chasee," which passed through a small hole in a barrier that was too small for the chaser to pass through. Consequently, the chaser went around the barrier to continue its pursuit of the chasee. After habituating to this stimulus, infants were shown one of two possible actions: a *congruent* (schema-consistent) action and an *incongruent* (schema-violating) action. Both action scenarios differed from the habituation stimulus in that the gap in the barrier was now sufficiently wide for the chaser to pass through. The congruent action showed the chaser doing exactly that: Both chaser and chasee passed through the opening in the barrier, a motion pattern different from that to which the infants had been habituated. The incongruent action showed the *same* motion trajectory to which the infants had been habituated: The chasee passed through the opening in the barrier, but the chaser went around the barrier despite the fact that the opening was now large enough to pass through.

Csibra et al. (2003) found that rather than dishabituate to the motion trajectory that was least similar to the habituation trajectory—that is, the congruent action—the infants dishabituated more often to the *similar* trajectory, that is, the incongruent action. The most plausible explanation for this finding is that infants make the assumption that a chaser will pursue the most direct possible path toward the chasee (reflecting the goal of catching the chasee). The method is elegant because it rules out the possibility that infants are simply learning trajectories through experience and dishabituating to deviations from the learned trajectories, because in this case they dishabituated to a trajectory that was most *similar* to the one they had learned and were unsurprised by a trajectory they had not seen before (because, by hypothesis, it conformed to the predictions of the inference system). This makes sense only if infants possess assumptions about the goals of the agents in question and about how agents will attempt to achieve those goals: The predicted behavior of the agents changes when the circumstances change so as to render a new trajectory best to achieve the chaser's goal. It thus appears that at least this part of the predator-prey inference system, the portion that generates predictions about the motion trajectories of predators and prey, is present by 12 months of age.

Several other studies support these results, demonstrating the existence of a pursuit-evasion schema in young children, in adults across cultures, and even in individuals with autism. Blythe, Todd, and Miller (1999) generated motion stimuli for several different types of goal-directed interaction by asking naïve subjects to act out these goals in a computer game and playing the recordings for other subjects. They found that adult subjects were reliably able to distinguish pursuit and evasion (chasing) from fighting, playing, leading and following, courtship, and territorial guarding. Barrett et al. (in press) replicated these results with German children ages 3 to 5 and with Shuar adults, suggesting that these schemas are universal components of the agency system.

Castelli et al. (2000) conducted an fMRI study of adult subjects who were asked to watch motion stimuli, including a pursuit and evasion event, and make intentionality judgments about the stimuli. Castelli et al. found that watching and making judgments about goal-directed interactions, including pursuit and evasion, activated common areas for each of several kinds of trajectories. For some trajectories, interpretation required attribution of belief states to the interacting agents (e.g., deception), requiring full-blown theory of mind. Other trajectories, including the pursuit and evasion trajectory, did not require attribution of beliefs, but only attribution of goals or intentions. This is consistent with models of the development of intentional inference such as Baron-Cohen's (1995) model, in which the capacity to reason about goal-directed behavior develops quite early and prior to full-blown, belief-based, theory of mind. If this is correct, the most elementary forms of predator-prey reasoning require only reasoning about goals and intentions, not beliefs. This is supported by a study of persons with autism by Castelli, Frith, Happé, and Frith (2002), which found that autistic subjects were able to identify goal-directed sequences including pursuit and evasion but not sequences that required attribution of belief. This is consistent with the idea that the predator-prey inference system, while part of an agency system that uses the intentional stance to predict behavior, evolved prior to the capacity to engage in belief-based reasoning and might be present in many mammalian species, not just those with full-blown theory of mind (Barrett, 1999).

AGENCY AND DEATH UNDERSTANDING

It is widely held that children acquire an understanding of death gradually, via domain-general learning mechanisms, and that children's early understanding of death is relatively poor in the sense that reflects a poor or nonexistent understanding of the physiological causes and entailments of death (Carey, 1985;

Speece & Brent, 1984, 1996). Indeed, at first glance there appears to be little reason, from an evolutionary perspective, to expect a reliably developing general understanding of death, especially one's own death, or to possess a general "death anxiety" or "fear of death" (Buss, 1997).

However, there are reasons to suspect that the agency system might contain a very specialized device whose function is to distinguish living agents from dead ones (Barrett, 1999; Barrett & Behne, in press; Barrett et al., forthcoming). There is clearly an advantage to being able to distinguish agents from nonagents, because agents can behave in goal-directed ways—including inflicting harm—and nonagents cannot. When considered as a signal detection problem, there is an asymmetry in the costs of different types of errors that might favor an error management bias towards assuming an object might be an agent in cases of uncertainty (Guthrie, 1993; Haselton & Buss, 2000; Öhman & Mineka, 2001). However, because assuming that something is an agent entails costs such as vigilance, allocation of cognitive resources, and the activation of potential danger responses, there will also be selection for accuracy. For example, upon discovering that an object is a stick and not a snake, the agency system should be deactivated.

For some objects, merely categorizing the object to kind is sufficient to rule out agency: Pieces of wood, for example, can never be agents. Animals, however, are agents when they are alive and cease to be agents when they die. Why would there be any selection to detect this transition? Because children in ancestral environments frequently encountered living animals, there would have been selection to monitor them as possible sources of danger and to understand their capacity to react to stimulus and possibly to cause harm. But children also frequently interacted with *dead* agents, including food animals that had been killed. If children were unable to discriminate living from dead animals, error management considerations would suggest that they should *always* assume the animal was an agent, a potential source of harm, and that it might react if touched or bitten into. This would clearly be disadvantageous and would cause children to fear their food.

Based on this reasoning, Barrett and Behne (in press) proposed that there should be a "switch," activated by particular kinds of cues, which would cause a living agent to be recategorized as a dead agent, and for the agency system to be switched off for that object. Again, an error management perspective suggests that this switch should be difficult to flip and that unreliable cues to death—lying down and being immobile, for example—should be poor at flipping it. The switch should be designed to be activated by sufficiently reliable cues such as severe disruptions of the body envelope (e.g., decapitation), cooking, or by knowledge of events highly likely to have caused death. Barrett and Behne reasoned that examining the sleep versus death distinction would be a particularly good means of testing this hypothesis. Sleep and death share many perceptual cues so, all else equal, would be likely to be confused. Children are often said in the death literature to confuse sleep and death (Speece & Brent, 1984). However, the *cessation of agency* hypothesis presented here suggests that children should strongly distinguish between these two states if presented with sufficiently reliable cues to activate the proposed death detection device.

To test this hypothesis, Barrett and Behne (in press) designed an experiment in which children heard brief stories about animals either going to sleep or being killed. Crucially, information hypothesized to be sufficient to trigger the death detection device was presented in death conditions, for example, being cooked, being attacked by a lion, or being shot. In the sleep condition, the cause of sleep was tiredness. After each manipulation, children were tested with agency questions such as, "If you touched the animal, could it move?" By age 4, children in both populations reliably distinguished between sleep and death, attributing agency properties to sleeping animals, but not to dead ones. The study found no population differences in the developmental trajectory of this ability, suggesting that development of the mechanism for recategorizing dead agents is robust to large differences in culture and individual experiences with animals and death. This finding stands in contrast to the majority of literature on children's understanding of death, which finds differences in death understanding between populations and between studies employing different methods to assess it (Speece & Brent, 1984, 1996). Part of the reason for this variation may be the failure to use stimuli that reliably trigger a living versus dead discrimination mechanism and to assess patterns of inference related to agency.

In a recent follow-up study, Barrett (unpublished data) has replicated these results among the Shuar using a different method (see also Barrett et al., forthcoming, for converging results), also showing that when the agency system is turned off, a system for making inferences about biological substances—in this case, meat—is turned on, and that when an animal dies, children begin to think of it in the same way that they think of meat. This reliably activated change in modes of construal makes sense in a species in which meat from prey animals constituted a significant portion of the diet.

INTENTIONAL INFERENCE IN HUNTING

In the anthropological literature on hunting in traditional societies, it is often remarked that hunters "anthropomorphize" animals, attributing to them humanlike mental states, intentions, goals, and even personalities to make predictions and inferences about their behavior (Blurton Jones & Konner, 1976; Liebenberg, 1990; Marks, 1976; Mithen, 1996; Silberbauer, 1981). However, there are at least two senses in which the word *anthropomorphic* is being used: (1) to describe the attribution to nonhuman animals of traits that are *strictly* human, or (2) simply to describe the attribution of *any* mental states to animals, whether correctly or not. In the former case, the attributions must, by definition, be incorrect; in the latter case, they might not be.

From the perspective developed here, we might expect hunters to use the inferential power of the agency system, including theory of mind, to make inferences about the behavior of prey animals during the course of a hunt and, indeed, for this to be part of the system's proper domain. The term *anthropomorphism* carries with it the flavor of irrational overattribution of human traits to animals, attributions that would lead to mistakes as often as correct inferences. However, when anthropomorphic strategies are mentioned in the hunter-gatherer literature, it is often remarked that these strategies are effective in predicting behavior. For example, Silberbauer (1981) reports that the G/wi of the Kalahari desert predict animal behavior through a complicated system of personality types and psychological predispositions. Silberbauer claimed that this led to accurate predictions of animal behavior, although he was unable to master the system himself. In other words, the hunters might have been using causally accurate attributions to animals, not irrational, fantasylike attributions of human-specific traits. This would parallel the child data from Barrett et al. (forthcoming), which contained remarkably few unrealistic attributions even in 3- to 5-year-olds.

In a recent study of Shuar hunters in the Ecuadorian Amazon, Barrett (2003) found that virtually no attributions of mental states to animals were anthropomorphic in terms of definition one. All were attributions that would be considered potentially correct by an ethologist or biologist such as, "The animal saw me" or "The animal knew I was there." Shuar hunters mimic animal calls explicitly to manipulate the beliefs of prey (the animal comes because it *believes* the call is coming from a conspecific). Hunters often claim to be exquisitely aware of the mental states of animals while pursuing them (Nelson, 1998). Barrett's (2003) data suggest that Shuar hunters constantly monitor the attention of the prey animal and adjust their own behavior to minimize the probability of detection. As Liebenberg (1990) found for Kalahari hunter-gatherers, Shuar hunters also use detailed observations of animal tracks to generate hypotheses about the internal states of the animals they are tracking, for example, that an animal intended to head for a particular refuge site, that an animal detected another animal at a certain point, or that an animal was startled and began to run. These data suggest that hunting is part of the proper domain of evolved systems for intentional inference and is a domain in which protoscientific hypothesis testing skills are applied (Liebenberg, 1990). Shuar hunters, like the G/wi, also appear to use personality-like psychological profiles of individual species in constraining their hypotheses; for example, some species are more skittish than others, some are more aggressive than others, and some have more sensitive smell or hearing.

FEAR

A discussion of predator-prey adaptations would not be complete without a discussion of fear. While the fear system is clearly distinct from the agency system, the two systems are likely to interact. The evolved function of fear is to organize responses to danger (Cosmides & Tooby, 2000; LeDoux, 1996; Öhman & Mineka, 2001). Fear not only organizes escape and avoidance responses to dangers but also deactivates certain cognitive processes (e.g., food search) and activates others (e.g., predator-prey routines) and may alter sensitivity thresholds of many systems. As an adaptive problem, predator avoidance shares some features with other danger-avoidance problems such as avoiding cliffs or sharp objects but also has some unique characteristics such as the fact that predators are intentional agents (note also that for some dangers, in particular, toxins and pathogens, there is a distinct emotional response, namely disgust). It is an open question to what extent animals that are dangerous for reasons of self-defense rather than predation, such as snakes and spiders, mobilize components of the agency system. To date, snake and spider fears have been the primary targets of research on evolved fear responses.

Öhman and Mineka (2001) have suggested that the fear system has at least four distinguishing characteristics: (1) it is stimulus-specific, being preferentially activated by evolutionarily prepared danger stimuli such as snakes, spiders, and falling objects; (2) its triggering by such stimuli is automatic; (3) it is relatively impenetrable to conscious control; and (4) it has dedicated neural circuitry, particularly in the amygdala. The fact that the input conditions of the fear system are centered on particular, evolutionarily relevant danger stimuli has been demonstrated in several ways. First, a large number of experiments have been conducted with humans using classical conditioning paradigms to measure the specificity of the fear response. Many of these studies compare conditioning stimuli such as snakes and spiders with fear-irrelevant controls such as houses, flowers, and mushrooms to demonstrate that conditioned associations between picture items and aversive conditioning stimuli such as shocks occur much more readily for dangerous than nondangerous items (Öhman, 1993). A second line of evidence for selectivity comes from observational fear-conditioning paradigms. In these experiments, humans or nonhuman primates are conditioned while observing conspecifics exhibiting fear responses to evolutionarily relevant dangerous items such as snakes and nondangerous items such as flowers. Under these conditions, fears are acquired very rapidly and much more readily for snakes than for flowers (Mineka et al., 1984). A third line of evidence comes from illusory correlation studies. In these studies, subjects are presented with photographs of, for example, snakes, spiders, flowers, and mushrooms, accompanied by events such as chimes (nonaversive) and shocks (aversive), and are later asked to estimate the degree of association between the photos and the events. Subjects tend to overestimate the conditional probability of the aversive events for the danger stimuli, a tendency known as a covariation bias (Tomarken, Mineka, & Cook, 1989).

Another feature of the fear system is automaticity. When the proper input conditions for the fear system are encountered, it is activated automatically even if subjects are not consciously aware of the triggering stimulus. The backward-masking paradigm has been used to show that fear can be activated by presentation of stimuli that are so rapid that subjects are unable to report what they were (Öhman & Soares, 1994). Additionally, Öhman and Mineka (2001) suggest that the fear system is *encapsulated* in the sense that the fear response is immune to higher level cognitive processes or expectations on the part of the subject. Upon seeing a snake, the automatic fear response runs its course even if subjects quickly become aware that the snake is not a threat. Hugdahl and Öhman (1977) examined the effect of explicit instructions to subjects in influencing their reactions to conditioned stimuli. When subjects were conditioned to expect a shock for fear-irrelevant stimuli such as circles and triangles and then told that there would be no more shocks, their skin conductance responses to circles and triangles immediately extinguished. When conditioned to expect shocks upon presentations of snake photos, however, the instruction that there would be no more shocks had no effect on subjects' skin conductance responses; in other words, the explicit knowledge that shocks would cease did not prevent the fear reaction.

The evolved function of fear is to influence behavior. Many fear responses—such as the rapid, reflexive pulling back that occurs when a snake is detected in one's path of movement—occur so rapidly that conscious awareness of the triggering stimulus and higher level cognitive processes occur only afterwards. Öhman and Mineka (2001) suggest that in the most evolutionarily ancient fear systems, perceptual threat detectors were directly connected to motor reflexes designed to move the organism away from danger and that intervening control systems (e.g., a predator-prey inference system) evolved later. In humans, it seems likely that fear is recruited in response to predators, but that higher level processes can mediate predator evasion strategies, especially for classes of animals for which optimal evasion strategies vary by taxon and must be learned.

THE PREDATOR-PREY KNOWLEDGE
ACQUISITION SYSTEM

How is knowledge about predators, prey, and other dangerous animals acquired? A moment's reflection suggests that generalized, feedback-based learning might not be well suited to this task. A child that requires attack or injury to learn that an animal is dangerous is unlikely to survive for long. For this reason, we might expect natural selection to have created a specialized learning system with one or more of the following features:

- Learning about dangerous animals might occur without extrinsic motivation such as actual injury or explicit instruction from parents. During childhood, children might be intrinsically motivated to seek out and acquire information about animals. Anecdotal observation suggests there might be something akin to a critical period of childhood interest in animals (e.g., the age when children become obsessed with dinosaurs), with interest shifting to other matters such as mating later in life. In traditional societies, acquisition of animal knowledge continues through adulthood (Kaplan & Robson, 2001), but might become motivated by practical concerns such as food acquisition, which are not motivating in early childhood.

- Something akin to "one-trial" learning, not dependent on feedback might occur, in which minimal information is required for the child to acquire a new animal concept (minimally, some identifying features and perhaps a name) along with information relevant to its dangerousness (e.g., mode of attack, places of encounter).

- The system might rely heavily on social learning. Cultural transmission is expected to be especially important in cases where individual learning is particularly costly or error prone and where important ecological knowledge can be stored and transmitted from individual to individual (Boyd & Richerson, 1985). In the case of animal knowledge, it is much less costly to learn from a peer or parent that a lion is dangerous than to learn this individually, the hard way. The experiments of Mineka et al. (1984) show that social transmission of animal fear is important in nonhuman primates, and there is anecdotal reason to suspect the same in humans. Indeed, the propensity to easily acquire new animal concepts without direct experience might lead to cultural by-products such as imaginary animal concepts that persist despite total lack of evidence (Sasquatch, the Loch Ness monster, and extraterrestrials), exploitation of imaginary animals as disciplinary tools (e.g., the bogey man), and acquisition of ecologically useless knowledge about, for example, *Pokémon* creatures (Balmford, Clegg, Coulson, & Taylor, 2002).

- The system might contain content biases or procedures that help to guide learning and to structure the input in useful ways such as a minimal set of prespecified cues to dangerousness (e.g., size, sharp teeth), conceptual "templates" with parameters that are set by learning (dangerous versus safe, carnivore versus herbivore; Boyer, 2001), or heuristic assumptions about category structure, for example, that animals are expected to be grouped into nested hierarchies (Atran, 1990).

- Acquisition of procedural knowledge—practical skills relevant to predation—may also depend on specialized evolved systems. Chase play, for example, may reflect the operation of an evolved system for training predator-prey pursuit and evasion skills (Boulton & Smith, 1992; Steen & Owens, 2001). As Steen and Owens observe, children are intrinsically motivated to engage in such play, as well as other predator-prey related play such as target practice (Blurton Jones & Marlowe, 2002), and this intrinsic motivation may be the result of selection because of the benefits of such play for real-world practical skills. Even in modern predator-free environments, these motivations may cause people to enjoy predator-prey related entertainment such as films and video games (Steen & Owens, 2001), which might be dubbed the "Jurassic Park hypothesis" (see Grimes, 2002).

PREDATOR-PREY BEHAVIOR

Compared to laboratory studies, data on actual antipredator behavior in humans are relatively scarce. We know quite a bit about the physiological responses induced by fear, but less about how these would affect actual behavior in an encounter. Antipredator behaviors in other species have been studied extensively and include specialized behaviors such as alarm calls and evasion behaviors tailored to specific predator types (Cheney & Seyfarth, 1990), broken wing displays (Ristau, 1991), death feigning and tonic immobility as responses to capture (Gallup, 1998), predator inspection, predator mobbing, and attempts to confuse predators while fleeing. Whether similar responses occur in humans is less certain.

A few studies have examined the responses of children to actual animals (Kidd & Kidd, 1987; Myers, 1996; Nielsen & Delude, 1989) and have found, as expected, greater fear toward dangerous animals than to safe ones, indicating that children are sensitive to danger and even to cues such as the direction a snake's head is pointing (Myers, 1996). A study by Coss (1999) attempted to assess how children would behave in response to a predator in a hypothetical scenario, by asking children to point to where they would go in a virtual environment presented on a computer screen. Coss found a sex difference in children's reports of where they would take refuge, with girls climbing trees significantly more often than boys. Coss suggests that this is due to "relic sexual dinichism": In ancestral hominids such as *Australopithecus,* females may have taken refuge more often in the branches of trees than males. Several converging lines of evidence in favor of this hypothesis are sex differences in playground-climbing behaviors and injury rates, with girls climbing more and falling less than boys, and sex differences in nighttime fears, with girls reporting greater fear of attacking agents coming from underneath them and boys from the side (Coss, 1999; Coss & Goldthwaite, 1995).

Several sources of behavioral evidence suggest that when confronted with predators, human antipredator behaviors can have an effect on reducing mortality, but the ability to escape from predators is by no means certain. Treves and Naughton-Treves (1999) studied the Ugandan Game Department's records of encounters between agropastoralists and predators (lions and leopards) in a period between 1923 and 1994. These records indicated that, consistent with data on ancestral hominid behavioral ecology, attacks by predators were common when humans attempted to scavenge carnivore kills. Men were most often targeted by predators, especially while hunting, but attacks on women and children, while rarer, more often lead to death, suggesting differences in predator evasion abilities. In cases where humans and predators coexist, frequently interact, and even compete for resources, predators still kill humans, as in areas of India where the ranges of tigers and people overlap, where attacks and deaths are frequent (Kruuk, 2002). Mountain lion attacks in California are another example (it is interesting that these appear to be directed preferentially toward children).

CONCLUSIONS

Given the importance of predators and prey in human evolution, it is likely that we have only begun to uncover the full array of predator-prey adaptations that the mind contains. Until very recently, attack by formidable alien beasts was a real and constant possibility in everyday life. The word *alien* means creatures whose bodies and minds were not human, but who were exquisitely adept at finding, stalking, and killing primates who were weak, slow, and perceptually deficient in comparison to many other species. Selection to be aware of these creatures, of their thoughts, plans, and intentions, as well as a strategic intelligence to take advantage of this awareness, would have been strong. Here, we need to think in science fiction terms. Imagine the human mind as an exquisitely designed computer, armed with state-of-the-art sensors, trackers, detectors, and inference engines all engineered for the purpose of predator defense and evasion. What would these look like? Without doubt, the best equipment designed by military science does not even come close. Yet, relatively little attention has been paid to predator detection and evasion as adaptive problems that could shed light on the design of our minds.

On the other side of the coin, humans are predators by nature. We have been hunters of other animals for millions of years. Far from diminishing with time, selection for the skills necessary to stalk and kill animals has accelerated over the course of human evolution, as hunting has played an ever-increasing role in human subsistence. For those who have never hunted, the difficulty of the task is easy to underestimate. Dawkins (1976) coined the term *the life/dinner principle* to refer to the asymmetry in fitness payoffs to predators and prey for the two possible outcomes of a predation event: If the predation event is a success, the predator wins dinner, but the prey loses his life; vice versa, if it fails. There is another asymmetry, which might be called the *anywhere but here* principle: For a predator to succeed, the predator must manage to be in exactly the same place as the prey at exactly the same time; for the prey to succeed, it need only be anywhere else. Obviously, it is much easier to satisfy the latter condition than the former. This means that whereas prey can use all kinds of "dumb" tactics to avoid predation, including hiding, crypsis, and living in holes or trees, predators must be designed to bring about a very unlikely and nonrandom physical state of the world, which prey are expressly designed to avoid. For tool-using predators, there is an added complication: We must either cause our own position to converge with that of the prey or cause the position of a projectile or trap to do so. This poses other adaptive problems such as the perceptual and motor problems involved in successfully aiming a projectile. Our minds are likely to be full of many detection, tracking, and behavior anticipation mechanisms of which we might not be fully aware.

For psychology, there likely remains much to discover about human predator-prey adaptations. There might be as-yet undiscovered mechanisms for detecting predators using motion and other perceptual cues, including perceptual templates for common predators such as big cats; mechanisms for assessing formidability of animals (predators, prey, and even other humans) using cues such as size, muscularity, and so on; early-developing responses to dangerous animals that require little or no learning; aspects of the fear system that have not been discovered using only snakes and spiders as stimuli; undiscovered mood or emotion states specific to stalking or being stalked; and more. The notion of intentional schemas that I have proposed here—specific, prepared, content domains within the domain of intentional reasoning, of which predator-prey would be only one— has scarcely been investigated, but it would be surprising if intentional reasoning were not rich with evolved, content-specific procedures. In addition, we might find predator-prey adaptations operating in unusual contexts, coopted to deal with problems outside their proper domains, from detecting oncoming objects in traffic to strategic reasoning in games or business. Finally, it is possible that investigating evolutionarily relevant problem domains such as predation, which are rarely considered by most contemporary cognitive and developmental psychologists, could lead to drastic reconsideration of how the domains of thought are organized: Rather than thinking of broad domains such as social cognition and theory of mind, we might realize that the mind is not organized around a few large problems but around many small ones such as agency detection, tracking objects, and inferring intention from motion, which do not map neatly onto the categories of contemporary psychology.

REFERENCES

Abell, F., Happé, F., & Frith, U. (2000). Do triangles play tricks? Attribution of mental states to animated shapes in normal and abnormal development. *Journal of Cognitive Development, 15,* 1–20.

Atran, S. (1990). *Cognitive foundations of natural history.* New York: Cambridge University Press.

Balmford, A., Clegg, L., Coulson, T., & Taylor, J. (2002). Why conservationists should heed Pokémon. *Science, 295,* 2367.

Barlow, H. B. (1953). Summation and inhibition in the frog's retina. *Journal of Physiology, 119,* 69–88.

Baron-Cohen, S. (1995). *Mindblindness: An essay on autism and theory of mind.* Cambridge, MA: MIT Press.

Barrett, H. C. (1999). Human cognitive adaptations to predators and prey. Dissertation, University of California at Santa Barbara.

Barrett, H. C. (2003). *Hunting and theory of mind.* 2003 Meetings of the Human Behavior and Evolution Society, Lincoln, NE.

Barrett, H. C. (2004). Cognitive development and the understanding of animal behavior. In B. Ellis & D. Bjorklund (Eds.), *Origins of the social mind.* New York: Guilford Press.

Barrett, H. C., & Behne, T. (in press). Children's understanding of death as the cessation of agency: A test using sleep versus death. *Cognition.*

Barrett, H. C., Todd, P. M., Miller, G. F., & Blythe, P. (in press). Accurate judgments of intention from motion alone: A cross-cultural study. *Evolution and Human Behavior.*

Barrett, H. C., Tooby, J., & Cosmides, L. (forthcoming). *Children's understanding of predator-prey interactions and death.*

Bertenthal, B. I., & Pinto, J. (1994). Global processing of biological motions. *Psychological Science, 5,* 221–225.

Blumenschine, R. J. (1987). Characteristics of an early hominid scavenging niche. *Current Anthropology, 28,* 383–407.

Blumstein, D. T., Daniel, J. C., Griffin, A. S., & Evans, C. S. (2000). Insular tammar wallabies (*Macropus eugenii*) respond to visual but not acoustic cues from predators. *Behavioral Ecology, 11,* 528–535.

Blurton Jones, N. G., & Konner, M. J. (1976). Kung knowledge of animal behavior. In R. B. Lee & I. DeVore (Eds.), *Kalahari hunter gatherers* (pp. 325–348). Cambridge, MA: Harvard University Press.

Blurton Jones, N. G., & Marlowe, F. W. (2002). Selection for delayed maturity: Does it take 20 years to learn to hunt and gather? *Human Nature, 13,* 199–238.

Blythe, P. W., Todd, P. M., & Miller, G. F. (1999). How motion reveals intention: Categorizing social interactions. In G. Gigerenzer, P. M. Todd, and the ABC Research Group (Eds.), *Simple heuristics that make us smart* (pp. 257–286). New York: Oxford University Press.

Boulton, M. J., & Smith, P. K. (1992). The social nature of play fighting and play chasing: Mechanisms and strategies underlying cooperation and compromise. In J. H. Barkow, L. Cosmides, & J. Tooby (Eds.), *The adapted mind: Evolutionary psychology and the generation of culture.* New York: Oxford.

Boyd, R., & Richerson, P. (1985). *Culture and the evolutionary process.* Chicago: University of Chicago Press.

Boyer, P. (2001). *Religion explained.* New York: Basic Books.

Brain, C. K. (1981). *The hunters or the hunted? An introduction to African cave taphonomy.* Chicago: University of Chicago Press.

Brantingham, P. J. (1998). Hominid-carnivore coevolution and invasion of the predatory guild. *Journal of Anthropological Archaeology, 17,* 327–353.

Bunn, H. T. (1994). Early Pleistocene hominid foraging strategies along the ancestral Omo River at Koobi Fora, Kenya. *Journal of Human Evolution, 27,* 247–266.

Buss, D. M. (1997). Human motivation in evolutionary perspective: Grounding terror management theory. *Psychological Inquiry, 8,* 22–26.

Byers, J. A. (1997). *American pronghorn: Social adaptations and the ghosts of predators past.* Chicago: University of Chicago Press.

Byrne, R. W., & Whiten, A. (1988). *Machiavellian intelligence.* New York: Oxford University Press.

Carey, S. (1985). *Conceptual change in childhood.* Cambridge, MA: MIT Press.

Carrier, D. R. (1984). The energetic paradox of human running and hominid evolution. *Current Anthropology, 25,* 483–495.

Castelli, F., Frith, C. D., Happé, F., & Frith, U. (2002). Autism, Asperger syndrome and brain mechanisms for the attribution of mental states to animated shapes. *Brain, 125,* 1839–1849.

Castelli, F., Happé, F., Frith, U., & Frith, C. D. (2000). Movement and mind: A functional imaging study of perception and interpretation of complex intentional movement patterns. *NeuroImage, 12,* 314–325.

Caviness, J. A., Schiff, W., & Gibson, J. J. (1962). Persistent fear responses in rhesus monkeys to the optical stimulus of "looming." *Science, 136,* 982–983.

Cheney, D., & Seyfarth, R. (1990). *How monkeys see the world: Inside the mind of another species.* Chicago: University of Chicago Press.

Cosmides, L. (1989). Has natural selection shaped how humans reason? Studies with the Wason Selection Task. *Cognition, 31,* 187–276.

Cosmides, L., & Tooby, J. (2000). Evolutionary psychology and the emotions. In M. Lewis & J. M. Haviland-Jones (Eds.), *Handbook of emotions* (2nd ed.). New York: Guilford Press.

Coss, R. G. (1999). Effects of relaxed natural selection on the evolution of behavior. In S. A. Foster & J. A. Endler (Eds.), *Geographic variation in behavior: Perspectives on evolutionary mechanisms.* Oxford, England: Oxford University Press.

Coss, R. G., & Goldthwaite, R. O. (1995). The persistence of old designs for perception. *Perspectives in Ethology, 11,* 83–148.

Coss, R. G., Guse, K. L., Poran, N. S., & Smith, D. G. (1993). Development of antisnake defenses in California ground squirrels (*Spermophilus beecheyi*): II. Microevolutionary effects of relaxed selection from rattlesnakes. *Behaviour, 124,* 137–164.

Csibra, G., Bíró, S., Koós, O., & Gergely, G. (2003). One-year-old infants use teleological representations of actions productively. *Cognitive Psychology, 27,* 111–133.

Csibra, G., Gergely, G., Bíró, S., Koós, O., & Brockbank, M. (1999). Goal attribution without agency cues: The perception of "pure reason" in infancy. *Cognition, 72,* 237–267.

Dawkins, R. (1976). *The selfish gene.* New York: Oxford University Press.

Gallup, G. G. (1998). Tonic immobility. In G. Greenberg & M. M. Haraway (Eds.), *Comparative psychology: A handbook* (pp. 777–782). New York: Garland.

Gergely, G., Nádasdy, Z., Csibra, G., & Bíró, S. (1995). Taking the intentional stance at 12 months of age. *Cognition, 56,* 165–193.

Gopnik, A., & Meltzoff, A. N. (1987). The development of categorization in the second year and its relation to other cognitive and linguistic developments. *Child Development, 58,* 1523–1531.

Grimes, K. (2002). Hunted. *New Scientist, 2238,* 34–37.

Guthrie, S. (1993). *Faces in the clouds.* New York: Oxford.

Haselton, M. G., & Buss, D. M. (2000). Error management theory: A new perspective on biases in cross-sex mind reading. *Journal of Personality and Social Psychology, 78,* 81–91.

Heider, F., & Simmel, M. (1944). An experimental study of apparent behavior. *American Journal of Psychology, 57,* 243–259.

Hugdahl, K., & Öhman, A. (1977). Effects of instruction on acquisition and extinction of electrodermal responses to fear-relevant stimuli. *Journal of Experimental Psychology: Human Learning and Memory, 3,* 608–618.

Humphrey, N. (1976). The social function of intellect. In P. P. G. Bateson & R. A. Hinde (Eds.), *Growing points in ethology.* Cambridge, England: Cambridge University Press.

Isaac, G. L. (1968). Traces of Pleistocene hunters: An East African example. In R. B. Lee & I. DeVore (Eds.), *Man the hunter.* Chicago: Aldine.

Johansson, G. (1973). Visual perception of biological motion and a model for its analysis. *Perception and Psychophysics, 14,* 201–211.

Johnson, S. C. (2000). The recognition of mentalistic agents in infancy. *Trends in Cognitive Science,* 4(1), 22–28.

Johnson, S. C., Booth, A., & O'Hearn, K. (2001). Inferring the unseen goals of a non-human agent. *Cognitive Development, 16,* 637–656.

Johnson, S. C., Slaughter, V., & Carey, S. (1998). Whose gaze will infants follow? Features that elicit gaze-following in 12-month-olds. *Developmental Science, 1,* 233–238.

Kaplan, H. S., & Robson, A. (2002). The co-evolution of intelligence and longevity and the emergence of humans. *Proceedings of the National Academy of Sciences, 99,* 10221–10226.

Kidd, A., & Kidd, R. (1987). Reactions of infants and toddlers to live and toy animals. *Psychological Reports, 61,* 455–464.

Kruuk, H. (2002). *Hunter and hunted: Relationships between carnivores and people.* Cambridge, England: Cambridge University Press.

LeDoux, J. E. (1996). *The emotional brain.* New York: Simon & Schuster.

Leslie, A. M. (1994). ToMM, ToBy, and agency: Core architecture and domain specificity. In L. A. Hirschfeld & S. A. Gelman (Eds.), *Mapping the mind: Domain specificity in cognition and culture* (pp. 119–148). Cambridge, England: Cambridge University Press.

Liebenberg, L. W. (1990). *The art of tracking: The origin of science.* Cape Town, South Africa: David Philip.

Mandler, J. M., & McDonough, L. (1998). Inductive inference in infancy. *Cognitive Psychology, 37,* 60–96.

Marks, S. A. (1976). *Large mammals and a brave people: Subsistence hunters in Zambia.* Seattle, WA: University of Washington Press.

Mather, G., & West, S. (1993). Recognition of animal locomotion from dynamic point-light displays. *Perception, 22,* 759–766.

Michotte, A. (1963). *The perception of causality.* London, England: Methuen.

Mineka, S., Davidson, M., Cook, M., & Keir, R. (1984). Observational conditioning of snake fear in rhesus monkeys. *Journal of Abnormal Psychology, 93,* 355–372.

Mithen, S. J. (1996). *The prehistory of the mind: The cognitive origins of art, religion and science.* London, England: Thames and Hudson.

Myers, O. E. (1996). Child-animal interaction: Nonverbal dimensions. *Society and Animals, 4,* 19–35.

Nelson, R. K. (1998). *Heart and blood: Living with deer in America.* New York: Vintage.

Nielsen, J. A., & Delude, L. (1989). Behavior of young children in the presence of different kinds of animals. *Anthrozoös, 3,* 119–129.

Neuhoff, J. G. (2001). An adaptive bias in the perception of looming auditory motion. *Ecological Psychology, 13,* 87–110.

New, J., Cosmides, L., & Tooby, J. (2003). *A content-specific attenuation of change blindness: Preferential attention to animate beings in natural scenes.* Vision Sciences Society, Sarasota, FL.

Öhman, A. (1986). Face the beast and fear the face: Animal and social fears as prototypes for evolutionary analyses of emotion. *Psychophysiology, 23,* 123–145.

Öhman, A. (1993). Stimulus prepotency and fear learning: Data and theory. In N. Birbaumer & A. Öhman (Eds.), *The organization of emotion: Cognitive, clinical and psychophysiological aspects.* Toronto: Hogrefe and Huber.

Öhman, A., Flykt, A., & Esteves, F. (2001). Emotion drives attention: Detecting the snake in the grass. *Journal of Experimental Psychology, General, 130,* 466–478.

Öhman, A., & Mineka, S. (2001). Fear, phobias and preparedness: Toward an evolved module of fear and fear learning. *Psychological Review, 108,* 483–522.

Öhman, A., & Soares, J. J. F. (1994). "Unconscious anxiety": Phobic responses to masked stimuli. *Journal of Abnormal Psychology, 103,* 231–240.

Opfer, J. E. (2003). Identifying living and sentient kinds from dynamic information: The case of goal-directed versus aimless autonomous movement in conceptual change. *Cognition, 86,* 97–122.

Peckarsky, B. L., & Penton, M. A. (1988). Why do *Ephemerella* nymphs scorpion posture: A "ghost of predation past"? *Oikos, 53,* 185–193.

Potts, R. (1989). *Early hominid activities at Olduvai.* Chicago: Aldine de Gruyter.

Quinn, P. C., & Eimas, P. D. (1996). Perceptual cues that permit categorical differentiation of animal species by infants. *Journal of Experimental Child Psychology, 63,* 189–211.

Rakison, D. H., & Poulin-Dubois, D. (2001). Developmental origin of the animate-inanimate distinction. *Psychological Bulletin, 127,* 209–228.

Ristau, C. (1991). Aspects of the cognitive ethology of an injury-feigning bird, the piping plover. In C. Ristau (Ed.), *Cognitive ethology: The minds of other animals.* Hillsdale, NJ: Erlbaum.

Rose, L., & Marshall, F. (1996). Meat eating, hominid sociality, and home bases revisited. *Current Anthropology, 37*(2), 307–338.

Scholl, B., & Tremoulet, P. (2000). Perceptual causality and animacy. *Trends in Cognitive Sciences, 4,* 299–308.

Seligman, M. E. P. (1971). Phobias and preparedness. *Behavior Therapy, 2,* 307–320.

Shipman, P. (1986). Scavenging or hunting in early hominids: Theoretical framework and tests. *American Anthropologist, 88,* 27–43.

Silberbauer, G. (1981). *Hunter and habitat in the Central Kalahari Desert.* Cambridge, England: Cambridge University Press.

Speece, M. W., & Brent, S. B. (1984). Children's understanding of death: A review of three components of a death concept. *Child Development, 55,* 1671–1686.

Speece, M. W., & Brent, S. B. (1996). The development of children's understanding of death. In C. A. Corr & D. M. Corr (Eds.), *Handbook of childhood death and bereavement.* New York: Springer.

Spelke, E. S. (1990). Principles of object perception. *Cognitive Science, 14,* 29–56.

Stanford, C. B. (1999). *The hunting apes: Meat eating and the origins of human behavior.* Princeton: Princeton University Press.

Stanford, C. B., & Bunn, H. T. (Eds.). (2001). *Meat-eating and human evolution.* New York: Oxford University Press.

Steen, F., & Owens, S. (2001). Evolution's pedagogy: An adaptationist model of pretense and entertainment. *Journal of Cognition and Culture, 1,* 289–321.

Sumi, S. (1984). Upside down presentation of the Johansson moving light spot pattern. *Perception, 13,* 283–286.

Sun, H., & Frost, B. J. (1998). Computation of different optical variables of looming objects in pigeon nucleus rotundus neurons. *Nature Neuroscience, 4,* 296–303.

Thorpe, S. J., Gegenfurtner, K. R., le Fabre-Thorpe, M., & Bulthoff, H. H. (2001). Detection of animals in natural images using far peripheral vision. *European Journal of Neuroscience, 14,* 869–876.

Todd, P. M., Barrett, H. C., Miller, G. F., & Blythe, P. (Under review). Accurate judgments of intention from motion cues alone.

Tomarken, A. J., Mineka, S., & Cook, M. (1989). Fear-relevant selective associations and covariation bias. *Journal of Abnormal Psychology, 98,* 381–394.

Tremoulet, P., & Feldman, J. (2000). Perception of animacy from the motion of a single object. *Perception, 29,* 943–951.

Treves, A., & Naughton-Treves, L. (1999). Risk and opportunity for humans coexisting with large carnivores. *Journal of Human Evolution, 36,* 275–282.

Van Valen, L. (1973). A new evolutionary law. *Evolutionary Theory, 1,* 1–30.

CHAPTER 8

Adaptations to Dangers from Humans

JOSHUA D. DUNTLEY

I am more and more convinced that Man is a dangerous creature, and that power whether vested in many or a few is ever grasping, and like the grave cries give, give. The great fish swallow up the small, and he who is most strenuous for the Rights of the people, when vested with power, is as eager after the prerogatives of Government. You tell me of degrees of perfection to which Humane Nature is capable of arriving, and I believe it, but at the same time lament that our admiration should arise from the scarcity of the instances.

—Abigail Adams, First Lady of the United States
from 1797 to 1801, in a letter dated 1775

OTHER HUMANS AS A HOSTILE FORCE OF NATURE

Dangers from humans manifest themselves in many different guises, including insults, robbery, violence, rape, and murder. All of the various dangers from other humans jeopardize survival. Many hostile human activities have been proposed to be the result of psychological adaptations. Researchers have found evidence for adaptations in the derogation of intrasexual competitors (Buss & Dedden, 1990), spousal violence (Buss & Shackelford, 1997b), aggression (Buss & Shackelford, 1997a; Campbell, 1993; Daly & Wilson, 1988; Wilson, Daly, & Pound, 2002), and rape (Thornhill & Palmer, 2000). At the core of the selection pressures that shaped these adaptations is conflict between individuals for limited resources. In this chapter, I (1) survey the sources of conflict between individuals, (2) discuss how natural selection has shaped strategies to best competitors in contexts of conflict, and (3) explain why one of those strategies is the infliction of costs on conspecifics, making other humans one of the most pervasive hostile forces of nature in our evolutionary history. Because of the great fitness consequences of being killed, discussion will focus on defenses against homicide.

WINNING COMPETITIONS FOR LIMITED RESOURCES

Three strategies an individual can adopt to win conflicts with rivals are: cooperate with them, outcompete them without directly inflicting costs on them, or directly inflict costs on rivals as a strategy to outcompete them. W. D. Hamilton (1964) demonstrated that selection can favor cooperation in contexts where the benefits of cooperative efforts flow to genetic relatives. Trivers (1971) argued that selection can favor cooperation in contexts of reciprocal altruism, where each of the cooperating individuals benefits from gains in trade. Finally, Tooby and Cosmides (1996) have proposed situations in which selection would favor cooperation even in the absence of costs to the individual who bestows benefits, as when, for example, a lumberjack lets a lost hiker follow him out of the woods.

The second strategy is outcompeting others for reproductively relevant resources without directly inflicting costs on them. This type of competition, often called *scramble* competition (Hassell, 1975; Nicholson, 1954), does not involve face-to-face interaction with a rival. Who acquires more of a limited resource, such as wild berries or tubers, determines the winner of scramble competitions. Any genes that may have contributed to the reliable development of the characteristics leading to greater success in scramble competitions would be passed to subsequent generations with greater frequency than competing alleles, slowly shaping the form and function of adaptations for scramble competition over deep time (Buss, 2004).

The third general strategy for winning contests for limited resources is inflicting costs on rivals. When the inclusive fitness costs of competing for a contested resource become greater than the benefits of controlling that resource, an individual should disengage from the competition. Such conditions would have selected for the purposeful infliction of costs as a strategy to outcompete rivals, leaving the winner in control of the reproductively relevant resources.

ZERO SUM AND NON-ZERO SUM COMPETITIONS

One form of competition is a zero sum game in which the amount of resources is fixed. The resources lost by one individual in a zero sum game are gained by the other, such that the sum of the resources gained and the resources lost is zero. The second form of competition can be considered non-zero sum games. In non-zero sum games, the amount that each player can gain is variable. There may be a clear winner and loser. But it is also possible that both players may win (e.g., through cooperation) or both players may lose (e.g., global nuclear war). Over evolutionary time, different strategies employed in competition with rivals would likely have yielded predictably different results. Scramble competition for resources would most often lead to non-zero sum outcomes where there is no clear winner or loser. Competitive strategies involving the direct infliction of costs would be more likely to lead to a zero sum outcome or a clear winner and loser. These competitive strategies are also more likely to lead to a situation in which both competitors lose. It is interesting that the strategy with the highest probability of a zero sum outcome is homicide. If a competitor is dead, he or she can no longer control any amount of resources.

Strategies likely to produce zero-sum outcomes have different effects on the winner and loser of a competition than strategies likely to produce non-zero sum outcomes. These different outcomes would have created different selection pressures on strategies likely to produce zero sum and non-zero sum outcomes, shaping distinct psychological adaptations for each.

SOURCES OF CONFLICT

To identify which individuals are most likely to be in conflict with one another, it is necessary to explore the adaptive problems that lead to conflict. Based on the scarcity and fitness value of a contested resource, it is possible to predict the likely range of strategies that evolved to obtain and control it. Conflict between two individuals is tempered by genetic relatedness (Hamilton, 1963). Closer genetic relatives should experience less conflict over resources than more distant relatives or unrelated individuals. A unit of food resource acquired and defended by adaptations specific to that purpose would benefit the genes that contributed to the adaptations' development whether the genes resided in the body of the person who acquired the food or the body of a genetic relative.

Conflict over Status

One broad context of conflict is for position in status hierarchies. All available evidence indicates that high-status men have sexual access to a larger number of women (Perusse, 1993). Men who are high in status also seek out younger and more fertile women (Grammer, 1992) and marry women who are more attractive (Taylor & Glenn, 1976; Udry & Eckland, 1984) than their low-status rivals. Although no comprehensive evolutionary theory of the importance of status over evolutionary history has been proposed (Buss, 2004), the potential for large fitness gains associated with increases in status would have created selection pressure for specialized cognitive adaptations that function to produce specific desires and behaviors that lead to hierarchy ascension and prevent large status falls.

Conflict over Material Resources

A second context of ancestrally recurrent conflict is conflict over *material resources* that helped to solve recurrent adaptive problems. Such resources include territory, food, weapons, and tools. There is also conflict over individuals who are the suppliers of material resources, such as conflict between siblings for investment from their parents and elder kin (Parker, Royle, & Hartley, 2002) and conflict between women for men with resources (Buss, Larsen, & Westen, 1996; Buss, Larsen, Westen, & Semmelroth, 1992).

Conflict over Mating Resources

Whereas the minimum obligatory parental investment for women is nine months, the minimum investment for men can be as little as a few minutes. Because women's minimum investment in reproduction is greater, the costs of a poor mate choice are higher (Trivers, 1972). As a result, there is conflict between the sexes about the timing of sexual activity. Because sex is less costly for men, they desire sexual activity much earlier in a relationship than do women (Werner-Wilson, 1998). Men also desire a greater number of sexual partners than women

(Schmitt, Shackelford, Duntley, Tooke, & Buss, 2002) and are more amenable to short-term, uncommitted sex (Buss, 2003).

Each of the sources of conflict between individuals discussed here is the result of evolved strategies. Selection blindly sculpted the adaptations that produce these strategies because of their benefits to individual reproductive success. That there are at least two individuals involved in any conflict is important to note when considering the selection pressures that sculpted adaptations for competition with conspecifics.

THE COEVOLUTION OF COST-INFLICTION AND DEFENSES AGAINST COSTS

Antagonistic coevolutionary arms races are part of the evolutionary history of all species. They can occur between species, as with the fox and the hare, or within species between competing adaptations in contexts of social conflict. They can create massive selection pressures, capable of producing rapid evolutionary change (see Phillips, Brown, & Shine, 2004). Any recurrent context of conflict between individuals has the potential to be a hotbed for the coevolution of competing strategies to best a competitor or defend against being bested.

The evolution of adaptations to inflict costs creates selection pressures for the coevolution of counteradaptations to avoid or prevent incurring the costs. The amount of selection pressure is a function of the magnitude of the costs and the frequency with which the costs occurred over evolutionary time. The evolution of adaptations to defend against incurring costs subsequently creates new selection pressure for refinements of adaptations designed to inflict costs or new adaptations for that end. These refined adaptations for cost-infliction, in turn, create new selection pressure for refinements in adaptations to defend against costs. This is an antagonistic, coevolutionary arms race between adaptations to inflict costs and adaptations to defend against them.

The existence of adaptations that are designed to counter the cost-inflicting strategy of a competitor is a source of evidence that the competitor's strategy is the product of adaptations. Counteradaptations to a given competitor's strategy can evolve only when the strategy has been sufficiently recurrent in predictable contexts over evolutionary time. Adaptations are more likely than by-products of adaptations or noise to produce evolutionarily recurrent, contextually predictable behaviors. Moreover, many evolved counteradaptations function by making a competitor's cost-inflicting behavior too costly to perform, which would create selection pressure against the cost-inflicting strategy. A cost-inflicting strategy that continues to persist over evolutionary time despite the costs suggests that it may, on average, be functional in producing a net benefit in a particular context. Evidence of such functionality is evidence of adaptation.

THE COEVOLUTION OF ENVIRONMENTAL DANGERS AND ADAPTATIONS TO DEFEND AGAINST THEM

Research suggests that the patterning of human fears of dangerous organisms is the result of adaptations to defend against costly interactions with them. For example, humans are more likely to develop fears of environmental hazards that were recurrent in past environments than of novel hazards that were introduced in our more recent history. Snakes are not a threat to human life in most of our modern environment, but automobiles, tobacco, and electricity are. Öhman, Lundqvist, and Esteves (2001) argue that humans lack the fear of cars, cigarettes, and electrical outlets that they have for snakes, spiders, and rodents because natural selection has not had enough time to fashion specific adaptations to produce fear of recent human inventions. Another example is the developmental timing of the emergence of fears of specific animals, which corresponds to the period in development when children begin to more widely explore their environment—about the age of 2. Understanding of death also emerges during this period, by the age of 3 or 4 (Barrett & Behne, in press). Fear or wariness of other humans may also develop because interactions between humans can be similarly antagonistic, even in relationships that intuitively may seem the closest.

THE COEVOLUTION OF DANGERS FROM HUMANS AND DEFENSES AGAINST THEM

A number of different strategies may be employed to inflict costs on others. To be effective, a cost-inflicting strategy must affect an individual or the individual's genetic relatives.

ASSAULTS ON STATUS

One strategy of cost-infliction is damaging the reputation of a rival, decreasing the rival's access to tangible resources and to mates. Given the importance of status, selection likely operated to produce adaptations for status hierarchy negotiation. An individual in a group cannot ascend in a status hierarchy without displacing someone above, bumping that person to a lower position than he or she occupied previously and inflicting costs associated with status loss. Higher status men have greater access to resources and more mating opportunities than lower status men (Betzig, 1993; Buss, 2003; Hill & Hurtado, 1996; Perusse, 1993). Because a larger number of mating opportunities enhances the reproductive success of men more than of women, there should be greater status striving among men than among women. Research across the life span has found that men place greater importance on coming out ahead and women are more focused on maintaining social harmony (Maccoby, 1990; Pratto, 1996; Whiting & Edwards, 1988).

A number of adaptations may have evolved to combat the danger of status loss caused by the cost-inflicting tactics of competitors. First, individuals should be armed with the ability to constantly track their own position in a status hierarchy, while also keeping track of their closest competitors (Buss, 2004). Individuals should be motivated to gather information about the strengths and weaknesses of their closest status rivals to inform strategies of status defense that may be required in the future. The strategic formation of alliances that will strengthen an individual's hold on a position in a status hierarchy can help defend against status assaults from others. Offensive tactics, such as competitor derogation (Buss & Dedden, 1990), can assault the status of those most likely to challenge an individual's position in the future, forestalling a status conflict. Competitor derogation may also be an effective strategy after a status loss has occurred. Recouping status that has been lost, however, can be a more formidable task than maintaining a position in a status hierarchy and may require more drastic measures. In response to public humiliation or challenges to status and social reputation, people may resort to violence and even murder. This made sense in the contexts of small group living in which we evolved (Tooby & DeVore, 1987), where a loss of status could have had devastating effects on survival and reproduction (Buss, 2004). The outcome of selection for status adaptations operating in small groups is evidenced today in our research on homicidal ideation, in which we find that the most frequent triggers of homicidal fantasies are status related (Buss & Duntley, 2005).

THEFT AND CHEATING

A second strategy of cost-infliction that may be used to gain an advantage in competition for resources is to steal the resources (see Cohen & Machalek, 1988) or cheat rivals out of them. A valuable weapon can be stolen and used against its owner. Valuable territory can be encroached on and its vegetation, water, shelter, and wildlife exploited (Chagnon, 1983). Mates can be poached from an existing relationship (Buss, 2000, 2003; Schmitt & Buss, 2001). Public knowledge that an individual has been cheated or had valuables stolen also can affect the person's reputation. The person may gain a reputation as one who is easy to exploit, perhaps increasing the likelihood that others will attempt to cheat or steal from the person in the future. An easily exploitable person may be less attractive to members of the opposite sex. Cheating or the theft of resources, in short, can be effective strategies of cost-infliction for individual gain.

To prevent the threat of material resource theft, individuals may have evolved adaptations that motivate them to keep valuable items under protection, conceal them, or make valuable commodities seem less desirable to rivals. They may have also evolved adaptations to detect those competitors who would cheat them. Deceiving rivals about the location of a valuable resource, such as food, has been shown to occur in other primate species, like tufted capuchin monkeys (*Cebus apella;* Fujita, Kuroshima, & Masuda, 2002), in pigs (Held, Mendl, Devereux, & Byrne, 2002), and in ravens (*Corvus corax;* Bugnyar & Kotrschal, 2004). The ability to detect cheaters in contexts of social exchange is another strategy to prevent the loss of resources to rivals. Sugiyama, Tooby, and Cosmides (2002) found evidence that the ability to detect cheaters is likely a cross-cultural universal. In their research, the Shiwiar hunter-horticulturalists of the Ecuadorian Amazon performed similarly to Harvard undergraduates in their ability to detect violations of conditional rules in contexts of social exchange. Both groups, however, performed poorly when asked to detect violations of conditional rules in contexts other than social exchange.

When the resource that is threatened is a mate rather than a material commodity, Buss and Shackelford (1997b) found that men and women engage in tactics that range from vigilance to violence to defend their relationships. Fueled by jealousy, an emotion absent from contexts of material resource theft, men's tactics of defending against mate poachers were found to be different from women's. Men are more likely to conceal their partners, display resources, and resort to threats and violence, especially against rivals. Men are also more likely to use tactics of submission and self-abasement, groveling, or promising their partners anything to get them to stay. Women are more likely to enhance their appearance and induce jealousy in their partners, demonstrating their desirability by showing that they have other mating prospects.

VIOLENCE

A third strategy for inflicting costs on rivals is to injure them. Healthy individuals can compete more effectively than the rivals they injure. Rivals may be more likely to avoid or drop out of competition with individuals who injured them in the past. Individuals who are capable of inflicting greater injuries on their competitors than the competitors inflict on them may gain a reputation of being difficult to exploit. This reputation may protect individuals against violent confrontations and grant easier access to resources with less resistance from their rivals.

The most effective strategy for preventing violence capable of producing injuries is to avoid the violent confrontation altogether. Because it is easier to attack an individual than a group, human adaptations to form alliances may provide one form of deterrence against violent rivals. Adaptations that lead to the avoidance of contexts likely to make an individual the target of violence may provide another kind of protection against being injured. Humans may also possess adaptations designed to attempt to reason with an attacker, emphasizing the costs of their violent behavior or offering some other possible resolution to the conflict. Finally, if an attack cannot be avoided, individuals may resort to violence or even murder to defend against an attack (Daly & Wilson, 1988).

RAPE

A fourth cost-inflicting strategy aimed directly at obtaining reproductive resources is rape. Rapists may benefit from the behavior by fathering offspring that they may not have otherwise produced. Rape inflicts not only terrible emotional costs (Block, 1990; Burgess & Holmstrom, 1974) and physical costs (Geist, 1988) on women but also fitness costs by bypassing female mechanisms of mate choice (Buss, 2004). Although scholars have concluded that there is not enough evidence to determine whether men have adaptations to rape (Buss, 2003, 2004; Symons, 1979), historical records and ethnographies suggest that rape occurs cross-culturally and was recurrent over deep time (Buss, 2003).

A number of researchers have proposed the existence of antirape adaptations. The formation of alliances with groups of men and other women for protection have been argued to be evolved counterstrategies to rapists' tactics (Smuts, 1992). The *bodyguard hypothesis* proposes that women's preference for mates who are physically formidable and high in social dominance is, at least in part, an adaptation to prevent rape (Wilson & Mesnick, 1997). Specialized fears that motivate women to avoid situations ancestrally predictive of an increased likelihood of being raped have been proposed to help preemptively defend against rape. To prevent conception resulting from rape, women may have evolved to avoid risky activities during ovulation (Chavanne & Gallup, 1998). Finally, the psychological pain of rape has been argued to motivate women to avoid being raped in the future (Thornhill & Palmer, 2000). In addition, women may possess adaptations to minimize the costs of rape after it has occurred. To avoid the reputational damage that can be associated with rape and decrease the risk of losing their romantic partner, women may feel motivated to keep their ordeal a secret. They may feel a strong urge to bathe themselves after the event, washing physical evidence of the forced encounter away so it cannot be detected, especially by their mate. Finally, women may seek revenge against their attacker by marshalling male relatives and allies to attack him, especially if the rapist represents a continuing threat to the women or their female relatives.

Some strategies employed to win competitions offer a potential solution to a wider variety of problems than others. For example, the use of violence to resolve conflict in contexts where the costs of aggression is low has the potential to solve a wider variety of problems than the clandestine theft of resources. Violence can be used as a strategy to simultaneously aid in theft, demonstrate the ability to acquire resources to potential mates, and intimidate rivals against retribution.

Strategies that evolved to defend against the dangers of other humans can be conceptualized in three temporal categories: (1) those that prevent or deter the event before it occurs, (2) those that try to stop or minimize the costs of the event while it is occurring, and (3) those capable of addressing the event after it has occurred. Just as some strategies of inflicting costs may simultaneously contribute to the solution of numerous adaptive problems, some evolved defenses can be used to combat a number of different strategies of cost-infliction.

> Scientists marvel at the predatory competence of the great white, praising its speed, brute strength, sensory acuity, and apparent determination, but man is a predator of far more spectacular ability. The shark does not have dexterity, guile, deceit, cleverness, or disguise. It also does not have our brutality, for man does things to man that sharks could not dream of doing. Deep in our cells we know this, so occasional fear of another human being is natural. (Gavin De Becker, *The Gift of Fear*, p. 283)

> She got out of the car and she saw me and she was frightened right away and she started to run. I ran after her and stabbed her twice in the back. Somebody yelled and I was frightened so I jumped back into the car . . . I had noticed as I was backing the car back that the woman had gotten up and appeared to be going around the corner, so I came back thinking that I would find her . . . The second door I tried opened, I opened, and there she was laying on the floor. When she saw me she started screaming again so I stabbed her a few more times. She seemed to quiet down a bit, so she wasn't really struggling with me that hard now. . . . (From Winston Moseley's confession for the murder of Kitty Genovese on March 16, 1964)

ADAPTATIONS FOR HOMICIDE

Homicide is a strategy capable of solving or contributing to the solution of conflict with other individuals. We propose that humans possess adaptations for murder (Buss & Duntley, 1998, 1999, 2003, in press; Duntley & Buss, 1999). According to Homicide Adaptation Theory, psychological adaptations for homicide were selected when they contributed to better solutions to adaptive problems, on average, than competing designs. Certain information processing adaptations in our brains were shaped by unique sets of selection pressures specifically to scrutinize and sometimes to produce *homicidal* behavior in adaptive problem contexts similar to those recurrently solvable by homicide in the past. Although some have suggested the possibility of adaptations for homicide (Ghiglieri, 1999; Pinker, 1997) and others have argued that humans may have an instinct to kill (e.g., Chagnon, 1988), no other theorists have gone into depth in exploring the likely design of adaptations for homicide (see a notable exception dealing with warfare: Tooby & Cosmides, 1988) despite the fact that most animal researchers take for granted that other species have adaptations to kill conspecifics (e.g., Ghiglieri, 1999; Hrdy, 1977; Wrangham & Peterson, 1996).

THE NATURE OF SELECTION PRESSURES FOR HOMICIDE ADAPTATIONS

We are *not* arguing that homicide would have evolved to be the *preferred strategy* for dealing with a given adaptive problem in all situations. In most sets of circumstances, the extremely high costs of committing murder would have outweighed its benefits. We propose, however, that homicidal behavior was the best solution for rare *combinations* of adaptive problems and circumstances, which provided selection pressure for the evolution of homicide adaptations. As a result, it is not possible to point to just one feature of a context that will activate a psychology of homicide in every instance in every person. Mitigating environmental factors (Gartner, 1990), heritable personality features (Rhee & Waldman, 2002), and the calibration of psychological mechanisms during development (Dodge, Bates, & Pettit, 1990) all contribute to determining whether homicide will be adopted. Many or all of these influences were part of the selection pressures that shaped homicide adaptations. It is through a combination of cues to the presence of an adaptive problem ancestrally solvable by murder that homicide adaptations are activated. The presence or absence of these cues, as well as their magnitude, can help us to predict when conspecific killing will be more or less likely to occur. Without complete knowledge of how human psychology produces homicidal behavior, however, it is not possible to make perfect predictions about whether homicide will occur in any individual case. The same is true of making predictions about any behavior.

RECURRENT ADAPTIVE PROBLEMS SOLVABLE BY HOMICIDE

We hypothesize that homicide was functional in solving a wide variety of adaptive problems. Specifically, the killing of a conspecific could have contributed to: (1) preventing the exploitation, injury, rape, or killing of self, kin, mates, and coalitional allies by conspecifics in the present and future; (2) reputation management against being perceived as easily exploited, injured, raped, or killed by conspecifics; (3) protecting resources, territory, shelter, and food from competitors; (4) eliminating resource-absorbing or costly individuals who are not genetically related (e.g., stepchildren); and (5) eliminating genetic relatives who interfere with investment in other vehicles better able to translate resources into genetic fitness (e.g., deformed infants, the chronically ill or infirmed).

THE FITNESS COSTS OF BEING KILLED

There are large and inalterable costs to the victims of homicide. It is bad to be murdered. Examining the costs of homicide through an evolutionary lens eluci- dates the true nature and magnitude of the costs incurred by victims of homicide and gives us a better understanding of how other humans were significant dan- gers over our evolutionary history. A murder victim's death has a much larger impact on his or her inclusive fitness than just the loss of the genes housed in the person's body. The inclusive fitness costs of dying at the hands of another human can cascade to the victim's children, spouse, kin, and coalitional allies. The spe- cific costs include the following.

LOSS OF FUTURE REPRODUCTION

A victim of murder cannot reproduce in the future with a current mate or with other possible mates. On average, this cost would have been greater for younger individuals than older individuals.

DAMAGE TO EXISTING CHILDREN

The child of a murdered parent receives fewer resources, is more susceptible to being exploited or injured by others, and may have more difficulty ascending sta- tus hierarchies or negotiating mating relationships, contributing to poorer fitness outcomes. Children of a murdered parent may see their surviving parent's invest- ment diverted away from them to a new mating relationship and to the children who are the product of that relationship. A single parent, who can invest only half of what two parents can invest, would be more likely to abandon his or her chil- dren in favor of better mating prospects in the future. And the children of a mur- dered parent risk becoming stepchildren, a condition that brings with it physical abuse and homicide rates 40 to 100 times greater than those found among chil- dren who reside with two genetic parents (Daly & Wilson, 1988).

DAMAGE TO EXTENDED KIN GROUP

A victim of homicide cannot protect or invest in extended kin. A victim's entire kin network can gain the reputation of being vulnerable to exploitation as a result of the murder. A homicide victim cannot influence the status trajectories or mat- ing relationships of family members. And the open position left by the murder victim in a kin network's status hierarchy could create a struggle for power among the surviving family members.

A MURDER VICTIM'S FITNESS LOSSES CAN BE A RIVAL'S FITNESS GAINS

Killers can benefit from the residual reproductive value and parenting value of the surviving mate of a homicide victim, sometimes at the expense of the vic- tim's children with that mate. Murderers can ascend into the vacancies in status hierarchies left by their victims. The children of killers would thrive relative to the children of murder victims, who would be deprived of the investment, pro- tection, and influence of two genetic parents. Many family members who would have survived if the person was not murdered will die before they can reproduce. And many children who would have been born to members of the family will never be born.

DEFENSES AGAINST HOMICIDE

Of all the dangers created by other humans, homicide can be the most devastating in terms of its effect on the inclusive fitness of its victims. If homicide recurred in predictable contexts over our evolutionary history, it would have created intense selection pressure to prevent or otherwise avoid being murdered. The heavy selection pressure created by the costs of being killed was powerful enough to shape distinct adaptations to defend against homicide (Buss & Duntley, 2005; Duntley & Buss, 1998, 2000, 2001, 2002).

The intensity of selection for any adaptation, including defenses against being killed, is a function of the *frequency* of the selective event and its *fitness costs.* Low base-rate events that impose heavy fitness costs, like homicide, can create intense selection pressure for adaptations to prevent or avoid them. Ancestral homicides, however, may not have been as infrequent as they are in many modern societies. Homicide rates in hunter-gatherer societies, which more closely resemble the conditions in which humans evolved, are far higher than those in modern state nations with organized law enforcement and judicial systems (Ghiglieri, 1999; Marshall & Block, 2004).

THE NATURE OF SELECTION PRESSURES FOR HOMICIDE DEFENSE ADAPTATIONS

Homicide defense adaptations would have been selected for only one function: to defend against the massive inclusive fitness costs incurred by murder victims and their kin. Adaptations against homicide could have accomplished this by leading individuals to: (1) avoid contexts that present an increased risk of becoming a murder victim, (2) manipulate these contexts so they are no longer dangerous, (3) defend against homicidal attacks, and (4) staunch the costs of homicide to genetic relatives after it has occurred.

AVOIDING CONTEXTS WHERE HOMICIDE IS LIKELY

One of the design features of homicide avoidance mechanisms is sensitivity to cues of high-risk contexts. Cues to the presence of such contexts include the following.

CONTROL OF TERRITORY

Individuals are more vulnerable to attack when away from their home territory. Being in a rival's territory or even a neutral territory would be a cue to an increased risk of attack. Chagnon (1983) reports that the Yanomamö Indians sometimes lure a rival group to their village under the auspices of having a celebratory feast. Away from their home, the rival group is at a strategic disadvantage. The Yanomamö attempt to lull their rivals into a false sense of security only to ambush them. Individuals should experience more fear of being killed in the presence of cues indicative of being in hostile territory.

CHARACTERISTICS OF THE PHYSICAL SURROUNDINGS

We hypothesize that characteristics of the physical surroundings are another source of ancestrally relevant cues to the likelihood of being murdered. It is easier for a competitor to hide in the shadows than the light. Individuals are more likely to be ambushed in areas where there are visual obstacles than on the open plains of a savannah. Individuals are more vulnerable to attack when their backs are to their competitors than when their backs are against a wall. Individuals should experience more fear of homicide and ideation that their life may be in danger in the presence of such cues to their vulnerability. This proposal is consistent with the Savanna Hypothesis. Kaplan (1992) argued that the process of evaluating landscape involves information gathering about places for surveillance, places for hiding, refuges from predators, and possible routes of escape. These forms of information gathering would have been beneficial strategies against dangerous conspecifics, including those with murderous intentions.

CHARACTERISTICS OF THE RIVAL

Over our evolutionary history, certain personality and life history characteristics of rivals were likely correlated with the likelihood that a rival would kill: high levels of narcissism, an antisocial personality, high impulsivity, low conscientiousness, high levels of hostility, and a history of committing acts of severe violence or homicide against others. Research has demonstrated that a history of violent behavior is often one of the strongest predictors of future violence (Douglas & Webster, 1999). The importance of the reputations of rivals in identifying conspecifics who pose an increased threat of killing cannot be underestimated. It is clear from many ethnographies, for example, that some men develop reputations as killers or thugs. The people who live in the same communities as these men give them a wide berth, trying to avoid antagonizing them (Chagnon, 1983; Ghiglieri, 1999).

FEATURES OF THE SITUATION

Specific adaptations likely evolved to be sensitive to circumstances ancestrally indicative of an increased probability of being murdered. These situations correspond to adaptive problem contexts solvable by homicide and include:

1. Injuring, raping, killing, or inflicting other serious costs on rivals, their kin, mates, or coalitional allies.
2. Damaging a rival's reputation, leading others to perceive the rival or genetic relatives as easily exploited, injured, raped, or killed.
3. Poaching the resources, mates, territory, shelter, or food that belongs to a rival.
4. Absorbing the resources of a nongenetic relative (e.g., stepchildren).
5. Interfering with parents' or kin's investment in other vehicles who are better able to translate resource investment into genetic fitness (e.g., deformed infants, the chronically ill or infirmed).

Perhaps the most effective defense against being killed is simply to avoid situations associated with an increased risk of being murdered. The experience of fear may be one adaptive mechanism that helps us to avoid such situations.

In his book *The Gift of Fear* (1997), Gavin De Becker argues that fear, when applied appropriately, can be considered a signal that exists to aid in our survival, protecting us from violent situations. It is adaptive to experience fear, he argues, when the fear is enabling—allowing individuals to effectively address the danger they face. Real fear, according to De Becker, "occurs in the presence of danger and will always easily link to pain or death" (p. 285).

Marks (1987) has argued that fear and anxiety can be protective in four primary ways. First, it can lead a person to freeze or become immobile, which could help to conceal a person, allow time to assess the situation, and perhaps decrease the likelihood of being attacked. This is a particularly valuable strategy when there is uncertainty about whether an individual has been spotted by a predator or hostile conpsecific, and when the exact location of the threat cannot be determined. Second, fear can provide motivation to escape or avoid danger in the environment, which can help move a person out of harm's way and perhaps find a location that provides some protection from future interactions with the source of the danger. Third, a strategy of aggression in self-defense may be adopted. A dangerous conspecific or predator can be frightened away or killed through the successful employment of an aggressive strategy. Finally, an individual can adopt a strategy of submission as a way to appease the source of the hostility, usually a member of the same species. Such strategies of submission are common among many species of social mammals, including humans (Buss, 2004).

Because homicide has unique fitness consequences, the fear of being murdered may be a distinct emotional state accompanied by specific decision rules that function to help individuals defend against being killed by conspecifics. Specifically, selection fashioned homicide defense adaptations that lead to the avoidance of:

- Visiting unfamiliar surroundings, particularly those controlled by rivals.
- Traveling through locations where homicidal competitors may be waiting in ambush.
- Traveling at night.
- Interacting with individuals who are more likely to murder.
- Inflicting costs likely to motivate a conspecific to kill you.

DEFENDING AGAINST HOMICIDAL ATTACKS

Another strategy for defending against being murdered is defending against the homicidal attacks of another individual. Such strategies can take three primary forms:

1. *Leaving the area that killers inhabit:* One strategy to decrease the likelihood of being murdered is to avoid living in locations inhabited by murderers. Some researchers have proposed that one explanation for human migration out of Africa, across Europe and Asia, and into the Americas was to avoid

hostile confrontations and warfare with conspecifics (Diamond, 1997; Richerson & Boyd, 1998). Fleeing homicidal rivals can be an effective strategy if their intended victims can move out of their reach.

2. *Manipulating the situation to make killing less beneficial and more costly:* People who believe they might be murdered may be able to alter aspects of the situation to increase the costs or decrease the benefits of a murderous conspecific's homicidal strategy, making murder less attractive than possible alternatives. Examples include:

   - Forging alliances with powerful and influential conspecifics.
   - Staying in the vicinity of coalitional allies who may serve as bodyguards.
   - Turning members of a group against the person who may intend to kill you.
   - Resolving the conflict with the conspecific through some form of repayment.
   - Helping a killer rival to salvage or restore the reputation you damaged.
   - Bargaining or begging for your life.
   - Threatening retaliation against a homicidal competitor by kin and coalitional allies.
   - Performing preemptive, perhaps homicidal, attacks against would-be killers, their kin, or their coalitional allies.

   Some of these strategies may be implemented up to the moment that an irreversible homicidal behavior is enacted on a victim. The implementation of these defensive strategies may not always be enough to derail a homicidal strategy in favor of a nonlethal alternative. If not, the person targeted by a killer would have no recourse but to defend against the attack.

3. *Defending against homicidal attacks:* At the point a rival is actively engaging in behaviors capable of killing someone, it may be too late to flee or otherwise derail the homicidal strategy. In such a face-to-face confrontation with a killer, the only two alternatives are to defend yourself or die. There are only two basic strategies of self-defense against a homicidal attack: call for help or physically incapacitate the killer so the intended victim can flee. Screams for help may be uniquely identifiable from other calls for assistance. Selection could have fashioned this kind of honest signal if fitness gains flowed to rescuers, such as kin or coalitional allies who might have benefitted from reciprocal exchange with the intended victim. References to "blood-curdling screams" and "screaming bloody murder" may refer to such uniquely identifiable screams for help by people battling off a rival's attempts to kill them. A "death scream" (Buss, personal communication, 2005) may represent another category of alarm that does not function as a call for help, but instead broadcasts a warning to kin and mates that a murderer is present as the victim dies.

   Incapacitating a killer is another strategy victims can use in self-defense. Invariably, this strategy involves a physical attack. At a minimum, the intended victims of a homicidal strategy must incapacitate the intended killer to such an extent that they can flee or buy enough time for help to arrive. In some confrontations with a murderer, the most practical strategy may be to kill in self-defense. Contexts leading victims to murder in self-defense are likely to include features such as some likelihood that the killer will continue to inflict costs in the future, a lack of kin or allies in close enough proximity to help, the failure of nonlethal strategies to incapacitate the killer, and a lack of other options.

One of the key differences between killers and victims in confrontations between the two is that killers are more often prepared to carry out their homicidal strategies than victims are to defend against them. Killers can select the time and place when it is best to commit murder. Natural selection would have favored adaptive design that led killers to catch victims alone and by surprise, reducing the possible costs of their homicidal strategy (e.g., being injured or killed by a victim or the victim's kin). As a result, it is likely that those most likely to die in the majority of face-to-face confrontations between would-be killers and their intended victims are the victims. Because the genetic relatives of murder victims also suffer fitness costs, adaptations to defend against being killed may also be found in murder victims' kin.

STAUNCHING THE COSTS OF HOMICIDE AMONG GENETIC RELATIVES ONCE IT HAS OCCURRED

At least two forces may have selected for adaptations in kin that function to staunch the negative consequences of a family member being murdered. First, damage to the reputation of a murder victim's family may be repaired by inflicting reciprocal costs on the killer. A family that is capable of striking back against the murderer of their kin may be able to demonstrate that it is no longer exploitable or that exploiters will pay with their lives. Second, killers will likely continue to be a source of danger in the future if they continue to live. Avenging the death of a family member by murdering the person responsible may eliminate a possible source of recurrent fitness costs.

All of the proposed adaptations for defending against homicide function by derailing or thwarting murderous strategies or by inflicting heavy costs on killers. The evolution of adaptations to defend against being murdered would have created selection pressure for the evolution of refined or additional adaptations for homicide that were capable of circumventing the evolved homicide defenses. The presence of refined and additional homicide adaptations, in turn, would have selected for refined or additional homicide defenses, and so on, setting up an antagonistic coevolutionary arms race between adaptations to kill and adaptations to defend against being murdered.

EVIDENCE OF ADAPTATIONS FOR HOMICIDE AND HOMICIDE DEFENSES

Homicide has the potential of occurring wherever there are humans interacting with other humans. This statement is as true of mother and child as it is of enemy nations. It is even true of the relationship between a pregnant mother and her developing fetus. For most women, a fetus they carry does not represent their last opportunity to reproduce. Women were selected to invest more in those offspring likely to yield the greatest reproductive benefit, even in utero. If a fetus is not viable, for example, it would make more sense for a pregnant woman to forgo her investment in its development in favor of investing in a subsequent pregnancy. Most successfully fertilized eggs do not result in a full-term pregnancy. Up to

78% of them fail to implant or are spontaneously aborted (Nesse & Williams, 1994). Most often, these outcomes occur because the mother detects chromosomal abnormalities in the fetus. The mother's ability to detect such abnormalities is the result of adaptations that function to prevent the mother from investing in offspring that will likely die young. Most miscarriages occur during the first 12 weeks of pregnancy (Haig, 1993), at a point where the mother has not invested heavily in a costly pregnancy and the spontaneously aborted fetus is less likely to lead to infection (Saraiya et al., 1999). The fetus, however, is not a passive pawn in its mother's evolved reproductive strategy. The fetus has only one chance to live. Selection would have favored fetal genes to resist its mother's attempt to abort it. The production and release of human chorionic gonadotropin (hCG) by the fetus into the mother's bloodstream, which is normally an honest signal of fetal viability, may be one adaptation against being spontaneously aborted. This hormone prevents the mother from menstruating, allowing the fetus to remain implanted. Maternal physiology seems to react to the production of hCG as a sign that the developing fetus is viable (Haig, 1993). Other humans do not cease to be dangerous at birth. For additional evidence, we focus on infanticide.

Researchers have hypothesized that the contested resource that leads to infanticide is often parental investment, leading to parent-offspring conflict (Trivers, 1974). There is conflict between a mother and her infant over the amount she invests in her child. The infant may desire greater investment than would be optimal, in the currency of inclusive fitness, for the mother to give. Additionally, the reproductive value of children is lowest at birth and increases as they age, a function of the likelihood they will survive to reproductive age.

A newborn infant has few options for defending itself from homicidal attacks perpetrated by adults. To defend against mother-perpetrated infanticide, a newborn's best strategy is to give off cues that it is a genetic vehicle worthy of investment. Immediately after birth, a newborn should give off cues to its health and vigor, cues capable of satisfying maternal adaptations that evolved to judge the probability of fitness payoffs for investing in the infant (Soltis, in press). Newborns who nurse in the first hour after birth stimulate a surge in maternal oxytocin levels, strengthening the bond between mother and newborn. Nursing mothers' priorities become shifted. They become less motivated to self-groom for the purposes of attracting a mate and more motivated to groom their infants (Insel, 1992). By contrast, new mothers who do not nurse are more likely to suffer from postpartum depression (Papinczak & Turner, 2000; Taveras et al., 2003), a condition associated with higher levels of mother-perpetrated infanticide (Knopps, 1993; Spinelli, 2004; see also Hagen, 1999) and significantly higher levels of maternal thoughts of harming their babies (Jennings, Ross, Popper, & Elmore, 1999; Kendall-Tackett, 1994). Newborns that are more active, as evaluated by APGAR scores, have been shown to be less likely to succumb to infant mortality (Chong & Karlberg, 2004; Morales & Vazquez, 1994) and would be a better object of maternal investment than newborns that were not active. Selection may have favored early nursing, the production of loud cries, and robust movements in newborns as defenses against mother-perpetrated infanticide.

As they grow older, infants are increasingly aware of their environment and able to move about on their own. As a result, they are increasingly likely to encounter dangers while outside the range of their caregivers' immediate protection. Infants who possess some ability to recognize potential dangers in the environment would have a significant advantage over infants with no such ability. Selection would have favored knowledge in advance, in the form of specific fears, to steer infants away from threats to their survival. The developmental timing of the emergence of fears provides evidence that selection played a part in shaping them. Many fears do not emerge in development until individuals first encounter adaptive problems. For example, the fear of heights first emerges when children begin to crawl during infancy. The emergence of this fear corresponds with infants' greater risk of falling as they move about on their own. Fear of strangers usually first emerges at about the same time (Scarr & Salapatek, 1970), corresponding with a greater risk of encountering hostile conspecifics. Stranger anxiety provides powerful protection against dangerous humans by preventing young children from approaching individuals they do not know and motivating them to seek parental protection. Stranger anxiety has been documented in a number of different cultures, from Guatemala and Zambia, to the !Kung and the Hopi Indians (P. K. Smith, 1979). Infant deaths at the hands of unrelated conspecifics have been documented among nonhuman primates (Ghiglieri, 1999; Hrdy, 1977; Wrangham & Peterson, 1996) and in humans (Daly & Wilson, 1988). Human children are more fearful of male strangers than female strangers, corresponding to the greater danger posed by male than female strangers over evolutionary time (Heerwagen & Orians, 2002). Even though the vast majority of strangers may not intend to inflict harm on children, if a fear of strangers prevented even a tiny fraction of children from being murdered over our evolutionary history, stranger anxiety would have been favored by selection.

Strangers are not the only threat to the lives of children. Children raised with a stepparent in the home are between 40 and 100 times more likely to be killed than children raised by two natural parents (Daly & Wilson, 1988). Stepfamilies were likely a recurrent feature of ancestral environments. Without modern medical treatments, diseases killed many adults. Fathers sometimes died in battles or on hunts. Mothers sometimes died during childbirth. After their partner's death, it was probably common for a surviving parent to find a new mate. Single parents may have evolved to prefer partners who posed the smallest risk to their existing children. Single parents' preferences for new partners may be, in part, evolved defenses against the murder of their existing children (Buss, 2005).

Stepchildren may also possess adaptations to help defend themselves against potentially murderous stepparents by recognizing characteristics of potential stepparents that may be predictive of their likelihood of inflicting costs on their new mate's children, including killing them. Children's evolved intuitions about potential stepparents could lead them to influence their surviving parent's mate choice, providing some measure of defense against being killed.

Selection also would have favored adaptations to guide the behavior of children living with a stepparent in the home. Stepchildren should take steps to minimize their costliness to their stepparent, such as keeping a low profile and demanding few resources. Stepchildren should also recognize opportunities to make themselves valuable to their stepparent, such as contributing to the care of children that result from the relationship between their genetic parent and stepparent. The best strategy of stepchildren who feel their life is in danger, however, may be to sabotage the relationship between their genetic parent and stepparent. This strategy may involve the infliction of costs by stepchildren on their stepparents in an attempt to get the stepparents to abandon their new romantic relationship. It may also involve stepchildren inflicting costs on themselves to influence their genetic parent to curb investment away from a new mateship and toward their children. Engaging in delinquent behaviors may be one strategy children use to inflict costs on themselves. Research has demonstrated that living in a stepfamily compared to living with two genetic parents more than doubles a child's risk of engaging in juvenile delinquent behavior (Coughlin & Vuchinich, 1996).

The presence of a stepparent in the home is a good example of a recurrent context of increased risk of homicide that may have selected for homicide defense adaptations in stepchildren and their kin. These adaptations become activated in stepchildren, but remain dormant in children who reside with both of their biological parents. Specialized adaptations to defend against homicide may exist for all contextual domains where there was a recurrent ancestral risk of being murdered. Many situations, however, do not provide complete information about the true probability that a person may fall victim to homicide. Because being killed is so costly, it is likely that selection fashioned adaptively patterned biases that lead people to systematically overestimate the likelihood that they will be killed in conditions of uncertainty.

MANAGING ERRORS TO AVOID BEING MURDERED

Goleman (1995) argued that people worry too much because most of what they worry about has a low probability of happening. However, a cognitive system that "irrationally" overestimated the likelihood of violence, thus reliably avoiding its costs, would be favored by selection over an unbiased, "rational" cognitive system that led an individual to incur heavy fitness costs, even a small amount of the time. Because many inferences about whether an individual will be targeted by a killer are obfuscated by varying degrees of uncertainty, contexts of homicide can be considered compatible with the logic of Error Management Theory (Haselton, 2003; Haselton & Buss, 2000). In situations involving uncertainty, making an erroneous inference about the intentions of others can carry high fitness costs. There are two types of errors a person can make when inferring the intentions of others: falsely inferring an intention that is not present or falsely inferring the absence of an intention that is present. In the case of avoiding homicide, selection pressure may have shaped cognitive biases that lead people to overinfer homicidal intent in others. It would be better, on average, to infer that someone might want to kill you when he or she really does not than to infer that someone does not want you dead when he or she actually does. In this way, people would avoid making the more costly of the two errors. In sum, one design feature of the psychology of homicide avoidance may be a cognitive bias that leads people to overinfer homicidal intent in the presence of cues to adaptive problems historically solvable by homicide.

The *amount* of uncertainty surrounding a potentially high-cost situation is likely to have an effect on the strength of the anti-homicide adaptive bias. Imagine a man walking home from a bar late on a rainy night. He decides to take a shortcut through a dark alley to shorten the distance he must walk in the rain. As he is walking, he notices another man limping slowly toward him down the alley . . . and immediately identifies the man as his brother. Assuming the two had a good, brotherly relationship, there would be little reason for the man to infer that his brother might want to kill him. Indeed, no fears of being killed should be triggered in this situation. Now imagine that another man takes a shortcut through an alley and sees a limping stranger slowly walking toward him.

Greater uncertainty about the intentions of the unknown man, in addition to the other features of the context, may lead to an overinference of the likelihood that this unknown man might have intentions to harm or kill. In conditions of complete uncertainty about the identity of another person, in situations lacking information about the motivations of others, and in the absence of information to the contrary, the safer error would be to overinfer a conspecific's hostile intentions. In fact, the safest error would be to assume that the other person intended to kill you. No costs that another person can inflict compare to the costs of being murdered. When facing uncertainty from environmental cues about the intentions of others, selection should mold psychological design to assume that the worst possible fitness event is going to occur, so its heavy costs can be avoided. People's evolved intuitions should lead them to fear being murdered. The strategies people employ to defend against homicide (e.g., avoiding the context, fleeing, or killing the attacker) would simultaneously defend against a number of non-lethal, cost-inflicting strategies. As a result, homicide defense adaptations may, to some degree, be a compromise between a pure defense against homicide and defenses against other significant dangers from conspecifics.

The strength of information processing biases that strategically overestimate the likelihood that another individual intends to inflict costs is proportional to the degree of uncertainty surrounding the individual and the context. In other words, *the bias toward inferring that another individual intends to inflict costs should increase as uncertainty about the individual and the context increases.* This is not to say that such an error management bias will be applied equally to all different individuals identified as a possible threat. The bias should be proportional to the ancestral threat that different individuals posed. It should be especially strong for those who posed the greatest threat, such as young adult males, and less strong or absent for others (e.g., infants, young children, the elderly).

There is evidence in the empirical literature that people's perceptions are skewed in precisely the direction predicted by Error Management Theory (Haselton & Buss, 2000). Experiments using schematic facial stimuli demonstrated that different facial expressions are not processed the same way (Öhman et al., 2001). Research participants viewed stimuli of threatening and friendly faces that were constructed from identical physical features. The threatening face was found more quickly than the happy face among neutral distracters. Additionally, faces with V-shaped eyebrows of a schematic angry facial display were more rapidly and accurately located than faces with inverted V-shaped eyebrows (friendly faces) in a visual search task. This research suggests a perceptual bias consistent with Error Management Theory that leads individuals to be especially sensitive to the presence of potentially hostile conspecifics. Natural selection would have favored a greater sensitivity to angry faces over friendly faces because those with hostile intentions would have posed an adaptive problem often requiring immediate action to avoid incurring potentially heavy costs.

More evidence consistent with adaptive cognitive biases to defend against being murdered comes from research of people's thoughts that someone might want to kill them. Corresponding to the greater danger posed by male strangers than female strangers, research participants were significantly more likely to report that a male stranger wanted to kill them than to report that a female stranger wanted them dead. In fact, not a single participant reported thinking that a female stranger had designs for their murder (Buss & Duntley, 2005).

Some final evidence that people overestimate the likelihood they will be killed comes from research that asked one group of participants to rate the likelihood they would murder when confronted with a situation (e.g., finding their romantic partner having sex with someone else) and asked another group of participants to rate the likelihood they would be killed if they were on the other side of the same situation (e.g., being caught having sex with someone else's romantic partner). Comparisons of participants' ratings of the likelihood they would kill versus ratings of the likelihood they would be killed show a consistent trend—people rate the likelihood they would be killed significantly higher. In other words, participants systematically overestimate the likelihood they would be murdered across a wide range of adaptive problems potentially solvable by homicide (Duntley & Buss, in preparation).

Many people still willingly enter into situations that could get them killed: People have extramarital affairs, derogate others to ascend status hierarchies, and poach material and mating resources from others. What makes them think they can get away with these things?

SECRECY

The answer may lie in the use of secrecy as a defense against being murdered. People become homicidal only if they are aware that they are being wronged. Ignorance can provide them bliss and provide those who sneak behind their backs some measure of protection from being killed. A sexual relationship conducted behind the back of an individual's partner, for example, has the potential to confer obvious fitness benefits to men in the form of more offspring. It can confer benefits to women as well, such as access to superior or more diverse genes and access to additional resources from an affair partner (Greiling & Buss, 2000). Selection should have favored the use of secrecy to defend against the costs of infidelity, which includes being killed by a jealous partner. The same logic applies to other behaviors that benefit one individual at a cost to another. In the case of sexual infidelity, there is a clear pattern in the risks of being killed. Men are more likely than women to kill their partner for a sexual infidelity. As a result, selection pressure may have been stronger on women to adopt clandestine tactics than it was on men. Women may have evolved to be more motivated and better at hiding their infidelities from their partners. This may help to explain why men indicate a greater amount of uncertainty about whether their romantic partner is having an affair than women do (Buss, 2000): Men encounter fewer cues to their partner's infidelity. Clandestine strategies, however, are not always effective. Sometimes men discover their partner's infidelity. As homicide statistics demonstrate (Buss, 2005; Daly & Wilson, 1988; Ghiglieri, 1999), perhaps the most dangerous human a woman will encounter in her lifetime is her own romantic partner.

KILLING IN SELF-DEFENSE: PREEMPTIVE HOMICIDE TO PREVENT BEING MURDERED

In a review of 223 appellate opinions of the homicide cases of battered women in Pennsylvania, 75% of the homicides occurred while the woman was being assaulted or abused by her romantic partner (Maguigan, 1991). In a study of mate homicides in North Carolina between 1991 and 1993, violence perpetrated by men against their romantic partners preceded 75% of cases where women killed them. In contrast, there is no evidence that violence perpetrated by women preceded any of the homicides committed by men (Smith, Moracco, & Butts, 1998). It can be argued that the majority of women who kill their romantic partners do so in self-defense. The example provided by these female-perpetrated mate homicides is vividly illustrative of the ultimate homicide defense: killing an attacker before the attacker kills you.

The costs of being murdered may have been substantial enough to select for adaptations designed to eliminate the threat of homicidal conspecifics by killing them. Selection for homicide defenses was unlike selection for the psychology of homicide. While adaptations for homicide were selected to favor nonlethal alternatives to solve adaptive problems in most circumstances (Buss & Duntley, 2005), selection likely favored psychological design to prefer murder as a strategy of self-defense in face-to-face confrontations with a killer. Killing someone to prevent the person from murdering you would have had distinct evolutionary advantages over strategies of nonlethal violence. By killing a murderous conspecific, you eliminate any future threat the person may have posed. While an injured rival can recuperate and attempt to kill you again, a dead rival cannot. By killing the person who would murder you, you also demonstrate a willingness and ability to kill, sending a powerful signal to others that attempts on your life will be met with the ultimate cost.

Most legal systems do not treat homicides committed in self-defense the same as other murders. The law considers killing in self-defense to be a form of justifiable homicide if the person who kills "reasonably believes that killing is a necessary response to a physical attack that is likely to cause serious injury or death" (Costanzo, 2004, p. 83). In the evolutionary history of adaptations to produce preemptive homicides, however, the management of errors under conditions of uncertainty would have played a pivotal role in determining what a person reasonably believes. It often may have been better for individuals in the past to overestimate the threat from hostile competitors and eliminate them permanently. Selection would have favored this strategy over nonlethal tactics that would allow threatening conspecifics to inflict costs in the future. The consequence of this overestimation is the preemptive murders of some people who would not have become killers. In the calculus of selection, however, it is better to be safe and alive than dead.

CONCLUSIONS

Dangers from other humans had a powerful effect on the survival of individuals in the past and the evolutionary history of our species. Conflict between individuals over limited resources was the source of selection pressures for the evolution of strategies to win the resources. One set of strategies for besting rivals in competition for resources is to directly inflict costs on them. These cost-inflicting strategies are what make other humans dangerous. The evolution of adaptations to inflict costs created selection pressure for the coevolution of counteradaptations to avoid or prevent incurring the costs. These coevolved counteradaptations, in turn, created selection pressure for the evolution of more refined and new adaptations for cost-infliction, creating an antagonistic, coevolutionary arms race between strategies to inflict costs and strategies to defend against them. Coevolutionary arms races can be extremely powerful. They can exert selection pressure on numerous physiological and psychological systems simultaneously, leading to rapid evolutionary change and great complexity of adaptive design. Adaptations for homicide and adaptations to defend against homicide may be results of an antagonistic coevolutionary arms race.

Homicide is different from all other, nonlethal strategies of cost-infliction because it has unique evolutionary effects that stem from the permanent elimination of another individual. The recurrent use of homicide to help solve adaptive problems would have created selection pressure for the evolution of adaptations that enable individuals to defend against being murdered. The costs of being killed are among the greatest an individual might incur at the hands of a conspecific. These tremendous costs may have created unique and powerful selection pressures for the evolution of homicide defense adaptations. Advances, refinements, and innovations in the design of homicide defenses may have created new selection pressure for reciprocal evolutionary change in psychological design for murder.

Evidence for the cognitive adaptations that resulted from the coevolutionary arms race between homicide and homicide defenses comes from varied sources, including research on the conflict between pregnant mothers and their fetuses, research on the specific fears of children, studies of what facial expressions are most quickly apprehended, research on the psychology of homicide defenses, patterns of self-defense homicides, and consistency with the logic of the process of natural selection. Though not conclusive, the available evidence suggests that coevolved adaptations for homicide and defenses against homicide may exist. If so, we are likely the only species that possess psychological adaptations that function specifically to kill humans. Other humans are the predators we should fear the most.

REFERENCES

Barrett, H. C., & Behne, T. (in press). Children's understanding of death as the cessation of agency: A test using sleep versus death. *Cognition*.

Betzig, L. L. (1993). Sex, succession, and stratification in the first six civilizations. In L. Ellis (Ed.), *Social stratification and socioeconomic inequality* (pp. 37–74). Westport, CT: Praeger.

Block, A. P. (1990). Rape trauma syndrome as scientific expert testimony. *Archives of Sexual Behavior, 19*, 309–323.

Bugnyar, T., & Kotrscha, K. (2004). Leading a conspecific away from food in ravens (Corvus corax)? *Animal Cognition, 7*, 69–76.

Burgess, A. W., & Holmstrom, L. L. (1974). Rape trauma syndrome. *American Journal of Psychiatry, 131*, 981–986.

Buss, D. M. (1996). Sexual conflict: Evolutionary insights into feminist and the "battle of the sexes." In D. M. Buss & N. M. Malamuth (Eds.), *Sex, power, conflict: Evolutionary and feminist perspectives* (pp. 296–318). New York: Oxford University Press.

Buss, D. M. (2000). *The dangerous passion: Why jealously is as necessary as love and sex.* New York: Free Press.

Buss, D. M. (2003). *The evolution of desire: Strategies of human mating (Revised Edition).* New York: Free Press.

Buss, D. M. (2004). *Evolutionary psychology: The new science of the mind.* (2nd ed.). Boston: Allyn & Bacon.

Buss, D. M. (2005). *The murderer next door: Why the mind is designed to kill.* New York: Penguin.

Buss, D. M., & Dedden, L. A. (1990). Derogation of competitors. *Journal of Social and Personal Relationships, 7*, 395–422.

Buss, D. M., & Duntley, J. D. (1998, July). *Evolved homicide modules.* Paper presented to the annual meeting of the Human Behavior and Evolution Society, Davis, CA. U.S.A.

Buss, D. M., & Duntley, J. D. (1999, June). *Killer psychology: The evolution of intrasexual homicide.* Paper presented to the annual meeting of the Human Behavior and Evolution Society, Salt Lake City, UT.

Buss, D. M., & Duntley, J. D. (2003). Homicide: An evolutionary perspective and implications for public policy. In N. Dess (Ed.), *Violence and public policy* (pp. 115–128). Westport, CT: Greenwood Publishing Group.

Buss, D. M., & Duntley, J. D. (in press). The evolution of gender differences in aggression. In S. Fein (Ed.), *Gender and aggression.* New York: Guilford Press.

Buss, D. M., & Duntley, J. D. (2005). *Homicide adaptation theory.* Manuscript submitted for publication.

Buss, D. M., Larsen, R. R., & Westen, D. (1996). Sex differences in jealousy: Not gone, not forgotten, and not explained by alternative hypotheses. *Psychological Science, 7,* 373–375.

Buss, D. M., Larsen, R. R., Westen, D., & Semmelroth, J. (1992). Sex differences in jealousy: Evolution, physiology, and psychology. *Psychological Science, 3,* 251–255.

Buss, D. M., & Shackelford, T. K. (1997a). Human aggression in evolutionary psychological perspective. *Clinical Psychology Review, 17,* 605–619.

Buss, D. M., & Shackelford, T. K. (1997b). From vigilance to violence: Mate retention tactics in married couples. *Journal of Personality and Social Psychology, 72,* 346–361.

Campbell, A. (1993). *Men, women, and aggression.* New York: Basic Books.

Chagnon, N. (1983). *Yanomamö: The fierce people* (3rd ed.). New York: Holt, Rinehart and Winston.

Chagnon, N. (1988). Life histories, blood revenge, and warfare in a tribal population. *Science, 239,* 985–992.

Chavanne, T. J., & Gallup, G. G., Jr. (1998). Variation in risk taking behavior among female college students as a function of the menstrual cycle. *Evolution and Human Behavior, 19,* 27–32.

Chong, D. S., & Karlberg, J. (2004). Refining the Apgar score cut-off point for newborns at risk. *Acta Paediatrica, 93,* 53–59.

Cohen, L. E., & Machalek, R. (1988). A general theory of expropriative crime: An evolutionary ecological approach. *American Journal of Sociology, 94,* 465–501.

Costanzo, M. (2004). *Psychology applied to law.* New York: ThomsonWadsworth.

Coughlin, C., & Vuchinich, S. (1996). Family experience in preadolescence and the development of male delinquency. *Journal of Marriage and the Family, 58,* 491–501.

Daly, M., & Wilson, M. (1988). *Homicide.* Hawthorne, NY: Aldine.

De Becker, G. (1997). *The gift of fear.* New York: Little, Brown, and Company.

Diamond, J. (1997). *Guns, germs, and steel: The fate of human societies.* New York: Norton.

Dodge, K. A., Bates, J. E., & Pettit, G. S. (1990). Mechanisms in the cycle of violence. *Science, 250,* 1678–1683.

Douglas, K. S., & Webster, C. D. (1999). Predicting violence in mentally and personality disordered individuals. In R. Roesch, S. D. Hart, & J. R. P. Oglof (Eds.), *Psychology and law: The state of the discipline* (pp. 175–239). New York: Kluwer/Plenum Press.

Duntley, J. D., & Buss, D. M. (1998, July). *Evolved anti-homicide modules.* Paper presented to the annual meeting of the Human Behavior and Evolution Society, Davis, CA. U.S.A.

Duntley, J. D., & Buss, D. M. (1999, June). *Killer psychology: The evolution of mate homicide.* Paper presented to the annual meeting of the Human Behavior and Evolution Society, Salt Lake City, UT.

Duntley, J. D., & Buss, D. M. (2000, June). *The killers among us: A co-evolutionary theory of homicide.* Invited paper presented at a special symposium organized by the Society for Evolution and the Law at the annual meeting of the Human Behavior and Evolution Society, Amherst, MA. U.S.A.

Duntley, J. D., & Buss, D. M. (2001, June). *Anti-homicide design: Adaptations to prevent homicide victimization.* Paper presented to the annual meeting of the Human Behavior and Evolution Society, London, UK.

Duntley, J. D., & Buss, D. M. (2002, July). *Homicide by design: On the plausibility of psychological adaptations for homicide.* Invited presentation for the First Annual AHRB Conference on Innateness and the Structure of the Mind, University of Sheffield, England.

Duntley, J. D., & Buss, D. M. (in press). Adaptations to defend against homicide.

Fujita, K., Kuroshima, H., & Masuda, T. (2002). Do tufted capuchin monkeys (Cebus apella) spontaneously deceive opponents? A preliminary analysis of an experimental food-competition contest between monkeys. *Animal Cognition, 5,* 19–25.

Gartner, R. (1990). The victims of homicide: A temporal and cross-national review. *American Sociological Review, 55,* 92–106.

Geist, R. F. (1988). Sexually related trauma. *Emergency Medical Clinics of North America, 6,* 439–466.

Ghiglieri, M. P. (1999). *The dark side of man: Tracing the origins of violence.* Reading, MA: Perseus Books.

Goleman, D. (1995). *Emotional intelligence: Why it can matter more than I.Q.* New York: Bantam.

Grammer, K. (1992). Variations on a theme: Age dependent mate selection in humans. *Behavioral and Brain Sciences, 15,* 100–102.

Greiling, H., & Buss, D. M. (2000). Women's sexual strategies: The hidden dimension of extra pair mating. *Personality and Individual Differences, 28,* 929–963.

Hagen, E. H. (1999). The functions of postpartum depression. *Evolution and Human Behavior, 20,* 325–359.

Haig, D. (1993). Genetic conflicts in human pregnancy. *Quarterly Review of Biology, 4,* 495–532.

Hamilton, W. D. (1963). The evolution of altruistic behavior. *American Naturalist, 97,* 354–356.

Hamilton, W. D. (1964). The genetical evolution of social behavior. I and, I. I. *Journal of Theoretical Biology, 7,* 1–52.

Haselton, M. G. (2003). The sexual overperception bias: Evidence of systematic bias in men from a survey of naturally occurring events. *Journal of Research on Personality, 37,* 34–47.

Haselton, M. G., & Buss, D. M. (2000). Error management theory: A new perspective on biases in cross-sex mind reading. *Journal of Personality and Social Psychology, 78,* 81–91.

Hassell, M. P. (1975). Density-dependence in single-species populations. *Journal of Animal Ecology, 44,* 283–295.

Heerwagen, J. H., & Orians, G. H. (2002). The ecological world of children. In P. H. Kahn, Jr. & S. R. Kellert (Eds.), *Children and nature: Psychological, socialcultural, and evolutionary investigations* (pp. 29–64). Cambridge, MA: MIT Press.

Held, S., Mendl, M., Devereux, C., & Byrne, R. W. (2002). Foraging pigs alter their behavior in response to exploitation. *Animal Behavior, 64,* 157–166.

Hill, K., & Hurtado, A. M. (1996). *Ache life history.* New York: Aldine De Gruyter.

Hrdy, S. B. (1977). Infanticide as a primate reproductive strategy. *American Scientist, 65,* 40–49.

Insel, T. R. (1992). Oxytocin—A neuropeptide for affiliation: Evidence from behavioral, receptor autoradiographic, and comparative studies. *Psychoneuroendocrinology, 17,* 3–35.

Jennings, K. D., Ross, S., Popper, S., & Elmore, M. (1999). Thoughts of harming infants in depressed and nondepressed mothers. *Journal of Affective Disorders, 54,* 21–28.

Kaplan, S. (1992). Environmental preference in a knowledge-seeking, knowledge-using organism. In J. Barkow, L. Cosmides, & J. Tooby (Eds.), *The adapted mind* (pp. 581–598). New York: Oxford University Press.

Kendall-Tackett, K. A. (1994). Postpartum depression. *Illness, Crisis, and Loss, 4,* 80–86.

Knopps, G. (1993). Postpartum mood disorders: A startling contrast to the joy of birth. *Postgraduate Medicine Journal, 103,* 103–116.

Maccoby, E. E. (1990). Gender and relationships: A developmental account. *American Psychologist, 45,* 513–520.

Maguigan, H. (1991). Myths and misconceptions in current reform proposals. *University of Pennsylvania Law Review, 140,* 379–486.

Marks, I. (1987). *Fears, phobias, and rituals: Panic, anxiety, and their disorders.* New York: Oxford University Press.

Marshall, I. H., & Block, C. R. (2004). Maximizing the availability of cross-national data on homicide. *Homicide studies, 8,* 267–310.

Morales, V. Z., & Vazquez, C. (1994). Apgar score and infant mortality in Puerto Rico. *Puerto Rico Health Science Journal, 13,* 175–181.

Moseley, W., see www.oldkewgardens.com/kitty_genovese-3-confession.pdf.

Nesse, R. M., & Williams, G. C. (1994). *Why we get sick.* New York: Times Books Random House.

Nicholson, A. J. (1954). An outline of the dynamics of animal populations. *Australian Journal of Zoology, 2,* 9–65.

Öhman, A., Lundqvist, D., & Esteves, F. (2001). The face in the crowd revisited: A threat advantage with schematic stimuli. *Journal of Personality and Social Psychology, 80,* 381–396.

Papinczak, T. A., & Turner, C. T. (2000). An analysis of personal and social factors influencing initiation and duration of breastfeeding in a large Queensland maternity hospital. *Breastfeeding Review, 8,* 25–33.

Parker, G. A., Royle, M. J., & Hartley, I. R. (2002). Intrafamilial conflict and parental investment: A synthesis. *Philosophical Transactions of the Royal Society of London, B., 357,* 295–307.

Perusse, D. (1993). Cultural and reproductive success in industrial societies: Testing the relationship at proximate and ultimate levels. *Behavioral and Brain Sciences, 16,* 267–322.

Phillips, B., Brown, G. P., & Shine, R. (2004). Assessing the potential for an evolutionary response to rapid environmental change: Invasive toads and an Australian snake. *Evolutionary Ecology Research, 6,* 799–811.

Pinker, S. (1997, November 2). Why they kill their newborns (pp. 52–54). *New York Times.*

Pratto, F. (1996). Sexual politics: The gender gap in the bedroom, the cupboard, and the cabinet. In D. M. Buss & N. M. Malamuth (Eds.), *Sex, power, conflict: Evolutionary and feminist perspectives* (pp. 179–230). New York: Oxford University Press.

Rhee, S. H., & Waldman, I. D. (2002). Genetic and environmental influences on antisocial behavior: A meta-analysis of twin and adoption studies. *Psychological Bulletin, 128,* 490–529.

Richerson, P. J., & Boyd, R. (1998). The evolution of human ultra-sociality. In I. Eibl-Eibesfeldt & F. K. Salter (Eds.), *Indoctrinability, warfare, and ideology* (71–95). New York: Berghahn Books.

Saraiya, M., Green, C. A., Berg, C. J., Hopkins, F. W., Koonin, L. M., & Atrash, H. K. (1999). Spontaneous abortion-related deaths among women in the United States, 1981–1991. *Obstetrical & Gynecological Survey, 54,* 172–176.

Scarr, S., & Salapatek, P. (1970). Patterns of fear development during infancy. *Merrill-Palmer Quarterly, 16,* 53–90.

Schmitt, D. P., & Buss, D. M. (2001). Human mate poaching: Tactics and temptations for infiltrating existing mateships. *Journal of Personality and Social Psychology, 80,* 894–917.

Schmitt, D. P., Shackelford, T. K., Duntley, J., Tooke, W., & Buss, D. M. (2001). The desire for sexual variety as a tool for understanding basic human mating strategies. *Personal Relationships, 8,* 425–455.

Smith, P. H., Moracco, K. E., & Butts, J. D. (1998). Partner homicide in context: A population-based perspective. *Homicide Studies, 2,* 400–421.

Smith, P. K. (1979). The ontogeny of fear in children. In W. Sluckin (Ed.), *Fear in animals and man* (pp. 164–168). London: Van Nostrand.

Smuts, B. B. (1992). Men's aggression against women. *Human Nature, 6,* 1–32.

Soltis, J. (in press). The signal functions of early infant crying. In *Behavioral and brain sciences.*

Spinelli, M. G. (2004). Maternal infanticide associated with mental illness: Prevention and the promise of saved lives. *American Journal of Psychiatry, 161,* 1548–1557.

Sugiyama, L. S., Tooby, J., & Cosmides, L. (2002). Cross-cultural evidence of cognitive adaptations for social exchange among the Shiwiar of Ecuadorian Amazonia. *Proceedings of the National Academy of Sciences of the United States of America, 99,* 11537–11542.

Symons, D. (1979). *The evolution of human sexuality.* New York: Oxford.

Taveras, E. M., Capra, A. M., Braveman, P. A., Jensvold, N. G., Escobar, G. J., & Lieu, T. A. (2003). Clinician support and psychosocial risk factors associated with breastfeeding discontinuation. *Pediatrics, 112,* 108–115.

Taylor, P. A., & Glenn, N. D. (1976). The utility of education and attractiveness for females' status attainment through marriage. *American Sociological Review, 41,* 484–498.

Thornhill, R., & Palmer, C. (2000). *A natural history of rape: Biological bases of sexual coercion.* Cambridge, MA: MIT Press.

Tooby, J., & Cosmides, L. (1988). *The evolution of war and its cognitive foundations.* Institute for Evolutionary Studies, Technical Report #88-1.

Tooby, J., & Cosmides, L. (1992). The psychological foundations of culture. In J. Barkow, L. Cosmides, & J. Tooby (Eds.), *The adaptedmind* (pp. 19–136). New York: Oxford University Press.

Tooby, J., & Cosmides, L. (1996). Friendship and the banker's paradox: Other pathways to the evolution of adaptations for altruism. *Proceedings of the British Academy, 88,* 119–143.

Tooby, J., & DeVore, I. (1987). The reconstruction of hominid behavioral evolution through strategic modeling. In W. G. Kinzey (Ed.), *The evolution of human behavior* (pp. 183–237). New York: State University of New York Press.

Trivers, R. L. (1971). The evolution of reciprocal altruism. *Quarterly Review of Biology, 46,* 35–57.

Trivers, R. L. (1972). Parental investment and sexual selection. In B. Campbell (Ed.), *Sexual selection and the descent of man: 1871–1971* (pp. 136–179). Chicago: Aldine.

Trivers, R. L. (1974). Parent–offspring conflict. *American Zoologist, 14,* 249–264.

Udry, R. R., & Eckland, B. K. (1984). Benefits of being attractive: Differential payoffs for men and women. *Psychological Reports, 54,* 47–56.

Werner-Wilson, R. J. (1998). Gender differences in adolescent sexual attitudes: The influence of individual and family factors. *Adolescence, 33,* 519–531.

Whiting, B., & Edwards, C. P. (1988). *Children of different worlds.* Cambridge, MA: Harvard University Press.

Wilson, M., Daly, M., & Pound, N. (2002). An evolutionary psychological perspective on the modulation of competitive confrontation and risk taking. In D. Pfaff et al. (Eds.), *Hormones, brain and behavior* (Vol. 5, pp. 381–408). San Diego, CA: Academic Press.

Wilson, M., & Mesnick, S. L. (1997). An empirical test of the bodyguard hypothesis. In P. A. Gowaty (Ed.), *Feminism and evolutionary biology: Boundaries, intersection, and frontiers.* New York: Chapman & Hall.

Wrangham, R. W., & Peterson, D. (1996). *Demonic males.* Boston: Houghton Mifflin.

PART III

MATING

DAVID M. BUSS

T HE STUDY OF human mating strategies must surely count as one of the first
empirical success stories in evolutionary psychology. The conceptual foundations of human mating can be traced to Darwin's monumentally important theory of sexual selection, which identified intrasexual competition and
preferential mate choice as key processes in the evolution of mating adaptations
(Darwin, 1871). Although largely ignored by biologists for many decades, sexual
selection theory was given new life by Robert Trivers a century later with his
seminal 1972 paper, "Parental Investment and Sexual Selection," in which he
identified relative parental investment as a driving force behind the two components of the process of sexual selection.

The next watershed in the study of human mating strategies was the publication in 1979 of Donald Symons's trenchant classic, *The Evolution of Human Sexuality.* Many of the foundations of human mating strategies described in this
section owe a great debt to Donald Symons. He was the first to articulate the
theoretical foundations of a fully adaptationist view of male and female mating
minds, arguing that they should be no less dimorphic than male and female
bodies. Symons was the first social scientist to take the writings of George C.
Williams (1966) to heart, applying rigorous standards for invoking the critical
but challenging concept adaptation. Indeed, although evolutionary psychologists are often accused of being "hyperadaptationist," Symons argued forcefully that certain aspects of human sexuality failed to meet the criteria needed
to invoke adaptation and were, therefore, likely to be by-products. Don
Symons's 1979 book can be regarded as the first major treatise on evolutionary
psychology proper, highlighting the centrality of psychological mechanisms as
adaptations and using human sexuality as a detailed vehicle for this more general argument.

David Schmitt in Chapter 9 furnishes a broad and insightful overview of
the foundations of human mating strategies. He considers the large menu of
evolved human mating strategies and outlines the evolutionary processes of

sexual selection by which they evolved. He reviews the ways that human mating strategies are highly sex-differentiated and exquisitely sensitive to context, in particular, the temporal dimension of short-term and long-term mating, as proposed by sexual strategies theory (Buss & Schmitt, 1993). He then discusses individual differences in mating strategies within sex. Finally, based on his own massive cross-cultural project and the prior work of others, he discusses the ways in which culture and ecology predictably activate human mating strategies from the universal menu.

Lawrence Sugiyama provides in Chapter 10 a comprehensive, up-to-date, and penetrating discussion on the evolutionary psychology of attractiveness. Conceptually, he locates the study of attractiveness within a broader framework of relationship value, including mate value, coalition value, and kin value. He provides the most compelling arguments to date for why attractiveness is important in all social relationships, not merely mating relationships (although they are especially critical in mating relationships). He then summarizes the voluminous empirical evidence on specific attributes that contribute to our standards of attractiveness, including skin condition, hair, symmetry, waist-to-hip ratio, and many others.

Steven Gangestad, Randy Thornhill, and Christine Garver-Apgar provide Chapter 11 on adaptations to ovulation—a long-ignored, but now burgeoning area of theoretical and empirical analysis. They place the study of adaptations to ovulation within the broader theoretical context of sexually antagonistic coevolution. Gangestad and his coauthors then discuss the theories and empirical evidence for the evolution of relatively concealed ovulation and extended female sexual receptivity across the menstrual cycle. This establishes the groundwork for conflicts of interest, the evolution of female infidelity, and cyclic changes in female mate preferences and sexual interests. Their chapter, highlighting the importance of the female ovulation cycle, heralds a sea change in the way scientists think about the evolution of human mating strategies. Simultaneously, it offers an example par excellence of the heuristic value of evolutionary hypotheses, guiding researchers to discover phenomena that otherwise would have remained entirely unexamined within nonevolutionary frameworks. Finally, it offers a serious challenge to mainstream nonevolutionary psychologists, whose theories currently cannot explain, even in principle, why males and females both would show such well-designed adaptations to ovulation.

Todd Shackelford, Nicholas Pound, Aaron Goetz, and Craig LaMunyon discuss the evolutionary psychology of sperm competition, a form of postcopulatory sexual selection, in Chapter 12. Starting with a brief review of the nonhuman literature on sperm competition, they assemble compelling evidence that sperm competition has been a recurrent phenomenon for humans. They discuss physiological, anatomical, and psychological evidence for sperm competition adaptations in men. Then they turn to hypothesized sperm competition adaptations in women, including precopulatory female choice and the timing of female orgasm. They conclude by suggesting that sperm competition has been an important, and relatively neglected, arena for sexually selected adaptations in humans. This excellent chapter again highlights the heuristic value of evolutionary thinking in discovering phenomena entirely missed by psychological theories that ignore evolutionary processes.

Neil Malamuth, Mark Huppin, and Bryant Paul provide in Chapter 13 an excellent discussion of another region of conflict between the sexes: sexual coercion by men. They furnish a judicious analysis of competing hypotheses about rape—whether it is caused by adaptations specifically designed for forced sex or instead is a by-product of more general adaptations to use force to achieve a variety of ends (e.g., stealing resources). They then focus on one potential candidate design feature of a rape adaptation—men's sexual arousal to forcing women into unwanted sex. In particular, they discuss individual differences among men in sexual arousal to force and identify the variables that lead some men, and not others, to adopt force in the context of sex. Strong conclusions about the conceptual status of rape are not possible at this point, but Malamuth and his coauthors provide a nuanced description of the possible psychological mechanisms involved and an up-to-date description of the relevant empirical evidence.

Lorne Campbell and Bruce Ellis conclude the mating section with Chapter 14, a stimulating discussion of love, commitment, and mate retention. They highlight the different adaptive benefits men and women would accrue from forming long-term pairbonds and delve into the underlying motivational and emotional mechanisms underlying such relationships. They nicely interweave theory and research emanating from mainstream nonevolutionary researchers with more functional analyses of long-term mating. Whereas they propose that an underlying psychological system captured by "love" motivates relationship formation, they suggest that anger and upset are motivational mechanisms designed to monitor signals of "strategic interference" with the relationship. Jealousy as an emotion and mate retention tactics as behaviors are proposed to serve relationship maintenance functions. Campbell and Ellis nicely illuminate the complexity of the evolutionary psychology of long-term mating, relationships formed and maintained by emotions ranging from love to rage.

While these chapters take stock of the current status of the science of mating, it is worthwhile to step back and see how far the field has come. In the mid-1980s, the field of mating was barely visible on the scientific map. Social psychologists had discovered a few things about attraction, but theories of mating were woefully simplistic. Most invoked single variables responsible for the selection of mates, such as similarity, proximity, or equity. Most theorists implicitly assumed that all mating was exclusively for the long term. Short-term mating was virtually ignored. Little was known about the processes of mate selection or mate attraction. Concepts such as mate retention, sexual conflict, adaptations to ovulation, sexually antagonistic coevolution, and many others were entirely absent.

Beginning in the mid- to late 1980s, the first raft of empirical studies on human mating appeared. In the 1990s, work on the evolutionary psychology of human mating mushroomed to become the most studied domain of evolutionary psychology. Although much scientific evidence has now cumulated supporting many hypothesized human mating adaptations, the area continues to be ripe for new discoveries. Because mating is so close to the reproductive engine of evolution, it follows that selection has fashioned a rich array of psychological adaptations to deal with the complex and recurrent adaptive problems that mating poses. The chapters in this section take stock of what we now know about human mating and point to fertile fields of mating adaptations yet to be discovered.

REFERENCES

Buss, D. M., & Schmitt, D. P. (1993). Sexual strategies theory: An evolutionary perspective on human mating. *Psychological Review, 100,* 204–232.

Darwin, C. (1871). *The descent of man and selection in relation to sex.* London: Murray.

Williams, G. C. (1966). *Adaptation and natural selection.* Princeton, NJ: Princeton University Press.

Adaptationism and Human Mating Psychology

DONALD SYMONS

A N ORCHID, *TRICHOCEROS ANTENNIFER*, that I tend on my back porch is gravid with lessons for students of human mating psychology. When a naïve houseguest first encounters a *T. antennifer* flower there usually is a brief moment of confusion followed by a burst of delighted laughter, as the guest realizes what he or she is seeing. While most orchids attract pollinators by offering them a food reward, *T. antennifer* is pollinated by the males of a certain type of Ecuadorian fly as they attempt to copulate with the orchid's flower. The males do this because *T. antennifer's* flower is an astonishingly realistic mimic of a female fly. (And if the flower is realistic to the *human* eye, how much more realistic is it likely to be to the eye of the male fly that it was designed by natural selection to bamboozle?)

The first lesson that I draw from this orchid's sex life is that we really should *not* be astonished by the complexity and precision of its flower's mimicry; rather, we should not be *more* astonished than we are by the complexity and precision of biological adaptations in general. What makes *T. antennifer's* mimicry seem so uncannily superb is that it is one of the rare cases in which we have immediately available in our mind's eye an image of optimal design (in this case a fly), and thus we can instantly and intuitively compare the actual adaptation (the orchid's flower) to this standard. For the vast majority of biological adaptations, however, we do *not* have an image of optimal design and thus cannot quickly or intuitively assess how closely most adaptations approximate optimality.

Human psychological mating adaptations, though buried deep between our ears rather than worn on our sleeves, were designed by the same evolutionary processes as was *T. antennifer's* flower, and there is no reason to expect these human adaptations to be less exquisitely adapted for their purposes than *T. antennifer's* flower is for its purpose. This adaptationist view of life informs the scientific imagination of Darwinian students of human mating psychology. The result—as represented in the following chapters—is a body of research that very

255

likely would never have been conceived or conducted absent an explicit, conscious Darwinism. Researchers innocent of Darwinism can palaver about learning, culture, gene-environment interaction, levels of analysis, and how complicated everything is until the cows come home, but they're unlikely to ask such a simple research question as the following: Do our brains contain species-typical devices whose functions are to (unconsciously) detect deviations from bilateral symmetry in the faces we observe and to cause us to prefer individuals with more symmetrical faces as mates (all else equal)? The twentieth-century histories of psychology and the social sciences do not encourage the belief that such a question ever would have been asked had evolutionary psychology not come along.

A nutshell summary of modern Darwinism is this: An organism is an integrated collection of problem-solving devices—that is, adaptations—that were shaped by natural selection over evolutionary time to promote, in some specific way, the survival of the genes that directed their construction. The "specific way" that an adaptation was designed to promote gene survival is that adaptation's *function* (or goal or purpose). The function of the heart is to pump blood, the function of pancreatic beta cells is to secrete insulin, and so forth. Unlike nonliving matter, living matter is not just complexly organized, it is *functionally* organized. The specific aspects of the environment to which an adaptation is adapted and on which its normal functioning and development depend are sometimes called its *environment of evolutionary adaptedness* (EEA).

The second lesson that I draw from *T. antennifer*'s sex life is that it is logically impossible to describe an adaptation without (at least implicitly) describing the adaptation's EEA. Without the EEA, there is no science of adaptation. Any scientifically useful description of *T. antennifer*'s flower will necessarily include a description of the morphology of certain female flies and the mating psychology of male flies found in *T. antennifer*'s natural habitat, the high-altitude cloud forests of Ecuador. Moreover, my brief description of *T. antennifer*'s flower would be intelligible only to those who already understood the nature and purpose of flowers and their evolved relationships with environmental vectors such as insects.

The EEAs of the vast majority of human adaptations still exist today and usually are too obvious to merit explicit mention. For example, a neurophysiologist describing the function of a certain component of the human visual system probably will simply assume that his or her colleagues know: (1) a great deal about the nature of electromagnetic radiation and (2) that the (natural) light falling on human retinas today is essentially identical to the light that fell on our ancestors' retinas during the evolution of our visual system. But human environments, especially those of modern industrialized societies, have changed in many ways in the brief period since the origin of agriculture 10,000 years ago, and some of these changes potentially affect the functioning of human mating adaptations. Darwinian students of human mating psychology thus have another advantage over other researchers: The Darwinian is alert to potentially significant differences between current and ancient environments, and this "EEA mindedness" can inform hypothesis formation. In some cases, it can even lead the Darwinian to posit the existence of adaptation where others perceive pathology or folly.

For example, a striking feature of human courtship—in its broadest sense—is the powerful effect that fear of rejection has on behavior. Sexual/romantic rejection hurts; the memory of being rejected hurts; the thought of being rejected hurts; hence, it is not surprising that the possibility of being rejected affects most people's mating behavior. Yet, on the face of it, fear of rejection seems to be astonishingly dysfunctional. The potential benefits of propositioning an attractive member of the other sex, which include everything from a sexual fling to a lifetime mateship, would appear to vastly outweigh the potential costs, which seem to consist mainly of a small amount of wasted time.

The potent effect that fear of rejection has on human courtship should inspire students of human mating psychology to consider whether this fear might have been adaptive during the vast majority of human evolution, even if it is not adaptive in many current environments. In other words, being rejected might have entailed real and significant costs in the human evolutionary past that it does not usually entail today. I propose the following hypothesis. During most of human evolutionary history, our ancestors lived in relatively small, face-to-face groups wherein sexual/romantic rejections were very likely to become common knowledge. When Ann the gatherer rejected Andy the hunter's proposition, everyone in their community probably found out about it before long (assuming that our ancestors were no less interested in other people's sex lives and no less prone to gossip than we are). The information that Ann had rejected Andy could diminish his perceived mate value in the eyes of others, including other potential mates (Ann may have rejected Andy because she had acquired mate-value-relevant information about him that others were not privy to). On a modern university campus, with thousands of students and enormous scope for anonymity, Bob's anxiety at the prospect of hitting on Bobbi is, perhaps, "irrational" in the sense that he has little to fear but fear itself; but the underlying motivational system may have been shaped by selection to function in an environment in which rejection had substantial costs.

Even if the historical, ethnographic, and archeological records did not unanimously indicate that humans evolved in, and are adapted to, life in much smaller groups than most of us encounter today, many aspects of our psychology, including fear of rejection, might allow us to infer the existence of such an ancestral world—just as Darwin correctly inferred that the orchid *Angraecum sesquipedale*, whose nectar-producing organ lies 30 cm inside it, must be pollinated by a then-unknown insect with a proboscis at least 30 cm long.

In conclusion, although Darwinism does not confer on its practitioners some sort of magical pipeline into human mating psychology, a conscious, explicit adaptationism does give the Darwinian at least two advantages in generating scientifically productive hypotheses. First, Darwinians expect the human brain to contain many complex, exquisitely engineered devices that were shaped by selection to solve the specific mating problems that our ancestors reliably encountered during the course of human evolutionary history. Second, Darwinians are ever mindful that these devices, whatever they may be, are adapted to a world that in some respects no longer exists. These are no mean advantages.

CHAPTER 9

Fundamentals of Human
Mating Strategies

DAVID P. SCHMITT

Primates are a diverse lot . . . some are monogamous, some polygynous, and some promiscuous. At least one—the human primate—is all of these.

—Mealey (2000, p. 262)

EVOLUTIONARY PSYCHOLOGISTS CURRENTLY disagree about the fundamental mating strategies of humans. Some contend that humans are exclusively designed for lifelong monogamy (Hazan & Zeifman, 1999). Others argue that humans are designed to mate with more than one person at a time, usually in the form of polygynous or extramarital relationships (Symons, 1979). Still others posit that humans possess a mixed or *pluralistic* mating repertoire (Belsky, Steinberg, & Draper, 1991) and that men and women each evolved facultative strategies of their own (Buss & Schmitt, 1993). Cross-species and cross-cultural comparisons by anthropologists, behavioral ecologists, human ethologists, primatologists, and reproductive biologists have produced conflicting accounts of human mating adaptations (Low, 2000; Mealey, 2000). As a result, a definitive characterization of humanity's fundamental mating strategy has remained elusive.

This chapter reviews cross-species and cross-cultural evidence regarding the mating strategies—and specialized mating psychologies—that may be fundamental to humans. Comparative features of social living, sexual dimorphism, and reproductive physiology across primate species reveal insights into our natural mating psychology (Dixson, 1998). Ethnological patterns and universals across foraging cultures—cultures that practice the hunting and gathering lifestyle that was prevalent for 99% of human history—also help to clarify human mating adaptations (Pasternak, Ember, & Ember, 1997). Overall, the extant evidence suggests humans evolved a pluralistic mating repertoire that differs in adaptive ways

258

across sex and temporal context, personal characteristics such as mate value and ovulatory status, and facultative features of culture and local ecology (Buss, 1994; Gangestad & Simpson, 2000).

MONOGAMOUS MATING STRATEGIES

Monogamous mating occurs when two individuals combine their reproductive efforts exclusively (Davies, 1991; Emlen & Oring, 1977). Monogamy may be *perennial*, when two members of the opposite sex form a lifelong mating bond, or *serial*, when members of the opposite sex are faithful to one another while they are paired, but the pairing does not last a lifetime (Fisher, 1989; see also Shuster & Wade, 2003). It was once thought that over 90% of bird species reproduce using monogamous mating strategies (Orians, 1969). Modern genetic testing of offspring and putative sires has shown that only about 10% of socially monogamous bird species are, in fact, genetically monogamous (Barash & Lipton, 2001; Birkhead & Møller, 1992).

Among mammals, both forms of monogamy are quite rare, emerging in perhaps 3% of all species (Clutton-Brock, 1989; Møller & Birkhead, 1989). This may be due to large sex differences in the obligatory parental investments of mammals (Trivers, 1972). Indeed, less than 10% of mammals show any signs of significant paternal investment at all (Geary, this volume; Woodroofe & Vincent, 1994). Among nonhuman primates, monogamy is found among some prosimians (e.g., lemurs), New World monkeys (e.g., marmosets and tamarins), and a few of the lesser apes (e.g., gibbons). Monogamy is rare or unseen among Old World monkeys (e.g., macaques and baboons) and the great apes (e.g., chimpanzees, gorillas, and humans). Humans are a terrestrial species, whereas all monogamous primates are arboreal (Dixson, 1998).

In humans, many men and women strive to form emotionally intimate relationships that are sexually monogamous (Hazan & Zeifman, 1999). Ethnological studies indicate, however, that only 16% of the world's preindustrial cultures have monogamous marriage systems (Frayser, 1985; Murdock, 1967). The official or preferred marriage system in most cultures (over 80%) is polygyny. Most men and women within preindustrial cultures are monogamously married (Hames, 1996; White, 1988; Whyte, 1980; see Table 9.1 on p. 260), a result of only men with high status and resources having the ability to provide for multiple women and their children (Betzig, 1986; Casimir & Aparna, 1995). When given a chance, most men prefer to have status and the multiple wives that status affords (Borgerhoff Mulder, 1988; E. A. Smith, 1998; Turke & Betzig, 1985; van den Berghe, 1979).

Comparative primate studies sometimes indicate that humans are designed for monogamy. Among the monogamous white-handed gibbon (*Hylobates lar*), the average body weight of an adult male is about 1,000 times the weight of the average male's testes (Dixson, 1998). Among humans, the average man's body weight is about 1,300 times the size of the average man's testes (Schultz, 1938), a ratio similar to the white-handed gibbon. In contrast, the more short-term-oriented common chimpanzee (*Pan troglodytes*) possesses extremely large testes with a body-testes ratio of only 350 (Dixson & Mundy, 1994), and the polygynous gorilla (*Gorilla gorilla*) has small testes with a body-testes ratio of over 5,000 (Hall-Craggs, 1962). Contradictory evidence regarding mating strategies exists in comparisons of primate seminal volume, sperm structure, and sperm

Table 9.1

Evidence Concerning Monogamy, Polygyny, and Short-Term Mating
as Fundamental Mating Strategies in Humans

Evidence of Monogamy in Humans

Most marriages in preindustrial cultures are socially monogamous (White, 1988).

Like most monogamous primates, humans are highly altricial (Lovejoy, 1981; T. M. Mueller, 1999).

Like most monogamous primates, mate desertion causes lower survival rates in human offspring (Hill & Hurtado, 1996).

Humans possess neurophysiological systems associated with pairbonding and attachment (Hazan & Zeifman, 1999; Young, 2003).

Evidence of Polygyny in Humans

Most marital systems in preindustrial cultures are socially polygynous (Frayser, 1985; Murdock, 1967).

Men with high status in foraging cultures often have multiple wives, and this is associated with increased reproductive success (Betzig, 1986; Borgerhoff Mulder, 1988).

Men with high mate value have more frequent copulations, more numerous partners, and more affairs once mated (Lalumière, Seto, & Quinsey, 1995; Perusse, 1993; Schmitt, 2004a).

Polygyny reliably emerges under adaptive ecological conditions (Low, 2000; Marlowe, 2003; Pasternak, Ember, & Ember, 1997).

Like most polygynous primates, human foragers live in relatively large bands (Lee & Daly, 1999).

Like most polygynous primates, human females are concentrated and guarded in foraging cultures (Chagnon, 1979).

Like most polygynous primates, human males vigorously compete for mates, display greater physical aggression, and have riskier life history strategies (R. D. Alexander, Hoogland, Howard, Noona, & Sherman, 1979; Archer & Lloyd, 2002; Clutton-Brock, 1988).

Evidence of Short-Term Mating in Humans

Infidelity, poaching, cuckoldry, and premarital sex are prevalent across cultures (Broude & Greene, 1976; Macintyre & Sooman, 1991).

Humans show evidence of sex-specific romantic jealousy adaptations across cultures (Buss et al., 1999; Buunk, Angleitner, Oubaid, & Buss, 1996).

Humans possess mate preference adaptations designed for short-term mating (Buss & Schmitt, 1993; Gangestad & Simpson, 2000).

Humans show evidence of adaptations to sperm competition (Baker & Bellis, 1995; Gallup et al., 2003; Shackelford, this volume).

Like most short-term oriented primates, humans have moderate sexual dimorphism (Dixson, 1998; Wolfe & Gray, 1982).

Like most short-term oriented primates, humans engage in frequent nonconceptive sex (Møller & Birkhead, 1989; Wrangham, 1993).

Like most short-term oriented primates, humans have moderate secondary sexual characteristics (Cartwright, 2000; Mealey, 2000).

quality (Baker & Bellis, 1995; Dixson, 1993; Møller, 1988). Overall, Dixson (1998) concluded that human male reproductive physiology is consistent with both monogamous and polygynous mating, providing only mixed support for the view that humans are monogamous.

Humans display extreme levels of altriciality compared to other primates, requiring large parental investments and possessing a relatively delayed adolescence (T. M. Mueller, 1999). These traits are indicative of monogamous mating (Lovejoy, 1981). Mate desertion is generally associated with lower infant survival in foraging cultures (Hill & Hurtado, 1996), another indication that humans are designed for monogamy. Finally, humans possess several neurophysiological systems of attachment linked with pairbonding and monogamy across species (Fisher, 1998; Hazan & Zeifman, 1999; Young, 2003).

Fisher (1992) suggests that human patterns of weaning, birth spacing, divorce, and remarriage all point to a system of serial monogamy. It takes about 4 years to wean a child in hunter-gatherer cultures, and birth spacing in a foraging environment averages about 4 years (Blurton Jones, 1986). Many divorces occur between the fourth and sixth year of marriage (Fisher, 1989, 1992), and men who practice serial monogamy are more reproductively successful than men who stay married to the same woman for a lifetime. Women who mate serially do not have a reproductive advantage over other women (Buckle, Gallup, & Rodd, 1996).

POLYGYNOUS MATING STRATEGIES

Polygynous mating strategies occur when individual males can mate with numerous females, whereas females tend to mate only with a single male. *Female-defense* or *harem* polygyny occurs when a single male mates with and defends numerous females against influxes of invading males (Emlen & Oring, 1977). *Resource-defense* polygyny occurs when a male is able to command and defend food supplies, territories, or other resources with regularity (Draper, 1989). Females preferentially desire and seek mateships with this high-resource male, even though he already is mated.

According to the polygyny threshold model (see Andersson, 1994; Orians, 1969), when the costs of mating polygynously with a given male (e.g., sharing his resources and having a rivalry with other females and their children) are outweighed by the benefits (e.g., acquiring a male with ample resources and high-quality genes), females tend to mate polygynously. This often occurs in species where males vary significantly in their genetic quality and in the resources they can accrue and monopolize. There is some evidence for the polygyny threshold model among human populations. For example, many women preferentially choose to mate with high-status men with ample resources rather than low-status men who would be unable to support a family (Borgerhoff Mulder, 1990, 1992), and polygyny is more likely to emerge in high-pathogen environments where genetic quality in men is important (Low, 2000).

In addition to the classic example of gorillas (Doran & McNeilage, 1998), polygynous mating occurs among several monkey species (e.g., proboscis monkeys), the hamadryas baboon, and occasionally among languars (Dixson, 1998). In polygynous species, male reproductive success is highly variable, due in part to highly dominant males monopolizing the reproductive capacity of females and leaving other males with no mating opportunities (L. Ellis, 1995). As a result, sexual selection processes are especially strong in polygynous species, and secondary sexual characteristics are often exaggerated (Dixson, 1998).

In humans, ethnological analyses of the world's preindustrial cultures find that over 80% allow or have allowed polygynous marriages (Frayser, 1985; Murdock, 1967; Whyte, 1980). Reproductive success for men living in foraging societies is significantly enhanced by securing multiple wives (Betzig, 1986; Borgerhoff Mulder, 1988; Casimir & Aparna, 1995; Chagnon, 1988; Heath & Hadley, 1998), providing evidence that historical selection pressures would have rewarded men who desired numerous mating partners (see also Schmitt, Alcalay, Allik, et al., 2003). Evidence also suggests that in foraging cultures, it is men who are dominant and, when possible, accrue the most resources who reap the benefits of marrying more than one woman (Betzig, 1988; Borgerhoff Mulder, 1990; Cronk, 1991; Irons, 1983). Men may defend not only status-linked resources but also the equitable distribution of resources and labor as a means of securing multiple partners. Some have argued that men may protect women against violence from other men, as a form of harem or female-defense polygyny, in foraging societies (Chagnon, 1979).

In modern cultures, men with high status and ample resources are often legally prohibited from obtaining additional wives. However, some evidence suggests modern men with high status still have a greater potential for fertility by copulating more often (Kanazawa, 2003; Perusse, 1993), having sex with more partners (Lalumière, Seto, & Quinsey, 1995; Perusse, 1993), engaging in more extrapair copulations or affairs (J. James, 2003; Schmitt, 2004a), and practicing legalized de facto polygyny (or "effective polygyny"; see Brown & Hotra, 1988; Daly & Wilson, 1983) by divorcing and remarrying a series of highly fertile women over time. These same high-fertility tendencies appear to hold true for men with other traits that women especially desire, including intelligence (Miller, 2000; Vining, 1986), dominance (Graziano, Jensen-Campbell, Todd, & Finch, 1997; Sadalla, Kenrick, & Vershure, 1987), athleticism (Faurie, Pontier, & Raymond, 2004), above-average height (Nettle, 2002; Pierce, 1996), and maturity (Kenrick & Keefe, 1992; White & Burton, 1988).

Polygyny displays adaptive patterning across the ecological conditions of foraging cultures (Flinn & Low, 1986; Low, 2000). Marlowe (2003) demonstrated that polygynous mating is more common in cultures with high pathogens (i.e., where genetic quality of males would be more important) and when gender equity exists in the contribution of calories to local food consumption (see also Gangestad & Simpson, 2000; Wood & Eagly, 2002). Monogamy, in contrast, is more prevalent in cultures with low levels of pathogens and when men contribute relatively more calories to the local diet (i.e., when a male's contribution to biparental care would be more important). The precise form of polygyny in humans also varies across cultures, coming in the form of *class-based or leader-only polygyny* where only men with ample resources obtain multiple wives, and *general polygyny* where number of wives is highly age-dependent and virtually all men who are elders have more than one wife (White & Burton, 1988). Indeed, anthropologists have found that many aspects of foraging culture, such as warfare, kinship, residence, and inheritance patterns, are systematically related to mating strategies in ways that suggest humans evolved to pursue polygynous mating strategies under particular conditions (see Low, 2000; Pasternak et al., 1997).

Human foragers, like other polygynous primates, reside in relatively large social groupings, with a typical band size between 15 and 50 (Lee & Daly, 1999). Women tend to be concentrated and guarded in foraging cultures (Chagnon, 1979), much like females in other polygynous species (Dixson, 1998). Human males also have high variance in status, intelligence, and reproductive success (Archer & Mehdikhani, 2003), and male-male competition for resources and mates is often violent and pronounced (Daly & Wilson, 1988; Daly, Wilson, & Weghorst, 1982). Finally, men are physically stronger and more aggressive than women, reach sexual maturity much later than women, have riskier life history strategies, and experience higher juvenile mortality (R. D. Alexander et al., 1979; Archer & Lloyd, 2002; Clutton-Brock, 1988; Geary, 1998; Mealey, 2000; Wolfe & Gray, 1982). All of these attributes are consistent with a polygynous mating strategy as fundamental to humans.

POLYANDROUS MATING STRATEGIES

Polyandrous mating systems are quite rare in the animal kingdom, especially among primates (Dixson, 1998). In *classic* or *serial* polyandry, females compete for access to numerous males and, after mating with an individual male, they desert the male and their offspring entirely. This mating system is found among several seahorse species (Alcock, 2001). In *cooperative* or *simultaneous* polyandry, a female mates with multiple males, stays with them over a long period of time, and all parents rear the offspring together. Among tamarins and marmosets, this is sometimes seen as a mating system secondary to monogamy (Dixson, 1998). In a few species, more than one female will mate with more than one male and all parents rear the offspring together. These systems are referred to as *polygynandrous*, though this form of mating is exceptionally rare.

Among humans, polyandry is found in less than 1% of preindustrial cultures (Murdock, 1967), and it is becoming less and less common (Trevithick, 1997). Typically, polyandry is not a preferred mating arrangement. Instead, it is regarded as a necessary tactic in response to poor or limited ecological conditions and peculiar inheritance rules. Polyandry is found among humans in areas of the Himalayas where the local ecology is harsh and does not easily support families. In some areas of Tibet, brothers inherit farming lands that cannot be divided into profitable subplots. In these cases, the brothers must pool their inherited resources in order to afford to marry a single woman and support their offspring (Beall & Goldstein, 1981; Crook & Crook, 1988). This form of mating is referred to as *fraternal* or *adelphic* polyandry and is the most common form of human polyandry. This appears not to be a preferred mating strategy in that when a man gains additional resources, he often marries another woman whom he does not share with others (E. A. Smith, 1998).

In some areas of Sri Lanka and among the Toda and Pahari Hindus of southern India, unrelated men occasionally marry the same woman in what is called *associated* or *nonadelphic* polyandry (Stephens, 1988). Normally, these polyandrous mateships occur alongside other forms of mating, including monogamy and polygyny. Overall, the extant evidence suggests that polyandry is not an evolved strategy in humans, but rather is a mating behavior that can emerge given harsh ecological circumstances, limited abilities for men to accumulate resources, and peculiar inheritance rules. There is evidence that women possess adaptations for sometimes mating with more than one partner, but these adaptations involve short-term mating.

SHORT-TERM MATING STRATEGIES

Short-term mating strategies, also called *multimale-multifemale* strategies, occur when females mate with numerous males and males mate with numerous females. Typically, these mateships are brief, lack the exclusivity of monogamous or polygynous unions, and long-term parenting demands fall primarily on a female and her relatives. Males and females in short-term-oriented species do not mate indiscriminately. Many of the same factors of intersexual selection found in monogamous and polygynous species—mate preferences for dominance, status, and health—occur in short-term-oriented species (Dixson, 1998).

In primates, short-term mating occurs in several of the prosimians (e.g., the ringtailed lemur, *Lemur catta*), New World monkeys (e.g., the squirrel monkey, *Saimiri sciureus*), Old World monkeys (e.g., the rhesus monkey, *Macaca mulatta*), and great apes (e.g., the common chimpanzee, *Pan troglodytes*). Short-term-oriented primates tend to show moderate sexual dimorphism, engage in frequent nonconceptive sex, and possess moderate secondary sexual characteristics (Dixson, 1998; Harvey & Harcourt, 1984; Martin, Willner, & Dettling, 1994).

In humans, no culture is known to exhibit short-term mating as an "official" strategy. However, numerous findings indicate humans are designed for at least some short-term mating. Ethnological investigations reveal that many short-term sexual behaviors—including premarital sex, extramarital sex, and mate poaching—are prevalent across most cultures (Barry & Schlegel, 1984; Broude & Greene, 1976; Jankowiak, Nell, & Buckmaster, 2002; Schmitt, Alcalay, Allik, et al., 2004). Among more developed societies, the occurrence rate of extramarital sex—defined as the percentage of people who have "ever" been unfaithful—ranges from 20% to 75% depending on age, type of relationship, and relationship duration (Laumann, Gagnon, Michael, & Michaels, 1994; Wiederman, 1997). Infidelity rates this high occur despite the fact that extramarital sex is met with more social disapproval in modern societies than in other cultures (Frayser, 1985; Pasternak et al., 1997).

Short-term mating within preindustrial cultures is highly prevalent. At least "occasional" extramarital sex takes place in over 70% of preindustrial cultures, occasional premarital sex prevails in 80% of preindustrial cultures, and in 50% of preindustrial cultures premarital sex is described as "universal" among both men and women (Broude & Greene, 1976). In several Amazonian cultures, there is a belief in "partible" paternity, the notion that all men who have sex with a pregnant woman impart some of their essence to the fetus (Beckerman & Valentine, 2002). In these cultures, married women receive extended benefits of protection and resources from the multiple men with whom they have sex (see also Hrdy, 1981). Women in foraging cultures who engage in short-term mating also benefit by obtaining immediate resources, securing a child if a current long-term mate is infertile, and gaining access to high-quality genes from a man whom she would be unable to obtain as a husband (Greiling & Buss, 2000; R. L. Smith, 1984).

In a recent cross-cultural study of 53 modern nations from North America, South America, Western Europe, Eastern Europe, Southern Europe, the Middle East, Africa, Oceania, South/Southeast Asia, and East Asia, Schmitt and his colleagues (Schmitt, Alcalay, Allik, et al., 2004) documented that human "mate poaching" (i.e., romantically attracting someone who is already in a relationship) is culturally universal (see Figure 9.1). Around 60% of men and 40% of women all around the world admit to having tried to attract someone else's partner (though short-term poaching is less common in East Asia). Approximately 10% of people report that their current romantic relationship resulted from mate poaching, and around 3% report that they and their current partner simultaneously poached each other away from a previous partner. Schmitt and his colleagues (Schmitt, Alcalay, Allik, et al., 2004) also found that frequent mate poachers and their targets have a specialized suite of personality traits. These traits, such as superficial

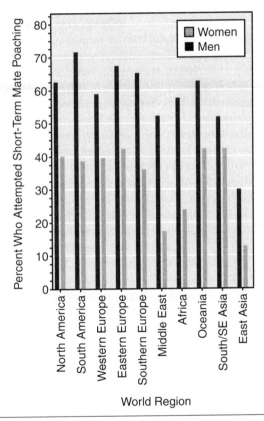

Figure 9.1 Percentage of Men and Women Who Attempted to Poach Another Person's Romantic Partner for a Short-Term Sexual Relationship across the 10 World Regions of the International Sexuality Description Project. *Source:* From "Patterns and Universals of Mate Poaching across 53 Nations: The Effects of Sex, Culture, and Personality on Romantically Attracting Another Person's Partner," by D. P. Schmitt et al., 2004a, *Journal of Personality and Social Psychology, 86*, pp. 560–584.

charm and a tendency toward deception, may constitute an adaptive life history strategy that is based, in part, on prolific short-term mating (Mealey, 1995).

Cuckoldry, when males are deceived into raising offspring that are genetically not their own, occurs in many primate species (van Schaik & Paul, 1996). In humans, it ranges from the relatively rare (i.e., 0.7% in Switzerland, see Sasse, Muller, Chakraborty, & Ott, 1994) to relatively common (i.e., around 30% in southeast England, see Philipp, 1973). Most population-based estimates of cuckoldry place the value between 10% and 15% in modern cultures (see Cerda-Flores, Barton, Marty-Gonzalez, Rivas, & Chakraborty, 1999; Macintyre & Sooman, 1991). Cuckoldry rates are somewhat lower among foraging cultures, ranging between 2% and 9% (see Baker & Bellis, 1995; Neel & Weiss, 1975). Cuckoldry rates of this magnitude suggest that short-term mating in the form of extramarital sex likely pays some reproductive dividends (especially for men who poach and women who obtain genetic quality) and has done so throughout our foraging past.

If our ancestors did routinely engage in infidelity and mate poaching, humans likely evolved countermeasures to thwart adulterous behavior. Evidence of these countermeasures can be seen in adaptations to romantic jealousy. According to Buss (2000), both men and women have evolved exquisite sensitivities to the possibility that mating partners might stray. In men, these sensitivities focus on *sexual* betrayal, in part because men, but not women, are susceptible to cuckoldry (Daly et al., 1982). In women, jealousy adaptations focus on *emotional* betrayal because women are always certain of maternity but are especially susceptible to a man emotionally connecting with another woman, deserting the current mateship, and eventually investing in offspring sired with the other woman (Buss, Larson, Weston, & Semmelroth, 1992).

This sex-specific adaptive design of romantic jealousy has been tested across numerous cultures (Buss, Shackelford, Choe, Buunk, & Dijkstra, 2000; Buss et al., 1999; Buunk et al., 1996) and has been documented as a cultural universal. Additional findings on sex-linked patterns of mate guarding (Buss, 1988; Buss & Shackelford, 1997; Flinn, 1985), mate deception (Bleske & Shackelford, 2001; Schmitt & Shackelford, 2003), marital conflict (Buss, 1989b; Shackelford & Weekes-Shackelford, 2004), and upset concerning mating rivals (Bleske-Rechek & Buss, 2001; Dijkstra & Buunk, 1998) support this interpretation of sex-differentiated jealousy adaptations. As such, these findings can be taken as indirect indicators of men's and women's ancestral tendencies to engage in short-term mating.

Men and women express highly specialized desires when seeking short-term mating partners (Buss & Schmitt, 1993; Gangestad, 2001; Regan, 1998), desires that may represent adaptations to short-term mating. For example, when women seek brief sexual relationships, they tend to express desires for, and consent to sex with, men who are physically symmetrical and possess high-quality genes indicative of low mutation load (Gangestad & Thornhill, 1997a; Rikowski & Grammer, 1999). Because women typically do not obtain long-term investments from brief sexual partners, genetic quality is one of the major benefits women reap from pursuing a short-term mating strategy (see also Cashdan, 1996; Greiling & Buss, 2000). Notably, women seeking a monogamous partner do not exhibit potent preferences for good genes and, instead, tend to seek traits in long-term partners—such as status, ambition, and generosity—that signal an ability and willingness of the man to devote resources to the woman and their offspring over the long haul (B. J. Ellis, 1992; Kenrick, Sadalla, Groth, & Trost, 1990). Moreover, when men pursue a short-term mating strategy, they do not particularly desire physical symmetry and instead desire potential partners who will be quick to consent to sex (Buss & Schmitt, 1993). When women exude this attribute, they are seen as especially effective at achieving a short-term relationship with a man (Greer & Buss, 1994; Schmitt & Buss, 1996, 2001). There is abundant evidence that men and women possess highly functional and sex-specific mate preferences that emerge when following a short-term mating strategy (Buss & Schmitt, 1993; Regan, Levin, Sprecher, Christopher, & Cate, 2000; Simpson, Gangestad, Christensen, & Leck, 1999), preferences that may represent dedicated psychological adaptations to short-term mating.

There is some evidence that humans are physiologically adapted for short-term mating (Baker & Bellis, 1995). In general, larger testes lead to more copious sperm production and are linked with more short-term mating, a trend that has been established across mammals (Harcourt, Harvey, Larson, & Short, 1981; Møller, 1989), including many species of primates (Baker & Bellis, 1995; Møller, 1988; Short, 1979). Compared to other primates, humans possess moderate size testes for their body size (Dixson, 1998). The location of testes is also indicative of a species' mating strategy, with external and scrotal locations being associated with higher sperm storage and more short-term mating (R. L. Smith, 1984). Among the great apes, humans and chimpanzees have external, scrotal testes with relatively little hair at the bottom, whereas the orangutan and the gorilla do not (Baker & Bellis, 1995). This suggests that humans, like the two species of chimpanzee, are physically adapted for short-term mating. Polymorphism in sperm structure and function, variability in sperm chemistry during different stages of ejaculation, and functional patterns of masturbation and orgasm also point to adaptive designs for short-term mating in humans (Baker & Bellis, 1995; Pound, 2002; see Shackelford, this volume; Thornhill, Gangestad, & Comer, 1995). Finally, the morphology of the human penis suggests that it has evolved to respond to sperm competition in that it is exceptionally long and exhibits sperm-displacing capabilities (Gallup et al., 2003).

Among monogamous primates, the average male is about 5% larger than the average female, whereas polygynous primates display bodily dimorphism over 50% (Dixson, 1998; Gaulin & Sailer, 1984; Martin et al., 1994). Among the 30 short-term-oriented primate species identified by Dixson (1998, table 3.6), the median sexual dimorphism in weight was approximately 33%, with our closest living relatives the common chimpanzee (*Pan troglodytes*) and the Bonobo or Pygmy chimpanzee (*Pan paniscus*) exhibiting 36% and 34% dimorphism, respectively. Human dimorphism in body size is also moderate (Wolfe & Gray, 1982), with men about 10% taller and 20% heavier than women (Gaulin & Boster, 1985). Thus, humans possess the moderate sexual dimorphism associated with short-term mating.

Short-term mating primates have two other distinctive characteristics. First, the frequency of nonconceptive sexual intercourse is very high among short-term-oriented primates. Hasegawa and Hiraiwa-Hasegawa (1990) report that female common chimpanzees (*Pan troglodytes*) might copulate over 100 times per successful conception. Similar rates are seen among other short-term mating primates, including humans (Møller & Birkhead, 1989; Wallen & Zehr, 2004; Wrangham, 1993). Second, humans are typical of short-term mating primates in terms of secondary sexual characteristics (Cartwright, 2000). Humans do not possess some of the extreme exaggerations of polygynous primates (e.g., the silver-back feature among dominant male gorillas; Doran & McNeilage, 1998). Neither are men and women nearly identical as with most monogamous primates (Dixson, 1998). Instead, men and women possess many moderate secondary sexual characteristics, including men's enhanced muscularity, wider shoulders, more prominent brow ridge, wider jaw, greater hairiness on the face and body, balding scalp, enlarged larynx, deeper voice, and lower levels of fat on the hips and buttocks (Barber, 1995; Geary, 1998; Low, Alexander, & Noonan, 1987; Mealey, 2000).

SEX AND CONTEXT DIFFERENCES IN HUMAN MATING STRATEGIES

What are evolutionary psychologists to conclude from the preceding account of human mating strategies? Humans clearly show design features associated with monogamy, including adaptations for pairbonding, preferential mate choice, and altriciality. At the same time, humans possess design features associated with polygyny such as sexually dimorphic life history tendencies and cross-culturally pervasive links among status, multiple mating, and differential reproductive success in men. Humans also show design features for short-term mating, including psychological and physiological adaptations to human sperm competition, infidelity, and short-term mate poaching.

One way to reconcile these apparently contradictory findings is to acknowledge that humans are designed and adapted for more than one mating strategy. In other words, humans as a species have a menu of mating strategies at their disposal (Buss, 1994, 1998; Buss & Schmitt, 1993) or, as more recent theorists have called them, *pluralistic* mating strategies (Gangestad & Simpson, 2000). According to this line of reasoning, humans come equipped with specialized mating adaptations for both long-term and short-term mating (Buss & Schmitt, 1993). Not all people pursue both mating strategies at all times. Instead, design features for long-term and short-term mating are differentially activated depending on the mating strategy that is currently being pursued (Schmitt, Shackelford, & Buss, 2001).

PARENTAL INVESTMENT THEORY

According to parental investment theory (Trivers, 1972), the relative proportion of parental investment—the time and energy devoted to the care of individual offspring (at the expense of other offspring)—varies across males and females. In some species, males provide more parental investment (e.g., the Mormon cricket; Alcock & Gwynne, 1991). In other species, females possess the heavy-investing parental burdens (e.g., most mammals; Clutton-Brock, 1991). Importantly, sex differences in parental investment burdens are systematically linked to the intrasexual and intersexual processes of sexual selection (Darwin, 1871). The sex that invests less in offspring is intrasexually more competitive, especially over gaining reproductive access to the opposite sex. The lesser investing sex also is more aggressive, tends to die earlier, tends to mature later, and generally competes with more vigor (see R. D. Alexander & Noonan, 1979). Furthermore, the lesser investing sex is intersexually less discriminating in mate choice; is willing to mate more quickly, at lower cost, and with more partners (Bateson,

1983; Clutton-Brock & Parker, 1992); and reproductively benefits from doing so (Bateman, 1948; Maynard Smith, 1977).

Much evidence in favor of parental investment theory (Trivers, 1972) comes from species where males are the lesser investing sex (e.g., Clutton-Brock, 1991). Males of these species display much more competitiveness with each other over sexual access to heavier investing females and to exhibit more intrasexual competition through greater aggressiveness, riskier life history strategies, and earlier death (Archer & Lloyd, 2002; Trivers, 1985). Lesser investing males also discriminate less in mate choice, often seeking multiple partners and requiring less time before consenting to sex (see Alcock, 2001).

Perhaps the most compelling support for parental investment theory (Trivers, 1972) has come from *sex-role reversed* species. In species where males are the heavy-investing parent (e.g., the red-necked phalarope; J. D. Reynolds, 1987), females are expected to vie more ferociously for sexual access to heavy-investing males and to require little from males before consenting to sex. This form of sexual differentiation exists among many sex-role reversed species including the red-necked phalarope, the Mormon cricket, katydids, dance flies, water bugs, seahorses, and a variety of fish species (Alcock, 2001; Alcock & Gwynne, 1991). Parental investment theory, therefore, is not a theory about males always having more interest in low-cost, indiscriminate sex than females. Instead, it is a theory about sex differences in parental investment systematically relating to sex differences in mating strategies.

Among humans, many males invest heavily as parents (Buss, 1994; Lovejoy, 1981). Nevertheless, men incur much lower levels of obligatory or "minimum" parental investment in offspring than women do (Symons, 1979). Women are obligated to incur the costs of internal fertilization, placentation, and gestation in order to reproduce. The minimum physiological obligations of men are considerably less—requiring only the contribution of sperm. Furthermore, all female mammals, including ancestral women, carried the obligations of lactation. Lactation can last several years in human foraging environments (Kelly, 1995), years during which it is more difficult for women to reproduce and invest in additional offspring than it is for men (Blurton Jones, 1986). Finally, across all known cultures, human males *typically* invest less in active parenting effort than females (Low, 1989; Quinn, 1977).

This human asymmetry in parental investment should result in the lesser investing sex (i.e., men) displaying greater intrasexual competitiveness and lower intersexual "choosiness" in mate preferences. Numerous studies have shown that men exhibit greater physical size and competitive aggression (Archer & Lloyd, 2002; Harvey & Reynolds, 1994), riskier life history strategies (Daly & Wilson, 1988), relatively delayed maturation (Geary, 1998), and earlier death than women do across cultures (R. D. Alexander & Noonan, 1979; Campbell, 2002). In addition, men's mate preferences are, as predicted, almost always less discriminating than women's, especially in the context of short-term mating (Kenrick et al., 1990).

Because men are the lesser investing sex of our species, they also should be more inclined toward low-cost, short-term mating than women. Human sex differences in the desire for short-term sex have been observed in studies of sociosexuality (Schmitt, in press; Wright & Reise, 1997), motivations for and prevalence of extramarital mating (Seal, Agostinelli, & Hannett, 1994; Wiederman, 1997), quality and quantity of sexual fantasies (B. J. Ellis & Symons, 1990), quality and quantity of pornography consumption (Malamuth, 1996), motivations for and use of prostitution (Burley & Symanski, 1981; McGuire & Gruter, 2003), willingness to have sex without commitment (Townsend, 1995), willingness to have sex with strangers (Clark & Hatfield, 1989), and in the fundamental differences between the short-term mating psychology of gay males and lesbians (Bailey, Gaulin, Agyei, & Gladue, 1994). Clearly, sex differences in parental investment obligations have an influence on men's and women's fundamental mating strategies (Hinde, 1984; Symons, 1979).

SEXUAL STRATEGIES THEORY

Buss and Schmitt (1993) extended Trivers' (1972) theory by proposing sexual strategies theory (SST). According to SST, men and women have evolved a complex repertoire of mating strategies. One strategy within this repertoire is *long-term* mating. Long-term mating is typically marked by extended courtship, heavy investment, pairbonding, the emotion of love, and the dedication of resources over a long temporal span to the mating relationship and any offspring that ensue. Another strategy within this repertoire is *short-term* mating, defined as a fleeting sexual encounter such as a hookup or one-night stand. Between the ends of this temporal continuum are brief affairs, prolonged romances, and other intermediate-term relationships. Which sexual strategy or mix of strategies an individual pursues is predicted to be contingent on factors such as opportunity, personal mate value, sex ratio in the relevant mating pool, parental influences, regnant cultural norms, and other features of social and personal context (see also Buss, 1994; Gangestad & Simpson, 2000; Schmitt, Alcalay, Allensworth, et al., 2003).

Sex Differences in Long-Term Mating   Although SST views both sexes as having long-term and short-term mating strategies, men and women are predicted to differ in what they desire and how they tactically pursue these strategies. In long-term mating, for example, the sexes are predicted to differ in their psychological adaptations of mate choice. Men place a greater premium on signals of fertility and reproductive value such as a woman's youth and physical appearance (Buss, 1989a; Cunningham, 1986; Cunningham, Roberts, Barbee, Druen, & Wu, 1995; Johnston & Franklin, 1993; Jones, 1995; Kenrick & Keefe, 1992; Singh, 1993; Symons, 1979; Townsend & Wasserman, 1998; Williams, 1975). In contrast, women place a greater premium on a man's status, resources, ambition, and maturity—cues relevant to his *ability* for long-term provisioning—and to his kindness, generosity, and emotional openness—cues to his *willingness* to provision women and their children (Buss & Barnes, 1986; Buunk et al., 2001; Cunningham, Barbee, & Pike, 1990; B. J. Ellis, 1992; Feingold, 1992; Kruger, Fisher, & Jobling, 2003).

Numerous studies have replicated or confirmed SST-related findings using national, cross-cultural, or multicultural samples (Bailey et al., 2000; Knodel, Low, Saengtienchai, & Lucas, 1994; Sprecher, Sullivan, & Hatfield, 1994; Walter, 1997). Other investigators have used nonsurvey techniques to study actual mate attraction, marriage, marital conflict, and divorce—including experimental, behavioral, and naturalistic methodologies—and have validated key SST hypotheses concerning sex differences in long-term mate preferences (Buss, 1989a; Hassebrauck, 1998; Kenrick, Neuberg, Zierk, & Krones, 1994; Li, Bailery, Kenrick, & Linsenmeier, 2002;

Schmitt, Couden, & Baker, 2001; Simpson et al., 1999; Speed & Gangestad, 1997; Wiederman & Dubois, 1998).

Sex Differences in Short-Term Mating   According to SST, both sexes are hypothesized to pursue short-term mateships in certain contexts but for different reproductive reasons (Buss & Schmitt, 1993). For women, the asymmetry in obligatory parental investment leaves them little to gain in reproductive output by engaging in indiscriminate, short-term sex with numerous partners. However, for men the potential reproductive benefits from promiscuous mating can be profound (Symons, 1979). A man can produce as many as 100 offspring by mating with 100 women over the course of a year, whereas a man who is monogamous tends to have only one child with his partner during that time. In evolutionary currencies, this represents a strong selective pressure—and a potent adaptive problem—for men's short-term mating strategy to favor a desire for sexual variety (Schmitt, Alcalay, Allik, et al., 2003). These 100 instances of only one-time mating between a man and 100 women would rarely, if ever, produce precisely 100 offspring (Fletcher & Stenswick, 2003). However, this selective pressure remains potent because a man mating with 100 women over the course of a year—particularly repeated matings when the women are nearing ovulation and are especially interested in short-term mating (Gangestad, 2001; Gangestad & Thornhill, this volume)—would likely have *significantly more* offspring than a man mating with only one woman over the course of a year.

Whether a woman mates with 100 men or is monogamously bonded with only one man, she still tends to produce only one child in a given year. The potential reproductive benefits from multiple mating with numerous partners, therefore, are much higher for men than women (Bateman, 1948; Symons, 1979). It is important to note that women can reap evolutionary benefits from short-term mating as well (Greiling & Buss, 2000). A key caveat, though, is that women's psychology of short-term mating appears to center more on obtaining men of high-genetic quality rather than numerous men in high-volume quantity (Gangestad & Thornhill, 1997a; R. L. Smith, 1984; Wilson, 1987).

A key premise of SST, therefore, is that both sexes can reap reproductive rewards from engaging in short-term mating under certain circumstances (Buss & Schmitt, 1993). Even though both sexes may adaptively pursue brief mateships, however, men and women are hypothesized by SST to differ in the evolved psychological design of their short-term mating strategies. According to SST, three of the more distinctive design features of men's short-term mating psychology are: (1) Men possess a greater desire than women do for a variety of sexual partners, (2) men require less time to elapse than women do before consenting to sexual intercourse, and (3) men tend to more actively seek short-term mateships than women do (Buss & Schmitt, 1993, p. 210). In each case, these hypothesized desires function to help solve men's adaptive problem of obtaining large numbers of short-term partners.

This suite of hypothesized sex differences has been well supported among studies of samples from the United States (Schmitt, Shackelford, & Buss, 2001). Recently, Schmitt and his colleagues (Schmitt, Alcalay, Allik, et al., 2003) replicated these fundamental sex differences across 10 major regions of the world. When people from North America were asked, "Ideally, how many different sexual partners would you like to have in the next month?" over 23% of men, but only 3% of women, indicated that they would like *more than one* sexual partner in the next month. This finding confirmed that many men desire sexual variety in the form of multiple sexual partners over brief time intervals, whereas very few women express such desires. Similar degrees of sexual differentiation were found all around the world. Moreover, when men and women actively pursuing short-term mates were asked whether they wanted more than one partner in the next month, over 50% of men, but less than 20% of women, expressed desires for multiple sexual partners (Schmitt, Alcalay, Allik, et al., 2003). This finding supports the key SST hypothesis that men's short-term mating strategy is very different from women's and is based, in part, on obtaining large numbers of sexual partners.

Other findings from the cross-cultural study by Schmitt and his colleagues (Schmitt, Alcalay, Allik, et al., 2003) documented that men universally agree to have sex after less time has elapsed than women do and that men from all world regions expend more effort on seeking brief sexual relationships than women do. For example, across all cultures nearly 25% of married men, but only 10% of married women, reported that they are actively seeking short-term, extramarital relationships. These culturally universal findings support the view that men evolved to seek large numbers of sex partners when they pursue a short-term mating strategy. Some women also pursue short-term mates, but when doing so they are more selective and tend to seek out men who are masculine, physically attractive, and otherwise possess high-quality genes (Buss & Schmitt, 1993; Gangestad & Thornhill, 1997b).

INDIVIDUAL DIFFERENCES IN HUMAN MATING STRATEGIES

The previous section addressed the evolutionary psychology of *how* men and women pursue short-term and long-term mating strategies. Another important question is *why* an individual man or woman would opt to pursue a long-term strategy versus a short-term strategy. Several theories have suggested that personal circumstances—including stage of life, personal characteristics, and physical attributes—play an adaptive role in shaping or evoking strategic mating choices (Buss, 1994; Buss & Schmitt, 1993; Gangestad & Simpson, 2000). Among the more important sex-specific features that affect mating strategies are men's overall mate value, women's ovulatory status, and women's age.

Sexual Strategy Pluralism

According to SST (Buss & Schmitt, 1993), whether a man pursues a short-term or long-term mating strategy depends, in part, on his status and prestige. In foraging cultures, men with higher status and prestige tend to possess multiple wives (Borgerhoff Mulder, 1988; Turke & Betzig, 1985), and in so doing polygynous men are able to satisfy aspects of both their long-term and short-term mating psychologies. In modern cultures, men with high status are usually unable to legally marry more than one woman. However, they are more likely to have extramarital affairs and to practice de facto polygyny in the form of serial marriage (Buss, 2000; Fisher, 1992). Given an equal sex ratio of men and women in a given culture, this results in other men—namely those with low status and prestige—being limited to monogamy in the form of one wife. In addition, some low-status men are left with no wives and may be forced to resort to coercive, promiscuous mating strategies (Malamuth, 1998; Thornhill & Palmer, 2000). Consequently, one important source of individual variation in mating strategy is male status.

Mating Differences within Men   Men's mating strategies depend on other factors as well, including their overall value in the mating marketplace (Gangestad & Simpson, 2000). A man's "mate value" is determined, in part, by his status and prestige. It is also affected by his current resource holdings, long-term ambition, intelligence, interpersonal dominance, social popularity, sense of humor, reputation for kindness, maturity, height, strength, and athleticism (Barber, 1995; Buss & Schmitt, 1993; B. J. Ellis, 1992; Smuts, 1995).

Most studies of men in modern cultures find that, when they are able to do so because of high mate value, men opt for short-term mating strategies. For example, Lalumière and his colleagues (1995) designed a scale to measure overall mating opportunities. This scale, similar to overall mate value, included items such as, "Relative to my peer group, I can get dates with ease." They found among North American men that those with higher mate value tended to have sex at an earlier age, to have a larger number of sexual partners, and to follow a more promiscuous mating strategy overall (see also J. James, 2003; Landolt, Lalumière, & Quinsey, 1995).

Another indicator of overall mate value is the social barometer of self-esteem (Kirkpatrick, Waugh, Valencia, & Webster, 2002). Similar to the results with mating opportunities, North American men who score higher on self-esteem scales tend to engage in more short-term mating strategies (Baumeister & Tice, 2001; Walsh, 1991). In a recent cross-cultural study by Schmitt (2004a), this revealing trend was evident across dozens of modern nations. The same relationship was usually not evident, and was often reversed, among women in modern nations (see also Mikach & Bailey, 1999). Women with high self-esteem were more likely to pursue monogamous, long-term mating strategies. These findings would seem to support parental investment theory (Trivers, 1972), in that when mate value is high and people are given a choice, men prefer short-term mating whereas women strategically opt for more monogamous mateships.

According to strategic pluralism theory (Gangestad & Simpson, 2000), men are more likely to engage in short-term mating strategies when they exhibit the physical characteristics most preferred by women, especially traits indicative of low genetic mutation load (Thornhill & Gangestad, 1994). Notably, higher facial symmetry is indicative of low mutation load in men (Gangestad & Thornhill, 1997b; Perrett et al., 1999), and women adaptively prefer facial symmetry when they follow a short-term mating strategy (Gangestad & Thornhill, 1997a) because one of the key benefits women can reap from short-term mating is to gain access to high-quality genes that they might not be able to secure from a long-term partner.

Evidence that physically attractive men adaptively respond to women's desires and become more promiscuous comes from several sources. For example, men who possess broad and muscular shoulders, a physical attribute preferred by short-term-oriented women (Frederick, Haselton, Buchanan, & Gallup, 2003), tend toward short-term mating as reflected in an earlier age of first intercourse, more sexual partners, and more extrapair copulations (Hughes & Gallup, 2003). In numerous studies of North American college students, Gangestad and his colleagues have shown that women who seek short-term mates place special importance on the physical attractiveness of their partners and that physically attractive men are more likely to pursue short-term mating strategies (Gangestad & Cousins, 2001; Gangestad & Thornhill, 1997a; Simpson et al., 1999). In a cross-cultural study of several dozen nations, Schmitt (2004b) replicated these results and found that men who consider themselves attractive in nearly all cultures are more likely than other men to engage in short-term mating strategies. In sum, evidence suggests that when men have the opportunity to pursue a short-term mating strategy, due to their high mate value and physical attractiveness, they tend to do so.

Some research suggests that genetic and hormonal predispositions may affect men's mating strategies (Bailey et al., 2000). Much of this research focuses on the mediating effects of testosterone. For example, compared to their same-age single peers, married men tend to have lower levels of testosterone (Booth & Dabbs, 1993; Burnham et al., 2003), and men who are expectant fathers and hope to have children only with their current partner have lower testosterone yet (Gray, Kahlenberg, Barrett, Lipson, & Ellison, 2002; Hirschenhauser, Frigerio, Grammer, & Magnusson, 2002). Men who are high in testosterone tend to have more sexual partners, to start having sex earlier, to have higher sperm counts, to be more interested in sex, to divorce more frequently, and are more likely to have affairs than other men in adulthood (G. M. Alexander & Sherwin, 1991; Booth & Dabbs, 1993; Manning, 2002; Udry & Campbell, 1994). The root cause of this mating strategy variability may lie in early testosterone exposure and its effects on the activation of men's short-term mating psychology. Exposure to high testosterone levels in utero causes increased masculinization of the human brain and increased testosterone in adulthood (Manning, 2002; Ridley, 2003). If men's brains are programmed for greater short-term mating in general (Symons, 1979), this would imply that those who are exposed to higher testosterone in utero would more likely develop short-term mating strategies in adulthood.

One clue to testosterone exposure can be found in the relative length of human fingers. Essentially, if an individual's ring fingers (fourth digits or 4D) are longer than his pointer fingers (second digits or 2D), high levels of in utero testosterone exposure and high circulating levels of testosterone in adulthood are implicated (Manning, 2002). In a recent study by Fowler and his colleagues (Fowler, Schmitt, Allensworth, & Hitchell, 2003), men with especially long ring fingers (i.e., those with a low 2D:4D ratio) were found to follow more short-term-oriented mating strategies (see also Stanik, 2003). Men with low 2D:4D ratios are also likely to have more children, to have more sperm motility, to be more competitive and assertive, and to be perceived as more attractive than other men (Manning, 2002). All of these findings implicate testosterone exposure as an activating factor in men's short-term strategies (cf. Putz, Gaulin, Sporter, & McBurney, 2004).

Mating Differences within Women   Women's desires for sex tend to peak during the late follicular phase, just before ovulation when the odds of becoming pregnant are maximized (Regan, 1996). It was once thought that this shift evolved because it increased the probability of conceptive intercourse in our monogamous female ancestors. However, several studies have documented that women's mating strategies change over the cycle, with short-term mating desires and behaviors peaking in the highly fertile days just before ovulation (Gangestad, 2001; Thornhill & Gangestad, in press).

Women who are interested in short-term mating tend to prefer men who are high in dominance and masculinity, as indicated by testosterone-related attributes such as prominent brows, large chins, and deeper voices (U. Mueller & Mazur, 1997; Penton-Voak & Chen, 2004; Perrett et al., 1999). Short-term-oriented women may prefer these attributes because markers of testosterone are honest indicators of immunocompetence quality in men (Gangestad & Thornhill, 2003; Thornhill & Gangestad, 1999). During the late follicular phase, women's preferences for masculine faces and voices conspicuously increase (Johnston, Hagel, Franklin, Fink, & Grammer, 2001; Penton-Voak & Perrett, 2000; Putz, 2004), precisely as though women are shifting to a short-term mating psychology.

A similar ovulatory shift occurs in women's preference for symmetrical faces. Women who generally pursue a short-term mating strategy express strong preferences for symmetrical male faces, perhaps because facial symmetry indicates low mutation load (Gangestad & Thornhill, 1997a). During the late follicular phase, women's preference for symmetrical faces increases even further (Gangestad & Cousins, 2001), again as though they have shifted their strategy to short-term mating. It has also been shown that women nearing ovulation find the pheromonal smell of symmetrical men more appealing than do less fertile women (Gangestad & Thornhill, 1998; Rikowski & Grammer, 1999; Thornhill & Gangestad, 1999), women who mate with more symmetrical men have more frequent and intense orgasms (Thornhill et al., 1995), and men with attractive faces have qualitatively better health (Shackelford & Larsen, 1999) and semen characteristics (Soler et al., 2003). Finally, women appear to dress more provocatively when nearing ovulation (Grammer, Renninger, & Fischer, 2004), though such women also reduce risky behaviors associated with being raped, especially if they are not taking contraception (Broder & Hohmann, 2003).

In addition to ovulatory shifts, there is also evidence that women's mating strategies change across their life span. A common assumption in the United States is that women's sexual desires, in general, reach a "sexual peak" shortly after the age of 30 (Barr, Bryan, & Kenrick, 2002). There are two related rationales for thinking an early-30s peak in female sexual desire may solve adaptive problems and increase women's reproductive success. First, the percentage of fertile ovulatory cycles—cycles that include an ovulation that could lead to pregnancy—varies tremendously over a woman's life span, reaching a peak at 70% in women during their early 30s (see Baker & Bellis, 1995; Döring, 1969). Second, the probability of giving birth to children with genetic disorders does not increase dramatically—as with many disorders and complications—until after a woman reaches 35 (Hook, 1981; Naeye, 1983). This powerful confluence of changes in the reproductive biology of women—a pending decrease in viable ovulations, alongside an imminent increase in offspring defects and birthing complications—would have presented women with adaptive problems in need of a solution. An early-30s peak in sexual desire would help to solve this problem by increasing women's rates of sexual intercourse when they were the most fertile and had not yet incurred age-heightened risks in giving birth.

In a study of 1,400 women from the United States and Canada, Schmitt and his colleagues (2002) found that women in their early 30s do experience a peak in sexual desire, as measured by subjective feelings of lust and behavioral manifestations of seductiveness and increased sexual activity. Along with evidence from social perceptions of sexual peak and suggestive findings from other large self-report surveys (Barr et al., 2002; Laumann et al., 1994), women's sexual desires appear to peak in their early 30s and may have the specific evolutionary function of either increasing reproduction with their primary long-term mating partner or leading women in their early 30s to engage in more extramarital affairs, perhaps in an effort to increase the genetic quality or diversity of their offspring (Baker & Bellis, 1995; R. L. Smith, 1984).

Other individual differences and personal situations may adaptively shift women's mating strategies. For example, short-term mating strategies are more likely to occur during adolescence, when her partner is of low mate value, when she desires to get rid of a mate, and after divorce—all situations where short-term mating serves adaptive functions (Betzig, 1989; Frayser, 1985; Greiling & Buss, 2000). In some cases, short-term mating seems to emerge as an adaptive reaction to early developmental experiences within the family (Belsky et al., 1991; Sulloway, 1996). For example, short-term mating is more likely to occur among women growing up in father-absent homes (Draper & Harpending, 1982; Moffitt, Caspi, Belsky, & Silva, 1992; Quinlan, 2003), especially in homes where a stepfather is present (B. J. Ellis & Garber, 2000). In these cases, the absence of a father may indicate to young women that mating-age men are unreliable. In such environments, short-term mating may serve as the more viable mating strategy in adulthood (but see Comings, Muhleman, Johnson, & MacMurray, 2002).

Finally, some have argued that frequency-dependent or other forms of selection have resulted in different heritable tendencies toward long-term versus short-term mating (Gangestad & Simpson, 1990; MacDonald, 1997). There is behavioral genetic evidence that age at first intercourse, lifetime number of sex partners, and sociosexuality—a general trait that varies from restricted long-term mating to unrestricted short-term mating—are somewhat heritable (Bailey et al., 2000; Lyons et al., 2004; Rowe, 2002). Findings often suggest mating strategy heritability is stronger in men than women (Dunne et al., 1997).

THE TRIVERS-WILLARD HYPOTHESIS

According to the Trivers-Willard hypothesis (Trivers & Willard, 1973), men and women differ in their potential for reproductive success. For any given man, his reproductive potential is much larger than a woman's because he can mate polygynously and can sire large quantities of offspring by following a short-term mating strategy. This is true, however, only if he has the qualities that women desire, such as high status and ample resources. If he has low status, he may be completely shut out of the mating marketplace. Women, in contrast, tend not to differ dramatically their total number of offspring. As a result, humans may have evolved to preferentially produce to sons when their offspring are likely to possess high status and resources, and daughters may be more likely when the reproductive outlook for offspring is relatively bleak. It is not the case that men or women consciously choose to manipulate the sex of their offspring. Rather, evolved mechanisms, involving hormonal factors and postnatal neglect, may function in this manner (Baker & Bellis, 1995; Grant, 1998).

On empirical examination, there is some support for the Trivers-Willard hypothesis among human populations (Gaulin & Robbins, 1991; W. H. James, 1987). For example, women from wealthy nations and women who have access to wealth themselves tend to have more sons than daughters (Mackey, 1993; U. Mueller, 1993), whereas low-status and single-parent women tend to have more daughters (Grant, 1998). In foraging cultures that practice polygyny, women who are monogamously married tend to have more sons than women who are polygynously married and have to share the husband's resources with his other wives and their children (Whiting, 1993). This evidence would seem to confirm that women adaptively shift their reproductive behavior in response to personal circumstances (cf. Keller, Nesse, & Hofferth, 2001; but see Webster, 2004).

CULTURAL DIFFERENCES IN HUMAN MATING STRATEGIES

In addition to sex and individual differences, human mating strategies vary in adaptive ways across cultures. Low (1990) has shown that tribal cultures with high pathogen stress tend to have polygynous marriage systems (see also Marlowe, 2003; White & Burton, 1988). Monogamous systems, in contrast, are relatively absent in high pathogen environments. This pattern of mating pluralism may be explained by high pathogen ecologies causing men to prefer genetic diversity in their offspring (diversity that would protect against pathogens and could be achieved through polygyny) while women prefer particularly healthy men who can support multiple wives, of which there are few in high pathogen areas of the world (Low, 2000). Mating adaptations designed to respond to pathogen levels may also give rise to different forms of polygyny. For example, in high-pathogen environments, polygynous men tend to marry exogamously, outside their local tribe, which further increases their offspring diversity. Sororal polygyny, when men marry women who are sisters, would provide less genetic diversity and rarely occurs in high-pathogen environments (Low, 2000).

OPERATIONAL SEX RATIOS AND MATING STRATEGIES

Pedersen (1991) has argued that a combination of sexual selection theory (Darwin, 1871) and parental investment theory (Trivers, 1972) leads to a series of predictions concerning the effects of sex ratio—the relative number of men versus women in a culture—on human mating. According to sexual selection theory, when males desire a particular attribute in mating partners, females must respond by competing in the expression and provision of that desired attribute. When there are many more females than males, males should become an especially scarce resource that females must compete for with even more intensity than normal (see also Guttentag & Secord, 1983).

When combined with the parental investment notion described earlier in which men tend to desire short-term mating (Buss & Schmitt, 1993; Symons, 1979; Trivers, 1972), this theory leads to the hypothesis in cultures with lower sex ratios (i.e., more women than men; traditionally ratios below 100) men become a scarce resource and can afford to demand from interested women that their desires for short-term sex be fulfilled. As a result, the culture as a whole should become more oriented toward short-term mating. Conversely, when sex ratios are high and men greatly outnumber women, men must enter into more intense competition for the limited number of potential female partners. Women's preferences for long-term monogamous relationships become the key desires that must be responded to if men are to remain competitive in the courtship marketplace. In cultures with higher sex ratios (i.e., more men than women; ratios above 100), people should possess more monogamous mating proclivities.

Using data from sex ratio fluctuations over time within the United States, Pedersen (1991) marshaled a compelling case for a causal link between sex ratios and human mating strategies. For example, high sex ratio fluctuations have been historically associated with increases in monogamy, as evidenced by lower divorce rates and men's greater willingness to invest in their children. Low sex ratios have been historically associated with indexes of short-term mating, such as an increase in divorce rates and a reduction in what he termed female "sexual coyness." In a recent cross-cultural study (Schmitt, in press), national sex ratios were correlated with direct measures of basic human mating strategies in an attempt to test Pedersen's (1991) theory. As expected, cultures with more men than women tended toward long-term mating, whereas cultures with more women than men tended toward short-term mating (see also Barber, 2000). As shown in Figure 9.2, women's sociosexuality tends to increase (i.e., become

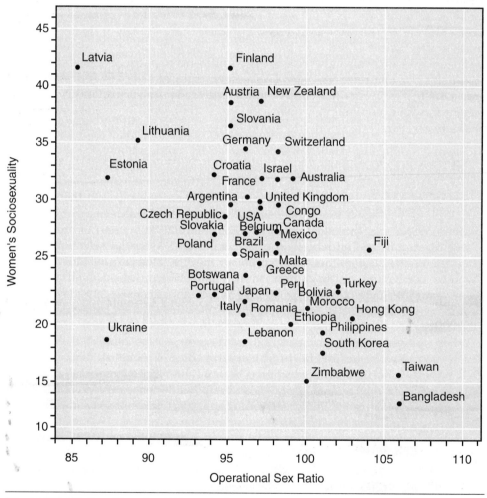

Figure 9.2   National Levels of Women's Sociosexuality Related to Operational Sex Ratios across 48 Nations of the International Sexuality Description Project. *Source:* From "Sociosexuality from Argentina to Zimbabwe: A 48-Nation Study of Sex, Culture, and Strategies of Human Mating," by D. P. Schmitt, in press, *Behavioral and Brain Sciences.*

more unrestricted or short-term oriented) as the operational sex ratio decreases (i.e., more women than men in the mating pool; scores below 100), $r(46) = -.50$, $< .001$. Overall, it appears that human mating strategies are facultatively responsive to the balance of men versus women in the local mating pool.

STRESS, FERTILITY, AND THE DEVELOPMENT OF MATING STRATEGIES

Several combinations of life history theory (Low, 1998) and attachment theory (Bowlby, 1969) have suggested that childhood experiences influence adult mating strategies (Belsky, 1999; Chisholm, 1996; Draper & Harpending, 1988). According to Belsky et al. (1991), early social experiences adaptively channel children down one of two reproductive pathways. Children who are socially exposed to high levels of stress—especially insensitive/inconsistent parenting, harsh physical environments, and economic hardship—tend to develop insecure parent-child attachment. These children also tend to physically mature earlier than children exposed to less stress. According to Belsky and his colleagues, attachment insecurity and early physical maturity subsequently lead to the adaptive development of what is called an "opportunistic" reproductive strategy (i.e., short-term mating). Conversely, children exposed to lower stress and less environmental hardship are more emotionally secure and physically mature later. These children develop a more "investing" reproductive strategy in adulthood (i.e., long-term mating) that pays evolutionary dividends in low stress environments.

A closely related theory has been proposed by Chisholm (1996), who argues that local mortality and fertility rates—presumably related to high stress and inadequate resources—act as cues that facultatively shift human mating strategies in evolutionary-adaptive ways (see also Weinrich, 1977). In cultures with high mortality rates and unpredictable resources, the optimal mating strategy is to reproduce early and often, a strategy related to insecure attachment, short-term temporal orientations, and promiscuous mating strategies. In cultures that are physically safe and have abundant resources, mortality rates are lower and the optimal strategy is to invest heavily in fewer numbers of offspring. In safer environments, therefore, individuals should pursue a long-term strategy associated with more monogamous mating.

Numerous studies have provided support for these developmental theories of human mating (Barber, 2003; Belsky, 1999; B. J. Ellis & Garber, 2000; Moffit et al., 1992; Quinlan, 2003). In a recent study, Schmitt and his colleagues (Schmitt, Alcalay, Allensworth, et al., 2004) measured the romantic attachment styles of over 17,000 people from 56 nations. They found, as expected, that insecure attachment styles were strongly related to various indexes of familial stress, economic resources, mortality, and fertility. Schmitt (2004a) also found that short-term mating was related to insecure attachment across cultures. As expected, the dismissing form of insecure attachment was linked to short-term mating in men, whereas the fearful/preoccupied forms of insecure attachment were linked to short-term mating in women. These findings support the view that stressful environments cause increases in insecure romantic attachment, increases linked to the facultative development of short-term mating strategies (Kirkpatrick, 1998).

CONCLUSIONS

Humans possess a pluralistic mating repertoire, organized in terms of basic long-term and short-term mating psychologies. The activation and pursuit of these mating psychologies differs in adaptive ways across sex, personal circumstance, and cultural context. Men's short-term strategy, for example, is based on obtaining large numbers of partners. Women's short-term strategy, in contrast, is more heavily rooted in obtaining men of high genetic quality, including men who possess masculine and symmetrical facial features. Men high in mate value tend to pursue short-term mating strategies more than other men, and when possible strive for polygynous or serial marriages. Women nearing ovulation express desires indicative of their short-term mating psychology, including being more sensitive to the pheromones of symmetrical men. In cultures with high stress and fertility, insecure attachment and short-term mating adaptively emerge, and female-biased sex ratios appear to adaptively generate short-term mating strategies as well.

An important area for future research will be to more precisely gauge the adaptive effects of culture on human mating strategies and find ways to apply these results to social problems and public policies. For example, based on the cross-cultural relationship between sex ratio and women's sociosexuality (see Figure 9.2), once women outnumber men at a sex ratio of about 95, women's sociosexuality conspicuously increases. In many American urban environments, women significantly outnumber men as a result of gang-related homicides and high rates of male imprisonment. Public policies that exacerbate excesses of women (e.g., drug laws that place large numbers of men in prison) may well serve to increase the short-term mating of local populations. Such a shift could have unintended secondary effects on single parenting (Burton, 1990; Lancaster, 1989), sexual aggression (Thornhill & Palmer, 2000), and risky sexual behavior associated with HIV/AIDS (Seal et al., 1994). Utilizing the facultative nature of mating strategy deployment and its adaptive calibration to local ecologies should prove useful for evolutionary-minded policymakers (Crawford & Salmon, 2004; McGuire & Gruter, 2003).

In the future, evolutionary perspectives on human mating strategies should become more fully integrated with other perspectives, including religious, historical, and feminist scholarship (see Buss & Malamuth, 1996; Gowaty, 1997). Religious teachings frequently address sexual and reproductive behavior, often in evolutionary-relevant ways (V. Reynolds & Tanner, 1983). The same may be true for other aspects of life that, at first glance, seem disconnected from human evolution. Political ideology, sexual orientation, gender identity, gender equality, education, climate, geography, ethnicity, and linguistic heritage may all impact human mating strategies (Barber, 2002; Broude, 1983; Hartung, 1985; Kelly, 1995; Wood & Eagly, 2002), yet none of these topics were adequately addressed in this chapter. The adaptationist perspective emphasized here represents a mere starting point for future theorizing and research on the broad spectrum of human sexual experience. Future efforts at manipulating and controlling human sexuality will be most effective, however, if they are rooted in the knowledge of our fundamental human mating strategies.

REFERENCES

Alcock, J. (2001). *Animal behavior* (7th ed.). Sunderland, MA: Sinauer Associates.

Alcock, J., & Gwynne, S. T. (1991). Evolution of insect mating systems: The impact of individual selectionist thinking. In W. J. Bailey & J. Ridsdill-Smith (Eds.), *Reproductive behavior in insects: Insects and populations.* New York: Chapman & Hill.

Alexander, G. M., & Sherwin, B. B. (1991). The association between testosterone, sexual arousal, and selective attention for erotic stimuli in men. *Hormones and Behavior, 25,* 367–381.

Alexander, R. D., Hoogland, J. L., Howard, R. D., Noonan, K. M., & Sherman, P. W. (1979). Sexual dimorphism and breeding systems in pinnipeds, ungulates, primates, and humans. In N. A. Chagnon & W. Irons (Eds.), *Evolutionary biology and human social behavior: An anthropological perspective* (pp. 402–435). North Scituate, MA: Duxbury.

Alexander, R. D., & Noonan, K. M. (1979). Concealment of ovulation, parental care, and human social interaction. In N. A. Chagnon & W. Irons (Eds.), *Evolutionary biology and human social behavior: An anthropological perspective* (pp. 436–453). North Scituate, MA: Duxbury.

Andersson, M. (1994). *Sexual selection.* Princeton, NJ: Princeton University Press.

Archer, J., & Lloyd, B. B. (2002). *Sex and gender* (2nd ed.). New York: Cambridge University Press.

Archer, J., & Mehdikhani, M. (2003). Variability among males in sexually selected attributes. *Review of General Psychology, 7,* 219–236.

Bailey, J. M., Gaulin, S., Agyei, Y., & Gladue, B. A. (1994). Effects of gender and sexual orientation on evolutionary relevant aspects of human mating psychology. *Journal of Personality and Social Psychology, 66,* 1081–1093.

Bailey, J. M., Kirk, K. M., Zhu, G., Dunne, M. P., & Martin, N. G. (2000). Do individual differences in sociosexuality represent genetic or environmentally contingent strategies? Evidence from the Australian twin registry. *Journal of Personality and Social Psychology, 78,* 537–545.

Baker, R. R., & Bellis, M. A. (1995). *Human sperm competition.* London: Chapman & Hall.

Barash, D. P., & Lipton, J. E. (2001). *The myth of monogamy.* New York: Freeman.

Barber, N. (1995). The evolutionary psychology of physical attractiveness: Sexual selection and human morphology. *Ethology and Sociobiology, 16,* 395–424.

Barber, N. (2000). On the relationship between country sex ratios and teen pregnancy rates: A replication. *Cross-Cultural Research, 34,* 26–37.

Barber, N. (2002). On the relationship between fertility and geographic latitude: A cross-national study. *Cross-Cultural Research, 36,* 3–15.

Barber, N. (2003). Paternal investment prospects and cross-national differences in single parenthood. *Cross-Cultural Research, 37,* 163–177.

Barr, A., Bryan, A., & Kenrick, D. T. (2002). Sexual peak: Socially shared cognitions about desire, frequency, and satisfaction in men and women. *Personal Relationships, 9,* 287–299.

Barry, H., & Schlegel, A. (1984). Measurements of adolescent sexual behavior in the standard sample of societies. *Ethnology, 23,* 315–329.

Bateman, A. J. (1948). Intra-sexual selection in Drosophila. *Heredity, 2,* 349–368.

Bateson, P. (Ed.). (1983). *Mate choice.* Cambridge, England: Cambridge University Press.

Baumeister, R. F., & Tice, D. M. (2001). *The social dimension of sex.* Needham Heights, MA.

Beall, C. M., & Goldstein, M. C. (1981). Tibetan fraternal polyandry: A test of sociobiological theory. *American Anthropologist, 83,* 5–12.

Beckerman, S., & Valentine, P. (Eds.). (2002). *Cultures with multiple fathers: The theory and practice of partible paternity in lowland South America.* Gainesville, FL: University Press of Florida.

Belsky, J. (1999). Modern evolutionary theory and patterns of attachment. In J. Cassidy & P. R. Shaver (Eds.), *Handbook of attachment* (pp. 141–161). New York: Guilford Press.

Belsky, J., Steinberg, L., & Draper, P. (1991). Childhood experience, interpersonal development, and reproductive strategy: An evolutionary theory of socialization. *Child Development, 62,* 647–670.

Betzig, L. (1986). *Despotism and differential reproduction: A Darwinian view of history.* New York: Aldine.

Betzig, L. (1988). Mating and parenting in Darwinian perspective. In L. Betzig, M. Borgerhoff Mulder, & P. Turke (Eds.), *Human reproductive behaviour: A Darwinian perspective* (pp. 49–63). Cambridge: Cambridge University Press.

Betzig, L. (1989). Causes of conjugal dissolution: A cross-cultural study. *Current Anthropology, 30,* 654–676.

Birkhead, T. R., & Møller, A. P. (1992). *Sperm competition in birds.* London: Academic Press.

Bleske, A. L., & Shackelford, T. K. (2001). Poaching, promiscuity, and deceit: Combating mating rivalry in same-sex friendships. *Personal Relationships, 8,* 407–424.

Bleske-Rechek, A. L., & Buss, D. M. (2001). Opposite-sex friendship: Sex differences and similarities in initiation, selection, and dissolution. *Personality and Social Psychology Bulletin, 27,* 1310–1323.

Blurton Jones, N. (1986). Bushman birth spacing: A test for optimal interbirth intervals. *Ethology and Sociobiology, 7,* 91–105.

Booth, A., & Dabbs, J. (1993). Testosterone and men's marriages. *Social Forces, 72,* 463–477.

Borgerhoff Mulder, M. (1988). Reproductive success in three Kipsigis cohorts. In T. H. Clutton-Brock (Ed.), *Reproductive success: Studies of individual variation in contrasting breeding systems* (pp. 419–435). Chicago: University of Chicago Press.

Borgerhoff Mulder, M. (1990). Kipsigis women's preferences for wealthy men: Evidence for female choice in mammals. *Behavioral Ecology and Sociobiology, 27,* 255–264.

Borgerhoff Mulder, M. (1992). Women's strategies in polygynous marriages. *Human Nature, 3,* 45–70.

Bowlby, J. (1969/1982). *Attachment and loss: Vol. I. Attachment.* New York: Basic Books.

Broder, A., & Hohmann, N. (2003). Variations in risk taking over the menstrual cycle: An improved replication. *Evolution and Human Behavior, 24,* 391–398.

Broude, G. J. (1983). Male-female relationships in cross-cultural perspective: A study of sex and intimacy. *Behavior Science Research, 18,* 154–181.

Broude, G. J., & Greene, S. J. (1976). Cross-cultural codes on twenty sexual attitudes and practices. *Ethnology, 15,* 409–403.

Brown, D. E., & Hotra, D. (1988). Are prescriptively monogamous societies effectively monogamous. In L. Betzig, M. Borgerhoff Mulder, & P. Turke (Eds.), *Human reproductive behavior: A Darwinian perceptive* (pp. 153–159). Cambridge: Cambridge University Press.

Buckle, L., Gallup, G. G., & Rodd, Z. A. (1996). Marriage as a reproductive contract: Patterns of marriage, divorce, and remarriage. *Ethology and Sociobiology, 17,* 363–377.

Burley, N., & Symanski, R. (1981). Women without: An evolutionary and cross-cultural perspective on prostitution. In R. Symanski (Ed.), *The immoral landscape: Female prostitution in western societies* (pp. 239–274). Toronto: Butterworth.

Burnham, T. C., Chapman, J. F., Gray, P. B., McIntyre, M. H., Lipson, S. F., & Ellison, P. T. (2003). Men in committed, romantic relationships have lower testosterone. *Hormones and Behavior, 44,* 119–122.

Burton, L. M. (1990). Teenage childbearing as an alternative life-course strategy in multigenerational black families. *Human Nature, 1,* 123–144.

Buss, D. M. (1988). From vigilance to violence: Tactics of mate retention in American undergraduates. *Ethology and Sociobiology, 9,* 291–317.

Buss, D. M. (1989a). Sex differences in human mate preferences: Evolutionary hypotheses tested in 37 cultures. *Behavioral and Brain Sciences, 12,* 1–49.

Buss, D. M. (1989b). Conflict between the sexes: Strategic interference and the evocation of anger and upset. *Journal of Personality and Social Psychology, 56,* 735–747.

Buss, D. M. (1994). *The evolution of desire.* New York: Basic Books.

Buss, D. M. (1998). Sexual strategies theory: Historical origins and current status. *Journal of Sex Research, 35,* 19–31.

Buss, D. M. (2000). *The dangerous passion.* New York: Free Press.

Buss, D. M., & Barnes, M. F. (1986). Preferences in human mate selection. *Journal of Personality and Social Psychology, 50,* 559–570.

Buss, D. M., Larsen, R. J., Westen, D., & Semmelroth, J. (1992). Sex differences in jealousy: Evolution, physiology, and psychology. *Psychological Science, 3,* 251–255.

Buss, D. M., & Malamuth, N. M. (Eds.). (1996). *Sex, power, and conflict: Evolutionary and feminist perspectives.* New York: Oxford University Press.

Buss, D. M., & Schmitt, D. P. (1993). Sexual strategies theory: An evolutionary perspective on human mating. *Psychological Review, 100,* 204–232.

Buss, D. M., & Shackelford, T. K. (1997). From vigilance to violence: Mate retention tactics in married couples. *Journal of Personality and Social Psychology, 72,* 346–361.

Buss, D. M., Shackelford, T. K., Choe, J., Buunk, B. P., & Dijkstra, P. (2000). Distress about mating rivals. *Personal Relationships, 7,* 235–243.

Buss, D. M., Shackelford, T. K., Kirkpatrick, L. A., Choe, J., Hasegawa, M., Hasegawa, T., et al. (1999). Jealousy and the nature of beliefs about infidelity: Tests of competing hypotheses about sex differences in the United States, Korea, and Japan. *Personal Relationships, 6,* 125–150.

Buunk, A. P., Angleitner, A., Oubaid, V., & Buss, D. M. (1996). Sex differences in jealousy in evolutionary and cultural perspective: Tests from the Netherlands, Germany, and the United States. *Psychological Science, 7,* 359–363.

Buunk, A. P., Dijkstra, P., Kenrick, D. T., & Warntjes, A. (2001). Age preferences for mates as related to gender, own age, and involvement level. *Evolution and Human Behavior, 22,* 241–250.

Campbell, A. (2002). *A mind of her own: The evolutionary psychology of women.* Oxford, England: Oxford University Press.

Cartwright, J. (2000). *Evolution and human behavior.* Cambridge, MA: MIT Press.

Cashdan, E. (1996). Women's mating strategies. *Evolutionary Anthropology, 5*, 134–143.

Casimir, M. J., & Aparna, R. (1995). Prestige, possessions, and progeny: Cultural goals and reproductive success among the Bakkarwal. *Human Nature, 6*, 241–272.

Cerda-Flores, R. M., Barton, S. A., Marty-Gonzalez, L. F., Rivas, F., & Chakraborty, R. (1999). Estimation of nonpaternity in the Mexican population of Nuevo Leon: A validation study of blood group markers. *American Journal of Physical Anthropology, 109*, 281–293.

Chagnon, N. A. (1979). Is reproductive success equal in egalitarian societies. In N. A. Chagnon & W. Irons (Eds.), *Evolutionary biology and human social behavior: An anthropological perspective* (pp. 374–401). North Scituate, MA: Duxbury Press.

Chagnon, N. A. (1988). Life histories, blood revenge, and warfare in a tribal population. *Science, 239*, 985–992.

Chisholm, J. S. (1996). The evolutionary ecology of attachment organization. *Human Nature, 7*, 1–38.

Clark, R. D., & Hatfield, E. (1989). Gender differences in receptivity to sexual offers. *Journal of Psychology and Human Sexuality, 2*, 39–55.

Clutton-Brock, T. H. (Ed.). (1988). *Reproductive success: Studies of individual variation in contrasting breeding systems.* Chicago: The University of Chicago Press.

Clutton-Brock, T. H. (1989). Mammalian mating systems. *Proceedings of the Royal Society of London. Series B, Biological Sciences, 236*, 339–372.

Clutton-Brock, T. H. (1991). *The evolution of parental care.* Princeton, NJ: Princeton University Press.

Clutton-Brock, T. H., & Parker, G. A. (1992). Potential reproductive rates and the operation of sexual selection. *The Quarterly Review of Biology, 67*, 437–456.

Comings, D. E., Muhleman, D., Johnson, J. P., & MacMurray, J. P. (2002). Parent-daughter transmission of the androgen receptor gene as an explanation of the effect of father absence on age of menarche. *Child Development, 73*, 1046–1051.

Crawford, C., & Salmon, C. (Eds.). (2004). *Evolutionary psychology, public policy, and personal decisions.* Mahwah, NJ: LEA.

Cronk, L. (1991). Wealth, status, and reproductive success among the Mukogodo of Kenya. *American Anthropologist, 93*, 345–360.

Crook, J. H., & Crook, S. J. (1988). Tibetan polyandry: Problems of adaptation and fitness. In L. Betzig, M. Borgerhoff Mulder, & P. Turke (Eds.), *Human reproductive behaviour: A Darwinian perspective* (pp. 97–114). Cambridge, England: Cambridge University Press.

Cunningham, M. R. (1986). Measuring the physical in physical attractiveness: Quasi-experiments on the sociobiology of female facial beauty. *Journal of Personality and Social Psychology, 50*, 925–935.

Cunningham, M. R., Barbee, A. P., & Pike, C. L. (1990). What do women want? Facialmetric assessment of multiple motives in the perception of male facial physical attractiveness. *Journal of Personality and Social Psychology, 59*, 61–72.

Cunningham, M. R., Roberts, R., Barbee, A. P., Druen, P. B., & Wu, C. (1995). Their ideas of attractiveness are, on the whole, the same as ours: Consistency and variability in the cross-cultural perception of female attractiveness. *Journal of Personality and Social Psychology, 68*, 261–279.

Daly, M., & Wilson, M. (1983). *Sex, evolution and behavior* (2nd ed.). Belmont, CA: Wadsworth.

Daly, M., & Wilson, M. (1988). *Homicide.* New York: Aldine de Gruyter.

Daly, M., Wilson, M., & Weghorst, S. J. (1982). Male sexual jealousy. *Ethology and Sociobiology, 3*, 11–27.

Darwin, C. R. (1871). *The descent of man and selection in relation to sex.* London: Murray.

Davies, N. B. (1991). Mating systems. In J. R. Krebs & N. B. Davies (Eds.), *Behavioural ecology: An evolutionary approach* (pp. 263–294). Oxford, England: Blackwell Scientific Publications.

Dijkstra, P., & Buunk, B. P. (1998). Jealousy as a function of rival characteristics: An evolutionary perspective. *Personality and Social Psychology Bulletin, 24*, 1158–1166.

Dixson, A. F. (1993). Sexual selection, sperm competition, and the evolution of sperm length. *Folia Primatologica, 61*, 221–227.

Dixson, A. F. (1998). *Primate sexuality: Comparative studies of the prosimians, monkeys, apes, and human beings.* New York: Oxford University Press.

Dixson, A. F., & Mundy, N. I. (1994). Sexual behavior, sexual swelling, and penile evolution in chimpanzees (*Pan troglodytes*). *Archives of Sexual Behavior, 23*, 267–280.

Doran, D. M., & McNeilage, A. (1998). Gorilla ecology and behavior. *Evolutionary Anthropology, 6*, 120–131.

Döring, G. K. (1969). The incidence of anovular cycles in women. *Journal of Reproductive Fertility, Suppl. 6*, 77–81.

Draper, P. (1989). African marriage systems: Perspectives from evolutionary ecology. *Ethology and Sociobiology, 10,* 145–169.

Draper, P., & Harpending, H. (1982). Father absence and reproductive strategy: An evolutionary perspective. *Journal of Anthropological Research, 38,* 255–273.

Draper, P., & Harpending, H. (1988). A sociobiological perspective on the development of human reproductive strategies. In K. MacDonald (Ed.), *Sociobiological perspectives on human development* (pp. 340–372). New York: Springer-Verlag.

Dunne, M. P., Martin, N. G., Statham, D. J., Slutske, W. S., Dinwiddie, S. H., Bucholz, K. K., et al. (1997). Genetic and environmental contributions to variance in age at first intercourse. *Psychological Science, 8,* 211–216.

Ellis, B. J. (1992). The evolution of sexual attraction: Evaluative mechanisms in women. In J. H. Barkow, L. Cosmides, & J. Tooby (Eds.), *The adapted mind* (pp. 267–288). New York: Oxford University Press.

Ellis, B. J., & Garber, J. (2000). Psychosocial antecedents of variation in girl's pubertal timing: Maternal depression, stepfather presence, and marital and family stress. *Child Development, 71,* 485–501.

Ellis, B. J., & Symons, D. (1990). Sex differences in sexual fantasy: An evolutionary psychological approach. *Journal of Sex Research, 27,* 527–556.

Ellis, L. (1995). Dominance and reproductive success: A cross-species comparison. *Ethology and Sociobiology, 16,* 257–333.

Emlen, S. T., & Oring, L. W. (1977). Ecology, sexual selection, and the evolution of mating systems. *Science, 197,* 215–223.

Faurie, C., Pontier, D., & Raymond, M. (2004). Student athletes claim to have more sexual partners than other students. *Evolution and Human Behavior, 25,* 1–8.

Feingold, A. (1992). Gender differences in mate selection preferences: A test of the parental investment model. *Psychological Bulletin, 112,* 125–139.

Fisher, H. E. (1989). Evolution of human serial pairbonding. *American Journal of Physical Anthropology, 78,* 331–354.

Fisher, H. E. (1992). *Anatomy of love: The natural history of monogamy, adultery, and divorce.* New York: Norton.

Fisher, H. E. (1998). Lust, attraction, and attachment in mammalian reproduction. *Human Nature, 9,* 23–52.

Fletcher, G. J. O., & Stenswick, M. (2003). The intimate relationship mind. In K. Sterelny & J. Fitness (Eds.), *From mating to mentality: Evaluating evolutionary psychology* (pp. 71–93). New York: Psychology Press.

Flinn, M. V. (1985). Mate guarding in a Caribbean village. *Ethology and Sociobiology, 9,* 1–28.

Flinn, M. V., & Low, B. S. (1986). Resource distribution, social competition, and mating patterns in human societies. In D. I. Rubenstein & R. W. Wrangham (Eds.), *Ecological aspects of social evolution: Birds and mammals* (pp. 217–243). Princeton, NJ: Princeton University Press.

Fowler, R., Schmitt, D. P., Allensworth, M., & Hitchell, A. (2003). *Anthropometric correlates of short-term mating in men and women: Finger length ratios, waist-to-hip ratios, and facial symmetry.* Unpublished manuscript.

Frayser, S. (1985). *Varieties of sexual experience: An anthropological perspective.* New Haven, CT: HRAF Press.

Frederick, D., Haselton, M. G., Buchanan, G. M., & Gallup, G. G. (2003). *Male muscularity as a good-genes indicator: Evidence from women's preferences for short-term and long-term mates.* Paper presentation to the 15th annual meeting of Human Behavior and Evolution Society, Lincoln, Nebraska.

Gallup, G. G., Burch, R. L., Zappieri, M. L., Parvez, R. A., Stockwell, M. L., & Davis, J. A. (2003). The human penis as a semen displacement device. *Evolution and Human Behavior, 24,* 277–289.

Gangestad, S. W. (2001). Adaptive design, selective history, and women's sexual motivations. In J. A. French, A. C. Kamil, & D. W. Leger (Eds.), *Evolutionary psychology and motivation* (pp. 37–74). Lincoln, Nebraska: University of Nebraska Press.

Gangestad, S. W., & Cousins, A. J. (2001). Adaptive design, female mate preferences, and shifts across the menstrual cycle. *Annual Review of Sex Research, 12,* 145–185.

Gangestad, S. W., & Simpson, J. A. (1990). Toward an evolutionary history of female sociosexual variation. [Special issue: Biological foundations of personality: Evolution, behavioral genetics, and psychophysiology.] *Journal of Personality, 58,* 69–96.

Gangestad, S. W., & Simpson, J. A. (2000). The evolution of human mating: Trade-offs and strategic pluralism. *Behavioral and Brain Sciences, 23,* 573–644.

Gangestad, S. W., & Thornhill, R. (1997a). The evolutionary psychology of extrapair sex: The role of fluctuating asymmetry. *Evolution and Human Behavior, 18,* 69–88.

Gangestad, S. W., & Thornhill, R. (1997b). Human sexual selection and developmental stability. In J. A. Simpson & D. T. Kenrick (Eds.), *Evolutionary social psychology* (pp. 169–195). Mahwah, NJ: Erlbaum.

Gangestad, S. W., & Thornhill, R. (1998). Menstrual cycle variation in women's preferences for the scent of symmetrical men. *Proceedings of the Royal Society of London. Series B, Biological Sciences, 265,* 927–933.

Gangestad, S. W., & Thornhill, R. (2003). Facial masculinity and fluctuating asymmetry. *Evolution and Human Behavior, 24,* 231–241.

Gaulin, S., & Boster, J. (1985). Cross-cultural differences in sexual dimorphism: Is there any variance to be explained? *Ethology and Sociobiology, 6,* 219–225.

Gaulin, S., & Robbins, C. J. (1991). Trivers-Willard effect in contemporary North American society. *American Journal of Physical Anthropology, 85,* 61–69.

Gaulin, S., & Sailer, L. D. (1984). Sexual dimorphism in weight among primates: The relative impact of allometry and sexual selection. *International Journal of Primatology, 5,* 515–535.

Geary, D. C. (1998). *Male, female: The evolution of human sex differences.* Washington, DC: American Psychological Association.

Geary, D. C., & Flinn, M. V. (2001). Evolution of human parental behavior and the human family. *Parenting: Science and Practice, 1,* 5–61.

Gowaty, P. A. (Ed.). (1997). *Feminism and evolutionary biology.* New York: Chapman & Hall.

Grammer, K., Renninger, L., & Fischer, B. (2004). Disco clothing, female sexual motivation, and relationship status: Is she dressed to impress? *Journal of Sex Research, 41,* 66–74.

Grant, V. J. (1998). *Maternal personality, evolution and the sex ratio.* London: Routledge.

Gray, P. B., Kahlenberg, S. M., Barrett, E. S., Lipson, S. F., & Ellison, P. T. (2002). Marriage and fatherhood are associated with lower testosterone in males. *Evolution and Human Behavior, 23,* 193–201.

Graziano, W. G., Jensen-Campbell, L. A., Todd, M., & Finch, J. F. (1997). Interpersonal attraction from an evolutionary perspective: Women's reactions to dominant and prosocial men. In J. A. Simpson & D. T. Kenrick (Eds.), *Evolutionary social psychology* (pp. 141–167). Mahwah, NJ: Erlbaum.

Greer, A. E., & Buss, D. M. (1994). Tactics for promoting sexual encounters. *Journal of Sex Research, 31,* 185–201.

Greiling, H., & Buss, D. M. (2000). Women's sexual strategies: The hidden dimension of short-term mating. *Personality and Individual Differences, 28,* 929–963.

Guttentag, M., & Secord, P. F. (1983). *Too many women? The sex ratio question.* Beverly Hills, CA: Sage.

Hall-Craggs, E. C. B. (1962). The testis of *Gorilla gorilla beringei. Proceedings of the Zoological Society of London, 139,* 511–514.

Hames, R. (1996). Costs and benefits of monogamy and polygyny for Yanomamö women. *Ethology and Sociobiology, 17,* 181–199.

Harcourt, A. H., Harvey, P. H., Larson, S. G., & Short, R. V. (1981). Testis weight, body weight, and breeding system in primates. *Nature, 293,* 55–57.

Hartung, J. (1985). Matrilineal inheritance: New theory and analysis. *Behavioral and Brain Sciences, 8,* 661–668.

Harvey, P. H., & Harcourt, A. H. (1984). Sperm competition, testes size, and breeding system in primates. In R. L. Smith (Ed.), *Sperm competition and the evolution of animal mating systems.* New York: Academic Press.

Harvey, P. H., & Reynolds, J. D. (1994). Sexual selection and the evolution of sex differences. In R. V. Short & E. Balaban (Eds.), *The difference between the sexes* (pp. 51–66). Cambridge, England: Cambridge University Press.

Hasegawa, T., & Hiraiwa-Hasegawa, M. (1990). Sperm competition and mating behavior. In T. Nishida (Ed.), *The chimpanzees of the Mahale mountains: Sexual and life history strategies* (pp. 115–132). Tokyo: University of Tokyo Press.

Hassebrauck, M. (1998). The visual process method: A new method to study physical attractiveness. *Evolution and Human Behavior, 19,* 111–123.

Hazan, C., & Zeifman, D. (1999). Pair bonds as attachments: Evaluating the evidence. In J. Cassidy & P. R. Shaver (Eds.), *Handbook of attachment* (pp. 336–354). New York: Guilford Press.

Heath, K. M., & Hadley, C. (1998). Dichotomous male reproductive strategies in a polygynous human society: Mating versus parental effort. *Current Anthropology, 39,* 369–374.

Hill, K., & Hurtado, A. M. (1996). *Ache life history: The ecology and demography of a foraging people.* New York: Aldine de Gruyter.

Hinde, R. A. (1984). Why do the sexes behave differently in close relationships? *Journal of Social and Personal Relationships, 1,* 471–501.

Hirschenhauser, K., Frigerio, D., Grammer, K., & Magnusson, M. S. (2002). Monthly patterns of testosterone and behavior in expectant fathers. *Hormones and Behavior, 42,* 172–181.

Hook, E. (1981). Rates of chromosomal abnormalities at different maternal ages. *Obstetrics and Gynecology, 58,* 282.

Hrdy, S. B. (1981). *The woman that never evolved.* Cambridge, MA: Harvard University Press.

Hughes, S. M., & Gallup, G. G. (2003). Sex differences in morphological predictors of sexual behavior: Shoulder to hip and waist to hip ratios. *Evolution and Human Behavior, 24,* 173–178.

Irons, W. (1983). Human female reproductive strategies. In S. K. Wasser (Ed.), *Social behavior of female vertebrates* (pp. 169–213). New York: Academic Press.

James, J. (2003). *Sociosexuality and self-perceived mate value: A multidimensional approach.* Poster presentation to the 15th annual meeting of Human Behavior and Evolution Society, Lincoln, Nebraska.

James, W. H. (1987). The human sex ratio: Part 1. A review of the literature. *Human Biology, 59,* 721–752.

Jankowiak, W., Nell, D., & Buckmaster, A. (2002). Extra-marital affairs: A reconsideration of the meaning and universality of the "double standard." *World Cultures, 13,* 2–21.

Johnston, V., & Franklin, M. (1993). Is beauty in the eye of the beholder? *Ethology and Sociobiology, 14,* 183–199.Jones, D. (1995). Sexual selection, physical attractiveness, and facial neoteny: Cross-cultural evidence and implications. *Current Anthropology, 36,* 723–748.

Johnston, V., Hagel, R., Franklin, M., Fink, B., & Grammer, K. (2001). Male facial attractiveness: Evidence for hormone-mediated adaptive design. *Evolution and Human Behavior, 22,* 251–267.

Kanazawa, S. (2003). Can evolutionary psychology explain reproductive behavior in the contemporary United States? *Sociological Quarterly, 44,* 291–302.

Keller, M. C., Nesse, R. M., & Hofferth, S. (2001). The Trivers-Willard hypothesis of parental investment: No effect in the contemporary United States. *Evolution and Human Behavior, 22,* 342–360.

Kelly, R. L. (1995). *The foraging spectrum: Diversity in hunter-gatherer lifeways.* Washington, DC: Smithsonian Institution Press.

Kenrick, D. T., & Keefe, R. C. (1992). Age preferences in mates reflect sex differences in human reproductive strategies. *Behavioral and Brain Sciences, 15,* 75–133.

Kenrick, D. T., Neuberg, S. L., Zierk, K. L., & Krones, J. M. (1994). Evolution and social cognition: Contrast effects as a function of sex, dominance, and physical attractiveness. *Personality and Social Psychology Bulletin, 20,* 210–217.

Kenrick, D. T., Sadalla, E. K., Groth, G., & Trost, M. R. (1990). Evolution, traits, and the stages of human courtship: Qualifying the parental investment model. [Special issue: Biological foundations of personality: Evolution, behavioral genetics, and psychophysiology.] *Journal of Personality, 58,* 97–116.

Kirkpatrick, L. A. (1998). Evolution, pair-bonding, and reproductive strategies: A reconceptualization of adult attachment. In J. A. Simpson & W. S. Rholes (Eds.), *Attachment theory and close relationships* (pp. 353–393). New York: Guilford Press.

Kirkpatrick, L. A., Waugh, C. E., Valencia, A., & Webster, G. D. (2002). The functional domain specificity of self-esteem and the differential prediction of aggression. *Journal of Personality and Social Psychology, 82,* 756–767.

Knodel, J., Low, B., Saengtienchai, C., & Lucas, R. (1997). An evolutionary perspective on Thai sexual attitudes and behavior. *Journal of Sex Research, 34,* 292–303.

Kruger, D. J., Fisher, M., & Jobling, I. (2003). Proper and dark heroes as dads and cads: Alternative mating strategies in British romantic literature. *Human Nature, 14,* 305–317.

Lalumière, M. L., Seto, M. C., & Quinsey, V. L. (1995). *Self-perceived mating success and the mating choices of males and females.* Unpublished manuscript.

Lancaster, J. B. (1989). Evolutionary and cross-cultural perspectives on single-parenthood. In R. W. Bell & N. J. Bell (Eds.), *Interfaces in psychology* (pp. 63–72). Lubbock: Texas Tech University Press.

Landolt, M. A., Lalumière, M. L., & Quinsey, V. L. (1995). Sex differences in intra-sex variations in human mating tactics: An evolutionary approach. *Ethology and Sociobiology, 16,* 3–23.

Laumann, E. O., Gagnon, J. H., Michael, R. T., & Michaels, S. (1994). *The social organization of sexuality.* Chicago: University of Chicago Press.

Lee, R. B., & Daly, R. (Eds.). (1999). *The Cambridge encyclopedia of hunters and gatherers.* Cambridge, MA: Cambridge University Press.

Li, N. P., Bailey, M. J., Kenrick, D. T., & Linsenmeier, J. A. (2002). The necessities and luxuries of mate preferences: Testing the tradeoffs. *Journal of Personality and Social Psychology, 82,* 947–955.

Lovejoy, O. (1981). The origin of man. *Science, 211,* 341–350.

Low, B. S. (1989). Cross-cultural patterns in the training of children: An evolutionary perspective. *Journal of Comparative Psychology, 103,* 313–319.

Low, B. S. (1990). Marriage systems and pathogen stress in human societies. *American Zoologist, 30,* 325–339.

Low, B. S. (1998). The evolution of human life histories. In C. Crawford & D. L. Krebs (Eds.), *Handbook of evolutionary psychology* (pp. 131–161). Mahwah, NJ: Erlbaum.

Low, B. S. (2000). *Why sex matters.* Princeton, NJ: Princeton University Press.

Low, B. S., Alexander, R. D., & Noonan, K. M. (1987). Human hips, breasts and buttocks: Is fat deceptive? *Ethology and Sociobiology, 8,* 249–257.

Lyons, M. J., Koenen, K. C., Buchting, F., Meyer, J. M., Eaves, L., Toomey, R. et al. (2004). A twin study of sexual behavior in men. *Archives of Sexual Behavior, 33,* 129–136.

MacDonald, K. (1997). Life history and human reproductive behavior: Environmental/contextual influences and heritable variation. *Human Nature, 8,* 327–359.

Macintyre, S., & Sooman, A. (1991). Non-paternity and prenatal genetic testing. *Lancet, 338,* 869–871.

Mackey, W. C. (1993). Relationships between the human sex ratio and the woman's microenvironment: Four tests. *Human Nature, 4,* 175–198.

Malamuth, N. M. (1996). Sexually explicit media, gender differences, and evolutionary theory. *Journal of Communication, 46,* 8–31.

Malamuth, N. M. (1998). An evolutionary-based model integrating research on the characteristics of sexually coercive men. In J. G. Adair, D. Belanger, & K. L. Dion (Eds.), *Advances in psychological science* (pp. 151–184). Hove: England Psychology Press.

Manning, J. T. (2002). *Digit ratio: A pointer to fertility, behavior, and health.* New Brunswick, NJ: Rutgers University Press.

Marlowe, F. M. (2003). The mating system of foragers in the standard cross-cultural sample. *Cross-Cultural Research, 37,* 282–306.

Martin, R. D., Willner, L. A., & Dettling, A. (1994). The evolution of sexual size dimorphism in primates. In R. V. Short & E. Balaban (Eds.), *The differences between the sexes* (pp. 159–200). Cambridge: Cambridge University Press.

Maynard Smith, J. (1977). Parental investment: A prospective analysis. *Animal Behavior, 25,* 1–9.

McGuire, M., & Gruter, M. (2003). Prostitution: An evolutionary perspective. In A. Somit & S. Peterson (Eds.), *Human nature and public policy: An evolutionary approach* (pp. 29–40). New York: Palgrave Macmillan.

Mealey, L. (1995). The sociobiology of sociopathy: An integrated evolutionary model. *Behavioral and Brain Sciences, 18,* 523–599.

Mealey, L. (2000). *Sex differences: Developmental and evolutionary strategies.* San Diego, CA: Academic Press.

Mikach, S. M., & Bailey, J. M. (1999). What distinguishes women with unusually high numbers of sex partners? *Evolution and Human Behavior, 20,* 141–150.

Miller, G. F. (2000). *The mating mind.* New York: Doubleday.

Moffitt, T. E., Caspi, A., Belsky, J., & Silva, P. A. (1992). Childhood experience and the onset of menarche: A test of a sociobiological model. *Child Development, 63,* 47–58.

Møller, A. P. (1988). Ejaculate quality, testes size, and sperm production in primates. *Journal of Human Evolution, 17,* 479–488.

Møller, A. P. (1989). Ejaculate quality, testes size, and sperm production in mammals. *Functional Ecology, 3,* 91–96.

Møller, A. P., & Birkhead, T. R. (1989). Copulation behavior in mammals: Evidence that sperm competition is widespread. *Biological Journal of the Linnean Society, 38,* 119–132.

Mueller, T. M. (1999). A multi-species comparison of time spent in adolescence. *American Journal of Primatology, 49,* 81–82.

Mueller, U. (1993). Social status and sex. *Nature, 363,* 490.

Mueller, U., & Mazur, A. (1997). Facial dominance in. *Homo sapiens* as honest signaling of male quality. *Behavioral Ecology, 8,* 569–579.

Murdock, G. P. (1967). *Ethnographic atlas.* Pittsburgh, PA: University of Pittsburgh Press.

Naeye, R. (1983). Maternal age, obstetric complications, and the outcome of pregnancy. *American Journal of Obstetrics and Gynecology, 61,* 210–216.

Neel, J. V., & Weiss, K. M. (1975). The genetic structure of a tribal population, the Yanomama Indians. XIII. Biodemographic studies. *American Journal of Physical Anthropology, 42,* 25–51.

Nettle, D. (2002). Height and reproductive success in a cohort of British men. *Human Nature, 13,* 473–491.

Orians, G. H. (1969). On the evolution of mating systems in birds and mammals. *American Naturalist, 103,* 589–603.

Pasternak, B., Ember, C., & Ember, M. (1997). *Sex, gender, and kinship: A cross-cultural perspective.* Upper Saddle, NJ: Prentice-Hall.

Pedersen, F. A. (1991). Secular trends in human sex ratios: Their influence on individual and family behavior. *Human Nature, 2,* 271–291.

Penton-Voak, I. S., & Chen, J. Y. (2004). High salivary testosterone is linked to masculine male facial appearance in humans. *Evolution and Human Behavior, 25,* 229–241.

Penton-Voak, I. S., & Perret, D. I. (2000). Female preference for male faces changes cyclically: Further evidence. *Evolution and Human Behavior, 20,* 295–307.

Perrett, D. I., Burt, D. M., Penton-Voak, I. S., Lee, K. J., Rowland, D. A., & Edwards, R. (1999). Symmetry and human facial attractiveness. *Evolution and Human Behavior, 20,* 295–307. Perrett, D. I., Lee, K. J., Penton-Voak, I. S., Rowland, D. R., Yoshikawa, S., Burt, D. M., et al. (1998). Effects of sexual dimorphism on facial attractiveness. *Nature, 394,* 884–887.

Perusse, D. (1993). Cultural and reproductive success in industrial societies: Testing the relationship at the proximate and ultimate levels. *Behavioral and Brain Sciences, 16,* 267–322.

Philipp, E. E. (1973). Discussion: Moral, social, and ethical issues. In G. E. W. Wolstenholme & D. W. Fitzsimons (Eds.), *Law and ethics of AID and embryo transfer* (pp. 663–666). Amsterdam: Associate Scientific Publishing.

Pierce, C. A. (1996). Body height and romantic attraction: A meta-analytic test of the male-taller norm. *Social Behavior and Personality, 24,* 143–149.

Pound, N. (2002). Male interest in visual cues of sperm competition risk. *Evolution and Human Behavior, 23,* 443–466.

Putz, D. A. (2004, July). *Women's preferences for men's voices vary cyclically with conception risk and predicted hormone levels.* Paper presentation to the 16th annual meeting of Human Behavior and Evolution Society, Berlin, Germany.

Putz, D. A., Gaulin, S. J. C., Sporter, R. J., & McBurney, D. H. (2004). Sex hormones and finger length: What does 2D:4D indicate? *Evolution and Human Behavior, 25,* 182–199.

Quinlan, R. J. (2003). Father absence, parental care, and female reproductive development. *Evolution and Human Behavior, 24,* 376–390.

Quinn, N. (1977). Anthropological studies on women's status. *Annual Review of Anthropology, 6,* 181–225.

Regan, P. C. (1996). Rhythms of desire: The association between menstrual cycle phases and female sexual desire. *The Canadian Journal of Human Sexuality, 5,* 145–156.

Regan, P. C. (1998). What if you can't get what you want? Willingness to compromise ideal mate selection standards as a function of sex, mate value, and relationship context. *Personality and Social Psychology Bulletin, 24,* 1294–1303.

Regan, P. C., Levin, L., Sprecher, S., Christopher, F. S., & Cate, R. (2000). Partner preferences: What characteristics do men and women desire in their short-term and long-term romantic partners? *Journal of Psychology and Human Sexuality, 12,* 1–21.

Reynolds, J. D. (1987). Mating system and nesting biology of the red-necked phalarope. *Phalaropus lobatus:* What constrains polyandry? *Isis, 129,* 225–242.

Reynolds, V., & Tanner, R. E. S. (1983). *The biology of religion.* London, England: Longman.

Ridley, M. (2003). *Nature via nurture.* New York: HarperCollins.

Rikowski, A., & Grammer, K. (1999). Human body odor, symmetry, and attractiveness. *Proceedings of the Royal Academy of London, B., 266,* 869–874.

Rowe, D. C. (2002). On genetic variation in menarche and age at first intercourse: A critique of the Belsky-Draper hypothesis. *Evolution and Human Behavior, 23,* 365–372.

Sadalla, E. K., Kenrick, D. T., & Vershure, B. (1987). Dominance and heterosexual attraction. *Journal of Personality and Social Psychology, 52,* 730–738.

Sasse, G., Muller, H., Chakraborty, R., & Ott, J. (1994). Estimating the frequency of nonpaternity in Switzerland. *Human Heredity, 44,* 337–343.

Schmitt, D. P. (2004a). *Sociosexuality, self-esteem, and romantic attachment.* Unpublished manuscript.

Schmitt, D. P. (2004b). *Sociosexuality related to finger length ratios, waist-to-hip ratios, body symmetry, and physical attractiveness in college-aged men and women: Evidence from the United States and 10 world regions.* Unpublished manuscript.

Schmitt, D. P. (in press). Sociosexuality from Argentina to Zimbabwe: A 48-nation study of sex, culture, and strategies of human mating. *Behavioral and Brain Sciences.*

Schmitt, D. P., Alcalay, L., Allensworth, M., Allik, J., Ault, L., Austers, I., et al. (2003). Are men universally more dismissing than women? Gender differences in romantic attachment across 62 cultural regions. *Personal Relationships, 10,* 307–331.

Schmitt, D. P., Alcalay, L., Allensworth, M., Allik, J., Ault, L., Austers, I., et al. (2004). Patterns and universals of adult romantic attachment across 62 cultural regions: Are models of self and other pancultural constructs? *Journal of Cross-Cultural Psychology, 35,* 367–402.

Schmitt, D. P., Alcalay, L., Allik, J., Angleitner, A., Ault, L., Austers, I., et al. (2004). Patterns and universals of mate poaching across 53 nations: The effects of sex, culture, and personality on romantically attracting another person's partner. *Journal of Personality and Social Psychology, 86,* 560–584.

Schmitt, D. P., Alcalay, L., Allik, J., Ault, L., Austers, I., Bennett, K. L., et al. (2003). Universal sex differences in the desire for sexual variety: Tests from 52 nations, 6 continents, and 13 islands. *Journal of Personality and Social Psychology, 85,* 85–104.

Schmitt, D. P., & Buss, D. M. (1996). Strategic self-enhancement and competitor derogation: Sex and context effects on the perceived effectiveness of mate attraction tactics. *Journal of Personality and Social Psychology, 70,* 1185–1204.

Schmitt, D. P., & Buss, D. M. (2001). Human mate poaching: Tactics and temptations for infiltrating existing mateships. *Journal of Personality and Social Psychology, 80,* 894–917.

Schmitt, D. P., Couden, A., & Baker, M. (2001). Sex, temporal context, and romantic desire: An experimental evaluation of Sexual Strategies Theory. *Personality and Social Psychology Bulletin, 27,* 833–847.

Schmitt, D. P., & Shackelford, T. K. (2003). Nifty ways to leave your lover: The tactics people use to entice and disguise the process of human mate poaching. *Personality and Social Psychology Bulletin, 29,* 1018–1035.

Schmitt, D. P., Shackelford, T. K., & Buss, D. M. (2001). Are men really more "oriented" toward short-term mating than women? A critical review of theory and research. *Psychology, Evolution and Gender, 3,* 211–239.

Schmitt, D. P., Shackelford, T. K., Duntley, J., Tooke, W., Buss, D. M., Fisher, M. L., et al. (2002). Is there an early-30's peak in female sexual desire? Cross-sectional evidence from the United States and Canada. *The Canadian Journal of Human Sexuality, 11,* 1–18.

Schultz, A. H. (1938). The relative weight of testes in primates. *Anatomical Record, 72,* 387–394.

Seal, D. W., Agostinelli, G., & Hannett, C. A. (1994). Extradyadic romantic involvement: Moderating effects of sociosexuality and gender. *Sex Roles, 31,* 1–22.

Shackelford, T. K., & Larsen, R. J. (1999). Facial attractiveness and physical health. *Evolution and Human Behavior, 20,* 71–76.

Shackelford, T. K., & Weekes-Shackelford, V. (2004). Why don't men pay child support. In C. Crawford & C. Salmon (Eds.), *Evolutionary psychology, public policy, and personal decisions* (pp. 231–248). Mahwah, NJ: LEA.

Short, R. V. (1979). Sexual selection and its component parts, somatic and genital selection, as illustrated in man and great apes. *Advances in the Study of Behavior, 9,* 131–158.

Shuster, S. M., & Wade, M. J. (2003). *Mating systems and strategies.* Princeton: Princeton University Press.

Simpson, J. A., Gangestad, S. W., Christensen, P. N., & Leck, K. (1999). Fluctuating asymmetry, sociosexuality, and intrasexual competitive tactics. *Journal of Personality and Social Psychology, 76,* 159–172.

Singh, D. (1993). Adaptive significance of female physical attractiveness: Role of waist-to-hip ratio. *Journal of Personality and Social Psychology, 65,* 293–307.

Smith, E. A. (1998). Is Tibetan polyandry adaptive? Methodological and metatheoretical analyses. *Human Nature, 9,* 225–261.

Smith, R. L. (1984). Human sperm competition. In R. L. Smith (Ed.), *Sperm competition and the evolution of animal mating systems* (pp. 601–659). New York: Academic Press.

Smuts, B. (1995). The evolutionary origins of patriarchy. *Human Nature, 6,* 1–32.

Soler, C., Núñez, M., Gutierrez, R., Nunez, J., Medina, P., Sancho, M., et al. (2003). Facial attractiveness in men provides clues to semen quality. *Evolution and Human Behavior, 24,* 199–207.

Speed, A., & Gangestad, S. W. (1997). Romantic popularity and mate preferences: A peer-nomination study. *Personality and Social Psychology Bulletin, 23,* 928–935.

Sprecher, S., Sullivan, Q., & Hatfield, E. (1994). Mate selection preferences: Gender differences examined in a national sample. *Journal of Personality and Social Psychology, 66,* 1074–1080.

Stanik, C. (2003, June). *An examination of the relationships between 2D:4D finger ratio and standard as well as sexual personality characteristics, dating patterns, guilt, and shame in college students.* Poster presentation to the 15th annual meeting of Human Behavior and Evolution Society, Lincoln, Nebraska.

Stephens, M. E. (1988). Half a wife is better than none: A practical approach to nonadelphic polyandry. *Current Anthropology, 29,* 354–356.

Sulloway, F. J. (1996). *Born to rebel.* New York: Pantheon.

Symons, D. (1979). *The evolution of human sexuality.* New York: Oxford University Press.

Thornhill, R., & Gangestad, S. W. (1994). Human fluctuating asymmetry and sexual behavior. *Psychological Science, 5,* 297–302.

Thornhill, R., & Gangestad, S. W. (1999). The scent of symmetry: A human sex pheromone that signals fitness? *Evolution and Human Behavior, 20,* 175–201.

Thornhill, R., & Gangestad, S. W. (in press). Do women have evolved adaptations for extra-pair copulation. In E. Voland & K. Grammer (Eds.), *Evolutionary aesthetics.* Heidelberg: Springer-Verlag.

Thornhill, R., Gangestad, S. W., & Comer, R. (1995). Human female orgasm and mate fluctuating asymmetry. *Animal Behaviour, 50,* 1601–1615.

Thornhill, R., & Palmer, C. T. (2000). *A natural history of rape.* Cambridge, MA: MIT Press.

Townsend, J. M. (1995). Sex without emotional involvement: An evolutionary interpretation of sex differences. *Archives of Sexual Behavior, 24,* 173–205.

Townsend, J. M., & Wasserman, T. (1998). Sexual attractiveness: Sex differences in assessment and criteria. *Evolution and Human Behavior, 19,* 171–191.

Trevithick, A. (1997). On a panhuman preference for monandry: Is polyandry an exception? *Journal of Comparative Family Studies, 28,* 154–181.

Trivers, R. (1972). Parental investment and sexual selection. In B. Campbell (Ed.), *Sexual selection and the descent of man: 1871–1971* (pp. 136–179). Chicago: Aldine.

Trivers, R. (1985). *Social evolution.* Menlo Park, CA: Benjamin/Cummings.

Trivers, R., & Willard, D. E. (1973). Natural selection of parental ability to vary the sex ratio of offspring. *Science, 179,* 90–92.

Turke, P., & Betzig, L. (1985). Those who can do: Wealth, status, and reproductive success on Ifaluk. *Ethology and Sociobiology, 6,* 79–87.

Udry, J. R., & Campbell, B. C. (1994). Getting started on sexual behavior. In A. S. Rossi (Ed.), *Sexuality over the life course* (pp. 187–207). Chicago: University of Chicago Press.

van den Berghe, P. L. (1979). *Human family systems: An evolutionary view.* New York: Elsevier.

van Schaik, C. P., & Paul, A. (1996). Male care in primates: Does it ever reflect paternity? *Evolutionary Anthropology, 5,* 152–156.

Vining, D. R. (1986). Social versus reproductive success: The central theoretical problem of human sociobiology. *Behavioral and Brain Sciences, 9,* 167–187.

Wallen, K., & Zehr, J. L. (2004). Hormones and history: The evolution and development of primate female sexuality. *Journal of Sex Research, 41,* 101–112.

Walsh, A. (1991). Self-esteem and sexual behavior: Exploring gender differences. *Sex Roles, 25,* 441–450.

Walter, A. (1997). The evolutionary psychology of mate selection in Morocco: A multivariate analysis. *Human Nature, 8,* 113–137.

Webster, G. D. (2004, July). *A non-linear approach to the Trivers-Willard hypothesis: Evidence from an archival analysis of inheritance data.* Paper presentation to the 16th annual meeting of Human Behavior and Evolution Society, Berlin, Germany.

Weinrich, J. (1977). Human sociobiology: Pairbonding and resource predictability (effects of social class and race). *Behavioral Ecology and Sociobiology, 2,* 91–118.

White, D. R. (1988). Rethinking polygyny: Co-wives, codes, and cultural systems. *Current Anthropology, 29,* 529–572.

White, D. R., & Burton, M. L. (1988). Causes of polygyny: Ecology, economy, kinship, and warfare. *American Anthropologist, 90,* 871–997.

Whiting, J. W. M. (1993). The effect of polygyny on sex ratio at birth. *American Anthropologist, 95,* 435–442.

Whyte, M. K. (1980). Cross-cultural codes dealing with the relative status of women. In H. Barry III & A. Schlegel (Eds.), *Cross-cultural samples and codes.* Pittsburgh, PA: University of Pittsburgh Press.

Wiederman, M. W. (1997). Extramarital sex: Prevalence and correlates in a national survey. *Journal of Sex Research, 34* 167–174.

Wiederman, M. W., & Dubois, S. L. (1998). Evolution and sex differences in preferences for short-term mates: Results from a policy capturing study. *Evolution and Human Behavior, 19*, 153–170.

Williams, G. C. (1975). *Sex and evolution.* Princeton: Princeton University Press.

Wilson, G. D. (1987). Male-female differences in sexual activity, enjoyment, and fantasies. *Personality and Individual Differences, 8*, 125–127.

Wolfe, L. D., & Gray, J. P. (1982). A cross-cultural investigation into the sexual dimorphism of stature. In R. L. Hall (Ed.), *Sexual dimorphism in* Homo Sapiens: *A question of size* (pp. 197–230). New York: Praeger.

Wood, W., & Eagly, A. H. (2002). A cross-cultural analysis of the behavior of men and women: Implications for the origins of sex differences. *Psychological Bulletin, 128*, 699–727.

Woodroofe, R., & Vincent, A. (1994). Mother's little helpers: Patterns of male care in mammals. *Trends in Ecology and Evolution, 9*, 294–297.

Wrangham, R. W. (1993). The evolution of sexuality in chimpanzees and bonobos. *Human Nature, 4*, 47–79.

Wright, T. M., & Reise, S. P. (1997). Personality and unrestricted sexual behavior: Correlations of sociosexuality in Caucasian and Asian college students. *Journal of Research in Personality, 31*, 166–192.

Young, L. J. (2003). The neural basis of pair bonding in a monogamous species: A model for understanding the biological basis of human behavior. In K. W. Wachter & R. A. Bulatao (Eds.), *Offspring: Human fertility behavior in biodemographic perspective* (pp. 91–103). Washington, DC: The National Academies Press.

CHAPTER 10

Physical Attractiveness in Adaptationist Perspective

LAWRENCE S. SUGIYAMA

THE LITERATURE ON human attractiveness spans the sciences, social sciences, and humanities, and dates back at least to the time of Plato. Consequently, scholars across the disciplines have proposed and investigated a variety of ideas about what makes some people more or less attractive than others (e.g., Etcoff, 1999). Addressing this vast literature from an adaptationist perspective is well beyond the scope of this chapter. This chapter limits itself to (1) outlining an adaptationist perspective on physical attractiveness, (2) presenting the basic questions that this perspective leads us to ask, (3) reviewing some important empirical advances in the answering of these questions, and (4) highlighting research avenues calling for increased attention. I argue that human physical attractiveness assessment is generated by adaptations functioning to evaluate evolutionarily relevant cues to human social value across multiple domains of interaction (e.g., kin, mating, cooperation) and that evolutionary human life history theory and data from small-scale foraging societies are instrumental in generating predictions about these domains of social value and the cues associated with them.

Multiple, converging lines of evidence are, therefore, useful to test whether a given phenotypic trait is an adaptation (e.g., Symons, 1989, 1992; Tooby & Cosmides, 1990, 1992). In the case of complex adaptations (e.g., immune systems, social exchange reasoning, or attractiveness-assessment psychologies), the most compelling case is made when there is evidence that: (1) the species in question recurrently faced a particular adaptive problem during recent evolutionary history, (2) the structure in question has a complex functional design that is so improbably well-suited to solving that adaptive problem that we are forced to reject pure chance as an alternative hypothesis, and (3) the organism in question shares with all normal conspecifics that design or a facultative developmental program that builds that design.

ATTRACTIVENESS ASSESSMENTS AS
MEASURES OF SOCIAL VALUE

We are powerfully attracted by some features (e.g., breasts, biceps, buttocks, lips, teeth) but less so by others (e.g., elbows, pinky fingers). We are repulsed by slightly different versions of things we are attracted to (e.g., wrinkled as opposed to smooth skin). Why do we find some features attractive and others not? The answer lies in what our preferences and revulsions cause us to do. Preference mechanisms motivate us to engage in behaviors that tended to increase fitness under the environmental conditions in which they were selected: Eating ripe fruit supplied our bodies with vital calories and nutrients; copulating with sexually mature conspecifics of the opposite sex increased our chances of reproducing. Conversely, revulsions discourage us from engaging in behaviors that were detrimental to survival and/or reproduction: Avoiding fetid swamps reduced our chances of contracting insect- or water-borne disease; being wary of snakes reduced our chances of being bitten by them. In short, preferences evolved because they increased the probability of an individual interacting with a stimulus in ways that tended to increase the distribution of the suite of alleles linked with that preference (Buss, 1992; Symons, 1979; Thornhill, 2003).

Attractiveness was a factor in many choices our ancestors had to make in daily life: what to eat, where to camp, with whom to ally themselves or mate. Each task involved a different adaptive problem and stimulus. In choosing a camp, for example, an individual would prefer a clear, level area with protective cover and good views in all directions, located near drinking water and plant and animal resources, and relatively free of pests (e.g., Appleton, 1975, 1984; S. Kaplan, 1992; Orians & Heerwagen, 1992). When choosing an ally, an individual would prefer good health, vigor, intelligence, generosity, reliability, and loyalty. Different suites of preference mechanisms are expected to have evolved in response to different adaptive problems and the stimuli associated with them. Because the cues associated with the relevant fitness-promoting aspects of ancestral environments varied from task to task, each preference suite is expected to target a different set of cues (although there may be some overlap between suites; see later discussion). Within each suite, selection is expected to have produced different assessment and preference mechanisms in response to each cue (e.g., Buss, 1992; Sugiyama, 1996, 2004a; Symons, 1979, 1995; Thornhill, 2003; Tooby & Cosmides, 1992). Thus, there is no general definition of attractiveness that applies to all stimuli. Consider sexual attraction: If we chose mates using the criteria for choosing food, we would find tubers, grubs, and buffalo as sexually arousing as healthy, fit, sexually mature members of our own species, and we would rapidly approach extinction.

Individuals may be attracted to objects that exhibit cues that were associated with a fitness-enhancing object under ancestral conditions but lack the fitness-enhancing properties themselves (Symons, 1987; Tooby & Cosmides, 1990). For example, our nonhuman primate and hominid ancestors lived in a world in which sweetness was a statistically reliable cue of nutritious, energy-packed foods (e.g., fruit, honey); consequently, our ancestors evolved a preference for sweetness, which motivated them to consume these healthy foods. Our preference psychology continues to attract us to sweet foods, but this often prompts a trip to the pastry shop instead of the fruit stand, a decidedly fitness-decreasing behavior (Eaton, Shostak, & Konner, 1988; Nesse & Williams, 1994).

Individuals may also be attracted to cues that have not been under selection per se. For example, finches have species-typical mate preferences for the color of bands put on their legs by researchers. Female zebra finches exhibit mate preferences for males with red rather than blue leg bands, while double-bar finches prefer light blue over red bands (Burley, 1986; Burley, Krantzberg, & Radman, 1982). At least some of these preferences appear to be a by-product of species-recognition mechanisms, since both double-bar and zebra finches prefer colors similar to their own species' plumage. Humans are certain to exhibit similar nonfunctional preferences, and complete understanding of human attractiveness will need to distinguish these preferences. However, because we lack principled guidelines for predicting such nonfunctional preferences, this chapter focuses primarily on hypothesized functional preferences whose features can potentially be predicted.

A leading alternate explanation of human attractiveness assessments is that our "capacity for culture" or a general-purpose learning psychology allows society, culture, or the media to tell us which sex to desire and/or what features are attractive (for discussion see Pinker, 2002; Tooby & Cosmides, 1992). On this view, who and what are attractive varies arbitrarily across cultures, individuals assess the physical attractiveness of both sexes based on local cultural dictates, and they tend to prefer the sex that society tells them to. If this view were correct, standards of attractiveness would vary randomly across the cultural and geographic landscapes of human experience. They do not (e.g., Buss, 1987; Cunningham, Barbee, & Pilhower, 2002; Jones & Hill, 1993; Langlois & Roggman, 1990; Rubenstein, Langlois, & Roggman, 2002; Sugiyama, 2004a; Symons, 1979, 1995).

There is considerable cross-cultural agreement on which faces are more attractive (e.g., Cunningham et al., 2002; Dion, 2002; Langlois & Roggman, 1990; Langlois, Roggman, Musselman, & Acton, 1991; Rubenstein et al., 2002; Thornhill & Gangestad, 1993; Zebrowitz, 1997). Galton (1879) noted that composite faces constructed by superimposing several individual photographs were more attractive than the faces from which they were made. Symons (1979) proposed that attractiveness-assessment mechanisms take as input the faces observed, then average those faces to produce templates of female and male facial attractiveness. All else equal, deviations from these templates decrease attractiveness. He reasoned that "the local populations' central tendency often approximates the naturally selected optimal design; hence selection is expected to have favored the ability to detect and prefer the central tendency" (Symons, 1995, p. 97). To test this hypothesis, Langlois and Roggman (1990) created computer-generated composites of up to 32 faces: Composites were rated more attractive than almost any of the individual faces from which they were made, and the more faces used in the composite, the more attractive the face was found (see also Jones & Hill, 1993 [Aché]; Pollard, 1995; Rhodes, Geddes, Jeffery, Dziurawiec, & Clark, 2002 [Japanese]; Rhodes, Sumich, & Byatt, 1999; Rhodes & Tremewan, 1996; Rhodes et al., 2001). Local population average is only one dimension of facial attractiveness. Subsequent research shows that facial attractiveness-assessment mechanisms may produce attraction to predictable deviations from the central tendency (e.g., Alley & Cunningham, 1991; Johnston & Franklin, 1993; Perrett, May, & Yoshikawa, 1994; Symons, 1995), and Symons has modified his hypothesis accordingly (1995). It is nevertheless clear that "averageness" is a cross-culturally recurrent feature affecting some of the variance in facial attractiveness assessment.

Perceptions of facial attractiveness emerge early in life in ways not easily explained by cultural learning theories. In a series of studies with children ranging in age from newborn to 25 months, infants noticed and preferred faces similar to those judged attractive by adults. Subjects were simultaneously presented with two faces; time spent gazing at each was recorded as a measure of attraction. Beginning at a few days old, infants look longer at faces that adults rated attractive than at those adults rated unattractive (Kramer, Zebrowitz, San Giovanni, & Sherak, 1995; Rubenstein, Langlois, & Kalakanis, 1999; Samuels & Ewy, 1985; Slater et al., 1998), regardless of whether the faces were Asian, African American, or Caucasian (Langlois, Ritter, Roggman, & Vaughn, 1991; Langlois et al., 1987). Babies also more frequently avoided and showed distress in response to an experimental confederate wearing an unattractive mask, but boys more often approached the confederate when she wore an attractive mask (Langlois, Roggman, Musselman, & Reiser-Danner, 1990).

Human Life History and the Domains of Social Value

Humans are an intensely social species, and our conspecifics are valuable to us for purposes other than mating (e.g., Sugiyama & Chacon, 2000; Sugiyama & Scalise Sugiyama, 2003; Tooby & Cosmides, 1996). Human evolutionary life history provides the key to understanding different domains of human social value (i.e., the value of individuals as potential interactants) and the physical cues correlated with them. Human survival and reproduction are dependent on solving adaptive problems associated with social interactions in four partially overlapping realms: reproductive, kin, cooperative, and coalitional relationships. Some individuals are more valuable to ego than others (e.g., as kin, mates, allies). Individuals who were attracted to individuals exhibiting relevant cues of high social value would have been more successful than those who were less discriminating. Human attractiveness-assessment psychology is therefore expected to index the social value of a potential partner using criteria correlated with the relevant category (e.g., descendant, mate, ally), depending on context. In other words, *cute, sexy, handsome, and dominant* are not exactly the same, and each appears to reflect a different aspect of social value (e.g., Cunningham, Druen, & Barbee, 1997; Keating, 2002; Zebrowitz & Rhodes, 2002). The question of how different attractiveness adaptations relate to each other and to different aspects of social value will be central to the next generation of adaptationist investigations of attractiveness. Anomalous findings and individual differences in attractiveness assessments may well resolve under this approach.

Scholars disagree about when and why key features of modern human life history came about (e.g., Flinn, Geary, & Ward, 2005; Hawkes, O'Connell, Blurton Jones, Alvarez, & Charnov, 1998; H. Kaplan et al., 2000;), but certain facts are clear: Humans have delayed reproduction; long life span; biparental investment; intergenerational care and provisioning of weaned juveniles and adults; coalitional child rearing, aggression, and foraging; and intense investment in skill and knowledge acquisition (e.g., Flinn et al., 2005; Hawkes, O'Connell, Blurton Jones, Alvarez, & Charnov, 2000; Hill & Kaplan, 1999; Hrdy, 1999; H. Kaplan et al., 2000; Tooby & DeVore, 1987). Human mating is flexible, exhibiting both long- and short-term mateships, serial monogamy, and a mild degree of polygyny (e.g., Beckerman & Valentine, 2002; Buss & Schmitt, 1993; Daly & Wilson, 1987; Fisher, 1992; Lancaster & Kaplan, 1994; van den Berghe, 1979). Extra-pair copulations also occur (e.g., Buss, 2000; Chagnon, 1997; Fisher, 1992; Thornhill & Gangestad, 2003). In small-scale societies, adult mortality is such that individuals frequently have multiple mates over their lifetime, and many children do not reside with both biological parents (e.g., Chagnon, 1997; Hill & Hurtado, 1996; Howell, 1979; Sugiyama, in press). Adults discriminate in their allocation of parental investment in juveniles depending on paternal certainty, phenotypic state of the juvenile, and local environmental parameters (e.g., Blurton Jones, Hawkes, & O'Connell, 1997; Gelles & Lancaster, 1987; Hewlett, 1992; Hrdy, 1999; Marlowe, 1999a, b, 2001). Lethal and sublethal violence between individuals and coalitions are also recurrent features of human existence across societies (e.g., Chagnon, 1988, 1997; Daly & Wilson, 1988; Descola, 1998; Ember & Ember, 1997; Hill & Hurtado, 1996; Keeley, 1996; Martin & Frayer, 1997). Evolution of each of these features of human life history presented our ancestors with numerous adaptive problems.

Life history theory examines how natural selection produced age-related allocation of resources between somatic (growth and maintenance) and reproductive (mating and parenting) effort (e.g., Charnov, 1993; Charnov & Schaffer, 1973; Hill & Hurtado, 1996; MacArthur & Wilson, 1967; Schaffer, 1974; Williams, 1966). Within a species' typical life history pattern, selection produces suites of reproductive, decision-making, and other motivational adaptations that generate adaptively "strategic" (usually unconscious) trade-offs in life effort in response to evolutionarily relevant environmental variables (e.g., Chisholm, 1993; Clutton-Brock, 1991; Daly & Wilson, 1984; Hill & Hurtado, 1996; Stearns, 1992; Trivers, 1972, 1974). Determining how individuals use local environmental cues to adjust their allocation of life resources is a main goal of understanding variation within a species' general life history parameters (e.g., Belsky, 1997; Betzig, Borgerhoff Mulder, & Turk, 1988; Blurton Jones et al., 1994; Draper & Harpending, 1982; Hill & Hurtado, 1996; Sugiyama, in press). Attractiveness-assessment mechanisms are a crucial component of the psychology involved in the processing of socioenvironmental cues relevant to the adaptive problems inherent in the life history traits listed earlier.

MATE VALUE

Reproductive effort includes identifying and acquiring mates. People differ in mate value, defined as the degree to which an individual would promote the reproductive success of another individual by mating with him or her. For example, copulation with an 8-year-old is ineffectual for reproduction; copulation with carriers of contagious disease is dangerous; copulation with individuals bearing severe genetic anomalies could result in costly pregnancies that produce nonviable offspring. Human mate value includes not only current fertility and fecundity but also reproductive value—the probable number of future offspring a person of a certain age and sex will produce. Over time, selection would spread genes that organized developmental properties motivating individuals to be attracted to conspecifics exhibiting cues of high mate value because these preferences likely led to more successful reproduction than alternative designs that may have arisen.

Components of human mate value appear to include phenotypic qualities such as health, fertility, fecundity, age, intelligence, status, parenting skill, kindness, and willingness and ability to invest in offspring (Buss, 1989; Gangestad & Simpson, 2000; Symons, 1979, 1992, 1995; Thornhill & Gangestad, 1999). Some variance in phenotypic qualities is heritable; therefore, some aspects of phenotypic quality may reflect underlying genotypic quality. Our mate-selection psychology must assess a potential mate for cues associated with each of these components, weigh their relative importance under current conditions, and then integrate these inputs to arrive at a comprehensive estimation of mate value (Buss, 1994; Miller, 2000; Sugiyama, 2004a; Symons, 1995). Some cues to mate value are physically observable, and the sum of these assessments contributes to our perception of potential mates' "physical attractiveness." Some features associated with high male mate value differ from those associated with high female mate value; criteria of male and female attractiveness are expected to differ when this is the case (e.g., Buss, 1987; Daly & Wilson, 1987; Symons, 1979, 1995).

Because individuals differ in the degree to which they possess the qualities associated with high mate value, some individuals make better mates than others. The result is competition for access to mates, especially high-quality mates. Darwin referred to the selective force created by this competition as sexual selection and identified two types. *Intrasexual selection* is the process whereby traits are selected that enable individuals to compete with members of the same sex for sexual access to the opposite sex (e.g., antlers, horns, tusks). *Intersexual selection* is the process whereby individuals with a given trait are preferred by the opposite sex as mating partners, with the result that said trait is spread, elaborated, or maintained in the population even if it has no survival value (e.g., Daly & Wilson, 1987; Darwin, 1872; Fisher, 1958; Miller, 2000; Ridley, 1993; Symons, 1979).

Costly signaling theory (also known as the handicap principle) posits that traits associated with good genes or the provision of material benefits can evolve into elaborate displays. On this view, elaborate displays can evolve as "honest" signals about underlying phenotypic and genotypic qualities of their bearers (Zahavi & Zahavi, 1997). When a trait signals information about its bearer that is useful for the bearer to transmit and for the recipient to receive, false signals might also be selected for, undermining the signal value of the trait to both sender and receiver. However, if the cost of sending the signal is such that only some individuals can afford to fully develop it and that cost is linked to the underlying phenotypic or genotypic quality being signaled, recipients can be assured of the signal's "honesty." Elaborate anatomical features, such as the peacock's tail, could evolve this way: Only high-quality males can produce the finest displays, so hens can reliably use male display in their mate choices, and the cost of the display to the cock is offset by his increased mating opportunities. Handicap signals are not restricted to mating: They can evolve whenever the conditions of costly signaling are met.

Because mating competition can be costly, it is often to an individual's advantage to assess the relative mate value of potential rivals before competing with them. Ancestral males capable of doing this could save time and energy by forgoing, avoiding, or subverting competition with those rivals they were unlikely to outcompete. Conversely, ancestral males could increase their mating access by focusing energies on driving off, dominating, outshining, undermining, or stealing mates from rivals against whom they had a reasonable chance of success. Similar benefits would accrue to females able to assess their competition and respond accordingly (e.g., Buss, 1994, 2000; Hess & Hagen, 2002; Pawlowski & Dunbar, 1999). This assessment amounts to an evaluation of the attractiveness of the same sex—not for the purpose of mating but to assess an individual's relative mate value (Pawlowski & Dunbar, 1999). Men are expected to use cues associated with male mate value to assess the fitness of their rivals, and women are expected to use cues associated with female mate value to assess the fitness of their rivals. Male and female assessments of a given individual's sexual attractiveness will, therefore, often concur, regardless of that individual's sex.

It follows that assessment and preference psychology are integrated but separable components of attractiveness psychology. In assessments of male sexual attractiveness, for example, women might experience feelings of desire (if the male were judged attractive), repugnance (if the male were judged unattractive), or indifference. In contrast, we might expect men to experience feelings such as submissiveness (if the male were judged attractive and dominant) or self-confidence and dominance (if the male were judged unattractive). Men and women have different adaptive objectives when evaluating the sexual attractiveness of a given male. Men must decide whether they should provoke, avoid a confrontation with, or cooperate with another male, and have, therefore, been under selection to evaluate the prowess of other males vis-à-vis their own. Women must decide whether they should copulate with, ally themselves with, or avoid a given male, and have, therefore, been under selection to evaluate males in terms of the fitness costs and benefits they present as mates and fathers. When it comes to evaluating female attractiveness, the tables are turned. Men must decide whether they should copulate with, cooperate with, or avoid a given female, and have, therefore, been under selection to evaluate females in terms of their fertility and sexual accessibility. Women must decide whether they should provoke, avoid a confrontation with, or befriend another female, and have, therefore, been under selection to evaluate the attractiveness and dominance of other females vis-à-vis their own.

Areas where we would expect to find sex differences in attractiveness assessment include the relative importance placed on different physical attractiveness cues. Overall, men place more value on good looks in a long-term mate than do women because female mate value is very closely linked to physiological condition (e.g., Buss, 1989; Buss & Schmitt, 1993; Symons, 1979; and see later discussion). Men may focus more on cues associated with potential rivals' physical formidability and dominance—size, strength, speed, physical agility, or their correlates—in assessing their own and their competitors' relative sexual attractiveness to women because these attributes could spell death or loss of a mate at the hands of a rival (e.g., Chagnon, 1988, 1997; Daly & Wilson, 1988). A host of data from psychological studies (e.g., Buss, Larson, Westen, & Semmelroth, 1992; Dijkstra & Buunk, 2001), homicide patterns (e.g., Daly & Wilson, 1988), and intratribal conflict (e.g., Chagnon, 1979, 1988, 1997) support the view that various aspects of mating competition are often causes of violence. For women, male mate value includes both: traits associated with genetic quality, health, and physical formidability, and traits associated with ability and willingness to invest in a woman and her offspring (e.g., Buss, 1987; Symons, 1979). Assessments based on these two criteria may diverge. Good looks appear to be relatively less important for women than for men in long-term mates because most women may have to trade off genetic quality and health for investment. However, these trade-offs are context-dependent: Women place more importance on physical characteristics in short-term and extra-pair sex partners (Buss & Schmitt, 1993; Greiling & Buss, 2000) and during the fertile phase of their ovulatory cycles. Women show increased preference for "masculine" male faces in prospective short-term mates (angular, deep brow; square jaw) but for less "masculine" male faces (softer, rounder) in a long-term mate (Penton-Voak et al., 1999; Perret et al., 1999; see later discussion).

Female Mate Value   Female mate value is linked to age, health, fertility, fecundity, and parity (e.g., Buss, 1992; Symons, 1979, 1995). In natural fertility foraging societies, women first give birth at about 17 to 20 years of age (Hill & Hurtado, 1996; R. L. Kelly, 1995; H. Kaplan et al., 2000). A woman's reproductive value—the probable number of future offspring a woman will have—is highest just before she begins fertile ovulatory cycles because she has all her reproductive years in front of her, yet the probability that she will die prior to reproduction is lowest. Fertility—the probability that copulation will result in pregnancy—varies across the reproductive life span. Peak age-specific female fertility in industrialized nations is around 22 years, but the best data from foraging populations indicate a peak age-specific fertility rate varying from about 22 years among the !Kung of Botswana and the Yanomamö of Venezuela to about 28 years among the Aché of Paraguay. Diet, work effort, stress, and social variables affect hormonal indices of female fertility and fecundity (ability to conceive when intercourse occurs during reproductive cycling), suggesting that within the reproductive life span, female reproduction varies with the socioecological contexts in which a woman finds herself (e.g., Ellison, 2001b, 2003; Hill & Hurtado, 1996).

The minimum investment necessary for women's successful reproduction is high. It includes accumulation of bodily reserves and maintenance of a positive energy balance, gestation, placentation, and the mortality risk associated with bearing a large-headed offspring via a relatively narrow pelvis (e.g., Bentley, Harrigan, & Ellison, 1998; Ellison, 2001a; Trevathan, 1987; Valeggia & Ellison, 2003a). Nursing, too, is energetically costly (Dewey, 1997). During this time, reproductive function is suppressed as a function of each woman's relative energy balance (e.g., Ellison, 2001a, 2001b; Jasienska & Ellison, 1998; Valeggia & Ellison, 2001, 2003b). R. L. Kelly (1995) lists the average weaning age for each of 30 hunter-gatherer groups: The mean average weaning age for these groups is 30.9 months. The interbirth interval for women in a mostly overlapping group of 11 foraging societies is 3.47 years, and the average total fertility rate is between five and six children. On average, forager women appear to get pregnant relatively soon after weaning the previous child.

Women, including forager women, may live well past their reproductive years, although maternal and grand-maternal investment of material and social support in descendants may continue after they reach adulthood (e.g., Hawkes et al., 1998, 2000; Hill & Hurtado, 1996; Hill & Kaplan, 1999; Hrdy, 1999). As a woman ages after menarche, she has progressively lower reproductive value, until fertility ceases altogether. Among Aché women, the average age of last birth is 42. By age 46, the yearly probability of birth is 0 (Hill & Hurtado, 1996). R. L. Kelly (1995) lists data on mean age at last birth for women in 10 foraging societies; the average mean is 34.9 years.

The human female reproductive environment of evolutionary adaptedness (EEA) was such that for most of the time between menarche and menopause a woman was not fecund. Based on Yanomamö data, Symons (1995) calculated that an ancestral woman could possibly conceive on just 78 of 8,030 days during her average reproductive life span. R. L. Kelly's (1995) data on foragers yield a similar conclusion. With average age at first birth of 17 and last birth by age 42 (for Aché), an average female forager's potential fertile life span is about 25 years, during which she is likely to have five children (Ellison, 2001b). She would have been pregnant or lactating for 5,985 days—almost two-thirds of her reproductive lifetime. With 3 fertile days per month, she could possibly be fecund on just 314 days in her 9125-day fertile lifetime, assuming she suffered no ill health, food constraints, failures of social support, or other stressors. For men, women's reproductive capacity itself is an extremely valuable fitness resource, access to which constitutes a primary constraint on men's relative reproductive success.

Because female reproductive value declines with age postmenarche, cues associated with advancing age are expected to be negatively correlated with female sexual attractiveness (e.g., Buss, 1989; Symons, 1979, 1995). Similarly, with each birth, the average forager woman loses another sixth of her reproductive value, on average. Thus, cues associated with parity are expected to be negatively correlated with female sexual attractiveness. Because some cues to fecundity are observable, selection is also expected to have produced adaptations to use statistically reliable cues to fecundity-related hormonal status in assessments of female mate attractiveness. Symons (1979, 1995) therefore argues that selection for preferences for cues of high reproductive value resulted in males being attracted to cues of nubility (i.e., female has begun ovulatory cycling but has not yet given birth), as indicated by cues to age, fertility, and parity. Because women do not advertise estrus, attraction to cues of nubility would dramatically increase a male's chances of reproducing, and a man who maintains exclusive mating access to a woman over her reproductive lifetime could on average sire five or six children with her. Finally, women with positive energy balance and good health are likely to be more fertile than those with negative energy balance and poor health; thus, men are expected to have evolved preference mechanisms that find cues of good health and nutrition attractive, and women are expected to use the same cues in assessments of their reproductive rivals. Even though selection may have produced attraction to cues of nubility, attraction to cues of nubility alone might compromise long-term mateships and would have the effect of concentrating male reproductive effort on fathering only the first of a woman's average six offspring. Other cues that a woman is resuming ovulatory cycling postpartum, such as lightening of the skin (Symons, 1995) or having a child approaching weaning age, should predict some of the variance in real-world female sexual attractiveness. Males face investment trade-offs between mate quantity and quality, and between mating and paternal investment. The costs and benefits associated with each will be affected by local paternal effects on offspring fitness and the relative costs and opportunities of obtaining multiple mates. The latter will be affected by a particular male's mate value, the degree of effective polygyny or operational sex ratio, and the relative value of long-term versus short-term mating for women.

Male Mate Value Women who mate with men with traits associated with high genetic quality are more likely to have high-quality offspring (i.e., via "good genes" sexual selection). Women's attractiveness-assessment psychology is thus predicted to include mechanisms for evaluating cues associated with male genotypic quality. One cue to genotypic quality is phenotypic condition, part of which is heritable. In addition to genetic quality, male mate value includes provision of material resources to mates, their offspring, and other adults (Gurven et al., 2000; Hewlett, 1992; Kaplan et al., 2000; Marlowe, 1999a, 1999b, 2001; Sugiyama & Chacon, 2000, in press). Across societies, women appear to assess and prefer men as long-term mates who evince cues of willingness and ability to invest in a woman and her offspring, such as kindness, intelligence, industriousness, and ability to acquire resources (e.g., Buss, 1989). Female mate choice for these traits is important in humans because of the long period of juvenile dependence and high cost of child rearing. Among the Aché, juveniles with father living suffer a third lower mortality than those whose father has died (Hill & Hurtado, 1996), although the relative contribution of males to their offsprings' fitness varies across social and ecological contexts (e.g., Hewlett, 1992; Marlowe, 1999a, 1999b).

Human males grow for a longer period, mature more slowly, and reproduce later than females (e.g., Bogin, 1999; Ellison, 2001b; Hill & Hurtado, 1996). They also exhibit higher variance in reproductive success across individuals than do females (e.g., Chagnon, 1997; Daly & Wilson, 1987; Hill & Hurtado, 1996). Because paternity is less certain than maternity, men's age at first reproduction is more difficult to track directly, but males in foraging societies typically do begin reproducing later than females, somewhere in their early 20s. Male fertility among the Aché, !Kung, and Yanomamö indicate a rise in fertility beginning in the late teens and peaking in the mid-30s to early 40s. Mean age at last birth for 23 Aché men who lived to at least 60 years old was 48 years: Although about half of the men stopped reproducing as early as women did, the other half continued reproduction for longer periods, including six men who continued reproduction past their mid-50s. Further, male foraging success peaks relatively late in life, around age 40 (Walker, Hill, Kaplan, & McMillan, 2002). Because male mate value is not so closely linked to youth, female choice is not expected to focus as much on male youth per se, but rather on cues of genotypic and phenotypic quality and productive ability (Buss, 1989; Symons, 1979). Selection is expected to have favored female assessment for phenotypic cues of male fertility. However, because one fertile male can potentially inseminate multiple females, preference for cues to fertility per se is perhaps less intense in women than in men.

Women can benefit from pursuing a mix of long- and short-term mating strategies in an effort to reduce trade-offs inherent in each (e.g., Buss & Schmitt, 1993; Thornhill & Gangestad, 2003). From a female perspective, poor health and/or genetic quality are liabilities in any prospective mating partner. However, women are expected to find physical traits linked to underlying genetic qualities relatively more important in short-term than in long-term mates. Long-term mateships entail child rearing; thus, prospective long-term partners must be evaluated for their parenting abilities as well as their physical attributes. Thus, size, strength, pugnacity, and physical dominance may be traded for ability and willingness to invest in the woman and her offspring. For women, parenting skills are less important in a short-term mate for obvious reasons. One ultimate benefit of a short-term mateship to a woman is an opportunity to provide better genes to her offspring than she can acquire through a long-term partner, and many of the traits associated with aggressive formidability—for example, size, strength, endurance—are proximate cues of good genes (e.g., Buss & Schmitt, 1993; Thornhill & Gangestad, 2003). In addition, some physical traits under the influence of testosterone are associated with differences in male mate value that may influence the male's propensity to pursue short- or long-term mating strategies. Females may use these traits as cues to probable male mating behavior. Women may be expected to use these same criteria in their assessments of the relative social value of their fathers, brothers, and other male kin to others, but to weight the criteria differently.

DESCENDANT VALUE

Juveniles differ in their social value to their parents and grandparents in their probable value as reproductively successful descendants. Parental investment (PI) theory focuses on how individuals allocate resources among existing offspring, current versus future offspring, and quantity versus quality of offspring (e.g., Trivers, 1972, 1974, 1985). In parentally investing species, we expect adaptations that generate parental allocation of resources to juveniles as if in response to three basic criteria: (1) the probability that the juvenile is the adult's progeny, (2) the probability that the juvenile will be able to translate investment into future reproductive success, and (3) the probable fitness outcomes of alternate potential uses of available resources (Trivers, 1972, 1974).

The probability that an individual is an adult's progeny is partially assessed via adaptations functioning to rapidly learn specific phenotypic (e.g., olfactory, visual, auditory) cues based on early postnatal exposure (Porter, 1991), and there is recent evidence that males may use facial resemblance to themselves to adduce probable paternity. Platek and colleagues (Platek, Burch, Panyavin, Wasserman, & Gallup, 2002; Platek et al., 2003) found that, when presented with different facial morphs created using each subjects' image and those of children, males were more likely to preferentially choose their own child/face morphs over those created using other subjects' faces as recipients of aid in hypothetical investment scenarios. Functional magnetic resonance imaging indicated that men's and women's neural activation patterns did not differ when viewing non-self-morphs, but did differ when viewing self-morphs, suggesting sex differences in neural processing of facial resemblance cues. In a similar study using color photographs, DeBruine (2004) found that both men and women used facial resemblance in investment decisions, while Apicella and Marlowe (2004) found that men self-reported greater investment in their children when they thought their children bore more resemblance to themselves.

The probability that a juvenile will translate investment into successful reproduction is in part related to his or her genotypic and phenotypic condition and contingent on socioecological context (e.g., Hrdy, 1999). Adaptations are expected that assess these features. Physical cues that were evolutionarily correlated with good health and high genetic quality provide physically observable correlates of a juvenile's probable ability to translate investment into reproduction and are expected to be found attractive in offspring. Physical cues of low genotypic or phenotypic quality are associated with reduction in parental care, suggesting these traits are unattractive to parents. For instance, physical deformity is a recurrent proximate cause for infanticide cross-culturally (Daly & Wilson, 1984); poor physical tone, lethargy, or lack of pedomorphic characteristics in infants may increase risk of abuse (McCabe, 1984, 1988) or maternal neglect when resources are scarce (e.g., Hrdy, 1999); and vocal qualities associated with premature birth are aversive to adults (Mann, 1992). Conversely, physical cues associated with infancy such as large eyes, small noses, and rounded head are attractive to parents and others (Alley, 1983; Sternglanz, Gray, & Murakami, 1977; Zebrowitz, 1997), and parents of attractive infants are more attentive and affectionate toward them (Hildebrandt & Fitzgerald, 1983; Langlois, Ritter, Casey, & Sawin, 1995).

KIN VALUE

Anthropologists have long recognized that in prestate, nonstratified societies (like those that characterized most of human evolution), social relationships fundamentally organized by kinship and kinship-like institutions (Chagnon, 1997). All known human cultures, past and present, include three basic kinds of social relationships based on kinship-like institutions: marriage, descent, and kinship classification systems. All kinship classification systems are based on three basic principles: sex, descent, and generation. These systems fall into seven basic types, depending on how precisely the kin terms divide kinship classification along these basic dimensions.

These common features of social organization reflect the value of kinship cross-culturally, and kin selection theory helps explain this value, even though classificatory kinship and biological kinship do not completely overlap. Individuals can increase the alleles they bear not only via their own reproduction but also via aid to those with whom they share those alleles by virtue of recent common descent (Hamilton, 1964; Maynard Smith, 1964; Williams, 1957). Kin selection theory shows how this kin-based altruism may be selected for: when the cost to the altruist of providing the aid is less than the benefit to the recipient devalued by the probable degree to which they are related (Hamilton, 1964). From ego's perspective, others vary in probable kin value. They differ in (1) their probable degree of relatedness to ego, (2) the probability that they will translate any investment by ego into future reproductive success, and (3) the probable fitness outcomes ego might reap from alternate uses of any available investment. Some individuals have higher kin value, and to the degree that they exhibit reliable cues to this value, they are expected to be more attractive than others. Adaptations for recognizing kin in humans include ones that appear to assess the likelihood of close biological relatedness based on relative proximity during critical stages of the life course (Lieberman, Tooby, & Cosmides, 2003; Shepher, 1971; Westermarck, 1926; Wolf & Huang, 1980). As with offspring, the probability that kin can translate investment into successful reproduction is affected by their phenotypic and genotypic quality, including the related variables of health, age, fertility, fecundity, and sex, all of which are associated with physically observable cues.

COOPERATIVE AND COALITIONAL VALUE

Although he overstated the case, Levi-Strauss (1969) saw marriage in traditional societies as an alliance or exchange primarily between men (the consanguineal male relatives of the bride and groom). Certainly, who mates with whom is of interest not only to the principals. With its concomitant social, economic, and reproductive rights, duties, and obligations, the universal institution of marriage reflects the fundamental interests of individuals in the mateships of their offspring, siblings, and close relatives. Mateships build and bind alliances, sons- and daughters-in-law play integral social and economic roles, and reproductive unions serve as vehicles for a descent group's reproductive future. Accordingly, family members regularly assess potential daughters- and sons-in-law with respect to their coalitional, productive, and reproductive assets, and the ethnographic literature reveals that many marriages, especially first marriages, are arranged (e.g., Chagnon, 1997; Frayser, 1985).

Another basic feature of human life history is the high degree of investment in juveniles provided by individuals other than the biological mother, including biological and social fathers, aunts, uncles, and grandparents. Hrdy (2002) argues that humans are essentially cooperative breeders, with multiple females and males cooperating in the raising of offspring. If this is the case, humans may cultivate relationships with others based on their suitability as alloparents. Relevant cues in making this choice may overlap with cues of long-term mate value but will diverge in some areas. Sex of alloparent is less important than sex of mate. Fertility and fecundity might oppositely affect relative mate and alloparent value: A postmenopausal woman has low reproductive value but could provide valuable benefits (e.g., resources, knowledge) as an alloparent (Hawkes et al., 1998, 2000). Moreover, she would not face a trade-off between investment in allochildren and her own current reproduction. Similarly, prereproductive females often provide alloparental care for younger siblings. But the opportunity costs of doing so increase as they have children of their own, thus decreasing their alloparental value to their parents.

Based on data from foraging societies, other ancestral cooperative activities include foraging (e.g., Alvard, 2004; Hill, 2002; Sosis, 2000), information transmission (e.g., Mithen, 1990; Scalise Sugiyama, 2001; Sugiyama & Scalise Sugiyama, 2003), and aid during health crises (Gurven et al., 2000; Sugiyama, 2004b; Sugiyama & Scalise Sugiyama, 2003). Health, physical abilities, generosity, cooperativeness, and intelligence provide at least some cues to an individual's value in the realms of foraging, coalitional aggression, health aid, and child rearing.

Finally, even individuals with whom ego does not directly cooperate can have social value when they yield positive externalities such as increasing ego's food supply, attracting potential mates to ego's proximity, deterring attacks, serving as sources of information, or helping ego's allies (e.g., Etcoff, 1999; Sugiyama & Scalise Sugiyama, 2003; Tooby & Cosmides, 1996). Conversely, individuals may have unintended negative effects on us. Unhealthy individuals may increase disease exposure. In small-scale societies, impulsively aggressive individuals may incite conflict, and the mentally ill might act unpredictably in ways that harm others' interests (e.g., Chagnon, 1988, 1997; Sugiyama, unpublished ethnographic data).

Coalitional Value As noted above, humans engage in a considerable amount of conflict, some of which results in homicide. And in a world of close-range, non-mechanized weaponry, individual strength, size, speed, and agility are highly advantageous. The word for headman often translates as "big" or "big man," and tribal leaders are often bigger than average (e.g., Brown, 1991). Leadership, organizational abilities, strategic acumen, and motivational skill are also valued in coalitional politics (e.g., Chagnon, 1997; Patton, 2000; Sugiyama & Scalise

Sugiyama, 2003) and may be assessed through observation or reputation. In addition, the value of a coalitional partner is based in part on his or her reliability, loyalty, strategic intelligence, and willingness and ability to back up coalitional interests with force (e.g., Chagnon, 1997; Patton, 2000).

Some of these abilities may be assessed through physical and behavioral cues, and adaptations for assessing the attractiveness of males as mates and allies are expected to target them. For example, reliability and ability to help defend coalitional interests will be affected by an individual's health: All else equal, individuals in frail health will be less reliable and less able defenders. Further, immune-compromised individuals may increase disease transmission among coalition members. Because physical prowess furthers success in foraging, fighting, and deterrence of violence, cues of physical prowess are likely to be important in assessments of male attractiveness by males. For men, physical prowess and aggressive formidability are linked to survival, social status, and, consequently, their social value to other males. Thus, males are expected to display these qualities to other males and to be adept at predicting the outcomes of physical conflicts based on assessment of the traits correlated with these qualities (e.g., dominance, tenacity, pugnacity, pain tolerance, agility, strength, endurance). All else equal, men should find males who exhibit these cues attractive coalition partners. Because successful coalition building and maintenance also require certain social and mental skills, traits associated with these qualities are expected to be found attractive in potential coalition partners as well. Male coalitional assessment psychology must, therefore, be able to weigh the degree to which a given male possesses these abilities and their relative importance to the coalition in question. A coalition of brawny, athletic warriors lacking planning ability could benefit from adding to its ranks a man who is physically deficient but strategically brilliant. My ethnographic observations indicate that shamans are often important political players even after they can no longer go on raids (see also Chagnon, 1997).

ORGANIZATION OF ATTRACTIVENESS-ASSESSMENT MECHANISMS

Mates and kin are often cooperative and coalitional allies; thus, some cues of mate, offspring, kin, and coalitional value may overlap. Others may not; for example, an individual may desire kindness in a mate but ruthlessness in a war ally. We must, therefore, understand how adaptations generating our perceptions of attractiveness are organized and why we see cross-cultural and individual variability in assessments of attractiveness.

A critical variable in the deployment of many adaptations is the phenotypic state of the assessor. For mating, parenting, and alliance formation, this state includes developmental stage, sex, health, nutritional, reproductive, and mating status. Other variables these adaptations must assess include:

1. How many coresident kin do I have (e.g., Chagnon, 1975, 1979, 1997; Hill & Hurtado, 1996; Sugiyama, in press)?
2. How many people value me, how much do they value me, and for what (Sugiyama, 1996; Sugiyama & Chacon, 2000; Sugiyama & Scalise Sugiyama, 2003; Tooby & Cosmides, 1996)?

3. Are my father and/or mother alive (e.g., Hagen, Hames, Craig, Lauer, & Price, 2001; Hill & Hurtado, 1996; Sugiyama, in press)?
4. How aggressively formidable am I compared to others (e.g., Chagnon, 1988, 1997; Patton, 2000)?
5. How attractive am I to others as a mate (e.g., Buss, 2000; Gangestad & Simpson, 2000)?
6. How attractive am I as friend or ally (Gurven et al., 2000; Sugiyama, 1996; Sugiyama & Chacon, 2000; Sugiyama & Scalise Sugiyama, 2003; Tooby & Cosmides, 1996)?

Even though the underlying functional design of attractiveness-assessment adaptations are expected to be universal, we should expect to see strategic variation in their behavioral expressions at the population, group, and individual levels.

Certain cues are expected to be weighted differently in arriving at an assessment of overall physical attractiveness. Variance in these weightings will be based on: (1) which features are statistically more likely to be associated with a particular aspect of the social value in question; (2) local environmental features (e.g., famine, health risk) that reliably change the relative value of attractiveness cues; (3) ecologically variable cues most highly cross-correlated with each other in the local environment; and (4) the phenotypic condition of the assessor. Overall judgment may reflect a compromise between the outputs of each of these components. Additionally, outputs of different assessment components may conflict with or enhance others in the production of a final perception of attractiveness (e.g., Grammer, Fink, Thornhill, Juette, & Runzal, 2002; Manning, Trivers, Singh, & Thornhill, 1999; Møller & Pomiankowski, 1993; Sugiyama, 2004a; Symons, 1995).

Each assessment mechanism can vastly reduce the computational complexity of its task by processing only a minute set of the information available in its environment. Nevertheless, each mechanism must be deployed under the appropriate conditions, and doing this requires information intake and analysis. This analysis implies a hierarchically organized but parallel processing system of feedback loops that inform the system based on cues received and instantiated (for a lens model, see Miller & Todd, 1998). It might look (in verbal terms) something like this:

1. Is this an animate object? (For example, is it unitary? Does it exhibit self-propelled motion?) If yes, go on; if no, inhibit systems associated with analysis of animate objects.
2. Is this a person? If yes, go on; if no, inhibit systems associated with person perception.
3. What sex is this person? If male, inhibit female assessment systems.
4. Is this person a potential threat?

And the questions would continue down the chains of assessment. This sketch should not be taken too literally. For one, the computer program metaphor is simply that—a metaphor, not a theory of neurobiological instantiation of these functional processes. And the verbal description of mate value criteria simply describes the higher-order conclusion based on specific traits assessed. For instance, the stimulus cue of an hourglass-shaped torso or a certain gait may leap through the system to "woman" such that some chains of analysis—"self-propelled," "short arms, long legs," "big ovoid head"—are bypassed entirely if the cue feedback is sufficiently unambiguous to reach levels critical for activation of the conclusion. The criterion "sufficiently unambiguous" itself evolved via selection and will be different for different domains and for different contextual cues in the local environment (which themselves are analyzed by parallel mental operations). Parallel processing—that is, the simultaneous performance of multiple information-processing tasks, the solution to each of which is codeterminate and requisite to reaching a final judgment—is continuously and routinely performed by perceptual adaptations (Pinker, 1997). This view of attractiveness-assessment cognition markedly differs from the view that attractiveness-assessment mechanisms will produce cross-culturally uniform standards, with some criteria always weighted more than others (e.g., Singh, 1993a; Tovée & Cornielsson, 1999; Yu & Shephard, 1998; but see Marlowe & Wetsman, 2001; Sugiyama, 2004a).

ASSESSMENT OF CUES TO HUMAN SOCIAL VALUE: HEALTH, PHENOTYPIC, AND GENOTYPIC QUALITY

Phenotypic condition refers to an individual's ability to efficiently acquire resources and convert them into fitness. Across all domains of social value, all else equal, an individual's value is higher if he or she is more likely than not to survive and maintain health—that is, if he or she exhibits good phenotypic condition. Health risk is a ubiquitous adaptive problem in current and prehistoric societies (e.g., Steckel, Rose, Larsen, & Walker, 2002; Sugiyama, 2004b). Hill and Hurtado (1996) note that illness and disease are the leading cause of death among the Yanomamö (74%) and !Kung (80%) and caused about a quarter of all precontact Aché deaths. Some of these deaths were due to introduced diseases, but many were not. For the precontact forest-living Aché, accidents were the second leading cause of death, followed by degenerative and congenital diseases. Although male and female mortality rates differ somewhat, in general, age-specific mortality rates show a U-shaped function across the life span, with high mortality during infancy dropping steeply until around age 15 and then creeping upward until they tail rapidly upward between about 60 and 65 years of age. While humans have relatively lower extrinsic mortality compared with chimpanzees, almost half of Aché foragers nevertheless die before their 50th birthday.

Potential death is not the only fitness cost of health risk. Poor nutrition, sickness, and injury reduce fertility, growth, and fitness, and can significantly interfere with ability to provide for self, offspring, and allies (e.g., Sugiyama, 2004a; Sugiyama & Chacon, 2000). Endemic intestinal parasites are commonly found among modern foraging peoples, and diarrheal disease remains a leading cause of juvenile mortality worldwide. Among Shiwiar forager-horticulturalists of Ecuador, lacerations are common across the life span (Sugiyama, 2004b, 2004c). Among the Yora of Peru, topical bacterial infection accounted for the majority of days on which individuals were disabled and could not forage or garden (Sugiyama & Chacon, 2000). Bites or infestation from ectoparasitic insects (e.g., mosquitoes, no-see-ums, ticks, chiggers) are ubiquitous among the Shiwiar, and many of them leave observable scars (Sugiyama, 2004b). Bot flies and sand fleas parasitize human hosts. If left untreated, open wounds from sand flea larvae can result in infection, making walking difficult and in extreme cases leading to death (Chagnon, 1997; Hagen et al., 2001). On a worldwide scale, ectoparasitic insects are major disease vectors causing high morbidity and mortality. Malaria, spread by anopheles mosquitoes, is a prominent culprit. In some areas, selection pressure from *Malaria falciperum* is so intense it maintains sickle cell trait, even though in the homozygous condition sickle cell anemia is fatal (Nesse & Williams, 1994). Parasite resistance is a critical feature in the evolution of mate choice, and sexual reproduction itself may have evolved in an arms race against rapidly coevolving pathogens (e.g., Hamilton & Zuk, 1982; Tooby, 1982).

Individuals vary in susceptibility to accidents and disease due to (1) differences in immune function, (2) chemical and behavioral factors associated with an individual's attractiveness and exposure to insects that are disease vectors, and (3) personality factors associated with risk taking, coordination, and so on (e.g., D. W. Kelly, 2001; Knols, De Jong, & Takken, 1995; Lindsay, Adiamah, Miller, Pleass, & Armstrong, 1993; Mukabana, Takken, Coe, & Knols, 2002; Sugiyama, 2004b). At least some of this variance is heritable. Moreover, individuals who are less susceptible to disease are less effective sources of transmission and thus should be preferable as group members and cooperative allies. Cues associated with the related factors of health, phenotypic, and genotypic quality are, therefore, expected to be attractive across all social value domains, even though relative preference for their cues might vary somewhat across them and across environmental condition (e.g., Low, 1990; Symons, 1979, 1995; Trivers, 1972). Gangestad and Buss (1993) analyzed cross-cultural data collected from thousands of individuals and found that, even controlling for income and distance from the equator (where pathogen prevalence is generally higher), the relative value of physical attractiveness in potential mates was greater in areas with higher pathogen prevalence.

Skin Quality   Given the close link among insect bites, disease, infection, and skin lesions and/or scars, it is no wonder that clear skin is assumed to be associated with attractiveness (Symons, 1995). Skin quality provides not only a cue to age (Symons, 1979, 1995) but also a partial record of an individual's current and lifetime health (e.g., Sugiyama, 2004b). In small-scale ancestral societies where the range of skin color variation is constrained compared to modern Western societies, relative skin tone can signal health. For example, hepatitis, iron deficiency, and parasitic infection can produce a yellowish or washed-out skin cast. Individuals with clear, unblemished skin tend to be relatively less exposed to or affected by parasites or the diseases they transmit (Sugiyama, 2004b). Clear skin also indicates absence of skin-damaging disease (e.g., measles, pox, leishmaniasis) and/or "good genes" for immune function indicated by an individual's ability to heal without infection (e.g., Singh & Bronstad, 1997). Finally, in women, dermatoses are correlated with elevated sex hormone and ovarian disorder (Schiavone, Reitschel, Sgoutas, & Harris, 1983; Steinberger, Rodriguez-Rigau, Smith, & Held, 1981; in Grammer et al., 2002).

Although the evolutionary prediction that smooth skin should be found attractive (because it is linked with youth, fertility, and reproductive value in females) has been made repeatedly (e.g., Symons, 1979, 1995), direct studies of skin texture/quality and attractiveness are few, perhaps because it is intuitively clear that wrinkled skin (a cue of older age), open sores, oozing pustules, and disfiguring scars are unattractive (e.g., Etcoff, 1999; Symons, 1995). In a study of facial symmetry (see later discussion), symmetrical faces constructed by putting together one side of a face and its mirror image were not found as attractive as their unsymmetrical originals (Swaddle & Cuthill, 1995). However, Perrett et al. (1999) showed that this was an artifact of the fact that the mirror images increased skin blemishes. When they controlled for skin blemishes, the symmetrical faces were rated more attractive. Jones et al. (2004) found that subjects' ratings of skin health were positively correlated with ratings of male facial attractiveness. Fink et al. (2001) presented subjects with faces whose shapes were standardized and found that skin texture significantly influenced attractiveness ratings. Grammer et al. (2002) had men rate the attractiveness of front, back, and facial digital photographs of 92 nude Caucasian women, standardized for size and orientation, on a seven-point scale. The photographs were measured for 36 physical traits predicted to be associated with attractiveness. As predicted, skin homogeneity was positively correlated with rated facial, front view, and total attractiveness. Although the correlations did not reach conventional levels of statistical significance, multidimensional measures on so complex a trait as attractiveness are such that any one trait may account for only a small portion of the variance in attractiveness (Grammer et al., 2002). Skin texture might be such a trait, or it could be that the relative value of skin texture in health appraisal (and, therefore, attractiveness) in a population with few ectoparasitic infections is relatively low. I would predict that natural levels of variation in skin quality among natural fertility, forager or horticulturalist peoples (i.e., peoples regularly exposed to parasitic, pathological, and outdoor causes of skin damage) would account for a higher proportion of the variance in attractiveness assessments than among Western subjects rating images of Western models.

Hair Quality   Grammer et al. (2002) found that hair length was significantly correlated with female attractiveness. Hair grows at the rate of about one-half inch per month, until it falls out upon reaching 2 to 3 feet in length. Starvation causes loss of hair, nutritional deficiencies in vitamins and minerals cause damaged hair, and malnourishment causes observable changes in hair color (e.g., dark hair takes on a reddish tone). Hair, therefore, provides an observable record of an individual's recent health and nutrition (serving as an indicator of diet and health over a 2- to 3-year period) and reflects heritable genotypic quality (Etcoff, 1999). Shiny, strong hair provides a cue to recent good health, developmental condition, and genotypic quality. Tellingly, long hair is often preferred across cultures, and long, lustrous hair is often associated with beauty (Etcoff, 1999). Hinsz, Matz, and Patience (2001) collected hair samples and contributor information from over 200 women ages 13 to 73 and found that younger, higher reproductive value women tended to have longer hair than older women, as predicted if higher reproductive value women were more likely to use their hair as an advertisement of that fact. And hair samples that beauticians rated as higher quality came from women who self-reported to be in better health, although age of donor probably contributes significantly to that result. It is interesting that hair grows fastest among women around the ages of peak fertility (Etcoff, 1999), with the result that evidence of environmental damage has less time to accumulate before new hair grows in, and evidence of health or dietary problems reflects a shorter period of time.

Oral Health   Diet is closely linked to health and fitness, and an individual's nutrition can be compromised by masticatory inefficiency, poor dentition, or dental disease (e.g., Symons, 1995; Walker, Sugiyama, & Chacon, 1998). Caries rates and periodontal disease can be affected by small differences in diet, developmental stress, and heritable genotypic variation (e.g., Hillson, 1996; Walker et al., 1998). Even though dental development is relatively well buffered against environmental disturbances, linear enamel hypoplasia (horizontal grooves in the enamel caused by developmental stress during enamel formation) provides visible evidence of developmental stress (Hillson, 1996; Skinner & Goodman, 1992). Left untreated, painful caries can reduce feeding efficiency. Left untreated long enough, they can result in dental abscess, infection and inflammation of bone tissue, and even death. Strong, even, white teeth thus provide a constellation of cues to health, developmental history, masticatory efficiency, and genotypic quality, and are thus predicted to be attractive (e.g., Symons, 1995). While most academics rarely confront individuals with untreated dental disease, in my experience conducting dental surveys among indigenous Amazonian groups, the breath of individuals with abscessed teeth or multiple carious lesions is far more aversive than that of others in the same population, even when no toothbrushes, toothpaste, or modern dentistry are available. Common halitosis stems from bacterial growth on the back of the tongue. While this growth probably doesn't have much direct negative effect on fitness, it might provide a cue to an individual's overall resistance to bacterial infection. Olfactory cues can, therefore, provide cues to oral health and hygiene and, less directly, to developmental integrity and genetic quality. However, despite the fact that dental hygiene is a multimillion-dollar industry, I found no direct tests of these predictions in the evolutionary literature.

Movement Patterns   Grammer et al. (2002) explain that movement patterns depend on motor control of biomechanical structures. Bone, muscle, and neuronal motor control are affected by heritable, developmental, and current physiological state, and there are biomechanical energetic optima of movements (Grammer et al., 2002). Individuals vary on these traits, such that individuals can be reliably identified by gait (Stevenage, Nixon, & Vince, 1999). Symons (1979) predicted that sprightly gait would be attractive in females because it was correlated with youth and nubility. Attaching lights to critical parts of the body allows movement to be studied without being confounded with other visual cues. These techniques have shown that relative youth can be predicted from gait (Montpare, Zebrowitz, & McArthur, 1988). Similarly, biomechanical features of health or other aspects of genetic or phenotypic quality should be assessable by movement. For instance, symmetry affects biomechanical efficiency (Manning & Pickup, 1998), and symmetry appears to be a correlate of genotypic and phenotypic quality (e.g., Thornhill & Gangestad, 1993; see later discussion). Animal studies have shown that movement differs between sick and healthy individuals. In particular, ability to move consistently through repeated motions (e.g., walking) may provide information about phenotypic condition, including health (Grammer et al., 2002). And motion is used in assessments of attractiveness for members of the opposite sex (Grammer et al., 2002). In particular, when digitally masked or pixilated images of men and women dancing were shown to subjects, they were found more attractive and erotic the larger and more sweeping their movement. Women who made slow, more fluid movements were found more attractive. In addition to information about sex, age, and identity (which subjects are able to predict from movement alone), Grammer et al. (2002) suggest that these motions also convey information about underlying genetic quality and resistance to developmental disturbances.

Fluctuating Asymmetry and Developmental Stability   Externally visible features of many animals' bodies are designed to be bilaterally symmetrical. However, environmental stress can disrupt developmental pathways. On average, random developmental disturbances are expected to affect development on both sides of the body equally, but mutational load or homozygosity may increase small random variations from symmetry during development, known as *fluctuating asymmetry* (FA; Mather, 1953; Palmer & Stobeck, 1986; Van Valen, 1962; Watson & Thornhill, 1994). FA thus provides a potential observable indicator of developmental instability: Individuals with lower FA appear to have either higher genetic quality, less exposure to developmental disturbances, or both. As an indicator of genotypic quality and ability to withstand developmental stress, pathogens, and genetic anomalies via more efficient use of developmental resources or enhanced immune function, FA has been hypothesized as one cue to genotypic and phenotypic quality. Because maintaining symmetrical development in the face of developmental disturbances is costly, FA may be an "honest" signal of genotypic and phenotypic quality related to a number of aspects of fitness. This signal quality is thought to be accentuated in males by display of physical features under developmental control of testosterone. Testosterone has negative effects on immune function, so only males with high genetic quality and immune function can have both high testosterone and high degrees of symmetry. Selection for preference for low FA opposite-sex individuals is therefore predicted (e.g., Gangestadt & Thornhill, 1999; Møller & Swaddle, 1997; Palmer & Stobeck, 1986; Thornhill & Gangestadt, 1993; Thornhill & Møller, 1997; Watson & Thornhill, 1994).

Research on a variety of species shows that FA is negatively correlated with fitness-related measures of growth, survival, fecundity, intrasexual competitiveness, and mating success (Lagesen & Folstad, 1998; Møller, 1990, 1992a, 1992b, 1993, 2002; Thornhill, 1992a, 1992b). FA appears to be heritable, such that offspring are likely to exhibit these advantages to some extent, although the degree of heritability is debated (Fuller & Houle, 2003; Gangestad & Thornhill, 1999). In men and women, symmetry appears to be associated with correlates of genotypic and phenotypic quality, including physical, cognitive, and mental health. More symmetrical men are more muscular (Gangestad & Thornhill, 1997b), are larger (Manning, 1995), have a lower resting metabolic rate (Manning, Koukourakis, & Brodie, 1997), and have a greater degree of testosterone-related facial cues of dominance and reproductive health (Gangestad & Thornhill, 2003) than do less symmetric males. Body weight, musculature, and testosterone levels may be condition-dependent: Higher genetic quality males are best able to develop and maintain large size, musculature, and high testosterone (Gangestad & Thornhill, 1997a, 1997b, 2003)—costly signals of "masculine" traits that pay off in intrasexual competition and intersexual attraction. Women reported finding these masculine traits particularly desirable in short-term mates and extra-pair sex partners (Buss & Schmitt, 1993; Greiling & Buss, 2000). They also appear to be more attracted to and more likely to have sex with men exhibiting these "masculine" traits during the fertile phase of their ovulatory cycle, as was predicted if female short-term mating is strategically deployed to increase the genetic quality of their offspring (Bellis & Baker, 1990; Johnston, Hagel, Franklin, Fink, & Grammer, 2001; Penton-Voak & Perrett, 2000; Penton-Voak et al., 1999; Thornhill & Gangestad, 2003).

FA is also negatively correlated with aspects of female health. Manning (1995) show an association between body weight and FA in women. In a large study of

26-year-old men and women, Milne et al. (2003) found female FA was significantly associated with body mass index (BMI) and overall reported number of medical conditions. Although FA was not significantly associated with blood pressure, cholesterol, or cardiorespiratory fitness, the authors suggest this could simply be the result of relatively low levels of environmental stressors in Westernized societies, leading to more homogeneity in FA (Milne et al., 2003). Among Hadza foragers, FA is higher than in U.S. college students, suggesting the Hadza do experience more developmental stress (Gray & Marlowe, 2002).

Given these associations between FA and poorer phenotypic condition, Gangestad, Thornhill, and Yeo (1994) predicted that symmetrical individuals would be perceived as more attractive than less symmetrical individuals. To the extent that individuals in better phenotypic condition should have, higher kin, coalitional, and offspring value, we should expect low FA to be more attractive across these domains of social value. Given that male FA is inversely related to cues of masculinity mediated by testosterone—for example, dominance, aggressiveness, large size, and musculature—we should expect males to find low FA and its correlates particularly attractive in their close male allies (as opposed to their enemies), at least as long as the benefit the ally provides is greater than the cost he imposes as a mating competitor. Sexual and coalitionary rivals are also likely to be assessed in part based on FA, but we would expect a negative emotional response to low FA and higher testosterone individuals that would increase in proportion to their formidability as sexual or coalitionary competitors (i.e., the greater the threat, the more intense the negative emotional response).

Relative symmetry is associated with facial attractiveness, as well as mating behavior and opportunities. FA is negatively correlated with facial attractiveness ratings of both males and females (Baker, 1997; Gangestad et al., 1994; Thornhill & Gangestad, 1993, 1994, 1999a). The clearest demonstrations of the link between attractiveness and symmetry use natural stimuli, rather than composites (e.g., Cunningham et al., 1991) or mirrored chimeras (e.g., Kowner, 1996; Langlois, Roggman, & Musselman, 1994), because the latter manipulations confound FA with either averageness or skin texture and may create unnatural-looking faces by exaggerating or reducing some features, particularly those that show directional asymmetry (DA; or nonrandom asymmetry not indicative of developmental disturbance; Farkas & Cheung, 1981; Little, Penton-Voak, Burt, & Perrett, 2002; Symons, 1995). Image manipulations of symmetry have led to contradictory results. Symmetrical faces created by taking half a facial image (split on the vertical midline) and joining it with its mirror image are not more attractive than the original, although averaging these first two chimera images does yield increased attractiveness (Kowner, 1996; Langlois et al., 1994; Rhodes et al., 1999; Swaddle & Cuthill, 1995).

Most studies on natural variation in facial symmetry show a positive relationship between symmetry and attractiveness (Grammer & Thornhill, 1994; Langlois et al., 1994; Mealey, Bridgestock, & Townsend, 1999; Rhodes, Proffitt, Grady, & Sumich, 1998; Rhodes et al., 1999; Rikowski & Grammer, 1999; Scheib, Gangestad, & Thornhill, 1999; but see Jones & Hill, 1993).

If low FA is associated with the ability to withstand developmental disturbance, such that symmetry is correlated with other cues of phenotypic condition, then low FA individuals may be found attractive because of those other cues, in addition to symmetry per se. If so, the link between symmetry and attractiveness would not be direct. Sheib et al. (1999) found that, when presented with male half-faces (split along the vertical midline), women's attractiveness ratings of half-face images were associated with symmetry of the full face, just as strongly as the women's ratings of the full faces. More symmetrical men had longer lower jaws and more prominent cheekbones, features that appear to reflect developmental influence of testosterone (see later discussion). Jones et al. (2001) also found that the relationship between attractiveness and facial symmetry is not direct, but mediated by the association of symmetry and apparent health (see also Shackelford et al., 2000). The direct effect of facial symmetry on attractiveness was small.

Body symmetry is also associated with facial symmetry and ratings of attractiveness, health, and fitness, supporting the idea that FA is related to underlying features of phenotypic condition. Thornhill and Gangestad (1994) measured seven nonfacial body traits of 122 undergraduates and found a positive correlation between age at first copulation and degree of asymmetry. They also found negative correlation between FA and self-reported number of lifetime sex partners, even when age, height, ethnicity, marital status, physical attractiveness, and physical anomalies were controlled. FA was important in evaluations of both male and female attractiveness. Gangestad measured FA of men from a small village on Dominica using 10 different body traits. Both male and female college students rated facial photographs of the more symmetrical men more attractive (Thornhill & Gangestad, 2002). Waynforth (1995) found FA related to higher morbidity and lower fecundity and marginally associated with higher age at first reproduction and fewer lifetime sex partners among Mayan men in Belize. Hume and Montgomerie (2001) studied the relationship among facial attractiveness ratings, FA (based on 22 traits), BMI, health, and age among almost 100 male and 100 female subjects, whose attractiveness was then rated by a large number of other men and women. For both males and females, there was a negative association between attractiveness and FA. For females, BMI and past health problems were the best predictors of female attractiveness; for males, it was the socioeconomic status of the environment in which they were raised.

Men with low FA report earlier age of first intercourse, higher numbers of sex partners, higher number of extra-pair copulation partners, and shorter time elapsed until sex with a new partner (Gangestad & Thornhill, 1997a; Thornhill & Gangestad, 1994, 2003). This pattern appears to be the product of individual differences in male mating strategy depending on males' relative attractiveness (and thus opportunities based on female mate choices) and hormone-mediated sociosexual strategies that covary with FA. This may exacerbate the trade-off women face between choice for good genes and for likely investment. As predicted, female attraction to low-FA males increases with woman's current fecundity and in short-term (or extra-pair) mating contexts (as does preference for male physical attractiveness and its correlates generally; see, e.g., Buss & Schmitt, 1993; Greiling & Buss, 2000). Degree of male symmetry predicts a significant amount of their partners' copulatory orgasms (Thornhill, Gangestad, & Comer, 1995), which may bias paternity toward symmetrical males via increased sperm retention (Baker & Bellis, 1995), and women experience more frequent orgasm with extra-pair mates (Thornhill & Gangestad, 2003). In the study of FA and attractiveness among Dominica men, women showed greater preference for symmetrical male faces as a function of the woman's probability of conception based on the phase of her ovulatory cycle. Finally, body scent may be associated with phenotypic condition, and when women were presented with T-shirts worn by different men, women not using hormonal contraceptives preferred the body scent of more symmetrical men, but only during the fertile times in their cycle. Hormonally contracepting women showed no shift (Gangestad & Thornhill, 1998; Rikowski & Grammer, 1999; Thornhill & Gangestad, 1999b). These studies indicate that all future research on female mate preferences must distinguish not only between short- and long-term female mating preferences but also between preferences during the fertile and nonfertile phases of the ovulatory cycle.

HORMONAL AND SEXUALLY DIMORPHIC CUES TO HEALTH, PHENOTYPIC, AND GENOTYPIC QUALITY

Some cues to social value differ between the sexes. Sexually dimorphic features develop partially under the influence of testosterone and estrogens. Sexual dimorphism in body size, strength, and physical weaponry typically evolves because of higher levels of intrasexual competition in one sex than in the other. Sexual dimorphism in ornamentation is usually the result of intersexual selection or mate choice. Sexually dimorphic traits therefore provide a variety of possible cues to the relative social value of both men and women, although the cues associated with each sex are expected to differ in certain predictable ways. Different morphological traits may be associated with relatively higher or lower social value in a given domain in different environments and be more or less important depending on local context. The underlying psychology generating attractiveness assessments for each assessed feature of body morphology is thus expected to generate differing assessments of attractiveness based on local environmental features. This discussion focuses on cues of social value related to the face, height, body mass, and bodily proportions.

Because mammalian female reproductive potential is usually less than that of males, intrasexual competition is typically higher among males, and males are correspondingly larger. If females preferentially mate with larger (or better-armed) males, the selective benefit of larger size is increased. In primates, dimorphism corresponds roughly with a species' mating pattern: Single-male/multifemale groups tend to have higher dimorphism than those living in "monogamous" pairs. In between are those, like humans, who live in multimale/multifemale groups and show mild size dimorphism in height, weight, and upper body musculature. A closer predictor of dimorphism is the species' operational sex ratio, or the ratio of reproductively active males to females expected in a given group at a given time (Mitani, Gros-Louis, & Richards, 1996).

In primates with multimale/multifemale groups, such as common chimpanzees and baboons, males may form coalitions to prevent solitary males or other coalitions from gaining sexual access to group females. For humans, having larger, stronger, more physically adept and aggressively formidable allies can be beneficial in these circumstances. However, an individual's coalition members are also his sexual rivals in the contest to mate with female group members: More formidable coalitional allies mean more formidable potential intrasexual competitors. For males, then, there are trade-offs between preferred size of allies and preferred size of competitors.

For females, one adaptive problem presented by sexual dimorphism is that males may use their size and strength advantage coercively. One solution to this problem is for females to obtain physical protection from other males (Buss & Schmitt, 1993). All else equal, females who preferred larger, stronger, more dominant males as sires for their offspring would tend to have sons who inherited these qualities. Females who preferred males exhibiting ability and willingness to invest in their offspring would tend to rear more offspring to maturity.

Formal modeling of these trade-offs is necessary to predict evolutionarily stable mixes of strategies within specific constraints. However, among Jivaroan-speaking indigenous Amazonians, living groups tend to include one or a few *juunt* (i.e., big men), whose coalitional ties to other groups form the basis for larger, intergroup coalitions and around whom aggregate a coalition of (usually) younger, smaller, less dominant, affinally or consanguineally related males (e.g., Descola, 1998; Patton, 2000). Younger men may jockey for status among themselves, but as they approach *juunt* age and status, they may increasingly conflict with established big men. Chagnon (1975, 1979, 1997) clearly shows that among the Yanomamö, when status or mating conflict increases to the point that the stability of intragroup coalitions is too frequently perturbed, the group fissions. As group size increases, group formidability increases, but so do internal conflicts.

Throughout the juvenile period, individuals face a trade-off between investment in immune function and growth. Adult size is partially heritable, but nutrition, pathogen exposure, and immune function affect how much energy is available for growth (e.g., Bogin, 1999; Gunnell, Smith, Ness, & Frankel, 2000; Read & Allen, 2000; Rivera, Martorell, Ruel, Habicht, & Haas, 1995; Roberts et al., 2000; Silventoinen, 2003). All else equal, in subsistence societies, larger individuals have higher phenotypic quality: They are more likely to survive and are better able to resist pathogens and to convert available ecological resources into somatic resources (e.g., Hill & Hurtado, 1996). Further, human growth is determinate: Growth ends when reproduction begins because the energetic costs of doing both simultaneously are too high (Hill & Hurtado, 1996). For women, the fitness benefit of additional growth includes the accumulation of somatic resources for later reproductive effort, increasing probability of survival (Jousilahti, Tuomilehto, Vartiainen, Eriksson, & Puska, 2000), lower offspring mortality (Sear et al., 2004), and lower maternal and infant mortality (taller women tend to have wider pelvises, easier births, and higher infant birthweights; see Kirchengast, Hartmann, Schweppe, & Husslein, 1998; Martorell, Delgado, Valverde, & Klein, 1981; Rosenberg, 1992). The potential benefits of earlier reproduction include lower prereproductive mortality risk and a longer time span in which to reproduce (Hill & Hurtado, 1996; Hill & Kaplan, 1999).

Height   Men tend to have partners who are shorter than themselves and vice versa (Gillis & Avis, 1980). In modern populations, there is generally a positive association between male height and health (Kuh & Ben Shlomo, 1997; Kuh & Wadsworth, 1993; Macintyre & West, 1991; Silventoinen, Lahelma, & Rahkonen, 1999) and reproductive success (RS; Mueller & Mazur, 2001; Nettle, 2002; Pawlowski, Dunbar, & Lipowicz, 2000). As noted earlier, relative height provides some information about phenotypic quality. However, extreme shortness and tallness may be associated with health problems in both sexes (e.g., Mueller & Mazur, 2001; Nettle, 2002). Height is associated with the rated attractiveness of men (e.g., Feingold, 1982; Gillis & Avos, 1980; Hensley, 1994), with American women rating short men undesirable for either long- or short-term mates. Tall, strong, athletic men are strongly desired as marriage partners (Buss & Schmitt, 1993), and taller-than-average men are preferred to men of short or average stature as dates and mating partners (Ellis, 1992). In analyses of personal ads, 80% of women who stated height preferences wanted men 6 feet tall or taller (Cameron, Oskamp, & Sparks, 1977). Ads placed by taller men receive more responses (Lynn & Shurgot, 1984; Pawlowski & Koziel, 2002). Women even seem to take height into consideration in sperm donors (Scheib, Kristiansen, & Wara, 1997).

Preference for tall men does not appear to be limited to intersexual choice. Coalitional leadership and height seem to be associated in both small-scale and state societies. In U.S. presidential elections, the taller candidate is more likely to win, with the margin of victory positively correlated with height (McCann, 2001). Senators and CEOs appear to be taller than the average American man (Etcoff, 1999; Keyes, 1980). Further, there appears to be a positive association between height and socioeconomic success (Bielicki & Szklarska, 1999; Frieze, Olson, & Good, 1990; Frieze, Olson, & Russell, 1991; Hensley & Cooper, 1987; Jackson, 1992). In an experimental study, 72% of recruiters for sales positions preferred the taller of two job applicants, but only one recruiter preferred the shorter candidate (the remainder had no preference; Kurtz, 1969). Among a large sample of British men, taller-than-average men had higher numbers of live-in partners and lower chance of either being childless or having had no significant mating relationship (Nettle, 2002). However, Nettle found no significant association between total number of offspring and height, although the men had not yet completed fertility: They were not yet of the age where they were likely to have had all children from a second marriage, and they had ready access to contraceptives.

If male size is positively associated with aggressive formidability, yet involves energetic or other trade-offs, then a reliable, efficient solution to these trade-offs would include a context-sensitive height-assessment adaptation functioning such that intensity of male height preference increases with increasing levels of intragroup conflict and intergroup coalitional conflict. Intensity of preference for taller males is also expected to vary with resource stress: Because taller males are those who could better afford the costs of growing larger, relative height provides a costly signal of phenotypic quality, amplified under resource and pathogen stress.

In their study of the intercorrelation of 36 female physical traits, Grammer et al. (2002) found a significant correlation between a woman's height and her attractiveness, which in factor analysis loaded highly with traits associated with their factor of nubility. Conversely, Hensley (1994) found no evidence that men use height in assessments of females. Sear et al. (2004) investigated the relationship between height and RS in a natural fertility population of Gambian women, providing evidence that ancestral males could have benefited from mate choice for locally taller women under some conditions. They found the expected trade-off between growth and age of sexual maturity, with taller women having later age at first birth. But the physiological benefits of increased growth paid off during their reproductive life span in higher RS: Offspring of taller women exhibited lower mortality.

Conversely, using data from Britain's National Child Development Study (a longitudinal study of socioeconomic and health among all children born in Britain during one week in 1958) to investigate the relationship between female height and lifetime RS, Nettle (2002) found a weak but highly significant inverted

U-shaped relationship between relative female height (at age 23) and RS at age 42, controlling for own or husband's socioeconomic status. Highest RS was for women between 0.7 and 1.7 standard deviations below the mean. Women of mean height had the highest number of marriages or long-term mates and were least likely never to have had a long-term mating relationship. Nettle also found the expected trade-off between growth and age of sexual maturity, with taller women beginning to reproduce later. However, age of the British sample corresponds with widespread availability of hormonal contraceptives, and the mean fertility was low for all heights observed, so later first reproduction of taller women cannot account for their lower RS. As predicted, given the life history trade-offs involved, female height preferences appear to change with (mild) socioecological risk. Pettijohn and Jungeberg (2004) found a significant positive correlation between yearly indicators of economic stress (predicted to covary with perceived ecological risk) and the height of *Playboy* Playmates chosen to be the *Playboy* magazine Playmate of the Year.

Weight, Body Fat, and BMI   Body fat provides a potential cue to female mate value because fertility, pregnancy, and lactation are supported by substantial fat stores (Frisch, 1990; Frisch & McArthur, 1974). Fat reserves may buffer decrease in female reproductive function related to arduous work regimes (Jasienska & Ellison, 1998) and seasonal negative protein-energy balance (Bentley, Harrigan, & Ellison, 1998), as well as the mortality risk and reproductive decline associated with illness/injury and poor health (e.g., Anderson et al., 1992; Brown & Konner, 1987; Sugiyama, 2004b; Sugiyama & Chacon, 2000). Workload, resource availability, and health risks are ecologically variable, so if psychological adaptations evolved to use body weight in assessments of attractiveness, they are expected to embody features that adjust preferred level of female body fat to these and other relevant features of the local environment during development and to update assessments with changes in these variables across the life span (Sugiyama, 1996, 2004a). Cold-adapted populations tend to have higher subcutaneous body fat, so factors such as climate are likely to affect local body fat preferences as well. Among the Aché, there is a positive linear relationship between female body weight and fertility at 30 years of age (Hill & Hurtado, 1996) similar to the pattern of height and fertility for Gambian women. Variance in Aché women's age-specific weight is higher than variance in male weight. And, in contrast to the increase in weight associated with age in contracepting, industrialized societies, Aché women show a common mammalian pattern in which they achieve peak weight just before reproductive maturity (age at first birth), followed by a decline in weight over the reproductive life span. In foraging populations, then, high weight is not a reliable cue of middle age, old age, or parity; rather, it can covary with nubility. Females among Shiwiar forager-horticulturalists of Ecuador show a similar pattern (Sugiyama, 1996).

Cross-culturally, preferred female body fat level increases with risk of local food shortages (Anderson et al., 1992). Studies show that preference for plumper women is common in non-Western societies with subsistence-based economies and/or higher risk of food shortages (Anderson et al., 1992; Brown & Konner, 1987; Ford & Beach, 1951; Sobal & Stunkard, 1989). All claims about attractiveness-assessment adaptations related to body weight must take this ecological variability—as well as age-related changes in body weight—into account. When North

American subjects rate the attractiveness of standardized female line drawings depicting low, normal, and high (but not obese) body weight, normal-weight figures are regularly preferred by North American White and Hispanic subjects (Singh, 1993a, 1993b, 1994c). Among 12 line drawing stimulus figures ranging from anorexic to obese, British, Kenyan, and Ugandan subjects rated normal-weight figures most attractive (Furnham & Radley, 1989), but Kenyans and Ugandans rated high-weight figures significantly more attractive than did British subjects or Kenyans living in Britain (Furnham & Alibhai, 1983; Furnham & Baguma, 1994). My Shiwiar informants regularly express preference for higher female body fat (within the local range), and experimental results confirm that higher-weight line drawings are found more sexually attractive, healthy, fertile, young, and preferable as spouses (Sugiyama, 2004a). Studies among Hadza foragers of Tanzania and Machiguenga forager-horticulturalists of Peru show similar results (Wetsman & Marlowe, 1999; Yu & Shepard, 1999). However, measures of subcutaneous body fat indicate that even the "fattest" Shiwiar woman has lower body fat than average U.S. female college students. Most Shiwiar (and Machiguenga) have probably never seen an obese individual, and their assessment system has never observed the link between obesity and other cues of poor phenotypic quality, such as shortness of breath, impaired gait and mobility, and increased susceptibility to disease. Pettijohn and Jungeberg's (2004) Playmate study indicates that within societies, preferences for higher weight correlate with economic indicators of "hard times." So, while body-weight preference varies across cultures and time, it does so in predictable ways, and nowhere have experimental studies found obesity considered the height of attractiveness. Conversely, even among Western college students, extreme thinness is not found most attractive, nor preferred (e.g., Tovée & Cornelissen, 2001).

BMI, or weight scaled for height (measured as kg/m^2), captures two relevant features of somatic growth: determinate skeletal growth and more fluctuating changes in body weight. In a series of experimental studies in which subjects were presented with female body images produced in various ways, BMI was reported to account for about 80% of the variance in female body attractiveness (e.g., Tovée & Cornelisson, 1999, 2001; Tovée et al., 1998, 1999, 2002). Tovée and Cornelisson (2001) had male and female undergraduates rate color digital 24-bit photos of 50 real women (18 to 42 years of age, mean age 26, s.d. 8 years) standing in uniform poses wearing standard tight gray leotards and leggings on a zero (lowest) to nine (highest) point attractiveness scale. Each subject rated 10 women's front and side view pictures from each of five BMI categories taken from obesity literature: emaciated (BMI <15), underweight (15 to 19), acceptable (20 to 24), overweight (25 to 30), and obese (>30). Men and women showed an indistinguishable pattern of results. Peak attractiveness ratings were for BMI of 19, with ratings falling precipitously for both higher and lower BMI figures. Front and side view results were highly correlated, suggesting they were generated by the same underlying assessment. However, this study has limited evolutionary ecological validity (EEV): It presents subjects with a narrow range of evolutionarily relevant morphological variation by presenting a limited range of female age, parity, fecundity, and current pregnancy (see Tovée & Cornelisson, 1999, 2001).

The actual perceptual cues used in weight-related assessment are not currently known. Fan, Liu, Wu, and Dai (2004) suggest that it is assessed via analysis of volume-to-height index (VHI), and that low female VHI is preferred. This is unlikely given the well documented preferences for higher body weight in some cultures. Given, however, that marriage arrangements are often made prior to female reproductive maturity and wooing a long-term mate may take some time, we might alternatively hypothesize that low VHI is associated with female pre-pubescence and that adaptations generating attraction to this female life stage would under some circumstances increase male fitness by targeting females when their reproductive value is high and there is still time enough to secure mating access before fertility onset (see, e.g., Symons, 1979, 1995). The observed male preference for relatively long legs to height (Fan et al., 2004), a ratio that in females is most pronounced at the onset of puberty, would support this contention. In industrialized societies, low VHI (and BMI) is associated with prepubescence (and nubility); in some forager societies, however, relatively higher BMI or VHI is associated with nubility. In sum, female body weight (or close correlates thereof) is an important cue to female reproductive value but what it indicates about reproductive value varies between populations. Relative weight preferences vary across populations in evolutionarily predictable ways and may vary within populations in predicted ways as well.

For males, fitness effects of growth differ from those for females. There is a positive relationship between Aché male body weight and fertility. The increase in fertility with body weight is steeper for males than for females to about 66 kg, upon which it declines with the few males over 67 kg. While 65 kg is the predicted optimal weight for Aché males to stop growing and begin reproduction given the mortality, growth rate, and impact of body size on fertility in this group, there may be a trade-off between optimal reproduction and foraging body size. Large Aché males could be more effective in intrasexual conflict, but they achieve lower hunting return rates (kg/hr) than average-size males, probably due to problems that larger men have moving efficiently in dense tropical forest (Hill & Hurtado, 1996).

Chagnon (1988) reports that Yanomamö men who are *unokai* (i.e., men who have undergone ritual ceremony as a result of participation in a killing) have higher RS than men who have not. In a society in which reputations for fierceness are valued, *unokai* status is public recognition that an individual is willing and able to defend his coalitional interests. Similar evidence is reported for Jivaroan men (Patton, 2000). Nevertheless, it is clear that willingness and ability to defend one's interests is an important component of male political leadership in small-scale societies. One venue where possible correlates of male aggressive formidability have been investigated is sports performance. Ritualized fighting such as Yanomamö chest pounding, side slapping, or club fighting are duals with normative rules that can reduce mortality risk, yet can serve to settle disputes and provide a (usually) sublethal outlet for physical aggression (Chagnon, 1997). Androgens, particularly testosterone, have developmental effects on spatial abilities, cardiovascular efficiency, speed, endurance, strength, muscle mass, and personality traits associated with aggressiveness (Bardin & Catterall, 1981; Dabbs & Dabbs, 2000; Manning & Bundred, 2000)—traits expected to be correlated with fighting formidability and physical dominance. Physical contests (e.g., wrestling, racing, weight throwing or carrying, ritualized fighting) are common cross-culturally and may serve as proxies of, training for, and/or advertisements of fighting ability (e.g., Chagnon, 1997; Chick & Loy, 2001; Hill, 1984; Manning & Taylor, 2001). Manning and Taylor (2001) suggest that sports serve as useful proxies for fighting ability because they require speed, endurance, strength, and good spatial skills. These traits are expected to correlate with phenotypic quality more generally and are required to some extent in hunting, although knowledge-based skills may be more important in determining hunting success (Kaplan et al., 2000), and strength peaks earlier than hunting return rates (Walker et al., 2002).

Faurie et al. (2004) found that male and female college students who participated in competitive sports or were enrolled in sports curricula reported higher numbers of opposite-sex sex partners than those who were not involved with sports. High-level competitors reported more previous-year opposite-sex partners than lower level competitors. For males but not females, BMI was positively associated with reported previous-year mates, although it could not be analytically separated from the sports participation variable. Manning and Taylor (2001) found evidence that level of sports performance is positively associated with testosterone markers. The ratio of the second to fourth digit, 2d:4d (index finger/ring finger), is generally lower in males than in females and appears to be a correlate of prenatal testosterone concentration (Manning, 2002; Manning, Scutt, & Lewis-Jones, 1998; Manning et al., 1999). Lower 2d:4d ratio is associated with higher level performance or competition in middle distance running (Manning & Pickup, 1998); running speed (Manning, 2002); sports generally (including running, football, and soccer); and martial arts, rugby, racquet sports, swimming, and hockey (Manning & Taylor, 2001). It is also associated with better mental rotation performance (Manning, 2002). Low 2d:4d is associated with testosterone-related personality traits such as aggression but also with intelligence (Manning, 2002). Both men and women can rate the attractiveness of hands. Longer fourth digits are also associated with prenatal testosterone, and when photocopied dorsal and ventral hand surfaces were presented to subjects, digit length was positively correlated with rated attractiveness and sexiness of male and female hands (Manning, 2002). In men, fourth-digit length, attractiveness, and height are positively associated, but there was a negative association between fourth-digit length and male weight. Since the stimuli were fromWestern subjects, the latter result could be due to obesity. Replication among a natural-fertility population of foragers or subsistence horticulturalists (among whom weight will be more closely associated with muscle mass and height) is warranted because other studies show positive correlations among size, strength, and attractiveness.

Sexual jealousy adaptations are expected to be expressed in situations where an individual perceives a threat to his or her relationship (Buss, Shackelford, Cloe, Buunk, & Dijkstra, 2000). The traits expected to evoke jealousy are therefore expected to reflect the outcome of self-to-other comparisons based on cues of relative mate value. Dijkstra and Buunk (2001) had subjects list the traits in a mating rival that would make them feel most jealous. The only specific morphological traits listed as jealousy-evoking in a rival were those cues associated with intrasexual competition. Among the traits listed as jealousy-provoking by males were rivals being bigger, stronger, taller, more heavily built, more muscular, and having broader shoulders than self (Dijkstra & Buunk, 2001). In line with predictions about sex differences in the value placed on certain cues to mate value (e.g., Buss, 1989; Buss & Schmitt, 1993; Symons, 1979), heterosexual males regarded each of these traits as being significantly more jealousy-provoking in a sexual rival than did females. Moreover, these traits loaded together in a principal components analysis of 56 different jealousy-evoking traits, suggesting that they are important interrelated features of male intrasexual competition.

Waist-to-Hip Ratio   There are pronounced postpubertal sex differences in the ratio of waist circumference to hip circumference (WHR; Jones, Hunt, Brown, & Norgan, 1986; Singh, 1993a, 1993b). In females, estrogen during puberty stimulates fat deposition on the thighs, hips, and buttocks, and inhibits deposition around the abdomen. It is also associated with the widening of the female pelvis. Women's WHR increases with pregnancy, number of births, and high intestinal parasite loads. Western women with normal WHR (.67–.80) are at reduced risk for primary infertility and various health problems (e.g., cardiovascular disorders, female carcinoma), independent of overall level of body fat (Bjorntorp, 1988; Marti et al., 1991; Singh, 1993a, 1993b). Conversely, adult male WHR averages about 0.9 and is associated with androgen hormonal profile. Singh therefore argues that selection shaped men's mating psychology to prefer low female WHR, regardless of overall preferences for body fat (Singh, 1993a, 1993b) and women's mating psychology to prefer male WHR of 0.9. To test these ideas, Singh had subjects examine 12 line drawings of female figures depicting four levels of WHR (0.7, 0.8, 0.9, and 1.0) and three levels of body weight (normal [N], low [L], and overweight [0]). When young White and Hispanic men ranked the figures for attractiveness, youthfulness, healthiness, sexiness, and capability of and desire for reproduction, they strongly preferred the normal weight figures (Singh, 1993a, 1993b, 1994a, 1994b). Within each body-weight category, lower WHR was preferred to higher WHR, with 0.7 WHR preferred overall (Singh, 1993a, 1993b, 1994a, 1994b). Ratings of college-age males and females agreed on the relative attractiveness of stimuli based on WHR (Singh, 1993b). Results were not simply the by-product of current fashion trends (in the simplistic cultural determinist sense). Analyses of body weight and WHR of *Playboy* Playmates, Miss America Contest winners (Singh, 1993a), and British fashion models (Morris et al., 1989) show that while weight decreased over time, WHR remained in the .68 to .72 range (Singh, 1993a). British males and African American, Hispanic, White, and Indonesian males in the United States also prefer lower WHR among women of normal weight within the normal Western range, but some variability exists in the preferred level of WHR across studies depending on the method used, specific questions asked, and population tested: Average-weight female figures with 0.7 WHR are usually judged most positively, but WHRs of 0.6 and 0.8 are sometimes judged most attractive as well (Furnham, Tan, & McManus, 1997; Henss, 1995; Singh, 1993a, 1993b, 1994a, 1994c, 1999; Singh & Luis, 1995). Idealized female WHR depicted in art also varies across cultures, but within cultures is consistently lower than idealized male WHR (Singh & Haywood, 1999). As predicted, subjects also rate male figures with 0.9 WHR (in the normal range for Western males) most attractive (Henss, 1995; Singh, 1994c).

Ancestral environmental variability and empirical data suggest that WHR assessment is more complex than an "invariant preference" for a specific WHR, or a rule specifying "the lower a woman's WHR, the better" (e.g., Marlowe & Wetsman, 2000; Singh, 1993a, 1993b; Sugiyama, 1996, 2004a; Symons, 1995; Tassinary & Hansen, 1998; Wetsman & Marlowe, 1999; Yu & Shepard, 1998). By Western standards, women in foraging populations have high numbers of pregnancies, high parasite loads, and high caloric dependence on fibrous foods (e.g., R. L. Kelly,

1995), all of which can increase WHR. These factors vary cross-culturally, suggesting that, across ancestral populations: (1) the normal range of female WHR was often higher than in Western populations, (2) what constituted locally "low" WHR varied, and (3) average WHR of nubile females and of females at peak fertility varied. Thus, a WHR that indicates pubertal onset, sex, fertility, parity, hormonal irregularities, and/or differentiates male from female in one population may not do so in another. Environmental conditions that fluctuate over an individual's lifetime could affect the relationship between local cues of reproductive value associated with age, sex, health, fertility, and body morphology, including WHR. WHR preference likely targets local distribution of female WHR and updates and recalibrates preferences as local conditions change. WHR of *Playboy* Playmates of the Year does appear to positively correlate with yearly indicators of economic stress, but so, too, does weight, and the effect of WHR controlling for weight was not addressed in that study (Pettijohn & Jungeberg, 2004).

The hypothesis that WHR affects assessments of attractiveness does not necessarily mean that WHR assessment is based on output from a psychological WHR calculation device of waist to hip per se. WHR could be assessed by a curve-detector mechanism, for instance. And because health and reproductive studies measure WHR in circumference, but experimental stimuli predominantly use front and back views, they lack some of the relevant health and reproductive value cues that WHR is hypothesized to provide. Further, the cues to female health and reproductive value hypothesized to be indexed by WHR are multidimensional. For example, pelvic width and angle were critical changes in female hominid morphology to accommodate the passage of large-headed babies through the pelvic opening. The developmental widening of women's pelvic bones is not complete until about 18 years of age, and it then increases with parity, while gynoid fat distribution appears at puberty. Yet, among Shiwiar and Aché women, body fat appears to decrease with age after first reproduction. These two aspects of WHR may therefore index different aspects of female mate value and independently contribute some of the variance in attractiveness assessment.

A reliable, efficiently functional mate-preference psychology using cues associated with WHR or body shape more generally should take as input the observable range of female WHR and body fat, based on analysis of the following critical WHR subcomponents: (1) pelvic width, shape, and angle; (2) hip width and circumference; (3) hip shape; (4) buttocks extension; (5) buttocks shape; (6) waist width and circumference; (7) waist shape; (8) stomach shape; and (9) stomach extension in relation to (10) other aspects of skeletal structure—such as shoulder and/or ribcage width, distance from pelvis to shoulder, and length of long bones (which provide reference points for assessing pelvic width and fat deposition)—in relation to overall growth, developmental health, and biomechanical efficiency (e.g., Sugiyama, 1996, 2004a). In sum, instead of uniform, cross-cultural preference for a specific WHR, lower WHR relative to the normal female range to which a man is exposed should be preferred. Because at some level low WHR will appear as a deformity, lower limits of WHR attractiveness are also expected (Symons, 1995). Additionally, men exposed to a higher range of healthy nubile female WHR should find higher WHR more acceptable than men exposed to a lower range of female WHR, and lowering the natural range of WHR to which men are exposed should predictably lower their expressed WHR preference, at least within the limits of the reaction norm for these adaptations (Sugiyama, 2004a).

The only studies that have tested WHR preferences in EEV small-scale, subsistence-economy populations report conflicting results (Marlowe, 2001; Sugiyama, 2004a; Wetsman & Marlowe, 1999; Yu & Shepard, 1998). These studies provide a useful illustration of the need for, but potential pitfalls of, cross-cultural testing of hypotheses about psychological adaptations (for an in-depth discussion, see Sugiyama, 2004a). The Matsiguenka are a case in point. Of six female line drawings depicting two WHRs (0.7 and 0.9) and three body weights (overweight, normal, and low weight), more isolated Matsiguenka men of Peruvian Amazonia ranked figures O.9, O.7, N.9, N.7, U.9, and U.7 in order of descending preference for attractiveness, health, and desirability as spouse (Yu & Shepard, 1998, 1999). In contrast, more acculturated Matsiguenka ranked the figures O.7, O.9, N.7, N.9, U.7, and U.9 in descending order for attractiveness and desirability as spouse. Yu and Shepard (1998) conclude that the Matsiguenka preference for low WHR is an artifact of "culture"—namely, Western media exposure. However, this argument fails to explain why Matsiguenka men should prefer the body shape of women from a foreign culture to that of women from their own—that is, how and why exposure to another culture interacts with the psychological design that produces WHR preferences.

Experimental stimuli must reflect local conditions. WHR of Matsiguenka women is higher than that of Western women (Yu & Shepard, 1998), yet the experimental stimuli used did not symmetrically bracket this range. The WHR considered "high" in the Matsiguenka study is the Shiwiar female average (Sugiyama, 2004a). No Shiwiar females had WHRs lower than 0.8, and the mean female WHR was 0.92. Labeling 0.9 WHR "high" under these circumstances is misleading, and using only 0.7 and 0.9 WHR (i.e., abnormally low and average) increases the probability that high body-weight preference will swamp any effects of WHR preference (Sugiyama, 1996, 2004a). Moreover, acculturated Matsiguenka are exposed to a lower range of female WHR than are unacculturated Matsiguenka. This exposure presents lower WHR in association with other cues to high female mate value in the bodies and faces of the nubile young women on beer posters and similar advertisements to which acculturated Matsiguenka are exposed. We should expect WHR assessments to be updated across the life span in response to changes in the local cue structure of WHR. Yu and Shepard's (1998) finding that more acculturated Matsiguenka are exposed to a lower range of and prefer lower relative female WHR than less acculturated Matsiguenka is consistent with the context-sensitive WHR-assessment algorithm outlined above.

When I presented the standard 12-stimuli array to Shiwiar men, I found significant effects of weight on a series of attractiveness-related measures, but no significant effects of WHR. However, when I reduced the variance in weight of line drawings presented, and compared preferences to local distribution of female and male WHR, Shiwiar men chose lower- than- locally average WHR figures as more sexually desirable, youthful, and healthy than locally high-WHR figures. When asked to pick the most sexually attractive, fertile, best mother, and wife, Shiwiar men never chose locally high-WHR figures more often than locally low-WHR figures, and when asked to pick the least desirable on these traits, locally low-WHR figures were always chosen more often than locally high-WHR figures. However, sample size was small and replication with a larger sample is necessary (Sugiyama, 2004a).

Marlowe et al. (in press) hypothesized that waist-to-buttocks ratio (WBR) was a critical feature used in female body shape attractiveness assessment. Their results show that Hadza men, who show no preference based on frontal views of WHR, do find lower WBR more attractive: Specifically, buttocks extension was found to be a variable in attractiveness assessment. Although I did not test this dimension directly, my Shiwiar informants spontaneously noted that low WHR drawings had "no buttocks"—that is, low buttocks extension—and "no" or "straight waists." Cross-cultural tests of preferences for this aspect of female morphology are warranted, but no more so than pelvic angle detection, relative pelvic width to shoulder width, and so on.

WHR does explain some of the variance in attractiveness ratings of women's bodies, both in static front, back, and side views (Grammer et al., 2002; Thornhill & Grammer, 1999; Tovée & Cornelisson, 2001; Tovée et al., 2002) and in three-dimensional rotation (Fan et al., 2004), but body shape accounts for less of the variance in attractiveness ratings than BMI. Tovée and colleagues have reported a series of studies in which subjects assess the attractiveness of women's bodies. They conclude that female WHR, and body shape generally, accounts for relatively little of the variance in female body attractiveness, perhaps, they suggest, because BMI and WHR covary, and BMI assessment is less variable than WHR depending on an individual's view (front versus side versus back). Conversely, when photos of men are assessed using the same methods, upper body shape accounts for the largest amount of variance in rated attractiveness (Maisey et al., 1999).

As noted earlier, studies based on photos of Western women over 18 (mean age 26, s.d. 8 years) present a limited range of the morphological variance to which WHR assessment is a hypothesized mate choice solution. WHR is hypothesized to distinguish pre- from postpubertal females, males from postpubertal females, pregnant from nonpregnant postpubertal females, relative parity, postpubertal females who are fertile from those suffering primary infertility, and fertile from postmenopausal women. Only the latter three issues could even potentially be tested in the Tovée and similar studies (e.g., Fan et al., 2004). In the population of women used as models, moreover, the number of women suffering primary infertility, the number of postmenopausal women, and variability in parity are all small. Determining the variance in reproductive value assessments accounted for by WHR requires subjects to compare figures encompassing the entire range of relevant stimuli: males and females of all ages and females of all levels of parity, primary infertility, and stages of pregnancy in a natural fertility population. In addition, the ecological reality of mating (and other social value) decisions seems to be better captured by choices between people, not abstract relative ratings along a Likert scale. Forced-choice methods may reveal effects of cues to social value that are obscured by having subjects rate stimuli on a scale.

Finally, the fitness effects of differences in attractiveness produced by particular reproductive value assessment adaptations targeting a specific cue can be associated with significant behavioral and fitness effects, even if the cue in question accounts for a relatively small proportion of the variance in attractiveness. Hughes and Gallup (2002) measured WHR of college men and women (none of whom were pregnant) and asked them to fill out a sexual history survey. Females with low WHR and males with WHR closest to 0.9 reported earlier age at first intercourse and more sex partners, extrapair copulations (EPC), and sex with individuals who were already in a relationship. This concurs with a study by Mikach and Bailey

(1999) finding that women with lower WHRs engage in more short-term sex than those with higher WHR. In related research that replicated and extended Hughes and Gallup (2002) to test relationships between vocal attractiveness and body morphology, the only association found between BMI and sexual behavior was that female age of first sexual intercourse was later among college women with higher BMI (Hughes et al., 2004).

Upper Body Morphology: Shoulders, Chest, and Breasts   Males and females exhibit sexual dimorphism in skeletal morphology and muscle mass as well as body fat distribution. One such feature is the circumference of the shoulders relative to that of the hips (shoulder-to-hip ratio [SHR]). Broad shoulders are associated with developmental effects of testosterone, such that men tend to have broader shoulders than women (Evans, 1972; Kasperk et al., 1997). In their sexual history study, Hughes and Gallup (2002) measured SHR as well as WHR of college men and women. Male SHR accounted for more of the variance in reported sexual behavior than did WHR. Men with high SHR reported earlier age at first intercourse, more sex partners, more EPCs, and more instances of being the extra-pair partner of a woman's EPC. Conversely, there was no association between female SHR and any of the sexual history measures. These findings bolster the claim that women find moderately broad shoulders and chests in men attractive (i.e., an inverted triangular shape of the upper torso) as long as they are not too "muscle bound" and that male shoulder width is a feature used by men in assessment of their rivals (e.g., Dijkstra & Buunk, 2001; Franzoi & Hertzog, 1987). Horvarth (1979) found shoulder width positively correlated with male attractiveness, and female ratings of color photos of male bodies show that waist-to-chest ratio (WCR) accounted for more of the variance in male body attractiveness than either WHR or BMI (see also Maisey et al., 1999). In their study of jealousy-provoking traits, Dijkstra and Buunk (2001) found that high SHR men were perceived as more attractive, and rivals with high SHR provoked greater jealousy in men than in women. But both sexes found rivals with higher SHR more physically and socially dominant.

While female SHR shows little effect on ratings of female attractiveness, breast shape and size do. Human breasts are highly sexually dimorphic, and women's breasts are large compared to closely related primate species. As such, they are likely the product of sexual selection. In natural fertility populations, breast morphology provides more powerful cues to age, parity, and pregnancy status than in nonnatural fertility populations (Symons, 1979): Budding breasts are associated with pubescence; developed, firm, high breasts are associated with nubility; engorged breasts indicate lactation; and degree of breast "sagginess" and lack of fullness tracks increasing parity and declining reproductive value. The changes before and after first pregnancy are particularly striking. Large breasts may more clearly manifest these changes, such that larger breasts could provide honest cues to reproductive value. Symons (1979) predicted that firm breasts that point slightly up and out (angle of axis) with small areola would be more attractive because they are associated with young women (i.e., high reproductive value). All else equal, larger breasts show higher levels of asymmetry, so breast size may provide honest (costly) signals to phenotypic quality (Manning et al., 1997; Møller et al., 2004). In a study presenting college men with female line drawings that varied in WHR, weight, and breast size, Singh and Young (1995) found that

slender, low-WHR figures with large breasts were judged most attractive, feminine, healthy, and desirable for both short- and long-term relationships. In their
study of attractiveness based on body and facial traits of nude female photographs, Grammer et al. (2002) found significant positive correlations between
breast size and attractiveness and negative association between areola size and
attractiveness. Principal components factor analysis for 36 traits predicted to be
associated with attractiveness showed that in a four-factor solution, there was
high positive loading of breast size and angle of axis and negative loading of areola size on the factor Grammer et al. conclude is associated with nubility. Møller
et al. (2004) looked at the relation among breast size, FA, and measures of female
attractiveness and fecundity in two populations (United States and Spain). They
found higher breast FA in women with large breasts than in women with small
breasts and negative association between breast FA and age-independent fecundity (Manning et al., 1997, 2004). However, when expected symmetry was allo-
metrically scaled to breast size, larger breast volume was associated with lower
than expected symmetry (Manning et al., 1997). Breast asymmetry appears to be
negatively associated with fitness (number of offspring) and positively associated
with later age at first reproduction (Manning et al., 1997). Manning et al. (1997)
conclude that women with higher levels of body fat have higher levels of estrogen
(which reduces immune function), producing larger breasts, but that this tends to
increase asymmetry. Only women with high phenotypic quality can produce
large symmetrical breasts, so large symmetrical breasts provide honest (costly)
signals of high phenotypic quality.

CONCLUSIONS

My goal in presenting an outline of social value in human life history perspective
was to present the foundation on which physical (and nonphysical) attractiveness
across different domains of social value can most usefully be based and from
which those conducting research on physical attractiveness could generate more
specific adaptationist hypotheses and empirical tests. This should be axiomatic:
Understanding of the mating preferences, differential parental solicitude, kin-
based cooperation, and coalitional dynamics of all other species except *Homo sapiens sapiens* is based on advances in evolutionary life history theory, particularly
those developed over the past 40 years. Adaptationist hypotheses about male and
female mate value assessment explicitly start with consideration of this aspect of
social value in evolutionary life history perspective (e.g., Buss, 1989; Buss &
Schmitt, 1993; Gangestad & Thornhill, 1997a; Grammer et al., 2002; Manning,
1997; Møller et al., 2004; Sugiyama, 2004a; Symons, 1979, 1995; Thornill & Gangestad, 1994, 1999; Thornhill & Grammer, 1999), just as hypotheses about offspring
phenotypic condition assessment explicitly start from parental investment theory
(e.g., Apicella & Marlowe, 2004; Daly & Wilson, 1988; DeBruine, 2004; Hrdy, 1999,
2002; Mann, 1992; Platek et al., 2002, 2003, 2004; Trivers, 1972, 1974).

The study of physical attractiveness has gained significantly in theoretical and
methodological sophistication over the past quarter century. Research on sexual
attractiveness has progressed most (arguably) because theoretical development on
mate choice in biology has a long history and because the adaptationist approach
provided a clear, cross-species, theoretical basis for its investigation in humans.
The adaptationist approach explicitly links theory and evidence that are normally

disciplinarily partitioned (e.g., by departments or fields of biology, anthropology, psychology), which gives it a powerful integrated dimension. Symons's *The Evolution of Human Sexuality* (1979) is a benchmark in this regard: Since its publication, an explicitly adaptationist approach to sexual attractiveness has increasingly informed research on human attractiveness in psychology. Further development of theory concerning the trade-offs involved in alternate sexual strategies in humans (e.g., Buss & Schmitt, 1993) has focused attention on context-sensitive mate selection for specific cues of reproductive value and phenotypic quality. For example, research on potential fitness trade-offs between female short-term and extra-pair mating strategies on the one hand and long-term mating strategies on the other led to the prediction and finding that women's mate preferences shift in the importance given to "good genes" traits and "good father" traits during the fertile and nonfertile phases of the ovulatory cycle (e.g., Franklin & Johnston, 2000; Johnston et al., 2001; Penton-Voak & Perrett, 2000). Prior to these predictions, research on female assessment of male attractiveness yielded contradictory results: Sometimes women preferred masculine and sometimes feminine faces. From now on, all research on women's attractiveness preferences must include data on ovulatory phase or else results will be confounded by these changes in preference. Similarly, Gangestad has shown individual differences in general mating strategies—what he calls *sociosexual orientation*. People with more "closed" sociosexual orientation tend to seek long-term mateships, have fewer mates, and begin having sex later in relationships, while those who have more "open" orientations show opposite tendencies. These tendencies could be mediated by hormonal effects during embryonic development and/or in "strategic" response to environmental effects during juvenile development (e.g., Belsky et al., 1991; Gangestad, 1993). Because mate choice preferences change along the short- to long-term strategy continuum, all future research should include a soci-sexual orientation measure, or else results from open and closed orientation subjects may wash out the results. In sum, we have identified numerous adaptive problems associated with mate-value assessment, which have been used to generate hypotheses regarding the physical cues targeted by mate-value assessment mechanisms. Tests of these hypotheses have yielded a rich data base for further exploration. Researchers are beginning to address how much of the variance in sexual attractiveness each of these cues accounts for, as well as the context-sensitive design of the mechanisms that take these cues as input. A next stage of research would profit from including a more evolutionarily relevant range of variation in experimental stimuli and regularly including subject data on known sources of systematic variability in mating preferences (e.g., fertility, sociosexual orientation, own attractiveness, short- versus long-term mateship).

Research into the relationship between attractiveness and cooperative, kin, and coalitional social value has progressed slowly, partly because an explicitly life history evolutionary approach has not been employed. Cunningham, Barbee, and Pilhower (2002) present a *multiple fitness model* of attractiveness assessment, based on the observation that different physical traits may signal different qualities, but they do not explicitly organize their model in terms of different domains of human sociality in evolutionary life history perspective, nor do they ground their predictions in the relevant data from human evolutionary ecology. Keating (2002) and others note that social and physical dominance are important features in attractiveness assessment that can be assessed via physical cues, but they haven't grounded this observation in the evolutionarily relevant aspects of dominance be-havior. Zebrowski and Rhodes (2002) suggest that because there are many types of attractiveness, measurement instruments should distinguish among them, yet most studies rely on "global 'attractiveness' rating scales" (p. 264).

In this chapter, I have tried to indicate what is known about the evolution of human life history as it relates to social value, in the hope that more psycholo-gists will be stimulated to read the primary anthropological literature on this topic. The value of this approach to the study of attractiveness is highlighted by the questions that no study has asked, yet that seem obvious to evolutionary an-thropologists interested in parsing social relations in small-scale, egalitarian so-cieties (e.g., Patton, 2000; Sugiyama, 1999; Sugiyama & Scalise Sugiyama, 2003). Distal concepts such as physical cues to physical and social dominance have been investigated, but no study of attractiveness has asked whom subjects would rather be attacked by, attack, fight, go to war with, seek revenge against, or have on their side in a fight. No study has asked whom subjects would rather have seeking vengeance against them or whom they would rather have defend them against attackers. Although a few studies have asked whom subjects would rather have as friend or roommate and a number have investigated the hiring, salary, and other advantages of physical attractiveness, no one has yet asked with whom subjects would most like to share food or who would be most likely to share food with the subject. No study has asked subjects whom they would rather have take care of their children, aid them in childbirth or in time of temporary disability, or establish trade relations with. And I have yet to find a study asking parents whom they would prefer their daughters or sons to have as friends, date, marry, have sex with, and so on based on physical appearance.

Complex information-processing adaptations are often expected to use infor-mational cues from the environment to generate different psychological and be-havioral outputs in response to different conditions. Therefore, hypotheses concerning such adaptations must delineate specific psychological properties (or their by-products) that process local social and environmental cues to generate the intra- and intercultural similarities and differences found in attractiveness standards for different domains of evolutionarily relevant social value. Among the contextual variables that social value assessment adaptations are expected to include in their calculations are assessor's and assessee's sex, developmental stage, health, reproductive and mating status, aggressive formidability, alterna-tive social options, and social value in different domains, which should influence the social strategies being deployed by the individual. Even though the underly-ing functional design of attractiveness-assessment adaptations is expected to be universal, we should expect to see strategic variation in its behavioral expression at the population, group, and individual levels.

Human physical attractiveness assessment is generated by adaptations func-tioning to evaluate evolutionarily relevant cues to human social value across mul-tiple domains of interaction. Evolutionary human life history theory is instrumental in generating predictions about these domains and their associated cues. Unfortunately, the field of psychology continues to pay little attention to our best sources of data concerning the life history trade-offs that formed the se-lective parameters in which the adaptations comprising our social adaptations evolved and the likely range of variability across which they were selected to function: the ethnographic, archaeological, and paleo-anthropological record of natural fertility, small-scale societies. With relatively few exceptions (e.g., Gray & Marlow, 2004; Jones & Hill, 1993; Sugiyama, 2004a; Wetsman & Marlowe, 1999; Yu & Shepard, 1999), direct tests of adaptationist hypotheses concerning physical attractiveness have not been conducted in small-scale, natural fertility populations, and anthropologists either conducted or collaborated on all of these studies. Conversely, the vast majority of anthropologists have not been trained to think about psychological processes in a way that would allow them to produce reasonable procedural hypotheses about how psychological adaptations might plausibly function (in a procedural cognitive sense). Of those who have, human behavioral ecologists have the scientific, empirical, and adaptationist expertise (see Hill & Hurtado, 1996; Smith et al., 2001) that make them natural research allies for psychologists (e.g., Barrett et al., 2004; Jones & Hill, 1993; Sugiyama, Tooby, & Cosmides, 2002; Wetsman & Marlowe, 1999). An apparent impediment to this kind of collaboration seems to be a common misperception that an evolutionary psychological approach predicts universality at the level of psychological or behavioral output instead of at the level of the functional organization of the information-processing system.

For example, in their interpretation of the observed cross-cultural variation in female height, RS, and marriage patterns, Sear et al. (2004) contrast their interpretation of the evolutionary psychology argument that complex cognitive adaptations will usually be universally distributed in a species with their (behavioral ecological) approach, stating:

> We believe that a much more satisfactory approach to the study of human behavior is to take social and ecological conditions into account, and to test evolutionary hypotheses across a variety of different cultures.... Given ... the ... wide range of ecological conditions that humans are able to live in, we think that human variation is, in any case, far more interesting to research than are human universals. (Sear et al., 2004, p. 12)

It is indeed true that more cross-cultural research is needed to test hypotheses about evolved mental function, and it is also true that the hypotheses about psychological design must include consideration of the ancestral range of variability in socioecological environments that constitute selection pressures and the cue structures with which the adaptations function to produce locally contingent behavioral expression (e.g., Sugiyama, 1996, 2004a; Sugiyama et al., 2002; Tooby & Cosmides, 1989, 1992). However, the larger message of Sear et al. (2004) mischaracterizes the evolutionary psychology approach, leading to what appears to be wholesale dismissal of the programme. To reiterate, evolutionary psychology predicts or expects the following: (1) complex information processing adaptations of the mind will usually be universally distributed in the species, (2) these adaptations will take local environmental information as input such that their outputs will differ depending on specific features of local conditions (what behavioral ecologists refer to as "reaction norms"), and (3) adequately characterized cognitive adaptations will specify how specific kinds of local environmental information are used by the adaptation in question to produce the variability in behavior that we observe (e.g., Sugiyama, 2004a; Tooby & Cosmides, 1989, 1992). My discussion of the design features necessary in a WHR-like assessment adaptation provides a case in point, as does research on menstrual shift in mating preferences and variation in weight preferences. Cross-cultural research is critical to this enterprise (e.g., Buss, 1989; Jones & Hill, 1993; Marlowe & Wetsman, 2001; Sugiyama, 2004a; Sugiyama et al., 2002; Tooby & Cosmides, 1989, 1992). Studying variability without considering it in terms of underlying information-processing regularities (and their decision-making outcomes) makes understanding of the generation of cross-cultural variation impossible. What is needed, then, is for psychologists to collaborate in cross-cultural research with evolutionary anthropologists and, conversely, for evolutionary anthropologists to more generally recognize that evolutionary psychological hypotheses *should often* predict context-dependent variation (e.g., Sugiyama, 2004a; Sugiyama et al., 2002; Tooby & Cosmides, 1992) just as behavioral ecological models do (e.g., Hill & Hurtado, 1996; Smith et al., 2002). Anthropologists can advance psychologists' appreciation of variability in local cues and behavioral outputs; in turn, psychologists can design their hypotheses to account for this variability and design their studies to include an ecologically relevant range of stimuli. I can't think of any aspect of human attractiveness research, evolutionary psychology, or psychology more generally, that wouldn't benefit from this approach. Because all normal conspecifics are expected to share complex adaptations or a facultative developmental programs that builds them, for evolutionary psychologists, this cross-cultural testing is a requisite component of our research program.

REFERENCES

Alley, T. (1983). Growth-produced changes in body shape and size as determinants of perceived age and adult caregiving. *Child Development, 54,* 241–248.

Alley, T., & Cunningham, M. R. (1991). Averaged faces are attractive, but very attractive faces are not average. *Psychological Science, 2,* 123–125.

Alvard, M. (2004). Carcass ownership and meat distribution by big-game cooperative hunters. In M. Alvard (Ed.), *Socioeconomic aspects of human behavioral ecology* (Vol. 23, pp. 99–131). Greenwich, CT: Elsevier.

Anderson, J. L., Crawford, C. B., Nadeau, J., & Lindberg, T. (1992). Was the Duchess of Windsor right? A cross-cultural review of the socioecology of ideals of female body shape. *Ethology and Sociobiology, 13,* 197–277.

Apicella, C. L., & Marlowe, F. W. (2004). Perceived mate fidelity and paternal resemblance predict men's investment in children. *Evolution and Human Behavior, 25,* 371–378.

Appleton, J. (1975). *The experience of landscape.* New York: Wiley.

Appleton, J. (1984). Prospects and refuges revisited. *Landscape Journal, 3,* 91–103.

Baker, R. R. (1997). Copulation, masturbation and infidelity: State-of-the-art. In A. Schmitt, K. Atzwanger, K. Grammer, & K. Schafer (Eds.), *New aspects of human ethology* (pp. 163–188). New York: Plenum Press.

Baker, R. R., & Bellis, M. A. (1995). *Human sperm competition: Copulation, masturbation and infidelity.* London: Chapman and Hall.

Bardin, C. W., & Catterall, J. F. (1981). Testosterone: A major determinant of extragenital sexual dimorphism. *Science, 211*(4488), 1285–1294.

Beckerman, S., & Valentine, P. (2002). *Cultures of multiple fathers: The theory and practice of partible paternity in lowland South America.* Gainesville: University of Florida Press.

Bellis, M. A., & Baker, R. R. (1990). Do females promote sperm competition? Data for humans. *Animal Behavior, 40,* 997–999.

Belsky, J. (1997). Attachment, mating, and parenting: An evolutionary interpretation. *Human Nature, 8*(4), 361–381.

Belsky, J., Steinberg, L., & Draper, P. (1991). Childhood experience, interpersonal development, and reproductive strategy: An evolutionary theory of socialization. *Child Development, 62,* 647–670.

Bentley, G. R., Goldberg, T., & Jasienska, G. (1993). The fertility of agricultural and nonagricultural traditional societies. *Population studies: A journal of demography, 47*(2), 269–281.

Bentley, G. R., Harrigan, A. M., & Ellison, P. T. (1998). Dietary composition and ovarian function among Lese horticulturalist women of the Ituri Forest, Democratic Republic of Congo. *European Journal of Clinical Nutrition, 52,* 261–270.

Betzig, L., Borgerhoff Mulder, M., & Turke, P. (Eds.). (1988). *Human reproductive behavior: A Darwinian perspective.* Cambridge, England: Cambridge University Press.

Bielicki, T., & Szklarska, A. (1999). Secular trends in stature in Poland: National and social class-specific. *Annals of Human Biology, 26,* 251–258.

Bjorntorp, P. (1988). The association between obesity, adipose tissue distribution and disease. *Acta Medica Scandinavica Supplement, 723,* 121–134.

Blurton Jones, N. G., Hawkes, K., & Draper, P. (1994). Difference between Hadza and !Kung children's foraging: Original affluence or practical reason. In E. S. Burch (Ed.), *Key issues in hunter-gatherer research* (pp. 189–215). Oxford, England: Berg.

Blurton Jones, N. G., Hawkes, K., & O'Connell, J. F. (1997). Why do Hadza children forage. In N. L. Segal, G. E. Weisfeld, & C. C. Weisfeld (Eds.), *Uniting psychology and biology: Integrative perspectives on human development* (pp. 279–313). Washington, DC: American Psychological Association.

Bogin, B. (1999). *Patterns of human growth.* Cambridge, England: Cambridge University Press.

Bronstad, P., & Singh, D. (1999, June). *Why did Tassinary and Hansen fail to replicate the relationship between WHR and female attractiveness?* Paper presented at the Annual meeting of the Human Behavior and Evolution Society, Salt Lake City, UT.

Brown, D. E. (1991). *Human universals.* New York: McGraw-Hill.

Brown, P. J., & Konner, M. (1987). An anthropological perspective on obesity. *Annals of the New York Academy of Sciences, 499,* 29–46.

Burley, N. (1986). Comparison of the band colour preferences of two estrildid finches. *Animal Behavior, 34,* 1732–1741.

Burley, N., Krantzberg, G., & Radman, P. (1982). Influences of colour-banding on the conspecific preferences of zebra finches. *Animal Behavior, 30,* 444–455.

Buss, D. M. (1987). Sex differences in human mate selection criteria: An evolutionary perspective. In C. Crawford, M. Smith, & D. Krebs (Eds.), *Sociobiology and psychology: Ideas, issues, and applications* (pp. 335–351). Hillsdale, NJ: Erlbaum.

Buss, D. M. (1989). Sex differences in human mate preferences: Evolutionary hypotheses tested in 37 cultures. *Behavioral and Brain Sciences, 12,* 1–49.

Buss, D. M. (1992). Mate preference mechanisms: Consequences for partner choice and intrasexual competition. In J. Barkow, L. Cosmides, & J. Tooby (Eds.), *The adapted mind: Evolutionary psychology and the generation of culture* (pp. 556–579). New York: Oxford University Press.

Buss, D. M. (1994). *The evolution of desire: Strategies of human mating.* New York: Basic Books.

Buss, D. M. (2000). *The dangerous passion: Why jealousy is as necessary as love and sex.* New York: Free Press.

Buss, D. M., Larsen, R. J., Westen, D., & Semmelroth, J. (1992). Sex differences in jealousy: Evolution, physiology, and psychology. *Psychological Science, 3,* 251–255.

Buss, D. M., & Schmitt, D. (1993). Sexual strategies theory: An evolutionary perspective on human mating. *Psychological Review, 100,* 204–232.

Buss, D. M., Shackelford, T. K., Cloe, J., Buunk, B. P., & Dijkstra, P. (2000). Distress about mating rivals. *Personal Relationships, 7,* 235–243.

Cameron, C., Oskamp, S., & Sparks, W. (1977). Courtship American style. *Family Coordinator, 26,* 27–30.

Chagnon, N. A. (1975). Genealogy, solidarity and relatedness: Limits to local group size and patterns of fissioning in an expanding population. *Yearbook of Physical Anthropology, 19,* 95–110.

Chagnon, N. A. (1979). Mate competition, favoring close kin, and village fissioning among the Yanomamö Indians. In N. A. Chagnon & W. Irons (Eds.), *Evolutionary biology and human social behavior* (pp. 86–131). North Scituate, MA: Duxbury Press.

Chagnon, N. A. (1988). Life histories, blood revenge, and warfare in a tribal population. *Science, 139,* 985–992.

Chagnon, N. A. (1997). *Yanomamö* (5th ed.). New York: Harcourt Brace.

Charnov, E. L. (1993). *Life history invariants: Some explanations of symmetry in evolutionary ecology.* Oxford, England: Oxford University Press.

Charnov, E. L., & Schaffer, W. M. (1973). Life-history consequences of natural selection: Cole's result revisited. *American Naturalist, 107,* 791–793.

Chick, G., & Loy, J. W. (2001). Making men of them: Male socialization for warfare and combative sports. *World Cultures, 12*(1), 2–17.

Chisholm, J. S. (1993). Death, hope, and sex: Life-history theory and the development of reproductive strategies. *Current Anthropology, 34*(1), 1–24.

Clutton-Brock, T. H. (1991). *The evolution of parental care*. Princeton: Princeton University Press.

Cunningham, M. R., Barbee, A. P., & Pike, C. L. (1991). What do women want? Facialmetric assessment of multiple motives in the perception of male facial physical attractiveness. *Journal of Personality and Social Psychology, 59*, 61–72.

Cunningham, M. R., Barbee, A. P., & Pilhower, C. L. (2002). Dimensions of facial physical attractiveness: The intersection of biology and culture. In G. Rhodes & L. A. Zebrowitz (Eds.), *Facial attractiveness: Evolutionary, cognitive, and social perspectives* (pp. 193–238). Westport, CT: Ablex.

Cunningham, M. R., Druen, P. B., & Barbee, A. P. (1997). Angels, mentors, and friends: Trade-offs among evolutionary, social, and individual variables in physical appearance. In J. A. Simpson & D. T. Kenrick (Eds.), *Evolutionary social psychology* (pp. 109–140). Hove, England: Erlbaum.

Dabbs, J. M., Jr., & Dabbs, M. G. (2000). *Heroes, rogues and lovers: Testosterone and behavior*. New York: McGraw-Hill.

Daly, M., & Wilson, M. (1984). A sociobiological analysis of human infanticide. In G. Hausfater & S. B. Hrdy (Eds.), *Infanticide: Comparative and evolutionary perspectives* (pp. 487–502). New York: Aldine.

Daly, M., & Wilson, M. (1987). *Sex evolution and behavior*. New York: Aldine.

Daly, M., & Wilson, M. (1988). *Homicide*. New York: Aldine.

Darwin, C. (1872). *The descent of man and selection in relation to sex*. London: John Murray.

DeBruine, L. M. (2004). Resemblance to self increases the appeal of child faces to both men and women. *Evolution and Human Behavior, 25*, 142–154.

Descola, P. (1998). *Spears of twilight: Life and death in the Amazon Jungle*. New York: New Press.

Dewey, K. G. (1997). Energy and protein requirements during lactation. *Annual Review of Nutrition, 17*, 19–36.

Dijkstra, P., & Buunk, B. P. (2001). Sex differences in the jealousy-evoking nature of a rival's body build. *Evolution and Human Behavior, 22*, 335–341.

Dion, K. (2002). Cultural perspectives on facial attractiveness. In G. Rhodes & L. A. Zebrowitz (Eds.), *Facial attractiveness: Evolutionary, cognitive, and social perspectives* (pp. 239–259). Westport, CT: Ablex.

Draper, P., & Harpending, H. (1982). Father absence and reproductive strategy: An evolutionary perspective. *Journal of Anthropological Research, 38*, 255–273.

Eaton, S. B., Shostak, M., & Konner, M. (1988). *The Paleolithic prescription: A program of diet and exercise and a design for living*. New York: Harper & Row.

Ellis, B. (1992). The evolution of sexual attraction: Evaluative mechanisms in women. In J. Barkow, L. Cosmides, & J. Tooby (Eds.), *The adapted mind: Evolutionary psychology and the generation of culture* (pp. 267–288). New York: Oxford University Press.

Ellison, P. T. (2001a). *On fertile ground*. Cambridge, MA: Harvard University Press.

Ellison, P. T. (Ed.). (2001b). *Reproductive ecology and human evolution*. New York: Aldine de Gruyter.

Ellison, P. T. (2003). Energetics and reproductive effort. *American Journal of Human Biology, 15*, 342–351.

Ellison, P. T., Painter-Brick, C., Lipson, S. F., & O'Rourke, M. T. (1993). The ecological context of human ovarian function. *Human Reproduction, 8*, 2248–2258.

Ember, C. R., & Ember, M. (1997). Violence in the ethnographic record: Results of cross-cultural research on war and aggression. In D. L. Martin & D. W. Frayer (Eds.), *Troubled times: Violence and warfare in the past* (pp. 1–20). Amsterdam, the Netherlands: Gordon and Breach.

Etcoff, N. (1999). *Survival of the prettiest*. New York: Doubleday.

Evans, R. B. (1972). Physical and biochemical characteristics of homosexual men. *Journal of Consulting and Clinical Psychology, 39*(1), 140–147.

Fan, J., Liu, F., Wu, J., & Dai, W. (2004). Visual perception of female physical attractiveness. *Proceedings of the Royal Society of London. Series B, Biological Sciences, 271*, 347–352.

Farkas, L. G., & Cheung, G. (1981). Facial asymmetry in healthy North American caucasians: An anthropometric study. *Angle Orthodontics, 51*, 70–77.

Faurie, C., Pontier, D., & Raymond, M. (2004). Student athletes claim to have more sexual partners than other students. *Evolution and Human Behavior, 25*, 1–8.

Feingold, A. (1982). Do taller men have prettier girlfriends? *Psychology Reports, 50*, 810.

Fink, B., Grammer, K., & Thornhill, R. (2001). Human (*Homo sapiens*) facial attractiveness in relation to skin texture and color. *Journal of Comparative Psychology, 115*, 92–99.

Fisher, H. E. (1992). *Anatomy of love: The natural history of monogamy, adultery and divorce*. New York: Norton.

Fisher, R. A. (1958). *The genetical theory of natural selection.* New York: Dover.

Flinn, M., Geary, D. C., & Ward, C. V. (2005). Ecological dominance, social competition, and coalitionary arms races: Why humans evolved extraordinary intelligence. *Evolution and Human Behavior, 26,* 10–46.

Ford, C. S., & Beach, F. A. (1951). *Patterns of sexual behavior.* New York: Harper.

Franklin, M., & Johnston, V. (2000, June). *Hormone markers and beauty.* Paper presented at meeting of the Human Behavior and Evolution Society, Amherst, MA.

Franzoi, S. L., & Hertzog, M. E. (1987). Judging physical attractiveness: What body aspects do we use? *Personality and Social Psychology Bulletin, 13,* 19–33.

Frayser, S. (1985). *Varieties of sexual experience: An anthropological perspective on human sexuality.* New Haven, CT: HRAF Press.

Frieze, I. H., Olson, J. E., & Good, D. C. (1990). Perceived and actual discrimination in the salaries of male and female managers. *Journal of Applied Social Psychology, 20,* 46–67.

Frieze, I. H., Olson, J. E., & Russell, J. (1991). Attractiveness and income for men and women in management. *Journal of Applied Social Psychology, 21,* 1039–1057.

Frisch, R. E. (1990). Body fat, menarche, fitness and fertility. In R. E. Frisch (Ed.), *Adipose tissue and reproduction* (pp. 1–26). Basel, Switzerland: Karger.

Frisch, R. E., & McArthur, J. W. (1974). Menstrual cycles: Fatness as a determinant of minimum weight necessary for their maintenance and onset. *Science, 185,* 554–556.

Fuller, R. C., & Houle, D. (2003). Inheritance of developmental instability. In M. Polak (Ed.), *Developmental instability: Causes and consequences* (pp. 157–183). New York: Oxford University Press.

Furnham, A., & Alibhai, N. (1983). Cross-cultural differences in the perception of female body shapes. *Psychological Medicine, 13,* 829–837.

Furnham, A., & Baguma, P. (1994). Cross-cultural differences in the evaluation of male and female body shapes. *International Journal of Eating Disorders, 15,* 81–89.

Furnham, A., & Radley, S. (1989). Sex differences in the perception of male and female body shapes. *Personality and Individual Differences, 10,* 653–662.

Furnham, A., Tan, T., & McManus, C. (1997). Waist-to-hip ratio and preferences for body shape: A replication and extension. *Personality and Individual Differences, 22,* 540–549.

Galton, F. (1879). Composite portraits, made by combining those of many different persons in a single resultant figure. *Journal of the Anthropological Institute, 8,* 132–144.

Gangestad, S. W. (1993). Sexual selection and physical attractiveness: Implications for mating dynamics. *Human Nature, 4,* 205–236.

Gangestad, S. W., & Buss, D. M. (1993). Pathogen prevalence and human mate preferences. *Ethology and Sociobiology, 14,* 89–96.

Gangestad, S. W., & Simpson, J. A. (2000). The evolution of human mating: The role of trade-offs and strategic pluralism. *Behavior and Brain Sciences, 23,* 573–644.

Gangestad, S. W., & Thornhill, R. (1997a). The evolutionary psychology of extra-pair sex: The role of fluctuating asymmetry. *Evolution and Human Behavior, 18,* 69–88.

Gangestad, S. W., & Thornhill, R. (1997b). Human sexual selection and developmental stability. In J. A. Simpson & D. T. Kenrick (Eds.), *Evolutionary social psychology* (pp. 169–195). Hillsdale, NJ: Erlbaum.

Gangestad, S. W., & Thornhill, R. (1998). Menstrual cycle variation in women's preference for the scent of symmetrical men. *Proceedings of the Royal Society of London. Series B, Biological Sciences, 265,* 927–933.

Gangestad, S. W., & Thornhill, R. (1999). Individual differences in developmental precision and fluctuating asymmetry: A model and its implications. *Journal of Evolutionary Biology, 12,* 402–416.

Gangestad, S. W., & Thornhill, R. (2003). Fluctuating asymmetry, developmental instability, and fitness: Toward model-based interpretation. In M. Polak (Ed.), *Developmental instability: Causes and consequences* (pp. 62–80). New York: Oxford University Press.

Gangestad, S. W., Thornhill, R., & Yeo, R. A. (1994). Facial attractiveness, developmental stability, and fluctuating asymmetry. *Ethology and Sociobiology, 15,* 73–85.

Gelles, R. J., & Lancaster, J. B. (1987). *Child abuse and neglect: Biosocial dimensions.* New York: Aldine de Gruyter.

Gillis, J. S., & Avis, W. E. (1980). The male-taller norm in mate selection. *Personality and Social Psychology Bulletin, 6,* 396–401.

Grammer, K., & Thornhill, R. (1994). Human (*Homo sapiens*) facial attractiveness and sexual selection: The role of symmetry and averageness. *Journal of Comparative Psychology, 108,* 233–242.

Grammer, K., Fink, B., Thornhill, R. R., Juette, A., & Runzal, G. (2002). Female faces and bodies: N-dimensional feature space and attractiveness. In G. Rhodes & L. A. Zebrowitz (Eds.), *Facial attractiveness: Evolutionary, cognitive and social perspectives* (pp. 91–126). Westport, CT: Greenwood.

Gray, P., & Marlowe, F. (2002). Fluctuating asymmetry of a foraging population: The Hadza of Tanzania. *Annals of Human Biology, 29*(5), 495–501.

Greiling, H., & Buss, D. M. (2000). Women's sexual strategies: The hidden dimension of extra pair mating. *Personality and Individual Differences, 28,* 929–963.

Gunnell, D., Smith, G., Ness, A., & Frankel, S. (2000). The effects of dietary supplementation on growth and adulty mortality: A re-analysis and follow-up of a pre-war study. *Public Health, 114,* 109–116.

Gurven, M., Allen-Arave, W., Hill, K., & Hurtado, A. M. (2000). It's a wonderful life: Signaling generosity among the Ache of Paraguay. *Evolution and Human Behavior, 21*(4), 263–282.

Hagen, E., Hames, R., Craig, N. M., Lauer, M. T., & Price, M. E. (2001). Parental investment and child health in a Yanomamö village suffering short-term food stress. *Journal of Biosocial Science, 33,* 503–528.

Hamilton, W. D. (1964). The genetical evolution of social behaviour, I, II. *Journal of Theoretical Biology, 7*(1/16), 17–52.

Hamilton, W. D., & Zuk, M. (1982). Heritable true fitness and bright birds: A role for parasites? *Science, 218,* 384–387.

Hawkes, K., O'Connell, J. F., & Blurton Jones, N. G. (1997). Hadza women's time allocation, offspring provisioning, and the evolution of long post-menopausal lifespans. *Current Anthropology, 38,* 551–557.

Hawkes, K., O'Connell, J. F., Blurton Jones, N. G., Alvarez, H., & Charnov, E. L. (1998). Grandmothering, menopause, and the evolution of human life histories. *Proceedings of the National Academy of Sciences, 95,* 1336–1339.

Hawkes, K., O'Connell, J. F., Blurton Jones, N. G., Alvarez, H., & Charnov, E. L. (2000). The grandmother hypothesis and human evolution. In L. Cronk, N. A. Chagnon, & W. Irons (Eds.), *Human behavior and adaptation: An anthropological perspective* (pp. 371–395). New York: Aldine.

Hensley, W. E. (1994). Height as a basis for interpersonal attraction. *Adolescence, 29,* 469–474.

Hensley, W. E., & Cooper, R. (1987). Height and occupational success: A review and critique. *Psychology Reports, 60,* 843–849.

Henss, R. (1995). Waist-to-hip ratio and attractiveness: Replication and extension. *Personality and Individual Differences, 19,* 479–488.

Hess, N. H., & Hagen, E. H. (2002). Informational warfare. *CogPrints.*

Hewlett, B. S. (Ed.). (1992). *Father-child relations: Cultural and biosocial contexts.* New York: Aldine.

Hildebrandt, K. A., & Fitzgerald, H. E. (1983). The infant's physical attractiveness: Its effect on bonding and attachment. *Infant Mental Health Journal, 4,* 3–12.

Hill, K. (2002). Altruistic cooperation during foraging by the Ache, and the evolved human predispostion to cooperate. *Human Nature, 13,* 105–128.

Hill, K., Boesch, C., Goodall, J., Pusey, A., Williams, J., & Wrangham, R. (2001). Mortality rates among wild chimpanzees. *Journal of Human Evolution, 40,* 437–450.

Hill, K., & Hurtado, A. M. (1996). *Ache life history: The ecology and demography of a foraging people.* New York: Aldine de Gruyter.

Hill, K., & Kaplan, H. (1999). Life history traits in humans: Theory and empirical studies. *Annual Review of Anthropology, 28,* 397–430.

Hillson, S. (1996). *Dental anthropology.* Cambridge, England: Cambridge University Press.

Hinsz, V. B., Matz, D. C., & Patience, R. A. (2001). Does women's hair signal reproductive potential? *Journal of Experimental Social Psychology, 37,* 166–172.

Horvarth, T. (1979). Correlates of physical beauty in men and women. *Social Behavior and Personality, 7,* 145–151.

Howell, N. (1979). *Demography of the Dobe Kung.* New York: Academic.

Hrdy, S. B. (1992). Fitness tradeoffs in the history and evolution of delegated mothering with special reference to wet-nursing, abandonment, and infanticide. *Ethology and Sociobiology, 13*(5–6), 409–442.

Hrdy, S. B. (1999). *Mother nature: A history of mothers, infants and natural selection.* New York: Pantheon.

Hrdy, S. B. (2000). The optimal number of fathers: Evolution, demography, and history in the shaping of female mate preferences. *Annals of the New York Academy of Sciences, 907,* 75–96.

Hrdy, S. B. (2002). *Cooperative breeding: An evolutionary and comparative perspective.* CHAGS9, Edinburgh, Scotland.

Hughes, S. M., Dispenza, F., & Gallup, G. G. (2004). Ratings of voice attractiveness predict sexual behavior and body configuration. *Evolution and Human Behavior, 25,* 295–304.

Hughes, S. M., & Gallup, G. G. (2002). Sex differences in morphological predictors of sexual behavior. *Evolution and Human Behavior, 24*(3), 173–178.

Hume, D. K., & Montgomerie, R. (2001). Facial attractiveness signals different aspects of "quality" in women and men. *Evolution and Human Behavior, 22*(2), 93–112.

Jackson, L. A. (1992). *Physical appearance and gender: Sociobiological and sociocultural perspective.* Albany: State University of New York Press.

Jasienska, G., & Ellison, P. T. (1998). Physical work causes suppression of ovarian function in women. *Proceedings of the Royal Society of London. Series B, Biological Sciences, 265,* 1847–1851.

Johnston, V. S., & Franklin, M. (1993). Is beauty in the eye of the beholder? *Ethology and Sociobiology, 14,* 183–199.

Johnston, V. S., Hagel, R., Franklin, M., Fink, B., & Grammer, K. (2001). Male facial attractiveness: Evidence for hormone mediated adaptive design. *Evolution and Human Behavior, 22,* 251–267.

Jones, B. C., Little, A. C., Feinberg, D. R., Penton-Voak, I. S., Tiddeman, B. P., & Perrett, D. I. (2004). The relationship between shape symmetry and perceived skin condition in male facial attractiveness. *Evolution and Human Behavior, 25,* 24–30.

Jones, B. C., Little, A. C., Penton-Voak, I. S., Tiddeman, B. P., Burt, D. M., & Perrett, D. I. (2001). Facial symmetry and judgements of apparent health: Support for a "good genes" explanation of the attractiveness-symmetry relationship. *Evolution and Human Behavior, 22,* 417–429.

Jones, D. (1995). Sexual selection, physical attractiveness, and facial neotony. *Current Anthropology, 5,* 723–748.

Jones, D. (2000). Group nepotism and human kinship. *Current Anthropology, 41*(5), 779–810.

Jones, D., & Hill, K. (1993). Criteria of facial attractiveness in five populations. *Human Nature, 4*(3), 271–296.

Jones, P. R. M., Hunt, M. J., Brown, T. P., & Norgan, N. G. (1986). Waist-hip circumference ratio and its relation to age and overweight in British men. *Clinical Nutrition, 40,* 239–247.

Jousilahti, P., Tuomilehto, J., Vartiainen, E., Eriksson, J., & Puska, P. (2000). Relation of adult height to cause-specific and total mortality: A prospective follow-up study of 31,199 middle-aged men and women in Finland. *American Journal of Epidemiology, 151,* 1112–1120.

Kaplan, H., Hill, K., Lancaster, J. J., & Hurtado, A. M. (2000). A theory of human life history evolution: Diet, intelligence, and longevity. *Evolutionary Anthropology, 9,* 156–185.

Kaplan, S. (1992). Environmental preference in a knowledge-seeking, knowledge-using organism. In J. Barkow, L. Cosmides, & J. Tooby (Eds.), *The adapted mind: Evolutionary psychology and the generation of culture* (pp. 581–600). New York: Oxford University Press.

Kasperk, C., Helmboldt, A., Borcsok, I., Heuthe, S., Cloos, O., Niethard, F., et al. (1997). Skeletal site-dependent expression of the androgen receptor in human osteblastic cell populations. *Calcified Tissue International, 61,* 464–473.

Keating, C. F. (2002). Charismatic faces: Social status cues put face appeal in context. In G. Rhodes & L. A. Zebrowitz (Eds.), *Facial attractiveness: Evolutionary, cognitive, and social perspectives* (pp. 153–192). Westport, CT: Ablex.

Keeley, L. H. (1996). *War before civilization.* New York: Oxford University Press.

Kelly, D. W. (2001). Why are some people bitten more than others? *Trends in Parasitology, 17,* 578–581.

Kelly, R. L. (1995). *The foraging spectrum: Diversity in hunter-gatherer lifeways.* Washington, DC: Smithsonian Institution Press.

Keyes, R. (1980). *The height of your life.* Boston: Little, Brown.

Kirchengast, S., Hartmann, B., Schweppe, K., & Husslein, P. (1998). Impact of maternal body build characteristics on newborn size in two different European populations. *Human Biology, 70,* 761–774.

Knols, B. G. J., De Jong, R., & Takken, W. (1995). Differential attractiveness of isolated humans to mosquitoes in Tanzania. *Transactions of the Royal Society of Tropical Medicine, 89,* 604–606.

Konner, M. J., & Worthman, C. (1980). Nursing frequency, gonadal function, and birth spacing among !Kung hunter-gatherers. *Science, 207,* 788–791.

Kowner, R. (1996). Facial asymmetry and attractiveness judgment in developmental perspective. *Journal of Experimental Psychology: Human Perception and Performance, 22,* 662–675.

Kramer, S., Zebrowitz, L. A., San Giovanni, J. P., & Sherak, B. (1995). Infant preferences for attractiveness and babyfaceness. In B. G. Bardy, R. J. Botsma, & Y. G. Guiard (Eds.), *Studies in perception and action III* (pp. 389–392). Hillsdale, NJ: Erlbaum.

Kuh, D., & Ben-Shlomo, Y. (1997). *Life course influences on adult disease.* Oxford, England: Oxford University Press.

Kuh, D., & Wadsworth, M. E. (1993). Physical health status at 36 years in a British national birth cohort. *Social Science and Medicine, 37,* 905–916.

Lagesen, K., & Folstad, I. (1998). Antler asymmetry and immunity in reindeer. *Behavioral Ecology and Sociobiology, 44*(2), 135–142.

Lancaster, J. B., & Kaplan, H. (1994). Human mating and family formation strategies: The effects of variability among males in quality and the allocation of mating effort and parental investment. In T. Nishida, W. C. McGrew, P. Marler, M. Pickford, & F. B. M. de Waal (Eds.), *Topics in primatology. Vol. 1: Human origins* (pp. 21–33). Tokyo: University of Tokyo Press.

Lancaster, J. B., & Kaplan, H. (2000). Parenting other men's children: Costs, benefits, and consequences. In L. Cronk, N. A. Chagnon, & W. Irons (Eds.), *Adaptation and human behavior: An anthropological perspective* (pp. 179–201). New York: Aldine.

Langlois, J. H., Ritter, J. M., Casey, R. J., & Sawin, D. B. (1995). Infant attractiveness predicts maternal behaviors and attitudes. *Developmental Psychology, 31,* 464–472.

Langlois, J. H., Ritter, J. M., Roggman, L. A., & Vaughn, L. S. (1991). Facial diversity and infant preferences for attractive faces. *Developmental Psychology, 27,* 79–84.

Langlois, J. H., & Roggman, L. A. (1990). Attractive faces are only average. *Psychological Science, 1,* 115–121.

Langlois, J. H., Roggman, L. A., Casey, R. J., Ritter, J. M., Reiser-Danner, L. A., & Jenkins, V. Y. (1987). Infant preferences for attractive faces: Rudiments of a sterotype? *Developmental Psychology, 23,* 363–369.

Langlois, J. H., Roggman, L. A., & Musselman, L. (1994). What is average and what is not average about attractive faces? *Psychological Science, 5,* 214–220.

Langlois, J. H., Roggman, L. A., Musselman, L., & Acton, S. (1991). A picture is worth a thousand words: Reply to "On the difficulty of averaging faces." *Psychological Science, 5,* 214–220.

Langlois, J. H., Roggman, L. A., Musselman, L., & Reiser-Danner, L. A. (1990). Infant's differential social responses to attractive and unattractive faces. *Developmental Psychology, 26,* 153–159.

Levi-Strauss, C. (1969). *The elementary structures of kinship.* Boston: Beacon Press.

Lieberman, D., Tooby, J., & Cosmides, L. (2003). Does morality have a biological basis? An empirical test of the factors governing moral sentiments relating to incest. *Proceedings of the Royal Society of London. Series B, Biological Sciences, 270,* 819–826.

Lindsay, S. W., Adiamah, J. H., Miller, J. E., Pleass, R. J., & Armstrong, J. R. M. (1993). Variation in attractiveness of human subjects to malaria mosquitoes (*Diptera: Culicidae*) in the Gambia. *Journal of Medical Entomology, 30,* 368–373.

Little, A. C., Penton-Voak, I. S., Burt, D. M., & Perrett, D. I. (2002). Evolution and individual differences in the perception of attractiveness: How cyclic hormonal changes and self-perceived attractiveness influence female preferences for male faces. In G. Rhodes & L. A. Zebrowitz (Eds.), *Facial attractiveness: Evolutionary, cognitive and social perspectives* (pp. 59–89). Westport, CT: Greenwood.

Low, B. S. (1990). Marriage systems and pathogen stress in human societies. *American Zoologist, 30,* 325–339.

Lynn, M., & Shurgot, B. A. (1984). Responses to lonely hearts advertisements: Effects of reported physical attractiveness, physique, and coloration. *Personality and Social Psychology Bulletin, 10,* 349–357.

MacArthur, R. H., & Wilson, E. O. (1967). *The theory of island biogeography.* Princeton, NJ: Princeton University Press.

Macintyre, S., & West, P. (1991). Social, developmental and health correlates of attractiveness in adolescence. *Sociology of Health and Illness, 13,* 149–167.

Maggioncalda, A. N., Sapolsky, R. M., & Czekala, N. M. (1999). Reproductive hormone profiles in captive male orangutans: Implications for understanding developmental arrest. *American Journal of Physical Anthropology, 109,* 19–32.

Maisey, D. M., Vale, E. L. E., Cornelissen, P. L., & Tovée, M. J. (1999). Characteristics of male attractiveness for women. *Lancet, 353,* 1500.

Mann, J. (1992). Nurturance or negligence: Maternal psychology and behavioral preference among preterm twins. In J. Barkow, L. Cosmides, & J. Tooby (Eds.), *The adapted mind: Evolutionary psychology and the generation of culture* (pp. 367–390). New York: Oxford University Press.

Manning, J. T. (1995). Fluctuating asymmetry and body weight in men and women: Implications for sexual selection. *Ethology and Sociobiology, 16,* 145–153.

Manning, J. T. (2002). *Digit ratio: A pointer to fertility, behavior and health.* New Brunswick, NJ: Rutgers University Press.

Manning, J. T., & Bundred, P. E. (2000). The ratio of 2nd to 4th digit length: A new predictor of disease predisposition? *Medical Hypotheses, 54*(5), 855–857.

Manning, J. T., Koukourakis, K., & Brodie, D. A. (1997). Fluctuating asymmetry, metabolic rate and sexual selection in human males. *Evolution and Human Behavior, 18,* 15–21.

Manning, J. T., & Pickup, L. J. (1998). Symmetry and performance in middle distance runners. *International Journal of Sports Medicine, 19*(3), 205–209.

Manning, J. T., Scutt, D., & Lewis-Jones, D. I. (1998). Developmental stability, ejaculate size and sperm quality in men. *Evolution and Human Behavior, 19,* 273–282.

Manning, J. T., Scutt, D., Whitehouse, G. H., & Leinster, S. J. (1997). Breast asymmetry and phenotypic quality in women. *Evolution and Human Behavior, 18,* 2223–2236.

Manning, J. T., & Taylor, R. P. (2001). Second to fourth digit ratio and male ability in sport: Implications for sexual selection in humans. *Evolution and Human Behavior, 22*(1), 61–69.

Manning, J. T., Trivers, R. L., Singh, D., & Thornhill, R. (1999). The mystery of female beauty. *Nature, 399,* 214–215.

Marlowe, F. (1999a). Male care and mating effort among Hadza foragers. *Behavioral Ecology and Sociobiology, 45,* 57–64.

Marlowe, F. (1999b). Showoffs or providers? The parenting effort of Hadza men. *Evolution and Human Behavior, 20*(6), 391–404.

Marlowe, F. (2001). Male contribution to diet and female reproductive success among foragers. *Current Anthropology, 42*(5), 755–763.

Marlowe, F. W., Apicella, C. L., & Reed, D. (in press). Men's preferences for women's waist-to-buttock ratio in two societies. *Evolution and Human Behavior.*

Marlowe, F., & Wetsman, A. (2001). Preferred waist-to-hip ratio and ecology. *Personality and Individual Differences, 30,* 481–489.

Marti, B., Tuomilehto, J., Salomaa, V., Kartovaara, L., Lorhonen, H. J., & Pietinen, P. (1991). Body fat distribution in the Finnish population: Environmental determinants and predictive power for cardiovascular risk factor levels. *Journal of Epidemiology and Community Health, 45,* 131–137.

Martin, D. L., & Frayer, D. W. (Eds.). (1997). *Troubled times: Violence and warfare in the past.* Amsterdam, the Netherlands: Gordon and Breach.

Martorell, R., Delgado, H. L., Valverde, V., & Klein, R. E. (1981). Maternal stature, fertility and infant mortality. *Human Biology, 53,* 303–312.

Mather, K. (1953). Genetical control of stability in development. *Heredity, 7,* 297–336.

Maynard Smith, J. (1964). Group selection and kin selection. *Nature, 20,* 1145–1147.

McCabe, V. (1984). Abstract perceptual information for age level: A risk factor for maltreatment? *Child development, 55,* 267–276.

McCabe, V. (1988). Facial proportions, perceived age, and caregiving. In T. R. Alley (Ed.), *Social and applied aspects of perceiving faces* (pp. 89–95). Mahwah, NJ: Earlbaum.

McCann, S. J. (2001). Height, societal threat, and the victory margin in presidential elections, 1824–1992. *Psychology Reports, 88,* 741–742.

Mealey, L., Bridgestock, R., & Townsend, G. (1999). Symmetry and perceived facial attractiveness. *Journal of Personality and Social Psychology, 76,* 151–158.

Mikach, S. M., & Bailey, M. (1999). What distinguishes women with unusually high numbers of sex partners? *Evolution and Human Behavior, 20,* 141–150.

Miller, G. (2000). *The mating mind.* New York: Doubleday.

Miller, G. F., & Todd, P. M. (1998). Mate choice turns cognitive. *Trends in Cognitive Sciences, 2*(5), 190–198.

Milne, B. J., Belsky, J., Poulton, R., Thomson, W. M., Caspi, A., & Kieser, J. (2003). Fluctuating asymmetry and physical health among young adults. *Evolution and Human Behavior, 24*(1), 53–63.

Mitani, J., Gros-Louis, J., & Richards, A. (1996). Sexual dimorphism, the operational sex ratio, and the intensity of male competition among polygynous primates. *American Naturalist, 147,* 966–980.

Mithen, S. J. (1990). *Thoughtful foragers: A study of prehistoric decision making.* Cambridge, England: Cambridge University Press.

Møller, A. P. (1990). Fluctuating asymmetry in male sexual ornaments may reliably reveal male quality. *Animal Behaviour, 40*(6), 1185–1187.

Møller, A. P. (1992a). Female swallow preference for symmetrical male sexual ornaments. *Nature, 357,* 238–240.

Møller, A. P. (1992b). Patterns of fluctuating asymmetry in weapons: Evidence for reliable signaling of quality in beetle horns and bird spurs. *Proceeding of the Royal Society of London. Series B, Biological Sciences, 245,* 1–5.

Møller, A. P. (1993). Patterns of fluctuating asymmetry in sexual ornaments predict female choice. *Journal of Evolutionary Biology, 6,* 481–491.

Møller, A. P. (2002). Developmental instability and sexual selection in stag beetles from Chernobyl and a control area. *Ethology, 108*(3), 193–204.

Møller, A. P., & Pomiankowski, A. (1993). Why have birds got multiple sexual ornaments? *Behavioral Ecology and Sociobiology, 32,* 167–176.

Møller, A. P., Soler, M., & Thornhill, R. (1995). Breast asymmetry, sexual selection and human reproductive success. *Ethology and Sociobiology, 16,* 207–219.

Møller, A. P., & Swaddle, J. P. (1997). *Asymmetry developmental stability and evolution.* Oxford, England: Oxford University Press.

Montpare, J. M., Zebrowitz, M., & McArthur, L. (1988). Impressions of people created by age-related qualities of their gaits. *Journal of Personality and Social Psychology, 55,* 547–556.

Morris, A., Cooper, T., & Cooper, P. J. (1989). The changing shape in female fashion models. *International Journal of Eating Disorders, 8*(5), 593–596.

Mueller, U., & Mazur, A. (2001). Evidence of unconstrained directional selection for male tallness. *Behavioral Ecology and Sociobiology, 50*(4), 302–311.

Mukabana, W. R., Takken, W., Coe, R., & Knols, B. G. J. (2002). Host-specific cues cause differential attractiveness of Kenyan men to the African malaria vector. *Anopheles gambiae, Malaria Journal, 1,* 17.

Nesse, R. M., & Williams, G. C. (1994). *Why we get sick: The new science of Darwinian medicine.* New York: Vintage Books.

Nettle, D. (2002). Women's height, reproductive success and the evolution of sexual dimorphism in modern humans. *Proceedings of the Royal Society of London. Series B, Biological Sciences, 269*(1503), 1919–1923.

Orians, G. H., & Heerwagen, J. H. (1992). Evolved responses to landscapes. In J. Barkow, L. Cosmides, & J. Tooby (Eds.), *The adapted mind: Evolutionary psychology and the generation of culture* (pp. 412–426). New York: Oxford University Press.

Palmer, A. C., & Stobeck, C. (1986). Fluctuating asymmetry: Measurement, analysis, pattern. *Annual Review of Ecology Systems, 17,* 391–421.

Patton, J. Q. (2000). Reciprocal altruism and warfare: A case from the Ecuadorian Amazon. In L. Cronk, N. Chagnon, & W. Irons (Eds.), *Adaptation and human behavior: An anthropological perspective* (pp. 417–436). Hawthorne, NY: Aldine de Gruyter.

Pawlowski, B., & Dunbar, R. (1999). Impact of market value on human mate choice. *Proceedings of the Royal Society of London. Series B, Biological Sciences, 266,* 281–285.

Pawlowski, B., Dunbar, R., & Lipowicz, A. (2000). Tall men have more reproductive success. *Nature, 403,* 156.

Pawlowski, B., & Koziel, S. (2002). The impact of traits offered in personal advertisements on response rates. *Evolution and Human Behavior, 23*(2), 139–149.

Penton-Voak, I. S., Jacobson, A., & Trivers, R. (2004). Populational differences in attractiveness judgements of male and female faces: Comparing British and Jamaican samples. *Evolution and Human Behavior, 25*(6), 355–370.

Penton-Voak, I. S., & Perrett, D. I. (2000). Female preference for male faces changes cyclically: Further evidence. *Evolution and Human Behavior, 21,* 39–48.

Penton-Voak, I. S., Perrett, D. I., Castles, D. L., Kobayashi, T., Burt, D. M., Murray, L. K., et al. (1999). Female preference for male faces changes cyclically. *Nature, 399,* 741–742.

Perrett, D. I., Burt, D. M., Penton-Voak, I. S., Lee, K. J., Rowland, D. A., & Edwards, R. (1999). Symmetry and human facial attractiveness. *Evolution and human behavior, 20,* 295–307.

Perrett, D. I., May, K. A., & Yoshikawa, S. (1994). Facial shape and judgement of female attractiveness. *Nature, 386,* 239–242.

Pettijohn, T. F., & Jungeberg, B. J. (2004). Playboy playmate curves: Changes in facial and body feature preferences across social and economic conditions. *Personality and Social Psychology Bulletin, 30*(9), 1186–1197.

Pinker, S. (1997). *How the mind works.* New York: Norton.

Pinker, S. (2002). *The blank slate: The modern denial of human nature.* New York: Viking.

Platek, S. M., Burch, R. L., Panyavin, I. S., Wasserman, B. H., & Gallup, G. G., Jr. (2002). Reactions to children's faces: Resemblance affects males more than females. *Evolution and Human Behavior, 23,* 159–166.

Platek, S. M., Critton, S. R., Burch, R. L., Frederick, D. A., Meyers, T. E., & Gallup, G. G., Jr. (2003). How much paternal resemblance is enough? Sex differences in hypothetical investment decisions but not in the detection of resemblance. *Evolution and Human Behavior, 24,* 81–87.

Platek, S. M., Raines, D. M., Gallup, G. G., Mohamed, F. B., Thomson, J. W., Myers, T., et al. (2004). Reactions to children's faces: Males are more affected by resemblance than females are, and so are their brains. *Evolution and Human Behavior, 25*(6), 394–405.

Pollard, J. S. (1995). Attractiveness of composite faces: A comparative study. *International Journal of Comparative Psychology, 8,* 77–83.

Porter, R. H. (1991). Mutual mother-infant recognition in humans. In P. G. Hepper (Ed.), *Kin recognition* (pp. 413–432). Cambridge, England: Cambridge University Press.

Read, A., & Allen, J. (2000). Evolution and immunology: The economics of immunity. *Science, 290,* 1104–1105.

Rhodes, G., Geddes, K., Jeffery, L., Dziurawiec, S., & Clark, A. (2002). Are average and symmetric faces attractive to infants? Discrimination and looking preferences. *Perception, 31,* 315–321.

Rhodes, G., Proffitt, F., Grady, J. M., & Sumich, A. (1998). Facial symmetry and the perception of beauty. *Psychonomic Bulletin and Review, 5*(4), 659–669.

Rhodes, G. F., Sumich, A., & Byatt, G. (1999). Are average facial configurations attractive only because of their symmetry? *Psychological Science, 10*(1), 52–58.

Rhodes, G. F., & Tremewan, T. (1996). Averageness, exaggeration, and facial attractiveness. *Psychological Science, 7*(2), 105–110.

Rhodes, G. F., Yoshikawa, S., Clark, A., Lee, K., McKay, R., & Akamatsu, S. (2001). Attractiveness of facial averageness and symmetry in non-western cultures. In search of biologically based standards of beauty. *Perception, 30*(5), 611–625.

Ridley, M. (1993). *The red queen: Sex and the evolution of human nature.* New York: Macmillan.

Rikowski, A., & Grammer, K. (1999). Human body odour, symmetry and attractiveness. *Proceedings of the Royal Society of London. Series B, Biological Sciences, 266,* 869–874.

Rivera, J., Martorell, R., Ruel, M., Habicht, J., & Haas, J. (1995). Nutritional supplementation during the preschool years influences body size and composition of Guatemalan adolescents. *Journal of Nutrition, 125,* 1068–1077.

Roberts, S. B., Pi-Sunyer, X., Kuler, L., Lane, M., Ellison, P., Prior, J. C., et al. (2000). Physiologic effects of lowering caloric intake in non-human primates and non-obese humans. *Journal of Gerontology: Biological Sciences, 56A,* 1–10.

Rosenberg, K. R. (1992). Evolution of modern human childbirth. *Yearbook of Physical Anthropology, 35,* 89–124.

Rubenstein, A. J., Langlois, J. H., & Kalakanis, L. E. (1999). Infant preferences for attractive faces: A cognitive explanation. *Developmental Psychology, 35,* 848–855.

Rubenstein, A. J., Langlois, J. H., & Roggman, L. A. (2002). What makes a face attractive and why: The role of averageness in defining facial beauty. In G. Rhodes & L. A. Zebrowitz (Eds.), *Facial attractiveness: Evolutionary, cognitive and social perspectives* (pp. 1–33). Westport, CT: Greenwood Publishers Group.

Samuels, C. A., & Ewy, R. (1985). Aesthetic perception of faces during infancy. *British Journal of Developmental Psychology, 3,* 221–228.

Scalise Sugiyama, M. (2001). Food, foragers, and folklore: The role of narrative in human subsistence. *Evolution and Human Behavior, 22,* 221–240.

Schaffer, W. M. (1974). Selection for optimal life histories: The effects of age structure. *Ecology, 55,* 291–303.

Scheib, J. E., Gangestad, S. W., & Thornhill, R. (1999). Facial attractiveness, symmetry and cues of good genes. *Proceedings of the Royal Society of London. Series B, Biological Sciences, 266,* 1913–1917.

Scheib, J. E., Kristiansen, A., & Wara, A. (1997). A Norwegian note on "sperm donor selection and the psychology of female mate choice." *Evolution and Human Behavior, 18,* 143–149.

Schiavone, F. E., Rietschel, R. L., Sgoutas, D., & Harris, R. (1983). Elevated free testosterone levels in women with acne. *Archives of Dermatology, 119,* 799–802.

Sear, R., Allal, N., & Mace, R. (2004). Height, marriage, and reproductive success in Gambian women. In M. Alvard (Ed.), *Socioeconomic aspects of human behavioral ecology* (Vol. 23). Greenwich, CT: Elsevier.

Shepher, J. (1971). Mate selection among second generation Kibbutz adolescents and adults: Incest avoidance and negative imprinting. *Archives of Sexual Behavior, 1,* 293–307.

Silventoinen, K. (2003). Determinants of variation in adult body height. *Journal of Biosocial Science, 35,* 263–285.

Silventoinen, K., Lahelma, E., & Rahkonen, O. (1999). Social background, adult body-height and health. *International Journal of Epidemiology, 28,* 911–918.

Singh, D. (1993a). Adaptive significance of female physical attractiveness: Role of waist-to-hip ratio. *Journal of Personality and Social Psychology, 65,* 293–307.

Singh, D. (1993b). Body shape and women's attractiveness: The critical role of waist-to-hip ratio. *Human Nature, 4,* 297–321.

Singh, D. (1994a). Body fat distribution and perception of desirable female body shape by young black men and women. *International Journal of Eating Disorders, 16,* 289–294.

Singh, D. (1994b). Ideal female body shape: Role of weight and waist-to-hip ratio. *International Journal of Eating Disorders, 16,* 283–288.

Singh, D. (1994c). Is thin really beautiful and good? Relationship between waist-to-hip ratio (WHR) and attractiveness. *Personality and Individual Differences, 16,* 123–132.

Singh, D. (1995a). Female health, attractiveness, and desirability for relationships: Role of breast asymmetry and waist-to-hip ratio. *Ethology and Sociobiology, 16,* 465–481.

Singh, D. (1995b). Female judgement of male attractiveness and desirability for relationships: Role of waist-to-hip ratio and financial status. *Journal of Personality and Social Psychology, 69(6),* 1089–1101.

Singh, D., & Bronstad, P. M. (1997). Sex differences in the anatomical locations of human body scarification and tattooing as a function of pathogen prevalence. *Evolution and Human Behavior, 18(6),* 403–416.

Singh, D., & Haywood, M. (1999, July). *Waist-to-hip ratio representation in ardent sculptures from four cultures.* Paper presented at the Annual meeting of the Human Behavior and Evolution Society, Salt Lake City, UT.

Singh, D., & Luis, S. (1995). Ethnic and gender consensus for the effects of waist-to-hip ratio on judgment of women's attractiveness. *Human Nature, 6,* 51–65.

Singh, D., & Young, R. K. (1995). Body weight, waist-to-hip ratio, breasts, and hips: Role in judgments of female attractiveness and desirability for relationships. *Ethology and Sociobiology, 16,* 483–507.

Skinner, M., & Goodman, A. H. (1992). Anthropological uses of developmental defects of enamel. In S. R. Saunders & M. A. Katzenberg (Eds.), *Skeletal biolog of past peoples: Research methods.* New York: Wiley-Liss.

Slater, A., Von der Schulennurg, C., Brown, E., Badenoch, M., Butterworth, G., Parsons, S., et al. (1998). Newborn infants prefer attractive faces. *Infant Behavior and Development, 21,* 345–354.

Smith, E. A., Borgerhoff Mulder, M., & Hill, K. (2001). Controversies in the evolutionary social sciences: A guide to the perplexed. *Trends in Ecology & Evolution, 16,* 128–135.

Sobal, J., & Stunkard, A. J. (1989). Socioeconomic status and obesity: A review of the literature. *Psychological Bulletin, 105,* 260–275.

Sosis, R. (2000). The emergence and stability of cooperative fishing on Ifaluk. In L. Cronk, N. Chagnon, & W. Irons (Eds.), *Adaptation and human behavior: An anthropological perspective* (pp. 437–472). New York: Aldine.

Stearns, S. (1992). *The evolution of life histories.* Oxford, England: Oxford University Press.

Steckel, R. H., Rose, J. C., Larsen, C. S., & Walker, P. L. (2002). Skeletal health in the Western Hemisphere from 4000 B. C. to the present. *Evolutionary Anthropology, 11,* 142–155.

Steinberger, E., Rodriguez-Rigau, L. J., Smith, K. D., & Held, B. (1981). The menstrual cycle and plasma testosterone level in women with acne. *Journal of the American Academy of Dermatology, 4(1),* 54–58.

Sternglanz, S. H., Gray, J. L., & Murakami, M. (1977). Adult preferences for infantile facial features: An ethological approach. *Animal Behaviour, 25,* 108–115.

Stevenage, S. V., Nixon, M. S., & Vince, K. (1999). Visual analysis of gait as a cue to identity. *Applied Cognitive Psychology, 13,* 513–526.

Sugiyama, L. S. (1996). *In search of the adapted mind: A study of human psychological adaptations among the Shiwiar of Ecuador and the Yora of Peru.* Unpublished PhD dissertation, University of California, Santa Barbara.

Sugiyama, L. S. (1999, June). *Preliminary analysis of status and social recognition among the Shiwiar.* MacArthur Foundation Risk Research Initiative, Economics Preferences Group, Risk preference roundtable. Salt Lake City, UT.

Sugiyama, L. S. (2004a). Is beauty in the context-sensitive adaptations of the beholder?: Shiwiar use of waist-to-hip ration in assessments of female mate value. *Evolution and Human Behavior, 25*(1), 51–62.

Sugiyama, L. S. (2004b). Illness, injury, and disability among Shiwiar forager-horticulturalists: Implications of health-risk buffering for the evolution of human life history. *American Journal of Physical Anthropology, 123,* 371–389.

Sugiyama, L. S. (2004c). Patterns of Shiwiar health insults indicate that provisioning during health crises reduces juvenile mortality. In M. Alvard (Ed.), *Socioeconomic aspects of human behavioral ecology: Research in economic anthropology* (Vol. 23, pp. 377–400). Greenwich, CT: Elsevier.

Sugiyama, L. S., & Chacon, R. (2000). Effects of illness and injury on foraging among the Yora and Shiwiar: Pathology risk as adaptive problem. In L. Cronk, N. A. Chagnon, & W. Irons (Eds.), *Human behavior and adaptation: An anthropological perspective* (pp. 371–395). New York: Aldine.

Sugiyama, L. S., & Chacon, R. (in press). Juvenile responses to household ecology among the Yora of Peruvian Amazonia. In B. Hewlett & M. Lamb (Eds.), *Hunter-gatherer childhoods: Evolutionary, developmental, and cultural perspectives* (pp. 237–261). New York: Aldine.

Sugiyama, L. S., & Scalise Sugiyama, M. (2003). Social roles, prestige, and health risk: Social niche specialization as a risk-buffering strategy. *Human Nature, 14,* 165–190.

Sugiyama, L. S., Tooby, J., & Cosmides, L. (2002). Cross-cultural evidence of cognitive adaptations for social exchange among the Shiwiar of Ecuadorian Amazonia. *Proceedings of the National Academy of Sciences, 99*(17), 11537–11542.

Swaddle, J. P., & Cuthill, I. C. (1995). Asymmetry and human facial attractiveness: Symmetry may not always be beautiful. *Proceedings of the Royal Society of London. Series B, Biological Sciences, 261,* 111–116.

Symons, D. (1979). *The evolution of human sexuality.* New York: Oxford University Press.

Symons, D. (1989). A critique of Darwinian anthropology. *Ethology and Sociobiology, 10,* 131–144.

Symons, D. (1992). On the use and misuse of Darwinism in the study of human behavior. In J. Barkow, L. Cosmides, & J. Tooby (Eds.), *The adapted mind: Evolutionary psychology and the generation of culture* (pp. 137–162). New York: Oxford University Press.

Symons, D. (1995). Beauty is in the adaptations of the beholder. In P. R. Abramson & S. D. Pinkerson (Eds.), *Sexual nature, sexual culture* (pp. 80–118). Chicago: University of Chicago Press.

Tassinary, L. G., & Hansen, K. A. (1998). A critical test of the waist-to-hip-ratio hypothesis of female physical attractiveness. *Psychological Science, 9,* 150–155.

Thornhill, R. (1992). Fluctuating asymmetry and the mating system of the Japanese scorpionfly (*Panorpa japonica*). *Animal Behaviour, 44,* 867–879.

Thornhill, R. (2003). Darwinian aesthetics informs traditional aesthetics. In K. Grammer & E. Voland (Eds.), *Evolutionary aesthetics* (pp. 9–38). Berlin, Germany: Springer-Verlag.

Thornhill, R., & Gangestad, S. W. (1993). Human facial beauty: Averageness, symmetry and parasite resistance. *Human Nature, 4,* 237–269.

Thornhill, R., & Gangestad, S. W. (1994). Human fluctuating asymmetry and human sexual behavior. *Psychological Science, 5,* 297–302.

Thornhill, R., & Gangestad, S. W. (1999a). Facial attractiveness. *Trends in Cognitive Science, 3,* 452–460.

Thornhill, R., & Gangestad, S. W. (1999b). The scent of symmetry: A human sex pheromone that signals fitness? *Evolution and Human Behavior, 20,* 175–201.

Thornhill, R., & Gangestad, S. W. (2003). Do women have evolved adaptation for extra-pair copulation. In E. Voland & K. Grammer (Eds.), *Evolutionary aesthetics* (pp. 341–368). Heidelberg, Germany: Springer–Verlag.

Thornhill, R., Gangestad, S. W., & Comer, R. (1995). Human female orgasm and mate fluctuating asymmetry. *Animal Behavior, 50,* 1601–1615.

Thornhill, R., & Grammer, K. (1999). The body and face of woman: One ornament that signals quality? *Evolution and Human Behavior, 20,* 105–120.

Thornhill, R., & Møller, A. P. (1997). Developmental stability, disease and medicine. *Biology Review, 72,* 497–528.

Tooby, J. (1982). Pathogens, polymorphism, and the evolution of sex. *Journal of Theoretical Biology, 97*, 557–576.

Tooby, J., & Cosmides, L. (1989). Evolutionary psychology and the generation of culture. Part I: Theoretical considerations. *Ethology and Sociobiology, 10*, 29–50.

Tooby, J., & Cosmides, L. (1990). The past explains the present: Emotional adaptations and the structure of ancestral environments. *Ethology and Sociobiology, 11*, 375–424.

Tooby, J., & Cosmides, L. (1992). The psychological foundations of culture. In J. Barkow, L. Cosmides, & J. Tooby (Eds.), *The adapted mind: Evolutionary psychology and the generation of culture* (pp. 19–136). New York: Oxford University Press.

Tooby, J., & Cosmides, L. (1996). Friendship and the banker's paradox: Other pathways to the evolution of adaptations for altruism. *Proceedings of the British Academy, 88*, 119–143.

Tooby, J., & DeVore, I. (1987). The reconstruction of hominid behavioral evolution through strategic modeling. In W. Kinzey (Ed.), *The evolution of human behavior: Primate models* (pp. 183–237). Albany: SUNY Press.

Tovée, M. J., & Cornelissen, P. L. (1999). The mystery of female beauty. *Nature, 399*, 215–216.

Tovée, M. J., & Cornelissen, P. L. (2001). Female and male perceptions of female physical attractiveness in front-view and profile. *British Journal of Psychology, 92*, 391–402.

Tovée, M. J., Hancock, P. J. B., Mahmoodi, S., Singleton, B. R. R., & Cornelissen, P. L. (2002). Human female attractiveness: Waveform analysis of body shape. *Proceedings of the Royal Society of London. Series B, Biological Sciences, 269*, 2205–2213.

Tovée, M. J., Maisey, D., Emery, J. L., & Cornelissen, P. L. (1999). Visual cues to human female attractiveness. *Proceedings of the Royal Society of London. Series B, Biological Sciences, 266*, 211–218.

Tovée, M. J., Reinhardt, S., Emery, J. L., & Cornelissen, P. L. (1998). Optimal BMI and maximum sexual attractiveness. *Lancet, 352*, 548.

Trevathan, W. (1987). *Human birth: An evolutionary perspective.* New York: Aldine de Gruyter.

Trivers, R. L. (1972). Parental investment and sexual selection. In B. Campbell (Ed.), *Sexual selection and the descent of man* (pp. 1871–1971). Chicago: Aldine.

Trivers, R. L. (1974). Parent offspring conflict. *American Zoologist, 14*, 249–263.

Trivers, R. L. (1985). *Social evolution.* Menlo Park, CA: Benjamin/Cummings.

Valeggia, C. R., & Ellison, P. T. (2001). Lactation, energetics, and postpartum fecundity. In P. T. Ellison (Ed.), *Reproductive ecology and human evolution* (pp. 85–106). New York: Aldine de Gruyter.

Valeggia, C. R., & Ellison, P. T. (2003a). Energetics, fecundity, and human life history. In J. Rodgers & H. P. Koehler (Eds.), *Biodemography of fertility* (pp. 87–103). Boston: Kluwer Academic.

Valeggia, C. R., & Ellison, P. T. (2003b). Impact of breastfeeding on anthropometric changes in peri-urban Toba women (Argentina). *American Journal of Human Biology, 15*, 717–724.

van den Berghe, P. L. (1979). *Human family systems: An evolutionary view.* Westport, CT: Greenwood Press.

Van Valen, L. (1962). A study of fuctuating asymmetry. *Evolution, 16*, 125–142.

Walker, P. L., Sugiyama, L. S., & Chacon, R. (1998). Diet, dental health, and cultural change among recently contacted South American Indian hunter-horticulturalists. In J. Lukacs & B. E. Hemphill (Eds.), *Human dental development, morphology and pathology: Essays in honor of Albert Dahlberg.* Eugene: University of Oregon Anthropological Papers.

Walker, R., Hill, K., Kaplan, H., & McMillan, G. (2002). Age-dependency in hunting ability among the Ache of Eastern Paraguay. *Journal of Human Evolution, 42*, 639–657.

Watson, P. J., & Thornhill, R. (1994). Fluctuating asymmetry and sexual selection. *Trends in Ecology and Evolution, 9*, 21–25.

Waynforth, D. (1995). Fluctuating asymmetry and human male life-history traits in rural Belize. *Proceedings of the Royal Society of London. Series B, Biological Sciences, 22/261*(1360), 111–116.

Westermarck, E. (1926). *The history of human marriage* (Vols. 1–3). London: Macmillan.

Wetsman, A., & Marlowe, F. (1999). How universal are preferences for female waist-to-hip ratios? Evidence from the Hadza of Tanzania. *Evolution and Human Behavior, 20*, 219–228.

Williams, G. C. (1957). Pleiotropy, natural selection, and the evolution of senescence. *Evolution, 11*, 298–411.

Williams, G. C. (1966). *Adaptation and natural selection.* Princeton, NJ: Princeton University Press.

Wolf, A., & Huang, C. (1980). *Marriage and adoption in China, 1845–1945.* Stanford, CA: Stanford University Press.

Yu, D., & Shepard, G. H. (1998). Is beauty in the eyes of the beholder? *Nature, 396*, 321–322.

Yu, D., & Shepard, G. H. (1999). The mystery of female beauty. *Nature, 399,* 216.

Zahavi, A., & Zahavi, A. (1997). *The handicap principle: A missing piece of Darwin's puzzle.* Oxford, England: Oxford University Press.

Zebrowitz, L. A. (1997). *Reading faces: Window to the soul?* Boulder, CO: Westview Press.

Zebrowitz, L. A., & Rhodes, G. (2002). Nature let a hundred flowers bloom: The multiple ways and wherefores of attractiveness. In G. Rhodes & L. A. Zebrowitz (Eds.), *Facial attractiveness: Evolutionary, cognitive and social perspectives* (pp. 261–293). Westport, CT: Greenwood Publishers Group.

CHAPTER 11

Adaptations to Ovulation

STEVEN W. GANGESTAD, RANDY THORNHILL, and
CHRISTINE E. GARVER-APGAR

HUMANS REPRODUCE SEXUALLY. They also have sex throughout the female menstrual cycle. Yet, copulation has a chance of resulting in conception only about 20% of days during a monthly cycle. Normally ovulating women are fertile up to 6 days of each month during which they ovulate: from 5 days before ovulation to the day of ovulation itself (Wilcox, Weinberg, & Baird, 1995).

In comparison with our closest primate relatives, women's cycles possess two noteworthy features. First, human females do not have conspicuous sexual swellings that vary across the cycle. Bonobos and chimpanzees do; hence, this feature possibly evolved in the hominid line. Second, humans have sex throughout the cycle. In the wild, male-female sex in chimpanzees and bonobos is largely specific to the period of swellings (e.g., Stanford, 1998). Because humans appear to be the only species characterized by both features (Alexander, 1987), they are probably keys to understanding important selection pressures that forged sexual relations in hominids.

Women's continuous sexual receptivity across the cycle need not imply lack of variation in female sexual interests or preferences across the cycle. Indeed, because copulation can potentially result in successful conception on very few, specific days, it would be surprising if selection had *not* forged psychological adaptations in one or both sexes to be sensitive to the timing of conception risk. Recent evidence strongly suggests that it has.

The selection pressures that we argue played prominent roles in forging human menstrual cycle variation involve *sexually antagonistic coevolution*. In this chapter, we discuss theory and research on sexually antagonistic coevolution, consider human sexuality in light of major sexual conflicts, and describe recent research on psychological changes across women's cycles.

SEXUALLY ANTAGONISTIC COEVOLUTION: THEORETICAL BACKGROUND

Through sexual reproduction, two individuals' genes are passed on to an offspring they jointly conceive; hence the offspring is a vehicle through which each individual's genes can be propagated. Nonetheless, reproduction should not be thought of as a purely cooperative enterprise between mates. Selection will favor individuals' treating their mates' outcomes just as important as their own when each individual can reproduce only with that particular mate—that is, when there is exclusive lifelong monogamy with no chance of remating. In such a case, the death of the mate ends an individual's reproductive career just as surely as does the individual's own death. By creating living groups of just two individuals—one member of each sex—experimental biologists have created these circumstances in laboratory populations. In natural populations, however, they rarely, if ever, exist. Instead, the events that would optimize one partner's reproductive outcomes do not perfectly match those that would optimize the other's. Mismatches reflect genetic conflicts of interest between the sexes within mateships, which can generate selection for features that promote the fitness of one sex at the expense of the fitness of the other sex. The outcome of such selection is referred to as *sexually antagonistic adaptation.*

Demonstrations of Sexually Antagonistic Coevolution

Rice (1996) conducted a spectacular demonstration of sexually antagonistic adaptation fueled by sexual conflicts of interest. Through an ingenious procedure, he allowed *Drosophila melanogaster* males to evolve while preventing females from evolving counteradaptations. Tests performed after 30 generations clearly demonstrated male adaptation to target females. Wild *melanogaster* typically mate promiscuously, and males make frequent attempts to induce remating on the part of females. Males in the experimental line had increased capacity for remating with females who had previously mated with competitor males taken from the control line. Moreover, competitor males were less able to remate with females previously mated with experimental males and to displace sperm inseminated by experimental males, even when experimental males were not present. In mixed groups, the reproductive success of experimental males was 24% greater than that of control males.

Male adaptation evolved at the expense of female fitness. Females mated to experimental males had higher mortality than those mated to controls, with no compensating increase in fecundity. Proteins in male *melanogaster* seminal fluid are a low-level toxin to females. The increased female mortality rate was likely mediated by a greater exposure to and enhanced toxicity of male seminal proteins. This effect is likely an incidental by-product of beneficial effects on male reproductive success. The proteins can harm other males' sperm. Some may enter the female's circulatory system and influence her neuroendocrine system in ways that benefit the male (e.g., by reducing her remating rate; see Rice, 1996).

Enforced monogamy should relax sexual conflict and increase the benefits of male benevolence toward females. One study established two replicate populations: a control population, in which a single female was housed with three males and a monogamous population, in which a single female was housed with a single male. When monogamy was enforced, male seminal fluid proteins evolved to be less toxic to females, male remating efforts were less intense, and the number of adult progeny produced per female was greater.[1]

---

[1] As Holland and Rice (1999) note, in some species polyandry probably has benefits due to mate choice that outweigh the costs of sexually antagonistic adaptation, but they did not observe that outcome in their own experiment.

MAJOR IMPLICATIONS OF SEXUALLY ANTAGONISTIC COEVOLUTION

It has long been recognized that species may coevolve with other species in an antagonistic fashion, for example, the coevolution of predator-prey, host-pathogen, or competitors for the same food source. Through antagonistic coevolution, new adaptations in one species (e.g., a trait in predators that increases their ability to capture prey) evoke selection on the other species (e.g., prey) to evolve counteradaptations (e.g., defenses)—which may then produce selective pressures on the first species to counter those counteradaptations, and so on. Antagonistic coevolution of adaptation and counteradaptation can span long stretches of evolutionary time, resulting in persistent evolutionary change in both species. Antagonistic coevolution is now widely known as the Red Queen process (Van Valen, 1973): This character in *Alice in Wonderland* claimed that she had to keep running simply to stay in the same place, so, too, species must continually evolve to effectively compete against enemies.

Genes within a single species can coevolve in an antagonistic fashion. Sexually antagonistic coevolution is a prime example of such interlocus contest evolution (ICE; Rice & Holland, 1997). Consider, for simplicity's sake, genes that are sex-limited and, therefore, expressed in only one sex. Such genes will be selected for benefits they provide to the sex in which they are expressed. Alleles at male sex-limited genes that have negative effects on their male carriers' mates may nonetheless spread in the population if they benefit males. The adaptations they beget (e.g., seminal proteins that affect female remating), however, set the stage for the evolution of female counteradaptations (e.g., resistance to the effects of the seminal proteins), which may then evoke selection for male counters to those counteradaptations (e.g., production of a more intense form or dose of seminal proteins), and so on. Persistent antagonistic coevolution of male and female sex-limited genes (and adaptations) within a single species' genome—an *intraspecific* Red Queen process—results.[2]

Red Queen processes lead to some predictable evolutionary outcomes. For one, loci affected by them tend to be subject to *relatively rapid evolution*. In fact, reproductive traits (e.g., mammalian gamete proteins, e.g., Swanson, Clark, Waldrip-Dail, Wolfner, & Aquadro, 2001; reproductive tracts, e.g., Gavrilets, 2000) do evolve at rapid rates. The reproductive genes of chimpanzees and humans have diverged markedly, largely due to positive selection for new alleles (as expected if antagonistic coevolution is involved), not random drift (Wyckoff, Wang, & Wu, 2000).

A related outcome is a *nonnegligible level of maladaptation*. Humans will never evolve surefire immunity to pathogen-mediated disease. The pathogens against which we defend ourselves evolve new ways to defeat our defense; any solution to their attacks is thus likely to be only temporary. Similarly, solutions to the other

---

[2] Sex limitation is not required nor necessarily expected of genes evolved through sexually antagonistic coevolution. Perhaps not atypically, genes that benefit one sex in intersexual conflicts impose costs when expressed in the other sex (e.g., genes that adaptively increase hormone action in one sex may maladaptively do so in the other sex). These *sexually antagonistic genes* may be selected if the net benefits to one sex outweigh the costs to the other. Selection should favor modifier genes that suppress expression of the gene to the sex hurt by it. Because genes involved in sexually antagonistic adaptations rapidly evolve, however, periods of stable selection on the sex necessary for the evolution of complete sex limitation may not be common. Sexually antagonistic genes compromise the design of each sex away from its optimum. See Chippendale, Gibson, and Rice (2001).

sex's antagonistic adaptations are typically temporary and, as a result, at no time is either sex likely to be perfectly adapted to the other.

Finally, Red Queen processes maintain *interindividual variation.* When selection leads to evolutionary stable solutions (e.g., adaptations to fixed environmental features), selection may drive out functional variation in alleles that map onto adaptations. But when solutions are unstable, new beneficial alleles emerge frequently and selection may not persist in one direction long enough to drive alleles to fixation. Fitness traits typically possess much more genetic variation than traits under stabilizing selection (with additive genetic coefficients of variation differing by a factor of 3 to 4; Houle, 1992). At least half of the genetic variation in fitness traits is probably due to mutations (e.g., Charlesworth & Hughes, 1998), but sexually antagonistic coevolution may account for a meaningful amount of variation in reproductive traits.[3]

HUMAN MATING AND SEXUALLY ANTAGONISTIC COEVOLUTION

Sexually antagonistic coevolution has likely played a key role in the sexual adaptations that distinguish humans from close ancestors, as well as those that account for cyclic variations. This coevolution must be understood in a broader context of human mating and reproduction, characterized by a high level of cooperation between the sexes. When cooperating individuals' interests do not perfectly match, one party can potentially benefit at the expense of the other and antagonistic selection may ensue (nicely illustrated by maternal-fetal conflict; Haig, 1993).

BIPARENTAL CARE OF OFFSPRING

With the expansion of the African savannas between 2.5 and 1.5 mya, early humans may have entered a feeding niche in which animal meat became a primary source of food, which both required and provided a high-quality diet. Forager diets contrast sharply with those of our nearest ancestors, with 30% to 80% of calories from vertebrate meat (versus 2% of the chimpanzee diet). This niche may have selected for a variety of characteristics that distinguish humans from their nearest relatives (e.g., an extended juvenile period of growth and learning, an extended lifespan, new forms of sociality fostering cooperative hunting and other alliances; Kaplan, Hill, Lancaster, & Hurtado, 2000).

It also had implications for male-female relations. Although both men and women contribute substantially to their own subsistence, the average adult male in most foraging societies generates more calories than he consumes, which benefits reproductive women and juveniles (e.g., Marlowe, 2001). The role of paternal investment in human evolution is debatable (e.g., Hawkes, O'Connell, & Blurton Jones, 2001), but much evidence suggests that paternal care has been an important feature of the human adaptive landscape (e.g., Geary, 2000; Kaplan et al., 2000).

---

[3] Rapid evolution may also result in a higher rate of mutation and a lack of canalizing processes that modify and narrow the range of gene expression, further promoting variation (e.g., Williams and Hurst, 2000). See also footnote 2.

THE POTENTIAL FOR EXTRA-PAIR MATING

Although polygyny is permitted in most societies in the cross-cultural record, social monogamy is by far and away the most common marital arrangement even in these societies (Murdock, 1949). But social monogamy need not imply sexual monogamy. Both men and women could potentially have benefited from engaging in sex with someone other than a primary partner—extra-pair copulation (EPC)—under some circumstances.

In species in which females have obligate investment in offspring greatly exceeding that of males, males can benefit from multiple mating. On average, men express greater interest in noncommitted sex than women (e.g., Buss & Schmitt, 1993). Male pursuit of EPC entails costs: the cost of mating effort[4] (e.g., investment in signals that display qualities preferred by females in noninvesting mates, courtship effort, intrasexual competition, search time), risks of injury or even death at the hands of primary partners of EPC partners (Buss, 2000), and potential desertion by dissatisfied mates. Male pursuit of EPC should hence be conditional on personal circumstances and socioecological context (Gangestad & Simpson, 2000).

Females may also benefit from EPC. Extra-pair paternity in many species of socially monogamous birds is common, accounting, on average, for 10% to 15% of offspring. The benefits that may account for female EPC fall into two broad categories (e.g., Jennions & Petrie, 2000). First, females can potentially garner a number of *direct benefits* that influence their own reproductive success through multiple matings (e.g., Greiling & Buss, 2000): direct exchange of sex for material benefits; confusion of paternity, which may inhibit aggression by males against offspring not their own; and male sperm quality and ability to conceive. Second, females may obtain *genetic benefits* for offspring, including:

1. *Intrinsically good genes:* genes with additive effects on offspring fitness (either through increased viability or mating ability; Kokko, Brooks, Jennions, & Morley, 2003) and that, therefore, affect offspring fitness independent of maternal phenotypic and genotypic features. Genetic differences between individuals are probably largely due to variation in the extent to which individuals carry mildly deleterious mutations and variation maintained by potent Red Queen processes (e.g., host-pathogen coevolution).
2. *Compatible genes:* genes that match well with the mother's to enhance offspring fitness.
3. *Diverse genes:* genes different from those of other offspring of the mother, which may thereby increase total fitness through bet hedging. For example, by diversifying a brood's self-recognition components of the immune system, a female may lower the probability that the entire brood will be wiped out by a single epidemic (see Jennions & Petrie, 2000).

In a number of systems, evidence points to intrinsic genetic benefits to extra-pair mating (e.g., zebra finches, dusky warblers, black-capped chickadees, great reed warblers, collared flycatchers, barn swallows, bearded tits; for a review, see Gangestad & Thornhill, 2004). In species in which the extra-pair paternity rate is

---

[4] Mating effort is allocation of time and energy to obtain mates, whereas parental effort is allocation of time and energy to enhance offspring fitness (Low, 1978).

high (yielding multiple opportunities for males to obtain extra-pair matings), more attractive males tend to engage in less parental effort, in accord with the good genes hypothesis (Møller & Thornhill, 1998b). At the same time, studies in other species in which extra-pair mating is common (e.g., razorbills, hooded warblers, sedge warblers) have yielded negative or equivocal evidence for intrinsic genetic benefits. The genetic benefits of EPC in some species may be better understood in terms of compatible genes (e.g., bluethroats; pied flycatchers) or diverse genes (e.g., great tits; see Gangestad & Thornhill, 2004; Jennions & Petrie, 2000).

MALE-FEMALE CONFLICTS OF INTEREST

In human mating pairs, two primary sexual conflicts of interest exist: conflict over male EPC mating efforts and conflict over female EPC. Sexually antagonistic coevolution should have produced adaptations in both sexes to selectively engage in or seek EPC and counteradaptations to prevent or discourage EPC by partners. These conflicts of interest are particularly important in humans due to biparental care. Although sexual conflicts of interest are ubiquitous, the specific nature of human sexual conflicts of interest is unusual if not unique among mammals and probably explains distinctive features of human sexuality.[5]

THE EVOLUTION OF CONCEALED OVULATION AND EXTENDED FEMALE SEXUALITY

The selective pressures that led to *concealed ovulation* and extended female sexuality in humans have been debated for more than two decades. Two major theories explain them in terms of sexual conflicts—but different ones.

THE MALE INVESTMENT HYPOTHESIS

One theory argues that these features evolved to promote bonding between a male-female pair and to keep an investing male close, thereby increasing levels of paternal investment (Alexander & Noonan, 1979). Concealed ovulation purportedly prohibits males from being able to engage selectively in efforts to obtain copulations from either their own primary partner or other women. The net benefits of male effort to seek matings outside a pair bond decreased and accordingly led men to allocate greater effort to parenting. Extended sexuality interacts synergistically with concealed ovulation to diminish interest in outside matings by preventing sexual receptivity as a cue to ovulation and permitting sexual access to a primary partner throughout the cycle when, from the male's point of view,

---

[5] No doubt, a host of additional important sexual conflicts of interest in humans that arise due to lack of obligate lifelong monogamy have been important in human evolutionary history. For instance, there may have historically existed a conflict over the mating rate. Men may have ancestrally benefited from a rate of mating greater than that optimal for females in light of the differential costs of sex and the fact that men do not know when females are fertile. Even nonreproductive sex may be more costly to females, on average, due to the fact that sperm may have untoward effects on immune function (see section on immunological effects), the greater male-to-female rate of transmission of sexually transmitted disease (STD), and the greater costs of STD to females (as STD more often leads to infertility in females).

there is always (outside menstruation) a nonzero probability of conception. Recent cost-benefit game-theoretic modeling confirms that sexuality extended outside the fertile period can favor increased male provisioning of material benefits (Rodríguez-Gironés & Enquist, 2001). In sum, Alexander and Noonan's model suggests that prominent features of female sexuality evolved as *adaptations revolving around conflicts of interest over male extra-pair mating effort.*

Females may be more likely to secure investment from single males when they synchronize menstruation. Synchrony has been argued to prevent dominant males from monopolizing females (Nunn, 1999b) as well as suppress extra-pair mating effort by an investing male. Despite many studies examining menstrual synchrony in humans, this literature is marked by controversy and not conclusive (e.g., Schank, 2002; Weller & Weller, 2002).

THE CUCKOLDRY HYPOTHESIS

Another theory (Benshoof & Thornhill, 1979; Symons, 1979) argues that the function of concealed ovulation in humans is to prevent men from being able to guard a primary partner during the few critical days prior to ovulation, thereby increasing women's ability to selectively choose a sire other than the investing male for genetic benefits through EPC. This theory, then, argues that prominent features of female sexuality evolved as *sexually antagonistic adaptations revolving around conflicts of interest over female extra-pair mating.*

ADDITIONAL VIEWS

Concealed ovulation may evolve as a means by which females confuse paternity, thereby reducing the incidence of infanticide or harmful aggression by males other than the genetic father (Hrdy, 1979). Like the EPC theory, this idea attributes the benefit of concealed ovulation to its effect on males' knowledge of paternity; unlike the EPC theory, it does not assume substantial paternal care by a primary partner. Paternity confusion has been an influential idea in primatology, though more often to explain why female sexual swellings do not perfectly covary with the period of fertility. Female baboons, for instance, display a graded sexual swelling across a time period extending outside the fertile window—most prominent at peak fertility and less intense otherwise—and mate with males throughout that period. The display may function to incite competition between males by signaling female quality (particularly at peak intensity; Domb & Pagel, 2000; but see Nunn, van Schaik, & Zinner, 2001) while at the same time confusing paternity because lower quality males gain access at lower fertility times (Nunn, 1999a). Chimpanzee's sexual swellings may function similarly (Burt, 1992). Complete lack of conspicuous swellings associated with ovulation combined with sexuality that extends beyond the fertile window could potentially function to confuse paternity in yet other primate species (e.g., Sillen-Tullberg & Møller, 1993).

Nonetheless, data and theory give reason to doubt that human concealed ovulation has been maintained by suppression of male aggression against offspring via paternity confusion. Female paternity confusion functions to suppress male aggression when females mate promiscuously. Despite claimed exceptions (e.g., the Canula and other small groups of Brazil; Hrdy, 1999), widespread female promiscuity (as opposed to highly selective EPC) is not characteristic of human groups. Female promiscuity is not compatible with the view that male parental investment has been an important component of recent human evolution; not surprisingly, it does not characterize nonhuman primate species in which males heavily invest in offspring (Dixson, 1998).

The term *concealed* ovulation itself may be misleading. It implies active selection to *hide* signs of ovulation. Sexual swellings are energetically costly, however; thus, a reduction in benefits derived from them could lead to selection for their absence *without* any distinctive benefit of "concealment" (Burt, 1992; Pawlowski, 1999). Swellings probably largely function to display quality (Domb & Pagel, 2000) and thereby incite competition involving the best males, evoke interest of high-quality males at a distance (e.g., Burt, 1992), or affect investment (e.g., protection). In some species such as gorillas, there is less benefit from a signal because groups often have a single adult male.[6] For reasons discussed later, however, we suspect that there has been active selection on human females for concealment of signals of ovulation.

Comparative Data

Comparative data indicate that absence of visual signs of ovulation has more often evolved in nonmonogamous than monogamous anthropoid primates (Sillen-Tullberg & Møller, 1993). At the same time, monogamy has more often evolved when signs of ovulation are absent than when they are present. Possibly, concealed ovulation can acquire new benefits in the context of monogamy, facilitating its evolution. In the evolutionary history of the apes, loss of conspicuous sexual swellings could have evolved prior to the evolution of biparental care, but acquired new benefits in the context of monogamy, thereby promoting monogamy. As well, ovulatory cycle phenomena may have been secondarily modified and reshaped in response to new selection pressures that emerged with monogamy.

Summary

Two leading theories explain concealed ovulation and female sexual receptivity extended across the cycle in humans (if not their original evolution, their maintenance in hominids): the male investment and the female EPC hypotheses. These theories need not be incompatible or mutually exclusive.[7] The male investment hypothesis focuses on the fact that, when lacking knowledge of a mate's ovulation, men's efforts to mate with primary partners become distributed across a span of time extending outside the fertile period, which biases men to expend *greater* paternal effort *during periods other than female mates' fertile period*. The female EPC hypothesis, by contrast, focuses on the fact that men are *less* able to concentrate effort to monopolize female mates *when they are fertile*. With loss of stimuli associated

---

[6] Adult female gorillas do not display a swelling, although adolescent female gorillas do. The latter do not signal ovulation because they are subfertile. They probably signal future reproductive value. Females in some single male groups signal; the function of signaling is probably to compete with other females for male investment by displaying quality.

[7] Alexander and Noonan's hypothesis, as explicitly stated, is inconsistent with the EPC theory in one important sense. They argued that females conceal ovulation from self as well as others (see also Burley, 1979). The EPC theory allows that changes across the cycle may be apparent to women themselves (though they need not be interpreted as changes related to fertility).

with ovulation recognizable to males, both can occur: Greater time allocation to a female outside a fertile period and less time allocation to a female during the fertile period. The conflicts of interest core to these hypotheses may very well help explain both concealed ovulation and extended female sexuality.

CYCLIC CHANGES IN FEMALE SEXUAL INTERESTS AND MATE PREFERENCES

In this section, we discuss psychological changes in female sexuality across the cycle. These features, we argue, are compatible with the female EPC hypothesis of concealed ovulation and extended sexuality only.

CHANGES IN SEXUAL INTEREST ACROSS THE CYCLE

Willingness to have sex throughout the cycle need not imply equal levels of interest in sexual activity across the cycle. In fact, women's interest in sex appears to vary across the cycle. Many normally ovulating (non-pill-using) women report increased sexual desire near ovulation (see Regan, 1996, for a review). Moreover, women are physiologically more aroused by and responsive to sexually explicit visual stimuli midcycle (Slob, Bax, Hop, Rowland, & van der Werflen Bosch, 1996). When near ovulation, women report more positive feelings to visual depictions of nude males (though not to babies, people occupied with body care, or other pictures of people) and respond with a greater late positive event-related EEG potential to nude males (a change in brain activity claimed to indicate greater emotional valence), particularly during a task that encourages deeper emotional processing (Krug, Pietrowsky, Fehm, & Born, 1994; Krug, Plihal, Fehm, & Born, 2000; cf. Meuwissen & Over, 1992). For unknown reasons, the peak near ovulation may be more pronounced for some women (e.g., those who experience premenstrual symptoms; for example, Van Goozen, Weigant, Endert, Helmond, & VandePoll, 1997). Several studies show that women initiate sex with their partners more midcycle; others have failed to detect this effect (see Gangestad & Cousins, 2001, for a review; see also Wilcox et al., 2004).

THE GOOD GENES EXTRA-PAIR COPULATION THEORY OF CHANGES IN FEMALE SEXUALITY ACROSS THE OVULATORY CYCLE

The good genes EPC theory is a recent evolutionary approach to understanding and exploring variations in female sexuality across the ovulatory cycle (e.g., Gangestad & Thornhill, 1998, 2004; Thornhill & Gangestad, 1999, 2003). It argues that women do not experience generalized increases in libido midcycle. Rather, their sexual desire is selective, and the precise features of men in whom they have sexual interest shift at this time, specifically:

- Ancestrally, not all women could have a primary social partner or a mate who, relative to other men, provided genetic benefits. Those whose partners lacked indicators of genetic fitness could potentially gain good genes for offspring through EPC with men possessing them.
- Women who had EPCs did so at a potential cost. EPCs could lead to the loss of parental investment from a primary mate as well as violence from mates (Buss, 2000).

- During infertile phases, women could not acquire genetic benefits through EPCs but could suffer its costs. Hence, selection should have shaped female attraction to indicators of genetic benefits for offspring to be *contingent on women's fertility status:* maximal when women are in the fertile phase of the cycle and less pronounced when infertile.[8]

This theory is obviously related to Benshoof and Thornhill's (1979) theory of concealed ovulation. Whereas that theory explains the relative *absence* of signs of ovulation, however, this one predicts that women's sexuality does vary across the cycle in important ways. Though these changes are not concealed to women themselves, women should not generally advertise them to primary male partners.

Tests of the Good Genes Extra-Pair Copulation Theory: Shifts in Female Attraction to Purported Indicators of Genetic Fitness

The good genes EPC theory yields a number of predictions. The first concerns the features that stimulate female sexual interest: *Normally ovulating women (e.g., women of reproductive age not using hormonal contraceptives) should be more attracted to male indicators of genetic benefits when in the fertile phase of their cycle than when non-fertile.* The theory further implies that *the shift should be specific to women's attraction to men as potential sex partners* (Penton-Voak et al., 1999). It predicts that fertile women should find male indicators of genetic benefits especially "sexy"; it offers no reason to expect changes in the features women find attractive in long-term, investing partners.

Female Preference for the Scent of Symmetry   Indicators of genetic fitness ancestrally are not fully known. Traits that covary with longevity and fecundity in modern environments may not have done so in ancestral environments and vice versa. Hence, investigators have typically relied on theory to identify traits purportedly associated with ancestral fitness.

One such trait is developmental instability—the imprecise expression of design due to developmental perturbations. These perturbations importantly include mutations and pathogens, factors that contribute to genetic variation in fitness. In many species, males who exhibit low developmental instability experience higher mating success (Møller & Thornhill, 1998a). The primary measure of developmental instability used in biology is fluctuating asymmetry (FA), absolute asymmetry in bilateral traits due to random errors in the development of the two sides. Most human studies measure and aggregate 7 to 10 asymmetries on bilateral traits (e.g., ears, elbows, wrists, ankles, feet, fingers). These asymmetries are very small and hence not cues by which individuals assess others' developmental instability; rather, the developmental instability they reveal to researchers is presumably signaled to others through other traits (see Gangestad & Thornhill, 2004). It appears that these cues include (though are by no means limited to) chemical signatures in sweat that can be detected through olfaction (see later discussion). The heritability of human developmental instability is unknown, but

---

[8] We do not imply here that women could not obtain other kinds of benefits (e.g., material benefits) through extra-pair sex throughout the cycle (e.g., Greiling & Buss, 2000). This hypothesis speaks only to extra-pair sex that functions to obtain genetic benefits.

data are consistent with moderate additive genetic variance, much of which is assumed to have related to fitness (e.g., health) ancestrally (see Gangestad & Thornhill, 2003b).

The initial test of the EPC theory examined whether women prefer the scent of symmetrical men more strongly when fertile than not. Four studies have tested this prediction; all support it (Gangestad & Thornhill, 1998; Rikowski & Grammer, 1999; Thornhill & Gangestad, 1999; Thornhill et al., 2003). In each study, men wore T-shirts for two nights. Normally ovulating women then rated the attractiveness of shirts' scents. As illustrated in Figure 11.1, women preferred the scent of symmetrical men only during the fertile period.

What chemical substance (or substances) in men's sweat is associated with symmetry and mediates this result is unknown. Theory and data suggest something androgen derived, as testosterone may be elevated in men who exert greater mating effort (e.g., Gray, Kahlenberg, Barrett, Lipson, & Ellison, 2002) and sweat glands in human skin have high levels of 5-alpha reductase activity, which converts the weak androgen testosterone into a powerful androgen, dihydrotestosterone (Luuthe et al., 1994). Women have greater preference for (or less aversion to) androstenone, an androgen-related substance in sweat, when midcycle, but not other scents tested (nicotine, alcohol; Hummel, Gollisch, Wildt, & Kobal, 1991; see also Grammer, 1993).

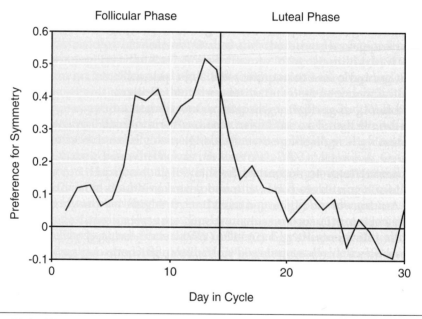

Figure 11.1 Women's Preference for the Scent of Symmetrical Men as a Function of Their Day in the Cycle. $N = 141$. Each point represents a three-day moving average. These data are compiled from three separate studies: "Menstrual Cycle Variation in Women's Preference for the Scent of Symmetrical Men," by S. W. Gangestad and R. Thornhill, 1998, *Proceedings of the Royal Society of London B, 262*, pp. 727–733; "The Scent of Symmetry: A Human Pheromone That Signals Fitness?," by R. Thornhill and S. W. Gangestad, 1999, *Evolution and Human Behavior, 20*, pp. 175–201; and "MHC, Symmetry and Body Scent Attractiveness in Men and Women (*Homo Sapiens*)," by R. Thornhill et al., 2003, *Behavioral Ecology*.

Female Preference for Facial Masculinity Compared to women, men have larger jaws, longer lower faces, and heavier brow ridges. The development of these features is affected by androgen production (see Swaddle & Reierson, 2002) and may have signaled better condition ancestrally (Thornhill & Gangestad, 1993; see also Getty, 2001). On average, men with masculine features are perceived to be more socially dominant but less willing to invest in a mateship than those with feminine faces, and some evidence suggests that these attributions may be accurate (see V. S. Johnston, Hagel, Franklin, Fink, & Grammer, 2001). Women are not uniformly more attracted to highly masculine faces. In different populations and using different methodologies, researchers have found masculine faces to be more (e.g., V. S. Johnston et al., 2001), less (e.g., Penton-Voak et al., 1999), or near equal (e.g., Swaddle & Reierson, 2002) in attractiveness relative to feminine faces. Possibly, women's preference for facial masculinization depends on the relative value they place (implicitly) on genetic fitness and male investment qualities. Consistent with this interpretation, women prefer more masculinized faces when evaluating men as short-term as opposed to long-term partners (Little, Jones, Penton-Voak, Burt, & Perrett, 2002). Male facial masculinity may also be associated with symmetry (e.g., Gangestad & Thornhill, 2003a; but see Koehler et al., 2004).

Penton-Voak et al. (1999) hypothesized that women find masculine faces more attractive when fertile than during infertile phases of their cycles. Multiple faces of the same sex were digitized and morphed to create average male and female faces. By blending or exaggerating differences between sex-specific averages, they created an array of faces that vary from androgynous to hypermasculine. Four different studies (conducted in the United Kingdom, Japan, United States, and Austria) using these or related stimuli have found the predicted shift toward favoring masculine faces midcycle (V. S. Johnston et al., 2001; Penton-Voak et al., 1999; Penton-Voak & Perrett, 2000).

In one study, Penton-Voak et al. (1999) added an important twist. They asked women to separately evaluate men's attractiveness as a short-term sex partner and as a long-term partner. As predicted, relationship status significantly moderated the fertility status effect. Fertility status affected preference for masculinity in a sex partner *only*, not in a long-term, investing partner.

The cues in scent that signal developmental stability may covary with other cues of developmental stability. Normally ovulating women from the United States rated the attractiveness of photos of men from a rural village in Dominica, West Indies. Women's preference for the faces of men with low body-fluctuating asymmetry was stronger when they were fertile (as estimated from day in the cycle) than when infertile (Thornhill & Gangestad, 2003). Koehler, Rhodes, and Simmons (2002), however, found no evidence that women find facial symmetry particularly attractive when midcycle, suggesting that these preferences are due to features other than symmetry (e.g., male facial masculinity; e.g., Gangestad & Thornhill, 2003a).

Macrae, Alnwick, Milne, and Schloerscheidt (2002) found that women recognized faces as being male more quickly when fertile (see also L. Johnston, Arden, Macrae, & Grace 2003). This effect, we suspect, is a by-product of greater salience of masculine features in male faces associated with their preference when women are fertile. The magnitude of the P300 response of the evoked potential (which covaries with the emotional salience of the stimulus) of women in the fertile cycle phase has been found to correlate with their rating of male facial attractiveness, but not their ratings of female facial beauty (Oliver-Rodriguez, Guan, & Johnston, 1999).

Female Preference for Men's Behavioral Displays   Simpson, Gangestad, Christensen, and Leck (1999) found that symmetrical men were more likely than asymmetrical men to explicitly put down competitors in a situation in which men competed for a potential lunch date with an attractive woman. Gangestad, Simpson et al. (2004) asked whether women are more attracted to men who exhibit these and related displays when fertile. The behaviors of the men being interviewed were coded for a host of verbal and nonverbal qualities, and two major dimensions differentiating men's performance were identified: social presence (e.g., composure) and direct intrasexual competitiveness (e.g., explicit derogation of a competitor). Normally ovulating women whose fertility status was estimated from day in the cycle rated the attractiveness of men in the videotapes as short-term and long-term partners. As predicted, women were particularly attracted to men who exhibited social presence and direct intrasexual competitiveness when fertile and evaluating them as sex partners; no shift was detected when women evaluated men as long-term partners (see Figure 11.2).

Gangestad, Simpson et al. (2004) did additional analyses on this data set. Men were rated for a variety of characteristics potentially valued in a mate. Women did not prefer all such features as short-term partners when fertile. While they particularly preferred as short-term partners fertile men who were rated as confrontative with other men, arrogant, muscular, physically attractive, and socially influential, they showed no preference shifts for men's kindness, intelligence,

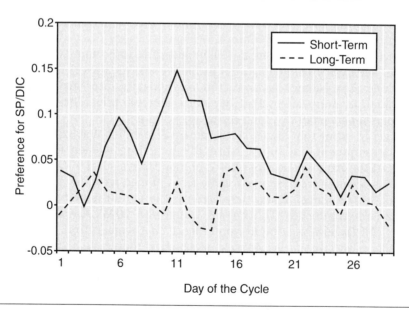

Figure 11.2   Women's Preference for Men Who Display Social Presence and Direct Intrasexual Competitiveness as Short-Term Partners (Solid Line) and Long-Term Partners (Dotted Line) as a Function of Day of Their Cycle. *N* = 238. *Source:* From "Women's Preferences for Male Behavioral Displays Change across the Menstrual Cycle," by S. W. Gangestad, J. A. Simpson, A. J. Cousins, C. E. Garver-Apgar, & P. N. Christensen, 2004, *Psychological Science, 15*, pp. 203–207.

and tendency to be a good father; men who appeared sexually faithful were seen as less sexy when women were midcycle.

Creative Talent   Haselton and Miller (2002) reasoned that creative talent may be an indicator of genetic fitness and, hence, preferred midcycle. They presented women sets of vignettes describing two men and asked them to choose one as more attractive, both within a short-term and long-term mating context. Within each set, one man had superior creativity (in painting works of art or in starting and running a small business), whereas the second had superior earning potential (as a talentless but successful abstract painter or an adopted inheritor of a large corporation). As predicted, fertile women particularly preferred the more creative men in the short-term, but not long-term, mating context.

Major Histocompatibility Complex (MHC) Traits   Research on shifts in women's preferences across the cycle have generally been inspired by ideas about the benefits of obtaining *intrinsically* good genes (e.g., relative lack of mutation in the genome or genes currently associated with pathogen resistance). One study (Thornhill et al., 2003) partly addressed the question of whether women also have design to selectively seek *compatible* or *diverse* genes through extra-pair sex,and hence, have stronger preferences for indicators of these benefits midcycle. MHC genes code for cell-surface markers used by the immune system to identify self and, by implication, foreign entities. The MHC system is highly polymorphic, which could be due to selection for heterozygosity or negative frequency-dependent selection: More complex and rare self-recognition markers may confer an advantage in the fight against pathogens. Wedekind, Seebeck, Bettens, and Paepke (1995) and Wedekind and Füri (1997) found that individuals prefer the scent of others who possess dissimilar MHC alleles (cf. Jacob, McClintock, Zelano, & Ober, 2002; Thornhill et al., 2003), which could be due to selection for inbreeding avoidance or producing disease-resistant offspring (via production of heterozygotes)—in either case, a preference for compatible genes. Thornhill et al. (2003) examined menstrual cycle variations in women's preference for the scent of MHC dissimilarity. They detected no hint of cyclic variation.

Women preferred the scent of men who were heterozygous at all three MHC loci. Two historical benefits possibly explain this preference: (1) Heterozygotes may have been healthier and hence better investors in offspring; (2) a heterozygotic mate produces a family with a given female that is more diverse at MHC alleles than does a homozygotic mate; within-family diversity of MHC may be favored because if a pathogen adapts well to the MHC markers of one family member, it is advantageous for others to have different ones (Tooby, 1982). These benefits can be obtained from a *long-term partner* with whom a female will have multiple offspring, but not from a noninvesting mate with whom she has a single offspring. It is interesting that women tended to prefer particularly the scent of heterozygotic males *outside* the fertile period (though this effect was only marginally significant, it was significantly different from the pattern for the preference for symmetry). Possibly, women particularly prefer indicators specifically important in a long-term mate outside the fertile period. In any event, these findings indicate that fertility status does not enhance all female preferences. Rather, only specific preferences are enhanced—perhaps those for ancestral indicators of genetic benefits.

Summary   Women's preferences shift across the cycle in a number of ways. When fertile, they particularly prefer the scent of more symmetrical men, more masculine faces, more assertive, intrasexually competitive displays, and creativity. Furthermore, attractiveness of these features in potential sex partners (i.e., evaluations of men's sexiness) is particularly affected; evaluations of men as long-term partners shift little if at all. There is little evidence of similar shifts in the preferences of women taking hormone-based contraception (e.g., Gangestad & Thornhill, 1998; Penton-Voak et al., 1999; Thornhill & Gangestad, 1999). No finding to date indicates that women particularly prefer markers of compatible genes or diverse genes when fertile.

TESTS OF THE EXTRA-PAIR COPULATION THEORY: SHIFTS IN FEMALE SEXUAL INTEREST ACROSS THE CYCLE

The EPC theory leads to a second prediction: *On average, women should report greater sexual attraction to and interest in men other than primary partners when fertile than when nonfertile. Furthermore, women whose primary partners lack indicators of genetic fitness should be particularly likely to show increased sexual attraction to and interest in men other than primary partners when fertile.* Changes in women's responses to their primary partners are predicted to depend on their partners' qualities: Women with partners who possess favored indicators midcycle should experience increased sexual attraction to them when fertile, whereas women paired with men who lack these indicators may be less attracted to them when fertile.

Shifts in Sexual Interests across the Cycle   Gangestad, Thornhill, and Garver (2002) asked normally ovulating women about their sexual interests and fantasies twice: once when fertile (as assessed by a luteinizing hormone [LH] surge) and once during the luteal phase (an infertile period). The average effect of fertility status on women's sexual attraction to and fantasy about *primary* partners was small and statistically insignificant. By contrast, women reported substantially greater attraction to and fantasy about men *other than primary partners* when fertile and, to a degree, significantly larger than changes in women's attraction to primary partners—findings replicated in a larger sample by Gangestad, Thornhill et al. (2004).

Relatedly, Haselton and Gangestad (2004) asked women to keep daily diaries about their attraction to men other than primary partners (friends, acquaintances, and strangers). Women reported that they were more attracted to and flirted more often with men other than primary partners on higher fertility days than during the luteal phase.

By contrast, Pillsworth, Haselton, and Buss (2004) did not find this pattern of results. Rather, normally ovulating, mated women reported greater in-pair sexual attraction when fertile. The authors noted that the relationships of women in their sample were generally new and satisfying. As relationship length increased, there was a tendency for greater extra-pair interests. Possibly, most relationships in this study were characterized by a period of infatuation with partners. Additional research is needed to examine the factors that moderate these effects more fully (see next section).

Bellis and Baker (1990) solicited responses to a survey on sexual behavior from a large sample of women through a popular magazine. Of those having primary partners, 6% reported that their last sex was an EPC. Whereas in-pair sex occurred at a fairly constant rate across the cycle, EPCs tended to occur more often on high-fertility days.

Male Partner Characteristics That Moderate the Relationship between Fertility Risk and Sexual Interests   The good genes EPC theory predicts that changes in sexual interests across the cycle depend on the features of a primary male partner. The effects of fertility status on female extra-pair interest should be driven by women with partners who lack purported indicators of genetic fitness.

Gangestad, Thornhill et al. (2004) tested whether these effects are moderated by male partners' fluctuating asymmetry. Both partners of romantically involved couples privately filled out questionnaires about events in the past 2 days twice, once on a high fertility day and once during the luteal phase. Overall, women with less symmetrical men reported greater sexual interest in men other than primary partners. The predicted moderator effect also emerged: Women paired with relatively asymmetrical men were substantially more attracted to extra-pair men when fertile than when infertile. By contrast, those with symmetrical men were not.

Women's sexual interest in their own partners yielded an opposite pattern: When fertile, women paired with symmetrical men reported greater attraction to their partners than women paired with asymmetrical men and to an extent greater than when women were infertile.

In their diary study, Haselton and Gangestad (2004) tested related predictions. Women rated their partners' attractiveness as short-term mates and long-term mates. The difference between the ratings reflected the extent to which a partner was viewed as sexually attractive but not particularly investing. As predicted, men's sexual attractiveness moderated the effect of fertility status on women's extra-pair interest: Women paired with men whose assets were as a good long-term, but not sexually attractive, partner reported greater sexual attraction to and flirtation with men other than their partners on high-fertility days. Women paired with sexy but not particularly good long-term partners showed no such pattern.

ALTERNATIVE EXPLANATIONS FOR FERTILITY STATUS EFFECTS ON FEMALE SEXUAL INTERESTS

Several lines of evidence, then, are consistent with the theory that women have adaptations that evolved to obtain genetic benefits through EPC. But a number of alternative explanations must be considered.

Women's Shifts in Sexual Interests Were Selected because of the Cost of Sex for Women   Sex is costly for women. Although sex outside the fertile period presumably had benefits ancestrally (accounting for the evolution of extended sexuality), perhaps when women are not fertile the optimal rate of sex with a long-term partner is less than when they are fertile, leading women to have greater sexual desire when fertile. This possibility cannot explain why cycle shifts are most marked for preferences concerning short-term partners rather than long-term partners, why at least one characteristic that women should prefer in long-term mates (MHC heterozygosity) shows a different pattern of menstrual cycle variation, and why women's increased sexual interest in nonpartner men at midcycle does not seem to be accompanied, in general, by an expression of lust toward the primary partner.

Women Seek Extra-Pair Sex Midcycle with Men Who Are Physical Protectors Rather than Sires with Good Genes   Ethnographic data indicate that protection by a primary mate may reduce sexual coercion by other males (e.g., Thornhill & Palmer, 2000). Possibly, women prefer short-term mates who can provide physical protection. Although symmetrical men appear to invest less time in and are less faithful to their primary relationship partners, they may be better able to provide physical protection (Gangestad & Thornhill, 1997); masculine features may function similarly. Female preference for male protection is not necessarily an explanation that is exclusive of good genes mate choice; women may obtain benefits of protection *and good genes* by selecting masculine, symmetrical sex partners. Physical protection may be more important midcycle because the cost of sexual coercion is greater when women are fertile (see later discussion). Nonetheless, it is not obvious how physical protection benefits themselves explain the observed pattern of sexual interests across the cycle. It seems unlikely that the physical protection women could gain from a short-term partner offsets the potential harm and cost they risk from their long-term partner. Related hypotheses that women seek extra-pair mates to obtain food or short-term transfer of material benefits similarly cannot account for menstrual cycle shifts.

Female Interest in Extra-Pair Sex Midcycle Functions to Give Many Males in the Social Group a Probability of Paternity, Thereby Reducing the Likelihood That Subsequent Offspring Will Be Injured or Killed by Males   This hypothesis does not predict that EPCs will occur at higher rates during the fertile phase; EPCs throughout the cycle confuse paternity.

Female Preferences for Extra-Pair Mates Target Men Who Provide Adequate Sperm and Hence Increase the Probability of Successful Conception Rather than Intrinsic Genetic Benefits   Possibly, women seek partners with high sperm quality when midcycle. Manning, Scutt, and Lewis-Jones (1998) found positive associations of body symmetry with ejaculate size and sperm motility in a sample of men attending a fertility clinic, though other studies examining associations among symmetry, ejaculate size, and sperm motility in samples of men not selected for fertility problems have yielded mixed results (Ellis, 2002; Firman, Simmons, Cummins, & Matson, 2003). Even if associations exist, it is unclear that selection of symmetrical men as short-term partners provides large reproductive benefits due to sperm quality benefits. Dominant male chickens, preferred by females, have poorer sperm quality (presumably because, relative to subordinate males, their reproductive success is less sensitive to having good sperm on the occasions they are able to inseminate females; Pizzari, Froman, & Birkhead, 2002).

Female Increase in Sexual Desire Midcycle Is a Phylogenetic Holdover from Ancestral Females Who Limited Sex to Days around Ovulation   Possibly, variation in female sexual interests across the cycle is a holdover from an ancestral species in which females were sexually receptive only close to and in the fertile period. This hypothesis, too, fails to explain several key details of the shifts—preferences for specific male features, increases in sexual desires particularly for nonpartner men, and shifts contingent on partner qualities. Moreover, given that selection has apparently extended female sexuality and modified ovulation-related stimuli to which males respond, it is unclear why it could not have similarly modified shifts in female sexual desires if those shifts lacked fitness benefits in humans. The hypothesis may, nonetheless, be correct in a limited sense: Ovulatory cycle shifts may have preceded adaptation for sire choice through EPC and, hence, these shifts need not have been constructed de novo. Previously existing ovulatory variations may have been secondarily modified for the function of sire choice through EPC.

Summary   Although each of the alternative explanations might account for one or another of the empirically documented design features, none but the EPC theory successfully explains *all* of the documented design features. The EPC theory currently best explains these features.

CHANGES IN MALE MATE GUARDING ACROSS THE CYCLE

We have discussed female adaptations entrained to their own ovulatory status. We now turn to discuss male adaptations sensitive partners' ovulatory status.

SEXUALLY ANTAGONISTIC COEVOLUTIONARY SELECTION ON MALE ADAPTATIONS

The good genes EPC theory states that selection has operated on women to be particularly attracted to male features ancestrally associated with genetic fitness when midcycle, particularly in the context of short-term sexual relationships. Hence, women experience shifts in sexual interests and attraction across the cycle, but—in accord with Benshoof and Thornhill's (1979) explanation of concealed ovulation—selection has suppressed the outward signs of ovulation. From the perspective of sexually antagonistic coevolutionary theory, however, selection should have favored *male* counteradaptations to detect their partners' ovulatory status—even if imperfectly—using whatever cues have not been fully suppressed and monitor their partners' activities when their partners have the greatest chances and motivation of producing an offspring with someone other than them.

Can Men Detect Women's Fertility Status?   Despite selection for suppression of outward cues of fertility status, subtle by-products of adaptive hormonal and other changes that occur across the cycle may not be fully suppressed. Evidence suggests that men can detect and prefer odors associated with women's fertile period. Singh and Bronstad (2001) had women wear T-shirts twice: near ovulation and during a nonfertile phase. Men preferred the scent of the shirts worn midcycle. Thornhill et al. (2003) replicated this effect (cf. Thornhill & Gangestad, 1999). Doty, Ford, Preti, and Huggins (1975) found that men preferred scents of vaginal swabs taken from ovulating women to those of nonovulating women.

Changes in Male Mate Guarding across the Cycle   Gangestad et al. (2002) asked women to report their primary partners' mate retention activities (Buss, 1988) over the previous 2 days twice: Once when fertile and once during the luteal phase. Two major dimensions, proprietariness and attentiveness, were assessed. As predicted, women claimed their partners were both more proprietary and attentive when fertile. Moreover, men whose partners reported enhanced attraction to extra-pair men midcycle especially enhanced the mate guarding midcycle. Changes in women's attraction to their own partners did not predict changes in men's mate guarding. Factors that might provoke increased male attention and mediate these effects include chemical signatures in scent and female behaviors associated with attraction to extra-pair men.

Moderators of Changes in Male Mate Guarding across the Cycle Men who lack features that women particularly prefer midcycle are at greatest risk of their partners experiencing extra-pair sexual attraction and, accordingly, might be expected to especially step up mate guarding midcycle. Haselton and Gangestad (2004) examined whether men's sexual attractiveness (relative to their attractiveness as a long-term mate) moderates the effect of female fertility status on men's jealousy and possessiveness. They found that it does: Men seen as good, long-term investors but relatively unsexy mates drove the effects of fertility status on mate guarding in this study; no change in the jealousy of sexy but not particularly good long-term mates was detected.

Women's physical attractiveness also moderated the effect of fertility status on men's jealousy and possessiveness. Highly attractive women reported relatively high levels of partner mate guarding throughout the cycle (see also Buss & Shackelford, 1997). The partners of less attractive women were possessive of them when they were fertile, but appreciably less so when they were infertile. Mate guarding can function to prevent both "mate poaching" (Buss, 1994) and cuckoldry. Men may engage in anticuckoldry tactics—which should be intensified midcycle—regardless of their partners' attractiveness, but step up antipoaching tactics— which should be more constant across the cycle—when their partners are more attractive.[9]

Some research hints that mated men's testosterone production varies as a function of their partners' ovulatory cycle (Hirschenhauser, Frigerio, Grammer, & Magnusson, 2002; Persky, Lief, O'Brien, Strauss, & Miller, 1977), though it is unclear in what direction it might change. The possibility that male endocrine function modulates and accounts for changes in their behavior across the cycle deserves investigation.

THE IMPLICATIONS OF COEVOLUTIONARY PROCESSES FOR
FREQUENCY OF EXTRA-PAIR SEX

The frequency of female EPC in humans appears to be, on average, modest and variable across populations. Of a large random sample of married women in the United States interviewed face-to-face, 15% admitted to extramarital sex (Laumann, Gagnon, Michael, & Michaels, 1994); anonymous questionnaire studies have yielded a mean rate of about 30% (see Thompson, 1983). Studies using DNA or blood markers to ascertain paternity indicate that extra-pair paternity is rare in a Swiss population (1%; Sasse, Muller, Chakraborty, & Ott, 1994), moderate in Monterrey, Mexico (12%; Cerda-Flores, Barton, Marty-Gonzalez, Rivas, & Chakraborty, 1999), and high in that city's low-income subpopulation (20%; though only 5% in its high socioeconomic status subsample).

---

[9] Neither Gangestad et al. (2002) nor Haselton and Gangestad (2003) questioned men about their mate-guarding efforts. Future research should investigate whether the cycle variation in women's reports reflect changes in men's actual mate guarding or changes in women's perception of and sensitivity to men's mate guarding.

Are these modest levels consistent with the good genes EPC theory? Imagine an experiment that will never be done, one that parallels Rice's (1996) seminal work on sexually antagonistic coevolution. Suppose that women were allowed to evolve in response to men but men not allowed to adapt to women. After many generations, women would likely gain an edge in the conflicts between the sexes—possibly evolving better means of circumventing male vigilance, reducing the costs of obtaining genetic benefits through extra-pair mating and, accordingly, doing so more often. Alternatively, if men but not women were allowed to evolve, men might evolve better means of detecting women's ovulation and avoiding cuckoldry, thereby reducing the frequency of women's extra-pair sex. Neither scenario has occurred; the sexes have coevolved and, most likely, both sexes' genetic interests are compromised by adaptations of the other sex. The mating strategies and tactics of *both* sexes have possibly undergone substantial revision through rounds of adaptation, counteradaptation, counter-counter adaptation, and so on—without, ironically, the actual extra-pair paternity rate ever having been extraordinary. Whether 2% or 20% or, as we suspect, somewhere between (and probably variable across ecological contexts), current estimates of extra-pair paternity are consistent with the good genes EPC theory.

FEMALE RISK-REDUCTION ACROSS THE CYCLE

Another major approach has guided research on ovulatory cycle shifts. Women may have evolved to avoid circumstances or sexual activities that would have led to undesirable reproductive outcomes.

ANTIRAPE ADAPTATION

The antirape hypothesis (Chavanne & Gallup, 1998) states: (1) Ancestrally, men sometimes circumvented female choice and forced copulation with women; (2) selection forged female antirape adaptations (e.g., wariness of going alone to places where women risk being raped); (3) although rape was always costly to female victims, women paid higher costs of rape during the fertile phase—possibly having a child sired by a father they didn't choose and who may not invest in the child; (4) because efforts to avoid rape entail costs (e.g., by limiting movement), the effort that women put into antirape tactics has been shaped to be most intense when the costs of rape are most devastating.[10]

Consistent with this hypothesis, normally ovulating women appear to particularly avoid putting themselves into situations perceived to entail high risk of rape (e.g., walking alone at night) when fertile (Bröder & Hohmann, 2003; Chavanne & Gallup, 1998)—despite being more likely to go out in public places when ovulating (Fessler, 2003). Moreover, women asked to imagine being

---

[10] This hypothesis does *not* require that men have evolved specialized adaptations for rape. Evidence that men have adaptation for forced copulation (i.e., rape was an adaptive even if rare contingent tactic, through which men's reproductive success shaped rape adaptations) remains inconclusive (see Thornhill & Palmer, 2000). Ancestral women, however, may have been at risk of rape even if men had not evolved adaptation for rape; rape could have been (and currently could be) an unselected-for by-product of men's desire for sexual variety, for instance. Regardless of whether rape was an adaptive contingent tactic for men, women may have evolved antirape adaptations if they were at risk of rape ancestrally.

sexually assaulted reveal greater hand strength when fertile; no such effect is observed when they are asked to imagine other events demanding strength (Petralia & Gallup, 2002).

AVOIDANCE OF OTHER SUBOPTIMAL MATING BEHAVIORS

Humans (and possibly many other species) experience disgust in response to a variety of sexual behaviors that are suboptimal, such as incest, which thereby functions to suppress those behaviors (e.g., Lieberman, Tooby, & Cosmides, 2002). Fessler and Navarrete (2003) reasoned that, because women ancestrally paid larger costs for engaging in suboptimal sexual behaviors when fertile, selection may have shaped sexual disgust to peak at that time. Women responded to a questionnaire that assessed disgust in several domains (sex, food, filth). Fertility risk positively predicted disgust only in the sexual domain.

CRYPTIC CHOICE MECHANISMS AND MENSTRUAL CYCLE VARIATION

The EPC theory argues that women have adaptations to seek, under certain conditions, a sire other than a primary partner through multiple mating. On occasion, women may have mated with multiple men within a single cycle or consecutive cycles. In this context, cryptic choice mechanisms—adaptations that affect choice of a sire during mating or postmating—may have evolved. These mechanisms should be designed to vary across the cycle.

MALE INDUCTION OF OVULATION

Jöchle (1973) argued that females may have adaptation to ovulate in response to sex with certain males (as in some other species; e.g., Smith, 1992). Recently, Preti, Wysocki, Barnhart, Sondheimer, and Leyden (2003) found that men's axillary sweat affects the LH pulses of normally ovulating women, which reflect hypothalamic responses regulating fertility and ovulation. Potentially, selection could favor females whose ovulation is induced by male cues as a means of biasing paternity. This view requires that females be sensitive to signals that differentiate men (e.g., chemical cues associated with quality). Future research should explore what male features (if any) influence women's ovulation.

IMMUNOLOGICAL EFFECTS ON FERTILITY

Though conventional wisdom suggests that the maternal immune system presents a danger to foreign sperm, it now appears that an immune response to sperm can facilitate favorable reproductive outcomes. Prior exposure to a man's sperm in the reproductive tract facilitates proper implantation of the zygote in the uterine wall (see Robertson, Bromfield, & Tremellen, 2003). Maternal immune system recognition of paternal MHC alleles (and possibly other proteins) in sperm may lead to tolerance of them in a conceptus. Consistent with this interpretation, MHC allele sharing between partners is associated with lower couple-specific fertility. The facilitating effect of maternal immune recognition of foreign MHC may be an adaptation to choose cryptically a compatible mate.

This mechanism would also tend to disfavor conception by men who have not had prior sexual relations with a female, which could include instances of sexual coercion as well as short-term sex partners. In addition, however, this system has possibly evolved to favor the sperm of a selective set of men.

Seminal fluid contains a rich variety of immunomodulatory factors that apparently function to induce female tolerance of male antigens. Broadly, the active immune system has two components: the cell-mediated system, which attacks viruses and bacteria that get inside cells, and the humoral system, which attacks normal bacteria, parasites, toxins, and other foreign bodies. Allocation of effort to one system detracts from the other. Components of seminal fluid (e.g., TGF-ß, prostaglandins, cortisol) bias the female reproductive tract toward humoral immunity (e.g., Denison, Grant, Calder, & Kelly, 1999; Robertson et al., 2003). It is interesting that the female reproductive tract appears to be biased *away from* humoral immunoactivity prior to ovulation (e.g., Franklin & Kutteh, 1999; Gravitt et al., 2003).

Sexually antagonistic selection may explain why the female reproductive tract is biased at midcycle in a direction opposing the effects of male sperm. If male fertility is enhanced by female immune recognition of sperm antigens, selection should favor seminal products that enhance that recognition (through humoral immunoactivity). The effects of those products may not optimize female immune functioning, cryptic choice, investment in nonoptimal offspring, and so on. Small differences in genetic interests between the sexes could drive a coevolutionary process through which male seminal products are selected for their powerful effects on female immune responsivity and the female reproductive tract is selected to counter these effects. That is, some males' seminal products (and, possibly, proteins on the sperm acrosome) may more effectively lead to conception and be sexually selected, whereas some females may be better able to control activities in their reproductive tract in their own interests, leading to selection for resistance.

In such a chase-away selection process, males who are most fit overall may have an edge in producing the most effective sperm (e.g., Kokko et al., 2003). Hence, sexual selection of this sort may ultimately be an instance of good genes sexual selection. If so, then female resistance is maintained by the fact that men whose semen is best able to overcome it offer genetic benefits and thereby functions as a cryptic choice mechanism for good genes.

One requirement for sexual selection to be potent is that the cost of the evolved female preference (here, resistance to male seminal products) must not be highly costly. Hence, female resistance should not markedly compromise fertility or optimal resistance to disease. It does not seem plausible that human females would pay the costs of EPC simply to run sperm competition races blind to explicit choice based on perceived features. Hence, the possibility that differences in semen properties themselves importantly drive female EPC behavior seems highly unlikely, though they could augment selection for EPC to obtain genetic benefits.[11]

---

[11] In addition, Baker and Bellis (1995) proposed that women's orgasm functions as a cryptic choice mechanism, as it purportedly facilitates transfer of sperm into the uterus. Thornhill, Gangestad, and Comer (1995) found that women with more symmetrical partners tend to orgasm during intercourse more frequently (see also Møller, Gangestad, & Thornhill, 1999; but for a failure to replicate, see Montgomerie & Bullock, 1999). It is unknown whether fertility status interacts with partner characteristics to predict orgasm frequency, though this issue is worthy of investigation. More fundamentally, the theory that orgasm facilitates sperm transport remains controversial (Levin, 2002).

CONCLUSIONS

The study of variation in women's sexuality across the cycle from an evolutionary perspective has historically emphasized the *lack* of variation (concealed ovulation and extended sexuality). As we noted at the outset, however, because copulation can potentially result in successful conception on very few, specific days, it would be surprising if selection had *not* forged psychological adaptations in one or both sexes to be sensitive to the timing of conception risk. And we now know that it has.

The footprints left by selection in ovulatory cycle shifts in female sexuality and male vigilance reveal important lessons about the historical process forging male and female sexual relations—lessons consistent with both intense cooperative investment in offspring and marked conflicts of interest between the sexes. Evolutionary psychologists, however, have only recently read and interpreted these footprints. Ovulatory cycle shifts are currently exciting topics of study. The story they tell, we suspect, has just begun to unfold.

REFERENCES

Alexander, R. D. (1987). *The biology of moral systems.* New York: Aldine de Gruyter.

Alexander, R. D., & Noonan, K. (1979). Concealment of ovulation, parental care, and human social evolution. In N. A. Chagnon & W. Irons (Eds.),*Evolutionary biology and human behavior: An anthropological perspective* (pp. 402–435). North Scituate, MA: Duxbury.

Baker, R. R., & Bellis, M. A. (1995). *Human sperm competition: Copulation, masturbation, and infidelity.* London: Chapman & Hall.

Bellis, M. A., & Baker, R. R. (1990). Do females promote sperm competition? Data for humans. *Animal Behaviour, 40,* 997–999.

Benshoof, L., & Thornhill, R. (1979). The evolution of monogamy and loss of estrus in humans. *Journal of Social and Biological Structures, 2,* 95–106.

Bröder, A., & Hohmann, N. (2003). Variations in risk-taking across the menstrual cycle: An improved replication. *Evolution and Human Behavior, 24,* 391–398.

Burley, N. (1979). The evolution of concealed ovulation. *American Naturalist, 114,* 835–858.

Burt, A. (1992). Concealed ovulation and sexual signals in primates. *Folia Primatologica, 58,* 1–6.

Buss, D. M. (1988). From vigilance to violence: Mate retention tactics in American undergraduates. *Ethology and Sociobiology, 9,* 291–317.

Buss, D. M. (1994). *The evolution of desire.* New York: Basic Books.

Buss, D. M. (2000). *The dangerous passion.* New York: Free.

Buss, D. M., & Schmitt, D. P. (1993). Sexual strategies theory: A contextual evolutionary analysis of human mating. *Psychological Review, 100,* 204–232.

Buss, D. M., & Shackelford, T. K. (1997). From vigilance to violence: Mate retention tactics in married couples. *Journal of Personality and Social Psychology, 72,* 346–361.

Cerda-Flores, R. M., Barton, S. A., Marty-Gonzalez, L. F., Rivas, F., & Chakraborty, R. (1999). Estimation of nonpaternity in the Mexican population of Nueveo Leon: A validation study with blood group markers. *American Journal of Physical Anthropology, 109,* 281–293.

Charlesworth, B., & Hughes, K. A. (1998). The maintenance of genetic variation in life history traits. In R. S. Singh & C. B. Krimbas (Eds.), *Evolutionary genetics from molecules to morphology.* Cambridge, England: Cambridge University Press.

Chavanne, T. J., & Gallup, G. G. (1998). Variation in risk taking behavior among female college students as a function of the menstrual cycle. *Evolution and Human Behavior, 19,* 27–32.

Chippendale, A. K., Gibson, J. R., & Rice, W. R. (2001). Negative genetic correlation between adult fitness for the sexes reveals ontogenetic conflict in *Drosophila. Proceedings of the National Academy of Sciences, USA, 98,* 1671–1675.

Denison, F. C., Grant, V. E., Calder, A. A., & Kelly, R. W. (1999). Seminal plasma components stimulate interleukin-8 and interleukin-10 release. *Molecular Human Reproduction, 5,* 220–226.

Dixson, A. F. (1998). *Primate sexuality: Comparative studies of the prosimians, monkeys, apes, and humans.* Oxford, England: Oxford University Press.

Domb, L. G., & Pagel, M. (2000). Sexual swellings advertise female quality in wild baboons. *Nature, 410,* 204–206.

Doty, R. L., Ford, M., Preti, G., & Huggins, G. R. (1975). Changes in the intensity and pleasantness of human vaginal odors during the menstrual cycle. *Science, 190,* 1316–1317.

Ellis, P. (2002, June). *FA and sperm quality in a sample of Boston men.* Paper presented at the annual meeting of the Human Behavior and Evolution Society, New Brunswick, NJ.

Fessler, D. M. T. (2002). Reproductive immunosuppression and diet: An evolutionary perspective on pregnancy sickness and meat. *Current Anthropology, 43,* 19–61.

Fessler, D. M. T. (2003). No time to eat: An adaptationist account of periovulatory behavioral changes. *Quarterly Review of Biology, 78,* 3–21.

Fessler, D. M. T., & Navarrete, C. D. (2003). Domain-specific variation in disgust sensitivity across the menstrual cycle. *Evolution and Human Behavior, 324,* 406–417.

Firman, R. C., Simmons, L. W., Cummins, J. M., & Matson, P. L. (2003). Are body fluctuating asymmetry and the ratio of 2nd to 4th digit length reliable predictors of semen quality? *Human Reproduction, 18,* 808–812.

Franklin, R. D., & Kutteh, W. H. (1999). Characterization of immunoglobulins and cytokines in human cervical mucus: Influence of exogenous and endogenous hormones. *Journal of Reproductive Immunology, 42,* 93–106.

Gangestad, S. W., & Cousins, A. J. (2001). Adaptive design, female mate preferences, and shifts across the menstrual cycle. *Annual Review of Sex Research, 12,* 145–185.

Gangestad, S. W., Garver-Apgar, C. E., Simpson, J. A., & Cousins, A. J. (2004). Changes in women's general mate preferences across the ovulatory cycle. Unpublished manuscript, University of New Mexico.

Gangestad, S. W., & Simpson, J. A. (2000). The evolution of human mating: The role of trade-offs and strategic pluralism. *Behavioral and Brain Sciences, 23,* 675–687.

Gangestad, S. W., Simpson, J. A., Cousins, A. J., Garver-Apgar, C. E., & Christensen, P. N. (2004). Women's preferences for male behavioral displays change across the menstrual cycle. *Psychological Science, 15,* 203–207.

Gangestad, S. W., & Thornhill, R. (1997). Human sexual selection and developmental stability. In J. A. Simpson & D. T. Kenrick (Eds.), *Evolutionary personality and social psychology* (pp. 169–195). Hillsdale, NJ: Erlbaum.

Gangestad, S. W., & Thornhill, R. (1998). Menstrual cycle variation in women's preference for the scent of symmetrical men. *Proceedings of the Royal Society of London. Series B, Biological Sciences, 262,* 727–733.

Gangestad, S. W., & Thornhill, R. (2003a). Facial masculinity and fluctuating asymmetry. *Evolution and Human Behavior, 24,* 231–241.

Gangestad, S. W., & Thornhill, R. (2003b). Fluctuating asymmetry, developmental instability, and fitness: Toward model-based interpretation. In M. Polak (Ed.), *Developmental instability: Causes and consequences.* Cambridge, England: Cambridge University Press.

Gangestad, S. W., & Thornhill, R. (2004). Female multiple mating and genetic benefits in humans: Investigations of design. In P. M. Kappeler & C. P. van Schaik (Eds.), *Sexual selection in primates: New and comparative perspectives.* Cambridge, England: Cambridge University Press.

Gangestad, S. W., Thornhill, R., & Garver, C. E. (2002). Changes in women's sexual interests and their partners' mate retention tactics across the menstrual cycle: Evidence for shifting conflicts of interest. *Proceedings of the Royal Society of London. Series B, Biological Sciences, 269,* 975–982.

Gangestad, S. W., Thornhill, R., & Garver-Apgar, C. E. (2004). Female sexual interests across the ovulatory cycle depend on primary partner developmental instability. Unpublished manuscript, University of New Mexico.

Gavrilets, S. (2000). Rapid evolution of reproductive barriers driven by sexual conflict. *Nature, 403,* 886–889.

Geary, D. C. (2000). Evolution and proximate expression of human paternal investment. *Psychological Bulletin, 126,* 55–77.

Getty, T. (2001). Signaling health versus parasites. *American Naturalist, 159,* 363–371.

Grammer, K. (1993). 5-α-androst-16en-3α-on: A male pheromone? A brief report. *Ethology and Sociobiology, 14,* 201–214.

Gravitt, P. E., Hildesheim, A., Herrero, R., Schiffman, M., Sherman, M. E., Bratti, M. C., et al. (2003). Correlates of IL-10 and IL-12 concentrations in cervical secretions. *Journal of Clinical Immunology, 23,* 175–183.

Gray, P. B., Kahlenberg, S. M., Barrett, E. S., Lipson, S. F., & Ellison, P. T. (2002). Marriage and fatherhood are associated with lower testosterone in males. *Evolution and Human Behavior, 23,* 193–201.

Greiling, H., & Buss, D. M. (2000). Women's sexual strategies: The hidden dimension of short-term extra-pair mating. *Personality and Individual Differences, 28,* 929–963.

Haig, D. (1993). Genetic conflicts in human pregnancy. *Quarterly Review of Biology, 68,* 495–532.

Haselton, M. G., & Gangestad, S. W. (2004). *Conditional expression of female desires and male mate retention efforts across the human ovulatory cycle.* Unpublished manuscript, UCLA.

Haselton, M. G., & Miller, G. F. (2002, June). *Evidence for ovulatory shifts in attraction to artistic and entrepreneurial excellence.* Paper presented at the annual meeting of the Human Behavior and Evolution Society Conference, Rutgers, New Jersey.

Hawkes, R., O'Connell, J. F., & Blurton Jones, N. G. (2001). Hunting and nuclear families: Some lessons from the Hadza about men's work. *Current Anthropology, 42,* 681–709.

Hirschenhauser, K., Frigerio, D., Grammer, K., & Magnusson, M. S. (2002). Monthly patterns of testosterone and monthly behavior in prospective fathers. *Hormones and Behavior, 42,* 172–181.

Holland, B., & Rice, W. R. (1999). Experimental removal of sexual selection reverses intersexual antagonistic coevolution and removes a reproductive load. *Proceedings of the National Academy of Sciences USA, 96,* 5083–5088.

Houle, D. (1992). Comparing evolvability and variability of traits. *Genetics, 130,* 195–204.

Hrdy, S. B. (1979). Infanticide among animals: A review, classification, and examination of the implications for the reproductive strategies of females. *Ethology and Sociobiology, 1,* 13–40.

Hrdy, S. B. (1999). *Mother nature: A history of mothers, infants, and natural selection.* New York: Pantheon.

Hummel, T., Gollisch, R., Wildt, G., & Kobal, G. (1991). Changes in olfactory perception during the menstrual cycle. *Experientia, 47,* 712–715.

Jacob, S., McClintock, M. K., Zelano, B., & Ober, C. (2001). Paternally inherited alleles are associated with women's choice of male odor. *Nature Genetics, 30,* 175–179.

Jennions, M. D., & Petrie, M. (2000). Why do females mate multiply? A review of the genetic benefits. *Biological Reviews, 75,* 21–64.

Jöchle, W. (1973). Coitus induced ovulation. *Contraception, 7,* 523–564.

Johnston, L., Arden, K., Macrae, C. N., & Grace, R. C. (2003). The need for speed: The menstrual cycle and person construal. *Social Cognition, 21,* 89–100.

Johnston, V. S., Hagel, R., Franklin, M., Fink, B., & Grammer, K. (2001). Male facial attractiveness: Evidence for hormone mediated adaptive design. *Evolution and Human Behavior, 23,* 251–267.

Kaplan, H. S., Hill, K., Lancaster, J. B., & Hurtado, A. M. (2000). A theory of human life history evolution: Diet, intelligence, and longevity. *Evolutionary Anthropology, 9,* 156–185.

Koehler, N., Rhodes, G., & Simmons, L. W. (2002). Are human female preferences for symmetrical male faces enhanced when conception is likely? *Animal Behavior, 64,* 233–238.

Koehler, N., Simmons, L. W., Rhodes, G., & Peters, M. (2004). The relationship between sexual dimorphism in human faces and fluctuating asymmetry. *Proceedings of the Royal Society of London. Series B, Biological Sciences, 271,* [Suppl. 4], S233–S236.

Kokko, H., Brooks, R., Jennions, M. D., & Morley, J. (2003). The evolution of mate choice and mating biases. *Proceedings of the Royal Society of London. Series B, Biological Sciences, 270,* 653–664.

Krug, R., Pietrowsky, R., Fehm, H. L., & Born, J. (1994). Selective influence of menstrual cycle on perception of stimuli of reproductive significance. *Psychosomatic Medicine, 56,* 410–417.

Krug, R., Plihal, W., Fehm, H. L., & Born, J. (2000). Selective influence of the menstrual cycle on perception of stimuli with reproductive significance: An event-related potential study. *Psychophysiology, 37,* 111–122.

Laumann, E. O., Gagnon, J. H., Michael, R. T., & Michaels, S. (1994). *The social organization of sexuality.* Chicago: University of Chicago Press.

Levin, R. J. (2002). The physiology of sexual arousal in the human female: A recreational and procreational synthesis. *Archives of Sexual Behavior, 31,* 405–411.

Lieberman, D., Tooby, J., & Cosmides, L. (2003). Does morality have a biological basis? An empirical test of the factors governing moral sentiments relating to incest. *Proceedings of the Royal Society of London. Series B, Biological Sciences, 270,* 819–826.

Little, A. C., Jones, B. C., Penton-Voak, I. S., Burt, D. M., & Perrett, D. I. (2002). Partnership status and the temporal context of relationships influence human female preferences for sexual dimorphism in male face shape. *Proceedings of the Royal Society of London. Series B, Biological Sciences, 269,* 1095–1100.

Low, B. S. (1978). Environmental uncertainty and the parental strategies of marsupials and placentals. *American Naturalist, 112,* 197–213.

Luuthe, V., Sugimoto, Y., Puy, L., Labrie, Y., Solache, I. L., Singh, M., et al. (1994). Characterization, expression, and immunohistochemical localization of 5-alpha-reductase activity in human skin. *Journal of Investigative Dermatology, 102,* 221–226.

Macrae, C. N., Alnwick, K. A., Milne, A. B., & Schloerscheidt, A. M. (2002). Person perception across the menstrual cycle: Hormonal influences on social-cognitive functioning. *Psychological Science, 13,* 532–536.

Manning, J. T., Scutt, D., & Lewis-Jones, D. I. (1998). Developmental stability, ejaculate size and sperm quality in men. *Evolution and Human Behavior, 19,* 273–182.

Marlowe, F. (2001). Male contribution to diet and female reproductive success among foragers. *Current Anthropology, 42,* 755–760.

Meuwissen, I., & Over, R. (1992). Sexual arousal across the menstrual phases of the human menstrual cycle. *Archives of Sexual Behavior, 21,* 101–119.

Møller, A. P., Gangestad, S. W., & Thornhill, R. (1999). Nonlinearity and the importance of fluctuating asymmetry as a predictor of fitness. *Oikos, 86,* 366–368.

Møller, A. P., & Thornhill, R. (1998a). Bilateral symmetry and sexual selection: A meta-analysis. *American Naturalist, 151,* 174–192.

Møller, A. P., & Thornhill, R. (1998b). Male parental care, differential parental investment by females and sexual selection. *Animal Behaviour, 55,* 1507–1515.

Montgomerie, R., & Bullock, H. (1999, June). Fluctuating asymmetry and the human female orgasm. Paper presented at the annual meetings of the Human Behavior and Evolution Society, Salt Lake City, UT.

Murdock, G. P. (1949). *Social structure.* New York: Macmillian.

Nunn, C. L. (1999a). The evolution of exaggerated sexual swellings in primates and the graded-signal hypothesis. *Animal Behaviour, 58,* 229–246.

Nunn, C. L. (1999b). The number of males in primate social groups: A comparative test of the socioecological model. *Behavioral Ecology and Sociobiology, 46,* 1–13.

Nunn, C. L., van Schaik, C. P., & Zinner, D. (2001). Do exaggerated sexual swellings function in female mating competition in primates? A comparative test of the reliable indicator hypothesis. *Behavioral Ecology, 12,* 646–654.

Oliver-Rodriguez, J. C., Guan, Z., & Johnston, V. S. (1999). Gender differences in late positive components evoked by human faces. *Psychophysiology, 36,* 176–185.

Pawlowski, B. (1999). Loss of oestrus and concealed ovulation in human evolution: The case against the sexual-selection hypothesis. *Current Anthropology, 40,* 257–275.

Penton-Voak, I. S., & Perrett, D. I. (2000). Female preference for male faces changes cyclically: Further evidence. *Evolution and Human Behavior, 21,* 39–48.

Penton-Voak, I. S., Perrett, D. I., Castles, D., Burt, M., Koyabashi, T., & Murray, L. K. (1999). Female preference for male faces changes cyclically. *Nature, 399,* 741–742.

Persky, H., Lief, H. I., O'Brien, C. P., Strauss, D., & Miller, W. R. (1977). Reproductive hormone levels and sexual behaviors of young couples during the menstrual cycle. In R. Gemme & C. C. Wheeler (Eds.), *Progress in sexology* (pp. 293–310). New York: Plenum Press.

Petralia, S. M., & Gallup, G. G. (2002). Effects of a sexual assault scenario on handgrip strength across the menstrual cycle. *Evolution and Human Behavior, 23,* 3–10.

Pillsworth, E. G., Haselton, M. G., & Buss, D. M. (2004). Ovulatory shifts in female sexual desire. *Journal of Sex Research, 41,* 55–65.

Pizzari, T., Froman, D. P., & Birkhead, T. R. (2002). Pre- and post-insemination episodes of sexual selection in the fowl *Gallus g. domesticus. Heredity, 88,* 112–116.

Preti, G., Wysocki, C. J., Barnhart, K. T., Sondheimer, S. J., & Leyden, J. J. (2003). Male axillary extracts contain pheromones that affect pulsatile secretion of luteinizing hormone and mood in women recipients. *Biology of Reproduction, 68,* 2107–2116.

Regan, P. C. (1996). Rhythms of desire: The association between menstrual cycle phases and female sexual desire. *Canadian Journal of Human Sexuality, 5,* 145–156.

Rice, W. R. (1996). Sexually antagonistic male adaptation triggered by experimental arrest of female evolution. *Nature, 381,* 232–234.

Rice, W. R., & Holland, B. (1997). The enemies within: Intragenomic conflict, Interlocus Contest Evolution (ICE), and the intraspecific Red Queen. *Behavioral Ecology and Sociobiology, 41,* 1–10.

Rikowski, A., & Grammer, K. (1999). Human body odour, symmetry and attractiveness. *Proceedings of the Royal Society of London. Series B, Biological Sciences, 266*, 869–874.

Robertson, S. A., Bromfield, J. J., & Tremellen, K. P. (2003). Seminal "priming" for protection from preeclampsia: A unifying hypothesis. *Journal of Reproductive Immunology, 59*, 253–265.

Rodríguez-Gironés, M. A., & Enquist, M. (2001). The evolution of female sexuality. *Animal Behaviour, 61*, 695–704.

Sasse, G., Muller, H., Chakraborty, R., & Ott, J. (1994). Estimating the frequency of nonpaternity in Switzerland. *Human Heredity, 44*, 337–343.

Schank, J. C. (2002). A multitude of errors in menstrual-synchrony research: Replies to Weller and Weller (2002) and Graham (2002). *Journal of Comparative Psychology, 116*, 319–322.

Sillen-Tullberg, B., & Møller, A. P. (1993). The relationship between concealed ovulation and mating systems in anthropoid primates: A phylogenetic analysis. *American Naturalist, 141*, 1–25.

Simpson, J. A., Gangestad, S. W., Christensen, P. N., & Leck, K. (1999). Fluctuating asymmetry, sociosexuality, and intrasexual competitive tactics. *Journal of Personality and Social Psychology, 76*, 159–172.

Singh, D., & Bronstad, P. M. (2001). Female body odour is a potential cue to ovulation. *Proceedings of the Royal Society of London. Series B, Biological Sciences, 268*, 797–801.

Slob, A. K., Bax, C. M., Hop, W. C., Rowland, D. L., & van der Werflen Bosch, J. J. (1996). Sexual arousability and the menstrual cycle. *Psychoneuroendocrinology, 21*, 545–558.

Smith, M. J. (1992). Evidence from the estrous cycle for male-induced ovulation in Bettongia-penicillata (*Marsupialia*). *Journal of Reproduction and Fertility, 95*, 283–289.

Stanford, C. B. (1998). The social behavior of chimpanzees and bonobos. *Current Anthropology, 39*, 399–419.

Swaddle, J. P., & Reierson, G. W. (2002). Testosterone increases perceived dominance but not attractiveness of human males. *Proceedings of the Royal Society of London. Series B, Biological Sciences, 269*, 2285–2289.

Swanson, W. J., Clark, A. G., Waldrip-Dail, H. M., Wolfner, M. F., & Aquadro, C. F. (2001). Evolutionary EST analysis identifies rapidly evolving male reproductive proteins in *Drosophila*. *Proceedings of the National Academy of Sciences, USA, 98*, 7375–7379.

Symons, D. (1979). *The evolution of human sexuality.* New York: Oxford University Press.

Thompson, A. P. (1983). Extramarital sex: A review of the research literature. *Journal of Sex Research, 19*, 1–22.

Thornhill, R., & Gangestad, S. W. (1993). Human facial beauty: Averageness, symmetry, and parasite resistance. *Human Nature, 4*, 237–270.

Thornhill, R., & Gangestad, S. W. (1999). The scent of symmetry: A human pheromone that signals fitness? *Evolution and Human Behavior, 20*, 175–201.

Thornhill, R., & Gangestad, S. W. (2003). Do women have evolved adaptation for extra-pair copulation. In E. Voland & K. Grammer (Eds.), *Darwinian aesthetics*. Cambridge, MA: MIT Press.

Thornhill, R., Gangestad, S. W., & Comer, R. (1995). Human female orgasm and mate fluctuating asymmetry. *Animal Behavior, 50*, 1601–1615.

Thornhill, R., Gangestad, S. W., Miller, R., Scheyd, G., McCollough, J., & Franklin, M. (2003). MHC, symmetry and body scent attractiveness in men and women (*Homo sapiens*). *Behavioral Ecology, 14*, 668–678.

Thornhill, R., & Palmer, C. T. (2000). *A natural history of rape: Biological bases of sexual coercion.* Cambridge, MA: MIT Press.

Tooby, J. (1982). Pathogens, polymorphism, and the evolution of sex. *Journal of Theoretical Biology, 97*, 557–576.

Van Goozen, S. H. M., Weigant, V. M., Endert, E., Helmond, F. A., & VandePoll, N. E. (1997). Psychoendocrinological assessment of the menstrual cycle: The relationship between hormones, sexuality, and mood. *Archives of Sexual Behavior, 26*, 359–382.

Van Valen, L. (1973). A new evolutionary law. *Evolutionary Theory, 1*, 1–30.

Wedekind, C., & Füri, S. (1997). Body odor preference in men and women: Do they aim for specific MHC combinations or simply heterozygosity? *Proceedings of the Royal Society of London. Series B, Biological Sciences, 264*, 1471–1479.

Wedekind, C., Seebeck, T., Bettens, F., & Paepke, A. J. (1995). MHC-dependent mate preferences in humans. *Proceedings of the Royal Society of London. Series B, Biological Sciences, 260*, 245–249.

Weller, A., & Weller, L. (2002). Menstrual synchrony can be assessed, inherent cycle variability notwithstanding: Commentary on Schank (2001). *Journal of Comparative Psychology, 116*, 316–318.

Wilcox, A. J., Baird, D. D., Dunson, D. B., McConnaughey, D. R., Kesner, J. S., & Weinberg, C. R. (2004). On the frequency of intercourse around ovulation: Evidence for biological influences. *Human Reproduction, 19*, 1539–1543.

Wilcox, A. J., Duncan, D. B., Weinberg, C. R., Trussell, J., & Baird, D. D. (2001). Likelihood of conception with a single act of intercourse: Providing benchmark rates for assessment of postcoital contraceptives. *Contraception, 63*, 211–215.

Wilcox, A. J., Weinberg, C. R., & Baird, B. D. (1995). Timing of sexual intercourse in relation to ovulation. *New England Journal of Medicine, 333*, 1517–1521.

Williams, E. J. B., & Hurst, L. D. (2000). The proteins of linked genes evolve at similar rates. *Nature, 407*, 900–903.

Wyckoff, G. J., Wang, W., & Wu, C. I. (2000). Rapid evolution of male reproductive genes in the descent of man. *Nature, 403*, 304–309.

CHAPTER 12

Female Infidelity and Sperm Competition

TODD K. SHACKELFORD, NICHOLAS POUND, AARON T. GOETZ,
and CRAIG W. LAMUNYON

THE TERM *SPERM COMPETITION* brings to mind an image of tiny sperm, battling with one another to fertilize a female's egg. The first definition of sperm competition—"the competition within a single female between the sperm from two or more males for the fertilization of the ova" (Parker, 1970, p. 527)—implies that sperm competition is an interaction among males' sperm, devoid of male and female anatomy, physiology, psychology, and behavior. Nothing could be further from the truth. An interactive competition among sperm is just one of many aspects of sperm competition. Broadly defined, sperm competition is sexual selection after the initiation of copulation, or *post*copulatory sexual selection (influences during copulation are still referred to as postcopulatory; see Eberhard, 1996; LaMunyon & Eisner, 1993). As with *pre*copulatory sexual selection, the postcopulatory form can occur intrasexually (male-male interactions) or intersexually (male-female interactions).

Whereas Darwin (1871) and others (see Andersson, 1994, for a review) have identified precopulatory adaptations associated with intrasexual competition and intersexual selection, sperm competition investigators aim to identify postcopulatory adaptations. The study of sperm competition, therefore, involves examining (1) how males compete to fertilize a female's egg(s) once the initiation of copulation has occurred and (2) how females nonrandomly bias paternity between two or more males' sperm (Eberhard, 1996).

SPERM COMPETITION IN NONHUMAN SPECIES

Sperm competition has been documented or inferred to exist in many species, ranging from molluscs (Baur, 1998) and insects (Simmons, 2001) to birds (Birk-

The authors are grateful to David Buss and Gordon Gallup for comments that improved this chapter. Address correspondence to Todd K. Shackelford, Florida Atlantic University, Department of Psychology, 2912 College Avenue, Davie, Florida 33314, USA, tshackel@fau.edu.

head & Møller, 1992) and mammals (Gomendio, Harcourt, & Roldán, 1998). In species with internal fertilization, there is the potential for sperm competition to occur whenever a female mates with multiple males in a sufficiently short period of time so that live sperm from two or more males are present in her reproductive tract. The outcome of such competition may depend on many factors, including mating order effects; male accessory secretions; the shape, number, and size of female sperm storage organs; and female manipulation of sperm. However, the number of sperm transferred may be one of the most important factors. A particular male can increase the probability of siring a female's offspring by inseminating more sperm, and a male that transfers very few sperm will generally experience little success in sperm competition (Parker, 1970, 1990a).

Although sperm are normally thought of as inexpensive to produce, the metabolic costs of ejaculate production are nontrivial. Across many species, these costs are attributable to the sheer numbers of sperm ejaculated, in addition to costs associated with the production and maintenance of the requisite physiological machinery (Dewsbury, 1982; Nakatsuru & Kramer, 1982). It is not uncommon for investment in sperm to depend on male body size in invertebrates (LaMunyon & Ward, 1998; Pitnick & Markow, 1994), suggesting that sperm production is limited by available resources. Repeated ejaculation can even lead to sperm depletion in some mammals (Ambriz et al., 2002). For males, therefore, there is a trade-off between ejaculate production costs and the potential benefits of delivering large numbers of sperm in any particular ejaculate.

One of the first hypotheses generated by sperm competition theory was that males deliver more sperm when the risk of sperm competition is higher (Parker, 1982, 1990a). Across species, therefore, investment in sperm production is predicted to depend on the risk of sperm competition. Within species, males are predicted to allocate their sperm in a prudent fashion and to inseminate more sperm when the risk of sperm competition is higher. In accordance with hypotheses generated by sperm competition theory, investment in sperm production is greater in species for which the risk of sperm competition is higher (e.g., Gage, 1994; Harcourt, Harvey, Larson, & Short, 1981; Møller, 1988). In nematodes, where sperm size correlates with sperm competitiveness, species with greater risk of sperm competition produce larger, but more costly, sperm (LaMunyon & Ward, 1998, 1999). Recent work, in addition, has demonstrated experimentally that exposure to mating environments with high levels of sperm competition can produce significant increases in testis size after only 10 generations in yellow dung flies (*Scathophaga stercoraria*; Hosken & Ward, 2001). The reverse is also true: Experimental removal of sperm competition in fruit flies has resulted in the evolution of lower investment in sperm production (Pitnick, Miller, Reagan, & Holland, 2001).

In addition to the evidence that investment in sperm production depends on the risk of sperm competition across species, evidence is accumulating that individual males are capable of prudent sperm allocation (Parker, Ball, Stockley, & Gage, 1997; Wedell, Gage, & Parker, 2002). Males in many species are capable of adjusting the number of sperm they deliver from one insemination to the next in response to cues of sperm competition risk. Males need to rely on cues predictive of sperm competition risk because this risk often cannot be assessed directly. Any auditory, chemosensory, tactile, or visual stimuli that reliably predict whether a female's reproductive tract (in the case of internal fertilizers) or the spawning area (in the case of external fertilizers) contains or will soon contain sperm from rival males could be used as cues to the risk of sperm competition.

There is experimental evidence that males of various species respond to cues of elevated sperm competition risk in an adaptive fashion (e.g., Gage, 1991; Gage & Baker, 1991). Of most relevance to humans is the finding that male rats (*Rattus norvegicus*) adjust the number of sperm they inseminate depending on the amount of time they have spent with a particular female prior to copulation (Bellis, Baker, & Gage, 1990). In this experiment, rats were housed in mixed-sex pairs but prevented from mating by wire mesh dividing each cage. When allowed to mate, males inseminated less sperm when copulating with a female that they had accompanied during the 5 days preceding her estrus than when mating with a female accompanied by a different male during those 5 days. Bellis et al. (1990) interpreted this finding as evidence of prudent sperm allocation, because time spent with a female prior to copulation can be thought of as "guarding" time, and "unguarded" females are more likely to contain sperm from one or more rival males.

Sperm competition can be far more costly than the loss of fertilizations to other males. Males of many species invest more than sperm during and/or after mating, and the loss of a fertilization may result in cuckoldry. Cuckoldry is a reproductive cost inflicted on a male by a female's sexual infidelity or promiscuity. In some species, the losses incurred extend after copulation due to long-term investment in unrelated offspring. This is the case for species that practice social monogamy, the mating system in which males and females form long-term pair bonds. Although it was once thought that sperm competition was rare in species that are socially monogamous, it is now clear that both males and females in these species pursue extra-pair copulations, and female sexual infidelity creates the primary context for sperm competition (Birkhead & Møller, 1992; Smith, 1984). In addition to the resources lost providing paternal care for an unrelated offspring, a male suffers the loss of the time, effort, and resources spent attracting his partner (Buss, 2004; Trivers, 1972). Because cuckoldry is so costly, males of paternally investing species are expected to have adaptations that decrease the likelihood of being cuckolded.

HAS SPERM COMPETITION BEEN AN ADAPTIVE PROBLEM FOR HUMANS?

The issue of whether sperm competition has been an important selective force during human evolution is controversial. Smith (1984) argued that facultative polyandry (i.e., female infidelity) would have been the most common context for the simultaneous presence of live sperm from two or more men in the reproductive tract of an ancestral woman. Other contexts in which sperm competition might have occurred include consensual communal sex, courtship, rape, and prostitution, but Smith (1984) argued that these contexts may not have occurred with sufficient frequency over human evolutionary history to provide selection pressures for adaptations to sperm competition equivalent to female infidelity.

Male morphology can also provide evidence of an evolutionary history of sperm competition. Across primate species, relative testicular size correlates positively with the degree of polyandry, which determines sperm competition (Harcourt et al., 1981; Harcourt, Purvis, & Liles, 1995; Short, 1979). Among gorillas (*Gorilla gorilla*), for instance, female promiscuity and sperm competition are rare, and the male gorilla's testes are relatively tiny, composing 0.018% of body weight.

Orangutans (*Pongo pygmaeus*), whose mating system falls between dispersed and polygyny and results in intermediate risk of sperm competition, have testes that compose 0.047% of body weight. Chimpanzees (*Pan troglodytes*) are highly promiscuous and males have relatively large testes, composing 0.268% of body weight. Because human testes are of intermediate size compared to other primates, composing 0.062% of body weight (Dixson, 1998; Harcourt et al., 1981), Smith (1984) argued that polyandry, and, therefore, sperm competition, was an important selection pressure during human evolution.

Evidence of an evolutionary history of female infidelity and sperm competition also is provided by the ubiquity and power of male sexual jealousy. Male sexual jealousy could only evolve if female sexual infidelity was a recurrent feature of human evolutionary history (see, e.g., Buss, Larsen, Westen, & Semmelroth, 1992; Daly, Wilson, & Weghorst, 1982; Symons, 1979), and female sexual infidelity increases the likelihood that sperm from two or more men simultaneously occupied the reproductive tract of a single woman. Based on past and present infidelity rates of men and women, it may be concluded that, although humans practice social monogamy, they are somewhat sexually promiscuous. Because of female sexual infidelity, males are likely to face the adaptive problems associated with sperm competition (Birkhead & Møller, 1992; Smith, 1984).

Evidence of adaptations to sperm competition in men and women indicates that sperm competition has been a continuous selection pressure during human evolution. This chapter reviews evidence of physiological, psychological, and behavioral mechanisms that are most parsimoniously explained as evolutionary responses to sperm competition.

Do Women Generate Sperm Competition?

Evolutionary accounts of human sexual psychology have emphasized the benefits to men of short-term mating and sexual promiscuity (e.g., Buss & Schmitt, 1993; Symons, 1979). For men to pursue short-term sexual strategies, however, there must be women who mate nonmonogamously (Greiling & Buss, 2000). Moreover, if ancestral women never engaged in short-term mating, men could not have evolved a strong desire for sexual variety in the absence of coercion or rape—contexts that would not require females to voluntarily engage in short-term mating (Schmitt et al., 2003; Smith, 1984).

Ancestral women may have benefited from facultative polyandry in several ways (for a review, see Greiling & Buss, 2000). Some of the most important potential benefits include the acquisition of resources, either in exchange for sex with multiple men (Symons, 1979) or by creating paternity confusion as a means to elicit investment (Hrdy, 1981). Ancestral women also may have benefited by accepting resources and parental effort from a primary mate while copulating opportunistically with men of superior genetic quality (Smith, 1984; Symons, 1979). Jennions and Petrie (2000) provide a comprehensive review of the genetic benefits to females of multiple mating.

Multiple mating by women is a prerequisite for sperm competition to occur, but not all patterns of polyandry are sufficient for postcopulatory competition among men. For sperm competition to occur, women must copulate with two or more men in a sufficiently short period of time such that there is overlap in the competitive life spans of the rival ejaculates. The length of this competitive window might be as short as 2 to 3 days (Gomendio & Roldán, 1993) or as long as 7 to 9 (Smith,

1984). Using an intermediate estimate of 5 days, Baker and Bellis (1995) argued that the questionnaire data they collected on female sexual behavior indicated that 17.5% of British women "double-mated" in such a way as to generate sperm competition (in the absence of barrier contraception) at some point during the first 50 copulations in their lifetimes. Although questions have been posed about the accuracy of this estimate (e.g., Gomendio et al., 1998), it is clear that women in contemporary human populations do frequently mate in a polyandrous fashion and thus potentially generate sperm competition in their reproductive tracts.

Large-scale studies of sexual behavior have not collected data on the frequency with which women double-mate specifically, but many have recorded how often they engage in concurrent sexual relationships, more generally. Laumann, Gagnon, Michael, and Michaels (1994), for example, found that 83% of respondents who report having had five or more sexual partners in the past year also report that at least two of these relationships were concurrent. Not all concurrent sexual relationships involve copulations with different men within a sufficiently short space of time to be considered double-matings, but it is likely that many do. Moreover, a major study of sexual behavior in Britain—the National Survey of Sexual Attitudes and Lifestyles conducted between 1999 and 2001 (Johnson et al., 2001)—revealed that 9% of women overall and 15% of those ages 16 to 24 years reported having had concurrent sexual relationships with men during the preceding year.

Bellis and Baker (1990) argued that women "schedule" their copulations in a way that *actively promotes* sperm competition. Active promotion of successive insemination by two or more men may allow a woman to be fertilized by the most competitive sperm. Bellis and Baker documented that women are more likely to double-mate when the probability of conception is highest, suggesting that women may promote sperm competition. When the probability of conception is lower, in contrast, women separate in time in-pair and extra-pair copulations over a 5-day period, making sperm competition less likely. Bellis and Baker argued that the results cannot be attributed to men's preferences for copulation with women at peak fertility. According to Bellis and Baker, if the results were due to men's preferences for copulation during peak fertility and not to women's active promotion of sperm competition, then in-pair copulations should occur more often during fertile phases of the menstrual cycle, just as was found for extra-pair copulations.

Bellis and Baker (1990) may have been too quick to dismiss the possibility that men prefer to copulate with a woman during peak fertility, however. Because women may be attempting to secure genetic benefits from their extra-pair partners (see, e.g., Gangestad & Simpson, 2000), women are predicted to prefer to copulate with extra-pair partners when conception is highest. A woman might simultaneously avoid copulation with a genetically inferior in-pair partner, although her in-pair partner might prefer to copulate with her precisely during the peak fertility phase of her cycle. Therefore, Bellis and Baker's finding that women are more likely to double-mate when the probability of conception is highest is consistent with the hypothesis that women sometimes actively promote sperm competition, but does not rule out the possibility that both in-pair and extra-pair partners prefer to copulate with a woman during her peak fertility.

POLYANDROUS SEX IN WOMEN'S FANTASIES

Sexual fantasy may provide a window through which to view the evolved psychological mechanisms that motivate sexual behavior (Ellis & Symons, 1990; Symons, 1979). A large empirical literature has addressed sex differences in sexual fantasy, and much of this work has been conducted from an evolutionarily informed perspective (see, e.g., Ellis & Symons, 1990; Wilson, 1987; and see Leitenberg & Henning, 1995, for a broad review of empirical work on sexual fantasy). This work documents several marked sex differences in the content of sexual fantasies, consistent with hypotheses generated from Trivers' (1972) theory of parental investment and sexual selection. Given the asymmetric costs associated with sexual reproduction, female reproduction is limited by the ability to bear and rear offspring, whereas males are limited by sexual access to females. Consequently, it has been hypothesized that men more than women have sexual fantasies that involve multiple, anonymous sexual partners who do not require an investment of time, energy, or resources prior to granting sexual access (e.g., Ellis & Symons, 1990), and empirical investigations have confirmed this hypothesis. Indeed, one of the largest sex differences occurs for fantasies about having sex with two or more members of the opposite sex concurrently: Men report this fantasy much more than do women (Leitenberg & Henning, 1995).

Tests of the hypothesis that men more than women fantasize about concurrent sex with two or more partners have inadvertently provided data on women's polyandrous sexual fantasies. Although this work clearly indicates that men are more likely than women to report fantasies of concurrent sex with multiple partners, polyandrous sex is certainly something about which women fantasize. In a large survey study, for example, Hunt (1974) found that 18% of women report fantasies of polyandrous sex, imagining themselves as a woman having sex with two or more men concurrently. Wilson (1987) surveyed nearly 5,000 readers of Britain's top-selling daily newspaper about their favorite sexual fantasy and performed content analyses on the responses of a random subsample of 600 participants. Polyandrous sex was the key element of the favorite sexual fantasy reported by 15% of female participants.

Studies using smaller samples of participants also provide evidence that polyandry is a common theme of women's sexual fantasies. For example, Rokach (1990) reported that, although sex with more than one partner accounted for 14% of the sexual fantasies reported by a sample of 44 men, it accounted for 10% of the fantasies reported by a sample of 54 women. Person, Terestman, Myers, Goldberg, and Salvadori (1989) and Pelletier and Herold (1988) documented that 27% and 29%, respectively, of the women sampled report fantasies of polyandrous sex. And fully 41% of women sampled by Arndt, Foehl, and Good (1985) report fantasies involving sex with two men at the same time. Davidson (1985) and Sue (1979) report that smaller but still sizable percentages (17% and 15%, respectively) of women recall fantasies involving sex with two or more men concurrently, and Price and Miller (1984) report that polyandrous sex was among the 10 most frequently reported fantasies in a small sample of college women. Indeed, polyandrous sex ranked as the third most frequent fantasy of African American women and as the eighth most frequent fantasy of European American women in this study.

If sexual fantasy reflects sexual desires and preferences that might sometimes be acted on, then previous research indicates that polyandrous sex is not an unlikely occurrence, particularly given the well-established finding that women more than men are the "gatekeepers" of sexual access—including when, where, and the conditions under which sex occurs (see, e.g., Buss, 2004; Symons, 1979). If, as Symons (1979) has argued, sexual fantasy provides a window through which to view evolved human psychology, then human female sexual psychology may include design features dedicated to the pursuit of polyandrous sex, with the consequence of promoting sperm competition.

MEN'S ADAPTATIONS TO SPERM COMPETITION

Sperm competition can take one of two forms: *contest competition,* in which rival ejaculates actively interfere with each other's ability to fertilize an ovum or ova, and *scramble competition,* which is akin to a race or lottery. In mammals, there are theoretical reasons to believe that most sperm competition takes the form of a scramble, and modeling studies and experimental findings support this view (Gomendio et al., 1998). Male adaptations to scramble competition are likely to take the form of physiological, anatomical, and behavioral features that increase the male's chances of fertilizing an ovum or ova in a competitive environment in which the ability to deliver large numbers of sperm is a crucial determinant of success.

IS THERE EVIDENCE OF PRUDENT SPERM ALLOCATION BY MEN?

Sperm competition theory predicts that, across species, investment in adaptations to sperm production varies with the risk of sperm competition (Parker, 1982, 1990a, 1990b), and adaptations to *high* levels of sperm competition include anatomical, physiological, and behavioral traits that facilitate the delivery of large numbers of highly competitive sperm. Sperm competition theory also predicts that, where the risk of sperm competition varies from mating to mating and where male adaptations to sperm are costly, individual males modulate their adaptations to sperm competition in a prudent fashion. When the risk varies, the modulations are likely to take the form of adjustments in the number of sperm inseminated. It is possible that the ability to modulate sperm competition adaptations will be seen even in species where the overall levels of sperm competition are not especially high—but where the costs of the adaptations are sufficiently pronounced to cause the evolution of mechanisms that allows prudent sperm allocation. Across primate species, relative testicular size (and, therefore, sperm numbers) correlates positively with the degree of polyandry (Harcourt et al., 1981; Short, 1979). Human ejaculates contain intermediate numbers of sperm compared to other primates (Short, 1979; Smith, 1984). Although much variation exists, the mean number of sperm per ejaculate for gorillas, orangutans, humans, and chimpanzees is 65, 91, 175, and 603 million, respectively (Smith, 1984).

Ejaculates do appear to be costly for human males to produce. Frequent ejaculation, especially occurring more frequently than every other day, results in decreased sperm counts (Tyler, Crockett, & Driscoll, 1982), suggesting limits to sperm production. Men hardly seem limited by sperm production, however, given the apparent wastage of sperm that occurs in humans. Sperm are continuously lost in the urine, and entire ejaculates are lost during nocturnal emissions and masturbation, although masturbatory ejaculates contain fewer sperm than do copulatory ejaculates (Zavos & Goodpasture, 1989). It has been suggested, however, that these lost sperm are older and less competitive (Baker & Bellis, 1993a) and that noncopulatory ejaculations increase the number of younger, highly competitive sperm ejaculated at the next copulation. Given the cost of human ejaculates and the fact that sperm competition risk varies from copulation to copulation depending on the sociosexual context, human males may have evolved the ability to modulate adaptations to sperm competition. The number of sperm contained in a man's ejaculate varies considerably from one ejaculate to the next (Mallidis, Howard, & Baker, 1991; Schwartz, Laplanche, Jouannet, & David, 1979). Although clinicians treat this intraindividual variability as "noise" or as a barrier to determining the "true" values of a man's semen parameters, predictions generated by sperm competition theory have led researchers to examine the possibility that some of this variability might reflect prudent sperm allocation in the face of variations in the temporal risk of sperm competition. Whether or not such variation is patterned adaptively in contemporary environments, it is possible that it may reflect the functioning of mechanisms that evolved to deal with variations in the risk of sperm competition in ancestral environments.

Men display prudent sperm allocation in at least one fundamental sense: Sperm are not emitted continuously but, instead, are ejected during discrete ejaculatory events that occur in response to sexual stimulation of sufficient intensity and duration. The only published evidence, however, indicating that men adjust ejaculate composition in response to adaptively relevant aspects of the sociosexual environment was reported in a series of papers by Baker and Bellis.

In 1989, Baker and Bellis first reported that the number of sperm inseminated by men varied according to hypotheses generated by sperm competition theory (Baker & Bellis, 1989b). For this study, 10 couples provided semen specimens collected via masturbation and others collected during copulation. In each case, participants used nonspermicidal condoms to collect the specimens and provided information about the time since their last ejaculation, the time since their last copulation, and the percentage of time spent together with their partner since the last copulation. The analysis was restricted to the first specimen provided in each of the two experimental contexts: masturbatory and copulatory. For the 10 copulatory specimens, there was a significant negative rank-order correlation ($r_s = -.95$) between the percentage of time the couple had spent *together* since their last copulation and the estimated number of sperm in the ejaculate. No such relationship was identified for masturbatory ejaculates. If the percentage of time spent apart from a partner is a reliable cue of the risk of female double-mating, then these findings are consistent with the hypothesis that there is a positive association between the number of sperm inseminated and the risk of sperm competition (Parker 1970, 1982).

What Baker and Bellis (1989b) reported, however, was a between-subjects relationship between sperm competition risk and ejaculate composition—an observation that, for a sample of 10 couples, men who had spent the most time apart from their partners since their last copulation produced copulatory ejaculates containing the most sperm. Baker and Bellis did not provide direct evidence of prudent sperm allocation by men from one specimen to the next in response to variation in sperm competition risk. It could be that men who tended to produce larger ejaculates also tended to spend a greater proportion of their time between copulations apart from their partners. Moreover, this relationship could be mediated by between-male differences in testicular size and associated levels of testosterone production if variability in these variables predicts semen parameters and certain aspects of sexual behavior.

In a follow-up to this initial report, Baker and Bellis (1993a) addressed the aforementioned problems by including in their analyses more than one ejaculate from each couple that participated in this second study. Twenty-four couples provided a total of 84 copulatory ejaculates. To assess whether the number of sperm inseminated by a man depended on the percentage of time spent together since the last copulation with his partner, only those copulatory specimens that were preceded by an ejaculation also produced during an in-pair copulation (IPC) were included in the analyses (IPC-IPC ejaculates). Forty specimens produced by five men were included in the final analysis, and for these a nonparametric test based on ranks indicated a significant negative association between the number of sperm inseminated and the proportion of time the couple had spent together since their last copulation.

Aside from the small sample size used in Baker and Bellis's (1993a) demonstration of prudent sperm allocation by individual men, there are methodological issues that may threaten the reliability, validity, and generalizability of the results. Recruited from the staff and postgraduate students in a biology department, the participants might have had some knowledge of the experimental hypothesis. It is not clear, however, how such knowledge could affect semen parameters. Knowledge about the experimental hypothesis could have affected the sexual behavior of the participants, and there is some evidence that semen parameters are subject to behavioral influences (Pound, Javed, Ruberto, Shaikh, & Del Valle, 2002; Zavos, 1988; Zavos, Kofinas, Sofikitis, Zarmakoupis, & Miyagawa, 1994). However, evidence that men are able to adjust their semen parameters in response to the demand characteristics of an experiment would perhaps be more remarkable than evidence of prudent sperm allocation in the face of cues of sperm competition risk.

Baker and Bellis (1993a) argued that increases in the number of sperm inseminated by a man in response to a decrease in the proportion of time spent together with his partner since the couple's last copulation reflects prudent sperm allocation in response to a cue of increased sperm competition risk. Several alternative interpretations are possible, however. For example, changes in ejaculate composition may be secondary to changes in female sexual behavior induced by partner absence. Women who have spent a smaller proportion of time together with their partner since the couple's last copulation may behave differently during intercourse and thus provide different stimuli prior to, and at the time of, ejaculation. This may be significant because evidence that human ejaculates obtained via uninterrupted coitus have higher semen volume, total sperm number, and sperm motility than those obtained via *coitus interruptus* (Zavos et al., 1994) indicates that sexual stimuli present at the moment of ejaculation may be important determinants of ejaculate composition.

Also, changes in semen parameters following a period of partner absence might not function primarily as a response to the risk that a partner contains sperm from a rival male but as a consequence of an extra-pair copulation during that period of absence. It is possible that changes in semen parameters occur following a period of partner absence because past absence may predict future absence (Gomendio et al., 1998). Thus, increases in the number of sperm delivered might serve simply to maximize the chances of conception during a future period of partner absence during which ovulation might occur.

PHYSIOLOGICAL MECHANISMS ASSOCIATED WITH PRUDENT
SPERM ALLOCATION

The findings of Baker and Bellis (1993a, 1995) suggest that men may be capable of prudent sperm allocation, but it is not clear how men accomplish this. The physiological mechanisms involved in the regulation of ejaculate composition are poorly understood, but clues to their possible nature might be derived from observations of the factors known to affect semen parameters.

In studies in which men provide multiple semen specimens over several days or weeks, there is substantial intraindividual variability in parameters such as ejaculate volume and sperm concentration (Mallidis et al., 1991; Schwartz et al., 1979), in part because both parameters are affected by the duration of ejaculatory abstinence (Blackwell & Zaneveld, 1992; Matilsky et al., 1993). There also is evidence that the context in which an ejaculate is produced is important. For example, ejaculates produced during copulation and collected in nonspermicidal condoms are generally superior to those produced via masturbation (Zavos, 1985). Compared to masturbatory ejaculates, copulatory ejaculates have greater volumes, greater total sperm numbers, and a higher grade of sperm motility (Zavos & Goodpasture, 1989). The percentage of motile and morphologically normal sperm also is higher for copulatory ejaculates, and these ejaculates consequently perform better on various sperm function tests (Sofikitis & Miyagawa, 1993).

The mechanisms that cause copulatory ejaculates to contain more sperm than masturbatory ejaculates are not fully understood, but the difference may be attributable, in part, to the greater intensity and duration of sexual arousal that typically precedes copulatory ejaculation. One study indicated that sexual stimulation, in the form of sexually explicit videotapes, can improve semen parameters for masturbatory ejaculates (Yamamoto, Sofikitis, Mio, & Miyagawa, 2000), but this contradicts a previous finding (van Roijen et al., 1996). An increase in the duration of precoital stimulation increases the number of motile sperm with normal morphology in copulatory ejaculates (Zavos, 1988). There also is a positive association between the duration of preejaculatory sexual arousal and sperm concentration for masturbatory ejaculates (Pound et al., 2002).

Relationships between semen quality and the duration of sexual arousal also have been documented in domesticated farm animals when specimens are collected for artificial insemination (e.g., bulls: Almquist, 1973; boars: Hemsworth & Galloway, 1979; and stallions: Weber, Geary, & Woods, 1990). Given the relationship between duration of preejaculatory sexual arousal and variation in ejaculate sperm counts across species, it is possible that males achieve adaptive changes in ejaculate composition through behavioral changes that prolong arousal prior to ejaculation. The idea that males delay intromission and ejaculation in response to cues of sperm competition risk is counterintuitive, however, because it is known that they are likely to experience increased sexual motivation at such times (see Pound, 2002). Perhaps more important, mammalian sperm competition is likely a race as well as a lottery. It, therefore, may be costly to prolong ejaculatory latency and thus delay insemination. Whether the increase in sperm numbers with prolonged arousal has an adaptive function is not clear, but this increase may depend on the same physiological mechanisms involved in adaptive increases in sperm numbers in other circumstances. An understanding of how sexual arousal can improve semen quality, therefore, can shed light on some of the possible sites where adaptive regulation might take place.

PSYCHOLOGICAL MECHANISMS ASSOCIATED WITH PRUDENT SPERM ALLOCATION

Males in many nonhuman species are capable of adjusting the number of sperm they inseminate in response to cues of sperm competition risk, and the available evidence indicates that this is something that men also are able to do

(Baker & Bellis, 1993a). Shackelford et al. (2002) investigated the psychological responses of men to cues of sperm competition risk, arguing that there must be psychological mechanisms in men that evolved to motivate behavior that would have increased the probability of success in sperm competition in ancestral environments.

Baker and Bellis (1993a, 1995) operationalized risk of sperm competition as the proportion of time a couple has spent together since their last copulation and examined changes in semen parameters associated with variations in this index, which, they argued, is inversely related to the risk of sperm competition. The proportion of time spent apart since the couple's last copulation is correlated negatively with the proportion of time that they have spent together and is arguably a more intuitive index of the risk of sperm competition. Shackelford et al. (2002) argued that the proportion of time spent apart is information that is processed by male psychological mechanisms that subsequently motivate a man to inseminate his partner as soon as possible to combat the increased risk of sperm competition.

Total time since last copulation is not clearly linked to the risk of sperm competition. Instead, it is the proportion of time a couple has spent apart since their last copulation—time during which a man cannot account for his partner's activities—that is linked to the risk that his partner's reproductive tract might contain the sperm of rival males (Baker & Bellis, 1995). Nevertheless, total time since last copulation might have important effects on a man's sexual behavior. As the total time since last copulation increases, a man might feel increasingly sexually frustrated whether that time has been spent apart or together. To address the potential confound, Shackelford et al. (2002) assessed the relationships between male sexual psychology and behaviors predicted to be linked to the risk of sperm competition (as assessed by the proportion of time spent apart since last copulation), controlling for the total time since a couple's last copulation.

Shackelford et al. (2002) suggested that men might respond differently to cues of sperm competition risk depending on the nature of their relationship with a particular woman. Satisfaction with, and investment in, a relationship are likely to be linked, with the result that a man who is more satisfied may have more to lose in the event of cuckoldry. For this reason, when examining the responses of men to increases in the proportion of time spent apart from their partner since their last copulation, Shackelford et al. controlled for the extent to which the participants were satisfied with their relationships.

Consistent with their predictions, Shackelford et al. (2002) found that a man who spends a greater proportion of time apart from his partner since their last copulation (and, therefore, faces a higher risk of sperm competition) rates his partner as more attractive, feels that other men find his partner more attractive, reports greater interest in copulating with his partner, and believes that his partner is more interested in copulating with him. The effects of the proportion of time spent apart are independent of the total time since the last copulation and independent of relationship satisfaction. These findings support the hypothesis that men, like males of other socially monogamous but not sexually exclusive species, have psychological mechanisms designed to solve the adaptive problems associated with a partner's sexual infidelity.

THE INFLUENCE OF SPERM COMPETITION ON MEN'S REPRODUCTIVE
ANATOMY AND COPULATORY BEHAVIOR

Human testis size suggests an evolutionary history of intermediate levels of sperm competition (Smith, 1984), and other aspects of male reproductive anatomy may provide insights as well. Human males have a penis that is longer than in any other species of ape (Short, 1979), but in relation to body weight it is no longer than the chimpanzee penis (Gomendio et al., 1998). Several arguments have been offered to explain how the length and shape of the human penis might reflect adaptation to sperm competition. A long penis may be advantageous in the context of scramble competition, which combines elements of a race and a lottery, because being able to place an ejaculate deep inside the vagina and close to the cervix may increase the chance of fertilization (Baker & Bellis, 1995; Short, 1979; Smith, 1984).

Using artificial genitals and simulated semen, Gallup et al. (2003) empirically tested Baker and Bellis's (1995) hypothesis that the human penis may be designed to displace semen deposited by other men in the reproductive tract of a woman. Gallup et al. documented that artificial phalluses that had a glans and a coronal ridge that approximated a real human penis displaced significantly more simulated semen than did a phallus that did not have a glans and a coronal ridge. When the penis is inserted into the vagina, the frenulum of the coronal ridge makes possible semen displacement by allowing semen to flow back under the penis alongside the frenulum and collect on the anterior of the shaft behind the coronal ridge. Displacement of simulated semen occurred, however, only when a phallus was inserted at least 75% of its length into the artificial vagina, suggesting that successful displacement of rival semen may require specific copulatory behaviors. Following allegations of female infidelity or separation from their partners (contexts in which the likelihood of rival semen being present in the reproductive tract is relatively greater), both sexes report that men thrusted deeper and more quickly at the couple's next copulation (Gallup et al., 2003). Such copulatory behaviors are likely to increase semen displacement.

In an independent test of the hypothesis that successfully displacing rival semen may require specific copulatory behaviors, Goetz et al. (2003) investigated whether and how men under a high risk of sperm competition might attempt to "correct" a female partner's sexual infidelity. Using a self-report survey, men in committed, sexual relationships reported their use of specific copulatory behaviors arguably designed to displace the semen of rival men. As hypothesized, men mated to women who place them at a high recurrent risk of sperm competition were more likely to perform semen-displacing behaviors such as an increase in number of thrusts, deepest thrust, average depth of thrusts, duration of sexual intercourse, and number of sexual positions initiated by the male, suggesting that men perform specific copulatory behaviors apparently designed to correct female sexual infidelity by displacing rival semen that may be present in the woman's reproductive tract.

One concern with the hypothesis that the human penis has evolved as a semen displacement device is that, during copulation, the penis would frequently remove a man's own semen, even if the least conservative estimates of the frequency of extra-pair copulations are accepted. The consequences of such an effect might be minimized, however, if thrusting is terminated immediately after ejaculation, and if the temporal spacing between successive in-pair copulations is much greater than the spacing between copulations involving different men. Indeed, the refractory period may have been designed for this purpose (Gallup, personal communication, July 2002). The inability to maintain an erection following ejaculation may function to minimize self-semen displacement. In addition, the costs of displacing a portion of one's own semen may have been outweighed by the tremendous reproductive benefits of displacing successfully a rival male's semen (for a review of evolutionary cost-benefit analyses, see Tooby & Cosmides, 1992).

THE INFLUENCE OF SPERM COMPETITION ON MEN'S MATE SELECTION

As Baker and Bellis (1995) noted, an evolutionary history of sperm competition may be responsible for myriad male behaviors related directly and indirectly to mating. Research informed by sperm competition theory is just beginning to uncover these behaviors. Aspects of men's short-term mate selection, for example, may have their origins in sperm competition.

To avoid sperm competition or to compete more effectively, men may have evolved mate preferences that function to select as short-term sexual partners women who present the lowest risk of current or future sperm competition (Shackelford, Goetz, LaMunyon, Quintus, & Weekes-Shackelford, 2004). The risk of sperm competition for a man increases with a prospective short-term partner's involvement in one or more relationships. Women who are not in a long-term relationship and do not have casual sexual partners, for example, present a low risk of sperm competition. Consequently, such women may be perceived as desirable short-term sexual partners. Women who are not in a long-term relationship but who engage in short-term matings may present a moderate risk of sperm competition, because women who engage in short-term matings probably do not experience difficulty obtaining willing sexual partners. Women in a long-term relationship may present the highest risk of sperm competition. The primary partner's frequent inseminations might, therefore, make women in a long-term relationship least attractive as short-term sexual partners.

As predicted, Shackelford et al. (2004) found that men's sexual arousal and reported likelihood of pursuing a short-term sexual relationship were lowest when imagining that the potential short-term partner is married, next lowest when imagining that she is not married but involved in casual sexual relationships, and highest when imagining that she is not married and not involved in any casual sexual relationships. These results suggest that, when selecting short-term sexual partners, men do so in part to avoid sperm competition.

THE INFLUENCE OF SPERM COMPETITION ON MEN'S SEXUAL AROUSAL AND SEXUAL FANTASIES

It is well documented that men's sexual fantasies often involve multiple, anonymous partners (Ellis & Symons, 1990), but men's sexual fantasies include more than sexual variety. Because sperm competition seems to have been a recurrent feature of human evolutionary history, it may be useful to interpret some facets of men's sexual fantasies in the light of sperm competition.

Anecdotal evidence suggests that many men are sexually aroused by the exclusive sexual interaction between two women. Indeed, a common scenario in movies and television shows involves two women (often implied or explicit heterosexuals) kissing or performing other sexual acts with each other while an audience of one or more men observe the acts and become sexually aroused. It could be argued that the sight of two heterosexual women engaging in sexual behaviors is sexually arousing because it suggests both women are sexually available and copulation with both is imminent. An interpretation informed by sperm competition theory, however, might argue that the sight of two heterosexual women engaging in sexual behaviors is sexually arousing because it may signal to men that the women are without male partners and, therefore, pose no risk of sperm competition.

Although the absence of sperm competition in a potential sexual partner is expected to be sexually arousing, it also has been argued that the *presence* of sperm competition may result in sexual arousal. Pound (2002) argued that men should find cues of increased sperm competition risk sexually arousing because frequent copulation can be an effective method of paternity assurance. Pound hypothesized that men, therefore, should be more aroused by pornography that incorporates cues of sperm competition than by comparable material in which such cues are absent. Content analyses of pornographic images on web sites and of commercial "adult" video releases revealed that depictions of sexual activity involving a female and multiple males are more prevalent than those involving a male and multiple females. An online survey of self-reported preferences and an online preference study that unobtrusively examined image selection behavior yielded corroborative results.

The idea that men might experience increased sexual motivation in response to cues of sperm competition risk also is supported by anecdotal accounts of men who engage in "swinging" or "partner-swapping." Such men often report that they find the sight of their partner interacting sexually with other men to be sexually arousing (Talese, 1981). Moreover, they report that they experience increased sexual desire for their partner following her sexual encounters with other men, and some men indicate that this increase in desire is particularly acute when they have witnessed their partner having sexual intercourse with another man (T. Gould, 1999).

IS THERE EVIDENCE OF CONTEST COMPETITION BETWEEN MEN'S EJACULATES?

Apart from the remarkable feat of traversing a hostile reproductive tract to fertilize an ovum or ova, sperm do some astonishing things. Sperm of the common wood mouse (*Apodemus sylvaticus*) have a hook that allows the sperm to adhere to one another to form a motile "train" of several thousand sperm (Moore, Dvorakova, Jenkins, & Breed, 2002). These trains display greater motility and velocity than single sperm, facilitating fertilization. This cooperative behavior among sperm of a single male reveals that sperm are capable of complex behavior. Might mammalian sperm display equally complex behavior *in the presence of rival sperm*?

Baker and Bellis (1988) proposed that, in mammals, postcopulatory competition among rival male ejaculates might involve more than just scramble competition and that rival sperm might interfere actively with each other's ability to fertilize ova. Mammalian ejaculates contain sperm that are polymorphic (i.e., existing in different morphologies or shapes and sizes). Previously interpreted as the result of developmental error (Cohen, 1973), Baker and Bellis proposed that sperm polymorphism was not due to meiotic errors, but instead reflected a functionally adaptive "division of labor" among sperm. Baker and Bellis proposed two categories of sperm: "egg-getters" and "kamikaze" sperm. Egg-getters comprise the small proportion of sperm programmed to fertilize ova. Baker and Bellis argued that most of the ejaculate is composed of kamikaze sperm that function to prevent other males' sperm from fertilizing the ova by forming a barrier at strategic positions within the reproductive tract. Preliminary evidence for the kamikaze sperm hypothesis came from the observation that the copulatory plugs of bats are composed of so-called "malformed" sperm (Fenton, 1984) and from documentation that, in laboratory mice, different proportions of sperm morphs are found reliably at particular positions within the female reproductive tract (Cohen, 1977).

Harcourt (1989) argued that "malformed" sperm were unlikely to have adaptive functions, citing evidence that, in lions, inbreeding results in an increase in the proportion of deformed sperm (Wildt et al., 1987). Harcourt also argued that the presence of malformed sperm in the copulatory plugs of bats is a consequence of the malformed sperm's poor mobility and, therefore, that plug formation was not a designed function of deformed sperm. Following Cohen (1973), Harcourt (1989, p. 864) concluded that "abnormal sperm are still best explained by errors in production."

Baker and Bellis (1989a) responded to Harcourt's (1989) objections and elaborated on the kamikaze sperm hypothesis. In their elaboration, Baker and Bellis (1989a) proposed a more active role for kamikaze sperm, speculating that evolutionary arms races between ejaculates could result in kamikaze sperm that incapacitate rival sperm with acrosomal enzymes or by inducing attack by female leucocytes. Baker and Bellis (1995) proposed specialized roles for kamikaze sperm and identified two categories of kamikaze sperm: "blockers" and "seek-and-destroyers." Baker and Bellis (1995) reported that, when mixing ejaculates from two different men in vitro, agglutination and mortality of sperm increased. Baker and Bellis (1995) interpreted these findings as an indication that, when encountering sperm from another male, some sperm impede the progress of rival sperm (blockers) and some sperm attack and incapacitate rival sperm (seek-and-destroyers).

Moore, Martin, and Birkhead (1999) performed the first and, thus far, only attempt to replicate some of Baker and Bellis's (1995) work, but failed to find incapacitation affects associated with the presence of rival sperm. After mixing sperm from different men and comparing these heterospermic samples to self-sperm (i.e., homospermic) samples, Moore et al. observed no increase in aggregation and no greater incidence of incapacitated sperm in the heterospermic samples. Moore et al. did not replicate precisely the methodological procedures used by Baker and Bellis (1995), however. Heterospermic and homospermic samples, for example, were allowed to interact for just 1 to 3 hours, whereas Baker and Bellis (1995) allowed them to interact for fully 3 to 6 hours. Moore et al. offered theoretical reasons for this shorter interactive window (i.e., because 1 to 3 hours is the time that sperm normally remain in the human vagina), but perhaps this interval was too short. Upon insemination, sperm have one of two initial fates: Some are ejected or secreted from the vagina, and some travel quickly from the vagina to the cervix and uterus. Perhaps the majority of sperm warfare takes place in the cervix and uterus, locations in the reproductive tract where sperm are able to interact for a prolonged period. If this is the case, Baker and Bellis's (1995) longer, 3- to 6-hour interactive window is more valid ecologically.

Aside from Moore et al.'s (1999) failure to replicate Baker and Bellis's (1995) findings, additional skepticism is generated by Baker and Bellis's failure to clearly specify how sperm can differentiate self-sperm from non-self-sperm. Given that sperm consist of a diminutive single-cell devoid of many of the cytoplasmic contents found in their somatic counterparts, a self-recognition system that must differentiate among not just different genes (because even sperm from a single male contain different combinations of genes), but different *sets* of competing genes (i.e., genes from another male), may be unlikely to have evolved. Moore et al.'s failure to replicate Baker and Bellis's (1995) findings and the absence of a clear self-recognition system is not necessarily fatal to the kamikaze sperm hypothesis, but such concerns are cause for skepticism about its plausibility, especially for the proposed seek-and-destroy sperm morphs. More work remains before we can draw a conclusion about the status of the hypothesis.

WOMEN'S ADAPTATIONS TO SPERM COMPETITION

If sperm competition was a recurrent feature of human evolutionary history, we would expect to identify adaptations not only in men but also in women. Given that selection will produce adaptations in females that allow them to influence paternity, the role of the female in sperm competition is as important as the role of the male. Female influence may be exerted before, during, and after copulation. Female choice that precedes copulation is known as "precopulatory female choice," whereas "postcopulatory female choice" refers to female influence that follows initiation of copulation (Eberhard, 1996). An evolutionary history of sperm competition, therefore, is expected to have produced precopulatory and postcopulatory female adaptations.

PRECOPULATORY FEMALE CHOICE: PROMOTING AND AVOIDING SPERM COMPETITION

Bellis and Baker (1990) documented that women are more likely to engage in successive copulations with in-pair and extra-pair partners in a short time interval when the probability of conception is highest, suggesting that women may have psychological adaptations that motivate active promotion of sperm competition, thus allowing their eggs to be fertilized by the most competitive sperm. It is possible that human female psychology also includes mechanisms designed to motivate the avoidance of sperm competition under certain conditions. Gangestad, Thornhill, and Garver (2002), for example, documented that, as women enter the high conception phase of their menstrual cycle, they are sexually attracted to, and fantasize about, men *other than* their regular partner. These results suggest that women are sensitive to the fact that favoring genes of an extra-pair partner over a primary partner is accomplished by copulation with only the extra-pair partner and not the primary partner when the likelihood of conception is high. Thus, women's sexual attraction to and fantasy about men other than their regular partner may qualify as a precopulatory female adaptation. But because men, in turn, have been selected to be sensitive to their partner's increased interest in extra-pair copulation near ovulation (Gangestad et al., 2002), women may possess postcopulatory adaptations designed to selectively favor sperm from one man over another.

POSTCOPULATORY FEMALE CHOICE: A FUNCTION FOR FEMALE COITAL ORGASM?

One such postcopulatory adaptation in women may be orgasm. Both the female clitoris and the male penis develop from the same embryonic organ, prompting Symons (1979) and S. J. Gould (1987) to argue that female orgasm is a by-product of male orgasm. Others have hypothesized, however, that female orgasm has an adaptive function (e.g., Alexander, 1979; Baker & Bellis, 1993b; Fox, Wolff, & Baker, 1970; Hrdy, 1981; Smith, 1984). A leading functional hypothesis is that female coital orgasm was designed in the context of sperm competition as a mechanism of selective sperm retention (Baker & Bellis, 1993b; Smith, 1984). Female orgasm causes the cervix to dip into the seminal pool deposited by the male at the upper end of the vagina, and this may result in the retention of a greater number of sperm (see research reviewed in Baker & Bellis, 1993b, 1995). Baker and Bellis (1993b) and Smith (1984) contend that by strategic timing of orgasm, women may select preferentially the sperm of extra-pair partners, who are likely to be of higher genetic quality than in-pair partners.

In a test of this hypothesis, Baker and Bellis (1993b) estimated the number of sperm in ejaculates collected by condoms during copulation and by vaginal "flowbacks" (i.e., ejected seminal and vaginal fluids) when condoms were not used and documented that women influence the number of sperm retained in their reproductive tract through the presence and timing of a coital orgasm. Coital orgasms that occurred between one minute before and 45 minutes after their partner ejaculated were linked with significantly greater sperm retention than coital orgasms that occurred earlier than one minute before their partner ejaculated. Analyzing women's copulatory behavior, Baker and Bellis also provided evidence that women with a regular partner and one or more extra-pair partners had significantly fewer high sperm retention orgasms with their regular, primary partner and more high sperm retention orgasms with their extra-pair partners.

Missing from Baker and Bellis's (1993b) study, however, was the explicit demonstration of higher sperm retention associated with partners of higher genetic quality. Thornhill, Gangestad, and Comer (1995) established this link. Thornhill et al. documented that women mated to men with low fluctuating asymmetry (indicating relatively high genetic quality) reported significantly more copulatory orgasms than did women mated to men with high fluctuating asymmetry (indicating relatively low genetic quality). Women mated to men with low fluctuating asymmetry did not simply have more orgasms, but specifically reported more copulatory orgasms likely to result in greater sperm retention. Another indicator of high genetic quality and related to fluctuating asymmetry is physical attractiveness. Replicating Thornhill et al.'s work, Shackelford et al. (2000) found that women mated to more physically attractive men were more likely to report having a copulatory orgasm at their most recent copulation than were women mated to less attractive men.

Although the hypothesis that female orgasm is an adaptation for postcopulatory female choice between rival ejaculates is plausible, the functional significance of the female orgasm is still hypothetical (Pound & Daly, 2000). While Baker and Bellis (1995) documented that women retain more sperm if they experience orgasm between one minute before and 45 minutes after their partner ejaculates than if they orgasm earlier than one minute before or not at all, Baker and Bellis assume that the number of sperm ejaculated is identical regardless of whether or when the woman has an orgasm. This assumption may be false, however, particularly because the duration of preejaculatory sexual arousal has been shown to correlate positively with the number of sperm ejaculated (Pound, 1999; Zavos, 1988). Moreover, it has yet to be demonstrated that female orgasm influences conception rates. If female orgasm causes the cervix to dip into the seminal pool, causing greater numbers of sperm to be retained, it would follow that the likelihood of conception will increase accordingly, but this has not been tested empirically. The observation that men are often concerned with whether their partner achieves orgasm and the observation that women often fake orgasm to appease their partner further suggests that female orgasm may have adaptive value (see Thornhill et al., 1995).

Direct evidence of preferential use of sperm by females is absent in humans, particularly because it is methodologically difficult to study female influence of sperm behavior within the female reproductive tract. Even in nonhuman animals, evidence of female manipulation of sperm is scarce and circumstantial. Although there have been rare observations of females discarding stored sperm when mating with a new partner (Davies, 1985; Etman & Hooper, 1979), most studies infer female manipulation based on patterns of sperm storage or patterns of offspring paternity (see, e.g., Eberhard, 1996). Because much of postcopulatory competition is played out in the reproductive tract, it is likely that human females have evolved a host of adaptations in response to sperm competition.

Far fewer adaptations to sperm competition have been proposed in women than in men. The fact that the bulk of this chapter focuses on men's adaptations is an accurate reflection of the historical and current state of research and theory in the field. Intersexual conflict between ancestral males and females produces a co-evolutionary arms race between the sexes, in which an advantage gained by one sex selects for counteradaptations in the other sex (see, e.g., Rice, 1996). Thus, men's numerous adaptations to sperm competition are likely to be met by numerous adaptations in women.

CONCLUSIONS

In this chapter, we have attempted to describe the far-reaching consequences of female infidelity, specifically sperm competition. Sperm competition and its effects were not discussed directly in the nonhuman literature until the 1970s and were ignored in humans well into the 1980s. Evolutionary-minded researchers are only beginning to uncover the anatomical, physiological, and psychological features produced by an evolutionary history of sperm competition. Sperm competition may have influenced men's and women's reproductive anatomy and physiology, men's attraction to and sexual interest in their partners, men's copulatory behaviors, men's short-term mate selection, and men's sexual arousal and sexual fantasies. Discovering the ways in which sperm competition may have designed human anatomy, physiology, and psychology will be challenging but necessary if we are to achieve a comprehensive understanding of human sexuality.

REFERENCES

Alexander, R. D. (1979). Sexuality and sociality in humans and other primates. In A. Katchadourian (Ed.), *Human sexuality* (pp. 81–97). Berkeley: University of California Press.

Almquist, J. O. (1973). Effects of sexual preparation on sperm output, semen characteristics and sexual activity of beef bulls with a comparison to dairy bulls. *Journal of Animal Science, 36,* 331–336.

Ambriz, D., Rosales, A. M., Sotelo, R., Mora, J. A., Rosado, A., & Garcia, A. R. (2002). Changes in the quality of rabbit semen in 14 consecutive ejaculates obtained every 15 minutes. *Archives of Andrology, 48,* 389–395.

Andersson, M. (1994). *Sexual selection.* Princeton, NJ: Princeton University Press.

Arndt, W. B., Jr., Foehl, J. C., & Good, F. E. (1985). Specific sexual fantasy themes: A multidimensional study. *Journal of Personality and Social Psychology, 48,* 472–480.

Baker, R. R., & Bellis, M. A. (1988). "Kamikaze" sperm in mammals? *Animal Behaviour, 36,* 936–939.

Baker, R. R., & Bellis, M. A. (1989a). Elaboration of the kamikaze sperm hypothesis: A reply to Harcourt. *Animal Behaviour, 37,* 865–867.

Baker, R. R., & Bellis, M. A. (1989b). Number of sperm in human ejaculates varies in accordance with sperm competition theory. *Animal Behaviour, 37,* 867–869.

Baker, R. R., & Bellis, M. A. (1993a). Human sperm competition: Ejaculate adjustment by males and the function of masturbation. *Animal Behaviour, 46,* 861–885.

Baker, R. R., & Bellis, M. A. (1993b). Human sperm competition: Ejaculate manipulation by females and a function for the female orgasm. *Animal Behaviour, 46,* 887–909.

Baker, R. R., & Bellis, M. A. (1995). *Human sperm competition.* London: Chapman & Hall.

Baur, B. (1998). Sperm competition in molluscs. In T. R. Birkhead & A. P. Møller (Eds.), *Sperm competition and sexual selection* (pp. 255–305). San Diego, CA: Academic Press.

Bellis, M. A., & Baker, R. R. (1990). Do females promote sperm competition: Data for humans. *Animal Behaviour, 40,* 197–199.

Bellis, M. A., Baker, R. R., & Gage, M. J. G. (1990). Variation in rat ejaculates consistent with the Kamikaze Sperm Hypothesis. *Journal of Mammalogy, 71,* 479–480.

Birkhead, T. R., & Møller, A. P. (1992). *Sperm competition in birds.* London: Academic Press.

Blackwell, J. M., & Zaneveld, L. J. (1992). Effect of abstinence on sperm acrosin, hypoosmotic swelling, and other semen variables. *Fertility and Sterility, 58,* 798–802.

Buss, D. M. (2004). *The evolution of desire* (Rev. ed.). New York: Basic Books.

Buss, D. M., Larsen, R. J., Westen, D., & Semmelroth, J. (1992). Sex differences in jealousy: Evolution, physiology and psychology. *Psychological Science, 3,* 251–255.

Buss, D. M., & Schmitt, D. P. (1993). Sexual strategies theory: An evolutionary perspective on human mating. *Psychological Review, 100,* 204–232.

Cohen, J. (1973). Cross-overs, sperm redundancy and their close association. *Heredity, 31,* 408–413.

Cohen, J. (1977). *Reproduction.* London: Butterworth.

Daly, M., Wilson, M., & Weghorst, J. (1982). Male sexual jealousy. *Ethology and Sociobiology, 3,* 11–27.

Darwin, C. (1871). *The descent of man and selection in relation to sex.* London: Murray.

Davidson, J. K. (1985). The utilization of sexual fantasies by sexually experienced university students. *Journal of American Health, 34,* 24–32.

Davies, N. B. (1985). Cooperation and conflict among dunnocks: *Prunella modularis,* in a variable mating system. *Animal Behaviour, 33,* 628–648.

Dewsbury, D. A. (1982). Ejaculate cost and male choice. *American Naturalist, 119,* 601–610.

Dixson, A. F. (1998). *Primate sexuality.* New York: Oxford University Press.

Eberhard, W. G. (1996). *Female control.* Princeton, NJ: Princeton University Press.

Ellis, B. J., & Symons, D. (1990). Sex differences in sexual fantasy: An evolutionary psychological approach. *Journal of Sex Research, 27,* 527–555.

Etman, A. A. M., & Hooper, G. H. S. (1979). Sperm precedence of the last mating in *Spodoptera litura. Annals of the Entomological Society of America, 72,* 119–120.

Fenton, M. B. (1984). The case of vepertilionid and rhinolophid bats. In R. L. Smith (Ed.), *Sperm competition and the evolution of animal mating systems* (pp. 573–587). London: Academic Press.

Fox, C. A., Wolff, H. S., & Baker, J. A. (1970). Measurement of intra-vaginal and intra-uterine pressures during human coitus by radio-telemetry. *Journal of Reproduction and Fertility, 22,* 243–251.

Gage, M. J. G. (1991). Risk of sperm competition directly affects ejaculate size in the Mediterranean fruit fly. *Animal Behaviour, 42,* 1036–1037.

Gage, M. J. G. (1994). Associations between body-size, mating pattern, testis size and sperm lengths across butterflies. *Proceedings of the Royal Society of London. Series B, 258,* 247–254.

Gage, M. J. G., & Baker, R. R. (1991). Ejaculate size varies with sociosexual situation in an insect. *Ecological Entomology, 16,* 331–337.

Gallup, G. G., Burch, R. L., Zappieri, M. L., Parvez, R. A., Stockwell, M. L., & Davis, J. A. (2003). The human penis as a semen displacement device. *Evolution and Human Behavior, 24,* 277–289.

Gangestad, S. W., & Simpson, J. A. (2000). The evolution of human mating: Trade-offs and strategic pluralism. *Behavior and Brain Sciences, 23,* 573–587.

Gangestad, S. W., Thornhill, R., & Garver, C. E. (2002). Changes in women's sexual interests and their partner's mate-retention tactics across the menstrual cycle: Evidence for shifting conflicts of interest. *Proceedings of the Royal Society of London, 269,* 975–982.

Goetz, A. T., Shackelford, T. K., Weekes-Shackelford, V. A., Euler, H. A., Hoier, S., & Schmitt, D. P. (2003). *Mate retention, semen displacement, and human sperm competition: A preliminary investigation of tactics to prevent and correct female infidelity.* Manuscript under review.

Gomendio, M., Harcourt, A. H., & Roldán, E. R. S. (1998). Sperm competition in mammals. In T. R. Birkhead & A. P. Møller (Eds.), *Sperm competition and sexual selection* (pp. 667–756). New York: Academic Press.

Gomendio, M., & Roldán, E. R. S. (1993). Mechanisms of sperm competition: Linking physiology and behavioral ecology. *Trends in Ecology and Evolution, 8,* 95–100.

Gould, S. J. (1987). Freudian slip. *Natural History, 96,* 14–21.

Gould, T. (1999). *The lifestyle.* New York: Firefly.

Greiling, H., & Buss, D. M. (2000). Women's sexual strategies: The hidden dimension of extra-pair mating. *Personality and Individual Differences, 28,* 929–963.

Harcourt, A. H. (1989). Deformed sperm are probably not adaptive. *Animal Behaviour, 37,* 863–865.

Harcourt, A. H., Harvey, P. H., Larson, S. G., & Short, R. V. (1981). Testis weight, body weight, and breeding system in primates. *Nature, 293,* 55–57.

Harcourt, A. H., Purvis, A., & Liles, L. (1995). Sperm competition: Mating system, not breeding season, affects testes size of primates. *Functional Ecology, 9,* 468–476.

Hemsworth, P. H., & Galloway, D. B. (1979). The effect of sexual stimulation on the sperm output of the domestic boar. *Animal Reproduction Science, 2,* 387–394.

Hosken, D. J., & Ward, P. I. (2001). Experimental evidence for testis size evolution via sperm competition. *Ecology Letters, 4,* 10–13.

Hrdy, S. B. (1981). *The woman that never evolved.* Cambridge, MA: Harvard University Press.

Hunt, M. (1974). *Sexual behavior in the 1970's.* Chicago: Playboy Press.

Jennions, M. D., & Petrie, M. (2000). Why do females mate multiply? A review of the genetic benefits. *Biological Reviews of the Cambridge Philosophical Society, 75,* 21–64.

Johnson, A. M., Mercer, C. H., Erens, B., Copas, A. J., McManus, S., Wellings, K., et al. (2001). Sexual behaviour in Britain: Partnerships, practices, and HIV risk behaviours. *Lancet, 358,* 1835–1842.

LaMunyon, C. W., & Eisner, T. (1993). Post-copulatory sexual selection in an arctiid moth (*Utetheisa ornatrix*). *Proceedings of the National Academy of Sciences, USA, 90,* 4689–4692.

LaMunyon, C. W., & Ward, S. (1998). Larger sperm outcompete smaller sperm in the nematode C. *elegans. Proceedings of the Royal Society of London. Series B, 265,* 1997–2002.

LaMunyon, C. W., & Ward, S. (1999). Evolution of sperm size in nematodes: Sperm competition favours larger sperm. *Proceedings of the Royal Society of London. Series B, 266,* 263–267.

Laumann, E. O., Gagnon, J. H., Michael, R. T., & Michaels, S. (1994). *The social organization of sexuality.* Chicago: University of Chicago Press.

Leitenberg, H., & Henning, K. (1995). Sexual fantasy. *Psychological Bulletin, 117,* 469–496.

Mallidis, C., Howard, E. J., & Baker, H. W. G. (1991). Variation of semen quality in normal men. *International Journal of Andrology, 14,* 99–107.

Matilsky, M., Battino, S., Benami, M., Geslevich, Y., Eyali, V., & Shalev, E. (1993). The effect of ejaculatory frequency on semen characteristics of normozoospermic and oligozoospermic men from an infertile population. *Human Reproduction, 8,* 71–73.

Møller, A. P. (1988). Testes size, ejaculate quality and sperm competition in birds. *Biological Journal of the Linnean Society, 33,* 273–283.

Moore, H., Dvorakova, K., Jenkins, N., & Breed, W. (2002). Exceptional sperm cooperation in the wood mouse. *Nature, 418,* 174–177.

Moore, H. D., Martin, M., & Birkhead, T. R. (1999). No evidence for killer sperm or other selective interactions between human spermatozoa in ejaculates of different males in vitro. *Proceedings of the Royal Society of London. Series B, 266,* 2343–2350.

Nakatsuru, K., & Kramer, D. L. (1982). Is sperm cheap: Male fertility and female choice in the lemon tetra (Pisces characidae). *Science, 216,* 753–755.

Parker, G. A. (1970). Sperm competition and its evolutionary consequences in the insects. *Biological Reviews, 45,* 525–567.

Parker, G. A. (1982). Why are there so many tiny sperm? Sperm competition and the maintenance of two sexes. *Journal of Theoretical Biology, 96,* 281–294.

Parker, G. A. (1990a). Sperm competition games: Raffles and roles. *Proceedings of the Royal Society of London. Series B, 242,* 120–126.

Parker, G. A. (1990b). Sperm competition games: Sneaks and extra-pair copulations. *Proceedings of the Royal Society of London. Series B, 242,* 127–133.

Parker, G. A., Ball, M. A., Stockley, P., & Gage, M. J. G. (1997). Sperm competition games: A prospective analysis of risk assessment. *Proceedings of the Royal Society of London. Series B, 264,* 1793–1802.

Pelletier, L. A., & Herold, E. S. (1988). The relationship of age, sex guilt, and sexual experience with female sexual fantasies. *Journal of Sex Research, 24,* 250–256.

Person, E. S., Terestman, N., Myers, W. A., Goldberg, E. L., & Salvadori, C. (1989). Gender differences in sexual behaviors and fantasies in a college population. *Journal of Sex and Marital Therapy, 15,* 187–198.

Pitnick, S., & Markow, T. A. (1994). Large-male advantages associated with costs of sperm production in *Drosophila hidey,* a species with giant sperm. *Proceedings of the National Academy of Sciences, USA, 91,* 9277–9281.

Pitnick, S., Miller, G. T., Reagan, J., & Holland, B. (2001). Males' evolutionary responses to experimental removal of sexual selection. *Proceedings of the Royal Society of London. Series B, 268,* 1071–1080.

Pound, N. (1999). Effects of morphine on electrically evoked contractions of the vas deferens in two congeneric rodent species differing in sperm competition intensity. *Proceedings of the Royal Society of London. Series B, 266,* 1755–1858.

Pound, N. (2002). Male interest in visual cues of sperm competition risk. *Evolution and Human Behavior, 23,* 443–466.

Pound, N., & Daly, M. (2000). Functional significance of human female orgasm still hypothetical. *Behavioral and Brain Sciences, 23,* 620–621.

Pound, N., Javed, M. H., Ruberto, C., Shaikh, M. A., & Del Valle, A. P. (2002). Duration of sexual arousal predicts semen parameters for masturbatory ejaculates. *Physiology and Behavior, 76,* 685–689.

Price, J. H., & Miller, P. A. (1984). Sexual fantasies of Black and of White college students. *Psychological Reports, 54,* 1007–1014.

Rice, W. R. (1996). Sexually antagonistic male adaptation triggered by experimental arrest of female evolution. *Nature, 381,* 232–234.

Rokach, A. (1990). Content analysis of sexual fantasies of males and females. *Journal of Psychology, 124,* 427–436.

Schmitt, D. P., Alcalay, L., Allik, J., Ault, L., Austers, I., Bennett, K. L., et al. (2003). Universal sex differences in the desire for sexual variety: Tests from 52 nations, 6 continents, and 13 islands. *Journal of Personality and Social Psychology, 85,* 85–104.

Schwartz, D., Laplanche, A., Jouannet, P., & David, G. (1979). Within-subject variability of human semen in regard to sperm count, volume, total number of spermatozoa and length of abstinence. *Journal of Reproduction and Fertility, 57,* 391–395.

Shackelford, T. K., Goetz, A. T., LaMunyon, C. W., Quintus, B. J., & Weekes-Shackelford, V. A. (2004). Sex differences in sexual psychology produce sex similar preferences for a short-term mate. *Archives of Sexual Behavior, 33,* 405–412.

Shackelford, T. K., LeBlanc, G. J., Weekes-Shackelford, V. A., Bleske-Rechek, A. L., Euler, H. A., & Hoier, S. (2002). Psychological adaptation to human sperm competition. *Evolution and Human Behavior, 23,* 123–138.

Shackelford, T. K., Weekes-Shackelford, V. A., LeBlanc, G. J., Bleske, A. L., Euler, H. A., & Hoier, S. (2000). Female coital orgasm and male attractiveness. *Human Nature, 11,* 299–306.

Short, R. V. (1979). Sexual selection and its component parts, somatic and genital selection as illustrated by man and the great apes. *Advances in the Study of Behavior, 9,* 131–158.

Simmons, L. W. (2001). *Sperm competition and its evolutionary consequences in the insects.* Princeton, NJ: Princeton University Press.

Smith, R. L. (1984). Human sperm competition. In R. L. Smith (Ed.), *Sperm competition and the evolution of animal mating systems* (pp. 601–660). New York: Academic Press.

Sofikitis, N. V., & Miyagawa, I. (1993). Endocrinological, biophysical, and biochemical parameters of semen collected via masturbation versus sexual intercourse. *Journal of Andrology, 14,* 366–373.

Sue, D. (1979). Erotic fantasies of college students during coitus. *Journal of Sex Research, 15,* 299–305.

Symons, D. (1979). *The evolution of human sexuality.* New York: Oxford University Press.

Talese, G. (1981). *Thy neighbor's wife.* New York: Ballantine Books.

Tooby, J., & Cosmides, L. (1992). The psychological foundations of culture. In J. H. Barkow, L. Cosmides, & J. Tooby (Eds.), *The adapted mind* (pp. 19–136). New York: Oxford University Press.

Thornhill, R., Gangestad, S. W., & Comer, R. (1995). Human female orgasm and mate fluctuating asymmetry. *Animal Behaviour, 50,* 1601–1615.

Trivers, R. L. (1972). Parental investment and sexual selection. In B. Campbell (Ed.), *Sexual selection and the descent of man* (pp. 139–179). London: Aldine.

Tyler, J. P., Crockett, N. G., & Driscoll, G. L. (1982). Studies of human seminal parameters with frequent ejaculation: I. Clinical characteristics. *Clinical Reproduction and Fertility, 1,* 273–285.

van Roijen, J. H., Slob, A. K., Gianotten, W. L., Dohle, G. R., vander Zon, A. T. M., Vreeburg, J. T. M., et al. (1996). Sexual arousal and the quality of semen produced by masturbation. *Human Reproduction, 11,* 147–151.

Weber, J. A., Geary, R. T., & Woods, G. L. (1990). Changes in accessory sex glands of stallions after sexual preparation and ejaculation. *Journal of the American Veterinary Medical Association, 196,* 1084–1089.

Wedell, N., Gage, M. J. G., & Parker, G. A. (2002). Sperm competition, male prudence and sperm-limited females. *Trends in Ecology and Evolution, 17,* 313–320.

Wildt, D. E., Bush, M., Goodrowe, K. L., Packer, C., Pusey, A. E., Brown, J. L., et al. (1987). Reproductive and genetic consequences of founding isolated lion populations. *Nature, 329,* 328–331.

Wilson, G. D. (1987). Male-female differences in sexual activity, enjoyment and fantasies. *Personality and Individual Differences, 8,* 125–127.

Yamamoto, Y., Sofikitis, N., Mio, Y., & Miyagawa, I. (2000). Influence of sexual stimulation on sperm parameters in semen samples collected via masturbation from normozoospermic men or cryptozoospermic men participating in an assisted reproduction programme. *Andrologia, 32,* 131–138.

Zavos, P. M. (1985). Seminal parameters of ejaculates collected from oligospermic and normospermic patients via masturbation and at intercourse with the use of a Silastic seminal fluid collection device. *Fertility and Sterility, 44,* 517–520.

Zavos, P. M. (1988). Seminal parameters of ejaculates collected at intercourse with the use of a seminal collection device with different levels of precoital stimulation. *Journal of Andrology, 9,* 36.

Zavos, P. M., & Goodpasture, J. C. (1989). Clinical improvements of specific seminal deficiencies via intercourse with a seminal collection device versus masturbation. *Fertility and Sterility, 51,* 190–193.

Zavos, P. M., Kofinas, G. D., Sofikitis, N. V., Zarmakoupis, P. N., & Miyagawa, I. (1994). Differences in seminal parameters in specimens collected via intercourse and incomplete intercourse (coitus interruptus). *Fertility and Sterility, 61,* 1174–1176.

CHAPTER 13

Sexual Coercion

NEIL M. MALAMUTH, MARK HUPPIN, and BRYANT PAUL

I N THIS CHAPTER, we discuss evolutionary psychological (EP) perspectives on sexual coercion, defined as acts that involve sexual behaviors whereby one of the individuals does not fully consent to the acts. Usually some use of physical force, threat, or some other form of coercion is used. EP perspectives seek to identify ultimate causes, complementing the focus on proximate causes only characteristic of other psychological theorizing. In addressing ultimate causation, evolutionary psychologists have often asked whether the ability to inflict sexual coercion and/or to avoid it contributed to reproductive success in our species' ancestral history, possibly giving rise to dedicated psychological mechanisms pertaining to coercive sex. Although addressing such questions is typical in EP theorizing, some critics have raised concerns that this might imply that sexual coercion is "natural" in the sense of inevitable or morally neutral, an implication we clearly wish to avoid (i.e., the naturalistic fallacy).

The observable behaviors encompassed within the category of sexual coercion may include acts with considerably differing motivations and causal antecedents (Buss, 2003; Mealey, 1995). Nevertheless, in applying the EP paradigm, we might begin by considering clues to motivational differences between males and females that may "set the stage" for the potential occurrence of sexual coercion generally. In particular, differences in minimal parental investment (Trivers, 1972) may contribute to a greater likelihood that on average a male will be motivated to have sexual relations with certain females than vice versa and that, for males, sex may be more easily separated from intimate emotions associated with long-term mating (Buss & Schmitt, 1993). Such differences may create conflicts that in certain contexts result in some men using coercion to overcome female reluctance and resistance. In keeping with the predictions derived from parental investment theory is the finding that across various societies and recorded human history, as well as across species where sexual aggression occurs, there are large sex differences in the use of sexual coercion. An illustrative example of research in current environments is that of Hines and Saudino (2003), who found sex differences not only in

The authors thank Eugenie Dye, Gad Horowitz, and Tamara Malamuth for their valuable comments on earlier drafts of this manuscript.

the frequency of sexual coercion but also in the type used. They found that "...
unlike men who were sexually coercive, sexually coercive females did not use
threats or force to make their partners have sex with them; they insisted on the
acts instead ..." (p. 214).

Much EP theorizing on sexual coercion has focused on models that directly or
indirectly implicate condition-dependent psychological mechanisms affecting an
individual's propensity to coerce. Environmental experiences, particularly in certain critical early stages, are said to result in the *calibration* of mechanisms at relatively fixed values, which can lead to lifelong differences in thresholds for
evoking sexually coercive responses. In contrast, EP theorizing typically has not
stressed any direct links between genetic differences and sexual coercion. However, there has been some consideration of the possibility that some genetic differences underlie certain personality and other characteristics that indirectly
affect the propensity to sexually coerce (L. Ellis, 1989; Malamuth, 1998). Lending
support to the potential usefulness of also considering genetic factors is evidence
of the ability to genetically breed mice that are either more or less sexually aggressive (Canastar & Maxson, 2003).

In this chapter, we center our attention on the male perpetrator's psychology.
Although such a focus is in keeping with the emphasis to date in EP theorizing and
research, it is more likely that specialized mechanisms for avoiding being sexually
coerced would have evolved in females than that specialized mechanisms for engaging in sexual coercion might have evolved in males. Buss (2003) reviewed several such proposed mechanisms for avoiding being victimized. Within the calculus
of evolutionary currency predicted from parental investment theory, in ancestral
environments the likely reproductive costs to females of losing the ability to choose
among potential mating partners due to sexual coercion would have been greater
than the potential reproductive increase to males of, at times, using coercive sex.
This may help explain why it has been found that in current environments victims
of sexual coercion suffer relatively higher trauma from sexual violence compared to
other types of physical assaults, even after controlling for the degree of physical
severity of the various assaults (e.g., Bennice, Resick, Mechanic, & Astin, 2003).

SEXUAL COERCION IN OTHER SPECIES

Sexual coercion, physical force, harassment, and other intimidation to obtain sex
have been reported in many species, although there appear to be far more species
where sexual coercion has not been reported. Clutton-Brock and Parker (1995)
suggested that three general forms of sexual coercion occur in other species: (1)
intimidation, where males punish females who refuse to mate and thus increase
the probability of securing future matings; (2) forced copulation, where physical
force is used to achieve intromission; and (3) harassment, where male aggression
imposes costs on females that increase the probability of immediate mating. More
recently, based on an in-depth review of the research literature on forced copulation among nonhumans, Lalumière, Harris, Quinsey, and Rice (in press) distilled
a number of specific characteristics that are regularly found to exist in those
species that exhibit some form of sexual coercion. Across all nonhuman species,
forced copulation is always perpetrated by males on female victims. Despite the
tendency of females in some species to be rather assertive in the mating process,
the authors could not find one instance of a female forcing sex on a male. Further,

fertile females are far more likely to be the target of forced copulation than those who are infertile. Relatedly, evidence suggests that forced copulation does occasionally result in insemination, fertilization, and offspring. Also, the male members of most species tend not to engage solely in coercive sexual behaviors. In fact, most males that engage in forced copulation are, at other times, typically also seen courting females.

Finally, Lalumière et al. (in press) recognized the role of individual differences within members of particular species in sexual coercion. Certain males are more likely than others to engage in forced copulation. Some males are more successful at sexual coercion than others. After reviewing the wide range of data available and alternative explanations, Lalumière et al. concluded that sexual coercion (particularly in the form of forced copulation) ". . . is a tactic used by some males under some conditions to increase reproduction" (p. 59).

The clearest indication of sexual coercion in other species would be evidence of a specific morphological adaptation for coercive sex. R. Thornhill and Sauer (1991) describe such a phenotypic feature in certain scorpion flies that appears to serve solely to allow a male scorpion fly to copulate with an unwilling female. The feature, a nodal organ, or clamplike device, is used to pin down one of the female's forewings during mating and has been observed to be used only for this purpose. Rendering the nodal organ inoperational renders the male scorpion fly unable to forcibly copulate with a female. The nodal organ in this species does not appear to serve any purpose other than rape.

Morphology specifically designed to facilitate coercive mating has been found to occur not only in scorpion flies but also in other insect species (e.g., Arnqvist, 1989). However, it is noteworthy that the number of examples of specialized mechanisms for sexual coercion that have been well identified in other species is very limited, particularly in species more similar to humans than insects.

A particularly interesting species to consider is the orangutan, one of the few nonhuman primate species where sexual coercion appears to be common (occurring in about one-third of all copulations; Crofoot & Knott, in press). There is some evidence for two distinct classes of orangutan males: large males as compared to small ones. Forced copulations appear to be more often perpetrated by the small males. Wrangham and Peterson (1996) propose that orangutan females are less attracted to the smaller males, resulting in more frequent rejection. However, their small size may give these smaller males an advantage in implementing coercive sex because in the rainforest trees, females can more easily escape from the larger males (Wrangham & Peterson, 1996). Some smaller males who have relatively little success in courting females may, therefore, gradually become "specialists" in using sexual coercion and relatively easily resort to using this alternative in their attempts to mate. Buss (2003) concludes that there is some evidence in this species suggestive of evolved specialized mechanisms pertaining to sexual coercion.

Although individual differences may be of some importance, research by Nadler (1977, 1999) highlights the importance of situational dynamics in the use of sexual coercion among orangutans. Nadler found that when males and females were placed in one cage together and the females could not avoid the males, males generally forced the females to have sex. However, when the females were given control over whether the males could enter into their area of the cage, males engaged in elaborate courting, and no forced sex occurred.

The evidence from orangutans may be contrasted with other similar species where sexual coercion does not appear to occur, particularly the Bonobos and common chimpanzees. This suggests the importance of factors such as the isolated social system unique to orangutans among the apes (see Smuts, 1995, and Smuts & Smuts, 1993, for analyses emphasizing the importance of female coalitions as a deterrent for male sexual aggression across various primate species and potential implications for humans).

SEXUAL COERCION IN HUMANS

An issue relevant to an evolutionary-based model of sexual coercion is its frequency in human history because regularly occurring events are more likely to have a ". . . logic embedded in the dynamics of natural selection for reproductive success" (Wrangham & Peterson, 1996, p. 138). Sexual coercion does appear to have occurred at many times throughout human history (e.g., Chagnon, 1994), and cross-cultural surveys reveal that it occurs with considerable frequency in most societies today (Basile, 2002; Broude & Greene, 1978; Levinson, 1989; Monson & Langhinrichsen-Rohling, 2002). Moreover, it is interesting that even relatively rape-free societies described in such surveys (e.g., Sanday, 1981) have various mixes of common internal and external mechanisms counteracting male tendencies for sexual aggression, suggesting that there may be a universal risk for such behavior.

Several sources of data suggest that when fear of punishment is reduced, many men do rape. This is particularly evident in times of war (see Allen, 1996; Brownmiller, 1975; Stiglmayer, 1994). In addition, research indicates that at least one-third of males admit some likelihood of sexual coercion if they could be assured that they would not suffer any negative consequences (e.g., Malamuth, 1981, 1989a, 1989b). Related to these data are findings that sexually coercive fantasies are common among men (Greendlinger & Byrne, 1987) and that such imagined sexual aggression is one of the key factors predictive of actual sexual aggression (Dean & Malamuth, 1997; Malamuth, 1981, 1988; Knight & Sims-Knight, 2003; Seto & Kuban, 1996). Imagined aggression may reveal important information about evolved mental mechanisms (B. Ellis & Symons, 1989; Kenrick & Sheets, 1993).

ADAPTATION, BY-PRODUCTS, OR NOISE

The most controversial evolutionary analysis of rape was presented by R. Thornhill and Palmer (2000). They sought to consider whether sexual coercion may be the result either of adaptations or by-products of adaptations. Adaptations were naturally selected for (i.e., they resulted in increased reproductive success). Criteria for establishing adaptation within evolutionary models include attributes of economy, efficiency, complexity, precision, reliability of development, and functionality in solving a specific problem (Buss, 1998; see also Tooby & Cosmides, 1992). By-products are incidental characteristics that did not evolve because they solved adaptive problems. For example, male nipples, which appear to have no design functionality of their own, may be by-products of the adaptive value of nipples in women (Symons, 1979).

The question of whether rape and other sexually coercive acts show evidence of adaptations or of by-products was first discussed extensively by Symons (1979). He concluded that the available data were insufficient to find rape as a facultative adaptation in the human male. Rather, rape was posited as a by-product of evolved male-female differences in sexual desire that promoted male reproductive success in contexts other than rape.

Later evolutionary models of rape have extended Symons's proposal to include rape as a by-product of both sexual desire and a generalized possessiveness or desire to control others (L. Ellis, 1989). Still other evolutionary models conceive of rape as a manifestation of an alternative strategy, for example, psychopathy, whereby rape is simply a by-product of the use of coercion in other areas (Mealey, 1995).

THE ADAPTATION HYPOTHESIS AND RELEVANT FINDINGS

The adaptation hypothesis suggests that in ancestral environments being sexually coercive under some circumstances (and, for women, having the capacity to avoid being sexual coerced) contributed to reproductive success sufficiently frequently to have resulted in some change in the evolved psychological architecture that would not have occurred without the recurring fitness consequences of sexual coercion. Therefore, this hypothesis posits specific psychological mechanisms pertaining to sexual coercion. Such specialized mechanisms might include reactions such as emotions or arousal patterns that in the proximate environment mediate between relevant environmental cues and behaviors.

From an EP perspective, the question is not whether sexual coercion is a better strategy for males than engaging in mutually consenting sex but whether for some ancestral males, under some circumstances, it may have been reproductively effective to use sexual coercion as compared to not using it. In other words, were there recurring ancestral conditions under which for some men, some of the time, there was an overall fitness increase resulting from sexual coercion? While the hypothesis that sexual coercion could have contributed to reproductive success has been criticized on grounds that rape rarely leads to conception, Gottschall and Gottschall (2003) estimated pregnancy rates resulting from penile-vaginal rape among women of reproductive age to be twice that of comparative consensual per-incident rates (6.42% to 3.1%). Controlling for age, rape pregnancy rates per incident remained 2% higher than consensual rates. This is a particularly interesting result considering that women are less likely to be raped near ovulation than at other times in the ovarian cycle, presumably due to female counteradaptations to the risk of rape. Indeed, Bröder and Hohmann (2003) found that during the ovulatory phase, naturally cycling women reduced risky behaviors and increased nonrisky behaviors, whereas women using contraceptives causing hormonal suppression did not show either effect. Other evidence suggestive of antirape adaptations among ovulating women comes from Petralia and Gallup (2002), who found that ovulating women demonstrated greater handgrip strength than nonfertile women in response to imagined sexual assault.

Various types of adaptation hypotheses have been proposed in respect of men's sexually aggressive behaviors, although this does not imply that the activation of specialized mechanisms and/or their manifestation in behavior are inevitable. An example of a relatively indirect version of the adaptation hypothesis has been suggested by Smuts and Smuts (1993) as a model similar to the feminist idea that the primary purpose of sexual coercion is male control over females. According to this model, the adaptation that evolved is a desire for general domination of females; this would have indirectly resulted in control of female sexuality and ultimately contributed to male reproductive success.

For their model, R. Thornhill and Palmer (2000) proposed several possible adaptive mechanisms, including mechanisms that (1) may aid males in evaluating the vulnerability of females to rape, (2) may serve to potentiate rape in men who lack sexual access to females, (3) may influence the evaluation of sexual attractiveness in potential rape victims, (4) may optimize sperm counts produced during rape, (5) may produce arousal specific to opportunities of rape, and (6) may motivate men to rape under conditions of sperm competition.

R. Thornhill and Palmer's vulnerability hypothesis supposes that rape may have been channeled toward activation in contexts in which potential costs to the prospective rapist (e.g., injury to the rapist from the victim, her social allies, or extant social sanctions) would have been outweighed by potential reproductive benefits. In modern society, there is some circumstantial evidence to support this analytical framework. For example, when fear of punishment is reduced and women are thus rendered more vulnerable to male aggression, many men do rape, with war prototypical of this phenomenon. Still, theft as well as rape occurs with elevated frequency during times of war, and many men indicate that they would steal if they could be assured of not getting caught (although there is evidence for specificity for sexual coercion once a general tendency to report some likelihood to commit any antisocial acts is controlled for, i.e., Malamuth, 1989a, 1989b). To support the hypothesis of a mechanism specifically designed to influence men to rape under conditions of increased female vulnerability, more evidence is needed showing how such a decision rule is selectively constituted.

Regarding R. Thornhill and Palmer's (2000) hypothesis that psychological mechanisms may exist to motivate rape in men who recurrently lack sexual access to females, it is true that men of lower socioeconomic status comprise a disproportionately large percentage of rapists (e.g., Amir, 1971). However, research has generally not supported the "sexually deprived" or "loser" model as characteristic of sexual coercers (Lalumière et al., in press; Malamuth, 1998). A variant of such a mechanism whereby "perceived relative deprivation" based on a person's expectations is better supported by the available data (Malamuth, 1998). Data do show that more sexually aggressive men and men who reported some likelihood of committing rape relatively frequently endorse statements such as, "I have been rejected by too many women in my life" (e.g., Check, Malamuth, Elias, & Barton, 1985) or "Many women get a kick out of teasing men by seeming sexually available and then refusing male advances" (Glick & Fiske, 1996) or "I feel that many women flirt with men just to tease or hurt them" (Check et al., 1975; Lonsway & Fitzgerald, 1995), but they do not necessarily support a simple mate deprivation prediction of fewer sexual opportunities. Such responses may be due to actual greater frequency of rejection experiences and/or to greater sensitivity to rejection. Lower socioeconomic level is also correlated with greater frequency of antisocial acts other than rape.

Another psychological mechanism specific to rape proposed by R. Thornhill and Palmer (2000) concerns a possible adaptation for targeting the most fertile females as rape victims. Since rape is likely to be a one-time act, it may be particularly crucial from a fitness perspective to identify highly fertile women in order to yield the highest likelihood of viable offspring. Research does indicate that young women are more likely to be raped than young girls or older women (Kilpatrick, Edmonds, & Seymour, 1992; Perkins, Klaus, Bastian, & Cohen, 1996), which is not equally true for other forms of physical assault (e.g., Acierno, Resnick, Saunders, & Best, 1999). During war, the preponderance of female rape victims are young and, ostensibly, highly fertile (Brownmiller, 1975; Niarchos, 1995). Additionally, the average age of victims who are both raped and robbed has been found to be significantly younger (28 years old) than that of female victims who are only robbed (35 years old; Felson & Krohn, 1990), and young women have been found to be overrepresented as victims of rape-murder but underrepresented as victims of theft-murder (e.g., Shackelford, 2002a, 2002b).[1] These last two observations run contrary to a "routine activities" perspective (see Mustaine & Tewksbury, 1999), which would suggest that young, reproductive-age women are sexually victimized more often than other women not because of any male motivation particular to raping young women, but simply because of these women's greater association with young men, the demographic group responsible for most crime, sexual and otherwise. However, because men may have evolved adaptations to be attracted to young fertile women (Symons, 1995), the fact that rapists target such women is not direct evidence for a rape adaptation any more than the fact that men prefer to look at pictures containing young fertile women would be evidence for a "picture looking" adaptation. The more compelling evidence required would show that fertility-related cues are particularly focused on by assailants in coercive sex as contrasted to the same men engaging in consensual sex.

Other possible adaptive mechanisms to rape that have been offered by R. Thornhill and Palmer (2000) pertain to sperm competition and men's patterns of sexual arousal. For example, if the sperm counts of ejaculates produced during rape differed from those produced during consensual copulation, such that men delivered larger ejaculates during rape, this might indicate an adaptation to rape associated with sperm competition, designed to increase probability of insemination during rape. There is currently little to back this assumption, although R. Thornhill and Palmer proposed that investigators might show men two conditions of sexually explicit stimuli, depictions of rape and of consensual sex, and measure their ejaculate. A related adaptation would be a mechanism causing men to be more aroused and thus to ejaculate more quickly during rape than during consensual sex to aid in avoiding apprehension. Finally, R. Thornhill and Palmer have suggested that marital rape may be adaptive in the sense that it appears to occur more frequently under conditions of sperm competition. At this point, these are untested hypotheses.

Conceptualizing Sexual Coercion as Either the Result of an Adaptation or as a By-product

While the distinction between an adaptation and a by-product of an adaptation is certainly an important key idea in evolutionary theory, we contend that there is a need to clarify at least two different possibilities. One usage, which appears the intended one by theorists such as R. Thornhill and Palmer (2000), refers to the "capitalizing" or "parasitizing" of mechanisms that evolved for other functions. For example, eating processed sugar may be pleasurable because of the parasitizing of psychological mechanisms designed to discriminate between ripe fruit and

---

[1] As suggested earlier, the fact that the victims are murdered is contrary to an evolutionary-based prediction, but this may be a function of the differences between ancestral conditions and modern environments where murders are sometimes committed following the rape to decrease the likelihood of detection.

other, less nutritious foods. There are some specialized psychological mechanisms being activated here, but their evolutionary development had nothing to do with the fitness consequences of eating processed sugar. When applied to sexual coercion, the idea is that whether rape could or could not be used as a conditional strategy had no consequences on the perpetrator's reproductive success. An example of this is interspecies rapes among some marine mammals (Palmer, 1989). Copulation with a female of another species cannot be the product of the intended target of an adaptive mechanism that contributed to anyone's reproductive success because no pregnancy can result. Rather, such acts clearly constitute side effects, probably a by-product of the low threshold of male sexual arousal that is calibrated to ensure that opportunities with potential mates are not missed.

Another way of reading a by-product concept doesn't fit well with the preceding description but may relate more to the possibility of multiplicity of functions. Consider the following example pertaining to plants:

> . . . the contention that apparently defensive traits of plants have actually evolved in response to natural selection imposed by natural enemies is more controversial. For some traits, it is clear that the only function is defense. Thorns and urticating hairs, for example, almost certainly function primarily to protect plants from mammalian herbivores. But in most cases, characteristics that confer resistance may have additional physiological or ecological functions. For example, although various flavonoids exhibit antifungal and antibacterial properties, most also absorb ultraviolet radiation efficiently and are believed to protect the plant from this environmental hazard. . . . Other functions performed by plant secondary chemicals include conferring frost tolerance, allelopathy, nutrient storage, structural reinforcement, mediation of stigmapollen interactions, regulation of biochemical processes, and signalling to mutualists. (Rausher, 2001, pp. 857–864)

Similarly, the ability to sexually coerce may have operated in a context of multiplicity of functions of coercion as a means of overcoming barriers or conflicts of interests in various arenas. Rape may indeed have been one of the areas where such coercive tactics paid off in fitness, but the psychological mechanisms that evolved may also have resulted in fitness consequences when they influenced acts such as killing or stealing. Differing behaviors may require the activation of differing combinatorial mechanisms (Malamuth, 1998; Pinker, 2000; e.g., sexual coercion may be the product of a combination of psychological mechanisms underlying coercion and those underlying sexuality, while murder does not require sexual mechanisms). The central point here is that the conceptual distinction between adaptations and by-products of adaptations that has guided much of the evolutionary debate on sexual coercion (e.g., R. Thornhill & Palmer, 2000) may need to be extended considerably to encompass other types of models (see Buss, Haselton, Shackelford, Bleske, & Wakefield, 1998, for a detailed discussion of various conceptualizations of by-products of adaptations).

SEXUAL AROUSAL TO FORCE

One hypothesized candidate for a specialized psychological mechanism motivating sexual coercion that has received the most focused attention is sexual arousal specific to forced sex, referred to here as *sexual arousal to force* (SAF). It is likely that such arousal is a manifestation of a broader category of sexual gratification from controlling or dominating women, which can be readily and visibly accomplished by the use of force.

Using an adaptation model, R. Thornhill and Thornhill (1992) discussed SAF extensively and argued that relatively higher sexual arousal to coercive sex among men should be associated with greater success in using coercive sexual tactics, thereby contributing to reproductive fitness under some circumstances. They noted that given the costs of forced mating in ancestral environments, including possible loss of status or life, males generally might be expected *not* to have evolved a preference for forced sex and, therefore, *not* to evidence SAF. If, however, under some recurrent ancestral environments the potential reproductive benefits of forced mating repeatedly outweighed the costs, psychological mechanisms enabling sexual arousal (e.g., an erect penis) despite a woman's lack of consent may have evolved.

Buss (2003) suggests that the model pertaining to SAF outlined and the data presented by Thornhill and Palmer (2000) do not enable differentiation among alternative hypotheses. In consideration of such criticisms, we elaborate both theoretically and empirically on the possibility that SAF might have evolved as a conditional specialized mechanism for sexual coercion in a manner to enable better testing of alternative explanations. In this context, we note an important point made by Hagen (2004). He argues that theoretically specialized mechanisms pertaining to rape would not be expected unless the problems involved in "successfully" committing such an act in ancestral environments were not the same problems as with the use of aggression in other contexts. The occurrence of sexual arousal in the context of coercive acts may be an important distinguishing characteristic. In the context of most aggressive acts, the occurrence of sexual arousal would be irrelevant or even detrimental. Because the preferred evolutionary strategy for most men in most circumstances would be to engage in consensual sex, the most common calibration of sexual arousal mechanisms should be to become inhibited by indications of lack of responsiveness by females. However, if an individual is to effectively engage in rape in ancestral environments, such aggression may require reversing of the default arousal pattern. This problem may indeed be hypothesized as a potentially unique adaptive problem associated with sexually coercive acts as contrasted with the use of coercion in other ancestral contexts.

In considering the following empirical data, we primarily rely on studies actually measuring such SAF (often by direct genital measures), and we believe that studies using related measures such as reported Dominance as a Motive for Sex (Nelson, 1979) and Rape Fantasies (Greendlinger & Byrne, 1987) assess highly related constructs that are also relevant to the present analysis.

PROPOSED EVOLVED FUNCTION OF SEXUAL AROUSAL TO FORCE

Within some ancestral circumstances, the inhibition or occurrence of sexual arousal in response to cues associated with using force might have been an important mediating mechanism affecting the likelihood of successfully dominating and exerting sexual control over an unwilling mating partner. Just as fear of spiders may serve as an avoidance emotion that increases the likelihood of avoiding certain specific potential threats, sexual arousal cued to the use of force may serve as an approach emotion that increases the likelihood of engaging in sexually coercive behavior. Such a conclusion is supported by the meta-analysis of

Allen, D'Alessio, and Emmers-Sommer (2000) indicating that sexual arousal is generally associated with positive psychological affect. Relatedly, after reviewing relevant findings, Lalumière, Quinsey, Harris, Rice, and Trautrimas (2003) asked, "Could it be that many theoreticians and clinicians are reluctant to consider the idea that many rapists do what they do because it is sexually arousing or gratifying?" (p. 222).

This hypothesis may be contrasted with nonevolutionary proposals in the research literature that seek to explain SAF. For example, Marshall and Fernandez (2000) proposed that SAF is not designed to facilitate sexual coercion but that the casual connection is in the opposite direction: They argue that SAF and other forms of "deviant" sexual arousal are the result of experience with repeated sexual offending. This model suggests that because the offender lacks the requisite social skills and confidence to engage in mutually consenting sex, he uses coercive tactics repeatedly, eventually resulting in the conditioning of SAF. Other hypotheses have also typically conceptualized such arousal as an "abnormality" that is likely to be evidenced by a relatively small percentage of men (e.g., Abel, Barlow, Blanchard, & Guild, 1977). An evolutionary-based model uniquely suggests that due to calibrating mechanisms grounded in the consequences in ancestral environments, a considerable percentage of "normal" men may reveal the type of sexual arousal patterning that could facilitate sexual coercion.

How might such calibration occur? In keeping with a common evolutionary proposition that humans share a common evolved psychology that enables relevant developmental experiences to "set" mechanisms at different levels (Belsky, Steinberg, & Draper, 1991; Draper & Harpending, 1982; Trivers, 1972), the model we outline here (which we label the *evolutionary functional* [EF] model) emphasizes some relevant perceived negative experiences with women that may set the sexual arousal versus sexual inhibition to force mechanism more in one direction or the other. Although full testing of such a process would require a longitudinal study that would be difficult to conduct, it should be feasible to temporarily prime similar processes to create a *state condition* related to the *trait condition*. Relevant data have been reported by Yates, Marshall, and Barbaree (1984), who found that college men who were insulted by a woman became subsequently relatively more sexually aroused by rape portrayals as compared to portrayals of consensual sex. Creating general arousal by physiological exercise instead of an insult by a woman did not result in a similar increase. Other relevant data are available that pertain to the trait rather than the state of anger and hostility toward women. These studies indicate that men who are hostile to women, typically on measures that include items referring to perceived rejection from women[2] (e.g., Check et al., 1985), show relatively high SAF as contrasted with men who are relatively low on such measures of hostility toward women. For example, many studies focusing on the *confluence model of sexual aggression* (e.g., Malamuth, Sockloskie, Koss, & Tanoka, 1991; Malamuth et al., 1995) have found that there is a strong connection between measures of individual differences in men's hostility toward women and their SAF or similar constructs such as Dominance as a Motive for Sex (e.g., Malamuth et al., 1991, 1995) and Rape Fantasies (Dean &

---

[2] We are not suggesting that perceived rejection is the only relevant potential antecedent that may affect the calibration of sexual arousal patterns, but one that is likely to operate in confluence with other factors.

Malamuth, 1997). Various other studies examining differences between behaviorally sexually nonaggressive men and sexual aggressors (some of whom are likely to have the relevant calibration of increased SAF) have found similar results (e.g., Lisak & Roth, 1988; Murnen, Wright, & Kaluzny, 2002). Several priming studies have revealed that sexually aggressive men may be more prone to "automatically" cognitively associate women with hostility, sex, and power (Bargh, Raymond, Pryor, & Strack, 1995; Leibold & McConnell, 2004). Barbaree (1990) reported a study with a rapist who was asked to imagine raping women for whom he held different emotional feelings. It was found that the greater the hostility to the woman, the greater the sexual arousal to rape cues. Forbes, Adams-Curtis, and White (2004) found that the key component linking various measures of male dominant ideology (e.g., attitudes supporting aggression or sexism) to aggression against women is hostility toward women. It is interesting that these investigators found that while for men a measure of hostile sexism was associated with increased sexual coercion, this was not true for women. Further, Baumeister, Catanese, and Wallace (2002) have summarized considerable data indicating that experiencing rejection by women, particularly by men who are relatively narcissistic, contributes to sexually coercive behavior. Taken together, these findings provide some support for the hypothesis that perceived blocked access to desired women and associated hostility toward women may affect the calibration of men's sexual arousal patterns in ways that could affect the likelihood of committing sexually coercive acts.

How might a mechanism of SAF operate to affect the likelihood of committing sexually coercive acts? Consider a simplistic distinction between two types of men: one for whom the best prospects for overall reproductive fitness involve mating only with a consenting partner and the other a man whose reproductive success could be augmented by using sexual coercion. (Rather than a simple dichotomy, we prefer a more dimensional conceptualization but use a dichotomy to facilitate explication.) If we were to design a psychological mechanism that provided the best decision rule (for total fitness) for each of these men, what might be its general properties? For the first man, there would be sensitivity to cues when a sexually desired female indicated disinterest, disgust, or other negative responses. This would be an effective mechanism for inhibiting approach tendencies where persisting in sex with an unwilling female would have high costs compared to pursuing consensual sex with alternative mating prospects. However, for the second type of individual, it could have been adaptive to have this inhibiting mechanism disengaged. Potentially, for this latter type, there may even have been some fitness benefit to increased SAF relative to consenting sex because engaging in coercion may require relatively high persistence and energy to overcome the resistance of an unwilling partner. This analysis suggests that type 1 men should show inhibited SAF sex, whereas type 2 men should show at least equal sexual arousal to both consensual and coercive sex (i.e., the shutting off of the inhibiting mechanism) or even greater arousal to some types of coercive sex (the activation of a mechanism creating greater sexual arousal). Such a distinction between two types of men may have some similarity to the distinction between large and small orangutans insofar as that distinction may serve as a useful illustration of how differently situated individuals may respond based on their unique developmental and current circumstances. In summary, if there were ancestral conditions under which for some men, some of the time, there was an overall fitness increase resulting from sexual coercion, then for these individuals it may well have been important not to be inhibited by cues of a woman's unwillingness and to potentially be sexually aroused by dominating and controlling the victim.

CONVICTED RAPISTS AS GENERALISTS

How might we choose two groups of men for comparison purposes to correspond roughly to the hypothesized two types described earlier? In the past, researchers have assumed that comparing convicted rapists to other men was appropriate (e.g., N. Thornhill & Thornhill, 1991; R. Thornhill & Palmer, 2000). This is in fact not the most desirable comparison. When such groups are used as the comparisons, the evidence is ambiguous (e.g., Baxter, Barbaree, & Marshall, 1986; Lalumière et al., 2003; Marshall & Kennedy, 2003).

Convicted rapists may encompass both men who rape because they are "generalists" vis-à-vis antisocial behavior and/or "specialists." The latter would have the psychological mechanisms calibrated to increase the likelihood of sexual coercion. The former group may include many individuals who have not had the relevant psychological mechanism calibrated but may use sexual coercion due to the workings of other psychological mechanisms. These men are relatively likely to engage in various forms of antisocial acts because they differ from other men not necessarily on the specific mechanism of SAF (or other specialized mechanisms for sexual coercion) but on mechanisms underlying general antisocial behaviors (e.g., lack of inhibitory self-control, high impulsivity, low empathy, and/or callousness). They may be more likely than others to steal or to use coercion for obtaining any desired goal, whether that be stealing a car or stealing sex. Accordingly, convicted rapists have been found to be comparable to other types of violent criminals on most measures of antisocial traits and behaviors (Lalumière et al., in press), most rapists have a history of nonsexual offenses, and the criminal records of rapists often resemble those of other offenders (Serin & Mailloux, 2003).

However, some rapists do appear to be specialists in their criminality. The Massachusetts Treatment Center Rapist Typology (see Knight & Prentky, 1990) does include two types more motivated than nonsexual subtypes by sexual gratification and a paraphilic interest in rape, whereas nonsexual subtypes are believed to be higher in hostility and anger, but the supporting evidence for such a typology has not been very strong. Barbaree, Seto, Serin, Amos, and Preston (1994) have shown that rapists classified as sexual subtypes demonstrate larger relative responses to rape than rapists deemed nonsexual. Other support for this argument comes from the research of Looman (2001). When this investigator classified rapists based on whether they reported a high level of "deviant fantasies" (e.g., rape fantasies and, therefore, relatively high SAF), she found that high fantasizers were much more likely to have committed multiple sexual offenses than rapists who did not report relatively high levels of such fantasies (5.0 sexual offenses versus 1.2 sexual offenses), and these rapists also had a considerably higher average number of victims (6.2 versus 1.6). Moreover, rapists who had reported having the deviant fantasies had lower general antisocial personality characteristics (as indicated on psychopathy measures) than men who did not report high levels of such fantasies. This finding again serves to illustrate that the search for evidence of a specialized mechanism would be better served by identifying comparison groups differing on the psychological mechanism of interest rather than focusing on the behavioral outcome of sexual coercion.

SPECIALIZATION AND COERCIVE POTENTIAL

Classifying rapists into subtypes, as the Massachusetts Treatment Center Rapist Typology has done, provides one potentially valuable means to identify men who may engage in sexual coercion partly because of the activation of specialized psychological mechanisms, but excludes most men from its sample. The data indicate that it is among noncriminal samples, particularly those drawn from college populations, that specialization may be most evident. Relevant data indicate that among general community samples, those men who self-identify as having committed sexual coercion show more evidence for "specialization" than convicted rapists. Knight and Prentky (under review) found that self-identified sexually coercive subgroups of community men exceeded incarcerated rapists on diverse measures of sexual and paraphilic fantasies, including sadism, sexual preoccupation, and bondage. It is interesting that self-identified sexual coercers among criminals who had not been convicted of sexual crimes also showed higher scores on such sexual and paraphilic fantasy than convicted rapists, suggesting that even among criminals, self-identification might be a better way to identify specialists for sexual coercion than simply looking at the crime for which the person was convicted. Although there were not significant differences between the community and criminal self-identified sexual coercers on these sexual and paraphilic fantasy measures, the community sample evidenced the highest scores. Overall, these data support the conclusion that most of those currently identified by the judicial system and convicted of acts of sexual coercion display less evidence of specialized psychological mechanisms than other self-identified sexually coercive men. However, particular caution may be necessary in interpreting the data from convicted rapists who might seek to portray a positive image because of the belief that it may affect their likelihood of being paroled.

As noted by Lalumière et al. (in press), in the published literature, researchers focusing on noncriminal samples generally have not addressed the question of whether sexually aggressive men engage in other forms of antisocial behavior as well. For this chapter, therefore, we conducted analyses specifically focusing on this issue in our longitudinal database (Malamuth, Linz, Heavey, Barnes, & Acker, 1995) of close to 150 men. In this research, we first assessed various measures on the same men at about age 20 (Time 1) and then again 10 years later (Time 2). We examined whether measures assessing SAF showed a pattern supporting specialization. We found clear support for such a specialized mechanism. For example, Time 1 physiological sexual arousal to rape versus nonrape as well as dominance as a motive for sex predicted Time 2 sexual aggression (at about average age 30; $r = .45$, $p < .01$, $r = .39$, $p < .01$, respectively), but these measures of SAF and dominance did not predict a variety of measures of later general antisocial behavior (e.g., drug use, lying, stealing, hitting, fraud, or killing; correlations ranging from .09 to .20, $p > .05$). Similarly, Time 1 sexual aggression correlated strongly and significantly with Time 2 sexual aggression, but neither of these was significantly associated with various measures of general antisocial behavior at Time 2 (ranging from .04 to .13). However, as consistently found in our various research studies on the confluence model of sexual aggression, there is a significant relationship between having adolescent delinquent friends and engaging in mild antisocial behavior and later sexual aggression, as reported in Malamuth et al. (1995).

Another strategy used by Malamuth, Check, and Briere (1986) to identify those men in community populations in whom the psychological mechanism of SAF has been calibrated to increase the likelihood of their using sexual coercion was to directly ask a sample of 359 undergraduate men how sexually aroused they would be by forced sex. The researchers discovered that indeed there were meaningful differences in their responses, with a considerable number reporting that coercion would be sexually stimulating. On the basis of the men's responses, they were classified into three levels of SAF, with approximately equal numbers in each group.

In an attempt to validate these self-reports, the researchers conducted a separate lab session, which included about a third of the participants. They were about equally drawn from each of the groups. In the lab, the researchers assessed on a direct genital measure of sexual arousal how aroused the participants were to depictions involving consensual sex, coercive sex, or nonsexual coercion where a man physically assaulted a woman. They found that the self-reports were indeed valid indicators of the men's sexual arousal pattern. Those who had earlier reported higher SAF did in fact show much higher physiologically measured SAF. The high SAF group also had significantly more sexual arousal to the aggressive than to the nonaggressive sexual portrayals ($p < .02$), whereas the no-arousal and moderate SAF groups showed the opposite effect, being less aroused by the aggressive than the nonaggressive depictions ($p < .03$). Also consistent with the specificity possibility, higher levels of SAF were predictive of men's reports that they found the idea of forcing a woman into sexual acts attractive and that they would actually do so if they could be assured that they would not be caught or punished (e.g., low arousal to force men reported an average of 1.06 on this five-point scale whereas the high arousal to force men reported an average of 3.19), but there were no significant differences on reported attractiveness and other measures pertaining to noncoercive intercourse. This finding supports the prediction that the psychological mechanism does not create a reduction in the propensity to engage in consensual sex (or is merely symptomatic of men with generally higher sexual propensities) but activates the increased potential of using coercive sex. To a smaller yet discernible degree, higher "trait" reported SAF was also associated with higher sexual arousal to the depiction of a man assaulting a woman physically without any sexual content. These findings indicate that it is feasible to identify men who have the psychological mechanism of sexual arousal calibrated in a direction that may facilitate sexually coercive behavior.

Similarly, in two studies of subjects recruited from university and community sources, Malamuth (1989b) found SAF measured by penile tumescence correlated with various measures of attraction to sexual aggression, including the multi-item Attraction to Sexual Aggression scale (in Study 1, $r = .21$, $p < .05$, in Study 2, $r = .27$, $p < .02$) as well as key individual items such as reported likelihood to rape if assured of not being punished (in Study 1, $r = .25$, $p < .02$, in Study 2, $r = .25$, $p < .02$), but not with identically worded questions (i.e., if assured of not being punished) inquiring about likelihood to rob (in Study 1, $r = .06$, $p =$ ns, in Study 2, $r = .12$, $p =$ ns) or murder (in Study 1, $r = -.08$, $p =$ ns, in Study 2, $r = .16$, $p =$ ns).[3] Relatedly, Malamuth (unpublished study) has found that among a sample of close to 200 men from the general population, SAF (measured by penile tumescence) and a measure of dominance as a motive for sex (Nelson, 1979) showed a high degree of evidence for specificity. These measures did not correlate significantly with a variety of measures of general antisocial behavior (e.g., drug use, lying, stealing, hitting, fraud, or killing), but they did correlate with reported sexual aggression. The finding regarding behavior is consistent with a considerable number of studies showing that relatively high SAF can predict sexual aggression (e.g., see Lalumière et al., 2003, for a summary) as well as attraction to or likelihood of aggressing sexually.

Other support for the specificity of SAF was obtained by Malamuth (1988), who showed that men who were higher in such arousal were more likely to engage in higher levels of laboratory aggression against a woman who had mildly insulted them but not against a man who had behaved in the same way. Similarly, Malamuth and Thornhill (1994) found that men's levels of Dominance as a Motive for Sex predicted domineeringness in a conversation with a woman who had insulted them, but such differences did not similarly predict domineeringness against a man. In sum, while more research is needed, measures assessing SAF and its correlates show an emerging pattern supporting the hypothesis of specialization for sexual coercion rather than alternatives such as reflecting generalized deviance or antisociality.

CONCEPTUALIZING SEXUAL AROUSAL TO FORCE

Models that seek to identify men who become sexually aroused to forced sex may examine one of two mechanisms: Such men are thought to either lack the inhibitions of other men (e.g., Baxter et al., 1986; Malamuth, Heim, & Feshbach, 1980; Seto & Kuban, 1996) or to be sexually excited by cues to force (e.g., Malamuth et al., 1980; Quinsey, Chaplin, & Upfold, 1984). The data from Malamuth et al. (1986), as well as cumulative evidence from various other sources, strongly indicate that both mechanisms may be valid: While some of these individuals appear to have the inhibitory aspect of SAF disengaged (Lohr, Adams, & Davis, 1997), a considerable number find force in the context of sex to be a stimulant of greater sexual arousal than consenting sex. Although both types of individuals also show a lower threshold for becoming sexually aroused and a greater interest in sexual cues per se, the data reveal that this can by no means fully account for either the

---

[3] A measure of antisocial characteristics/psychoticism, however (examples of items included "Have you always been a loner?" and "Would you like to think other people are afraid of you?"), correlated in both studies not only with likelihood to rape but also with likelihood to rob or murder, consistent with the idea that the use of sexual coercion may involve the workings of psychological machinery reflecting both some general antisocial tendencies and some mechanisms specific to rape motivation (Malamuth, 2003). Research assessing the relative contribution of both types of psychological mechanisms with general population samples highlights the far greater importance of specialized mechanisms (e.g., Vega & Malamuth, 2003).

inhibition pattern or the increased SAF (e.g., Lohr et al., 1997; Wilson, Holm, Bishop, & Borowiak, 2002).

In support of the conclusion that some men are more sexually aroused by the introduction of force, Bernat, Calhoun, and Adams (1999) found that the penile tumescence of self-identified sexually aggressive men who also held callous sexual beliefs increased when force was introduced into a sexual scenario. Seto and Kuban (1996) tested sexually coercive fantasizers, rapists, courtship-disordered men, and community controls[4] and observed that sexually coercive fantasizers preferred rape to consenting sex (with the other groups either responding more to consenting sex or responding equally to consenting and deviant stimuli; see also Barnes, Malamuth, & Check, 1984; Lalumière et al., 2003; Malamuth & Check, 1981, for a review). Related research indicates that for men from the general population who indicate some likelihood to sexually aggress or who are sexually aggressive, but not other participants, the addition of power cues makes females over whom they have power more sexually attractive (Bargh et al., 1975; Leibold & McConnell, 2004).

IS SEXUAL AROUSAL TO FORCE A SPECIALIZED MEDIATOR OF SEXUAL COERCION?

Malamuth and Impett (1999) conducted a series of mediational analyses to attempt to directly test the hypothesis that high SAF is a specific mediator of forced sex. Researchers from various disciplines have emphasized the usefulness of conducting such mediational analyses (e.g., Baron & Kenny, 1986). For example, Mirowsky (1999) indicates that it is ". . . the single most valuable procedure for explaining associations. The technique is to sociological research what anatomical dissection is to biological research" (p. 106). Mediators reveal the "generative mechanisms" or "processes" through which the identified variable influences the outcome. In their mediational analyses, Malamuth and Impett examined the role of various psychological characteristics of men who varied in their levels of Hostile Masculinity (Malamuth et al., 1991, 1995) to assess which of these psychological characteristics were predictive of different types of behaviors. The mediators assessed included those associated with general antisocial behaviors, namely general impulsivity and anger-proneness, as well as mediators associated with nonsexual conflict and aggression toward women such as low ability to feel intimate emotions or closeness. The analyses conducted examined the mediational role of each of six factors while controlling for overlap among these factors.

Using a general population sample, these researchers found evidence supportive of SAF as a specific mediator of coercive sexual behavior. Sexually coercive behaviors were mediated only by Sexually Coercive Fantasies and Attitudes Accepting of Violence against Women, a factor also shown to have a considerable specificity vis-à-vis sexual aggression against women (e.g., Dominic & Zeichner, 2003; Malamuth, 1988; see Figure 13.1 on p. 410). In contrast, other more general characteristics such as Impulsivity and Anger-Proneness were typically the

---

[4] Courtship-disordered men are those who have been diagnosed with exhibitionism, voyeurism, toucheurism/frotteurism, or multiple paraphilias. Fantasizers reported 6 or more months of recurrent intense, sexual fantasies or urges in which the suffering of the victim is deemed sexually exciting (corresponding to the *DSM-IV* definition of sexual sadism; American Psychiatric Association, 1994), but professed that they had not acted on their urges.

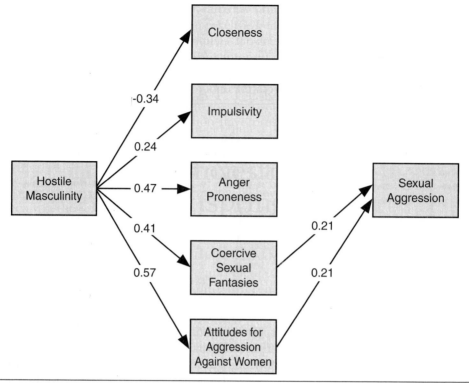

Figure 13.1 Results of Mediation Analysis Suggesting That "Specialized" Mechanisims Mediate the Association between Hostile Masculinity and Sexual Aggression.

mediators between Hostile Masculinity and other outcomes (e.g., general stress in relationships with women); Sexually Coercive Fantasies was not a mediator in those instances (see Figure 13.2).

Although these data are clearly consistent with the specificity of mediational mechanisms, the one somewhat unexpected finding was that Sexually Coercive Fantasies also mediated the relationship between Hostile Masculinity and Non-Sexual Aggression against women. This mediation remained after controlling for the possibility that men who were relatively high on nonsexual aggression against women were also sexually coercive. These data corroborate earlier findings that some of the men who report high SAF also evidence sexual arousal to a depiction of a man assaulting a woman in a nonsexual manner (Malamuth et al., 1986). Such findings are consistent with hypotheses that controlling a woman in a nonsexual context via physical aggression and domination may affect the likelihood of being able to control her sexually (e.g., Smuts, 1992). For some men, SAF may become generalized to the use of force and physical control over women more generally and not require any sexual stimuli.

Other studies support the mediational role of SAF and similar constructs as a key element motivating sexual coercion. Malamuth (2003) has reviewed various studies with noncriminal samples indicating that sexual coercers do not reveal a high level of general antisocial characteristics or adult antisocial behavior but that characteristics such as impulsivity, callousness, and lack of empathy may

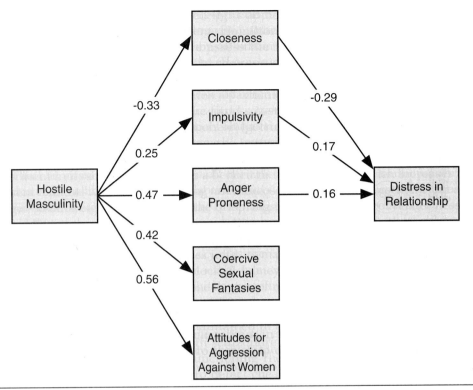

Figure 13.2 Example of Results of Mediation Analysis for Outcomes Other than Sexual Coercion Suggesting That the Mechanisims Mediating the Association between Hostile Masculinity and Outcomes such as Distress in Relationship Are More "General" Factors.

exert only an indirect impact on the use of sexual coercion. In such general population samples, only if the man also has relatively high scores on elements associated with power-oriented sexuality is he likely to be sexually aggressive (e.g., Bourg, 2001; Lim & Howard, 1998). Similarly, using three separate general population samples from differing countries, Chiroro, Bohner, Viki, and Jarvis (2004) conducted an analysis to examine what factors mediate between rape myth acceptance and a measure of rape proclivity (i.e., men's reports that they might behave the same way as the rapist in a written scenario). The researchers included in their mediation analysis two measures pertaining to SAF in response to the rape scenario. One inquired how sexually aroused the man was by the rape scenario, and the other, labeled by the investigators as Expected Enjoyment of Dominance, specifically asked how much participants would have "enjoyed getting their way in this situation." While sexual arousal to the rape scenario was consistently found to be highly correlated with Expected Enjoyment of Dominance, such anticipated dominance enjoyment was also the single factor that was consistently and strongly the significant predictor of rape proclivity.

CONCLUSIONS

EP theory and research seek to better understand the ultimate causes and the design of evolved psychological mechanisms underlying manifest behavior. In addressing the topic of sexual coercion, there has, therefore, been considerable focus on whether there may have been, on average, fitness consequences in recurring ancestral environments of the ability to successfully avoid and/or inflict sexual coercion. The discussion in this chapter focusing primarily on perpetrators suggests three competing models:

1. There were no recurring fitness consequences of using sexual coercion; therefore, the mind's architecture does not include any psychological mechanisms relevant to sexual coercion.

2. Fitness consequences were a function of the ability to selectively use coercion in various arenas, with sexual conflict being one of many, but there weren't any specific adaptive problems unique to using coercion in the sexual arena. The evolved architecture of the mind, therefore, includes psychological mechanisms designed specifically to potentiate using coercion in various arenas, including but not limited to sexual coercion.

3. Because there were unique adaptive problems associated with the use of coercion in the sexual context (e.g., how to maintain an erection and subdue a victim who is fighting back), specialized psychological mechanisms may have evolved that enabled the effective use of such coercion in that sexual context. Such specialized modules evolved because there were some fitness benefits in ancestral environments specific to the selective use of sexual coercion that differed from the use of coercion in nonsexual contexts.

In seeking to identify potential candidates for such specialized modules, it is useful to reiterate that sexual coercion may be a manifest act that encompasses differing motivations and antecedents. We suggested that rapists identified by the legal system are typically generalists who commit various types of antisocial behavior and often may not reveal the activation of any specialized psychological mechanisms motivating sexual coercion. In contrast, among sexual aggressors in the general population, there appear to be a considerably larger percentage of men who are specialists and may be particularly useful for studying such mechanisms. We particularly explored herein the possibility that SAF may be a candidate for an evolved specialized mechanism for engaging in sexual coercion. The viability of the EF model for such arousal must be determined by its ability to generate empirically testable predictions. It is important, therefore, to examine how this model has fared in its predictions in contrast to other models. The following is a summary of our conclusions in comparing the EF model to others focusing only on proximate causes as well as to a by-product evolutionary model.

FREQUENCY

How many men in the general population would be expected to show relatively high SAF? In conceptualizing sexual coercion as either the result of sexual pathology or general antisocial characteristics, proximate models typically predict that only the few "sick" or "antisocial" would fail to inhibit SAF and/or show increased arousal by the inclusion of force. It is not clear to us whether a by-product model would make any predictions regarding the expected frequency of differing sexual arousal patterns.

The EF model suggests that some psychological mechanisms may have evolved that when activated by environmental conditions (e.g., repeated rejection from desired females, early experiences with exploitative relationships as opposed to cooperative nurturing, and environmental messages via the mass media that communicate favorable images of sexual violence) increase the likelihood of effectively implementing a coercive sexual act. Although the calibration of their arousal mechanism would not be expected to depend only on these experiences, and the relevant environmental conditions would need to be better described, it may be expected that within the general population a substantial minority of men would show lack of inhibition and/or increased SAF. The various sources of data described earlier appear to indicate that a substantial minority (e.g., as much as one-third of the population) reveal the type of arousal pattern that indicates the disengagement of the inhibitory mechanism and/or increased arousal to force and are, therefore, arguably most consistent with the EF model rather than the other models.

CORRELATES WITH OTHER CHARACTERISTICS OF MEN

In addition to the expectations regarding frequency of sexual arousal patterns, various models may have differing expectations about which characteristics of men would be associated with the differing arousal patterns. Proximate models typically would predict that men who show greater SAF would reveal general sexual deviance, a lower threshold for sexual arousal in general, and/or general antisocial characteristics. The data do not support these predictions: SAF is not associated with increased antisocial or deviant characteristics and behavior generally nor is it fully explainable by a general lower threshold for becoming sexually aroused. A by-product model might not predict any systematic association between SAF and any characteristics or behaviors.

The EF model predicts that the degree of perceived blocked access to desired females and resultant emotional responses (e.g., anger, hostility) would be relevant to the development of SAF. The data pertaining to correlates of SAF described earlier and elsewhere (e.g., Malamuth, 1998; Malamuth et al., 1986) are strongly consistent with the EF model by showing strong connections with hostility to women and perceived rejection.

CORRELATES WITH BEHAVIOR

Different predictions arise from the various models regarding the function of SAF and, therefore, its association with sexually coercive behaviors. Some nonevolutionary proximate models (but not all) argue that responses such as fantasies of rape and SAF have no association to behavioral inclinations. Similarly, a by-product model would not make any clear predictions one way or the other about an association between SAF and actual coercion. The EF model suggests a direct role for SAF with energizing and potentiating behavioral tendencies. Inhibited arousal would be expected to discourage sexual persistence in response to a woman's lack of responsiveness; in contrast, the disengagement of such inhibition and increased arousal would be expected to facilitate sexually aggressive tendencies and, under some conditions, the actual manifestation of increased sexual aggression. The data showing that SAF is one of the important predictors of reported likelihood of raping and of actual sexual coercion as well as the findings that such arousal is a critical mediator between hostile masculinity characteristics and sexual aggression are consistent with the EF model.[5]

Much further theoretical development and empirical testing are needed to assess the viability of the type of EF model we have described. The difference in the type of questions raised by such a model is apparent when we contrast it to that raised by proximate models. For example, Barbaree and Marshall (1991) published a thorough attempt to compare differing models focusing on SAF. Although they describe the purpose of the models as designed to ". . . account for men's sexual arousal to descriptions of rape" (p. 621), all of the six models essentially provide descriptive analyses designed to identify the critical features distinguishing sexual aggressors from nonaggressors (e.g., the ability to suppress sexual arousal or the augmentation of sexual arousal by other emotional states such as hate). None of these models ever raise the question of why there might be certain design features that might lead to observed recurring patterns of individual differences in SAF (e.g., why it is that some men, but not others, who perceive rejection from desired females develop a pattern of SAF whereas women who are similarly rejected by men do not show such a pattern). While we recognize that such questions should be asked with sensitivity to their potential misunderstanding and misuse within certain political contexts, we believe that they may provide useful insights to horrible acts and possibly better preventative policies.

REFERENCES

Abel, G. G., Barlow, D. H., Blanchard, E., & Guild, D. (1977). The components of rapists' sexual arousal. *Archives of General Psychiatry, 34,* 895–903.

Acierno, R., Resnick, K. D., Saunders, B., & Best, C. L. (1999). Risk factors for rape, physical assault, and posttraumatic stress disorder in women: Examination of differential multivariate relationships. *Journal of Anxiety Disorders, 13,* 541–563.

Allen, B. (1996). *Rape warfare: The hidden genocide in Bosnia-Herzegovina and Croatia.* Minneapolis, MN: University of Minnesota Press.

Allen, M., D'Alessio, D., & Emmers-Sommer, T. M. (2000). Reactions of criminal sexual offenders to pornography: A meta-analytic summary. In M. Roloff (Ed.), *Communication yearbook 22* (pp. 139–169). Thousand Oaks, CA: Sage.

American Psychiatric Association. (1994). *Diagnostic and statistical manual of mental disorders* (4th ed.). Washington, DC: Author.

Amir, M. (1971). *Patterns in forcible rape.* Chicago: University of Chicago Press.

Arnqvist, G. (1989). Sexual selection in a water strider: The function, mechanism and selection and heritability of a male grasping apparatus. *Oikos, 56,* 344–350.

Barbaree, H. E. (1990). Stimulus control of sexual arousal: Its role in sexual assault. In W. L. Marshall, D. Laws, & H. E. Barbaree (Eds.), *Handbook of sexual assault: Issues, theories, and treatment of the offender* (pp. 115–142). New York: Plenum Press.

Barbaree, H. E., & Marshall, W. L. (1991). The role of male sexual arousal in rape: Six models. *Journal of Consulting and Clinical Psychology, 59,* 621–630.

Barbaree, H. E., Seto, M. C., Serin, R., Amos, N., & Preston, D. (1994). Comparisons between sexual and nonsexual rapist subtypes: Sexual arousal to rape, offense precursors, and offense characteristics. *Criminal Justice and Behavior, 21,* 95–114.

---

[5] We do not present here a systematic comparison between the EF model and various feminist models, although we believe that there are many similar predictions from certain feminist models that emphasize the link among sexual dominance, hostility, and aggression against women. Certainly, though, there are some key differences in the etiological paths emphasized.

Bargh, J. A., Raymond, P., Pryor, J. B., & Strack, F. (1995). Attractiveness of the underling: An automatic power → sex association and its consequences for sexual harassment and aggression. *Journal of Personality and Social Psychology, 68*, 768–781.

Barnes, G., Malamuth, N., & Check, J. (1984). Psychoticism and sexual arousal to rape depictions. *Personality and Individual Differences, 5*, 273–279.

Baron, R. M., & Kenny, D. A. (1986). The moderator-mediator variable distinction in social psychological research: Conceptual, strategic, and statistical considerations. *Journal of Personality and Social Psychology, 51*(6), 1173–1182.

Basile, K. C. (2002). Prevalence of wife rape and other intimate partner sexual coercion in a nationally representative sample of women. *Violence and Victims, 17*, 511–524.

Baumeister, R. F., Catanese, K. R., & Wallace, H. M. (2002). Conquest by force: A narcissistic reactance theory of rape and sexual coercion. *Review of General Psychology, 6*, 92–135.

Baxter, D. J., Barbaree, H. E., & Marshall, W. L. (1986). Sexual responses to consenting and forced sex in a large sample of rapists and nonrapists. *Behaviour Research and Therapy, 24*, 513–520.

Belsky, J., Steinberg, L., & Draper, P. (1991). Childhood experience, interpersonal development, and reproductive strategy: An evolutionary theory of socialization. *Child Development, 62*, 647–670.

Bennice, J. A., Resick, P., Mechanic, M., & Astin, M. (2003). The relative effects of intimate partner physical and sexual violence on post-traumatic stress disorder symptomatology. *Violence and Victims, 18*, 87–94.

Bernat, J. A., Calhoun, K. S., & Adams, H. E. (1999). Sexually aggressive and nonaggressive men: Sexual arousal and judgments in response to acquaintance rape and consensual analogues. *Journal of Abnormal Psychology, 108*, 662–673.

Bourg, S. N. (2001). Sexual and physical aggression within a dating/acquaintance relationship: Testing models of perpetrator characteristics. Unpublished doctoral dissertation, Auburn University.

Bröder, A., & Hohmann, N. (2003). Variations in risk taking behavior over the menstrual cycle: An improved replication. *Evolution and Human Behavior, 24*, 391–398.

Broude, G. J., & Greene, S. J. (1978). Cross-cultural codes on 20 sexual attitudes and practices. *Ethnology, 15*, 409–430.

Brownmiller, S. (1975). *Against our will: Men, women, and rape.* New York: Simon & Schuster.

Buss, D. M. (1998). Sexual strategies theory: Historical origins and current status. *Journal of Sex Research, 35*, 19–31.

Buss, D. M. (2003). *The evolution of desire: Strategies of human mating.* New York: Basic Books. (Original work published 1994)

Buss, D. M., Haselton, M. G., Shackelford, T. K., Bleske, A. L., & Wakefield, J. C. (1998). Adaptations, exaptations, and spandrels. *American Psychologist, 53*, 533–548.

Buss, D. M., & Schmitt, D. P. (1993). Sexual strategy theory: An evolutionary perspective on human mating. *Psychological Review, 100*, 204–232.

Canastar, A., & Maxson, S. (2003). Sexual aggression in mice: Effects of male strain and of female estrous state. *Behavior Genetics, 33*, 521–528.

Chagnon, N. A. (1994, August). How important was "marriage by capture" as a mating strategy in the EEA? *Human Behavior and Evolution Society Newsletter, 3*, 1–2.

Check, M. V. P., Malamuth, N., Elias, B., & Barton, S. (1985). On hostile ground. *Psychology Today, 19*, 56–61.

Chiroro, P., Bohner, G., Viki, G. T., & Jarvis, C. I. (2004). Rape myth acceptance and rape proclivity: Expected dominance versus expected arousal as mediators in acquaintance-rape situations. *Journal of Interpersonal Violence, 19*, 427–442.

Clutton-Brock, T., & Parker, G. (1995). Sexual coercion in animal societies. *Animal Behaviour, 49*, 1345–1365.

Crofoot, M. C., & Knott, C. D. (in press). What we do and don't know about orangutan male dimorphism. In B. M. F. Galdikas, N. Briggs, L. K. Sheeran, & G. L. Shapiro (Eds.), *Great and small apes of the world: Vol. II. Orangutans and Gibbons.*

Dean, K., & Malamuth, N. (1997). Characteristics of men who aggress sexually and of men who imagine aggressing: Risk and moderating variables. *Journal of Personality and Social Psychology, 72*, 449–455.

Dominic, J. P., & Zeichner, A. (2003). Effects of trait anger and negative attitudes toward women on physical assault in dating relationships. *Journal of Family Violence, 18*(5), 301–307.

Draper, P., & Harpending, H. (1982). Father absence and reproductive strategy: An evolutionary perspective. *Journal of Anthropological Research, 38*, 255–273.

Ellis, B., & Symons, D. (1989). Sex differences in sexual fantasy. *Journal of Sex Research, 27,* 527–555.

Ellis, L. (1989). *Theories of rape: Inquiries into the causes of sexual aggression.* New York: Hemisphere.

Felson, R. B., & Krohn, M. (1990). Motives for rape. *Journal of Research in Crime and Delinquency, 1*(27), 222–242.

Forbes, G. B., Adams-Curtis, L. E., & White, K. B. (2004). First- and second-generation measures of sexism, rape myths and related beliefs, and hostility toward women. *Violence Against Women, 10,* 236–261.

Glick, P., & Fiske, S. T. (1996). The Ambivalent Sexism Inventory: Differentiating hostile and benevolent sexism. *Journal of Personality and Social Psychology, 70,* 491–512.

Gottschall, J., & Gottschall, T. (2003). Are per-incident rape-pregnancy rates higher than per-incident consensual pregnancy rates? *Human Nature, 14,* 1–20.

Greendlinger, V., & Byrne, D. (1987). Coercive sexual fantasies of college men as predictors of self-reported likelihood to rape and overt sexual aggression. *Journal of Sex Research, 23,* 1–11.

Hagen, E. H. (2004). Is rape an adaptation. *The Evolutionary Psychology FAQ* Retrieved January 25, 2004 from www.anth.ucsb.edu/projects/human/evpsychfaq.html.

Hines, D. A., & Saudino, K. J. (2003). Gender differences in psychological, physical, and sexual aggression among college students using the Revised Conflict Tactics Scales. *Violence and Victims, 18,* 197–217.

Kenrick, D. T., & Sheets, V. (1993). Homicidal fantasies. *Ethology and Sociobiology, 14,* 231–246.

Kilpatrick, D., Edmunds, C., & Seymour, A. (1992). *Rape in America: A report to the nation.* Arlington, VA: National Victim Center.

Knight, R. A., & Prentky, R. A. (1990). Classifying sexual offenders: The development and corroboration of taxonomic models. In W. L. Marshall, D. R. Laws, & H. E. Barbaree (Eds.), *Handbook of sexual assault: Issues, theories, and treatment of the offender* (pp. 23–52). New York: Plenum Press.

Knight, R. A., & Prentky, R. A. (2004, March). *The role of sexual motivation in sexually coercive behavior.* Manuscript under review.

Knight, R. A., & Sims-Knight, J. E. (2003). The developmental antecedents of sexual coercion against women: Testing alternative hypotheses with structural equation modeling. *Annals of the New York Academy of Sciences, 989,* 72–85.

Lalumière, M. L., Harris, G. T., Quinsey, V. L., & Rice, M. E. (in press). *The nature of rape: Understanding male propensity for sexual aggression.* Washington, DC: American Psychological Association.

Lalumière, M. L., Quinsey, V. L., Harris, G. T., Rice, M. E., & Trautrimas, C. (2003). Are rapists differentially aroused by coercive sex in phallometric assessments? *Annals of the New York Academy of Sciences, 989,* 211–224.

Leibold, J. M., & McConnell, A. R. (2004). Women, sex, hostility, power, and suspicion: Sexually aggressive men's cognitive associations. *Journal of Experimental Social Psychology, 40,* 256–263.

Leibold, J. M., & McConnell, A. R. (2004, January). The consequences of powerlessness on aggression and on attraction toward women by sexually aggressive men. Manuscript under review.

Levinson, D. (1989). *Family violence in cross-cultural perspective.* Thousand Oaks, CA: Sage.

Lim, S., & Howard, R. (1998). Antecedents of sexual and non-sexual aggression in young Singaporean men. *Personality and Individual Differences, 25,* 1163–1182.

Lisak, D., & Roth, S. (1988). Motivational factors in nonincarcerated sexually aggressive men. *Journal of Personality and Social Psychology, 55,* 795–802.

Lohr, B. A., Adams, H. E., & Davis, M. J. (1997). Sexual arousal to erotic and aggressive stimuli in sexually coercive and noncoercive men. *Journal of Abnormal Psychology, 106*(2), 230–242.

Lonsway, K. A., & Fitzgerald, L. F. (1995). Attitudinal antecedents of rape myth acceptance: A theoretical and empirical reexamination. *Journal of Personality and Social Psychology, 68,* 704–711.

Looman, J. (2001). Sexual arousal in rapists and child molesters. *Dissertation Abstracts International: B. The Physical Sciences and Engineering, 61*(10-B), 5571. (UMI No. AAT 3059657)

Malamuth, N. (1981). Rape proclivity among males. *Journal of Social Issues, 37,* 138–157.

Malamuth, N. (1988). Predicting laboratory aggression against female vs. male targets: Implications for research on sexual aggression. *Journal of Research in Personality, 22,* 474–495.

Malamuth, N. (1989a). The attraction to sexual aggression scale: Part one. *Journal of Sex Research, 26,* 26–49.

Malamuth, N. (1989b). The attraction to sexual aggression scale: Part two. *Journal of Sex Research, 26,* 324–354.

Malamuth, N. (1995). Using the confluence model of sexual aggression to predict men's conflict with women: A 10-year follow-up study. *Journal of Personality and Social Psychology, 69,* 353–369.

Malamuth, N. (1998). An evolutionary-based model integrating research on the characteristics of sexually aggressive men. In J. G. Adair & D. Belanger (Eds.), *Advances in psychological science: Vol. 1. Social, personal, and cultural aspects* (pp. 151–184). Hove, England: Psychology Press/Erlbaum.

Malamuth, N. (2003). Criminal and non-criminal sexual aggressors: Integrating psychopathy in a hierarchical-mediational confluence model. In R. A. Prentky, E. Janus, & M. Seto (Eds.), *Understanding and managing sexually coercive behavior: Annals of the New York Academy of Sciences* (Vol. 989, pp. 33–58). New York: New York Academy of Sciences.

Malamuth, N. (unpublished study). Sexual arousal to dominance and force shows evidence of specificity. Manuscript in preparation, University of California, Los Angeles.

Malamuth, N., & Check, J. (1981). The effects of mass media exposure on acceptance of violence against women: A field experiment. *Journal of Research in Personality, 15,* 436–446.

Malamuth, N., Check, J., & Briere, J. (1986). Sexual arousal in response to aggression: Ideological, aggressive and sexual correlates. *Journal of Personality and Social Psychology, 50,* 330–340.

Malamuth, N., Heim, M., & Feshbach, S. (1980). The sexual responsiveness of college students to rape depictions: Inhibitory and disinhibitory effects. *Journal of Personality and Social Psychology, 38,* 399–408.

Malamuth, N., & Impett, E. (June, 1999). Mechanisms mediating the relation between hostile masculinity and sexual aggression. Paper presented at the Annual Meetings of the Human Behavior and Evolution Society, Salt Lake City, Utah.

Malamuth, N., Linz, D., Heavey, C., Barnes, G., & Acker, M. (1995). Using the confluence model of sexual aggression to predict men's conflict with women: A 10-year follow-up study. *Journal of Personality and Social Psychology, 69,* 353–369.

Malamuth, N., Sockloskie, R. J., Koss, M. P., & Tanaka, J. S. (1991). Characteristics of aggressors against women: Testing a model using a national sample of college students. *Journal of Consulting and Clinical Psychology, 59,* 670–681.

Malamuth, N., & Thornhill, N. (1994). Hostile masculinity, sexual aggression and gender-biased domineeringness in conversations. *Aggressive Behavior, 20,* 185–193.

Marshall, W. L., & Fernandez, Y. M. (2000). Phallometric testing with sexual offenders: Limits to its value. *Clinical Psychology Review, 20,* 807–822.

Marshall, W. L., & Kennedy, P. (2003). Sexual sadism in sexual offenders: An elusive diagnosis. *Aggression and Violent Behavior, 8,* 1–22.

Mealey, L. (1995). The sociobiology of sociopathy: An integrated evolutionary model. *Behavioral and Brain Sciences, 995*(18), 523–541.

Mirowsky, J. (1999). Analyzing associations between mental health and social circumstances. In C. S. Aneshensel & J. C. Phelan (Eds.), *Handbook of sociology and social research* (pp. 105–123). Dordrecht, Netherlands: Kluwer Academic.

Monson, C. M., & Langhinrichsen-Rohling, J. (2002). Sexual and nonsexual dating violence perpetration: Testing an integrated perpetrator typology. *Violence and Victims, 17,* 403–428.

Murnen, S., Wright, C., & Kaluzny, G. (2002). If "boys will be boys," then girls will be victims? A meta-analytic review of the research that relates masculine ideology to sexual aggression. *Sex Roles, 46,* 359–375.

Mustaine, E. E., & Tewksbury, R. (1999). A routine activities theory explanation for women's stalking victimizations. *Violence Against Women, 5,* 43–62.

Nadler, R. D. (1977). Sexual behavior of captive orangutans. *Archives of Sexual Behavior, 6,* 457–475.

Nadler, R. D. (1999). Sexual aggression in the great apes: Implications for human law. *Jurimetrics Journal, 39,* 149–155.

Nelson, D. A. (1979). Personality, sexual functions, and sexual behavior. An Experiment in methodology. *Dissertation Abstracts International, 995*(39), 6134. (UMI No. AAT 7913307)

Niarchos, C. (1995). Women, war and rape: Challenges facing the international tribunal for the former Yugoslavia. *95 Human Rights Quarterly, 17,* 649–690.

Palmer, C. (1989). Rape in nonhuman species: Definitions, evidence, and implications. *Journal of Sex Research, 26,* 353–374.

Perkins, C., Klaus, P., Bastian, L., & Cohen, R. (1996). *Criminal victimization in the United States, 1993.* [National Crime Victimization Survey Report]. Washington, DC: Bureau of Justice Statistics, U.S. Department of Justice.

Petralia, S. M., & Gallup, G. G. (2002). Effects of a sexual assault scenario on handgrip strength across the menstrual cycle. *Evolution and Human Behavior, 23,* 3–10.

Pinker, S. (2000). *How the mind works.* New York: Norton.

Quinsey, V. L., Chaplin, T. C., & Upfold, D. (1984). Sexual arousal to nonsexual violence and sadomasochistic themes among rapists and non-sex offenders. *Journal of Consulting and Clinical Psychology, 52,* 651–657.

Rausher, M. D. (2001). Co-evolution and plan resistance to natural enemies. *Nature, 44,* 857.

Sanday, P. R. (1981). The sociocultural context of rape: A cross-cultural study. *Journal of Social Issues, 37,* 5–27.

Serin, R., & Mailloux, D. (2003). Assessment of sex offenders: Lessons learned from the assessment of non-sex offenders. *Annals of the New York Academy of Sciences, 989,* 185–197.

Seto, M. C., & Kuban, M. (1996). Criterion-related validity of a phallometric test for paraphilic rape and sadism. *995 Behaviour Research and Therapy, 34,* 175–183.

Shackelford, T. K. (2002a). Are young women the special targets of rape-murder? *Aggressive Behavior, 28,* 224–232.

Shackelford, T. K. (2002b). Risk of multiple-offender rape-murder varies with female age. *Journal of Criminal Justice, 30,* 135–141.

Smuts, B. (1992). Male aggression against women: An evolutionary perspective. *Human Nature, 3,* 1–44.

Smuts, B. (1995). The evolutionary origins of patriarchy. *Human Nature, 6,* 1–32.

Smuts, B., & Smuts, R. (1993). Male aggression and sexual coercion of females in nonhuman primates and other mammals: Evidence and theoretical implications. *Advances in the Study of Behavior, 22,* 1–63.

Stiglmayer, A. (Ed.). (1994). *Mass rape.* Arkansas, NE: University of Nebraska Press.

Symons, D. (1979). *The evolution of human sexuality.* New York: Oxford University Press.

Symons, D. (1995). Beauty is in the adaptations of the beholder: The evolutionary psychology of human female sexual attractiveness. In P. R. Abramson & S. D. Pinkerton (Eds.), *Sexual nature/sexual culture* (pp. 80–118). Chicago: University of Chicago Press.

Thornhill, N., & Thornhill, R. (1991). An evolutionary analysis of psychological pain following human (Homo sapiens) rape: IV. The effect of the nature of the sexual assault. *Journal of Comparative Psychology, 105,* 243–252.

Thornhill, R., & Palmer, C. T. (2000). *A natural history of rape: Biological bases of sexual coercion.* Cambridge, MA: MIT Press.

Thornhill, R., & Sauer, K. (1991). The notal organ of the scorpionfly (*Panorpa vulgaris*): An adaptation to coerce mating duration. *Behavioral Ecology, 2,* 156–164.

Thornhill, R., & Thornhill, N. (1983). Human rape: An evolutionary analysis. *Ethology and Sociobiology, 4,* 137–173.

Thornhill, R., & Thornhill, N. (1992). The evolutionary psychology of men's coercive sexuality. *Behavioral and Brain Sciences, 15,* 363–421.

Tooby, J., & Cosmides, L. (1992). Psychological foundations of culture. In J. Barkow, L. Cosmides, & J. Tooby (Eds.), *The adapted mind* (pp. 19–136). Chicago: Aldine.

Trivers, R. (1972). Parental investment and sexual selection. In B. Campbell (Ed.), *Sexual selection and the descent of man, 1871–1971.* (pp. 136–179). Chicago: Aldine.

Vega, V., & Malamuth, N. (2003). *Predicting sexual aggression: The role of mass media exposure in the context of general and specific antisocial characteristics.* Paper presented at the meetings of the International Communication Association, San Diego, 2003.

Wilson, B. A., Holm, J. E., Bishop, K. L., & Borowiak, D. M. (2002). Predicting responses to sexually aggressive stories: The role of consent, interest in sexual aggression, and overall sexual interest. *Journal of Sex Research, 39,* 275–283.

Wrangham, R. W., & Peterson, D. (1996). *Demonic males: Apes and the origins of human violence.* Boston: Houghton Mifflon.

Yates, E., Marshall, W. L., & Barbaree, H. E. (1984). Anger and deviant sexual arousal. *Behavior Therapy, 15*(3), 287–294.

CHAPTER 14

Commitment, Love, and Mate Retention

LORNE CAMPBELL and BRUCE J. ELLIS

Love is kind; love is not easily provoked, it thinks no evil; love does not rejoice in iniquity, but rejoices in the truth; love believes all things, hopes all things, and endures all things; love never fails.

—1 Corinthians 13: 4–7

IN A LETTER TO THE CHURCH of Corinth written almost 2,000 years ago, Paul the Apostle put into words what most people only feel in their hearts. He spoke of the necessity, character, and permanence of love, attempting to capture the essence of the emotional bond that brings people together to form relationships and make relationships last. The centrality of love in human life is reflected across time and culture in stories, poems, plays, and music. Although it has been suggested that romantic love is an invention of Western civilization (e.g., Stone, 1988), it has been convincingly demonstrated that romantic love and pair bonding transcend time and culture (e.g., Daly & Wilson, 1983; Jankowiak & Fischer, 1992). The ubiquity of love suggests it has played an important role in human evolution, having close ties to reproductive success (e.g., Buss, 1988b; Mellen, 1981).

Although love has been a focal point for poets and philosophers for thousands of years, it has been largely ignored by scientists until recent times. Researchers in the social sciences only began to seriously investigate love and romantic relationships in the 1970s. A large proportion of relationship research during this time focused not on relationship processes but on interpersonal attraction. Great strides were subsequently made in the study of relationship processes, identifying behavioral and emotional exchanges between partners that presaged satisfaction and stability (see Gottman, 1994, for a review). This research was principally descriptive, however, and over 20 years ago a strong theoretical approach to the study of love and close relationships was called for by Harold Kelley and his colleagues

419

(1983). Many researchers took up this challenge, establishing over the past 2 decades what has recently been labeled the *new science of intimate relationships* (Fletcher, 2002).

Drawing on the power of evolutionary theory to explain behavior across cultures and species, particularly in the domains of sex and reproduction, evolutionary psychology has now emerged as a major perspective in the study of intimate relationships (Fletcher, 2002). This chapter applies this perspective to the study of love, commitment, and mate retention. We begin with an overview of the evolutionary basis of long-term mating and high parental investment in humans. Next we discuss two emotional-motivational systems—love and anger-upset—that play major roles in regulating relationship feelings and behavior. Then we highlight recent evolutionary research on the love system and its links to relationship ideals, investment, and dependence. Finally, we review the anger-upset system and its links to jealousy, mate-retention strategies, and relationship violence.

THE ROLE OF PAIR BONDING IN HUMAN REPRODUCTION

In sexually reproducing species, attracting mates, retaining mates, successfully copulating with them, and ensuring the survival of offspring to reproductive age are all fundamental to successful reproduction (e.g., Buss, 1988b). Although men and women differ in many aspects of their mating strategies, both men and women face the adaptive challenge of successfully rearing offspring. Offspring survival became increasingly dependent on extended and intensive parental investment during human evolution because of the onset of bipedalism and concomitant increases in brain size. This heightened dependency increased levels of parental investment needed to ensure offspring survival and development, placing large demands on the mother's time, ability to collect food, and ability to defend herself and her infant. The increasing immaturity of human infants thus created a strong selection pressure for biparental care.

Many theorists have posited that romantic love evolved as a commitment device to maintain relational bonds between mothers and fathers and facilitate mutual investment in offspring (e.g., Kirkpatrick, 1998; Mellen, 1981). Increased infant dependency placed greater burdens on mothers and increased the value of paternal support in feeding and protecting young. Given that men have a genetic interest in the survival of their offspring, they were able to benefit reproductively by forming committed, investing relationships that would have reliably increased the probability of offspring survival (e.g., Barash, 1977; Fisher, 1998; Kenrick & Trost, 1997). The formation of pair bonds, therefore, should translate into fitness, and an excellent review of the literature on paternal investment by Geary (2000) reported a great deal of evidence in support of this claim. For instance, paternal investment in the form of pair bonds has been linked in preindustrial times with increased infant health and decreased infant mortality (e.g., Hed, 1987) not only because a working father allowed a mother to spend more time with a young infant that required breast feeding (Reid, 1997) but also because a couple with a working father enjoyed a relatively higher socioeconomic status (SES) and thus was able to provide better food and shelter (H. Schultz, 1991). Paternal investment is also related to improved social competitiveness for children, such as higher SES in adulthood (e.g., Kaplan, Lancaster, & Anderson, 1998), later onset of pubertal timing in girls (Ellis, McFadyen-Ketchum, Dodge, Pettit, & Bates,

1999), and increased educational achievement for adolescents (e.g., Amato & Keith, 1991). It is clear that children born and raised within pair bonds have been more likely to survive to reproductive age and to be more socially competitive later in life when they are attempting to attract mates (Geary, 2000).

The prevalence of sexually transmitted diseases (STDs) may have created another selection pressure for the formation of long-term pair bonds. At least 50 STDs have been documented, ranging from viruses, bacteria, fungi, protozoa, and ectoparasites (see Centers for Disease Control and Prevention, 2002). Although many of these STDs have been recently introduced to humans (e.g., AIDS), Mackey and Immerman (2000) suggest that humans have been vulnerable to these types of diseases over evolutionary history. The fertility of women in particular is severely compromised when they contract an STD, and often the disease can spread to the fetus or to the infant as he or she passes through the birth canal. For example, women with syphilis have a heightened risk of miscarriage, premature delivery, stillbirth, and infant death, and the chances that the fetus will contract the disease are almost 100% if it is not treated (e.g., K. F. Schulz, Murphy, Patamasucon, & Meheus, 1990). The strongest predictor of contracting STDs is the number of sexual partners (e.g., Moore & Cates, 1990); therefore, the best way to limit the risk of contracting a disease that could have lethal effects on reproductive success is to limit the number of sexual partners. Because women are much more susceptible than men to contracting STDs (e.g., Glynn et al., 2001; Moore & Cates, 1990), ancestral women would have differentially benefited from a more restrictive attitude toward uncommitted sex. If more inhibited women contracted fewer STDs and experienced greater reproductive success, they would have been more attractive as long-term mates, and the proclivity to desire fewer sexual partners would have been selected for. STDs may have been one important factor in the development of pair bonds over evolutionary history by enhancing the benefits of sexual exclusivity and increasing the reproductive success of both men and women (Mackey & Immerman, 2000).

EVIDENCE OF PAIR BONDING

In every known culture, formal marriage arrangements between men and women exist (Brown, 1991; Buss, 1985; Daly & Wilson, 1983). An analysis of 166 societies by Jankowiak and Fischer (1992) concluded that romantic love is found worldwide, and over 90% of people in the world will marry at least once during their lives (Buss, 1985). Whereas a large proportion of cultures permit polygyny (i.e., having more than one wife; van den Berghe, 1979), very few men in these cultures engage in this practice (Lancaster & Kaplan, 1994). Less than 1% of cultures, though, permit a woman to take more than one husband at a time (i.e., polyandry), and this practice is extremely rare (van den Berghe, 1979). Therefore, marital attachment is a universal feature of human existence, and most people in the world marry only one person at a time (Fisher, 1992).

Recent research indicating different neural activities related to pair bonding emphasizes proximate mechanisms that promote the development and maintenance of relationships. Fisher summarizes some of this research in her model of mating, reproduction, and parenting. The model posits that mating behaviors are guided by three distinct emotion systems—lust, attraction, and attachment—and that behaviors related to each set of emotions are governed by a unique set of neural activities (Fisher, 1998, 2000). The lust system is proposed to motivate individuals to locate sexual opportunities and is mainly associated with estrogens and androgens in the brain. The attraction system directs an individual's attention toward specific mates, makes him or her crave emotional union with this person, and is associated with high levels of dopamine and norepinephrine and low levels of serotonin in the brain. The attachment system is distinguished by the maintenance of close proximity, feelings of comfort and security, and feelings of emotional dependency and is associated with oxytocin (for women) and vasopressin (for men; Carter, 1998; Insel, Winslow, Wang, & Young, 1998). Additionally, when both men and women who are deeply in love are asked to think of their partners while their brain is being scanned, regions of the brain that are associated with reward become activated (the same regions activated by cocaine), whereas they do not become activated when thinking of an acquaintance (Bartels & Zeki, 2000). Overall, there are likely to be many neural circuits in the brain that function to promote attraction to specific individuals and to forming and maintaining long-term relationships.

Fisher's attraction and attachment systems are conceptually similar to Bowlby's attachment theory (1969). Bowlby proposed that the process of evolution by natural selection equipped infants with a repertoire of behaviors that serves to facilitate proximity to caregivers, particularly in situations when support is required, and that these behaviors are essential for survival. Bowlby believed that the bond forged between mother and infant in childhood provides a cognitive and affective foundation for later attachments and that the attachment system serves a similar affect-regulatory function in adulthood as it did in infancy. Zeifman and Hazan (1997; see also Shaver, Hazan, & Bradshaw, 1988) have proposed that attachment is one of the psychological mechanisms that have evolved to solve the adaptive problem of keeping parents together to raise offspring. The secure feelings that partners experience in each other's presence, the lonely feelings while they are apart, and the desire to be together after separations are hallmarks of the attachment system, as well as emotions that serve to keep people together in committed relationships. Importantly, the hormone oxytocin plays a central role in the formation of attachment bonds between mother and infant (see Hrdy, 1999, for a review), as well as between romantic partners (Carter, 1992), suggesting a mechanism that functions to promote attachments at all stages of life.

Pair bonds are not only a universal phenomenon in humans but also associated with psychological and physical health. For example, broken social ties or poor relationships correlate with increased vulnerability to disease; heart attack victims are more likely to have a recurring attack when they live alone; the happiest university students are those that feel satisfied with their love life; those who enjoy close relationships cope better with various stresses, including bereavement, rape, job loss, and illness; and happily married individuals are less likely to experience depression than unhappily married or unmarried individuals (for a review, see Myers, 1999). Moreover, married men and women report more happiness than people who have never married, have separated, or have divorced (Myers & Diener, 1995). This research suggests a link between the theoretical benefits of pair bond formation and the practical benefits people derive from them. Humans may be designed to respond positively when a long-term mate is secured and relationships endure.

Although it is widely accepted that long-term mating relationships are an integral part of human reproduction, the primacy of long-term mating remains a matter of debate. Zeifman and Hazan (1997) have postulated that humans have evolved to maintain relationships primarily over long periods of time (perhaps a lifetime). Fisher (1998), however, suggests that although long-term relationships have obvious reproductive benefits, the desire to stay in one relationship wanes as a function of the amount of time it takes an infant to become less dependant on parental investment (approximately 4 years). Indeed, across cultures, most marriages do not last a lifetime, and most societies have established divorce procedures (Betzig, 1989; Brown, 1991). Moreover, approximately 30% of men and women have had extramarital sex at least once (Thompson, 1983), and infidelity is the most frequently cited reason for divorce across cultures (Betzig, 1989). That humans are inclined to form pair bonds does not deny that they are sometimes motivated to dissolve these pair bonds or seek additional mating opportunities while in long-term romantic relationships (Kirkpatrick, 1998). The *lust, attraction,* and *attachment* systems are capable of being activated independently, implying that even after attachments are formed partners may find potential mates and relationships very appealing (e.g., Fisher, 1998, 2000). That is, humans have a menu of mating strategies that includes long-term commitment, short-term opportunistic copulation, extra-pair copulation, and so forth (see Buss, 1994; Buss & Schmitt, 1993). This variation in mating strategies suggests the importance of understanding the factors that arouse both feelings of love for the partner, lust for alternative mates, and relationship discontent.

Even though men and women share some reproductive goals that motivate them to *form* long-term relationships, they also possess different goals *in* these romantic relationships (e.g., Buss, 1995; Kenrick & Trost, 1997; Trivers, 1972). Women tend to be more concerned about securing resources from their partners to aid in child rearing and should, therefore, be dissatisfied with husbands who have few resources, do not possess traits related to the ability to acquire resources (e.g., ambition, leadership), or are directing resources elsewhere (e.g., outside mating opportunities; Ellis, 1992). Men should be concerned with optimizing paternity certainty. Raising unrelated offspring to reproductive age adds no value to a person's reproductive success, and men should, for example, be especially vigilant of their partners' activities with other men (Buss & Shackelford, 1997).

In summary, romantic relationships function to increase the reproductive success of both men and women, and a number of proximate mechanisms have been hypothesized to motivate people to form and maintain relatively long-term relationships. Although the study of relationship processes is relatively new, evolutionary psychologists are at the vanguard of examining subjective experiences of love and discontent in ongoing romantic relationships. In the following section, we outline an organizing framework for research on relationship process from an evolutionary perspective.

EMOTIONAL-MOTIVATION SYSTEMS IN RELATIONSHIPS: LOVE AND ANGER-UPSET

Romantic partners have the capacity to elicit both extremely positive and negative emotions, from love and elation to jealousy and rage. This duality has been validated by extensive research highlighting positive and negative emotional experiences in relationships. What is surprising, however, is that these two classes of emotions have been studied predominantly in isolation (cf. Ellis & Malamuth, 2000). One body of research has focused on the psychological experience and expression of love, such as individuals' subjective experiences of love (Fehr, 1988) and how they display their love to their partners (Buss, 1988b). A different body of research has addressed aggressive and abusive behaviors in relationships, with much of this research focusing on the role of anger in predicting relationship outcomes (e.g., Buss, 1989a). Although experiences of love and anger often coexist in romantic relationships (e.g., Bookwala, Frieze, & Grote, 1994), the fact that little research has addressed both sets of emotions simultaneously makes it difficult to determine the extent to which these emotions constitute opposite or independent systems, both in terms of covariation and functions.

Bridging the study of emotions in relationships, the *discrete systems model* of love and anger-upset, developed by Ellis and Malamuth (2000; see also Ellis, 1998), provides an organizing framework for characterizing relationship processes that are related to the experience of positive and negative emotions. Positive and negative emotions constitute largely orthogonal dimensions, suggesting that the processes related to the experience of either set of emotions are generally independent (Watson & Clark, 1997). Feelings of love and anger that arise in romantic relationships, therefore, may have separate (rather than opposite) causes and consequences. This view is consistent with evolutionary theorizing on the function of emotions, which conceptualizes emotions as adaptations that track important costs and benefits in the environment and function to adjust behavior in ways that increase the individual's capacity and tendency to respond adaptively to those costs and benefits (Nesse, 1990). From this perspective, different emotion systems are activated by distinct sources of information from the environment, and these systems transform that information into specific physiological and behavioral outputs that are relevant to the situation that brought the system online.

The discrete systems model posits that variations in characteristic levels of love and anger-upset experienced in different relationships track specific, largely independent fitness-relevant features of those relationships. When people feel that their partners and relationships are facilitating their relationship needs, they should experience heightened feelings of love toward those partners and relationships, whereas when people feel that their partners or relationships are interfering with their relationship needs, they should experience high levels of anger and upset (see Buss's model of strategic interference, 1989a). The discrete systems model posits that feelings of love should be related to increased commitment and satisfaction with the relationship and to prorelationship behaviors directed toward the partner, whereas feelings of anger and upset should be related to lower satisfaction with the relationship and more aggressive behaviors directed toward the partner.

Testing these predictions with a sample of 124 dating couples, Ellis and Malamuth (2000) found that variations in strategic facilitation (but not strategic interference) contributed uniquely to the prediction of love in both men and women, whereas variations in strategic interference (but not strategic facilitation) contributed uniquely to the prediction of anger-upset in both men and women. For example, the frequency with which a person's partner "takes care of me when I am sick" or "displays concern for my problems" uniquely predicted feelings of love but *not* intensity of anger-upset. Conversely, the frequency with which the partner "cancels dates with me at the last minute" or "treats me like I am stupid or inferior" uniquely predicted anger-upset but *not* love. Contrary to intuition, being in a relationship characterized by relatively high levels of strategic interference did not jeopardize love, nor did being in a relationship characterized by relatively high levels of strategic facilitation soften anger-upset. This is not to say that strategic facilitation and strategic interference were themselves independent, but rather that strategic facilitation and strategic interference were largely independent and domain-specific at the emotional level in their contributions to either love or anger.

The discrete systems model states that, because the emotions of love and anger-upset correspond to different adaptive problems in close relationships (securing strategic facilitation versus reducing strategic interference), they prepare and motivate the individual to engage in different forms of partner-directed behavior. Consistent with the model, feelings of love for an individual's partner uniquely predicted commitment-promoting behavior (but not partner-directed aggression), whereas typical levels of anger-upset experienced during conflict with the partner uniquely predicted aggression (but not commitment). For example, individuals who felt more love for their partners were more likely to propose marriage or maintain dating exclusivity but were *not* less likely to shout at their partners or throw objects at them. These data do not imply that aggression and commitment are themselves independent (there was a tendency for individuals who were more aggressive toward their partners to also perform more commitment-promoting behaviors and vice versa). Rather, anger-upset and love appear to be largely independent and domain-specific in their direct effects on either aggression or commitment.

In sum, the discrete systems model suggests that experiences of love and anger-upset within romantic relationships are largely independent because they were shaped by natural selection to solve different adaptive problems encountered in those relationships during human evolution. The independence of emotion systems may help explain why individuals can be simultaneously in love with their partner, infuriated over their partner's condescending behavior, mad with jealousy, and sexually attracted to someone else. This model also provides a useful way of organizing existing research on relationship processes, an organizational system that we use in the following sections to discuss research adopting an evolutionary approach to the study of relationships.

RELATIONSHIP PROCESSES AND THE LOVE SYSTEM

One theoretical approach that has been very successful in predicting the development and maintenance of satisfaction in romantic relationships is *interdependence theory* (Kelley & Thibault, 1978; Thibault & Kelley, 1959). According to this perspective, individuals evaluate their partners and relationships based on the perceived consistency between a priori standards or expectations and perceptions of the current partner and relationship. In making these evaluations, individuals rely on two standards: the comparison level (CL) and the comparison level for alternatives (CLalt; see Rusbult & Arriaga, 1997). The CL is the standard that individuals use to evaluate the attractiveness of their relationship and how satisfactory it is (Thibaut & Kelley, 1959). Hence, CL is a measure of the degree to which general outcomes (i.e., rewards minus costs) in a relationship exceed the outcomes an individual believes he or she deserves. CLalt, in contrast, reflects the level of outcomes that individuals believe they can obtain from their best available alternative partners-relationships. Individuals with higher CLalts perceive that the outcomes attainable in their best alternative relationships are better than those found in their current relationships.

Interdependence theory proposes that people should become dissatisfied with their relationship when they think they are receiving less than they "deserve." When people feel that they have superior alternatives to their current relationship, they should feel less dependent on their partners-relationships and be less likely to remain in the relationship over time. One strength of interdependence theory is that it can explain why some people leave apparently rewarding relationships, while some people stay in apparently poor relationships. A limitation of the theory is that it does not specify the content of individuals' CL or CLalt and, therefore, does not address the possibility that individuals may evaluate their partners or relationships on content-specific standards or dimensions. Specifically, it speaks little to the evolved goals of men and women in relationships, a topic that evolutionary theory specifically addresses (e.g., Ellis, 1992; Shackelford & Buss, 1997; Symons, 1979). In this section, we discuss three programs of research that have investigated feelings of love and satisfaction in relationships by combining elements of interdependence and evolutionary theories.

THE IDEAL STANDARDS MODEL

The ideal standards model (ISM; Fletcher, Simpson, Thomas, & Giles, 1999; Simpson, Fletcher, & Campbell, 2001) proposes that people possess images of their ideal partner or an abstract concept of the qualities that they would like their potential or current romantic partner to have. Ideals comprise three interlocking components: perceptions of the self, partner, and relationships (Baldwin, 1992). Individuals' images of their ideal partners reflect their self-perceptions, the qualities they would like their partner to possess, and the type of relationship that they would like to have.

According to the ISM, the ideals that people use as evaluative criteria for their romantic partners should reflect evolutionary-relevant relationship goals. Principles derived from evolutionary theories (see Buss & Schmitt, 1993; Gangestad & Simpson, 2000) suggest that people ought to judge ideal partners on three basic dimensions: (1) their capacity for intimacy and commitment, (2) their attractiveness and general health, and (3) their social status and resources. These three dimensions make good theoretical sense in light of recent evolutionary models that integrate *good provider* and *good genes* theories of human mating (see Gangestad & Simpson, 2000). Each dimension represents a different "route" to obtaining a mate and promoting the individual's own reproductive fitness (see Buss & Schmitt, 1993). By being attentive to a partner's capacity for intimacy and commitment, individuals should increase their chances of finding a cooperative, committed partner who is likely to be a devoted parent. By focusing on attractiveness and health, individuals are more likely to acquire a mate who is younger, healthier, and perhaps more fertile (especially in the case of men choosing women). And by considering a partner's resources and status, individuals should be more likely to obtain a mate who can ascend social hierarchies and form coalitions with other people who have, or can acquire, valued social status or other resources (especially in the case of women choosing men). Factor analyses of data collected from two independent samples confirmed this tripartite factor structure regarding how individuals evaluate romantic partners (Fletcher et al., 1999).

According to the model, comparisons between these ideal standards and perceptions of the current partner or relationship should serve three basic functions. The magnitude of the discrepancies between ideal standards and perceptions of the current partner-relationship (hereafter referred to as *partner discrepancies*) allows individuals to (1) estimate and *evaluate* the quality of their partners and relationships (e.g., to assess the appropriateness of potential or current partners-relationships), (2) *explain* what happens in relationships (e.g., give causal accounts explaining relationship satisfaction, problems, or conflicts), and (3) *regulate* and make adjustments in relationships (e.g., to predict and possibly control current partners-relationships). Large partner discrepancies should indicate to people that they are in an unsatisfactory relationship, which may motivate them to make adjustments in the current relationship (e.g., lower their ideals or enhance their partners) or end the relationship. When people fall short of their partners' ideals, they are in a qualitatively different situation. Such persons may have to engage in different regulatory behaviors to reduce the size of their *partners'* discrepancy. For instance, an individual may have to avoid conflict and showcase his or her best qualities in an effort to more closely meet his or her partner's standards.

To test the hypothesis that smaller partner discrepancies should be associated with more positive relationship evaluations, Fletcher et al. (1999) had people rank the importance of various ideal attributes along with their perceptions of their current partner-relationship on items taken from the ideal partner scales. Consistent with the model, individuals with smaller partner discrepancies rated their relationships more favorably. To test and make inferences about possible causal relations, Fletcher, Simpson, and Thomas (2000) tracked a large sample of individuals in newly formed dating relationships over time and demonstrated that comparisons between ideals and perceptions of the current partner have a causal impact on later relationship evaluations. These results suggest that cognitive comparisons between ideal standards and perceptions of the current partner-relationship influence the way in which partners and relationships are evaluated over time, at least in the early stages of relationship development.

The magnitude of partner discrepancies should affect not only how individuals evaluate their relationships but also how the partners of the individuals feel about the relationship (e.g., Sternberg & Barnes, 1985). Campbell, Simpson, Kashy, and Fletcher (2001) tested this hypothesis by asking both members of a large sample of dating couples to report their ideal standards and how closely their partners matched their ideals. Smaller partner discrepancies predicted greater relationship quality as reported by both members of the dyad. Individuals whose partners more closely matched their ideals reported greater perceived relationship quality, as did the partners of the individuals. This "partner" effect suggests that individuals can sense how well they are living up to their partners' ideal standards. Over time, those who are faring poorly may feel threatened or insecure about the long-term status of the relationship or their position within it, which should lower their evaluations.

The three ideal dimensions reflect the adaptive problems that men and women have faced over evolutionary history. Whereas men should be more focused on the youth and attractiveness of their long-term mates, women should be more keenly attuned to their partners' status and prospects for acquiring status (e.g., Buss & Shackelford, 1997). Perceiving that a partner falls short of an individual's vitality-attractiveness ideals should, therefore, have a more deleterious effect on men's relationship evaluations, whereas perceiving that a partner does not meet the individual's status-resources ideals should be more detrimental to women's relationship evaluations. Additionally, men should be more concerned when their own level of status and resources falls short of their partners' ideals because this discrepancy may suggest an unhappy partner who may seek other mating opportunities. Similarly, women should be more worried when their attractiveness does not match their partners' ideals. These gender differences, however, have not been rigorously investigated in the few studies that have tested predictions derived from the ISM.

INVESTMENTS IN RELATIONSHIPS

When relationships end, it is possible to recover items left at a partner's apartment or divide marital assets, but it is not possible to retrieve the time spent doing things with, or for, partners. These types of "unbankable" relationship investments play a pivotal role in interdependence and social exchange theories of relationship commitment. Specifically, the more people invest in their relationships, the more likely they are to stay in those relationships (Rusbult & Buunk, 1993).

There are some limitations to traditional research on relationship investments, most notably the failure to distinguish between the different types of investments that people make in their relationships. Investment has been treated as a unitary construct and measured with a few items that tap overall investment size. Global measurement of investment, however, does not enable content-oriented research on investment. For example, individuals have many choices regarding where to allocate money for future savings. Money can be funneled into work-sponsored pension accounts, a bank account, registered retirement plans, mutual funds, individual stocks, savings bonds, and so on, depending on the perceived value of the investment for the individual. A person nearing retirement may benefit most from investing in low-risk savings bonds to secure the stability of capital, whereas a younger person may benefit most from investing in the stock market to take advantage of the greater potential for growth. The sum of all investments reflects the overall investment of an individual, but without looking at specific investments little can be gleaned about the value and utility of that person's portfolio. Similarly, in romantic relationships people have many different options for their investments (e.g., time spent with partner, resource allocation, parental investment, emotional investment), with different options having potentially greater returns.

Traditional models also tend to focus on the impact of investments on the individual making the investments and not on the beneficiary of these investments (i.e., the partner). According to these models, investment serves to increase an individual's own commitment to his or her partner and relationship; thus the return on investment is reflected solely in the commitment of the individual to his or her relationship. Investments can be made, though, to elicit returns from others, such as when a helpful act directed toward another person is reciprocated

(Trivers, 1971). Investments should thus serve to increase the commitment of the recipient, meaning the return on investment is the assurance that the partner will remain loyal and committed to the relationship (Ellis, 1998).

Ellis's (1998) model of partner-specific investment (PSI) was developed in part to address the shortcomings of traditional research on investment and commitment. Grounded in evolutionary theory, this model conceptualizes the psychological mechanisms that underlie decisions about allocation of PSI as components of specialized problem-solving machinery designed by natural selection to serve particular functions (cf. Williams, 1975). Ellis (1998) posited that PSIs function to secure access to the long-term social, physical, and energetic resources of a specific mate. There are two related types of PSIs: tangible and symbolic. Tangible investments reflect effort on the part of the investor (the "sender") to bestow immediate benefits on the investee (the "receiver"; e.g., buying something for a partner, providing emotional support); symbolic investments display the sender's willingness to continue investing in the relationship in the future (e.g., discussing the future of the relationship; showing concern for a partner's problems). Drawing on the individual's desire to feel secure in the affections of his or her partner (Bowlby, 1969; Murray, 2001), symbolic investment functions to secure access to a given receiver by enhancing levels of trust and security in the relationship. Investment, by indicating a sender's level of commitment to the relationship, serves to induce trust in, and extract commitment from, the receiver.

The purported functions of investments are similar to the hypothesized functions of mate-retention behaviors discussed by Buss (1988a)—they both serve to keep a specific romantic relationship intact. However, these two models emphasize different strategies for reaching this goal. Investments are defined as behavioral contributions to a partner, whereas mate-retention behaviors are defined as behaviors people engage in to prevent their partner from forming a relationship with someone else. As conceptualized by Ellis (1998), mate-retention behaviors are, therefore, grounded more in feelings of jealousy and insecurity and are activated by cues signaling strategic interference, often in the form of real or perceived infidelity or abandonment. Investment behaviors, by contrast, reflect the individual's expression of love while serving to increase the commitment of the partner to the relationship. PSI thus involves facilitation of the receiver's relationship goals. Consistent with this distinction between PSI and mate retention, research has shown that feelings of love and jealousy in relationships are largely uncorrelated (see White & Mullen, 1989).

Ellis (1998) employed an evolutionary perspective to identify a delimited set of historically important adaptive problems that men and women solved in part through formation of long-term alliances with mates. Modeling the nature of these adaptive problems provided a basis for developing hypotheses about the salient forms of PSI that would have historically solved them. It is just these forms of PSI that we should be selected to evaluate and respond to in close romantic relationships:

- *The problem of provisioning* (e.g., supplying food, shelter, and territory for themselves and their families).
- *The problem of protection* (e.g., avoiding physical domination or harm from other individuals).

- *The problem of parental nurturance* (e.g., caring for and socializing offspring).
- *The problem of sexual access* (e.g., maintaining sexual access to the reproductive capacity of their partners).
- *The problem of commitment* (e.g., securing consistent delivery of PSI from the partner over an extended time period).

This approach suggests that evolution has equipped us with psychological mechanisms that detect and encode information about the degree to which romantic partners are willing and able to solve these adaptive problems. Investment acts should, therefore, be specific, mapping onto the types of adaptive problems facing men and women.

To develop a set of investment acts that correspond to the key adaptive problems identified by the theory, as well as to identify and domain-sample the range of investment acts that men and women direct toward one another, Ellis (1998) employed both *top-down* and *bottom-up* procedures. The top-down procedure involved theory-driven nomination of investment acts by the experimenter to correspond to the five adaptive problems specified earlier. The bottom-up procedure involved having undergraduates nominate particular acts that reflect investment in a relationship, as defined by inputs of time, energy, and resources. The pool of items was then subjected to factor analysis, and 10 dimensions of investment were identified and scaled to form the PSI Inventory (Ellis, 1998). These PSI factors were labeled Expressive-Nurturing, Future-Oriented, Giving of Time, Sexually Proceptive, Monetarily Investing, Honest, Physically Protective, Socially Attentive, Good Relationship with Partner's Family, and Not Sexualizing of Others. The PSI Inventory afforded two levels of assessment. First, at the individual level, the PSI scales assessed the specific forms of investment that flow between dating partners. These individual scales were at best only moderately correlated, suggesting the existence of largely independent constructs. Second, at the group level, the PSI scales formed a coherent subset of variables that (despite their relative independence) loaded together on a common factor. The general PSI factor provided a means of assessing overall investment levels by combining the specific scales into a general index.

Further development and validation of the PSI Inventory was based on a series of studies comprising a total of 227 dating couples (Ellis, 1998). This work embedded PSI in a theoretical framework, specifying its meaning, distinguishing it from other constructs, and indicating how measures of PSI should and should not relate to other variables. Participants completed both self- and partner-report versions of the PSI Inventory and Buss's (1988a) mate-retention inventory, as well as measures of love for the partner, security felt in the relationship, and amount of sexual attention directed toward others. The pattern of results largely supported the main predictions, showing that (1) the overall index of investment was not correlated with the overall mate-retention index, (2) love was positively related to overall partner investments but not to overall levels of mate-retention behavior, (3) security felt was positively related to overall partner investments and negatively related to overall partner mate-retention behaviors, and conversely (4) amount of sexual attention directed toward others was negatively related to overall partner investments and positively related to overall partner mate-retention behaviors.

In sum, levels and types of investments that are received by individuals from their partners provide valuable information about the degree that their relationship goals are being facilitated. Research on PSIs, however, does not directly address why individuals choose to invest more or less in their relationships. One possibility is that people who feel their partners more closely match their ideals may feel more inclined to invest in their relationship as an expression of their love and commitment. That is, investments may be linked with the perceived mate value of partners. Future research needs to investigate individuals' motivation to invest, the unique information men and women obtain from different investments, and the relationship between investments and relationship longevity.

Dependence in Relationships

As specified by interdependence theory (Kelley & Thibaut, 1978; Thibaut & Kelley, 1959), *dependence* reflects the degree to which outcomes obtained in an individual's current relationship surpass his or her CLalt. By definition, therefore, questions such as, "All things considered, how do your potential dating alternatives compare to your current relationship?" and "If you and your current partner broke up, how difficult would it be to find another partner of comparable quality?" assess dependence. Research on dependence has shown that individuals who believe they could replace their partners more easily are more likely to terminate their relationships, whereas those who believe that their partners would be more difficult to replace feel more satisfied with their relationships and engage in behaviors that promote greater long-term relationship well-being (Drigotas & Rusbult, 1992). People are more satisfied with their relationship when they perceive their partners to have valuable personal attributes and when they feel their partners' qualities surpass their best available alternatives.

The concept of dependence can help explain why people often stay in relationships that are of objectively poor quality. Although it may be disheartening to perceive a partner as relatively low on attractiveness, it may be extremely difficult for a person to obtain a partner who is more attractive. Thus, from the perspective of interdependence theory, the most important question in evaluating current and potential mates is not, "What qualities does this person have?" but rather, "How does this person's qualities compare with those of my best alternative partner(s)?" Although most evolutionary research on interpersonal attraction and relationship satisfaction has addressed the first question, recent evolutionary research by Ellis, Simpson, and Campbell (2002) has demonstrated the utility of focusing on subjective dependence in predicting relationship feelings and behavior. Specifically, Ellis et al. (2002) developed and validated a new construct and self-report inventory—the Trait-Specific Dependence Inventory (TSDI)—which assesses the personality traits of romantic partners in relation to an individual's own level of dependence. The TSDI was developed to (1) identify the major dimensions on which current and potential mates are evaluated and (2) assess beliefs about how easily the outcomes obtained from a person's current partner or relationship could be met by alternative partners or relationships on each dimension.

Selection of items for the TSDI was based both on the Big Five model of personality and evolutionary models of mate selection. The Big Five traits have been given various labels but are widely known as Surgency, Agreeableness, Conscientiousness, Neuroticism, and Openness to Experience. Buss (1991b) has proposed that these dimensions have been invented, have evolved, and are used because they efficiently summarize the most important features of the social landscape, including major dimensions of human mate value. To the extent that specific attributes, such as those indexed by the Big Five, were reliably associated with the capacity to promote reproductive success in members of the other sex in ancestral environments, sexual selection should have shaped psychological mechanisms to detect and prefer these attributes in mates. Such attributes should form the central components of "mate value" and constitute basic domains of comparison between current and alternative partners.

Based on a series of factor analytic studies of both Big Five markers and personal attributes that were theoretically linked to mate value, Ellis et al. (2002) derived six major domains of comparison between current and alternative partners, each of which were theoretically linked to adaptively important questions about mates (as expressed in the questions following each trait description):

1. *Agreeable-committed* (altruism, cooperation, trust, fidelity, and commitment): Who is likely to share resources? Who will be a good cooperator and reciprocator? Who will remain faithful and committed to a long-term relationship?
2. *Resource-accruing potential* (dependability, perseverance, achievement orientation, intelligence, and economic success): Who has the will and perseverance to achieve important goals? Who can reliably obtain economic and nutritional resources for me and my family?
3. *Physical prowess* (physical strength and prowess): Who is a good hunter and fighter? Who can retain the resources they have and expropriate resources from others?
4. *Emotional stability* (calmness and stability): Who can cope with adversity without being overwhelmed by it? Who is mentally healthy and stable?
5. *Surgency* (dominance, leadership, and ascendance): Who is high or low in the present social hierarchy? Who is likely to aggressively pursue available resources and opportunities?
6. *Physical attractiveness* (beauty and sex appeal): Who is healthy? Who is fertile? Who has "good genes" that could be passed on to my children?

The TSDI constituted the six summated rating scales based on these dimensions (Ellis et al., 2002). To assess subjective dependence to partners, each TSDI item was worded in the following manner: "If you and your current partner broke up, how difficult would it be for you to find another partner who is as [*adjective*]?" Thus, for each personality adjective (trait), respondents were asked to make *explicit* comparisons between their current partner and their best available alternative partner(s).

Three different samples of individuals in romantic relationships completed the TSDI, which enabled us to confirm the six-factor structure, demonstrate convergent and discriminant validity of the inventory, and examine how subjective feelings of dependence on these six dimensions uniquely related to relationship feelings and behavior, after statistically controlling for how people perceived their partners' absolute standing on each dimension. The six TSDI dimensions successfully predicted three relationship outcomes—love, time investment, and anger-upset—above and beyond matched sets of traditional personality trait measures. In fact, perceptions of partners in absolute terms on these six dimensions were weakly related to individuals' relationship evaluations, with most of these links becoming statistically nonsignificant after taking into account the individuals' subjective dependence on their partners on these dimensions. Taken together, these results suggest that the TSDI is a reliable, valid, and unique construct that represents a new trait-specific method of assessing dependence in romantic relationships along major dimensions of mate value (Ellis et al., 2002).

RELATIONSHIP PROCESSES AND THE ANGER-UPSET SYSTEM

Whereas the love system is sensitive to cues signaling the facilitation of relationship-oriented goals and underpins positive relationship emotions, a function of the anger-upset system is to monitor cues to strategic interference and regulate negative relationship emotions. Negative emotions should be triggered by cues signaling that relationship goals are threatened and motivate the individual to remove these threats. One form of strategic interference involves inadequate support and investment by a partner within the context of an ongoing relationship. Another form of strategic interference involves diversion of investment by an individual's partner away from the primary relationship toward a rival. Evolutionary psychological research has documented that perceived threats to relationship fidelity arouse feelings of jealousy (e.g., Buss, Larsen, Westen, & Semmelroth, 1992) and, in some instances, motivate individuals to acts of psychological and physical abuse that are designed to preclude further strategic interference by their partners (Daly & Wilson, 1988b).

Given the amount of time and energy that individuals invest in developing and maintaining romantic relationships and the substantial fitness costs associated with mate defection, the thought of losing a valued partner and relationship can arouse considerable anxiety and concern. Whereas locating and securing a partner may solve the problem of mate selection, there are still many hurdles to overcome in the process of mate retention. In situations where the subjective probability of losing a mate to potential rivals is high, individuals should be motivated to enact behaviors designed to prevent the loss of the partner and relationship (Buss & Shackelford, 1997).

JEALOUSY

Jealousy is defined as a negative emotional experience that results from the potential loss of valued relationships to real or imagined rivals (Salovey, 1991). The three feelings that best describe jealousy are hurt, anger, and fear (e.g., Guerrero & Anderson, 1998). Buss (2000) suggests that over evolutionary history individuals that were vigilant to interlopers experienced greater reproductive success than those who were less concerned about rivals. If jealousy has played an important role in the evolution of human relationships, it should be a universal human emotion, and recent research suggests that it is (Buss et al., 1999). Additionally, men and women do not differ in the frequency or intensity of their jealousy (e.g., Buss, 2000; Buunk, 1995; Shackelford, LeBlanc, & Drass, 2000), suggesting that it has played an important role in the retention of partners and relationships for both sexes.

There are differences, however, between men and women in their experiences of jealousy, and these differences neatly overlap with their different goals in relationships. Whereas women can be confident that they are in fact the mother of their children, men cannot be certain that they are the father. Paternity uncertainty should make men more sensitive to cues of sexual infidelity of their partners and wary of rivals that are friendly or flirtatious with their partners (Symons, 1979). Natural selection may have even favored men who have a low threshold to cues of sexual infidelity, as the benefits of being cautious outweigh the costs of not being cautious enough (e.g., Haselton & Buss, 2000; see also Haselton, Nettle, & Andrews, Chapter 25, this volume). Although maternity uncertainty has not been an issue for women, securing the resources to raise highly dependent offspring was a challenge for ancestral women. The ability to raise offspring to reproductive age would be severely compromised if paternal investment were to be directed elsewhere; therefore, women should be sensitive to cues indicating emotional infidelity of their partners. If a man falls in love with another women and subsequently leaves the relationship to form another, his resources will be largely directed away from the abandoned woman. Natural selection may have, therefore, favored women who underestimate the amount of commitment men have to relationships and are particularly sensitive to signals that their partners are forming emotional bonds with other women (Haselton & Buss, 2000).

A great deal of research supports the notion that men's jealousy is particularly responsive to cues of sexual infidelity, whereas women's jealousy is principally related to cues of emotional infidelity (for a review, see Buss, 2000; but see DeSteno, Bartlett, Braverman, & Salovey, 2002, and Harris, 2003, for challenges to these data). For example, Buss et al. (1992) asked men and women to imagine a close romantic relationship and then to imagine the partner becoming involved with someone else. When asked what sort of involvement would bother them the most, men selected imagining their partner enjoying passionate sexual intercourse with another person, whereas women selected imagining their partner forming a deep emotional attachment to another person. This basic pattern of effects was replicated with physiological data showing that men displayed greater electrodermal activity (EDA) and increased pulse, as well as greater muscular tensions measured by electromyography (EMG) activity of the *corrugator supercilii* muscle (a muscle associated with "furrowing" of the brow and expressing negative emotion), when imagining a partner's sexual relative to emotional infidelity, whereas the pattern was reversed for women. Men also report more difficulty in forgiving a sexual infidelity than women and a greater likelihood of ending a relationship following a partner's sexual rather than emotional infidelity (Shackelford, Buss, & Bennet, 2002). Evidence obtained across cultures suggests that husbands are more likely to divorce wives who have engaged in sexual infidelities, whereas wives are less likely to divorce husbands who have engaged in similar behaviors (Betzig, 1989). This general pattern of results is not surprising given that men's relationship goals center on directing resources to their own, and not somebody else's, children, and women's relationship goals concentrate on retaining the resources that men bring to the relationship.

VIOLENCE IN RELATIONSHIPS

Cost-inflicting behaviors are often directed toward the ones we love (Miller, 1997b), and this is also true of physical violence. For instance, in Canada, between 16% and 35% of women surveyed say they have experienced at least one physical assault by a male dating partner (Kelly & DeKeseredy, 1993). Statistics Canada also reported that in 1993 approximately 30% of Canadian women reported at least one incident of physical or sexual violence at the hands of a marital partner. Of the women who had been abused, one-third had feared for their lives during the abusive relationship (Statistics Canada, 1994). In the United States, approximately 1.8 million wives are beaten by their husbands in any given year (Meloy, 1998). Although women do physically abuse their husbands, and oftentimes at rates commensurate with male-to-female violence (e.g., Kwong, Bartholomew, & Dutton, 1999), women relative to men experience much more severe physical injury at the hands of their partners. Additionally, abuse seems to be directed toward women with higher reproductive value—women who are younger are 10 times more likely to be the victim of spousal abuse than older women (Peters, Shackelford, & Buss, 2002).

The source of a great deal of conflict and physical abuse in relationships is male sexual jealousy experienced as the result of wifely infidelity (e.g., Daly & Wilson, 1988b; Wilson & Daly, 1992). In fact, the most frequently cited cause of spousal homicide worldwide is male sexual jealousy (e.g., Daly & Wilson, 1988a, 1988b; Shackelford, 2000). Thus, men not only experience increased jealousy and assorted negative emotions regarding partners' sexual infidelities but also are more likely than women to physically harm (even murder) their partners. Women, though, rarely kill their partners because of sexual transgressions, but generally in defense against a jealous husband or after a prolonged period of abuse where no alternative ways of leaving the relationship are perceived (Daly & Wilson, 1988a).

MATE-RETENTION STRATEGIES

When people form a relationship, there still exists a number of potential mates in their ecological environment, and they or their partner may be the target of mate-poaching tactics of others (Schmitt & Buss, 2001). There is, therefore, a perennial danger to the stability of relationships. As a result, relationships can dissolve as partners seek out other mating opportunities, or they can remain intact but with the behaviors of each spouse interfering with the reproductive success of the other. For instance, sexual infidelities on the part of wives can result in men directing resources to children that are not genetically related to them, a phenomenon that exists at rates as high as 10% in some cultures (Baker & Bellis, 1995). Additionally, women can lose valued resources if husbands direct them to other women or their offspring. These threats should have motivated ancestral men and women to engage in activities that function to retain mates after they have been obtained.

Buss and Shackelford (1997) suggested that situations more closely aligned with the relationship goals of men and women should be related to their mate-retention behaviors. For instance, men and women rely on different qualities of their partners to aid in their own reproductive success. Men are capable of producing sperm from puberty until well into old age, whereas women are born with a limited number of ovum that can be fertilized only during a circumscribed period of time, with fertility peaking in the mid-20s and decreasing significantly over time to essentially zero in the later 40s. Younger women are, therefore, more reproductively valuable. Also, physical features related to increased fertility (e.g., low waist-to-hip ratio; Singh, 1993) are rated as universally attractive to men

(Buss, 1989b; Symons, 1979), making physical attractiveness—in addition to age—another component of women's mate value. Younger, more physically attractive women are more desirable mates because of their increased fertility, but are also more attractive to potential mate poachers, who may attempt to woo them into extra-pair copulations or to leave their partner. Men married to women higher in mate value (i.e., younger, more physically attractive women) should, therefore, devote more time to mate-retention behaviors.

Men's mate value as long-term partners rests largely on their ability and willingness to provide external resources to the partner and relationship (Buss, 1989b; but see Gangestad & Simpson, 2000, for a discussion of physical cues associated with mate value in men). Men that possess many resources or have the ability to acquire resources and are more willing to share these resources (Graziano, Jensen-Campbell, Todd, & Finch, 1997) should be more desirable as mates, and they may be the target of mate-poaching tactics of other women. Women married to men with more resources should, therefore, devote more time to mate-retention behaviors.

Buss and Shackelford (1997) tested these hypotheses with a sample of 107 married couples. Participants completed Buss's (1989a) scale of mate retention that contains 19 different mate-retention acts, as well as various other measures associated with the perceived mate value of partners, and satisfaction with the relationship. In general, men reported using resource display more than women as a mate-retention tactic, whereas women reported using appearance enhancement more as a mate-retention tactic. Furthermore men's use of mate-retention tactics was strongly related to the youth and perceived physical attractiveness of their partners, whereas women's mate-retention behaviors were weakly related to their husbands' age and perceived physical attractiveness. However, women's mate-retention behaviors were positively correlated with their husbands' income and husbands' reported status-striving behaviors, while men's mate-retention behaviors were not related to their wives' income or status-striving behaviors. Confirming predictions, men and women appeared more motivated to maintain their relationships and thus prevent the interference of their relationship goals when they had partners that possessed the qualities most closely aligned with the success of their relationship goals.

CONCLUSIONS

In this chapter, we discussed several research programs demonstrating the significant contributions of evolutionary theory to the understanding of relationship processes. An important conceptual advance was the recent introduction of the discrete systems model (Ellis & Malamuth, 2000), establishing the relative independence of factors related to the experience of positive and negative emotions in relationships. According to this model, the love and anger-upset systems are largely independent, responsible for tracking different cues that signify relationship success or trouble, and motivating behavior designed to solve different sets of problems recurrent over evolutionary history.

In discussing the love system, we overviewed three programs of research that have blended concepts from interdependence and evolutionary theory to predict relationship evaluations, feelings of love, and interpersonal behaviors. Each program of research shared a common theme, focusing on cognitions and behaviors that signal the degree to which partners are facilitating relationship goals. Additionally, in each program, concepts from interdependence theory that were originally posited as broad, general constructs (e.g., "Does my partner meet my general needs?") were broken down into adaptively relevant, domain-specific constructs (e.g., "Does my partner meet my needs for warmth, status, and/or attractiveness?"). The development of scales that assess ideal standards, investments in relationships, and different facets of dependence will allow for a greater understanding of how men and women calibrate their feelings of love, how they behave toward their partners, and the stability of relationships.

In discussing the anger-upset system, it was shown that negative emotions are aroused when people fear that their romantic relationship goals are being impeded and when their relationship is threatened by rivals. Specifically, men seek to avoid cuckoldry, becoming jealous and potentially violent at the thought of their partners engaging in extra-pair sex with rivals. Men are also more vigilant of partners that are younger and more attractive, cues to increased fertility that rivals would also find particularly appealing. Women seek to avoid the loss of resources required for the raising of immature offspring and become jealous at the thought of their partners developing an emotional attachment with another woman that may threaten their access to resources. When women are vigilant of their partners, their partners generally have a handsome income and are more ambitious.

Although an impressive array of research currently exists focusing on relationship processes from an evolutionary perspective, the relative youth of the science of intimate relationships (cf. Fletcher, 2002) suggests that much more remains to be discovered. Based on the theoretical and empirical foundations developed in this chapter, we foresee the following key directions for the future of relationship research from an evolutionary perspective. First, the factors that uniquely facilitate the experience of positive and negative emotions in relationships need to be more fully investigated. Although self-reports of love and anger-upset are differentially correlated with the perceived facilitation and interference of relationship goals, these results do not directly support the notion that the love and anger-upset systems are sensitive to the perceived facilitation and interference of relationship goals, respectively.

Second, even though preliminary research supports the basic tenets of the three models discussed in the overview of the love system, a number of key hypotheses from each model remain to be tested. For example, research on partner-specific investments has not yet addressed why individuals choose to invest more or less in their relationships. Additionally, the regulatory behaviors of individuals when they feel their partners do not match their ideals, or when they fall short of their partners' ideals, on different ideal-partner dimensions has not been investigated. The importance of testing these and other untested hypotheses of these models is paramount.

Third, research should begin to focus on psychological processes designed to keep people in relationships or suppress activation of the "lust" system in the presence of attractive alternative partners. For instance, research has shown that individuals that are more committed to their partners are more likely to pay less attention to potential attractive alternative partners (Miller, 1997a), and when they do notice these alternative partners, they are more likely to devalue them

(Johnson & Rusbult, 1989). Individuals may, therefore, be equipped with psychological mechanisms designed to promote relationship stability when relationship goals are being facilitated. How people regulate perceptions of, and feelings for, alternative partners needs to be incorporated into evolutionary-informed research on romantic relationships.

Fourth, the impact of other evolutionary-relevant relationships on romantic relationship processes should also be examined. The presence or absence of extended kin networks, for example, and the quality of these relationships may aid in either the facilitation or interference of relationship goals. Additionally, the number and "quality" of offspring (e.g., physical health) and the bonds forged with children can be the source of both marital satisfaction and marital troubles. Problems with conceiving, the death of infants due to illness or accident, or disagreements in the number of children desired may motivate partners to seek other options to optimize their reproductive success. Many middle-level evolutionary theories focus on relationships with extended family and offspring, but at present the interconnections between these different relationships are not understood.

Paul the Apostle's musings on love reflect an early attempt to describe a set of emotions that humans have been experiencing for thousands of years. Through the rigorous research of evolutionary psychologists, we are beginning to understand the importance of love and associated behaviors to reproductive success. Future research that addresses the key points discussed earlier, in addition to many other unmentioned topic areas, will greatly assist in this process, making the study of relationship processes from an evolutionary perspective a standard practice in the science of intimate relationships.

REFERENCES

Amato, P. R., & Keith, B. (1991). Parental divorce and the well-being of children: A meta-analysis. *Psychological Bulletin, 110,* 26–46.

Baker, R. R., & Bellis, M. A. (1995). *Human sperm competition.* London: Chapman & Hall.

Baldwin, M. W. (1992). Relational schemas and the processing of social information. *Psychological Bulletin, 112,* 461–484.

Barash, D. (1977). *Sociobiology and behavior.* New York: Elsevier.

Bartels, A., & Zeki, S. (2000). The neural basis of romantic love. *NeuroReport, 11,* 3829–3834.

Betzig, L. (1989). Causes of conjugal dissolution: A cross-cultural study. *Current Anthropology, 30,* 654–676.

Bookwala, J., Frieze, I. H., & Grote, N. K. (1994). Love, aggression, and satisfaction in dating relationships. *Journal of Social and Personal Relationships, 11,* 625–632.

Bowlby, J. (1969). *Attachment and loss: Vol. 1. Attachment.* New York: Basic Books.

Brown, D. E. (1991). *Human universals.* New York: McGraw-Hill.

Buss, D. M. (1985). Human mate selection. *American Scientist, 73,* 47–51.

Buss, D. M. (1988a). From vigilance to violence: Mate-guarding tactics: *Ethology and Sociobiology, 9,* 291–317.

Buss, D. M. (1988b). Love acts: The evolutionary biology of love. In R. J. Sternberg & M. L. Barnes (Eds.), *The psychology of love* (pp. 100–118). New Haven, CT: Yale University Press.

Buss, D. M. (1989a). Conflict between the sexes: Strategic interference and the evocation of anger and upset. *Journal of Personality and Social Psychology, 56,* 735–747.

Buss, D. M. (1989b). Sex differences in human mate preferences: Evolutionary hypotheses tested in 37 cultures. *Behavioral and Brain Sciences, 12,* 1–49.

Buss, D. M. (1991a). Conflict in married couples: Personality predictors of anger and upset. *Journal of Personality, 59,* 663–688.

Buss, D. M. (1991b). Evolutionary personality psychology. *Annual Review of Psychology, 42,* 459–491.

Buss, D. M. (1994). *The evolution of desire: Strategies of human mating.* New York: Basic Books.

Buss, D. M. (1995). Evolutionary psychology: A new paradigm for psychological science. *Psychological Inquiry, 6,* 1–30.

Buss, D. M. (2000). *The dangerous passion: Why jealousy is as necessary as love and sex.* New York: Free Press.

Buss, D. M. (2004). *Evolutionary psychology: The new science of the mind* (2nd ed.). Boston: Allyn & Bacon.

Buss, D. M., Larsen, R. J., Westen, D., & Semmelroth, J. (1992). Sex differences in jealousy: Evolution, physiology, and psychology. *Psychological Science, 3,* 251–255.

Buss, D. M., & Schmitt, D. P. (1993). Sexual strategies theory: A contextual evolutionary analysis of human mating. *Psychological Review, 100,* 204–232.

Buss, D. M., & Shackelford, T. K. (1997). From vigilance to violence: Mate retention tactics in married couples. *Journal of Personality and Social Psychology, 72,* 346–361.

Buss, D. M., Shackelford, T. K., Kirkpatrick, L. A., Choe, J. C., Lim, H. K., Hasegawa, M., et al. (1999). Jealousy and the nature of beliefs about infidelity: Tests of competing hypotheses about sex differences in the United States, Korea, and Japan. *Personal Relationships, 6,* 125–150.

Buunk, B. P. (1995). Sex, self-esteem, dependency and extradyadic sexual experiences as related to jealousy responses. *Journal of Social and Personal Relationships, 12,* 147–153.

Campbell, L., Simpson, J. A., Kashy, D. A., & Fletcher, G. J. O. (2001). Ideal standards, the self, and flexibility of ideals in close relationships. *Personality and Social Psychology Bulletin, 27,* 447–462.

Carter, C. S. (1992). Oxytocin and sexual behavior. *Neuroscience and Biobehavioral Reviews, 16,* 131–144.

Carter, C. S. (1998). Neuroendocrine perspectives on social attachment and love. *Psychoneuroendocrinolgy, 23,* 779–818.

Centers for Disease Control and Prevention. (2002). *Sexually transmitted disease surveillance, 2001.* Atlanta, GA: U. S. Department of Health and Human Services.

Daly, M., & Wilson, M. (1983). *Sex, evolution, and behavior* (2nd ed.). Belmont, CA: Wadsworth.

Daly, M., & Wilson, M. (1988a). Evolutionary social psychology and family homicide. *Science, 242,* 519–524.

Daly, M., & Wilson, M. (1988b). *Homicide.* New York: Aldine de Gruyter.

DeSteno, D., Bartlett, M. Y., Braverman, J., & Salovey, P. (2002). Sex differences in jealousy: Evolutionary mechanism or artifact of measurement? *Journal of Personality and Social Psychology, 83,* 1103–1116.

Drigotas, S. M., & Rusbult, C. E. (1992). Should I stay or should I go? A dependence model of breakups. *Journal of Personality and Social Psychology, 62,* 62–87.

Ellis, B. J. (1992). The evolution of sexual attraction: Evaluative mechanisms in women. In J. H. Barkow, L. Cosmides, & J. Tooby (Eds.), *The adapted mind: Evolutionary psychology and the generation of culture* (pp. 267–288). London: Oxford University Press.

Ellis, B. J. (1998). The partner-specific investment inventory: An evolutionary approach to individual differences in investment. *Journal of Personality, 66,* 383–442.

Ellis, B. J., & Malamuth, N. M. (2000). Love and anger in romantic relationships: A discrete systems model. *Journal of Personality, 68,* 525–556.

Ellis, B. J., McFadyen-Ketchum, S., Dodge, K. A., Pettit, G., & Bates, J. (1999). Quality of early family relationships and individual differences in the timing of pubertal maturation in girls: A longitudinal test of an evolutionary model. *Journal of Personality and Social Psychology, 77,* 387–401.

Ellis, B. J., Simpson, J. A., & Campbell, L. (2002). Trait-specific dependence in romantic relationships. *Journal of Personality, 70,* 611–659.

Fehr, B. (1988). Prototype analysis of the concepts of love and commitment. *Journal of Personality and Social Psychology, 55,* 557–579.

Fisher, H. E. (1992). *Anatomy of love: A natural history of mating, marriage, and why we stray.* New York: Fawcett Columbine.

Fisher, H. E. (1998). Lust, attraction and attachment in mammalian reproduction. *Human Nature, 9,* 23–52.

Fisher, H. E. (2000). Lust, attraction, attachment: Biology and evolution of the three primary emotion systems for mating, reproduction, and parenting. *Journal of Sex Education Therapy, 25,* 96–104.

Fletcher, G. J. O. (2002). *The new science of intimate relationships.* Oxford, England: Blackwell.

Fletcher, G. J. O., Simpson, J. A., & Thomas, G. (2000). The role of ideals in early relationship development. *Journal of Personality and Social Psychology, 79,* 933–940.

Fletcher, G. J. O., Simpson, J. A., Thomas, G., & Giles, L. (1999). Ideals in intimate relationships. *Journal of Personality and Social Psychology, 76,* 72–89.

Gangestad, S. W., & Simpson, J. A. (2000). The evolution of human mating: Trade-offs and strategic pluralism. *Behavior and Brain Sciences, 23,* 573–587.

Geary, D. C. (2000). Evolution and proximate expression of human paternal investment. *Psychological Bulletin, 126,* 55–77.

Glynn, J. R., Carael, M., Auvert, B., Kahindo, M., Chege, J., Musonda, R., et al. (2001). Why do young women have a much higher prevalence of HIV than young men? A study of Kisumu, Kenya and Ndola Zambia. *AIDS, 15,* S51–S60.

Gottman, J. M. (1994). *What predicts divorce? The relationship between marital processes and marital outcomes.* Hillsdale, NJ: Erlbaum.

Graziano, W. G., Jensen-Campbell, L. A., Todd, M., & Finch, J. F. (1997). Interpersonal attraction from an evolutionary perspective: Women's reactions to dominant and prosocial men. In J. A. Simpson & D. T. Kenrick (Eds.), *Evolutionary social psychology* (pp. 141–168). Mahwah, NJ: Erlbaum.

Guerrero, L. K., & Anderson, P. A. (1998). Jealousy experience and expression in romantic relationships. In P. A. Anderson & L. K. Guerrero (Eds.), *Handbook of communication and emotion* (pp. 155–188). San Diego, CA: Academic Press.

Harris, C. R. (2003). A review of sex differences in sexual jealousy, including self-report data, psychophysiological responses, interpersonal violence, and morbid jealousy. *Personality and Social Psychology Review, 7,* 102–128.

Haselton, M. G., & Buss, D. M. (2000). Error management theory: A new perspective on biases in cross-sex mind reading. *Journal of Personality and Social Psychology, 78,* 81–91.

Hed, H. M. E. (1987). Trends in opportunity for natural selection in the Swedish population during the period 1650–1980. *Human Biology, 59,* 785–797.

Hrdy, S. B. (1999). *Mother nature: A history of mothers, infants, and natural selection.* New York: Pantheon Books.

Insel, T. R., Winslow, J. T., Wang, Z., & Young, L. J. (1998). Oxytocin, vasopressin, and the neuroendocrine basis of pair bond formation. *Advances in Experimental and Medical Biology, 449,* 215–224.

Jankowiak, W. R., & Fischer, E. F. (1992). A cross-cultural perspective on romantic love. *Ethnology, 21,* 149–155.

Johnson, D. J., & Rusbult, C. E. (1989). Resisting temptation: Devaluation of alternative partners as a means of maintaining commitment in close relationships. *Journal of Personality and Social Psychology, 57,* 967–980.

Kaplan, H. S., Lancaster, J. B., & Anderson, K. G. (1998). Human parental investment and fertility: The life histories of men in Albuquerque. In A. Booth & A. C. Crouter (Eds.), *Men in families: When do they get involved? What difference does it make?* (pp. 55–109). Mahway, NJ: Erlbaum.

Kelley, H. H., Berscheid, E., Christensen, A., Harvey, J. H., Huston, T. L., Levinger, G. et al. (1983). Analyzing close relationships. In H. H. Kelley, E. Berscheid, A. Christensen, et al. (Eds.), *Close relationships* (pp. 20–67). New York: Freeman.

Kelley, H. H., & Thibaut, J. W. (1978). *Interpersonal relations: A theory of interdependence.* New York: Wiley.

Kelly, K., & DeKeseredy, W. (1993). The incidence and prevalence of woman abuse in Canadian university and college dating relationships. *Journal of Human Justice, 4,* 25–52.

Kenrick, D. T., & Trost, M. R. (1997). Evolutionary approaches to relationships. In S. Duck (Ed.), *Handbook of personal relationships: Theory, research and interventions* (2nd ed., pp. 151–177). New York: Wiley.

Kirkpatrick, L. A. (1998). Evolution, pair bonding, and reproductive strategies: A reconceptualization of adult attachment. In J. A. Simpson & W. S. Rholes (Eds.), *Attachment theory and close relationships* (pp. 353–393). New York: Guilford Press.

Kwong, M. J., Bartholomew, K., & Dutton, D. G. (1999). Gender differences in patterns of relationship violence in Alberta. *Canadian Journal of Behavioral Science, 31,* 150–160.

Lancaster, J. B., & Kaplan, H. (1994). Human mating and family formation strategies: The effects of variability among males in quality and the allocation of mating effort and parental investment. In T. Nishida, W. C. McGrew, P. Marler, M. Pickford, & F. B. M. De Waal (Eds.), *Topics in primatology: Vol. 1. Human origins* (pp. 21–33). Tokyo: University of Tokyo Press.

Mackey, W. C., & Immerman, R. S. (2000). Sexually transmitted diseases, pair bonding, fathering, and alliance formation disease avoidance behaviors as a proposed element in human evolution. *Psychology of Men and Masculinity, 1,* 49–61.

Mellen, S. L. W. (1981). *The evolution of love.* Oxford, England: Freeman.

Meloy, J. R. (Ed.). (1998). *The psychology of stalking: Clinical and forensic perspectives*. New York: Academic Press.

Miller, R. S. (1997a). Inattentive and contented: Relationship commitment and attention to alternatives. *Journal of Personality and Social Psychology, 73,* 758–766.

Miller, R. S. (1997b). We always hurt the ones we love: Aversive interactions in close relationships. In R. Kowalski (Ed.), *Aversive interpersonal interactions* (pp. 11–29). New York: Plenum Press.

Moore, D. E., & Cates, W. (1990). Sexually transmitted diseases and infertility. In K. K. Holmes, P. A. Mardh, P. F. Sparling, & P. J. Wiesner (Eds.), *Sexually transmitted diseases* (2nd ed., pp. 19–29). New York: McGraw-Hill.

Murray, S. L. (2001). Seeking a sense of conviction: Motivated cognition in close relationships. In G. J. O. Fletcher & M. S. Clark (Eds.), *Blackwell handbook of social psychology: Interpersonal process* (pp. 107–126). Oxford, England: Blackwell.

Myers, D. G. (1999). Close relationships and quality of life. In D. Kahneman, E. Diener, & N. Schwarz (Eds.), *Well-being: The foundations of hedonic psychology* (pp. 374–391). New York: Russell Sage Foundation.

Myers, D. G., & Diener, E. (1995). Who is happy? *Psychological Science, 6,* 10–19.

Nesse, R. M. (1990). Evolutionary explanations of emotions. *Human Nature, 1,* 261–289.

Peters, J., Shackelford, T. K., & Buss, D. M. (2002). Understanding domestic violence against women: Using evolutionary psychology to extend the feminist functional analysis. *Violence and Victims, 17,* 255–264.

Reid, A. (1997). Locality or class? Spatial and social differentials in infant and child mortality in England and Wales, 1895–1911. In C. A. Corsini & P.P Viazzo (Eds.), *The decline of infant and child mortality* (pp. 129–154). The Hague, The Netherlands: Martinus Nijhoff.

Rusbult, C. E., & Arriaga, X. B. (1997). Interdependence theory. In S. Duck (Ed.), *Handbook of personal relationships* (2nd ed., pp. 221–250). New York: Wiley.

Rusbult, C. E., & Bunnk, A. P. (1993). Commitment processes in close relationships: An interdependence analysis. *Journal of Social and Personal Relationships, 10,* 175–204.

Salovey, P. (Ed.). (1991). *The psychology of jealousy and envy*. New York: Guilford Press.

Schmitt, D. P., & Buss, D. M. (2001). Human mate poaching: Tactics and temptations for infiltrating existing mateships. *Journal of Personality and Social Psychology, 80,* 894–917.

Schultz, H. (1991). Social differences in mortality in the eighteenth century: An analysis of Berlin church registers. *International Review of Social History, 36,* 232–248.

Schulz, K. F., Murphy, F. K., Patamasucon, P., & Meheus, A. Z. (1990). Congenital syphilis. In K. K. Holmes, P. A. Mardh, P. F. Sparling, & P. J. Wiesner (Eds.), *Sexually transmitted diseases* (2nd ed., pp. 821–842). New York: McGraw-Hill.

Shackelford, T. K. (2000). Reproductive age women are over-represented among perpetrators of husband-killing. *Aggressive Behavior, 26,* 309–317.

Shackelford, T. K., & Buss, D. M. (1997). Marital satisfaction in evolutionary psychological perspective. In R. J. Sternberg & M. Hojjat (Eds.), *Satisfaction in close relationships* (pp. 7–25). New York: Guilford Press.

Shackelford, T. K., Buss, D. M., & Bennet, K. (2002). Forgiveness or breakup: Sex differences in response to a partner's infidelity. *Cognition and Emotion, 16,* 299–307.

Shackelford, T. K., LeBlanc, G. J., & Drass, E. (2000). Emotional reactions to infidelity. *Cognition and Emotion, 14,* 643–659.

Shaver, P., Hazan, C., & Bradshaw, D. (1988). Love as attachment: The integration of three behavioral systems. In R. J. Sternberg & M. L. Barnes (Eds.), *The psychology of love* (pp. 68–99). New Haven, CT: Yale University Press.

Simpson, J. A., Fletcher, G. J. O., & Campbell, L. (2001). The structure and function of ideal standards in close relationships. In G. J. O. Fletcher & M. Clark (Eds.), *Blackwell handbook of social psychology: Interpersonal processes* (pp. 86–106). Oxford, England: Blackwell.

Singh, D. (1993). Adaptive significance of female physical attractiveness: Role of waist-to-hip ratio. *Journal of Personality and Social Psychology, 65,* 293–307.

Statistics Canada. (1994). Wife assault: The findings of a national survey. *Juristat Service Bulletin, 14,* 1–22.

Sternberg, R. J., & Barnes, M. L. (1985). Real and ideal others in romantic relationships: Is four a crowd? *Journal of Personality and Social Psychology, 49,* 1586–1608.

Stone, L. (1988). Passionate attachments in the West in historical perspective. In W. Gaylin & E. Person (Eds.), *Passionate attachments*. New York: Free Press.

Symons, D. (1979). *The evolution of human sexuality*. New York: Oxford University Press.

Thibaut, J. W., & Kelley, H. H. (1959). *The social psychology of groups.* New York: Wiley.

Thompson, A. P. (1983). Extramarital sex: A review of literature. *Journal of Sex Research, 19,* 1–22.

Trivers, R. L. (1971). The evolution of reciprocal altruism. *Quarterly Review of Biology, 46,* 35–57.

Trivers, R. L. (1972). Parental investment and sexual selection. In B. Campbell (Ed.), *Sexual selection and the descent of man* (pp. 136–179). New York: Aldine de Gruyter.

van den Berghe, P. L. (1979). *Human family systems: An evolutionary view.* Westport, CT: Greenwood Press.

Watson, D., & Clark, L. A. (1997). Measurement and mismeasurement of mood: Recurrent and emergent issues. *Journal of Personality Assessment, 68,* 267–296.

White, G. L., & Mullen, P. E. (1989). *Jealousy: Theory, research, and clinical strategies.* New York: Guilford Press.

Wiggins, J. S. (Ed.). (1996). *The five-factor model of personality: Theoretical perspectives.* New York: Guilford Press.

Williams, G. C. (1975). *Sex and evolution.* Princeton, NJ: Princeton University Press.

Wilson, M., & Daly, M. (1992). The man who mistook his wife for chattel. In J. Barkow, L. Cosmides, & J. Tooby (Eds.), *The adapted mind* (pp. 289–322). New York: Oxford University Press.

Zeifman, D., & Hazan, C. (1997). Attachment: The bond in pair bonds. In J. A. Simpson & D. T. Kenrick (Eds.), *Evolutionary social psychology* (pp. 237–264). Mahwah, NJ: Erlbaum.

PART IV

PARENTING AND KINSHIP

MARTIN DALY and MARGO WILSON

More than 40 years have passed since Hamilton (1964) published his theory of inclusive fitness, suggesting that organisms and all their constituent adaptations can best be understood as functionally nepotistic. And more than 30 years ago, it was already apparent to some biologists (Alexander, 1974; Ghiselin, 1974; Trivers, 1974; Williams, 1966; Wilson, 1975) that the sociobiological revolution launched by Hamilton must transform the ways in which psychologists think about social relations, especially family relations. Unfortunately, like other domain-general areas of psychology that have been slow to incorporate evolutionary insights, traditional social and developmental psychology had a lot of inertia and were not quick to exploit the heuristic potential of Hamilton's analysis. But the long-awaited revolution is at last well underway, as the chapters in this part demonstrate.

Jeffrey Kurland and Steven Gaulin (Chapter 15) provide a clear introduction to inclusive fitness theory and related evolutionary theoretical developments and make a cogent case for their value for organizing existing knowledge and directing new discovery in the realm of human family affairs. David Geary (Chapter 16) explores what is known about the unusual role of human fathers in light of these same theoretical ideas. Catherine Salmon (Chapter 17) focuses on what theory and data say about the ways in which limited parental resources are allocated and on the implications for sibling relations. Eugene Burnstein (Chapter 18) is mainly concerned with the evidence for nepotistic bias in the allocation of social benefits and with how kin are recognized. Mark Flinn, Carol Ward, and Robert Noone (Chapter 19) then integrate the data of behavioral endocrinology with evolutionary theoretical ideas introduced in previous chapters. All five chapters drive home by example a point that we, too, have stressed (Daly & Wilson, 1995): Evolutionary theoretical analysis is not an alternative to the more "proximate" theories favored by most social and developmental psychologists but is of value precisely because it helps in the ordinary business of psychological scientists, namely, the quest to discover and correctly characterize psychological structures and processes and their developmental determinants.

Early efforts to apply the Hamiltonian worldview to human affairs (e.g., several chapters in Chagnon & Irons, 1979) were mainly concerned to demonstrate the reality and specificity of human nepotism and paid little attention to its psychological mediation. But nepotism isn't magic—it is accomplished by means of "kin recognition" mechanisms and behavioral decision rules—so the psychological issues eventually came to the fore. In addition to circumstantial cues of familial relationship, for example, do people respond to olfactory, visual, and perhaps other phenotypic kinship cues, too? Reasons to think they might, including paternal uncertainty and the problem of distinguishing full siblings from maternal half siblings, have long been discussed, but it's only in the past decade that strong evidence for phenotype matching has accrued (see Burnstein, Chapter 18). This area of research provides some nice examples of exactly why sophisticated evolutionary theorizing is more powerful than the domain-general theories that remain popular with many psychologists. For example, Burnstein discusses the considerable evidence supporting an old domain-general proposition that mere exposure breeds positive affect and suggests that this affective response to familiarity may be "designed" to subserve nepotism, but the evidence for special design becomes really persuasive when it is shown that the phenomenon in question is not, after all, so domain-general. By manipulating subliminal cues of facial similarity, for example, DeBruine (in press) has shown that the resemblance of others to one's self simultaneously elevates willingness to trust and invest resources in them and yet decreases their sexual attractiveness, as we might expect in view of the distinct requirements for responses to be adaptive in the distinct domains of nepotism and mate choice.

There is a great deal still to be discovered about the evolutionary psychology of human kinship. As Kurland and Gaulin (Chapter 15) note, we have scarcely scratched the surface of the potentially rich topics of sibling relationships and grandparenthood. Whether psychological adaptations for grandparenting even exist is unclear, but one result that would strongly suggest the existence of such adaptations would be if even grandparents who invest preferentially in sons over daughters nevertheless show a subsequent preference for their daughters' (certain) children over their sons' (putative) children.

Another rather obvious question for the future is whether children are sensitive to cues of full versus half sibship. Studies of contemporary hunter-gatherers suggest that the successive offspring of an ancestral woman often had the same father but perhaps nearly equally often did not, and Trivers's (1974) parent-offspring conflict theory implies that a 4-year-old would do well to assess whether a newborn maternal sibling is a relative of degree $r = .5$ versus $r = .25$ and to adjust tactics of sib competition accordingly. But whether toddlers actually do this remains unknown.

The discovery of imprinted gene effects (see Burnstein, Chapter 18) has triggered what is perhaps the only truly revolutionary advance in evolutionary understanding of sociality since Hamilton made fitness inclusive (Haig, 2002). Despite some early appreciation of the potential importance of intragenomic conflict (e.g., Cosmides & Tooby, 1981), Hamilton's theory had let us all get away with conceptualizing individual organisms as integrated systems with a unity of purpose, namely, the promotion of inclusive fitness. However, because genes that are regularly expressed only when inherited from one's mother are selected to produce different phenotypic effects than other genes expressed only when inherited from father (as well as from ordinary, nonimprinted autosomal genes), and because we now know that such imprinted genes influence social phenotypes, engage in arms races, and are perhaps especially active in the brain, we have to face the fact that even individual phenotypes cannot always be expected to evolve toward the elimination of conflict and waste. Many exciting discoveries about imprinted gene effects in nervous system development and neuropsychology can be expected in the near future, and these effects are likely to be focused in the domains of filial and fraternal/sororal behavior.

A final topic that is not mentioned in any of this part's chapters deserves attention here, namely, the question of what sort of evolved cognitive processes underpin human kinship systems. Descent reckoning and kin terminology have been cornerstones of anthropological inquiry, and their enormous cross-cultural variability has provided many anthropologists with an apparent rationale for scoffing at the very notion of an evolved human nature. It therefore behooves evolutionary psychologists to identify what it is that all human kinship systems share and to elucidate how a panhuman kinship psychology could generate the diversity that we see, much as evolution-minded psycholinguists have clarified the nature of our "language instinct" (Pinker, 1994). In a recent tour de force, Jones (2004a, 2004b) claims to have done just that, presenting a theory of kinship cognition that purportedly derives all extant human kinship systems from a "universal grammar" that is closely akin to (and perhaps homologous with) that which generates languages. The near future should tell us whether Jones's theory is indeed the "universal acid" that explains kinship systems and their diversity or whether it needs major amendment, but in either case, it constitutes an important step forward for evolutionary psychology.

Less than a decade ago, we (Daly, Salmon, & Wilson, 1997) could justly complain that the subject matter of social psychology was overwhelmingly the study of stranger interactions and that even the subfield concerned with "close relationships" dealt solely with mates and friends, never with blood kin. It is a great pleasure to see that, thanks to the interdisciplinary efforts of anthropologists, biologists, and, yes, even psychologists, the grounds for this complaint are at last fading.

REFERENCES

Alexander, R. D. (1974). The evolution of social behavior. *Annual Review of Ecology and Systematics, 5,* 325–283.

Chagnon, N. A., & Irons, W. I. (Eds.). (1979). *Evolutionary biology and human social behavior.* North Scituate, MA: Duxbury Press.

Cosmides, L., & Tooby, J. (1981). Cytoplasmic inheritance and intragenomic conflict. *Journal of Theoretical Biology, 89,* 83–129.

Daly, M., & Wilson, M. (1995). Discriminative parental solicitude and the relevance of evolutionary models to the analysis of motivational systems. In M. S. Gazzaniga (Ed.), *The cognitive neurosciences* (pp. 1269–1286). Cambridge, MA: MIT Press.

Daly, M., Salmon, C. A., & Wilson, M. (1997). Kinship: The conceptual hole in psychological studies of social cognition and close relationships. In J. A. Simpson & D. T. Kenrick (Eds.), *Evolutionary social psychology* (pp. 265–296). Mahwah, NJ: Erlbaum.

DeBruine, L. M. (in press). Trustworthy, but not lust-worthy: Context-specific effects of facial resemblance. *Proceedings of the Royal Society of London. Series B, Biological Sciences.*

Ghiselin, M. T. (1974). *The economy of nature and the evolution of sex.* Berkeley: University of California Press.

Haig, D. (2002). *Genomic imprinting and kinship.* New Brunswick, NJ: Rutgers University Press.

Hamilton, W. D. (1964). The genetical evolution of social behaviour I and II. *Journal of Theoretical Biology, 7,* 1–52.

Jones, D. M. (2004a). The generative psychology of kinship: Part I. Cognitive universals and evolutionary psychology. *Evolution and Human Behavior, 24,* 303–319.

Jones, D. M. (2004b). The generative psychology of kinship: Part II. Generating variation from universal building blocks with optimality theory. *Evolution and Human Behavior, 24,* 320–350.

Pinker, S. (1994). *The language instinct.* New York: Morrow.

Trivers, R. L. (1974). Parent-offspring conflict. *American Zoologist, 14,* 249–264.

Williams, G. C. (1966). *Adaptation and natural selection.* Princeton, NJ: Princeton University Press.

Wilson, E. O. (1975). *Sociobiology: The new synthesis.* Cambridge, MA: Belknap Press.

CHAPTER 15

Cooperation and Conflict among Kin

JEFFREY A. KURLAND and STEVEN J. C. GAULIN

THE EVOLVED PSYCHOLOGY of conflict and cooperation among kin depends on the ultimate causes of kin interaction. Despite the centrality of kin selection theory (Hamilton, 1963, 1964) to studies of sociality among nonhuman animals, this theory has inspired relatively little research in psychology. A recent search of the PsycINFO database produced only 165 articles with the phrases "kin selection" or "inclusive fitness" in their titles or abstracts. A mere 10% of these attempted to test predictions from the theory; the remainder merely alluded to it. In contrast, a parallel search of the Biological Abstracts database produced more than 800 hits. Based on a sample, about 40% tested some aspect of the theory, which suggests that the application of kin selection to human behavior is still in its infancy.

Although agreeing on little else, anthropologists acknowledge that kinship is one of the central organizing features of human society (Lowie, 1948; Murdock, 1949). Yet, social psychology remains almost exclusively the study of interactions among strangers. Daly, Salmon, and Wilson (1997) suggest two reasons for this. First, much of what we know about human psychology derives from the college students who take an introductory psychology course. When these people meet in the psychology lab, they are typically strangers. Second, the real social relationships that dominate our lives are complex and riddled with "confounding variables" that play havoc with experimental designs. No wonder they are understudied. In addition, the empirical thrust of modern psychology has been guided more by proximate than ultimate causal questions. Thus, psychologists have felt no compelling need to keep up with developments in the evolutionary sciences. Had they done so, they would have noticed the explosive impact of kin selection theory on biology (e.g., Dawkins, 1989).

We thank R. L. Trivers for generous early mentorship and continuing inspiration. We also thank Martin Daly for many helpful suggestions, Joonghwan Joen for critical comments, David Buss for inviting us to contribute and, of course, our parents, offspring, and siblings for teaching us about the complexities of kin dynamics. Research was supported by the Henry Luce Foundation to JAK.

Although Daly et al. (1997) argue for the importance of an evolutionarily grounded kinship theory for psychology, there has been little research in this area (but see Fagen, 1976; Partridge & Nunney, 1977). Perhaps, because of the complexities of kinship theory in general and parent-offspring conflict models in particular, kinship theory has been comparatively ignored (e.g., in contrast to sexual selection; cf. Buss, 1999, and Chapters 9 through 14, this volume) by evolutionary psychologists. To set the stage for a future equalization of research effort, we begin with a review of the relevant evolutionary theory and then proceed to outline its potential application to the study of human kin interactions and concomitant psychology, within and beyond the nuclear family.

A TAXONOMY OF SOCIALITY

We use *competition* or *conflict* to include *selfish* behavior that confers a fitness benefit on the actor, while placing a fitness cost on the recipient. We ignore problematic, *spiteful* behavior that results in costs to both participants. *Cooperation* involves mutual fitness benefits for both actors, whereas *altruism* refers to interactions where the actor incurs a fitness cost while benefiting the recipient. Although it is unfortunately common to refer to both altruism and cooperation by the term *cooperation*, it is essential to distinguish these interaction types because the evolutionary conditions that favor each differ. Despite their connotations in ordinary parlance, these terms refer to fitness effects, not to psychological states. However, it is a premise of evolutionary psychology that social evolution profoundly affects the design of the human nervous system and hence its associated psychologies.

THE EVOLUTION OF ALTRUISM

The problem for sociobiology and allied fields has been to provide an explanation for the evolution of altruism and sociality (Krebs & Davies, 1993; Nakamura, 1980; Quellar, 1983; Wilson, 1975). A variety of models have been proposed and tested. These models allow the evolution of altruism by means of different life-historical and demographic mechanisms: (1) multilevel, nonnaïve *group selection* for indiscriminate altruism (Reeve & Keller, 1999; Chapter 29, this volume); (2) inclusive fitness maximization through *kin selection* (Charlesworth, 1980; Hamilton, 1964); (3) return benefit, delayed benefit, and strong *reciprocity* (Fehr and Fischbacher, in press; Gintis, 2000; Trivers, 1971); (4) incidental altruism and cooperation by *by-product mutualism* (Brown, 1983a); (5) *nepotistic manipulation* of helpers by exploitative parents and other kin (Alexander, 1974, 1987; Trivers, 1974); (6) signaling by costly and hence reliable *handicaps* (Grafen, 1990a, 1990b; Zahavi, 1975; Zahavi & Zahavi, 1997); and (7) misfiring and elicitation of benefits by social *parasitism* (Wilson, 1975). It is natural that our discussion of conflict and cooperation among human kin focuses on Hamiltonian kinship theory.

KINSHIP THEORY

You might expect the products of Darwinian evolution to be self-centered (Dawkins, 1976). However, kin selection theory (1964) emphasizes that this view is too simplistic. The essence of kin selection was foreshadowed by Darwin (1859) in his discussion of sterility among the social insects on analogy with artificial sib selection for meat quality among domesticated beef. A full account had to await the analysis of W. D. Hamilton (1963, 1964), who, not by chance, was pondering Darwin's problem of eusociality in hymenopterans. The problem is that the workers in these species have atrophied ovaries and are active helpers to the queen in rearing new colony members. If natural selection favors traits that enhance reproduction, how could reproductively self-sacrificing sterility evolve?

THE PARADOX OF ALTRUISM

As is often the case, the answer to this paradox lies in recognizing that the problem has been imprecisely specified. Selection favors or eliminates traits, but only by favoring or eliminating the alleles that importantly shape those traits. So the question is: "How can alleles that cause sterility ever spread?" Alleles can have different effects in different somatic and genetic environments, and they can have effects that are not limited to the body where they reside, so-called *extended phenotypes* (Dawkins, 1982). Animal architecture provides a large class of examples of physical extended phenotypes (Dewey, 1991; Hansell, 1984; von Frisch, 1983). Genes can also have extended-phenotypic effects in the social realm, aiding or hindering reproduction of conspecifics.

Hamilton demonstrated in population genetics terms that an allele causing sterility, or any fitness-debilitating trait, could spread if it had certain extended-phenotypic effects. To be perpetuated, such an allele must cause sufficient compensatory benefits to the fitness of conspecifics, who themselves are likely to carry that same allele due to genealogical relatedness. In essence, its social effects must produce a net benefit to the allele. Hamilton's analysis shows that altruism will spread in the population as long as $r_{ij} B_j > C_i$, where C_i is the fitness cost to the individual (i) expressing the allele, B_j is the fitness benefit to a neighbor (j), and r_{ij} is their *degree of relatedness*, that is, the likelihood that the recipient and the altruist carry the same allele due to immediate common ancestry. This inequality is known as *Hamilton's rule*.

Hamilton's theory also makes predictions about competition. The naïve expectation is that alleles that induce altruism will be eliminated and alleles that induce selfishness will spread. However, kin selection theory reveals that these predictions are wrong, because the evolutionary consequences of altruism or selfishness depend on the values of B_i, C_j, and r_{ij}. Just as alleles with altruistic effects can spread if they give sufficiently significant benefits to copies of themselves, so, too, alleles with selfish effects will be eliminated if they confer significant costs on copies of themselves. Selection will remove selfish alleles whenever $r_{ij} C_j > B_i$, where now B_i is the fitness benefit to the individual expressing the selfish allele, C_j is the fitness cost to the related neighbor, and r_{ij} is as before. Hence, Hamilton offered a general theory for the evolution of social behavior.

Although kinship theory is typically used to account for the evolution of altruism, the propinquity of close kin entails competition over fitness-limiting resources (West, Murray, Machado, Griffin, & Herre, 2001; West, Pen, & Griffin, 2002). Dispersal patterns, habit selection, and ontogenetic imprinting may cause close relatives to spend their lives in proximity. When this occurs, competition among kin over mates, food, space, nesting sites, and other resources will be common. Thus, we should expect to see (sometimes deadly) conflict among kin, not just harmony and cooperation.

Relatedness Asymmetries

We have treated r_{ij} as a probability, not a certainty, but one that is symmetric by sex. Internal fertilization potentially changes all that. Due to gestation, parturition, and lactation, women will be unambiguously related to their children whereas (putative) fathers will not. This sex difference in parent-offspring relatedness has been referred to as *paternal confidence* or *paternity certainty,* terms with cognitive implications (Alexander, 1974; Hartung, 1985; Kurland, 1979). To be relevant to the topic at hand—the psychology of kinship—this relatedness asymmetry must be established somewhere in the actor's psychology, though it need not be represented consciously. To better mark our agnosticism about the precise psychological mechanisms, we prefer the term *paternal probability.* This asymmetry is expected to generate evolutionary forces that will ramify beyond parents, offspring, and the nuclear family.

KIN SELECTION CONUNDRUMS

Beyond Darwinian Fitness

There are two alternate ways of thinking about kinship effects in evolution: One uses Hamilton's concept of *inclusive fitness,* and the other, less appreciated approach employs *neighbor-modulated fitness* (Frank, 1998; Hamilton, 1970). Basic *Darwinian fitness* is free of kinship effects beyond parent and offspring. Darwinian fitness measures either the absolute or relative rate of gene transmission solely in terms of progeny production: parent to offspring, offspring to grandoffspring, and so on. However, Hamilton realized that neighbors exchange fitness-relevant costs and benefits. Some of Ego's neighbors may be genealogically connected to her and hence share genes with her as parameterized by r_{ij}. However, in deriving the conditions for adaptive social evolution by means of total fitness effects, Hamilton had to avoid double counting benefits and costs during social interactions from Ego toward her neighbors and from her neighbors toward her.

Thus, inclusive fitness measures gene transmission via (1) unaided offspring production by Ego (*personal fitness effect*) plus (2) Ego's incremental and decremental effects on the offspring production of relatives (*inclusive fitness effect*). Both components are frequently misunderstood. For example, if Bobbi has two offspring and two nephews via her full sister Polly, Bobbi's inclusive fitness is *not* the sum of her *r*'s to these four children. Her personal fitness effect must not include any reproductive benefits she received from her kin. And her inclusive fitness effect does not automatically include all of Polly's appropriately devalued offspring. It includes only that component of Polly's devalued fitness that is due to Bobbi's efforts. In other words, Bobbi can augment her inclusive fitness by either having more offspring through her own efforts or by helping Polly have more offspring than she otherwise would. Bobbi cannot increase her inclusive fitness by letting her kin boost her reproduction or by standing by and letting Polly reproduce. This framework is consistent. Any reproductive gain Bobbi gets from a relative is part of that relative's inclusive fitness, and any reproduction Polly does on her own is part of hers. The inclusive fitness effect refers to actual investment in kin. This effect must not be double counted in the fitness of donor and recipient, as has sometimes been done (e.g., Jones, 2000; see Grafen, 1982, 1984, 1991).

Defined correctly, absolute inclusive fitness is not easily measured without experimental intervention. Nevertheless, we can compare the inclusive fitness from different social interactions by the same actors or types of actors to determine which of the alternatives is more adaptive. This is a common procedure in behavioral ecology, where the appropriate genealogies or DNA data and reproductive histories exist (reviewed in Alcock, 2001). Due to both methodological difficulties and ethical concerns, inclusive fitness estimates have never been undertaken in a human proband.

Neighbor-modulated fitness offers a different framework for conceptualizing kin selection. Here we consider not Ego's effects on her neighbors, but Ego's neighbor's effects on her. Within this framework, altruistic alleles pile up benefits because their carriers tend to have neighboring relatives who are also carriers and who, therefore, donate aid to Ego. This neighbor-modulated fitness is directly estimated by counting Ego's lifetime reproductive success. In several helpful papers, Grafen (1982, 1984, 1991) neatly differentiates the inclusive-fitness and neighbor-mediated metrics. He also demonstrates that, properly applied, these two accounting methods yield the same result, both collapsing to Hamilton's rule. The inclusive fitness method is more transparent than the population-genetic, neighbor-modulated model, but not necessarily more tractable for fieldwork.

PARADOXES OF RELATEDNESS

Another frequent muddle concerns the correct metric for relatedness. Sometimes r_{ij} is defined as a correlation, a regression, or a simple conditional probability (Grafen, 1991; Kurland & Gaulin, 1979; Michod & Hamilton, 1980). These diverse relatedness measures are derived from the theory of inbreeding, which was inspired by the need to track changes in allele frequency at evolving loci (e.g., Crow & Kimura, 1970). This literature stresses that it is essential to distinguish two kinds of allelic similarity: (1) *identity by descent* (IBD) and (2) *identity by state* (IBS). Let us assume that two friends, Betsy and Helen, are both AB at the ABO locus. They share the same alleles due to a random draw from the North American deme, where both alleles exist at appreciable frequency. Their alleles are physically the same, but not because of immediate shared ancestry. Betsy and Helen are IBS, but not IBD, at the ABO locus.

Failure to appreciate the IBS/IBD distinction will produce dangerous confusion. In population genetics, relatedness has little to do with an allele's physical structure or function and everything to do with its origin and pedigree. Genetic similarity is not equivalent to relatedness, and this distinction has implications for the evolution of social behavior (Dickinson & Koenig, 2003; Sinervo & Clobert, 2003). For example, within our species, the majority of loci are monomorphic. Is r_{ij} minimally ½ between any two humans? No, at least as regards what r_{ij} must measure for kin selection theory to be coherent. It is alleles in common, IBD, that are the *predictable* part of the genomes shared between interacting organisms. The other, random part of their genomes contains alleles for altruism and nonaltruism at exactly their population frequency. Thus, the beneficial and detrimental effects of social acts will strike *both* kinds of alleles equally; hence the net result will be no change in the frequency of these alleles' IBS. Hamilton (1964) refers to that part of the genome that is IBS as *the diluting effect* and shows that it can affect the rate of evolution of sociality genes but not the ultimate outcome.

EVOLUTIONARY SPECULATIONS ABOUT THE FAMILY

Parent-Offspring Conflict

In a seminal paper, R. L. Trivers (1974) identifies the evolutionary basis of cooperation and conflict among kin. His use of the Hamiltonian theory reveals a zone of *parent-offspring conflict*, perhaps misnamed because it also extends to other kin. Despite the putative symmetries in relatedness between members of the nuclear family (parents, offspring, and siblings), Trivers notes that any individual ego will confront asymmetries. The mother is equally related to her offspring. However, the offspring is completely related to itself, but only half as related to its full siblings. A Hamiltonian offspring should value its personal fitness twice as much as its values any full sib's fitness.

Parental investment (Trivers, 1972) is anything a parent does that increases the recipient offspring's fitness at a cost to some (hypothetical) other offspring (see Chapters 16 and 17, this volume). For simplicity's sake, Trivers considers a single parental act. In this case, because the parent (p) is equally related to all its offspring, it will continue to invest as long as the benefit of the parental resources for the offspring (o) outweighs the cost of deferring future reproduction (C_p), that is, $B_o > C_p$. All things being equal, it should allocate resources equally to its progeny. However, and this is Trivers's key insight, from the perspective of the offspring, investment in itself should ideally continue as long as $B_o > \frac{1}{2} C_p$. Trivers thus identifies a zone of conflict within the nuclear family. This occurs because parental and progeny genes "calculate" their inclusive fitness from any act of parental investment in different ways. The zone of conflict is precisely defined as $1 < B_o/C_p < 2$.

The same inclusive-fitness analysis can be performed for any kin triad. For example, suppose a "rational gene" in the parent is evaluating the fitness repercussions of an interaction between its offspring and its sister's offspring, a *nibling* (z). Assume a completely outbred population such that the parent-offspring, parent-nibling, and offspring-cousin relatedness values are $r_{po} = \frac{1}{2}$, $r_{pz} = \frac{1}{4}$, and $r_{oz} = \frac{1}{8}$, respectively. Suppose the parent invests in a nibling rather than its offspring whenever $\frac{1}{4} B_z > \frac{1}{2} C_o \rightarrow B_z > 2C_o$. From the offspring's perspective, its inclusive fitness increases whenever $\frac{1}{8} B_z > C_o \rightarrow B_z > 8C_o$. There is a much wider zone of evolutionary conflict between parent and offspring over the latter's altruistic tendencies toward cousins, in particular, whenever $2 < B_z/C_o < 8$. Therefore, all things equal, the ratio of conflict to cooperation will increase as r_{ij} decreases within extended families.

All in the Family

Sibling conflict is an obvious corollary of Trivers's model. Each sibling benefits by taking parental resources away from its brother or sister and directing them to itself, whenever $B_o > \frac{1}{2} C_s$, where the subscript s refers to a full sibling of Ego, referred to by o. The intensity of sibling conflict may sometimes lead to outright siblicide, as in many shore birds (Mock & Parker, 1997). Schwabl, Mock, and Gieg

(1997) demonstrate that cattle egret mothers endow first-laid eggs with extra androgens, enhance the aggressiveness of senior nestlings, and hence act in concert with their selfish, first-born offspring's sibling conflict. Such hormonal favoritism influences sibling rivalry and implies that parents and offspring can evolve mechanisms for mutually adaptive brood reduction. Indeed, some biologists suggest that the production of supernumerary offspring among birds and mammals may be, in effect, a parental insurance policy: If circumstances are good, all offspring will survive (Godfray, 1995b; Godfray, Harvey, & Partridge, 1991; MacNair & Parker, 1979; Mock, 1987).

Except for twinning, humans do not have clutches. However, there can be considerable overlap between siblings during the extended period of human parental investment. There are many implications of Trivers's (1974) family-conflict model for psychiatry, socialization theory, and the politics of the family. Sib conflict and homicide among royalty competing for the throne are made famous in Shakespeare's tragedies. These themes have certainly been a source of poignant literary analysis in the West for millennia: from tragic Oedipus to kvetch Portnoy. Indeed, some humanists have found in our peculiarly intensive family ecology the source of all neurosis, psychosis, and the world's troubles (Freud, 1930; Laing, 1971). To what extent birth-order effects, homosexual celibacy, or various psychiatric disorders arise from human sibling conflict remains to be seen (e.g., Sulloway, 1995).

BATTLEGROUND VERSUS RESOLUTION

From its inception, Trivers's parent-offspring conflict was challenged because any fitness advantage accruing to offspring would supposedly be eliminated by their own production of contentious children (Alexander, 1974; Bateson, 1994; Brown, 1983b; Hartung, 1977; Mock & Forbes, 1992). However, whether we use sophisticated mathematical models or more intuitive Evolutionarily Stable Strategy (ESS) analyses, as long as we maintain a gene perspective on evolution, optimally selfish-offspring alleles will spread (Blick, 1977; Dawkins, 1976). If so, who, if anyone, wins? As Godfray (1995a, 1999) points out, parent-offspring conflict models are *battleground* models; they describe ideal levels of investment for parent and offspring. However, they do not specify the outcome. For that, we seek *resolution* models to tell us what to expect in the hive, nest, or suburban split-level. Resolution models generate testable predictions.

RESOLUTION MODELS

Without Parental Care A trivial but reasonable resolution to parent-offspring conflict occurs among animals without parental care, that is, without postparturitional effort (Kurland & Gaulin, 1984). For parasitoid wasps laying eggs on hosts, the mother should win. This would seem to vindicate Alexander's (1974) prediction that offspring are caught in a kind of *trophic trap* where the parent has control of resources. However, selfish offspring might engage in sibling conflict over resources, reducing the parent's optimal fitness (Godfray & Parker, 1992; Harper, 1986; Rodríguez-Gironés, 1999; Rodríguez-Gironés, Cotton, & Kacelnik, 1996). The parent could evolve to reduce clutch size, hence lowering competition among the brood, short-circuiting offspring selfishness. Although the parent always wins control of clutch size, the offspring always wins control of resource consumption. Thus, we return to a dynamic evolutionary process where either party might win. In game-theory terms, this kind of conflict is analogous to coordination games with two pure Nash-equilibria: Either the parent or the offspring wins. In species with postparturitional interaction, such a resolution is moot (Godfray, 1999).

With Parental Care   For humans we need to assume postparturitional investment and significant interaction, perhaps for life. Finding the solution to this kind of parent-offspring conflict is no mean task. Using traditional population-genetic models is a formidable undertaking with often indeterminate results (Feldman & Eshel, 1982; MacNair & Parker, 1978; Metcalf & Stamps, 1979; Parker & MacNair, 1978, 1979; Stamps, Metcalf, & Kirshnan, 1978). Neither the analytic procedure nor the results are transparent. Instead, a more intuitive inclusive-fitness approach combined with ESS analysis can help find the equilibria or optima of parent-offspring conflict, if there are any.

Four modeling schemes have been used to predict resolution of this family conflict. Each makes different assumptions about which parental and offspring traits are evolving and hence which optima are possible. The first type assumes fixed parental and offspring behaviors (MacNair & Parker, 1978, 1979; Parker & MacNair, 1978, 1979). The second permits variable but costly parental and progeny manipulations of resource allocation (Yamamura & Higashi, 1992). The third allows the offspring, but not the parent, to alter how efficiently it turns parental resources into personal fitness (Eshel & Feldman, 1991). Finally, some models make offspring communication costly, supposedly guaranteeing honest signaling and allowing accurate parental assessment of offspring need (Godfray, 1991; Godfray & Johnstone, 2000). The complex workings of these models are usefully reviewed by Godfray (1995a, 1999), who introduced the metaphors of battleground and resolution. Parker, Royle, and Hartley (2002) also provide a primer on models of parent-offspring conflict and resolution based on neighbor-mediated rather than inclusive fitness.

It is not surprising, given their assumption of evolutionarily fixed parent and offspring behavior, that the Parker-MacNair resolution is an intermediate level of investment between the parent's and offspring's optima, contingent on the value of r_{ij}. The Yamamura-Higashi model, which is a general model of conflict resolution among relatives, generates a range of optima. That is, it establishes optimal parental investment as a function of the costs that the two parties incur in manipulating the outcome. The cheaper the costs to one party, the more the evolutionary equilibrium favors that party's optimum level of investment. Hence, without details of natural history, there is no single winner and loser. The Eshel-Feldman approach confirms that costly communication of need (begging) can elicit extra investment. In that sense the offspring wins, but then so, too, must the parent, because offspring are signaling genuine need. Again, the exact outcome depends on assumptions about how efficiently offspring can use and influence resource allocation. This model has limited applicability because it allows offspring to influence parents, but not vice versa.

Begging to Know   The most fertile theoretical work on parent-offspring conflict involves signaling equilibria, which promise to predict observable outcomes. Signaling theorists explicitly model offspring communicative ploys and parental counterploys (Godfray, 1991, 1999; Godfray & Johnstone, 2000; Harper, 1986; Johnstone & Grafen, 1993). By taxing offspring, costly begging provides the parent with reliable information about its progeny's need, especially about the offspring's *cryptic condition* (Godfray, 1995a, 1999). Parents presumably can assess offspring's age, size, competitive ability, and the like, but internal states of motivation, hunger, thirst, and fear must be communicated by cries and begging. If these signals are costly, out-and-out lying should be eliminated. In that sense, parents win, but so do young whose real needs are satisfied. There are both field observations and experiments that corroborate this view of conflict: Parents respond to increased begging, and offspring become sated (Godfray, 1995a, 1999; Kilner & Johnstone, 1997).

Trivers (1974) addressed this signaling perspective, suggesting that offspring will be keen psychological manipulators of parents by begging and extorting because the parents' only indication of the offspring's cryptic condition comes from the offspring itself and can thus be exaggerated for gain. Zahavi (1977) suggests that a nestling can cry "fox, fox!" out of context, blackmailing the parent: "Take care of me or your inclusive fitness will suffer!" Modeling suggests that, when that offspring can afford to misrepresent their need and if most signals are reliable most of the time, deceptive communication by offspring can evolve (Johnstone & Grafen, 1993). Parents may control a trophic trap, but offspring run an extortion racket.

Cheap Talk   These models assume that every type of offspring need is signaled by a unique begging signal, and thus they seek *separating equilibria*. But if different types of needy offspring evince the same begging signal, then parents cannot distinguish degrees of need, but must respond in some average or discrete way to classes of begging progeny. In that case, the parent-offspring system will evolve toward *pooled equilibria* (Bergstrom & Lachmann, 1997, 1998; Lachmann & Bergstrom, 1998). The result may be infinitely many equilibria, including cost-free begging (defined in terms of the relative or marginal cost of altering a signal) or no signaling. Some research suggests that the costly signaling ESSs found by researchers such as Grafen, Johnstone, and others are globally unstable and easily collapse to a nonsignaling equilibrium (Rodríguez-Gironés et al., 1996). Given this, Rodríguez-Gironés et al. (1996) claim that, because offspring signaling must have evolved from a nonsignaling state, it probably arose out of sibling conflict and the advantage to the parent of responding. Such a system implies lots of noise and hence the evolution of what economists call *cheap talk*. This makes for a complex and shifting arena of kin interactions.

TOWARD AN EVOLUTIONARY THEORY OF THE FAMILY

ANYTHING GOES

Do these evolutionary conflict models collectively suggest that "anything goes" among parents, offspring, and siblings? One limitation of the ESS model is that, because such a model is not dynamic, it establishes only local equilibria. The derived equilibria cannot automatically be reached from any point in the parent-offspring parameter space. It is important to remember that the resulting diverse optima reported earlier are not globally stable; they are not necessarily basins of attraction. To demonstrate that requires *replicator-dynamic* analysis, which can be messy.

In an overlooked paper, Harpending (1979) uses standard Volterra, nonlinear, predator-prey equations, rather than the ESS analysis, to model the tactics and countertactics of parents and offspring embroiled in Triversian conflict. He finds that if parental investment is very low, selfish-offspring genes will spread, because of the high cost of parental monitoring and control. If investment and care are very high, generous offspring will evolve, because there's enough to go around. However, if parental investment is intermediate and offspring selfishness has an appreciable cost (e.g., from predation on whining progeny), then slow, undamped cycles of parent and progeny behavior will evolve. In that case, the current state of the real world "would seem completely indeterminate" (Harpending, 1979, p. 629).

Much of the disagreement among kin-conflict theoreticians results from their different assumptions about the behavior, life history, ecology, and environment of idealized parents and offspring. Model results are typically sensitive to initial conditions and parameter values (Eshel & Feldman, 1991; Feldman & Eshel, 1982; Stamps et al., 1978). Moreover, there is great difficulty in understanding the actual genetics underlying kin conflict (Godfray, 1995a). However, with an appropriate experimental system, such as insects, we can show that parents respond differentially to offspring signals of need. These differences result from genetic differences among mothers in their responsiveness to progeny signals and among progeny in their ability to elicit care (Agrawal, Brodie, & Brown, 2001).

The available models offer psychologists only broad guidelines about cooperative and competitive behavior among kin. Thus, kin researchers should inform the theoreticians about what environmental boundary conditions, what features of behavior, and what aspects of kin dynamics need to be specified in the battleground and resolution models. Indeed, Godfray (1995a, 1999) and Parker et al. (2002) are well aware of these methodological issues and the importance of collaboration between modelers and empiricists. Only by accurately and realistically defining the parameterization of kin dynamics will more perspicacious models emerge.

QUO VADIS?

Despite the current indeterminacy of parent-offspring conflict models, it is important to extrapolate even tentative predictions beyond the nuclear family. The most robust outcome of Trivers's (1974) original model and its recent extensions is that the evolutionary zone of conflict becomes exacerbated as relatedness between actors decreases. Thus, with the usual *ceteris paribus* clause:

- Altruistic nuclear family relations will dominate kin relationships.
- Determinate maternal and probabilistic paternal links will lead to a female laterality bias.
- Conflict will increase and cooperation will decrease with decreasing relatedness.
- Kin will track relatedness differences within the family.
- Kin will track the benefit-to-cost ratio of interactions.
- Reciprocity will increase as relatedness decreases between kin.
- Deceit, manipulation, and exploitation will increase as relatedness decreases among kin.

The importance of nuclear kin may be too obvious to mention. For example, when theoreticians address family dynamics, *family* always means parent, offspring, and siblings. More distant kin are rarely considered (cf. Fagen, 1976; Partridge & Nunney, 1977) and for good reason. Temper tantrums, begging, and other demanding gestures are usually reserved for parents and, to a lesser degree, for siblings (and mates). These signals of need, whether honest or dishonest, unfold ontogenetically within the confines of the nuclear family, suggesting they are adaptations to that environment. This raises a critical issue: How important were nonnuclear kin to inclusive (or neighbor) fitness during our evolutionary history?

The Evolutionary Environment of Kin

Based on estimated age-specific birth and death rates for the Paleolithiclike populations of Archaic Native Americans, we can estimate the expected number of relatives in each kin category (Kurland & Sparks, 2003). Over a range of demographic assumptions, the odds are about $9:1$ against a 20-year-old woman having her 40-year-old mother alive for possible help rearing her offspring and $4:1$ against her 5-year-older sib being alive. These calculations imply that reproductively active Paleolithic individuals would potentially have had many more distant than nuclear kin available for interaction. However, such relations may have been especially intense and valuable, because altruism would have been more potent among nuclear than distant kin. This also suggests increased mutualism or strong reciprocity among distant kin (cf. Fehr & Gächter, 2002), which may, in part, explain why human kinship systems are classificatory rather than genealogical: The metaphor of kinship perhaps allows easier manipulation of distant kin and nonkin.

Investigating cooperation and conflict among kin should help us uncover the mental modules, if any, that represent the evolved psychology of human kinship, family, and sociality (Daly et al., 1997; see also Chapters 15 and 17, this volume). There is rather good evidence for an evolved psychology of reciprocity in the form of a cheater-detection module (Cosmides & Tooby, 1992). How good then is the evidence for kinship modules?

HUMAN KINSHIP PSYCHOLOGY

What do the evolutionary dynamics of hypothetical altruism alleles tell us about the expected behavior of social humans? Hamilton's (1964) prediction is:

> The social behavior of a species evolves in such a way that in each distinct behavior-evoking situation the individual will seem to value his neighbor's fitness against his own according to the coefficients of relationship appropriate to that situation. (Hamilton, 1964, p. 23)

However, this theory does not tell us what we ought to observe about the relevant proximate psychology.

Psychological Assessment and Hamilton's Rule

We should not conflate analytic descriptions with proximate mechanisms. Hamilton's theory is not a psychological theory. Nevertheless, the operation of kin selection requires mechanisms for the (possibly unconscious) assessment of r, B, and C.

Estimating B *and* C   Benefit and cost are situational: They depend on the nature of the resource and the actors' relative ability to convert the resource into progeny. Kin selection is not the only evolutionary force that requires accurate resource assessment. Theories of foraging and aggressive competition also assume the evolution of such abilities (Krebs, 1978; Maynard Smith, 1974; Schoener, 1971). When the considerations exchanged (food, assistance, information) among kin are regular features of the species' natural history, individuals should evolve to value them accurately. Different values typically attach to C and B in any given exchange due to structural or situational asymmetries (age, status, sex, or even location), because C and B are not properly measured in dollars or calories but in reproductive consequences.

Life history is a reliable feature of a species' biology, and individuals will be sensitive to the effects of life history variables, such as age, on B and C. Due to senescence, older individuals are less efficient at converting resources into offspring. Moreover, benefits passed to younger individuals tend to exert their effects over a longer part of the life span. Thus, aid is expected to flow from older to younger individuals because the two differ in reproductive value (the age-specific expectation of future offspring; Fisher, 1958). Other predictions follow from this line of analysis: Due to differential resource access, high-status individuals might experience less cost for any given benefit than lower status individuals would. Moreover, C or B could vary with sex in complex ways; this is the premise of the Trivers-Willard hypothesis (Trivers & Willard, 1973). In the existing literature, some of these predicted effects are clear and recurrent, whereas others have yet to be tested.

Estimating r   There are two kinds of data available for estimating *r*—contextual data and similarity data—and both vary in quality. High-quality contextual information derives from birth events. Women who give birth to viable offspring are related to those offspring by .5. Other individuals can exploit this regularity. Because a woman generally gives significant parental investment only to children satisfying this birth criterion, her younger progeny can cue on her behavior for information about who their probable order siblings are (Holmes & Sherman, 1983; Kurland, 1977; Lehmann & Perrin, 2002). At progressively lower reliability, larger webs of inference can be developed about mother's siblings (aunts and uncles) and their offspring (cousins). Males, too, can use birth information, but it will always be less reliable for them (see earlier Relatedness Asymmetries section). A woman's behavior and reputation can also provide information about her partner's likely relatedness to her progeny. In addition, certain ecological and demographic parameters, such as population viscosity and dispersal patterns, will predictably affect the degree of relatedness among neighbors (reviewed in Alcock, 2001).

The issues surrounding similarity cues to *r* are often misunderstood. For example, Rushton, Russell, and Wells' (1984) *genetic similarity theory* assumes that altruism is favored in proportion to the level of overall genetic similarity between the actors. But this is not what Hamilton (1964) proved; altruistic alleles spread if they sufficiently benefit copies of *themselves*, not copies of other alleles that happen to be shared by the altruist and recipient. Because of (largely) independent assortment of alleles at meiosis, extensive genetic similarity gives information about the sharing of a *particular* allele (i.e., the allele inducing altruism) only when similarity reveals genealogical relatedness. Organisms could adaptively modulate their altruism based on phenotypic similarity *if* similarity reliably reflects closeness of ancestry. There is a family context where selection might latch onto variation of this type. All of a mother's offspring are equally related to her. But they may not be equally related to each other: Some may be full and others half siblings. Because *r* differs between the two, there would be a reason to discriminate. This is an ecologically realistic situation where phenotypic similarity could provide a cue to genealogical closeness (Daly et al., 1997). Several studies (see following discussion) support the predicted discrimination but are mute about its psychological mediation. Various kinds of *phenotypic matching* are possible, but few have been convincingly demonstrated for humans. Odor-based kin recognition is an exception (Porter & Moore, 1981).

In evaluating kin recognition systems, we ignore *greenbeard alleles* (Dawkins, 1976), which both produce a distinct phenotypic marker and predispose altruism toward other bearers of the marker. Such effects are possible though rare (Keller & Ross, 1998; Krieger & Ross, 2002; Queller et al., 2003) and have never been demonstrated for humans. More importantly, even if they existed, they would not, strictly speaking, be kin effects because it is the sharing of the greenbeard allele, not recent genealogical linkage, that induces the altruism.

Some research has explicitly evaluated the effects of phenotypic similarity. DeBruine (2002) tested subjects in a two-stage trust game, where they had an opportunity to win larger rewards but also risked being cheated, if and only if they trusted their partner in the first stage. Computer morphing techniques were used to create different facial images of "partners" for 16 such two-stage games. For each subject, one-half of these facial morphs blended two stranger faces, but the other half blended the subject's own face with a stranger's. Subjects were significantly more likely to trust their self-morph partners. Controls ruled out differential attractiveness and familiarity as explanations for these results. Studies by Platek and colleagues (reviewed in later section) demonstrate an effect of phenotypic similarity on male investment decisions.

IS HUMAN BEHAVIOR HAMILTONIAN?

ETHNOGRAPHIC AND BEHAVIORAL STUDIES

The ethnography studies of helping (Berte, 1988; Chagnon & Bugos, 1979; Hames, 1987; Hawkes, 1983; Turke, 1988) and food-sharing behavior (Betzig, 1988; Betzig & Turke, 1986; Kaplan & Hill, 1985) demonstrate discrimination in favor of kin. Though there are other dimensions of human alliance besides kinship (e.g., Gurven, 2000; Hawkes, O'Connell, & Blurton Jones, 2001), relatedness organizes much everyday helping and sharing among traditional peoples. Sahlins (1977) explicitly criticized this conclusion, arguing that human kinship is defined by arbitrary cultural conventions, not by genetic relatedness. But as Morgan pointed out, the "issue is not whether the terms humans use to describe social kinship precisely reflect their biological relationships, but whether the structure of human activities is such that kin selection might in fact operate" (Morgan, 1979, p. 83). Morgan presented data on the composition of Yupic Eskimo whaling crews, operating five-man *umiaks* in the Bering Sea. Although cultural norms about crew membership are stated in terms of social kinship, crew members are closely related genetically, and more highly related crews tend to mount more hunts.

Kinship doesn't just provide the backbone of human social structure; sufficiently fine-grained ethnographic studies show how it shapes the details of day-to-day interaction and exchange in traditional societies.

If the kin-favoring bias predicted by theory rests on an underlying nepotistic psychology, it should be manifest even in exotic places like late twentieth century North America. Essock-Vitale and McGuire (1985) did in-depth interviews with 300 White, middle-class Los Angeles women, and one of the focal topics was helping behavior. The women were 35 to 45 years old and thus nearing the end of their child-bearing (but not necessarily their child-rearing) years. The subjects sorted helping events into major and minor instances, weighing both the amount of help received and the difficulty of giving it, and they reported both help they had received and help they had given. Essock-Vitale and McGuire found that major helping to or from nonkin was significantly more likely to be reciprocal (the amount of help given was equal to the amount of help received) than was helping among kin. This follows from the fact that inclusive fitness effects should mitigate the need for reciprocity (Trivers, 1971). Major help was significantly more likely to come from close (high r) kin. Likewise, the larger the amount of help given, the more likely it was to have come from kin. Help was much more likely to flow from individuals of lower reproductive value to individuals of higher reproductive value than to flow in the opposite direction. (See Estimating B and C section.) Notions of paternity probability suggest a further prediction: Help should more often come from matrilateral than patrilateral kin. This prediction was also supported.

Jankowiak and Diderich (2000) offered a fine-grained test of Hamiltonian theory by comparing full- and half-sib relationships in a polygynous Mormon community. They measured four dimensions of solidarity, which they termed *normative, functional, affectual,* and *associational.* Examples of tasks, questions, or observations associated with each are: Draw your family; Who lends you money? Which sibling do you feel closest to? and observations of attendance at birthday parties, respectively. For all four dimensions, associations were significantly stronger between full than half sibs. Mormon church teachings heavily emphasize family harmony and solidarity. If implemented behaviorally, these tenets would eliminate the full/half sibling distinction, but they seem not to.

Segal's (1984) report of greater solidarity between identical than fraternal twins may provide a parallel example, but there are reasons to be more skeptical. Mixed families of full and half sibs were probably a reasonably common feature of hominid family life. But identical twins would have been rare—and their joint survival vanishingly so—yielding few opportunities for selection to build mechanisms for distinguishing identical twins from other siblings. Yet, Segal's results require explanation. If sibling adaptations include a capacity to distinguish full and half sibs, perhaps based on similarity, identical twins may present a supernormal stimulus to this mechanism (Daly et al., 1997).

We asked University of Pittsburgh undergraduates about their relationships with full siblings, maternal and paternal half sibs, stepsibs, and maternal and paternal cousins. Not all students had every type of kin, but for each occupied category we asked when they last saw a member of that category and when they last did a favor for a member of the category. The study provided six categorical responses to each of the two questions: over the past weekend, over the recent semester break, during the past semester, during the calendar year just ended, prior to that, never. Based on our sample, full sibs have more frequent contact than do

Table 15.1
Most Recent Contact and Favor among Different Classes of Kin

	Week-End	Holiday	Past Term	Past Year	Prior Year	Never
Contact						
Full sib[acd]	77	79	2	4	1	0
Half sib[a]	8	17	3	2	12	2
Maternal half[b]	7	7	1	0	3	0
Paternal half[b]	1	10	2	2	9	2
Stepsib[c]	2	11	2	1	4	0
Cousin[d]	23	168	28	41	56	10
Maternal cuz[e]	15	96	13	20	14	5
Paternal cuz[e]	8	72	15	21	42	5
Favor						
Full sib[acd]	55	97	6	3	1	1
Half sib[a]	6	16	6	2	9	5
Maternal half	5	6	3	1	2	1
Paternal half	1	10	3	1	7	4
Stepsib[c]	1	8	0	3	4	3
Cousin[d]	10	122	23	56	66	49
Maternal cuz	6	72	11	29	26	19
Paternal cuz	4	50	12	27	40	30

Kin categories marked with the same superscript differ significantly in behavior ($p < .05$, by likelihood ratio χ).

half sibs, stepsibs, or cousins (Table 15.1). Maternal half sibs have more contact than paternal half sibs, and the same laterality bias appears among cousins. The same patterns were replicated in the favor data, with the exception that the difference between paternal and maternal relatives, though in the same direction, did not reach statistical significance.

Littlefield and Rushton (1986) evaluated several predictions from kin selection theory by examining the magnitude of grief experienced when a child dies. Grief is expected to be proportionate to magnitude of lost (inclusive) fitness prospects. Parents answered demographic questions about a deceased child, reported their own levels of grief, and estimated the bereavement of other relatives. Parents experienced more grief than less closely related relatives. Controlling for parental age, the death of an older child caused more grief than the death of a younger child. Likewise, the death of a healthy child caused more grief than the death of a sickly or impaired child, but this difference did not reach statistical significance. There were also significant laterality effects. Mothers grieved more than fathers, and maternal aunts and uncles grieved more than paternals. Grandparents grieved in proportion to the number of certain links between them and the grandchild: Maternal grandmothers (0 uncertain links) grieved more than maternal grandfathers and paternal grandmothers (both with one uncertain link), who grieved more than paternal grandfathers (two uncertain links).

According to the sociological literature on support networks, people seek companionship and everyday support among nonkin—friends and associates—but tend to rely on kin for more substantial help (Fischer, 1982). For example, Shavit, Fischer, and Koresh (1994) studied support networks among urban Israelis during the 1991 Gulf War. Their subjects were about equally likely to seek emotional support—through discussing their plans or fears—with friends and with kin. But when they moved to seek temporary residence in less threatened areas or checked on how others had fared in an attack, they systematically turned to kin.

Postmortem bequests allow a window on the differential valuation of various possible recipients (Judge & Hrdy, 1992; Smith, Kish, & Crawford, 1987). Taking the thousand most recently probated wills in British Columbia, Canada, as their sample, Smith et al. (1987) analyzed the testator's disbursement of dollars. On average, 46.5% was willed to individuals related by .5 to the testator (38.6% to offspring plus 7.9% to siblings), 8.3% went to individuals related by .25 (5.1% to nieces and nephews plus 3.2% to grandchildren), and 0.6% to individual related by .125 (cousins). Surviving spouses received 36.9%, and 7.7% went to nonkin, including charitable organizations. The declining disbursement with decreasing r was highly significant. The fact that offspring received significantly larger bequests than siblings can be interpreted as a reproductive-value effect, though a bias toward grandchildren over nieces and nephews was not observed. Based on a sample of 1,538 wills from Sacramento, California, Judge and Hrdy (1992) found that spouses and children received 92% of the average estate, leaving very little for more distant kin or nonrelatives.

"WHAT IF?" STUDIES

Burnstein, Crandall, and Kitayama (1994) used hypothetical scenarios to explore inclinations toward high- and low-benefit helping in both the United States and Japan. A high-cost example is entering a burning building to save someone; a low-cost scenario is helping someone load furniture. (These scenarios confound B and C: Saving someone from a fire is both more beneficial and more costly than loading furniture.) All the scenarios were structured such that three different categories of potential recipients were available, but there was time to help only one of these people. The categories of recipients were formed by mixing various levels of r (four levels from .0 to .5), age (five levels from 3 days to 75 years), and sex (two levels, female and male). The resulting data showed that willingness to help dropped off sharply as degree of relatedness declined. The magnitude of the benefit (and cost) had the predicted impact: The slope of willingness to help on relatedness was significantly steeper for life-and-death situations than for everyday situations. As in the Essock-Vitale and McGuire (1986) study, younger individuals were seen as more appropriate targets of help than older ones. The only exception was for everyday helping aimed at 75-year-olds, where subjects rated themselves as quite likely to help.

Webster (2003) asked his subjects to distribute hypothetical lottery winnings with the constraint that they couldn't keep any money and could give it only to biological kin. This method will not show whether people value their kin over nonkin, but it will reveal whether all kin are treated as equivalent. Webster's key variables were r, size of the hypothetical lottery, and certainty of genetic relationship. Closeness of genetic relationship was by far the strongest predictor of how much subjects allocated, with closer kin being allocated more. The wealth variable also had a significant impact: The less subjects had to distribute, the more they favored close kin over distant kin. Recall that Burnstein et al. (1994) found a stronger kin-favoring bias in the life-and-death scenarios. This might seem counter to Webster's observation, where small lotteries are more heavily allocated to close kin, but the two situations are not parallel. In the Burnstein et al. (1994) scenarios, the cost and the benefit covary, so the proper summary is that when both costs and benefits are high, kin are more heavily favored. In Webster's study there are no costs because subjects are not permitted to keep any of their winnings. One summary of his finding is that when resources are scarce, kin are more strongly favored. Finally, and independently, Webster observed a paternity probability effect. Remember that links through males are uncertain compared to links through females. Webster found that the more male links between a subject and a particular kinsperson, the less that kinsperson was allocated.

RESTRAINED COMPETITION AMONG KIN

The theory of kin selection predicts not only increased altruism toward genetic relatives but also decreased selfishness among kin. Daly and Wilson (1988b) suggested that tactics of conflict resolution should be responsive to selection. Homicide is the most extreme such tactic and thus should be rare among kin. This hypothesis is tricky to evaluate. For any real homicide, there is some pool of potential victims available to the killer. The pool includes both relatives and nonrelatives. If relatives comprise 5% of the victim pool, we would expect 5% of the real-world victims to be relatives, unless being a relative affects the chance of being killed. Unfortunately, it is virtually impossible to define the victim pool for most real homicides. Daly and Wilson's (1988b) solution was to examine domestic homicides, where one member of a household killed another. They examined all 98 solved domestic homicides in Detroit for 1972. In 1970 (the nearest census year), the average Detroit resident, age 14 years or older, lived with 3.0 other persons. Age 14 was used as a cutoff because fewer than 1% of the homicides in Detroit were committed by people under 14, but 12% were committed by older teenagers. In column A, Table 15.2 shows the composition of the average household. For example, the average potential homicide offender lived with 0.6 spouses (i.e., 60% of Detroiters over 14 lived with a spouse). How many domestic homicides would

Table 15.2
An Analysis of Homicide Risk to Kin and Nonkin

	Coresidents		Homicides		Relative
	N	Percentage	Expected	Actual	Risk
	A	B = (A/3.0)	C = (B × 98)	D	E = (D/C)
Nonkin					
Spouses	0.60	0.20	19.60	65.00	3.32
Other nonkin	0.10	0.03	3.27	11.00	3.37
Total nonkin	0.70	0.23	22.87	76.00	3.32
Kin					
Offspring	0.90	0.30	29.40	8.00	0.27
Parents	0.40	0.13	13.07	9.00	0.69
Other kin	1.00	0.33	32.67	5.00	0.15
Total kin	2.30	0.77	75.13	22.00	0.29
Grand total	3.00	1.00	98.00	98.00	1.00

Adapted from *Homicide*, Table 2.1, by M. Daly and M. Wilson, 1988, Chicago: Aldine deGuryter.

have been spousal homicides if homicide was randomly distributed within house-holds? Given the mean number of coresidents (3.0), spouses constituted 0.6/3.0 = 20% of the coresidents of the average Detroiter. Thus, on a chance basis, 20% of the 98 domestic homicide victims, or 19.6 victims, would have been spouses. In fact, 65 of the 98 domestic homicide victims were spouses. Thus, the relative risk to spouses (the number of actual homicides divided by the number of homicides expected on the basis of chance) is 65/19.6 = 3.32, meaning that spouses were killed more than three times as often as we would expect, based on how many spouses there are in the average household.

Similar calculations for each category of coresident produce a clear pattern. Nonrelatives are killed more often than expected by chance, and blood relatives are killed less often than expected by chance. Collectively, nonkin have a relative risk of 3.32; they are killed more than three times as often as expected. The same calculation for kin yields a relative risk of .29; kin are killed less than ⅓ as often as expected. Dividing 3.32 by .29 = 11.35; coresident nonkin are at 11 times greater risk of domestic homicide than coresident kin. Daly and Wilson (1988b) note that even this 11-fold difference underestimates the differential risk to kin and nonkin because some of the "kin" in Table 15.2 are not genetically related (i.e., they are stepkin).

The angry hand is often less restrained when the targets are fictive rather than genetic kin. The case of stepchildren is especially well documented. In a variety of large, or small and carefully controlled, data sets, the effects are overwhelming: Stepchildren are many times more likely to be abused and killed than are genetic children (Daly & Wilson, 1985, 1988a, 1988b, 1998, 2001; Lightcap, Kurland, & Burgess, 1982). It now appears that living with a stepparent is the single greatest risk factor for child abuse.

Cognitive Mediation of Nepotism

Two recent studies explored the cognitive or affective mediation of these kin-favoring biases. Korchmaros and Kenny (2001) targeted emotional closeness (Cunningham, 1986), "a sense of concern, trust and caring for another individual, and enjoyment of the relationship with that individual" (Korchmaros & Kenny, 2001, p. 262), as a candidate mediator of kin-directed altruism. They collected information about family members, including names, relationships (e.g., mother), and perceived emotional closeness from undergraduates. Then they selected subjects who had given information on at least five family members who varied in r and emotional closeness. These subjects were asked to make life-and-death assistance choices in hypothetical scenarios that pitted every possible pairwise combination of five family members against each other. It is not surprising that r was a powerful predictor of which family member they chose to help. When emotional closeness was added to the model, it reduced the explanatory power of r by about 33%. In other words, emotional closeness explained about one-third of the subjects' preference for closer kin. Other, as yet unspecified, mediators seem to be at work.

Kruger (2003) asked more than 600 subjects to picture themselves in a possibly life-threatening situation with a target individual: a sibling close in age and, separately, a close friend. Drawing on the existing literature on altruism, Kruger assessed feelings of empathy (Batson et al., 1997), feelings of self-other overlap or "oneness" (Cialdini, Brown, Lewis, Luce, & Neuberg, 1997), and expectations of reciprocity (Trivers, 1971) between the subject and the target individual. Path analysis indicated that the subjects' stated helping intentions were not fully explained by these three variables: Kinship made a significant unique contribution, and its effect was greater than that for empathetic concern. Oneness and empathetic concern were not higher for sib targets than for friend targets, again indicating that the effects of kinship on altruism are independent of the established psychological mediators of helping behavior.

RELATIONSHIP-SPECIFIC PSYCHOLOGY

Recognizing the important principle of modularity—the idea that psychological adaptations are likely to be specialized for rather narrow functions—we can sketch the landscape of human kinship psychology. Kin relationships are not homogeneous, nor are they differentiated merely in terms of degree of relatedness (Daly et al., 1997). For example, mothers and daughters are symmetrically related by .5 and linked via a single meiotic event, but the psychological mechanisms that would best organize a mother's behavior are different from the ones that would best serve a daughter. Likewise, mothers and fathers face somewhat different evolutionary challenges and thus should evolve different adaptive psychologies. Sibling relations pose different problems than grandparent-grandchild relations. To the extent that each of these relationships was common and important in the Environment of Evolutionary Adaptedness (EEA) (Kurland & Sparks, 2003; Tooby & DeVore, 1987), we can expect different sets of psychological adaptations, specialized for optimal behavior in each context.

KINSHIP PSYCHOLOGY OF MOTHERHOOD

Mothers are arbiters of resource flow to children. Given this, the inherent relatedness asymmetries in the family (Trivers, 1974) will profoundly influence the psychological dynamics underlying mother-child interactions. The divergence of evolutionary objectives begins at zygote formation, and evidence of parent-offspring conflict is present from very early in gestation (Haig, 1993). Although these gestational struggles are not psychological, they demonstrate that, even in the intimate context of pregnancy, there are fundamental conflicts of interest among kin.

Early termination of investment is the most extreme manifestation of parent-offspring conflict. Evolution should build psychological mechanisms to prevent mothers from investing in offspring unlikely to reproduce. Theory predicts that any such "decisions" would involve implicit "comparisons" with plausible reproductive alternatives (Alexander, 1979): A given offspring or situation represents a good or bad reproductive opportunity only in terms of some probabilistic set of other options. Although there may be mechanisms for the evaluation of offspring quality in utero (e.g., maternal responsiveness to fetal chorionic gonadotropin production; Haig, 1993), new data and options are available to a mother after parturition.

Infanticide poses moral and ethical dilemmas, but the ethnographic record suggests it has long provided a means of adjusting the allocation of parental effort (e.g., Bugos & McCarthy, 1984; Daly & Wilson, 1988b; Howell, 1979; Williamson, 1978). Infanticide would be a doomed reproductive strategy if it were obligate. A review of the circumstances that elicit facultative infanticide in non-human animals (Daly & Wilson, 1988b) suggests three predisposing factors: lack of genetic relatedness, unpromising offspring, and unpropitious circumstances. The first is irrelevant to mothers. The second refers to infants who would be inefficient recipients of maternal investment; due to some defect, they would require inordinate amounts of investment or would be unlikely to translate such investment into progeny. The third focuses not on the infant but on the circumstances of its birth. For example, in many species an offspring born at the wrong season would be unlikely to survive. Perhaps more significantly for humans, an offspring born too soon after a sibling or one without a willing pater would have faced greater challenges and imposed more costs on its mother. Mothers should be designed to assess perinatally the quality of their offspring and the various environmental predictors of success and failure. When the combination of factors was sufficiently negative, early termination of investment would have been the best strategy. What evidence exists for the kind of psychological mechanisms predicted by this analysis?

Indirect evidence comes from observations suggesting that, behaviorally, the suggested facultative relationship exists. Using the 60-society "probability sample" of the Human Relations Area Files, Daly and Wilson (1984, 1988b) tabulated the ethnographic evidence and found 112 reasons, justifications, or explanations for infanticide; in other words, the average society in this database presented just under two such justifications. Of these 112 justifications, 15 were not clearly related to any of the three hypothesized precipitating factors. But most of these 15 seem to be infanticides committed or coerced by individuals other than the mother and thus are irrelevant to the discussion here. Likewise, an additional 20 reasons concern paternity issues, a topic relevant to the psychology of fatherhood (see later discussion). But 77 of the justifications highlight the two issues most relevant to maternal investment strategies: offspring quality and environmental predictors of offspring survival. For 21 of these societies, the ethnographic sources note that deformed or very ill infants were killed. A further 56 justifications targeted unfavorable rearing circumstances. These reasons included twinning, too short an interbirth interval, too many children to support, absence of an investing male, and economic hardship.

Bugos and McCarthy (1984) provided an analysis of the circumstances surrounding more than 50 infanticides in an indigenous South American population, the Ayoreo. They argue that if infanticide is viewed as a strategy for maximizing lifetime reproductive success, its incidence should be inversely correlated with mother's age. This is partly due to certain circumstances correlated with youth: Young mothers tend to be inexperienced in procuring resources and as caretakers, and they are more likely to be unmarried or uncertain about the reliability of ongoing male parental investment. In short, they tend to be unprepared to provision an infant. It also follows from life history theory. The younger a woman is, the more likely she is to experience a better reproductive opportunity in the future. To make the point from the other end of the curve, a 45-year-old woman holding her newborn is probably staring at all of her residual reproductive value. Thus, examining age-specific infanticide rates in a group of Ayoreo women who had committed at least one infanticide, Bugos and McCarthy (1984) found a dramatic negative association with mother's age.

Infanticides are much rarer in the modern West—probably for a variety of reasons, including the rule of law and the embedding of parturition in the medical context. Nevertheless, infanticides still do occur, and they are probably substantially underreported (McClain, Sacks, Froehlke, & Ewigman, 1993). Do they exhibit the same patterns as the Ayoreo infanticides? Both youth, through its effects on a mother's future options, and unmarried status, through its effects on resource supply, can be expected to influence the likelihood of infanticide. Although correlated, these two effects can be disentangled in large data sets. Daly and Wilson (1984, 1988b) evaluated these predictions for a large, multiyear sample of Canadian infanticides. They found the effects to be independent, large, and highly significant. For example, over the years sampled, 88.3% of the women giving birth in Canada were married; but only 39.5% of the mothers who committed infanticide were married. Likewise, only 3.1% of new mothers were under 18 years of age, but 15.7% of infanticidal mothers were.

Most contemporary analyses of infanticide highlight legal and ethical issues and, when they discuss causes, generally treat the behavior as pathological (e.g., Spinelli, 2003). Nevertheless, epidemiological studies consistently replicate Daly and Wilson's findings. One recent study of the risk factors for infanticide drew on the nearly 35 million infants born in the United States between 1983 and 1991 (Overpeck, Brenner, Trumble, Trifiletti, & Berendes, 1998). Of these, 2,776 infants died during the first year of life from intentional or suspicious causes. Overpeck et al. analyzed these 35 million births in terms of relative-risk categories. For example, taking mothers 25 years old or older as the baseline, infants whose mothers were under 15 years of age were 6.8 times as likely to be killed. Several of the most potent risk factors are summarized in Table 15.3 on page 468. Although the authors offered no such analysis, all these factors can be interpreted as proxies either of infant quality or the propitiousness of the reproductive venture. Youthful mothers are not only more likely to kill their infants but also progressively more likely to do so when they are already burdened by an older child. Unmarried mothers and those with little education presumably find themselves in a poor position to invest. Handicapped or otherwise less-than-perfect infants are everywhere at elevated risk of infanticide (Horan & Delahoyde, 1982). This demographic study presents only indirect evidence; infants born at early gestational ages are more at risk of infanticide. These factors operate in a monotonic, dose-dependent way that matches the predictions first laid out by Daly and Wilson (1984).

More direct evidence on the psychological bases of maternal investment concerns postpartum depression (PPD). Depression is a "psychopathology" often held up as a "cause" of infanticide (Spinelli, 2003). Parturition has long been recognized as a major risk factor for depression (Paffenberg & McCabe, 1966). On the theory that mood constitutes an internal system of rewards and punishments calibrated to likely fitness outcomes (Nesse, 1990; Tooby & Cosmides, 1990), this may be surprising because postpartum women have just sustained a significant fitness increase. Maladaptive, side-effect explanations are possible given the dramatic peripartum shift in hormone regimes. PPD has also been given adaptive interpretations (Daly & Wilson, 1988b; Hagen, 1999). Daly and Wilson (1988b) suggested that a mild peripartum depression could function to neutralize any elation a new mother might feel and thus permit a more objective evaluation of offspring quality and environmental conditions. If this were the whole explanation, all mothers would presumably benefit equally; how could we explain individual differences in the susceptibility to or the severity of PPD? According to Daly and Wilson (1995, p. 1282), more severe PPD is "especially likely when the mother is young, single, at odds with the father, or otherwise lacking in social

Table 15.3
Evolutionarily Relevant Factors Affecting
the Risk of Infanticide

Factor	Relative Risk
Mother's Age	
<15 years	6.8
15–16 years	5.3
17–19 years	4.6
20–24 years	2.6
≥ 25 years*	1.0
Mother's Age × Infant's Birth Order	
<17 years	
Second or subsequent	10.9
First	6.6
17–19 years	
Second or subsequent	9.3
First	4.6
20–24 years	
Second or subsequent	4.3
First	2.2
≥ 25 years	
Second or subsequent	1.4
First*	1.0
Mother's Marital Status	
Unmarried	4.3
Married*	1.0
Mother's Education	
<11 years	8.4
12 years	3.9
13-15 years	2.3
≥ 16 years*	1.0
Gestational Age at Birth	
< 28 weeks	3.6
28–36 weeks	2.2
≥ 37 weeks*	1.0

Note: * = Baseline category for calculating relative risks.
Source: From "Risk Factors for Infant Homicide in the United States," by M. D. Overpeck et al., 1998, *New England Journal of Medicine, 339*, pp. 1211–1216.

support . . . and when the infant is suffering from poor health." Hagen (1999) explicitly links his model of PPD to Daly and Wilson's (1984, 1988b, 1995) cost/benefit analysis of maternal investment decisions. He suggests that individual differences are expected because mothers differ in how much social support they have, how promising their infant is, and how adequate their resources are for child rearing. In essence, he argues and supports through a comprehensive literature review that PPD is most likely in the kinds of cases that would have led to infanticide in the EEA. On this view, the psychological pain of PPD would have alerted mothers that a particular birth was not a fitness-enhancing opportunity.

KINSHIP PSYCHOLOGY OF FATHERHOOD

In some ways the psychological demands of fatherhood and motherhood are similar. Both face the problem of evaluating whether any given infant or reproductive opportunity warrants their parental investment; and both face the problem of adaptively allocating investment among their genetic progeny. But because women alone gestate, fathers and mothers face somewhat different challenges. The primary relevance of paternal probability to male psychology lies in the risk of cuckoldry. Men who broadcast their investment indiscriminately to members of the next generation are vulnerable to exploitation by others who fertilize and abandon their mates. In this selective environment, relevant evolved mechanisms could include anticuckoldry tactics and offspring discrimination mechanisms (Daly & Wilson, 1998).

Male sexual proprietariness may be an example of the first (Betzig, 1989; Daly, Wilson, & Weghorst, 1982). A woman stands to forfeit some of her husband's resources when he is sexually unfaithful. But cuckolded men may invest for decades in unrelated "children." It is not surprising, then, that historical and ethnographic sources reveal a widespread double standard in the punishment of sexual infidelity. Adultery is universally defined based on the marital status of the female actor, and adulterous women are viewed as having collaborated in a property crime against their husbands (Daly, Wilson, & Weghorst, 1982). Betzig (1989) surveyed the causes of divorce reported for the 186 societies of the Standard Cross-Cultural Sample. Infidelity (or lack of virginity) justifies divorce in 94 cases, but does it do so equally for both sexes? In 25 cases it does; but the remaining cases distribute very unequally. For two societies, the ethnographic materials indicate that a woman can divorce an unfaithful husband, whereas in 60 societies, unfaithful wives are subject to divorce. Evidence suggests that male sexual proprietariness motivates a large proportion of spousal homicides (Daly & Wilson, 1988b).

What psychology underlies these patterns? Both sexes experience jealousy, but the substance of that jealousy seems to be different (Daly et al., 1982). Buss, Larsen, Westen, and Semmelroth (1992) asked subjects to imagine a serious romantic relationship they had had or would like to have and then presented two scenarios. One involved their partner forming an emotional attachment to someone else, and the other involved their partner having a sexual encounter with someone else. Subjects were asked to report which of these two scenarios would be more distressing to them. Males were significantly more likely than females to find the sexual scenario more distressing. In a parallel study, these researchers used physiological measures of distress—electrodermal activity, pulse rate, and contraction of the brow (*corrugator supercilii*) muscle. The same pattern of results emerged with males, but not females, exhibiting more dramatic physiological responses to the sexual infidelity scenario, though not all predicted differences reached statistical significance. These studies have been criticized because they use a forced-choice response format (Harris, 2000). Thus, a recent replication is helpful: Pietrzak, Laird, Stevens, and Thompson (2002) studied jealousy responses using forced-choice, rating-scale, and physiological measures on a single group of subjects. All three measures exhibited the same pattern of sex differences initially reported by Buss et al. (1992). To the extent that emotions form the affective components of motivational systems (Gaulin & McBurney, 2001; Nesse, 1989; Plutchik, 1980; Tooby & Cosmides, 1990), male jealousy seems adapted to guard against cuckoldry.

Phenotypic resemblance cues might provide evidence about a man's genetic relatedness to his putative offspring. Because maternity is never in doubt, we might expect a sex effect in this domain. Men might be better at detecting resemblance than women, or men might be more sensitive to resemblance when making investment decisions. Curiously then, most studies have explored whether people in general are better at diagnosing father-child relatedness than mother-child relatedness. There are two problems with this idea. First, there may be some benefit from detecting the relatedness of other males to their various children, but an egocentric mechanism allowing the recognition of an individual's own offspring would be more valuable. Second, some authors suggest (Christenfeld & Hill, 1995) that infants might benefit from ontogenetic mechanisms that produced elevated levels of paternal resemblance. This, too, is a dubious claim because such mechanisms would be a double-edged sword: Advertising who your father is could advertise cuckoldry (Pagel, 1997). To work well, any such mechanisms would have to be facultatively dependent on whether Dad was Mom's current partner, the problem being the shortage of relevant cues from the perspective of the fetus. Thus, it is not surprising that these studies have produced inconsistent results. Christenfeld and Hill (1995) found that men and women were able to match photographs of 1-year-olds to photographs of their (putative) fathers but not to their mothers. But several other studies have failed to replicate this sex difference (Bredért & French, 1999; Nesse, Silverman, & Bortz, 1990) or found significant effects in the opposite direction (McClain, Setters, Moulton, & Pratt, 2000).

In addition, most resemblance studies face a methodological challenge. Their stimulus materials typically come from family photo albums. Pictures of mom, dad, and children are collected from various families and then shuffled together to produce stimulus sets in which some parent-child dyads are related and some are not. The subjects' task is to identify the genetic parent-child dyads. Unfortunately, the stimulus sets are contaminated by the phenomenon under investigation: The mothers are genetic parents but the fathers may not be. Some unspecified portion of "mistakes" by subjects are correct due to cuckoldry.

Recent work by Platek and his collaborators avoids this problem by manipulating resemblance experimentally. It also goes beyond recognition to the effect of physical resemblance on men's and women's investment inclinations. Platek used computer imaging techniques to morph the faces of adults with those of children. Some of the children's faces were morphed with subjects' faces, and some were morphed with those of other, randomly chosen adults. All morphs were 50/50 mixes of the adult and the child, and both male and female adult faces were morphed with both sexes of children. Then, selections of five such adult-child faces were presented to the subjects along with positive and negative investment questions, such as: "Which of these children would you be most likely to adopt?" and "Which of these children would you spend the least time with?" If subjects had selected faces at random, then they would have picked faces that had been morphed with their own 20% of the time for both positive and negative questions. But male subjects tended to pick their self-morphed faces significantly more often—up to 90% of the time—for positive questions and showed a tendency to choose self-morphed faces less often than chance for the negative questions (Platek, Burch, Panyavin, Wasserman, & Gallup, 2002). These deviations from randomness were nearly absent for female subjects.

How much resemblance is necessary to trigger men's investment inclinations? In the previous study, all faces were a 50/50 blend. In a follow-up study, a variety of more dilute morphs were also created, including faces with 25%, 12.5%, 6.25%, and 3.125% of the adult image (Platek et al., 2003). Again, a strong sex difference emerged with males more likely to choose self-morphed faces for the positive investment questions. There was also a relatively clear threshold, with this bias appearing for morphs that included 25% or more of the subject's image. A parallel experiment asked whether men and women are equally skilled at detecting resemblance. Again, various adult-child morphs including 50% to 3.125% of the adult image were used. Subjects were asked to select from an array the adult face that most resembled the adult-child morph (i.e., the face that was morphed with the child's face). In some trials the correct choice was the subject's own image, and in others it was a stranger's. The only effect was a main one for level of morph: Both sexes could detect the source face for 50% adult-child morph, regardless of whether the face was their own. Sex of subject, sex of adult face, and sex of child face made no difference, and more dilute morphs could not be accurately detected. These results suggest two conclusions. First, men and women are equally good at detecting resemblance, but only men seem to use resemblance in making investment decisions. This makes adaptive sense: Women can't be cuckolded and thus don't need a psychology that links investment decisions to phenotypic cues of relatedness. Second, in making investment decisions, men respond to lower levels of resemblance (e.g., 25% morphs) than they can consciously detect. One final finding is relevant. In debriefing, subjects were asked how difficult it was to answer the hypothetical investment questions. Men found the decisions significantly easier than women, suggesting that the faces offered some cue relevant to their decision (Platek et al., 2002, 2003).

Functional magnetic resonance imaging (fMRI) offers the possibility of studying modularity directly. Recently, Platek (2003) employed fMRI while male and female subjects viewed infant faces, some of which had been morphed with the subject's image and some of which were morphed with images of strangers. When viewing stranger-morphed faces, men and women showed the same pattern of neural activation, but when viewing self-morphed faces, there was a significant sex difference in the brain areas being used. This suggests that men, but not women, have evolved particular neurocognitive machinery for processing children's phenotypic resemblance to them (Platek, 2003).

Experimental studies offer good control, but they often sacrifice ecological validity. Though important, the studies just outlined assume that computer morphing provides an adequate analogue of gene expression in sexually reproduced diploids. And indeed they may, at least for studying the effects of resemblance on investment. But it is useful to have parallel data from the real world. Burch and Gallup (2000) studied a group of 55 men mandated for domestic violence treatment. Most of the men had putative offspring in their homes, and some also had stepchildren. Among many other variables, the men rated how much each of their children resembled them and the quality of their relationship with each child. These two variables were strongly and significantly correlated for the putative children ($r = .6$) but not for the stepchildren. Likewise, men also reported how often others told them each of their children resembled them and this, too, was significantly correlated with the quality of their relationship, but only for the putative children ($r = .54$). Similar but weaker correlations linked how much the men resembled their own fathers and the quality of their relationship with them, but no such pattern existed for their resemblance of and relationship with their mothers.

Burch and Gallup (2000) noted that paternal resemblance claims by others were highly correlated with the men's own evaluations of how much their children resembled them ($r = .87$), labeling this effect a "social mirror." If men use the social mirror in parental investment decisions, actors who have an interest in these decisions might attempt to warp the mirror to their advantage. Thus, several studies have tested the hypothesis that mothers and other matrilateral kin allege paternal investment more that fathers and patrilateral kin (Daly & Wilson, 1982; McLain et al., 2000; Regalski & Gaulin, 1993). These studies, conducted in the United States, Canada, and Mexico, all found that paternal resemblance was alleged significantly more often than maternal, but that this was entirely due to the paternal resemblance claims of mothers. In addition, all of the studies found either a trend or a significant effect of the father's presence: Mothers were more likely to claim paternal resemblance when the father could hear their remarks. The possibility that mothers' claims influence fathers' perceptions is supported because mothers' and fathers' resemblance claims tend to agree (Regalski & Gaulin, 1993), possibly because infants differ in how much they resemble one or the other parent, with these differences being apparent to both. Thus, one study sought an external standard for evaluating mothers' and fathers' resemblance (McLain et al., 2000). In a counterbalanced design, each infant's photograph was presented with photographs of candidate mothers and fathers. Raters performed better than chance at identifying actual parents and were significantly better at matching mothers to infants than fathers to infants, suggesting that many paternal resemblance claims were exaggerated. Overall, the parents' resemblance claims accorded well with the performance of the raters: Raters more often correctly identified the parent whom the infant had been alleged to resemble. This was equally true for fathers' allegations and mothers' allegations when made out of the fathers' earshot. But the mothers' allegations made when the fathers were present—preponderantly claims of paternal resemblance—accorded significantly less well with the performance of the raters. These studies suggest that the social mirror is indeed being warped by mothers (and to a lesser degree by other matrilateral relatives).

PARENTAL PROBABILITY AND MORE DISTAL KIN RELATIONS:
THE LATERALITY BIAS

Hartung (1985) documented the roots of the notion that, when marital infidelity is frequent, men often invest in their sisters' rather than their wives' children. Alexander (1974) brought this idea to the attention of evolutionary psychologists, and Kurland (1979) was the first to model it broadly. The avunculate—wherein men have primary responsibilities for their sisters' children rather than their wives'—and matrilineal inheritance are just special cases of an apparently more general phenomenon. Links through males are less certain than links through females, and this asymmetry impacts on probabilities of relatedness beyond the nuclear family. A maternal grandmother is connected to her grandchild through two certain (female) links: She is her daughter's mother and the grandchild is her daughter's child. Maternal grandfathers and paternal grandmothers are each connected to the grandchild though one certain and one uncertain (male) link. Paternal grandfathers are connected through two uncertain links. Similarly for collateral relatives, matrilateral aunts and uncles (related through the mother) are more closely related to their nieces and nephews than are patrilateral aunts and uncles (related through the father). With p representing the populationwide mean probability of paternity, the actual degree of relatedness among relatives can be specified. Mother's mother (MoMo) is related to her grandchild by $\frac{1}{4}$, but father's mother is related to hers by only $\frac{1}{4}p$. Likewise, mother's sister (MoSis) is related to her niece or nephew by $\frac{1}{8}(1 + p^2)$, whereas father's sister (FaSis) is related by only $\frac{1}{8}p(1 + p^2)$; see Gaulin, McBurney, & Brakeman-Wartell, 1997, for explicit derivations). Because p is less than 1, matrilateral grandparents, aunts, and uncles are more closely related and hence expected to be more solicitous than the equivalent patrilateral relatives.

A number of studies, including some summarized earlier, have reported such a bias. Essock-Vitale and McGuire (1985) noted that the women in their sample were more likely to receive help from their matrilateral kin. In Webster's (2003) study of hypothetical lottery distributions, the uncertainty effect was highly significant: Smaller shares went to relatives connected through a larger number of uncertain links. Littlefield and Rushton (1986) found that a systematic bias is the magnitude of grief following the death of a child: Across the various types of grandparents, aunts, and uncles, the greater the number of uncertain links, the less grief the relative experienced. Frequency of contact between Pittsburgh undergraduates and their sibs and cousins also shows a matrilateral bias (Table 15.1). Note that laterality biases are not sex biases. Women generally invest more in kin than men. But that is not a laterality bias because both sexes can, simultaneously, be matrilateral and patrilateral relatives (e.g., a woman is aunt to her brother's and to her sister's children).

Euler and Weitzel (1996) asked German adults to rate the levels of grandparental solicitude they had experienced for each of their four grandparents. Results strongly followed actual relatedness, with MoMos showing the highest solicitude, MoFas and FaMos showing intermediate levels, and FaFas showing the least (Table 15.4). Their large sample permitted some fine-grained analysis. In the

Table 15.4
Solicitude Ratings for Four Classes of Grandparents

Grandparent	Living with Spouse		Widowed		Living Separately	
	Mean	*N*	Mean	*N*	Mean	*N*
Mother's mother	5.09	633	5.10	602	5.06	48
Mother's father	4.51	551	4.17	517	2.06	34
Father's mother	4.20	595	4.41	571	3.25	36
Father's father	3.80	470	3.89	487	1.77	30

Data from "Discriminative Grandparental Solicitude as Reproductive Strategy," by H. Euler and B. Weitzel, 1996, *Human Nature, 7,* pp. 39–59.

group of grandparents that lived together, MoFas invested more than FaMos, but in the widowed subset the pattern for these two intermediate cases ($r = \frac{1}{4}p$) was reversed. Likewise, for the subset of grandparents who were living but separated or divorced, all solicitude ratings fell off sharply, except for the MoMos. Investment of the MoFa seems to be strongly influenced by his partner, the MoMo: When that relationship is dissolved, his investment declines. Considering the frequent role of infidelity in divorce (Betzig, 1989) and the parallel effect of infidelity on p, it is interesting that divorce has a much more drastic effect on MoFa's investment than his partner's death does.

With smaller samples, Pashos (2000) replicated this study in three populations: urban Germans, urban Greeks, and rural Greeks. The urban populations showed the same ordering of solicitude seen in the leftmost column of Table 15.4: from most to least solicitous, MoMo, MoFa, FaMo, FaFa. However, the rural Greek sample was different, showing a strong patrilateral bias, with FaMos investing the most, followed by FaFas and MoMos, and with MoFas investing the least. Pashos attributes this difference to the significant patrilineal influence in traditional Greek culture, a feature that apparently does not penetrate the urban context. On the argument advanced earlier, matrilineal bias would be expected to be cross-culturally variable only to the extent that p varied. This remains an open question.

Demographic data support the predicted matrilateral bias. Beise and Voland (2002) examined a 150-year-sample of German births from the eighteenth and nineteenth centuries. They used multilevel event-history models to explore the impact of grandmothers' survival on infant survival. The question was: Were infants whose grandmothers were alive more likely to survive during the first 5 years than those whose grandmothers were dead? It depends on which grandmother—those without a living MoMo are, in various age intervals, up to 60% more likely to die, compared to those without a living FaMo.

The behavior of mated grandparents is not independent. Although MoMo and MoFa are mates and often live together as grandparents, MoSis and MoBro would never constitute a mated pair; nor would FaSis and FaBro. Thus, aunts and uncles, approximately equally closely related to their nieces and nephews as grandparents are to grandchildren, allow further exploration of the effects of p on kin relations. Using multivariate controls for age and distance effects, Gaulin et al. (1997) found significant matrilateral biases in both aunts' and uncles' investment. A subsequent study (McBurney, Simon, Gaulin, & Geliebter, 2002) applied the same methods to a sample of orthodox Jews, a population thought to have especially high paternity probability. The orthodox aunts and uncles showed a weaker matrilateral bias than did the unselected sample of Gaulin et al. (1997), but not significantly so. Why might this be? Perhaps the greater investment of matrilateral relatives is not facultatively dependent on p; the level of matrilateral bias could simply be a constant, adjusted to mean levels of p over the past few 100,000 years. Alternatively, even if matrilateral bias were facultative—as Hartung's (1985) analysis on matrilineal inheritance suggests—the range of responsiveness would probably be bounded by the maximum and minimum p during the EEA (Tooby & DeVore, 1987). If this is correct, the data for Germans, urban Greeks, Pennsylvanians, and orthodox Jews agree in suggesting that the prehistoric maximum p was approximately .9 (Gaulin et al., 1997), though data from rural Greeks (Pashos, 2000) contradict this interpretation. These questions might be partially resolved by measuring the level of matrilateral bias in societies where p is significantly lower than .9.

THE PSYCHOLOGY OF SIBLING RELATIONS

The empirical studies reviewed earlier reveal a clear nepotistic bias in favor of siblings, but that is not the only prediction from theory. If "functional families" exhibit no conflict, then all families are predicted to be dysfunctional because siblings will not agree on the optimal allocation of parental resources: Depending on the mating system, each member of a sibship should view itself as two to four times more worthy of parental investment than the others (Trivers, 1974). That such sibling rivalry occurs is old news, but tests of evolutionary predictions about its form, nature, and extent are completely lacking at present, primarily because the battleground and resolution models do not yet provide clear and testable predictions.

A comparison with maternal-fetal conflict (Haig, 1993) is informative. The strategies of the mother and fetus are identifiable based on the genotype of the tissues involved (e.g., trophoblast) or the interplay of maternal and fetal hormones (e.g., human placental lactogen from the fetus versus insulin from the mother). A history of protracted arms races is strongly suggested by shifts in the physical boundary between mother and fetus (as when fetal cells invade the endometrium) and by the elevated levels of the relevant hormones in pregnant compared to nonpregnant women. The battleground and tactics are relatively conspicuous in this physical realm. But what are the psychological equivalents of these tactics in the struggle between siblings for parental resources?

THE PSYCHOLOGY OF GRANDPARENTHOOD

There is considerable debate about the demography of our hominid ancestors, and this casts a shadow over the analysis of grandparental behavior. Should we expect to find specific grandparental, as distinct from parental, adaptations? This depends on how frequently hominid survival produced three-generation overlap. Kristen Hawkes has argued that female menopause is a life-historical adaptation specifically designed to allow grandmaternal investment (Hawkes, O'Connell, & Blurton Jones, 1989, 1997; Hawkes, O'Connell, Blurton Jones, Alvarez, & Charnov, 1998), though some models of life history evolution (Rogers, 1993, 2003) and hunter-gatherer demography (Kurland & Sparks, 2003) argue against this scenario. The criticisms are that (1) early cessation of reproduction in the form of menopause would have cost more in offspring production than it returned in grandchild survival and (2) few hominid women would have lived to an age where they had grandchildren to invest in. These significant issues notwithstanding, grandparents—most especially maternal grandmothers (see earlier discussion)—do lavish both time and energy on their grandchildren and take great pleasure in the process. An internal reward system seems to drive their behavior. This suggests either adaptations for grandmaternal care or the "parasitization" of some other adaptive (e.g., maternal) caregiving system. The laterality biases discussed earlier, if sufficiently general, would be evidence for grandparental adaptations.

CONCLUSION

The study of kinship psychology must be grounded in Hamilton's (1964) theory of kin selection, as distilled through the lenses of Trivers's (1974) parent-offspring conflict theory and paternal probability theory (Alexander, 1974; Kurland, 1979). The few applications of these evolutionary theories in the social sciences and humanities have often failed to recognize that Hamilton's r does not map precisely onto either genotypic or phenotypic similarity and that any predictions are sensitive to the benefit-to-cost ratios of social interactions (Dawkins, 1979; Grafen, 1982, 1984, 1991).

Evolutionary models significantly revise Darwin's (1859) predictions about the distribution of both selfish and altruistic traits, though they are mute on the phenomenological instantiation of these tendencies. Theoretical explorations of parent-offspring conflict imply that parents, offspring, and their siblings will always disagree about the optimal distribution of parental resources and that no single outcome of this disagreement will be evolutionarily stable. These results can be extended to more distant kin beyond the nuclear family, though there has been little theoretical research in this area. Both battleground and resolution models of kin conflict and cooperation are abstract, and testable predictions are few. Moreover, because they are sensitive to starting assumptions, the different models often come to contradictory conclusions. These models focus on parent-offspring and sibling conflict neglecting more distant kin, despite their importance in human societies.

Numerous empirical studies show that human behavior is decidedly nepotistic, as predicted by Hamilton's theory. A growing number of studies are unpacking the psychological underpinnings of kin-biased behavior, though much remains to be done in terms of both motivational and cognitive research. As suggested by Daly et al. (1997), the focus should be on relationship-specific psychological adaptations. Considerable evidence shows that this approach has borne fruit in the study of maternal and paternal behavior. Much less evidence exists for relationship-specific adaptations among siblings and more distant relatives such as grandparents, aunts, and uncles. However, the laterality bias in kinship interactions, due to the paternity probability, is a good candidate for further study.

REFERENCES

Agrawal, A. F., Brodie, E. D., III, & Brown, J. (2001). Parent-offspring coadaptation and the dual genetic control of maternal care. *Science, 292,* 1710–1712.

Alcock, J. (2001). *Animal behavior: An evolutionary approach.* Sunderland, MA: Sinauer.

Alexander, R. D. (1974). The evolution of social behavior. *Annual Review of Ecology and Systematics, 5,* 325–383.

Alexander, R. D. (1979). *Darwinism and human affairs.* Seattle: University of Washington Press.

Alexander, R D. (1987). *The biology of moral systems.* New York: Aldine De Gruyter

Bateson, P. (1994). The dynamics of parent-offspring relationships in mammals. *Trends in Ecology and Evolution, 9,* 399–403.

Batson, C. D., Sager, K., Garst, E., Kang, M., Rubchinsky, K., & Dawson, K. (1997). Is empathy-induced helping due to self-other merging? *Journal of Personality and Social Psychology, 73,* 495–509.

Beise, J., & Voland, E. (2002). A multilevel event history analysis of the effects of grandmothers on child mortality in a historical German population (Krummhorn, Ostfriesland, 1720–1874). *Demographic Research, 7,* 469–498.

Bergstrom, C., & Lachmann, M. (1997). Signalling among relative: I. Is costly signaling *too* costly. *Proceedings of the Royal Society of London. Series B, Biological Sciences, 352,* 609–617.

Bergstrom, C., & Lachmann, M. (1998). Signalling among relatives. III. Talk is cheap. *Proceedings of the National Academy of Science of the United States of America, 95,* 5100–5105.

Berte, N. (1988). K'ekchi' horticultural labor exchange: Productive and reproductive implications. In L. Betzig, M. Borgerhoff Mulder, & P. Turke (Eds.), *Human reproductive behavior: A Darwinian perspective* (pp. 83–96). Cambridge, England: Cambridge University Press.

Betzig, L. L. (1988). Redistribution: Equity or exploitation. In L. Betzig, M. Borgerhoff Mulder, & P. Turke (Eds.), *Human reproductive behavior: A Darwinian perspective* (pp. 49–63). Cambridge, England: Cambridge University Press.

Betzig, L. L. (1989). Causes of conjugal dissolution: A cross-cultural study. *Current Anthropology, 30,* 654–676.

Betzig, L., & Turke, P. (1986). Food sharing on Ifaluk. *Current Anthropology, 27,* 397–400.

Blick, J. (1977). Selection for traits which lower individual reproduction. *Journal of Theoretical Biology, 67,* 597–601.

Bredért, S., & French, R. (1999). Do babies resemble their fathers more than their mothers? A failure to replicate Christenfeld and Hill. *Evolution and Human Behavior, 20,* 129–135.

Brown, J. L. (1983a). Cooperation: A biologist's dilemma. In J. S. Rosenblatt (Ed.), *Advances in the study of behavior* (pp. 1–37). New York: Academic Press.

Brown, J. L. (1983b). Parental facilitation: Parent-offspring relations in communal breeding birds. *Behavioral Ecology and Sociobiology, 10,* 111–117.

Bugos, P. E., & McCarthy, L. M. (1984). Ayoreo infanticide: A case study. In G. Hausfater & S. B. Hrdy (Eds.), *Infanticide: Comparative and evolutionary perspectives* (pp. 503–520). New York: Aldine.

Burch, R. L., & Gallup, G. G. (2000). Perceptions of paternal resemblance predict family violence. *Evolution and Human Behavior, 21,* 429–435.

Burnstein, E., Crandall, C., & Kitayama, S. (1994). Some neo-Darwinian decision rules for altruism: Weighing cues for inclusive fitness as a function of the biological importance of the decision. *Journal of Personality and Social Psychology, 67,* 773–789.

Buss, D. M. (1999). *Evolutionary psychology: The new science of the mind.* Boston, MA: Allyn & Bacon.

Buss, D. M., Larsen, R. J., Westen, D., & Semmelroth, J. (1992). Sex differences in jealousy: Evolution, physiology and psychology. *Psychological Science, 3,* 251–255.

Chagnon, N., & Bugos, P. (1979). Kin selection and conflict: An analysis of a Yanomamö ax fight. In N. Chagnon & W. Irons (Eds.), *Evolutionary biology and human social behavior* (pp. 213–237). North Scituate, MA: Duxbury.

Charlesworth, B. (1980). Models of kin selection. In H. Markl (Ed.), *Evolution of social behavior: Hypotheses and empirical tests* (pp. 77–88). Weinheim: Verlag Chemie.

Christenfeld, N. J. S., & Hill, E. A. (1995). Whose baby are you? *Nature, 378,* 669.

Cialdini, R., Brown, S., Lewis, B., Luce, C., & Neuberg, S. (1997). Reinterpretation of the empathy-altruism relationship: When one into one equals oneness. *Journal of Personality and Social Psychology, 73,* 481–494.

Cosmides, L., & Tooby, J. (1992). Cognitive adaptations for social exchange. In J. H. Barkow, L. Cosmides, & J. Tooby (Eds.), *The adapted mind: Evolutionary psychology and the generation of culture* (pp. 163–228). Oxford, England: Oxford University Press.

Crow, J. F., & Kimura, M. (1970). *An introduction to population genetics theory.* New York: Harper & Row.

Cunningham, M. R. (1986). Levites and brother's keepers: A sociogenetic perspective on prosocial behavior. *Humbolt Journal of Social Relations, 13,* 35–67.

Daly, M., Salmon, C., & Wilson, M. (1997). Kinship: The conceptual hole in psychological studies of social cognition and close relationships. In J. A. Simpson & D. T. Kenrick (Eds.), *Evolutionary social psychology* (pp. 265–296). Mahwah, NJ: Erlbaum.

Daly, M., & Wilson, M. (1982). Whom are newborn babies said to resemble? *Ethology and Sociobiology, 3,* 69–78.

Daly, M., & Wilson, M. (1984). A sociobiological analysis of human infanticide. In G. Hausfater & S. Hrdy (Eds.), *Infanticide: Comparative and evolutionary perspectives* (pp. 487–505). New York: Aldine.

Daly, M., & Wilson, M. (1985). Child abuse and other risks of not living with both parents. *Ethology and Sociobiology, 6,* 197–210.

Daly, M., & Wilson, M. (1988a). Evolutionary social psychology and family homicide. *Science, 242,* 519–524.

Daly, M., & Wilson, M. (1988b). *Homicide.* Chicago: Aldine deGruyter.

Daly, M., & Wilson, M. (1995). Discriminative parental solicitude and the relevance of evolutionary models to the analysis of motivational systems. In M. Gazzaniga (Ed.), *The cognitive neurosciences* (pp. 1269–1286). Cambridge, MA: MIT Press.

Daly, M., & Wilson, M. (1998). *The truth about Cinderella: A Darwinian view of parental love.* New Haven, CT: Yale University Press.

Daly, M., & Wilson, M. (2001). An assessment of some proposed exceptions to the phenomenon of nepotistic discrimination against stepchildren. *Annales Zoologici Fennici, 38,* 287–296.

Daly, M., Wilson, M., & Weghorst, S. J. (1982). Male sexual jealousy. *Ethology and Sociobiology, 3,* 11–27.

Darwin, C. R. (1859). *On the origin of species.* London: John Murray.

Dawkins, R. (1976). *The selfish gene.* Oxford, England: Oxford University Press.

Dawkins, R. (1979). Twelve misunderstandings of kin selection. *Zeitschrift fur Tierpsychologie, 51,* 184–200.

Dawkins, R. (1982). *The extended phenotype.* Oxford, England: Oxford University Press.

Dawkins, R. (1989). *The selfish gene, new edition.* Oxford, England: Oxford University Press.

DeBruine, L. M. (2002). Facial resemblance enhances trust. *Proceedings of the Royal Society of London. Series B, Biological Sciences, 269,* 1307–1312.

Dewey, J. O. (1991). *Animal architecture.* New York: Orchard.

Dickinson, J. L., & Koenig, W. D. (2003). Desperately seeking similarity. *Science, 300,* 1887–1889.

Eshel, I., & Feldman, M. W. (1991). The handicap principle in parent-offspring conflict: Comparison of optimality and population-genetic analyses. *American Naturalist, 137,* 167–185.

Essock-Vitale, S., & McGuire, M. (1985). Women's lives viewed from an evolutionary perspective. II. Patterns of helping. *Ethology and Sociobiology, 6,* 155–173.

Euler, H., & Weitzel, B. (1996). Discriminative grandparental solicitude as reproductive strategy. *Human Nature, 7,* 39–59.

Fagen, R. M. (1976). Three-generation family conflict. *Animal Behaviour, 24,* 874–879.

Fehr, E., & Gächter, S. (2002). Altruistic punishment in humans. *Nature, 415,* 137–140.

Fehr, E., & Fischbacher, U. (in press). The nature of human altruism: Proximate patterns and evolutionary origins. *Nature.*

Feldman, M. W., & Eshel, I. (1982). On the theory of parent-offspring conflict: A two-locus model. *American Naturalist, 119,* 285–292.

Fischer, C. S. (1982). *To dwell among friends: Personal networks in town and city.* Chicago: University of Chicago Press.

Fisher, R. A. (1958). *The genetical theory of natural selection* (2nd ed.). New York: Dover.

Frank, S. A. (1998). *Foundations of social evolution.* Princeton, NJ: Princeton University.

Freud, S. (1930). *Civilization and its discontents.* London: Hogarth Press.

Gaulin, S. J. C., & McBurney, D. H. (2001). *Psychology: An evolutionary approach.* Upper Saddle River, NJ: Prentice-Hall.

Gaulin, S. J. C., McBurney, D. H., & Brakeman-Wartell, S. (1997). Matrilateral biases in the investment of aunts and uncles: A consequence and measure of paternity uncertainty. *Human Nature, 8,* 139–151.

Gintis, H. (2000). Strong reciprocity and human sociality. *Journal of Theoretical Biology, 206,* 169–179.

Godfray, H. C. J. (1991). The signalling of need by offspring to their parents. *Nature, 352,* 328–330.

Godfray, H. C. J. (1995a). Evolutionary theory of parent-offspring conflict. *Nature, 376,* 133–138.

Godfray, H. C. J. (1995b). Signalling of need between parents and young: Parent-offspring conflict and sibling rivalry. *American Naturalist, 146,* 1–24.

Godfray, H. C. J. (1999). Parent-offspring conflict. In L. Keller (Ed.), *Levels of selection in evolution* (pp. 100–120). Princeton, NJ: Princeton University Press.

Godfray, H. C. J., Harvey, P. H., & Partridge, L. (1991). Clutch size. *Annual Review of Ecology and Systematics, 22,* 409–429.

Godfray, H. C. J., & Johnstone, R. A. (2000). Begging and bleating: The evolution of parent-offspring signalling. *Philosophical Transactions of the Royal Society, London, B., 355,* 1581–1591.

Godfray, H. C. J., & Parker, G. A. (1992). Sibling competition, parent-offspring conflict and clutch size. *Animal Behaviour, 43,* 473–490.

Grafen, A. (1982). How not to measure inclusive fitness. *Nature, 298,* 425–426.

Grafen, A. (1984). Natural selection, kin selection and group selection. In J. R. Krebs & N. B. Davies (Eds.), *Behavioral ecology: An evolutionary approach* (2nd ed., pp. 62–84). Sunderland, MA: Sinauer.

Grafen, A. (1990a). Biological signals as handicaps. *Journal of Theoretical Biology, 144,* 517–546.

Grafen, A. (1990b). Sexual selection unhandicapped by the Fisher process. *Journal of Theoretical Biology, 144*, 473–516.

Grafen, A. (1991). Modelling in behavioural ecology. In J. R. Krebs & N. B. Davies (Eds.), *Behavioral ecology: An evolutionary approach* (3rd ed., pp. 5–31). Sunderland, MA: Sinauer.

Gurven, M. (2000). "It's a Wonderful Life": Signaling generosity among the Ache of Paraguay. *Evolution and Human Behavior, 21*, 263–282.

Hagen, E. (1999). The functions of post-partum depression. *Evolution and Human Behavior, 20*, 325–359.

Haig, D. (1993). Genetic conflicts in human pregnancy. *Quarterly Review of Biology, 68*, 495–532.

Hames, R. (1987). Garden labor exchange among the Ye'kwana. *Ethology and Sociobiology, 8*, 259–284.

Hamilton, W. D. (1963). The evolution of altruistic behaviour. *American Naturalist, 97*, 354–356.

Hamilton, W. D. (1964). The genetical evolution of social behaviour. *Journal of Theoretical Biology, 7*, 1–52.

Hamilton, W. D. (1970). Selfish and spiteful behavior in an evolutionary model. *Nature, 228*, 1218–1220.

Hansell, M. H. (1984). *Animal architecture and building behavior.* London: Longman.

Harpending, H. C. (1979). The population genetics of interaction. *American Naturalist, 113*, 622–630.

Harper, A. B. (1986). The evolution of begging: Sibling competition and parent-offspring conflict. *American Naturalist, 128*, 99–114.

Harris, C. R. (2000). Psychophysiological response to imagined infidelity: The specific innate modular view of jealousy reconsidered. *Journal of Personality and Social Psychology, 78*, 1082–1091.

Hartung, J. (1977). An implication about human mating systems. *Journal of Theoretical Biology, 66*, 737–745.

Hartung, J. (1985). Matrilineal inheritance: New theory and analysis. *Behavioral and Brain Sciences, 8*, 661–688.

Hawkes, K. (1983). Kin selection and culture. *American Ethnologist, 10*, 346–363.

Hawkes, K., O'Connell, J. F., & Blurton Jones, N. G. (1989). Hardworking Hadza grandmothers. In V. Standen & R. Foley (Eds.), *Comparative socioecology: The behavioural ecology of humans and other mammals* (pp. 341–366). Oxford, England: Blackwell.

Hawkes, K., O'Connell, J. F., & Blurton Jones, N. G. (1997). Hadza women time allocation, offspring provisioning, and the evolution of post-menopausal life spans. *Current Anthropology, 38*, 551–578.

Hawkes, K., O'Connell, J. F., & Blurton Jones, N. G. (2001). Hadza meat sharing. *Evolution and Human Behavior, 22*, 113–142.

Hawkes, K., O'Connell, J. F., Blurton Jones, N. G., Alvarez, H., & Charnov, E. L. (1998). Grandmothering, menopause, and the evolution of human life histories. *Proceedings of the National Academy of Sciences of the United States of America, 95*, 1336–1339.

Holmes, W. G., & Sherman, P. W. (1983). Kin recognition in animals. *The American Scientist, 71*, 46–55.

Horan, D. J., & Delahoyde, M. (1982). *Infanticide and the handicapped newborn.* Provo: Brigham Young University Press.

Howell, N. (1979). *Demography of the Dobe !Kung.* New York: Academic Press.

Jankowiak, W., & Diderich, M. (2000). Sibling solidarity in a polygamous community in the USA: Unpacking inclusive fitness. *Evolution and Human Behavior, 21*, 125–139.

Johnstone, R. A., & Grafen, A. (1993). The continuous Sir Philip Sidney Game: A simple model of biological signalling. *Journal of Theoretical Biology, 156*, 215–234.

Johnstone, R. A., & Grafen, A. (1993). Dishonesty and the handicap principle. *Animal Behaviour, 46*, 759–764.

Jones, D. (2000). Group nepotism and human kinship. *Current Anthropology, 41*, 779–809.

Judge, D. S., & Hrdy, S. B. (1992). Allocation of accumulated resources among close kin: Inheritance in Sacramento, California, 1890–1984. *Ethology and Sociobiology, 13*, 495–522.

Kaplan, H., & Hill, K. (1985). Food sharing among Ache foragers: Tests of explanatory hypotheses. *Current Anthropology, 26*, 233–245.

Keller, L., & Ross, K. G. (1998). Selfish genes: A green beard in the red fire ant. *Nature, 394*, 573–575.

Kilner, R., & Johnstone, R. A. (1997). Begging the question: Are offspring solicitation behaviors signals of need? *Trends in Ecology and Evolution, 12*, 11–15.

Korchmaros, J. D., & Kenny, D. A. (2001). Emotional closeness as a mediator of the effect of genetic relatedness on altruism. *Psychological Science, 12*, 262–265.

Krebs, J. R. (1978). Optimal foraging. In J. R. Krebs & N. B. Davies (Eds.), *Behavioural ecology: An evolutionary approach* (pp. 23–63). Oxford, England: Blackwell.

Krebs, J. R., & Davies, N. B. (1993). *An introduction to behavioural ecology.* Sunderland, MA: Sinauer.

Krieger, M. J. B., & Ross, K. G. (2002). Identification of a major gene regulating complex social behavior. *Science, 295,* 328–332.

Kruger, D. J. (2003). Evolution and altruism: Combining psychological mediators with naturally selected tendencies. *Evolution and Human Behavior, 24,* 118–125.

Kurland, J. A. (1977). Kin selection in the Japanese monkey. *Contributions to Primatology, 12,* 1–145. Basel, Switzerland: Karger.

Kurland, J. A. (1979). Paternity, mother's brother and human sociality. In N. Chagnon & W. Irons (Eds.), *Evolutionary biology and human social behavior* (pp. 145–180). North Scituate, MA: Duxbury.

Kurland, J. A., & Gaulin, S. J. C. (1979). Testing kin selection: Problems with r. *Behavioral Ecology and Sociobiology, 6,* 81–82.

Kurland, J. A., & Gaulin, S. J. C. (1984). The evolution of male parental investment: Effects of genetic relatedness and feeding ecology on the allocation of reproductive effort. In D. M. Taub (Ed.), *Primate paternalism* (pp. 259–308). New York: Van Nostrand Reinhold.

Kurland, J. A., & Sparks, C. S. (2003, June). *Is there a Paleolithic demography: Implications for evolutionary psychology and sociobiology.* Paper presented at the 15th annual meeting of the Human Behavior and Evolution Society Meetings, Lincoln, NE.

Lachmann, M., & Bergstrom, C. (1998). Signalling among relatives: II. Beyond the Tower of Babel. *Journal of Theoretical Population Biology, 54,* 146–160.

Laing, R. D. (1971). *The politics of the family and other essays.* London: Tavistock Publications.

Lehmann, L., & Perrin, N. (2002). Altruism, dispersal and phenotypic-matching kin recognition. *American Naturalist, 159,* 452–468.

Lightcap, J. L., Kurland, J. A., & Burgess, R. L. (1982). Child abuse: A test of some predictions from evolutionary theory. *Ethology and Sociobiology, 3,* 61–67.

Littlefield, C. H., & Rushton, J. P. (1986). When a child dies: The sociobiology of bereavement. *Journal of Personality and Social Psychology, 51,* 797–802.

Lowie, R. H. (1948). *Social organization.* New York: Rinehart.

MacNair, M. R., & Parker, G. A. (1978). Models of parent-offspring conflict: 2. Promiscuity. *Animal Behaviour, 26,* 111–122.

MacNair, M. R., & Parker, G. A. (1979). Models of parent-offspring conflict: 3. Intra-brood conflict. *Animal Behaviour, 27,* 1202–1209.

Maynard Smith, J. (1974). The theory of games and the evolution of animal conflicts. *Journal of Theoretical Biology, 47,* 209–221.

McBurney, D., Simon, J., Gaulin, S. J. C., & Geliebter, A. (2002). Matrilateral biases in the investment of aunts and uncles: Replication in a population presumed to have high paternity certainty. *Human Nature, 13,* 391–401.

McClain, P. W., Sacks, J. J., Froehlke, R. G., & Ewigman, B. G. (1993). Estimates of fatal child abuse and neglect, United States, 1979 through 1988. *Pediatrics, 91,* 338–343.

McLain, D. K., Setters, D., Moulton, M. P., & Pratt, A. E. (2000). Ascription of resemblance of newborns. *Evolution and Human Behavior, 21,* 11–23.

Metcalf, R. A., & Stamps, J. A. (1979). Parent-offspring conflict that is not limited by degree of kinship. *Journal of Theoretical Biology, 76,* 99–107.

Michod, R. E., & Hamilton, W. D. (1980). Coefficients of relatedness in sociobiology. *Nature, 288,* 694–697.

Mock, D. W. (1987). Siblicide, parent-offspring conflict and unequal parental investment by egrets and herons. *Behavioral Ecology and Sociobiology, 20,* 247–256.

Mock, D. W., & Forbes, L. S. (1992). Parent-offspring conflict: A case of arrested development. *Trends in Ecology and Evolution, 7,* 409–413.

Mock, D. W., & Parker, G. A. (1997). *The evolution of sibling rivalry.* Oxford, England: Oxford University Press.

Morgan, C. (1979). Eskimo hunting groups, social kinship and the possibility of kin selection in humans. *Ethology and Sociobiology, 1,* 83–86.

Murdock, G. P. (1949). *Social structure.* New York: Macmillan.

Nakamura, R. R. (1980). Plant kin selection. *Evolutionary Theory, 5,* 113–117.

Nesse, R. (1990). Evolutionary explanations of emotions. *Human Nature, 1,* 261–289.

Nesse, R., Silverman, A., & Bortz, A. (1990). Sex differences in ability to recognize family resemblance. *Ethology and Sociobiology, 11,* 11–21.

Overpeck, M. D., Brenner, R. A., Trumble, A. C., Trifiletti, L. B., & Berendes, H. W. (1998). Risk factors for infant homicide in the United States. *New England Journal of Medicine, 339,* 1211–1216.

Paffenberg, R. S., & McCabe, L. J. (1966). The effect of obstetric and perinatal events on risk of mental illness in women of childbearing age. *American Journal of Public Health, 56,* 400–407.

Pagel, M. (1997). Desperately concealing father: A theory of parent-infant resemblance. *Animal Behavior, 53,* 973–981.

Parker, G. A., & MacNair, M. R. (1978). Models of parent-offspring conflict: 1. Monogamy. *Animal Behaviour, 26,* 97–110.

Parker, G. A., & MacNair, M. R. (1979). Models of parent-offspring conflict: 4. Suppression: Evolutionary retaliation by the parent. *Animal Behaviour, 27,* 1210–1235.

Parker, G. A., Royle, N. J., & Hartley, I. R. (2002). Intrafamilial conflict and parental investment: A synthesis. *Philosophical Transactions of the Royal Society, London, B., 357,* 295–307.

Partridge, L., & Nunney, L. (1977). Three-generation family conflict. *Animal Behaviour, 25,* 785–786.

Pashos, A. (2000). Does paternity uncertainty explain discriminative grandparental solicitude? A cross-cultural study in Greece and Germany. *Evolution and Human Behavior, 21,* 97–109.

Pietrzak, R. H., Laird, J. D., Stevens, D. A., & Thompson, N. S. (2002). Sex differences in human jealousy: A coordinated study of forced-choice, continuous rating-scale and physiological responses on the same subjects. *Evolution and Human Behavior, 23,* 83–94.

Platek, S. M. (2003, June). *Paternal uncertainty, the brain, and children's faces: Neural correlates of child facial resemblance.* Paper presented at the 15th annual meeting of the Human Behavior and Evolution Society, Lincoln, NE.

Platek, S. M., Burch, R. L., Panyavin, I. S., Wasserman, B. H., & Gallup, G. G. (2002). Reactions to Children's faces: Resemblance affects males more than females. *Evolution and Human Behavior, 23,* 159–166.

Platek, S. M., Critton, S. R., Burch, R. L., Frederick, D. A., Myers, T. E., & Gallup, G. G. (2003). How much paternal resemblance is enough? Sex differences in hypothetical investment decisions but not in the detection of resemblance. *Evolution and Human Behavior, 24,* 81–87.

Plutchik, R. (1980). A general psychoevolutionary theory of emotion. In R. Plutchik & H. Kellerman (Eds.), *Emotion: Theory, research and experience: Vol. 1. Theories of emotion* (pp. 3–24). New York: Academic Press.

Porter, R. H., & Moore, J. D. (1981). Human kin recognition by olfactory cues. *Physiology and Behavior, 27,* 493–495.

Queller, D. C. (1983). Kin selection and conflict in seed maturation. *Journal of Theoretical Biology, 100,* 153–172.

Queller, D. C., Ponte, E., Bozzaro, S., & Strassmann, J. E. (2003). Single-gene greenbeard effects in the social amoeba *Dictyostelium discoideum. Science, 299,* 105–106.

Regalski, J., & Gaulin, S. J. C. (1993). Whom are Mexican infants said to resemble? Monitoring and fostering paternal confidence in the Yucatan. *Ethology and Sociobiology, 14,* 97–113.

Reeve, H. K., & Keller, L. (1999). Levels of selection. In L. Keller (Ed.), *Levels of selection in evolution* (pp. 3–14). Princeton, NJ: Princeton University Press.

Rodríguez-Gironés, M. A. (1999). Sibling competition stabilizes signalling resolution models of parent-offspring models. *Philosophical Transactions of the Royal Society, London, B., 266,* 2399–2402.

Rodríguez-Gironés, M. A., Cotton, P. A., & Kacelnik, A. (1996). The evolution of begging: Signaling and sibling competition. *Proceedings of the National Academy of Sciences of the United States of America, 93,* 14637–14641.

Rogers, A. (1993). Why menopause? *Evolutionary Ecology, 7,* 406–420.

Rogers, A. (2003). *The extended post-reproductive life-span: Why humans have it and chimpanzees don't.* Paper presented at the Luce Conference on Evolutionary Models of Economic and Social Behavior, April 11–13, State College, PA.

Rushton, J. P., Russell, R. J. H., & Wells, P. A. (1984). Genetic similarity theory: Beyond kin selection. *Behavior Genetics, 14,* 179–193.

Sahlins, M. (1977). *The use and abuse of biology: An anthropological critique of sociobiology.* Chicago: University of Chicago Press.

Schoener, T. W. (1971). Theory of feeding strategies. *Annual Review of Ecology and Systematics, 2,* 369–404.

Schwabl, H., Mock, D. W., & Gieg, J. A. (1997). A hormonal mechanism for parental favouritism. *Nature, 386,* 231.

Segal, N. (1984). Cooperation, competition and altruism within twin sets: A reappraisal. *Ethology and Sociobiology, 5,* 163–177.

Shavit, Y., Fischer, C. S., & Koresh, Y. (1994). Kin and nonkin under collective threat: Israeli networks during the Gulf War. *Social Forces, 72,* 1197–1215.

Sinervo, B., & Clobert, J. (2003). Morphs, dispersal behavior, genetic similarity and the evolution of cooperation. *Science, 300,* 1949–1951.

Smith, M. S., Kish, B. J., & Crawford, C. B. (1987). Inheritance of wealth as human kin investment. *Ethology and Sociobiology, 8,* 171–182.

Spinelli, M. G. (2003). *Infanticide: Psychosocial and legal perspectives on mothers who kill.* Washington, DC: American Psychiatric Publishing.

Stamps, J. A., Metcalf, R. A., & Krishnan, V. V. (1978). A genetic analysis of parent-offspring conflict. *Behavioural Ecology and Sociobiology, 3,* 369–392.

Sulloway, F. J. (1995). Birth order and evolutionary psychology: A meta-analytic overview. *Psychological Inquiry, 6,* 75–80.

Tooby, J., & Cosmides, L. (1990). The past explains the present: Emotional adaptations and the structure of ancestral environments. *Ethology and Sociobiology, 11,* 375–424.

Tooby, J., & DeVore, I. (1987). The reconstruction of hominid behavioral evolution through strategic modeling. In W. Kinzey (Ed.), *Primate models for the origin of human behavior.* New York: SUNY Press.

Trivers, R. L. (1971). The evolution of reciprocal altruism. *Quarterly Review of Biology, 46,* 35–57.

Trivers, R. L. (1972). Parental investment and sexual selection. In B. G. Campbell (Ed.), *Sexual selection and the descent of man, 1871–1971* (pp. 136–179). Chicago: Aldine Publishing Company.

Trivers, R. L. (1974). Parent-offspring conflict. *The American Zoologist, 14,* 249–264.

Trivers, R. L., & Willard, D. E. (1973). Natural selection of parental ability to vary the sex ratio of offspring. *Science, 179,* 90–92.

Turke, P. (1988). Helpers at the nest: Childcare networks on Ifaluk. In L. Betzig, M. Borgerhoff Mulder, & P. Turke (Eds.), *Human reproductive behavior: A Darwinian perspective* (pp. 173–188). Cambridge, England: Cambridge University Press.

von Frisch, K. (1983). *Animal architecture.* New York: Van Nostrand Reinhold.

Webster, G. D. (2003). Prosocial behavior in families: Moderators of resource sharing. *Journal of Experimental Social Psychology, 39,* 644–652.

West, S. A., Murray, M. G., Machado, C. A., Griffin, A. S., & Herre, E. A. (2001). Testing Hamilton's rule with competition between relatives. *Nature, 409,* 510–512.

West, S. A., Pen, I. I., & Griffin, A. S. (2002). Cooperation and competition between relatives. *Science, 296,* 72–75.

Williamson, L. (1978). Infanticide: An anthropological analysis. In M. Kohl (Ed.), *Infanticide and the value of life* (pp. 61–75). Buffalo, NY: Prometheus.

Wilson, E. O. (1975). *Sociobiology: The new synthesis.* Cambridge, MA: The Belknap Press of Harvard University.

Yamamura, N., & Higashi, M. (1992). An evolutionary theory of conflict resolution between relatives: Altruism, manipulation and compromise. *Evolution, 46,* 1236–1239.

Zahavi, A. (1975). Mate selection: A selection for a handicap. *Journal of Theoretical Biology, 53,* 205–214.

Zahavi, A. (1977). Reliability in communication systems and the evolution of altruism. In B. Stonehouse & C. Perrins (Eds.), *Evolutionary ecology* (pp. 253–259). Baltimore: University Park Press.

Zahavi, A., & Zahavi, A. (1997). *The handicap principle: A missing piece of Darwin's puzzle.* Oxford, England: Oxford University Press.

CHAPTER 16

Evolution of Paternal Investment

DAVID C. GEARY

R EPRODUCTION INVOLVES TRADE-OFFS between mating and parenting (Trivers, 1972; Williams, 1966) and attendant conflicts between males and females and parents and offspring (Hager & Johnstone, 2003; Trivers, 1974). Conflicts arise because the ways in which each sex and each parent distribute limited reproductive resources is not always in the best interest of the other sex or offspring. Still, males and females have overlapping interests, as do parents and offspring; thus the evolution and proximate expression of reproductive effort reflects a coevolving compromise between the best interest of the two sexes and of parents and offspring. For the majority of species, males invest more in mating (typically competition for access to reproductive females) than in parenting, and females invest more in parenting than in mating (Andersson, 1994; Darwin, 1871), although there are readily understandable exceptions (Reynolds & Székely, 1997). Females benefit from male-male competition and the male focus on mating because their offspring are sired by the most fit males, and successful males benefit because they produce more offspring by competing for access to multiple mates than by investing in parenting. The basic pattern is especially pronounced in mammals, where male parenting is found in less than 5% of species and where females invest heavily in offspring (Clutton-Brock, 1991). The reasons for the large mammalian sex difference are related to the biology of internal gestation and obligatory postpartum suckling and the associated sex differences in the opportunity and potential benefits of seeking multiple mating partners (Clutton-Brock & Vincent, 1991; Trivers, 1972).

Given this, the phenomenon of human paternal investment is extraordinary and the focus of this chapter (see also Draper & Harpending, 1988; Flinn & Low, 1986; Geary, 2000; Geary & Flinn, 2001; Marlowe, 2000). Human paternal investment is considered in terms of the benefits of providing care to children and the costs of investment from the males' perspective, as well as cost-benefit trade-offs from the females' perspective. In the first section, I provide an introduction to these trade-offs in nonhuman species and discuss them in relation to human paternal investment in the second section. In the third section, I discuss the proximate correlates of men's parenting, and the final section focuses on their potential ultimate correlates.

PARENTAL INVESTMENT

Parents invest in offspring indirectly and directly (Qvarnström & Price, 2001). Indirect investment is genetic inheritance, although the quality of this investment (e.g., as it affects growth rate) often varies from one parent to the next (Savalli & Fox, 1998). Direct investment involves providing offspring with nutrients during gestation or egg production and postnatally, as well as protecting them from predators (Clutton-Brock, 1991). For highly social species, direct investment can also involve assistance in establishing position in the social hierarchy and navigating social discourse (Alberts & Altmann, 1995; Buchan, Alberts, Silk, & Altmann, 2003). Separating the effects of direct from indirect parental investment is complicated by potential interactions between genetic and environmental influences on offspring. Indirect, genetic influences can, for instance, affect the traits of offspring and thus the quantity and quality of direct investment provided by parents (Moore, Wolf, & Brodie, 1998).

The details of these potential genotype-environment interactions are not well understood; thus my discussion of direct parental effects must be tempered by the possibility of indirect effects. Despite these complications, parenting is generally associated with lower offspring mortality due to protection from predators and conspecifics (i.e., member of the same species) and parental provisioning (Clutton-Brock, 1991). The result is healthier adults that are better able to compete for mates and that produce larger and healthier offspring themselves (Clutton-Brock, Albon, & Guinness, 1988). In short, parents pay the cost of investing in offspring because these offspring are more likely to survive and reproduce than are offspring that receive reduced or no direct parental investment.

PATERNAL INVESTMENT

Although uncommon in mammals, paternal investment is found in many species of bird and fish and in some species of insect (Perrone & Zaret, 1979; Thornhill, 1976; Wolf, Ketterson, & Nolan, 1988). The study of the attendant cost-benefit trade-offs is complicated by the evolutionary history of the species, as well as by whether paternal investment is *obligate* or *facultatively* expressed (Arnold & Owens, 2002; Clutton-Brock, 1991; Fishman, Stone, & Lotem, 2003). Obligate investment means that male care is necessary for the survival of his offspring. In these species, selection favors males who invest in offspring and could eventually result in males showing high levels of paternal investment, independent of proximate conditions (Westneat & Sherman, 1993).

Human paternal investment and that of many other species is facultatively expressed; that is, it is not always necessary for offspring survival and thus can vary with proximate conditions (Westneat & Sherman, 1993). The facultative expression of paternal investment is typically found when there is a high degree of paternity certainty, when investment improves offspring survival rates, and when it does not severely restrict opportunities to mate with multiple females (Birkhead & Møller, 1996; Møller & Cuervo, 2000; Perrone & Zaret, 1979; Trivers, 1972). The facultative expression of male parenting thus reflects trade-offs between the costs and benefits of this direct investment in the social and ecological contexts in which the male is situated.

TRADE-OFFS

Male parenting in fish species is typically associated with external fertilization and male defense of nesting sites to exclude competitors (Perrone & Zaret, 1979). Under these conditions, paternal certainty is high. Males are also able to fertilize the eggs of more than one female; thus investment does not reduce mating opportunities. In contrast, paternal investment is uncommon in fish species with internal fertilization, presumably because paternity is not certain and because males can abandon females after fertilization and avoid the cost of investment.

Paternal investment does occur in some species with internal fertilization, including most species of bird and a few mammals, mostly carnivores and some primates (Dunbar, 1995; Mock & Fujioka, 1990). Again, the degree of paternal investment varies with potential benefits to offspring, paternity certainty, and availability of other mates. The former benefit of paternal investment has been demonstrated by removing fathers from nests, which results in lower offspring survival rates. In an analysis across 31 bird species, Møller (2000) determined that 34% of the variability in offspring survival was due to paternal investment. In some species, removal of the male results in the death of all nestlings (obligate investment); in other species, male removal has lesser effects, as females compensate for lost provisions (facultative investment).

As noted, variability in male provisioning is related to the likelihood of paternity (Arnold & Owens, 2002; Møller, 2000). For many species, female cuckoldry of their social partner involves trade-offs between the risk of losing his investment and gaining better genes and thus healthier offspring from another male (Møller & Tegelström, 1997). In species in which male investment is obligate, cuckoldry rates are very low; that is, females do not risk losing paternal investment (Birkhead & Møller, 1996). For species in which male investment is not obligate, cuckoldry rates vary with male quality; females often risk loss of male investment and copulate with healthier males if they are paired with low-quality males (Møller & Tegelström, 1997). These cross-species relations have been supported by some (Dixon, Ross, O'Malley, & Burke, 1994; Sheldon, Räsänen, & Dias, 1997), but not all (Kempenaers, Lanctot, & Robertson, 1998) studies of the within-species relation between paternal investment and extra-pair paternity. Some of the inconsistencies may be related to the ability of males to detect their partner's extra-pair copulations or extra-pair paternity of offspring (Neff & Sherman, 2002). Ewen and Armstrong (2000) studied this relation in the socially monogamous stitchbird (*Notiomystis cincta*); males provide between 16% and 32% of the food to the nestlings, depending on age of the brood. Extra-pair copulations occur in the pair's territory and are thus easily monitored by the male. Males counter this paternity threat by chasing off extra-pair males. Despite this male strategy, extra-pair copulations do occur. In this study, as the frequency of female extra-pair copulations increased, male provisioning of the brood decreased ($r = -.72$).

Neff (2003) studied these relations in the bluegill sunfish (*Lepomis macrochirus*), where parental males defend a territory, externally fertilize, and then fan and protect eggs. One type of cuckolder male hides behind rocks or plants and attempts to sneak into the nest to fertilize the eggs. Before the eggs hatch, threats to paternity can thus be determined by presence or absence of cuckolder males. After the eggs hatch, parental males can determine paternity based on olfactory cues from fry urine. As predicted, parental males reduced fanning and protecting of eggs if cuckolder males were present. Once the fry hatched and parental males could determine paternity, they protected them only if they were the father, whether or not cuckolder males were present before the fry hatched. This and other well-controlled studies (Ewen & Armstrong, 2000) suggest that when males detect nonpaternity risks, they reduce their level of paternal investment and often do so in direct relation to the magnitude of the risk (Møller, 2000). However, provisioning and protecting offspring are not always parental investment, as male provisioning is sometimes related to mating effort, specifically, to obtain sexual access to the offspring's mother (Rohwer, Herron, & Daly, 1999; Smuts & Gubernick, 1992).

In any case, paternity certainty and an improvement in the survival rate of his offspring are not sufficient for the evolution or facultative expression of paternal investment. The benefits of paternal investment must also be greater than the benefits of siring offspring with more than one female (Dunbar, 1995). For instance, social monogamy and high levels of paternal investment are common in *canids* (e.g., coyotes, *Canis latrens*), who tend to have large litters (Asa & Valdespino, 1998). Large litter sizes, prolonged offspring dependency, and the ability of the male to provide food during this dependency result in *canid* males being able to sire more offspring with a monogamous, high parental investment strategy than with a polygynous strategy. Paternal investment might also evolve if females are ecologically dispersed, and thus males do not have the opportunity to pursue multiple mating partners, as with *callitrichid* monkeys such as marmosets (*Callithrix*; Dunbar, 1995). In these species, paternal investment is related to male-female joint defense of a defined territory, which limits the male's ability to expand his territory to include other females; female-on-female aggression that prevents males from forming harems; concealed ovulation, which prolongs the pairs' relationship to ensure conception; and females often having twins, which increases the benefits of paternal care.

INTEGRATION

The patterns associated with the facultative expression of paternal investment are described in Table 16.1. Male's reproductive behavior is especially complicated when paternal investment improves offspring survival rate and offspring quality and when the reproductive benefits of seeking additional mates do not always outweigh the reproductive benefits of paternal investment. These dynamics appear to parallel those found in humans. Under these conditions, selection will favor a mixed reproductive strategy, with different males varying in their emphasis on mating and parenting and individual males varying in emphasis on mating and parenting in their relationship with different females. Individual differences in paternal investment, in turn, are likely to be related to male condition (e.g., social status), ecological factors (e.g., available mates), female strategies to induce paternal investment, female quality, and genetically based differences in male reproductive strategy (Krebs & Davies, 1993).

Table 16.1
Factors Associated with the Evolution and Facultative Expression
of Paternal Investment

Offspring Survival

1. If paternal investment has little or no effect on offspring survival rate or quality, selection will favor male abandonment if additional mates can be found (Trivers, 1972;
   Westneat & Sherman, 1993; Williams, 1966).
2. If paternal investment results in relative but not an absolute improvement in offspring
   survival rate or quality, selection will favor males that show a mixed reproductive
   strategy. Males can vary in degree of emphasis on mating and parenting, contingent
   on social (e.g., male status, availability of mates) and ecological (e.g., food availability) conditions (Westneat & Sherman, 1993; Wolf et al., 1988).

Mating Opportunities

1. If paternal investment is not obligate and mates are available, selection will favor:
   A. Male abandonment, if paternal investment has little effect on offspring survival
      rate and quality (Clutton-Brock, 1991).
   B. A mixed male reproductive strategy, if paternal investment improves offspring sur-
      vival rate and quality (Perrone & Zaret, 1979; Wolf et al., 1988).
2. Social and ecological factors that reduce the mating opportunities of males, such as
   dispersed females or concealed (or synchronized) ovulation, will reduce the opportunity cost of paternal investment. Under these conditions, selection will favor paternal
   investment, if this investment improves offspring survival rate or quality or does not
   otherwise induce heavy costs on the male (Clutton-Brock, 1991; Dunbar, 1995; Perrone & Zaret, 1979; Thornhill, 1976; Westneat & Sherman, 1993).

Paternity Certainty

1. If the certainty of paternity is low, selection will favor male abandonment (Clutton-
   Brock, 1991; Møller, 2000, Westneat & Sherman, 1993).
2. If the certainty of paternity is high, selection will favor paternal investment if:
   A. Investment improves offspring survival or quality, and
   B. The opportunity costs of investment (i.e., reduced mating opportunities) are lower
      than the benefits associated with investment (Dunbar, 1995; Thornhill, 1976;
      Westneat & Sherman, 1993).
3. If the certainty of paternity is high and the opportunity costs, in terms of lost mating
   opportunities, are high, selection will favor males with a mixed reproductive strategy,
   that is, the facultative expression of paternal investment, contingent on social and
   ecological conditions (Dunbar, 1995; Westneat & Sherman, 1993).

Adapted from "Evolution and Proximate Expression of Human Paternal Investment," by D. C.
Geary, 2000, *Psychological Bulletin, 126,* p. 60. Copyright 2000 by the American Psychological
Association. Reprinted with permission.

HUMAN PATERNAL INVESTMENT

The evolution and maintenance of human paternal investment must involve trade-
offs between benefits to children, paternity certainty, and lost mating opportunities. The relation between paternal investment and the well-being of children is
reviewed in the first subsection, whereas paternity certainty and the reproductive strategies of women and associated mating opportunities of men are reviewed in the second subsection.

Physical and Social Well-Being of Children

As noted in Table 16.1, to evolve, human paternal investment and its facultative expression must reduce child mortality rates or improve in child quality (e.g., as it enhances their social competitiveness). Support is found in the relation between paternal investment and children's well-being in extant populations and the historical record (Hill & Hurtado, 1996; Richner, Christe, & Oppliger, 1995; Schultz, 1991).

Physical Well-Being   In traditional and developing societies and in the historical record, there is a consistent relation between paternal investment and children's mortality rates, but a strong causal relation cannot be drawn. First, higher quality men are typically paired with higher quality (e.g., better gatherers) women (Blurton Jones, Hawkes, & O'Connell, 1997); thus the higher survival rates of their children cannot be attributed solely to men's parenting. Second, the interaction between indirect genetic and direct parental effects on children is not well understood (e.g., Caspi et al., 2002) and thus complicates the assessment of direct investment. Finally, men's parenting may at times be mating effort and is thus not paternal investment per se (Borgerhoff Mulder, 2000; Marlowe, 2000).

Despite these complications, men's providing of care, food, and other resources lowers infant and child mortality risks in some contexts and generally improves the physical health of children. In the hunter-gatherer Ache (Paraguay), about 1 of 3 children die before reaching the age of 15 years, with highly significant differences in mortality rates for father-present and father-absent children (Hill & Hurtado, 1996). Father absence triples the probability of child death due to illness and doubles the risk of the child being killed by other Ache. Overall, father absence at any point prior to the child's 15th birthday is associated with a mortality rate of more than 45%, as compared to a mortality rate of about 20% for children whose father resides with them until their 15th birthday.

There is a consistent relation between marital status and infant and child mortality rates in developing countries. "Both univariate and multivariate results show that mortality of children is raised if the woman is not currently married, if she has married more than once or if she is in a polygamous union. . . . Overall, it appears that there is a strong, direct association between stable family relationships and low levels of child mortality, although the direction of causation cannot be inferred from the data" (United Nations, 1985, p. 227). The same pattern was found throughout preindustrial and industrializing Europe and the United States (Herlihy, 1965; Klindworth & Voland, 1995; Morrison, Kirshner, & Molho, 1977; Schultz, 1991). In an analysis of demographic records from eighteenth century Berlin, Schultz found a strong correlation ($r = .74$) between socioeconomic status (SES, a composite of income, educational level, and occupational status) and infant and child mortality rates; SES was defined in part by paternal occupation. During the 1437 to 1438 and 1449 to 1450 epidemics in Florence, Italy, child mortality rates increased 5- to 10-fold and varied inversely with SES (Morrison et al., 1977). In nineteenth century Sweden, infant mortality rates were 1½ to 3 times higher for children born to unmarried mothers than children born to married couples (Brändström, 1997).

An analysis of mortality risks in early twentieth century England and Wales suggested that "a child's chance of survival was strongly conditioned by . . . what job its father did" (A. Reid, 1997, p. 151). Children of professional fathers had a 54% lower mortality rate than children whose fathers were unskilled laborers. Even when SES, environment (urban versus agricultural setting), maternal age, and other factors were controlled, infants and young children of working mothers had a 34% higher mortality rate than did children whose mothers did not work because women married to men with a sufficient income often stayed home to breast-feed, which was associated with significantly lower infant mortality (Rollet, 1997). Resources provided by fathers also allowed the family to live in healthier environments and provide a more stable food supply, which contributed to the relation between SES and infant and child mortality rates (A. Reid, 1997). In keeping with paternal effects, within-family studies—which control for maternal and child characteristics—indicate increased infant and child mortality rates following paternal death in developing nations today and in preindustrial Europe (Klindworth & Voland, 1995; Kok, van Poppel, & Kruse, 1997; United Nations, 1985).

The relation between SES and the physical well-being of children is still found in industrial nations today (e.g., I. Reid, 1998), even with low infant and child mortality. Adler et al. (1994, p. 22) concluded that "individuals in lower social status groups have the highest rates of morbidity and mortality within most human populations. Moreover, studies of the entire SES hierarchy show that differences in social position relate to morbidity and mortality even at the upper levels of the hierarchy." The relation between SES and health holds for all members of the family and is not simply related to access to health care or to differences in health-related behaviors (e.g., smoking). In addition, SES appears to influence how well an individual is treated by other individuals and the degree to which he or she can control the activities of everyday life, which appear to influence physical health (Lachman & Weaver, 1998). Across industrial societies today, paternal income and occupational status are an important, and sometimes the sole, determinant of the family's SES and are thus correlated with the physical well-being of the children.

Social Well-Being   Because human paternal investment is not obligate, men have the option of focusing their reproductive energies on mating or on parenting. Given that some level of paternal investment is found in most human societies (Geary, 2000), it is almost certain that under some conditions, and at some point in our evolutionary past, men benefited by shifting some portion of reproductive effort from mating to parenting (Lovejoy, 1981). Men's parenting is, nonetheless, puzzling in contexts with low infant and child mortality rates. Under these conditions, selection should favor men who reduced or eliminated parenting in favor of mating. Evolutionary inertia is one potential reason for the continuation of paternal investment in these environments; specifically, it reflects selection for such investment in environments with high infant and child mortality. If so, then men may no longer experience benefits from paternal investment, and successful high-investment men may be disadvantaged in terms of lost mating opportunities. A second potential reason is that men's parenting provides social-competitive advantages to children; that is, it is designed to improve the "quality" of offspring (Davis & Daly, 1997). If so, then paternal investment should improve social competitiveness, and a smaller number of socially competitive children should result in reproductive advantages.

COMPETITIVENESS In industrial societies, one trait associated with social competitiveness is educational achievement, which is related to heritable individual differences in cognitive ability and to home environment (Cleveland, Jacobson, Lipinski, & Rowe, 2000; Geary, 2005). In these societies, paternal investment, including income provided to the family and direct care, is correlated with better academic skills in children and higher SES in adulthood (Kaplan, Lancaster, & Anderson, 1998; Pleck, 1997). However, a causal relation between paternal investment and these outcomes has not been established (Parke & Buriel, 1998). Indirect, genetic influences cannot be ruled out, nor can the effects of assortative mating. With respect to the latter, high investing men tend to marry women who are more competent, intelligent, and better educated and thus more effective parents than women married to lower investing men (Luster & Okagaki, 1993). Indeed, the strength of the relation between paternal characteristics and child outcomes is reduced considerably, once maternal characteristics are controlled (Amato, 1998). There are, however, unique relations between paternal investment and some child outcomes. Paternal investment of time (e.g., helping with homework) and income (e.g., for tutoring or college) is associated with upward social mobility of children, even when maternal characteristics (e.g., years of education) are controlled (Amato, 1998; Kaplan, Lancaster, Bock, & Johnson, 1995; Kaplan et al., 1998).

Moreover, withdrawal of paternal investment is correlated with decrements in children's later social success. In industrial societies, investment is typically reduced or withdrawn following divorce, and there are consistent differences in the social and educational competencies of children from divorced as compared to intact families, favoring the latter. However, causal relations are again difficult to determine. Many of the differences between children from divorced and intact families can be traced to differences in family functioning before the divorce (Cherlin et al., 1991; Furstenberg & Teitler, 1994). Still, some differences between children from intact and divorced families are found, after controlling for pre-divorce levels of family conflict and other confounding variables. It appears that divorce results in small to moderate increases in aggressive and noncompliant behaviors, especially in boys; an early onset of sexual activity for adolescent boys and girls; and lowered educational achievement in adulthood for men and women (Amato & Keith, 1991; Belsky, Steinberg, & Draper, 1991; Ellis et al., 2003; Florsheim, Tolan, & Gorman-Smith, 1998). These findings suggest paternal investment can improve children's later social competitiveness, given the strong relation between delayed sexual activity, educational outcomes, and later SES (Belsky et al., 1991; Parke & Buriel, 1998).

There is also evidence for direct paternal effects on the well-being of children (Parke, 1995; Pleck, 1997). Paternal involvement in play is associated with children's skill at regulating their emotional states and their later social competence. For instance, children who have fathers who regularly engage them in physical play are more likely to be socially popular than are children who do not regularly engage in this type of play (Carson, Burks, & Parke, 1993). Qualitative features of fathers' relationships with their children, such as positive emotional tone of the interactions, are also associated with greater social and academic competencies in children (Parke & Buriel, 1998) and with fewer behavioral (e.g., aggression) and psychological (e.g., depression) difficulties (Florsheim et al., 1998; Pleck, 1997).

Girls with a warm relationship with their father and a father who is highly invested in the family experience menarche later than do girls living in father-absent homes or with an emotionally distant father (Ellis, McFadyen-Ketchum, Dodge, Pettit, & Bates, 1999); high familial stress and presence of a stepfather or mother's boyfriend also contribute to early sexual maturation in girls (Ellis & Garber, 2000). Later sexual maturation should enable girls to acquire additional social-competitive competencies (e.g., more education) and thus greater ability to eventually invest in their children. The associated traits may also include competencies that support high cooperation with a spouse and thus high paternal investment in their children (MacDonald, 1992).

All of these relations are, however, confounded by genetic and child evocative effects and by the earlier mentioned maternal effects (Comings, Muhleman, Johnson, & MacMurray, 2002; Park & Buriel, 1998; Scarr & McCarthy, 1983). Motivated and intelligent children are more likely to receive education-related paternal investment than are other children (Kaplan et al., 1998), and even these effects might be due to shared genes (e.g., for intelligence). Genetic influences on personality traits, such as impulsivity, might contribute to the relation between parental divorce and children's later reproductive relationships, rather than simply the experience of parental conflict and divorce (McGue & Lykken, 1992). Studies that incorporate genetic influences, as well as simultaneously assessing maternal and paternal effects, are needed to more firmly establish a causal relation between paternal investment and child outcomes (Reiss, 1995).

SELECTION In industrial societies, a man's SES influences his mating options before marriage but is unrelated to reproductive success, due to socially imposed monogamy and birth control (Perusse, 1993). The finding that SES is unrelated to reproductive outcomes suggests that paternal investment in the competitiveness of children does not result in reproductive advantages. In fact, under these conditions, high levels of paternal investment might be associated with reproductive disadvantages due to the costs of investment. However, prior to the substantive reductions in infant and child mortality in Western culture, higher SES was associated with lower mortality, as described earlier.

When SES and social competitiveness reduce child mortality risks, paternal investment can be a viable strategy if it enables children to maintain or improve their SES and competitiveness in adulthood. Improved social competitiveness would enhance children's ability to acquire resources in adulthood (e.g., generating wealth), which would reduce the mortality risks of their children and the investor's grandchildren. Such investment would have been particularly advantageous in populations subject to frequent but unpredictable population crashes and when mortality varied inversely and strongly with SES, as it often did (Post, 1985). Because fluctuating mortality risks were unpredictable and disproportionately affected lower SES children, selection would have favored paternal investment that enabled their children to maintain or improve their later SES. To be effective, this investment would have to be provided even when current mortality risks are low.

Although not certain, the pattern suggests that paternal investment is an evolved reproductive strategy that enhances the physical well-being of children and their social competitiveness. In environments with intense social competition over scarce resources and with unpredictable mortality risks, paternal investment in children's social competitiveness is, in effect, insurance against unforeseen risks (Boone & Kessler, 1999; Geary, 2000; Geary & Flinn, 2001; Lancaster & Lancaster, 1987). Given the uneven distribution of social capital (e.g., intelligence) and wealth, not all men have the means to improve children's social competitiveness. And, some resource-holding men will invest in multiple wives rather than in their children's social competitiveness (Borgerhoff Mulder, 2000; Marlowe, 2000).

PATERNITY CERTAINTY AND WOMEN'S REPRODUCTIVE STRATEGIES

Men's parenting appears to reduce infant and child mortality risks and improve children's social competitiveness, but these outcomes are not sufficient for the evolution of paternal investment. As described in Table 16.1, the evolution and facultative expression of paternal investment is also related to paternity certainty and alternative mating opportunities.

Paternity Certainty   Because human paternal investment is not obligate in many contexts, some women may attempt to cuckold their partners. The benefits would include additional social and material support from the extra-pair man and perhaps higher quality genes for her children (Geary, Vigil, & Byrd-Craven, 2004). As with other species, the risks include mate guarding, male-on-female aggression, and abandonment (Betzig, 1989; Daly & Wilson, 1988). The definitive study of human cuckoldry has not been conducted, although it clearly happens. Bellis and Baker (1990), for example, found that when women initiated an infidelity it often occurred around the time of ovulation. For this sample, 7% of the copulations during the time of ovulation were with an extra-pair man and were less likely to involve use of contraceptives than copulations with their social partner.

Definitive conclusions cannot be reached, but it appears that men are cuckolded about 10% of the time (Bellis & Baker, 1990; Flinn, 1988; Gaulin, McBurney, & Brakeman-Wartell, 1997; McBurney, Simon, Gaulin, & Geliebter, 2002). The issues are complex, however, as the rate varies significantly across cultural settings and SES. Sasse, Muller, Chakraborty, and Ott (1994) reported that nonpaternity rates were 1% in Switzerland, but others have reported rates greater than 20% in low SES settings (Cerda-Flores, Baron, Marty-Gonzalez, Rivas, & Chakraborty, 1999; Potthoff & Whittinghill, 1965). Still, paternity certainty is higher in humans than in our two closest relatives (chimpanzees, *pan troglodytes*, and bonobos, *pan paniscus*), suggesting that most women do not cuckold their social partners. The pattern is consistent with coevolving reproductive strategies, whereby women's tendency toward sexual fidelity is traded for men's paternal investment.

Women's Reproductive Strategies   Several features of women's sexuality might be considered strategies, at least in part, to reduce men's mating opportunities and thus create conditions that could facilitate the evolution and facultative expression of paternal investment. These include concealed ovulation, aversion to casual sex, and female-on-female aggression (Geary, 1998; Oliver & Hyde, 1993). To ensure conception, concealed ovulation requires men to maintain a longer relationship with women than is necessary in most other primate species (Dunbar, 1995), but this is not sufficient to ensure paternal investment. If other proximate mechanisms were not operating, such as pairbonding (Miller & Fishkin,

1997), then once physical signs of pregnancy were evident men could easily abandon women. Concealed ovulation and the period of extended sexual activity may, in fact, be one mechanism that fosters pairbonding and later paternal investment (MacDonald, 1992).

Women's aversion to casual sex greatly restricts men's mating opportunities (Buss & Schmitt, 1993) and thus the opportunity cost of paternal investment. And finally, women compete over mates, often through relational aggression. This involves gossiping about and attempting to socially manipulate other women (Crick, Casas, & Mosher, 1997) and excluding potential competitors (over mates) from the social group (Geary, 2002b). When effective, the strategy reduces men's mating opportunities and thus lowers the opportunity cost of parenting.

FACULTATIVE EXPRESSION OF HUMAN PATERNAL INVESTMENT

The first subsection describes potential proximate influences on facultative expression of men's parenting, and the second describes wider social correlates of this investment.

PROXIMATE CORRELATES

The respective subsections provide reviews of the genetic, hormonal, social, and developmental correlates of men's parenting.

Genetic and Hormonal Correlates   Across species, sex differences and within-sex individual differences in parental behavior are associated with a suite of hormonal and neuroendocrine mechanisms (Wynne-Edwards, 2001), some of which are genetically mediated (Schneider et al., 2003; Young, Roger, Waymire, MacGregor, & Insel, 1999). Men's parenting also appears to be influenced by many of these same mechanisms, but it is not known if individual differences in these mechanisms (e.g., sensitivity to oxytocin) are heritable in humans. In any case, maternal and paternal cortisol levels are correlated with attentive and sensitive parenting of newborns (Corter & Fleming, 1995; Stallings, Fleming, Corter, Worthman, & Steiner, 2001), although there are also hormonal correlates that differ across mothers and fathers (Fleming, Ruble, Krieger, & Wong, 1997; S. E. Taylor et al., 2000). Expectant fathers who respond to infant distress cues (e.g., crying) with concern and a desire to comfort the infant have higher prolactin levels and lower testosterone levels than other men (Storey, Walsh, Quinton, & Wynne-Edwards, 2000). "Men with more pregnancy symptoms (couvade) and men who were most affected by the infant reactivity test had higher prolactin levels and greater post-test reduction in testosterone" (Storey et al., 2000, p. 79).

Based on a parenting survey administered to twins, Pérusse and colleagues found evidence for modest genetic contributions to two features of parental investment, care (e.g., sensitivity to emotional state) and protection (e.g., keeping the child close; Perusse, Neale, Heath, & Eaves, 1994). Genetic models explained 18% to 25% of the individual differences on these dimensions of paternal parenting and 23% to 39% of the individual differences in maternal parenting. These same models suggested unique environmental effects account for the majority of the individual differences in both paternal and maternal care and protection, at least as measured by this survey. A similar study found parental reports of positive support (e.g., affection, encouragement) of their children were moderately heritable, although separate estimates were not provided for mothers and fathers (Losoya, Callor, Rowe, & Goldsmith, 1997).

These results are intriguing but in need of replication with more direct measures of parental investment. Moreover, the reported effects might not reflect genetic influences on paternal investment per se but rather heritable personality factors that are not directly related to the evolution of paternal care but nonetheless influence parenting. Particularly important are heritable personality factors such as conscientiousness, associated with the stability of long-term relationships, especially with a spouse, and factors such as irritability that would affect responsiveness to children (Graziano & Eisenberg, 1997; Jockin, McGue, & Lykken, 1996; Rowe, 2002). Still, it is likely that individual differences in both paternal and maternal investment reflect some degree of heritable variability in the hormonal and neuroendocrine systems associated with parenting behavior. At the same time, parental behavior and the underlying hormonal and neuroendocrine systems are almost certainly influenced by social factors, including the child's behavior, the nature of the spousal relationship, and wider ecological conditions (S. E. Taylor et al., 2000; Geary & Flinn, 2002), although the relative influence of these factors cannot be determined from existing studies.

Social Correlates　The quality of the spousal relationship is related to the ways in which both mothers and fathers interact with their children (Amato & Keith, 1991; Cox, Owen, Lewis, & Henderson, 1989; Davies & Cummings, 1994; Howes & Markman, 1989), but "paternal parenting is more dependent on a supportive marital relationship than maternal parenting" (Parke, 1995, p. 37). Observational studies have found that "the quality of the marital dyad, whether reported by the husband or wife, is the one most consistently powerful predictor of paternal involvement (with his infant) and satisfaction (with the parenting role)" (Feldman, Nash, & Aschenbrenner, 1983, p. 1634; see also Belsky, Gilstrap, & Rovine, 1984). Basically, marital conflict often results in fathers' withdrawal from children and spouse (Christensen & Heavey, 1990), although this is sometimes more pronounced for daughters than for sons (Kerig, Cowan, & Cowan, 1993) and varies with the nature of the interpersonal dynamics between husband and wife (Gottman, 1998).

In sum, men in satisfying spousal relationships show higher levels of paternal investment than other men do. It is possible that women's efforts to maintain an intimate and cooperative spousal relationship is a strategy to induce and maintain paternal investment. It is also possible that men biased toward paternal investment are more cooperative and prone to monogamy and thus less likely to incite conflict with their wives than other men, or it is possible that the relation between marital satisfaction and paternal investment reflects genetic and not social effects. Most likely, it is a combination of heritable biases and reactivity to marital dynamics that influence paternal investment, but definitive answers must await research designs that assess social and genetic factors and their interaction (Parke & Buriel, 1998).

Developmental Correlates Childhood experiences have been proposed as influencing later reproductive strategies (Belsky et al., 1991; Chisholm, 1993; Miller & Fishkin, 1997). Local mortality risks and low resource availability, in particular, are hypothesized to be associated with how men later distribute their reproductive effort. When mortality risks are high and/or resources are scarce, investment in more rather than fewer offspring is assumed to ensure that at least some will survive to adulthood. Specifically, Belsky et al. and Chisholm argued that mortality risks and low resource availability influence the nature of parent-child relationships. In risky, low resource environments, the psychological and physiological stressors on parents are high, resulting in less attentive and more conflicted parent-child relationships. The prediction is that these relationships will be associated with a later tendency to form unstable, low parental investment relationships, that is, a focus on mating rather than parenting. In less risky, high resource environments, parent-child relationships are warmer and reflect higher levels of paternal and maternal investment (MacDonald, 1992). The prediction is that these relationships will be associated with a tendency to later form stable, high parental-investment relationships.

Aspects of the model have been supported in several recent studies. Wilson and Daly (1997) found age of first reproduction, number of children born per woman, mortality risks, and local resource availability are interrelated in modern-day Chicago. With low resource availability, men compete intensely for resource control. The result is higher premature death rates and an average life span difference of 23 years (54 versus 77 years) comparing the least and most affluent neighborhoods. Shorter life spans are associated with earlier age of first reproduction for both sexes and nearly twice as many children born per woman comparing the least and most affluent neighborhoods. In other words, the early and frequent reproduction of women and men in these contexts might be, at least in part, a facultative response to high mortality rates (see also Geary, 2002a; Korpelainen, 2000).

Consistent with the Belsky et al. (1991) model, paternal absence and marital conflict are also associated with reproductive events. For boys, paternal absence and marital conflict are associated with more risk taking and higher age-specific mortality rates, due largely to more accidents and violent deaths (Peterson, Seligman, Yurko, Martin, & Friedman, 1998). In relation to men whose parents had not divorced, these men are also more likely to divorce and thus show reduced paternal investment themselves (Tucker et al., 1997), but, again, genetic and social contributions to these effects were not separated.

Other studies, however, are inconsistent with the psychosocial stress model. For Ache and Mayan men, Waynforth, Hurtado, and Hill (1998, p. 383) found that "measures of family stress and violence were unsuccessful in predicting age at first reproduction, and none of the psychosocial stress indicators predicted lifetime number of partners." Father absence was related to less "willingness to pay time and opportunity costs to maintain a sexual relationship" (Waynforth et al., 1998, p. 383), although this could easily reflect genetic and not psychosocial effects. Other studies of human populations and of other species suggest low resource availability and other stressors are associated with delayed, not early, reproduction (Krebs & Davies, 1993; MacDonald, 1997). In all, there appears to be a relation between early experiences and men's later focus on mating or parenting. However, without studies that control for genetic effects and conditions (e.g., reproductive opportunity) at the time of reproduction, causal relations between developmental experiences and later reproductive activities cannot be drawn.

CULTURAL AND ECOLOGICAL CORRELATES

Draper and Harpending (1988) described human cultures as tending to be father-absent or father-present, reflecting differences in the relative emphasis of men on mating or parenting, respectively. I contrast father-absent and father-present societies in the first subsection (see also Marlowe, 2000) and discuss how men's reproductive strategies vary with mating opportunities in the second.

Cultural Correlates   Father-absent societies are characterized by aloof spousal relationships, polygynous marriages, local warfare, male social displays, and inconsistent direct paternal investment (Draper & Harpending, 1988; Hewlett, 1988; Marlowe, 2000; West & Konner, 1976; Whiting & Whiting, 1975). These conditions "are particularly prevalent in so-called middle-range societies, that is, those where agriculture is practiced at a very low level" (Draper & Harpending, 1988, p. 349) and in resource-rich ecologies. In the latter, women can often provision their children without the direct contribution of the father (Draper, 1989), although the father may control the land and other resources women use to feed their children (Borgerhoff Mulder, 2000). In these societies, polygynous marriages are not prohibited, and wealthy men often invest resources or social power in attempting to secure additional wives, often to their reproductive advantage (Chagnon, 1988) and often at a risk of increased child mortality and thus a reproductive cost to individual wives (Marlowe, 2000).

Father-present societies are common in harsh ecologies and in industrial societies (Draper & Harpending, 1988). These societies are characterized by ecologically or socially imposed monogamy (Flinn & Low, 1986). In harsh ecologies, most men are unable to acquire the resources (e.g., meat) needed to support more than one wife and family; thus their reproductive options are restricted to monogamy. In many industrial societies, legal and moral prohibitions against polygynous marriages, combined with women's preference for monogamous marriages (Geary, 1998), limit men's mating opportunities and thereby reduce the opportunity cost of paternal investment. The result is a relative shift in men's reproductive efforts from mating to parenting.

Ecological Correlates   The ratio of reproductive-age men to reproductive-age women in the local ecology is called the operational sex ratio (OSR). In human populations, the OSR is determined by sex differences in birth rates, death rates, and migration patterns. One factor that particularly skews the OSR in industrial societies is population growth rate, with expanding populations yielding an "oversupply" of women. This results from a preference of women for slightly older marriage partners (Kenrick & Keefe, 1992). With an expanding population, the younger generation of women compete for marriage partners among a smaller cohort of older men.

With an oversupply of women (e.g., from 1965 through the 1970s in the United States), men are better able to pursue their reproductive preferences. These historical periods are generally characterized by liberal sexual mores, high divorce rates, an increase in the number of out-of-wedlock births and the number of families headed by single women, an increase in women's participation in the workforce, and lower levels of paternal investment (see Guttentag & Secord, 1983). During these periods, men, on average, are able to express their preference for a variety of sexual partners and relatively low levels of paternal investment (Pedersen, 1991), although some men remain monogamous (Miller & Fishkin, 1997). When there is an oversupply of men (Guttentag & Secord, 1983), women are better able to enforce their preference for a monogamous, high-investment spouse. These periods are generally characterized by an increase in the level of commitment of men to marriage, as indexed by declining divorce rates and greater levels of paternal investment.

Hurtado and Hill (1992) reported a similar pattern in the Ache and Hiwi (hunter-gatherers in southwestern Venezuela). In the Ache, there are more reproductive-age women than men (OSR of 1.3), whereas in the Hiwi, there are more reproductive-age men than women (OSR of .78). These differences "in levels of mating opportunities between the Ache and the Hiwi occur alongside marked contrasts in marital stability. Whereas serial monogamy and extramarital promiscuity are very common among the Ache, stable lifetime monogamous unions with almost no extramarital copulation is the normative mating pattern among the Hiwi" (Hurtado & Hill, 1992, p. 40). These patterns are found despite high infant and child mortality risks associated with paternal abandonment with the Ache and low risks with the Hiwi, suggesting some men are more influenced by mating opportunities than child mortality risks (Marlowe, 2000).

EVOLUTIONARY PRESSURES

The construction of models of the evolution of human paternal behavior can be guided by the proximate and evolutionary correlates of paternal investment in other species (see Table 16.1) and by comparative analyses of evolutionarily related species. For humans, the most appropriate comparisons would involve other species of *Homo* and australopithecine species, but these are all extinct. Thus, a common approach is to use patterns in the two species most closely related to humans, chimpanzees and bonobos. However, it is not clear that these are appropriate comparison species because males show little to no paternal investment, among other differences in reproductive dynamics. If our ancestors were like chimpanzees or bonobos, multiple changes in male (e.g., increase in parenting) and female (e.g., emergence of concealed ovulation) reproductive behavior would have had to occur to create the current human pattern. Geary and Flinn (2001) proposed the reproductive dynamics of our ancestors might instead have been more similar to that of our distant cousin, the gorilla (*Gorilla gorilla*), because moving from a gorillalike pattern to the current human pattern would require fewer evolutionary changes.

The modal social organization of gorillas is single-male harems, which typically include one reproductive male, many females, and their offspring (Fossey, 1984; Stewart & Harcourt, 1987; A. B. Taylor, 1997). In lowland gorillas (*Gorilla gorilla gorilla*), several families may occupy the same geographical region and are often in proximity, whereas in mountain gorillas (*Gorilla gorilla beringei*) they are geographically isolated. In both cases, adult male and female gorillas often form long-term social relationships, and male gorillas show high levels of affiliation with their offspring, presumably due to high levels of paternity certainty associated with single-male harems. "Associated males hold, cuddle, nuzzle, examine, and groom infants, and infants turn to these males in times of distress" (Whitten, 1987, p. 346).

If the launching point was a gorillalike pattern, then current patterns of human parenting and family structure (i.e., one adult male, one or several adult females and their children), as well as long-term male-female relationships, have been a feature of the hominid social structure for millions of years. The primary evolutionary change needed to move from a single-male harem to the multimale, multifemale communities found with humans is the formation of male kin-based coalitions. The first evolutionary step to multimale communities would simply involve greater stability and cooperation among adult males. Such coalitions could easily arise from a gorillalike system, with the formation of father-son coalitions or coalitions among brothers. In fact, groups of bachelor males are common in mountain gorillas (Robbins, 1996). Among lowland gorillas, several families will occupy the same geographical region and encounters between groups are often friendly, especially among the males (Bradley et al., 2004). Bradley et al.'s DNA fingerprinting of male and female relatedness among these families indicates that males tend to be organized as clusters of kin, whereas females tend to be unrelated to other group members. This form of social organization provides the social context from which kin-based male coalitions could evolve. Once formed, stable groups of cooperating males could easily displace a lone male (Wrangham, 1999). As with chimpanzees, once they evolved early hominid communities were likely characterized by coalitions of related males that defended a territory against groups of conspecific males (Foley & Lee, 1989; Goodall, 1986). Unlike chimpanzees, the gorillalike family structure would have been retained.

Unlike female chimpanzees or bonobos, female gorillas do not typically have conspicuous sexual swellings, although they often have minor swellings and primarily solicit copulations behaviorally (Stewart & Harcourt, 1987). Thus, moving from a gorillalike pattern of female sexual solicitation to the current human pattern (e.g., concealed ovulation) requires fewer changes than evolving from the promiscuous chimpanzeelike or bonobolike pattern. Still, there may have been a strengthening of male-female pairbond during hominid evolution to reduce cuckoldry risks and maintain male parenting in a multimale, multifemale community. Evolution from a gorillalike pattern would simply require a quantitative change in the strength of the pairbond, whereas evolution from a chimpanzeelike or bonobolike pattern would require a more substantive and qualitative change in the nature of male-female relationships. If correct, male parenting, long-term female-male relationships, and a family structure following the gorillalike pattern may have been in place since the emergence of our australopithecine ancestors (Lovejoy, 1981).

CONCLUSIONS

When viewed from the perspective of mammalian reproduction, the most extraordinary feature of human parental care is men's parenting. Although definitive conclusions cannot be drawn at this time, what is known suggests the evolution and proximate expression of human paternal investment is related to many of the same factors associated with such investment in other species (e.g., Perrone & Zaret, 1979; Thornhill, 1976). These factors include reductions in infant and child mortality rates and improvements in children's social competitiveness

(Kaplan et al., 1998). As with other species where males parent, men's parenting appears to be related to comparatively high levels of paternity certainty and reduced mating opportunities. The latter likely resulted from physical (e.g., concealed ovulation) and social (e.g., aversion to casual sex) adaptations in our female ancestors, as appears to be the case with socially monogamous primates (Dunbar, 1995).

The net result is that men and women benefit from paternal investment, but this investment is not obligate. Rather, men's parenting is facultatively expressed, contingent on personal, social, and ecological conditions. Among these conditions are heritable individual differences in emphasis on mating or parenting, personality, the quality of the spousal relationship, and child characteristics (Kaplan et al., 1998; Luster & Okagaki, 1993; Rowe, 2002). Childhood experiences such as parental divorce, as well as wider social and ecological factors such as laws against polygynous marriages, are also correlated with the degree to which men invest in the well-being of their children (Belsky et al., 1991; Flinn & Low, 1986; Miller & Fishkin, 1997). However, the relative contribution of each of these factors is not currently known. For instance, it is not clear whether early experiences in conflicted households cause later low investment parenting, whether shared genes cause unstable relationships across generations, or whether some interaction between heritable risks and early stressors are involved (Losoya et al., 1997; Reiss, 1995). The challenge for researchers is to design evolutionarily informed studies that enable the simultaneous assessment of many of these factors and to more critically explore the causes and correlates of individual differences in men's parenting.

REFERENCES

Adler, N. E., Boyce, T., Chesney, M. A., Cohen, S., Folkman, S., Kahn, R. L., et al. (1994). Socioeconomic status and health: The challenge of the gradient. *American Psychologist, 49,* 15–24.

Alberts, S. C., & Altmann, J. (1995). Preparation and activation: Determinants of age at reproductive maturity in male baboon. *Behavioral Ecology and Sociobiology, 36,* 397–406.

Amato, P. R. (1998). More than money? Men's contributions to their children's lives. In A. Booth & A. C. Crouter (Eds.), *Men in families: When do they get involved? What difference does it make?* (pp. 241–278). Mahwah, NJ: Erlbaum.

Amato, P. R., & Keith, B. (1991). Parental divorce and the well-being of children: A meta-analysis. *Psychological Bulletin, 110,* 26–46.

Andersson, M. (1994). *Sexual selection.* Princeton, NJ: Princeton University Press.

Arnold, K. E., & Owens, I. P. F. (2002). Extra-pair paternity and egg dumping in birds: Life history, parental care and the risk of retaliation. *Proceedings of the Royal Society of London. Series B, Biological Sciences, 269,* 1263–1269.

Asa, C. S., & Valdespino, C. (1998). Canid reproductive biology: An integration of proximate mechanisms and ultimate causes. *American Zoologist, 38,* 251–259.

Bellis, M. A., & Baker, R. R. (1990). Do females promote sperm competition? Data for humans. *Animal Behaviour, 40,* 997–999.

Belsky, J., Gilstrap, B., & Rovine, M. (1984). The Pennsylvania infant and family development project: I. Stability and change in mother-infant and father-infant interaction in a family setting at one, three, and nine months. *Child Development, 55,* 692–705.

Belsky, J., Steinberg, L., & Draper, P. (1991). Childhood experience, interpersonal development, and reproductive strategy: An evolutionary theory of socialization. *Child Development, 62,* 647–670.

Betzig, L. (1989). Causes of conjugal dissolution: A cross-cultural study. *Current Anthropology, 30,* 654–676.

Birkhead, T. R., & Møller, A. P. (1996). Monogamy and sperm competition in birds. In J. M. Black (Ed.), *Partnerships in birds: The study of monogamy* (pp. 323–343). New York: Oxford University Press.

Blurton Jones, N. G., Hawkes, K., & O'Connell, J. F. (1997). Why do Hadza children forage. In N. L. Segal, G. E. Weisfeld, & C. C. Weisfeld (Eds.), *Uniting psychology and biology: Integrative perspectives on human development* (pp. 279–313). Washington, DC: American Psychological Association.

Boone, J. L., & Kessler, K. L. (1999). More status or more children? Social status, fertility reduction, and long-term fitness. *Evolution and Human Behavior, 20,* 257–277.

Borgerhoff Mulder, M. (2000). Optimizing offspring: The quantity-quality tradeoff in agropastoral Kipsigis. *Evolution and Human Behavior, 21,* 391–410.

Bradley, B. J., Doran-Sheehy, D. M., Lukas, D., Boesch, C., & Vigilant, L. (2004).Dispersed male networks in Western gorillas. *Current Biology, 14,* 510–513.

Brändström, A. (1997). Life histories of lone parents and illegitimate children in nineteenth-century Sweden. In C. A. Corsini & P. P. Viazzo (Eds.), *The decline of infant and child mortality* (pp. 173–191). Hague, Netherlands: Martinus Nijhoff.

Buchan, J. C., Alberts, S. C., Silk, J. B., & Altmann, J. (2003, September 11). True paternal care in a multi-male primate society. *Nature, 425,* 179–181.

Buss, D. M., & Schmitt, D. P. (1993). Sexual strategies theory: An evolutionary perspective on human mating. *Psychological Review, 100,* 204–232.

Carson, J., Burks, V., & Parke, R. D. (1993). Parent-child physical play: Determinants and consequences. In K. MacDonald (Ed.), *Parent-child play: Descriptions and implications* (pp. 197–220). Albany: State University of New York Press.

Caspi, A., McClay, J., Moffitt, T. E., Mill, J., Martin, J., Craig, I. W., et al. (2002, August 2). Role of genotype in the cycle of violence in maltreated children. *Science, 297,* 851–854.

Cerda-Flores, R. M., Barton, S. A., Marty-Gonzalez, L. F., Rivas, F., & Chakraborty, R. (1999). Estimation of nonpaternity in the Mexican population of Nuevo Leon: A validation study with blood group markers. *American Journal of Physical Anthropology, 109,* 281–293.

Chagnon, N. A. (1988, February 26). Life histories, blood revenge, and warfare in a tribal population. *Science, 239,* 985–992.

Cherlin, A. J., Furstenberg, F. F., Jr., Chase-Lansdale, P. L., Kiernan, K. E., Robins, P. K., Morrison, D. R., et al. (1991, June 7). Longitudinal studies of effects of divorce on children in Great Britain and the United States. *Science, 252,* 1386–1389.

Chisholm, J. S. (1993). Death, hope, and sex: Life-history theory and the development of reproductive strategies. *Current Anthropology, 34,* 1–24.

Christensen, A., & Heavey, C. L. (1990). Gender and social structure in the demand/withdraw pattern of marital conflict. *Journal of Personality and Social Psychology, 59,* 73–81.

Cleveland, H. H., Jacobson, K. C., Lipinski, J. J., & Rowe, D. C. (2000). Genetic and shared environmental contributions to the relationship between the home environment and child and adolescent achievement. *Intelligence, 28,* 69–86.

Clutton-Brock, T. H. (1991). *The evolution of parental care.* Princeton, NJ: Princeton University Press.

Clutton-Brock, T. H., Albon, S. D., & Guinness, F. E. (1988). Reproductive success in male and female red deer. In T. H. Clutton-Brock (Ed.), *Reproductive success: Studies of individual variation in contrasting breeding systems* (pp. 325–343). Chicago: University of Chicago Press.

Clutton-Brock, T. H., & Vincent, A. C. J. (1991, May 2). Sexual selection and the potential reproductive rates of males and females. *Nature, 351,* 58–60.

Comings, D. E., Muhleman, D. D., Johnson, J. P., & MacMurray, J. P. (2002). Parent-daughter transmission of the androgen receptor gene as an explanation of the effect of father absence on age of menarche. *Child Development, 73,* 1046–1051.

Corter, C. M., & Fleming, A. S. (1995). Psychobiology of maternal behavior in human beings. In M. H. Bornstein (Ed.), *Handbook of parenting: Vol. 2. Biology and ecology of parenting* (pp. 87–116). Mahwah, NJ: Erlbaum.

Cox, M. J., Owen, M. T., Lewis, J. M., & Henderson, V. K. (1989). Marriage, adult adjustment, and early parenting. *Child Development, 60,* 1015–1024.

Crick, N. R., Casas, J. F., & Mosher, M. (1997). Relational and overt aggression in preschool. *Developmental Psychology, 33,* 579–588.

Daly, M., & Wilson, M. (1988). *Homicide.* New York: Aldine de Gruyter.

Darwin, C. (1871). *The descent of man, and selection in relation to sex.* London: John Murray.

Davies, P. T., & Cummings, E. M. (1994). Marital conflict and child adjustment: An emotional security hypothesis. *Psychological Bulletin, 116,* 387–411.

Davis, J. N., & Daly, M. (1997). Evolutionary theory and the human family. *Quarterly Review of Biology, 72,* 407–435.

Dixon, A., Ross, D., O'Malley, S. L. C., & Burke, T. (1994, October 20). Paternal investment inversely related to degree of extra-pair paternity in the reed bunting. *Nature, 371,* 698–700.

Draper, P. (1989). African marriage systems: Perspectives from evolutionary ecology. *Ethology and Sociobiology, 10,* 145–169.

Draper, P., & Harpending, H. (1988). A sociobiological perspective on the development of human reproductive strategies. In K. B. MacDonald (Ed.), *Sociobiological perspectives on human development* (pp. 340–372). New York: Springer-Verlag.

Dunbar, R. I. M. (1995). The mating system of callitrichid primates: I. Conditions for the coevolution of pair bonding and twinning. *Animal Behaviour, 50,* 1057–1070.

Ellis, B. J., Bates, J. E., Dodge, K. A., Fergusson, D. M., Horwood, J. L., Pettit, G. S., et al. (2003). Does father absence place daughters at special risk for early sexual activity and teenage pregnancy? *Child Development, 74,* 801–821.

Ellis, B. J., & Garber, J. (2000). Psychosocial antecedents of variation in girls' pubertal timing: Maternal depression, stepfather presence, and marital and family stress. *Child Development, 71,* 485–501.

Ellis, B. J., McFadyen-Ketchum, S., Dodge, K. A., Pettit, G. S., & Bates, J. E. (1999). Quality of early family relationships and individual differences in the timing of pubertal maturation in girls: A longitudinal test of an evolutionary model. *Journal of Personality and Social Psychology, 77,* 387–401.

Ewen, J. G., & Armstrong, D. P. (2000). Male provisioning is negatively correlated with attempted extrapair copulation in the stitchbird (or hihi). *Animal Behaviour, 60,* 429–433.

Feldman, S. S., Nash, S. C., & Aschenbrenner, B. G. (1983). Antecedents of fathering. *Child Development, 54,* 1628–1636.

Fishman, M. A., Stone, L., & Lotem, A. (2003). Fertility assurance through extrapair fertilizations and male paternity defense. *Journal of Theoretical Biology, 221,* 103–114.

Fleming, A. S., Ruble, D., Krieger, H., & Wong, P. Y. (1997). Hormonal and experiential correlates of maternal responsiveness during pregnancy and the puerperium in human mothers. *Hormones and Behavior, 31,* 145–158.

Flinn, M. V. (1988). Mate guarding in a Caribbean village. *Ethology and Sociobiology, 9,* 1–28.

Flinn, M. V., & Low, B. S. (1986). Resource distribution, social competition, and mating patterns in human societies. In D. I. Rubenstein & R. W. Wrangham (Eds.), *Ecological aspects of social evolution: Birds and mammals* (pp. 217–243). Princeton, NJ: Princeton University Press.

Florsheim, P., Tolan, P., & Gorman-Smith, D. (1998). Family relationships, parenting practices, the availability of male family members, and the behavior of inner-city boys in single-mother and two-parent families. *Child Development, 69,* 1437–1447.

Foley, R. A., & Lee, P. C. (1989, February 17). Finite social space, evolutionary pathways, and reconstructing hominid behavior. *Science, 243,* 901–906.

Fossey, D. (1984). *Gorillas in the mist.* Boston: Houghton Mifflin Co.

Furstenberg, F. F., Jr., & Teitler, J. O. (1994). Reconsidering the effects of marital disruption. *Journal of Family Issues, 15,* 173–190.

Gaulin, S. J. C., McBurney, D. H., & Brakeman-Wartell, S. L. (1997). Matrilateral biases in the investment of aunts and uncles: A consequence and measure of paternity uncertainty. *Human Nature, 8,* 139–151.

Geary, D. C. (1998). *Male, female: The evolution of human sex differences.* Washington, DC: American Psychological Association.

Geary, D. C. (2000). Evolution and proximate expression of human paternal investment. *Psychological Bulletin, 126,* 55–77.

Geary, D. C. (2002a). Sexual selection and human life history. In R. Kail (Ed.), *Advances in child development and behavior* (Vol. 30, pp. 41–101). San Diego, CA: Academic Press.

Geary, D. C. (2002b). Sexual selection and sex differences in social cognition. In A. V. McGillicuddy-De Lisi & R. De Lisi (Eds.), *Biology, society, and behavior: The development of sex differences in cognition* (pp. 23–53). Greenwich, CT: Ablex/Greenwood.

Geary, D. C. (2005). *The origin of mind: Evolution of brain, cognition, and general intelligence.* Washington, DC: American Psychological Association.

Geary, D. C., & Flinn, M. V. (2001). Evolution of human parental behavior and the human family. *Parenting: Science and Practice, 1,* 5–61.

Geary, D. C., & Flinn, M. V. (2002). Sex differences in behavioral and hormonal response to social threat: Commentary on Taylor et al. (2000). *Psychological Review, 109,* 745–750.

Geary, D. C., Vigil, J., & Byrd-Craven, J. (2004). Evolution of human mate choice. *Journal of Sex Research, 41,* 27–42.

Goodall, J. (1986). *The chimpanzees of Gombe: Patterns of behavior.* Cambridge, MA: The Belknap Press.

Gottman, J. M. (1998). Toward a process model of men in marriages and families. In A. Booth & A. C. Crouter (Eds.), *Men in families: When do they get involved? What difference does it make?* (pp. 149–192). Mahwah, NJ: Erlbaum.

Graziano, W. G., & Eisenberg, N. (1997). Agreeableness: A dimension of personality. In R. Hogan, J. Johnson, & S. Briggs (Eds.), *Handbook of personality psychology* (pp. 795–824). San Diego, CA: Academic Press.

Guttentag, M., & Secord, P. (1983). *Too many women?* Beverly Hills, CA: Sage.

Hager, R., & Johnstone, R. A. (2003, January 30). The genetic basis of family conflict resolution in mice. *Nature, 421,* 533–535.

Herlihy, D. (1965). Population, plague and social change in rural Pistoia, 1201–1430. *Economic History Review, 18,* 225–244.

Hewlett, B. S. (1988). Sexual selection and paternal investment among Aka pygmies. In L. Betzig, M. Borgerhoff Mulder, & P. Turke (Eds.), *Human reproductive behaviour: A Darwinian perspective* (pp. 263–276). Cambridge, England: Cambridge University Press.

Hill, K., & Hurtado, A. M. (1996). *Ache life history: The ecology and demography of a foraging people.* New York: Aldine de Gruyter.

Howes, P., & Markman, H. J. (1989). Marital quality and child functioning: A longitudinal investigation. *Child Development, 60,* 1044–1051.

Hurtado, A. M., & Hill, K. R. (1992). Paternal effect on offspring survivorship among Ache and Hiwi hunter-gatherers: Implications for modeling pair-bond stability. In B. S. Hewlett (Ed.), *Father-child relations: Cultural and biosocial contexts* (pp. 31–55). New York: Aldine de Gruyter.

Jockin, V., McGue, M., & Lykken, D. T. (1996). Personality and divorce: A genetic analysis. *Journal of Personality and Social Psychology, 71,* 288–299.

Kaplan, H. S., Lancaster, J. B., & Anderson, K. G. (1998). Human parental investment and fertility: The life histories of men in Albuquerque. In A. Booth & A. C. Crouter (Eds.), *Men in families: When do they get involved? What difference does it make?* (pp. 55–109). Mahwah, NJ: Erlbaum.

Kaplan, H. S., Lancaster, J. B., Bock, J. A., & Johnson, S. E. (1995). Does observed fertility maximize fitness among New Mexican men? A test of an optimality model and a new theory of parental investment in the embodied capital of offspring. *Human Nature, 6,* 325–360.

Kempenaers, B., Lanctot, R. B., & Robertson, R. J. (1998). Certainty of paternity and paternal investment in eastern bluebirds and tree swallows. *Animal Behaviour, 55,* 845–860.

Kenrick, D. T., & Keefe, R. C. (1992). Age preferences in mates reflect sex differences in human reproductive strategies. *Behavioral and Brain Sciences, 15,* 75–133.

Kerig, P. K., Cowan, P. A., & Cowan, C. P. (1993). Marital quality and gender differences in parent-child interaction. *Developmental Psychology, 29,* 931–939.

Klindworth, H., & Voland, E. (1995). How did the Krummhörn elite males achieve above-average reproductive success? *Human Nature, 6,* 221–240.

Kok, J., van Poppel, F., & Kruse, E. (1997). Mortality among illegitimate children in mid-nineteenth-century the Hague. In C. A. Corsini & P. P. Viazzo (Eds.), *The decline of infant and child mortality* (pp. 193–211). Hague, Netherlands: Martinus Nijhoff.

Korpelainen, H. (2000). Fitness, reproduction and longevity among European aristocratic and rural Finnish families in the 1700s and 1800s. *Proceedings of the Royal Society of London. Series B, Biological Sciences, 267,* 1765–1770.

Krebs, J. R., & Davies, N. B. (1993). *An introduction to behavioural ecology* (3rd ed.). Oxford, England: Blackwell Science Ltd.

Lachman, M. E., & Weaver, S. L. (1998). The sense of control as a moderator of social class differences in health and well-being. *Journal of Personality and Social Psychology, 74,* 763–773.

Lamb, M. E., & Elster, A. B. (1985). Adolescent mother-infant-father relationships. *Developmental Psychology, 21,* 768–773.

Lancaster, J. B., & Lancaster, C. S. (1987). The watershed: Change in parental-investment and family-formation strategies in the course of human evolution. In J. B. Lancaster, J. Altmann, A. S. Rossi, & L. R. Sherrod (Eds.), *Parenting across the life span: Biosocial dimensions* (pp. 187–205). New York: Aldine de Gruyter.

Losoya, S. H., Callor, S., Rowe, D. C., & Goldsmith, H. H. (1997). Origins of familial similarity in parenting: A study of twins and adoptive siblings. *Developmental Psychology, 33,* 1012–1023.

Lovejoy, C. O. (1981). The origin of man. *Science, 211,* 341–350.

Luster, T., & Okagaki, L. (1993). Multiple influences on parenting: Ecological and life-course perspectives. In T. Luster & L. Okagaki (Eds.), *Parenting: An ecological perspective* (pp. 227–250). Hillsdale, NJ: Erlbaum.

MacDonald, K. (1992). Warmth as a developmental construct: An evolutionary analysis. *Child Development, 63,* 753–773.

MacDonald, K. (1997). Life history theory and human reproductive behavior: Environmental/contextual influences and heritable variation. *Human Nature, 8,* 327–359.

Marlowe, F. (2000). Paternal investment and the human mating system. *Behavioural Processes, 51,* 45–61.

McBurney, D. H., Simon, J., Gaulin, S. J. C., & Geliebter, A. (2002). Matrilateral biases in the investment of aunts and uncles: Replication in a population presumed to have high paternity certainty. *Human Nature, 13,* 391–402.

McGue, M., & Lykken, D. T. (1992). Genetic influence on risk of divorce. *Psychological Science, 3,* 368–373.

Miller, L. C., & Fishkin, S. A. (1997). On the dynamics of human bonding and reproductive success: Seeking windows on the adapted-for-human-environmental interface. In J. A. Simpson & D. T. Kenrick (Eds.), *Evolutionary social psychology* (pp. 197–235). Mahwah, NJ: Erlbaum.

Mock, D. W., & Fujioka, M. (1990). Monogamy and long-term pair bonding in vertebrates. *Trends in Ecology and Evolution, 5,* 39–43.

Møller, A. P. (2000). Male parental care, female reproductive success, and extrapair paternity. *Behavioral Ecology, 11,* 161–168.

Møller, A. P., & Cuervo, J. J. (2000). The evolution of paternity and paternal care. *Behavioral Ecology, 11,* 472–485.

Møller, A. P., & Tegelström, H. (1997). Extra-pair paternity and tail ornamentation in the barn swallow *Hirundo rustica. Behavioral Ecology and Sociobiology, 41,* 353–360.

Moore, A. J., Wolf, J. B., Brodie, E. D., III (1998). The influence of direct and indirect genetic effects on the evolution of behavior: Social and sexual selection meet maternal effects. In T. A. Mousseau & C. W. Fox (Eds.), *Maternal effects as adaptations* (pp. 22–41). New York: Oxford University Press.

Morrison, A. S., Kirshner, J., & Molho, A. (1977). Life cycle events in 15th century Florence: Records of the *Monte Delle Doti. American Journal of Epidemiology, 106,* 487–492.

Neff, B. D. (2003, April 17). Decisions about parental care in response to perceived paternity. *Nature, 422,* 716–719.

Neff, B. D., & Sherman, P. W. (2002). Decision making and recognition mechanisms. *Proceedings of the Royal Society of London. Series B, Biological Sciences, 269,* 1435–1441.

Oliver, M. B., & Hyde, J. S. (1993). Gender differences in sexuality: A meta-analysis. *Psychological Bulletin, 114,* 29–51.

Parke, R. D. (1995). Fathers and families. In M. H. Bornstein (Ed.), *Handbook of parenting: Vol. 3. Status and social conditions of parenting* (pp. 27–63). Mahwah, NJ: Erlbaum.

Parke, R. D., & Buriel, R. (1998). Socialization in the family: Ethnic and ecological perspectives. In W. Damon & E. Eisenberg (Eds.), *Handbook of children psychology* (5th ed., Vol. 3, pp. 463–552). New York: Wiley.

Pedersen, F. A. (1991). Secular trends in human sex ratios: Their influence on individual and family behavior. *Human Nature, 2,* 271–291.

Perrone, M., Jr., & Zaret, T. M. (1979). Parental care patterns of fishes. *American Naturalist, 113,* 351–361.

Perusse, D. (1993). Cultural and reproductive success in industrialized societies: Testing the relationship at the proximate and ultimate levels. *Behavioral and Brain Sciences, 16,* 267–322.

Perusse, D., Neale, M. C., Heath, A. C., & Eaves, L. J. (1994). Human parental behavior: Evidence for genetic influence and potential implication for gene-culture transmission. *Behavior Genetics, 24,* 327–335.

Peterson, C., Seligman, M. E. P., Yurko, K. H., Martin, L. R., & Friedman, H. S. (1998). Catastrophizing and untimely death. *Psychological Science, 9,* 127–130.

Pleck, J. H. (1997). Paternal involvement: Levels, sources, and consequences. In M. E. Lamb (Ed.), *The role of the father in child development* (3rd ed., pp. 66–103). New York: Wiley.

Post, J. D. (1985). *Food shortage, climatic variation, and epidemic disease in preindustrial Europe: The mortality peak in the early 1740s.* Ithaca, NY: Cornell University Press.

Potthoff, R. F., & Whittinghill, M. (1965). Maximum-likelihood estimation of the proportion of nonpaternity. *American Journal of Human Genetics, 17,* 480–494.

Qvarnström, A., & Price, T. D. (2001). Maternal effects, paternal effects and sexual selection. *Trends in Ecology and Evolution, 16,* 95–100.

Reid, A. (1997). Locality or class? Spatial and social differentials in infant and child mortality in England and Wales, 1895–1911. In C. A. Corsini & P. P. Viazzo (Eds.), *The decline of infant and child mortality* (pp. 129–154). Hague, Netherlands: Martinus Nijhoff.

Reid, I. (1998). *Class in Britain.* Cambridge, Great Britain: Polity Press.

Reiss, D. (1995). Genetic influences on family systems: Implications for development. *Journal of Marriage and the Family, 57,* 543–560.

Reynolds, J. D., & Székely, T. (1997). The evolution of parental care in shorebirds: Life histories, ecology, and sexual selection. *Behavioral Ecology, 8,* 126–134.

Richner, H., Christe, P., & Oppliger, A. (1995). Paternal investment affects prevalence of malaria. *Proceedings of the National Academy of Sciences USA, 92,* 1192–1194.

Robbins, M. M. (1996). Male-male interactions in heterosexual and all-male wild mountain gorilla groups. *Ethology, 102,* 942–965.

Rohwer, S., Herron, J. C., & Daly, M. (1999). Stepparental behavior as mating effort in birds and other animals. *Evolution and Human Behavior, 20,* 367–390.

Rollet, C. (1997). Childhood mortality in high-risk groups: Some methodological reflections based on French experience. In C. A. Corsini & P. P. Viazzo (Eds.), *The decline of infant and child mortality* (pp. 213–225). Hague, Netherlands: Martinus Nijhoff.

Rowe, D. C. (2002). What twin and adoption studies reveal about parenting. In J. G. Borkowski, S. L. Ramey, & M. Bristol-Power (Eds.), *Parenting and the child's world: Influences on academic, intellectual, and social-emotional development* (pp. 21–34). Mahwah, NJ: Erlbaum.

Sasse, G., Muller, H., Chakraborty, R., & Ott, J. (1994). Estimating the frequency of nonpaternity in Switzerland. *Human Heredity, 44,* 337–343.

Savalli, U. M., & Fox, C. W. (1998). Genetic variation in paternal investment in a seed beetle. *Animal Behaviour, 56,* 953–961.

Scarr, S., & McCarthy, K. (1983). How people make their own environments: A theory of genotype—>environment effects. *Child Development, 54,* 424–435.

Schneider, J. S., Stone, M. K., Wynne-Edwards, K. E., Horton, T. H., Lydon, J., O'Malley, B., et al. (2003). Progesterone receptors mediate male aggression toward infants. *Proceedings of the National Academy of Sciences USA, 100,* 2951–2956.

Schultz, H. (1991). Social differences in mortality in the eighteenth century: An analysis of Berlin church registers. *International Review of Social History, 36,* 232–248.

Sheldon, B. C., Räsänen, K., & Dias, P. C. (1997). Certainty of paternity and paternal effort in the collared flycatcher. *Behavioral Ecology, 8,* 421–428.

Smuts, B., & Gubernick, D. J. (1992). Male-infant relationships in nonhuman primates: Paternal investment or mating effort. In B. S. Hewlett (Ed.), *Father-child relations: Cultural and biosocial contexts* (pp. 1–30). New York: Aldine de Gruyter.

Stallings, J., Fleming, A. S., Corter, C., Worthman, C., & Steiner, M. (2001). The effects of infant cries and odors on sympathy, cortisol, and autonomic responses in new mothers and non-postpartum women. *Parenting: Science and Practice, 1,* 71–100.

Stewart, K. J., & Harcourt, A. H. (1987). Gorillas: Variation in female relationships. In B. B. Smuts, D. L. Cheney, R. M. Seyfarth, R. W. Wrangham, & T. T. Struhsaker (Eds.), *Primate societies* (pp. 155–164). Chicago: The University of Chicago Press.

Storey, A. E., Walsh, C. J., Quinton, R. L., & Wynne-Edwards, K. E. (2000). Hormonal correlates of paternal responsiveness in new and expectant fathers. *Evolution and Human Behavior, 21,* 79–95.

Taylor, A. B. (1997). Relative growth, ontogeny, and sexual dimorphism in Gorilla (*Gorilla gorilla gorilla* and *G. g. beringei*): Evolutionary and ecological considerations. *American Journal of Primatology, 43,* 1–31.

Taylor, S. E., Klein, L. C., Lewis, B. P., Gruenewald, T. L., Gurung, R. A. R., & Updegraff, J. A. (2000). Biobehavioral responses to stress in females: Tend-and-befriend, not fight-or-flight. *Psychological Review, 107,* 411–429.

Thornhill, R. (1976). Sexual selection and paternal investment in insects. *American Naturalist, 110,* 153–163.

Trivers, R. L. (1972). Parental investment and sexual selection. In B. Campbell (Ed.), *Sexual selection and the descent of man 1871–1971*(pp. 136–179). Chicago: Aldine Publishing.

Trivers, R. L. (1974). Parent-offspring conflict. *American Zoologist, 14,* 249–264.

Tucker, J. S., Friedman, H. S., Schwartz, J. E., Criqui, M. H., Tomlinson-Keasey, C., Wingard, D. L., et al. (1997). Parental divorce: Effects on individual behavior and longevity. *Journal of Personality and Social Psychology, 73,* 381–391.

United Nations. (1985). *Socio-economic differentials in child mortality in developing countries.* New York: Author.

Waynforth, D., Hurtado, A. M., & Hill, K. (1998). Environmentally contingent reproductive strategies in Mayan and Ache males. *Evolution and Human Behavior, 19,* 369–385.

West, M. M., & Konner, M. J. (1976). The role of father: An anthropological perspective. In M. E. Lamb (Ed.), *The role of the father in child development* (pp. 185–217). New York: Wiley.

Westneat, D. F., & Sherman, P. W. (1993). Parentage and the evolution of parental behavior. *Behavioral Ecology, 4,* 66–77.

Whiting, B. B., & Whiting, J. W. M. (1975). *Children of six cultures: A psycho-cultural analysis.* Cambridge, MA: Harvard University Press.

Whitten, P. L. (1987). Infants and adult males. In B. B. Smuts, D. L. Cheney, R. M. Seyfarth, R. W. Wrangham, & T. T. Struhsaker (Eds.), *Primate societies* (pp. 343–357). Chicago: The University of Chicago Press.

Williams, G. C. (1966). Natural selection, the costs of reproduction, and a refinement of Lack's principle. *American Naturalist, 100,* 687–690.

Wilson, M., & Daly, M. (1997). Life expectancy, economic inequality, homicide, and reproductive timing in Chicago neighbourhoods. *British Medical Journal, 314,* 1271–1274.

Wolf, L., Ketterson, E. D., & Nolan, V., Jr. (1988). Paternal influence on growth and survival of dark-eyed junco young: Do parental males benefit? *Animal Behaviour, 36,* 1601–1618.

Wrangham, R. W. (1999). Evolution of coalitionary killing. *Yearbook of Physical Anthropology, 42,* 1–30.

Wynne-Edwards, K. E. (2001). Hormonal changes in mammalian fathers. *Hormones and Behavior, 40,* 139–145.

Young, L. J., Nilsen, R., Waymire, K. G., MacGregor, G. R., & Insel, T. R. (1999, August 19). Increased affiliative response to vasopressin in mice expressing the V_{1a} receptor from a monogamous vole. *Nature, 400,* 766–768.

CHAPTER 17

Parental Investment and Parent-Offspring Conflict

CATHERINE SALMON

M
ANY SPECIES DO NOT engage in parental care (Alcock, 2001). Part of the reason is that parental care is costly. By investing in offspring, parents lose out on resources that could be devoted to themselves, used in the pursuit of a larger territory, or finding additional mates. Some parents even risk their own survival in an effort to improve the survival of their offspring. So when we do see parental care, the reproductive benefits must have been great enough to outweigh the costs of providing not only the physical means for survival (food, shelter, protection) but also fostering the development of the skills required for success across the lifespan.

From the parental perspective, each individual's overall reproductive effort is a combination of mating effort (courtship, etc.) and parental effort or investment. Trivers (1972) defined *parental investment* as any investment by the parent in an individual offspring that increases the offspring's chance of surviving (and hence reproductive potential) at the cost of the parent's ability to invest in other offspring (either current or future). In many species, it involves actions such as food provisioning and protection from predators. In humans, it involves a great deal more, ranging from providing food and shelter to an education, music lessons, taking the kids to hockey or gymnastics, or providing them with braces. In general, an offspring's fitness increases with the amount of parental investment it receives. We can assume that in species that have parental care, extremely low levels of parental investment may result in the loss of offspring as a certain minimal amount of investment is required for survival. However, a point of diminishing return is also eventually met at very high levels of parental investment because the offspring are unable to capitalize on investment over and above a certain amount.

Financial support for the author's own work on family dynamics has come from the Social Sciences and Humanities Research Council of Canada. Thanks to Martin Daly, David Buss, and Frank Sulloway for their helpful comments and to Jennifer Davis, who was to write this chapter with me originally, but is currently allocating her resources to parental investment.

506

Hamilton's rule (1964) can shed light on how parents and offspring behave with regard to parental investment. Hamilton developed the concept of inclusive fitness, noting that when we assess the fitness of a trait or behavior, we need to consider its contribution to the reproduction of that individual and to whether it influences the reproductive prospects of its kin. The inequality that sums up the conditions under which a particular behavior would be expected to spread is $c < rb$, where c equals the fitness cost of the action (such as providing food) to the actor, b is the fitness benefit (getting to eat) to the recipient, and r is the degree of relatedness between the actor and recipient (.5 for parent-offspring, .5 for full siblings, .25 for half-siblings, etc.). Obviously, a parent's investment in its offspring provides a benefit to the offspring, which increases the parent's inclusive fitness. As long as the cost of parental investment doesn't begin to outweigh the benefit to the offspring times the degree of relatedness, it should continue.

Similarly, in a brood of two equal siblings, A and B, from Hamilton's rule (1964), A should continue to take resources until its marginal gains drop to ½ those of B, who gets the remainder (Parker, Mock, & Lamey, 1989). For half siblings, marginal gains drop to ¼. The key point is the degree of relatedness. A child shares a given gene with itself with a probability of 1.0, but it shares the same gene with a probability of only .5 with a sibling. For this reason, a child is expected to try to obtain resources (or continue to monopolize them in the case of nursing, for example) unless the value of that resource to that child drops below the value, multiplied by the degree of relatedness, of giving that resource to its sibling. Parents, in contrast, are equally related (0.5) to each of their offspring. As a result, they are motivated to distribute resources equally unless one child is better able to benefit from the resources than others. Our offspring are the way our genes get into the next generation, but not all offspring are equally good fitness vehicles. Some offspring will be better able to survive or be more likely to mate. Such offspring are a better investment risk. Certain offspring may be more likely to benefit from some forms of parental care than others (an infant compared to a teenager, perhaps). As a result, selection has favored mechanisms of parental care that have the effect of increasing the fitness of the parent by favoring offspring who are likely to provide a higher reproductive return on their parents' investment (Daly & Wilson, 1995). But the costs, degree of relatedness, and benefits to parents can be influenced by a variety of factors that in turn influence the amount of parental investment given. The conflict these factors can cause between parent and offspring is discussed later.

FACTORS AFFECTING THE AMOUNT OF PARENTAL INVESTMENT

There are numerous factors that can have an impact on the amount of parental resources invested in any particular child.

FACTORS INFLUENCING COSTS TO PARENTS

Parental age is one factor that influences the costs of parental investment. As parents themselves grow older, the fitness value of an offspring of any given age and phenotype increases relative to the parent's residual reproductive value.

Thus, in any species in which expected future reproduction is a declining function of parental age, older parents will have been selected to invest more in offspring, all else being equal, than younger parents (Pugesek, 1995; Salmon & Daly, 1998; Voland & Gabler, 1994). Evidence from various studies suggests that in many species, this is the case (Clark, Moghaddas, & Galef, 2002; Clutton-Brock, 1984). For example, Clark et al.'s (2002) study of parental effort in female Mongolian gerbils found that older mothers provided more parental investment than younger mothers.

If young women have many years in which to give birth to and invest in children, sacrificing one may not be too costly. Older women, nearing the end of their reproductive capacity who pass up an opportunity to bear and invest in children, may not have another chance. As opportunities for reproduction diminish, postponing childbearing and rearing would be reproductively costly. From this perspective, we expect that natural selection would favor older women who invest immediately and to a significant degree in children rather than postponing. Dramatic decreases in rates of maternally perpetrated infanticide as a function of maternal age appear to be one reflection of age-related changes in the relative weights that the maternal psyche places on a woman's infant versus her future reproduction (Bugos & McCarthy, 1984; Daly & Wilson, 1995; Lee & George, 1999; Overpeck, Brenner, Trumble, Trifiletti, & Berendes, 1998).

The *number of offspring* at any given time is also expected to have an impact on parental investment. Because parental investment is a limited resource (food, time, money) that must be allocated among offspring, it seems clear that with the possible exception of protection from predators, most parental resources will be in shorter supply when there are multiple young (not necessarily all the same age) present at the same time. An increased number of children means fewer resources for each child.

Parental resource circumstances are also predicted to have an impact on the amount of parental investment. When resources are in short supply or difficult to obtain, any particular investment is more costly from the parent's perspective than when resources are abundant. Davis and colleagues (Davis & Todd, 1999; Davis, Todd, & Bullock, 1999) modeled the success of a variety of parental investment decision rules in the Western bluebird and found that the success of different rules is highly dependent on the amount of resources available to parents. The less parents have, the more biased they ought to be in their allocation of investments. Parents faced with extremely poor resources ought to invest heavily in a single offspring, ignoring the others. As resources become more abundant, parents do best by becoming more egalitarian (which seems counter to the Trivers-Willard hypothesis, which is discussed later). At a very general level, we could argue that the degree to which parents divide current investment unequally among offspring is a function of the amount of resources available to them.

FACTORS INFLUENCING BENEFITS TO PARENTS

The *age of the child* can have a significant impact on the benefit to parents of parental investment. In many ways, we would predict a greater payoff from investing in older children. An individual's expected contribution to parental fitness resides mainly in his or her reproductive value (expected future reproduction; Fisher, 1930), and this quantity increases with age until at least puberty, making an older, immature offspring more valuable from the parental perspective than a younger one (Montgomerie & Weatherhead, 1988). This increase occurs primarily because in non-technological societies some percentage of children die. As a result, the average 14-year-old, for example, has a higher reproductive value than the average infant because some infants don't survive to their teenage years. Surviving to puberty was more difficult over most of human ancestral history, when rates of infant mortality were high. However, the older an individual offspring gets, in many cases, the less valuable parental investment (especially certain kinds of investment) will be in terms of the offspring's ability to utilize it when compared to its utility to other offspring. In particular, a great deal of parental investment is often critical to the survival and future of young offspring. For them, significant parental investment can make a huge difference.

In the human case, parents clearly respond to the changing needs and abilities of their children. But when one child must be sacrificed so others can be saved, it is apparently a cross-cultural universal that the youngest is the likeliest victim (Daly & Wilson, 1984). Data on Canadian homicides also suggests that older children are more highly valued. When Daly and Wilson (1988) looked at the risk of the homicide of a child by a biological parent in relation to the child's age, infants were at a much higher risk of being killed than any other group of children. After 1 year, the rates drop off dramatically until they reach zero at age 17. And it is not only that infants are easier to kill because the risk of a child being killed by a non-relative shows a different pattern, with 1-year-olds more likely to be killed than infants, and teenagers being the most likely to be killed.

A *child's expected future prospects* will also be expected to have an impact on the benefits of parental investment. In other words, future survival and reproductive success influence the benefit to parents. If there is unlikely to be a fitness return on their investment, natural selection would be unlikely to favor mechanisms to invest in such offspring. Like offspring age, offspring's expected future prospects are related to an offspring's ability to convert parental investment into fitness. Thus, we would expect evolved psychological mechanisms of parental care to be sensitive to cues of offspring "quality" or ability to convert parental care into future reproductive success. For example, children who are disabled in some way, all else being equal, are less likely to have future reproductive success than children who are healthy.

In humans, poor infant quality clearly has an impact on parental investment. Offspring born with a severe physical deformity are likely to be the victims of infanticide, especially in traditional societies where institutional care of the handicapped is not available (Daly & Wilson, 1984, 1988). The increased level of care such children require for a low evolutionary payoff (they are unlikely to reproduce even if they do survive) means that parents are better off if they terminate investment early on and begin to invest in a new offspring. Even in North America, handicapped children are at greater risk of abuse and more likely to suffer injuries requiring a visit to hospital at the hands of their parents than healthy children (Daly & Wilson, 1984).

In addition, Hill and Ball (1996) examined the ethnographic literature for the reasons given cross-culturally for infanticide shortly after birth. Most involved abnormal circumstances surrounding the birth, including the baby born breech, feet first, or with teeth. They noted that many of the characteristics mentioned were associated with conditions that increase childhood morbidity.

But infanticide is not the only phenomenon that reveals the importance of a child's future prospects to parental investment. Trivers and Willard (1973) have argued that when one sex has a greater variance in lifetime reproductive success than the other and parents (specifically mothers) vary in their physical condition or access to resources, differences in preferences for offspring of the two sexes are likely to evolve. If male reproductive success depends on the individual's condition (bigger males get more mates), mothers in good condition who are able to invest heavily will be able to influence the reproductive success of their sons more successfully than mothers in poor condition (or with few resources). They should, therefore, prefer to have sons or to invest more in their sons (Bercovitch, Widdig, & Nurnberg, 2000; Trivers & Willard, 1973). In contrast, mothers in poor condition should prefer daughters because daughters are reproductively less risky (lower variance). This is known as the Trivers-Willard effect.

Cameron and Linklater's (2000) study of feral horses illustrated that mares in good condition invested more in their sons (measured by time spent in close proximity and amount of sucking, etc.) while mares in poor condition invested more in daughters. However, there are situations where it might be advantageous for good condition females to invest in daughters. Silk (1983) has suggested that when females are philopatric (remain in their natal territory) and compete for resources and rank, high-ranking mothers should invest more in daughters and low-ranking mothers should invest more in sons. There is evidence that, in rhesus macaques, this is indeed what occurs (Maestripieri, 2001).

There are several human examples of the Trivers-Willard effect (but see Sieff, 1990, and Keller et al., 2001 for studies that failed to confirm the effect). Dickemann's (1979) historical review of infanticide within the Indian caste system indicated that, before the twentieth century, infanticide was extremely common among the highest castes with female infants the victims. Daughters in such castes had few options. They could only marry within their own caste, not a lower one. Among high caste families, investment in males (who could marry females from their own or lower subcastes) was a better bet in terms of numbers of grandchildren and, as a result, parents invested significantly more in sons than daughters (Das Gupta, 1987). Amongst those of lower social status, the fact that males, on average, would marry down led to daughters outreproducing sons. Correspondingly, parents biased their investment toward daughters (seen in a much lower rate of female infanticide). Studies in the United States (Gaulin & Robbins, 1991) and Kenya (Cronk, 1989) have suggested that female infants from low-income families are nursed more than infant boys.

Studies of Hungarian Gypsy populations actually show a female-biased sex ratio (Bereczkei & Dunbar, 1997, 2002). Unlike the native Hungarian population, Gypsies have many more daughters than sons and, like the lower caste Indians, are considered to be of low social status. Gypsy women are much more likely to marry up the social scale than men, outreproducing their brothers, and tending to have healthier babies than Gypsy women who marry other Gypsies. Unsurprisingly, Gypsy parents invest more heavily in their daughters than their sons. Bereczkei and Dunbar (1997) found that compared to native Hungarians, Gypsy women spent more time nursing their firstborn daughters than sons and provided more paid education for their daughters than sons. Recent work (Bereczkei & Dunbar, 2002) suggests that rural Gypsies may invest more in daughters to facilitate a helping-at-the-nest strategy (this occurs in birds when a sexually mature offspring remains at the natal nest and "helps" to raise its siblings, usually when breeding territory is scarce) to improve mothers' reproductive success while urban Gypsies may be investing more in daughters because of their greater probability of reproductive success.

There are also examples in humans where investment favors sons. In societies where the possession of resources has a significant impact on male reproductive success, a preference for sons (or for investing highly in them) is seen among the affluent. This has been the case in eighteenth-century northern German villages (Voland, 1998) and has been noted in the records of probated wills among Canadians living in British Columbia (Smith, Kish, & Crawford, 1987).

FACTORS AFFECTING RELATEDNESS

Three main factors influence relatedness in this context: paternity certainty, stepparenting, and adoption.

Paternity uncertainty plays a significant role in why females invest more in parental care than males. From a genetic perspective, individual males should invest in an offspring only if they can be sure that the offspring is their own. Mammalian females (with internal gestation and fertilization) have always been certain that their offspring are their own. Males do not have such certainty and, as a result, should be attuned to signs of paternity and inclined to invest only when such signs are present. In many bird species, in particular, male parental care is influenced by the likelihood that the male is the genetic father of the offspring (Green, 2002; Lifjeld, Slagsvold, & Ellegren, 1998; Osorio-Beristain & Drummond, 2001).

There are a variety of results that suggest that paternity uncertainty does have an impact on human paternal investment. Mothers attempt to reassure fathers about their putative paternity. Daly and Wilson's (1982) study of the spontaneous comments made by Canadian parents and grandparents after a baby's birth indicates that grandparents make many more comments about the paternal resemblance in the baby's face than any maternal resemblance ("Look, he has his dad's chin."). Similar findings have been reported for Mexican infants (Regalski & Gaulin, 1993). It seems that everyone (except the father) wants to present the image of the baby as looking just like him. For further discussion, see Kurland and Gaulin (Chapter 15, this volume).

Stepparenting also affects relatedness in that stepparents are not related biologically to any stepchildren they may have. In species with biparental care, when one parent dies or disappears and is replaced by a new mate, any offspring now have a stepparent. As with paternity uncertainty, we would expect mechanisms of parental allocation of investment to be sensitive to whether an offspring is a person's biological child, with resources being directed away from stepchildren toward biological children.

In some species, being unrelated to a new mate's offspring means not just a lack of inclination to invest parentally, but a motivation to eliminate them from the picture. When a male Hanuman langur takes over a troop, he is likely to attempt to kill the infants present. Hanuman langurs live in bands, often consisting of one large reproductive male and a group of smaller adult females and their offspring. Hrdy (1977) has suggested that this infanticidal behavior evolved as a result of sexual competition. When a female's infant is killed, she returns to a state of sexual receptivity. The new male will then gain almost immediate sexual access to the females in the troop. In lions, infanticide often occurs when a new group of males takes over a pride containing females with young cubs (Ebensperger, 1998; Pusey & Packer, 1994). The new males will hunt down cubs and attempt to kill them, despite the efforts of the lionesses to protect them. Lionessess with cubs give birth at approximately 2 year intervals. If a cub dies, the mother will become sexually receptive right away and mate with one of the new males. From the males' perspective, there are clear reproductive benefits to infanticide. If they are likely to control a pride for, on average, 2 years, they should not waste that window of mating opportunity by letting the females nurse cubs that are not theirs. Correspondingly, in species where sexual access to males limits female reproductive success, like the jacana, females practice infanticide, destroying another female's clutch so that the male will abandon it, mate with her, and care for her eggs (Emlen, Demong, & Emlen, 1989).

Daly and Wilson (1984, 1988, 2001) have spent 20 years exploring the nature of discriminative parental solicitude, paying particular attention to the dynamics of stepparenting in humans. Parental care can be viewed as a continuum with self-sacrifice at one end while at the other end are acts that inflict costs on the child, including child abuse and homicide. Inclusive fitness theory tells us that genetic relatedness to a child is one predictor of infanticide; the less genetically related the adult is to the child, the higher the probability of infanticide. Daly and Wilson (1988) have tested this theory. Their study of child abuse in Hamilton, Ontario, demonstrated that children living with one genetic parent and one stepparent are about 40 times more likely to be physically abused than children living with both genetic parents. This occurs even when controlling for poverty and socioeconomic status (to control for the higher rate of child abuse in low-income families).

Data on child infanticide tell the same story. The rates of child murder are far higher for stepparents than for genetic parents. The risk is highest for the very young, particularly children under 2 years of age. Daly and Wilson (1988) found that the risk of a preschool-age child being killed ranged from 40 to 100 times higher for stepchildren than for children living with two genetic parents.

A less extreme example involves amount of investment, rather than termination. Stepfathers invest fewer monetary resources in their stepchildren. In a study of men living in Albuquerque, New Mexico, Anderson, Kaplan, and Lancaster (1999) reported that genetic children were 5.5 times more likely to receive some money for college than stepchildren. On average, genetic children received $15,500 more for college and had 65% more of their college expenses paid for than stepchildren. There have also been suggestions that when stepparental investment is seen, it may reflect mating effort on the part of males (intended to make themselves more attractive to their new mate) rather than parental effort (Anderson et al., 1999; Hofferth & Anderson, 2003; Rowher, Herron, & Daly, 1999).

Adoption is another factor that changes relatedness. We also need to distinguish between the adoption of related and unrelated individuals. With an individual's own offspring, relatedness is .5. The adoption of any other kin (niece, cousin's child, etc.) involves a lesser degree of relatedness but there would still be some genetic common interest. Under these circumstances, we would expect a lesser degree of parental investment than in an individual's own biological child. From this perspective, we would expect very little to no parental investment in an adopted child because they are not genetically related at all. With stepparent situations, at least one parent is the biological parent; in adopted situations, there is no biological parent present.

However, there is little evidence that the adoption of unrelated individuals has ever occurred with any frequency over most of human evolutionary history. Nonhuman primates, who often live in close-knit kin groups like humans, tend not to adopt orphaned young (Silk, 1990). In most animal species, parents recognize their own young, especially ones where parents are exposed to the offspring of many individuals, such as in colonially nesting birds (Medvin & Beecher, 1986; Medvin, Stoddard, & Beecher 1993), bats (Balcombe, 1990; McCracken, 1993) or herd animals like horses and sheep. In ones where parents are solitary or the offspring are not very mobile (like some cliff nesting birds), parental recognition tends to be less common or less accurate, and accidental adoptions occur (Beecher, 1982; Knudsen & Evans, 1986; Medvin, Stoddard, & Beecher, 1993).

Most human historical adoption and adoption practices in traditional societies have been of genetically related individuals. Those individuals who cannot have their own children have often adopted their siblings' extra children ($r = .25$; Pennington & Harpending, 1993; Silk, 1980, 1987). In Stack's (1974) study of a Chicago urban Black community, most of the fostered children were with maternal kin, older sisters, aunts, and grandmothers. There is no reason to expect that we would have a mechanism designed specifically to deal with the adoption of unrelated individuals. It may be that in our current environment, strong biological and cultural desires lead some individuals to adopt unrelated offspring. The relationship between adopted children and parents typically functions in the same way as that between genetic parents and children, particularly when they are adopted as very young infants.

CONFLICT WITHIN THE FAMILY

Parker and colleagues (Parker, Royle, & Hartley, 2002) have suggested that we need to consider the conflicts of interest that exist among all family members. The potential for conflict exists between parents over how much parental investment each should give to their shared genetic offspring. Offspring compete amongst themselves for access to parental resources. Conflict can also occur between parents and offspring or even between offspring and future offspring. The parental investment that occurs is the outcome of all these conflicts. It is influenced not only by differences in relatedness between siblings, but by whether one parent's investment costs affect the reproductive success of the other parent (Lessells & Parker, 1999).

PARENT-OFFSPRING CONFLICT

At the core of inclusive fitness theory is the idea that kin are valuable and that we share a commonality of interest. In a genetic sense, what enhances the fitness of a person's kin enhances his or her own fitness. The more closely related two relatives are, the more common their genetic cause. But the inevitable consequence of social living is that at some point, individuals who interact will experience some conflict. Individuals act so as to increase his or her own inclusive fitness, even when it has fitness costs to others. Parent-offspring interaction can be highly cooperative but it can also involve significant conflict. There may be agreement about the general goal of offspring fitness, but conflict over amounts of investment in one offspring versus another.

Being closely related does not mean that two individuals' interests are identical. As much as the degree of genetic similarity is a source of unity, the degree of genetic difference is a source of possible conflict. This becomes obvious when individuals are competing for scarce resources (mates, food, or territory). Conflicts can also happen in cooperative relationships (between mates, for example), when disagreement occurs over to the optimal distribution of resources (to shared offspring, offspring of a previous union or mating effort). Such conflicts can also occur between parent and offspring.

Parent-offspring conflict can arise because some actions that advance the fitness of an offspring can potentially reduce the lifetime success of the parent and just as some actions that benefit parental fitness can reduce the lifetime fitness of a particular offspring. Siblicide is a good illustration of such actions. Siblicide is common in some boobies, colonially nesting seabirds. Typically, the older, or "A," chick eliminates its younger "B" chick sibling within the first few days post hatching. Forced from the nest, the younger chick will die of exposure or starvation. Masked booby parents "allow" siblicide, because they are unable to prevent it or because it is in the best interests of the parents themselves as well as the surviving chick. But there is much less siblicide in the blue-footed booby. This could be the result of differences in either chick or parent behavior. In fact, when blue-footed booby chicks are placed in a masked booby nest, the A chick will kill its sibling (Lougheed & Anderson, 1999). When masked chicks are placed in a blue-footed nest, the foster parents seem to prevent siblicide from occurring. The assumption is that, in the blue-footed species, the benefits to parents of having both chicks survive outweigh the cost to the A chick, from the parental perspective.

In general, we would expect individuals to allocate their parental investment among their offspring in ways that optimize their own inclusive fitness. All other things being equal, parents are equally related to all their offspring. However, we would expect offspring to have a somewhat different take on that matter. They are more closely related to themselves than to their siblings (Trivers, 1974). As a result, we might expect each offspring to want to extract more than its own share of parental investment. Conflicts arise over the level of investment considered to be appropriate. This zone of conflict can be predicted from kin selection theory. When the costs to parents are less than the benefits, both parents and offspring benefit from parental investment and there is no conflict. When the costs becomes greater than the benefits but not more than twice the benefits, parents lose but offspring still gain, so there is conflict. When the costs become greater than twice the benefit, both lose, so there is no conflict, and parental investment ends. (For a review of parent-offspring conflict in nonhuman primates, see Maestripieri, 2002.)

MATERNAL-FETAL CONFLICT

Parental investment by mothers begins long before birth. The mother's own resources provide nutrients and a safe environment for the developing child over the 9 month gestational period. Although, at first glance, this would seem a very harmonious relationship with mother and fetus sharing the same goals, the genetic interests of both parties are not identical. Because the fetus is more closely related to itself than either its mother or any future siblings, the process of pregnancy becomes a sensitive balance between the developing fetus' tendency to secure as large a share of maternal resources as possible and the mother's tendency to preserve some resources for herself and future offspring. Often this balancing act results in a variety of unpleasant symptoms for the mother and occasionally serious complications. Haig (1993, 1998) has analyzed pregnancy complications from a maternal-fetus conflict perspective, suggesting that such conflicts are responsible for some puzzling aspects of pregnancy and its complications. For a more in-depth discussion, see Kurland and Gaulin (Chapter 15, this volume).

WEANING CONFLICT

Conflict over weaning in mammals (Trivers, 1974) is a very clear example of parent-offspring conflict. As Figure 17.1 illustrates, parents are selected to continue to invest in their offspring up to the point when the cost in terms of reduced reproductive success (the more parents invest in a current offspring, the less they have to invest in future offspring) begins to outweigh the benefits of increased survival for the current offspring. Or, as soon as the costs begin to exceed the benefits (B/C < 1), parents should stop investing in the current offspring and start to work on the next (Trivers, 1974).

At this point, the offspring would still like investment to continue, being more closely related to itself than to any future siblings; it has been selected to demand investment until the cost-benefit ratio drops below .5. After that point, continued demands for investment would lead to a reduction in indirect fitness because the parent would produce fewer siblings with whom the offspring would share genes. But until that point is reached, offspring should attempt to

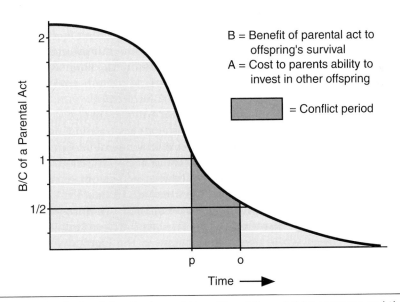

Figure 17.1 Analysis of the Costs and Benefits of Parental Investment and the Parent Offspring Conflict That Results. Adapted from "Parent-Offspring Conflict," by R. L. Trivers, 1974, *American Zoologist, 14,* pp. 249–264.

obtain as much parental investment as possible, enhancing its own reproductive fitness in the process. As a result, weaning conflict tends to involve a gradual shift in parental investment.

Attachment

In a sense, attachment type can be seen as the result of the type of parental investment a child receives. Bowlby (1969) characterized attachment as reflecting a child's "internal working model" of the self, others, and relationships, emphasizing the importance of early experience on adult personality and behavior. Harlow's (1958) well-known work on motherless monkeys was an unpleasant illustration. Current attachment theory suggests that individual differences in the quality of infant-parent attachment are largely shaped by the quality of care provided to the child, and that a secure relationship early in life influences future development (Belsky, 1997). It has been suggested that variation in attachment security evolved to increase reproductive fitness under variable conditions and that environmentally modified life history traits generally serve our reproductive fitness (Belsky, Steinberg, & Draper, 1991). The argument has been that attachment styles evolved as psychological mechanisms for converting information about an individual's environment into fitness-promoting reproductive strategies (Belsky, 2000; Bjorklund & Pellegrini, 2002; Chisholm, 1996; Wiley & Carlin, 1999). This theory relies on two assumptions: (1) Patterns of attachment are relatively stable from infancy to early adulthood, and (2) environmental conditions were relatively stable across the first 20 to 30 years of human life in the ancestral environment (Belsky, 1997).

Foley (1992) claimed that attachment functioned in the EEA to deal with risks that were recurrent but whose timing was uncertain, requiring a flexible developmental path. If offspring success depended on the quality and quantity of parental investment received, the biggest risks to that investment would be either an inability or unwillingness on the part of parents to invest. For parents in certain circumstances, the best long term fitness outcome might involve reductions or termination of investment in a particular offspring. This would allow resources to be allocated elsewhere, to other offspring, future mating, or survival (Chisholm, 1996; Draper & Harpending, 1982; Main, 1990).

According to Chisholm's life history model of attachment (1996), the type of attachment seen is a facultative adaptation to the style of parenting. Consistently responsive attentive parenting produces secure attachment because, in the ancestral environment, such parenting was evidence of access to resources and a commitment to provide the necessities of life to that offspring. Non-responsive or rejecting parenting produces insecure attachment. In the EEA, such parents would have been unable or unwilling to invest in their offspring. The suggestion has been that insecure-avoidant represents the facultative adaptation to parental unwillingness to invest while insecure-resistant is the facultative adaptation to parental inability to invest (Chisholm, 1996).

Attachment is normally classified as secure, insecure-avoidant, and insecure-resistant. If individual differences in attachment organization represent facultative adaptations to conditions of risk and uncertainty that were recurrent in the EEA (Chisholm, 1996), we can examine the nature of styles of attachment in a new light. Secure attachment would develop under ecological conditions that indicated that resources were reasonably abundant and would remain so. This would foster the belief that the world is a relatively safe place, other people can be trusted, and relationships last. The result would be the emphasis of parenting over mating.

The psychological and behavioral data on secure individuals is consistent in terms of adult relationships and parenting. Secure men have more positive and encouraging relationships with their spouses than insecure men (Cohn, Cowan, Cowan, & Pearson, 1992) while secure women under stress are more likely to seek emotional support and comfort from their male partner (Simpson, Rhodes, & Nelligan, 1992). Conflict and negative affect are common in married couples where both are insecure (Cohn et al., 1992), but when both partners are secure, negative interactions are rare (Senchak & Leonard, 1992). In general, lower levels of conflict and more skilled ways of managing conflict occur in relationships involving secure individuals. Secure individuals report greater relationship satisfaction when dating (Simpson, 1990) and their romantic relationships are longer lasting whether dating or married (Hazan & Shaver, 1987; Kirkpatrick & Davis, 1994; Shaver & Hazan, 1993). A history of secure attachment encourages the development of satisfying stable mateships that in turn focus on high investment parenting (Van Ijzendoorn, 1995; Ward & Carlson, 1995), resulting in a quality versus quantity approach to reproduction.

Belsky et al. (1991) and Chisholm (1996) have suggested when the flow of resources is chronically low or unpredictable, it may be (or have been) biologically adaptive to reduce parental investment and allocate resources not to parenting but to offspring production (Borgerhoff Mulder, 1992). Limited unpredictable resources would result in a parenting style that crafts an offspring worldview of people as untrustworthy and uncaring. In such a world, individuals would do best if they were themselves opportunistic and exploitative. Under such conditions, individuals will have many partners and mateships will be unstable with many kids and little paternal care.

The data suggest that insecure-avoidant individuals are more promiscuous and less committed (Kirkpatrick & Hazan, 1994; Simpson, 1990) and more likely to split up when in a relationship (Feeney & Noller, 1992). As well, avoidant mothers are less responsive (Van Ijzendoorn, 1995), less supportive and helpful, less concerned and more remote, and controlling (Crowell & Feldman, 1988, 1991).

The insecure-resistant case is a little different. Children with this attachment style tend to inflate their need for care and attention (Cassidy & Berlin, 1995) in response to inconsistently responsive care. One suggestion as to why this develops has been related to the helpers at the nest phenomenon (Bogerhoff Mulder, 1992; Emlen, Wrenge, & Demong, 1995). Inconsistently responsive parenting seems to produce a dependency in their children, which has been suggested to promote the parent's reproductive fitness. Kunce and Shaver (1994) noted that insecure-resistant women are compulsive caregivers, particularly toward younger siblings. Being separated from their small children is difficult for resistant mothers (Crowell & Feldman, 1988), and they often believe their older offspring are unable to cope away from home (Kobak, Ferenz-Gillies, Everhart, & Seabrook, 1994). They keep their children close and dependent, increasing the possibility of helping at the nest behavior. Such an attachment style might occur more frequently in certain environments (e.g., firstborn females), particularly if the mother's ability to care for her offspring is impaired due to a lack of resources or assistance (Belsky, 1997).

Attachment, whether secure (reliable parental investment) or insecure (the consequences of early stress), might have evolved to function as a barometer of future social relations. Data on early menarche, father absence, and sexual activity (Ellis, McFadyen-Ketchum, Dodge, Pettit, & Bates, 1999; Graber, Brooks-Gunn, & Warren, 1995; Surbey, 1990, 1998; Trickett & Putnam, 1993; Wierson, Long, & Forehand, 1993) suggest that this may be the case. When girls grow up in father-absent homes (cues that the local males may be unlikely to stay and invest or that long-term life prospects are poor), they tend to mature faster and follow a strategy of quantity over quality. Under some circumstances, it's adaptive to reproduce early and often. In a similar vein, data suggest that boys that grow up in father-absent homes may exhibit increased promiscuity and criminality as well as a general increase in "macho" behavior (Bereczkei & Csanaky, 1996). Such a strategy of increased aggression might serve under some circumstances to intimidate rivals and attract women interested in protection (Kim, Smith, & Palermiti, 1997).

SIBLING RELATIONS

The other side to parent-offspring conflict is how the battle for resources plays itself out among a group of siblings. Natural selection has shaped strategies for sibling competition just as it shaped mechanisms for discriminative parental solicitude. Many factors play a role in the approach individual siblings may take, but two are of particular interest: birth order and birth spacing (interbirth interval).

BIRTH ORDER

Theoretical models of the evolution of parental inclinations predict that parents often treat their offspring differently. There are grounds for predicting discriminative parental solicitude in relation to a number of factors including offspring age, parental age, birth order, offspring sex, cues of phenotypic quality, and cues of parentage (Clutton-Brock, 1991; Daly & Wilson, 1995; Trivers & Willard, 1973). The unifying notion behind these theories is that natural selection has shaped parental psychologies to function as if they "value" individual offspring and investments in their development in proportion to the expected impacts of such investments on parental fitness (genetic posterity) in ancestral environments.

The question of how parents may be biased in their investment can be informed by a consideration of models of parental investment in other species. At some level, the problem faced by human parents trying to figure out how to divide investment among multiple children is the same as the problem faced by any species in which multiple dependent offspring of differing ages (or birth orders) are raised simultaneously. It is important to note that in most animal models, parental investment is primarily understood in terms of provisioning (Clutton-Brock, 1991; Davis & Todd, 1999). While this assumption is true for humans as well, it does not capture the range of other types of human parental investment, which include education (though we could argue that many animals expend resources in teaching their offspring to hunt, e.g.), sports, and other activities. The connection to survival here seems less clear. But one answer may be that it reflects parental investment in children's social competitiveness, which seems to correlate positively with reproductive outcomes and negatively with mortality risks (Boone & Kessler, 1999; Hertwig, David, & Sulloway, 2002).

Another important point is that parent birds, for example, can face extreme resource shortages where it will be impossible for all the chicks to survive. In Davis et al.'s bluebird model (1999), as soon as there were enough resources to keep them all alive, egalitarian division rules did best. If we assume that human parents typically have enough resources available to them to raise all of their children to adulthood (as presumably most do in Western societies), this assumption leads to the expectation that human parents may use a decision rule that divides investment equally among all of their children. Such a rule is called the *equity heuristic* (Hertwig et al., 2002).

However, the equity heuristic is not the only model of the allocation of parental investment. There are times when the equal allocation of resources may not provide the optimal result, perhaps because most of the time all else is not equal and some offspring may be more valuable fitness vehicles than others.

The anticipated relevance of birth order to the allocation of parental investment is a corollary of the importance of offspring age. An individual's expected contribution to parental fitness resides mainly in its reproductive value (expected future reproduction), and this quantity increases with age until at least puberty, making an older, immature offspring more valuable from the parental perspective than a younger one (Montgomerie & Weatherhead, 1988). In the human case, parental favoring of older offspring can be masked by changing parental response to children with changing needs and abilities, but it becomes apparent when tough choices have to be made. When one child must be sacrificed so others can be saved, it appears to be a cross-cultural universal that the youngest is the likeliest victim (Daly & Wilson, 1984).

In addition to enjoying the relative security of parental preference in a pinch, firstborn children have always benefited from an early absence of sibling contenders for a share of parental investment. Even in the modern West, where parental resources are presumably less stretched than in noncontracepting, premodern societies, firstborn children still receive more parental caretaking and attention in infancy than laterborns (Jacobs & Moss, 1976), and they grow faster, such that despite being smaller at birth, they are larger by 1 year of age (Meredith, 1950; Wingerd, 1970).

There is, however, a countervailing effect: As parents themselves grow older, the fitness value of an offspring of any given age and phenotype increases relative to the parent's residual reproductive value. Thus, in any species in which expected future reproduction is a declining function of parental age, older parents will have been selected to invest more in offspring, all else being equal, than younger parents (Pugesek, 1995). Thanks to menopause, this argument certainly applies to the human female, and dramatic decreases in maternally perpetrated infanticide as a function of maternal age appear to be one reflection of age-related changes in the relative weights that the maternal psyche places on the female's infant versus her future (Bugos & McCarthy, 1984; Daly & Wilson, 1995).

Impact of Birth Order on Personality and Development   Sulloway and others (Salmon, 1999; Salmon & Daly, 1998; Sulloway, 1996, p. 305) have suggested that the favoring of firstborns (due to their greater reproductive value) and lastborns (due to older parents and lack of younger rival) means that middleborns are the birth order that loses out on average in the parental investment game. Certainly middleborns seem to report lesser levels of financial and emotional support from parents (Janicki & Salmon, 2002; Kennedy, 1989; Salmon & Daly, 1998) than firstborns or lastborns (who tend to be more parentally and familially oriented). As a result, they seem to focus more on developing nonkin reciprocal relationships outside the family unit (Salmon, 2003), and their personality traits seem to be a reflection of that. They are often noted for their skills in getting along with other people and in being excellent negotiators, traits that would have tended to serve them well in trying to find their niche within the family and a network of support outside it (Sulloway, 1999).

Sulloway (1996) has summed up many of the birth order differences with regard to personality in terms of the five-factor model of personality (which posits five basic personality dimensions: conscientiousness, agreeableness, openness to experience, extraversion, and neuroticism). He states that:

> By itself, competition among siblings does not lead to birth order differences in personality. But birth order provides a powerful proximate (and environmental) source of sibling strategies. These tactical differences arise because birth order is correlated with differences in age, size, power, and status within the family. These physical and social disparities cause siblings to experience family relationships in dissimilar ways and to pursue differing ways of optimizing their parents' investment in their welfare. (Sulloway, 1999, p. 190)

The literature on birth order and personality is huge (more than 2,000 studies), but Sulloway's (1995) meta-analysis of those studies that control for related background variables reveals consistent birth order differences across the five factor model. Firstborns are typically noted to be more responsible. In fact, the related big five trait of conscientiousness is one that shows consistent birth order differences with firstborns tending to score higher than laterborns. Even IQ scores seem to experience a minor impact in terms of birth order with firstborns having a slightly higher IQ than their younger siblings. It corresponds to about 1 IQ point per birth position so that a firstborn's IQ would be one point higher than their second born sibling and two points higher than their third, and so on (Zajonc & Mullally, 1997).

Even if parents do not actively favor one child over another (Hertwig et al., 2002), siblings compete with each other for a greater share of parental resources. Sulloway (1995) suggested that they do so by carving out unique niches, or roles, within the family that are influenced by their birth order. Secure in their expectation of parental favoritism (and benefiting from an early absence of competitiors for parental investment), firstborns tend to have their choice of niches. Motivated to fulfill parental expectations, they typically become supporters of parental values and the status quo. Laterborns cannot compete as effectively in the same roles (being smaller in size and less experienced), so they seek out different niches, other routes to sources of parental (or other) investment. Personality traits that facilitate this include openness to experience and unconventionality, traits that sometimes mark them as rebels. Michalski and Shackelford (2002) have also suggested that firstborns are more likely to follow long-term mating strategies than laterborn children, with laterborn children desiring a greater variety of sexual partners in the future.

Siblings are not only different in the ways they approach parental investment and cultivating niches, but also in the strategies they use in interacting with each other. Human siblings have dominance hierarchies much like those of other mammals (Sulloway, 2001a). Anyone who watches a litter of puppies can observe the largest using physical strength or the threat of it to get their own way. Firstborn humans are very similar, tending to dominate their younger siblings. Smaller siblings (or laterborn humans) have to resort to alternative strategies, finding ways to get parental assistance or forming bonds with other siblings to unite against their oppressor. What eldest sibling hasn't been occasionally frustrated at having their plans thwarted by a junior sib who has gone whining or crying to a parent?

Only children (those with no siblings) are an example of what happens without sibling competition. In a sense, they are firstborns who never had a sibling come along to compete for parental resources. Like firstborns, they tend to have a drive for success and respect for parental values. But on many other measures, they fall somewhere in between first and laterborns (Sulloway, 2001b). Birth intervals can also affect the correlation between birth order and personality as well as levels of parental investment. Large age spacing (six or more years) can make a firstborn more like an only child. The same is true for lastborns born long after their other siblings.

One of the best methods for examining birth order effects on personality involves studies where siblings are asked questions about each other's personality traits (Paulhus, Chen, & Trapnel, 1999; Sulloway, 1999). In addition, because these sibling strategies are adopted for competition within the family, within family data would be the most appropriate to evaluate these processes. Such within family designs typically produce significant birth order effects, with more conscientious firstborns and more agreeable laterborns.

Birth Spacing

The influence of birth order is decreased when the birth interval is so short that the siblings are on almost equal footing or when the interval is so large that they are not competing for the same resources from parents. For example, a middleborn with a sibling seven years older and another sibling one year younger may have a personality more representative of a firstborn than a typical middleborn (Sulloway, 1999).

Parents invest in their offspring based on many things, including offspring quality, reproductive value, their own residual reproductive value, and the amount of available resources. There is a cost-benefit analysis going on. And for siblings, their brothers and sisters also entail costs and benefits, which vary in proportion to the birth interval. Substantially older offspring, no longer dependent on parental care, experience minimal costs from additional siblings. Close age spacing increases competition for parental investment, promoting greater parent-offspring conflict as well as increased sibling rivalry. As well, the costs represented by a younger sibling are greatest when both are infants, requiring the same high levels of parental investment. In traditional societies, birth intervals of less than 5 years are associated with increased infant mortality (Daly & Wilson, 1988, p. 46; Lindstrom & Berhanu, 2000; Muhuri & Menken, 1997).

The influence of birth order on sibling strategies should be greatest for offspring who are spaced within 5 years. Under these circumstances, older siblings should tend to highlight their own worth and run down the value of their younger siblings. Younger siblings should respond by trying to minimize direct comparisons with older siblings, diverging in their interests and perhaps searching out nonparental sources of investment as they get older (Salmon & Daly, 1998). For example, in terms of openness to experience, the greatest disparities are among offspring separated by moderate age differences. Those that are more distant or very close are less polarized (Koch, 1956; Sulloway, 1996). The reasons for this seem clear in terms of large birth intervals but less intuitive for close ones until we consider the issue of benefit, not just the cost of the sibling. If we look at the relative differences in the likelihood of survival of offspring, those that are close in age are more equal. The cost of the sibling may be high, but the benefit is also high because the other is equally likely to survive. For large intervals, the cost is much less because the older sibling needs less parental investment, though the benefit may be lower because the younger sibling may be less likely to survive simply by virtue of the fact that it is young. At middle age spacings, the adjusted costs of having a younger sibling are elevated in relation to the benefits. As a result, moderate age gaps result in more polarization between siblings (Sulloway, 1996).

CONCLUSION

Basic human relationships and characteristic conflicts show a startling consistency across time and space, and it is reasonable to expect that psychological adaptations have evolved to deal with them that are particular to each type of relationship. Evolutionary psychology contributes to our understanding of parent-offspring relations, as well as sibling relations, allowing us to predict and explain the behavior of parents and offspring with regard to social and ecological variables.

Parental investment in humans shares a great deal with parental investment by other mammals. Females invest substantially more than males, the amount of investment given is influenced by the availability of resources and the likelihood of their successful use, and male investment reflects genetic certainty of paternity. But human parental investment also differs from that of other mammals, largely due to our greater cognitive ability, social complexity, and the resulting extended period of childhood dependency. Human children require greater investment than other primate offspring and, in particular, fathers must contribute more than they do in many species. The conflicts between parent and offspring and between siblings are also seen in many other species, weaning conflict perhaps the most frequently cited example, and are reflections of the fact that though all these individuals have shared genetic interests, they are not identical genetic interests.

Maternal investment begins in utero as do conflicts over levels of investment. Conditions such as preeclampsia can be seen as the result of a tug of war between mother and fetus over the amount of fetal growth that is appropriate. Differential investment in offspring is common and reflects the factors that affect the costs and benefits of parental investment to parents, including parental age, number of offspring, parental resources, age of offspring, offspring's expected future prospects, paternity certainty, and stepparenthood. Sibling conflict can be seen as an extension of parent-offspring conflict, and the degree of conflict is influenced by birth spacing (exacerbated by small intervals) and birth order (in that parents may bias their investment toward a particular birth order).

REFERENCES

Alcock, J. (2001). *Animal behavior: An evolutionary approach* (7th ed.). Sunderland, MA: Sinauer.

Anderson, J. G., Kaplan, H. S., & Lancaster, J. B. (1999). Paternal care by genetic fathers and stepfathers: 1. reports from Albuquerque men. *Evolution and Human Behaviour, 20*, 405–431.

Balcombe, J. P. (1990). Vocal recognition of pups by mother Mexican free-tailed bats, Tadarida brasiliensis mexicana. *Animal Behaviour, 39,* 960–966.

Beecher, M. D. (1982). Signature systems and kin recognition. *American Zoologist, 22,* 477–490.

Belsky, J. (1997). Attachment, mating, and parenting: An evolutionary interpretation. *Human Nature, 8,* 361–381.

Belsky, J. (2000). Conditional and alternative reproductive strategies: Individual differences in susceptibility to rearing experience. In J. Rodgers & D. Rowe (Eds.), *Genetic influences on fertility and sexuality* (pp. 127–146). Boston: Kluwer Academic.

Belsky, J., Steinberg, L., & Draper, P. (1991). Childhood experience, interpersonal development, and reproductive strategy: An evolutionary theory of socialization. *Child Development, 62,* 647–670.

Bercovitch, F. B., Widdig, A., & Nurnberg, P. (2000). Maternal investment in rhesus Macaques (*Macaca mulatto*): Reproductive costs and consequences on raising sons. *Behavioral Ecology and Sociobiology, 48,* 1–11.

Bereczkei, T., & Csanaky, A. (1996). Evolutionary pathway of child development: Lifestyles of adolescents and adults from father-absent families. *Human Nature, 7,* 257–280.

Bereczkei, T., & Dunbar, R. I. M. (1997). Female-biased reproductive strategies in a Hungarian Gypsy population. *Proceedings of the Royal Society of London. Series B, Biological Sciences, 264,* 17–22.

Bereczkei, T., & Dunbar, R. I. M. (2002). Helping-at-the-nest and sex-biased parental investment in a Hungarian Gypsy population. *Current Anthropology, 43,* 804–809.

Bjorklund, D. F., & Pellegrini, A. D. (2002). *The origins of human nature: Evolutionary developmental psychology.* Washington, DC: American Psychological Association.

Boone, J. L., & Kessler, K. L. (1999). More status or more children? Social status, fertility reduction, and long-term fitness. *Evolution and Human Behavior, 20,* 257–277.

Borgerhoff Mulder, M. (1992). Reproductive decisions. In E. A. Smith & B. Winterholder (Eds.), *Evolutionary ecology and human behavior* (pp. 147–179). New York: Aldine de Gruyter.

Bowlby, J. (1969). *Attachment and loss* (Vol. 1). New York: Basic Books.

Bugos, P. E., & McCarthy, L. M. (1984). Ayoreo infanticide: A case study. In G. Hausfater & S. B. Hrdy (Eds.), *Infanticide: Comparative and evolutionary perspectives* (pp. 503–520). New York: Aldine.

Cameron, E. Z., & Linklater, W. L. (2000). Individual mares bias investment in sons and daughters in relation to their condition. *Animal Behaviour, 60,* 359–367.

Cassidy, J., & Berlin, L. (1995). The insecure/ambivalent pattern of attachment: Theory and research. *Child Development, 65,* 971–991.

Chisholm, J. S. (1996). The evolutionary ecology of attachment organization. *Human Nature, 7,* 1–38.

Clark, M. M., Moghaddas, M., & Galef, B. G., Jr. (2002). Age at first mating affects parental effort and fecundity of female Mongolian gerbils. *Animal Behaviour, 63,* 1129–1134.

Clutton-Brock, T. H. (1984). Reproductive effort and terminal investment in iteroparous animals. *American Naturalist, 123,* 25–35.

Clutton-Brock, T. H. (1991). *The evolution of parental care.* Princeton, NJ: Princeton University Press.

Cohn, D., Cowan, P., Cowan, C., & Pearson, J. (1992). Working models of Childhood attachment and couples relationships. *Journal of Family Issues, 13,* 432–449.

Cronk, L. (1989). Low socioeconomic status and female-based parental investment: The Mokogodo example. *American Anthropologist, 91,* 414–429.

Crowell, J., & Feldman, S. (1988). Mother's internal models of relationships and children's behavioral and developmental status: A study of mother-child interaction. *Child Development, 59,* 1273–1285.

Crowell, J., & Feldman, S. (1991). Mother's working models of attachment Relationships and mother and child behavior during separation and reunion. *Developmental Psychology, 27,* 597–605.

Daly, M., & Wilson, M. (1982). Whom are newborn babies said to resemble? *Ethology and Sociobiology, 3,* 69–210.

Daly, M., & Wilson, M. (1984). A sociobiological analysis of human infanticide. In G. Hausfater & S. B. Hrdy (Eds.), *Infanticide: Comparative and evolutionary perspectives* (pp. 487–502). New York: Aldine.

Daly, M., & Wilson, M. (1988). *Homicide.* Hawthorne, NY: Aldine.

Daly, M., & Wilson, M. (1995). Discriminative parental solicitude and the relevance of evolutionary models to the analysis of motivational systems. In M. Gazzaniga (Ed.), *The cognitive neurosciences* (pp. 1269–1286). Cambridge, MA: MIT Press.

Daly, M., & Wilson, M. (2001). An assessment of some proposed exceptions to the phenomenon of nepotistic discrimination against stepchildren. *Annales Zoologici Fennici, 38,* 287–296.

Das Gupta, M. (1987). Selective discrimination against female children in rural Punjab. *Indian Population and Development Review, 13,* 77–100.

Davis, J. N., & Todd, P. M. (1999). Parental investment by decision rules. In G. Gigerenzer, P. M. Todd, & The ABC Research Group (Eds.), *Simple heuristics that make us smart* (pp. 309–324). New York: Oxford University Press.

Davis, J. N., Todd, P. M., & Bullock, S. (1999). Environment quality predicts parental provisioning decisions. *Proceedings of the Royal Society of London. Series B, Biological Sciences, 266,* 1791–1797.

Dickemann, M. (1979). Female infanticide, reproductive strategies, and social stratification: A preliminary model. In N. A. Chagnon & W. Irons (Eds.), *Evolutionary biology and human social behavior* (pp. 321–367). North Scituate, MA: Duxbury Press.

Draper, P., & Harpending, H. (1982). Father absence and reproductive strategy: An evolutionary perspective. *Journal of Anthropological Research, 38,* 255–273.

Ebensperger, L. A. (1998). Strategies and counterstrategies to infanticide in mammals. *Biological Reviews, 73,* 321–346.

Ellis, B. J., McFadyen-Ketchum, S., Dodge, K. A., Pettit, G. S., & Bates, J. E. (1999). Quality of early family relationships and individual differences in the timing of pubertal maturation in girls: A longitudinal test of an evolutionary model. *Journal of Personality and Social Psychology, 77,* 387–401.

Emlen, S. T., Demong, N. J., & Emlen, D. J. (1989). Experimental induction of infanticide in female wattled jacanas. *Auk, 106,* 1–7.

Emlen, S. T., Wrenge, P. H., & Demong, N. J. (1995). Making decisions in the family: An evolutionary perspective. *American Scientist, 83,* 148–157.

Feeney, J., & Noller, P. (1992). Attachment style and romantic love: Relationship dissolution. *Australian Journal of Psychology, 44,* 69–74.

Fisher, R. A. (1930). *The genetical theory of natural selection.* Oxford, England: Clarendon Press.

Foley, R. (1992). Evolutionary ecology of fossil hominids. In E. Smith & B. Winterhalder (Eds.), *Evolutionary ecology and human behavior* (pp. 131–164). New York: Aldine de Gruyter.

Gaulin, S. J. C., & Robbins, C. J. (1991). Trivers-Willard effect in contemporary North American society. *American Journal of Physical Anthropology, 85,* 61–69.

Graber, J., Brooks-Gunn, J., & Warren, M. (1995). The antecedents of menarcheal age: Heredity, family environment, and stressful life events. *Child Development, 66,* 346–359.

Green, D. J. (2002). Pair bond duration influences paternal provisioning and the primary sex ratio of brown thornbill broods. *Animal Behaviour, 64,* 791–800.

Haig, D. (1993). Genetic conflicts in human pregnancy. *The Quarterly Review of Biology, 68,* 495–532.

Haig, D. (1998). Genetic conflicts of pregnancy and childhood. In S. C. Stearns (Ed.), *Evolution in health and disease* (pp. 77–90). Oxford, England: Oxford University Press.

Hamilton, W. D. (1964). The genetic evolution of social behavior, I. *Journal of Theoretical Biology, 7,* 1–16.

Harlow, H. (1958). The nature of love. *American Psychologist, 3,* 673–685.

Hazan, C., & Shaver, P. (1987). Romantic love conceptualized as an attachment process. *Journal of Personality and Social Psychology, 52,* 511–524.

Hertwig, R., Davis, J. N., & Sulloway, F. J. (2002). Parental investment: How an equity motive can produce inequity. *Psychological Bulletin, 128,* 728–745.

Hill, C. M., & Ball, H. L. (1996). Abnormal births and other "ill omens": The adaptive case of infanticide. *Human Nature, 7,* 381–401.

Hofferth, S., & Anderson, K. G. (2003). Are all dads equal? Biology versus marriage as basis for paternal investment. *Journal of Marriage and Family, 65,* 213–232.

Hrdy, S. B. (1977). Infanticide as a primate reproductive strategy. *American Scientist, 65,* 40–49.

Jacobs, B. S., & Moss, H. A. (1976). Birth order and sex of sibling as determinants of Mother-infant interaction. *Child Development, 47,* 315–322.

Janicki, M., & Salmon, C. A. (2002, June). *Friend and family dynamics: Relationships between birth order, exchange orientation and perceptions of exchange.* Paper presented at the Human Behavior and Evolution Society's annual meeting, Rutgers, NJ.

Keller, M. C., Nesse, R. M., & Hofferth, S. (2001). The Trivers-Willard hypothesis of parental investment. *Evolution and Human Behavior, 22,* 343–360.

Kennedy, G. E. (1989). Middleborns' perceptions of family relationships. *Psychological Reports, 64,* 755–760.

Kim, F., Smith, P. K., & Palermiti, A. (1997). Conflict in childhood and reproductive development. *Ethology and Sociobiology, 18,* 107–142.

Kirkpatrick, L. A., & Davis, K. (1994). Attachment style, gender and relationship stability: A longitudinal analysis. *Journal of Personality and Social Psychology, 66,* 502–512.

Kirkpatrick, L. A., & Hazan, C. (1994). Attachment styles and close relationships: A four year prospective study. *Personal Relationships, 1,* 123–142.

Knudsen, B., & Evans, R. M. (1986). Parent-young recognition in herring gulls (*Larus argentatus*). *Animal Behaviour, 34,* 77–80.

Kobak, R., Ferenz-Gillies, R., Everhart, E., & Seabrook, L. (1994). Maternal attachment strategies and emotion regulation with adolescent offspring. *Journal of Research on Adolescence, 4,* 553–566.

Koch, H. L. (1956). Some emotional attitudes of the young child in relation to characteristics of his sibling. *Child Development, 27,* 393–426.

Kunce, L., & Shaver, P. (1994). An attachment-theoretical approach to caregiving in romantic relationships. In K. Bartholomew & D. Perlman (Eds.), *Advances in personal relationships* (Vol. 5, pp. 205–237). London: Jessica Kingsley.

Lee, B. J., & George, R. M. (1999). Poverty, early childbearing and child maltreatment: A multinomial analysis. *Children and Youth Services Review, 21,* 755–780.

Lessells, C. M., & Parker, G. A. (1999). Parent-offspring conflict: The full-sib-half-sib fallacy. *Proceedings of the Royal Society of London. Series B, Biological Sciences, 266,* 1637–1643.

Lifjeld, J. T., Slagsvold, T., & Ellegren, H. (1998). Experimentally reduced paternity affects paternal effort and reproductive success in Pied Flycatchers. *Animal Behaviour, 55,* 319–329.

Lindstrom, D. P., & Berhanu, B. (2000). The effects of breastfeeding and birth spacing on infant and early childhood mortality in Ethiopia. *Social Biology, 47,* 1–17.

Lougheed, L. W., & Anderson, D. J. (1999). Parent blue-footed boobies suppress siblicidal behavior of offspring. *Behavioral Ecology and Sociobiology, 45,* 11–18.

Maestripieri, D. (2001). Female-biased maternal investment in rhesus macaques. *Folia Primatologia, 72,* 44–47.

Maestripieri, D. (2002). Parent-offspring conflict in primates. *International Journal of Primatology, 23,* 923–951.

Main, M. (1990). Cross-cultural strategies of attachment and attachment organization: Recent studies, changing methodologies, and the concept of conditional strategies. *Human Development, 33,* 48–61.

McCracken, G. F. (1993). Locational memory and female-pup reunions in Mexican free-tailed bat maternity colonies. *Animal Behaviour, 45,* 811–813.

Medvin, M. B., & Beecher, M. D. (1986). Parent-offspring recognition in the barn swallow (*Hirundo rustica*). *Animal Behaviour, 34,* 1627–1639.

Medvin, M. B., Stoddard, P. K., & Beecher, M. D. (1993). Signals for parent-offspring recognition: A comparative analysis of the begging calls of cliff swallows and barn swallows. *Animal Behaviour, 45,* 841–850.

Meredith, H. V. (1950). Birth order and body size: Neonatal and childhood materials. *American Journal of Physical Anthropology, 8,* 195–224.

Michalski, R. L., & Shackelford, T. K. (2002). Birth order and sexual strategy. *Personality and Individual Differences, 33,* 661–667.

Montgomerie, R. D., & Weatherhead, P. J. (1988). Risks and rewards of nest defense by parent birds. *Quarterly Review of Biology, 63,* 167–187.

Muhuri, P. K., & Menken, J. (1997). Adverse effects of next birth, gender, and family composition on child survival in rural Bangladesh. *Population Studies, 51,* 279–294.

Osorio-Beristain, M., & Drummond, H. (2001). Male boobies expel eggs when paternity is in doubt. *Behavioral Ecology, 12,* 16–21.

Overpeck, M. D., Brenner, R. A., Trumble, A. C., Trifiletti, L. B., & Berendes, H. W. (1998). Risk factors for infant homicide in the United States. *New England Journal of Medicine, 339,* 1211–1216.

Parker, G. A., Mock, D. W., & Lamey, T. C. (1989). How selfish should stronger sibs be? *American Naturalist, 133,* 846–868.

Parker, G. A., Royle, N. J., & Hartley, I. R. (2002). Intrafamilial conflict and parental investment: A synthesis. *Philosophical Transactions of the Royal Society of London, B., 357,* 295–307.

Paulhus, D. L., Chen, D., & Trapnell, P. D. (1999). Birth order and personality within families. *Psychological Science, 10,* 482–488.

Pennington, R., & Harpending, H. (1993). *The structure of an African Pastoralist community: Demography, history, and ecology of the Ngamiland Herero.* Oxford, England: Oxford University Press.

Pugesek, B. H. (1995). Offspring growth in the California gull: Reproductive effort and parental experience hypotheses. *Animal Behavior, 49,* 641–647.

Pusey, A. E., & Packer, C. (1994). Infanticide in lions. In S. Parmigiani & F. S. vom Saal (Eds.), *Infanticide and parental care* (pp. 277–299). Chur, Switzerland: Harwood Academic Press.

Regalski, J. M., & Gaulin, S. J. C. (1993). Whom are Mexican infants said to resemble? Monitoring and fostering paternal confidence in the Yucatan. *Ethology and Sociobiology, 14,* 97–113.

Rohwer, S., Herron, J. C., & Daly, M. (1999). Stepparental behavior as mating effort in birds and other animals. *Evolution and Human Behavior, 20,* 367–390.

Salmon, C. A. (1999). On the impact of sex and birth order on contact with kin. *Human Nature, 10,* 183–197.

Salmon, C. A. (2003). Birth order and relationships: Family, friends, and sexual partners. *Human Nature, 14,* 73–88.

Salmon, C. A., & Daly, M. (1998). Birth order and familial sentiment: Middleborns are different. *Evolution and Human Behavior, 19,* 299–312.

Senchak, M., & Leonard, K. (1992). Attachment style and marital adjustment among newlywed couples. *Journal of Social and Personality Development, 9,* 51–64.

Shaver, P., & Hazan, C. (1993). Adult romantic attachment: Theory and evidence. In D. Perlman & W. Jones, (Eds.), *Advances in personal relationships* (Vol. 4). Greenwich, CT: SAI.

Sieff, D. F. (1990). Explaining biased gender ratios in human populations. *Current Anthropology, 31,* 25–48.

Silk, J. B. (1980). Adoption and kinship in Oceania. *American Anthropologist, 82,* 799–820.

Silk, J. B. (1983). Local resource competition and facultative adjustment of sex ratios in relation to competitive ability. *American Naturalist, 121,* 56–66.

Silk, J. B. (1987). Adoption among the Inuit. *Ethos, 15,* 320–330.

Silk, J. B. (1990). Which humans adopt adaptively and why does it matter? *Ethology and Sociobiology, 11,* 425–426.

Simpson, J. (1990). Influences of attachment styles on romantic relationships. *Journal of Personality and Social Psychology, 59,* 971–980.

Simpson, J., Rhodes, W., & Nelligan, J. (1992). Support seeking and support giving within couples in an anxiety-provoking situation: The role of attachment styles. *Journal of Personality and Social Psychology, 62,* 434–446.

Smith, M. S., Kish, B. J., & Crawford, C. B. (1987). Inheritance of wealth and human kin investment. *Ethology and Sociobiology, 8,* 171–182.

Stack, C. B. (1974). *All Our Kin.* New York: Harper and Row.

Sulloway, F. J. (1995). Birth order and evolutionary psychology: A meta-analytic overview. *Psychological Inquiry, 6,* 75–80.

Sulloway, F. J. (1996). *Born to rebel.* New York: Pantheon.

Sulloway, F. J. (1999). Birth order. In M. A. Runco & S. Pritzker (Eds.), *Encyclopedia of creativity* (Vol. 1, pp. 189–202). San Diego, CA: Academic Press.

Sulloway, F. J. (2001a). Birth order, sibling competition, and human behavior. In H. R. Holcomb III (Ed.), *Conceptual challenges in evolutionary psychology: Innovative research strategies* (pp. 39–83). Boston: Kluwer Academic.

Sulloway, F. J. (2001b). Sibling-order effects. In N. J. Smelser & P. B. Baltes (Eds.), *International Encyclopedia of Social and Behavioral Sciences* (Vol. 21, pp. 14058–14063). Oxford: Elsevier.

Surbey, M. (1990). Family composition, stress, and human menarche. In F. Bercovich & T. Zeigler (Eds.), *The socioendocrinology of primate reproduction* (pp. 11–32). New York: Liss.

Surbey, M. (1998). Parent and offspring: Strategies in the transition at adolescence. *Human Nature, 9,* 67–94.

Trickett, P., & Putman, F. (1993). The impact of child sexual abuse on females: Toward a developmental psychobiological integration. *Psychological Science, 4*(2), 81–87.

Trivers, R. L. (1972). Parental investment and sexual selection. In B. Campbell (Ed.), *Sexual selection and the descent of man: 1871–1971* (pp. 136–179). Chicago: Aldine.

Trivers, R. L. (1974). Parent-offspring conflict. *American Zoologist, 14,* 249–264.

Trivers, R. L., & Willard, D. (1973). Natural selection of parental ability to vary the sex-ratio of offspring. *Science, 179,* 90–92.

Van Ijzendoorn, M. (1995). Adult attachment representations, parental responsiveness, and infant attachment: A meta-analysis on the predictive validity of the adult attachment interview. *Psychological Bulletin, 117,* 387–403.

Voland, E. (1998). Evolutionary ecology of human reproduction. *Annual Review of Anthropology, 27,* 347–374.

Voland, E., & Gabler, S. (1994). Differential twin mortality indicates a correlation between age and parental effort in humans. *Naturwissenschaften, 81,* 224–225.

Ward, M. J., & Carlson, E. (1995). Associations among adult attachment representations: Maternal sensitivity, and infant-mother attachment in a sample of adolescent mothers. *Child Development, 66,* 69–79.

Wierson, M., Long, P. J., & Forehand, R. L. (1993). Toward a new understanding of early menarche: The role of environmental stress in pubertal timing. *Adolescence, 23,* 913–924.

Wiley, A. S., & Carlin, L. C. (1999). Demographic contexts and the adaptive role of mother-infant attachment: A hypothesis. *Human Nature, 10,* 135–161.

Wingerd, J. (1970). The relation of growth from birth to 2 years to sex, parental size, and other factors, using Rao's method of transformed time scale. *Human Biology, 42,* 105–131.

Zajonc, R. B., & Mullally, P. R. (1997). Birth order: Reconciling conflicting effects. *American Psychologist, 52,* 685–699.

CHAPTER 18

Altruism and Genetic Relatedness

EUGENE BURNSTEIN

TWO PEOPLE ARE kin if one is the ancestor or the descendant of the other, or they have a common ancestor. No human relationship is more precise, enduring, and inescapable. Nor is there a more intimate and taxing relationship, aside from those to create additional kin. Yet, the behaviorist orthodoxy, particularly its unbending commitment to learning, which informed psychological theory during much of the twentieth century, assumed there is nothing inherent to genetic relatedness that precludes unrelated individuals from developing equally close and demanding ties. Although the shortcomings of behaviorism have become widely recognized, its view of kinship has remained well ensconced. However, Hamilton's (1964) formulation of *inclusive fitness,* by expanding natural selection to offer a coherent explanation of social processes inexplicable within the "standard paradigm," may well require psychology to reconsider this view—and much else.

HAMILTON'S THEORY OF KIN ALTRUISM

By inextricably linking kinship and altruism, the notion of inclusive fitness provides a compelling explanation of how altruism evolved and, by extension, why our concern about others' fate increases with their genetic relatedness to us. It is also a conceptual guide for anyone interested in the computational mechanisms involved in altruistic behavior. Fitness in general refers to gene transmission via offspring. *Darwinian* fitness is the number of offspring an individual produces independent of the contributions of others in the community or the rate of unaided gene transmission from parents to progeny. *Inclusive* fitness equals an individual's Darwinian fitness plus his or her contribution to the reproductive success of relatives (Dawkins, 1982, chap. 10).

Prior to Hamilton, altruism was a major paradox: If natural selection disfavors traits that impose a cost on fitness (reduces reproductive success) while favoring

528

those that benefit fitness (increases reproductive success), and altruism, while benefiting the recipient, reduces the fitness of the altruist, then how could altruism have evolved? Hamilton's solution: Suppose altruism's costs are *C* and its benefits, *B*. Darwinian fitness does predict a trait causing its possessor reproductive harm, that is, $C > B$ must be selected against except, however, when altruist and recipient are related. Then *due to sharing one or more ancestors, they also are likely to share the genes underlying the trait.* In fact, the exact probability that relatives have a gene in common is given by their degree of relatedness, *r*. It follows that genes coding for altruism can experience a *net* benefit when the cost to the altruist of helping is less than the benefit to the recipient weighted by their degree of relatedness, that is, $C < rB$.

Estimates of the extent to which traits such as altruism are favored by natural selection have to be *inclusive* so that they reflect not only the trait's (negative) impact on the fitness of the altruist but also its (positive) impact on the fitness of kin. Hence, relatives can influence the fate of altruism to the same or greater degree than the altruist, depending on the probability, *r*, they share the genes coding for the trait of altruism and the extent to which *B* exceeds *C*. Hamilton's formulation has enormous significance for psychological theory because it requires that we think of the mind as an organ *designed by natural selection (1) to categorize people by their degree of genetic relatedness and (2) to compute the costs and benefits of interacting with them.*

THE RANGE OF KIN ALTRUISM: HOW INCLUSIVE?

In parts of China and among the Nuer and Tiv, individuals identify thousands of people beyond "near" distant kin as "distant" distant kin (Palmer & Steadman, 1997). Because the return to fitness of altruism toward distant distant kin is minuscule, typically less than helping an unrelated person with whom another has a profitable exchange, it may be surprising that such groups often have norms obliging members to favor these distant distant relatives over nonkin. Fortes (1969) remarks that prescriptive altruism, which he labels the "axiom of kinship amity," applies to the *whole* Tiv population, meaning all those who trace their descent from a single founding ancestor, some 800,000 individuals. When prescriptive altruism extends to a very large number of tenuously related individuals, as in the axiom of kinship amity, and trumps reciprocity, inclusive fitness is certain to be violated. According to Burch (1975), the "moral compulsion" among the Inuit to discriminate in favor of unfamiliar distant distant kin over unrelated neighbors who have been trustworthy partners is sufficiently powerful that ". . . even the strongest non-kin tie was considered weaker than the weakest kin relationship. In times of crisis, such as famine or war, one always had to opt for a kinsman in favor of a partner, and one knew one's partner would have to do likewise" (p. 198).

If altruism is prescriptive even on occasions when the degree of genetic relatedness is very small, the altruist's fitness will decline depending on the frequency of such occasions. What is most likely, however, is that a mutual understanding exists between nonkin partners that when certain events occur kinship is privileged. Given these events are as infrequent as those cited by Burch—famine and war—suspending reciprocity "for the duration" may not be perceived as a betrayal and will not incur costs. Even models postulating innate generative kinship schemas assume genealogical distance, the extent distant distant kin are represented in a group's classificatory system, is flexible and allows for collective action (Jones, 2003). Furthermore, given that kin altruism is inherently risky and that reciprocity can minimize its costs, the two strategies may be functionally linked, perhaps with common genetic roots. Reciprocity assumes individuals are selected to behave altruistically in the short term as long as there is a net return in the long term. This requires familiarity; people need to recognize each other and remember who owes whom what. In ancestral environments, familiarity implies genetic relatedness, which means reciprocity probably evolved in kin networks. As a result, it inevitably served to correct common violations of inclusive fitness—human judgments of costs and benefits as well as genetic relatedness are error prone, particularly in crises when they are hurried if not automatic. However, altruism becomes less risky and, hence, a more robust strategy if altruists, should they miscalculate and do too much, will be made whole by the recipient, kin, or third parties.

KIN RECOGNITION: CATEGORIZING PEOPLE BY THEIR DEGREE OF GENETIC RELATEDNESS

Assortative pairing is often cited as evidence for a human capacity to detect family resemblances (see review and comments in Rushton, 1989). Based on assessment of blood antigens, spouses turn out to be genetically more similar than randomly chosen couples—resource retention and other benefits of nepotism tend to make the risk of inbreeding depression tolerable for marriages between cousins or more distant kin (van den Berghe, 1983). Also, long-term friends are genetically more similar than unacquainted pairs. There are, however, a few problems in evaluating these effects. At the theoretical level, it can be argued that a comparable relationship among blood group similarity, trait similarity, and heritability could be obtained under the hypothesis that mate preferences are the result of exposure to parents or other relatives rather than an ability to detect similar genes. As Daly remarked (1989),"If men marry the images of their mothers . . . then men . . . [will not just resemble their wives but] . . . will most resemble their wives in those traits which they themselves most resemble their mothers, hence the most heritable traits" (p. 520). However, the most common criticism of assortative pairing as evidence for a kin recognition mechanism is that people cannot be assigned at random to being spouses (friends) or strangers. Even in modern societies, those of similar ethnicity and nationality tend to live near one another (Glazer, 1975). Because ethnicity and nationality are predictors of blood group type and propinquity is one of the better predictors of marital and friendship choice, it is not surprising that spouses and friends have the same blood type whether or not they are capable of detecting genetic similarity. At the same time, however, experiments with random assignment find that even when the prospect of mating or lasting friendship is nonexistent, people are attracted to others with similar psychological traits and, maybe, even more strongly repelled by others who differ from them in these respects—suggesting there is a tendency to disadvantage dissimilar (competing) phenotypes as well as to advantage those that are similar (Berscheid, 1985; Kenrick & Trost, 1987; Rosenbaum, 1986). Finally, Newcomb (1961) had randomly paired strangers live together in the same residence for several months and found a marked increase in friendships based on similarity in values comparable to those found to have high heritability (Tesser, 1993).

SINGLE LOCUS KIN RECOGNITION SYSTEMS

Hamilton (1964) conjectured if a gene gave rise to a recognizable phenotype and at the same time induced the bearer to benefit individuals sharing that phenotype, it would spread faster and prevail over competing genes—Dawkins (1976) labeled this signaling function the *greenbeard* effect. But if alleles at other loci are capable of generating their own recognition systems to counter the action of competing recognition alleles and there is no reason they are not, the upshot would be an intragenic "tug of war" (Alexander & Borgia, 1978). In any event, discriminative altruism based on the workings of a single-locus recognition system has weak empirical support. Indeed, among vertebrates when preferential actions are associated with a single distinct genetic character, social experience has been shown to play a key role in shaping the preference (e.g., when mate choice is based on plumage color, individuals select mates of the same color as the family in which they were reared; Waldman, 1988).

A celebrated instance of what might approximate a single-locus recognition system is a group of genes called the *major histocompatibility complex* (MHC). Early evidence from experiments with mice indicated the MHC facilitated disassortative mating, an adaptive strategy since the ability to recognize and avoid mating with a sib or half sib reduces the likelihood of harmful recessive genes combining. However, later findings demonstrated the importance of familiarity; namely, male mice cross-fostered at birth to parents genetically dissimilar from themselves later prefer to mate with females differing from their foster parents' rather than their own MHC type (Yamazaki, Beauchamp, Curran, Bard, & Boyse, 2000; Yamazaki, Beauchamp, Kupniewski, & Bard, 1988). Nonetheless, odors encoded by MHC genes do differ between families, and in normal environments they would, therefore, contribute to disassortative mating by serving as informative kin recognition labels. Experiments with humans by Wedekind and colleagues (Milinski & Wedekind, 2001; Wedekind & Füri, 1997; Wedekind, Seebeck, Bettens, & Paepke, 1995; see review in Kohl, Atzmueller, Fink, & Grammer, 2001) find evidence for just such a function. In these studies women who rated T-shirts worn for a few days by men judged the body odor of those differing from them in MHC as more attractive (e.g., reporting they were reminded of current or former mates) than that of males similar in MHC, *but* only if they were ovulating. Among females taking oral contraceptives, the effect was *reversed*, the odor of MHC-similar males being judged more attractive than that of MHC-dissimilar males. Apparently, women recognize nonfamilial men and find them desirable primarily when being nonfamilial reduces chances of inbreeding. The reverse effect in women avoiding reproduction suggests detecting MHC similarities may serve cooperative ties.

Whether or not a single-locus kin recognition systems exists in humans, its implementation assumes a set of operations common to all judgments of phenotypic similarity, namely, a comparison between two kinds of knowledge corresponding roughly to a *stimulus* and a *standard*. Researchers, however, traditionally distinguish between these operations according to the origin of the standard. Kin recognition based on *familiarity* or its ecological correlate, *proximity*, implies a comparison between a perceptual representation of the person's traits (the input code) and a memory trace (the mnemonic code) of the same or similar persons' traits. The alternative mechanism, *phenotype matching*, is assumed to operate when individuals recognize unfamiliar kin on first encounter or when they discriminate among equally familiar people according to their degree of relatedness. However, both familiarity and phenotype matching require individuals to compare a person's features with a standard set derived from experience with others in appropriate social situations (e.g., where a person learns those features typical of kin) or a set internally derived either from self-observation, as had been assumed in MHC olfactory signals, or directly given in a genetically programmed template. Nonetheless, following tradition, we consider these two mechanisms separately.

FAMILIARITY

Social learning probably has a significant role whatever the kin recognition mechanism, especially in humans who commonly match relatively abstract, amorphous, and malleable phenotypes (e.g., personality traits and attitudes). Indeed, there is impressive evidence that, early in development, humans need only a small amount of experience to identify kin. An infant discriminates between mother and unrelated women by their voices within 24 hours after birth, by the odor of their breasts within 6 days after birth, and by their faces (photographs) 2 weeks after birth. Nor are mothers less adept. They can identify their offspring in a set of several matched photographs of infant faces after about 5 hours of postnatal contact, in a crowded nursery by odor following a single exposure 6 hours after birth, and by voice 2 days after birth (see reviews in Bjornlund & Pellegrini, 2002). In a striking demonstration of precocious kin detection, Kisilevsky et al. (2003) measured fetal heart rate while exposing term fetuses to tape recordings of their mother's voice or that of a female stranger. They found heart rate increased in response to the mother's voice but decreased in response to the stranger's. As to the prenatal impact on the recognition of fathers, Trivers (2002) observed a few hours after he and his 7-month-pregnant wife had a heated dispute that she noticed the fetus ". . . was unusually active within her, which she attributed to our recent argument. I [Trivers] will never forget the sensation I experienced, a kind of mental shudder. I thought we were arguing in private—no witnesses! My crime loomed up larger in my mind. I knew the child could hear perfectly well in the womb, and I imagined that he could easily associate maternal stress hormones experienced via the placenta with my loud and ugly voice, in effect forming a hypothesis about me before meeting me!" (p. 152). The "looming" no doubt was compounded by the knowledge that the placenta itself was designed to serve his fitness interest more than that of his wife's (Haig, 2002).

To the extent familiarity is a cue to genetic relatedness, it should increase disassortative behavior in situations where familiarity raises the possibility of inbreeding. In research on human disassortativity, pairs of unrelated coreared males and females are contrasted with pairs reared apart in respect to mutual sexual interest or anxiety about having sexual relations. The earliest of these studies found that when time came to marry, Israelis born on kibbutzim and raised together communally in nurseries chose unfamiliar mates from outside the kibbutz rather than those who were highly familiar, namely, each other (Shepher, 1971). Parallel effects were found in analyses of Taiwanese minor marriages, an arrangement whereby mothers hand over a daughter shortly after birth to another family to be coreared with its son, whom she is destined to marry (Wolf, 1995). As in the kibbutz, corearing reduces interest in mating, which casts a pall over reproduction: The minor marriage fertility rate was 31% lower and its divorce rate 300% higher than in marriages among those not coreared. In Canadian and Californian samples, corearing predicts anxieties about or intensity of condemnation of incest as well as the likelihood of individuals actually engaging in it (Bevc & Silverman, 2000; Liebermann, Tooby, & Cosmides, 2002; Thornhill, 1991). Liebermann et al. (2002) found familiarity, as measured by length of coresidence, was correlated ($r = .61$) with feelings that consensual brother-sister sex and consensual brother-sister marriage were "morally wrong" among respondents who were coreared but *knew they were unrelated*. One obvious implication is that male-female familiarity automatically primes a sense of genetic relatedness (and fear of mating) despite knowledge to the contrary.

The psychological effect of familiarity on interpersonal attraction was summarized by Homans (1950): "If the frequency of interaction between two or more persons increases, the degree of liking for one another will increase" (p. 112). Others go further to assert interaction is unnecessary, the essential condition for attraction being "mere exposure"—an idea initially proposed by Titchner (1910), who conjectured that familiarity produces "a glow of warmth" and unfamiliarity "an uneasy restlessness" (pp. 408–409). The classic demonstration of the affective consequences of familiarity due to mere exposure was by Zajonc (1968) using photographs of faces. Later research found these effects are general, occurring not only with people (faces or names) as stimuli but also with food, words (meaningful as well as nonsensical), or geometrical forms and regardless of whether the context in which stimuli were presented is pleasant or unpleasant. Moreover, mere exposure seems to increase attractiveness most readily under conditions characteristic of group life, namely, when encoding complex rather than simple stimuli, with brief exposure intervals, with longer rather than shorter intervals between stimulus exposure and expression of feeling, and when the critical stimuli are presented in a heterogeneous series with many other noisy events interspersed rather than in a homogeneous series with nothing interspersed (see the review in Bornstein, 1989). These, together with the purely cognitive effects of mere exposure, such as an increased sensitivity to details of appearance and a heightened ability to identify individuals (Gibson, 1969), would seem well designed to abet kin recognition.

PHENOTYPE MATCHING

In phenotype matching, individuals compare another's trait (e.g., odor or voice) with a memory code representing the same trait in themselves or in a close relative. Besides pheromones, much of the work on adult human phenotype matching and detection of genetic relatedness involves the face. This is consistent with the conventional wisdom that facial resemblance is highly diagnostic of kinship. Thus, when comparing the face of newborns to that of an adult, family members typically remark on resemblances to the father or, less frequently, another paternal relative (Daly & Wilson, 1982; Regalski & Gaulin, 1993). Whether this is a ploy to reduce uncertainty of paternity or the objective truth—infants who look like their father are obviously advantaged—remains to be seen (Bressan & Dal Martello, 2002). What is important in respect to kin recognition, however, is to determine the extent to which facial resemblances by themselves, absent maternal tactics or social norms, cause us to trust or help others as if they were kin.

A standard technique used to manipulate facial resemblance involves digital morphing whereby the experimenter melds photographs of two source faces into a virtual face with specific features of the source faces. Studies have compared the impact of self-morphs (virtual faces combining the subject's features with those of a stranger) and non-self-morphs (virtual faces combining the facial features of two strangers) or of several self-morphs with different proportions of the subject's features. DeBruine (2002) had people play an anonymous one-shot sequential bargaining game with a hypothetical partner known to them only from a photograph. In one condition, the photographs were self-morphs and in the other, non-self-morphs. The game required the first player to decide whether to dictate an equitable division of a small sum or to forego it and trust the second player to divide another much larger sum equitably even though the latter is perfectly free to behave selfishly. In such circumstances, game theory recommends a distrustful strategy by first players. Instead, DeBruine found that those with a self-morphed partner tended to forego the certain sum and rely on their partner to be generous in dividing up the larger sum whereas those with non-self-morphs did not. Facial resemblance, in short, increases trust.

Although it may behoove mothers to reassure their mate about paternity, Platek and his coworkers (Platek, Burch, Panyavin, Wasserman, & Gallup, 2002; Platek et al., 2003) argue that deliberately pointing out resemblances can be interpreted as masking uncertainty about paternity or as a cuckolding stratagem. Hence, Platek et al. (2002) hypothesize that as a countertactic, men are likely to have evolved a capacity to detect resemblances. To test these ideas, they morphed the faces of female and male young adults with those of 2-year-old strangers. The self-morphed faces were then repeatedly shown on a monitor in an array of four other non-self-morphed faces of 2-year-olds. During each trial, subjects decided which one of the five children they would benefit in a specific fashion. Platek et al. found that men decide to benefit their self-morph both more often than chance and more often than women. The decision items follow (percentage choosing the self-morph is given in parenthesis; the first value is for male subjects, the second, female subjects):

- "Which one of these children would you be most likely to adopt?" (90% versus 35%)
- "Which one . . . do you find to be the most attractive?" (85% versus 35%)
- "Which one . . . would you be comfortable spending the most time with?" (70% versus 35%)
- "Which one . . . would you least resent paying child support for?" (40% versus 25%)
- "Which one . . . would you spend $50 on if you could spend it on only one child?" (80% versus 40%)

The decision also was easier for men, and their decision time was shorter than women's. In other experiments, Platek et al. (2003) presented a series of self-morphs that varied in the degree of resemblance to the subject from about 3% to 50%. They found no sex difference in the frequency with which individuals discriminated in favor of their self-morph nor was this frequency greater than chance for the 3% and 6% self-morphs. However, at 25% and 50% resemblance, men favored their self-morph more than chance and more than women. This suggests either that (1) men are more sensitive to resemblances and recognize them more readily than women or (2) men give more weight to them in decisions similar to paternal investing but not otherwise. To examine these two possibilities, Platek et al. (2003) asked subjects to merely *match* child morphs to an adult photograph of themselves or to a photograph of a strange adult. When the child morphs contained at least 50% of either their own or the strangers' features, both men and women achieved reliable and equal levels of accuracy. Thus, in deciding on facial resemblances when the decision is *irrelevant to fitness,* men are no more sensitive than women. However, when fitness is relevant, namely, deciding who benefits and at what cost, men are more likely than women to use facial resemblance as grounds for discriminating. Finally, when identifying which morph looks most like them, men are unable to perceive a resemblance until morphs contain at least 50% of their facial features; but if deciding which morph to benefit, men overwhelmingly pick their self-morph even though it contains no more than 25% of their facial features. As Platek et al. point out, this finding suggests that, given a payoff to fitness, men process facial resemblances without awareness. While research on phenotype matching using facial morphs is relatively new, the findings make a strong case that humans are sensitive to resemblances and use this information to assess genetic relatedness in deciding whom to benefit. Whether the decision approximates that predicted by inclusive fitness, however, depends on how costs and benefits are computed.

COMPUTING THE COSTS AND BENEFITS OF ALTRUISM

In ethnographic studies, the extent to which a computational procedure conforms to inclusive fitness predictions is inferred from changes in people's behavior as their own or others' contributions to fitness change. For instance, according to the *grandmother hypothesis* (Hawkes, O'Connell, Blurton Jones, Alvarez, & Charnov, 1998), variations in a woman's reproductive career require a two-part strategy for her to maximize fitness over the life span. The first part assumes that evolution of menopause is the result of the demands that bearing and rearing of children put on women. The second part is based on menopause functioning to increase the reproductive success of offspring: With increasing age, women get a greater return to fitness by avoiding pregnancy, thereby minimizing the mortality risk associated with reproduction among older women and instead assisting in the rearing of their grandchildren. The cross-cultural evidence that older women further the reproductive success of their daughters and sons is considerable. Among the Hadza, grandmothers provide more food for the household by toiling extra hours (with the same efficiency as younger women), and, importantly, the more hours they work, the greater the rate of growth of their grandchildren (Hawkes et al., 1998). Sears, Mace, and McGregor (2000) also found that

Gambian children with a living maternal grandmother are heavier, taller, and have better chances of survival than other children, the effect being considerably augmented if grandmothers are past childbearing age. The importance of the grandmothers' reproductive value in how they distribute help had been suggested earlier by Hames (1988). He observed among the Ye' kwana that mothers' postmenopausal kin provide more child care than premenopausal kin even though both were equally related to the child. Reproduction also elicits solicitousness in normally indifferent males. For instance, Hazda wives provide more food for the household than husbands do if there are no young children; as soon as there are offspring, however, husbands begin to contribute more than wives (Marlowe, 2003).

The grandmother hypothesis is only one of many themes in the ethnography of kin altruism. There are, in addition, analyses of political coalitions (e.g., Dunbar, Clark, & Hurst, 1997) as well as of spontaneous alliances in deadly quarrels and emergencies (e.g., Chagnon & Bugos, 1979; Sime, 1983), demonstrating that their cohesion, durability, and effectiveness depend on the density of kinship ties. Sime (1983), for example, interviewed a large number of people at an English seaside vacation complex soon after a fire in which 50 died. In his analysis, he assumed that faced with "... an impending physical threat ... and access to an escape route diminishing rapidly ... individuals will not be concerned solely with self-preservation. They will be even more concerned than usual to retain contact or make contact with other group members with whom they have close psychological ties and who are also threatened" (p. 21). Sime uses the phrase "close psychological ties" to mean kinship. Hence, he pits self-preservation against inclusive fitness. Nearly two-thirds of the respondents went to the complex with their immediate families and a third with friends. Of the groups whose members were together when the fire started, over two-thirds of the families but only about a quarter of the nonfamilies emerged together. There were also a good number of families and nonfamilies whose members were separated at the time they perceived themselves in peril. Of these initially separated groups, half of the families risked taking time to find one another and emerged from the burning building together, whereas none of the nonfamily groups did so (for other examples of kin altruism in life or death situations, see Buss, 2003).

Probably the largest number of studies of kin altruism focuses on the role of genetic relatedness in resource distribution. Thus, we know when estates are settled in North America (Judge, 1995), when fishermen divide their catch on a Pacific atoll (Betzig & Turke, 1986), or in South American horticultural tribes when free labor is given (Berte, 1988) that a disproportionately large share goes to close relatives. Field studies, therefore, not only provide arresting evidence in support of Hamilton's model but also are critical in showing its computational assumptions are ecologically valid. At the same time, however, field studies do not lend themselves to control groups, and random assignment is virtually impossible. Hence, experimental analyses, if not sufficient, are necessary. Fortunately, social psychologists, while having a deaf ear for kinship, have long been interested in the ability of group members to assess who among them can help and whether he or she is willing to incur the cost. As a result, we know humans are adept at ranking one another according to their ability to benefit the group (e.g., the amount each member contributes to group problem solving) and their willingness to do this (e.g., each members' degree of cooperativeness or friendliness). Indeed, ability and willingness to help are by far the two most important traits individuals use to differentiate themselves (Hare, 1976); and they seem to do so automatically because individual differences are detected with minimal incentive and early in the interaction, probably within the first minute (Fisek & Ofshe, 1970).

Additional evidence comes from experiments on mixed-motive games, especially those that make the stark comparison between interacting with partners that have fitness (or self-) interests, namely, another person, and partners without such interests, namely, a computer. In the earliest of these, Abric, Faucheux, Moscovici, and Plon (1967) programmed both types of partners to play the identical strategy, TIT-FOR-TAT (TFT) in an iterated Prisoner's Dilemma Game (PDG). Under these conditions, TFT typically produces increasingly high levels of cooperation, as it did in this experiment *if* the partner was thought to be another person. Subjects who played against a computer increasingly defected with cooperative choices reaching its nadir, about 15%, during the final third of the trials. In the PDG and like situations, individuals "mind read" to decide whether the partner's intentions are benign or malevolent; and if the latter, they may play TFT to persuade the partner to change (Hedden & Zhang, 2002; for similar effects in coordination games, see Burnstein, 1969). However, *theory of mind* processing, that is, analyzing others' output in terms of their intentions or persuasibility, is unlikely when they are programmed agents. Instead, subjects in Abric et al. who played against a computer adopted a minimax strategy, consistently defecting to protect themselves from the worst outcome the partner could inflict. A striking demonstration of such reasoning is observed using the ultimatum game where, unlike the PDG, it is impossible to avoid being taken advantage of should the partner decide to do so. The game is played by two people only once and under conditions of total anonymity. They are shown a sum of money and then one of them, the proposer, says how the sum should be divided between the two. Once the division is proposed, the other person, the responder, can either accept or reject it. If the responder rejects it, neither individual gets anything; if the responder accepts it, the money is divided accordingly. Responders typically take umbrage at lopsided proposals and, irrationally, reject them out of hand so both players take home nothing. But you get this "go to hell" effect only if responders think the proposer is another person. When it is a computer, they invariably accept the proposal regardless of how lopsided (Blount, 1995).

According to inclusive fitness theory, players should be more trusting and cooperative to the extent they are genetically related. Indirect support for this hypothesis is provided by DeBruine's (2002) and Platek et al.'s (2002, 2003) research on facial resemblances that found self-morphs elicit greater trust and altruism than morphs of strangers. A direct test was made by Segal and Hershberger (1999), who compared the behavior of monozygotic (MZ) and dizygotic (DZ) twins in a PDG. They found MZ cooperated appreciably more than DZ partners, which complements earlier observations that MZ twins maintain equality of performance on lexical and mathematical tasks (e.g., one twin will slow down to allow the cotwin to catch up) whereas DZ twins try to outdo each other; MZ twins also free-ride less often, work harder for a cotwin, and, as a result, complete joint tasks more quickly than DZ twins (Von Bracken, 1934). It is these kinds of effects that are said to explain the belief in a *twin bond phenomenon*—that genetic identity confers deeper mutual understanding on twins than on normal mortals. At the same time, however, should this belief be sufficiently widespread, it would raise the disquieting possibility of a self-fulfilling prophecy: Rather than a capacity to detect genetic similarities, the twin bond phenomenon is the result of MZ twins and, to a lesser extent, DZ twins (plus family and friends) being themselves convinced of a twin bond phenomenon.

Until several years ago, the social perception literature considered it a settled issue that, to understand the cause of someone's action, observers discount context and explain what was said or done by attributing it to an underlying disposition or trait that corresponds to or is directly implied by the person's action (e.g., Reeder, Fletcher, & Furman, 1989). When it comes to computing the return to fitness, this means altruists would systematically err because they are prone to ignore situational pressures that might tempt the recipient to deceive them about genetic relatedness or the cost and benefits of altruism. Since then, however, cross-cultural experiments indicate that humans do take context into account and judge the sincerity of a statement or action accordingly (Miyamoto & Kitayama, 2002; Morris, Menon, & Ames, 2001). Thus, in cultures that value conformity, observers tend to discount dispositions or traits and to explain another's behavior in terms of situational pressures (e.g., family obligations), whereas in cultures that value independence, observers discount situational pressures as an explanation and tend to attribute another's behavior to a disposition or trait (e.g., ambitiousness). Recent research (e.g., Mealey, Daood, & Krage, 1996; Oda, 1997; Yamagishi, Tanida, Mashima, Shimoma, & Kanazawa, 2003) also indicates that the human cognitive system is particularly sensitive when encoding actions in suspicious circumstances (e.g., those associated with deception) and cautious to the point of automatically considering the opposite of what is asserted (Schul, Mayo, & Burnstein, in press). More generally, given sufficient familiarity with another, people are sensitive to the other's trustworthiness. They predict better than chance whether someone will cooperate or defect in a PDG after interacting with them for about half an hour (Frank, Gilovich, & Regan, 1993). And after watching a film of individuals engage in a discussion of an irrelevant topic, people can distinguish those who are typically helpful from those who rarely help (W. M. Brown, Palamenta, & Moore, 2003).

Some of the strongest evidence of an inclusive fitness psychology comes from experiments systematically varying genetic relatedness and the costs and benefits of altruism. Bear in mind that when researchers impose large payoffs, the decision task is invariably hypothetical, so the strategies displayed could be different from those observed in real decision making. Nonetheless, they can claim their findings do indicate whether humans are able to (and, hence, are probably designed to) behave in a manner consistent with inclusive fitness theory. However, we begin with a study of real decisions with tangible costs and tangible benefits. Fieldman, Plotkin, Dunbar, Robertson, and McFarland (described in Barrett, Dunbar, & Lycett, 2002) paid subjects to perform an isometric skiing exercise doable for about a minute without much discomfort but increasingly painful thereafter. Pay depended on the time the exercise was maintained and, thus, the pain endured. The exercise was repeated on successive days; each day the cash earned went either to the subject, a parent or sibling, a grandparent, a niece or nephew, a cousin, or a good friend. As inclusive fitness predicts, the length of time subjects performed the exercise, the pain they endured, and the money thereby provided to another varied directly with the latter's genetic relatedness.

There are also nonfindings in Fieldman et al. whose absence is informative: Willingness to endure pain did not depend on either the affection for or actual contact with recipients of the cash. This is not the first time researchers discovered that contact and emotional ties are unnecessary for kin altruism. Korchmaros and Kenny (2001) measured the "emotional closeness" individuals felt toward a relative as well as the risk they would take to save the relative's life. They found the variance in risk taking was only partly mediated by emotional closeness and an appreciable amount depended directly on genetic relatedness. Similarly, Kruger (2003) had individuals indicate their "empathic concern" (an index based on rating of liking and similarity) for a sibling or a close friend, after which they estimated their willingness to help either in a life-threatening situation. Again, individuals were more likely to help siblings than friends regardless of whether they felt empathic concern for them. Segal, Hershberger, and Arad (2003) observed comparable effects with MZ and DZ twins separated at birth and reunited as adults. After similar amounts of contact, MZ twins are more likely to feel "closer than best friends" and "more familiar than best friends" than are DZ twins, who in turn are more likely to feel this way than nonbiological siblings with whom they were coreared. Equally interesting, there is a positive correlation between the twins' perception of physical similarity to their cotwin and their feelings of closeness to and familiarity with the latter, suggesting that resemblance itself can produce an emotional bond. At the same time, genetic relatedness has a unique effect on a twin's willingness to help his or her cotwin unmediated by feelings of closeness. One obvious implication is that genetic relatedness may spontaneously prime an impulse to behave altruistically. To the extent emergencies were common in the ancestral environment, computing cost and benefits automatically, not bothering to check for liking or disliking, might well contribute to fitness.

Burnstein, Crandall, and Kitayama (1994; also see Cunningham, 1986) tried to analyze cost-benefit computations in more detail by presenting respondents with sets of two or three people and requiring them to choose from each set the one they would most likely help. These choices are made under either of two conditions (Burnstein et al., 1994, Study 2). One involves a scenario in which benefits are large relative to costs (e.g., respondents imagine a relative asleep in a burning house who is certain to perish unless they are willing to risk injury to rescue him or her); the other, a scenario in which benefits are relatively small (e.g., respondents imagine a relative who has forgotten some items while shopping and will have to do without unless they are willing to risk being late for a meeting to go to the store for the relative). Recipients in the scenarios vary in age, sex, and degree of kinship. In Japanese and American samples, the likelihood of receiving help increased with genetic relatedness. But more importantly, the rate of increase is greater under the life or death scenario, especially between $r = .50$ and $r = 1.0$, than under the ordinary favor scenario. This confirms a straightforward prediction of inclusive fitness theory that the larger the ratio of benefits to costs, the more likely altruists will discriminate in favor of close kin. A replication of this effect using a much larger sample (Burnstein et al., 1994, Study 4) is shown in Figure 18.1 on page 540. As Chagnon and Bugos (1979) remarked regarding an Yanamamo axe fight they filmed, it is in just such interactions that "... the axiomatic qualities of human kinship as prescriptive altruism take on form

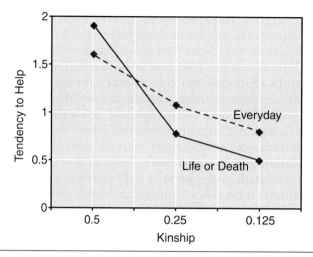

Figure 18.1 Tendency to Help under Life or Death versus Everyday Conditions.

and substance. . . . If we are interested in . . . understanding the extent to which . . . [human] behavior is 'tracking' biologically relevant dimensions of kinship . . . crisis or conflict situations . . . are a reasonable place to begin" (p. 215).

Burnstein et al. (1994) also found that female relatives are favored over male relatives by respondents of both sexes. One obvious explanation for this effect is the existence of a norm about helping females in distress. That this norm should be equally strong among Japanese and Americans is less obvious. Alternatively, male respondents may have given more weight to the recipient's reproductive (or mate) value while female respondents may have given more weight to the possibilities of cooperation with the recipient—women seem to cooperate more readily than men do (Essock-Vitale & McGuire, 1985). Consistent with the reproductive value hypothesis, around 45, the age level in study closest to the onset of menopause, the tendency to favor females vanishes. Regardless of sex, however, the very young and very old are most vulnerable to accident, disease, and abuse. The very old also have less reproductive value as do the very young at least until they reach puberty, far from a sure thing in the ancestral environment. According to inclusive fitness theory, when the benefits of altruism are significant, very old relatives are least likely to receive help; very young relatives, depending on time to puberty, moderately likely; and those of intermediate age, most likely. In life or death situations, therefore, kin altruism is *curvilinear*, that is, inverted-U shaped, with the recipient's age. Burnstein et al. do find this effect after priming respondents to discount for time to puberty (e.g., they have to imagine living in a parlous environment with high infant mortality rates). When the benefits of altruism are nil, this relationship should attenuate. In fact, it reversed and became a U-shaped function with the very young and very old having a decidedly better chance of receiving help than relatives of intermediate age (Burnstein et al., 1994, Study 3). This effect is conjectured to stem from knowledge that refusing to help damages a person's reputation, particularly when helping is inexpensive and benefits the most vulnerable. Hence, by choosing to aid very young or very old relatives—those least able to reciprocate—we advertise our generosity as well as our resources (Zahavi & Zahavi, 1997).

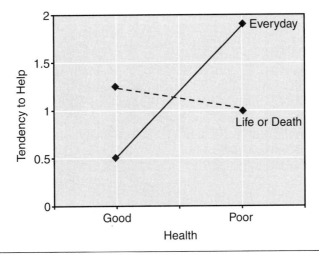

Figure 18.2 Tendency to Help as a Function of the Relative's Health under Life or Death versus Everyday Conditions.

In assessing the contribution to fitness of relatives' health and wealth, note that wealth, unlike health, can be transferred or otherwise used by its owners to manipulate others. Presumably, then, an altruist is more likely to think strategically when relatives differ in wealth than when they differ in health. A reasonable hypothesis, therefore, is that health functions like age with good health corresponding to the least vulnerable kin and poor health to the most vulnerable. In the case of differences in wealth, however, individuals should ingratiate themselves with wealthy relatives—an instance of self-interest emerging in kin altruism—by favoring them over poor relatives. At the same time, according to Hamilton, close kin are more predisposed to share resources than distant kin *unless* they particularly like or are obligated to the recipient. Burnstein et al. (1994, Studies 4 & 5) found considerable support for this line of reasoning. In life or death situations, altruists tend to discriminate in favor of healthy kin at the expense of those in poor health; but if it is an everyday favor, they do the reverse, favoring those in poor health over those in good health (see Figure 18.2). Given differences in wealth, however, when help is a matter of life or death, altruists do not discriminate between rich and poor *close* kin, but they do between rich and poor *distant* kin; that is, rich siblings are helped as often as poor ones but rich cousins are helped more often than poor ones. However, if benefits are trivial, reputation again seems to come into play with help increasing as recipients' wealth *decreases* and as relatedness increases. Altruists not only choose to do everyday favors for siblings rather than for cousins but also, in contrast to life or death situations, prefer to do them for poor siblings and cousins rather than for rich ones.

There is also some evidence in Burnstein et al. (1994, Study 6) that when altruists decide between kin *groups*, they discriminate in favor of those with the greater overall reproductive return, defined as the sum of the members' degrees of genetic relatedness or *r*-values (e.g., groups containing either four cousins, two nieces, or one sib would have a reproductive value of .50; groups containing either eight cousins, four nieces, and two sibs, a reproductive value of 1.0; see

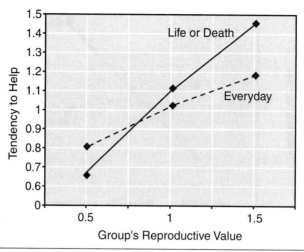

Figure 18.3 Tendency to Help a Group of Relatives as a Function of the Group's Reproductive Value.

Figure 18.3). A more extensive and important series of experiments on kin groups was performed by Wang (1996a, 1996b, 1996c, 2002; Wang & Johnston, 1995). He hypothesized an evolved *kith-and-kin* rationality attuned to ecologically significant constants in the social environment such as group structure and size. According to Wang, human computational strategies are designed to process a collection of individuals as a social unit or "true group" when the number of members approximates either that of primordial groups or groups typical of the person's environment, depending on whether we assume the concept of a true group is innate or learned. Roughly, the range might extend from several (e.g., family or friends) to 100 or 200 individuals (e.g., a community). Once a collection exceeds this size, it is no longer represented as a coherent, organized, or true group and instead is processed as an undifferentiated mass. Wang uses decision tasks that typically show an irrational reversal of preferences called the *framing effect* (Tversky & Kahneman, 1981). This is a bias in choice occurring when a person has to decide between a certain outcome and a probabilistic or risky one. Choices of this sort can be either positively or negatively framed. Positive framing expresses the outcomes in terms of gains (e.g., "Imagine 600 people are infected by a fatal disease. There are two medical procedures that can be used. If procedure A is used, 200 of them will be saved for certain. If procedure B is used, there is a one-third probability of saving all 600 and a two-thirds probability that none will be saved."). Negative framing expresses the identical outcomes in terms of losses (e.g., ". . . If procedure A is used, 400 of them will die for certain. If procedure B is used, there is a two-thirds probability of all 600 dying and a one-third probability that none will die."). The standard finding is that with positive framing people are risk averse, preferring the certain outcome over the probabilistic one; but when the decision is negatively framed, they are risk seeking, preferring the probabilistic outcome over the sure thing.

Wang's prediction is that the framing effect occurs only for relatively large collectivities because they are not true groups. Members of true groups are perceived as belonging together or even inseparable; and such groups evoke a "live or die together" decision rule especially when the true group consists of kin. To

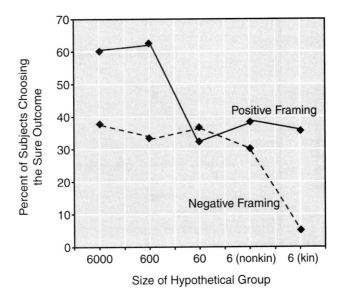

Figure 18.4   Risk Proneness as a Function of Group Size and Kinship. *Source:* From "A Kith-and-Kin Rationality in Risky Choices: Empirical Examinations and Theoretical Modeling" (pp. 47–70), by X. T. Wang, in *Risky Transactions: Trust, Kinship, and Ethnicity*, F. Salter (Ed.), 2002, Oxford, UK: Berghahn Books.

test this notion, subjects made either negatively or positively framed decisions for groups of 6,000, 600, 60, or 6 individuals with the 6 in some conditions specified as close kin. Standard framing effects were found for the 6,000- and 600-member groups with most choosing the certain over the risky outcome under positive framing and the risky over the certain outcome under negative framing. However, when group size decreased to 60, risk seeking dominated under either kind of framing with around 70% of the subjects preferring the probabilistic choice over the sure thing for both the 60- and the 6-person groups; and strikingly, when the 6 were relatives, over 90% chose the probabilistic outcome (see Figure 18.4).

Wang also uses six-member kin groups containing two close relatives of the same sex, two distant relatives of the opposite sex, and two unspecified relatives (e.g., a group with mother, daughter, uncle, nephew, and two other relatives or father, son, aunt, niece, and two other relatives). Choices are always positively framed so subjects decide between a medical procedure certain to save the two male kin or the two female kin who were either close or distant kin and a procedure with a one-third probability of saving the whole group. As a final wrinkle, half the subjects imagine the group members are their own relatives and half that they are another person's relatives. With their own kin in mind, about 40% of the subjects chose the sure thing to save a pair of close relatives, whereas only about 20% did so to save a pair of distant relatives. This difference disappears when it's someone else's relatives; then the certain outcome is preferred over the uncertain one in about 30% of the cases regardless of the degree of genetic relatedness. Rather amazingly, even when the sure thing's expected value is appreciably greater than probabilistic outcome (e.g., saving four of six with certainty versus a one-third chance of saving all six), only about 33% choose the sure thing if

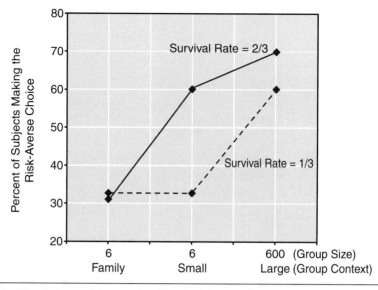

Figure 18.5 The Effects of Increasing Survival Rates of Hypothetical Patients on Subjects' Risk Preference across Social Group Contexts. *Source:* From "A Kith-and-Kin Rationality in Risky Choices: Empirical Examinations and Theoretical Modeling" (pp. 47–70), by X. T. Wang, in *Risky Transactions: Trust, Kinship, and Ethnicity,* F. Salter (Ed.), 2002, Oxford, UK: Berghahn Books.

the group members are kin whereas about 60% do so if the group members are strangers (Wang, 1996a, 1996c; see Figure 18.5). These experimental findings plus those from field studies of life-threatening emergencies such as Sime (1983) are consistent with a kith-and-kin rationality that is distinctly different from the calculus used in decisions about unrelated individuals. In perilous situations, kin tend to think of themselves as a social unit or true group and behave according to a "live-or-die-together" rule.

ALTRUISM IN THE ABSENCE OF KINSHIP?

According to inclusive fitness theory, altruism as specified in Hamilton's inequality will not evolve in the absence of genetic relatedness (i.e., if $r = 0$). Trivers (1971) does not dispute the point but proposes that even when self-interest dominates, reciprocal altruism, if not Hamiltonian altruism, can evolve among nonkin to the extent (1) the benefits one party provides another are returned at a later date, and thereby (2) all parties experience a net increase in fitness. This is also implicit in Alexander's (1987, p. 3) analysis of morality where he proposes, ". . . human conduct and the human psyche are to be understood only if societies are seen as collections of individuals seeking their own self-interest . . ." and blatant in Ghiselin's (1974, p. 247) analysis where he concludes, "Scratch an altruist and watch a hypocrite bleed." Nonetheless, there is a body of findings that shows altruisticlike risk taking, trust, and generosity occur among unrelated individuals. Dawes and colleagues (e.g., Caporael, Dawes, Orbell, & van de Kragt, 1989) used a step-level public goods problem in which some number of individual members (the quota) have to contribute their own money for all group members to be awarded additional money. If the quota isn't met, contributors lose their contribution while noncontributors keep what they have; if the quota is met, each member gains the same amount. In the standard form, the game is one-shot; players are strangers and play anonymously. Free-riding, therefore, is a dominant strategy. Yet, over many experiments, on average around 50% of the members risk the sucker's payoff and contribute. If anonymity is briefly lifted for discussion but restored before members make their decisions, around 85% of them contribute even though many believe there are already more than enough contributors to meet the quota, arguably the height of irrationality (for a review of the most recent experimental evidence for nonkin altruism, see Gintis, Bowles, Boyd, & Fehr, 2003).

Two kinds of explanations for the evolution of nonkin altruism have been advanced. One assumes it to be a pleiotropism—that nonkin and kin altruism are related traits influenced by a common genetic system or the former is a side effect of a system coding for the latter. Intuitively this explanation doesn't seems unreasonable. A gene can code for numerous traits, and a trait, particularly a behavioral strategy, can be influenced by numerous genes. Moreover, the psychological mechanisms supporting kin altruism, in particular, theory of mind processing and empathy, seem easily, if not spontaneously, activated by unrelated individuals (Batson, 1991; Batson & Moran, 1999; Stotland, 1969). In modern communities where nonkin ties are common, these mechanisms probably cause frequent and potentially costly false alarms; but in the ancestral environment, such mistakes might well have been rare enough not to encourage free-riding. In any event, Boehm (1999; also see Jones, 2000) has suggested how such a pleiotropic effect might be sustainable: If there are frequent occasions on which related and unrelated individuals are benefited *simultaneously,* then a nonkin pleiotropism could be established, especially were kin to gain more thereby (e.g., arbitrating costly disputes between relatives and unrelated individuals when the former has more at stake than the latter).

The other explanation of nonkin altruism claims it is a product of group selection (Boehm, 1999; Wilson & Sober, 1994). It assumes communities of altruists tend to reproduce, grow, and fission at a greater rate than communities of selfish individuals and will eventually replace the latter. More generally, the argument for group selection is that when altruism is the property of a group (e.g., the proportion of members who are altruists) and influences selection, then any explanation of changes in fitness of its individual members requires this group property be taken into account. However, the conditions necessary for group selection are stringent: (1) Between-group variance in altruism should be large relative to within-group variance, (2) the rate of group extinction should be high, and (3) group boundaries should be relatively impermeable.

How often these circumstances occur is difficult to say (but see Boehm, 1999; Wilson & Sober, 1994). Some are readily produced in the laboratory, however. In particular, consensual decision making, common among hunter-gatherers as well as in more developed societies, has effects consistent with group selection. Suppose, for instance, members initially differ on the maximum risk deemed acceptable to pursue a particular strategy and after discussing the issue, they arrive at a consensus. Then two changes in the group will be observed: First, individual prediscussion choices shift toward the group consensus inevitably reducing within-group variance. Second, the group decision is more extreme than that favored by the average member prior to discussion; hence small prediscussion differences between risk-prone and risk-averse groups become larger (see the review of group polarization in R. Brown, 1986). Finally, high rates of group extinction result primarily from intergroup warfare (Boehm, 1999; Knauft, 1991). Again, while the frequency of such conflicts in the ancestral environment is unknown, social dilemma research demonstrates an upsurge in altruism among members, as measured by the number contributing to the public good, when their group competes with another group (Bornstein & Ben-Yossef, 1994). This is at least consistent with the hypothesis that group selection, propelled by intergroup conflict and high rates of group extinction, favored collectivities whose members were predisposed to sacrifice for one another.

A standard objection to these kinds of experimental findings is that in the ancestral environment most transactions had as context the "shadow of the future"; few were one-shot or anonymous. The behaviors deemed unselfish or irrational in the laboratory, therefore, would have been over most of human history self-interested and fitness enhancing. As a result, a sense that we are known to our partners or that we may interact with them in the future could have evolved as a default expectation and be difficult to suppress. The same criticism cannot be made about findings from ethnographic studies. Nonetheless, they have inherent ambiguities that allow questions to be raised about their observations of nonkin altruism. For instance, Hill's (2002) rich analysis of "altruistic cooperation" among the Ache indicates both men and women spend about 10% of their foraging time in activities such as climbing a tree to shake down fruit for others or building a bridge so that others can cross a river. The vast majority of these efforts increase the recipient's gain from foraging but do nothing for the benefactor, and the two individuals are very rarely related. Most remarkable is the high degree of food sharing where the amount individuals receive depends more on need (e.g., size of family) than their contribution to foraging and little, if at all, on genetic relatedness. Yet, there are signs the computations involved are not quite altruistic in Hamilton's sense. Rather, they seem to reflect a concern with equity, a principle of conduct that requires intricate policing with individuals being rewarded in some circumstances, for example, when they overfulfill and do more than is expected, and punished in others, for example, when they underfulfill and do less than is expected (Brosnan & de Waal, 2003; Messick & Cook, 1983; Walster, Walster, & Berscheid, 1978). If the function of generosity among unrelated individuals is to maintain or restore equity, the psychological mechanisms involved are likely to be different from those supporting kin altruism. A number of findings suggest this is the case. For example, worker output in anonymous, one-shot worker-boss games is markedly influenced by the possibility of workers being rewarded or punished afterward. Most bosses actually deliver even though it is costly, the work is already done, and they (as well as workers) know they will have no future contact (see Gintis et al., 2003). It is difficult to imagine efforts to aid an offspring being similarly manipulated; instead, kin altruism occurs not merely in the absence of rewards but when the payoff to the altruist could easily be negative, either deadly (e.g., Sime, 1983), physically painful, or hypothetically both (e.g., Burnstein et al., 1994).

To establish and maintain an effective system of foraging, or any other division of labor, equity would seem a more useful strategy than Hamiltonian self-sacrifice. In any event, according to Hill (2002), the Ache have made a social bargain whose guiding principle is the maintenance of a fair balance between a forager's contribution and return while taking into account differences in needs, abilities, and resources—"If you make an effort to forage, then you have a right to a share of the food." What individuals perceive to be a fair balance probably involves computing the effort most foragers like themselves (e.g., those similar in age, experience, numbers of dependents) make relative to the food shares they receive and varies within imprecise limits—narrow when food is scarce and wide when it is plentiful. The key theoretical point, however, is that social bargains demand policing; kin altruism does not. According to Hamilton's model, whether individuals feel their relatives are unfairly advantaged or disadvantaged is irrelevant to helping them. Indeed, we seem designed to benefit kin at a cost to ourselves independent of their deservingness.

CONCLUSIONS

Hamilton in his theory of inclusive fitness proposed that altruism will evolve to the extent that the reproductive costs to the altruist are less than the reproductive benefits to the recipient weighted by their degree of relatedness ($C < rB$). This general formulation is well supported by ethnographic and experimental research, both of which consistently demonstrate that individuals are more likely to sacrifice for close kin than for distant kin and least likely to do so for unrelated individuals. Moreover, the tendency to discriminate as a function of relatedness is particularly strong when stakes are high, for example, in a life or death emergency. The implication is that individuals somehow estimate not only the degree of relatedness but also the costs and benefits of altruism. How these computations are performed and what mechanisms are involved are less clear.

Studies on assortative behavior, while not free of methodological problems, suggest individuals choose mates and friends as if they recognize family resemblances. While the process might suggest a genetically programmed template, for example, when assortative mating and friendship appear to involve a single-locus recognition system, familiarity is critical. This is readily demonstrated in studies on the Westermarck (1891) effect where, for example, it is not so much knowledge of kinship but rather the length of corearing that decreases the likelihood of mating and increases abhorrence of sexual relations between close kin. Moreover, the process of familiarization often begins early during infancy (e.g., recognizing mother's face) and in some cases prior to birth (e.g., recognizing mother's voice). In addition to familiarity, there is good evidence of a kin recognition mechanism based on phenotype matching. Experiments using facial self-morphs demonstrate that an observer can detect resemblances to self or to people who look like the observer (hence, are likely to be kin) without being aware of it and that they will use this information to benefit them with no expectation of repayment. Whatever the nature of the computational mechanism, its prowess seems considerable so that in assessing the costs and benefits of altruism we are capable of taking into account the reproductive value of relatives as reflected in their age, state of health, or resources. Indeed, some argue that kin altruism is based on a calculus qualitatively different from that of classic self-interest. Evidence for a distinct kith-and-kin rationality comes from experiments showing, for example, that individuals are risk averse when deciding on a course of action to save a group of unrelated individuals, but they become decidedly risk prone when it's a group of close kin, even if the expected value of the certain course of action is considerably greater than that of the risky one.

Finally, although according to Hamilton's formulation genetic relatedness is a necessary condition for the evolution of altruism, there are numerous findings indicating something very like it occurs among unrelated individuals. However, the fact that generosity on the part of nonkin often depends on policing to suppress free-riding suggests its function is to maintain equity in a division of labor rather than altruism, at least as it is specified in the theory of inclusive fitness.

REFERENCES

Abric, J. C., Faucheux, C., Moscovici, S., & Plon, M. (1967). Role de l'image du partenaire sur la cooperation en situation de jeu. *Psychologie Francaise, 12,* 267–275.

Alexander, R. D. (1987). *The biology of moral systems.* New York: Aldine de Gruyter.

Alexander, R. D., & Borgia, G. (1978). Group selection, altruism, and the levels of organization of life. *Annual Review of Ecology and Systematics, 9,* 449–474.

Barrett, L., Dunbar, R., & Lycett, J. (2002). *Human evolutionary psychology.* Princeton, NJ: Princeton University Press.

Batson, C. D. (1991). *The altruism question: Toward a social-psychological answer.* Hillsdale, NJ: Erlbaum.

Batson, C. D., & Moran, T. (1999). Empathy-induced altruism in a prisoner's dilemma. *European Journal of Social Psychology, 29,* 909–924.

Berscheid, E. (1985). Interpersonal attraction. In G. Lindzey & E. Aronson (Eds.), *Handbook of social psychology* (3rd ed., Vol. 2, pp. 413–484). New York: Random House.

Berte, N. A. (1988). K'ekchi horticultural labor exchange: Productive and reproductive implications. In L. Betzig, M. Borgerhoff Mulder, & P. Turke (Eds.), *Human reproductive behavior: A Darwinian perspective* (pp. 83–96). Cambridge, UK: Cambridge University Press.

Betzig, L., & Turke, P. (1986). Food sharing on Ifaluk. *Current Anthropology, 27,* 397–400.

Bevc, I., & Silverman, I. (2000). Early separation and sibling incest: A test of the revised Westermarck theory. *Evolution and Human Behavior, 21,* 151–162.

Bjorklund, D. F., & Pellegrini, A. D. (2002). *The origins of human nature: Evolutionary developmental psychology.* Washington, DC: American Psychological Association.

Blount, S. (1995). When social outcomes aren't fair: The effect of causal attributions on preferences. *Organizational Behavior and Human Decision Processes, 63,* 131–144.

Boehm, C. (1999). The natural selection of altruistic traits. *Human Nature, 10,* 205–252.

Bornstein, G., & Ben-Yossef, M. (1994). Cooperation in intergroup and single-group social dilemmas. *Journal of Experimental Social Psychology, 30,* 52–67.

Bornstein, R. F. (1989). Exposure and affect: Overview and meta-analysis of research. *Psychological Bulletin, 106,* 231–262.

Bressan, P., & Dal Martello, M. F. (2002). *Talis pater, talis filius:* Perceived resemblance and the belief in genetic relatedness. *Psychological Science, 13,* 213–218.

Brosnan, S. F., & de Waal, F. B. M. (2003). Monkeys reject unequal pay. *Nature, 425,* 297–299.

Brown, R. (1986). *Social psychology* (2nd ed.). New York: Free Press.

Brown, W. M., Palameta, B., & Moore, C. (2003). Are there nonverbal cues to commitment? An exploratory study using the zero-acquaintence video presentation paradigm. *Evolutionary Psychology, 1,* 42–69.

Burch, E. S., Jr. (1975). *Eskimo kinsmen: Changing family relationships in northwest Alaska.* St. Paul, MN: West Co.

Burnstein, E. (1969). Reward and punishment in behavioral interdependence. In J. Mills (Ed.), *Experimental social psychology* (pp. 341–370). New York: Macmillan.

Burnstein, E., Crandall, C., & Kitayama, S. (1994). Some neo-Darwinian decision rules for altruism: Weighting cues for inclusive fitness as a function of the biological importance of the decision. *Journal of Personality and Social Psychology, 67,* 773–789.

Buss, D. M. (2003). *Evolutionary psychology: The new science of the mind* (2nd ed.). Boston: Allyn & Bacon.

Caporael, L. R., Dawes, R. M., Orbell, J. M., & van de Kragt, A. J. C. (1989). Selfishness examined: Cooperation in the absence of egoistic incentives. *Behavioral and Brain Sciences, 12,* 683–739.

Chagnon, N. A., & Bugos, P. E., Jr. (1979). Kin selection and conflict: An analysis of a Yanomamo ax fight. In N. A. Chagnon & W. Irons (Eds.), *Evolutionary biology and human social behavior: An anthropological perspective* (pp. 213–249). North Sciutate, MA: Duxbury Press.

Cunningham, M. R. (1986). Levites and brother's keeper: A sociobiological perspective on prosocial behavior. *Humbolt Journal of Social Relations, 13,* 35–67.

Daly, M. (1989). On distinguishing evolved adaptation from epiphenomena. *Behavioral and Brain Sciences, 12,* 520.

Daly, M., & Wilson, M. (1982). Whom are newborn babies said to resemble? *Ethology and Sociobiology, 3,* 69–78.

Dawkins, R. (1976). *The selfish gene.* Oxford, England: Oxford University Press.

Dawkins, R. (1982). *The extended phenotype.* Oxford, England: Freeman.

DeBruine, L. M. (2002). Facial resemblance enhances trust. *Proceedings of the Royal Society of London. Series B, Biological Sciences, 269,* 1307–1312.

Dunbar, R. I. M., Clark, A., & Hurst, N. L. (1997). Conflict and cooperation among the Vikings: Contingent behavioral decisions. *Ethology and Sociobiology, 16,* 233–246.

Essock-Vitale, S., & McGuire, M. T. (1985). Women's lives viewed from an evolutionary perspective. II. Patterns of helping. *Ethology and Sociobiology, 6,* 155–173.

Fisek, M. H., & Ofshe, R. (1970). The process of status evolution. *Sociometry, 33,* 327–346.

Fortes, M. (1969). *Kinship and social order.* Chicago: Aldine.

Frank, R. H., Gilovich, T., & Regan, D. T. (1993). The evolution of one-shot cooperation—an experiment. *Ethology and Sociobiology, 14,* 247–256.

Ghiselin, M. T. (1974). *The economy of nature and the evolution of sex.* Berkeley: University of California Press.

Gibson, E. J. (1969). *Principles of perceptual learning and development.* New York: Appleton-Century-Crofts.

Gintis, H., Bowles, S., Boyd, R., & Fehr, E. (2003). Explaining altruistic behavior in humans. *Evolution and Human Behavior, 24,* 153–172.

Glazer, N. (1975). *Affirmative discrimination.* New York: Basic Books.

Haig, D. (2002). *Genomic imprinting and kinship.* New Brunswick, NJ: Rutgers University Press.

Hames, R. (1988). The allocation of parental care among the Ye'kwana. In L. Betzig, M. Borgerhoff Mulder, & P. Turke (Eds.), *Human reproductive behavior: A Darwinian perspective* (pp. 237–252). Cambridge, UK: Cambridge University Press.

Hamilton, W. D. (1964). The genetical evolution of social behavior, I and II. *Journal of Theoretical Biology, 7,* 1–52.

Hare, A. P. (1976). *Handbook of small group research* (2nd ed.). New York: Free Press.

Hawkes, K., O'Connell, J. F., Blurton Jones, N. G., Alvarez, H., & Charnov, E. L. (1998). Grandmothering, menopause, and the evolution of human life histories. *Proceedings of the National Academy of Sciences of the United States, 95,* 1336–1339.

Hedden, T., & Zhang, J. (2002). What do you think I think you think?: Strategic reasoning in matrix games. *Cognition, 85,* 1–36.

Hill, K. (2002). Altruistic cooperation during foraging by the Ache, and the evolved human predisposition to cooperate. *Human Nature, 13,* 105–128.

Homans, G. C. (1950). *The human group.* New York: Harcourt, Brace.

Jones, D. (2000). Group nepotism and human kinship. *Current Anthropology, 41,* 779–809.

Jones, D. (2003). The generative psychology of kinship: Part I. Cognitive universals and evolutionary psychology. *Evolution and Human Behavior, 24,* 303–319.

Judge, D. S. (1995). American legacies and the variable life histories of women and men. *Human Nature, 6,* 291–324.

Kenrick, D. T., & Trost, M. R. (1987). A biosocial theory of heterosexual relationships. In K. Kelley (Ed.), *Females, males, and sexuality: Theory and research* (pp. 59–100). New York: State University of New York Press.

Kisilevsky, B. S., Hains, S. M. J., Lee, K., Xie, X., Huang, H., Ye, H. H., et al. (2003). Effects of experience on fetal voice recognition. *Psychological Science, 14,* 220–224.

Knauft, B. B. (1991). Violence and sociality in human evolution. *Current Anthropology, 32,* 391–428.

Kohl, J. V., Atzmueller, M., Fink, B., & Grammer, K. (2001). Human pheromones: Integrating neuroendocrinology and ethology. *Neuroendocirnology Letters, 22,* 309–321.

Korchmaros, J. D., & Kenny, D. A. (2001). Emotional closeness as a mediator of the effect of genetic relatedness on altruism. *Psychological Science, 12,* 262–265.

Kruger, D. J. (2003). Evolution and altruism: Combining psychological mediators with naturally selected tendencies. *Evolution and Human Behavior, 24,* 118–125.

Lanzetta, J. T., & Englis, B. G. (1989). Expectations of cooperation and competition and their effects on observers' vicarious emotional responses. *Journal of Personality and Social Psychology, 56,* 543–554.

Lieberman, D., Tooby, J., & Cosmides, L. (2003). Does morality have a biological basis?: An empirical test of the factors governing moral sentiments relating to incest. *Proceedings of the Royal Society of London. Series B, Biological Sciences, 10.*

Marlowe, F. (2003). A critical period for provisioning by Hadza men: Implications for pair bonding. *Evolution and Human Behavior, 24,* 217–229.

Mealey, L., Daood, C., & Krage, M. (1996). Enhanced memory for faces of cheaters. *Ethology and Sociobiology, 17,* 119–128.

Messick, D. M., & Cook, K. S. (Eds.). (1983). *Equity theory: Psychological and sociological perspectives.* New York: Praeger.

Milinski, M., & Wedekind, C. (2001). Evidence for MHC-correlated perfume preferences in humans. *Behavioral Ecology, 12,* 140–149.

Miyamoto, Y., & Kitayama, S. (2002). Cultural variation in correspondence bias: The critical role of attitude diagnosticity of socially constrained behavior. *Journal of Personality and Social Psychology, 83,* 1239–1248.

Morris, M. W., Menon, T., & Ames, D. R. (2001). Culturally conferred conceptions of agency: A key to social perception of persons, groups, and other actors. *Personality and Social Psychology Review, 5,* 169–182.

Newcomb, T. M. (1961). *The acquaintance process.* New York: Holt, Rhinehart and Winston.

Oda, R. (1997). Biased face recognition in the prisoner's dilemma game. *Evolution and Human Behavior, 18,* 309–316.

Palmer, C. T., & Steadman, L. B. (1997). Human kinship as a descendant-leaving strategy: A solution to an evolutionary puzzle. *Journal of Social and Evolutionary Systems, 20,* 39–51.

Platek, S. M., Burch, R. L., Panyavin, I. S., Wasserman, B. H., & Gallup, G. G., Jr. (2002). Reactions to children's faces: Resemblance matters more for males than females. *Evolution and Human Behavior, 23,* 159–166.

Platek, S. M., Critton, S. R., Burch, R. L., Frederick, D. A., Myers, T. E., & Gallup, G. G., Jr. (2003). How much paternal resemblance is enough?: Sex differences in hypothetical investment decisions but not in the detection of resemblance. *Evolution and Human Behavior, 24,* 81–87.

Reeder, G. D., Fletcher, G. J. O., & Furman, K. (1989). The role of observers' expectations in attitude attribution. *Journal of Experimental Social Psychology, 25,* 168–188.

Regalski, J. M., & Gaulin, S. J. C. (1993). Whom are Mexican infants said to resemble? Monitoring and fostering paternal confidence in the Yucatan. *Ethology and Sociobiology, 11,* 11–21.

Rosenbaum, M. E. (1986). The repulsion hypothesis: On the nondevelopment of relationships. *Journal of Personality and Social Psychology, 51,* 1156–1166.

Rushton, J. P. (1989). Genetic similarity, human altruism, and group selection. *Behavioral and Brain Sciences, 12,* 503–559.

Schul, Y., Mayo, R., & Burnstein, E. (in press). Encoding under trust and distrust: The spontaneous activation of incongruent cognitions. *Journal of Personality and Social Psychology.*

Sears, R., Mace, R., & McGregor, I. A. (2000). Maternal grandmothers improve nutritional status and survival of children in rural Gambia. *Proceedings of the Royal Society of London. Series B, Biological Sciences, 267,* 1641–1647.

Segal, N. L., & Hershberger, S. L. (1999). Cooperation and competition in adolescent twins: Findings from a prisoner's dilemma game. *Evolution and Human Behavior, 20,* 29–51.

Segal, N. L., & Hershberger, S. L., & Arad, S. (2003). Meeting one's twin: Perceived social closeness and familiarity. *Evolutionary Psychology, 1,* 70–95.

Shepher, J. (1971). Mate selection among second generation kibbutz adolescents and adults: Incest avoidance and negative imprinting. *Archives of Sexual Behavior, 1,* 293–307.

Sime, J. D. (1983). Affiliative behavior during escape to building exits. *Journal of Environmental Psychology, 3,* 21–41.

Stotland, E. (1969). Exploratory investigations of empathy. In L. Berkowitz (Ed.), *Advances in experimental social psychology* (Vol. 4, pp. 271–313). New York: Academic Press.

Tesser, A. (1993). The importance of heritability in psychological research: The case of attitudes. *Psychological Review, 100,* 129–142.

Thornhill, N. W. (1991). An evolutionary analysis of rules regulating human inbreeding and marriage. *Behavioral and Brain Sciences, 14,* 247–293.

Titchener, E. B. (1910). *A text-book of psychology* (Rev. ed.). New York: Macmillan.

Trivers, R. L. (1971). The evolution of reciprocal altruism. *Quarterly Review of Biology, 46*, 35–57.

Trivers, R. L. (2002). *Natural selection and social theory.* New York: Oxford.

Tversky, A., & Kahneman, D. (1981). The framing of decisions and the psychology of choice. *Science, 211*, 453–458.

van den Berghe, P. L. (1983). Human inbreeding avoidance: Culture in nature. *Behavioral and Brain Sciences, 6*, 91–123.

Von Bracken, H. (1934). Mutual intimacy in twins. *Character and Personality, 2*, 293–309.

Waldman, B. (1988). The ecology of kin recognition. *Annual Review of Ecology and Systematics, 19*, 543–571.

Walster, E., Walster, G. W., & Berscheid, E. (1978). *Equity: Theory and research.* Boston: Allyn & Bacon.

Wang, X. T. (1996a). Domain-specific rationality in human choices: Violations of utility axioms and social contexts. *Cognition, 60*, 31–63.

Wang, X. T. (1996b). Evolutionary hypotheses of risk-sensitive choice: Age differences and perspective change. *Ethology and Sociobiology, 17*, 1–15.

Wang, X. T. (1996c). Framing effects: Dynamics and task domains. *Organizational Behavior and Human Decision Processes, 68*, 145–157.

Wang, X. T. (2002). A kith-and-kin rationality in risky choices: Empirical examinations and theoretical modeling. In F. Salter (Ed.), *Risky transactions: Trust, kinship, and ethnicity* (pp. 47–70). Oxford, England: Berghahn.

Wang, X. T., & Johnston, V. S. (1995). Perceived social context and risk preferences: A re-examination of framing effects in a life-death decision problem. *Journal of Behavioral Decision Making, 8*, 278–293.

Wedekind, C., & Füri, S. (1997). Body odour preferences in men and women: Aims for specific MHC-combinations or simply heterozygosity? *Proceedings of the Royal Society of London. Series B, Biological Sciences, 264*, 1471–1479.

Wedekind, C., Seebeck, T., Bettens, F., & Paepke, A. J. (1995). MHC-dependent mate preferences in humans. *Proceedings of the Royal Society of London. Series B, Biological Sciences, 260*, 245–249.

Westermarck, E. A. (1891). *The history of human marriage.* New York: Macmillan.

Wilson, D. S., & Sober, E. (1994). Reintroducing group selection to the human behavioral sciences. *Behavioral and Brain Sciences, 17*, 585–654.

Wolf, A. P. (1995). *Sexual attraction and childhood association in China: A Chinese brief for Edward Westermarck.* Stanford: Stanford University Press.

Yamagishi, T., Tanida, S., Mashima, R., Shimona, E., & Kanazawa, S. (2003). You can judge a book by its cover: Evidence that cheaters may look different from cooperators. *Evolution and Human Behavior, 24*, 290–301.

Yamazaki, K., Beauchamp, G. K., Curran, M., Bard, J., & Boyse, E. A. (2000). Parent-progeny recognition as a function of MHC-odor type identity. *Proceedings of the National Academy of Sciences of the United States of America, 97*, 10500–10502.

Yamazaki, K., Beauchamp, G. K., Kupniewski, D., & Bard, J. (1988). Familial imprinting determines selective mating preferences. *Science, 240*, 1331–1332.

Zahavi, A., & Zahavi, A. (1997). *The handicap principle: A missing part of Darwin's puzzle.* Oxford, England: Oxford University Press.

Zajonc, R. B. (1968). Attitudinal effects of mere exposure. *Journal of Personality and Social Psychology Monograph Supplement, 9*(2, Pt. 2), 2–27.

CHAPTER 19

Hormones and the Human Family

MARK V. FLINN, CAROL V. WARD, and ROBERT J. NOONE

Hormones and neurotransmitters help shape important aspects of our lives, including growth, differentiation, sexuality, physiology, emotion, and cognition. From romantic thoughts to jealous rage, from the release of gametes to lactation and parent-offspring bonding, the extraordinary molecules produced and released by tiny and otherwise seemingly insignificant cells and glands orchestrate our reproductive strategies. A key research objective is to understand the evolutionary functions of this chemical language.

Endocrine and neuroendocrine systems may be viewed as complex sets of mechanisms designed by natural selection to communicate information among cells and tissues. This chapter focuses on an area of particular importance for evolutionary psychology: the behavioral endocrinology of the human family. Steroid and peptide hormones, associated neurotransmitters, and other chemical messengers guide mating and parental behaviors of mammals in many important ways (Curtis & Wang, 2003; Rosenblatt, 2003; Young & Insel, 2002). Cross-species comparisons among primates require careful analysis (Bercovitch & Ziegler, 2002) because of the apparent rapid evolutionary changes in patterns of reproductive behaviors and increased phenotypic flexibility involving intricate mental processes. *Homo sapiens* presents special problems in these regards (Fisher, 2004; Maestripieri, 1999; Marler, Bester-Meredith, & Trainor, 2003; Wynne-Edwards, 2001, 2003).

Here we first provide a theoretical scenario for the evolution of human patterns of mating and parenting behaviors. We test our model by examining the phylogenetic trajectories of associated traits such as sexual dimorphism and life history stages from the hominin fossil record. We then turn to a description and functional analysis of the endocrine mechanisms that may influence these remarkable reproductive behavioral characteristics of our species.

EVOLUTION OF THE HUMAN FAMILY

The human family is extraordinary and unique in many respects (Alexander, 1990b; Geary & Flinn, 2001). Humans are the only species to live in multimale groups with complex coalitions and extensive paternal care. Humans have concealed (or "cryptic") ovulation, physically altricial but mentally precocial infants,

552

lengthy child development, female orgasm, and menopause. Hormones are involved in the development (ontogeny) and regulation of these and other components of reproduction, including the neurobiology that underpins the associated psychological competencies (e.g., Bartels & Zeki, 2004). Understanding the proximate causes, phylogenetic relations, and adaptive functions of the hormonal and neurotransmitter mechanisms may provide important steps toward reconstructing the evolutionary history of our (human) unusual patterns of mating and parenting and their variability in different environmental contexts.

The altricial (helpless) infant is indicative of a protective environment provided by intense parental and alloparental care in the context of kin groups (Alexander, 1987; Chisholm, 1999; Flinn, 2004a, 2004b; Flinn & Ward, 2004; Hrdy, 1999, 2004). The human baby does not need to be physically precocial. Rather than investing in the development of locomotion, defense, and food acquisition systems that function early in ontogeny, the infant can work instead toward building a more effective adult phenotype. The brain continues rapid growth, and the corresponding cognitive competencies largely direct attention toward the social environment. Plastic neural systems enable adaptation to the nuances of the local community, such as its language (Alexander, 1990a; Bjorklund & Pellegrini, 2002; Bloom, 2000; Geary & Bjorklund, 2000; Geary & Huffman, 2002; Small, 1998, 2001). In contrast to the slow development of ecological skills of movement, fighting, and foraging, the human infant rapidly acquires skill with the complex communication system of human language (Pinker, 1994) and other social competencies such as facial recognition (de Haan, Johnson, & Halit, 2003), eye contact (Farroni, Mansfield, Lai, & Johnson, 2003), and smiling (Bornstein & Arterberry, 2003). The extraordinary information-transfer abilities enabled by linguistic competency provide a conduit to the knowledge available in other human minds. This emergent capability for intensive and extensive communication potentiates the social dynamics characteristic of human groups (Dunbar, 1997, 2004) and provides a new mechanism for social learning and culture. The recursive pattern recognition and abstract symbolic representation central to linguistic competencies may facilitate the open-ended, creative, and flexible information processing characteristic of humans—especially of children (Flinn & Ward, 2004; cf. Ranganath & Rainer, 2003).

The advantages of intensive parenting, including paternal protection and other care, require a most unusual pattern of mating relationships: moderately exclusive pair bonding in multiple-male groups. No other primate (or mammal) that lives in large, cooperative multiple-reproductive-male groups has extensive male parental care, although some protection by males is evident in multimale troops of baboons (Buchan, Alberts, Silk, & Altmann, 2003), and extensive care is provided by males in small monogamous family groups in indris, marmosets, tamarins, night monkeys, titi monkeys, and, to a lesser degree, gibbons. Although some group-living species of birds have paternal care, there appear to be special mechanisms enhancing confidence of paternity (e.g., mate guarding and the lack of long gestation periods), and they lack the coalitionary cooperation characteristic of humans (for reviews, see LeBlanc, 2003; Wrangham & Peterson, 1996). Among primates, competition for females in multiple-male groups usually results in low confidence of paternity (e.g., chimpanzees). Males and females forming exclusive pair bonds in multiple-male primate groups would provide cues of nonpaternity for other males and hence place their offspring at higher risk for infanticide (Hrdy, 1999). Paternal care is most likely to be favored by natural selection in conditions where males can identify their offspring with sufficient probability to offset the costs of investment (Alexander, 1974; Flinn, 1981), although reciprocity with potential mates is also likely to be involved (Buss, 1994; Flinn, 1988; Smuts, 1985). Humans exhibit a unique "nested family" social structure, involving complex reciprocity among males and females embedded in kin networks that restricts direct competition for mates among group members. It is difficult to imagine how this system could be maintained in the absence of another unusual human trait: concealed or "cryptic" ovulation (Alexander, 1990b; Alexander & Noonan, 1979). Although many other primates lack estrus swellings and other obvious visual signals of female reproductive condition (Pawlowski, 1999; Sillen-Tullberg & Møller, 1993), humans appear especially oblivious to the timing of ovulation, although frequency of intercourse (Wilcox et al., 2004), mate-guarding activities (Flinn, 1988), and mate choice discrimination (Gangestad, Simpson, Cousins, Garver-Apgar, & Christensen, 2004) may be higher during midcycle in some conditions.

Human groups tend to be male philopatric (men reside in the group in which they were born, although they may also emigrate), resulting in extensive male kin alliances, useful for competing against other groups of male kin (Chagnon, 1988; LeBlanc, 2003; Wagner, Flinn, & England, 2002; Wrangham & Peterson, 1996). Patterns of kinship residence, however, are variable (Murdock, 1949) and associated with different aspects of mating and marriage systems (Flinn & Low, 1986; Rohner & Veneziano, 2001). Females also have complex social networks, but usually are not involved directly in the overt physical aggression and alliances characteristic of intergroup relations (Campbell, 2002; Geary & Flinn, 2002; for an insightful case of indirect competitive activities by females, see Biella, Chagnon, & Seaman, 1997).

Across extant primates, a long developmental period and intensive parenting are associated with a long life span (Allman & Hasenstaub, 1999; Allman, Rosin, Kumar, & Hasenstaub, 1998; Leigh, 2004; van Schaik & Deaner, 2003). One unique feature of the life history and long life span of women is menopause. Menopause results in an extended period during which women can invest in the well-being of their later born children as part of a potential adaptation that enables the long-term investment in a smaller number of children and other relatives such as grandchildren. It allows them to focus on children they have already produced, avoiding the costs of additional pregnancies at a time when their health and the likelihood of their survival to the end of later born children's dependency are diminishing (Alexander, 1974; Hawkes, 2003; Williams, 1957). The increasing probability of mother's death with age has especially significant effects on the reproductive value of later born children if long-term maternal investment is important. Orphans have low reproductive value in many societies. A parallel is found in some preindustrial societies, whereby parents sometimes commit infanticide to reduce the risks to their older children (Daly & Wilson, 1988; Hill & Hurtado, 1996). Infanticide, as well as reduced fertility associated with breastfeeding and increasing age (Ellison, 2001), enables parents to reduce the number of dependent offspring and direct more parental investment to older children. When this pattern is combined with a substantial increase in the length of the developmental period, menopause follows as a logical evolutionary adaptation that serves the same function, that is, to reduce the number of dependent children and thus free parental resources that can be invested in a smaller number of children and other kin. Empirical tests demonstrating such advantages, however, have proven difficult (Hill & Hurtado, 1991, 1996; Hill & Kaplan, 1999; cf. Hawkes, 2003; Hawkes, O'Connell, Blurton Jones, Alvarez, & Charnov, 1998).

Men, with different, less risky parental activities, would not have been subject to the same selective pressures for terminating reproductive potential, although they, too, may have been selected to adjust reproductive behavior from mating to parenting with increased age (Draper & Harpending, 1988). From this perspective, older females may have had important effects on the success of their developing children, perhaps in part because of the importance of their accumulated knowledge for negotiating the social environment. Socially skilled and well-connected older mothers and grandmothers may have been especially valuable teachers of social and political wisdom, with associated reproductive benefits (Alexander, 1990b; Caspari & Lee, 2004; Coe, 2003; cf. O'Connell, Hawkes, & Blurton Jones, 1999). In short, the doubling of the maximum life span of humans, involving an increased period of prereproductive development on the one hand and an increased period of postreproductive parental and kin investment on the other, suggests the importance of parent-offspring relationships for acquiring and mastering sociocompetitive information (Bjorklund & Pellegrini, 2002; Flinn & Ward, 2004; Geary, 2005).

These characteristics of the human family—extensive biparental and kin care, physically altricial but linguistically and cognitively precocial infants, lengthy childhood and adolescence, concealed ovulation, variably exclusive pair bonds in multiple-male coalitionary groups, and menopause—are a unique combination of traits with associated morphological, physiological, and psychological mechanisms (Flinn, Geary, & Ward, 2005). In the following section, we review the paleontological evidence of the selective pressures that produced this complex set of adaptations.

THE FOSSIL RECORD

The temporal sequence of changes in hominin anatomy documented in the fossil record provides evidence of the sequence of morphological changes that occurred in human evolution. Unfortunately, it is difficult to directly infer hominin social structures and associated neurobiological and endocrinological mechanisms from fossils. Some evidence comes from changes in the pattern of human sexual dimorphism and shifts in life history strategies that would impact social interactions, in particular, reduction in the magnitude of body size sexual dimorphism, threefold increase in brain volume, near doubling of the length of the developmental period, and disappearance of related species of hominins. Covariation among these variables and social and ecological differences across living primates provide data from which inferences can be made about the nature of social dynamics in human evolution (Alexander, Hoogland, Howard, Noonan, & Sherman, 1979; Clutton-Brock, 1977; Dunbar, 1998; Foley, 1999; Plavcan, van Schaik, & Kappeler, 1995), although associated models may not be definitive (Plavcan, 2000).

The best indicators of the increasing stability of male-female pair bonds and associated male coalitionary behavior in the fossil record are sexual dimorphism and life history patterns. Reduced body size dimorphism is associated with both monogamy (Plavcan, 2000, 2001) and male coalitionary behavior (Pawlowski, Lowen, & Dunbar, 1998; Plavcan & van Schaik, 1997; Plavcan et al., 1995) in extant primates. Although the large canine size dimorphism that characterizes all living and fossil great apes had greatly diminished in *Australopithecus* (Ward, Leakey, & Walker, 2001; Ward, Walker, & Leakey, 1999), the reduced body mass dimorphism typical of modern humans did not occur until sometime during the evolution of *Homo erectus* (McHenry, 1992a, 1992b, 1994; cf. Reno, Meindl, McCollum, & Lovejoy, 2003).

It is tempting to assume that the behavioral characteristics of the ancestor common to the australopithecine species and humans were similar to those observed in modern chimpanzees or bonobos (de Waal & Lanting, 1997; Kano, 1992; Wrangham, 1999; Wrangham & Peterson, 1996; Zihlman, Cronin, Cramer, & Sarich, 1978). This appears a reasonable assumption in some respects, as relative brain sizes of chimpanzees, bonobos, and australopithecines are very similar (McHenry, 1992a, 1992b). In addition, sexual dimorphism in body weight is about 20% for chimpanzees and bonobos (Goodall, 1986; Kano, 1992), as it is in humans. Thus, it might appear that the large multimale, multifemale group structures characterizing all three species would have been found in the last common ancestor and thus in earliest hominins. Chimpanzees and humans display coalitional aggression (Wrangham, 1999), and although this is not documented for the less studied bonobos, it has been hypothesized to be a homologous trait shared with the common ancestor of chimpanzees and humans (Wrangham & Peterson, 1996).

Size dimorphism was substantially greater in *Australopithecus* than in *Pan* or *Homo*, although less than in gorillas and orangutans (McHenry, 1992b; Ward et al., 1999, 2001; but see Reno et al., 2003). The contrast suggests that reproductive strategies of australopithecines may have differed in important respects from that of male chimpanzees, bonobos, and humans. *Australopithecus* body mass dimorphism suggests that these early hominins were polygynous, as significant mass dimorphism is not associated with monogamy in any extant primate (Plavcan, 2001). Body mass dimorphism is inconsistent with both monogamy and extensive coalitionary behaviors in extant primates (Plavcan, 2000; Plavcan & van Schaik, 1997). Therefore, the social structure of *Australopithecus* was unlikely to have been characterized by either monogamy or extensive male coalitions.

At some point during the evolution of *Homo erectus,* body size sexual dimorphism became reduced to near-modern human levels. The reduction in sexual dimorphism resulted in spite of a slight increase in male size, because of an even more substantial increase in female body size (McHenry, 1994). Body mass dimorphism in early *H. erectus* is difficult to estimate accurately, but disparities in size and robusticity among even early *H. erectus* crania are less than in australopithecine species, signaling a reduction in body size sexual dimorphism. By the early mid-Pleistocene (approximately 800 k), body mass dimorphism was similar to that found in modern humans (McHenry, 1994; Ruff, Trinkaus, & Holliday, 1997), consistent with either an increase in pair bonding and/or male coalitionary behaviors.

Changes in social behavior accompanying the shift in mating and parenting strategies are likely to have presented novel cognitive challenges involving complex reciprocity among coalition members. Unlike gorillas, with one-male breeding groups, and chimps, with promiscuous mating and little male parental behavior, at some point the evolving hominids were faced with the difficulties of managing increasingly exclusive pair bonds in the midst of increasingly large coalitions of potential mate competitors. These behavioral changes would be consistent with the documented decreases in dimorphism.

Prolongation of childhood, including secondarily altricial infants born early in their ontogenies coupled with extended juvenile periods, an adolescent growth spurt, and delayed maturation relative to apes (Bogin, 1991, 1999), seems to have broadly coevolved with changes in sexual dimorphism and reproductive behaviors. The first major changes in hominin infant altriciality probably occurred in *Homo erectus*, concurrent or slightly behind changes in sexual dimorphism and cranial capacity—that is, more recently than 1.5 mya (Antòn & Leigh, 2003; Nelson, Thompson, & Krovitz, 2003). Female pelvic dimensions are constrained by mechanical-locomotor as well as thermoregulatory constraints, so birth canal size was not greatly expanded over australopithecine levels (Begun & Walker, 1993; Ruff, 1995), yet adult brain sizes were nearly doubled. This means that to have appropriate neonatal proportions relative to the size of the mother's pelvic inlet, infants must have been born at a relatively small size and were relatively altricial early (Martin, 1990; Portman, 1941; Rosenberg & Trevathan, 1996) with rapid rates of brain growth (Antòn & Leigh, 2003; Martin, 1983). They do not appear to have attained large adult brain size simply by prolonging overall growth (Deacon, 1997; Dean et al., 2001; Leigh, 2004). Increasingly altricial infants would have required more intensive parenting by the mother, and, given the decrease in sexual dimorphism occurring at this time, which may indicate pair bonding, perhaps parental care by the father and/or alloparents (Flinn & Ward, 2004; Rosenberg, 1992; Rosenberg & Trevathan, 1996).

Despite these ontogenetic shifts associated with the timing of birth, delayed maturation does not appear to have occurred until later in human evolution (summary in Nelson et al., 2003). Dental development is coupled to life history variables such as age at sexual maturity, and thus can be used to infer the timing of important life history stages. Early *Homo erectus* appears to have had relatively rapid development, similar in rate to *Australopithecus* and great apes, whereas that of modern humans is much slower (Dean et al., 2001). Coincident with its rapid rate of development, early *H. erectus* is predicted to have lacked a humanlike adolescent growth spurt, based on the fact that the single known juvenile skeleton, KNM-WT 15000, appears to have had a more rapid rate of dental development than that of his postcranial skeleton when compared with humans (Antòn & Leigh, 2003; Smith, 1993). There are no comprehensive data on rates of child development for hominins between 1.6 mya and 60 k, but the single Neandertal specimen examined by Dean and colleagues (2001) was modern in its developmental trajectory, indicating a humanlike extended childhood had occurred by this time. A modern human pattern of dental development was present by 800 k (Bermudez de Castro et al., 1999, 2003), but this may or may not imply a similar rate (Dean et al., 2001). Relatively large brains in some Neandertals compared to their dental development stages (Dean, Stringer, & Bromage, 1986) may reflect the overall larger brains of at least some individuals, rather than significant maturational differences. If it does, it might be reasonable to hypothesize that the human adolescent growth spurt was already in place by this time as well (Bermudez de Castro et al., 2003). Neandertals and modern humans probably shared similar stages of development, including an adolescent growth spurt, that would have been present in their mutual ancestry, perhaps by 500 kya (Krovitz, 2003). Longevity appears to have gradually increased from *Australopithecus* to modern humans with a higher proportion of individuals living to old age in the last 50 k (Caspari & Lee, 2004). If ecological dominance reduced mortality from extrinsic causes, this would allow for selection for delayed reproduction and extended life histories (Chisholm, 1999; Stearns, 1992; Williams, 1957).

Taking all the data together, it appears that the evolution of altriciality may have begun after the initial brain expansion but that delayed maturation and an adolescent growth spurt may have evolved later in human evolution, perhaps as brain size increase continued throughout the Pleistocene.

Thus, it appears that modern human social structures, and likely human family structures, developed gradually during the early to mid-Pleistocene. Integrated adaptations included more altricial infants, delayed maturation, increasingly stable mating relationships between males and females, increasing paternal and alloparental care of offspring, and more significant nonkin coalitionary behaviors. All of these changes roughly cooccurred with brain size expansion, which began increasing with early Homo and continued through the mid-Pleistocene where it reached modern human levels (Lee & Wolpoff, 2003). Evidence for coevolution among all of these variables broadly supports a model in which increasing social

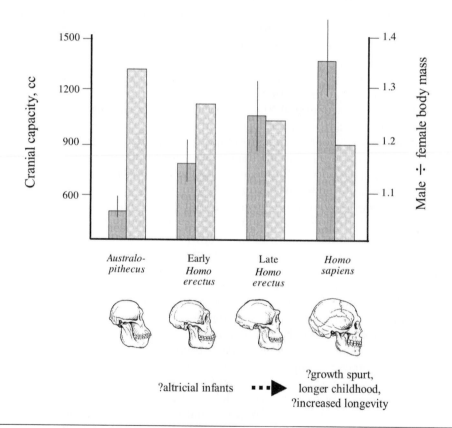

Figure 19.1 Bar Graphs Depicting Mean Cranial Capacity (dark gray with sample ranges). Data from "The Pattern of Evolution in Pleistocene Human Brain Size," by S. H. Lee and M. H. Wolpoff, 2003. *Paleobiology 29*, pp. 186–196. Also includes estimated body size sexual dimorphism for each group of hominins. Data from "Body Size and Proportions in Early Hominids," by H. M. McHenry 1992a, *American Journal of Physical Anthropology, 87*, pp. 407–431. Time of first appearance for evidence of changes in maturation and development rates indicated below. Crania illustrations modified from *Primate Evolution and Adaptations*, by J. G. Fleagle, 1999, New York: Academic Press.

complexity favored sociocognitive competencies, necessitating a longer childhood and more parental care of children (Figure 19.1).

In the following sections, we examine the hormonal mechanisms that may be involved with the ontogeny and regulation of this unique combination of life history, reproductive, and social traits suggested by the fossil and comparative primate evidence.

HORMONAL AND NEUROTRANSMITTER MECHANISMS

The constellation of behaviors associated with the human family and the dynamics of social competition described in previous sections require complex regulatory systems. In this section, we first briefly review the potential mechanisms for human pair bonding, maternal and paternal attachment to offspring, kin attachment, and male coalitions. Much of the research on the basic mechanisms has been done with nonhuman models and is not easily applied directly to some aspects of human psychology. We then turn to a more detailed analysis of how the neuroendocrine stress response system functions to enable acquisition of social competencies during childhood in the context of the human family environment.

The chemical messenger systems that orchestrate the ontogeny and regulation of sexual differentiation, metabolism, neurogenesis, immune function, growth, and other complex somatic processes tend to be evolutionarily conservative among primates and more generally among mammals. Hence rodent and nonhuman primate models provide important comparative information about the functions of specific human neuroendocrine systems, for which we often have little direct empirical research. It is the particular balance of human mechanisms and abilities that is unique and reflects the history of selection for complex social interactions that shaped the human lineage.

THE CHEMISTRY OF AFFECTION

Some of the most precious of all our human feelings are stimulated by close social relationships: a mother holding her newborn infant for the first time, brothers reunited after a long absence, or lovers entangled in each other's arms. Natural selection has designed our neurobiological mechanisms, in concert with our endocrine systems, to generate potent sensations in our interactions with these most evolutionarily significant individuals. We share with our primate relatives the same basic hormones and neurotransmitters that underlie these mental gifts. But our unique evolutionary history has modified us to respond to different circumstances and situations; we are rewarded and punished for somewhat different stimuli than our phylogenetic cousins. Chimpanzees and humans delight in biting into a ripe, juicy mango. But the endocrine, neurological, and associated emotional responses of a human father to the birth of his child (e.g., Storey, Walsh, Quinton, & Wynne-Edwards, 2000) are likely to be quite different from the responses of a chimpanzee male. Happiness for a human (Buss, 2000) has many unique designs, such as romantic love (Fisher et al., 2002), that involve shared endogenous messengers from our phylogenetic heritage.

Attachments are central in the lives of the social mammals. Basic to survival and reproduction, these interdependent relationships are the fabric of the social networks that permit individuals to maintain cooperative relationships over time. Although attachments can provide security and relief from stress, close relationships also exert pressures on individuals to which they continuously respond. It should not be surprising, therefore, that the neuroendocrine mechanisms underlying attachment and stress are intimately related to one another. And although at the present time a good deal more is known about the stress response systems than the affiliative systems, some of the pieces of the puzzle are beginning to fall into place.

The mother-offspring relationship is at the core of mammalian life, and it appears that the biochemistry at play in the regulation of this intimate bond was also selected to serve in primary mechanisms regulating bonds between mates, paternal care, the family group, and even larger social networks (Fisher et al., 2002; Hrdy, 1999). Although a number of hormones and neurotransmitters are involved in attachment and other components of relationships, the two peptide hormones, oxytocin (OT) and arginine-vasopressin (AVP), appear to be primary (Carter, 2002; Curtis & Wang, 2003; Lim et al., 2004; Young & Insel, 2002), with dopamine, cortisol, and other hormones and neurotransmitters having mediating effects.

The hypothalamus is the major brain site where OT and AVP, closely related chains of nine amino acids, are produced. From there they are released into the central nervous system (CNS) as well as transported to the pituitary where they are stored until secreted into the bloodstream. OT and AVP act on a wide range of neurological systems, and their influence varies among mammalian species and stage of development. The neurological effects of OT and AVP appear to be key mechanisms (e.g., Bartels & Zeki, 2004) involved in the evolution of human family behaviors. The effects of OT and AVP in humans are likely to be especially context dependent, because of the variable and complex nature of family relationships.

PARENTAL CARE

Along with OT and AVP, prolactin, estrogen, and progesterone are involved in parental care among mammals (Insel & Young, 2001). The involvement of these hormones varies across species and between males and females. The effects of these hormones are influenced by experience and context. Among rats, for example, estrogen and progesterone appear to prime the brain during pregnancy for parental behavior. Estrogen has been found to activate the expression of genes that increase the receptor density for OT and prolactin, thus increasing their influence (Young & Insel, 2002).

OT is most well known for its role in regulating birth and lactation, but along with AVP, it has also been found to play a central role in maternal care and attachment (Carter, 2002; Fleming, O'Day, & Kraemer, 1999). Just prior to birth, an increase in OT occurs, which is seen as priming maternal care. An injection of OT to virgin rats has been found to induce maternal care, while an OT antagonist administered to pregnant rats interferes with the development of maternal care (Carter, 2002).

The new rat mother seems to require hormonal activation to stimulate maternal behavior. Once she has begun to care for her pups, however, hormones are not required for maternal behavior to continue. Olfactory and somatosensory stimulation from interactions between pups and mother are, however, required for the parental care to continue (Fleming et al., 1999). The stimulation from suckling raises OT levels in rodents and breastfeeding women, which then results in not only milk letdown but also a decrease in limbic hypothalamic-anterior pituitary-adrenal cortex system (HPA) activity and a shift in the autonomic nervous system (ANS) from a sympathetic tone to a parasympathetic tone (Uvnas-Moberg, 1998). This results in a calmness seen as conducive to remaining in contact with the infant. It also results in a shift from external-directed energy toward the internal activity of nutrient storage and growth (Uvnas-Moberg, 1998).

Experience also influences parental behavior and the hormonal activity associated with it. In animal studies, a significant body of evidence demonstrates that early life experience influences later parental behavior (Champagne & Meaney, 2001; Fairbanks, 1989). And a number of studies demonstrate that this experience influences the neurohormonal biology involved in the expression of maternal care (Champagne & Meaney, 2001; Fleming et al., 1999). The HPA system of offspring during development is influenced by variation in maternal care, which then influences their maternal behavior as adults. Such changes involve the production of, and receptor density for, stress hormones and OT.

HPA-modulated hormones and maternal behavior are related in humans during the postpartum period (Fleming, Steiner, & Corter, 1997). During this time, cortisol appears to have an arousal effect, focusing attention on infant bonding. Mothers with higher cortisol levels were found to be more affectionate, more attracted to their infant's odor, and better at recognizing their infant's cry during the postpartum period.

FMRI studies of brain activity involved in maternal attachment in humans indicate that the activated regions are part of the reward system and contain a high density of receptors for OT and AVP (Bartels & Zeki, 2004; Fisher, 2004). These studies also demonstrate that the neural regions involved in attachment activated in humans are similar to those activated in nonhuman animals. Among humans, however, neural regions associated with social judgment and assessment of the intentions and emotions of others exhibited some deactivation during attachment activities, suggesting possible links between psychological mechanisms for attachment and management of social relationships. Falling in love with a mate and offspring may involve temporary deactivation of psychological mechanisms for maintaining an individual's social "guard" in the complex reciprocity of human social networks. Dopamine levels are likely to be important for both types of relationship but may involve some distinct neural sites. It will be interesting to see what fMRI studies of attachment in human males indicate because that is where the most substantial differences from other mammals would be expected. Similarly, fMRI studies of attachment to mothers, fathers, and alloparental caretakers in human children may provide important insights into the other side of parent-offspring bonding.

Paternal Care Paternal care is not common among mammals. For evolutionary reasons noted earlier, it is found among some rodent and primate species, including humans. The extent and types of paternal care vary among species. The hormonal influence in parental care among males appears to differ somewhat from that found among females. Vasopressin appears to function as the male counterpart to OT (Young & Insel, 2002). Along with prolactin and OT, vasopressin prepares the male to be receptive to and care for infants (Bales, Kim, Lewis-Reese, & Carter, 2004).

Paternal care is more common in monogamous than polygamous mammals and is often related to hormonal and behavioral stimuli from the female. In the monogamous California mouse, disruption of the pair bond does not affect maternal care but does diminish paternal care (Gubernick, 1996). In other species with biparental care, however, paternal care is not as dependent on the presence of the female (Young & Insel, 2002). Experience also plays a role in influencing hormonal activation and paternal behavior. Among tamarins, experienced fathers have higher levels of prolactin than first-time fathers (Ziegler & Snowdon, 1997).

Pair Bonding   Like male parental care, bonding between mates is also uncommon among mammals but has been selected for when it has reproductive advantages for both parents (Carter, 2002; Clutton-Brock, 1991; Young, Wang, & Insel, 2002). Monogamy is found across many mammalian taxa, but most of the current knowledge related to the neuroendocrine basis of this phenomenon has been obtained from the comparative study of two closely related rodent species. The prairie vole (*Microtus ochrogaster*) mating pair nest together and provide prolonged biparental care, while their close relatives, the meadow vole (*Microtus pennsylvanicus*), do not exhibit these behaviors (Young et al., 2002). As with other social behaviors in rodents, OT and AVP have been found to be central in the differences these related species exhibit with respect to pair bonding.

Pair bonding occurs for the prairie vole following mating. Vagino-cervical stimulation results in a release of OT and the development of a partner preference for the female (Carter, 2002; Young et al., 2002). For the male, it is an increase in AVP following mating and not just OT that results in partner preference. Exogenous OT injected in the female and exogenous AVP in the male prairie vole result in mate preference even without mating. This does not occur with meadow voles (Young et al., 2002).

The receptor density for OT and AVP in specific brain regions might provide the basis for mechanisms underlying other social behaviors. Other neurotransmitters, hormones, and social cues also are likely to be involved, but slight changes in gene expression for receptor density, such as those found between the meadow and prairie voles in the ventral palladium (located near the nucleus accumbens, an important component of the brain's reward system), might demonstrate how such mechanisms could be modified by selection (Lim et al., 2004). The dopamine D2 receptors in the nucleus accumbens appear to link the affiliative OT and AVP pair-bonding mechanisms with positive rewarding mental states (Aragona, Liu, Curtis, Stephan, & Wang, 2003; Wang et al., 1999). The combination results in the powerful addiction that parents have for their offspring.

Given the adaptive value of extensive biparental care and prolonged attachment found in the mating pair and larger family network, it is not surprising that similar neurohormonal mechanisms active in the maternal-offspring bond would also be selected to underlie these other attachments. Though there is some variation among species and between males and females, the same general neurohormonal systems active in pair bonding in other species are found in the human (Wynne-Edwards, 2003). The challenge before evolutionary psychologists is to understand how the general systems have been modified and linked with other special human cognitive systems (e.g., Allman, Hakeem, Erwin, Nimchinsky, & Hof, 2001; Blakemore, Winston, & Frith, 2004) to produce the unique suite of human family behaviors.

THE CHEMISTRY OF STRESS, FAMILY,
AND THE SOCIAL MIND

The evolutionary scenario proposed in previous sections posits that the family is of paramount importance in a child's world. Throughout human evolutionary history, parents and close relatives provided calories, protection, and information necessary for survival, growth, health, social success, and eventual reproduction. The human mind, therefore, is likely to have evolved special sensitivity to interactions with family caretakers, particularly during infancy and early childhood (Baumeister & Leary, 1995; Belsky, 1997, 1999; Bowlby, 1969; Daly & Wilson, 1995; Geary & Flinn, 2001).

The family and other kin provide important cognitive "landmarks" for the development of a child's understanding of the social environment. The reproductive interests of a child overlap with those of its parents more than with any other individuals. Information (including advice, training, and incidental observation) provided by parents is important for situating oneself in the social milieu and developing a mental model of its operations. A child's family environment may be an especially important source and mediator of stress, with consequent effects on health.

Psychosocial stressors are associated with increased risk of infectious disease (Cohen, Doyle, Turner, Alper, & Skoner, 2003) and a variety of other illnesses (Ader, Felten, & Cohen, 2001). Physiological stress responses regulate the allocation of energetic and other somatic resources to different bodily functions via a complex assortment of neuroendocrine mechanisms. Changing, unpredictable environments require adjustment of priorities. Digestion, growth, immunity, and sex are irrelevant while being chased by a predator (Sapolsky, 1994). Stress hormones help shunt blood, glucose, and so on to tissues necessary for the task at hand. Chronic and traumatic stress can diminish health, evidently because resources are diverted away from important health functions. Such diversions may have special significance during childhood because of the additional demands of physical and mental growth and development and possible long-term ontogenetic consequences.

STRESS RESPONSE MECHANISMS AND THEORY

Physiological response to environmental stimuli perceived as stressful is modulated by the limbic system (amygdala and hippocampus) and basal ganglia. These components of the CNS interact with the sympathetic and parasympathetic nervous systems and two neuroendocrine axes, the sympathetic—adrenal medullary system (SAM) and the HPA. The SAM and HPA systems affect a wide range of physiological functions in concert with other neuroendocrine mechanisms and involve complex feedback regulation. The SAM system controls the catecholamines norepinephrine and epinephrine (adrenalin). The HPA system regulates glucocorticoids, primarily cortisol (for reviews, see McEwen, 1995; Sapolsky, Romero, & Munck, 2000; Weiner, 1992).

Cortisol is a key hormone produced in response to physical and psychosocial stressors (Mason, 1968; Selye, 1976). It is produced and stored in the adrenal cortex. Release into the plasma is primarily under the control of pituitary adrenocorticotropic hormone (ACTH). The free or unbound portion of the circulating cortisol may pass through the cell membrane and bind to a specific cytosolic glucocorticoid receptor. This complex may induce genes coding for at least 26 different enzymes involved with carbohydrate, fat, and amino acid metabolism in brain, liver, muscle, and adipose tissue (Yuwiler, 1982).

Cortisol modulates a wide range of somatic functions, including: (1) energy release (e.g., stimulation of hepatic gluconeogenesis in concert with glucagon and inhibition of the effects of insulin), (2) immune activity (e.g., regulation of inflammatory response and the cytokine cascade), (3) mental activity (e.g., alertness, memory, and learning), (4) growth (e.g., inhibition of growth hormone and somatomedins), and (5) reproductive function (e.g., inhibition of gonadal steroids, including testosterone). These complex multiple effects of cortisol muddle understanding of its adaptive functions. The demands of energy regulation must orchestrate with those of immune function, attachment bonding, and so forth. Mechanisms for localized targeting (e.g., glucose uptake by active *versus* inactive muscle tissues and neuropeptide-directed immune response) provide fine-tuning of the preceding general physiological effects. Cortisol regulation allows the body to respond to changing environmental conditions by preparing for *specific* short-term demands (Mason, 1971; Munck, Guyre, & Holbrook, 1984; Weiner, 1992).

These temporary beneficial effects of glucocorticoid stress response, however, are not without costs. Persistent activation of the HPA system is associated with immune deficiency, cognitive impairment, inhibited growth, delayed sexual maturity, damage to the hippocampus, and psychological maladjustment (Ader, Felten, & Cohen, 2001; Dunn, 1995; Glaser & Kiecolt-Glaser, 1994). Chronic stress may diminish metabolic energy (Ivanovici & Wiebe, 1981; Sapolsky, 1991, 1992b) and produce complications from autoimmune protection (Munck & Guyre, 1991). Stressful life events—such as divorce, death of a family member, change of residence, or loss of a job—are associated with infectious disease and other health problems (Herbert & Cohen, 1993; Maier, Watkins, & Fleschner, 1994).

Current psychosocial stress research suggests that cortisol response is stimulated by uncertainty that is perceived as significant and for which behavioral responses will have unknown effects (Kirschbaum & Hellhammer, 1994; Weiner, 1992). That is, important events are going to happen; the child does not know how to react but is highly motivated to figure out what should be done. Cortisol release is associated with unpredictable, uncontrollable events that require full alert readiness and mental anticipation. In appropriate circumstances, temporary moderate increases in stress hormones (and associated neuropeptides) may enhance mental activity for short periods in localized areas, potentially improving cognitive processes for responding to social challenges (Beylin & Shors, 2003; cf. Breier et al., 1987). Other mental processes may be inhibited, perhaps to reduce external and internal "noise" (Servan-Schreiber, Printz, & Cohen, 1990; cf. Kirschbaum, Wolf, May, Wippich, & Hellhammer, 1996; Newcomer, Craft, Hershey, Askins, & Bardgett, 1994).

Relations between cortisol production and emotional distress, however, are difficult to assess because of temporal and interindividual variation in HPA response (Kagan, 1992; Nachmias, Gunnar, Mangelsdorf, Parritz, & Buss, 1996). Habituation may occur to repeated events for which a child acquires an effective mental model. Attenuation and below-normal levels of cortisol may follow a day or more after emotionally charged events. Chronically stressed children may develop abnormal cortisol response, possibly via changes in binding globulin levels and/or reduced affinity or density of glucocorticoid or corticotropin releasing hormone (CRH)/vasopressin receptors in the brain (Fuchs & Flugge, 1995). Early experience—such as perinatal stimulation of rats (Meaney et al., 1991), prenatal stress of rhesus macaques (Clarke, 1993; Schneider, Coe, & Lubach, 1992), and sexual abuse among humans (de Bellis et al., 1994; Heim et al., 2000)—may permanently alter HPA response. And personality may affect HPA response (and vice versa) because children with inhibited temperaments tend to have higher cortisol levels than extroverted children (Kagan, Resnick, & Snidman, 1988; cf. Gunnar, Porter, Wolf, Rigatuso, & Larson, 1995; Hertsgaard, Gunnar, Erickson, & Nachmias, 1995; Nachmias et al., 1996).

Further complications arise from interaction between HPA stress response and a wide variety of other neuroendocrine activities, including modulation of catecholamines, melatonin, testosterone, serotonin, ß-endorphins, cytokines, and enkephalins (de Kloet, 1991; Saphier et al., 1994; Sapolsky, 1992a). Changes in cortisol for energy allocation and modulation of immune function may be confused with effects of psychosocial stress. As reviewed in the previous section, OT and vasopressin intracerebral binding sites are associated with familial attachment in mammals and may influence distress involving caretaker-child relationships. Other components of the HPA axis such as CRH and melanocyte stimulating hormone have effects that are distinct from cortisol.

STRESS RESPONSE AND FAMILY ENVIRONMENT

Composition of the family or caretaking household may have important effects on child development (Kagan, 1984; Whiting & Edwards, 1988). For example, in Western cultures, children with divorced parents may experience more emotional tension or "stress" than children living in a stable two-parent family (Gottman & Katz, 1989; Pearlin & Turner, 1987; Wallerstein, 1983).

Investigation of physiological stress responses in the human family environment has been hampered by the lack of noninvasive techniques for measurement of stress hormones. Frequent collection of plasma samples to assess temporal changes in endocrine function is not feasible in nonclinical settings. The development of saliva immunoassay techniques, however, presents new opportunities for stress research. Saliva is relatively easy to collect and store, especially under adverse field conditions faced by anthropologists (Ellison, 1988). In this section we review results from a longitudinal, 17-year study of child stress and health in a rural community on the island of Dominica (for reviews see Flinn, 1999, 2005; Flinn & England, 1995, 1997, 2003). The research design uses concomitant monitoring of a child's daily activities, stress hormones, and psychological conditions to investigate the effects of naturally occurring psychosocial events in the family environment (Figure 19.2).

Associations between average cortisol levels of children and household composition are presented in Figure 19.3 on page 567. Children living with nonrelatives, stepfathers and half-siblings (stepfather has children by the stepchild's mother), or single parents without kin support had higher average levels of cortisol than children living with both parents, single mothers with kin support, or grandparents. A further test of this hypothesis is provided by comparison of step- and genetic children residing in the same households (Figure 19.4 on p. 567).

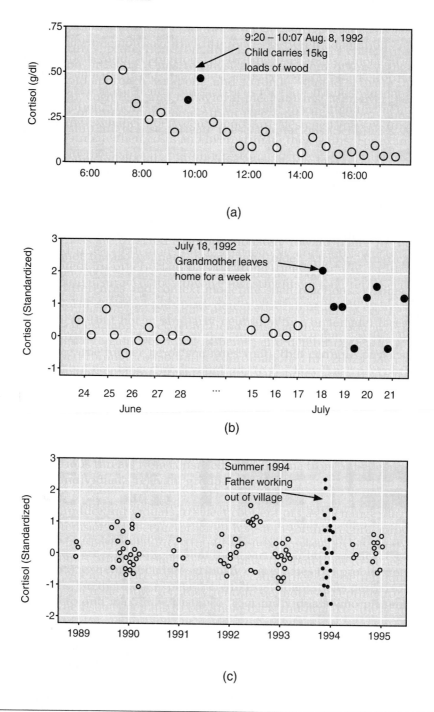

Figure 19.2 Longitudinal Monitoring of Cortisol Levels as a Tool for Investigating Stress Response among Children in a Caribbean Village. (A) Hourly sampling of a 12 year-old male demonstrating elevation of cortisol levels associated with carrying heavy loads of wood; (B) Twice-daily sampling of a 13 year-old girl demonstrating change in pattern of cortisol levels associated with temporary absence of caretaking grandmother; (C) Twice-daily sampling over a seven-year period of a male born in 1985 demonstrating the change in pattern of cortisol levels associated with the absence of his father.

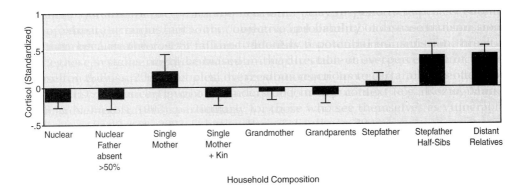

Figure 19.3 Household Composition and Cortisol. Vertical bars represent 95% confidence intervals (1.96 SE). Sample sizes (*N* of children, *N* of cortisol saliva assays) are 89, 6905; 28, 2234; 30, 2296; 31, 2581; 32, 2645; 16, 1341; 5, 279; 24, 1870; 9, 482. Adapted from "Childhood Stress: Endocrine and Immune Responses to Psychosocial Events" (pp. 107–147), by M. V. Flinn and B. G. England, in J. M. Wilce (Ed.), *Social and Cultural Lives of Immune Systems*, 2003, London: Routledge Press.

Stepchildren had higher average cortisol levels than their half-siblings residing in the same household who were genetic offspring of both parents.

Several caveats need emphasis. First, not all children in difficult family environments have elevated cortisol levels. Second, household composition is not a uniform indicator of family environment. Some single-mother households, for example, appear more stable, affectionate, and supportive than some two-parent households. Third, children appear differentially sensitive to different aspects of their caretaking environments, reflecting temperamental and other individual differences.

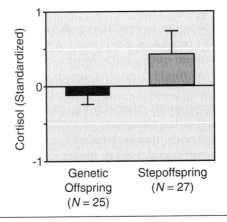

Figure 19.4 Average (Mean) Cortisol Levels of Step and Genetic Children Residing in the Same Household. In 38 of 43 dyads, stepchildren had higher mean cortisol levels than their co-resident half-siblings who are genetic offspring of both resident parents. Average age of stepchildren is 11.3 years, genetic children 8.4 years. Ninety-five percent confidence intervals are shown by vertical lines. Adapted from "Social Economics of Childhood Glucocorticoid Stress Response and Health," by M. V. Flinn and B. G. England, 1997, *American Journal of Physical Anthropology, 102*(1), pp. 33–53.

These caveats, however, do not invalidate the general association between household composition and childhood stress. There are several possible reasons underlying this result. Children in difficult caretaking environments may experience chronic stress resulting in moderate-high levels of cortisol (i.e., a child has cortisol levels that are above average day after day). They may experience more acute stressors that substantially raise cortisol for short periods of time. They may experience more frequent stressful events (e.g., parental chastisement or marital quarreling—see Finkelhor & Dzuiba-Leatherman, 1994; Flinn, 1988; Wilson, Daly, & Weghorst, 1980) that temporarily raise cortisol. There may be a lack of reconciliation between parent and child. And they may have inadequate coping abilities, perhaps resulting from difficult experiences in early development. The following case examples present temporal analyses of family relations and cortisol levels that illustrate some of these possibilities.

Case 1: Acute Stress Response

"Jenny" was a 12-year-old girl who lived with her grandparents, aunt, and uncle. Her mother had lived in Guadeloupe for the past 10 years. At 9:17 A.M. on July 17, 1994, MVF observed the following events: "Wayonne," a 6-year-old male cousin who was visiting for the week, threw a stone at Jenny, who was sweeping in front of the house. She responded by scolding Wayonne, who pouted and retreated behind a mango tree. Wayonne found a mango pit and lobbed it toward Jenny but missed and hit a dress hanging on a clothesline, marking it with a streak of red dirt. Jenny ran to Wayonne and struck him on the legs with her broom. He began

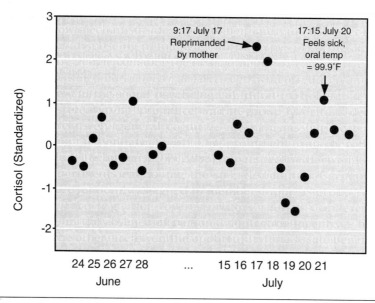

Figure 19.5 Morning and Afternoon Cortisol Levels of "Jenny" during Summer 1994. Late June cortisol levels are normal, but after being reprimanded by her grandmother on the morning of July 17, she has elevated cortisol levels for one day, followed by depressed cortisol levels for two days. Jenny exhibits symptoms of an upper respiratory infection with slight fever (common cold, probably rhinovirus) on the afternoon of July 20. Adapted from "Family Environment, Stress, and Health during Childhood" (pp. 105–138), by M. V. Flinn, in *Hormones, Health, and Behavior*, C. Panter-Brick and C. Worthman (Eds.), 1999, Cambridge: Cambridge University Press.

to cry, arousing the interest of "granny Ninee," who emerged from the cooking room asking what happened. Upon hearing the story, granny Ninee scolded Jenny for "beating" Wayonne. Jenny argued that she was in the right, but granny Ninee would not hear of it and sent her into the house. Jenny appeared frustrated but looked down and kept quiet despite a quivering lip.

Jenny's cortisol levels were substantially elevated that afternoon, followed by subnormal levels the next day (a possible recovery period?). Three days after the incident, she reported feeling ill and had a runny nose and oral temperature of 99.9°F (Figure 19.5).

Case 2:

On June 28, 1992, a serious marital conflict erupted in the "Franklin" household. "Amanda" was a 34-year-old mother of six children, five of whom (ages 2, 3, 5, 8, and 14) were living with her and their father/stepfather, "Pierre Franklin." Amanda was angry with Pierre for spending money on rum. Pierre was vexed with Amanda for "shaming" him in front of his friends. He left the village for several weeks, staying with a relative in town. His three genetic children (ages 2, 3, and 5) showed abnormal cortisol levels (in this case, elevated) for a prolonged period following their father's departure (Figure 19.6). This pattern is typical: children usually became habituated to stressful events, but absence of a parent

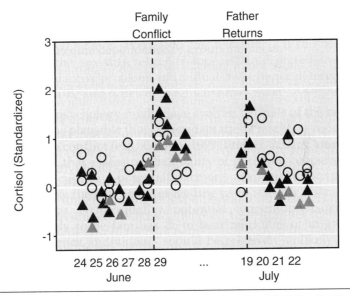

Figure 19.6 Marital Conflict and Cortisol Levels in the "Franklin" Family. Three genetic children (2-, 3-, and 5-year-old males) are represented by triangles and two stepchildren (8- and 14-year-old females) are represented by dots respectively. Cortisol levels of three genetic children are normal before the conflict, rise during the conflict and during father's absence, briefly rise upon his return, and return to normal (lower) levels. The younger of the two stepchildren has a pattern of abnormally high cortisol, although her levels are moderate during stepfather's absence. The older stepdaughter has a similar, but more normal pattern of cortisol levels. Adapted from "Social Economics of Childhood Glucocorticoid Stress Response and Health," by M. V. Flinn and B. G. England, 1997, *American Journal of Physical Anthropology, 102*(1), pp. 33–53.

often resulted in abnormal patterns of elevated and/or subnormal cortisol levels. Following the return of their father, the Franklin children's cortisol levels resumed a more normal profile. Again, this pattern is typical: children living in families with high levels of marital conflict (observed and reported serious quarreling, fighting, residence absence) were more likely to have abnormal cortisol profiles than children living in more amiable families were.

The events in children's lives that are associated with elevated cortisol are not always traumatic or even "negative." Eating meals; hard physical work; routine competitive play such as cricket, basketball, and "king of the mountain" on ocean rocks; and return of a family member that was temporarily absent (e.g., father returning from a job in town for the weekend) were associated with temporary moderate increases (about 10% to 100%) in cortisol among healthy children. These moderate stressors usually had rapid attenuation (< one hour) of cortisol levels (some stressors had characteristic temporal "signatures" of cortisol level and duration).

High-stress events (cortisol increases from 100% to 2000%), however, most commonly involved trauma from family conflict or change (Flinn & England, 2003; Flinn, Quinlan, Turner, Decker, & England, 1996). Punishment, quarreling, and residence change substantially increased cortisol levels, whereas calm, affectionate contact was associated with diminished (−10% to −50%) cortisol levels. Of all cortisol values that were more than two standard deviations above mean levels (i.e., indicative of substantial stress), 19.2% were temporally associated with traumatic family events (residence change of child or parent/caretaker, punishment, "shame," serious quarreling, and/or fighting) within a 24-hour period. In addition, 42.1% of traumatic family events were temporally associated with substantially elevated cortisol (i.e., at least one of the saliva samples collected within 24 hours was > 2 SD above mean levels). Chronic elevations of cortisol levels, as in the example of the Franklin family (case #2), may also occur, but are more difficult to assess quantitatively.

There was considerable variability among children in cortisol response to family disturbances. Not all individuals had detectable changes in cortisol levels associated with family trauma. Some children had significantly elevated cortisol levels during some episodes of family trauma but not during others. Cortisol response is not a simple or uniform phenomenon. Numerous factors, including preceding events, habituation, specific individual histories, context, and temperament, might affect how children respond to particular situations.

Nonetheless, traumatic family events were associated with elevated cortisol levels for all ages of children more than any other factor that we examined. These results suggest that family interactions were a critical psychosocial stressor in most children's lives, although the sample collection during periods of intense family interaction (early morning and late afternoon) may have exaggerated this association.

Although elevated cortisol levels are associated with traumatic events such as family conflict, long-term stress may result in diminished cortisol response. In some cases, chronically stressed children had blunted response to physical activities that normally evoked cortisol elevation. Comparison of cortisol levels during "nonstressful" periods (no reported or observed crying, punishment, anxiety, residence change, family conflict, or health problem during 24-hour period before saliva collection) indicates a striking reduction and, in many cases, reversal of the family environment-stress association (Flinn & England, 2003). Chronically stressed children sometimes had subnormal cortisol levels when they were not in stressful situations. For example, cortisol levels immediately after school (walking home from school) and during noncompetitive play were lower among some chronically stressed children (cf. Long, Ungpakorn, & Harrison, 1993). Some chronically stressed children appeared socially "tough" or withdrawn and exhibited little or no arousal to the novelty of the first few days of the saliva collection procedure.

Glucocorticoid stress response may be viewed as an adaptive mechanism that allocates energy resources to different bodily functions, including immunity, growth, muscle action, and cognition (Maier et al., 1994; McEwen, 1995; Sapolsky, 1994). Understanding the algorithms for stress response allocation decisions is important because of consequences for health and psychological development (Tinbergen, 1974). Release of cortisol and other stress hormones in response to traumatic family events may modulate energy and mental activity to resolve perceived psychosocial problems but may diminish immunity and other health functions.

Relations between family environment and cortisol stress response appear to result from a combination of factors including frequency of traumatic events, frequency of positive "affectionate" interactions, frequency of negative interactions such as irrational punishment, frequency of residence change, security of "attachment," development of coping abilities, and availability or intensity of caretaking attention. Probably the most important correlate of household composition that affects childhood stress is maternal care. Mothers in socially "secure" households (i.e., permanent amiable coresidence with mate and/or other kin) appeared more able and more motivated to provide physical, social, and psychological care for their children. Mothers without mate or kin support were likely to exert effort attracting potential mates and may have viewed dependent children as impediments to this. Hence coresidence of father may provide not only direct benefits from paternal care but also may affect maternal care (Belsky, Steinberg, & Draper, 1991; Flinn, 1992; Hurtado & Hill, 1992; Lamb, Pleck, Charnov, & Levine, 1987; Scheper-Hughes, 1988). Young mothers without mate support usually relied extensively on their parents or other kin for help with child care.

Children born and raised in household environments in which mothers have little or no mate or kin support were at greatest risk for abnormal cortisol profiles and associated health problems. Because socioeconomic conditions influence family environment, they have consequences for child health that extend beyond direct material effects. And because health in turn may affect an individual's social and economic opportunities, a cycle of poor health and poverty may be perpetuated generation after generation.

CONCLUSIONS

People in difficult social environments tend to be less healthy in comparison with their more fortunate peers (e.g., Cohen et al., 2003; Dressler & Bindon, 2000; Flinn, 1999; Wilkinson, 2001). Social support has reproductive consequences (e.g., Silk, Alberts, & Altmann, 2003). If the brain evolved as a social tool, then the expenditure of somatic resources to resolve psychosocial problems makes sense. Relationships, especially family relationships, are of paramount importance. They have been a key factor affecting human reproductive success at least for over half a million years, and selection has shaped our hormonal, neural, and psychological mechanisms to respond to this critical selective pressure. Children elevate their stress hormone (cortisol) levels much more frequently and extensively in response to psychosocial stimuli than to challenges associated with the physical environment. The adaptive effects of the major stress hormones (Huether, 1996, 1998) and affiliative neurotransmitters on neural reorganization are consistent with the observation that children are especially sensitive to their social worlds (Flinn, 1999).

Social competence is extraordinarily difficult because the target is constantly changing and similarly equipped with theory of mind and other cognitive abilities. The sensitivity of the stress-response and affiliative systems to the social environment may enable adaptive neural reorganization to this most salient and dynamic puzzle. Childhood is necessary and useful for acquiring the information and practice to build and refine the mental algorithms critical for negotiating the social coalitions that are key to success in our species. The human family provides critical support for the developing child in this regard. Traumatic early environments may result in diminished abilities to acquire social competencies as a consequence of glucocorticoid hypersensitivity disrupting neurogenesis, particularly in the hippocampus (Mirescu, Peters, & Gould, 2004; Weaver et al., 2004). An improved understanding of the hormonal and neurological mechanisms that facilitate the intensive and extensive relationships involved with human families and broader kin coalitions, including comparisons between humans and our close primate relatives, may provide important insights into the selective pressures that shaped human psychology.

REFERENCES

Ader, R., Felten, D. L., & Cohen, N. (Eds.). (2001). *Psychoneuroimmunology* (3rd ed.). New York: Academic Press.

Alexander, R. D. (1974). The evolution of social behavior. *Annual Review of Ecology and Systematics, 5*, 325–383.

Alexander, R. D. (1987). *The biology of moral systems.* Hawthorne, NY: Aldine de Gruyter.

Alexander, R. D. (1990a). Epigenetic rules and Darwinian algorithms: The adaptive study of learning and development. *Ethology and Sociobiology, 11*(3), 1–63.

Alexander, R. D. (1990b). *How did humans evolve? Reflections on the uniquely unique species.* Museum of Zoology [Special Publication No. 1]. Ann Arbor: The University of Michigan.

Alexander, R. D., Hoogland, J. L., Howard, R. D., Noonan, K. M., & Sherman, P. W. (1979). Sexual dimorphisms and breeding systems in pinnipeds, ungulates, primates, and humans. In N. A. Chagnon & W. Irons (Eds.), *Evolutionary biology and human social behavior: An anthropological perspective* (pp. 402–435). North Scituate, MA: Duxbury Press.

Alexander, R. D., & Noonan, K. M. (1979). Concealment of ovulation, parental care, and human social evolution. In N. A. Chagnon & W. Irons (Eds.), *Evolutionary biology and human social behavior: An anthropological perspective* (pp. 436–453). North Scituate, MA: Duxbury Press.

Allman, J., & Hasenstaub, A. (1999). Brains, maturation times and parenting. *Neurobiology of Aging, 20*(6), 447–454.

Allman, J., Hakeem, A., Erwin, J. M., Nimchinsky, E., & Hof, P. (2001). The anterior cingulate cortex: The evolution of an interface between emotion and cognition. *Annals of the New York Academy of Sciences, 935*, 107–117.

Allman, J., Rosin, A., Kumar, R., & Hasenstaub, A. (1998). Parenting and survival in anthropoid primates: Caretakers live longer. *Proceedings of the National Academy of Sciences, USA, 95*, 6866–6869.

Antòn, S. C., & Leigh, S. R. (2003). Growth and life history in *Homo erectus*. In J. L. Thompson, G. E. Krovitz, & A. J. Nelson (Eds.), *Patterns of growth and development in the genus* Homo (pp. 219–245). Cambridge, UK: Cambridge University Press.

Aragona, B. J., Liu, Y., Curtis, J. T., Stephan, F. K., & Wang, Z. (2003). A Critical Role for Nucleus Accumbens Dopamine in Partner-Preference Formation in Male Prairie Voles. *Journal of Neuroscience, 23*(8), 3483–3490.

Bales, K. L., Kim, A. J., Lewis-Reese, A. D., & Carter, C. S. (2004). Both oxytocin and vasopressin may influence alloparental behavior in male prairie voles. *Hormones and Behavior 45*(5), 354–361.

Bartels, A., & Zeki, S. (2004). The neural correlates of maternal and romantic love. *NeuroImage, 21,* 1155–1166.

Baumeister, R. F., & Leary, M. R. (1995). The need to belong: Desire for interpersonal attachment as a fundamental human motive. *Psychological Bulletin, 117,* 497–529.

Begun, D. R., & Walker, A. (1993). The endocast. In A. Walker & R. Leakey (Eds.), *The Nariokotome* Homo erectus *skeleton* (pp. 326–358). Cambridge, MA: Harvard University Press.

Belsky, J. (1997). Attachment, mating, and parenting: An evolutionary interpretation. *Human Nature, 8,* 361–381.

Belsky, J. (1999). Modern evolutionary theory and patterns of attachment. In J. Cassidy & P. R. Shaver (Eds.), *Handbook of attachment: Theory, research, and clinical applications* (pp. 141–161). New York: Guilford Press.

Belsky, J., Steinberg, L., & Draper, P. (1991). Childhood experience, interpersonal development, and reproductive strategy: An evolutionary theory of socialization. *Child Development, 62*(4), 647–670.

Bercovitch, F. B., & Ziegler, T. E. (2002). Current topics in primate socioendocrinology. *Annual Reviews in Anthropology, 31,* 45–67.

Bermudez de Castro, J. M., Rosas, A., Carbonee, E., Nicolás, M. E., Rodríguez, J., & Arsuaga, J.-L. (1999). A modern human pattern of dental development in Lower Pleistocene hominids from Atapuerca-TD6 (Spain). *Proceedings of the National Academy of Sciences, 96,* 4210–4213.

Bermudez de Castro, J. M., Ramírez Rossi, F., Marinón-Torres, M., Sarmiento Pérez, S., & Rosas, A. (2003). Patterns of dental development in Lower and Middle Pleistocene hominins from Atapuerca (Spain). In J. L. Thompson, G. E. Krovitz, & A. J. Nelson (Eds.), *Patterns of growth and development in the genus* Homo (pp. 246–270). Cambridge, UK: Cambridge University Press.

Beylin, A. V., & Shors, T. J. (2003). Glucocorticoids are necessary for enhancing the acquisition of associative memories after acute stressful experience. *Hormones and Behavior, 43,* 124–131.

Biella, P., Chagnon, N. A., & Seaman, G. (1997). *Yanomamo interactive: The ax fight.* Fort Worth, TX: Harcourt Brace.

Bjorklund, D. F., & Pellegrini, A. D. (2002). *The origins of human nature: Evolutionary developmental psychology.* Washington, DC: American Psychological Association Press.

Blakemore, S.-J., Winston, J., & Frith, U. (2004). Social cognitive neuroscience: Where are we heading? *Trends in Cognitive Neurosciences, 8*(5), 216–222.

Bloom, P. (2000). *How children learn the meaning of words.* Cambridge, MA: MIT Press.

Bogin, B. (1991). The evolution of human childhood. *BioScience, 40,* 16–25.

Bogin, B. (1999). *Patterns of human growth* (2nd ed.). Cambridge, UK: Cambridge University Press.

Bornstein, M. H., & Arterberry, M. E. (2003). Recognition, discrimination and categorization of smiling by 5-month-old infants. *Developmental Science, 6*(5), 585–599.

Bowlby, J. (1969). *Attachment and loss: Vol. 1. Attachment.* London: Hogarth.

Breier, A., Albus, M., Pickar, D., Zahn, T. P., Wolkowitz, O. M., & Paul, S. M. (1987). Controllable and uncontrollable stress in humans: Alterations in mood and neuroendocrine and psychophysiological function. *American Journal of Psychiatry, 144,* 1419–1425.

Buchan, J. C., Alberts, S. C., Silk, J. B., & Altmann, J. (2003). True paternal care in a multi-male primate society. *Nature, 425,* 179–181.

Buss, D. M. (1994). *The evolution of desire: Strategies of human mating.* New York: Basic Books.

Buss, D. M. (2000). The evolution of happiness. *American Psychologist, 55,* 15–23.

Campbell, A. (2002). *A mind of her own: The evolutionary psychology of women.* London: Oxford University Press.

Carter, C. S. (2002). Neuroendocrine perspectives on social attachment and love. In J. T. Caciooppo, G. G. Berntson, R. Adolphs, C. S. Carter, R. J. Davidson, M. K. McClintock, et al. (Eds.), *Foundations in social neuroscience* (pp. 853–890). Cambridge, MA: MIT Press.

Caspari, R., & Lee, S.-H. (2004). Older age becomes common late in human evolution. *Proceedings of the National Academy of Sciences, USA, 101,* 10895–10900.

Chagnon, N. A. (1988). Life histories, blood revenge, and warfare in a tribal population. *Science, 239,* 985–992.

Champagne, F., & Meaney, M. J. (2001). Like mother, like daughter: Evidence for non-genomic transmission of parental behavior and stress responsivity. *Progress in Brain Research, 133,* 287–302.

Chisholm, J. S. (1999). *Death, hope and sex.* Cambridge, UK: Cambridge University Press.

Clarke, A. S. (1993). Social rearing effects on HPA axis activity over early development and in response to stress in rhesus monkeys. *Developmental Psychobiology, 26*(8), 433–446.

Clutton-Brock, T. H. (1977). Sexual dimorphism, socionomic sex ratio and body weight in primates. *Nature, 269,* 797–800.

Clutton-Brock, T. H. (1991). *The evolution of parental care.* Princeton, NJ: Princeton University Press.

Coe, K. (2003). *The ancestress hypothesis: Visual art as adaptation.* New Brunswick, NJ: Rutgers University Press.

Cohen, S., Doyle, W. J., Turner, R. B., Alper, C. M., & Skoner, D. P. (2003). Emotional style and susceptibility to the common cold. *Psychosomatic Medicine, 65*(4), 652–657.

Curtis, T. J., & Wang, Z. (2003). The neurochemistry of pair bonding. *Current Directions in Psychological Science, 12*(2), 49–53.

Daly, M., & Wilson, M. (1988). *Homicide.* Hawthorne, NY: Aldine de Gruyter.

Daly, M., & Wilson, M. (1995). Discriminative parental solicitude and the relevance of evolutionary models to the analysis of motivational systems. In M. S. Gazzaniga (Ed.), *The cognitive neurosciences* (pp. 1269–1286). Cambridge, MA: MIT Press.

Deacon, T. W. (1997). What makes the human brain different? *Annual Review of Anthropology, 26,* 337–357.

Dean, M. C., Leakey, M. G., Reid, D., Schrenk, F., Schwartz, G. T., Stringer, C., et al. (2001). Growth processes in teeth distinguish modern humans from *Homo erectus* and earlier hominins. *Nature, 414,* 628–631.

Dean, M. C., Stringer, C. B., & Bromage, T. G. (1986). Age at death of the Neanderthal child from Devil's Tower, Gibraltar, and the implications for studies of general growth and development in Neanderthals. *American Journal of Physical Anthropology, 70,* 301–310.

de Bellis, M., Chrousos, G. P., Dorn, L. D., Burke, L., Helmers, K., Kling, M. A., et al. (1994). Hypothalamic-pituitary-adrenal axis dysregulation in sexually abused girls. *Journal of Clinical Endocrinology and Metabolism, 78,* 249–255.

de Haan, M., Johnson, M. H., & Halit, H. (2003). Development of face-sensitive event-related potentials during infancy: A review. *International Journal of Psychophysiology, 51*(1), 45–58.

de Kloet, E. R. (1991). Brain corticosteroid receptor balance and homeostatic control. *Frontiers in Neuroendocrinology, 12*(2), 95–164.

de Waal, F. B. M., & Lanting, F. (1997). *Bonobo: The forgotten ape.* Berkeley: University of California Press.

Draper, P., & Harpending, H. (1988). A sociobiological perspective on the development of human reproductive strategies. In K. MacDonald (Ed.), *Sociobiological perspectives on human development* (pp. 340–372). New York: Springer-Verlag.

Dressler, W., & Bindon, J. R. (2000). The health consequences of cultural consonance: Cultural dimensions of lifestyle, social support, and arterial blood pressure in an African American community. *American Anthropologist, 102*(2), 244–260.

Dunbar, R. I. M. (1997). *Gossip, grooming, and evolution of language.* Cambridge, MA: Harvard University Press.

Dunbar, R. I. M. (1998). The social brain hypothesis. *Evolutionary Anthropology, 6,* 178–190.

Dunbar, R. I. M. (2004). *The human story.* London: Faber & Faber.

Dunn, A. J. (1995). Interactions between the nervous system and the immune system: Implications for psychopharmacology. In F. R. Bloom & D. J. Kupfer (Eds.), *Psychopharmacology: The fourth generation of progress.* New York: Raven Press.

Ellison, P. (1988). Human salivary steroids: Methodological considerations and applications in physical anthropology. *Yearbook of Physical Anthropology, 31,* 115–142.

Ellison, P. (2001). *On fertile ground: A natural history of human reproduction.* Cambridge, MA: Harvard University Press.

Fairbanks, L. A. (1989). Early experience and cross-generational continuity of mother-infant contact in vervet monkeys. *Developmental Psychobiology, 22*(7), 669–681.

Farroni, T., Mansfield, E. M., Lai, C., & Johnson, M. H. (2003). Infants perceiving and acting on the eyes: Tests of an evolutionary hypothesis. *Journal of Experimental Child Psychology, 85*(3), 199–212.

Finkelhor, D., & Dzuiba-Leatherman, J. (1994). Victimization of children. *American Psychologist, 49*(3), 173–183.

Fisher, H. (2004). *Why we love: The nature and chemistry of romantic love.* New York: Henry Holt.

Fisher, H., Aron, A., Mashek, D., Strong, G., Li, H., & Brown, L. L. (2002). Defining the brain systems of lust, romantic attraction and attachment. *Archives of Sexual Behavior, 31*(5), 413–419.

Fleagle, J. G. (1999). *Primate evolution and adaptations.* New York: Academic Press.

Fleming, A. S., O'Day, D. H., & Kraemer, G. W. (1999). Neurobiology of mother-infant interactions: Experience and central nervous system plasticity across development and generations. *Neuroscience and Biobehavioral Reviews, 23,* 673–685.

Fleming, A. S., Steiner, M., & Corter, C. (1997). Cortisol, hedonics, and maternal responsiveness in human mothers. *Hormones and Behavior, 32,* 85–98.

Flinn, M. V. (1981). Uterine and agnatic kinship variability. In R. D. Alexander & D. W. Tinkle (Eds.), *Natural selection and social behavior: Recent research and new theory* (pp. 439–475). New York: Blackwell Press.

Flinn, M. V. (1988). Mate guarding in a Caribbean village. *Ethology and Sociobiology 9*(1), 1–28.

Flinn, M. V. (1992). Paternal care in a Caribbean village. In B. Hewlett (Ed.), *Father-child relations: Cultural and biosocial contexts* (pp. 57–84). Hawthorne, NY: Aldine.

Flinn, M. V. (1999). Family environment, stress, and health during childhood. In C. Panter-Brick & C. Worthman (Eds.), *Hormones, health, and behavior* (pp. 105–138). Cambridge, UK: Cambridge University Press.

Flinn, M. V. (2004). Culture and developmental plasticity: Evolution of the social brain. In K. MacDonald & R. L. Burgess (Eds.), *Evolutionary perspectives on child development* (pp. 73–98). Thousand Oaks, CA: Sage.

Flinn, M. V. (2005). Alloparental care and the ontogeny of glucocorticoid stress response among stepchildren. In G. Bentley & R. Mace (Eds.), *Alloparental care in human societies.* Cambridge, UK: Cambridge University Press.

Flinn, M. V., & England, B. G. (1995). Childhood stress and family environment. *Current Anthropology, 36,* 854–866.

Flinn, M. V., & England, B. G. (1997). Social economics of childhood glucocorticoid stress response and health. *American Journal of Physical Anthropology, 102*(1), 33–53.

Flinn, M. V., & England, B. G. (2003). Childhood stress: Endocrine and immune responses to psychosocial events. In J. M. Wilce (Ed.), *Social and cultural lives of immune systems* (pp. 107–147). London: Routledge Press.

Flinn, M. V., Geary, D. C., & Ward, C. V. (2005). Ecological dominance, social competition, and coalitionary arms races: Why humans evolved extraordinary intelligence. *Evolution and Human Behavior, 26*(1).

Flinn, M. V., & Low, B. S. (1986). Resource distribution, social competition, and mating patterns in human societies. In D. Rubenstein & R. Wrangham (Eds.), *Ecological aspects of social evolution* (pp. 217–243). Princeton, NJ: Princeton University Press.

Flinn, M. V., Quinlan, R., Turner, M. T., Decker, S. D., & England, B. G. (1996). Male-female differences in effects of parental absence on glucocorticoid stress response. *Human Nature, 7*(2), 125–162.

Flinn, M. V., & Ward, C. V. (2004). Evolution of the social child. In B. Ellis & D. Bjorklund (Eds.), *Origins of the social mind: Evolutionary psychology and child development* (pp. 19–44). London: Guilford Press.

Foley, R. A. (1999). Hominid behavioral evolution: Missing links in comparative primate socioecology. In P. C. Lee (Ed.), *Comparative primate socioecology* (pp. 363–386). Cambridge, UK: Cambridge University Press.

Fuchs, E., & Flugge, G. (1995). Modulation of binding sites for corticotropin-releasing hormone by chronic psychosocial stress. *Psychoneuroendocrinology, 30*(1), 33–51.

Gangestad, S. W., Simpson, J. A., Cousins, A. J., Garver-Apgar, C. E., & Christensen, P. (2004). Women's preferences for male behavioral displays change across the menstrual cycle. *Psychological Science, 15*(3), 203–206.

Geary, D. C. (2005). *The origin of mind.* Washington, DC: American Psychological Association.

Geary, D. C., & Bjorklund, D. F. (2000). Evolutionary developmental psychology. *Child Development, 71*(1), 57–65.

Geary, D. C., & Flinn, M. V. (2001). Evolution of human parental behavior and the human family. *Parenting: Science and Practice, 1,* 5–61.

Geary, D. C., & Flinn, M. V. (2002). Sex differences in behavioral and hormonal response to social threat. *Psychological Review, 109*(4), 745–750.

Geary, D. C., & Huffman, K. J. (2002). Brain and cognitive evolution: Forms of modularity and functions of mind. *Psychological Bulletin, 128,* 667–698.

Glaser, R., & Kiecolt-Glaser, J. K. (Eds.). (1994). *Handbook of human stress and immunity.* New York: Academic Press.

Goodall, J. (1986). *The chimpanzees of Gombe.* Cambridge, MA: Harvard University Press.

Gottman, J. M., & Katz, L. F. (1989). Effects of marital discord on young children's peer interaction and health. *Developmental Psychology, 25*(3), 373–381.

Gubernick, D. (1996). A natural family system. *Family Systems, 3,* 109–124.

Gunnar, M., Porter, F. L., Wolf, C. M., Rigatuso, J., & Larson, M. C. (1995). Neonatal stress reactivity: Predictions to later emotional temperament. *Child Development, 66,* 1–13.

Hawkes, K. (2003). Grandmothers and the evolution of human longevity. *American Journal of Human Biology, 15*(3), 380–400.

Hawkes, K., O'Connell, J. F., Blurton Jones, N. G., Alvarez, H., & Charnov, E. I. (1998). Grandmothering, menopause, and the evolution of human life histories. *Proceedings of the National Academy of Sciences, USA, 95,* 1336–1339.

Heim, C., Newport, D. J., Heit, S., Graham, Y. P., Wilcox, M., Bonsall, R., et al. (2000). Pituitary-adrenal and autonomic responses to stress in women after sexual and physical abuse in childhood. *Journal of the American Medical Association, 284*(5), 592–597.

Herbert, T. B., & Cohen, S. (1993). Stress and immunity in humans: A meta-analytic review. *Psychosomatic Medicine, 55,* 364–379.

Hertsgaard, L., Gunnar, M., Erickson, M. F., & Nachmias, M. (1995). Adrenocortical responses to the strange situation in infants with disorganized/disoriented attachment relationships. *Child Development, 66,* 1100–1106.

Hill, K., & Hurtado, A. M. (1991). The evolution of reproductive senescence and menopause in human females. *Human Nature, 2*(4), 315–350.

Hill, K., & Hurtado, A. M. (1996). *Ache life history: The ecology and demography of a foraging people.* Hawthorne, NY: Aldine de Gruyter.

Hill, K., & Kaplan, H. (1999). Life history traits in humans: Theory and empirical studies. *Annual Reviews of Anthropology, 28,* 397–430.

Hrdy, S. B. (1999). *Mother nature: A history of mothers, infants, and natural selection.* New York: Pantheon.

Hrdy, S. B. (2004). Evolutionary context of human development: The cooperative breeding model. In C. S. Carter & L. Ahnert (Eds.), *Attachment and bonding: A New Synthesis* Dahlem Workshop, 92. Cambridge, MA: MIT Press.

Huether, G. (1996). The central adaptation syndrome: Psychosocial stress as a trigger for adaptive modifications of brain structure and brain function. *Progress in Neurobiology, 48,* 568–612.

Huether, G. (1998). Stress and the adaptive self organization of neuronal connectivity during early childhood. *International Journal of Developmental Neuroscience, 16*(3/4), 297–306.

Hurtado, A. M., & Hill, K. R. (1992). Paternal effect on offspring survivorship among Ache and Hiwi hunter-gatherers: Implications for modeling pair-bond stability. In B Hewlett (Ed.), *Father-child relations: Cultural and biosocial contexts* (pp. 31–55). Hawthorne, NY: Aldine de Gruyter.

Insel, T. R., & Young, L. R. (2001). The neurobiology of attachment. *Nature Reviews: Neuroscience, 2,* 129–136.

Ivanovici, A. M., & Wiebe, W. J. (1981). Towards a working "definition" of "stress": A review and critique. In G. W. Barrett & R. Rosenberg (Eds.), *Stress effects on natural ecosystems* (pp. 13–17). New York: Wiley.

Kagan, J. (1984). *The nature of the child.* New York: Basic Books.

Kagan, J. (1992). Behavior, biology, and the meanings of temperamental constructs. *Pediatrics, 90,* 510–513.

Kagan, J., Resnick, J. S., & Snidman, N. (1988). The biological basis of childhood shyness. *Science, 240,* 167–171.

Kano, T. (1992). *The last ape: Pygmy chimpanzee behavior and ecology.* Stanford: Stanford University Press.

Kirschbaum, C., & Hellhammer, D. H. (1994). Salivary cortisol in psychneuroendocrine research: Recent developments and applications. *Psychoneuroendocrinology, 19,* 313–333.

Kirschbaum, C., Wolf, O. T., May, M., Wippich, W., & Hellhammer, D. H. (1996). Stress- and treatment-induced elevations of cortisol levels associated with impaired declarative memory in healthy adults. *Life Sciences, 58*(17), 1475–1483.

Krovitz, G. E. (2003). Shape and growth differences between Neanderthals and modern humans: Grounds for a species-level distinction. In J. L. Thompson, G. E. Krovitz, & A. J. Nelson (Eds.), *Patterns of growth and development in the genus* Homo (pp. 320–342). Cambridge, UK: Cambridge University Press.

Lamb, M., Pleck, J., Charnov, E., & Levine, J. (1987). A biosocial perspective on paternal behavior and involvement. In J. B. Lancaster, J. Altmann, A. Rossi, & L. Sherrod (Eds.), *Parenting across the lifespan: Biosocial dimensions* (pp. 111–142). Hawthorne, NY: Aldine de Gruyter.

LeBlanc, S. A. (2003). *Constant battles: The myth of the peaceful, noble savage.* New York: St. Martin's Press.

Lee, S.-H., & Wolpoff, M. H. (2003). The pattern of evolution in Pleistocene human brain size. *Paleobiology, 29*, 186–196.

Leigh, S. R. (2004). Brain growth, cognition, and life history in primate and human evolution. *American Journal of Primatology, 62*, 139–164.

Lim, M. M., Wang, Z., Olazabal, D. E., Ren, X., Terwilliger, E. F., & Young, L. J. (2004). Enhanced partner preference in a promiscuous species by manipulating the expression of a single gene. *Nature, 429*, 754–757.

Long, B., Ungpakorn, G., & Harrison, G. A. (1993). Home-school differences in stress hormone levels in a group of Oxford primary school children. *Journal of Biosocial Sciences, 25*, 73–78.

Maestripieri, D. (1999). The biology of human parenting: Insights from non-human primates. *Neuroscience and biobehavioral reviews, 23*, 411–422.

Maier, S. F., Watkins, L. R., & Fleschner, M. (1994). Psychoneuroimmunology: The interface between behavior, brain, and immunity. *American Psychologist, 49*, 1004–1007.

Marler, C. A., Bester-Meredith, J., & Trainor, B. C. (2003). Paternal behavior and aggression: Endocrine mechanisms and nongenomic transmission of behavior. In P. J. B. Slater, J. S. Rosenblatt, C. T. Snowden, & T. J. Roper (Eds.), *Advances in the study of behavior, 32*, 263–323. San Diego, CA: Academic Press.

Martin, R. D. (1983). *Human brain evolution in an ecological context.* 52nd James Arthur lecture on the evolution of the human brain. New York: American Museum of Natural History.

Martin, R. D. (1990). *Primate origins and evolution.* Princeton: Princeton University Press.

Mason, J. W. (1968). A review of psychoendocrine research on the pituitary-adrenal cortical system. *Psychosomatic Medicine, 30*, 576–607.

Mason, J. W. (1971). A re-evaluation of the concept of "non-specificity" in stress theory. *Journal of Psychosomatic Research, 8*, 323–334.

McEwen, B. S. (1995). Stressful experience, brain, and emotions: Developmental, genetic, and hormonal influences. In M. S. Gazzaniga (Ed.), *The cognitive neurosciences* (pp. 1117–1135). Cambridge, MA: MIT Press.

McHenry, H. M. (1992a). Body size and proportions in early hominids. *American Journal of Physical Anthropology, 87*, 407–431.

McHenry, H. M. (1992b). How big were early hominids? *Evolutionary Anthropology, 1*, 15–20.

McHenry, H. M. (1994). Behavioral ecological implications of early hominid body size. *Journal of Human Evolution, 27*, 77–87.

Meaney, M., Mitchell, J., Aitken, D., Bhat Agar, S., Bodnoff, S., Ivy, L., & Sarriev, A. (1991). The effects of neonatal handling on the development of the adrenocortical response to stress: Implications for neuropathology and cognitive deficits later in life. *Psychoneuroendocrinology, 16*, 85–103.

Mirescu, C., Peters, J. D., & Gould, E. (2004). Early life experience alters response of adult neurogenesis to stress. *Nature Reviews: Neuroscience, 7*(8), 841–846.

Munck, A., & Guyre, P. M. (1991). Glucocorticoids and immune function. In R. Ader, D. L. Felten, & N. Cohen (Eds.), *Psychoneuroimmunology.* San Diego, CA: Academic Press.

Munck, A., Guyre, P. M., & Holbrook, N. J. (1984). Physiological functions of glucocorticoids in stress and their relation to pharmacological actions. *Endocrine reviews, 5*, 25–44.

Murdock, G. P. (1949). *Social structure.* New York: Macmillan.

Nachmias, M., Gunnar, M., Mangelsdorf, S., Parritz, R. H., & Buss, K. (1996). Behavioral inhibition and stress reactivity: The moderating role of attachment security. *Child Development, 67*, 508–522.

Nelson, A. J., Thompson, J. L., & Krovitz, G. E. (2003). Conclusions: Putting it all together. In J. L. Thompson, G. E. Krovitz, & A. J. Nelson (Eds.), *Patterns of growth and development in the genus* Homo (pp. 436–445). Cambridge, UK: Cambridge University Press.

Newcomer, J. W., Craft, S., Hershey, T., Askins, K., & Bardgett, M. E. (1994). Glucocorticoid-induced impairment in declarative memory performance in adult humans. *Journal of Neuroscience, 14*(4), 2047–2053.

O'Connell, J. F., Hawkes, K., & Blurton Jones, N. G. (1999). Grandmothering and the evolution of *Homo erectus. Journal of Human Evolution, 36,* 461–485.

Pawlowski, B. (1999). Loss of oestrus and concealed ovulation in human evolution: The case against the sexual-selection hypothesis. *Current Anthropology, 40*(3), 257–275.

Pawlowski, B., Lowen, C. B., & Dunbar, R. I. M. (1998). Neocortex size, social skills and mating success in primates. *Behaviour, 135,* 357–368.

Pearlin, L. I., & Turner, H. A. (1987). The family as a context of the stress process. In S. V. Kasl & C. L. Cooper (Eds.), *Stress and health: Issues in research methodology.* New York: Wiley.

Pinker, S. (1994). *The language instinct.* New York: Morrow.

Plavcan, J. M. (2000). Inferring social behavior from sexual dimorphism in the fossil record. *Journal of Human Evolution, 39,* 327–344.

Plavcan, J. M. (2001). Sexual dimorphism in primate evolution. *Yearbook of Physical Anthropology, 44,* 25–53.

Plavcan, J. M., & van Schaik, C. P. (1997). Interpreting hominid behavior on the basis of sexual dimorphism. *Journal of Human Evolution, 32*(4), 345–374.

Plavcan, J. M., van Schaik, C. P., & Kappeler, P. M. (1995). Competition, coalitions and canine size in primates. *Journal of Human Evolution, 28,* 245–276.

Portman, A. (1941). Die tragzeiten der primaten und die dauer der schwangerschaft beim menschen: Ein roblem der vergleichenden biologie. *Revue Suisse de Zoologie, 48,* 511–518.

Ranganath, C., & Rainer, G. (2003). Neural mechanisms for detecting and remembering novel events. *Nature Reviews: Neuroscience, 4,* 193–202.

Reno, P. L., Meindl, R. S., McCollum, M. A., & Lovejoy, C. O. (2003). Sexual dimorphism in *Austrolopithecus afarensis* was similar to that of humans. *Proceedings of the National Academy of Sciences, 100*(16), 9404–9409.

Rohner, R. P., & Veneziano, R. A. (2001). The importance of father love: History and contemporary evidence. *Review of General Psychology, 5,* 382–405.

Rosenblatt, J. S. (2003). Outline of the evolution of behavioral and nonbehavioral patterns of parental care among the vertebrates: Critical characteristics of mammalian and avian parental behavior. *Scandinavian Journal of Psychology, 44*(3), 265–271.

Rosenberg, K. (1992). The evolution of modern human childbirth. *Yearbook of Physical Anthropology, 35,* 89–134.

Rosenberg, K., & Trevathan, W. (1996). Bipedalism and human birth: The obstetrical dilemma revisited. *Evolutionary Anthropology, 4,* 161–168.

Ruff, C. B. (1995). Biomechanics of the hip and birth in early *Homo. American Journal of Physical Anthropology, 98,* 527–574.

Ruff, C. B., Trinkaus, E., & Holliday, T. W. (1997). Body mass and encephalization in Pleistocene *Homo. Nature, 387,* 173–176.

Saphier, D., Welch, J. E., Farrar, G. E., Ngunen, N. Q., Aguado, F., Thaller, T. R., et al. (1994). Interactions between serotonin, thyrotropin-releasing hormone and substance P in the CNS regulation of adrenocortical secretion. *Psychoneuroendocrinology, 19,* 779–797.

Sapolsky, R. M. (1991). Effects of stress and glucocorticoids on hippocampal neuronal survival. In M. R. Brown, G. F. Koob, & C. Rivier (Eds.), *Stress: Neurobiology and neuroendocrinology* (pp. 293–322). New York: Dekker.

Sapolsky, R. M. (1992a). Neuroendocrinology of the stress-response. In J. B. Becker, S. M. Breedlove, & D. Crews (Eds.), *Behavioral endocrinology* (pp. 287–324). Cambridge, MA: MIT Press.

Sapolsky, R. M. (1992b). *Stress, the aging brain, and the mechanisms of neuron death.* Cambridge, MA: MIT Press.

Sapolsky, R. M. (1994). *Why zebras don't get ulcers.* New York: Freeman.

Sapolsky, R. M., Romero, L. M., & Munck, A. U. (2000). How do glucocorticoids influence stress responses? *Endocrine Reviews, 21*(1), 55–89.

Scheper-Hughes, N. (Ed.). (1988). *Child survival: Anthropological perspectives on the treatment and maltreatment of children.* Boston: Reidel.

Schneider, M. L., Coe, C. L., & Lubach, G. R. (1992). Endocrine activation mimics the adverse effects of prenatal stress on the neuromotor development of the infant primate. *Developmental Psychobiology, 25,* 427–439.

Servan-Schreiber, D., Printz, H., & Cohen, S. D. (1990). A network model of catecholamine effects: Gain, signal-to-noise ratio, and behavior. *Science, 249,* 892–895.

Seyle, H. (1976). *The stress of life* (Rev. ed.). New York: McGraw-Hill.

Silk, J. S., Alberts, S. C., & Altmann, J. (2003). Social bonds of female baboons enhance infant survival. *Science, 302,* 1231–1234.

Sillen-Tullberg, B., & Møller, A. P. (1993). The relationship between concealed ovulation and mating systems in anthropoid primates: A phylogenetic analysis. *American Naturalist, 141*(1), 1–25.

Small, M. F. (1998). *Our babies, ourselves.* New York: Random House.

Small, M. F. (2001). *Kids.* New York: Doubleday.

Smith, B. H. (1993). The physiological age of KNM-WT15000. In A. Walker & R. E. Leakey (Eds.), *The Nariokotome* Homo erectus *skeleton* (pp. 195–220). Cambridge, MA: Harvard University Press.

Smuts, B. (1985). *Sex and friendship in baboons.* Hawthorne, NY: Aldine de Gruyter.

Stearns, S. C. (1992). *The evolution of life histories.* Oxford, England: Oxford University Press.

Storey, A. E., Walsh, C. J., Quinton, R. L., & Wynne-Edwards, K. E. (2000). Hormonal correlates of paternal responsiveness in new and expectant fathers. *Evolution and Human Behavior, 21*(2), 79–95.

Tinbergen, N. (1974). Ethology and stress diseases. *Science, 185,* 20–27.

Uvnas-Moberg, K. (1998). Oxytocin may mediate the benefits of positive social interaction and emotions. *Psychoneuroendocrinology, 23,* 819–835.

van Schaik, C., & Deaner, R. (2003). Life history and cognitive evolution in primates. In F. de Waal & P. Tyack (Eds.), *Animal social complexity: Intelligence, culture and individualized societies* (pp. 5–25). Cambridge, MA: Harvard University Press.

Wagner, J. D., Flinn, M. V., & England, B. G. (2002). Hormonal response to competition among male coalitions. *Evolution and Human Behavior, 23*(6), 437–442.

Wallerstein, J. S. (1983). Children of divorce: Stress and developmental tasks. In N. Garmezy & M. Rutter (Eds.), *Stress, coping, and development in children* (pp. 265–302). New York: McGraw-Hill.

Ward, C. V., Walker, A., & Leakey, M. G. (1999). The new hominid species *Australopithecus anamensis. Evolutionary Anthropology, 7,* 197–205.

Ward, C., Leakey, M. G., & Walker, A. (2001). Morphology of *Australopithecus anamensis* from Kanapoi and Allia Bay, Kenya. *Journal of Human Evolution, 41,* 255–368.

Weaver, I. C. G., Cervoni, N., Champagne, F. S., D'Alessio, A. C. D., Sharma, S., Seckl, J. R., et al. (2004). Epigenetic programming by maternal behavior. *Nature Reviews: Neuroscience, 7*(8), 847–854.

Weiner, H. (1992). *Perturbing the organism.* Chicago: University of Chicago Press.

Whiting, B. B., & Edwards, C. P. (1988). *Children of different worlds.* Cambridge, MA: Harvard University Press.

Wilcox, A. J., Baird, D. D., Dunson, D. B., McConnaughey, D. R., Kesner, J. S., & Weinberg, R. L. (2004). On the frequency of sexual intercourse around ovulation: Evidence for biological influences. *Human Reproduction, 19*(7), 1539–1543.

Wilkinson, R. G. (2001). *Mind the gap: Hierarchies, health, and human evolution.* New Haven, CT: Yale University Press.

Williams, G. C. (1957). Plieotropy, natural selection, and the evolution of senescence. *Evolution, 11,* 398–411.

Wilson, M. I., Daly, M., & Weghorst, S. J. (1980). Household composition and the risk of child abuse and neglect. *Journal of Biosocial Sciences, 12,* 333–340.

Wrangham, R. W. (1999). Evolution of coalitionary killing. *Yearbook of Physical Anthropology, 42,* 1–30.

Wrangham, R. W., & Peterson, D. (1996). *Demonic males.* New York: Houghton Mifflin Company.

Wynne-Edwards, K. E. (2001). Hormonal changes in mammalian fathers. *Hormones and Behavior, 40,* 139–145.

Wynne-Edwards, K. E. (2003). From dwarf hamster to daddy: The intersection of ecology, evolution, and physiology that produces paternal behavior. In P. J. B. Slater, J. S. Rosenblatt, C. T. Snowden, & T. J. Roper (Eds.), *Advances in the study of behavior, 32,* 207–261. San Diego, CA: Academic Press.

Young, L. J., & Insel, T. R. (2002). Hormones and parental behavior. In J. B. Becker, S. M. Breedlove, D. Crews, & M. M. McCarthy (Eds.), *Behavioral endocrinology* (pp. 331–369). Cambridge, MA: MIT Press.

Young, L., Wang, Z., & Insel, T. R. (2002). Neuroendocrine bases of monogamy. In J. T. Cacioppo, G. G. Berntson, R. Adolphs, C. S. Carter, R. J. Davidson, M. K. McClintock, et al. (Eds.), *Foundations in social neuroscience* (pp. 809–816). Cambridge, MA: MIT Press.

Yuwiler, A. (1982). Biobehavioral consequences of experimental early life stress: Effects of neonatal hormones on monoaminergic systems. In L. J. West & M. Stein (Eds.), *Critical issues in behavioral medicine* (pp. 59–78). Philadelphia: J. P. Lippincott.

Ziegler, T. E., & Snowdon, C. T. (1997). Role of prolactin in paternal care in a monogamous New World primate, Saguinus oedipus. *The integrative neurobiology of affiliation. Annals of the New York Academy of Sciences, 807,* 599–601.

Zihlman, A., Cronin, J., Cramer, D., & Sarich, V. M. (1978). Pygmy chimpanzee as a possible prototype for the common ancestor of humans, chimpanzees and gorillas. *Nature, 275,* 744–746.

PART V

GROUP LIVING

DAVID M. BUSS

Homo sapiens has been called "the social animal" for a good reason. Living in groups defines a key mode of human existence. Groups contain a bounty of resources critical to survival and reproduction. They afford safety and protection from predators and from other humans. They are populated with potential friends for mutually beneficial social exchange. They contain reproductively valuable mates. And they are inhabited with kin, precious carriers of our genetic cargo, from whom we can receive aid and in whom we can invest. At the same time, group living intensifies competition over precisely those reproductively relevant resources, creating sources of conflict not faced by more solitary creatures. The chapters in this part describe many of the complexities of the evolutionary psychology of group living.

Leda Cosmides and John Tooby in Chapter 20 provide a comprehensive review of the extensive body of research, much of it conducted by them and their students, on neurocognitive adaptations for social exchange. They elucidate the many design features that such adaptations theoretically should possess and provide compelling arguments that domain-general mechanisms cannot achieve the specific outcomes needed for successful social exchange. They review competing theories of the content effects on the Wason selection task and marshal empirical evidence relevant to adjudicating among those theories. In a display of the sort of methodological pluralism advocated by Simpson and Campbell (Chapter 4, this volume), Cosmides and Tooby describe cross-cultural studies, studies using traditional methods of cognitive psychology, and studies using neurocognitive techniques.

Anne Campbell in Chapter 21 provides an overview of theory and research on human aggression, the ways in which humans inflict costs on other humans. The domains include aggression against kin (e.g., maternal infanticide), aggression against mates, aggression against intrasexual rivals, aggression through defection, and aggression of coalitions against rival coalitions. She provides a detailed analysis of the underlying adaptations for aggression, the ways in which they are sex-differentiated in design, and the contextual and ecological variables to which they respond. Her impressive chapter, following the chapter on social exchange, highlights the view that humans are neither "good" nor "bad," neither exclusive cooperators nor exclusive aggressors, but rather contain complex mechanisms of mind designed to confer benefits *and* to inflict costs on other humans in highly situation-contingent ways.

Robert Kurzban and Steven Neuberg in Chapter 22 approach problems of group living through a different lens—adaptations for managing in-group and out-group relationships. Specifically, they focus on discrimination, stigmatization, and social exclusion. Whereas most mainstream psychologists treat these pervasive human social phenomena as by-products of domain-general cognitive mechanisms, Kurzban and Neuberg argue that they are products of more specialized cognitive, affective, and behavioral adaptations designed to solve adaptive problems of group living. Proprietary categorization systems for identifying coalitions, subcoalitions, and enemies, for example, help to solve problems of managing group-on-group conflict. These important insights lead to a deeper understanding of coalitional psychology and of how humans handle conflicts that inevitably arise within and between groups.

All known social groups contain status or dominance hierarchies, either formal or informal. Reproductively relevant resources are closely linked with position in these hierarchies. Denise Cummins provides in Chapter 23 a fascinating evolutionary psychological analysis of dominance, status, and social hierarchies at several levels of analysis—neuroendocrinological, cognitive, and behavioral. She shows connections between reciprocity (see Cosmides & Tooby, Chapter 20, this volume) and social status and explores the mind-reading adaptations necessary for successful negotiation of status hierarchies. Cummins provides an insightful analysis of development—when certain adaptations for hierarchy negotiation come "on line" in individual's lives—as well as the emergence of sex differences in status striving.

Peter MacNeilage and Barbara Davis in Chapter 24 provide an exciting discussion on the evolution of language, an ability that must have massively changed the nature of group living. Whereas some evolutionary psychologists, such as Steven Pinker and Paul Bloom, argue that language has all the hallmarks of an adaptation, MacNeilage and Davis question this view, arguing that language originated as a by-product of adaptations designed for other functions. They stress the importance of phylogeny in the emergence of language and argue for the importance of self-organization. As such, this chapter exemplifies the diversity of theoretical positions within evolutionary psychology, illustrating healthy debate within the field. It shows that evidence for adaptation has to be assembled on a case-by-case basis, not assumed a priori.

Martie Haselton, Daniel Nettle, and Paul Andrews present theory and empirical research on the evolution of cognitive biases in social interaction in Chapter 25. They provide sound arguments that certain social cognitive biases are in fact designed and functional, resulting in better solutions to adaptive problems than cognitive mechanisms that "accurately" detected social signals. They call for an evolutionary reformulation of the entire "heuristics and biases" literature, which typically cast humans as making illogical and unfounded errors. This new line of work has already led to the discovery of new cognitive biases and offers much promise for the future discovery of additional adaptive biases. It also may lead to the detumescence of decades of work that has cast humans erroneously as fundamentally irrational and hopelessly muddled in their judgment and decision making.

The part ends with Chapter 26 by Dennis Krebs on the evolution of morality. He begins by distinguishing between selfishness at the level of the gene and the level of the individual and argues that moral dispositions at the level of the individual can and almost certainly have evolved. He provides a complex and nuanced analysis of many facets of morality, including the functions of moral judgment, impression management and deception of others about one's morality, and how morality is linked to social exchange, mating, kin investment, and status hierarchies. Along the way, Krebs provides fascinating insights into the evolutionary psychology of friendship, deference, forgiveness, contrition, and the moral emotions that underlie these actions.

Group living is what we do as a species. It offers a bounty of benefits through cooperation and an abundance of costs through social conflict. As a consequence, it is reasonable to expect that humans have evolved a large number of specialized adaptations for dealing with other humans, both for within-group interactions and for dealing with other groups. Collectively, these seven chapters highlight the complexity of human evolutionary psychology for group living and pave the way for the discovery of many more adaptations for grappling with the challenges posed by other humans.

CHAPTER 20

Neurocognitive Adaptations Designed for Social Exchange

LEDA COSMIDES and JOHN TOOBY

If a person doesn't give something to me, I won't give anything to that person. If I'm sitting eating, and someone like that comes by, I say, "Uhn, uhn. I'm not going to give any of this to you. When you have food, the things you do with it make me unhappy. If you even once in a while gave me something nice, I would surely give some of this to you."

Nisa from *Nisa: The Life and Words of a !Kung Woman*, Shostak, 1981, p. 89

Instead of keeping things, [!Kung] use them as gifts to express generosity and friendly intent, and to put people under obligation to make return tokens of friendship. . . . In reciprocating, one does not give the same object back again but something of comparable value.

Eland fat is a very highly valued gift . . . Toma said that when he had eland fat to give, he took shrewd note of certain objects he might like to have and gave their owners especially generous gifts of fat.

Marshall, 1976, pp. 366–369

NISA AND TOMA WERE hunter-gatherers, !Kung San people living in Botswana's inhospitable Kalahari desert during the 1960s. Their way of life was as different from that in an industrialized, economically developed society as any on earth, yet their sentiments are as familiar and easy to comprehend as those of your neighbor next door. They involve *social exchange*, interactions in which one party provides a benefit to the other conditional on the recipient's providing a benefit in return (Cosmides, 1985; Cosmides & Tooby, 1989; Tooby & Cosmides, 1996). Among humans, social exchange can be implicit or explicit, simultaneous or sequential, immediate or deferred, and may involve alternating actions by the two parties or follow more complex structures. In all these cases, however, it is a way people cooperate for mutual benefit. Explicitly agreed-to forms of social exchange are the focus of study in economics (and are known as exchange or trade), while biologists and anthropologists focus more on implicit, deferred cases of exchange, often called *reciprocal altruism* (Trivers, 1971), *reciprocity,* or *reciprocation.* We will refer to the inclusive set of cases of the mutually conditioned provisioning of benefits as social exchange, regardless of subtype. Nisa and Toma are musing about social exchange interactions in which the expectation of reciprocity is implicit and the favor can be returned at a much later date. In their society, as in ours, the benefits given and received need not be physical objects for exchange to exist, but can be services (valued actions) as well. Aid in a fight, support in a political conflict, help with a sick child, permission to hunt and use water holes in your family's territory—all are ways of doing or repaying a favor. Social exchange behavior is both panhuman and ancient. What cognitive abilities make it possible?

For 25 years, we have been investigating the hypothesis that the enduring presence of social exchange interactions among our ancestors has selected for cognitive mechanisms that are specialized for reasoning about social exchange. Just as a lock and key are designed to fit together to function, our claim is that the proprietary procedures and conceptual elements of the social exchange reasoning specializations evolved to reflect the abstract, evolutionarily recurring relationships present in social exchange interactions (Cosmides & Tooby, 1989).

We picked social exchange reasoning as an initial test case for exploring the empirical power of evolutionary psychological analysis for a number of reasons. First, the topic is intrinsically important: Exchange is central to all human economic activity. If exchange in our species is made possible by evolved, neurocomputational programs specialized for exchange itself, this is surely worth knowing. Such evolved programs would constitute the foundation of economic behavior, and their specific properties would organize exchange interactions in all human societies; thus, if they exist, they deserve to be mapped. The discovery and mapping of such mechanisms would ground economics in the evolutionary and cognitive sciences, cross-connecting economics to the rest of the natural sciences. Social exchange specializations (if they exist) also underlie many aspects of a far broader category of implicit social interaction lying outside economics, involving favors, friendship, and self-organizing cooperation.

There was a second reason for investigating the computational procedures engaged by social exchange: The underlying counterhypothesis about social exchange reasoning that we have been testing against is the single most central assumption of the traditional social and behavioral sciences—the blank slate view of the mind that lies at the center of what we have called the *standard social science model* (Tooby & Cosmides, 1992). On this view, humans are endowed with a powerful, general cognitive capacity (intelligence, rationality, learning, instrumental reasoning), which explains human thought and the great majority of human behavior. In this case, humans putatively engage in successful social exchange through exactly the same cognitive faculties that allow them to do everything else: Their general intelligence allows them to recognize, learn, or reason out intelligent, beneficial courses of action. Despite—or perhaps because—this hypothesis has been central to how most neural, psychological, and social scientists conceptualize human behavior, it is almost never subjected to potential empirical falsification (unlike theories central to physics or biology). Investigating reasoning about social exchange provided an opportunity to test the blank slate hypothesis empirically in domains (economics and social behavior) where it had previously been uncritically accepted by almost all traditional researchers. Moreover, the results of these tests would be powerfully telling for the general issue of whether an evolutionary psychological program would lead to far-reaching and fundamental revisions across the human sciences. Why? If mechanisms of general rationality exist and are to genuinely explain anything of significance, they should surely explain social exchange reasoning as one easy application. After all, social exchange is absurdly simple compared to other cognitive activities such as language or vision, it is mutually beneficial and intrinsically rewarding, it is economically rational (Simon, 1990), and it should emerge spontaneously as the result of the ability to pursue goals; even artificially intelligent agents capable of pursuing goals through means-ends analysis should be able to manage it. An organism that was in fact equipped with a powerful, general intelligence would not *need* cognitive specializations for social exchange to be able to engage in it. If it turns out that humans nonetheless have adaptive specializations for social exchange, it would imply that mechanisms of general intelligence (if they exist) are relatively weak, and natural selection has specialized a far larger number of comparable cognitive competences than cognitive and behavioral scientists had anticipated.

Third, we chose reasoning because reasoning is widely considered to be the quintessential case of a content-independent, general-purpose cognitive competence. Reasoning is also considered to be the most distinctively human cognitive ability—something that exists in opposition to, and as a replacement for, instinct. If, against all expectation, even human reasoning turned out to fractionate into a diverse collection of evolved, content-specialized procedures, then adaptive specializations are far more likely to be widespread and typical in the human psychological architecture, rather than nonexistent or exceptional. Reasoning presents the most difficult test case, and hence the most useful case to leapfrog the evolutionary debate into genuinely new territory. In contrast, the eventual outcome of debates over the evolutionary origins and organization of motivation (e.g., sexual desire) and emotion (e.g., fear) are not in doubt (despite the persistence of intensely fought rearguard actions by traditional research communities). No blank slate process could, even in principle, acquire the human complement of motivational and emotional organization (Cosmides & Tooby, 1987; Tooby, Cosmides, & Barrett, 2005). Reasoning will be the last redoubt of those who adhere to a blank slate approach to the human psychological architecture.

Fourth, logical reasoning is subject to precise formal computational analysis, so it is possible to derive exact and contrasting predictions from domain-general and domain-specific theories, allowing critical tests to be devised and theories to be potentially or actually falsified.

Finally, we chose the domain of social exchange because it offered the opportunity to explore whether the evolutionary dynamics newly charted by evolutionary game theory (e.g., Maynard Smith, 1982) could be shown empirically to have sculpted the human brain and mind and, indeed, human moral reasoning. If it could be empirically shown that the kinds of selection pressures modeled in evolutionary game theory had real consequences on the human psychological architecture, then this would help lay the foundations of an evolutionary approach to social psychology, social behavior, and morality (Cosmides & Tooby, 2004). Morality was considered by most social scientists (then as now) to be a cultural product free of biological organization. We thought on theoretical grounds there should be an evolved set of domain-specific grammars of moral and social reasoning (Cosmides & Tooby, 1989) and wanted to see if we could clearly establish at least one rich empirical example—a grammar of social exchange. One pleasing feature of the case of social exchange is that it can be clearly traced step by step as a causal chain from replicator dynamics and game theory to details of the computational architecture to specific patterns of reasoning performance to specific cultural phenomena, moral intuitions, and conceptual primitives in moral philosophy—showcasing the broad integrative power of an evolutionary psychological approach. This research is one component of a larger project that includes mapping the evolutionary psychology of moral sentiments and moral emotions alongside moral reasoning (e.g., Cosmides & Tooby, 2004; Lieberman, Tooby, & Cosmides, 2003; Price, Cosmides, & Tooby, 2002).

What follows are some of the high points of this 25-year research program. We argue that social exchange is ubiquitously woven through the fabric of human life in all human cultures everywhere, and has been taking place among our ancestors for millions and possibly tens of millions of years. This means social exchange interactions are an important and recurrent human activity with sufficient time depth to have selected for specialized neural adaptations. Evolutionary game theory shows that social exchange can evolve and persist only if the cognitive programs that cause it conform to a narrow and complex set of design specifications. The complex pattern of functional and neural dissociations that we discovered during a 25-year research program reveal so close a fit between adaptive problem and computational solution that a neurocognitive specialization for reasoning about social exchange is implicated, including a subroutine for cheater detection. This subroutine develops precocially (by ages 3 to 4) and appears cross-culturally—hunter-horticulturalists in the Amazon detect cheaters as reliably as adults who live in advanced market economies. The detailed patterns of human reasoning performance elicited by situations involving social exchange correspond to the evolutionarily derived predictions of a specialized logic or grammar of social exchange and falsify content-independent, general-purpose reasoning mechanisms as a plausible explanation for reasoning in this domain. A developmental process that is itself specialized for social exchange appears to be responsible for building the neurocognitive specialization found in adults: As we show, the design, ontogenetic timetable, and cross-cultural distribution of social exchange are not consistent with any known domain-general learning process. Taken together, the data showing design specificity, precocious development, cross-cultural universality, and neural dissociability implicate the existence of an evolved, species-typical neurocomputational specialization.

In short, the neurocognitive system that causes reasoning about social exchange shows evidence of being what Pinker (1994) has called a *cognitive instinct:* It is complexly organized for solving a well-defined adaptive problem our ancestors faced in the past, it reliably develops in all normal humans, it develops without any conscious effort and in the absence of explicit instruction, it is applied without any conscious awareness of its underlying logic, and it is functionally and neurally distinct from more general abilities to process information or behave intelligently. We briefly review the evidence that supports this conclusion, along with the evidence that eliminates the alternative by-product hypotheses that have been proposed. (For more comprehensive treatments, see Cosmides, 1985, 1989;

Cosmides & Tooby, 1989, 1992, 2005; Fiddick, Cosmides, & Tooby, 2000; Stone, Cosmides, Tooby, Kroll, & Knight, 2002; Sugiyama, Tooby, & Cosmides, 2002.)

SOCIAL EXCHANGE IN ZOOLOGICAL AND CULTURAL PERSPECTIVE

Living in daily contact affords many opportunities to see when someone needs help, to monitor when someone fails to help but could have, and, as Nisa explains, to withdraw future help when this happens. Under these conditions, reciprocity can be delayed, understanding of obligations and entitlements can remain tacit, and aid (in addition to objects) can be given and received (Shostak, 1981). But when people do not live side by side, social exchange arrangements typically involve explicit agreements, simultaneous transfer of benefits, and increased trade of objects (rather than intimate acts of aid). Agreements are explicit because neither side can know the other's needs based on daily interaction, objects are traded because neither side is present to provide aid when the opportunity arises, and trades are simultaneous because this reduces the risk of nonreciprocation—neither side needs to trust the other to provide help in the future. Accordingly, explicit or simultaneous trade is usually a sign of social distance (Tooby & Cosmides, 1996). !Kung, for example, will trade hides for knives and other goods with Bantu people but not with fellow band members (Marshall, 1976).

Explicit trades and delayed, implicit reciprocation differ in these superficial ways, but they share a deep structure: X provides a benefit to Y conditional on Y doing something that X wants. As humans, we take it for granted that people can make each other better off than they were before by exchanging benefits—goods, services, acts of help and kindness. But when placed in zoological perspective, social exchange stands out as an unusual phenomenon whose existence requires explanation. The magnitude, variety, and complexity of our social exchange relations are among the most distinctive features of human social life and differentiate us strongly from all other animal species (Tooby & DeVore, 1987). Indeed, uncontroversial examples of social exchange in other species are difficult to find, and despite widespread investigation, social exchange has been reported in only a tiny handful of other species, such as chimpanzees, certain monkeys, and vampire bats (see Dugatkin, 1997; Hauser, in press, for contrasting views of the non-human findings).

Practices can be widespread without being the specific product of evolved psychological adaptations. Is social exchange a recent cultural invention? Cultural inventions such as alphabetic writing systems, cereal cultivation, and Arabic numerals are widespread, but they have one or a few points of origin, spread by contact, and are highly elaborated in some cultures and absent in others. Social exchange does not fit this pattern. It is found in every documented culture past and present and is a feature of virtually every human life within each culture, taking on a multiplicity of elaborate forms, such as returning favors, sharing food, reciprocal gift giving, explicit trade, and extending acts of help with the implicit expectation that they will be reciprocated (Cashdan, 1989; Fiske, 1991; Gurven, 2002; Malinowski, 1922; Mauss, 1925/1967). Particular methods or institutions for engaging in exchange—marketplaces, stock exchanges, money, the Kula Ring—are recent cultural inventions, but not social exchange behavior itself.

Moreover, evidence supports the view that social exchange is at least as old as the genus *Homo* and possibly far older than that. Paleoanthropological evidence indicates that before anatomically modern humans evolved, hominids engaged in social exchange (see, e.g., Isaac, 1978). Moreover, the presence of reciprocity in chimpanzees (and even certain monkeys; Brosnan & de Waal, 2003; de Waal, 1989, 1997a, 1997b; de Waal & Luttrell, 1988) suggests it may predate the time, 5 to 7 million years ago, when the hominid line split from chimpanzees. In short, social exchange behavior has been present during the evolutionary history of our line for so long that selection could well have engineered complex cognitive mechanisms specialized for engaging in it.

Natural selection retains and discards properties from a species' design based on how well these properties solve adaptive problems—evolutionarily recurrent problems whose solution promotes reproduction. To have been a target of selection, a design had to produce beneficial effects, measured in reproductive terms, in the environments in which it evolved. Social exchange clearly produced beneficial effects for those who successfully engaged in it, ancestrally as well as now (Cashdan, 1989; Isaac, 1978). A life deprived of the benefits that reciprocal cooperation provides would be a Hobbesian nightmare of poverty and social isolation, punctuated by conflict. But the fact that social exchange produces beneficial effects is not sufficient for showing that the neurocognitive system that enables it was designed by natural selection for that function. To rule out the counterhypothesis that social exchange is a side effect of a system that was designed to solve a different or more inclusive set of adaptive problems, we need to evaluate whether the adaptation shows evidence of special design for the proposed function (Williams, 1966).

So what, exactly, is the nature of the neurocognitive machinery that enables exchange, and how specialized is it for this function? Social exchange is zoologically rare, raising the possibility that natural selection engineered into the human brain information processing circuits that are narrowly specialized for understanding, reasoning about, motivating, and engaging in social exchange. On this view, the circuits involved are neurocognitive adaptations *for* social exchange, evolved cognitive instincts designed by natural selection for that function—the *adaptive specialization hypothesis*. An alternative family of theories derives from the possibility that our ability to reason about and engage in social exchange is a by-product of a neurocognitive system that evolved for a different function. This could be an alternative specific function (e.g., reasoning about obligations). More usually, however, researchers expect that social exchange reasoning is a by-product or expression of a neurocognitive system that evolved to perform a more general function—operant conditioning, logical reasoning, rational decision making, or some sort of general intelligence. We call this family of explanations the *general rationality hypothesis*.

The general rationality hypothesis is so compelling, so self-evident, and so entrenched in our scientific culture that researchers find it difficult to treat it as a scientific hypothesis at all, exempting it from demands of falsifiability, specification, formalization, consistency, and proof they would insist on for any other scientific hypothesis. For example, in dismissing the adaptive specialization hypothesis of social exchange without examining the evidence, Ehrlich (2002) considers it sufficient to advance the folk theory that people just "figure it out." He makes no predictions nor specifies any possible test that could falsify his view. Orr (2003) similarly refuses to engage the evidence, arguing that perhaps "it just pays to behave in a certain way, and an organism with a big-enough brain reasons this out, while evolved instincts and specialized mental modules are beside the point" (p. 18). He packages this argument with the usual and necessarily undocumented claims about the low scientific standards of evolutionary psychology (in this case, voiced by unnamed colleagues in molecular biology).

What is problematic about this debate is not that the general rationality hypothesis is advanced as an alternative explanation. It is a plausible (if hopelessly vague) hypothesis. Indeed, the entire social exchange research program has, from its inception, been designed to systematically test against the major predictions that can be derived from this family of countertheories, to the extent they can be specified. What is problematic is that critics engage in the pretense that tests of the hypothesis they favor have never been carried out; that their favored hypothesis has no empirical burden of its own to bear; and that merely stating the general rationality hypothesis is enough to establish the empirical weakness of the adaptive specialization hypothesis. It is, in reality, what Dawkins (1986) calls the *argument from personal incredulity* masquerading as its opposite—a commitment to high standards of hypothesis testing.

Of course, to a cognitive scientist, Orr's conjecture as stated does not rise to the level of a scientific hypothesis. "Big brains" cause reasoning only by virtue of the neurocognitive programs they contain. Had Orr specified a reasoning mechanism or a learning process, we could empirically test the proposition that it predicts the observed patterns of social exchange reasoning. But he did not. Fortunately, however, a number of cognitive scientists have proposed some well-formulated by-product hypotheses, all of which make different predictions from the adaptive specialization hypothesis. Moreover, even where well-specified theories are lacking, one can derive some general predictions from the class of general rationality theories about possible versus impossible patterns of cultural variation, the effects of familiarity, possible versus impossible patterns of neural dissociation, and so on. We have tested each by-product hypothesis in turn. None can explain the patterns of reasoning performance found, patterns that were previously unknown and predicted in advance by the hypothesis that humans have neurocognitive adaptations designed for social exchange.

SELECTION PRESSURES AND PREDICTED DESIGN FEATURES

To test whether a system is an adaptation that evolved for a particular function, one must produce design evidence. The first step is to demonstrate that the system's properties solve a well-specified adaptive problem in a well-engineered way (Tooby & Cosmides, 1992, Chapter 1, this volume; Dawkins, 1986; Williams, 1966). This requires a well-specified theory of the adaptive problem in question.

For example, the laws of optics constrain the properties of cameras and eyes: Certain engineering problems must be solved by any information processing system that uses reflected light to project images of objects onto a 2-D surface (film or retina). Once these problems are understood, the eye's design makes sense. The transparency of the cornea, the ability of the iris to constrict the pupillary opening, the shape of the lens, the existence of photoreactive molecules in the retina, the resolution of retinal cells—all are solutions to these problems (and have their counterparts in a camera). Optics constrain the design of the eye, but the design of programs causing social behavior is constrained by the behavior of other agents—more precisely, by the design of the behavior-regulating programs in other agents and the fitness consequences that result from the interactions these programs cause. These constraints can be analyzed using evolutionary game theory (Maynard Smith, 1982).

An *evolutionarily stable strategy* (ESS) is a strategy (a decision rule) that can arise and persist in a population because it produces fitness outcomes greater than or equal to alternative strategies (Maynard Smith, 1982). The rules of reasoning and decision making that guide social exchange in humans would not exist unless they had outcompeted alternatives, so we should expect that they implement an ESS.[1] By using game theory and conducting computer simulations of the evolutionary process, one can determine which strategies for engaging in social exchange are ESSs.

Selection pressures favoring social exchange exist whenever one organism (the provider) can change the behavior of a target organism to the provider's advantage by making the target's receipt of that benefit *conditional* on the target acting in a required manner. In social exchange, individuals agree, either explicitly or implicitly, to abide by a particular *social contract*. For ease of explication, let us define a social contract as a conditional (i.e., *If-then*) rule that fits the following template: "If you accept a benefit from X, then you must satisfy X's requirement" (where X is an individual or set of individuals). For example, Toma knew that people in his band recognize and implicitly follow a social contract rule: *If you accept a generous gift of eland fat from someone, then you must give that person something valuable in the future.* Nisa's words also express a social contract: *If you are to get food in the future from me, then you must be individual Y* (where Y = an individual who has willingly shared food with Nisa in the past). Both realize that the act of accepting a benefit from someone triggers an obligation to behave in a way that somehow benefits the provider, now or in the future.

This mutual provisioning of benefits, each conditional on the other's compliance, is usually modeled by game theorists as a repeated Prisoners' Dilemma (Axelrod & Hamilton, 1981; Boyd, 1988; Trivers, 1971; but see Stevens & Stephens, 2004; Tooby & Cosmides, 1996). The results show that the behavior of cooperators must be generated by programs that perform certain specific tasks very well if they are to be evolutionarily stable (Cosmides, 1985; Cosmides & Tooby, 1989). Here, we focus on one of these requirements: cheater detection. A *cheater* is an individual who fails to reciprocate—who accepts the benefit specified by a social contract without satisfying the requirement that provision of that benefit was made contingent on.

The ability to reliably and systematically detect cheaters is a necessary condition for cooperation in the repeated Prisoners' Dilemma to be an ESS (e.g.,

---

[1] If the rules regulating reasoning and decision-making about social exchange do not implement an ESS, it would imply that these rules are a by-product of some other adaptation that produces fitness benefits so huge that they compensate for the systematic fitness costs that result from its producing non-ESS forms of social exchange as a side effect. Given how much social exchange humans engage in, this alternative seems unlikely.

Axelrod, 1984; Axelrod & Hamilton, 1981; Boyd, 1988; Trivers, 1971; Williams, 1966).[2] To see this, consider the fate of a program that, because it cannot detect cheaters, bestows benefits on others unconditionally. These unconditional helpers will increase the fitness of any nonreciprocating design they meet in the population. But when a nonreciprocating design is helped, the unconditional helper never recoups the expense of helping: The helper design incurs a net fitness cost while conferring a net fitness advantage on a design that does not help in return. As a result, a population of unconditional helpers is easily invaded and eventually outcompeted by designs that accept the benefits helpers bestow without reciprocating them. Unconditional helping is not an ESS.

In contrast, program designs that cause *conditional* helping—that help those who reciprocate the favor, but not those who fail to reciprocate—can invade a population of nonreciprocators and outcompete them. Moreover, a population of such designs can resist invasion by designs that do not reciprocate (cheater designs). Therefore, conditional helping, which requires the ability to detect cheaters, is an ESS.

Engineers always start with a task analysis before considering possible design solutions. We did, too. By applying ESS analyses to the behavioral ecology of hunter-gatherers, we were able to specify tasks that an information processing program would have to be good at solving for it to implement an evolutionarily stable form of social exchange (Cosmides, 1985; Cosmides & Tooby, 1989). This task analysis of the required computations, *social contract theory*, specifies what counts as good design in this domain.

Because social contract theory provides a standard of good design against which human performance can be measured, there can be a meaningful answer to the question, "Are the programs that cause reasoning about social exchange well engineered for the task?" Well-designed programs for engaging in social exchange—if such exist—should include features that execute the computational requirements specified by social contract theory, and do so reliably, precisely, and economically (Williams, 1966).

From social contract theory's task analyses, we derived a set of predictions about the design features that a neurocognitive system specialized for reasoning about social exchange should have (Cosmides, 1985; Cosmides & Tooby, 1989). The following six design features (D1-D6) were among those on the list:

---

[2] Detecting cheaters is necessary for contingent cooperation to evolve, even when providing a benefit is cost free (i.e., even for situations that do not fit the payoff structure of a Prisoners' Dilemma; Tooby & Cosmides, 1996). In such cases, a design that cooperates contingently needs to detect when someone has failed to provide a benefit because it needs to know when to shift partners. In this model (just as in the Prisoners' Dilemma), a design that cannot shift partners will have lower fitness than a design that detects cheaters and directs future cooperation to those who do not cheat. Fitness is lower because of the opportunity cost associated with staying, not because of the cost of providing a benefit to the partner. Failure to understand that social exchange is defined by contingent provision of benefits, not by the suffering of costs, has resulted in some irrelevant experiments and discussion in the psychological literature. For example, showing that cheater detection can still occur when the requirement is not costly (e.g., Cheng & Holyoak, 1989) is a prediction of social contract theory, not a refutation of it (Cosmides, 1985; Cosmides & Tooby, 1989). For the same reason, there is no basis in social contract theory for Cheng and Holyoak's (1989) distinction between "social exchanges" (in which satisfying the requirement involves transferring a good, at some cost) and "social contracts" (in which satisfying a requirement may be cost free). For further discussion, see Fiddick et al. (2000).

D1. Social exchange is cooperation for mutual *benefit.* If there is nothing in a conditional rule that can be interpreted as a rationed benefit, then interpretive procedures should not categorize that rule as a social contract. To trigger the inferences about obligations and entitlements that are appropriate to social contracts, the rule must be interpreted as restricting access to a benefit to those who have met a requirement. (This is a necessary, but not sufficient, condition; Cosmides & Tooby, 1989; Gigerenzer & Hug, 1992.)

D2. Cheating is a specific way of violating a social contract: It is taking the benefit when you are not entitled to do so. Consequently, the cognitive architecture must define the concept of *cheating* using contentful representational primitives, referring to illicitly taken *benefits.* This implies that a system designed for cheater detection will not know what to look for if the rule specifies no benefit to the potential violator.

D3. The definition of cheating also depends on which agent's point of view is taken. Perspective matters because the item, action, or state of affairs that one party views as a benefit is viewed as a requirement by the other party. The system needs to be able to compute a cost-benefit representation from the perspective of each participant and define cheating with respect to that perspective-relative representation.

D4. To be an ESS, a design for conditional helping must not be outcompeted by alternative *designs.* Accidents and innocent mistakes that result in an individual being cheated are not markers of a design difference. A cheater detection system should look for cheaters: individuals equipped with programs that cheat by design.[3] Hence, intentional cheating should powerfully trigger the detection system whereas mistakes should trigger it weakly or not at all. (Mistakes that result in an individual being cheated are relevant only insofar as they may not be true mistakes.)

D5. The hypothesis that the ability to reason about social exchange is acquired through the operation of some general-purpose learning ability necessarily predicts that good performance should be a function of experience and familiarity. In contrast, an evolved system for social exchange should be designed to recognize and reason about social exchange interactions no matter how unfamiliar the interaction may be, provided it can be mapped onto the abstract structure of a social contract. Individuals need to be able to reason about each new exchange situation as it arises, so rules that fit the template of a social contract should elicit high levels of cheater detection, even if they are unfamiliar.

D6. Inferences made about social contracts should not follow the rules of a content-free, formal logic. They should follow a content-specific adaptive logic, evolutionarily tailored for the domain of social exchange (described in Cosmides & Tooby, 1989).

---

[3] *Programs that cheat by design* is a more general formulation of the principle, which does not require the human ability to form mental representations of intentions or to infer the presence of intentional mental states in others. An analogy to deception may be useful: Birds that feign a broken wing to lure predators away from their nests are equipped with programs that are designed to deceive the predator, but the cognitive procedures involved need not include a mental representation of an *intention* to deceive.

Cheating does involve the violation of a conditional rule, but note that it is a particular *kind* of violation of a particular *kind* of conditional rule. The rule must fit the template for a *social contract;* the violation must be one in which an individual *intentionally* took what *that* individual considered to be a *benefit* and did so without satisfying the requirement.

Formal logics (e.g., the propositional calculus) are content blind; the definition of *violation* in standard logics applies to all conditional rules, whether they are social contracts, threats, or descriptions of how the world works. But, as shown later, the definition of cheating implied by design features D1 through D4 does not map onto this content-blind definition of violation. What counts as cheating in social exchange is so content sensitive that a detection mechanism equipped only with a domain-general definition of violation would not be able to solve the problem of cheater detection. This suggests that there should be a program specialized for cheater detection. To operate, this program would have to function as a subcomponent of a system that, because of its domain-specialized structure, is well designed for detecting social conditionals involving exchange, interpreting their meaning, and successfully solving the inferential problems they pose: *social contract algorithms.*

CONDITIONAL REASONING AND SOCIAL EXCHANGE

Reciprocation is, by definition, social behavior that is conditional: You agree to deliver a benefit *conditionally* (conditional on the other person doing what you required in return). Understanding it therefore requires conditional reasoning.

Because engaging in social exchange requires conditional reasoning, investigations of conditional reasoning can be used to test for the presence of social contract algorithms. The hypothesis that the brain contains social contract algorithms predicts a dissociation in reasoning performance by *content:* a sharply enhanced ability to reason adaptively about conditional rules when those rules specify a social exchange. The null hypothesis is that there is nothing specialized in the brain for social exchange. This hypothesis follows from the traditional assumption that reasoning is caused by content-independent processes. It predicts no enhanced conditional reasoning performance specifically triggered by social exchanges as compared to other contents.

A standard tool for investigating conditional reasoning is the Wason selection task, which asks you to look for potential violations of a conditional rule of the form *If P, then Q* (Wason, 1966, 1983; Wason & Johnson-Laird, 1972). Using this task, an extensive series of experiments has been conducted that addresses the following questions:

- Do our minds include cognitive machinery that is *specialized* for reasoning about social exchange (alongside other domain-specific mechanisms, each specialized for reasoning about a different adaptive domain involving conditional behavior)? Or,
- Is the cognitive machinery that causes good conditional reasoning general—does it operate well regardless of content?

If the human brain had cognitive machinery that causes good conditional reasoning regardless of content, then people should be good at tasks requiring conditional reasoning. For example, they should be good at detecting violations of

Ebbinghaus disease was recently identified and is not yet well understood. So an international committee of physicians who have experience with this disease were assembled. Their goal was to characterize the symptoms, and develop surefire ways of diagnosing it.

Patients afflicted with Ebbinghaus disease have many different symptoms: nose bleeds, headaches, ringing in the ears, and others. Diagnosing it is difficult because a patient may have the disease, yet not manifest all of the symptoms. Dr. Buchner, an expert on the disease, said that the following rule holds:

"If a person has Ebbinghaus disease, then that person will be forgetful."
If   *P*   *then*   *Q*

Dr. Buchner may be wrong, however. You are interested in seeing whether there are any patients whose symptoms violate this rule.

The cards below represent four patients in your hospital. Each card represents one patient. One side of the card tells whether or not the patient has Ebbinghaus disease, and the other side tells whether or not that patient is forgetful.

Which of the following card(s) would you definitely need to turn over to see if any of these cases violate Dr. Buchner's rule: "If a person has Ebbinghaus disease, then that person will be forgetful." Don't turn over any more cards than are absolutely necessary.

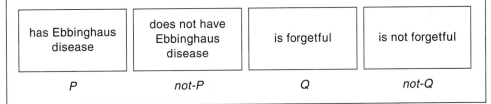

Figure 20.1   The Wason Selection Task (Descriptive Rule, Familiar Content). In a Wason task, there is always a rule of the form, *If P then Q,* and four cards showing the values *P, not-P, Q,* and *not-Q* (respectively) on the side that the subject can see. From a logical point of view, only the combination of *P* and *not-Q* can violate this rule, so the correct answer is to check the *P* card (to see if it has a *not-Q* on the back), the *not-Q* card (to see if it has a *P* on the back), and no others. Few subjects answer correctly, however, when the conditional rule is descriptive (indicative), even when its content is familiar; e.g., only 26% of subjects answered the above problem correctly (by choosing "has Ebbinghaus disease" and "is not forgetful"). Most choose either *P* alone, or *P* and *Q.* (The italicized *P*s and *Q*s are not in problems given to subjects.)

conditional rules. Yet studies with the Wason selection task show that they are not. Consider the Wason task in Figure 20.1. The correct answer (choose *P,* choose *not-Q*) would be intuitively obvious if our minds were equipped with reasoning procedures specialized for detecting *logical* violations of conditional rules. But this answer is not obvious to people. Studies in many nations have shown that reasoning performance is low on descriptive (indicative) rules like the rule in Figure 20.1: Only 5% to 30% of people give the logically correct answer, even when the rule involves familiar terms drawn from everyday life (Cosmides, 1989; Manktelow & Evans, 1979; Sugiyama et al., 2002; Wason, 1966, 1983). Interestingly, explicit instruction in logical inference does not boost performance: People who have just completed a semester-long college course in logic perform no better than people without this formal training (Cheng, Holyoak, Nisbett, & Oliver, 1986).

Formal logics, such as the propositional calculus, provide a standard of good design for content-general conditional reasoning: Their inference rules were constructed by philosophers to generate true conclusions from true premises, regardless of the subject matter one is asked to reason about. When human performance is measured against this standard, there is little evidence of good design: Conditional rules with descriptive content fail to elicit logically correct performance from 70% to 95% of people. Therefore, one can reject the hypothesis that the human mind is equipped with cognitive machinery that causes good conditional reasoning across all content domains.

A DISSOCIATION BY CONTENT

People are poor at detecting violations of conditional rules when their content is descriptive. Does this result generalize to conditional rules that express a social contract? No. People who ordinarily cannot detect violations of if-then rules can do so easily and accurately when that violation represents cheating in a situation of social exchange. This pattern—good violation detection for social contracts but not for descriptive rules—is a dissociation in reasoning elicited by differences in the conditional rule's *content*. It provides (initial) evidence that the mind has reasoning procedures specialized for detecting cheaters.

More specifically, when asked to look for violations of a conditional rule that fits the social contract template—"If you take benefit B, then you must satisfy requirement R" (e.g., "If you borrow my car, then you have to fill up the tank with gas")—people check the individual who accepted the benefit (borrowed the car; P) and the individual who did not satisfy the requirement (did not fill the tank; *not-Q*). These are the cases that represent potential cheaters (Figure 20.2a). The adaptively correct answer is immediately obvious to most subjects, who commonly experience a pop-out effect. No formal training is needed. Whenever the content of a problem asks one to look for cheaters in a social exchange, subjects experience the problem as simple to solve, and their performance jumps dramatically. In general, 65% to 80% of subjects get it right, the highest performance found for a task of this kind (for reviews, see Cosmides, 1985, 1989; Cosmides & Tooby, 1992, 1997; Fiddick et al., 2000; Gigerenzer & Hug, 1992; Platt & Griggs, 1993).

Given the content-blind syntax of formal logic, investigating the person who borrowed the car (P) and the person who did not fill the gas tank (*not-Q*) is logically equivalent to investigating the person with Ebbinghaus disease (P) and the person who is not forgetful (*not-Q*) for the Ebbinghaus problem in Figure 20.1. But everywhere it has been tested (adults in the United States, United Kingdom, Germany, Italy, France, Hong Kong, Japan; schoolchildren in Quito, Ecuador; Shiwiar hunter-horticulturalists in the Ecuadorian Amazon), people do not treat social exchange problems as equivalent to other kinds of conditional reasoning problems (Cheng & Holyoak, 1985; Cosmides, 1989; Hasegawa & Hiraishi, 2000; Platt & Griggs, 1993; Sugiyama et al., 2002; supports D5, D6). Their minds distinguish social exchange content from other domains, and reason as if they were translating their terms into representational primitives such as *benefit, cost, obligation, entitlement, intentional,* and *agent* (Figure 20.2b; Cosmides & Tooby, 1992; Fiddick et al., 2000). Reasoning problems could be sorted into indefinitely many categories

A.

Teenagers who don't have their own cars usually end up borrowing their parents' cars. In return for the privilege of borrowing the car, the Carter's have given their kids the rule,

"If you borrow my car, then you have to fill up the tank with gas."

Of course, teenagers are sometimes irresponsible. You are interested in seeing whether any of the Carter teenagers broke this rule.

The cards below represent four of the Carter teenagers. Each card represents one teenager. One side of the card tells whether or not a teenager has borrowed the parents' car on a particular day, and the other side tells whether or not that teenager filled up the tank with gas on that day.

Which of the following card(s) would you definitely need to turn over to see if any of these teenagers are breaking their parents' rule: "If you borrow my car, then you have to fill up the tank with gas." Don't turn over any more cards than are absolutely necessary.

borrowed car	did not borrow car	filled up tank with gas	did not fill up tank with gas

B.

The mind translates social contracts into representations of benefits and requirements, and it inserts concepts such as "entitled to" and "obligated to", whether they are specified or not.

How the mind "sees" the social contract above is shown in **bold italics**.

"If you borrow my car, then you have to fill up the tank with gas."

If you take the benefit, then you are obligated to satisfy the requirement.

borrowed car	did not borrow car	filled up tank with gas	did not fill up tank with gas
= accepted the benefit	*= did not accept the benefit*	*= satisfied the requirement*	*= did not satisfy the requirement*

Figure 20.2 Wason Task with a Social Contract Rule. (A) In response to this social contract problem, 76% of subjects chose *P and not-Q* ("borrowed the car" and "did not fill the tank with gas")—the cards that represent potential cheaters. Yet only 26% chose this (logically correct) answer in response to the descriptive rule in Figure 20.1. Although this social contract rule involves familiar items, unfamiliar social contracts elicit the same high performance. (B) How the mind represents the social contract shown in (A). According to inferential rules specialized for social exchange (but not according to formal logic), "If you take the benefit, then you are obligated to satisfy the requirement" implies "If you satisfy the requirement, then you are entitled to take the benefit". Consequently, the rule in (A) implies: "If you fill the tank with gas, then you may borrow the car" (see Figure 20.4, switched social contracts).

Table 20.1
Alternative (By-product) Hypotheses Eliminated

B1. That familiarity can explain the social contract effect.

B2. That social contract content merely activates the rules of inference of the propositional calculus (logic).

B3. That any problem involving payoffs will elicit the detection of logical violations.

B4. That permission schema theory can explain the social contract effect.

B5. That social contract content merely promotes "clear thinking."

B6. That a content-independent deontic logic can explain social contract reasoning.

B7. That a single mechanism operates on all deontic rules involving subjective utilities.

B8. That relevance theory can explain social contract effects (see also Fiddick et al., 2000).

B9. That rational choice theory can explain social contract effects.

B10. That statistical learning produces the mechanisms that cause social contract reasoning.

based on their content or structure (including the propositional calculus's two content-free categories, antecedent and consequent). Yet, even in remarkably different cultures, the same mental categorization occurs. This cross-culturally recurrent dissociation by content was predicted in advance of its discovery by social contract theory's adaptationist analysis.

This pattern of good performance on reasoning problems involving social exchange is what we would expect if the mind reliably develops neurocognitive adaptations for reasoning about social exchange. But more design evidence is needed. Later we review experiments conducted to test for design features D1 through D6: features that should be present if a system specialized for social exchange exists.

In addition to producing evidence of good design for social exchange, recall that one must also show that the system's properties are not better explained as a solution to an alternative adaptive problem or by chance (Tooby & Cosmides, 1992, Chapter 1, this volume). Each experiment testing for a design feature was also constructed to pit the adaptive specialization hypothesis against at least one alternative by-product hypothesis, so by-product and design feature implications are discussed in tandem. As we show, reasoning performance on social contracts is not explained by familiarity effects, by a content-free formal logic, by a permission schema, or by a general deontic logic. Table 20.1 lists the by-product hypotheses that have been tested and eliminated.

DO UNFAMILIAR SOCIAL CONTRACTS ELICIT CHEATER DETECTION? (D5)

An individual needs to understand each new opportunity to exchange as it arises, so it was predicted that social exchange reasoning should operate even for unfamiliar social contract rules (D5). This distinguishes social contract theory strongly from theories that explain reasoning performance as the product of general learning strategies plus experience: The most natural prediction for such skill-acquisition theories is that performance should be a function of familiarity.

The evidence supports social contract theory: Cheater detection occurs even when the social contract is wildly unfamiliar (Figure 20.3a). For example, the rule, "If a man eats cassava root, then he must have a tattoo on his face," can be made to fit the social contract template by explaining that the people involved consider eating cassava root to be a benefit (the rule then implies that having a tattoo is the requirement an individual must satisfy to be eligible for that benefit). When given this context, this outlandish, culturally alien rule elicits the same high level of cheater detection as highly familiar social exchange rules. This surprising result has been replicated for many different unfamiliar rules (Cosmides, 1985, 1989; Cosmides & Tooby, 1992; Gigerenzer & Hug, 1992; Platt & Griggs, 1993).

ELIMINATING FAMILIARITY (B1)

The dissociation by content—good performance for social contract rules but not for descriptive ones—has nothing to do with the familiarity of the rules tested.

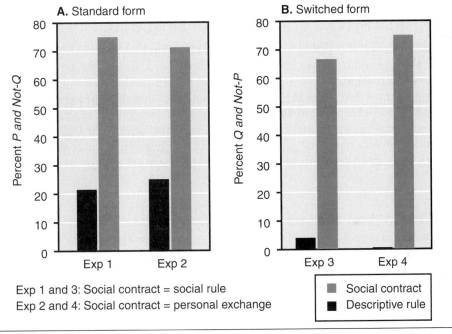

Figure 20.3 Detecting Violations of Unfamiliar Conditional Rules: Social Contracts versus Descriptive Rules. In these experiments, the same, unfamiliar rule was embedded either in a story that caused it to be interpreted as a social contract or in a story that caused it to be interpreted as a rule describing some state of the world. For social contracts, the correct answer is always to pick the *benefit accepted* card and the *requirement not satisfied* card. (A) For standard social contracts, these correspond to the logical categories *P* and *not-Q*. *P and not-Q* also happens to be the logically correct answer. Over 70% of subjects chose these cards for the social contracts, but fewer than 25% chose them for the matching descriptive rules. (B) For switched social contracts, the *benefit accepted* and *requirement not satisfied* cards correspond to the logical categories *Q* and *not-P*. This is not a logically correct response. Nevertheless, about 70% of subjects chose it for the social contracts; virtually no one chose it for the matching descriptive rules (see Figure 20.4).

Familiarity is neither necessary nor sufficient for eliciting high performance (B1 of Table 20.1).

First, familiarity does not produce high levels of performance for descriptive rules (Cosmides, 1989; Manktelow & Evans, 1979). Note, for example, that the Ebbinghaus problem in Figure 20.1 involves a familiar causal relationship (a disease causing a symptom) embedded in a real-world context. Yet only 26% of 111 college students that we tested produced the logically correct answer, *P & not-Q*, for this problem. If familiarity fails to elicit high performance on descriptive rules, then it also fails as an explanation for high performance on social contracts.

Second, the fact that unfamiliar social contracts elicit high performance shows that familiarity is not necessary for eliciting violation detection. Third (and most surprising), people are just as good at detecting cheaters on culturally unfamiliar or imaginary social contracts as they are for ones that are completely familiar (Cosmides, 1985). This provides a challenge for any counterhypothesis resting on a general-learning skill acquisition account (most of which rely on familiarity and repetition).

ADAPTIVE LOGIC, NOT FORMAL LOGIC (D3, D6)

As shown earlier, it is possible to construct social contract problems that will elicit a logically correct answer. But this is not because social exchange content activates logical reasoning.

Good cheater detection is not the same as good detection of logical violations (and vice versa). Hence, problems can be created in which the search for cheaters will result in a logically incorrect response (and the search for logical violations will fail to detect cheaters; see Figure 20.4). When given such problems, people look for cheaters, thereby giving a logically incorrect answer (*Q* and *not-P*).

PERSPECTIVE CHANGE

As predicted (D3), the mind's automatically deployed definition of cheating is tied to the perspective you are taking (Gigerenzer & Hug, 1992). For example, consider the following social contract:

> [1] If an employee is to get a pension, then that employee must have worked for the firm for over 10 years.

This rule elicits different answers depending on whether subjects are cued into the role of employer or employee. Those in the employer role look for cheating by employees, investigating cases of *P* and *not-Q* (employees with pensions; employees who have worked for fewer than 10 years). Those in the employee role look for cheating by employers, investigating cases of *not-P* and *Q* (employees with no pension; employees who have worked more than 10 years). *Not-P & Q* is correct if the goal is to find out whether the employer is cheating employees. But it is not *logically* correct.[4]

In social exchange, the benefit to one agent is the requirement for the other: For example, giving pensions to employees benefits the employees but is the require-

---

[4] Moreover, the propositional calculus contains no rules of inference that allow *If P, then Q* to be translated as *If Q, then P* (i.e., no rule for translating [1] as [2]; see text) and then applying the logical definition of violation to [2] to arrive at the employee perspective answer (see Fiddick et al., 2000).

Consider the following rule:

Standard format:

*If you take the **benefit,** then satisfy my **requirement*** (e.g., "If I give you $50, then give
                                                                  me your watch.")

| *If* | *P* | *then* | *Q* |

Switched format:

*If you satisfy my **requirement,** then take the **benefit*** (e.g., "If you give me your watch,
                                                                then I'll give you $50.")

| *If* | *P* | *then* | *Q* |

The cards below have information about four people to whom this offer was made.
Each card represents one person. One side of a card tells whether the person accepted the benefit, and the other side of the card tells whether that person satisfied
the requirement. Indicate only those card(s) you definitely need to turn over to see
if any of these people have violated the rule.

	✔			✔
	Benefit accepted	Benefit not accepted	Requirement satisfied	Requirement not satisfied
Standard:	*P*	*not-P*	*Q*	*not-Q*
Switched:	*Q*	*not-Q*	*P*	*not-P*

Figure 20.4   Generic Structure of a Wason Task When the Conditional Rule Is a Social
Contract. A social contract can be translated into either social contract terms (benefits
and requirements) or logical terms (*P*s and *Q*s). Check marks indicate the correct card
choices if one is looking for cheaters—these should be chosen by a cheater detection
subroutine, whether the exchange was expressed in a standard or switched format. This
results in a logically incorrect answer (*Q* and *not-P*) when the rule is expressed in the
switched format, and a logically correct answer (*P* and *not-Q*) when the rule is expressed
in the standard format. By testing switched social contracts, one can see that the reasoning procedures activated cause one to detect cheaters, not logical violations (see Figure
20.3B). Note that a logically correct response to a switched social contract—where *P* =
requirement satisfied and *not-Q = benefit not accepted*—would fail to detect cheaters.

ment the employer must satisfy (in exchange for > 10 years of employee service).
To capture the distinction between the perspectives of the two agents, rules of inference for social exchange must be content sensitive, defining benefits and requirements relative to the agents involved. Because logical procedures are blind
to the content of the propositions over which they operate, they have no way of
representing the values of an action to each agent involved.

SWITCHED SOCIAL CONTRACTS

By moving the benefit from the antecedent clause (*P*) to the consequent clause
(*Q*), one can construct a social exchange problem for which the adaptively correct
cheater detection response is logically incorrect.

According to the propositional calculus (a formal logic), *If P then Q* does not imply *If Q then P*; therefore, "If you take the benefit, then you are obligated to satisfy the requirement," does not imply, "If you satisfy the requirement, then you are entitled to take the benefit." But inferential rules specialized for social exchange do license the latter inference (Cosmides & Tooby, 1989). Consequently, social exchange inferences (but not logical ones) should cause rule [1] above to be interpreted as implying:

> [2] If an employee has worked for the firm for over 10 years, then that employee gets a pension.

Assume you are concerned that employees have been cheating and are asked to check whether any employees have violated the rule. Although [2] and [1] are not logically equivalent, our minds interpret them as expressing the same social contract agreement. Hence, in both cases, a subroutine for detecting cheaters should cause you to check employees who have taken the benefit (gotten a pension) and employees who have not met the requirement (worked < 10 years).

But notice that these cards fall into different logical categories when the benefit to the potential cheater is in the antecedent clause versus the consequent clause (standard versus switched format, respectively; Figure 20.4). When the rule is expressed in the switched format, "got a pension" corresponds to the logical category Q, and "worked less than 10 years" corresponds to the logical category *not-P*. This answer will correctly detect employees who are cheating, but it is logically incorrect. When the rule is expressed in the standard format, the same two cards correspond to P and *not-Q*. For standard format social contracts, the cheater detection subroutine will produce the same answer as logical procedures would—not because this response is logically correct, but because it will detect cheaters.

When given switched social contracts like [2], subjects overwhelmingly respond by choosing *Q & not-P*, a logically incorrect answer that correctly detects cheaters (Figure 20.3b; Cosmides, 1985, 1989; Gigerenzer & Hug, 1992; supports D2, D6). Indeed, when subjects' choices are classified by *logical* category, it looks like standard and switched social contracts elicit different responses. But when their choices are classified by *social contract* category, they are invariant: For both rule formats, people choose the cards that represent an agent who took the benefit and an agent who did not meet the requirement.

This robust pattern occurs precisely because social exchange reasoning is sensitive to content: It responds to a syntax of agent-relative benefits and requirements, not antecedents and consequents. Logical procedures would fail to detect cheaters on switched social contracts. Being content blind, their inferential rules are doomed to checking P and *not-Q*, even when these cards correspond to potential altruists (or fools)—that is, to people who have fulfilled the requirement and people who have not accepted the benefit.

ELIMINATING LOGIC (B2, B3)

Consider the following by-product hypothesis: The dissociation between social contracts and descriptive rules is not caused by a cheater detection mechanism.

Instead, the human cognitive architecture applies content-free rules of logical inference, such as *modus ponens* and *modus tollens.* These logical rules are activated by social contract content but not by other kinds of content, and that causes the spike in *P & not-Q* answers for social contracts.

The results of the switched social contract and the perspective change experiments eliminate this hypothesis. Social contracts elicit a logically incorrect answer, *Q & not-P,* when this answer would correctly detect cheaters. Logical rules applied to the syntax of the material conditional cannot explain this pattern, because these rules would always choose a true antecedent and false consequent (*P & not-Q*), never a true consequent and false antecedent (*Q & not-P*).

There is an active debate about whether the human cognitive architecture includes content-blind rules of logical inference, which are sometimes dormant and sometimes activated (e.g., Bonatti, 1994; Rips, 1994; Sperber, Cara, & Girotto, 1995). We are agnostic about that issue. What is clear, however, is that such rules cannot explain reasoning about social contracts (for further evidence, see Fiddick et al., 2000).

DEDICATED SYSTEM OR GENERAL INTELLIGENCE?

Social contract reasoning can be maintained in the face of impairments in general logical reasoning. Individuals with schizophrenia manifest deficits on virtually any test of general intellectual functioning they are given (McKenna, Clare, & Baddeley, 1995). Yet their ability to detect cheaters can remain intact. Maljkovic (1987) tested the reasoning of patients suffering from positive symptoms of schizophrenia, comparing their performance with that of hospitalized (nonpsychotic) control patients. Compared to the control patients, the schizophrenic patients were impaired on more general (non-Wason) tests of logical reasoning, in a way typical of individuals with frontal lobe dysfunction. But their ability to detect cheaters on Wason tasks was unimpaired. Indeed, it was indistinguishable from the controls and showed the typical dissociation by content. This selective preservation of social exchange reasoning is consistent with the notion that reasoning about social exchange is handled by a dedicated system, which can operate even when the systems responsible for more general reasoning are damaged. It provides further support for the claim that social exchange reasoning is functionally and neurally distinct from more general abilities to process information or behave intelligently.

HOW MANY SPECIALIZATIONS FOR CONDITIONAL REASONING?

Social contracts are not the only conditional rules for which natural selection should have designed specialized reasoning mechanisms (Cosmides, 1989). Indeed, good violation detection is also found for conditional rules drawn from two other domains: threats and precautions. Is good performance across these three domains caused by a single neurocognitive system or by several functionally distinct ones? If a single system causes reasoning about all three domains, then we should not claim that cheater detection is caused by adaptations that evolved for that specific function.

The notion of multiple adaptive specializations is commonplace in physiology: The body is composed of many organs, each designed for a different function. Yet many psychologists cringe at the notion of multiple adaptive specializations when these are computational. Indeed, evolutionary approaches to psychology foundered in the early 1920s on what was seen as an unfounded multiplication of "instincts."

That was before the cognitive revolution, with its language for describing what the brain does in information processing terms and its empirical methods for revealing the structure of representations and processes. Rather than relying on a priori arguments about what should or could be done by a single mechanism, we can now empirically test whether processing about two domains is accomplished by one mechanism or two. We should not imagine that there is a separate specialization for solving each and every adaptive problem. Nor should real differences in processing be ignored in a misguided effort to explain all performance by reference to a single mechanism. As Einstein once said, "Make everything as simple as possible, but no simpler."

CONDITIONAL REASONING ABOUT OTHER SOCIAL DOMAINS

Threats specify a conditional rule (*If you don't do what I require, I will harm you*), which the threatener can violate in two ways: by bluffing or by double-crossing. It appears that people are good at detecting bluffs and double-crosses on Wason tasks that test threats (with an interesting sex difference never found for social exchange problems; Tooby & Cosmides, 1989). However, these violations do not map onto the definition of cheating and, therefore, cannot be detected by a cheater detection mechanism. This suggests that reasoning about social contracts and threats is caused by two distinct mechanisms. (So far, no theory advocating a single mechanism for reasoning about these two domains has been proposed. Threats are not deontic; see later discussion.)

Also of adaptive importance is the ability to detect when someone is in danger by virtue of having violated a precautionary rule. These rules have the general form, "*If one is to engage in hazardous activity H, then one must take precaution R*" (e.g., "If you are working with toxic gases, then wear a gas mask"). Using the Wason task, it has been shown that people are very good at detecting potential violators of precautionary rules; that is, individuals who have engaged in a hazardous activity without taking the appropriate precaution (e.g., those working with toxic gases [P] and those not wearing a gas mask [not-Q]). Indeed, relative to descriptive rules, precautions show a spike in performance, and the magnitude of this content effect is about the same as that for detecting cheaters on social contracts (Cheng & Holyoak, 1989; Fiddick et al., 2000; Manktelow & Over, 1988, 1990, 1991; Stone et al., 2002).

A system well designed for reasoning about hazards and precautions should have properties different from one for detecting cheaters, many of which have been tested for and found (Fiddick, 1998, 2004; Fiddick et al., 2000; Pereyra & Nieto, in press; Stone et al., 2002). Therefore, alongside a specialization for reasoning about social exchange, the human cognitive architecture should contain computational machinery specialized for managing hazards, which causes good violation detection on precautionary rules. Obsessive-compulsive disorder, with its compulsive worrying, checking, and precaution taking, may be caused by a misfiring of this precautionary system (Cosmides & Tooby, 1999; Leckman & Mayes, 1998, 1999).

An alternative view is that reasoning about social contracts and precautionary rules is generated by a single mechanism. Some view both social contracts and precautions as deontic rules (i.e., rules specifying obligations and entitlements) and wonder whether there is a general system for reasoning about deontic conditionals. More specifically, Cheng and Holyoak (1985, 1989) have proposed that inferences about both types of rule are generated by a permission schema, which operates over a larger class of problems.[5]

Can positing a permission schema explain the full set of relevant results? Or are they more parsimoniously explained by positing two separate adaptive specializations, one for social contracts and one for precautionary rules? We are looking for a model that is as simple as possible, but no simpler.

SOCIAL CONTRACT ALGORITHMS OR A PERMISSION SCHEMA? LOOKING FOR DISSOCIATIONS *WITHIN* THE CLASS OF PERMISSION RULES (D1, D2, D4)

Permission rules are a species of conditional rule. According to Cheng and Holyoak (1985, 1989), these rules are imposed by an authority to achieve a social purpose, and they specify the conditions under which an individual is permitted to take an action. Cheng and Holyoak speculate that repeated encounters with such social rules cause domain-general learning mechanisms to induce a *permission schema*, consisting of four production rules (see Table 20.2 on p. 606). This schema generates inferences about any conditional rule that fits the following template: "If action A is to be taken, then precondition R must be satisfied."

Social contracts fit this template. In social exchange, an agent *permits* you to take a benefit from him or her, conditional on your having met the agent's requirement. There are, however, many situations other than social exchange in which an action is permitted conditionally. Permission schema theory predicts uniformly high performance for the entire class of permission rules, a set that is larger, more general, and more inclusive than the set of all social contracts (see Figure 20.5 on p. 607).

On this view, a neurocognitive system specialized for reasoning about social exchange, with a subroutine for cheater detection, does not exist. According to their hypothesis, a permission schema causes good violation detection for all permission rules; social contracts are a subset of the class of permission rules; therefore, cheater detection occurs as a by-product of the more domain-general permission schema (Cheng & Holyoak, 1985, 1989).

In contrast, the adaptive specialization hypothesis holds that the design of the reasoning system that causes cheater detection is more precise and functionally specialized than the design of the permission schema. Social contract algorithms should have design features that are lacking from the permission schema, such as responsivity to benefits and intentionality. As a result, removing benefits (D1, D2) and/or intentionality (D4) from a social contract should produce a permission rule that fails to elicit good violation detection on the Wason task.

---

[5] Cheng and Holyoak (1985) also propose an obligation schema, but permission and obligation schemas do not lead to different predictions on the kinds of rules usually tested (see Cosmides, 1989; Rips, 1994, p. 413).

Table 20.2
The Permission Schema Is Composed of Four Production Rules[a]

Rule 1: If the action is to be taken, then the precondition must be satisfied.[b]
Rule 2: If the action is not to be taken, then the precondition need not be satisfied.
Rule 3: If the precondition is satisfied, then the action may be taken.
Rule 4: If the precondition is not satisfied, then the action must not be taken.

[a] Cheng and Holyoak, 1985.
[b] Social contracts and precautions fit the template of Rule 1:
  If the benefit is to be taken, then the requirement must be satisfied.
  If the hazardous action is to be taken, then the precaution must be taken.

As Sherlock Holmes might put it, we are looking for the dog that did not bark: permission rules that do *not* elicit good violation detection. That discovery would falsify permission schema theory. Social contract theory predicts functional dissociations *within* the class of permission rules whereas permission schema theory does not.

NO BENEFITS, NO SOCIAL EXCHANGE REASONING: TESTING D1 AND D2

To trigger cheater detection (D2) and inference procedures specialized for interpreting social exchanges (D1), a rule needs to regulate access to benefits, not to actions more generally. Does reasoning performance change when benefits are removed?

BENEFITS ARE NECESSARY FOR CHEATER DETECTION (D1, D2)

The function of a social exchange for each participant is to gain access to benefits that would otherwise be unavailable to them. Therefore, an important cue that a conditional rule is a social contract is the presence in it of a desired benefit under the control of an agent. *Taking a benefit* is a representational primitive within the social contract template *If you take benefit B, then you must satisfy requirement R.*

The permission schema template has representational primitives with a larger scope than that proposed for social contract algorithms. For example, *taking a benefit* is *taking an action,* but not all cases of taking actions are cases of taking benefits. As a result, all social contracts are permission rules, but not all permission rules are social contracts. Precautionary rules can also be construed as permission rules (although they need not be; see Fiddick et al., 2000, exp. 2). They, too, have a more restricted scope: *Hazardous actions* are a subset of *actions; precautions* are a subset of *preconditions.*

Note, however, that there are permission rules that are neither social contracts nor precautionary rules (see Figure 20.5). This is because there are actions an individual can take that are not *benefits* (social contract theory) and that are not *hazardous* (hazard management theory). Indeed, we encounter many rules like this in everyday life—bureaucratic and corporate rules, for example, often state a procedure that is to be followed without specifying a benefit (or a danger). If the mind has a permission schema, then people should be good at detecting violations of

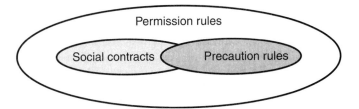

Figure 20.5 The Class of Permission Rules Is Larger Than, and Includes, Social Contracts and Precautionary Rules. Many of the permission rules we encounter in everyday life are neither social contracts nor precautions (white area). Rules of civil society (etiquette, customs, traditions), bureaucratic rules, corporate rules—many of these are conditional rules that do not regulate access to a benefit or involve a danger. Permission schema theory (see Table 20.2) predicts high performance for all permission rules; however, permission rules that fall into the white area do not elicit the high levels of performance that social contracts and precaution rules do. Neuropsychological and cognitive tests show that performance on social contracts dissociates from other permission rules (white area), from precautionary rules, and from the general class of deontic rules involving subjective utilities. These dissociations would be impossible if reasoning about social contracts and precautions were caused by a single schema that is general to the domain of permission rules.

rules that fall into the white area of Figure 20.5, that is, permission rules that are neither social contracts nor precautionary. But they are not. Benefits are necessary for cheater detection.

Using the Wason task, several labs have tested permission rules that involve no benefit (and are not precautionary). As predicted by social contract theory, these do not elicit high levels of violation detection. For example, Cosmides and Tooby (1992) constructed Wason tasks in which the elders (authorities) were creating laws governing the conditions under which adolescents are permitted to take certain actions. For all tasks, the law fit the template for a permission rule. The permission rules tested differed in just one respect: whether the action to be taken is a benefit or an unpleasant chore. The critical conditions compared performance on these two rules:

[3] "If one goes out at night, then one must tie a small piece of red volcanic rock around one's ankle."

[4] "If one takes out the garbage at night, then one must tie a small piece of red volcanic rock around one's ankle."

A cheater detection subroutine looks for benefits illicitly taken; without a benefit, it doesn't know what kind of violation to look for (D1, D2). When the permitted action was a benefit (getting to go out at night), 80% of subjects answered correctly; when it was a chore (taking out the garbage), only 44% did so. This dramatic decrease in violation detection was predicted in advance by social contract theory. Moreover, it violates the central prediction of permission schema theory: that being a permission rule is sufficient to facilitate violation detection. There are now many experiments showing poor violation detection with permission rules that lack a benefit (e.g., Barrett, 1999; Cosmides, 1989, exp. 5; Fiddick, 2003; Manktelow & Over, 1991; Platt & Griggs, 1993).

This is another dissociation by content, but this time it is *within* the domain of permission rules. To elicit cheater detection, a permission rule must be interpreted as restricting access *to a benefit*. It supports the psychological reality of the representational primitives posited by social contract theory, showing that the representations necessary to trigger differential reasoning are more content specific than those of the permission schema.

Benefits Trigger Social Contract Interpretations (D1)

The Wason experiments just described tested D1 and D2 in tandem. But D1—the claim that benefits are necessary for permission rules to be *interpreted* as social contracts—receives support independent of experiments testing D2 from studies of moral reasoning. Fiddick (2004) asked subjects what justifies various permission rules and when an individual should be allowed to break them. The rules were closely matched for surface content, and context was used to vary their interpretation. The permission rule that lacked a benefit (a precautionary one) elicited different judgments from permission rules that restricted access to a benefit (the social contracts). Whereas social agreement and morality, rather than facts, were more often cited as justifying the social contract rules, facts (about poisons and antidotes) rather than social agreement were seen as justifying the precautionary rule. Whereas most subjects thought it was acceptable to break the social contract rules if you were not a member of the group that created them, they thought the precautionary rule should always be followed by people everywhere. Moreover, the explicit exchange rule triggered very specific inferences about the conditions under which it could be broken: Those who had received a benefit could be released from their obligation to reciprocate, *but only by those who had provided the benefit to them* (i.e., the obligation could not be voided by a group leader or by a consensus of the recipients themselves). The inferences subjects made about the rules restricting access to a benefit follow directly from the grammar of social exchange laid out in social contract theory (Cosmides & Tooby, 1989). These inferences were not—and should not—be applied to precautionary rules (see also Fiddick et al., 2000). The presence of a benefit also predicts inferences about emotional reactions to seeing someone violate a permission rule: Social contract violations were thought to trigger anger whereas precautionary violations were thought to trigger fear (Fiddick, 2004). None of these dissociations within the realm of permission rules are predicted by permission schema theory.

INTENTIONAL VIOLATIONS VERSUS INNOCENT MISTAKES: TESTING D4

Intentionality plays no role in permission schema theory. Whenever the action has been taken but the precondition has not been satisfied, the permission schema should register that a *violation* has occurred. As a result, people should be good at detecting violations of permission rules, whether the violations occurred by accident or by intention. In contrast, social contract theory predicts a mechanism that looks for *intentional* violations (D4).

Program designs that cause unconditional helping are not evolutionarily stable strategies. Conditional helping can be an ESS because cheater detection provides a specific fitness advantage unavailable to unconditional helpers: By identifying cheaters, the conditional helper can avoid squandering costly cooperative efforts in the future on those who, by virtue of having an alternative program design, will not reciprocate. This means the evolutionary function of a cheater detection subroutine is to correctly connect an attributed disposition (to cheat) with a person (a cheater). It is not simply to recognize instances wherein an individual did not get what he or she was entitled to. Violations of social contracts are relevant only insofar as they reveal individuals disposed to cheat—individuals who cheat by design, not by accident. Noncompliance caused by factors other than disposition, such as accidental violations and other innocent mistakes, does not reveal the disposition or design of the exchange partner. Accidents may result in someone being cheated, but without indicating the presence of a cheater.[6]

Therefore, social contract theory predicts an additional level of cognitive specialization beyond looking for violations of a social contract. Accidental violations of social contracts will not fully engage the cheater detection subroutine; intentional violations will (D4).

A Dissociation for Social Contracts

Given the same social exchange rule, one can manipulate contextual factors to change the nature of the violation from intentional cheating to an innocent mistake. One experiment, for example, compared a condition in which the potential rule violator was inattentive but well meaning to a condition in which she had an incentive to intentionally cheat. Varying intentionality caused a radical change in performance, from 68% correct in the intentional cheating condition to 27% correct in the innocent mistake condition (Cosmides, Barrett, & Tooby, forthcoming; supports D4; disconfirms B1–B8). Fiddick (1998, 2004) found the same effect (as did Gigerenzer & Hug, 1992, using a different context manipulation).

In both scenarios, violating the rule would result in someone being cheated, yet high performance occurred only when being cheated was caused by a cheater. Barrett (1999) conducted a series of parametric studies to find out whether the drop in performance in the innocent mistake condition was caused by the violator's lack of intentionality (D4) or by the violator's failure to benefit from her mistake (D2; see earlier discussion, on the necessity of *benefits* to elicit cheater detection). He found that both factors independently contributed to the drop, equally and additively. Thus, the same decrease in performance occurred whether (1) violators would benefit from their innocent mistakes, or (2) violators wanted to break the rule on purpose but would not benefit from doing so. For scenarios missing both factors (i.e., accidental violations that do not benefit the violator), performance dropped by twice as much as when just one factor was missing. That is, the more factors relevant to cheater detection are removed, the more performance dropped.

In bargaining games, experimental economists have found that subjects are twice as likely to punish defections (failures to reciprocate) when it is clear that the defector intended to cheat as when the defector is a novice who might have simply made a mistake (Hoffman, McCabe, & Smith, 1998). This provides

---

[6] Mistakes can be faked, of course. Too many by a given individual should raise suspicion, as should a single mistake that results in a very large benefit. Although this prediction has not been tested yet, we would expect social contract algorithms to be sensitive to these conditions.

interesting convergent evidence, using entirely different methods, for the claim that programs causing social exchange distinguish between mistakes and intentional cheating.

NO DISSOCIATION FOR PRECAUTIONS

Different results are expected for precautionary rules. Intentionality should not matter if the mechanisms that detect violations of precautionary rules were designed to look for people in danger. For example, a person who is not wearing a gas mask while working with toxic gases is in danger, whether that person forgot the gas mask at home (accidental violation) or left it home on purpose (intentional violation). That is, varying the intentionality of a violation should affect social exchange reasoning but not precautionary reasoning. Fiddick (1998, 2004) tested and confirmed this prediction: Precautionary rules elicited high levels of violation detection whether the violations were accidental or intentional, but performance on social contracts was lower for accidental violations than for intentional ones. This functional distinction between precautionary and social exchange reasoning was predicted in advance based on the divergent adaptive functions proposed for these two systems.

ELIMINATING PERMISSION SCHEMA THEORY (B4)

The preceding results violate central predictions of permission schema theory. According to that theory, (1) all permission rules should elicit high levels of violation detection, whether the permitted action is a benefit or a chore; and (2) all permission rules should elicit high levels of violation detection, whether the violation was committed intentionally or accidentally. Both predictions fail. Permission rules fail to elicit high levels of violation detection when the permitted action is neutral or unpleasant (yet not hazardous). Moreover, people are bad at detecting accidental violations of permission rules that are social contracts. Taken together, these results eliminate the hypothesis that the mind contains or develops a permission schema of the kind postulated by Cheng and Holyoak (1985, 1989).

ELIMINATING CONTENT-FREE DEONTIC LOGICS (B6)

The same results also falsify hypothesis B6: that cheater detection on social contracts is caused by a content-free deontic logic (for discussion of this possibility, see Manktelow & Over, 1987). All the benefit and intentionality tests described in this section involved deontic rules, but not all elicited high levels of violation detection.

This same set of results also defeats a related claim by Fodor (2000): that "the putative cheater detection effect on the Wason task is actually a materials artifact" (p. 29). This sweeping conclusion is predicated on the (mistaken) notion that the only evidence for cheater detection comes from experiments in which the control problems are indicative (i.e., descriptive) conditional rules (a curious mistake because it is refuted by experiments with deontic controls, which are presented in the single source Fodor cites: Cosmides & Tooby, 1992). According to Fodor, reasoning *from* a deontic conditional rule that is stipulated to hold is more likely to elicit violation detection than reasoning *about* a rule whose truth is in question (even though in both cases the individual is asked to do the same thing: look for rule violations). Fodor's explanation for this purported difference is deeply flawed (among other things, it assumes what it seeks to explain). But instead of disputing Fodor's reasoning, let us consider whether his artifact explanation can account for the cheater detection results observed. After all, there are many experiments comparing reasoning on social contracts to reasoning about other deontic conditionals.

According to Fodor, high levels of violation detection will be found for any deontic rule that specifies what people are (conditionally) required to do (because all involve reasoning with the law of contradiction). All the permission rules described earlier had precisely this property, all were stipulated to hold, and, in every case, subjects were asked to reason *from* the rule, not about it. If Fodor's artifact hypothesis were correct, all of these rules should have elicited good violation detection. But they did not. Violation detection was poor when the deontic rule lacked a benefit; it was also poor for social contract rules when the potential violator was accused of making innocent mistakes rather than intentional cheating. This pattern is predicted by social contract algorithms, but not by Fodor's hypothesis that reasoning from a deontic conditional rule is sufficient to elicit good violation detection.

B5—that social contract rules elicit good performance merely because we understand what implications follow from them (e.g., Almor & Sloman, 1996)—is eliminated by the intention versus accident dissociation. The same social contract rule—with the same implications—was used in both conditions. If the rule's implications were understood in the intention condition, they should also have been understood in the accident condition. Yet the accident condition failed to elicit good violation detection. Understanding the implications of a social contract may be necessary for cheater detection (Fiddick et al., 2000), but the accident results show this is not sufficient.

In short, it is not enough to admit that moral reasoning, social reasoning, or deontic reasoning is special: The specificity of design for social exchange is far narrower in scope.

A NEUROPSYCHOLOGICAL DISSOCIATION BETWEEN SOCIAL CONTRACTS AND PRECAUTIONS

Like social contracts, precautionary rules are conditional, deontic, and involve subjective utilities. Moreover, people are as good at detecting violators of precautionary rules as they are at detecting cheaters on social contracts. This has led some to conclude that reasoning about social contracts and precautions is caused by a single more general mechanism (e.g., general to permissions, to deontic rules, or to deontic rules involving subjective utilities; Cheng & Holyoak, 1989; Manktelow & Over, 1988, 1990, 1991; Sperber et al., 1995). Most of these one-mechanism theories are undermined by the series of very precise, functional dissociations between social exchange reasoning and reasoning about other deontic permission rules (discussed earlier). But a very strong test, one that addresses *all* one-mechanism theories, would be to find a neural dissociation between social exchange and precautionary reasoning.

ONE MECHANISM OR TWO?

If reasoning about social contracts and precautions is caused by a single mechanism, then neurological damage to that mechanism should lower performance on both types of rule. But if reasoning about these two domains is caused by two functionally distinct mechanisms, then it is possible for social contract algorithms to be damaged while leaving precautionary mechanisms unimpaired, and vice versa.

Stone et al. (2002) developed a battery of Wason tasks that tested social contracts, precautionary rules, and descriptive rules. The social contracts and precautionary rules elicited equally high levels of violation detection from normal subjects (who got 70% and 71% correct, respectively). For each subject, a difference score was calculated: percentage correct for precautions minus percentage correct for social contracts. For normal subjects, these difference scores were all close to zero (Mean = 1.2 percentage points, $SD = 11.5$).

Stone et al. (2002) administered this battery of Wason tasks to R. M., a patient with bilateral damage to his medial orbitofrontal cortex and anterior temporal cortex (which had disconnected both amygdalae). R. M.'s performance on the precaution problems was 70% correct: equivalent to that of the normal controls. In contrast, his performance on the social contract problems was only 39% correct. R. M.'s difference score (precautions minus social contracts) was 31 percentage points. This is 2.7 standard deviations larger than the average difference score of 1.2 percentage points found for control subjects ($p < .005$). In other words, R. M. had a large deficit in his social contract reasoning, alongside normal reasoning about precautionary rules.

Double dissociations are helpful in ruling out differences in task difficulty as a counterexplanation for a given dissociation (Shallice, 1988), but here the tasks were perfectly matched for difficulty. The social contracts and precautionary rules given to R. M. were logically identical, posed identical task demands, and were equally difficult for normal subjects. Moreover, because the performance of the normal controls was not at ceiling, ceiling effects could not be masking real differences in the difficulty of the two sets of problems. In this case, a single dissociation licenses inferences about the underlying mental structures. R. M.'s dissociation supports the hypothesis that reasoning about social exchange is caused by a different computational system than reasoning about precautionary rules: a two-mechanism account.

Although tests of this kind cannot conclusively establish the anatomical location of a mechanism, tests with other patients suggest that damage to a circuit connecting anterior temporal cortex to the amygdalae was important in creating R. M.'s selective deficit.[7] Recent functional imaging (fMRI) studies also support the hypothesis that social contract reasoning is supported by different brain areas than precautionary reasoning, and imply the involvement of several brain areas in addition to temporal cortex (Wegener, Baare, Hede, Ramsoy, & Lund, 2004; Fiddick, Spampinato, & Grafman, forthcoming).

---

[7] Stone et al. (2002) tested two other patients with overlapping but different patterns of brain damage. R.B. had more extensive bilateral orbitofrontal damage than R. M., and had some anterior temporal damage as well, but his right temporal pole was largely spared (thus he did not have bilateral disconnection of the amygdalae): His scores were 85% correct for precautions and 83% correct for social contracts. B.G. had extensive bilateral temporal pole damage compromising (though not severing) input into both amygdalae, but his orbitofrontal cortex was completely spared: He scored 100% on both sets of problems.

Eliminating One-Mechanism Hypotheses (B6-B8; B1-B4)

Every alternative explanation of cheater detection proposed so far claims that reasoning about social contracts and precautions is caused by the same neurocognitive system. R. M.'s dissociation is inconsistent with all of these one-mechanism accounts. These accounts include mental logic (Rips, 1994), mental models (Johnson-Laird & Byrne, 1991), decision theory/optimal data selection (Kirby, 1994; Oaksford & Chater, 1994), permission schema theory (Cheng & Holyoak, 1989), relevance theory (Sperber et al., 1995),[8] and Manktelow and Over's (1991, 1995) view implicating a system that is general to any deontic rule that involves subjective utilities. (For further evidence against relevance theory, see Fiddick et al., 2000; for further evidence against Manktelow & Over's theory, see Fiddick & Rutherford, in press.)

Indeed, no other reasoning theory even distinguishes between precautions and social contract rules; the distinction is derived from evolutionary-functional analyses and is purely in terms of *content*. These results indicate the presence of a very narrow, content-sensitive cognitive specialization within the human reasoning system.

PRECOCIOUS DEVELOPMENT OF SOCIAL EXCHANGE REASONING

Children understand what counts as cheating on a social contract by age 3 (Harris & Núñez, 1996; Harris, Núñez, & Brett, 2001; Núñez & Harris, 1998a).[9] This has been shown repeatedly in experiments by Harris and Núñez using an evaluation task: a task in which the child must decide when a character is violating a rule. Consider, for example, a story in which Carol wants to ride her bicycle but her mom says, "If you ride your bike, then you must wear an apron." This rule restricts access to a benefit (riding the bike) based on whether the child has satisfied an arbitrary requirement. The child is then shown four pictures (Carol riding the bike wearing an apron, Carol riding without an apron, Carol wearing an apron but not riding, and Carol not riding or wearing an apron) and asked to choose the picture in which Carol is doing something naughty. British 3-year-olds chose the correct picture (Carol riding the bike with no apron) 72% to 83% of the time; 4-year-olds, 77% to 100% of the time (Harris & Núñez, 1996; Harris et al., 2001; Núñez & Harris, 1998a). These performance levels were found whether the social contract emanated from the mother or was a consensual swap between two children; that is, the rule did not have to be imposed by an authority figure. A variety of tests showed that, for social contracts, children understood that taking the benefit was *conditional* on meeting the requirement. They were not merely looking for cases in which the requirement was not met; they were looking for cases in which the benefit was taken *and* the requirement was not met. The same effects were found for preschoolers from the United Kingdom, Colombia, and (with minor qualifications) rural Nepal.

The performance of the preschoolers was adultlike in other ways. Like adults, the preschoolers did well whether the social contract was familiar or unfamiliar.

---

[8] For a full account of the problems relevance theory has explaining social contract reasoning, see Fiddick et al., 2000.

[9] Younger children have not been tested yet.

Also like adults, intentionality mattered to the children. Núñez and Harris (1998a) varied (1) whether the character had taken the benefit or not and (2) whether the character had failed to fulfill the requirement by accident or deliberately. Children were far more likely to say the character had been naughty when the breach was intentional than accidental. Four-year-olds deemed social contract violations naughty 81% of the time when they were intentional versus 10% of the time when they were accidental; for 3-year-olds, the figures were 65% versus 17%, respectively. Children also could match emotions to outcomes for reciprocal exchanges: Given an agreement to swap, they understood that the victim of cheating would feel upset, and that both children would be happy if the swap was completed (Núñez, 1999).

Moreover, the children tested by Harris and Núñez (1996) showed the same dissociation between social contract and descriptive rules as adults: 3- to 4-year-olds chose the correct violation condition only 40% of the time for descriptive rules but 72% to 83% of the time for social contracts. By age 5, children could solve a full-array Wason selection task when the rule was a social contract (Núñez & Harris, 1998b; performance limitations, rather than competence problems, interfered with the Wason performance of the preschoolers).[10]

CROSS-CULTURAL INVARIANCES AND DISSOCIATIONS IN SOCIAL EXCHANGE REASONING

Cognitive neuroscientists have long been aware that neural dissociations are useful for elucidating mental structure. But cultural dissociations may provide a uniquely informative source of converging evidence. Because the ontogenetic experience of people in different cultures varies widely, cross-cultural studies allow one to see whether differences in ontogenetic experience are associated with differences in mental structure.

Most psychologists and anthropologists believe that high-level cognitive competences emerge from general-purpose cognitive abilities trained by culturally specific activities, rather than as part of our evolved, reliably developing, species-typical design. That cheater detection should be well developed across cultures is a falsifiable prediction of the evolutionary account, which posits that this competence should be distributed in a species-typical, human universal fashion. More precisely, because detecting cheaters is necessary for social exchange to be an ESS, the development of cheater detection should be buffered against cultural variation and, therefore, be uniform. In contrast, the development of ESS-irrelevant aspects of performance (e.g., interest in acts of generosity) is under no selection to be uniform across cultures and should, therefore, be free to vary with cultural circumstance.

---

[10] Although the definitive experiments have not yet been done, existing evidence suggests that preschoolers also understand violations of precautionary rules. The rules used by Harris and Núñez (1996) fell into two categories: pure social contracts ("arbitrary permissions" and "swaps," in their terminology) and hybrid rules (ones that can be interpreted either as social contracts or precautionary). The hybrids were rules that restricted access to a benefit on the condition that a precaution was taken, for example, *If you play outside, you must wear a coat* (to keep warm). Cummins (1996) tested a more purely precautionary rule, but the context still involved restrictions on access to a benefit (playing outside).

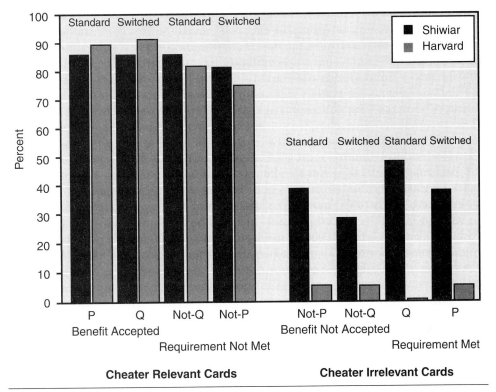

Figure 20.6 Performance of Shiwiar Hunter-Horticulturalists and Harvard Undergraduates on Standard and Switched Social Contracts. (Percent of subjects choosing each card.) There was no difference between the two populations in their choice of cheater relevant cards (*benefit accepted, requirement not satisfied*). They differed only in their choice of cheater-irrelevant cards (Shiwiar showing more interest in cards that could reveal acts of generosity or fair play). Shiwiar high performance on cheater-relevant cards is not caused by indiscriminate interest in all cards. Holding logical category constant, Shiwiar always chose a card more frequently when it was relevant to cheater detection than when it was not. This can be shown by comparing performance on standard versus switched social contracts. (E.g., the *P* card is cheater relevant for a standard social contract, but not for a switched one; see Figure 20.4.)

Sugiyama, Tooby, and Cosmides (2002) tested these predictions among the Shiwiar, a hunter-horticultural population in a remote part of the Ecuadorian Amazon. Good cheater detection had already been established in the United States, Europe, Hong Kong, and Japan. But adults in advanced market economies engage in more trade—especially with strangers—than people who hunt and garden in remote parts of the Amazon. Anonymity facilitates cheating; markets increase the volume of transactions experienced by each individual. If no evolved specialization is involved—that is, if general-purpose processes induce a cheater detection subroutine through repeated experience with cheating—then this subroutine might not be found outside the Western world.

The Shiwiar were raised and continue to live in a culture as different from that of American college students as any on the planet. Nevertheless, Shiwiar were just as good at detecting cheaters on Wason tasks as Harvard undergraduates were (Figure 20.6). For cheater-relevant cards, the performance of Shiwiar hunter-horticulturalists was identical to that of Harvard students. Shiwiar differed only in that they were more likely to also show interest in cheater-irrelevant cards—the ones that could reveal acts of generosity. (Their excellence at cheater detection did not result from indiscriminate interest in all cards. Controlling for logical category, Shiwiar were more than twice as likely to choose a card when it was cheater-relevant than when it was not; $p < .005$.) In short, there was no dissociation between cultures in the parts of the mechanism necessary to its performing its evolved function. The only "cultural dissociation" was in ESS-irrelevant aspects of performance.

Is cheater detection invariant because the sociocultural experience of Shiwiar and American subjects is too similar to cause differences in reasoning performance? Clearly not; if that were true, the two populations would perform identically on cheater-irrelevant cards as well as on cheater-relevant ones. That did not happen.

This is the only research we know of to show identical performance across very different cultural groups on those aspects of a reasoning problem that are relevant to a cognitive adaptation functioning as an evolutionarily stable strategy, yet different performance on those aspects that are irrelevant to the adaptation functioning as an ESS. That performance in detecting cheaters was invariant across very disparate cultural settings suggests that the brain mechanism responsible is a reliably developing neurocognitive system. That is, its development is canalized in a way that buffers it against idiosyncratic variations in ontogenetic experience.

DOES DOMAIN-GENERAL LEARNING BUILD THE SPECIALIZATION FOR SOCIAL EXCHANGE?

The empirical evidence reviewed earlier strongly supports the claim that reasoning about social exchange is caused by neurocognitive machinery that is specialized for this function in adults: social contract algorithms. This conclusion was supported not just by evidence from Wason tasks but also from experimental economics games, moral reasoning protocols, emotion attribution tasks, and developmental studies. What makes the Wason results particularly interesting, however, is that the Wason task requires information search. The Wason results indicate the presence of a subroutine that is narrowly specialized for *seeking out* information that would *reveal* the presence of cheaters. This subroutine is not designed to seek out information that would reveal the presence of cheating (when this occurs by mistake), or permission violations, or violations in general.

But how was this very precisely designed computational specialization produced? Are the developmental mechanisms that build social contract algorithms domain-specific and specialized for this function? Or are social contract specializations in adults built by domain-general learning mechanisms?

If computational specializations for social exchange are acquired via some general-purpose learning process, then we should not claim that the specialization is an evolved adaptation *for* social exchange. Instead, the social exchange specialization would be the product of a learning mechanism that evolved to solve a different, perhaps more general, adaptive problem.

GENERAL PURPOSE LEARNING IS A NONSTARTER

Evidence of an adaptive specialization in the adult human mind often meets the following rejoinder: Although the adult mechanism is specialized, the mechanisms that built it are not—the adult specialization was acquired via a general purpose learning process (e.g., Elman et al., 1996; Gauthier & Tarr, 2002; Orr, 2003; Rumelhart & McClelland, 1986; for discussion, see Duchaine, 2001; Pinker, 2002; Tooby & Cosmides, 1992).

There is a fundamental problem with this view: No general purpose learning process is known to science (Gallistel, 2000). This is not because scientists are in the dark about animal learning. Learning processes specialized for solving specific adaptive problems have been found in many species, including dead reckoning in desert ants, learned food aversions in rats, star navigation in birds, snake fear in primates, and language acquisition in humans (Gallistel, 1990, 2000; Garcia, 1990; Garcia & Koelling, 1966; Mineka & Cook, 1993; Pinker, 1994). Indeed, even classical conditioning, considered by many to be the premier example of general purpose learning, is anything but (Staddon, 1988). The empirical evidence shows that this form of learning is adaptively specialized for a specific computational task common in foraging and predator avoidance: multivariate nonstationary time series analysis (Gallistel & Gibbon, 2000).

Classical and operant conditioning are adaptive specializations, but it is true that they operate over inputs from many different domains (i.e., they are somewhat content-general). So let us reframe the rejoinder thus: Are adult specializations for reasoning about social exchange acquired via classical or operant conditioning?

At the root of operant and classical conditioning is the ability to respond contingently to reward and punishment (Gallistel & Gibbon, 2000; Staddon, 1988). Social exchange entails such contingencies: I offer to provide a benefit to you, contingent on your satisfying a requirement that I specify. I impose that requirement in the hope that your satisfying it will create a situation that benefits me in some way.

Yet the ability to respond contingently to reward and punishment is not sufficient for social exchange to emerge in a species. All animal species can be classically and operantly conditioned (Staddon, 1988), but few species engage in social exchange. If classical and/or operant conditioning caused the acquisition of social exchange specializations, then social exchange should be zoologically widespread. The fact that it is so rare means that it is not the consequence of any behavior-regulation or learning process that is zoologically common.

Although reciprocity is rare in the animal kingdom, it is found in a number of nonhuman primate species (Brosnan & de Waal, 2003; de Waal, 1989, 1997a, 1997b; de Waal & Luttrell, 1988). Its presence in other primates means that social exchange behavior can arise in the absence of language. This means the conditioning hypothesis cannot be rescued by arguing that the development of social exchange requires the joint presence of language and conditioning mechanisms.

NOT RATIONAL CHOICE (B9)

Can the development of neurocognitive specializations for reasoning about social exchange be accounted for by the fact that reciprocity is economically advantageous? An economic folk theory exists and was recently articulated by Orr (2003, p. 18):

An evolutionary psychologist might counter that the fact that a behavior conforms so closely to what's expected of an adaptive one is evidence that it's a bona fide biological adaptation. And here we arrive at another problem. For the same logic that makes a behavior evolutionarily advantageous might also make it "economically" advantageous.... The point is that when evolutionary and economic considerations yield the same prediction, conformity to Darwinian predictions cannot be taken as decisive.

This would be a good point if economists had a theory of the computations that give rise to economic learning and decision making. But they do not. Having no account of how economic reasoning is accomplished, economists rely on rational choice theory, an *as if* approach. According to rational choice theory, people reason *as if* they were equipped with neurocognitive mechanisms that compute (in some as yet unspecified way) the subjective expected utility of alternative actions, and choose the one that maximizes personal utility (Savage, 1954).

Rational choice theory makes very precise predictions about the choices people should make when engaging in social exchange and other economic games. Contrary to Orr's assumption, however, rational choice theory and the evolutionarily functional theory of social exchange make different predictions about human behavior (Hoffman, McCabe, & Smith, 1998). There is now a large body of results from experimental economics showing that people rarely behave as rational choice theory predicts and that this is not due to inexperience with the experimental situation—even experienced subjects violate rational choice theory predictions (e.g., Fehr & Gächter, 2000a, 2000b; Henrich et al., in press; Hoffman, McCabe, & Smith, 1998). For example, when given the opportunity to engage in social exchange, people routinely and systematically choose to cooperate with others when they would earn a higher payoff by defecting; they also punish acts of cheating when they would earn more by not doing so. That is, they cooperate and punish in circumstances, such as the one-shot Prisoners' Dilemma, where these choices are not utility maximizing (Hoffman, McCabe, & Smith, 1998). As Hoffman, McCabe, and Smith (1998) argue, these are precisely the responses one would expect of specializations designed to operate in small hunter-gatherer bands, where repeated interactions are the norm and one-shot interactions are rare. The results reported earlier on accidental versus intentional violations of social contracts are also inconsistent with economic prediction. Rational choice theory predicts mechanisms that respond to the payoff structure of situations, not to intentions, and cheating produces the same negative payoff whether it was accidental or intentional. Thus, a system designed for maximizing utility should detect cheating, not cheaters. Yet that is not the empirical finding.

Rational or *economically advantageous* has to refer to some kind of reasoning process if it is to serve as an explanation of anything, and the most completely axiomatized normative model of rational economic behavior fails to predict or explain the facts of when humans choose to cooperate and punish, either in social exchange (Hoffman, McCabe, & Smith, 1998) or in public goods games (Fehr & Gächter, 2000a, 2000b; Henrich et al., in press; Kurzban, McCabe, Smith, & Wilson, 2001). Because the facts of social exchange reasoning and behavior contradict central predictions of rational choice theory, this economic by-product hypothesis cannot explain the features of the neurocognitive specialization found in adults, or the development of these features (B9 eliminated). In light of this failure, a number of economists are turning to evolutionary psychological accounts of social exchange and judgment under uncertainty to explain human economic behavior (Gigerenzer & Selten, 2001; Hoffman, McCabe, & Smith, 2001; Romer, 2000).

STATISTICAL LEARNING AND CONTENT-FREE INDUCTIVE INFERENCE: MORE DOGS THAT DO NOT BARK (B10)

Various accounts of inductive learning have been proposed: Bayesian learning machines, connectionist systems that compute a multiple regression, contingency calculators. Some posit highly domain-specific, inductive learning systems (e.g., Marcus, 2001; Staddon, 1988), but most do not (e.g., Elman et al., 1996; Quartz & Sejnowski, 1997).

The domain-general proposals foreground the role of content-blind inductive inference procedures in the construction of mental content.[11] These extract statistical relationships from patterns that are objectively present in the external world. Indeed, they are constrained to do so: The world is the only source of content for these statistical learning mechanisms. As a result, we should see certain dogs barking. For example, twentieth-century Chicago schoolchildren should fear things that are dangerous to children living in twentieth-century urban Chicago—electric sockets, cars, streets, hot stoves. The content of their fears should reflect the frequency and statistical distribution of dangers in the modern world because it was constructed by content-free mechanisms operating on information derived from these distributions.

By contrast, domain-specific learning mechanisms are content rich: They allow inferences that go beyond the information given, so the mental content constructed may be richer than (or merely different from) the statistical distribution of information in the external world of individual experience. For example, when asked what they are most afraid of, Chicago schoolchildren name lions, tigers, wild animals, "monsters" (dangerous but unspecified animal or humanlike creatures), snakes, and spiders (Maurer, 1965). The content of their fears reflects the statistical distribution of dangers in an ancestral world they have never experienced (Marks, 1987). It does not reflect the statistical distribution of dangers in urban Chicago—that is, the modern dogs are not barking.

People reliably develop—apparently by age 3—social contract algorithms with the properties discussed in this review. These properties make that neurocognitive system very good at solving an adaptive problem of the ancestral world: seeking out information that would reveal cheaters. We know there is good design for this ancestral problem because very precise patterns of dissociations by content—both functional and neural—were predicted in advance of their discovery on the basis of ESS analyses applied to the behavioral ecology of hunter-gatherers. However, statistical learning theories cannot even retrodict this pattern of dissociations (let alone predict them in advance).

The explanatory variables that drive statistical learning are experience, repetition, and their consequence, familiarity. If these variables caused the development

---

[11] Attentional biases (e.g., for faces) play a role in some of the domain-general theories (e.g., Elman et al., 1996), but these are thought to be few in number and, crucially, to not contain the mental content that is eventually constructed (the source of which is patterns in the world).

of reasoning specializations, we should observe a different set of reasoning specializations than are found, including ones that produce good violation detection for permission rules and even descriptive ones. But these modern dogs are not barking.

Where Is the Specialization for Finding Violations of Descriptive Rules?   Descriptive rules are not rare, exotic occurrences. They are claims about how the world works, commonplaces of everyday conversation (*If you wait until November, the clinic will be out of flu shots. If she eats hot chili, she likes a cold beer. If you use that pan, the casserole will stick. If you wash with bleach, your clothes will be whiter.*). Actions are more likely to succeed when they are based on true rather than false information, so violations of these claims should be salient. Consistent with this, people do know what counts as a violation: They can tell you that cases in which *P* happens but *Q* does not violate a descriptive rule, even when the rule is abstract or unfamiliar (Manktelow & Over, 1987).

But this knowledge does not translate into efficacious information search. Although people *recognize* violations of descriptive rules when they occur, they do not *seek out* information that could reveal such violations, even when they are explicitly asked to do so on a Wason task (see instructions for Figure 20.1; for discussion, see Fiddick et al., 2000). That is, humans do not reliably develop reasoning specializations that cause them to *look for* potential violations of descriptive rules. This dissociation between people's knowledge and what information they search for is found for descriptive rules but not for social contracts. Descriptive rules are ubiquitous. If experience with a type of rule were sufficient for statistical learning to build a specialization for information search, then we should observe good violation detection on Wason tasks using descriptive rules (even unfamiliar ones), just as we do for social contracts.

Even worse, experience with *specific* descriptive rules does nothing to improve performance. Early research using the Wason task explored whether violation detection for descriptive rules was better when the rule, relation, or any of its terms were familiar. It was not (Cheng, Holyoak, Nisbett, & Oliver, 1986; Cosmides, 1985; Manktelow & Evans, 1979; Wason, 1983). Furthermore, people who had repeated experience with instances that violated a particular concrete rule performed no better than people who did not have these experiences (Manktelow & Evans, 1979). The impotence of repeated experience with concrete violations is mirrored in the social contract results, where high performance is observed regardless of experience. College students are intimately familiar with rules restricting access to alcohol (e.g., *If you drink beer, then you must be over 21*), yet Cosmides (1985) found they are no better at detecting violations of this familiar rule than they are for never-experienced rules about cassava root and tattoos.

Where Is the Specialization for Finding Violations of Permission Rules?   The failure of statistical learning theories becomes even clearer when we consider that social exchange rules are but a small subset of all permission rules (which are, in turn, a subset of deontic rules, which are themselves a subset of all conditional rules). By class inclusion, humans necessarily have far more experience with permission rules than with social contracts (legend, Figure 20.5). It was on this basis that Cheng and Holyoak (1985, 1989) argued that domain-general inductive processes *should* produce the more abstract and inclusive permission schema, rather than social contract algorithms, and that this schema should operate not only on social contracts but also on precautionary rules and indeed on any social norm that gives conditional permission. Yet careful tests showed that the permission schema they predicted does not exist.

Poor performance in detecting violations of conditional permission rules drawn from the white zone of Figure 20.5 cannot be explained by claiming that all the permission rules we happen to encounter are either social contracts or precautions. Conditional social norms that fit neither category permeate our society (*If one eats red meat, then one drinks red wine. If you live east of Milpas Street, then vote at Cleveland Elementary School. If the blue inventory form is filled out, file it in the metal bin.*). Yet we do not develop information search strategies specialized for detecting violations of such rules.

Where Is the Specialization for Detecting Negative Payoffs? Statistical learning theorists might respond by saying that learning occurs in response to negative payoffs (see Manktelow & Over, 1995, for a related proposal). This view predicts an information search specialization for detecting when a negative payoff might occur, whether it is produced by cheating on a social contract or failing to take precautions in hazardous situations (Manktelow & Over, 1991, 1995).

Fiddick and Rutherford (in press) show that no such specialization exists: Information search on Wason tasks using social contracts and related rules bears no relationship to subjects' judgments about which outcomes produce negative payoffs. Moreover, R. M.'s neural dissociation (preserved search for violations of precautionary rules with impaired search for cheaters) shows that the mind does not contain a unitary specialization for detecting negative payoffs.

Where Is the Specialization for Detecting Cheating, Rather than Cheaters? What if statistical learning is triggered by negative payoffs, but only within the domain of social exchange? (This is hardly a domain-general proposal, but never mind.) A person can be cheated—receive a negative payoff due to the violation of a social exchange agreement—by accident or by intention. Both kinds of violation damage personal utility, both are useful to detect, and both require detection if the participant in an exchange is to get what he or she wants and is entitled to. Moreover, because innocent mistakes and intentional cheating both result in someone being cheated, situations in which a person *was cheated* are statistically more common than situations in which someone was cheated *by a cheater*. Hence, this domain-restricted version of statistical learning predicts the development of an information search specialization that looks for acts in which someone was cheated, regardless of cause. This specialization would be easy to engineer: A mechanism that indiscriminately scrutinizes cases in which the benefit was accepted and cases in which the requirement was not met would reveal both accidental and intentional violations. But this specialization does not exist: People are not good at detecting acts of cheating when there is evidence that they occurred by accident rather than intention.

In contrast, it is specifically the detection of intentional cheaters that makes contingent exchange evolutionarily stable against exploitation by cheaters (i.e., an ESS). That people are good at detecting intentional cheating but not accidental mistakes is a unique prediction of the evolutionary task analysis of exchange.

Variables That Affect Statistical Learning Do Not Seem to Affect the Development of Cheater Detection An information search specialization for detecting cheaters reliably develops across large variations in experience, repetition, and familiarity. For example:

- Precocious performance is neither necessary nor sufficient for sustaining an adaptationist hypothesis (Cosmides & Tooby, 1997). It is, however, relevant for evaluating claims of content-free inductive learning because these predict that the development of reasoning skills will reflect the child's experience (e.g., Markman, 1989). The early age at which children understand social exchange reasoning undermines the hypothesis that social contract specializations were constructed by content-independent procedures operating on individual experience.

  Preschool-age children are not noted for the accuracy and consistency of their reasoning in many domains, even ones with which they have considerable experience. For example, many children this age will say that a raccoon can change into a skunk; that there are more daisies than flowers; that the amount of liquid changes when poured from a short fat beaker into a tall thin one; that they have a sister but their sister does not (Boden, 1980; Carey, 1984; Keil, 1989; Piaget, 1950). When reasoning about social exchange, however, preschool-age children show virtually all the features of special design that adults do.

  When a child has had experience in a number of domains, it is difficult to explain how or why a content-blind statistical learning mechanism would cause the early and uniform acquisition of a reasoning skill for one of these domains, yet fail to do so for the others. When one considers that adults have massive experience with permission rules, yet fail to develop specializations for detecting violations of this more general and, therefore, more common class, the presence of accurate cheater detection in 3- and 4-year-olds is even more surprising.

- Cultural experience is often invoked as a schema-building factor. Yet, despite a massive difference in experience with trade and cheating, there was no difference between Shiwiar and American adults in cheater detection.

Statistical Learning Summary   Neither experience, repetition, nor familiarity explain which reasoning skills develop and which do not, yet they should if specializations develop via statistical learning. In contrast, the hypothesis that social contract algorithms were built by a developmental process designed for that function neatly accounts for all the developmental facts: that cheater detection develops invariantly across widely divergent cultures (whereas other aspects dissociate); that social exchange reasoning and cheater detection develop precocially; that the mechanisms responsible operate smoothly regardless of experience and familiarity; that they detect cheaters and not other kinds of violators; and that the developmental process results in a social contract specialization rather than one for more inclusive classes such as permission rules.

CONCLUSIONS

There are strict standards of evidence for claiming that an organic system is an evolved adaptation. The system that causes reasoning about social exchange meets these standards. Reasoning about social exchange narrowly dissociates from other forms of reasoning, both cognitively and neurally. The pattern of results reveals a system equipped with exactly those computational properties necessary to produce an evolutionarily stable form of conditional helping (as opposed to the many kinds of unconditional helping that are culturally encouraged). These properties include, but are not limited to, the six design features discussed herein, all of which were predicted in advance from the task analyses contained in social contract theory (see Cosmides & Tooby, 1992, Fiddick et al., 2000 for others). Importantly, the pattern of results cannot be explained as a by-product of a reasoning adaptation designed for some different, or more general, function. Every by-product hypothesis proposed in the literature has been tested and eliminated as an explanation for social exchange reasoning (see Table 20.1).

The design of the computational specialization that causes social exchange reasoning in adults (and preschoolers) places limits on any theory purporting to account for its development. No known domain-general process can account for the fact that social contract specializations with these particular design features reliably develop across cultures, whereas specializations for more commonly encountered reasoning problems do not develop at all. Indeed, the social contract specialization has properties that are better adapted to the small-group living conditions of ancestral hunter-gatherers than to modern industrial societies. Experience of the world may well be necessary for its development during ontogeny, but the developmental process implicated appears to be a domain-specific one, designed by natural selection to produce an evolutionarily stable strategy for conditional helping.

The simplest, most parsimonious explanation that can account for all the results—developmental, neuropsychological, cognitive, and behavioral—is that the human brain contains a neurocognitive adaptation designed for reasoning about social exchange. Because the developmental process that builds it is specialized for doing so, this neurocognitive specialization for social exchange reliably develops across striking variations in cultural experience. It is one component of a complex and universal human nature.

REFERENCES

Almor, A., & Sloman, S. (1996). Is deontic reasoning special? *Psychological Review, 103,* 374–380.

Axelrod, R. (1984). *The evolution of cooperation.* New York: Basic Books.

Axelrod, R., & Hamilton, W. D. (1981). The evolution of cooperation. *Science, 211,* 1390–1396.

Barrett, H. C. (1999, June). *Guilty minds: How perceived intent, incentive, and ability to cheat influence social contract reasoning.* 11th annual meeting of the Human Behavior and Evolution Society, Salt Lake City, Utah.

Boden, M. (1980). *Jean Piaget.* New York: Viking.

Bonatti, L. (1994). Why should we abandon the mental logic hypothesis? *Cognition, 50,* 17–39.

Boyd, R. (1988). Is the repeated prisoner's dilemma a good model of reciprocal altruism? *Ethology and Sociobiology, 9,* 211–222.

Brosnan, S. F., & de Waal, F. B. M. (2003). Monkeys reject unequal pay. *Nature, 425,* 297–299.

Carey, S. (1984). Cognitive development: The descriptive problem. In M. S. Gazzaniga (Ed.), *Handbook of cognitive neuroscience.* (pp. 37–66). New York: Plenum Press.

Cashdan, E. (1989). Hunters and gatherers: Economic behavior in bands. In S. Plattner (Ed.), *Economic anthropology* (pp. 21–48). Stanford, CA: Stanford University Press.

Cheng, P., & Holyoak, K. (1985). Pragmatic reasoning schemas. *Cognitive Psychology, 17,* 391–416.

Cheng, P., & Holyoak, K. (1989). On the natural selection of reasoning theories. *Cognition, 33,* 285–313.

Cheng, P., Holyoak, K., Nisbett, R., & Oliver, L. (1986). Pragmatic versus syntactic approaches to training deductive reasoning. *Cognitive Psychology, 18,* 293–328.

Cosmides, L. (1985). *Deduction or Darwinian algorithms? An explanation of the "elusive" content effect on the Wason selection task.* Doctoral dissertation, Department of Psychology, Harvard University (UMI No. 86–02206).

Cosmides, L. (1989). The logic of social exchange: Has natural selection shaped how humans reason? Studies with the Wason selection task. *Cognition, 31,* 187–276.

Cosmides, L., Barrett, H. C., & Tooby, J. (forthcoming). *Social contracts elicit the detection of intentional cheaters, not innocent mistakes.*

Cosmides, L., & Tooby, J. (1987). From evolution to behavior: Evolutionary psychology as the missing link. In J. Dupre (Ed.), *The latest on the best: Essays on evolution and optimality.* Cambridge, MA: MIT Press.

Cosmides, L., & Tooby, J. (1989). Evolutionary psychology and the generation of culture: Part II. Case study: A computational theory of social exchange. *Ethology and Sociobiology, 10,* 51–97.

Cosmides, L., & Tooby, J. (1992). Cognitive adaptations for social exchange. In J. Barkow, L. Cosmides, & J. Tooby (Eds.), *The adapted mind* (pp. 163–228). New York: Oxford University Press.

Cosmides, L., & Tooby, J. (1997). Dissecting the computational architecture of social inference mechanisms. In *Characterizing human psychological adaptations (Ciba Foundation Symposium #208)* (pp. 132–156). Chichester, England: Wiley.

Cosmides, L., & Tooby, J. (1999). Towards an evoluationary taxonomy of treatable conditions. *Journal of Abnormal Psychology, 108,* 453–464.

Cosmides, L., & Tooby, J. (2004). Knowing thyself: The evolutionary psychology of moral reasoning and moral sentiments. In R. E. Freeman & P. Werhane (Eds.), *Business, science, and ethics: The Ruffin series* (No. 4, pp. 93–128). Charlottesville, VA: Society for Business Ethics.

Cosmides, L., & Tooby, J. (2005). Social exchange: The evolutionary design of a neurocognitive system. In M. S. Gazzaniga (Ed.), *The new cognitive neurosciences, III.* Cambridge, MA: MIT Press.

Cummins, D. D. (1996). Evidence of deontic reasoning in 3- and 4-year-old children. *Memory and Cognition, 24,* 823–829.

Dawkins, R. (1986). *The blind watchmaker.* New York: Norton.

de Waal, F. (1989). Food sharing and reciprocal obligations among chimpanzees. *Journal of Human Evolution, 18,* 433–459.

de Waal, F. (1997a). The chimpanzee's service economy: Food for grooming. *Evolution and Human Behavior, 18,* 375–386.

de Waal, F. (1997b). Food transfers through mesh in brown capuchins. *Journal of Comparative Psychology, 111,* 370–378.

de Waal, F., & Luttrell, L. (1988). Mechanisms of social reciprocity in three primate species: Symmetrical relationship characteristics or cognition? *Ethology and Sociobiology, 9,* 101–118.

Duchaine, B. (2001). *Computational and developmental specificity in face recognition: Testing the alternative explanations in a developmental prosopagnosic.* Doctoral dissertation, Department of Psychology, University of California, Santa Barbara.

Dugatkin, L. A. (1997). *Cooperation among animals: A modern perspective.* New York: Oxford.

Ehrlich, P. (2002). *Human natures: Genes, cultures, and the human prospect.* Washington, DC: Island Press.

Elman, J., Bates, E., Johnson, M. H., Karmiloff-Smith, A., Parisi, D., & Plunkett, K. (1996). *Rethinking innateness: Connectionism in a developmental context.* Cambridge, MA: MIT Press.

Fehr, E., & Gächter, S. (2000a). Cooperation and punishment in public goods experiments. *American Economic Review, 90,* 980–994.

Fehr, E., & Gächter, S. (2000b). Fairness and retaliation: The economics of reciprocity. *Journal of Economic Perspectives, 14,* 159–181.

Fiddick, L. (1998). *The deal and the danger: An evolutionary analysis of deontic reasoning.* Doctoral dissertation, Department of Psychology, University of California, Santa Barbara.

Fiddick, L. (2003). Is there a faculty of deontic reasoning? A critical re-evaluation of abstract deontic versions of the Wason selection task. In D. Over (Ed.), *Evolution and the psychology of thinking: The debate* (pp. 33–60). Hove, England: Psychology Press.

Fiddick, L. (2004). Domains of deontic reasoning: Resolving the discrepancy between the cognitive and moral reasoning literatures. *Quarterly Journal of Experimental Psychology, 57A*(4), 447–474.

Fiddick, L., Cosmides, L., & Tooby, J. (2000). No interpretation without representation: The role of domain-specific representations and inferences in the Wason selection task. *Cognition 77,* 1–79.

Fiddick, L., & Rutherford, M. (in press). Looking for loss in all the wrong places: Loss-avoidance does not explain cheater detection. *Evolution and Human Behavior.*

Fiddick, L., Spampinato, M., & Grafman, J. (forthcoming). Social contracts and precautions activate different neurological systems: An fMRI investigation of deontic reasoning.

Fiske, A. (1991). *Structures of social life: The four elementary forms of human relations.* New York: Free Press.

Fodor, J. (2000). Why we are so good at catching cheaters. *Cognition, 75,* 29–32.

Gallistel, C. R. (1990). *The organization of learning.* Cambridge, MA: MIT Press.

Gallistel, C. R. (2000). The replacement of general-purpose learning models with adaptively specialized learning modules. In M. S. Gazzaniga (Eds.), *The New Cognitive Neurosciences* (pp. 1179–1191). Cambridge, MA: MIT Press.

Gallistel, C. R., & Gibbon, J. (2000). Time, rate and conditioning. *Psychological Review, 107,* 289–344.

Garcia, J. (1990). Learning without memory. *Journal of Cognitive Neuroscience, 2*(4), 287–305.

Garcia, J., & Koelling, R. A. (1966). Relations of cue to consequence in avoidance learning. *Psychonomic Science, 4,* 123–124.

Gauthier, I., & Tarr, M. J. (2002). Unraveling mechanisms for expert object recognition: Bridging brain activity and behavior. *Journal of Experimental Psychology: Human Perception and Performance, 28,* 431–446.

Gigerenzer, G., & Hug, K. (1992). Domain specific reasoning: Social contracts, cheating, and perspective change. *Cognition, 43,* 127–171.

Gigerenzer, G., & Selten, R. (Eds.). (2001). *Bounded rationality: The adaptive toolbox.* Cambridge, MA: The MIT Press.

Gurven, M. (in press). To give and to give not: The behavioral ecology of human food transfers. *Behavioral and Brain Sciences,* ID code: bbs00001257.

Harris, P., & Núñez, M. (1996). Understanding of permission rules by preschool children. *Child Development, 67,* 1572–1591.

Harris, P., Núñez, M., & Brett, C. (2001). Let's swap: Early understanding of social exchange by British and Nepali children. *Memory and Cognition, 29,* 757–764.

Hasegawa, T., & Hiraishi, K. (2000). Ontogeny of the mind from an evolutionary psychological viewpoint. In S. Watanabe (Ed.), *Comparative cognitive science of mind* (pp. 413–427). Kyoto: Minerva Publications.

Hauser, M. D. (in press). *Ought! The inevitability of a universal moral grammar.* New York: Holt.

Henrich, J., Boyd, R., Bowles, S., Gintis, H., Fehr, E., Camerer, C., et al. (in press). 'Economic man' in cross-cultural perspective. *Behavioral and Brain Sciences.*

Hoffman, E., McCabe, K., & Smith, V. (1998). Behavioral foundations of reciprocity: Experimental economics and evolutionary psychology. *Economic Inquiry, 36,* 335–352.

Isaac, G. (1978). The food-sharing behavior of protohuman hominids. *Scientific American, 238,* 90–108.

Johnson-Laird, P., & Byrne, R. (1991). *Deduction.* Hillsdale, NJ: Erlbaum.

Keil, F. (1989). *Concepts, kinds, and cognitive development.* Cambridge, MA: MIT Press.

Kirby, K. (1994). Probabilities and utilities of fictional outcomes in Wason's four-card selection task. *Cognition, 51,* 1–28.

Kurzban, R., McCabe, K., Smith, V. L., & Wilson, B. J. (2001). Incremental commitment and reciprocity in a real time public goods game. *Personality and Social Psychology Bulletin, 27*(12), 1662–1673.

Leckman, J., & Mayes, L. (1998). Maladies of love: An evolutionary perspective on some forms of obsessive-compulsive disorder. In D. M. Hann, L. C. Huffman, I. I. Lederhendler, & D. Meinecke (Eds.), *Advancing research on developmental plasticity: Integrating the behavioral science and neuroscience of mental health* (pp. 134–152). Rockville, MD: U.S. Department of Health and Human Services.

Leckman, J., & Mayes, L. (1999). Preoccupations and behaviors associated with romantic and parental love: Perspectives on the origin of obsessive-compulsive disorder. *Obsessive-Compulsive Disorder, 8*(3), 635–665.

Lieberman, D., Tooby, J., & Cosmides, L. (2003). Does morality have a biological basis? An empirical test of the factors governing moral sentiments relating to incest. *Proceedings of the Royal Society London. (Biological Sciences), 270*(1517), 819–826.

Malinowski, B. (1922). *Argonauts of the Western Pacific.* New York: Dutton Press.

Maljkovic, V. (1987). *Reasoning in evolutionarily important domains and schizophrenia: Dissociation between content-dependent and content independent reasoning.* Unpublished honors thesis, Department of Psychology, Harvard University.

Manktelow, K., & Evans, J. St. B. T. (1979). Facilitation of reasoning by realism: Effect or noneffect? *British Journal of Psychology, 70,* 477–488.

Manktelow, K., & Over, D. (1987). Reasoning and rationality. *Mind and Language, 2,* 199–219.

Manktelow, K., & Over, D. (1988, July). Sentences, stories, scenarios, and the selection task. *First international conference on thinking.* Plymouth, UK.

Manktelow, K., & Over, D. (1990). Deontic thought and the selection task. In K. J. Gilhooly, M. T. G. Keane, R. H. Logie, & G. Erdos (Eds.), *Lines of thinking* (Vol. 1, pp. 153–164). London: Wiley.

Manktelow, K., & Over, D. (1991). Social roles and utilities in reasoning with deontic conditionals. *Cognition, 39,* 85–105.

Manktelow, K., & Over, D. (1995). Deontic reasoning. In S. E. Newstead & J. St. B. T. Evans (Eds.), *Perspectives on thinking and reasoning: Essays in honor of Peter Wason* (pp. 91–114). Hove, England: Erlbaum.

Marcus, G. (2001). *The algebraic mind: Reflections on connectionism and cognitive science.* Cambridge, MA: MIT Press.

Markman, E. (1989). *Categorization and naming in children.* Cambridge, MA: MIT Press.

Marks, I. (1987). *Fears, phobias, and rituals.* New York: Oxford University Press.

Marshall, L. (1976). Sharing, talking, and giving: Relief of social tensions among the !Kung. In R. Lee & I. DeVore (Eds.), *Kalahari hunter-gatherers: Studies of the !Kung San and their neighbors.* Cambridge, MA: Harvard University Press.

Maurer, A. (1965). What children fear. *Journal of Genetic Psychology, 106,* 265–277.

Mauss, M. (1967). *The gift: Forms and functions of exchange in archaic societies.* New York: Norton. (Original work published 1925)

Maynard Smith, J. (1982). *Evolution and the theory of games.* Cambridge, England: Cambridge University Press.

McKenna, P., Clare, L., & Baddeley, A. (1995). Schizophrenia. In A. D. Baddeley, B. A. Wilson, & F. N. Watts (Eds.), *Handbook of memory disorders* (pp. 271–292). New York: Wiley.

Mineka, S., & Cook, M. (1993). Mechanisms involved in the observational conditioning of fear. *Journal of Experimental Psychology: General, 122,* 23–38.

Núñez, M. (1999). Conditional agreements of reciprocal exchange and the emotions involved. *IX European Conference on Developmental Psychology.* Spetses, Greece, September 1999.

Núñez, M., & Harris, P. (1998a). Psychological and deontic concepts: Separate domains or intimate connections? *Mind and Language, 13,* 153–170.

Núñez, M., & Harris, P. (July 1998b). *Young children's reasoning about prescriptive rules: Spotting transgressions through the selection task.* Paper presented at the XVth Biennial Meeting of the International Society for the Study of Behavioral Development, Berne, Switzerland.

Oaksford, M., & Chater, N. (1994). A rational analysis of the selection task as optimal data selection. *Psychological Review, 101,* 608–631.

Orr, H. A. (2003). Darwinian storytelling. *New York Review of Books, L*(3), 17–20.

Pereyra, L., & Nieto, J. (in press). La especificidad del razonamiento sobre situaciones de peligro. (Reasoning specializations for situations involving hazards and precautions) *Revista Mexicana de Psicología.*

Piaget, J. (1950). *The psychology of intelligence.* (M. Piercy & D. E. Berlyne, Trans.). New York: Harcourt.

Pinker, S. (1994). *The language instinct.* New York: Morrow.

Pinker, S. (2002). *The blank slate.* New York: Viking.

Platt, R., & Griggs, R. (1993). Darwinian algorithms and the Wason selection task: A factorial analysis of social contract selection task problems. *Cognition, 48,* 163–192.

Price, M. E., Cosmides, L., & Tooby, J. (2002). Punitive sentiment as an anti-free rider psychological device. *Evolution and Human Behavior, 23,* 203–231.

Quartz, S., & Sejnowski, T. (1997). The neural basis of cognitive development: A constructivist manifesto. *Behavioral and Brain Sciences, 20*(4), 537–596.

Rips, L. (1994). *The psychology of proof.* Cambridge, MA: MIT Press.

Romer, P. (2000). Thinking and Feeling. *American Economic Review, 90*(2), 439–443.

Rumelhart, D., & McClelland, J. (1986). On learning the past tenses of English verbs: Implicit rules or parallel distributed processing. In D. Rumelhart, J. McClelland, & The PDP Research Group (Eds.), *Parallel distributed processing: Explorations in the microstructure of cognition* (Vol. 2, pp. 216–271). Cambridge, MA: MIT Press.

Savage, L. J. (1954). *The foundations of statistics.* New York: Wiley.

Shallice, T. (1988). *From neuropsychology to mental structure.* Cambridge, England: Cambridge University Press.

Shostak, M. (1981). *Nisa: The life and words of a !Kung woman.* Cambridge, MA: Harvard University Press.

Simon, H. (1990). A mechanism for social selection and successful altruism. *Science, 250,* 1665–1668.

Sperber, D., Cara, F., & Girotto, V. (1995). Relevance theory explains the selection task. *Cognition, 57,* 31–95.

Staddon, J. E. R. (1988). Learning as inference. In R. C. Bolles & M. D. Beecher (Eds.), *Evolution and learning.* Hillsdale, NJ: Erlbaum.

Stevens, J., & Stephens, D. (2004). The economic basis of cooperation: Trade-offs between selfishness and generosity. *Behavioral Ecology, 15*(2), 255–261.

Stone, V., Cosmides, L., Tooby, J., Kroll, N., & Knight, R. (2002, August). Selective impairment of reasoning about social exchange in a patient with bilateral limbic system damage. *Proceedings of the National Academy of Sciences, 99*(17), 11531–11536.

Sugiyama, L., Tooby, J., & Cosmides, L. (2002, August). Cross-cultural evidence of cognitive adaptations for social exchange among the Shiwiar of Ecuadorian Amazonia. *Proceedings of the National Academy of Sciences, 99*(17), 11537–11542.

Tooby, J., & Cosmides, L. (1989, August). *The logic of threat.* Paper presented at the Human Behavior and Evolution Society, Evanston, IL.

Tooby, J., & Cosmides, L. (1992). The psychological foundations of culture. In J. Barkow, L. Cosmides, & J. Tooby (Eds.), *The adapted mind* (pp. 19–136). New York: Oxford University Press.

Tooby, J., & Cosmides, L. (1996). Friendship and the banker's paradox: Other pathways to the evolution of adaptations for altruism. In W. G. Runciman, J. Maynard Smith, & R. I. M. Dunbar (Eds.), *Evolution of social behaviour patterns in primates and man. Proceedings of the British Academy, 88,* 119–143.

Tooby, J., Cosmides, L., & Barrett, H. C. (2005). Resolving the debate on innate ideas: Learnability constraints and the evolved interpenetration of motivational and conceptual functions. In P. Carruthers, S. Laurence, & S. Stich (Eds.), *The innate mind: Structure and content.* New York: Oxford University Press.

Tooby, J., & DeVore, I. (1987). The reconstruction of hominid behavioral evolution through strategic modeling. In W. G. Kinsey (Ed.), *Primate models of hominid behavior* (pp. 183–237). New York: SUNY Press.

Trivers, R. (1971). The evolution of reciprocal altruism. *Quarterly Review of Biology, 46,* 35–57.

Wason, P. (1966). Reasoning. In B. M. Foss (Ed.), *New horizons in psychology* (pp. 135–151). Harmondsworth, England: Penguin.

Wason, P. (1983). Realism and rationality in the selection task. In J. St. B. T. Evans (Ed.), *Thinking and reasoning: Psychological approaches* (pp. 44–75). London: Routledge.

Wason, P., & Johnson-Laird, P. (1972). *The psychology of reasoning: Structure and content.* Cambridge, MA: Harvard University Press.

Wegener, J., Baare, W., Hede, A., Ramsoy, T., & Lund, T. (2004, October). *Social relative to non-social reasoning activates regions within anterior prefrontal cortex and temporal cortex.* Paper presented at Abstracts of the Society for Neuroscience, San Diego, CA.

Williams, G. (1966). *Adaptation and natural selection.* Princeton, NJ: Princeton University Press.

CHAPTER 21

Aggression

ANNE CAMPBELL

THE ACADEMIC STUDY of aggression is a microcosm of the diversity of theoretical views, methodological predilections, and implicit politics of the social sciences generally. Aggression has been taken to be innate and learned, universal and culturally prescribed, a pervasive trait and a contextualized response, functional and dysfunctional, behavioral and cognitive, and a phenomenon to be measured and modeled or experienced and described.

Evolutionary theory offers a unifying framework that can structure our thinking, integrate findings, and generate predictions. Genes, under selection pressures, build brains that interact with the environment resulting in advantageous behavioral phenotypes. An evolutionary approach requires us to be explicit about the adaptive benefits of aggression. But as evolutionary psychologists, we must go further to identify the proximate mechanisms that regulate the use of aggression as a strategy.

AGGRESSION CONCEPTUALIZED

Darwin observed that most animals propagate rapidly, and their numbers are checked only by the availability of the resources in their habitat. Resources are commodities that enhance fitness in the form of increased survival and reproduction. They include food, shelter, territory, mates, dominance, and survival of self and blood kin. Aggression is one response to competition for resources. It is not the only one. For example, when food becomes scarce, an individual or group might abandon a territory and find a new one. But such a choice carries costs; it might establish a reputation for weakness and invite victimization, a location with sufficient resources might not be found before starvation, and indigenous groups might respond violently to incursion by strangers (Gat, 2000). Given such costs, there are payoffs for remaining and directly contesting the critical resources.

Because aggression is the most reliable elicitor of further aggression, it is a dangerous form of behavior and not one to be undertaken lightly. Any organism that engaged in it in a persistent and inflexible way would be unlikely to survive for long. The contingent nature of aggression and its reliance on net utility are central to an evolutionarily informed understanding of aggression. Because adaptations to aggression are selected when they confer a net benefit, we should expect that the resulting psychological design would be sensitive to rewards and costs. On the reward side are the twin incentives of achieving gains (acquiring resources) and avoiding losses (maintaining resources). On the cost side lies the prospect of injury or death. In any given situation of zero-sum competition, an individual can choose between attack and submission, withdrawal or flight. Which offers the better prospect? In each case, the net value is the reward multiplied by its probability minus the cost multiplied by its probability. Probabilities include the current status and physical capability of the organism relative to its competitor. If opponents are equally matched, aggression is the better choice when the value of the resource gained or maintained is greater than the cost of injury. Reciprocally, nonaggression is the better choice if the value of injury avoidance is greater than the cost of the lost resource. Evolutionary psychology does not propose that such a mathematical calculation is actually made. Rather, emotionally driven information processing mechanisms have been honed through evolutionary time to trip a decision in a way that can seem automatic and unreflective.

To the nonevolutionary-minded psychologist, the preceding reward-cost model may seem overly simple. Indeed, a plethora of subtypes of aggression have been proposed (see Weinshenker & Siegel, 2002), which have often served to confuse rather than enlighten. The most pervasive attempts at taxonomy have concentrated on motive and emotion, resulting in two broad classes of acts. On one hand, instrumental, proactive, or predatory aggression (Aronson, 1992; Meloy, 1988) identifies the acquisition of some extrinsic reward as the goal with harm inflicted merely as a tool to that end. Such acts are planned, not responsive to threat, and are characterized by an absence of anger and arousal. On the other hand, there is reactive, defensive, hostile, or affective aggression (Geen, 2001). Such aggression is "a response to antecedent conditions such as goal blocking and provocation, and responses are primarily interpersonal and hostile in nature" (Coie & Dodge, 1997, p. 784). The aim of the aggression is seen as the gratification of inflicting retaliatory harm, and anger is emphasized as an emotional precursor or concomitant.

These distinctions between proactive and reactive forms of aggression are problematic (Bushman & Anderson, 2001). There are correlations above .70 between instruments assessing the two forms in children (Vitaro, Brendgen, & Tremblay, 2002). Motivationally, reactive aggression can have extrinsic goals (e.g., self-defense), just as in instrumental aggression, in which harm delivery is a means to an end. Emotionally, one form of aggression can quickly give rise to another (e.g., a bully becomes enraged by his victim's refusal to submit). While the infliction of intentional harm *can* occur in the absence of anger (an executioner, a soldier), such rare acts are more usefully seen as a form of obedience rather than aggression. More usually, proactive aggression (e.g., issuing a challenge to a rival) is charged with anger (caused by that rivalry). With regard to proaction and reaction, the decision as to who is the attacker is often a matter of who is still standing at the end of the encounter. Ethnographic research confirms that, in any given fight, both protagonists will claim that they reacted "righteously" to unreasonable provocation (Katz, 1988).

It is conceptually and heuristically simpler to consider the rewards as a double-side coin. On one side are gains achieved (proactive aggression) and on the other, losses avoided (reactive aggression). Because anger is central to the motivation of both kinds of reward, the distinction becomes one of degree, not of kind.

OPPONENTS AND MOTIVE

The function or ultimate cause of aggression is to acquire or defend resources that are important in conferring reproductive or survival benefit. In this section I examine the proximate causes of aggression: the immediate impelling motives that drive aggressive acts. Motives vary chiefly as a function of opponent. The reasons for attacking a romantic rival are different from those that cause a tribe to patrol its territorial boundaries. The form of aggression also varies from silent genetic arms races to raucous outright brawls.

KIN AND NONKIN

Because blood relatives share genes, evolutionary theory predicts that kin should be less frequently a target of aggression than nonkin. Until the appearance of Daly and Wilson's (1988) seminal book, this prediction seemed to clash with prevailing social science wisdom that more murder victims are members of the same family than any other category of murder-victim relationship. Daly and Wilson's data from 508 nonaccidental Detroit homicides indicated that one-quarter involved relatives. However, closer examination revealed that only 6.3% of cases were murders of genetic kin. A popular explanation of family murder is simply that family victims are more available—we spend a greater amount of time with them. Daly and Wilson computed the family composition of the average Detroit household, comparing expected and actual rates of murder. Spouses and nonrelatives sharing a home are far more likely to be murdered (relative to their expected rate) than offspring, parents, and other blood relatives. The consanguinity index for victim-offender pairs is consistently lower than it is for cooffending partners for a range of societies and historical periods (Daly & Wilson, 1988, p. 35), indicating that kin are more likely to be conspirators in murder than targets.

Stepparents present an interesting case from an evolutionary perspective. The genetic bond between parent and child, manifested in parental solicitude, normally results in a considerable degree of tolerance for the unidirectional flow of care from parent to child. An absence of genetic bond characterizes the stepparental relationship where the child acquired by the new spouse is likely to be seen as a cost rather than a benefit. A child living with a stepparent in the United States or Canada is 70 times more likely to be physically abused and 100 times more likely to be fatally abused (Wilson, Daly, & Weghorst, 1980). This elevated risk is not attributable to the mother's age, size of family, socioeconomic situation, or reporting bias. There is, however, an effect of child's age with infants under the age of 2 being at particular risk. The traditional view that family conflict follows the child's rejection of the substitute parent predicts greater hostility with increasing age and independence of the child. The age effect, however, does conform to evolutionary predictions: The younger the child, the greater is the degree of care demanded and the more protracted the length of time over which it will be required.

Given a similar absence of genetic relationship, why do adoptive couples not show similarly high rates of abuse? Crucially the child is unrelated to either parent; hence the furtherance of one partner's genetic interest does not exploit the efforts of the other. Additionally, adoptions are a result of a positive desire to raise the child, adoptive parents are screened, couples are usually financially stable, and the child can be returned if the arrangements do not work out.

[handwritten margin note: Seems inadequate]

MATERNAL-INFANT CONFLICT AND INFANTICIDE

Competition exists even in those relationships that we have historically regarded as the most intimate—between a mother and her unborn child (see Gaulin & Kurland, Chapter 15, this volume). Because of women's high level of parental investment, women should be extremely careful about which pregnancies go to term and which newborns elicit investment (Hrdy, 1999). Early miscarriage may be a form of quality control of the embryo. In normally cycling women, only about 60% of fertilized eggs implant, and of these, 60% do not survive to the 12th day of pregnancy. A further 20% are miscarried in the first trimester (Baker, 1996). If conception takes place, the embryo produces human chorionic gonadotrophin, which prevents the regression of the corpus luteum and maintains progesterone levels. If the embryo is unable to produce sufficient hCG, progesterone levels drop and the pregnancy does not continue. Haig (1996) suggests that this ability may be an honest signal of fetal quality and the mechanism may be sensitive to environmental factors. Miscarriage rates increase with the outbreak of war or with the death or infidelity of a woman's partner.

[handwritten margin note: But not pregnancy trauma?]

Infanticide is an act that seems on the surface to be wholly incompatible with evolutionary theory because it involves a parent killing the vehicle responsible for transmitting his or her genes. Yet, given the high degree of human maternal investment, a woman is better off abandoning a nonviable infant as early as possible (Trivers, 1972). We would expect to see infanticide where the cost of continued investment exceeds the probable reward of a reproductively capable adult. Daly and Wilson (1988) consulted cross-cultural evidence from 60 societies around the world, noting the reasons given for infanticide. Some are features of infant quality (deformity or perinatal illness), quantity (twins), or timing (when an infant is born too soon after a previous birth, the mother, in line with evolutionary predictions, prefers the child in whom she has already invested). Economic circumstances also play a role. Fifty-six societies recognized infanticide as a response to the absence of male support and economic hardship. A baby that is the product of a clandestine extramarital union also poses a threat to the continued provisioning of older children by her husband. Infanticide rates drop with increasing maternal age and concomitant reduction in reproductive value (Daly & Wilson, 1988). Although abortion has effectively removed the need for infanticide in many societies, its correlates mirror those of infanticide: maternal youth, absence of a supporting male partner, or paternity uncertainty (Essock-Vitale & McGuire, 1988; Hill & Low, 1992).

Conversely, once a mother has committed herself to an infant, we would expect that she would be willing to fight to protect it. Although maternal aggression has been closely studied in rodents (Lonstein & Gammie, 2002), it has been barely addressed in humans. Nevertheless, it is an important area in which evolutionary theory is well placed to generate hypotheses.

MALE-FEMALE PARTNER AGGRESSION

Married or cohabiting partners are not genetically related although they each have a genetic interest in the children that are produced from the union. From an evolutionary perspective, we should not be surprised to find conflicts of interest between partners arising from attempts by one partner to exact greater investment from the other than that partner himself or herself provides and, among men, from issues relating to paternal certainty.

At a biological level, human's history of mild polygyny meant that a given fetus might be the only one that a male shared with this particular female. It was to his advantage to increase the woman's investment in this infant while a woman's optimal strategy was to apportion resources equally over her past, present, and future offspring. This conflict has been studied in the phenomenon of genomic imprinting in which the expression of genes depends on their maternal or paternal origin (Goos & Silverman, 2001). Paternal genes are expressed in the development of the placenta, which sequesters maternal resources for the fetus (Moore & Haig, 1991); in Igf2, which controls the growth of the embryo (Haig & Graham, 1991); and in the development of hypothalamic structures, which govern feeding after birth (Keverne, Fundele, Narashima, Barton, & Surani, 1996). To counter this paternal exploitation, maternally active genes code for a false receptor to block the uptake of lgf2 and for the development of the infant neocortex that can "control" the expression of limbic system demands. Early in pregnancy, the mother's blood pressure drops in what appears to be an attempt to reduce blood flow to the placenta. However, as the fetus grows it exerts greater control over blood flow and pre-eclipse may actually reflect a mother-father battle that the father is winning. Essentially, a conflict of interest between parents about the degree of maternal investment is fought out in genes that build the fetus.

Despite a polygynous history, monogamy or serial monogamy is currently the most common form of marriage. Monogamy offers rewards and costs to both sexes. For men, monogamy releases them from bachelor conflict, enhances male alliances, affords the opportunity of at least modest reproductive success, allows sexual intercourse ad libitum, increases certainty of paternity, allows monopoly of a woman's entire reproductive career, and enhances offspring survival and success. Male costs include the lost opportunity for extreme reproductive success, the price of mate guarding, protection and provisioning, and the possibility of cuckoldry and, consequently, wasted parental effort.

For women, monogamy means greater time and energy to invest in her young, extra calories, protection from sexual aggression and infant harassment by other males, energy saved by servicing a single partner rather than several, and an increase in offspring survival and success. On the debit side, she lowers the diversity of her children's genetic inheritance, forgoes potential "sexy sons" from higher quality genotypic males, exposes herself to the risk of jealousy-motivated violence, and incurs energy and time costs in guarding her partner from takeovers by unpartnered, younger women.

Given the delicate balance of rewards and costs, we would expect that spousal relationships would be vulnerable to attempts by one party to decrease their costs and improve their payoffs. Studies suggest that the specific foci of conflict involve perceived inequality in the division of labor, problematic drinking and drug use by one partner, and, for wives, perception of the husband spending their income foolishly (Fincham, 2003).

Women's economic dependence on males is believed to have been increased by patrilocality, consequent loss of female kin bonds, the evolution of male alliances, and a shift from a hunter-gatherer to an agriculture lifestyle (Smuts, 1995). Because provisioning and protection are central to a woman's payoffs, it is not surprising that conflict would arise where these are not provided. In a prospective study of divorce, Amato and Rogers (1997) found that economic profligacy on the husband's part increased the odds of divorce by 187% while women's foolish use of money increased divorce odds to a much lesser extent (77%). Divorce rates, which are higher among Black Americans than among other ethnic groups, may also reflect low levels of male support (Sampson, 1995; Tucker & Mitchell-Kernan, 1997). Anxiety about the ability to provide has been found to be a strong contributor to marital instability among African Americans (Tucker & Mitchell-Kernan, 1997). However, when the effects of poverty and family size are controlled, Black partners are *less* likely to separate than Whites (Hampton, 1975), underlining the importance of economic rather than cultural factors in mating tactics.

Another important source of marital conflict is infidelity (see Shackelford & LaMunyon, Chapter 12, this volume). Wifely infidelity has traditionally been subject to harsher punishment than a husband's (Betzig, 1989; Wilson & Daly, 1992) because a sexually unfaithful woman places her husband in danger of investing in another man's child. Of 214 jealousy-motivated partner homicides in Canada, the husband was the killer in 195 (Daly & Wilson, 1988). Jealousy may be the result of selection for extreme sensitivity to signs of sexual infidelity that is likely to evolve when the costs of failing to detect a true signal are greater than the costs of a false alarm (Buss, 2000). Such a finely tuned detection system can lead to unwarranted or pathological jealousy. Abused women report patterns of excessive male monitoring, which, early in the relationship, they interpreted as signs of devotion. These women may not be entirely deluded (Buss, 2000). Partners who express greater jealousy about their partner are more likely to marry them subsequently (Mathes, 1986). Jealousy also reveals a partner's estimation of their mate's market value. Because the probability of infidelity in both sexes is associated with their attractiveness relative to their spouse (Buss & Shackelford, 1997), attractive partners invite more mate guarding. Women are most likely to be killed by their husbands when they are younger and more attractive (Daly & Wilson, 1988).

Why do men predominate in jealousy-related homicides? Although sexual infidelity may be more provocative to men than women, studies in which participants are asked to rate independently the personal impact of emotional and sexual betrayal report no sex differences (Buss, 1989; Buunk & Hupka, 1987). Both sexes score between six and seven on a seven-point scale for each form of infidelity. Nor does it appear to be a difference in anger. Most studies find that women report as much (e.g., Paul, Foss, & Baenninger, 1996; Pines & Friedman, 1998) or more anger (e.g., Buss, 1989; De Weerth & Kalma, 1993; Paul, Foss, & Galloway, 1993) than men in response to betrayal. The plausible proposal that a partner's adultery is a more serious affront to a man's reputation than to a woman's has not been supported (Paul et al., 1993).

why more IPV perpetration by women in general?

The sex difference in intimate violence is confined to lethal and near-lethal acts of aggression. Archer's (2000) meta-analytic review of spousal aggression shows that men are more likely than women to kill and inflict serious injury on their partners. The proportion of spousal homicides in which women are victims is usually well above .50 with the highest values occurring in India and Africa. However, this gender imbalance is not true for sublethal attack. Archer's (2000) meta-analysis found a small effect size ($d = -.05$) in favor of women. This is supported by studies in which participants are asked to report on their probable reaction to infidelity; women score higher than men in reported likelihood of physical and verbal abuse of their partner (De Weerth & Kalma, 1993). Nor is women's partner aggression attributable to self-defense: More women than men report that they initiated an attack (DeMaris, 1992). Female assaults are most often initiated by younger women, typically students, in a dating relationship in which there is a low rate of male aggression. Archer (2000) proposes that these women have little fear of sanctions or retaliation by their partner. Here, as in other arenas of aggression, the magnitude of the sex difference rises in line with the lethality of the attack, and women's fear is negatively related to their aggression (Eagly & Steffen, 1986).

MALE SAME-SEX AGGRESSION

Worldwide, more than 99% of same-sex homicides are male on male (Daly & Wilson, 1988). Although men's homicidal response has been seen as disproportionate to the cause, ethnographic work (Katz, 1988) suggests that what might appear "trivial" to a dispassionate outsider is of central concern to the participants. What is at stake is variously called heart, face, balls, or honor—in short, a man's status vis-à-vis his peers. The interactional pattern of these disputes has been reconstructed (e.g., Felson, 1982) and takes a fairly predictable form. Man A behaves in a way that is read by B as a slight to his status (jostles him, reprimands him, makes hostile eye contact). B responds by demanding that A retract the affront. A refuses to comply and B threatens aggression. At this point, third parties may intervene to defuse or encourage the dispute. Once a threat has been issued, it is difficult for the protagonists to back down without loss of face. The dynamic that drives the escalation is the refusal by both parties to submit or withdraw even when neither one wants to proceed with the fight.

Daly and Wilson (1988) interpret men's extreme sensitivity to slight and loss of status in evolutionary terms. Polygyny represents a successful strategy for any man with good genetic or material resources because he is not constrained by the reproductive output of one woman as in monogamy. Effective polygyny exists where the fitness variance of males exceeds that of females. The extreme tails of the male distribution represent that exceptional reward in terms of resulting children available to successfully polygynous men and the catastrophic failure of losers. Males compete for females because of their greater parental investment, and competition is fierce because of the high fitness incentives. Men are sensitive to slights to their status because of the association between dominance and reproductive success. Contemporary men are not directly fighting *about* women (Fischer & Rodriguez Mosquera, 2001). Rather, they are fighting for status in relation to other men because in ancestral times this would have translated to increased reproductive success.

Evolutionary developmental psychologists have proposed that childhood sex differences reflect boys' preparation for the status contests of young adulthood. Boys are more assertive than girls by 13 months of age (Goldberg & Lewis, 1969). Between the ages of 2 and 4, boys more often attack people, fight, and destroy things than do girls (Koot & Verhulst, 1991). Boys prefer to compete while girls prefer to cooperate (Boehnke, Silbereisen, Eisenberg, Teykowski, & Palmonari, 1989), spending 65% of their free time in competitive games compared to 35% among girls (Lever, 1978). Sports reflect boys' preference for gross motor behavior and propulsion, which is evident cross-culturally (Whiting & Edwards, 1988) from infancy onward (Eaton & Enns, 1986). There is also a marked difference between the sexes, visible by age 3, in play that involves chasing, capturing, wrestling, and restraining. Boys engage in rough and tumble play three to six times as frequently as girls (DiPietro, 1981). Boys more than girls can tell who is strongest in rough and tumble play, try to win to show that they are tougher, and think it is important to be good at real fighting (Boulton, 1996). Rough play seems to be important in establishing social dominance, which boys rate as more important than girls (Jarvinen & Nicholls, 1996). Hierarchical dominance relations appear in boys' groups from the age of 6, and a boy's position at this age predicts his dominance 9 years later (Weisfeld, 1999).

FEMALE SAME-SEX AGGRESSION

Ecologically or socially imposed monogamy tends to equalize the fitness distribution of the sexes and creates two-way sexual selection. We, therefore, expect that women would compete with one another in the currency of attributes that are valued by men.

One of these is age. Because fertility declines after about the age of 25, adult males prefer younger partners, and marriage patterns indicate that the typical age gap is about 3 years (Buss & Schmitt, 1993). However, teenage boys rate a woman 5 years older than them to be the perfect partner (Kenrick, Keefe, Gabrielidis, & Cornelius, 1996) while by the age of 60, men prefer women who are on average 15 years younger than themselves (Kenrick & Keefe, 1992). Associated with age is physical attractiveness, ranked as more important in mate choice by men than women. Historically, women have used lead, mercury, lemon juice, egg whites, milk, vinegar, kohl, and dye to enhance their facial features. In the United States, 88% of women over the age of 18 wear makeup to correct asymmetries, signal sexuality, and mimic youth, and 91% of face lifts are performed on women (Etcoff, 1999). Because a narrow waist is associated with age and fertility (Zaadstra et al., 1993), women use bras, corsets, and surgery to "normalize" perceived size anomalies and to exaggerate the apparent narrowness of the waist. In evaluating their rivals, women attend particularly to their waist, hips, and legs (Dijkstra & Buunk, 2001). While men compete with rival men by exaggerating their superiority, promiscuity, and popularity, women compete with other women by alterations to their appearance, such as makeup, nail polish, fake tans, and tight clothing (Buss, 1988a, 1988b; Tooke & Camire, 1991). Even where there is no explicit mention of attracting mates, women more often compete with one another in the currency of appearance (Cashdan, 1998; Walters & Crawford, 1994).

Given paternity uncertainty (consequent on concealed ovulation, internal fertilization, and continuous female receptivity), men are concerned about future

[handwritten note at top: Hmn ... seems to contradict interest in pomo & "slutty girls" cost benefit diff in considering partner vs. temp. sexual mate]

fidelity in a long-term partner. Because the best predictor of future behavior is past behavior, a woman's past willingness to engage in casual sex is information that is likely to carry considerable weight. Terms such as *slag, tart,* or *whore* are powerful sources of reputation challenge among women (Brown, 1998; Campbell, 1995; Lees, 1993). Girls are reluctant to associate with girls who have developed a reputation (Lees, 1993). Women more than men enforce this double standard of sexual restraint (Baumeister & Twenge, 2002). Buss and Dedden's (1990) study found that young women were judged more likely than men to question a rival's fidelity and to draw attention to their promiscuity. Observational studies of female street gang members (Campbell, 1986; Hanna, 1999) indicate that this is not confined to middle-class women: "The girls have very distinct notions and expectations of other female members' appearance and conduct that are clearly tied to their sexual reputation ... we find gang girls spending a great deal of energy 'bitching' or casting doubt on others' reputations. This cross-cultural process operates not only as a mechanism of social control, but also of distancing and confirming one's own reputation" (Joe Laidler & Hunt, 2001, p. 668). Despite public acknowledgment of the double standard of sexual behavior, accusations of female promiscuity continue to be potent. As Lees (1993, p. 267) notes, "... a girl reacts by denying the accusation rather than by objecting to the use of the category. For them what is important is to prove that you are not a slag: what they unquestioningly accept is *the legitimacy of the category of slag.*"

DEFECTION AGGRESSION

Humans are characterized by uniquely high levels of cooperation between nonkin (Trivers, 1971). The chief threat to the evolvability of reciprocal altruism is cheaters or freeloaders who accept altruistic acts but do not repay them (see Cosmides & Tooby, Chapter 20, this volume). Incentive theories such as indirect reciprocity and costly signaling propose a net benefit to altruists over the long term. Deterrent theories, more relevant to aggression, highlight costs inflicted on individuals who fail to reciprocate.

In the short term, retribution is costly for the wronged party; a trifling loss may not be worth the energy and risk of locating and punishing the cheater. But retaliation must be inflicted (not merely threatened) if it is to be credible and act as an "honest" deterrence signal. A mechanism is required that ensures that the best long-term, rather than short-term, strategy is selected. Anger solves this "commitment problem" (Frank, 1988).

That humans are prepared to incur losses to avoid being exploited is demonstrated in the Ultimatum Bargaining Game. Player A is given a sum of money (e.g., $1) and must offer some proportion of it to Player B. If B accepts, the money is divided as agreed, but if B refuses neither party gets any money. Despite the fact that a minimum offer (1 cent) should rationally be accepted by Player B, most frequently it is not (Kahneman, Knetsch, & Thaler, 1986). Nor are such derisory offers usually made (Güth, Schmittberger, & Schwarze, 1982). Humans will incur an absolute cost provided it penalizes a "cheater" even more, and potential cheaters are sensitive to this likely "punishment." This is true even in "one-off" interactions with strangers. Punishment is associated with anger that is proportionate to degree of exploitation and is effective in deterring it (Fehr & Gächter, 2002).

COALITIONAL AGGRESSION

As Geary and Flinn (2002, p. 747) note, "In preindustrial societies, coalitional warfare is common and social politicking and alliance formation is a crucial element of the social life of men." High levels of intragroup cooperation provide a platform for intergroup competition. Such competition is chiefly undertaken by males. They compete for control of resources and the territories that contain them (van der Dennen, 2002) whether they are attractive to females (foraging areas) or they are advantageous to males (areas containing females from other groups). With respect to between-group territorial aggression, humans and chimpanzees are both similar and unusual: "Very few animals live in patrilineal male-bonded communities wherein females routinely reduce the risks of inbreeding by moving to neighboring groups to mate. And only two animal species are known to do so with a system of intense, male initiated territorial aggression, including lethal raiding into neighbouring communities in search of vulnerable enemies to attack and kill" (Wrangham & Peterson, 1996, p. 24). Female transfer, male cooperation, group territoriality, and "proto-ethnocentrism" appear to be the necessary conditions for intergroup aggression (van der Dennen, 1995; Wrangham, 1999).

Chagnon (1988) described the high levels of between-group violence among the Yanomamo, subsistence farmers of southern Venezuela and northern Brazil. The 20,000 Yanomamo live in groups of about 90 people. If disputes between individual members of different groups cannot be dealt with by a chest-pounding duel or a club fight, the entire village will wage war. This often involves raids in which 10 to 20 men make a 4- or 5-day walk to the enemy's village. At dawn, they shoot any undefended male that they can find with poison-tipped arrows. If they happen upon a woman, she is abducted, raped, and taken back to their own village—where the villagers wait for the inevitable retaliatory raid. About 40% of Yanomamo men are *unokais*—men who have killed—and they are celebrated as heroes, acquiring two and a half times the number of wives as other men and producing more than three times the number of children (Chagnon, 1988). Similar examples of raiding and retaliation are reported among other swidden agriculturalists and among hunter-gatherers (Robarchek & Robarchek, 1992).

Social identity theory provides a psychological account of the proto-ethnocentrism underpinning intergroup conflict. Social identity theorists (Hogg & Abrams, 1988) took the classic Robber's Cave study (Sherif, Harvey, White, Hood, & Sherif, 1961) as the basis for arguing that intergroup hostility results from realistic competition over resources. The minimal group paradigm is used to examine the process in the laboratory: Participants are randomly allocated to one of two groups and asked to choose (from a selection) an allocation of points to individuals (excluding themselves) in each group. Although the alternatives provide the opportunity to do this either fairly, in terms of maximum joint profit or maximum in-group profit, individuals actually choose to maximize the differences between the two groups even when this means penalizing the in-group in terms of absolute gains. Although not explicitly instructed to compete, participants aim to create the maximum difference between their resources and those of the other group. This effect rests on two processes. Social categorization allows individuals to categorize themselves as group members ("an accentuation of similarities between self and other in-groupers and differences between self and outgroupers," Hogg & Abrams, 1988, p. 21) while social comparison processes steer the individual toward the selection of dimensions on which the in-group excels (positive distinctiveness) resulting in enhanced social identity for the group and motivating the acquisition of group norms of behavior. Mere self-identification as a group member trips the switch that directs us toward in-group loyalty and competition with other groups.

There is a tension between individual 'selfish' selection, favoring nonpartici-pation in warfare, and group selection favoring participation. One approach em-phasizes the within-group benefits accruing to warriors: status, reproductive success, deference, and indebtedness. Along with these incentives, punishment or ostracism of nonparticipators can act as a deterrent (Boyd, Gintis, Bowles, & Richerson, 2003; Boyd & Richerson, 1992). Ostracism would have been a virtual death sentence in the Pleistocene. Even those who reject group selectionism do not deny that group membership is the single best individual strategy for sur-vival. Animals in many species flock or aggregate because an isolated individual is more vulnerable to attack or predation.

Maynard Smith (1998) addresses the tension between individual and group-level selection factors in terms of relative selection pressures:

> The essential point is that higher level entities (for example individuals carrying many genes, or societies comprising many individuals) will evolve characteristics favoring the success of the group, provided there are processes that reduce within-group selection. In human groups, the most important such process is the ho-mogenisation of behaviour by social norms. (p. 640)

This dovetails well with social identity theory's emphasis on subscription to common norms of mutual assistance and cooperation. Conformity to local norms can also account for the development of subgroups and group fission. Kenrick, Li, and Butner (2003) used dynamical systems theory to show that, even where the tendency to act in a cooperative way is randomly distributed, the simple rule, "Do what the majority of your immediate neighbors do," over time results in a clear bifurcation of the population into distinct strategies. This might engender group fission resulting in the extinction of groups composed of 'selfish' strategists either as a result of internal group dynamics or of between-group competition.

In summary, coalitional aggression will evolve where the value of the benefits (increased inclusive fitness, avoidance of punishment or ostracism) exceeds the costs (injury, death), each multiplied by its respective probability. (The probabil-ity of incurring life-threatening costs was likely minimized by a strong imbalance of power favoring the attacking group; Wrangham, 1999.) Under these conditions, warriors would do better than nonwarriors. Cultural transmission favoring imita-tion of the most successful (and subsequently the most common) strategy would increase male coalitional aggression. Consequent territorial expansion meant in-creased resources in terms of safety, nutrition, and mates. Once such effective groups evolved, less cohesive groups would be at a strong selective disadvantage. As van der Dennen (2002, p. 58) notes, "the only possible competitive strategy for survival in competition with a group practicing warfare is warfare itself," leading to a positive feedback loop.

SEX DIFFERENCES IN AGGRESSION

Daly and Wilson (1988) set out the evolutionary logic of heightened male relative to female aggression (see Male Same-Sex Aggression section). Theirs is an incentive position; the greater variance in male fitness associated with polygyny means that males have much to gain by aggression. Females cannot increase their reproductive output by mating with multiple partners; hence there is less incentive for competition. Daly and Wilson are agnostic as to the mediating psychological mechanisms underlying increased male aggression suggesting various possibilities, most of which increase appetitive motivation and a few of which suggest a reduction in inhibition.

Campbell (1999, 2002) argued that the sex difference in aggression can best be understood in terms of differences in parental investment. When females make the greater parental investment, the death of a mother has more serious consequences for the survival of her offspring than the death of a father. This would favor female avoidance of direct physical aggression except in those circumstances where failure to aggress posed even greater costs (i.e., maternal aggression in the face of infanticidal conspecifics). Studies suggest that the proximal psychological mechanism may be inhibition (fear and behavioral suppression of aggression) rather than incentives (anger in which sex differences are not found, Kring, 2000). The magnitude of sex differences in aggression rises in line with the dangerousness of the form and the extent of likely injury, provocation, emotional arousal, and fear reported by females (Bettencourt & Miller, 1996; Eagly & Steffen, 1986; Knight, Guthrie, Page, & Fabes, 2002). Females also show decreased risk taking where there is danger of immediate physical injury (Byrnes, Miller, & Schafer, 1999), higher levels of anxiety and fear (Arrindell, Kolk, Pickersgill, & Hageman, 1993), and stronger behavioral inhibition (Bjorklund & Kipp, 1996).

Campbell argues that females have strong incentives to compete (for long-term mates and resources) but that this is typically managed by employing indirect or relational strategies that pose less danger to the perpetrator (Bjorkqvist, Lagerspetz, & Kaukiainen, 1992). These strategies include rumor spreading, punitive friendship termination, gossiping, ostracism, and stigmatization. These forms of indirect aggression generally increase between the ages of 6 and 17 years, but the increase is more marked in girls than in boys (Archer, in press). In adulthood, at least in Western samples, the sex difference diminishes as males move toward less confrontational tactics.

Taylor et al. (2000) also proceed from the assumption that greater parental investment by females has increased their need to avoid exposing themselves and their offspring to danger. They propose that neuroendocrine responses may have developed in response to threats that make fight-or-flight less likely in females and instead enhance befriending other females in the service of tending the infant when danger is near. Although the HPA stress response does not differ substantially between the sexes, they propose that the associated behavioral response may. In males, testosterone rises in response to stress and mediates the relationship between sympathetic arousal and aggression. Because mothers cannot flee or fight without leaving their offspring fatally exposed, estrogen enhances the anxiolytic properties of oxytocin that is released in response to stress and is implicated in maternal bonding with the infant. With fight and flight both representing dangerous options, females tend to form strong affiliative bonds with one another for protection. Groups are better able to detect incipient threat, to confuse a predator, and to mount an effective defense.

MECHANISMS OF AGGRESSION

Although emotion has historically been seen as the enemy of reason, there is now considerable scholarly agreement that emotions act to promote the selection of adaptive strategies. For evolutionary psychologists, the function of emotions is to focus attention on immediate problems in the environment and to aid in winnowing down, evaluating, and selecting courses of action. Emotions, in short, solve the "frame problem" (Ketelaar & Todd, 2001), which appears whenever there are too many pieces of information available and no means of knowing which are relevant to the solution of a current problem. By the time an individual (even if it were computationally possible) has considered all the possible implications of every piece of information in a stimulus array in order to locate those that are relevant, they are likely to have incurred severe opportunity costs or even death. What is needed is a device that will prioritize relevant information and allow a fast and frugal decision to be taken that maximizes positive outcomes.

Emotions serve this function. Honed over evolutionary time, they equip us with guidance knowledge related to past outcomes that we have neither seen nor experienced. Emotions do not inflexibly produce a single automatic behavior, rather:

> . . . an emotion is a superordinate program whose function is to direct the activities and interactions of the subprograms governing perception; attention; inference; learning; memory; goal choice. . . . An emotion is not reducible to any one category of effects, such as effects on physiology, behavioural inclinations, cognitive appraisals, or feeling states, because it involves evolved instructions for all of them together. (Cosmides & Tooby, 2000, p. 93)

In situations of potential aggression, rewards and costs must both be calculated. The two corresponding emotional systems are anger and fear. At an anatomical level, the anger and fear systems run in parallel, linking the amygdala and the periaqueductal gray matter via the hypothalamus (Panksepp, 2002). Both systems entrain a variety of information processing subroutines including attentional bias, selective encoding of information, interpretation, and anticipation of likely consequences (Coie & Dodge, 1997). LeDoux's (1998) work on fear has shown that dangerous stimuli are processed by a fast "low road" from the sensory thalamus to the amygdala, and a slower "high road" through the sensory cortex that provides a fuller representation of the source of danger and, as with anger, allows for more sensitive processing of relevant information (Öhman, 2000). The output of these parallel processes is a conscious emotional experience, which may vary along a continuum between pure anger and pure fear. Impulses to aggress can be completely checked by fear, resulting in freezing or immobility where flight is impossible or unlikely to be successful. Inaction may turn off whatever signals are currently activating the opponent's anger.

While fear has an automatic inhibitory effect on ongoing activity, inhibition can also be instated through top-down or effortful commands (Gray, 1982). This is particularly true of human aggression; we are able to inhibit aggression against inappropriate targets (e.g., small children) despite an absence of fear. This distinction between motivational (fearful, subcortical) inhibition and effortful (goal-oriented, prefrontal) inhibition has been made by Derryberry and Rothbart (1997). The former develops early in life and is associated with the limbic system while the latter appears later, concurrent with anterior cortical structures. The acquisition of effortful control appears to be built on the fear response (Fowles, 1994), and individuals with higher levels of fearfulness demonstrate enhanced inhibitory control over their behavior (Rothbart & Bates, 1998). Weak motivational inhibition is thought to underlie the aggressive problems of conduct disorder. Quay (1993), following Gray (1982), argued that impulsive behavior results from a relatively underactive inhibition mechanism, encapsulated in the notion that aggressive individuals are "bad at fear." Low resting heart rate in children (a partially heritable index of fearlessness and low nervous system reactivity) is predictive of later aggression and adult violent crime (Raine, Venables, & Mednick, 1997). Conduct-disordered children and psychopaths perform poorly on passive avoidance tasks (that require response inhibition) as a result of their diminished sensitivity to and reflection on cues for adverse consequences (Patterson & Newman, 1993).

Self-control has attracted much interest in the field of criminology. Because the benefits of crime are immediate and appealing, an adequate theory must address why the majority of people desist from it. Gottfredson and Hirschi (1990) emphasized the importance of self-control (composed of impulsivity, risk seeking, present orientation, temper, and carelessness) in interaction with criminal opportunities. This proposal has been tested in 21 empirical studies with more than 49,727 participants. The effect size found for low self-control ranks as "one of the strongest known correlates of crime" (Pratt & Cullen, 2000, p. 952). Two of the component subscales (risk seeking and impulsivity) have been found to be as predictive of offending as the full scale (LaGrange & Silverman, 1999). These are the components most closely associated with inhibitory processes.

Self-control finds its psychological analogue in *behavioral impulsivity*. This was examined in a longitudinal study of the development of antisocial behavior (White et al., 1994). Factor analysis of 11 different impulsivity measures revealed two factors: cognitive (e.g., Stroop task performance) and behavioral (e.g., ratings of impulsive behavior). While the factors were intercorrelated at .53, it was behavioral impulsivity that was more strongly related to delinquency. Similar results have been found in other longitudinal studies (Loeber et al., 2001). Impulsivity is particularly relevant to violent offenses (Henry, Caspi, Moffitt, & Silva, 1996).

Sex differences have been found in social and behavioral inhibition (Bjorklund & Kipp, 1996), criminological measures of self-control (LaGrange & Silverman, 1999), impulsivity (Côté, Tremblay, Nagin, Zoccolillo, & Vitaro, 2002), and effortful control (Kochanska, Murray, & Harlan, 2000). There are also marked sex differences in pathologies of underregulation (Moffitt, Caspi, Rutter, & Silva, 2001). Moffitt et al. (2001) found that sex differences in antisocial behavior could be fully explained by personality variables including the higher order trait of constraint (self-control, harm avoidance, and traditionalism). At a neurochemical level, researchers have identified serotonin (5-HT) as the transmitter responsible for inhibitory control over aggression (Miczek, Weerts, Haney, & Tidey, 1994). Sex differences have been reported in serotonin uptake, especially in the frontal cortex responsible for behavioral inhibition (e.g., Biver et al., 1996).

CONTEXTUAL ADJUSTMENT OF AGGRESSION IN DEVELOPMENT

The phenotype is a product of epigenesis: the interaction of the genotype with its environment over time. Increasingly, evolutionary psychologists are exploring how conditional strategies may be affected by life history circumstances. We would expect that sustained immersion in a highly aggressive community should result in raised levels of aggression because failure to aggress (when this is the majority strategy) is likely to result in considerable costs. This section considers the evidence for this proposal.

THE ECOLOGICAL TRANSMISSION OF AGGRESSION

Violence is closely associated with community poverty where competition for essential resources is high. Neighborhood impoverishment explained 71% of the variance in violent crime across 171 census tracts (Coulton, Korbin, Su, & Chow, 1995). Children growing up in these neighborhoods are more frequently exposed to violence (Sampson & Lauritsen, 1994) and are more often victimized by it (Esbensen & Huizinga, 1991). Both experiences are associated with violent behavior (Salzinger, Feldman, Stockhammer, & Hood, 2002).

Within communities, family poverty is associated with high levels of partner violence. Witnessing parental violence increases child aggression (Widom, 1989). Jaffee, Moffitt, Caspi, Taylor, and Arseneault (2002) found that over and above common genetic effects, adult domestic violence accounted for 5% of the variation in children's externalizing behaviors. Poverty is also strongly associated with child maltreatment (Coulton et al., 1995), and researchers concur that the effect of poverty on children is mediated by parenting style (Zingraff, Leiter, Meyers, & Johnsen, 1993). Family poverty and descent into poverty increase parental stress, the use of harsh discipline, low levels of supervision, poor parent-child attachment, and noncompliant behavior, which in turn are associated with delinquency (Leventhal & Brooks-Gunn, 2000; McLoyd, 1998; Sampson & Laub, 1994). Aspects of family functioning that involve direct parent-child contact are the most powerful predictors of delinquency (Loeber & Southamer-Loeber, 1986). Dodge, Pettit, and Bates (1994) reported that physical discipline by parents explained about half the effect of low socioeconomic status on children's aggressive behavior. Sampson and Laub (1994, p. 536) found that family processes accounted for two-thirds of the relationship between poverty and delinquency and that "the significant effect of poverty on delinquency is eliminated when discipline, supervision and attachment are controlled."

Parents' style of child rearing is responsive to the temperament and behavior of the child (Lytton, 1990). Difficult children evoke lower levels of maternal supervision, more erratic and harsh discipline, and weakened attachment between parent and child (Sampson & Laub, 1994). They may also be more vulnerable to community effects. The impact of impulsivity on antisocial behavior is stronger in poorer neighborhoods with low community control (Lynam et al., 2000).

Child temperament suggests an additional complication for ecological analysis: the selective migration of *genetically* vulnerable families to poor neighborhoods. With regard to genetic effects, Carey's (1994) review of twin and adoption studies that assessed aggressive personality characteristics at various ages gave a heritability estimate of .44. Caspi, Taylor, Moffitt, and Plomin (2000) found that genetic effects accounted for 55% of the variance in 2-year-old children's problem behavior, shared family environment for 20%, and child-specific environment for 24%.

Moffitt (1993) presents an explicitly interactional model of the development of antisocial behavior. Some infants are neuropsychologically vulnerable as a result of poor prenatal and perinatal care or genetically inherited deficits. The problem behaviors of these children are compounded by passive (parental lifestyle), reactive (hostile parental response), and active (deviant peer choice) gene-environment correlations. The resulting difficult temperament manifests itself in *heterotypic continuity* across the life span (toddler tantrums, childhood aggression, adolescent high-risk sexual and lifestyle choices, adult spouse abuse, and child maltreatment).

As the preceding studies show, there is a clear association between growing up in a violent neighborhood or home and increased risk of violent behavior. The next section considers how such phenotypic alteration might take place.

PSYCHOLOGICAL MODELS OF ECOLOGICAL ADJUSTMENT

Dodge and Coie's (see Coie & Dodge, 1997) information processing model proposes that high levels of aggression are explained by deficits or biases at different stages in the transition between information reception and behavioral enactment.

With regard to *encoding,* aggressive children selectively attend to aggressive cues in the stimulus array. Todorov and Bargh (2002) describe this as an automatic priming effect, involving a spreading activation from the stimulus itself to associated physiological reactions, motor tendencies, feelings, thoughts, and memories. Semantic priming effects have been found for aggression even when stimuli are presented below perceptual threshold (Srull & Wyer, 1979, 1980). Chronic accessibility occurs where individuals have been exposed to consistently high levels of mundane aggression. Stimuli that cue chronically accessible constructs are detected even under conditions of information overload (Bargh & Pratto, 1986). As Coie and Dodge (1997, p. 797) note, ". . . growing up in an environment in which violence is normative will increase the accessibility of aggressive constructs in future situations."

Aggressive children (both clinical and nonclinical) more often make hostile attributions to ambiguous acts than do nonaggressive children (Coie & Dodge, 1997). This hostile attribution bias is largely confined to judgments about actions directed toward the self and is predictive of future aggressive behavior and violent crime. Hostile attributions can be veridical, as Coie and Dodge (1997) point out:

> It is only a short leap to suggest that attributions of hostile intent and experiences of anger in response to current provocative stimuli are more likely if a child is

growing under circumstances of pervasive violence, harm, and deprivation: when provocateurs regularly assault the child; when assaults regularly occur toward the child's family, peers and ethnic group; and when peer groups and family also interpret provocateurs as being hostile. These conditions characterize many environments of poverty and ethnic heterogeneity; and some subcultures (e.g., gangs). In such environments, hypervigilance to hostile cues and attributions of threat may occasionally be adaptive, and retaliatory aggression may be common. (p. 796)

In terms of *accessing possible responses,* elementary-age aggressive children generate relatively more antisocial and aggressive solutions to conflict. Experience of aggressive interchanges also contributes to the formation of scripts or event-specific memories that are used to guide behavior (Huesmann, 1988). Violent families and neighborhoods present repeated opportunities to learn aggressive scripts (Coie & Dodge, 1997).

Response selection depends in part on a child's experience of the payoffs for aggression. Among peers, children who successfully counteraggress against bullies become more likely to react aggressively in the future (Patterson, Littman, & Bricker, 1967), and within the family, children's aggressive behavior is negatively reinforced by the termination of aversive maternal nagging. Aggressive children anticipate more positive outcomes from aggression and expect fewer negative sanctions (punishment and unpopularity) than nonaggressive children (see Coie & Dodge, 1997). Empirically, it is difficult to distinguish between response selection and the final stage of the model *behavioral enactment.* Inhibitory deficits have been strongly implicated in both processes (see Mechanisms of Aggression section).

Other approaches to developmental adjustment focus on alterations in stress reactions. The threat of violence induces fear. In response to fear messages from the amygdala and hippocampus, the hypothalamic-pituitary-adrenal (HPA) axis releases corticosteroids to prepare the body for flight or fight reactions. Long-term or chronic exposure to fear-inducing stimuli is associated with dysregulation of the system (Glaser, 2000). Repeated exposure can lead to down-regulation of the biochemical response resulting in cortisol levels within the normal range and lower responsiveness to frightening situations (Yehuda, Giller, Southwick, Lowy, & Mason, 1991). Maltreated children show no rise in cortisol levels in response to a conflictual social interaction (Hart, Gunnar, & Cicchetti, 1995). Aggressive children and adolescents also show lower heart rates (Raine, 1993), suggestive of an underactive response to threat or danger.

Early mother-infant experiences may be implicated in this lowered response. Separation from the mother in monkey studies activates the HPA stress response. Gunnar (1998) suggests that because high cortisol levels can be damaging to the developing brain, security of attachment evolved as a mechanism to protect the brain by buffering the HPA axis. Maltreated children have been found to show lower levels of cortisol reactivity in stressful situations, suggesting down-regulation or blunting of the HPA axis. Paradoxically, they also show hypervigilance and hyperactive response to threatening cues (Perry, Pollard, Blakley, Baker, & Vigilante, 1995).

Information processing and physiological adjustments are unlikely to be independent of each other (Repetti, Taylor, & Seeman, 2002). Sustained mundane violence in the family can enhance attention to aggressive cues and increase hostile attributions while simultaneously altering the magnitude of the stress response and lowering behavioral inhibitions against aggression.

AGGRESSION AND CULTURE

To many evolutionary psychologists, culture means the social transmission of knowledge and behavior. In addition to specific mechanisms that prepare humans to meet recurrent challenges in the environment, we have evolved the capacity for cultural learning. While much has been written about gene-culture coevolution (see Janicki & Krebs, 1998), very little of this material has explicitly focused on aggression.

Evolutionary-minded social scientists approach the role of culture with caution. When geographical variability in a behavior is found, two candidate solutions present themselves: pure cultural transmission and facultative adaptation to an ecological niche (sometimes called *evoked culture*). The previous section outlined how such a facultative adaptation might be developmentally mediated. The process hinges on adjustment to prevailing levels of aggressive behavior in the surrounding community and especially the family—it does not argue that aggressive behavior itself has to be learned. Indeed, there is much evidence to the contrary (Archer & Côté, in press). Aggression is manifest from an early age in infants and children around the world. Children learn to modulate aggression, bringing it into line with community levels.

While culture is a problematic tool for explaining the acquisition of aggressive behavior, it is a stronger candidate for explaining how such acts are interpreted. Aggression can be valued or condemned according to its context and historical period. We honor men who kill in war but prosecute men who kill in peacetime. We tolerate a parent who hits his or her own child but not one who hits someone else's. Greek warrior heroes carried off women as prizes of war, but today rape by invading troops, though not uncommon, is condemned. Valuation of aggression is a stronger candidate for a cultural explanation because it shows variability. Variability does not imply arbitrariness. There are good reasons why a group might value acts of intergroup aggression while condemning the same acts when directed at in-group members or why males, living in monogamous relationships, might be outraged by rape.

Although the value accorded to aggression may influence its behavioral form and frequency, the failure of social psychology to establish significant relationships between attitudes and behavior should make us skeptical. Attitudes are poor predictors of behavior. Societal tolerance of aggression may be more likely to affect post hoc explanations than behavior itself. When acts are strongly condemned, people offer excuses for their behavior. Excuses are assertions that, though the act in question was wrong, the actor cannot be held fully accountable for his or her actions. Where there is greater tolerance, aggressors may seek to justify their action. Justifications consist of an admission of responsibility but an assertion that the act in question was necessary or laudable under the particular circumstances. These two forms of account may vary historically or regionally according to prevailing attitudes. Street gang members *justify* their aggression in terms of territorial defense, self-protection, or economics, that is, maintaining a monopoly on local drug sales (Campbell, 1986). Middle-class women *excuse* their aggression as a temporary lapse of self-control caused by stress, alcohol, or hormonal disturbance (Campbell, 1993).

Cultural learning is more than acquiring new behaviors as it is in other primates. The human abilities to assume an intentional stance, form symbolic mental representations, and communicate by language allow us to transmit values about behaviors, modify these evaluations as a function of context, entertain multiple interpretations of the same event, and even dispute the legitimacy of these various representations. We argue about the morality of a "just" war, codify social judgments in criminal law but accept mitigation, chide our children for fighting yet secretly hope that they will stand up for themselves, and seek the dividing line where "normal" aggression becomes pathological. These reflective and discursive abilities mark us out as human, but beneath our moral and political equivocation lies aggression as a basic, evolved tool of survival.

CONCLUSIONS

The psychology of aggression, prior to the advent of an evolutionary perspective, was often a fragmented and incoherent enterprise. Psychologists studying aggression in criminology, child development, sociology, neuroscience, and clinical work had no common language. Theories abounded and the selection of one over another appeared to reflect the personal or political predilection of the researcher. Variables examined in studies were as often based on common-sense pragmatics as on theory. Evolutionary theory provides a coherent way of thinking and talking about aggression in functional terms. Not only does it make sense of everyday emotional experiences such as jealousy, rivalry, competition and in-group loyalty, but in generates predictions, often novel, that are testable. Despite early critical misunderstanding ("genes for aggression"), the basic biological fact that DNA codes for proteins that build brains that affect and are affected by the environment is now widely understood by social scientists. Evolutionary psychology has progressed to the point of being as much about psychology as about evolution. Emotion and cognition have taken center stage as the proximal mediators of behavior. Like other species, we are the inheritors of brains equipped with primitive automatic hormonal, emotional, and behavioral responses designed to assist our survival under threat. Uniquely, the massive cortical expansion of the human brain has given us the ability to flexibly, consciously, and culturally tailor behavior to our circumstances.

REFERENCES

Amato, P. R., & Rogers, S. J. (1997). A longitudinal study of marital problems and subsequent divorce. *Journal of Marriage and the Family, 59,* 612–624.

Archer, J. (2000). Sex differences in aggression between heterosexual partners: A meta-analysis. *Psychological Bulletin, 126,* 651–680.

Archer, J. (in press). Are women or men the more aggressive sex. In S. Fein, A. Goethals, & M. Sandstrom (Eds.), *Gender and aggression.* Mahwah, NJ: Erlbaum.

Archer, J., & Côté, S. (2005). Sex differences in aggressive behaviour: A developmental and evolutionary perspective. In R. E. Tremblay, W. W. Hartup, & J. Archer (Eds.), *Developmental origins of aggression* (pp. 425–446). New York: Guilford Press.

Aronson, E. (1992). *The social animal*. New York: Freeman.

Arrindell, W. A., Kolk, A. M., Pickersgill, M. J., & Hageman, W. J. J. M. (1993). Biological sex, sex-role orientation, masculine sex role stress, dissimulation and self-reported fears. *Advances in Behaviour Research and Therapy, 15,* 103–146.

Baker, R. (1996). *Sperm wars*. London: Fourth Estate.

Bargh, J. A., & Pratto, F. (1986). Individual construct accessibility and perceptual selection. *Journal of Experimental Social Psychology, 22,* 293–311.

Baumeister, R. F., & Twenge, J. M. (2002). Cultural suppression of female sexuality. *Review of General Psychology, 6,* 166–203.

Bettencourt, B. A., & Miller, N. (1996). Gender differences in aggression as a function of provocation: A meta-analysis. *Psychological Bulletin, 119,* 422–447.

Betzig, L. L. (1989). Causes of marital dissolution: A cross-cultural study. *Current Anthropology, 30,* 654–676.

Biver, F., Lotstra, F., Monclus, M., Wikler, D., Damhaut, P., Mendlewicz, J., et al. (1996). Sex difference in 5HT(2) receptor in the living human brain. *Neuroscience Letters, 204,* 1–2.

Bjorklund, D. F., & Kipp, K. (1996). Parental investment theory and gender differences in the evolution of inhibition mechanisms. *Psychological Bulletin, 120,* 163–188.

Bjorkqvist, K., Lagerspetz, K., & Kaukiainen, A. (1992). Do girls manipulate and boys fight? Developmental trends in regard to direct and indirect aggression. *Aggressive Behavior, 18,* 117–127.

Boehnke, K., Silbereisen, R., Eisenberg, N., Teykowski, J., & Palmonari, A. (1989). Developmental patterns of prosocial motivation: A cross-national study. *Journal of Cross-Cultural Psychology, 20,* 219–243.

Boulton, M. (1996). A comparison of 8- and 11-year-old girls' and boys' participation in specific types of rough-and-tumble play and aggressive fighting: Implications for functional hypotheses. *Aggressive Behavior, 22,* 271–287.

Boyd, R., Gintis, H., Bowles, S., & Richerson, P. J. (2003). The evolution of altruistic punishment. *Proceedings of the National Academy of Sciences, 100,* 3531–3535.

Boyd, R., & Richerson, P. (1992). Punishment allows the evolution of cooperation (and just about anything else) in sizable groups. *Ethology and Sociobiology, 13,* 171–195.

Brown, L. M. (1998). *Raising their voices: The politics of girls' anger*. London: Harvard University Press.

Bushman, B. J., & Anderson, C. A. (2001). Is it time to pull the plug on the hostile versus instrumental aggression dichotomy? *Psychological Review, 108,* 273–279.

Buss, D. M. (1988a). The evolution of human intrasexual competition: Tactics of mate attraction. *Journal of Personality and Social Psychology, 54,* 616–628.

Buss, D. M. (1988b). From vigilance to violence: Tactics of mate retention in American undergraduates. *Ethology and Sociobiology, 9,* 291–317.

Buss, D. M. (1989). Conflict between the sexes: Strategic interference and the evocation of anger and upset. *Journal of Personality and Social Psychology, 56,* 735–747.

Buss, D. M. (2000). *The dangerous passion*. London: Bloomsbury.

Buss, D. M., & Dedden, L. A. (1990). Derogation of competitors. *Journal of Personal and Social Relationships, 7,* 395–422.

Buss, D. M., & Schmitt, D. (1993). Sexual strategies theory: An evolutionary perspective on human mating. *Psychological Review, 100,* 204–232.

Buss, D. M., & Shackelford, T. K. (1997). Susceptibility to infidelity in the first year of marriage. *Journal of Research in Personality, 31,* 193–221.

Buunk, B., & Hupka, R. B. (1987). Cross-cultural differences in the elicitation of jealousy. *Journal of Sex Research, 23,* 12–22.

Byrnes, J. P., Miller, D. C., & Schafer, W. D. (1999). Gender differences in risk taking: A meta-analysis. *Psychological Bulletin, 125,* 367–383.

Campbell, A. (1986). *The girls in the gang*. Oxford, England: Blackwell.

Campbell, A. (1993). *Out of control: Men, women and aggression*. London: Pandora.

Campbell, A. (1995). A few good men: Evolutionary psychology and female adolescent aggression. *Ethology and Sociobiology, 16,* 99–123.

Campbell, A. (1999). Staying alive: Evolution, culture and women's intrasexual aggression. *Behavioural and Brain Sciences, 22,* 203–252.

Campbell, A. (2002). *A mind of her own: The evolutionary psychology of women*. Oxford, England: Oxford University Press.

Carey, G. (1994). Genetics and violence. In A. J. Reiss, K. A. Miczek, & J. A. Roth (Eds.), *Understanding and preventing violence* (pp. 21–58). Washington, DC: National Academy Press.

Cashdan, E. (1998). Are men more competitive than women? *British Journal of Social Psychology, 37,* 213–229.

Caspi, A., Taylor, A., Moffitt, T. E., & Plomin, R. (2000). Neighborhood deprivation affects children's mental health: Environmental risks identified in a genetic design. *Psychological Science, 11,* 338–342.

Chagnon, N. A. (1988). Life histories, blood revenge, and warfare in a tribal population. *Science, 239,* 985–992.

Coie, J. D., & Dodge, K. A. (1997). Aggression and antisocial behaviour. In W. Damon & N. Eisenberg (Eds.), *Handbook of child psychology: Vol. 3. Social, emotional and personality development* (pp. 779–862). New York: Wiley.

Cosmides, L., & Tooby, J. (2000). Evolutionary psychology and the emotions. In M. Lewis & J. M. Haviland-Jones (Eds.), *Handbook of emotions* (2nd ed., pp. 91–115). New York: Guilford Press.

Côté, S., Tremblay, R. E., Nagin, D., Zoccolillo, M., & Vitaro, F. (2002). The development of impulsivity, fearfulness and helpfulness during childhood: Patterns of consistency and change in trajectories of boys and girls. *Journal of Child Psychology and Psychiatry, 43,* 609–618.

Coulton, C., Korbin, J., Su, N., & Chow, J. (1995). Community level factors and child maltreatment rates. *Child Development, 66,* 1262–1276.

Daly, M., & Wilson, M. (1988). *Homicide.* New York: Aldine de Gruyter.

DeMaris, A. (1992). Male versus female initiation of aggression: The case of courtship violence. In E. C. Viano (Ed.), *Intimate violence: Interdisciplinary perspectives* (pp. 111–120). Washington, DC: Hemisphere.

Derryberry, D., & Rothbart, M. K. (1997). Reactive and effortful processes in the organization of temperament. *Development and Psychopathology, 9,* 633–652.

De Weerth, C., & Kalma, A. (1993). Female aggression as a response to sexual jealousy: A sex role reversal? *Aggressive Behavior, 19,* 265–279.

Dijkstra, P., & Buunk, B. P. (2001). Sex differences in the jealousy-evoking nature of a rival's body build. *Evolution and Human Behavior, 22,* 335–341.

DiPietro, J. A. (1981). Rough and tumble play: A function of gender. *Developmental Psychology, 17,* 50–58.

Dodge, K. A., Pettit, G. S., & Bates, J. (1994). Socialization mediators of the relation between socioeconomic status and child conduct problems. *Child Development, 65,* 649–665.

Eagly, A. H., & Steffen, V. (1986). Gender and aggressive behavior: A meta-analytic review of the social psychological literature. *Psychological Bulletin, 100,* 309–330.

Eaton, W. O., & Enns, L. R. (1986). Sex differences in human motor activity level. *Psychological Bulletin, 100,* 19–28.

Esbensen, F., & Huizinga, D. (1991). Juvenile victimization and delinquency. *Youth and Society, 23,* 202–228.

Essock-Vitale, S. M., & McGuire, M. T. (1988). What 70 million years hath wrought: Sexual histories and reproductive success of a random sample of American women. In L. Betzig, M. Borgerhoff Mulder, & P. Turke (Eds.), *Human reproductive behaviour: A Darwinian perspective* (pp. 221–235). Cambridge, England: Cambridge University Press.

Etcoff, N. (1999). *Survival of the prettiest.* London: Little, Brown.

Fehr, E., & Gächter, S. (2002). Altruistic punishment of cheaters. *Nature, 415,* 136–140.

Felson, R. B. (1982). Impression management and the escalation of aggression and violence. *Social Psychology Quarterly, 45,* 245–254.

Fincham, F. D. (2003). Marital conflict: Correlates, structure and context. *Current Directions in Psychological Science, 12,* 23–27.

Fischer, A. H., & Rodriguez Mosquera, P. M. (2001). What concerns men? Women or other men? *Psychology, Evolution and Gender, 3,* 5–25.

Fowles, D. C. (1994). A motivational theory of psychopathology. In W. G. Spaulding (Ed.), *Nebraska symposium on motivation: Vol. 41. Integrative views of motivation, cognition and emotion* (pp. 181–238). Lincoln: University of Nebraska Press.

Frank, R. (1988). *Passions within reason: The strategic role of emotions.* New York: Norton.

Gat, A. (2000). The human motivational complex: Evolutionary theory and the causes of hunter-gatherer fighting. Part I: Primary somatic and reproductive causes. *Anthropological Quarterly, 73,* 20–34.

Geary, D. C., & Flinn, M. V. (2002). Sex differences in behavioural and hormonal response to social threat: Commentary on Taylor et al. (2000). *Psychological Review, 109,* 745–750.

Geen, R. G. (2001). *Human aggression* (2nd ed.). Buckingham: Open University Press.

Glaser, D. (2000). Child abuse and neglect and the brain: A review. *Journal of Child Psychology and Psychiatry, 41,* 97–116.

Goldberg, S., & Lewis, M. (1969). Play behavior in the year-old infant: Early sex differences. *Child Development, 40,* 21–31.

Goos, L. M., & Silverman, I. (2001). The influence of genomic imprinting on brain development and behaviour. *Evolution and Human Behavior, 22,* 385–407.

Gottfredson, M., & Hirschi, T. (1990). *A general theory of crime.* Stanford, CA: Stanford University Press.

Gray, J. A. (1982). *The neuropsychology of anxiety: An enquiry into the functions of the septo-hippocampal system.* New York: Oxford University Press.

Gunnar, M. (1998). Quality of early care and buffering of neuroendocrine stress reactions: Potential effects of the developing human brain. *Preventative Medicine, 27,* 208–211.

Güth, W., Schmittberger, R., & Schwarze, B. (1982). An experimental analysis if ultimatum bargaining. *Journal of Economic Behavior and Organizations, 3,* 367–388.

Haig, D. (1996). Placental hormones, genomic imprinting and maternal-fetal communication. *Journal of Evolutionary Biology, 9,* 357–380.

Haig, D., & Graham, C. (1991). Genomic imprinting and the strange case of the insulin-like growth factor II receptor. *Cell, 64,* 1045–1046.

Hampton, R. L. (1975). Marital disruption: Some social and economic consequences. In J. N. Morgan (Ed.), *Five thousand American families* (Vol. 3, pp. 163–188). Ann Arbor, MI: Institute for Social Research.

Hanna, C. (1999). Ganging up on girls: Young women and their emerging violence. *Arizona Law Review, 41,* 93–141.

Hart, J., Gunnar, M., & Cicchetti, D. (1995). Salivary cortisol in maltreated children: Evidence of relations between neuroendocrine activity and social competence. *Development and Psychopathology, 7,* 11–26.

Henry, B., Caspi, A., Moffitt, T. E., & Silva, P. A. (1996). Temperamental and familial predictors of violent and nonviolent criminal convictions: Age 3 to age 18. *Developmental Psychology, 32,* 614–623.

Hill, E. M., & Low, B. S. (1992). Contemporary abortion patterns: A life history approach. *Ethology and Sociobiology, 13,* 35–48.

Hogg, M. A., & Abrams, D. (1988). *Social identifications: A social psychology of intergroup relations and group processes.* London: Routledge.

Hrdy, S. B. (1999). *Mother nature: Natural selection and the female of the species.* London: Chatto and Windus.

Huesmann, L. R. (1988). An information-processing model for the development of aggression. *Aggressive Behavior, 14,* 13–24.

Jaffee, S. R., Moffitt, T. E., Caspi, A., Taylor, A., & Arseneault, L. (2002). Influence of domestic violence on children's internalizing and externalizing problems: An environmentally informative twin study. *Journal of the Academy of Child and Adolescent Psychiatry, 41,* 1095–1103.

Janicki, M. G., & Krebs, D. L. (1998). Evolutionary approaches to culture. In C. Crawford & D. L. Krebs (Eds.), *Handbook of evolutionary psychology: Ideas, issues and applications* (pp. 163–207). Mahwah, NJ: Lawrence Erlbaum.

Jarvinen, D. W., & Nicholls, J. G. (1996). Adolescents' social goals, beliefs about the causes of social success and dissatisfaction in peer relations. *Developmental Psychology, 32,* 435–441.

Joe Laidler, K., & Hunt, G. (2001). Accomplishing femininity among the girls in the gang. *British Journal of Criminology, 41,* 656–678.

Kahneman, D., Knetsch, J., & Thaler, R. (1986). Fairness and the assumptions of economics. *Journal of Business, 59,* 285–300.

Katz, D. (1988). *Seductions of crime: The moral and sensual attractions of doing evil.* New York: Basic Books.

Kenrick, D. T., & Keefe, R. C. (1992). Age preferences in mates reflect sex differences in human reproductive strategies. *Behavioral and Brain Sciences, 15,* 75–133.

Kenrick, D. T., Keefe, R. C., Gabrielidis, C., & Cornelius, J. S. (1996). Adolescents' age preferences for dating partners: Support for an evolutionary model of life-history strategies. *Child Development, 67,* 1499–1511.

Kenrick, D. T., Li, N. P., & Butner, J. (2003). Dynamical evolutionary psychology: Individual decision rules and emergent social norms. *Psychological Review, 110,* 3–28.

Ketelaar, T., & Todd, P. M. (2001). Framing our thoughts: Ecological rationality as evolutionary psychology's answer to the frame problem. In H. H. Halcombe, III (Ed.), *Conceptual challenges in evolutionary psychology* (pp. 179–211). London: Kluwer Press.

Keverne, E. B., Fundele, R., Narasimha, M., Barton, S. C., & Surani, M. A. (1996). Genomic imprinting and the differential roles of parental genomes in brain development. *Developmental Brain Research, 92,* 91–100.

Knight, G. P., Guthrie, I. K., Page, M. C., & Fabes, R. A. (2002). Emotional arousal and gender differences in aggression: A meta-analysis. *Aggressive Behavior, 28,* 366–393.

Kochanska, G., Murray, K. T., & Harlan, E. T. (2000). Effortful control in early childhood: Continuity and change, antecedents and implications for social development. *Developmental Psychology, 36,* 220–232.

Koot, H. M., & Verhulst, F. C. (1991). Prevalence of problem behavior in Dutch children aged 2–3. *Acta Psychiatrica Scandinavica, 83,* 1–37.

Kring, A. M. (2000). Gender and anger. In A. H. Fischer (Ed.), *Gender and emotion: Social psychological perspectives* (pp. 211–231). Cambridge: Cambridge University Press.

LaGrange, T. C., & Silverman, R. A. (1999). Low self control and opportunity: Testing the general theory of crime as an explanation for gender differences in delinquency. *Criminology, 37,* 41–72.

LeDoux, J. (1998). *The emotional brain.* London: Weidenfeld and Nicholson.

Lees, S. (1993). *Sugar and spice: Sexuality and adolescent girls.* London: Penguin.

Leventhal, T., & Brooks-Gunn, J. (2000). The neighbourhoods they live in: The effects of neighbourhood residence on child and adolescent outcomes. *Psychological Bulletin, 126,* 309–337.

Lever, J. (1978). Sex differences in the games children play. *Social Problems, 23,* 478–487.

Loeber, R., Farrington, D. P., Stouthamer-Loeber, M., Moffitt, T. E., Caspi, A., & Lynam, D. (2001). Male mental health problems, psychopathy, and personality traits: Key findings from the first 14 years of the Pittsburgh youth study. *Clinical Child and Family Psychology Review, 4,* 273–297.

Loeber, R., & Stouthamer-Loeber, M. (1986). Family factors as correlates and predictors of juvenile conduct problems and delinquency. In M. Tonry & N. Morris (Eds.), *Crime and justice: An annual review of research* (Vol. 7, pp. 29–149). Chicago: University of Chicago Press.

Lonstein, J. S., & Gammie, S. C. (2002). Sensory, hormonal and neural control of maternal aggression in laboratory rodents. *Neuroscience and Biobehavioral Reviews, 26,* 869–888.

Lynam, D. R., Caspi, A., Moffitt, T. E., Wikstrom, P. H., Loeber, R., & Novak, S. (2000). The interaction between impulsivity and neighbourhood context on offending: The effects of impulsivity are stronger on poorer neighbourhoods. *Journal of Abnormal Psychology, 109,* 563–574.

Lytton, H. (1990). Child and parent effects in boys conduct disorder: A reinterpretation. *Developmental Psychology, 26,* 683–697.

Mathes, E. W. (1986). Jealousy and romantic love: A longitudinal study. *Psychological Reports, 58,* 885–886.

Maynard Smith, J. (1998). The origin of altruism. *Nature, 393,* 639–640.

McLoyd, V. C. (1998). Socioeconomic disadvantage and child development. *American Psychologist, 53,* 185–204.

Meloy, J. R. (1988). *The psychopathic mind: Origins, dynamics and treatment.* Northvale, NJ: Aronson.

Miczek, K. A., Weerts, E., Haney, M., & Tidey, J. (1994). Neurobiological mechanisms controlling aggression: Preclinical developments for pharmacotherapeutic interventions. *Neuroscience and Biobehavioural Reviews, 18,* 97–110.

Moffitt, T. E. (1993). Adolescent limited and life course persistent antisocial behaviour: A developmental taxonomy. *Psychological Review, 100,* 674–701.

Moffitt, T. E., Caspi, A., Rutter, M., & Silva, P. A. (2001). *Sex differences in antisocial behaviour: Conduct disorder, delinquency and violence in the Dunedin longitudinal study.* Cambridge: Cambridge University Press.

Moore, T., & Haig, D. (1991). Genomic imprinting in mammalian development: A parental tug-of-war. *Trends on Genetics, 7,* 45–49.

Öhman, A. (2000). Fear and anxiety: Evolutionary, cognitive and clinical perspectives. In M. Lewis & J. M. Haviland-Jones (Eds.), *Handbook of emotions* (2nd ed., pp. 573–593). New York: Guilford Press.

Panksepp, J. (2002). Emotions as natural kinds in the mammalian brain. In M. Lewis & J. M. Haviland-Jones (Eds.), *Handbook of emotions* (2nd ed., pp. 137–156). New York: Guilford Press.

Patterson, C. M., & Newman, J. P. (1993). Reflectivity and learning from aversive events: Toward a psychological mechanism for the syndromes of disinhibition. *Psychological Review, 100,* 716–736.

Patterson, G. R., Littman, R. A., & Bricker, W. (1967). Assertive behaviour in children: A step toward a theory of aggression. *Monographs of the Society for Research in Child Development, 32*(5, Serial No. 113).

Paul, L., Foss, M. A., & Baenninger, M. (1996). Double standards for sexual jealousy: Manipulative morality or a reflection of evolved sex differences? *Human Nature, 7,* 291–321.

Paul, L., Foss, M. A., & Galloway, J. (1993). Sexual jealousy in young women and men: Aggressive responses to partner and rival. *Aggressive Behavior, 19,* 401–420.

Perry, B., Pollard, R., Blakley, T., Baker, W., & Vigilante, D. (1995). Childhood trauma, the neurobiology of adaptation and "use dependent" development of the brain: How "states" become "traits." *Infant Mental Health Journal, 16,* 271–291.

Pines, A. M., & Friedman, A. (1998). Gender differences in romantic jealousy. *Journal of Social Psychology, 138,* 54–71.

Pratt, T. C., & Cullen, F. T. (2000). The empirical status of Gottfredson and Hirschi's general theory of crime: A meta-analysis. *Criminology, 38,* 931–964.

Quay, H. C. (1993). The psychobiology of undersocialised aggressive conduct disorder: A theoretical perspective. *Development and Psychopathology, 5,* 165–180.

Raine, A. (1993). *The psychopathology of crime: Criminal behaviour as a clinical disorder.* San Diego, CA: Academic Press.

Raine, A., Venables, P. H., & Mednick, S. A. (1997). Low resting heart rate at age 3 predisposes to aggression at age 11 years: Evidence from the Mauritius child health project. *Journal of the American Academy of Child and Adolescent Psychiatry, 36,* 1457–1464.

Repetti, R. L., Taylor, S. E., & Seeman, T. E. (2002). Risky families: Social environments and the mental and physical health of offspring. *Psychological Bulletin, 128,* 330–366.

Robarchek, C. A., & Robarchek, C. J. (1992). Cultures of war and peace: A comparative study of Waorani and Semai. In J. Silverberg & J. P. Gray (Eds.), *Aggression and peacefulness in humans and other primates* (pp. 189–213). New York: Oxford University Press.

Rothbart, M. K., & Bates, J. E. (1998). Temperament. In W. Damon & N. Eisenberg (Eds.), *Handbook of child psychology: Vol. 3. Social, emotional and personality development* (5th ed., pp. 105–176). Chichester, England: Wiley.

Salzinger, S., Feldman, R. S., Stockhammer, T., & Hood, J. (2002). An ecological framework for understanding risk for exposure to community violence and the effects of exposure on children and adolescents. *Aggression and Violent Behavior, 7,* 423–451.

Sampson, R. (1995). Unemployment and imbalanced sex ratios: Race-specific consequences for family structure and crime. In M. B. Tucker & C. Mitchell-Kiernan (Eds.), *The decline in marriage among Afro-Americans: Causes, consequences and policy implications* (pp. 229–254). New York: Russell Sage Foundation.

Sampson, R. J., & Laub, J. H. (1994). Urban poverty and the family context of delinquency: A new look at structure and process in a classic study. *Child Development, 54,* 523–540.

Sampson, R. J., & Lauritsen, J. (1994). Violent victimization and offending: Individual, situational and community-level risk factors. In A. J. Reiss & J. A. Roth (Eds.), *Understanding and preventing violence: Social influences* (Vol. 3, pp. 1–114). Washington, DC: National Academy Press.

Sherif, M., Harvey, O. J., White, B. J., Hood, W. R., & Sherif, C. (1961). *Intergroup conflict and cooperation: The Robber's Cave experiment.* Norman, OK: Oklahoma Book Exchange.

Smuts, B. B. (1995). The evolutionary origins of patriarchy. *Human Nature, 6,* 1–32.

Srull, T. K., & Wyer, R. S. (1979). The role of category accessibility in the interpretation of information about persons: Some determinants and implications. *Journal of Personality and Social Psychology, 37,* 1660–1672.

Srull, T. K., & Wyer, R. S. (1980). Category accessibility and social perception: Some implications for the study of person memory and interpersonal judgments. *Journal of Personality and Social Psychology, 38,* 841–856.

Taylor, S. E., Klein, L. C., Lewis, B. P., Gruenewald, T. L., Gurung, R. A. R., & Updegraff, J. A. (2000). Biobehavioral responses to stress in females: Tend-and-befriend, not fight-or-flight. *Psychological Review, 107,* 411–429.

Todorov, A., & Bargh, J. A. (2002). Automatic sources of aggression. *Aggression and Violent Behavior, 7,* 53–68.

Tooke, W., & Camire, L. (1991). Patterns of deception in intersexual and intrasexual mating strategies. *Ethology and Sociobiology, 12*, 345–364.

Trivers, R. L. (1971). The evolution of reciprocal altruism. *Quarterly Review of Biology, 46*, 35–56.

Trivers, R. L. (1972). Parental investment and sexual selection. In B. Campbell (Ed.), *Sexual selection and the descent of man, 1871–1971* (pp. 136–179). Chicago: Aldine.

Tucker, M. B., & Mitchell-Kernan, C. (1997). Understanding marital decline among African Americans. *Perspectives, 3*, 1–5.

van der Dennen, J. M. G. (1995). *The origin of war: The evolution of male-coalitional reproductive strategy.* Groningen: Origin Press.

van der Dennen, J. M. G. (2002). Evolutionary theories if warfare in preindustrial foraging societies. *Neuroendocrinology Letters, 23*(4), 55–65.

Vitaro, F., Brendgen, M., & Tremblay, R. E. (2002). Reactively and proactively aggressive children: Antecedent and subsequent characteristics. *Journal of Child Psychology and Psychiatry, 43*, 495–505.

Walters, S., & Crawford, C. B. (1994). The importance of mate attraction for intrasexual competition in men and women. *Ethology and Sociobiology, 15*, 5–30.

Weinshenker, N. J., & Siegel, A. (2002). Bimodal classification of aggression: Affective defense and predatory attack. *Aggression and Violent Behavior, 7*, 237–250.

Weisfeld, G. E. (1999). *Evolutionary principles of human adolescence.* New York: Basic Books.

White, J. L., Moffitt, T. E., Caspi, A., Bartusch, D. J., Needles, D. J., & Stouthamer-Loeber, M. (1994). Measuring impulsivity and examining its relationship to delinquency. *Journal of Abnormal Psychology, 103*, 192–205.

Whiting, B. B., & Edwards, C. P. (1988). *Children of different worlds: The formation of social behavior.* Cambridge, MA: Harvard University Press.

Widom, C. S. (1989). The intergenerational transmission of violence. In N. A. Weiner & M. E. Wolfgang (Eds.), *Pathways to violence* (pp. 137–201). Newbury Park, CA: Sage.

Wilson, M., & Daly, M. (1992). The man who mistook his wife for a chattel. In J. H. Barkow, L. Cosmides, & J. Tooby (Eds.), *The adapted mind: Evolutionary psychology and the generation of culture* (pp. 289–322). New York: Oxford University Press.

Wilson, M., Daly, M., & Weghorst, S. J. (1980). Household composition and the risk of child abuse and neglect. *Journal of Biosocial Science, 12*, 333–340.

Wrangham, R. W. (1999). Evolution of coalitionary killing. *Yearbook of Physical Anthropology, 42*, 1–30.

Wrangham, R. W., & Peterson, D. (1996). *Demonic males: Apes and the origins of human violence.* New York: Houghton Mifflin.

Yehuda, R., Giller, E., Southwick, S., Lowy, M., & Mason, J. (1991). Hypothalamic-pituitary dysfunction in post-traumatic stress disorder. *Biological Psychiatry, 30*, 1031–1048.

Zaadstra, B. M., Seidell, J. C., Van Noord, P. A., te Velde, E. R., Habbema, J. D., Vrieswijk, B., et al. (1993). Fat and female fecundity: Prospective study of body fat distribution on conception rates. *British Medical Journal, 306*, 484–487.

Zingraff, M., Leiter J., Meyers, K., & Johnsen, M. (1993). Child maltreatment and youthful problem behaviour. *Criminology, 31*, 173–202.

CHAPTER 22

Managing Ingroup and Outgroup Relationships

ROBERT KURZBAN and STEVEN NEUBERG

Humans are distinctively "ultrasocial" (Campbell, 1983; Richerson & Boyd, 1998): Unlike the vast majority of other species, individuals who are not closely genetically related work cooperatively to achieve common goals. This cooperation takes diverse forms, including hunting of large game (Hawkes, 1993; Lee & DeVore, 1968), construction of goods for individual use (Chagnon, 1997), and large-scale military contests in which individuals sacrifice themselves to benefit others (Keegan, 1994).

Social interactions with conspecifics obviously carry large potential fitness benefits but also entail enormous potential fitness costs, such as agonistic conflict and communication of pathogens. Any given interaction also carries opportunity costs, as limits on the size of an individual's social network mean that a particular social interaction precludes some others (Dunbar, 1993; Tooby & Cosmides, 1996). Social organisms, therefore, should not be promiscuously social, interacting without selectivity. Choosing from among the possibilities for social interactions thus represents a critical class of adaptive problems, and natural selection would, therefore, have favored cognitive mechanisms designed to make good decisions about an individual's social interactions and social interactants.

In short, we should expect humans to exhibit *discriminate sociality* (Kurzban & Leary, 2001) and to possess psychological mechanisms designed to preserve the benefits of sociality and simultaneously limit its costs. We argue that these adaptations are complex and sensitive to various elements of social context and lead people to adopt specific criteria for selecting the members of their groups, attune themselves to threats arising from both within their groups and from other groups, and occasionally inflict costs on those who threaten the benefits of sociality. We suggest that these evolved, domain-specific mechanisms collectively lead to phenomena that fall under the rubrics of social exclusion, stigmatization, and discrimination.

FUNCTIONAL SPECIFICITY IN SOCIAL COGNITION

The traditional social-cognitive approach applies broad principles drawn from cognitive psychology—categorization, schemas, memory models—to stimuli in the social world: people. This approach takes the "functions" of cognitive systems to be very general ones: making sense of the world, storing information efficiently, generating inferences, and so on.

In contrast, we believe that the mechanisms underpinning social cognition have been designed to serve specifically *social* functions and that these functions are likely to be varied and numerous (Cosmides & Tooby, 1992; Tooby & Cosmides, 1992). For example, whereas many social scientists have traditionally conceptualized stigmatization and prejudice as simple devaluations of others, an implication of a functionally specific adaptationist view is that because different individuals and groups might be perceived to pose qualitatively different profiles of threats, they should also elicit qualitatively different profiles of stigmatizing and prejudicial reactions.

Another entailment of our view is that one prevalent conceptualization of "group"—most simply, two or more individuals who influence one another—is likely inadequate. For example, the intergroup relations literature within social psychology has focused on groups in a nonspecific way, as implied by general terms such as *in-group favoritism* and *outgroup homogeneity*. This literature implies that relations between members of different gender groups, families, ethnic groups, work teams, and college majors operate similarly: A group is a group is a group. In contrast, we believe it is important to recognize that there exist qualitatively different types of groups that the mind treats differently from one another (e.g., Lickel et al., 2000).

A good example is ethnicity. Gil-White (2001) has argued for a domain-specific species like construal of ethnic groups (or *ethnies*), suggesting that ethnies are essentialized in the same way that the mind essentializes species (Gelman, 1996). Other social categories, such as professions, for example, he argues, are not treated in this way (see also Rothbart & Taylor, 1992).

CHOOSING SOCIAL PARTNERS

Choices for social interactants are constrained by personal history because an individual is born to a particular kin group in a particular location, with preexisting alliances and political structures. Social life is complex, however, and opportunities arise for the restructuring of affiliations, the formation of subcoalitions, and the migration of individuals from one place to another. There is, and presumably historically has been, significant opportunity for individuals to choose their social partners.

Such choices are neither arbitrary nor random because individuals who were unable to extract the benefits of social interactions were disadvantaged relative to those better positioned to reap these benefits. Humans, who appear to be designed to cooperate in groups, should have adaptations for selecting carefully among possible groups and group members. In particular, we should expect humans to have adaptations designed to prefer associating with individuals who are likely to deliver fitness benefits because of either their ability or inclination to do so. Because skills, access to resources, and social networks make people more or less valuable to a particular individual, a well-designed cognitive system should seek out those individuals and those interactions that make the most out of others' idiosyncratic altruistic capacities and proclivities (Berscheid & Reis, 1998).

In short, individuals should have preferences for certain kinds of people over others—the basis of discrimination. In some instantiations—the hiring of employees based on ethnicity—discrimination is salient and controversial. In other forms—the selection of acquaintanceships based on apparent agreeableness—the discrimination is nearly invisible and noncontroversial. Yet, both are based on preferences and are fundamentally discriminatory. In this section, we consider some preferences that drive people as they choose social partners, drawing on theories designed to explain cooperation, including kin selection (Hamilton, 1964), reciprocal altruism (Trivers, 1971), and cultural group selection (Boyd & Richerson, 1985).

Kin

Numerous accounts of Hamilton's (1964) theory of kin selection are available (e.g., Dawkins, 1982), so we do not discuss it here. In general, natural selection leads to adaptations designed to deliver benefits to kin provided the associated costs are small relative to these benefits. Humans clearly possess such adaptations (Daly, Salmon, & Wilson, 1997; Daly & Wilson, 1988). Because an individual's kin are likely to be motivated to take opportunities to benefit the self, human preferences can be expected to make kin among the most appealing social partners, as observed in nepotistic inheritance and the selection of coalitional allies (Chagnon, 1975; Chagnon & Bugos, 1979; but see Patton, 2000). For a thorough review of human kin selected adaptations, see Kurland and Gaulin (Chapter 15, this volume).

Cooperative and Trustworthy Types

Because humans form groups with distantly related others, people should prefer to interact with those possessing traits likely to make them good partners for cooperative activity. Individuals differ substantially when faced with options to behave altruistically or selfishly. Research on "social value orientation," for example, suggests that some people consistently choose to behave cooperatively, competitively, or in a purely self-regarding fashion in experimental games (McClintock, 1972; Van Lange, Otten, De Bruin, & Joireman, 1997). Similarly, within the context of social dilemmas, some individuals seem predisposed to behave consistently selfishly (Kurzban & Houser, 2005). This tendency has important implications for group dynamics: When a small number of people choose to cooperate very little, this reluctance seems to spread over time to other group members (e.g., Komorita, Hilty, & Parks, 1991; Kurzban & Houser, 2005).

People care about these differences. Cottrell, Neuberg, and Li (2005) had students contemplate a range of different interdependent groups (work project team, basketball team, fraternity, etc.) and rate how important it is for members of these groups to possess a variety of personal characteristics. Regardless of the group's task, *trustworthiness* and, to a lesser extent, *cooperativeness* were rated as highly important, with very little across-group or within-group variance. Other characteristics (e.g., intelligence, extraversion, physical attractiveness, conscientiousness) did not show this consistency. These results highlight the particular importance of trustworthiness and cooperativeness in the context of interdependent coordination.

AVAILABILITY FOR FUTURE INTERACTION

Analyses of dyadic cooperation show that reciprocally cooperative strategies are more successful as the probability of future interaction increases (Axelrod, 1984). This might have an analog in multiindividual interactions: In some models of cooperation, variants of reciprocal strategies enjoy success when groups of individuals consistently interact with one another over time (Boyd & Richerson, 1985; Gintis, 2000; Nowak & Sigmund, 1998; Panchanathan & Boyd, 2003).

It therefore seems plausible that human psychology is tuned to cues suggesting that an individual is in a long-interacting group, conditioning his or her cooperation on these cues (Keser & van Winden, 1997; see also Gintis, et al., 2003). These considerations also highlight the importance of maintaining one's reputation as an altruist or cooperator and imply that we should expect people to choose to be more cooperative when they believe they are being observed: If reputations matter, people should have mechanisms designed to preserve them (e.g., Frank, 1988).

Indeed, selfish or antisocial behavior is more common under conditions of anonymity: When people feel "deindividuated," minimizing reputational concerns, they are more likely to take advantage of opportunities to be selfish (e.g., Prentice-Dunn & Rogers, 1980; Zimbardo, 1970). For example, children in Halloween costumes obscuring their identity take more candy than those who are identifiable (Diener, Fraser, Beaman, & Kelem, 1976). Similarly, when adult experimental subjects are assured of anonymity from other subjects and from experimenters, they behave more selfishly (Burnham, 2003; Hoffman, McCabe, Shachat, & Smith, 1994). Conversely, such subjects behave more altruistically when more identifiable (Andreoni & Petrie, 2004). The effects of identifiability suggest that prosocial behavior is motivated in part by the effects of having a positive reputation and the reciprocal benefits this entails.

Related to anonymity is the perception that an individual is involved in an interaction that will not continue, and the experimental economics literature suggests that people are sensitive to this factor (e.g., Fehr & Gächter, 2003). Evidence from the Prisoner's Dilemma suggests that people cooperate more when they believe their interactions will be repeated and exhibit "end game" effects, such that previously cooperative individuals choose to defect when the end of the game looms (Andreoni & Miller, 1993; Keser & van Winden, 1997).

Even under the worst conditions for cooperation, however—one-shot, anonymous interactions—people do sometimes choose to cooperate (e.g., see the "strangers" condition in Andreoni & Miller, 1993). It may be that the systems designed for altruism were designed for a world in which repeat interaction was common, therefore, reflecting a tendency to behave in a way that embodies the assumption that cooperation generally provides gains in trade (Burnham & Hare, in press; Burnham & Johnson, in press). If human psychology is designed to make inferences about the probability of additional future interactions, complementary adaptations might exist designed to persuade potential relationship partners that one is indeed going to be available for future interactions. In other words, there may exist adaptations designed to commit oneself to certain kinds of future behaviors. In formal analyses, commitment has long been recognized as an important parameter influencing a broad range of strategic interactions, and work continues in this area (Kerr & Kaufman-Gilliland, 1994; Kurzban, McCabe, Smith, & Wilson, 2001; Nesse, 2001; Schelling, 1960). Commitment to social groups can take the form of tattoos, scars, or even the public performance of rituals or the endorsement of beliefs idiosyncratic to the group; because such badges and behaviors reduce the likelihood that an individual will be accepted by a rival group, it serves as a signal of commitment to his or her present group.

Finally, familiarity—a sign that an individual has been around in the past, and thus perhaps a cue that he or she is likely to be around in the future—increases prosocial action. For example, people are socially attracted to those they believe to be familiar and are more likely to help them (Schroeder, Penner, Dovidio, & Piliavin, 1995). Further, parents not only appear to encourage their children to behave prosocially toward familiar others but also attempt to curb their children's prosociality toward those who are unfamiliar (Peterson, Reaven, & Homer, 1984).

In sum, when selecting group members, people seek those who exhibit cues suggesting they will be around in the future, such as familiarity and indices of commitment.

Ability to Coordinate

Multi-individual cooperation often requires computationally complex coordination. Individuals should thus prefer interaction partners with whom successful coordination is easier (due to shared language, etc.). Conversely, the importance of coordination might explain the stigma that attaches to certain kinds of conditions, such as mental illness, which undermine predictability and thus coordination (Kurzban & Leary, 2001). Indeed, along with trustworthiness and cooperativeness, emotional stability—one indicator of predictability—appears to be valued in partners across a range of interaction contexts (Cottrell et al., 2005).

Some have argued that the need for coordination explains the central position of *norms*—the rules that govern how social transactions are conducted—suggesting that people are often best served by adopting the norms that others are using, thereby allowing coordination with the largest number of possible others (Boyd & Richerson, 1985). Gil-White (2001) has extended this argument to the case of ethnicity, suggesting that the distaste for interacting with those outside an individual's ethnic group is a preference that evolved due to the fitness losses associated with the costs of attempting to coordinate with people with different norms.

Finally, the ability to coordinate might also be tied to individual histories with others. As people learn more about others' idiosyncratic traits and preferences, coordination should be made easier because of the ability to anticipate others' actions and read their intentions (Tooby & Cosmides, 1996). This should lead to momentum in social dynamics, as individuals become better interaction partners simply by virtue of shared history.

Taken together, these arguments suggest that selection pressures associated with coordination partners might have led to psychological systems designed to prefer those whose behavior is most predictable, including coethnics and familiar others.

GENERATION OF POSITIVE EXTERNALITIES

In the language of economics, externalities are unintended consequences to one agent that result from another agent's pursuit of his or her goals (Samuelson, 1970). For example, motorcyclists generate the negative externality of noise pollution when traveling from one place to another. When other people work toward their own idiosyncratic social goals, they generate positive and negative externalities. People benefit by associating with those who emit positive externalities, such as those with multiple skills, material resources, social connections, kin networks, and the like (Tooby & Cosmides, 1996). Conversely, human social psychology might be designed to avoid those who are likely to generate few positive externalities.

SUMMARY

Individuals who prefer associating with those who possess characteristics heuristically associated with the provision of fitness benefits should be at an advantage relative to individuals who are indiscriminately altruistic toward others. For example, because familiar individuals—those who have been seen frequently in the past—are also more likely to be around in the future, they should be more desirable as interactants than less familiar individuals, even though the link between familiarity and likelihood of prosocial future interaction is imperfect.

Evolved preferences for some types of interaction partners necessarily entail discrimination against the disfavored alternatives. In addition to discriminating in whom they interact with, humans also discriminate in how they interact with others, imposing costs and delivering or extracting benefits on some more than others. We now turn to this important issue.

MANAGING INGROUP RELATIONSHIPS

Humans have an array of evolved affective/cognitive mechanisms because different social threats, like different physical threats, must be recognized and responded to appropriately (e.g., Schaller & Neuberg, 2003). Physical threats (e.g., an incoming projectile) are identified through heuristically associated cues (e.g., rapid increase in an object's size), activating appropriate goals (e.g., escape) and action (e.g., jumping to the side). Social threats are no different. We identify the presence of a threat (e.g., disease by contagion) through its heuristically associated cues (e.g., bodily fluids), which then activate emotional reactions (e.g., disgust), beliefs (e.g., person is diseased, contaminated), goals (e.g., noncontact, distance), and behavioral inclinations (e.g., avoidance; Frijda, 1986; Izard, 1991; Plutchik, 1980; Roseman, Wiest, & Swartz, 1994; Tomkins, 1963).

Stigmatization must, therefore, be conceptualized as more than simple devaluation of another, as it has traditionally been conceived (e.g., Crocker, Major, & Steele, 1998). Although several perspectives recognize the multifaceted emotional texturing of stigma (e.g., Brewer & Alexander, 2002; Dijker, 1987; Fiske, Cuddy, Glick, & Xu, 2002; Goffman, 1963; Mackie, Devos, & Smith, 2000), we conceive of the different stigmatizing reactions as manifestations of function-specific adaptations designed to respond to individuals who pose different threats (Cottrell &

Neuberg, in press; Kurzban & Leary, 2001; Neuberg & Cottrell, 2002; Schaller, Park, & Faulkner, 2003).

Further, if different mechanisms are involved for different threats, then different contextual factors can be expected to moderate them. Just as loud noises are especially startling in the dark (Grillon, Pellowski, Merikangas, & Davis, 1997), in-group betrayal might elicit particularly intense reactions within the context of intergroup competition.

In this section, we discuss several threats group members can pose, the evolved mechanisms hypothesized to counter them, and individual difference and sociocontextual variables that potentially facilitate and attenuate these reactions.

FREE RIDING AND PUNISHMENT

The breadth of peoples' desire to punish those who enjoy cooperation's benefits without paying associated costs remains mysterious (Fehr & Gächter, 2002). For dyads, adaptations designed to punish those who defect are relatively well understood, as models of the evolution of cooperation in dyads that interact over time (Trivers, 1971) and subsequent simulations (Aktipis, 2004; Axelrod, 1984) have helped to inform the search for the cognitive mechanisms that underpin cooperation. Punishing cheaters in social exchanges is sensible if doing so prevents them from doing so again in the future (Cosmides & Tooby, 1992). Experimental evidence reliably shows that even in one-shot, two-person bargaining games, people will endure costs to inflict costs on those who are perceived to be insufficiently fair or generous (e.g., Roth, 1995), a result that obtains even when the stakes are high (Hoffman, McCabe, & Smith, 1996). Why people punish, even in nonrepeated interaction, remains the subject of debate, but data from a vast empirical enterprise investigating this issue testify to the strength of the human psychology of punishment (Fehr & Fischbacher, 2003; Henrich et al., 2001).

Findings from Public Goods games similarly indicate that anger and the desire to punish free riders emerge in group contexts. In a typical experiment using the "voluntary contribution mechanism" (e.g., Isaac & Walker, 1988), subjects are randomly assigned to groups of generally between four and eight people and must divide money provided by the experimenter into two accounts. Money placed into one of the accounts, the private account, is kept while money placed in the group account is increased by a commonly known constant ($h > 1$) but shared equally among all group members. For suitably chosen values of h, each unit invested in the group account increases the aggregate group payoff but decreases the investing individual's payoff. A player's contribution to the group account is, therefore, an index of cooperation.

When this game is repeated and players observe the total contribution by the group in previous rounds, a frequently replicated result is that the total contribution to the group account begins at roughly 50% of the total aggregate endowments. This initial inclination toward group contribution contrasts with the prediction derived from standard economic theory—that players will contribute nothing toward the group account—and is remarkably robust, being observed across relatively wide parameters of the game (Ledyard, 1995). Contributions to the group account do tend to decrease from round to round toward zero.

The ability to punish defectors, however, increases cooperation. Yamagishi (1986) introduced a sanctioning system so that after observing other players' contributions, individuals could, at a cost to themselves, reduce the income of the lowest contributor to the public good. When sanctioning was relatively inexpensive (costing the low contributors twice what punishers paid to sanction them), the sanctioning system was used and contributions were quite high, over 70% by the end of the series of rounds. These results have recently been replicated and extended (Carpenter, 2002; Fehr & Gächter, 2000, 2002), suggesting not only that people are willing to punish at a cost to themselves but also that this punishment is effective at removing much potential free riding.

Anger appears to be a critical force underlying the punishment of free riders. Fehr and Gächter (2002) found that in reacting to hypothetical scenarios, people estimated that they would be angry in proportion to the extent to which others contributed less than they themselves did. In the extreme hypothetical scenarios, nearly half of the participants were at ceiling on a seven-point Likert scale. Similarly, college students in a series of studies were asked to characterize the threats that different groups in the United States pose to the nation (e.g., to physical safety, property, values) and to report how they felt about these groups. Groups perceived to purposely take more than they contribute elicited anger (Cottrell & Neuberg, in press; Neuberg & Cottrell, 2002). And in a small groups competition experiment in which an experimental confederate posed one of several threats to the group's success, anger was the focal participant reaction toward confederates who free-rode on their teammates' efforts (Wilbur, Shapiro, Neuberg, Goldstein, & Hofer, 2003).

From the point of view of standard analyses of cooperation in groups, these results represent something of a puzzle. If public goods games are conceptualized as good models for understanding the evolution of cooperation in groups, then strategies that punish should be at a selective disadvantage relative to strategies that do not, as punishment entails a cost that benefits all group members, who stand to gain from the benefits that punishment brings to cooperative groups (Boyd & Richerson, 1988; Oliver, 1980). Because ostracism—excluding individuals from a group—is a subcategory of punishment, it is subject to the same problem.

The solution to this problem is the topic of considerable recent debate. Boyd, Gintis, Bowles, and Richerson (2003) presented one solution that turns on an interesting asymmetry: The fitness disadvantage of being a punisher depends on the number of free riders; if defectors are rare, punishers only infrequently have to punish and thus bear only a small fitness cost. Boyd et al.'s (2003) simulations show that the small individual disadvantage to punishing allows group selection to favor groups with substantial numbers of individuals who both cooperate and punish noncooperators.

Other possible explanations for punitive sentiments are on offer. Price, Cosmides, and Tooby (2002) argued that desires to punish those who are free-riding in the context of group cooperation seem to be designed to decrease the fitness advantage enjoyed by those who do not pay the costs of cooperating. Alternatively, some have suggested that anger at defection against the group—which motivates punishment—is a by-product of affective systems designed in the context of dyadic interactions (Neuberg & Cottrell, 2002). As indicated earlier, anger and desire for punishment might help support mechanisms designed for gains in trade by preventing individuals from being exploited (Cosmides & Tooby, 1992). Considerable debate continues surrounding these issues, detailed discussions of which are available elsewhere (e.g., Gintis, Bowles, Boyd, & Fehr, 2003).

In sum, the empirical evidence strongly suggests that there is a robust psychology of retribution in the context of both dyads and groups. Debate remains, however, about the correct theoretical explanation for adaptations designed to punish noncooperators.

INTENTIONAL FREE RIDING VIA INABILITY

Taking benefits without contributing to group welfare is not always voluntary. For instance, children fail to contribute proportionately to groups (e.g., Hill & Kaplan, 1999), yet elicit little anger or punishment (for failure in this particular respect). Similarly, individuals unable to contribute to group welfare because of disability might burden their groups, yet often elicit empathy and pity instead of anger (e.g., Dijker & Koomen, 2003; Weiner, Perry, & Magnusson, 1988).

On a strict cost-benefit analysis, the reason for a free rider's noncontribution shouldn't matter. However, if punishment psychology is designed to induce future cooperation (see earlier discussion), it should be designed to incur costs of sanctioning only if it is likely to do some good: Punishing those who can't contribute will obviously not cause increased contribution in the future.

Another possibility is that the inability to contribute is often a temporary state, and helping such individuals makes more likely returned help in the future. Indeed, helping people in need might be cost effective, as it is often possible to deliver benefits that come at a relatively small cost to self but that are very valuable to the recipient. Natural selection might, therefore, have favored affective and motivational systems designed to succor those in temporary need over a more indifferent system by virtue of the subsequent benefits in the form of reciprocal actions once the target individual is sufficiently recovered from his or her state (Tooby & Cosmides, 1996).

From this view, empathy, pity, and prosociality should be elicited more readily when helping the target is seen as a good investment, as when those with infirmities give cues that suggest that their infirmities are transient and remediable and/or are judged not responsible for their plight and, therefore, less likely to be in the needy position again (Weiner et al., 1988). In contrast, nonobvious infirmities (e.g., depression, learning disabilities) should less readily elicit empathy and pity and thus help (Weiner et al., 1988). However, help is context dependent: As the marginal cost of help increases, willingness to do so should decrease. For instance, some nomadic peoples kill the very young and very old if they interfere with the travel necessary for subsistence (e.g., Alvarsson, 1988; Condon, 1987; de Coccola & King, 1986; Graburn, 1969).

Laboratory experiments clearly show that differences in perceived defector intentions influence how they are treated. When players' moves are perceived as outside their control, both positive reciprocity—reward—and negative reciprocity—punishment—are reduced (Blount, 1995; Falk, Fehr, & Fischbacher, 2000; Rigdon, McCabe, & Smith, 2003).

In sum, anger and punishment in response to free riding might be deactivated under certain conditions, occasionally even replaced by empathy and prosociality, possibly in the service of future group cooperation.

PHYSICAL ATTACK

For social creatures, protection from attack by conspecifics constitutes an important selection pressure. Cues to physical threat from others—angry facial expressions, rapid approach, weapons, and so forth—should activate the appropriate emotional, cognitive, and behavioral mechanisms. Moreover, because of the importance of intergroup competition (see later discussion), cues to outgroup membership might also activate these adaptations (Schaller & Neuberg, 2003).

Ethnic outgroups indeed elicit distinctive physiological (Hart et al., 2000), cognitive (Judd & Park, 1988), and behavioral responses (Sidanius & Pratto, 1999). Furthermore, consistent with arguments that it is particularly male cooperative coalitions that constitute aggressive threat (Keegan, 1994; Tiger, 1969), prejudices of White Americans toward Black Americans, and the stereotypes of criminality and aggressiveness are directed disproportionately toward males in their teens and 20s—and not toward younger, female, and older African Americans (e.g., Quillian & Pager, 2001; see also Sidanius & Veniegas, 2000).

Individual differences and context moderate such reactions. Whites who believe that the world is a dangerous place detect anger in neutrally expressive male African American (but not in similarly neutral White or female) faces (Maner et al., 2005). Further, in a dark room, the more a person believes the world is a dangerous place, the higher he or she rates traits that connote physical danger (e.g., "hostile") but not danger-irrelevant traits (e.g., "lazy") as "part of the popular cultural stereotype of Blacks" (Schaller, Park, & Mueller, 2003; see also Schaller, Park, & Faulkner, 2003).

In sum, there exist powerful adaptations designed to counter physical threats in humans, and these influence intragroup relations. These adaptations also appear to be intimately bound together with in-group/outgroup psychology, suggesting that serious threats from conspecifics also came from outside, rather than just inside, an individual's relevant group.

HEALTH

Because parasites are selected to exploit their particular host species (e.g., Anderson & May, 1982), extreme sociality seriously exacerbates the problem of keeping free of parasites. We therefore expect there to exist adaptations designed to minimize exposure to and maximize distance from individuals who present cues to parasitic infection.

Disgust constitutes a critical affective element of this system, elicited most readily by those who exhibit external cues associated with disease—discharged bodily fluids, and, more generally, deviations from the species-typical morphology (e.g., skin conditions, facial and bodily asymmetries, absence of limbs, unusual behaviors; Ginsburg & Link, 1993; Kurzban & Leary, 2001; Park, Faulkner, & Schaller, 2003; Rozin, Markwith, & Nemeroff, 1992; Schaller, Park, & Faulkner, 2003).

These cues elicit physical disgust with its associated facial responses (narrowed eyes, protruding tongue, etc.; Rozin, Lowery, & Ebert, 1994) and the tendency to avoid contact with the apparently diseased individual and his or her bodily secretions.

These systems are cue-based and heuristic—they respond to imperfect cues in the proximate stimulus, not to the "objective" probability of disease transmission. Further, because the cost of failing to identify a potential transmission threat is high, these systems might be biased in the direction of overperception of threat (Haselton & Buss, 2000). Peoples' overzealous reactions to certain kinds of conditions (AIDS or cancer) might be understood in this context (e.g., Rozin, Markwith, & Nemeroff, 1992), particularly for those who see themselves as vulnerable to disease (Park et al., 2003; Schaller, Park, & Faulkner, 2003).

Potentially contagious others also elicit empathy and pity (see earlier discussion), sometimes leading to a certain degree of ambivalence (Cottrell & Neuberg, in press). Indeed, people report ambivalent feelings toward persons with physical disabilities (e.g., Katz, 1981; Katz, Wackenhut, & Hass, 1986), and avoidance appears to be the primary means of dealing with disabled individuals (e.g., Hardaway, 1991; Kleck, Ono, & Hastorf, 1966; Perlman & Routh, 1980; Snyder, Kleck, Strenta, & Mentzer, 1979; Stephens & Clark, 1987). As discussed earlier, perception of the severity and the degree to which someone is *intentionally* placing others at risk should mediate responses to potentially contagious others.

In sum, there seem to be mechanisms designed to protect people from contagion. These include an aesthetic system designed to prefer the normal phenotype and affective and behavioral systems designed to motivate avoidance of those seen as likely to transmit parasitic infections.

SOCIALIZATION THREATS

Common norms of behavior facilitate coordination and the gains from cooperation, and a signal feature of human groups is the transmission of information that enables norm sharing. This fact might partially explain why humans prefer to interact with those who share an individual's norms, to copy his or her group's norms, and, critically, to react negatively to those with different norms (Boyd & Richerson, 1985).

Value differences indeed create prejudices of many sorts (e.g., Biernat, Vescio, Theno, & Crandall, 1996; Katz & Hass, 1988; Rokeach, 1972), eliciting disgust and a desire to separate the violators from other group members (Cottrell & Neuberg, in press), mirroring physical disgust (Rozin, Haidt, & McCauley, 2000; Rozin, Lowery, Imada, & Haidt, 1999).

It is interesting that people respond negatively to norm violations that have no obvious effects on their own interests, suggesting that the underlying psychology is more specific than simple cost-benefit computations. These effects seem to be particularly pronounced, as we might expect, when those with discrepant norms have the potential to be models for subsequent social learners within the group (Neuberg, Smith, & Asher, 2000). For example, despite increasingly favorable attitudes in the past 25 years, people have remained relatively unenthusiastic about homosexuals in two potentially influential social positions—elementary school teachers and clergy ("Americans growing more tolerant of gays," 1996; Newport, 2001). Similarly, certain grade- and secondary-school movements away from public education and toward private religious schools, charter schools, and home schooling appear to be driven not only by traditional education concerns but also by concerns related to "value education."

SUMMARY

We've presented several threats that emerge in the context of human sociality; there no doubt exist many others. Our thesis is that just as humans have evolved mechanisms for choosing selectively among those who would likely be valuable versus costly group members, we also possess evolved mechanisms for addressing those threats often posed within social groups. These systems include sensitivity to features associated with these threats, conditions (both personal and socioenvironmental) under which certain threats may be especially likely to emerge or be damaging, and a functional set of emotional, cognitive, and behavioral responses designed to mitigate or eliminate these threats. Stigmatization is neither random nor arbitrary but designed to enhance the fitness benefits of highly interdependent group living.

INTERGROUP RELATIONS

Intergroup conflict seems a ubiquitous feature of human life (Keegan, 1994; Sumner, 1906), and the historical association between groups and the most severe forms of violence have led to multiple, evolution-based accounts of intergroup conflict (e.g., Alexander, 1987; Eibl-Eibesfeldt, 1979). Here we discuss three broad classes of explanations for the mechanisms that underlie this pervasive feature of social life. Two of these explanations suggest that adaptations designed for other purposes—general cognition and within-group cooperation—have the side effect of intergroup conflict. The third explanation posits that intergroup conflict is a result of evolved cognitive mechanisms designed for precisely this purpose.

INTERGROUP COMPETITION AS A BY-PRODUCT OF DOMAIN-GENERAL COGNITIVE MECHANISMS

A predominant view in the social psychological literature holds that intergroup processes such as stereotyping, prejudice, and in-group favoritism derive from a small number of relatively general cognitive mechanisms (e.g., categorization) and motivations (e.g., self-enhancement). One prominent example is Social Identity Theory (e.g., Tajfel & Turner, 1979, 1986), a perspective derived largely from the findings of experiments employing the so-called minimal group paradigm. Here, individuals are randomly assigned to membership in a "group" of no previous personal relevance (e.g., dot "overestimators" versus "underestimators") and, subsequently, in the absence of personal contact or incentives for favoring one group versus the other, are given the opportunity to allocate benefits or costs (often "points" with no economic value) to individual members of the groups. Findings suggest that some individuals discriminate in favor of those placed into the same category. From such findings, the conclusion is often drawn that the simple act of social categorization, coupled with relatively basic motivations for self-enhancement, can explain intergroup phenomena (Tajfel & Turner, 1986).

These findings and conclusions are vulnerable, however, on several grounds (Yamagishi, 2003). First, even when in-group favoritism is observed, it tends to be of only modest magnitude; indeed, many participants show a preference for equal splits of points when possible. Second, the effect is very fragile, breaking down, for example, when it is costs rather than benefits to be allocated (Mummendey et al., 1992) or when there are three groups rather than two (Hartstone & Augoustinos, 1995).

Further, categorization per se might not be as important as perceived interdependence in generating in-group favoritism. When participants believe they will receive their allocation from an outgroup member, they exhibit outgroup favoritism (Rabbie, Schot, & Visser, 1989), and when they believe that their allocations come not from a fellow in-group member but instead from the experimenter, they allocate rewards evenly (Karp, Jin, Shiotsuka, & Yamagishi, 1993). In another experiment, participants were asked the following question: "Did you think that your own group members would allocate you more if you allocated more to a member of your own group?" Only those who answered in the affirmative showed in-group favoritism, strongly suggesting a kind of groupwise, reciprocal psychology (Jin, Yamagishi, & Kiyonari, 1996). Taken together, these results suggest that, instead of categorization per se, the key element in peoples' decisions to favor fellow in-group members might be the perception that group members are mutually dependent on one another (Rabbie et al., 1989; Yamagishi, 2003).

More generally, although it is possible that relatively domain-general cognitive mechanisms are responsible for the exceedingly rich and complex dynamics that characterize intergroup relations, such a possibility strikes us as remote. While general cognitive processes related to categorization, storage, retrieval, and so on are relevant to social cognition, a full explanation of intergroup processes is likely to require that theoreticians move beyond simple considerations of domain-general processes to consider the specific domains of social life. The task of understanding the complexities of behavior in "minimal groups" provides a case in point: Categorization alone seems insufficient in the absence of considering the concept of mutual outcome dependence of group members.

Intergroup Competition as a By-product of Intragroup Cooperation

Human cooperative psychology might have evolved because of the benefits group living affords, but it is plausible that these adaptations might, as a side effect, contribute to intergroup conflict (e.g., Boehm, 1999; Brewer, 2001; Campbell, 1967).

Earlier we argued that assessing the quality of potential cooperation partners directs attention to cues to a potential partner's availability for future interactions. This might have the side effect of leading us to initially characterize members of other groups as low-quality, potential cooperation partners because outsiders are unlikely to be familiar or to bear markings of in-group commitment. As a consequence, individuals should be relatively unlikely to act prosocially toward outsiders. Indeed, Eibl-Eibesfeldt (1979) puts it simply: ". . . in all cultures, they [strangers] are met with a certain reserve. Fear and rejection of strangers develop even in the absence of bad experiences with them" (p. 105). In and of themselves, preferences for familiar in-group members do not imply the necessity of outgroup hostility (Brewer, 1979, 2001).

In a world in which groups come into contact with one another and compete for scarce resources, intragroup preference and cooperation can turn into intergroup hate and conflict. Research from the realistic group conflict theory tradition—the idea that intergroup conflict is driven by competition for scarce resources—indicates that intergroup prejudices and conflict increase as real competition between groups for valuable resources increases (e.g., Bonacich, 1972;

Brewer & Campbell, 1976; Sherif, Harvey, White, Hood, & Sherif, 1961/1988), and recent survey research reveals few prejudices in the absence of perceived tangible outgroup threats, but considerable prejudices in the presence of such threats (e.g., Cottrell & Neuberg, in press; Neuberg & Cottrell, 2002). This implies that the more an individual is invested in and dependent on his or her own group—and therefore, identifies with it—the more he or she should be prejudiced and discriminate against outgroups; this idea has received ample support (e.g., Branscombe, Ellemers, Spears, & Doosje, 1999; Hodson, Dovidio, & Esses, 2003; Perreault & Bourhis, 1999).

However, even in the absence of tangible threat or competition, when in-group norms are given moral weight—as Gil-White (2001) has argued that they are—outgroup members become the target of moral ire simply by following their own norms. Hence, Gil-White's (2001) model entails conflict between ethnies as a downstream consequence of the evolved preference for coethnics who share an individual's norms.

Finally, it has been argued that the same threat-based framework useful for predicting the suites of stereotypical beliefs, emotional reactions, and action tendencies elicited by threatening in-group members can predict the suites of stereotypical beliefs, emotional reactions, and action tendencies elicited by parallel outgroup threats. Just as individuals who are perceived to illegitimately take another's valuable resources elicit anger and the desire to aggress, outgroups perceived to threaten in-group resources elicit anger and the desire to aggress; just as individuals who hold differing values elicit moral disgust and the inclination to avoid, groups who hold differing values elicit disgust and the inclination to avoid (e.g., Neuberg & Cottrell, 2002; Schaller & Neuberg, 2003; Schaller, Park, & Faulkner, 2003). The parallel nature of the in-group stigma syndromes and intergroup prejudice syndromes is consistent with the possibility that intergroup conflict emerges as a by-product of adaptations designed to solve problems of intragroup relations.

INTRAGROUP COOPERATION AS AN ADAPTATION FOR INTERGROUP COMPETITION

Some have argued that multiindividual cooperation might be specifically designed for intergroup conflict. Models of this type face the usual difficulties associated with explaining free riding: Individuals are better off allowing others to bear the costs of competing, especially if competition entails violent competition in which injury or death is possible.

Tooby and Cosmides (1988) suggest that, under particular conditions—including uncertainty about who is likely to be killed and reasonably equitable division of the acquired fitness benefits—mechanisms designed to exploit the reproductive resources of other groups (i.e., reproductive females) might be selected for even when cooperation for this purpose places the lives of individual group members at risk. This model implies that intergroup conflict is a male phenomenon.

Whether this model is correct or not, it does seem plausible that the potential fitness gains obtainable through the particular forms of cooperative, coordinated activities in which males and females differentially engaged—including cooperative aggression (e.g., in warfare) and hunting among males—seem to have led to a more pronounced "coalitional psychology" among men (Kurzban & Leary, 2001).

Most transparently, warfare is a distinctly male phenomenon (Keegan, 1994). Females have occasionally assumed support roles in conflict, but males have historically been the exclusive participants as combatants in warfare.

Differential selection pressures such as these might help explain some sex differences, including the finding that males tend to be more prejudiced against outgroups than are females (e.g., Sidanius, Cling, & Pratto, 1991; Watts, 1996) and that males tend to be seen as the prototypical outgroup member (Zárate & Smith, 1990). It also might go some of the way toward explaining discrimination on the basis of sex. Clearly, such discrimination exists: Historically, women have been excluded from positions of political power (Sidanius & Pratto, 1999), excluded from or discriminated against in the context of economic production, and systematically barred from certain occupations or professions (Daly & Wilson, 1983) and particular kinds of groups and associations (Tiger, 1969). Male psychology might be designed to seek control of political power and resources and, moreover, seek out other males as cooperative partners in these activities (Sidanius & Pratto, 1999; Tiger, 1969).

There are a number of findings from the laboratory that link multi-individual cooperation and intergroup conflict. In a number of environments, people choose more competitive options when they are playing a Prisoner's Dilemma game as a member of a group rather than as an individual (Insko et al., 1987; Insko & Schopler, 1998), and groups are (often correctly) perceived to be competitive (Fiske & Ruscher, 1993).

Although intergroup conflict is apparently ubiquitous, widespread, violent conflict and intense emotions of hate are restricted to certain kinds of social identities. Gil-White (2001) points out that architects and lawyers do not riot one against the other. Kurzban and Leary (2001) make a similar point about groups such as the obese, who are, to be sure, the target of negative beliefs and prejudices, but have never been subject to the kind of attacks associated with nations, ethnies, or even supporters of athletic clubs. Not all kinds of groups elicit the desire for conquest or extermination, and not all kinds of groups motivate cooperation for the purpose of intergroup competition and conflict. The most severe forms of antisocial behavior seem, instead, to be restricted to groups that are construed as potentially coordinated, cooperative sets of individuals. This may frequently be true of ethnies, which share norms and practices that allow close coordination.

SUMMARY

It seems unlikely that intergroup prejudices and conflict emerge simply from a small constellation of simple domain-general cognitive and affective processes, as some traditional social science theorizing suggests. More likely, they derive both from adaptations designed specifically for this purpose and as a by-product of mechanisms designed for other purposes, including within-group cooperation. It seems unlikely, however, that intergroup conflict, with its attendant affective, cognitive, and behavioral components, derives solely from adaptations designed for within-group cooperation. The intensity of emotion associated with intergroup conflict and its historical omnipresence is consistent with the view that there are specific adaptations serving the function of group-based competition.

DOMAIN SPECIFICITY REVISITED AND EXTENDED

Mackie et al. (2000) asked: "Why does one outgroup attract fear or contempt while another becomes the target of anger?" (p. 602). Our answer is straightforward: Because different groups activate different adaptations designed to cope with different social problems. Those coalitions and ethnies perceived to threaten physical safety elicit fear, those perceived to threaten health or morals elicit disgust, and those perceived to free-ride on others or to take what is not rightly theirs elicit anger. As much as we might prefer parsimony, there is no single system that can address effectively the many social challenges people face. Rather, problems of sociality are addressed by a set of distinct, and functionally relevant, cognitive, affective, and behavioral adaptations.

Earlier we suggested that the monolithic concept *group* should be replaced by a set of more useful concepts. Wilder and Simon (1998) observed that "an overview of the various definitions of *group* employed by social psychologists reveals a tale not unlike that of the blind men trying to describe an elephant by touching only one part of the animal" (p. 29). We agree with this general assessment of the confusion in the literature but suggest a slightly different cause: There's more than one animal in the room.

Granted, we believe it possible, even likely, that perceivers apply categorization systems of relatively broad functional scope for classifying and understanding certain social groupings: "People wearing white shoes," for example, is a category that might well be constructed much the same way that categories such as "artifacts under 5 pounds" are constructed. Nonetheless, it's likely that perceivers bring to bear distinct and proprietary categorization systems for classifying and understanding other kinds of social groupings, such as cooperative coalitions and ethnies. If so, it should be possible to distinguish among these different types of groups by looking at the array of processes associated with social cognition—how targets are categorized, the inferences people make based on group membership, the affective systems that are engaged as a function of the nature of the outgroup, and the behaviors different types of outgroup members evoke.

Kurzban, Tooby, and Cosmides (2001) addressed specificity of this type by showing that, for coalitions, categorization may be driven less by perceptual similarity—as general categorization systems might be—than by cues to coordinated, cooperative action. Similarly, Gil-White (2001) suggested and provided evidence that the parsing of ethnies is performed by a proprietary system originally designed to categorize species. Sidanius and colleagues' recent work (Sidanius & Pratto, 1999; Sidanius & Veniegas, 2000) suggests that simple, and apparently straightforward, models of "cross-categorization" need to take into account the qualitative nature of the group categories being combined. For example, because both Blacks and females face discrimination, we might expect that Black females would face the greatest discrimination. Instead, discrimination is worst for Black males (Sidanius & Veniegas, 2000). This finding not only resonates with the argument that coalitional psychology is designed for predominantly male group conflicts, but also illustrates the more general principle that investigations of in-group favoritism and outgroup discrimination should take into account the nature of the particular groups involved and the threats they are seen to pose.

CONCLUSIONS

We have suggested throughout this chapter that social exclusion, stigma, and discrimination are far from monolithic constructs, defined simply in terms of negative affect and avoidance tendencies. Rather, they reflect an array of qualitatively discrete suites of affective, cognitive, and behavioral adaptations that have evolved to solve diverse problems associated with sociality. An important consequence is that there might be different underlying cognitive representational systems for handling different kinds of collections of people.

Additional work should continue to clarify the important distinctions that human psychology makes among the different ways in which people can be represented—as categories (obese people), coalitions (the Miami Dolphins), and ethnies (Jews). In short, just as *social exclusion, stigma, prejudice,* and *discrimination* represent more than just monolithic constructs, so, too, for the case of *groups*. Because each of these may lead to stigmatization, exclusion, or prejudices of different sorts, it is important to understand how cues to different kinds of groupings and the threats they may appear to pose map onto different stigma and prejudice syndromes (Schaller & Neuberg, 2003).

REFERENCES

Aktipis, C. A. (2004). When to walk away, contingent movement and the evolution of cooperation. *Journal of Theoretical Biology, 231,* 249–260.

Alexander, R. D. (1987). *The biology of moral systems.* New York: Aldine de Gruyter.

Alvarsson, J.-A. (1988). *The Mataco of the Gran Chaco: An ethnographic account of change and continuity in Mataco socio-economic organization.* Uppsala, Sweden: Academiae Upsaliensis.

Americans growing more tolerant of gays. (1996, November). In *Gallup Organization.* Available online at: http://www.gallup.com/poll/news/961214.html.

Anderson, R. M., & May, R. M. (1982). Coevolution of hosts and parasites. *Parasitology, 85,* 411–426.

Andreoni, J., & Miller, J. H. (1993). Rational cooperation in the finitely repeated prisoner's dilemma: Experimental evidence. *Economic Journal, 103,* 570–585.

Andreoni, J., & Petrie, R. (2004). Public goods experiments without confidentiality: A glimpse into fund-raising. *Journal of Public Economics, 88,* 1605–1623.

Axelrod, R. (1984). *The evolution of cooperation.* New York, Basic Books.

Berscheid, E., & Reis, H. T. (1998). Attraction and close relationships. In D. T. Gilbert, S. T. Fiske, & G. Lindzey (Eds.), *The handbook of social psychology* (4th ed., pp. 193–281). New York: McGraw-Hill.

Biernat, M., Vescio, T. K., Theno, S. A., & Crandall, C. S. (1996). Values and prejudice: Toward understanding the impact of American values on outgroup attitudes. In C. Seligman, J. M. Olson, & M. P. Zanna (Eds.), *Values: The Ontario Symposium* (Vol. 8). Hillsdale, NJ: Erlbaum.

Blount, S. (1995). When social outcomes aren't fair: The effect of causal attributions on preferences. *Organizational Behavior and Human Decision Processes, 63,* 131–144.

Boehm, C. (1999). *Hierarchy in the forest.* Cambridge, MA: Harvard University Press.

Bonacich, E. (1972). A theory of ethnic antagonism: The split labor market. *American Sociological Review, 37,* 547–559.

Boyd, R., Gintis, H., Bowles, S., & Richerson, P. J. (2003). The evolution of altruistic punishment. *Proceedings of the National Academy of Sciences, 100,* 3531–3535.

Boyd, R., & Richerson, P. J. (1985). *Culture and the Evolutionary Process.* Chicago: University of Chicago Press.

Boyd, R., & Richerson, P. J. (1988). The evolution of reciprocity in sizable groups. *Journal of Theoretical Biology, 132,* 337–356.

Branscombe, N. R., Ellemers, N., Spears, R., & Doosje, B. (1999). The context and content of social identity threat. In N. Ellemers, R. Spears, & B. Doosje (Eds.), *Social identity: Context, commitment, content* (pp. 35–58). Oxford, England: Blackwell.

Brewer, M. B. (1979). Ingroup bias in the minimal intergroup situations: A cognitive motivational analysis. *Psychological Bulletin, 86,* 307–324.

Brewer, M. B. (2001). Ingroup identification and intergroup conflict: When does ingroup love become outgroup hate. In R. D. Ashmore, L. Jussim, & D. Wilder (Eds.), *Social identity, intergroup conflict, and conflict reduction: Rutgers series on self and social identity* (Vol. 3, pp. 17–41). London: Oxford University Press.

Brewer, M. B., & Alexander, M. G. (2002). Intergroup emotions and images. In D. M. Mackie & E. R. Smith (Eds.), *From prejudice to intergroup relations: Differentiated reactions to social groups* (pp. 209–225). New York: Psychology Press.

Brewer, M. B., & Campbell, D. T. (1976). *Ethnocentrism and intergroup attitudes: East African evidence.* Beverly Hills, CA: Sage.

Burnham, T. C. (2003). Engineering altruism: A theoretical and experimental investigation of anonymity and gift giving. *Journal of Economic Behavior and Organization, 50,* 133–144.

Burnham, T. C., & Hare, B. (in press). Engineering human cooperation: Does involuntary neural activation increase public goods contributions in adult humans? *Human Nature.*

Burnham, T. C., & Johnson, D. (2003). *The puzzle of human cooperation: Adaptation or evolutionary legacy?* Unpublished manuscript, Harvard University.

Burnham, T. C., & Johnson, D. (in press). The biological and evolutionary logic of cooperation. *Analyse & Kritik.*

Campbell, D. T. (1967). Stereotypes and the perception of group differences. *American Psychologist, 22,* 817–829.

Campbell, D. T. (1983). Two distinct routes beyond kin selection to ultrasociality: Implications for the humanities and social sciences. In D. Bridgeman (Ed.), *The nature of prosocial development: Theories and strategies* (pp. 11–41). New York: Academic Press.

Carpenter, J. (in press). Punishing free riders: How group size affects mutual monitoring and the provision of public goods. *Games and Economic Behavior.*

Chagnon, N. A. (1975). Genealogy, solidarity, and relatedness: Limits to local group size and patterns of fissioning in an expanding population. *Yearbook of Physical Anthropology, 19,* 95–110.

Chagnon, N. A. (1997). *Yąnomamö.* Fort Worth, TX: Harcourt Brace.

Chagnon, N. A., & Bugos, P. (1979). Kin selection and conflict: An analysis of a Yanomamö ax fight. In N. A. Chagnon & W. Irons (Eds.), *Evolutionary biology and human social behavior: An anthropological perspective* (pp. 86–132). North Scituate, MA: Duxbury.

Condon, R. G. (1987). *Inuit youth: Growth and change in the Canadian Arctic.* New Brunswick, NJ: Rutgers University Press.

Cosmides, L., & Tooby, J. (1992). Cognitive adaptations for social exchange. In J. Barkow, L. Cosmides, & J. Tooby (Eds.), *The adapted mind* (pp. 163–228). New York: Oxford University Press.

Cottrell, C. A., & Neuberg, S. L. (in press). Different emotional reactions to different groups: A sociofunctional threat-based approach to "prejudice." *Journal of Personality and Social Psychology.*

Cottrell, C. A., Neuberg, S. L., & Li, N. P. (2005). *What do people want in a group member? A sociofunctional analysis of valued and devalued characteristics.* Manuscript under review, Arizona State University.

Crocker, J., Major, B., & Steele, C. (1998). Social stigma. In S. Fiske, D. Gilbert, & G. Lindzey (Eds.), *Handbook of social psychology* (Vol. 2, pp. 504–553). Boston: McGraw-Hill.

Daly, M., Salmon, C., & Wilson, M. (1997). Kinship: The conceptual hole in psychological studies of social cognition relationships. In J. A. Simpson & D. T. Kenrick (Eds.), *Evolutionary social psychology* (pp. 265–296). Mahwah, NJ: Erlbaum.

Daly, M., & Wilson, M. (1983). *Sex, evolution and behavior* (2nd ed.). Belmont, CA: Wadsworth.

Daly, M., & Wilson, M. (1988). *Homicide.* Hawthorne, NY: Aldine de Gruyter.

Dawkins, R. (1982). *The extended phenotype: The gene as the unit of selection.* Oxford, England: Oxford University Press.

de Coccola, R., & King, P. (1986). *The incredible Eskimo: Life among the barren land Eskimos.* Surry, British Columbia, Canada: Hancock House.

Diener, E., Fraser, S. C., Beaman, A. L., & Kelem, R. T. (1976). Effects of deindividuation variables on stealing among Halloween trick-or-treaters. *Journal of Personality and Social Psychology, 33,* 178–183.

Dijker, A. J. (1987). Emotional reactions to ethnic minorities. *European Journal of Social Psychology, 17,* 305–325.

Dijker, A. J., & Koomen, W. (2003). Extending Weiner's attribution-emotion model of stigmatization of ill persons. *Basic and Applied Social Psychology, 25,* 51–68.

Dunbar, R. (1993). Coevolution of neocortical size, group size and language in humans. *Behavioral and Brain Sciences, 16,* 681–735.

Eibl-Eibesfeldt, I. (1979). *The biology of peace and war.* New York: Viking Press.

Falk, A., Fehr, E., & Fischbacher, U. (2000). Testing theories of fairness: Intentions matter. *Institute for Empirical Research in Economics.* University of Zurich, Working Paper #63.

Fehr, E., & Fischbacher, U. (2003). The nature of human altruism. *Nature, 425,* 785–791.

Fehr, E., & Gächter, S. (2000). Fairness and retaliation: The economics of reciprocity. *Journal of Economic Perspectives, 14,* 159–181.

Fehr, E., & Gächter, S. (2002). Altruistic punishment in humans. *Nature, 415,* 137–140.

Fehr, E., & Gächter, S. (2003). The puzzle of human co-operation: A reply. *Nature, 421,* 912.

Fiske, S. T., Cuddy, A. J., Glick, P., & Xu, J. (2002). A model of (often mixed) stereotype content: Competence and warmth respectively follow from perceived status and competition. *Journal of Personality and Social Psychology, 82,* 878–902.

Fiske, S. T., & Ruscher, J. B. (1993). Negative interdependence and prejudice: Whence the affect. In D. M. Mackie & D. L. Hamilton (Eds.), *Affect, cognition, and stereotyping: Interactive processes in group perception* (pp. 239–268). San Diego, CA: Academic Press.

Frank, R. (1988). *Passions within reason: The strategic role of the emotions.* New York: Norton.

Frijda, N. H. (1986). *The emotions.* Cambridge, England: Cambridge University Press.

Gelman, S. A. (1996). Concepts and theories. In R. Gelman & T. Kit-Fong (Eds.), *Perceptual and cognitive development* (pp. 117–150). San Diego, CA: Academic Press.

Gil-White, F. J. (2001). Are ethnic groups biological "species" to the human brain?: Essentialism in our cognition of some social categories. *Current Anthropology, 42,* 515–554.

Ginsburg, I. H., & Link, B. G. (1993). Psychosocial consequences of rejection and stigma feelings in psoriasis patients. *International Journal of Dermatology, 32,* 587–591.

Gintis, H. (2000). Strong reciprocity and human sociality. *Journal of Theoretical Biology, 206,* 169–179.

Gintis, H., Bowles, S., Boyd, R., & Fehr, E. (2003). Explaining altruistic behavior in humans. *Evolution and Human Behavior, 24,* 153–172.

Goffman, E. (1963). *Stigma: Notes on the management of spoiled identity.* New York: Simon & Schuster.

Graburn, N. H. H. (1969). *Eskimos without igloos: Social and economic development in Sugluk.* Boston: Little, Brown.

Grillon, C., Pellowski, M., Merikangas, K. R., & Davis, M. (1997). Darkness facilitates acoustic startle reflex in humans. *Biological Psychiatry, 42,* 453–460.

Hamilton, W. D. (1964). The genetical evolution of social behavior. *Journal of Theoretical Biology, 7,* 1–16.

Hardaway, B. (1991). Imposed inequality and miscommunication between physically impaired and physically nonimpaired interactants in American society. *Howard Journal of Communications, 3,* 139–148.

Hart, A. J., Whalen, P. J., Shin, L. M., McInerney, S. C., Fischer, H., & Rauch, S. L. (2000). Differential response in the human amygdala to racial outgroup vs. ingroup face stimuli. *NeuroReport, 11,* 2351–2355.

Hartstone, M., & Augoustinos, M. (1995). The minimal group paradigm: Categorization into two versus three groups. *European Journal of Social Psychology, 25,* 179–193.

Haselton, M. G., & Buss, D. M. (2000). Error management theory: A new perspective on biases in cross-sex mind reading. *Journal of Personality and Social Psychology, 78,* 81–91.

Hawkes, K. (1993). Why hunter-gatherers work: An ancient version of the problem of public goods. *Current Anthropology, 34,* 341–361.

Henrich, J., Boyd, R., Bowles, S., Camerer, C., Gintis, H., McElreath, R., et al. (2001). In search of Homo economicus: Experiments in 15 small-scale societies. *American Economic Review, 91,* 73–79.

Hill, K., & Kaplan, H. (1999). Life history traits in humans: Theory and empirical studies. *Annual Review of Anthropology, 28,* 397.

Hodson, G., Dovidio, J. F., & Esses, V. M. (2003). Ingroup identification as a moderator of positive-negative asymmetry in social discrimination. *European Journal of Social Psychology, 33,* 215–233.

Hoffman, E. K., McCabe, K. K., Shachat, J., & Smith, V. L. (1994). Preferences, property rights and anonymity in bargaining games. *Games and Economic Behavior, 7,* 346–380.

Hoffman, E. K., McCabe, K., & Smith, V. L. (1996). On expectations and the monetary stakes in ultimatum games. *International Journal of Game Theory, 25,* 289–301.

Insko, C., Pinkley, R., Hoyle, R., Dalton, B., Hong, G., Slim, R., et al. (1987). Individual-group discontinuity: The role of intergroup contact. *Journal of Experimental Social Psychology, 23,* 250–267.

Insko, C., & Schopler, J. (1998). Differential distrust of groups and individuals. In C. Sedikides, J. Schopler, & C. A. Insko (Eds.), *Intergroup cognition and intergroup behavior* (pp. 75–107). Mahwah, NJ: Erlbaum.

Isaac, R. M., & Walker, J. (1988). Group size effects in public goods provision: The voluntary contribution mechanism. *Quarterly Journal of Economics, 103,* 179–199.

Izard, C. E. (1991). *The psychology of emotions.* New York: Plenum Press.

Jin, N., Yamagishi, T., & Kiyonari, T. (1996). Bilateral dependency and the minimal group paradigm. *Japanese Journal of Psychology, 67,* 77–85.

Judd, C. M., & Park, B. (1988). Outgroup homogeneity: Judgments of variability at the individual and group levels. *Journal of Personality and Social Psychology, 54,* 778–788.

Karp, D., Jin, N., Shinothuka, H., & Yamagishi, T. (1993). Raising the minimum in the minimum group paradigm (In English). *Japanese Journal of Experimental Psychology, 32,* 231–240.

Katz, I. (1981). *Stigma: A social psychological analysis.* Hillsdale, NJ: Erlbaum.

Katz, I., & Hass, R. G. (1988). Racial ambivalence and American value conflict: Correlational and priming studies of dual cognitive structures. *Journal of Personality and Social Psychology, 55,* 893–905.

Katz, I., Wackenhut, J., & Hass, R. G. (1986). Racial ambivalence, value duality, and behavior. In J. F. Dovidio & S. L. Gaertner (Eds.), *Prejudice, discrimination, and racism* (pp. 35–59). New York: Academic Press.

Keegan, J. (1994). *A history of warfare.* New York: Vintage.

Kerr, N. L., & Kaufman-Gilliland, C. M. (1994). Communication, commitment, and cooperation in social dilemmas. *Journal of Personality and Social Psychology, 66,* 513–529.

Keser, C., & van Winden, F. (1997). Partners contribute more to public goods than strangers: Conditional cooperation. *Tinbergen Institute Discussion Papers 97-018/1,* Tinbergen Institute.

Kleck, R., Ono, H., & Hastorf, A. H. (1966). The effects of physical deviance upon face-to-face interaction. *Human Relations, 19,* 425–436.

Komorita, S. S., Hilty, J. H., & Parks, C. D. (1991). Reciprocity and cooperation in social dilemmas. *Journal of Conflict Resolution, 35,* 494–518.

Kurzban, R., & Houser, D. (2005). An experimental investigation of cooperative types in human groups: A complement to evolutionary theory and simulations. *Proceedings of the National Academy of Sciences, 98.*

Kurzban, R., & Leary, M. R. (2001). Evolutionary origins of stigmatization: The functions of social exclusion. *Psychological Bulletin, 127,* 187–208.

Kurzban, R., McCabe, K., Smith, V. L., & Wilson, B. J. (2001). Incremental commitment and reciprocity in a real time public goods game. *Personality and Social Psychology Bulletin, 27,* 1662–1673.

Kurzban, R., Tooby, J., & Cosmides, L. (2001). Can race be erased? Coalitional computation and social categorization. *Proceedings of the National Academy of Sciences, 98,* 15387–15392.

Ledyard, J. (1995). Public goods: A survey of experimental research. In J. Kagel & A. E. Roth (Eds.), *Handbook of experimental economics* (pp. 11–194). Princeton, NJ: Princeton University Press.

Lee, R. B., & DeVore, I. (1968). Problems in the study of hunters and gatherers, in, R. B. Lee & I. DeVore (Eds.), *Man the hunter* (pp. 3–12). Chicago: Aldine.

Lickel, B., Hamilton, D. L., Wieczorkowska, G., Lewis, A., Sherman, S. J., & Uhles, A. N. (2000). Varieties of groups and the perception of group entitativity. *Journal of Personality and Social Psychology, 78,* 223–246.

Mackie, D. M., Devos, T., & Smith, E. R. (2000). Intergroup emotions: Explaining offensive action tendencies in an intergroup context. *Journal of Personality and Social Psychology, 79,* 602–616.

Maner, J. K., Kenrick, D. T., Becker, D. V., Delton, A. W., Hofer, B., Wilbur, C. J., et al. (2003). Sexually selective cognition: Beauty captures the mind of the beholder. *Journal of Personality and Social Psychology, 85,* 1107–1120.

Maner, J. K., Kenrick, D. T., Becker, D. V., Robertson, T., Hofer, B., Delton, A., et al. (2005). Functional projection: How fundamental social motives can bias interpersonal perception. *Journal of Personality and Social Psychology, 88,* 63–78.

McClintock, C. G. (1972). Social motivation—A set of propositions. *Behavioral Science, 17,* 438–454.

Mummendey, A., Simon, B., Dietze, C., Grünert, M., Haeger, G., Kessler, S., et al. (1992). Categorization is not enough: Intergroup discrimination in negative outcome allocations. *Journal of Experimental Social Psychology, 28,* 125–144.

Nesse, R. M. (2001). *Evolution and the capacity for commitment.* New York, NY: Russell Sage Foundation.

Neuberg, S. L., & Cottrell, C. A. (2002). Intergroup emotions: A sociofunctional approach. In D. M. Mackie & E. R. Smith (Eds.), *From prejudice to intergroup relations: Differentiated reactions to social groups* (pp. 265–283). New York: Psychology Press.

Neuberg, S. L., Smith, D. M., & Asher, T. (2000). Why people stigmatize: Toward a biocultural framework. In T. Heatherton, R. Kleck, J. G. Hull, & M. Hebl (Eds.), *The social psychology of stigma* (pp. 31–61). New York: Guilford Press.

Newport, F. (2001, June). *American attitudes toward homosexuality continue to become more tolerant.* Princeton, NJ: The Gallup Organization.

Nowak, M. A., & Sigmund, K. (1998). Evolution of Indirect Reciprocity by Image Scoring. *Nature, 393,* 573–577.

Oliver, P. (1980). Rewards and punishments as selective incentives for collective action: Theoretical investigations. *American Journal of Sociology, 85,* 1357–1375.

Panchanathan, K., & Boyd, R. (2003). A tale of two defectors: The importance of standing for the evolution of indirect reciprocity. *Journal of Theoretical Biology, 224,* 115–126.

Park, J. H., Faulkner, J., & Schaller, M. (2003). Evolved disease-avoidance processes and contemporary anti-social behavior: Prejudicial attitudes and avoidance of people with physical disabilities. *Journal of Nonverbal Behavior, 27,* 65–87.

Patton, J. Q. (2000). Reciprocal altruism and warfare: A case from the Ecuadorian Amazon. In L. Cronk, N. Changon, & W. Irons (Eds.), *Adaptation and human behavior: An anthropological perspective* (pp. 417–436). Hawthorn, NY: Aldine de Gruyter.

Perlman, J. L., & Routh, D. K. (1980). Stigmatizing effects of a child's wheelchair in successive and simultaneous interactions. *Journal of Pediatric Psychology, 5,* 43–55.

Perreault, S., & Bourhis, R. Y. (1999). Ethnocentrism, social identification, and discrimination. *Personality and Social Psychology Bulletin, 25,* 92–103.

Peterson, L., Reaven, N., & Homer, A. L. (1984). Limitations imposed by parents on children's altruism. *Merrill-Palmer Quarterly, 31,* 269–286.

Plutchik, R. (1980). *Emotion: A psychoevolutionary synthesis.* New York: Harper & Row.

Prentice-Dunn, S., & Rogers, R. W. (1980). Effects of deindividuating situational cues and aggressive models on subjective deindividuation and aggression. *Journal of Personality and Social Psychology, 39,* 104–113.

Price M., Cosmides, L., & Tooby, J. (2002). Punitive sentiment as an anti-free rider psychological device. *Evolution and Human Behavior, 23,* 203–231.

Quillian, L., & Pager, D. (2001). Black neighbors, higher crime? The role of racial stereotypes in evaluations of neighborhood crime. *American Journal of Sociology, 107,* 717–767.

Rabbie, J. M., Schot, J. C., & Visser, L. (1989). Social identity theory: A conceptual and empirical critique from the perspective of a behavioural interaction model. *European Journal of Social Psychology, 19,* 171–202.

Richerson, P. J., & Boyd, R. (1998). The evolution of human ultra-sociality. In I. Eibl-Eibisfeldt & F. Salter (Eds.), *Indoctrinability, ideology, and warfare: Evolutionary perspectives* (pp. 71–96). New York: Berghahn Books.

Rigdon, M., McCabe, K., & Smith, V. (2003). Positive reciprocity and intentions in trust games. *Journal of Economic Behavior and Organization, 52,* 267–275.

Rokeach, M. (1972). *Beliefs, attitudes, and values.* San Francisco: Jossey-Bass.

Roseman, I. J., Wiest, C., & Swartz, T. S. (1994). Phenomenology, behaviors, and goals differentiate discrete emotions. *Journal of Personality and Social Psychology, 67,* 206–221.

Roth, A. (1995). Bargaining experiments. In J. H. Kagel & A. Roth (Eds.), *The handbook of experimental economics* (pp. 253–348). Princeton, NJ: Princeton University Press.

Rothbart, M., & Taylor, M. (1992). Category labels and social reality: Do we view social categories as natural kinds. In G. Semin & K. Fiedler (Eds.), *Language, interaction, and social cognition* (pp. 11–36). London: Sage.

Rozin, P., Haidt, J., & McCauley, C. R. (2000). Disgust. In M. Lewis & J. M. Haviland-Jones (Eds.), *Handbook of emotions* (2nd ed., pp. 637–653). New York: Guilford Press.

Rozin, P., Lowery, L., & Ebert, R. (1994). Varieties of disgust faces and the structure of disgust. *Journal of Personality and Social Psychology, 66,* 870–881.

Rozin, P., Lowery, L., Imada, S., & Haidt, J. (1999). The CAD triad hypothesis: A mapping between three moral emotions (contempt, anger, disgust) and three moral codes (community, autonomy, divinity). *Journal of Personality and Social Psychology, 76,* 574–586.

Rozin, P., Markwith, M., & Nemeroff, C. (1992). Magical contagion beliefs and fear of AIDS. *Journal of Applied Social Psychology, 22,* 1081–1092.

Samuelson, P. A. (1970). *Economics.* New York: McGraw-Hill.

Schaller, M., & Neuberg, S. L. (2005). *The nature in prejudice(s).* Manuscript under review, Arizona State University.

Schaller, M., Park, J. H., & Faulkner, J. (2003). Prehistoric dangers and contemporary prejudices. *European Review of Social Psychology, 14,* 105–137.

Schaller, M., Park, J. H., & Mueller, A. (2003). Fear of the dark: Interactive effects of beliefs about danger and ambient darkness on ethnic stereotypes. *Personality and Social Psychology Bulletin, 29,* 637–649.

Schelling, T. C. (1960). *The strategy of conflict.* Cambridge, MA: Harvard University Press.

Schroeder, D. A., Penner, L. A., Dovidio, J. F., & Piliavin, J. A. (1995). *The psychology of helping and altruism.* New York: McGraw-Hill.

Sherif, M., Harvey, O. J., White, B. J., Hood, W. R., & Sherif, C. W. (1988). *The Robbers Cave experiment: Intergroup conflict and cooperation.* Middletown, CT: Wesleyan University Press. (Original work published 1961).

Sidanius, J., Cling, B. J., & Pratto, F. (1991). Ranking and linking behavior as a function of sex and gender: An exploration of alternative explanations. *Journal of Social Issues, 47,* 131–149.

Sidanius, J., & Pratto, F. (1999). *Social dominance: An intergroup theory of social hierarchy and oppression.* New York: Cambridge University Press.

Sidanius, J., & Veniegas, R. C. (2000). Gender and race discrimination: The interactive nature of disadvantage. In S. Oskamp (Ed.), *Reducing prejudice and discrimination: The Claremont Symposium on applied social psychology* (pp. 47–69). Mahwah, NJ: Erlbaum.

Snyder, M. L., Kleck, R. E., Strenta, A., & Mentzer, S. J. (1979). Avoidance of the handicapped: An attributional ambiguity analysis. *Journal of Personality and Social Psychology, 12,* 2297–2306.

Stephens, K. K., & Clark, D. W. (1987). A pilot study on the effect of visible physical stigma on personal space. *Journal of Applied Rehabilitation Counseling, 18,* 52–54.

Sumner, W. G. (1906). *Folkways.* New York: Ginn.

Tajfel, H., & Turner, J. C. (1979). An integrative theory of intergroup conflict. In W. G. Austin & S. Worchel (Eds.), *The social psychology of intergroup relations* (pp. 33–47). Monterey, CA: Brooks/Cole.

Tajfel, H., & Turner, J. C. (1986). The social identity theory of intergroup behaviour. In S. Worchel & W. G. Austin (Eds.), *Psychology of intergroup relations* (pp. 7–24). Chicago: Nelson-Hall.

Tiger, L. (1969). *Men in groups.* New York: Random House.

Tomkins, S. S. (1963). *Affect, imagery, and consciousness: Vol. 2. The negative affects.* New York: Springer.

Tooby, J., & Cosmides, L. (1988). The evolution of war and its cognitive foundations. *Institute for Evolutionary Studies Technical Report 88-1,* Palo Alto, CA.

Tooby, J., & Cosmides, L. (1992). The psychological foundations of culture. In J. Barkow, L. Cosmides, & J. Tooby (Eds.), *The adapted mind* (pp. 19–136). New York: Oxford University Press.

Tooby, J., & Cosmides, L. (1996). Friendship and the banker's paradox: Other pathways to the evolution of adaptations for altruism. *Proceedings of the British Academy, 88,* 119–143.

Trivers, R. L. (1971). The evolution of reciprocal altruism. *Quarterly Review of Biology, 46,* 35–57.

Van Lange, P. A. M., Otten, W., De Bruin, E. M., & Joireman, J. A. (1997). Development of prosocial, individualistic, and competitive orientations: Theory and preliminary evidence. *Journal of Personality and Social Psychology, 73,* 733–746.

Watts, M. W. (1996). Political xenophobia in the transition from socialism: Threat, racism, and ideology among East German youth. *Political Psychology, 17,* 97–126.

Weiner, B., Perry, R. P., & Magnusson, J. (1988). An attributional analysis of reactions to stigma. *Journal of Personality and Social Psychology, 55,* 738–748.

Wilbur, C., Shapiro, J., Neuberg, S. L., Goldstein, N., & Hofer, B. (2003). *Putting together the pieces: A sociofunctional account of intragroup relations.* Unpublished data, Arizona State University.

Wilder, D. A., & Simon, A. F. (1998). Categorical and dynamic groups: Implications for social perception and intergroup behavior. In C. Sedikides, J. Schopler, & C. A. Insko (Eds.), *Intergroup cognition and intergroup behavior* (pp. 27–44). Mahwah, NJ. Erlbaum.

Yamagishi, T. (1986). The provision of a sanctioning system as a public good. *Journal of Personality and Social Psychology, 51,* 110–116.

Yamagishi, T. (2003, January). *The group heuristic: A psychological mechanism that creates a self-sustaining system of generalized exchanges.* Santa Fe, NM: Santa Fe Institute Workshop on the Co-evolution of Institutions and Behavior.

Zárate, M. A., & Smith, E. R. (1990). Person categorization and stereotyping. *Social Cognition, 8,* 161–185.

Zimbardo, P. G. (1970). The human choice: Individuation, reason, and order versus deindividuation, impulse, and chaos. In W. J. Arnold & D. Levine (Eds.), *Nebraska symposium on motivation* (Vol. 17, pp. 237–307). Lincoln, NE: University of Nebraska.

CHAPTER 23

Dominance, Status, and Social Hierarchies

DENISE CUMMINS

O N JULY 7, 2003, THREE TEENAGE boys dressed like characters from the Matrix movies were charged with murder conspiracy, car jacking, and illegal weapons possession. Their plan was to steal a car, kill three middle school classmates, then carry out random attacks on as many people as possible through their hometown of Oaklyn, New Jersey. Their plans bore a striking resemblance to the shootings that took place in schools across the country in 1999, beginning with Colorado's Columbine high school in which two teens killed 13 people before taking their own lives. It was as though the Columbine students' actions had ignited a rage that had been simmering just below the collective surface of American teenage consciousness.

In the aftermath of these tragedies, schools responded in predictable ways. Collective action was taken to deter violence and make us feel safe once again. Surveillance cameras were installed in classrooms. Weapon checkpoints were set up in school entrances. Security guards were posted. Dress codes were instituted. Attempts were made to pass legislation allowing parents to access a list of books their children check out of the school library. Political pundits and social commentators filled the airwaves and print media with analyses of the tragedies. We wanted to know how something like this could happen and how it could have been prevented. The usual suspects were trotted out and held up for scrutiny: TV violence, the ready availability of guns, and the presumed "breakdown" of the American family values. The makers of violent video games were sued by crusading lawyers who sought to hold them accountable given that many of these violent teens spent hours playing (and, in some cases, designing) such games.

Pundits and wise men aside, the most telling insights came from the students themselves. They pointed the finger not at the usual suspects but instead squarely and directly at the source of so much teeming rage: the status hierarchies that completely define their lives in and out of school ("High School Hell," 1999; "Oaklyn Plot Investigators," 2003). As one student put it, "It's a rat race inside the school to see who's going to be more popular. Everybody's thinking: Am

I going to look cool to the popular kids? Are they going to accept me?" In the words of another, "The jocks rule the school, and they kind of get a big head and think they own the world." (The term *jock*, as it turns out, is used freely to refer to high-status, popular students.) And yet another, "It just makes you not want to go to school; you don't want to deal with those people." According to classmates, the ringleader of the Oaklyn teens was constantly tormented for a speech impediment caused by a cleft, his bow-legged and stooped gait, and even his clothes. As one student put it, he "was an easy target, but he never lashed out. He just took it." And still another, "Everybody picked on him." In the words of the Columbine shooters, "This is for all the people who made fun of us all these years!"

According to students, the popular—or high-status—kids make life hell for those they believe to be less popular and, therefore, lower status than themselves. They freely inflict verbal abuse (usually under the guise of teasing), cut in front of less popular kids in food lines or push them out of line and take their place, or deliberately bump into them in the halls and smirk while walking away. They act as though they have and deserve "priority of access to resources," including the teacher's attention, best places to sit on the bus or in the lunchroom, and the most attractive mates. The methods they use to assert these "entitlements" usually avoid detection by supervising adults because, as researcher Rachel Simmons (2002) puts it, high-status kids (particularly girls) have learned how to operate "below the radar." They know how to completely dominate and suppress those outside their own popular cliques in ways that are either difficult to detect or socially acceptable.

The students' analyses, however, were dismissed out of hand by school officials, social commentators, and political pundits because, after all, how could things so trivial as *status* and *popularity* possibly lead to such violent tragedies? The connection is not so incredible, however, when viewed against the backdrop of human evolutionary psychology. When explaining physical and behavioral traits, evolutionary scientists distinguish between ultimate and proximate causes. *The ultimate cause of* a trait is simply the survival or reproductive value it confers or (in the case of evolutionary lag) it conferred in the past. Proximate causes are the mechanisms and stimuli that subserve it or evoke it.

SOCIAL HIERARCHIES: ULTIMATE CAUSES

The key to understanding the impact of status lies in appreciating its relation to *survival and reproductive success* both during our evolutionary past and in our present lives. Status (or rank) is most frequently defined *as priority of access to resources in competitive situations*. Natural selection is a straightforward process: The genes of those who live long enough to reproduce remain in the gene pool. The genes of those who don't, don't. In most species, there is a direct relationship between social status and reproductive success, with higher status individuals being less likely to die of predation or starvation and more likely to leave living offspring (Clutton-Brock, 1988; Clutton-Brock & Harvey, 1976; Dewsbury, 1982; Ellis, 1995). Among species in which status is unstable, the level of reproductive success achieved by any individual is directly related to the length of time during which the individual is high ranking (Altmann et al., 1996). There is a direct relationship between status and *inclusive fitness,* where fitness is defined as the number of living offspring an individual has that go on to reproduce themselves, and inclusive

fitness is defined as the reproductive success of individuals and their closely related kin—or to put it more precisely, personal fitness plus *the effects of actions* on
the reproduction of genetic relatives, degraded by relatedness (see, e.g., Dawkins,
1982). Your status is directly tied to your ability to survive, reproduce, and take
care of yourself, your offspring, and your kin.

SOCIAL HIERARCHIES: PROXIMATE CAUSES

Proximate causes are the mechanisms or stimuli that directly subserve a trait.
With respect to status differences and status striving, we can distinguish among
several such causes.

SOCIAL STATUS AND NEUROENDOCRINE RESPONSES

Given the intimate and direct relationship among status, survival, and reproductive
success, it should come as no surprise that a loss in status (however trivial its manifestation may seem to our modern sensibilities) should send an alarm signal directly to our physiology. A loss in status can mean the difference between life and
death—or between merely surviving and having a life worth living. These "alarm
signals" manifest themselves as changes in our physiology, which motivate us to act
in ways that either keep them the way they are (in the case of pleasant-feeling
changes) or make them go away (in the case of unpleasant-feeling changes). These
changes take place in the neuroendocrine system, a sort of dialog between the nervous system and the endocrine system in which certain cells release hormones into
the blood in response to stimulation of the nervous system. When the individual is
challenged in some way, the brain activates the autonomic nervous system, which
stimulates the output of two hormones, cortisol from the adrenal cortex and adrenalin from the adrenal medulla. Adrenalin affects us immediately by increasing
heart rate and blood pressure and mobilizing stored energy reserves. Cortisol
works more slowly, replenishing energy supplies through fat storage. Collectively,
the cascade of events that occurs in the neuroendocrine system is referred to as
stress. If the stress is temporary, these responses help to put the body back into balance (or allostasis). If instead the stress is chronic, these responses can have deleterious effects on the individual's mental and physical health (McEwen & Wingfield,
2002). These deleterious effects manifest as altered fat storage and mobilization,
hormonal imbalances, sleep disturbances, cardiovascular disease, altered mood,
and altered neuroendocrine reactivity. A frequently used measure of stress level is
circulating cortisol.

The direct connection between status effects and neuroendocrine response is
plainly evident in research based on animal models, particularly research on individuals living in naturalistic ecologies in intact social groups. Hormones play a
large role in the development and expression of social status. Status correlates
with androgen and serotonin levels in many species of primates in that those
with higher levels are also higher ranking (Ellis, 1995; Sapolsky, 1990; Sapolsky &
Ray, 1989). This relationship is also bidirectional: Changes in social status produce marked changes in levels of these hormones. Following contests of rank, defeated males exhibit a drop in androgen levels while winners' levels rise;
serotonin levels rise in subordinates who improve their social status (Niehoff,
1999; Sapolsky, 1990, 1999; Sapolsky & Ray, 1989). Subordinates who receive frequent beatings from dominants suffer persistently elevated cortisol (stress hor-

mone) levels and impaired endocrine feedback responses to stress (Blanchard, Sakai, & McEwen, 1993). Cortisol levels of all members of a social group soar during periods of social instability resulting from upheavals in the dominance hierarchy, such as when unfamiliar individuals are introduced into a group or an alpha male is ousted (McEwen & Wingfield, 2002; Niehoff, 1999).

Are these effects seen in humans? The answer appears to be, decidedly, yes. The intimate relationship between social status and neuroendocrine responses is plainly evident in modern humans. You may believe you don't think much about status, but your endocrine system shows otherwise. Changes in status produce large changes in hormone levels. For example, following competitive games, male winners typically show elevated testosterone levels relative to losers (Booth, Shelly, Mazur, Tharp, & Kittok, 1989; Elias, 1981). This is true even when the competition involves little physical action, as in chess competitions (Mazur, Booth, & Dabbs, 1992) or contests in reaction time (Gladue, Boechler, & McCaul, 1989). Female winners have lower levels of cortisol (a hormone secreted by the adrenal glands in response to physical or social stressors) than female losers (Bateup, Booth, Shirtcliff, & Granger, 2001). An individual need not even participate in the game to show the effects; hormone levels in fans who watch the game mirror those of the team they support (Bernhardt, Dabbs, Fielden, & Lutter, 1989). The neuroendocrine responses that are evoked by human competitive games are, therefore, essentially the same as the responses seen in contests of rank in other species. In fact, it is often difficult for competitors and fans to remember that these contests are, after all, just games. Physiologically, they feel like the real thing: a competitive contest between rivals that will determine where we stand in the hierarchy and hence what our chances of long-term survival are likely to be.

A number of studies have demonstrated a reliable relationship between socioeconomic status and neuroendocrine reactivity. For example, adults and children of low socioeconomic status typically show higher cortisol levels than those of higher socioeconomic status (Kapuku, Treibner, & Davis, 2002; Lupien, King, Meaney, & McEwen, 2001). Several health indices reliably correlate with socioeconomic status, and these correlations cannot be explained simply in terms of differences in access to health care, smoking, or other objective factors (Adler, Boyce, Chesney, Folkman, & Syme, 1993; Adler et al., 1994; McEwen & Wingfield, 2002). We might be tempted to conclude that these results simply show that poverty is more stressful than wealth, but the picture emerging from this branch of research suggests the story is far more complex. What seems to matter instead is *perceived* social status vis-à-vis others. For example, among healthy White women, perceived social status is consistently and strongly related to a wide constellation of hormone-dependent health indices, including heart rate, sleep latency, body fat distribution, and cortisol habituation to repeated stress; this is true even after the contribution of *objective* socioeconomic status is partialed out (Adler, Epel, Casellazzo, & Ickovics, 2000). Compared to socially dominant individuals, subordinate or submissive individuals have higher baseline cortisol levels, display greater changes in physiological stress indices during conflict, and more slowly recover from conflict-induced changes in cardiovascular activity measures (Newton, Blane, Flores, & Greenfield, 1999; Rejeski, Gagne, Parker, & Koritnik, 1989). This is true even among married couples; perception of spouse dominance correlates with blood pressure reactivity during marital interactions (Brown, Smith, & Benjamin, 1998). Moreover, when frustrated by antagonists, stress indices (e.g., blood pressure and cortisol levels) can be made to return to baseline levels if the frustrated individuals are given the opportunity to aggress against their antagonists—but only if they believe their antagonists to be of lower status than themselves; when retaliating against antagonists they believe to be of higher status, these indices remain at their frustration-induced levels (Hokanson, 1961; Hokanson & Shetler, 1961).

Finally, the relationship between status and neuroendocrine responses appears to be bidirectional: Not only does perceived social status influence hormone levels, but also changes in hormone levels can change an individual's perceived social status and thereby his or her manner of interacting with the world. For example, in one double-blind study (Tse & Bondy, 2002), citalopram (a selective serotonin-reuptake inhibitor) or a placebo was administered to 10 volunteers while their roommates received no treatment. While on the drug, these volunteers were rated by their roommates as significantly less submissive and more cooperative. They also spontaneously adopted a dominant pattern of eye contact when interacting with strangers.

Neuroendocrine reactivity, therefore, is more than a simple correlative response to events in the social and physical environments. It comprises a signaling system that informs a person (and others) of his or her current relative status: How you feel tells you where you are in the social hierarchy, and how you react to social stressors informs others of your status as well (e.g., dominant eye patterns signal higher status than submissive eye patterns). And where you are in the hierarchy is a pretty good predictor of your chances of long-term survival and quality of life. As the Columbine and related tragedies show, life at the bottom of the hierarchy can be pretty grim emotionally, and, as this section shows, the constant emotional turmoil that those at the bottom suffer put them at high risk for illness, depression, or violence.

SOCIAL STATUS AND COGNITIVE-BEHAVIORAL STRATEGIES

At this point, we might ask what determines an individual's place in a social hierarchy; that is, what makes some people higher in status than others? It is plain that status hierarchies emerge early in development and with little assistance from caretakers. Status hierarchies are apparent in the play groups of preschool children as young as 2 years of age (Frankel & Arbel, 1980; Strayer & Trudel, 1984). Children in this age group differ among themselves on measures of social dominance. In fact, social dominance is the earliest stable dimension of peer group social organization and one of the earliest emerging and most enduring observable personality traits (Frankel & Arbel, 1980; Hold-Cavell & Boursutzky, 1986; Lemerise, Harper, & Howes, 1998). Even toddlers seem to be acutely aware of these differences in that they prefer to associate with and imitate high-status as opposed to low-status individuals (Boulton & Smith, 1990; LaFreniere & Charlesworth, 1983; Russon & Waite, 1991).

To explore this question, we again look at status striving in Darwin's laboratory—the natural world. Common wisdom has it that higher rank among animals means greater size, and indeed, size and dominance rank are correlated in many species (Ellis, 1995). But even in those showing such a correlation, size constitutes only one contributing to social rank. Investigations of social interactions in a variety of species suggest that dominance hierarchies are supported by a collection of specific *cognitive* functions and that those who achieve dominance are those who are particularly adept at them. *Selection favors those who have social and political intelligence.* This turns out to mean: (1) being adept at learning the implicit rules that constrain behavior in a person's social group and monitoring compliance with them, (2) forecasting and influencing the behavior of others, and (3) forming powerful alliances based on reciprocal obligations.

Social Status, Mind Reading, and Deception   Social living confers both costs and benefits to individuals. The costs are increased competition for food, shelter, mates, and the like. The benefits are increased access to mates and increased opportunities for cooperative action, including predator defense, caring for the young, and (in the case of humans, at any rate) collectively manipulating the physical environment to better suit their needs. In hierarchical social groups, how these costs and benefits cash out depend a good deal on an individual's status. Consider that from a cognitive standpoint, a social hierarchy is, essentially, a set of *social norms,* that is, *rules that constrain the behavior of individuals depending on their rank* (Cummins, 2000). In human societies, these may be implicit or explicitly codified as regulations or laws. In animal societies, these social norms are implicit yet reflected in virtually every activity, including who is allowed to sit next to, play with, share food with, groom, or mate with whom. Animal societies often resemble human feudal societies in that high-status individuals typically take on the role of enforcing these implicit social norms, aggressing against those who violate them and breaking up disputes between lower ranking individuals (Boehm, 1992). For example, high-ranking individuals often punish violations of social norms as benign as grooming or sharing food with forbidden individuals. In fact, perceived violation of the "social code" has been designated by many researchers as the single most common cause of aggression in primate societies (Hall, 1964).

Also as in feudal societies, animal societies that are characterized by rigid social hierarchies are more stable than those that lack them, and disruptions in social rankings (e.g., the ousting of an alpha male—or, in the case of humans, a local baron or king) constitute periods of intense social tension and conflict (Coates-Markel, 1997; de Waal, 1982). The social stability conferred by strict social hierarchies, however, carries a cost in terms of individual freedom. To avoid punishment (or ostracism, which can mean death due to predation or starvation), individuals must learn what is *permitted,* what is *forbidden,* and what is *obligated given their place in the hierarchy, and they must comply with these norms* (see Cummins, 1996a, 1998, 2000, for a more complete discussion). Individual behavior must be monitored with respect to them and violations responded to effectively.

While nonhierarchical societies (e.g., those of some aboriginal societies) can also be rigidly defined in terms of social norms that constrain behavior, the difference is that in social hierarchies, what an individual may, must, or must not do depends in large part on his or her status. In many cases, this is because the norms typically concern access to resources. *To be of high status means to have priority of access to resources in competition.* If high-status individuals fail to monitor the behavior of subordinates vis-à-vis available resources, then they cannot maintain priority of access to resources.

Among humans, this phenomenon is perhaps most clearly manifested in political-orientation scales that measure social dominance. People who score high on measures of social dominance tend to prefer hierarchical relationships in society, distribution of resources based on merit, conservative ideology, military programs, and punitive justice policies (Pratto, Tartar, & Conway-Lanz, 1999). These are all consistent with maintaining priority of access to resources. Those scoring low on social dominance measures tend to favor social equality, distribution of resources based on need, and social programs (Pratto et al., 1999). In fact, social dominance measures have been found to account for much of the sex-linked variability in political attitudes (Pratto, Stallworth, & Sidanius, 1997).

Effects like these can also be produced in contrived laboratory settings using simple but straightforward cognitive tasks. Participants are presented scenarios that describe arbitrary social rules and are required to monitor compliance of fictitious individuals. Under these circumstances, adults are far more likely to look for violators of the rules when they believe they are monitoring individuals who are *lower* status than themselves than when monitoring individuals of equally high, equally low, or higher status than themselves (Cummins, 1999a). Adults also exhibit better face recognition memory for low-status cheaters than high-status cheaters or noncheaters of any rank (Mealey, Daood, & Krage, 1996).

Because agents (as opposed to objects) move of their own volition and have internal states (physical, emotional, and mental), negotiating the demands of the social environment is several orders of magnitude more computationally complex than negotiating the demands of the physical environment. Imagine a computerized robot that must learn to negotiate a complex but stable physical environment versus one that must learn to negotiate an environment populated by other robots that move of their own accord and are motivated to seek goals based on internal states that are unobservable but presumably similar to its own (e.g., finding food and shelter). The computational demands of keeping track of events and objects in the former are trivial compared to keeping track of events and objects in the latter. If you encounter a rock in the former and move around it, you can be pretty sure that it will remain in the same place while your back is turned. If you encounter an agent in the latter and move around it, you can't be sure of where it will be a few seconds later. Nor can you be sure that it will not show up again in the place you are headed, with much the same goal in mind as you. Engaging in competitive or cooperative action requires, at the very least, keeping track of what the other is doing as well as keeping track of your own actions and their outcomes.

These characteristics of the social environment constitute evolutionary "pressure" for solving certain kinds of social problems, problems that are directly related to *fitness and are best solved through cognitive effort*, particularly cognitive effort involved in the forecasting and influencing of others' behavior. Social dominance has been found to correlate with deceptive ability and enhanced ability to decode nonverbal cues. Individuals who are perceived and rated as socially dominant are better at deceiving others, persuading others, and interpreting others' intentions (Hall, Halberstadt, & O'Brien, 1997; Keating & Heltman, 1994).

There is a large literature on deception among primates that suggests Machiavellian intent in some primate social interactions (Byrne, 1995; Whiten & Byrne, 1988a). The major outcome of most of these deceptions is *flouting social norms without getting caught,* a singularly effective strategy by which low-ranking individuals improve their access to resources (see Cummins, 2000, for examples). For example, dominant males monopolize reproduction opportunities by aggressing against or threatening to aggress against females and subordinate males who are caught socializing or consorting (Cheney & Seyfarth, 1990, p. 227). Because of the high risks involved in such forbidden liaisons, females and subordinate males often engage in deception, such as concealing their trysts behind obstacles and suppressing their copulation cries (de Waal, 1988; Kummer, 1988). Deceptions of this kind have also been observed for hiding other forbidden behaviors, such as stealing food, failing to share food, or grooming forbidden individuals (see Whiten & Byrne, 1988b, for numerous examples). For example, they conceal objects or behaviors from others by hiding them from view, acting quietly so as not to attract attention, avoiding looking at a desirable object themselves, or distracting attention away from the desired object or forbidden behaviors (Byrne, 1995; Whiten & Byrne, 1988a). Subordinates garner a larger share of resources through deception and form alliances with forbidden individuals through surreptitious food sharing or grooming, alliances that can be called on during contests of rank. Gagneux, Woodruff, and Boesch (1997) report that over 50% of the offspring born to female chimpanzees in their study group were fathered by males from *other troops*. The females in question had surreptitiously disappeared around the times of their estrus and reappeared a few days later. During these times, they had apparently engaged in clandestine matings. This observation perhaps offers the clearest testament to the impact greater intelligence can have on reproductive success. Variation in intelligence is a trait on which natural selection can operate. This situation seems to produce a kind of evolutionary arms race in that species that show the greatest capacity for this type of deception (e.g., chimpanzees) also have the most unstable dominance hierarchies relative to those that have stable hierarchies (e.g., macaques; Whiten & Byrne, 1988a, 1988b). It is difficult to dominate individuals who have the cognitive wherewithal to outwit you.

The impact of strategic deception on relative status has also been demonstrated in human cognitive experimental studies. These studies often themselves rely on deception. A group of participants are gathered into a room and given a hypothetical problem, such as determining how they would survive following a plane crash in a remote mountain area with only rope, matches, and 3 ounces of water. In reality, the solution they come up with is not of particular interest. What is of interest is how the decision making unfolds. Inevitably, one or more individuals come to dominate the group, steering the discussion down particular paths and emphasizing some offered solutions over others. These dominant individuals also turn out to be those who are best at deception. For example, when asked to take a sip of a truly foul-tasting liquid and then tell others that the liquid tastes great, dominant individuals are more convincing than subordinate individuals. It is on the whole more difficult to tell when they are lying or when they are telling the truth compared to subordinate individuals. Apparently, dominant individuals have (by nature or by learning) an arsenal of methods for leading, persuading, deceiving, or otherwise influencing others.

Social Status and Reciprocity   Outwitting the competition is only part of the story. To acquire and maintain a favorable position in the hierarchy, it is also necessary to form strong alliances with others. This is best accomplished through the formation of reciprocal obligations.

The study of reciprocity has a long and venerable history in evolutionary biology. The idea is that individuals cooperate for mutual benefit—I'll help you if you help me. According to *selfish gene* theories (Dawkins, 1976), reciprocity shouldn't exist. Natural selection operates at the level of the individual, or to be more precise, natural selection is differential gene replication but operates through differential reproductive success of individuals. There appears to be little benefit to cooperating with another individual if that means enhancing that individual's reproductive benefits at your expense, such as spending time grooming another individual rather than foraging or hunting to enhance your own survival or investing effort in caring for another's offspring instead of or in addition to your own. Yet, such cooperation does exist in nature in abundance. In his seminal paper on reciprocal altruism, Trivers (1971) cited cleaning symbioses (seen in over 45 species of fish and 6 species of shrimp), birdcalls (which often warn the entire flock of approaching predators), and extensive cooperative efforts among humans as examples of evolved reciprocity. Weighing heavily in this literature, evolutionary biologists Axelrod and Hamilton point out in the opening paragraph of their much-cited paper on models of reciprocity (1981, p. 1390): "The theory of evolution is based on the struggle for life and the survival of the fittest. Yet cooperation is common between members of the same species and even between members of different species."

Of the various explanations offered for this phenomenon, four have perhaps had the greatest impact: Hamilton's rule (Hamilton, 1964), communalism, mutualism, and reciprocal altruism. Hamilton's rule (sometime referred to as kin selection) shows that fitness benefits can accrue to those who preferentially aid individuals with whom they share genes (relatives or kin). Fitness is measured in terms of the number of copies of a gene passed on to subsequent generations (rather than simply number of offspring produced). When modeled in this way (by tracking genes), it can be shown that individuals can increase their fitness either by producing their own offspring *or* by aiding the reproduction of genetic relatives—as long as the degree of relatedness (number of genes shared) is high enough so that the benefits that accrue to the recipient are greater than the costs that accrue to the actor. In communalism, the interaction is beneficial for one and harmless to the other (e.g., birds eating insects off giraffes). In mutualism, both organisms benefit from the interactions (e.g., bees and flowers, clown fish and anemones).

Reciprocal altruism is a bit more complicated. Each individual helps another individual while also helping himself or herself (Trivers, 1971, p. 39). Conferring a benefit on the partner usually involves incurring a cost to oneself. The problem is that while a given individual can benefit from cooperating, he or she can usually do better by exploiting the cooperative efforts of others, that is, by accepting the benefits of the cooperative venture without reciprocating. In that case, the defector reaps the biggest reward, having gotten the offered benefit without reciprocating, while the cooperator suffers the costs involved in cooperating while reaping none of the benefits. The latter outcome is disadvantageous to survival. Failure to reciprocate is termed *cheating* (Trivers, 1971, p. 39), and in single-shot cooperative ventures, cheating (defection) is indeed an evolutionarily stable strategy (Axelrod & Hamilton, 1981). The situation changes dramatically, however, if (1) participants will have future opportunities to cooperate (as would be the case in a stable social group) and (2) participants can recognize each other. Under these conditions, reciprocity can evolve as an evolutionarily stable strategy *only if* those who fail to reciprocate are punished through exclusion from subsequent cooperative ventures. One of the most robust strategies to emerge in modeling research under these conditions is *Tit for Tat,* in which a party chooses to cooperate on the first round and then matches whatever the other player did on the preceding move in subsequent rounds.

Cooperation can have a marked impact on reproductive success by influencing the status of the cooperators. Changes in status typically occur when lower ranking individuals challenge higher ranking ones. Among male primates, rank within the dominance hierarchy is acquired and maintained through dyadic aggression, and alliances determine the fate of outranked individuals, including alpha males whose rank is usurped (Chapais, 1988, 1992; Harcourt & de Waal, 1992; Riss & Goodall, 1977; Uehara, Hiraiwa-Hasegawa, Hosaka, & Hamai, 1994). Alpha males who form or already possess strong alliances with other males maintain a relatively high, stable position within the group, while those who have no alliances or weak alliances are ostracized, maintaining a solitary existence outside the group (Goodall, 1986; Uehara et al., 1994). Importantly, these alliances are formed and maintained through cooperative effort, or more precisely, through the formation of reciprocal obligations. During agonistic encounters, individuals typically call for help, and *nonkin* allies are more likely to supply that help if the individual in question has groomed them, shared food with them, or assisted them in agonistic encounters in the past (de Waal, 1989; Seyfarth & Cheney, 1984). Similarly, they punish noncooperators by directly aggressing against them when they themselves request help (de Waal, 1989), failing to come to their aid, or by misinforming or failing to inform them about the location of food (Woodruff & Premack, 1979).

Not all alliances are equally effective, and, like human children, nonhuman primates often seem to focus their alliance-building efforts on higher status individuals. For example, baboons, macaques, and vervet monkeys form matrilineal hierarchies in which any female is dominant to all the females that are subordinate to her mother, and she is subordinate to all the females that are dominant to her mother (Cheney & Seyfarth, 1990). During agonistic encounters, support is typically given to the higher ranking females, who in turn intervene in conflicts when they themselves are dominant to the target of the aggression. By aiding higher ranking females, lower ranking females form strong alliances based on reciprocal obligations that enable them to move up in rank. As any eighth grader or high schooler can tell you, survival in a hierarchical social environment depends on having loyal and powerful friends, and acquiring such friends is facilitated by doing them favors.

What counts as sufficient reciprocation also depends on the relative status of the individuals involved. Among those close in rank, the rate of intervention by individual A on behalf of B is proportional to the rate of intervention of B on behalf of A (de Waal, 1992). But high-ranking individuals need not reciprocate as often as subordinates in order to maintain an alliance (Chapais, 1988, 1992; Seyfarth & Cheney, 1984). The most frequent explanation given for this is that greater benefits derive from their interventions due to their priority of access to physical and social resources.

Among humans, the majority of research on reciprocity has come from experimental economics in which partners are given the opportunity to cooperate or defect in Prison Dilemma-like scenarios. With few exceptions, these studies have tended to analyze reciprocity as though it existed in a social vacuum in which two anonymous agents with equal exogenous status and no prior social history reach a fair outcome. The striking thing about many of these studies is how frequently people's decisions appear inconsistent with rational choice theory. For example, Weg and Smith (1993) gave subjects the opportunity to win money in transactions based on repeated Prisoner's Dilemma scenarios. The subject's task was to decide whether to betray his or her collaborators and win a fixed amount of money or to trust them and possibly win more or less than the fixed amount. Subjects showed a greater willingness to trust and a greater unwillingness to forgive betrayals of that trust than would have been predicted by rational choice theory. The subjects' choices perhaps appear more rational when viewed through the lens of evolutionary biology models of reciprocity. These subjects seem to come to the task biased toward cooperation, then (as in Tit for Tat) respond in ways that reward fellow cooperators and punish defectors (through exclusion or retaliation). Indeed, studies by Fehr and his colleagues suggest that the ability to detect and punish cheaters has a large influence in producing cooperative outcomes that deviate from standard game-theoretic predictions (Fehr & Gächter, 2000; Fehr, Gächter, & Kirchsteiger, 1997; see also Güth & van Damme, 1998).

Even more striking are results of studies that employ the *dictator* game in which two people are jointly assigned a provisional sum of money. One person, the *dictator,* then decides how the money is to be split between the two. Standard self-interested economic analyses predict that dictators should award themselves the full amount, and many do; but a significant number of dictators and, in many cases, the majority will give the other person a nontrivial amount of the money (e.g., Forsythe, Howowitz, Savin, & Sefton, 1994; Hoffman, McCabe, Shachat, & Smith, 1994; Hoffman, McCabe, & Smith, 1996; Johannesson & Persson, 2000). In a variation of this game, called the *ultimatum* game, the other person is given the opportunity to either accept the proposed split or turn it down causing both players to walk away with nothing. In these studies, significantly more *proposers* (equivalent to dictators in the dictator game) offer the responder a nontrivial amount of the money with the modal offer usually being a 50-50 split. According to standard game-theoretic analyses, the addition of this second phase of play should make little difference to the proposed divisions. Given that the proposer has all the goods upfront, responders should favor a single penny over nothing at all (which is what they'll each get if the responder declines), and the proposers knowing this should offer the responders as little as possible.

These results suggest that individuals come to these tasks with normative standards of fairness, and behavior that departs significantly from these norms elicits retaliatory, spiteful, or other apparently "irrational" responses. In the case of strangers of presumably equal status but demonstrably unequal power (as in the dictator and ultimatum games), the normative expectation seems to be a 50-50 split. Proposers and dictators appear to take these implicit norms into consideration when making decisions, and *their decisions are guided in large part by distance from the expected normative division.* Use of this metric results in decisions that depart significantly from predictions based on simple self-interest.

The workings of this "implicit normative metric" is perhaps most apparent in a series of studies by van Dijk and Vermunt (2000). These researchers had people play the dictator and ultimatum game with a special twist: Proposers and dictators received twice the value of each token being divided, while their partners received the stated value of the tokens. In one version of the games, both players knew about the arrangement (symmetric information). In a second version, only the proposers/dictators knew that they would receive twice as much money for each token (asymmetric information). This manipulation had no effect in the dictator game; dictators made a modal offer of two-thirds of the tokens for their opponents under both information conditions. But it had a large impact in the ultimatum game; proposers made modal offers of two-thirds of the tokens (an equal monetary value distribution) for their opponents in the symmetric information condition, but they exploited their opponents' ignorance in the asymmetric information condition by making a seemingly fair offer to split the tokens in half (with more of the actual monetary surplus going to the proposers). Van Dijk and Vermunt interpreted these results to mean that differences in the distribution of power between these two games were responsible for participants acting more generously in the dictator game than in the ultimatum game. They suggested that in situations involving strong power asymmetries (as in the dictator game), normative considerations will predominate, whereas in situations involving more equal power relations (as in the ultimatum game), strategic considerations will predominate.

Perhaps the most interesting aspect of these results is that they suggest priority of access to resources (as in the dictator game) may sometimes elicit a sense of "pastoral responsibility" toward the other, more powerless party. Using a different methodological approach, Fiddick and Cummins (2001) explored the impact of differential status, economic resources, and social relationship on tolerance toward cheating. Subjects were asked to consider a carpooling arrangement in which one party agrees to pay for gasoline if the other party does all the driving. They were shown hypothetical ledgers showing gas payments that indicated varying degrees of compliance on the part of the gas-paying partner (from 100% compliance to as little as 25%) and were asked to indicate (1) their willingness to continue the arrangement and (2) their perception of how fairly they'd been treated. In some scenarios, the two parties were of equal status (both employees), and in some they were of unequal status in that one was an employee and the other a boss. Participants were found to be far more tolerant of cheating when they adopted the perspective of the higher status person (which the authors referred to as a "noblesse oblige effect"). These results could not be interpreted simply in terms of asymmetrical costs and benefits. Participants judged the employee to derive more of a benefit from the carpooling arrangement than the boss, and there was no difference in the perceived costs paid by the employee and the boss. Further, the results obtained even when the employee was described as making more money than the boss (due to other income sources for the employee). Only two factors seemed to attenuate this effect. The first was removal of the social relationship between the parties. If the parties were described as having met through a classified ad rather than one being the other's employee, noblesse oblige disappeared; equivalent levels of intolerance for cheating was found regardless of whether the reasoner took the perspective of employee or boss. This strongly suggested that it was asymmetries in the social relation and not asymmetries in costs and benefits that underlie the effect. The second factor was culture. European subjects (Germans and Britons) showed the effect more strongly than North American subjects (Americans and Canadians), presumably due to differences in political histories (e.g., a history of feudalism in Europe). Instead of asymmetrical costs and benefits, these results suggest that status impacts *expectations concerning appropriate behavior.* Cheating a person of lower status appears to be more unacceptable than cheating a person of higher status. Together with the results of Cummins (1999a) and Mealey et al. (1996), these results suggest that high status carries with it an expectation of pastoral responsibility; high-status individuals are expected to monitor compliance with laws and contracts, yet show tolerance during enforcement if the miscreant is of lower status than the cheated individual. It is too soon, however, to draw any definitive conclusions about the role played by status with this database. More research on this topic is needed, particularly research based on Prisoner Dilemma studies that allow actual (as opposed to imaginary) money to change hands.

HOW DEVELOPMENT INFORMS EVOLUTIONARY EXPLANATIONS OF SOCIAL DOMINANCE EFFECTS

The thesis of this chapter is that the necessity of surviving and thriving in a social environment yields evolutionary pressure that shapes the physiological systems involved in neuroendocrine reactivity, cognition, and emotion. With respect to the first and second of these, we have seen how subtle changes in perceived relative status can produce large neuroendocrine and emotional responses. These responses are (in the long run) predictive of overall health and mortality.

With respect to the cognition, the evolutionary effects of sociality are plainly evident in cognitive development. We are intensely social beings from the moment of birth. Newborns (no more than a few minutes old) show a distinct bias for looking at faces as compared to other equally complex stimuli (Goren, Sarty, & Wu, 1975). Ten-week-old infants have been found to distinguish among emotional facial expressions (D'Entremont & Muir, 1997). Within the first year of life, infants also engage in social referencing, looking at their caregivers' reactions to novel stimuli (e.g., Stenberg & Hagekull, 1997). And by 2 years of age, they can succeed at tasks that require them to grasp another's goals, desires, or preferences (e.g., Bartsch & Wellman, 1989). But, as we saw, becoming a fully functioning social agent involves more than preferring social stimuli. It also requires inducing the rules that constrain behavior in an individual's social group, monitoring the behavior of self and others with respect to them, and developing the skills necessary to compete and cooperate effectively with others to achieve social goals—even if that entails the use of deception.

Developmental research has shown that, like language acquisition, very young children show a marked *precocity* for acquiring social rules and monitoring compliance with them. Children as young as 16 months look longer at visual displays depicting violations of arbitrary social rules than at similar displays that do not constitute violations of social rules (Cummins, 1999b). Reference to social rules appears in children's justifications of their behavior as early as 24 months of age (Dunn, 1988), and by 2½ years of age, children distinguish between social conventions and moral rules, using these distinctions to discipline their inferences concerning acceptable behavior (Hollos, Leis, & Turiel, 1986; Nucci, Turiel, & Encarnacion-Gawrych, 1983). When asked to test compliance with social rules, 3-year-olds have been found to spontaneously seek out potential rule violations just as adults do (Cummins, 1996c), readily distinguish rule-violating behavior from compliant behavior (Harris & Núñez, 1996), and give cogent explanations as to why violating instances constitute violations of the rule (Harris & Núñez, 1996). In fact, their performance is equivalent to adults on these social reasoning tasks (Cummins, 1996c). In contrast, when asked to perform a nonsocial task of apparent equal complexity (test the truth of a rule rather than monitor compliance), children in this age group fail not only to seek out potentially falsifying evidence (Cummins, 1996b) but also to distinguish confirming from falsifying instances and cannot give coherent justifications for their decisions (Harris & Núñez, 1996).

And with respect to deception, dominant preschoolers (like their adult counter-parts) are more successful not only at directing the play activities of their peers but also at deceiving them (and adults) as well.

These striking differences in performance are important because, unlike other characteristics of cognitive development, they don't go away with maturity. For nearly 3 decades, psychologists have noted that adults reason more effectively about some domains than others. One of the most robust, domain-specific effects is seen in the realm of social reasoning. When reasoning about prescriptive rules (social norms), adults spontaneously look for possible violations of the rule; that is, they look to see who might be breaking the rule (Cheng & Holyoak, 1985; Cos-mides, 1989; Cummins, 1996c; Gigerenzer & Hug, 1992; Manktelow & Over, 1991). Violation detection is appropriate for other types of reasoning tasks, such as evaluating the truth of a statement or rule, yet is rarely observed. This reason-ing strategy seems to be triggered almost exclusively by problems with social content, particularly permissions, obligations, prohibitions, promises, and warnings. The magnitude of the difference in performance on truth-testing and violation-detection versions of these tasks in the adult literature is identical to that in the developmental literature (10% to 30% correct on truth testing versus 60% to 90% correct on social versions of the same tasks). This means that the ad-vantage for social reasoning emerges early in development and continues to color reasoning performance throughout the life span. The average 3-year-old appears to have as firm a grasp on the implications of socially prescriptive rules as the av-erage adult. As any parent knows, unfortunately, this hardly guarantees compli-ance; indeed, the ability to flout social rules increases as the ability to deceive emerges. For example, 2-year-old toddlers can appreciate others' intentions and goals and can effectively thwart them from reaching those goals through sabo-tage (e.g., locking a box or erasing footprints); it is not until later in development (after the emergence of a theory of mind at about 4 to 5 years of age) that they can effectively thwart others by manipulating their beliefs or other means of decep-tion (Sodian, 1991). As their ability to manipulate beliefs develops, so does their ability to flout social rules and influence others.

SEX DIFFERENCES IN STATUS STRIVING

Among mammals, there is a significant difference between potential reproductive success of males and females, namely, that the ceiling for male reproduction is much higher for males than females. This difference is because sperm are plenti-ful compared to eggs, and females necessarily invest more energy in reproduction than do males (e.g., pregnancy and lactation) and are typically more involved in the care of very young offspring (i.e., infants and toddlers). Male mammals are not obligated to invest heavily in their offspring. They can, in a sense, drop their genes and go.

Comparatively speaking, therefore, female reproduction is limited by access to resources while male reproduction is limited by access to mates. Once a preg-nancy has occurred, females cannot increase their reproductive success by engag-ing in further matings. Because of the greater cost to females in producing young, they instead can increase their lifelong reproductive success by investing in their offspring to ensure their survival. In contrast, males can increase their reproduc-tive success by maximizing the number of fertile females with whom they mate.

If the number of males in a population is approximately equal to that of females, then there exists enormous pressure for competition among males for access to fertile females, and there will exist greater variability among male reproductive success: For every male who gains reproductive access to a disproportionate share of females, other males lose opportunities to reproduce. It is here that status differences begin to have major impact. Generally speaking, the higher the status a male enjoys, the greater access to potential mates he also enjoys.

This point is perhaps most clearly demonstrated by the results of a large historical study of six early civilizations that spanned four continents and 4,000 years (Betzig, 1993). Despite numerous differences among the cultures, there existed a remarkably consistent pattern with respect to status-based differential sexual access among men. Rich nobles maintained harems that included dozens— sometimes hundreds—of women. In India, for example, Bhupinder Singh maintained 332 women in his harem, while many commoners were so poor they could not afford wives at all. Similar disproportionate mating systems were observed in China, where princes maintained harems of hundreds of women, generals had 30 or more, upper-class men housed 6 to 12, and middle-class men kept 3 or 4. Sometimes the number of women who could be "distributed" among the male populace was regulated by law. According to Incan law and custom, "principal persons" were given 50 young women; leaders of vassal nations, 30; heads of provinces of more than 100,000 people were given 20; governors of at least 100 people were given 8; petty chiefs, 7; smaller chiefs, 5; and so on. Women, in short, were distributed like property strictly according to the status of men.

Status appears to improve male sexual access even when women are given (relatively speaking) more choice in the matter. By definition, higher status men have access and control of greater resources than do lower status men, and, as was pointed out earlier, female reproduction is limited by access to resources necessary to support pregnancy, lactation, and caring for the young. This makes high-status men more desirable to females than low-status men (Buss, 1994; Hill & Hurtado, 1996). This is most starkly demonstrated by the fact that women in polygynous societies that restrict the avenues women may pursue to obtain resources typically prefer to be one of many cowives of a prosperous man than the only wife of a poor one (Betzig, 1986). In Western cultures that have legally enforced monogamy and relatively greater financial opportunities available to women, high-status men are nonetheless still preferred as mates and as partners in extramarital affairs (Baker & Bellis, 1995; Perusse, 1993). The key factor here seems to be differential distribution of resources between the sexes. In their study in Hungary, Bereczkei, Vorgos, Gal, and Bernath (1997) found that females did not seek mates with resources as frequently as females in other nations. Since the collapse of communism in Hungary, there are still relatively few men with an income sufficient enough to maintain a family. The researchers speculate that, as a result, females in this culture have shifted their attention to cues other than those referring to resources when seeking mates (Bereczkei et al., 1997). Related research indicates which cues women attend to depends in large part on what their goals are in the dating game.

Kelly and Dunbar (2001) had 120 subjects (ages 18 to 55 years) rate eight profiles of imaginary male personalities designed to portray the presence or absence of the qualities of altruism or bravery. They found that altruistic males were preferred for long-term relationships and friendships. But for short-term liaisons (i.e., flings or affairs), they found that females preferred nonaltruistic, risk-prone, and brave males to altruistic, risk-averse, or nonbrave males, and that men were aware of these preferences. It is not surprising, then, that men tend to engage in "display behavior" that signals these qualities. Sadalla, Kenrick, and Vershure (1987) found that dominant behavior in males increased females' sexual attraction to them, but such behavior in females was not related to sexual attraction in males. This was true despite the fact that male dominance was not related to general likeability. In other words, females in these studies found dominant males more sexually attractive even though they didn't like them much. Following up on this, Graziano, Jensen-Campbell, Todd, and Finch (1997; using structural equation modeling) found that men who were not likeable were not attractive regardless of their dominance status. For men who were perceived to be likeable, however, dominance enhanced their physical attractiveness significantly. In another set of studies, researchers employed computer graphic techniques to manipulate the "masculinity" or "femininity" of a composite male face (Penton-Voak et al., 1999). The same results obtained: Females found highly masculinized faces more attractive when they were in the most fertile segment of their menstrual cycles.

Given that women apparently reward men for these dominant personality traits, it should come as no surprise that men score higher in social dominance orientation than do women (Pratto, 1996): They tend to prefer social hierarchies and endorse an ideology that sanctions domination of one group over another and the allocation of more perks to one group than another. This sex difference has been observed in numerous cultures, including Sweden, which is one of the most egalitarian cultures in the world (Buss, 1994).

Intrasexual competition among females has received less attention from researchers than has intrasexual competition among males, partly because females compete in far subtler ways than do males, ways that are opaque to those who don't know the game. These differences are perhaps most starkly apparent in the results of studies of female middle and high school cliques (Crick, 1996; Crick & Grotpeter, 1995; Simmons, 2002). The overall profile of sex differences that is emerging from this body of research shows that males tend to use direct confrontation to dominate and subdue potential threats and rivals. Females, however, prefer to use indirect means that can easily go undetected by teachers and others not involved in the devious attack, such as spreading rumors aimed at ruining a potential rival's reputation; excluding, ignoring, and isolating her socially; staring to intimidate her into silence; and derogating the rival when "popular" boys are nearby. This is referred to as *relational aggression*. The effectiveness of these strategies lies in the fact that they hit the opponent "where they live": When threatened, males attempt to fight or flee, while females attempt to "tend and befriend," that is, engage in caretaking of their loved ones and strengthen social ties (Taylor, Klein, Lewis, Gruenewald, & Updegraff, 2002). To disable a rival, therefore, males tend to attack while females attempt to socially isolate her through exclusion, malicious gossip, and reputation damage. Females describe such strategies as "destroying" a rival.

EMOTIONAL, PSYCHOLOGICAL, AND STRATEGIC RESPONSES TO LOSS OF STATUS

Losses in status can have devastating consequences for social agents. Some are readily perceived and measured, such as demotion at work yielding a reduction in pay and the concomitant negative impact on an individual's family. Others are more subtle yet still profound.

A loss of status can produce a deep sense of shame in the individual, which is communicated tacitly by avoiding eye contact with others, lowering the chin, hunching body posture, and avoiding social encounters (Wicker, Payne, & Morgan, 1983). In some circumstances, loss of status can evoke feelings of rage and depression (Gilbert, 1990). While rage may motivate the individual to retaliate, depression may prompt submissive behavior to appease others or to prevent further humiliation (Forrest & Hokanson, 1975).

Envy is perhaps the most frequent and most destructive—yet least studied— emotional response to perceived losses or inequalities in status. People experience envy when someone else has something they desire for themselves. The things that evoke envy may be tangible objects (e.g., more money, a better house, a more desirable mate, more or better friends) or intangible qualities (e.g., being better looking, smarter, taller, or more popular). Such individuals are sometimes referred to as "tall poppies," or "one whose distinction, rank, or wealth attracts envious notice or hostility" (Ramson, 1988). As such, they are obvious targets for envy and for the destructive behavior that envy can unleash. For example, Feather (1994) found that the most common emotional reaction to tall poppies was envy, especially if the tall poppy's success was in a domain that was important to the individual. Moreover, the negative reaction respondents felt toward tall poppies depended in part on their own degree of satisfaction with themselves in that people with low self-esteem reported more envy and more delight at the apparent fall of tall poppies than did people with high self-esteem. Similarly, Salovey and Rodin (1984) conducted a study in which participants were told that their standing on a self-relevant characteristic was worse than that of a successful peer. After receiving this information, participants were found to verbally derogate the successful peer, were less likely to seek friendship with that person, and reported feeling more depressed and anxious about interacting with that person. That is, people like other people to the extent that they feel good about themselves when they're with them. Tall poppies make others feel diminished, and the dislike they attract is proportional to the discomfort others feel in their presence. This discomfort can provoke "retaliatory" behavior on the part of the "diminished" person, such as destroying the tall poppy's reputation through malicious gossip, social ostracism, or loss of job or other forms of income.

CONCLUSIONS

Does this mean that social hierarchies are a biological imperative? On the contrary, few aspects of human behavior are so rigidly determined. The breadth and depth of human cognitive functions enable us to reflect on the outcomes of our choices even before we make them. As Richard Dawkins (1976, p. 215) put it: "We have the power to defy the selfish genes of our birth."

And as philosopher Dan Dennett (1984, p. 45) further elaborates:

> So although we arrive on this planet with a built-in, biologically endorsed set of biases . . . we can nevertheless build lives from this base that overthrow those innate preferences. We can tame and rescind and (if need be) repress those preferences in favor of "higher" preferences . . .

The point of this chapter was to show how Darwinian processes have produced a complex network of cognitive, emotional, and physiological systems that bias us toward producing this kind of social structure, how we are wired from higher cognition right on down to our neuroendocrinology to detect minute changes in our status vis-à-vis others. From this perspective, the Columbine tragedy and its more recent counterparts should come as no surprise. When Darwinian processes are allowed full play—that is, when human beings are placed in competitive circumstances with very little oversight from benign governing bodies—there is a very high degree of risk that social dominance hierarchies will emerge in their ugliest incarnation. Human history and current newspapers are clear testaments to this on a grander scale than our high schools. In its most benign form, social dominance means nothing more than the fact that some individuals are more adept at influencing and, therefore, leading others. In its most malignant form, social dominance can mean despotism—the monopolization of resources by a privileged few who use their social advantages to oppress others. Ironically, the direction human societies take (including microsocieties such as corporate businesses, universities, and even human families) depends in large part on the beliefs and personalities of the dominant individuals within them. It has been effectively argued by historians that the major reason the American and French revolutions played out so immensely differently despite taking place during the same historical time period can be directly traced to the philosophical readings that influenced the architects of those revolutions (*Wall Street Journal*, July 14, 1989). The American Revolution was grounded in ideas of the Anglo-Scottish Enlightenment, particularly the writings of John Locke, David Hume, and Adam Smith. In this tradition, a person is a political creature some of the time but is primarily a private individual—a parent, spouse, worshiper, or worker. Accordingly, the American Revolution sought to weaken and fracture political power in favor of the individual right to privacy. In contrast, the French Revolution took its crucial ideas from the French Enlightenment, led by Jean Jacques Rousseau. This tradition sought to transform the human condition by strengthening the power of the central government into a single indivisible unit. All individual acts were seen in a broader political context.

If the analysis of social dominance, social hierarchies, and social power offered here is on track, then the steps that should be taken to avoid the malevolence that can erupt from unbridled Darwinian processes, such as the nation saw in the Columbine tragedy, are clear: It is the dominant individuals who must be identified and influenced to create a "kinder, gentler" social environment because it is they who wield the kind of social power that can effect true and lasting changes.

REFERENCES

Adler, N. E., Boyce, W. T., Chesney, M. A., Cohen, S., Folkman, S., Kahn, R. L., et al. (1994). Socioeconomic status and health: The challenge of the gradient. *American Psychologist, 49,* 15–24.

Adler, N. E., Boyce, W. T., Chesney, M. A., Folkman, S., & Syme, L. (1993). Socioeconomic inequalities in health: No easy solution. *Journal of the American Medical Association, 269,* 3140–3145.

Adler, N. E., Epel, E. S., Castellazzo, G., & Ickovics, J. R. (2000). Relationship between subjective and objective social status with psychological functioning: Preliminary data in healthy, white women. *Health Psychology, 19,* 586–592.

Altmann, J., Alberts, S. C., Haines, S. A., Dubach, J., Muruth, P., Coote, T., et al. (1996). Behavior predicts genetic structure in a wild primate group. *Proceedings of the National Academy of Sciences, 93,* 5795–5801.

Axelrod, R., & Hamilton, W. D. (1981). The evolution of cooperation. *Science, 211,* 1390–1396.

Baker, R. R., & Bellis, M. A. (1995). *Human sperm competition.* London: Chapman and Hall.

Bartsch, K., & Wellman, H. M. (1989). Young children's attribution of action to beliefs and desires. *Child Development, 60,* 946–964.

Bateup, H. S., Booth, L., Shirtcliff, E. A., & Granger, D. A. (2002). Testosterone, cortisol, and women's competition. *Evolution and Human Behavior, 23,* 181–192.

Berezckei, T., Vorgos, S., Gal, A., & Bernath, L. (1997). Resources, attractiveness, family commitment; reproductive decisions in human mate choice. *Ethology. ALQ: 103,* 681–699.

Bernhardt, P., Dabbs, J., Fielden, J., & Lutter, C. (1989). Testosterone changes during vicarious experiences of winning and losing among fans at sporting events. *Physiology and Behavior, 65,* 59–62.

Betzig, L. L. (1986). *Despotism and differential reproduction: A Darwinian view of history.* Hawthorne, NY: Aldine.

Betzig, L. L. (1993). Sex, succession, and stratification in the first six civilizations. In L. Ellis (Ed.), *Social stratification and socioeconomic inequality* (pp. 37–74). Westport, CT: Praeger.

Blanchard, D. C., Sakai, R. R., & McEwen, B. (1993). Subordination stress: Behavioral, brain, and neuroendocrine correlates. *Behavioral Brain Research, 58,* 113–121.

Boehm, C. (1992). Segmentary "warfare" and the management of conflict: Comparison of East African chimpanzees and patrilineal-patrilocal humans. In A. Harcourt & F. B. M. de Waal (Eds.), *Coalitions and alliances in humans and other animals* (pp. 137–175). Oxford, England: Oxford University Press.

Booth, A., Shelly, G., Mazur, A., Tharp, G., & Kittok, R. (1989). Testosterone and winning and losing in human competition. *Hormones and Behavior, 23,* 556–571.

Boulton, M. J., & Smith, P. K. (1990). Affective bias in children's perceptions of dominance relationships. *Child Development, 61,* 221–229.

Brown, P. C., Smith, T. W., & Benjamin, L. S. (1998). Perceptions of spouse dominance predict blood pressure reactivity during marital interactions. *Annals of Behavioral Medicine, 20,* 286–293.

Buss, D. M. (1994). The strategies of human mating. *American Scientist, 82,* 238–249.

Byrne, R. (1988). The manipulation of attention in primate tactical deception.

Byrne, R. (1995). *The thinking ape: Evolutionary origins of intelligence.* Oxford, England: Oxford University Press.

Chapais, B. (1988). Rank maintenance in female Japanese Macaques: Experimental evidence for social dependency. *Behavior, 104,* 41–59.

Chapais, B. (1992). Role of alliances in the social inheritance of rank among female primates. In A. Harcourt & F. B. M. de Waal (Eds.), *Cooperation in contests in animals and humans* (pp. 29–60). Oxford, England: Oxford University Press.

Cheney, D. L., & Seyfarth, R. M. (1990). *How monkeys see the world.* Chicago: University of Chicago Press.

Cheng, P. W., & Holyoak, K. J. (1985). Pragmatic reasoning schemas. *Cognitive Psychology, 17,* 391–416.

Clutton-Brock, T. H. (1988). Reproductive success. In T. H. Clutton-Brock (Ed.), *Reproductive success.* Chicago: University of Chicago Press.

Clutton-Brock, T. H., & Harvey, P. H. (1976). Evolutionary rules and primate societies. In P. P. G. Bateson & R. A. Hinde (Eds.), *Growing points in ethology* (pp. 195–238). Cambridge, England: Cambridge University Press.

Coates-Markle, L. (1997). Choosing to survive. *Equus, 231,* 34–41.

Cosmides, L. (1989). The logic of social exchange: Has natural selection shaped how humans reason? studies with the wason selection task. *Cognition, 31,* 187–276.

Crick, N. R. (1996). The role of overt aggression, relational aggression, and prosocial behavior in the prediction of children's future social adjustment. *Child Development, 67,* 2317–2327.

Crick, N. R., & Grotpeter, J. K. (1995). Relational aggression, gender, and social-psychological adjustment. *Child Development, 66,* 710–722.

Cummins, D. D. (1996a). Dominance hierarchies and the evolution of human reasoning. *Minds and Machines, 6,* 463–480.

Cummins, D. D. (1996b). Evidence of deontic reasoning in 3- and 4-year-olds. *Memory and Cognition, 24,* 823–829.

Cummins, D. D. (1996c). Evidence for the innateness of deontic reasoning. *Mind and Language, 11,* 160–190.

Cummins, D. D. (1998). Social norms and other minds: The evolutionary roots of higher cognition. In D. D. Cummins & C. A. Allen (Eds.), *The evolution of mind* (pp. 30–50). New York: Oxford University Press.

Cummins, D. D. (1999a). Cheater detection is modified by social rank. *Evolution and Human Behavior, 20,* 229–248.

Cummins, D. D. (1999b, June). *Early emergence of cheater detection in human development.* Presented at the 11th annual meeting of the Human Behavior and Evolution Society, Salt Lake City, UT.

Cummins, D. D. (2000). How the social environment shaped the evolution of mind. *Synthese, 122,* 1–26.

Dawkins, R. (1976). *The selfish gene.* Oxford, England: Oxford University Press.

Dawkins, S. (1982). *The extended phenotype.* Oxford, England: Freeman.

Dennett, D. (1984). *Elbow room.* Cambridge, MA: Bradford/MIT Press.

D'Entremont, B., & Muir, D. W. (1997). Five-month-olds attention and affective responses to still-faced emotional expressions. *Infant Behavior and Development, 20,* 563–568.

de Waal, F. (1982). *Chimpanzee politics.* Baltimore: Johns-Hopkins University Press.

de Waal, F. (1988). Chimpanzee politics. In R. W. Byrne & A. Whiten (Eds.), *Machiavellian intelligence* (pp. 122–131). Oxford, England: Oxford University Press.

de Waal, F. (1989). Food sharing and reciprocal obligations among chimpanzees. *Journal of Human Evolution, 18,* 433–459.

de Waal, F. (1992). Coalitions as part of reciprocal relations in the Arnhem chimpanzee colony. In A. H. Harcourt & F. de Waal (Eds.), *Coalitions and alliances in humans and other animals* (pp. 233–258). Oxford, England: Oxford University Press.

Dewsbury, D. A. (1982). Dominance rank, copulatory behavior and differential reproduction. *Quarterly Review of Biology, 57,* 135–159.

Dunn, J. (1988). *The beginnings of social understanding.* Oxford, England: Basil Blackwell.

Elias, M. (1981). Serum cortisol, testosterone, and testosterone-binding globulin responses to competitive fighting in human males. *Aggressive Behavior, 7,* 215–224.

Ellis, L. (1995). Dominance and reproductive success among nonhuman animals: A cross-species comparison. *Ethology and Sociobiology, 16,* 257–333.

Feather, N. T. (1994). Attitudes toward achievers and reactions to their fall: Theory and research concerning tall poppies. *Advances in Experimental Social Psychology, 26,* 1–73.

Fehr, E., & Gächter, S. (2000). Cooperation and punishment in public goods experiments. *American Economic Review, 90,* 980–994.

Fehr, E., Gächter, S., & Kirchsteiger, G. (1997). Reciprocity as a contract enforcement device: Experimental evidence. *Econometrica, 65,* 833–860.

Fiddick, L., & Cummins, D. D. (2001). Reciprocity in ranked relationships: Does social structure influence social reasoning? *Journal of Bioeconomics, 3,* 149–170.

Forrest, M. S., & Hokanson, J. E. (1975). Depression and autonomic arousal reduction accompanying self-punitive behavior. *Journal of Abnormal Psychology, 84,* 346–357.

Forsythe, R., Howowitz, J., Savin, N., & Sefton, M. (1994). Fairness in simple bargaining experiments. *Games and Economic Behavior, 6,* 347–369.

Frankel, D. G., & Arbel, T. (1980). Group formation by two-year-olds. *International Journal of Behavioral Development, 3,* 287–298.

Gagneux, P., Woodruff, D. S., & Boesch, C. (1997). Furtive mating in female chimpanzees. *Nature, 387,* 358–369.

Gigerenzer, G., & Hug, K. (1992). Domain specific reasoning: Social contracts, cheating, and perspective change. *Cognition, 43,* 127–171.

Gilbert, P. (1990). Changes: Rank, status, and mood. In S. Fischer & C. L. Cooper (Eds.), *On the move: The psychology of change and transition* (pp. 33–52). New York: Wiley.

Gladue, B., Boechler, M., & McCaul, K. (1989). Hormonal response to competition in human males. *Aggressive Behavior, 15,* 409–422.

Goodall, J. (1986). *The chimpanzees of Gombe.* Cambridge, MA: Belknap Press.

Goren, C. C., Sarty, M., & Wu, P. Y. K. (1975). Visual following and pattern discrimination of face-like stimuli by newborn infants. *Pediatrics, 59,* 544–549.

Graziano, W. G., Jensen-Campbell, L. A., Todd, M., & Finch, J. F. (1997). Interpersonal attraction from an evolutionary psychology perspective: Women's reactions to dominant and prosocial men. In J. A. Simpson & D. T. Kenrick (Eds.), *Evolutionary social psychology* (pp. 141–167). Hillsdale, NJ: Erlbaum.

Güth, W., & van Damme, E. (1998). Information, strategic behavior, and fairness in ultimatum bargaining: An experimental study. *Journal of Mathematical Psychology, 42,* 227–247.

Hall, J. A., Halberstadt, A. G., & O'Brien, C. E. (1997). "Subordination" and nonverbal sensitivity: A study and synthesis of findings based on trait measures. *Sex Roles, 37,* 295–317.

Hall, K. R. L. (1964). Aggression in monkey and ape societies. In J. Carthy & F. Ebling (Eds.), *The natural history of aggression* (pp. 51–64). London: Academic Press.

Hamilton, W. D. (1964). The genetical evolution of social behavior I and II. *Journal of Theoretical Biology, 7,* 1–52.

Harcourt, A. H., & de Waal, F. B. M. (Eds.). (1992). *Coalitions and alliances in humans and other animals.* Oxford, England: Oxford University Press.

Harris, P. L., & Núñez, M. (1996). Understanding of permission rules by preschool children. *Child Development, 67,* 1572–1591.

"High school hell: Shooters were ostracized by school cliques" (1999, April 23). ABCNEWS.com.

Hill, K., & Hurtado, A. M. (1996). *Ache life history: The ecology and demography of a foraging people.* New York: Aldine de Gruyter.

Hoffman, E., McCabe, K., Shachat, K., & Smith, V. (1994). Preferences, property rights, and anonymity in bargaining games. *Games and Economic Behavior, 7,* 346–380.

Hoffman, E., McCabe, K., & Smith, V. (1996). Social distance and other-regarding behavior in dictator games. *American Economic Review, 86,* 653–660.

Hokanson, J. E. (1961). The effect of frustration and anxiety on overt aggression. *Journal of Abnormal and Social Psychology, 62,* 346–351.

Hokanson, J. E., & Shetler, S. (1961). The effect of overt aggression on physiological arousal. *Journal of Abnormal and Social Psychology, 63,* 446–448.

Hold-Cavell, B. C., & Borsutzky, D. (1986). Longitudinal study of a group of preschool children. *Ethology and Sociobiology, 7,* 39–56.

Hollos, M., Leis, P. E., & Turiel, E. (1986). Social reasoning in Ijo children and adolescents in Nigerian communities. *Journal of Cross-Cultural Psychology, 17,* 352–374.

Johannesson, M., & Persson, B. (2000). Non-reciprocal altruism in dictator games. *Economics Letters, 69,* 137–142.

Kapuku, G. K., Treibner, F. A., & Davis, H. C. (2002). Relationships among socioeconomic status, stress induced changes in cortisol, and blood pressure in African American males. *Annals of Behavioral Medicine, 24,* 320–325.

Keating, C. F., & Heltman, K. R. (1994). Dominance and deception in children and adults: Are leaders the best misleaders? *Personality and Social Psychology Bulletin, 54,* 312–321.

Kelly, S., & Dunbar, R. I. M. (2001). Who dares, wins: Heroism versus altruism in women's mate choice. *Human Nature, 12,* 89–105.

Kummer, H. (1988). Tripartite relations in Hamadryas baboons. In R. W. Byrne & A. Whiten (Eds.), *Machiavellian intelligence* (pp. 113–121). Oxford, England: Oxford University Press.

La Freniere, P., & Charlesworth, W. R. (1983). Dominance, attention, and affiliation in a preschool group: A nine-month longitudinal study. *Ethology and Sociobiology, 4,* 55–67.

Lemerise, E. A., Harper, B. D., & Howes, H. M. (1998). The transition from kindergarten to ungraded primary: Longitudinal predictors of popularity and social reputation. *Early Education and Development, 9,* 187–210.

Lupien, S. J., King, S., Meaney, M., & McEwen, B. S. (2000). Child's stress hormone levels correlate with mother's socioeconomic status and depressive state. *Biological Psychiatry, 48,* 976–980.

Manktelow, K. I., & Over, D. E. (1991). Social roles and utilities in reasoning with deontic conditionals. *Cognition, 39,* 85–105.

Mazur, A., Booth, A., & Dabbs, J. (1992). Testosterone and chess competition. *Social Psychology Quarterly, 55,* 70–77.

McEwen, B. S., & Wingfield, J. C. (2002). The concept of allostasis in biology and biomedicine. *Hormones and Behavior, 43,* 2–15.

Mealey, L., Daood, C., & Krage, M. (1996). Enhanced memory for faces of cheaters. *Ethology and Sociobiology, 17,* 119–128.

Newton, T. L., Bane, C. M., Flores, A., & Greenfield, J. (1999). Dominance, gender, and cardiovascular reactivity during social interaction. *Psychophysiology, 36,* 245–252.

Niehoff, D. (1999). *The biology of violence.* New York: Free Press.

Nucci, L. P., Turiel, E., & Encarnacion-Gawrych, G. E. (1983). Children's social interactions and social concepts: Analyses of morality and convention in the Virgin Islands. *Journal of Cross-Cultural Psychology, 14,* 469–487.

Oaklyn plot investigators seize suspects' computers" (2003, July 8). *Philadelphia Inquirer Online,* A01.

Penton-Voak, I. S., Perrett, D. I., Castles, D. L., Kobayashi, T., Burt, D. M., Murray, L. K., et al. (1999). Menstrual cycle alters face preference. *Nature, 399,* 741–742.

Perusse, D. (1993). Cultural and reproductive success in industrial societies: Testing the relationship at proximate and ultimate levels. *Behavioral and Brain Sciences, 16,* 267–322.

Pratto, E. (1996). Sexual politics: The gender gap in the bedroom, the cupboard, and the cabinet. In D. M. Buss & N. M. Malamuth (Eds.), *Sex, power, conflict: Evolutionary and feminist perspectives* (pp. 179–230). New York: Oxford University Press.

Pratto, F., Tatar, D. G., & Conway-Lanz, S. (1999). Who gets what and why: Determinants of social allocations. *Political Psychology, 1,* 127–150.

Pratto, F., Stallworth, L. M., & Sidanius, J. (1997). The gender gap: Differences in political attitudes and social dominance relations. *British Journal of Social Psychology, 36,* 49–68.

Ramson, W. S. (1988). *Australian national dictionary.* Melbourne: Oxford University Press.

Rejeski, W. J., Gagne, M., Parker, P. E., & Koritnik, D. R. (1989). Acute stress reactivity from contested dominance in dominant and submissive males. *Behavioral Medicine, 15,* 118–124.

Riss, D. C., & Goodall, J. (1977). The recent rise to the alpha-rank in a population of free-living chimpanzees. *Folia Primatologica, 27,* 134–151.

Russon, A. E., & Waite, B. E. (1991). Patterns of dominance and imitation in an infant peer group. *Ethology and Sociobiology, 12,* 55–73.

Sadalla, E. K., Kenrick, D. T., & Vershure, B. (1987). Dominance and heterosexual attraction. *Journal of Personality and Social Psychology, 52,* 730–738.

Salovey, P., & Rodin, J. (1984). Some antecedents and consequences of social comparison jealousy. *Journal of Personality and Social Psychology, 47,* 780–792.

Sapolsky, R. M. (1990). Adrenocortical function, social rank, and personality among wild baboons. *Biological Psychiatry, 28,* 862–878.

Sapolsky, R. M. (1999). Hormonal correlates of personality and social contexts: From non-human to human primates. In C. Panter-Brick & C. M. Worthman (Eds.), *Hormones, health, and behavior: A socio-ecological and lifespan perspective* (pp. 18–46). New York: Cambridge University Press.

Sapolsky, R. M., & Ray, J. (1989). Styles of dominance and their physiological correlates among wild baboons. *American Journal of Primatology, 18,* 1–9.

Seyfarth, R. M., & Cheney, D. L. (1984). Grooming, alliances, and reciprocal altruism in vervet monkeys. *Nature, 308,* 541–543.

Simmons, R. (2002). *Odd girl out: The hidden culture of aggression among girls.* New York: Harcourt.

Sodian, B. (1991). The development of deception in young children. *British Journal of Developmental Psychology. Special issue: Perspectives on the Child's Theory of Mind, 9,* 173–188.

Stenberg, G., & Hagekull, B. (1997). Social referencing and mood modification in 1-year-olds. *Infant Behavior and Development, 20,* 209–217.

Strayer, F. F., & Trudel, M. (1984). Developmental changes in the nature and function of social dominance among young children. *Ethology and Sociobiology, 5,* 279–295.

Taylor, S. E., Klein, L. C., Lewis, B. P., Gruenewald, T. L., & Updegraff, J. A. (2002). Biobehavioral responses to stress in females: Tend-and-befriend, not fight-or-flight. *Psychological Review, 109,* 745–750.

Trivers, R. (1971). The evolution of reciprocal altruism. *Quarterly Review of Biology, 46,* 35–57.

Tse, W. S., & Bond, A. L. (2002). Serotonergic intervention affects both social dominance and affiliative behavior. *Psychopharmacology, 161,* 324–330.

Uehara, S., Hiraiwa-Hasegawa, M., Hosaka, K., & Hamai, M. (1994). The fate of defeated alpha male chimpanzees in relation to their social networks. *Primates, 35,* 49–55.

van Dijk, E., & Vermunt, R. (2000). Strategy and fairness in social decision making: Sometimes it pays to be powerless. *Journal of Experimental Social Psychology, 36,* 1–25.

Weg, E., & Smith, V. (1993). On the failure to induce meager offers in ultimatum games. *Journal of Economic Psychology, 14,* 17–32.

Whiten, A., & Byrne, R. W. (1988a). The manipulation of attention in primate tactical deception. In R. W. Byrne & A. Whiten (Eds.), *Machiavellian intelligence* (pp. 211–224). Oxford, England: Oxford University Press.

Whiten, A., & Byrne, R. W. (1988b). Tactical deception in primates. *Behavioral and Brain Sciences, 11,* 233–273.

Wicker, F. W., Payne, G. C., & Morgan, R. D. (1983). Participant descriptions of guilt and shame. *Motivation and Emotion, 7,* 25–39.

Woodruff, G., & Premack, D. (1979). Intentional communication in the chimpanzee: The development of deception. *Cognition, 7,* 333–362.

CHAPTER 24

The Evolution of Language

PETER F. MACNEILAGE and BARBARA L. DAVIS

OSMIDES AND TOOBY (1992), major contributors to *The Adapted Mind* (Barkow, Cosmides, & Tooby, 1992), a manifesto for the emerging discipline of evolutionary psychology, see their field as allied with the recent cognitive revolution. They reject behaviorism's view that the mind is, in effect, single-minded—that is, possessing just one domain-general capacity. They contend that the mind comprises a whole constellation of modules—functionally isolable subunits, each innate and each having evolved during hominid life on the savanna to do different kinds of computations. Typifying the misguided behaviorists, they say, is Fred Skinner; typifying the enlightened innatists (aka *nativists*) is Noam Chomsky. And, most significantly, they cite *generative grammar,* Chomsky's construct of a modular device underlying linguistic competence, as paradigmatic for their discipline.

It's a little ironic that they've chosen Chomsky as an inspiration for the new discipline, given his claim that "the complexity of language cannot be explained by natural selection" (Pinker & Bloom, 1992, p. 452). Natural selection is the cornerstone of modern evolutionary theory. In discussing innate mental structure, Chomsky has said, dismissively, "It is perfectly safe to attribute this development to 'natural selection' so long as we realize there is no substance to this assertion, that it amounts to nothing more than a belief that there is some naturalistic explanation for these phenomena" (Chomsky, 1972, p. 97). Thus, Chomsky rejects the notion that natural selection underpins the branch of the tree of life that led to language. Instead, he sees that branch as more like a graft, powered by other formative factors not yet understood—the causal effects of increasing pressure on an enlarging brain, for example, or even the operation of yet-undiscovered laws of physics.

Chomsky's stance on evolution arises from his belief that generative grammar is fundamentally innate and whole unto itself, functioning like a closed mathematical system (Tomasello, 2002), hence impervious to modification by external,

This chapter was prepared with the support of research grant HD-27733-11 from the Public Health Service. We thank John Trimble for much more than editorial assistance.

mundane forces operating over long periods of time. To this assumption, Pinker and Bloom (1992) have offered a spirited rebuttal, arguing that language is indeed subject to natural selection. Yet Pinker (1994), like Cosmides, Tooby, and others, gives a warm embrace to the Chomskyan perspective, which is basically non-Darwinian. That inconsistency in evolutionary psychology has unwittingly undercut the new discipline because it finds itself endorsing evolution but, like Chomsky, without phylogeny.

Darwin, let us remember, had postulated that all changes in life forms, without exception, have involved *descent with modification, powered by the mechanism of natural selection.* Evolutionary psychology accepts that postulate, at least in principle, but in practice it scants one-half of it. It postulates that the human brain evolved specialized modules as adaptive responses to natural selection pressures. But it glosses over their "descent with modification" by calling the modules *innate*—that is, built-in—without considering how the modules accomplished that feat, if indeed they did.

Here we feel the sway of Chomsky. His theory of universal grammar (UG) was so brilliant, and his core argument—that infants can't possibly sort out the grammatical complexities of language without having it available a priori—was so persuasive that it was easy to believe that UG, though literally man-made, epitomizes adaptive complexity in nature. And because, thanks to Darwin, evolution appears the only possible source of that complexity, evolutionary psychology has been willing to adopt UG as evolutionary without facing up to Chomsky's flat rejection of natural selection.

Cosmides and Tooby, for their part, have simply sidestepped the whole issue by claiming that "theories of phylogenetic constraint are not very useful or well developed" (1999, p. 297). Pinker and Bloom (1992) evade the issue in another way. They equate *language* with Chomsky's *grammar*, which primarily involves syntax—sentence structure—arguably the pinnacle of language but surely not its starting point. Most people believe single *words* preceded syntax, and for those, a capability of forming individual packets of meaning-sound pairs (or, if it was signed language, meaning-sign pairs) must have evolved. But Pinker and Bloom's stance is that because no other species has syntax, we aren't able to *do* a language phylogeny. So while Pinker and Bloom think Chomsky's grammar could result from natural selection, their adherence to his narrow conception of language results, in effect, in a *de novo* evolution scenario like Chomsky's, one that ignores the history of the meaning and signaling aspects of it.

This absence of a phylogenetic focus in the treatment of language by evolutionary psychologists, whatever the reason for it, helps reinforce the notion that language evolved *de novo*, as if by some miracle, as Chomsky feels free to suggest. It leaves the discipline with a lot of explaining to do. As Deacon noted, "The theory that innate knowledge of grammar is the heritage of all human children simply asserts the answers to these messy questions and leaves it to evolutionary biology and neuroscience to explain how the answers are to be derived" (1997, p. 103).

This chapter, heeding Deacon's challenge, has three main sections. The first section directly confronts the phylogenetic question of descent with modification—the trail of successful adaptations to selection pressures—which we place in the perspective of communication, broadly understood. The second section explores the actual *transmission* of language—both spoken and signed. The physical transmission system for language production and comprehension in both modalities is relatively accessible to observation and has a long and well-known history. Though neither modality's system is yet used for language by any nonhuman species, we believe that knowing their history and the history of the brain organization controlling them, obtainable from other species, helps illuminate language phylogeny. Our final section explores the relationship between biological and cultural influences on language history.

THE EVOLUTION OF COMMUNICATION: TINBERGEN'S FOUR QUESTIONS

We recommend four perspectives from which to approach any trait, such as language, in an organism's communication system. (A trait is an attribute that is reasonably consistent over time.) These perspectives, derived from the work of Nobel Laureate Nikko Tinbergen (1963), are distilled in a set of four wonderfully simple, pragmatic questions. They were later adapted by Hauser, who, in his monograph *The Evolution of Communication* (1996), contended that they provide "the only fully encompassing and explanatory approach to communication in the animal kingdom, including human language" (p. 2). The four perspectives are the mechanistic, the functional, the ontogenetic, and the phylogenetic. Of any trait—in this case, language—Tinbergen would have us ask:

1. *"How does it work?"* That is, what mechanisms (neural, physiological, psychological, etc.) underlie its expression?
2. *"What does it do for the organism?"* That is, how does any supposed *adaptation* affect the organism's functional capabilities—that is, its survival and reproduction?
3. *"How does it get that way in development?"* That is, what ontogenetic (genetic and postgenetic environmental) factors guide its development?
4. *"How did it get that way in evolution?"* That is, how does the phylogenetic (evolutionary) history of the species help us understand the trait's structure in light of ancestral features?

QUESTION 1: HOW DOES LANGUAGE WORK?

This question is important because if, as Darwin would have contended, language is evolution of *action* capabilities as a result of successful use, we need to understand the present stage of its development to have something concrete to work backward from.

Psycholinguists—that is, psychologists who work on language—refer to the production and comprehension of language as *language processing*. Chomsky's own term for these processes is *performance*. But in his generative grammar (e.g., 1965) performance is of secondary interest. Instead, he would have us go deeper and focus on what he calls *competence*—his notion of what underlies performance:

> By a generative grammar, I mean a description of the tacit competence of the speaker-hearer that underlies his actual performance in production and perception

(understanding) of speech. A generative grammar, ideally, specifies a pairing of semantic and phonetic representations over an infinite range; it thus constitutes a hypothesis as to how the speaker-hearer interprets utterances, abstracting away from the many factors that interweave with tacit competence to determine actual performance. (p. 75)

(Here, *generative* refers to how grammatical rules, acting on words of the language, can generate a large number of sentences; *semantic* refers to meaning; and *phonetic* refers to the observable surface level of speech.)

In Chomsky's conception, the generative grammar that lies between—and helps pair up—semantic and phonetic representations has two components: syntax (sentence structure), which is the main component, and phonology (sound patterns). All humans, he contends, share an innate basis for generative grammar. Hence he calls it a *universal grammar* (1966, p. 116). This innate component, he believes, was the first aspect of language to have originated and is independent of the semantic and phonetic levels that it eventually links—that is, it's a module. He considers it to have evolved for what he calls mental "expressions" (Chomsky, 2000, p. 19), not for communication.

While Chomsky himself has not been concerned with the performance level, his revolutionary view of language has inspired a huge amount of research on both production and comprehension. We are now fortunate, for example, to have a relatively well-accepted model of language production constructed by Levelt (e.g., 1999) that takes us from communicative intentions to fluent speech. A summary of the model, presented in his paper "A Blueprint of the Speaker," appears in Figure 24.1 on page 702. As we discuss how the model works, we include definitions of core concepts.

Consider first the upper box—the rhetorical/semantic/syntactic system. (*Rhetorical* refers to the effective use of speech.) At the conceptual preparation stage, speakers formulate some preverbal message using the resources available to them in the upper right ellipse. (*ToM*—theory of mind—refers to "our understanding of our minds and others"; Gopnik, 1999, p. 838.) Our ability to formulate a ToM is considered a crucial underpinning for language evolution. *Discourse* here refers to the context of communicative exchange in which a speech utterance occurs. *Preverbal* refers to the fact that the message at this particular point takes the form of lexical concepts—concepts attached to words (e.g., the concept of a dog) but not yet converted into words.

The lexical concepts activate their corresponding syntactic words, termed *lemmas*. The words are called *syntactic* here because they specify, or call for, aspects of sentence structure. For example, a normally transitive verb (e.g., *kissed*) calls for two noun phrases (e.g., *John* and *Mary*). In contrast, an intransitive verb (e.g., *dozed*) calls for only one (e.g., *John dozed*). Pronouns call for number agreement in their following verb: *she is, they are,* and so on. The result is the surface structure of the sentence.

Consider now the phonological/phonetic system box. *Morphological* refers to meaning units (morphemes). Some words, such as *black*, consist of only one morpheme; others, such as *blackboard* and *blacken*, consist of more. *Gestures* are movements of what are termed the *speech articulators*—lips, tongue, and soft palate. When a lemma is selected, the speaker accesses its morphological and phonological structure. In the phonetic encoding stage, each syllable must give rise to articulatory gestures—basically a pattern of movements of the speech apparatus. In

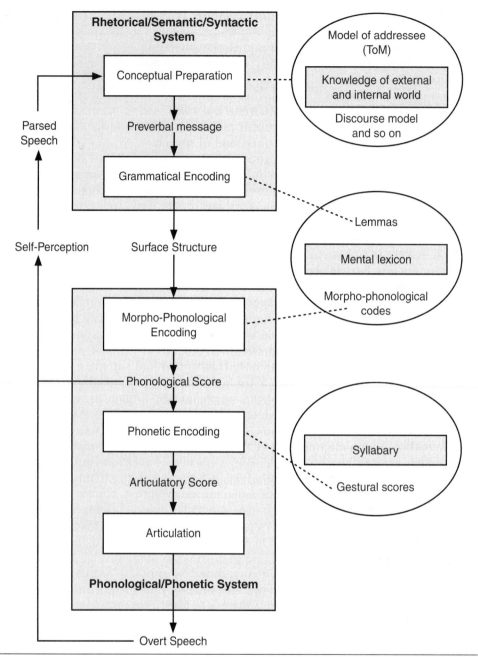

Figure 24.1   A Blueprint of the Speaker. *Source:* From "Producing Spoken Language: A Blueprint of the Speaker" (pp. 83–166), by W. J. M. Levelt, in *The Neurocognition of Language*, C. M. Brown and P. Hagoort (Eds.), 1999, Oxford: Oxford University Press.

the model, control patterns (articulatory scores) for several hundred frequently used syllables are considered to be stored as wholes, but less familiar syllables have to be constructed online.

In the articulation stage, these movement patterns are realized at two sites. One is the larynx, which controls the pitch of the voice and whether a sound is voiced or voiceless. The other is the supralaryngeal vocal tract (the air space between larynx and lips), the shape of which is controlled by the lips, jaw, tongue, and soft palate.

The loop on the left side of the figure labeled *self-perception* signifies our ability to listen to our own speech, not just others', and to monitor our impending output at the level of the phonological score, so we can detect errors before they reach the output stage.

One further aspect of the online organization of speech should be noted. Many years ago the renowned neuropsychologist Karl Lashley (1951) suggested that studying speech errors might help us better understand the serial order of speech—that is, how the sequence of events in speech is organized. A prominent finding in subsequent studies (e.g., Shattuck-Hufnagel, 1979) is that when speech *segments*—consonants and vowels—are misplaced, they invariably go into the same position in syllable structure that they came out of. Thus, an initial consonant in a syllable will go into an initial position in another syllable (e.g., *fast mapping* → *mast fapping*), and a vowel will go into the position for a vowel in another syllable (e.g., *ad hoc* → *odd hack*). These errors give us a key insight into the modern process of syllable production. Levelt contended that the discovery that segmental "content" elements go into what he called "syllable frame structure" is the main finding in the psycholinguistic study of speech errors (Levelt, 1992). It is also the starting point for the frame/content theory of the evolution of speech organization (MacNeilage, 1998b), which is discussed later.

Whereas Levelt (1999) gives us "A Blueprint of the Speaker," Cutler and Clifton (1999) offer "A Blueprint of the Listener" (see Figure 24.2 on p. 704). According to them, the listener functions as a "device for conversion of acoustic input into meaning" (p. 123). Listening begins with "auditory input"—input of the auditory signal and psychoacoustic-level processing. Next comes decoding. Here the listener must distinguish speech from other types of auditory input arriving simultaneously. Then the listener must convert this acoustic code into a more abstract level of representation that is independent of myriad variables—utterance contexts, rates of speech, differing ages and genders of speakers, and so on.

Complicating matters still further is the task of *segmentation*—that is, dividing the input into individual segments (consonants and vowels). Because the segments overlap and the incoming acoustic input stream has enormous variability, how do we discern the constituent segments to extract meaning from that stream? The solution may involve word-recognition and utterance-interpretation processes as well as explicit cues in the stream. (An *utterance* is a stretch of speech bounded by pauses.) Here the listener is helped by prosody ("the melody and rhythm of a sentence" [p. 145]) as well as segmental aspects of the signal. Prosodic cues may include a listener's ability to detect language-specific stress "unit boundaries" (as associated, e.g., with the characteristic strong-weak stress pattern in English disyllabic words such as *blackboard*). *Word recognition* involves concurrent activation and competition among available word representations. Candidate words compatible with portions of the incoming signal are simultaneously activated and compete for recognition. For example, a spoken word resembles other words and may even have words or parts of words embedded in it (e.g., *steak* can encompass lexical neighbors such as *stay, state, snake*). Winning strategies in the competition process include a combination of segmental and prosodic cues as well as word-frequency and utterance-level context effects.

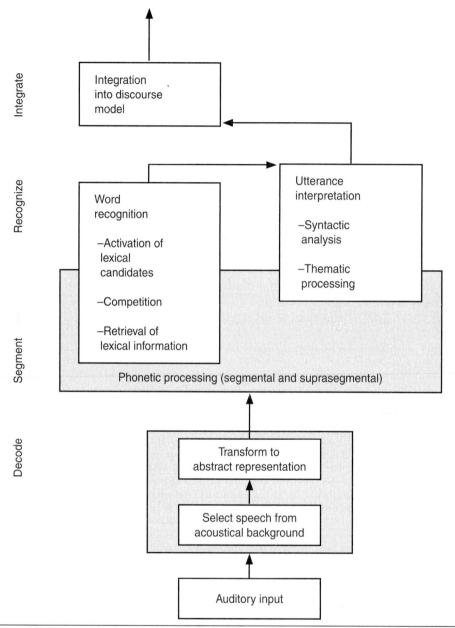

Figure 24.2 A Blueprint of the Listener. *Source:* From "Comprehending Spoken Language: A Blueprint of the Listener" (pp. 123–166), by A. Cutler and C. Clifton Jr., in *The Neurocognition of Language,* C. M. Brown and P. Hagoort (Eds), 1999, Oxford: Oxford University Press.

Once a particular word has "won," its morphological and semantic information is activated. Contemporary models indicate that full multimorphemic word forms are represented and linked in nodes based on common morphemes (e.g., a separate node for *counts, discount, unaccountability, counter*). Selection of the spoken word with accompanying morphological structure will constrain its integration into higher-level structures. At a semantic level, the competition process may include simultaneous cross-modal *priming* (activating) of all ambiguous meanings regardless of word frequency (e.g., each of the homonyms *weak* and *week* could prime both *month* and *strong*). The task of utterance interpretation and integration includes dividing each sentence into components, determining the relationships of parts to the whole sentence both syntactically and semantically, and determining the parts' role in discourse. Here, listeners are guided by their knowledge of language structure as well as by information provided by the particular words retrieved.

QUESTION 2: WHAT DOES LANGUAGE DO FOR THE ORGANISM?

Lurking behind this question is a most fundamental one: "What are the adaptations, and what selection pressures did they respond to?" Hauser finds that "rarely have researchers asked whether language could be considered an adaptation" (Hauser, 1996, pp. 3–4). As significant exceptions, he singles out Lieberman (e.g., Lieberman, 1984) and Pinker and Bloom (1992).

Lieberman was the first to suggest a specific adaptation associated with the evolution of language. Using fossil evidence, he argued that a shape change in hominids' supralaryngeal vocal tract, occurring some 350,000 years ago, enabled them to produce, for improved communication, a wider range of speech sounds—wide enough to make modern language possible. Until this time, he argued, the mouth cavity in all mammals was a single, basically horizontal tube. But the descent of the larynx created a second, basically vertical posterior tube behind the tongue. Lieberman's hypothesis has not been without its critics. Boe, Heim, Honda, and Maeda (2002) have disputed his acoustic assumptions, claiming that he underestimated the vocal capabilities of the single-tube tract. In addition, it has been pointed out that languages today can function with as few as 11 consonant and vowel sounds (Hawaiian, e.g., has just 13). Hauser, Chomsky, and Fitch (2002) question whether the descended larynx was indeed an adaptation for speech, noting that a number of other mammals also have one. They suggest that the descent of the larynx may have been a "classical Neodarwinian preadaptation" (p. 1574)—an adaptation later borrowed for a different use—which could have evolved as a self-protective acoustic device for exaggerating an animal's apparent size (longer tract, lower-pitched sounds). But perhaps most importantly, Lieberman's hypothesis says nothing about how speech became organized the way it did—the chief question, in our view. It's one thing to have a wider repertoire of sounds, but how do we get from there to the actual sound systems of language itself—syllables containing consonants and vowels?

Categorical perception of speech, another proposed speech-related adaptation of long standing, has had a fate similar to Lieberman's two-tube vocal tract. Liberman and Mattingly (1985) theorized that hominids had an innate module that segmented the continuous acoustic waveform of speech into consonant and vowel categories (hence categorical perception) by making reference to supposedly invariant motor commands underlying their production. But several researchers (e.g., Kluender, Diehl, & Killeen, 1987) have found homologs of this capacity in numerous other animals.

A putative adaptation that has so far survived critical scrutiny is embodied in Lindblom's (1986) hypothesis that languages with various numbers of vowels arrange these vowels in perceptual space to optimize the distance between them. Using a computer implementing an algorithm for perceptual-distance optimization, Lindblom was able to predict almost exactly the vowels actually used in languages with up to nine vowels in the system. Thus, vowels tend to space themselves the way people do in elevators. Is this property innate? Lindblom thinks not, believing it instead to be a self-organizational result of continually operating pressures on a language communication system to keep messages distinct from each other. A *self-organizing* system—say, a hurricane—is one in which a global-level pattern emerges solely from numerous local interactions among the lower-level components of that system without an external controller (see Camizon et al., 2001).

Considering speech production again, the adaptive significance of the frame/content mode of speech production, mentioned earlier, is clear. It's a relatively common conviction (e.g., Jackendoff, 2002) that the inaugural step for true language required the evolution of a *combinatorial phonology* whereby members of a relatively small set of meaningless units are concatenated to form patterns for a large number of words. The resultant system can be described as "open" in that it can be added to more or less indefinitely. Studdert-Kennedy and Lane (1980) have argued that this development was necessary to solve what they call the "impedence-matching" problem, which grew in proportion to the number of words being sent. According to this theory, users soon reached a point, with holistic word patterns, where they could no longer distinguish between similar words. But with a frame/content mode of organization, they could make do with a limited number of distinguishable consonants and vowels. Programming them into just a few syllable types lets users produce many thousands of different words—even words having few syllables.

A similar form of organization to that at the phonological level is present at the morphosyntactic level, leading to Hockett's (1978) characterization of language as a dualistic system. Given a finite inventory of morphemes/words and a few hundred syntactic rules, an astronomical number of sentences can be generated. But we don't yet have a comprehensive explanation of this "dual hierarchical structure of phonology and syntax," which Knight, Studdert-Kennedy, and Hurford (2000a) consider "language's most remarkable, distinctive and unprecedented feature" (p. 8).

One other property of syntax requires comment, namely, *recursion*. A structure can recur within another structure that has the same formal category. For example, in the nursery rhyme "The house that Jack built," relative clauses—each signaled by the relative pronoun "that"—contain, in effect, additional sentences that can continue to recur within the base sentence of "This is a house":

> This is the house that Jack built. ("This is a house." "Jack built it.")
> This is the malt that lay in the house that Jack built. (Adding "Malt lay in it.")
> This is the rat that ate the malt that lay . . . , etc.

This property enables a language to have an indefinite number of sentences. In a recent radical change of perspective, Chomsky has surmised that recursiveness may be the only aspect of language that is unique to it (Hauser et al., 2002). How Chomsky will reconcile this stance with his denial of natural selection remains to be seen.

The main reason Pinker and Bloom gave for their assertion that language indeed evolved by natural selection was its adaptive importance:

> Humans acquire a great deal of information during their lifetimes. Since this acquisition process occurs at a rate far exceeding that of biological evolution, it is invaluable in dealing with the causal contingencies of the environment that change within a lifetime, and provides a decisive advantage in competition with other species that can only defend themselves against new threats in evolutionary time. There is an obvious advantage in being able to acquire such information about the world second hand: By tapping into the vast repertoire of knowledge accumulated by some other individual, one can avoid having to duplicate the possibly time-consuming and dangerous trial-and-error process that won that knowledge. Furthermore, within a group of interdependent cooperating individuals, the states of other individuals are among the most important things in the world worth knowing about. Thus, communication of knowledge and internal states is useful to creatures who have a lot to say and who are on speaking terms. (Pinker & Bloom, 1992, p. 460)

They then enumerated several kinds of linguistic content "worthy of communication among humans" (p. 460).

Other researchers have offered more specific suggestions about the adaptive value of various aspects of language and the value of additional preadaptations that might have made language possible. Some of them are considered in the following discussion of ontogeny and phylogeny.

QUESTION 3: HOW DOES LANGUAGE GET THAT WAY IN ONTOGENY?

As mentioned earlier, Chomsky's conception of language acquisition has long dominated the field of cognitive science. It sprang from his attempt to solve what he called "Plato's problem"—the problem of "poverty of the stimulus" (Chomsky, 1966, p. xxv). Building on Plato's conception of the relationship of environment to mind, he felt that there isn't enough information in the linguistic environment to enable an infant to acquire language without formal instruction. And because few infants are given any systematic instruction, they must get their linguistic knowledge from some other source. That other source, Chomsky surmised, is UG, which functions as an innate *language acquisition device* (LAD; Chomsky, 1965).

One property of language whose acquisition seems to require innate guidance is *structure dependence.* According to a behaviorist view of language, the next word in a sentence tends to be the one that has occurred most often after the precursor word in the past. Thus, sequences are learned from previous occurrences. But take this sentence: "The man who is picking us up is here." The choice of the second *is* after *up* could not be a result of such a sequence having frequently occurred in the past. Its choice is a function of a hierarchical sentence *structure* in which the second *is* is most closely related to *man*, which occurs much further back in the sentence. Such structures must be innate, the argument goes, for an infant to produce sentences like this.

Pinker (1994) points out that even at a simpler level, word order is an unreliable guide to grammar's organization. He notes (p. 283) that infants, on hearing sentences such as:

Jane eats chicken.
  Jane eats fish.
  Jane likes fish.

might be able to construct sentences such as
  Jane likes chicken.

But suppose further sentences include
  Jane eats slowly.
  Jane might fish.

Using the same procedures, the infant is then likely to construct sentences such as
  Jane might slowly.
  Jane likes slowly.
  Jane might chicken.

Pinker argues that for infants to avoid such pitfalls, they "must couch rules in terms of grammatical categories like noun, verb, and auxiliary, not in actual words" (pp. 283–284). These categories, Pinker says, echoing Chomsky, are innate—or, as Pinker puts it, "hardwired."

Another argument for assuming that language acquisition rests on innate knowledge is that the typical infant's grammatical errors are corrected too seldom to enable him or her to eventually eliminate them. Mistakes in *meaning* are apt to be corrected, yes, but grammatical mistakes aren't. Nevertheless, infants manage to learn grammatically correct utterances. Pinker observes that "any no-feedback situation presents a difficult challenge to the design of a learning system" (p. 282). To cope with this problem, he suggests, "A good start would be to build in the basic organization of grammar" (p. 282), which, he believes, is exactly what happened.

Yet another complication seemingly calling for innateness is that certain grammatical constructions apply to some classes of verbs but not to others. For example, it's incorrect to apply the present progressive suffix *-ing* to verbs of desire such as *want,* as in "I am wanting to go now." Yet infants for some reason rarely make mistakes like this.

But how far do infants go beyond the data available to them? Conclusions as to their so-called "creativity" seem to depend on how closely we study their progress across time—in short, on what could be called the grain of analysis. In looking at an infant's output change over a period of months—a coarse-grained analysis—we typically see spectacular changes in output that seem unrelated to regularities in the input. For example, Pinker (1994) refers to an "All Hell Breaks Loose" stage "between the late twos and the mid threes" (p. 269). As he describes it: "Sentence length increases steadily, and because grammar is a discrete combinatorial system, the number of syntactic constructions increases exponentially, doubling each month and reaching the thousands before the third birthday. . . . A full range of sentence types flower—questions with words like *who, what,* and *where,* relative clauses, comparatives, negations, complements, conjunctions and passives" (p. 271).

But what if we use a finer grain of analysis? Lieven, Behrens, Speares, and Tomasello (2003) taped the output of a child learning English. They taped in hour-long sessions, 5 times a week, over a 6-week period. Then they traced the history of the set of more than 300 multiword utterances produced in the final taping session. Nearly two-thirds of these utterances, they found, had been produced before. Of the remainder, most consisted of repetitions of what they called an "utterance schema" (e.g., "Where's the _____ ?"), plus other linguistic content either filling in the empty slot in the schema or adding on to one end of a schema. Their conclusion? The child's "creativity" over this period primarily involved cutting and pasting of previously used material. (For an explication of the "cutting and pasting" metaphor, see Tomasello, 2002.)

Most of the evidence cited for grammatical innateness involves output patterns that seem unlearnable in terms of traditional behavioristic theories of learning. But Braine (1994) contends that the case for grammatical innateness, though plausible, needs a developmental theory that takes particular aspects of UG as a starting point and relates them to the facts of language development. In "Is Nativism Sufficient?" (1994), he concludes that "nativism is ultimately unsatisfactory because it systematically neglects the other task, which is to account for development, including the emergence of the postulated innate primitives" (p. 9). He points out that while "the current Chomskyan linguistic theory offers various universal principles that have arcane-sounding names—the projection principle, the theta-criterion, subjacency, the case filter, the empty category principle, to name a few, . . . there has been no discussion of how such principles would be embodied in mental operations or structures in the child's mind, so as to constrain the form of the linguistic system" (p. 20).

Building a developmental theory based on UG is complicated by the fact that Chomsky has produced no fewer than three versions: the standard theory in 1965, the government and binding theory in 1981, and the minimalist program in 1995 (see Jackendoff, 2002). Each version has very different implications for how an infant would connect its innate endowment with a real language.

Another problem concerns what is universal in languages. Normally, as Braine notes, only universal features are considered innate. According to Jackendoff (2002), "The open vocabulary, phonology, and word concatenation are surely universal. But then we start running into exceptions" (p. 261). Citing Van Valin and LaPolla's (1997) conclusion "that if a characteristic is not universal it is not part of Universal Grammar" (p. 263), Jackendoff responds that "if Universal Grammar is to be the unlearned basis from which language is learned, it better be available to help infants learn case systems, fixed word order, and grammatical functions in case the language in the environment happens to have them" (p. 263).

Acquisition of Speech   We consider now how *speech* gets the way it does in ontogeny. One explanation is the *frames, then content* conception of MacNeilage and Davis (1990; MacNeilage, 1998). In this view, the first step in acquiring the programmable syllabic frames of adult speech, described under Tinbergen's question 1, occurs when an infant, at roughly 7 months, begins to babble—that is, to produce rhythmic, repetitive series of consonant-vowel (CV) alternations such as "bababa." These close/open mouth alternations, which MacNeilage and Davis call "motor frames," eventually develop to enable the kind of frame programming that can go wrong when consonants and vowels are misplaced in adult speech, though they still preserve their positions in frames. But these frames are not initially subject to internal programming. For the typical repetitive sequences such as "bababa," the tongue is primarily inert, remaining in the same position throughout a babbling episode. Hence, babbling may be said to illustrate *frame dominance* (Davis & MacNeilage, 1995).

Languages employ a wide variety of C-V sequences within syllables and almost always have sequences of different syllables (e.g., "bodega"), so infants must eventually develop the internal programming of frames necessary to do this. Such an ability develops slowly over 3 or 4 years of word production, starting at about 12 months. There is broad agreement (MacNeilage & Davis, 2000) that a major initial step toward this in infants, clearly observable by age 2, is their learning to favor a sequence in which a *labial* or lip consonant (e.g., *b*) comes first and is followed after the vowel by a *coronal* or tongue-front consonant (e.g., *d*), as in "bado" for *bottle*. MacNeilage and Davis (2000) contend that these developments and others are not the result of innate proscriptions but are instead the *self-organizational* consequences of adult language input patterns interacting with factors such as articulatory ease, the problem of sequence initiation, and the functional load that results from the new (postbabbling) demands of interfacing the motor system with the mental dictionary. Self-organizational processes, together with learning, may prove sufficient to enable the entire subsequent process of acquisition of frame programming by means of insertion of consonant and vowel segments.

The Neurobiology of Innateness   Most of the issues regarding the ontogeny of language that we have discussed have involved inferences from infant behavior as to the possibility of language innateness. A more direct approach that might allay the concern of Deacon, mentioned earlier, that the innateness problem is being finessed, would be to show that there is indeed a genetic basis for language innateness. For Pinker:

> The grammar genes would be stretches of DNA that code for proteins, or trigger the transcription of proteins, in certain times and places in the brain, that guide, attract, or glue neurons into networks that, in combination with the synaptic tuning that takes place during learning, are necessary to compute the solution to some grammatical problem (like choosing an affix or a word). (1994, p. 322)

But can genes actually specify the detailed structure of the nervous system in this way? Not according to prominent scientists in molecular biology (Stent, 1981), neurobiology (Damasio, 1994), developmental neurophysiology (Singer, 1989), and neurology of language development itself (Elman et al., 1996). These scientists contend that the human complement of about 30,000 genes contains insufficient information to specify the structure of the human nervous system, which comprises about a hundred billion cells, each having, on average, several hundred connections with other cells. Besides the informational poverty of the genes, Stent (1981) also emphasizes what could be called the enormous causal distance between genes and the eventual structure of the nervous system, stating that "the role of the genes . . . is at too many removes from the processes that actually build nerve cells and specify neural circuits that underlie behavior to provide an appropriate conceptual structure for posing the developmental questions that need to be answered" (Stent, 1981, pp. 186–187). A more acceptable role of the genes in neurogenesis, Damasio suggests (1994), is that they assist in establishing the most primitive survival-related circuits in the vertebrate nervous system but not circuits related to high-level cognition.

Genetic hypotheses for UG tend to fit what Dawkins (1986) has called the *blueprint* metaphor. A blueprint, like an architect's drawing of a house, contains, from the very beginning, a representation of all the important parts of the end product. But the human body's organization, unlike that of a house, is far from fixed in advance, he says. While every cell in the body contains genetic instructions of some sort, body parts and brain parts differentiate in a context-dependent manner that is related to local cell growth in a multistage interactive process, the complexity of which still evades systematic description.

So Dawkins proposes, as an alternative, what he considers a better metaphor for human development—the *recipe*. Life starts with a number of ingredients that must be in the right proportions and assembled in the right order. Then, "To simulate the 'baking' of a baby, we should imagine not a single process in a single oven, but a tangle of conveyor belts, passing different parts of the dish through 10,000,000 different miniaturized ovens in series and in parallel, each oven bringing out a different combination of flavors from 10,000 basic ingredients" (p. 297).

All of this does not mean that there is *no* genetic basis for language. It simply means that there is, at present, no accepted scenario for how it might manifest itself in the nervous system's organization.

Inferring Genes from a Language Disorder: A Case Study   Another way to assess genetic theories of language is to seek genetically transmitted language disorders. If indeed we can find a specific genetic basis for some specific aspect of language in a particular, well-defined subpopulation, this would surely support an innatist view of evolution.

Recently, researchers have been investigating whether a particular familial pattern of language pathology reveals the genetic organization that underlies it. Gopnik and her colleagues (e.g., Gopnik & Crago, 1991) studied members of an English family who consistently produced, in Pinker's words, "grammatical errors such as misuse of pronouns, and of suffixes like the plural and the past tense" (Pinker, 1994, p. 49). Here are some of his examples:

> It's a flying finches they are.
> She remembered when she hurts herself the other day.
> The neighbors phone the ambulance because the man fall off the tree.

Gopnik and Crago (1991) concluded that "a single dominant gene controls for those mechanisms that result in a child's ability to construct paradigms that constitute morphology" (p. 47). But a more comprehensive examination of this same subpopulation by Vargha-Khadem, Watkins, Alcock, Fletcher, and Passingham (1995) led to a far different conclusion: "The inherited behavior has a broad phenotype which transcends impaired generation of syntactical rules and includes a striking articulatory impairment as well as deficits in intellectual, linguistic, and orofacial praxic [= motor skill] functions generally" (p. 930).

Subsequently, researchers studying the FOXP2 gene, underlying this syndrome, concluded that this gene "might be generally implicated in aspects of motor control in mammalian species, and was already playing a role in the development of motor-related brain regions *in the human-mouse common ancestor*" (Lai, Gerrelli, Monacom, Fisher, & Copp, 2003, p. 2461; italics added). However, a recent mutation in this gene that has become fixed in the human population in the past 200,000 years (Enard et al., 2002) has prompted much speculation regarding its importance in the ascendance of modern humans in general and language in particular (e.g., Ridley, 2003).

So we seem to still be at an early stage in our attempt to verify and clarify any proposed innate language capacity. It has not yet been shown that language is innate in the sense of having genetic preordination specific to it. Because a more detailed discussion of the issue is beyond the scope of this chapter, we refer the interested reader to a monograph titled *Rethinking Innateness* by Elman et al., which reviews 12 "lines of evidence that are frequently offered in favor of the genetic control of cortical representations that constitute linguistic knowledge" (1999, p. 371).

QUESTION 4: HOW DID LANGUAGE GET THAT WAY IN PHYLOGENY?

In this section we will consider three topics: evolution of grammar, precursors to language, and the frame/content theory of the evolution of speech.

Evolution of Grammar   The only detailed theory for how the grammatical component of language evolved is that of Bickerton (1995). (See also Calvin & Bickerton, 2000, for a more accessible discussion of this theory.) According to Bickerton, language evolved in two stages. First came a *protolanguage*—a single-word stage with minimal syntactic organization. This stage, Bickerton believes, evolved not for social-communication processes, as some believe (e.g., Humphrey, 1976), but in response to selection pressures for labeling objects in the environment, primarily to facilitate foraging and instruction of the young. Bickerton considers this stage to be represented today by three language genres: (1) the two-word stage of speech acquisition, (2) sign languages taught to apes, and (3) pidgin languages. He argues that all these varieties of protolanguages:

- Can only string together a small handful of words at a time.
- Can leave out any words they feel like leaving out.
- Often depart from the customary word order unpredictably and for no obvious reason.
- Cannot form any complex structures whether these be complex noun phrases or sentences more than a clause long.
- Contain, if they have any at all, only a tiny fraction of the inflexions and the "grammatical words"—things such as articles, prepositions, and the like that make up 50% of true language utterances (Calvin & Bickerton, 2000, p. 30).

The second stage, Bickerton believes, saw the evolution of basic syntactic form. He surmises that it evolved with reciprocal altruism, as in "When I scratch your back, you scratch mine" (Calvin & Bickerton, p. 125). To keep track of social interactions in this category, he believes, our ancestors had to develop various semantic concepts or "thematic roles"—for example, "AGENT (the performer of an action) and THEME (who- or whatever undergoes the action)" (Calvin & Bickerton, p. 130) as well as "GOAL (whoever the action was directed towards)" (Calvin & Bickerton, p. 130). He argues that "the practice of reciprocal altruism created the set of abstract categories and structures that, once they were joined to a structureless protolanguage, yielded the kind of syntax that all modern humans exhibited" (Calvin & Bickerton, p. 126).

The basic syntax that was created in this way contained a verb signifying the action and one, two or three "argument structures," or noun phrases, the syntactic equivalents of thematic roles.

Precursors to Language   As to other phylogenetic views, Dunbar (1996) theorizes that speech might have first evolved for vocal grooming (which eventually took the form of gossip), not for object labeling. He argues that as group sizes got larger in hominid evolution, actual grooming, which enhances social bonding, became impracticable, so vocal grooming evolved as a substitute for it. Commenting on the significance of this work, Knight, Studdert-Kennedy, and Hurford (2000a) state, "For the first time [it] specified concrete Darwinian selection pressures driving language evolution" (p. 7).

Donald (1994) offers a more general theory for how the expressive capabilities of hominids evolved. The great merit of Donald's work is that it helps us understand the remarkable, but usually neglected, action capabilities underlying a wide range of action-based performances of modern hominids—not only our ability at, but also our fascination with, singing and music in general, opera, ballet, games, and sports. He argues that these are consequences of the evolution of a general-purpose mimetic ability, probably in *Homo erectus*. He considers that they evolved in response to selection pressures for group solidarity and were manifest in earlier forms in tribal rituals. Donald argues that this development provided a basis for the later development of the action level of language—potentially either signed or spoken language, though he believes spoken language came first. In his opinion, this mimetic revolution must have preceded language, because language conferred such power on the species that had it evolved before these various action capabilities, they would never have evolved in the first place.

An important development in neurophysiology bears on Donald's theory. Rizzolatti and his colleagues (e.g., Rizzolatti, Fogassi, & Gallese, 2000) have discovered a class of "mirror neurons" in the monkey homolog of a language area—Broca's area. These neurons discharge both when a monkey performs a particular action, like grasping, and when the monkey observes others performing the same action. Circuits underlying the action of these neurons could have formed an initial phylogenetic basis for mimesis. It has also been suggested that use of this link between an animal's actions and the actions of others could have formed an initial basis for the evolution of ToM.

Evolution of Speech: The Frame/Content Theory   According to MacNeilage and Davis's frame/content (F/C) theory, the first speech may have taken the form of CV protosyllables—"motor frames"—similar to those heard today in the babbling of infants, as described earlier. Two reasons for this claim are the sheer rhythmic fluency of much babbling, which suggests a deep phylogeny, and the fact that the CV form is the only universal syllable type in languages today.

Another reason to believe that ontogeny has phylogenetic roots is that the inertial tendency for restricted tongue movement observed in babbling also appears in the structure of languages. Tongue position for a vowel in a CV syllable tends to correlate with that for the preceding consonant (MacNeilage & Davis, 2000; see also Rousett, 2003). The obvious fact that biomechanical inertia of the tongue co-evolved with it means that this inertia must have been present from the origin of speech. A long tradition in biology has emphasized that ontogeny and phylogeny share common physical constraints (Lock & Peters, 1996).

Another suggestive link between phylogeny and ontogeny is the fact that languages also tend to favor the initial pattern of intersyllabic variegation described earlier—labial consonant/vowel/coronal consonant sequences are favored over their opposite (MacNeilage & Davis, 2000; Rousett, 2003). Thus, the same self-organizational process that perhaps results in these forms in infants (described under Tinbergen's question 3) could have also occurred in earlier hominids, with one important qualification: Hominids were creating these forms, whereas modern infants usually have a model for them from adult input.

According to F/C theory, frames evolved by descent with modification in several stages. The mandibular cycle apparently first evolved for ingestive processes such as sucking, chewing, and licking in early mammals (Radinsky, 1987). Because many modern primates have visuofacial cyclicities involving mandibular oscillation (e.g., lip smacks, tongue smacks, teeth chatters), it suggests that hominids exapted (borrowed) the mandibular cycle of ingestion for communication (e.g., Van Hooff, 1967). With this phylogenetic base, protosyllables could have been formed by pairing visuofacial mandibular cyclicities with phonation—a pairing that is present in some other modern primates (Van Hoof, 1967). The possibility that frames evolved from ingestive cyclicities is increased by the fact that mammals' main cortical area for the control of ingestive cyclicities includes the homolog of the main cortical area for speech motor control—Broca's area and its immediate surround.

The plausibility of this theory is strengthened by the recent discovery of oral mirror neurons in the monkey homolog of Broca's area (Ferrari, Gallese, Rizzolatti, & Fogassi, 2003). Though most of these neurons are involved with both ingestion and orofacial communication, one neuron was reported to be solely involved in lip smacking. Ferrari et al. (2003) endorse the F/C view that, in their words, "Ingestive actions are the basis on which communication is built" (p. 1713).

It's often noted that monkeys do not actually imitate, nor do they speak. But there is evidence that monkeys have a human-like left hemisphere specialization for both the reception (Poremba et al., 2004) and the production (Hook-Costigan & Rogers, 1998) of vocal communication. The likely presence of this human-like, lateralized communicative capacity and oral mirror neurons in forms ancestral to humans may have provided an initial basis for the human vocal-imitation capacity, which makes the learning of diverse languages possible.

EVOLUTION OF LANGUAGE TRANSMISSION

In this section we consider various questions about language evolution that hinge on the existence of sign languages in addition to spoken languages.

DID A SIGNED LANGUAGE COME FIRST?

A persistent theme in the literature regarding the language-transmission process is that a gestural (i.e., signed) language may have been the first language. Most recently, Corballis (2002) has taken up the cause of Gordon Hewes (1973, 1996), who reintroduced this idea to the modern scientific community.

Researchers have advanced several arguments for a gestural origin of language. One argument is that earlier visual-gestural capacities were greater than vocal-auditory capacities (e.g., Givon, 2002). Our nearest living relatives, the great apes, have failed to learn speech, but they *have* learned sign systems, suggesting that sign was more readily available to our ancestors than speech. The theory that adequate oral capabilities had lagged behind manual ones has been bolstered by Lieberman's claim, described earlier, that not until some 350,000 years ago did the hominid vocal tract evolve an anatomical configuration allowing a multitude of speech sounds to be produced (Lieberman, 1984). Meantime, the advent of tool construction/use in *Homo Habilis* over 2 million years ago, perhaps associated with a preferred right hand/left hemisphere (Toth, 1985), has been taken to indicate a quantum jump in manual capacity, which could have facilitated manual communication, thus forming the left-hemisphere basis for the eventual emergence of spoken language (Kimura, 1979). The initial discovery of *manual* mirror neurons in the monkey homolog of Broca's area has led to the proposal that these neurons could have supported an initial *gestural* language (Rizzolatti & Arbib, 1998). But perhaps the main argument for considering sign language as our first language involves the property of *iconicity.* Because a sign can *look like* the object, event, or attribute it symbolizes, it seems a natural way to establish the concept-signal link for words.

Hockett (1978) has advanced a compelling counterargument to this scenario, however. Gestural communication could never have achieved the status of a true language, he says, because if it had, it would have conferred such advantages that the usually cited selection pressures for its subsequent abandonment (that it ties up the hands, isn't omnidirectional, and doesn't work in the dark) would be insufficient. In short, it would still be with us.

On the question of what exactly would have constituted a *true* language, proponents of a gestural origin are somewhat reticent, but from the perspective of the transmission process, we suggest it should minimally include a combinatorial phonological level (e.g., Jackendoff's protolanguage level, 2002), allowing the construction of an open lexicon out of a limited repertoire of phonological formatives—a presyntactic stage. Such a combinatorial phonology is in fact present in the signed languages of the deaf. Here, three major meaningless components—handshape, location (where the sign is made), and movement—are concatenated to form a large number of lexical items (Klima & Bellugi, 1979).

An additional problem for gestural-origins scenarios is that there have been, at best, only fragmentary accounts of what the necessary intermodal translation process would have been from the visual-gestural to the vocal-auditory modality. Hewes conceded (1996) that this is the weakest part of his scenario. What would a translation process have to contend with? First, there is the huge difference in the structure of the modalities, if we take modern signed language as a model for the putative original signed language. In speech, consonants are described in terms of three parameters: (1) place of articulation—where in the mouth the constriction for the consonant is made, (2) manner of articulation—how much of a constriction is made and how it is made, and (3) voicing—whether the vocal folds vibrate during the constriction. Vowels are primarily described in terms of the height of the tongue and its position in the front-back axis. An intermodal translation process would presumably involve getting from the handshapes, locations, and movements of signed language to these parameters of spoken language.

With few exceptions, the relation between a concept and its sound pattern across present-day spoken languages is arbitrary. This fact has always been a major stumbling block for vocal-origins scenarios. Falk (in press) revives the provocative suggestion that the concept-sound pairing may have arisen in the context of parent-infant interaction. She notes Goldman's (2001) finding that modern infants produce nasalized demand vocalizations and argues that these might have been interpreted by our ancestors as words for *mother*. This possibility is supported by Murdock's (1959) data showing that 78% of the words for *mother* in a corpus of 474 languages have a nasal consonant in their first syllable. This is in contrast to words for *father*, 66% of which have an oral consonant in their first syllable.

A third view is that neither manual nor vocal language came first, but instead the two media coevolved for communication purposes. This is in fact the dominant conception of the *modern* speech-gesture relationship in extended cultures. It comes from David MacNeill (1992), who suggests that gesture and speech form an inseparable unit in which the two modalities perform two different but complementary functions. While the mouth delivers the linguistic message using the combinatoric-sequential linguistic capability of the vocal-auditory modality, the hand simultaneously delivers an iconic imagistic message. Goldin-Meadow and MacNeill (1999) suggest that this may have been the way the hand and mouth have been related in hominids from the beginning.

THE SIGNIFICANCE OF MODERN SIGNED LANGUAGES

Modern signed languages have great importance for the understanding of the evolution of language and the human mind—importance that goes well beyond the hypothesis that language first evolved as a signed language. The modern presence of these languages, which are commonly deemed equal in their expressive power to spoken languages, has encouraged the belief of linguists in the Chomskyan tradition that UG is an amodal capacity—a high-level linguistic module independent of the medium of communication. This belief is consistent with Chomsky's view that language initially evolved as a tool for thought, not for communication. But the claim that signed language provides evidence for an amodal linguistic capacity remains controversial. We briefly examine this claim.

The question of whether there is an amodal language capacity has been considered with regard to three aspects of language: basic structure and function, brain organization, and acquisition. In none of these respects has amodality been convincingly demonstrated.

With regard to structure, no amodality claim has ever been able to reconcile a fundamental difference in the organization of spoken and signed languages. Spoken languages use *sequentiality*, because the auditory modality is by definition linked to the time domain, while signed languages use *simultaneity*. The two primary informational elements of speech—the consonants and vowels—are set out across time at the rate of about 15 per second. The three primary informational elements of signed language—handshape, location, and movement—are presented simultaneously in a single sign, and signs appear at the rate of only about 2 per second. In addition, whereas morphological complexity is usually handled in spoken language by introducing *successive* morphemes, in signed languages it's typically introduced within the time of presentation of the single base sign (Klima & Bellugi, 1979). This difference negates attempts to equate the sign with the spoken syllable in the grammar in general because single syllables are perhaps most characteristically submorphemic elements in spoken language.

In addition, at the level of phonological substructure, there are no agreed-on parallels between the concepts of syllable, segment (consonant and vowel), and distinctive feature in spoken syllables and signs (see Sandler & Lillo-Martin, 2001, for a discussion). At the level of function, a comparison of phonological serial-ordering order errors in the two modalities (Shattuck-Hufnagel, 1979, for speech; Hohenberger, Happ, & Leuninger, 2002, for sign) shows that while the main error unit in speech is the individual subsyllabic segment—the consonant or vowel—the main sign error unit is a component of the whole putative syllable—a handshape, a location, or a movement. Such differences and others led Hohenberger et al. (2002) to conclude that "the 'frame-content' metaphor," which, as we have seen, is a central metaphor for the organization of vowels and consonants in spoken syllables, "cannot be transferred to sign languages straightforwardly" (p. 134).

Another fundamental difference between spoken and signed language structure pointed out by Sandler and Lillo-Martin concerns the phenomenon of verb agreement. For example, English has only a single agreement marker. In a sentence such as "Hadar walks to school," the *s* on the verb agrees with third-person-singular properties of the proper noun, in the present tense. But not all spoken languages have verb agreement, and where it exists, it takes a variety of forms. In contrast, there is a form of verb agreement that appears universal in signed languages. It is illustrated by forms like the verb *look at* in which the hand moves from the viewer to the viewed and thus moves in opposite directions in "I look at you" and "You look at me." Here, apparently the grammar capitalizes on spatial cognition. The existence of a universal in signed language alone is inconsistent with the claim of a single amodal UG (Sandler & Lillo-Martin, 2001).

Klima and Bellugi and their colleagues, focusing on sign-language aphasia, have made a sustained attempt to show that "the left cerebral hemisphere in humans may have an innate predisposition for the central components of language independent of the modality" (Poizner, Klima, & Bellugi, 1987, p. 212; see also Hickok, Bellugi, & Klima, 1996). But a number of problems with this contention have been pointed out by MacNeilage (1998a), including the possibility that much of the claimed left-hemisphere specialization for signed language may be attributable to this hemisphere's control of the preferred right hand of signers. In addition, most recently, Newman, Bavelier, Corina, Zezzard, and Neville (2002) show that in signed-language comprehension by native signers, there is a mostly symmetrical activation of the left and right hemispheres, even though spoken-language comprehension primarily involves the left hemisphere.

Pettito (e.g., Pettito, Holowka, Sergio, & Ostry, 2001) has argued that language, whether spoken or signed, has an underlying amodal rhythmic organization (the origin of which is not discussed), and infants have a genetically determined amodal perceptual sensitivity to this rhythm and a natural propensity to produce it (again, the origin of which is not discussed), which allows them to acquire language. But the hypothesized rhythms of vocal babblers and sign babblers are apparently different, and each of them is different from the rhythms of spoken language and signed language of adults (insofar as these can be specified), which are also different from each other.

LANGUAGE TRANSMISSION AND THE QUESTION OF LANGUAGE INNATENESS

Let us now try to make good on our claim regarding the value of focusing on language transmission as a way to understand language phylogeny. We begin with the fact that the two transmission systems, spoken language and signed language, have equal status as fully expressive forms of language. On the basis of complexity of design, they must both be regarded as having an innate basis according to orthodox evolutionary psychology, and, as we have seen, generative linguistics sees in them a common innate amodal basis.

But signed language is not universally in culturewide use, which is significant because capacities are generally thought to become innate by solving species-wide problems. And as we have seen, the assumption that spoken and signed languages have an amodal basis has not been substantiated. That being so, we cannot say that amodality allows signed language to be as good as spoken language even though it's not universally selected for use today. Another possibility is to argue that signed language is as good as spoken language because it was the first language; therefore, the capabilities that underlie it are still available to us. But we agree with Hockett (1978) that if signed language had ever evolved, presumably it would still be universally with us. In addition, we pointed out that no adequate translation theory for the necessary shift to spoken language has ever been provided. So it remains possible that signed language results from the application of a general-purpose capability to the problem of a deficit in the input component of the universal linguistic transmission medium—audition. And if signed languages are just as good as spoken languages, although not innate, it becomes possible that spoken languages are not innate either.

BIOLOGICAL VERSUS SOCIOCULTURAL FACTORS IN LANGUAGE EVOLUTION

Because evolutionary psychology emphasizes the putative genetic consequences of biological adaptations, we have focused here on biological aspects of evolution of linguistic capacity in the individual. But language surely reflects both *biological* evolution and *sociocultural* developments. Any language existing today must have been worked out historically between its users. After all, however language originated, it's now a communicative device, and for it to work there must be "parity" (Liberman & Mattingly, 1985). That is, what counts for the speaker must count in the same way for the listener. This parity must have been achieved socially from the very beginning. (As we have seen, Falk, in press, offers us a possibility for how a socially established coding system began for spoken language.) An appropriate metaphor here may be that of an "interactive evolutionary spiral through which both individual language capacity and a communal system of symbolic communication must have more or less simultaneously involved" (Studdert-Kennedy, Knight, & Hurford, 1998, p. 4). The take of these authors on the biology/culture question is, "What had to get into the genes among other things was the capacity and motivation to enter into the processes of social interaction that led and still leads into language" (p. 2).

The biological versus sociocultural issue cannot simply be finessed with the claim that genes determine culture (see Ridley, 2003), even though there is obviously some truth to this. After all, we do have some 6,000 mutually unintelligible languages. So we're left with a vexing question: "What is *primarily* biological and what is *primarily* sociocultural, given that the two are correlated?"

A large group of "functional" or "cognitive" linguists (see Tomasello, 1998, for a compendium) emphasize the importance of the *communicative* function of language in its evolution and thus assert that semantics (meaning) must have been fundamental to the evolution of language from the beginning rather than being epiphenomenal to the evolution of a grammatical module, as Chomskyan linguists would have it. In their view, whether innate or not, language is quintessentially a matter of social communication. They focus on two aspects of language: language typology (cross-language similarities and differences) and historical linguistics.

To suggest the flavor of this enterprise, we briefly look at two principles that the generative linguist Newmayer (1998), following a careful review of the field, deemed worthy of special mention. One of them, considered to operate during comprehension, is *parsing pressure*—"pressure to identify the constituents of a sentence as quickly as possible" (Newmayer, 2002, p. 370). This proposed selection pressure tends to align syntax and semantics in a sentence to make it easier to parse (decompose). The second, more general but somewhat related, principle is *iconicity*—"the idea that form, length, complexity, or interrelationship of elements in a linguistic representation reflects the form, length, complexity, or interrelationships of elements in the concept, experience or communicative strategy that the representation encodes" (Newmayer, 1998, p. 114). Both principles pertain to the optimal transmission of meaning.

Generativists, in the effort to distinguish their own perspective from the functionalist one, often find themselves forced to *define* UG in terms of phenomena for which functional explanations seem least likely. For example, Chomsky has asserted that "structure dependence" seems to have no utility for communication (Chomsky, 1975, p. 58). Newmayer talks of an "arbitrary residue of formal patterns where there's *no* obvious direct link to function" (1998, p. 2). This insistence on the centrality of *lack of functionality* of UG is rather embarrassing for evolutionary psychology, which has selected UG as paradigmatic for its discipline, but which at the same time has adaptive function as its centerpiece.

As to the history of languages, any reconstructions that go back beyond 10,000 years are generally considered suspect in the orthodox language community (e.g., Dixon, 1997). But things that happen to language in its observable history may nevertheless provide clues to language origins. For example, one focus of study is "grammaticalization." This is the phenomenon whereby grammatical morphemes (e.g., inflexions such as *-ing* and *-ed* and so-called "function words" such as articles, prepositions, pronouns, conjunctions) arise by splitting off from, or taking on more generalized meaning relative to, the "content words" such as nouns and verbs that they historically derive from. This phenomenon seems to provide clues as to how grammatical morphemes might have arisen in the first place (e.g., Heine & Kuteva, 2002).

An important recent development in the language sciences is the advent of a diverse group of scientists who have built models that *simulate* various aspects of social interaction between speakers and listeners. These models have been featured in a three-volume series on language evolution based on biennial international conferences (Hurford, Studdert-Kennedy, & Knight, 1998; Knight, Studdert-Kennedy, & Hurford, 2000b; Wray, 2002; see, e.g., the work of Batali, De Boer, Kirby, Hurford, & Steels in these volumes). Reviewing some of these studies, Knight, Studdert-Kennedy, and Hurford (2000a) observe: "Here, aspects of linguistic structure are shown to arise by self-organization from the process of interaction itself, without benefit of standard selection pressures" (p. 11). They conclude that these approaches "promise a sharp reduction in the amount of linguistic structure that has to be attributed to natural selection" (p. 11). We could argue that this body of work is unimportant because it's operating above or beyond the level at which innate adaptations are formed, or because it's considering phenomena that occurred after basic language had evolved. But the ultimate issue here is this: If the most basic patterns of language were forced to emerge from the contingencies of the communication process in interaction with the nonlinguistic cognitive capabilities of the participants, there may be no reason to regard them as innate.

Finally, an extreme position regarding cultural evolution of language, though one increasingly deserving of note, is that units of imitation called "memes" (Dawkins, 1976), which can replicate themselves in culture in something like the way genes replicate in nature, could play a major role in language evolution (Blackmore, 1999). They certainly play a major role in language learning today. In this view, the aspect of the human mind involved in language would be like the rest of the mind as conceived by Donald (2001), namely, "a 'hybrid' product of biology and culture" (p. xiii).

CONCLUSIONS

Though Chomsky disavows natural selection, evolutionary psychology has chosen his universal grammar module as a paradigmatic hominid adaptation. That choice encourages a neglect of Darwin's core phylogenetic tenet of descent with modification, according to which language must have evolved from nonlanguage capabilities of ancestral forms. So this chapter has focused on the history of the manual and vocal transmission media as a wedge into the phylogenetic issue. We considered four questions, derived from Tinbergen (1963), regarding language as a communication system: (1) mechanistic: "How does it work?" (2) functional/adaptational: "What does it do for the organism?" (3) ontogenetic: "How does it get that way in development?" (4) phylogenetic: "How did it get that way in evolution?" We explored several possible precursors of language and putative paths toward language. Emerging as a recurring theme was the importance of self-organizational processes. Then we analyzed the relation between spoken and signed language transmission systems from a phylogenetic and contemporary perspective. Our analysis prompted us to ask whether it's prudent to continue to assume that language is innate. Finally, we noted a major role of cultural factors in the present form and perhaps the phylogeny of language.

REFERENCES

Barkow, J. H., Cosmides, L., & Tooby, J. (Eds.). (1992). *The adapted mind.* Oxford, England: Oxford University Press.

Bickerton, D. (1995). *Language and human behavior.* Seattle: University of Washington Press.

Blackmore, S. (1999). The *meme machine.* Oxford, England: Oxford University Press.

Boe, L.-J., Heim, J.-L., Honda, K., & Maeda, S. (2002). The potential Neanderthal vowel space was as large as that of modern humans. *Journal of Phonetics, 30,* 456–484.

Braine, M. D. S. (1994). Is nativism sufficient? *Journal of Child Language, 21,* 9–31.

Calvin, W. H., & Bickerton, D. (2000). *Lingua ex machina.* Cambridge, MA: MIT Press.

Camizon, S., Deneubourg, J.-F., Franks, N. R., Sneyd, J., Theraulaz, G., & Bonabeau, E. (2001). *Self-organization in biological systems.* Princeton, NJ: Princeton Univesity Press.

Chomsky, N. (1965). *Aspects of the theory of syntax.* Cambridge, MA: MIT Press.

Chomsky, N. (1966). *Cartesian linguistics.* New York: Harper & Row.

Chomsky, N. (1972). *Language and mind* (extended edition). New York: Harcourt, Brace and Jovanovich.

Chomsky, N. (1975). *Reflections on language.* New York: Pantheon.

Chomsky, N. (2000). *The architecture of language.* Oxford, England: Oxford University Press.

Corballis, M. C. (2002). *From hand to mouth: The Origins of language.* Princeton, NJ: Princeton University Press.

Cosmides, L., & Tooby, J. (1992). The psychological foundations of culture. In J. H. Barkow, L. Cosmides, & J. Tooby (Eds.), *The adapted mind* (pp. 19–136). Oxford, England: Oxford University Press.

Cosmides, L., & Tooby, J. (1999). Evolutionary psychology. In R. A. Wilson & F. Keil (Eds.), *The MIT encyclopedia of the cognitive sciences* (pp. 295–298). Cambridge, MA: MIT Press.

Cutler, A., & Clifton, C., Jr. (1999). Comprehending spoken language: A blueprint of the listener. In C. M. Brown & P. Hagoort (Eds.), *The neurocognition of language* (pp. 123–166). Oxford, England: Oxford University Press.

Damasio, A. (1994). *Descartes' error.* New York: Grosset/Putnam.

Davis, B. L., & MacNeilage, P. F. (1995). The articulatory basis of babbling. *Journal of Speech and Hearing Research, 38,* 1199–1211.

Dawkins, R. (1976). *The selfish gene.* Oxford, England: Oxford University Press.

Dawkins, R. (1986). The *blind watchmaker.* New York: Norton.

Deacon, T. W. (1997). *The symbolic species.* New York: Norton.

Dixon, R. M. W. (1997). The rise and fall of languages. Cambridge, England: Cambridge University Press.

Donald, M. (1994). *Origin of the modern mind.* Cambridge, MA: Harvard University Press.

Donald, M. (2001). *A mind so rare.* New York: Norton.

Dunbar, R. I. M. (1996). *Grooming, gossip and the evolution of language.* London: Faber and Faber.

Elman, J., Bates, E., Johnson, M., Karmiloff-Smith, A., Parisi, D., & Plunkett, K. (1996). *Rethinking innateness: A connectionist perspective on development.* Cambridge, MA: MIT Press.

Enard, W., Przeworski, M., Fisher, S. E., Lai, C. S. L., Wiebe, V., Kitano, T., et al. (2002). Molecular evolution of FOXP2, a gene involved in speech and language. *Nature, 418,* 869–872.

Falk, D. (in press). Prelinguistic evolution in early hominins: Whence motherese. *Behavioral and Brain Sciences.*

Ferrari, P. F., Gallese, V., Rizzolatti, G., & Fogassi, L. (2003). Mirror neurons responding to the observation of ingestive and communicative mouth actions in the monkey ventral premotor cortex. *European Journal of Neuroscience, 17,* 1703–1714.

Givon, T. (2002). The visual information system as an evolutionary precursor to human language. In T. Givon & B. F. Malle (Eds.), *The evolution of language out of pre-language* (pp. 3–50). Amsterdam: John Benjamins.

Goldin-Meadow, S., & MacNeill, D. (1999). The role of gesture and mimetic representation in making language the province of speech. In M. C. Corballis & S. E. G. Lea (Eds.), *The descent of mind* (pp. 155–172). Oxford, England: Oxford University Press.

Goldman, H. I. (2001). Parental reports of 'MAMA' sounds in infants: An exploratory study. *Journal of Child Language, 28,* 497–506.

Gopnik, A. (1999). Theory of mind. In R. A. Wilson & F. Keil (Eds.), *The MIT encyclopedia of the cognitive sciences* (pp. 838–840). Cambridge, MA: MIT Press.

Gopnik, M., & Crago, M. (1991). Familial aggregation of a developmental language disorder. *Cognition, 39,* 1–50.

Hauser, M. D. (1996). *The evolution of communication.* Cambridge, MA: MIT Press.

Hauser, M. D., Chomsky, N., & Fitch, W. T. (2002). The faculty of language: What is it, who has it, and how did it evolve? *Science, 298,* 1569–1579.

Heine, B., & Kuteva, T. (2002). On the evolution of grammatical forms. In A. Wray (Ed.), *The transition to language* (pp. 376–398). Cambridge, England: Cambridge University Press.

Hewes, G. W. (1973). Primate communication and the gestural origins of language. *Current Anthropology, 14,* 5–24.

Hewes, G. (1996). A history of the study of language origins and the gestural primacy hypothesis. In A. Lock & C. R. Peters (Eds.), *Handbook of human symbolic evolution* (pp. 571–595). Oxford, England: Clarendon Press.

Hickok, G., Bellugi, U., & Klima, E. (1996). The neurobiology of sign language and its implications for the neural basis of language. *Nature, 381,* 699–702.

Hockett, C. F. (1978). In search of Jove's brow. *American Speech, 53,* 243–319.

Hohenberger, A., Happ, D., & Leuninger, H. (2002). Modality-dependent aspects of sign language production: Evidence from slips of the hands and their repairs in German sign language. In R. Meier, K. Cormier, & D. Quinto-Pozos (Eds.), *Modality and structure in signed and spoken language* (pp. 112–142). Cambridge, England: Cambridge University Press.

Hook-Costigan, M. A., & Rogers, L. J. (1998). Lateralized use of the mouth in production of vocalizations by marmosets. *Neuropsychologia, 36,* 1265–1273.

Humphrey, N. (1976). The social function of intellect. In P. G. Bateson & R. A. Hinde (Eds.), *Growing points in ethology* (pp. 303–317). Cambridge, England: Cambridge University Press.

Hurford, J. R., Studdert-Kennedy, M., & Knight, C. (1998). *Approaches to the evolution of language: Social and cognitive bases.* Cambridge, England: Cambridge University Press.

Jackendoff, R. (2002). *Foundations of language: Brain, meaning, grammar, evolution.* Oxford, England: Oxford University Press.

Kimura, D. (1979). Neuromotor mechanisms in the evolution of human communication. In H. D. Steklis & M. J. Raleigh (Eds.), *Neurobiology of social communication in Primates* (pp. 197–220). New York: Academic Press.

Klima, E. S., & Bellugi, U. (1979). *The signs of language.* Cambridge, MA: Harvard University Press.

Kluender, K. R., Diehl, R., & Killeen, P. R. (1987). Japanese quail can learn phonetic categories. *Science, 237,* 1195–1197.

Knight, C., Studdert-Kennedy, M. G., & Hurford, J. R. (2000a). *The evolutionary emergence of language.* Cambridge, England: Cambridge University Press.

Knight, C., Studdert-Kennedy, M. G., & Hurford, J. R. (2000b). Language: A darwinian adaptation. In C. Knight, M. G. Studdert-Kennedy, & J. R. Hurford (Eds.), *The evolutionary emergence of language* (pp. 1–15). Cambridge, England: Cambridge University Press.

Lai, C., Gerrelli, D., Monacom, A. P., Fisher, S. E., & Copp, A. J. (2003). FOXP2 expression during brain development coincides with adult sites of pathology in a severe speech and language disorder. *Brain, 126,* 1–8.

Lashley, K. S. (1951). The problem of serial order in behavior. In L. A. Jeffress (Ed.), *Cerebral mechanisms in behavior* (pp. 112–136). New York: Wiley.

Levelt, W. J. M. (1992). Accessing words in speech production: Stages, processes and representations. *Cognition, 42,* 1–22.

Levelt, W. J. M. (1999). Producing spoken language: A blueprint of the speaker. In C. M. Brown & P. Hagoort (Eds.), *The neurocognition of language* (pp. 83–166). Oxford, England: Oxford University Press.

Liberman, A. M., & Mattingly, I. G. (1985). The motor theory of speech perception revised. *Cognition, 21,* 1–36.

Lieberman, P. (1984). *The biology and evolution of language.* Cambridge, MA: Harvard University Press.

Lieven, E., Behrens, H., Speares, J., & Tomasello, M. (2003). Early syntactic creativity: A usage-based approach. *Journal of Child Language, 30,* 333–370.

Lindblom, B. (1986). Phonetic universals in vowel systems. In J. J. Ohala & J. J. Jaeger (Eds.), *Experimental phonology* (pp. 13–37). Orlando, FL: Academic Press.

Lock, A., & Peters, C. R. (Eds.). (1996). *Handbook of human symbolic evolution.* Oxford, England: Clarendon Press.

MacNeilage, P. F. (1998a). Evolution of mechanisms of language output: Comparative neurobiology of vocal and manual communication. In J. R. Hurford, M. Studdert-Kennedy, & C. Knight (Eds.), *Approaches to the evolution of language: Social and cognitive bases* (pp. 222–241). Cambridge, England: Cambridge University Press.

MacNeilage, P. F. (1998b). The frame/content theory of evolution of speech production. *Behavioral and Brain Sciences, 21,* 499–546.

MacNeilage, P. F., & Davis, B. L. (1990). Acquisition of speech: Frames, then content. In M. Jeannerod (Ed.), *Attention and performance X111* (pp. 453–476). Hillsdale, NJ: Erlbaum.

MacNeilage, P. F., & Davis, B. L. (2000). Origin of the internal structure of word forms. *Science, 288,* 527–531.

MacNeill, D. (1992). *Hand and mind: What gestures reveal about thought.* Chicago: University of Chicago Press.

Murdock, G. P. (1959). Cross-language parallels in parental kin terms. *Anthropological Linguistics, 1,* 1–5.

Newman, A. J., Bavelier, D., Corina, D., Zezzard, P., & Neville, H. J. (2002). A critical period for right hemisphere recruitment in American Sign Language processing. *Nature Neuroscience, 5,* 76–80.

Newmayer, F. (1998). *Language form and language function.* Cambridge, MA: MIT Press.

Newmayer, F. (2002). Uniformitarian assumptions and language evolution research. In A. Wray (Ed.), *The transition to language* (pp. 359–375). Cambridge, England: Cambridge University Press.

Pettito, L. A., Holowka, S., Sergio, L. E., & Ostry, D. (2001). Language rhythms in baby hand movements. *Nature, 413,* 35.

Pinker, S. (1994). *The language instinct.* New York: Morrow.

Pinker, S., & Bloom, P. (1992). Natural language and natural selection. In J. H. Barkow, L. Cosmides, & J. Tooby (Eds.), *The adapted mind* (pp. 451–494). Oxford, England: Oxford University Press.

Poizner, H., Klima, E., & Bellugi, U. (1987). *What the hands reveal about the brain.* Cambridge, MA: MIT Press.

Poremba, A., Malloy, M., Saunders, R. E., Carson, R. E., Herscovitch, P., & Mishkin, M. (2004). Species-specific calls evoke asymmetric activity in the monkey's temporal poles. *Nature, 427,* 448–451.

Radinsky, L. B. (1987). *The evolution of vertebrate design.* Chicago: University of Chicago Press.

Ridley, M. (2003). *Nature via nurture.* New York: HarperCollins.

Rizzolatti, G., & Arbib, M. A. (1998). Language within our grasp. *Trends in Neurosciences, 21,* 188–194.

Rizzolatti, G., Fogassi, L., & Gallese, V. (2000). Cortical mechanisms subserving object grasping and action recognition: A new view of cortical motor functions. In M. S. Gazzaniga (Ed.), *The new cognitive neurosciences* (pp. 539–552). Cambridge, MA: MIT Press.

Rousett, I. (2003, August). From lexical to syllabic organization: Favored and disfavored co-occurrences. *Proceedings of the 15 International Congress of Phonetics, Barcelona, Vol. 1* 715–718.

Sandler, W., & Lillo-Martin, D. (2001). Natural sign languages. In M. Aronoff (Ed.), *The Blackwell handbook of linguistics* (pp. 533–562). Oxford, England: Blackwell.

Shattuck-Hufnagel, S. (1979). Speech errors as evidence for a serial ordering mechanism in sentence production. In W. E. Cooper & E. C. T. Walker (Eds.), *Sentence processing: Psycholinguistic studies presented to Merrill Garrett* (pp. 295–342). Hillsdale, NJ: Erlbaum.

Singer, W. (1989). The brain's self organizing learning system. In K. A. Klivington (Ed.), *The science of mind* (pp. 174–180). New York: MIT Press.

Stent, G. (1981). Strength and weakness of the genetic approach to the development of the nervous system. *Annual Review of Neuroscience, 4,* 163–194.

Studdert-Kennedy, M. G., Knight, C., & Hurford, J. R. (1998). In J. R. Hurford, M. Studdert-Kennedy, & C. Knight (Eds.), *Approaches to the evolution of language: Social and cognitive bases* (p. 4). Cambridge, England: Cambridge University Press.

Studdert-Kennedy, M. G., & Lane, H. (1980). Clues from the difference between signed and spoken languages. In U. Bellugi & M. G. Studdert-Kennedy (Eds.), *Biological constraints on linguistic form* (pp. 29–40). Berlin, Germany: Verlag Chemie.

Tinbergen, N. (1963). On the aims and methods of ethology. *Zeitschrift fur Tierpsychologie, 20,* 410–433.

Tomasello, M. (1998). Introduction: A cognitive-functional perspective on language structure. In M. Tomasello (Ed.), *The new psychology of language: Cognitive and functional approaches to language structure* (pp. vii–xxiii). Mahwah, NJ: Erlbaum.

Tomasello, M. (2002). The emergence of grammar in early child language. In T. Givon & B. F. Malle (Eds.), *The evolution of language out of pre-language* (pp. 309–328). Amsterdam: John Benjamins.

Toth, N. (1985). Archeological evidence for preferential right handedness in the lower and middle pleistocene and its possible implications. *Journal of Human Evolution, 14,* 607–614.

Van Hooff, J. A. R. A. M. (1967). Facial displays of the catarrhine monkeys and apes. In D. Morris (Ed.), *Primate ethology* (pp. 7–68). London: Weidenfield and Nicholson.

Van Valin, R., & LaPolla, R. (1997). *Syntax: Structure, meaning, and function.* Cambridge, England: Cambridge University Press.

Vargha-Khadem, F., Watkins, K., Alcock, K., Fletcher, P., & Passingham, R. (1995). Praxic and non-verbal cognitive deficits in a large family with a genetically transmitted speech and language disorder. *Proceedings of the National Academy of Sciences, 92,* 930–933.

Wray, A. (Ed.). (2002). *The transition to language.* Cambridge, England: Cambridge University Press.

CHAPTER 25

The Evolution of Cognitive Bias

MARTIE G. HASELTON, DANIEL NETTLE, and PAUL W. ANDREWS

Humans, like other animals, see the world through the lens of evolved adaptations. In vision, for example, the experience of color is mediated by the adaptations of the eye, which in the human case uses wavelengths of electromagnetic radiation between about 380 and 760 nanometers, allowing us to see hues ranging from red to violet. But, there are other possible colors on earth. Recent work on bird species demonstrates that "blue" tits are actually ultraviolet (Hunt, Bennett, Cuthill, & Griffiths, 1998). The feathers of the male blue tit reflect ultraviolet radiation (300 to 400 nm), and females display a preference for males with the brightest ultraviolet crests (Hunt et al., 1998). Some reptiles, such as rattlesnakes, see light in the infrared range (see Goldsmith, 1990, for a review). Color is not an inherent property of an object; it is constructed by the interaction of reflected radiation in the environment with evolved visual mechanisms in the perceiver (Bennett, Cuthill, & Norris, 1994).

Using faculties of social perception, humans construct images of the social world in similar ways. Like color, sexual attractiveness is not a feature of the world that preexists the mechanisms that perceive it, and what is sexually attractive varies depending on the perceiver. Within humans, what appears attractive in a man depends on adaptively relevant variables that differ between female perceivers and within individual perceivers at different points in time. Women who are higher in physical attractiveness themselves find facially masculine men more attractive than do less attractive women (Little, Burt, Penton-Voak, & Perrett, 2001). Even more dramatic, women's ratings of men's attractiveness vary across the menstrual cycle, with more facially masculine men preferred near ovulation and less masculine men preferred at other times (Penton-Voak et al., 1999). Thus, a man that a woman sees as particularly attractive on one day might seem less so on another, even though he has not changed at all.

We are grateful to David Buss for generous editorial feedback and for pointing out the auditory looming phenomenon and the idea that outbreaks of disease evoke error management biases. Thanks also to Craig Fox and David Funder for helpful comments on an earlier draft of this chapter.

It appears that the "there" of familiar experience is one that the mind has a role in constructing. The mind translates the properties of the world, such as electromagnetic radiation and the contours of objects, into useful units of information. One of the most dramatic demonstrations of the role of the mind in our apprehension of the world is the existence of cognitive biases. A wide range of biases, which we review in the next section, has been discovered by psychologists. Where biases exists, individuals draw inferences or adopt beliefs where the evidence for doing so in a logically sound manner is either insufficient or absent.

As well as being interesting in their own right, biases are important to study because they often reveal the design of the mind. In this chapter, we present a three-category framework for understanding cognitive biases from an evolutionary perspective, and we discuss what biases in each category can tell us about the evolved mind. We conclude by describing the implications of this evolutionary psychological perspective on biases. For example, the functional specificity of these biases reveals the intricacy of the mind's design and supports the key hypothesis that the mechanisms of mind are domain-specific. The conclusion that many biases are not the result of constraints or mysterious irrationalities also speaks to the ongoing debate about human rationality. Our perspective suggests that biases often are not *design flaws*, but *design features.*

THE EVOLUTIONARY FOUNDATIONS OF COGNITIVE BIAS

"Rational" decision-making methods . . . logic, mathematics, probability theory . . . are computationally weak: incapable of solving the natural adaptive problems our ancestors had to solve reliably in order to reproduce. . . . This poor performance on most natural problems is the primary reason why problem-solving specializations were favored by natural selection over general-purpose problem-solvers. Despite widespread claims to the contrary, the human mind is not worse than rational . . . but may often be better than rational.

—Cosmides & Tooby, 1994, p. 329

Cognitive biases present something of a challenge to the evolutionary psychologist. Because they depart from standards of logic and accuracy, they appear to be design flaws instead of examples of good engineering. Cognitive traits can be evaluated according to any number of performance criteria (logical sufficiency, accuracy, speed of processing, etc.), and the value of a criterion depends on the question the scientist is asking. The question facing the evolutionary scientist is to identify whether a feature has been shaped by selection and, if so, to determine what its function is. Often the scientist has information about only what the feature does— its effects. However, selection often generates a tight fit between the design features and their effects. To the evolutionary psychologist, therefore, the evaluative task is not whether the cognitive feature is accurate or logical, but how well it solves a particular problem relative to other problems that it could potentially solve (i.e., whether the trait solves a problem with proficiency and specificity).

In evolutionary psychology, proficiency and specificity interact in the concept of *domain specificity.* As Tooby and Cosmides (1992) and others have argued, it is likely that the mind is equipped with function-specific mechanisms adapted for special purposes—mechanisms with special design for solving problems of mating, which are separate, at least in part, from those involved in solving problems of food choice, predator avoidance, and social exchange (see Boyer & Barrett, Chapter 3, this volume). In the evaluation of cognitive biases, demonstrating domain specificity in solving a particular problem is a part of building a case that the trait has been shaped by selection to perform that function. The evolved function of the eye, for instance, is to facilitate sight because it does this well (it exhibits proficiency), the features of the eye have the common and unique effect of facilitating sight (it exhibits specificity), and there are no plausible alternative hypotheses that account for the eye's features.

Some design features that appear to be flaws when viewed in one way are revealed to be adaptations when viewed differently. If we only consider the fact that high fevers make people feel miserable, and in extreme cases can lead to death, the capacity to develop fever appears a terrible flaw in design. However, if we ask what the evolved function of fever is, we come to learn that elevated body temperature may be a natural defense against pathogens. This hypothesis led to research showing that fever-reducing medicines increase susceptibility to infection and prolong its resolution, thus challenging the common use of aspirin as a treatment for upper respiratory infections and influenza (see Williams & Nesse, 1991, for a review). Viewed in light of evolution, the capacity for fever may in fact be well-designed.

In sum, there may be many evolutionary reasons for apparent design flaws, and a close examination often provides insight into the evolutionary forces that shaped them and their functions. We propose that analogous logic may be applied to understanding cognitive biases. Cognitive biases can arise for three reasons: (1) Selection may discover useful shortcuts that tend to work in most circumstances, though they fall short of some normative standards (heuristics); (2) biases can arise if biased solutions to adaptive problems resulted in lower error costs than unbiased ones (error management biases); and (3) apparent biases can arise if the task at hand is not one for which the mind is designed (artifacts). Table 25.1 presents this

Table 25.1
Evolutionary Taxonomy of Cognitive Biases

Type of Bias	Examples
Heuristic: Bias results from evolutionary or information processing constraints; mechanisms work well in most circumstances, but are prone to break down in systematic ways.	1. Use of stereotypes 2. Fundamental attribution "error" 3. One-reason decision strategies
Error management bias: Selection favored bias toward the less costly error; although error rates are increased, net costs are reduced.	1. Auditory looming (Figure 1) 2. Sexual overperception by men (Figure 2) 3. Commitment underperception by women (Figure 3) 4. Positive illusions
Artifact: Apparent biases and errors are artifacts of research strategies; they result from the application of inappropriate normative standards or placement of humans in unnatural settings.	1. Some instances of base-rate neglect in statistical prediction 2. Some instances of the confirmation bias

taxonomy. We do not intend these categories to be fully exhaustive or mutually exclusive; we do propose that they are a useful way of organizing research on cognitive bias and gaining insight into why biases occur.

HEURISTICS

Perhaps the most commonly invoked explanation for bias is that they are a by-product of processing limitations—because information processing time and ability are limited, humans must use shortcuts or rules of thumb that are prone to breakdown in systematic ways. This explanation for biases can be traced in large part to the influential work of Kahneman and Tversky (e.g., Tversky & Kahneman, 1974; see Gilovich, Griffin, & Kahneman, 2002, for a recent review; see Kahneman, 2003, for a recent theoretical treatment). Kahneman and Tversky demonstrated that human judgments often departed substantially from normative standards based on probability theory or simple logic. In judging the sequences of coin flips, for example, people assessed the sequence HTHTTH to be more likely than the sequence HHHTTT or HHHHTH. As Tversky and Kahneman (1974) pointed out, while in some sense representative, the first sequence contains too many alternations and too few runs. The "gambler's fallacy" is the expression of a similar intuition. The more bets lost, the more the gambler feels a win is now due, even though each new turn is independent of the last (Tversky & Kahneman, 1974).

Another example is the famous "Linda problem" (Tversky & Kahneman, 1983). Subjects read a personality description: "Linda is 31 years old, single, outspoken, and very bright. She majored in philosophy. As a student, she was deeply concerned with issues of discrimination and social justice and participated in anti-nuclear demonstrations." They were then asked to determine which of two options was more probable: (a) Linda is a bank teller or (b) Linda is a bank teller and active in the feminist movement. Although the conjunction cannot be more likely than either of its constituents, between 80% and 90% of subjects tend to select (b) as the more probable option. Tversky and Kahneman (1983) dubbed this effect the "conjunction fallacy."

Tversky and Kahneman attributed these and other biases to the operation of mental shortcuts: "People rely on a limited number of heuristic principles which reduce the complex tasks of assessing probabilities and predicting values to simpler judgmental operations" (1974, p. 1124). The gambler's fallacy and the conjunction fallacy are attributed to one of the most commonly invoked heuristics, *representativeness*, or the way in which A resembles or is representative of B. According to this account, alternating heads and tails is more representative of randomness than are series containing runs. The description of Linda is representative of a feminist; thus participants choose feminist and bank teller rather than bank teller alone.

EFFECTS OF TIME AND MOTIVATION

The notion that biases result from the use of simplifying heuristics has logical appeal. As expressed by Arkes (1991), "The extra effort required to use a more sophisticated strategy is a cost that often outweighs the potential benefit of enhanced accuracy" (pp. 486–487). This cost can affect the evolution of cognitive mechanisms at two levels: (1) There may be costs in evolutionary terms because the development of certain brain circuits will either increase the length of ontogeny or remove potential energetic allocation away from the development of other mechanisms, and (2) there may be costs in real time because decisions using complex algorithms will take longer or require more attentional resources than decisions using simpler alternatives. Adaptive decisions often need to be made fast, and this may well constrain the type of strategies that are optimal. Evidence from a variety of sources demonstrates that people do indeed solve problems differently when under time pressure or when their motivations to be accurate are reduced.

Fiske (1993) proposed that the social perceptions of individuals occupying positions of higher power in social hierarchies are less accurate than those lower in the hierarchy. Those higher in power are more likely to endorse stereotypes about others than to attend to individuating information specific to the target being evaluated, which presumably enhances accuracy (Goodwin, Gubin, Fiske, & Yzerbyt, 2000). Individuals assigned more decision-making power in reviewing internship applications attend more to stereotype consistent information and less to stereotype disconfirming information (Goodwin et al., 2000). Similarly, in a study of two student groups competing for university funding, Ebenbach and Keltner (1998) found that individuals reporting more personal power judged their opponents' attitudes less accurately. A common interpretation of findings such as these is that lower power individuals occupy a more precarious social position and must, therefore, allocate more time and energy to social judgments; more powerful individuals enjoy the luxury of allocating their cognitive efforts elsewhere (Keltner, Gruenfeld, & Anderson, 2003).

Some of the best evidence for cognitive heuristics comes from the abundant literature on the *fundamental attribution error* (FAE). The FAE occurs when people are asked to make an inference about the mental state or underlying disposition of an actor. Although there are differences of opinion about the precise nature of the FAE (e.g., Sabini, Siepmann, & Stein, 2001), a relatively descriptive account is that people tend to infer that an actor's internal state corresponds to expressed behavior more than appears to be logically warranted by the situation (Andrews, 2001; Ross, 1977).

In the classic experiment, Jones and Harris (1967) gave subjects either a pro-Castro essay or an anti-Castro essay purportedly written by a student. In one set of variants (the choice variants), subjects were merely told that the student wrote the essay as part of a class. In the other variants (the no-choice variants), subjects were told that the professor assigned the student either the pro-Castro or the anti-Castro stance. In both variants, the corresponding inference is that the writer actually believes in the stance. In the no-choice variants, the situation suggests that the writer is less likely to believe in the stance than in the choice variants. Jones and Harris predicted that subjects would be agnostic about the writer's actual beliefs in the no-choice condition. However, subjects tended to make the corresponding inference even in the no-choice conditions—the so-called fundamental attribution error.

The FAE may result from a frugal cognitive heuristic that is usually effective. For example, personality does indeed exist, and when people make personality inferences, even about people with whom they have had only brief interactions, they have some predictive validity (e.g., Colvin & Funder, 1991). If the FAE is the result of a frugal cognitive heuristic, one prediction is that it should take cognitive effort to avoid it. People who avoid the FAE do take longer on the task (Yost & Weary, 1996), and they are more likely to commit the FAE under conditions of cognitive load (Trope & Alfieri, 1997). A second prediction is that incentives for more refined judgments should diminish reliance on the heuristic. Indeed, people are less likely to make the FAE when they are told they will be held accountable for their attributions (Tetlock, 1985) or when they are given a monetary incentive for making correct attributions (Vonk, 1999). Moreover, people in more interdependent societies (e.g., China or Korea) are less likely to make the FAE than people in the United States or Europe (Norenzayan, Choi, & Nisbett, 2002). A possible explanation is that greater interdependency makes it more important to make accurate attributions of others' mental states and internal dispositions (Neuberg & Fiske, 1987).

EFFECTIVENESS OF HEURISTICS

Heuristics and biases research has generated much debate, for example, about the ecological validity of the problems, the conclusions to be drawn about the adequacy of everyday decision making, and the precision of the heuristics proposed (Gigerenzer, 1996, 2000; Hertwig & Gigerenzer, 1999; Kahneman & Tversky, 1996; see also Biases as Artifacts section). From an evolutionary psychology perspective, though, what is of interest is the broad consensus that human decision making relies on a repertoire of simple, fast, heuristic decision rules to be used in specific situations. Much experimental work has focused on the cases where these rules lead to illogicality or error, but the assumption is that over a broad range of fitness-relevant past scenarios, they were highly effective.

The direct demonstration of the effectiveness of heuristic decision rules has only just begun. Gigerenzer and Goldstein (1996) showed that a family of simple decision-making rules that uses only one datum can work as well or better than more complex algorithms that use all available information, for example, the *recognition heuristic*. When asked to make judgments about which of two alternatives will be higher on some criterion variable (e.g., who will succeed in a sports contest or which city is larger), someone who uses the heuristic will choose the alternative that is most familiar. For example, when asked which city has a larger population, San Diego or San Antonio, German students tend to guess right: San Diego (Goldstein & Gigerenzer, 1999). Paradoxically, American students tend to get it wrong. This is the *less-is-more effect*—American students cannot use recognition because both cities are known, so they rely on other cues, which are often invalid.

Gigerenzer and Goldstein (1996) augmented these surprising results with formal simulations that pitted one-reason heuristics, in this case, the *take-the-best* algorithm, against computationally sophisticated algorithms suggested by other cognitive scientists. *Take-the-best* assumes a decision tree structure. It starts with recognition. If recognition is a predictor of the criterion variable and one item in the decision task is recognized but the other is not, the recognized option is selected. If recognition does not apply (e.g., both options are recognized), then you move to the next step in the tree, searching memory for the most valid cue that discriminates between the alternatives. If the cue has a positive value for one alternative but not for the other, *take-the-best* is completed. If both have a positive cue value, the next cue is retrieved from memory, and so on. The algorithm is fast because it is relatively simple, and it is frugal because it looks up only as much information as it needs. And, surprisingly, it performs as well or better than classically optimal algorithms that use all of the information available to the decision maker (e.g., multiple regression).

These results offer an existence proof. Decision-making adaptations can be simple but still as effective as complex strategies on real-world tasks. If researchers in the laboratory can exploit reliable features of the informational environment to create simple but highly effective reasoning strategies, natural selection can do so as well. Because selection has shaped different decision strategies for different adaptive problems, it seems unlikely that there is a single, general *take-the-best* or *recognition* adaptation. Rather, these simple strategies, and others like them, form the armamentarium that natural selection has tended to use in creating decision-making adaptations. We propose that combinations of these strategies are used by an array of distinct, domain-specific, evolved mental mechanisms. (For two interesting examples in the mate selection context, see Dugatkin, 1996; Miller & Todd, 1998.)

In sum, there is ample evidence of cognitive bias and error in humans. Some of these biases may result from the use of shortcuts, which are often effective. There is also evidence that relaxing constraints or increasing motivation for accuracy can improve reasoning in some domains. For these effects, it is important to note that the constraints explanation is not complete. Why are these biases the defaults? We have suggested that dispositional inference may be the default because personality has predictive power (also see Haselton & Buss, 2003). In the following section, we further suggest that the direction and content of biases is not arbitrary. Although these biases might arise in part because of the mind's limited computational power, the particular forms they assume serve the fitness interests of the perceiver (also see Kenrick & Maner, in press; Krebs & Denton, 1997).

ERROR MANAGEMENT BIASES

Laboratory research on "error" . . . attracts much attention because it appears to have dismal implications for social reasoning. These implications are illusory, however, because an error is not the same thing as a "mistake."

—Funder (1987)

ERROR MANAGEMENT THEORY

Error management theory (EMT; Haselton & Buss, 2000; Haselton & Nettle, 2004) applies the principles of signal detection theory (Green & Swets, 1966) to judgment tasks to make predictions about evolved cognitive design. The central idea is that any cognitive mechanism can produce two types of error: a false positive (adopting a belief that is false) and a false negative (failing to adopt a belief that is true). The equivalents couched in perceptual terms are detecting a stimulus that does not exist (false positive) and failing to detect a stimulus that is real (false negative), but the logic is the same in either formulation.

On the face of it, it would seem that an optimal mechanism would make no errors of either type. However, many real-world tasks of judgment are probabilistic and, therefore, include an irreducible amount of uncertainty. Auditory judgment, for example, is rendered uncertain by the presence of ambient noise, and some error is likely to occur however good the mechanism.

Crucially, the consequences for the organism of making the two types of error may not be the same. Fleeing from an area that contains no predator may be inconvenient but is much less costly than the failure to detect a predator that really is close by. EMT predicts that an optimal decision rule will minimize not the crude rate of error, but the net effect of error on fitness. Where one error is consistently more damaging to fitness than the other, EMT predicts that a bias toward making the less costly error will evolve; it is better to make *more* errors overall as long as they are of the relatively cheap kind. The magnitude and direction of bias are predicted to be affected by two factors: the asymmetry of the cost of the two errors (the bias will be toward making the less costly error, and larger asymmetries produce larger biases) and the amount of uncertainty in the task (biases are expected only when judgments are uncertain). For mathematical formalism of this logic and the expectations of EMT, see Haselton and Nettle (2004).

We have argued that many apparent biases may reflect the operation of mechanisms designed to make inexpensive, frequent errors rather than occasional disastrous ones (Haselton & Nettle, 2004). Table 25.2 on pages 732–733 provides examples by outlining the domain in which the effect occurs, the hypothesized costs of errors, and the expected outcome. In the following subsections, we discuss each of the entries in Table 25.2 along with other illustrative effects (for a complete review and analysis, see Haselton & Nettle, 2004).

PROTECTIVE BIASES

Broadly speaking, the possible error management effects we have identified fall into three somewhat overlapping clusters. The first are physically protective biases.

Auditory Looming   A perceptual example is *auditory looming* (Neuhoff, 2001). People judge a sound that is rising in intensity to be closer, and approaching more rapidly, than an equidistant sound that is falling in intensity. In a series of experiments involving speakers moving on cables, Neuhoff (2001) shows that auditory looming leads to biased perceptions of the proximity of moving sound sources, as well as a general tendency to underestimate the distance of sound sources. Subjects judge an approaching sound source to be closer by than a receding one, when in fact they are located at distances equally far away from the subject (see Figure 25.1 on p. 734). There is a clear error management interpretation of this effect: It is better to be ready for an approaching object too early than too late (Neuhoff, 2001).

Allergy, Cough, and Anxiety   Nesse (2001) argued for the *smoke detector principle* in bodily systems designed to protect from harm. He describes medical examples such as allergy and cough where a protective system is often mobilized in the absence of real threat. These defense systems appear to be overresponsive. Dampening them with drugs or treatment actually results in few troublesome effects on the recipient (Nesse, 2001). Psychological defense mechanisms such as anxiety are also easily evoked, especially in connection with things likely to have been dangerous in the ancestral environment, such as spiders, snakes, and potentially

Table 25.2
A Selection of Adaptive Biases

Category and Domain	False Positive (FP)	Costs of FP	False Negative (FN)	Costs of FN	Result
Protective: Approaching sounds	Ready too early	Low	Struck by source	High	Bias toward underestimating time to arrival
Protective: Foodstuffs	Eat a food type that is safe	Low	Ingest toxin or pathogen	High	Bias toward acquiring permanent aversion on the basis of one piece of evidence of toxicity
Protective: Diseased persons	Avoid noninfectious person	May be low, depending on relationship	Become infected	Often very high	Tendency to avoid persons with physical afflictions, even if noninfectious
Social: Men's inference of female sexual interest	Inferring sexual interest where there is none	Rejection—relatively low	Inferring no interest when there is interest	Missed reproductive opportunity—high	Sexual overperception by men
Social: Women's inference of commitment	Inferring interest to commit where there is none	Desertion—high	Inferring unwillingness to commit where there is willingness	Delayed start to reproduction—relatively low	Underperception of commitment by women.

Social: Social exchange	Attempt to free ride and get caught	Potential ostracism, especially in collectivist social situations—high	Cooperate when one could free ride	Give up an unnecessary benefit in exchange—relatively low	Bias toward cooperation
Self and Future: Beliefs about future achievements	Believe you can achieve things when you cannot	Low (if costs of failure are low)	Believe you cannot achieve things when you could	High (if benefit of success is high)	Optimistic bias (where benefits of success exceed costs of failure)
Self and Future: Control of events	Believe you control events that you have no control over	Low (if control behavior is inexpensive)	Believe your behavior ineffective when it is effective	Leads to passivity; potentially high	Illusion of control, superstitions

Adapted from *The Evolution of the Paranoid Optimist: An Integrative Model of Cognitive Biases*, by M. G. Haselton and D. Nettle, 2004, Manuscript under review, University of California, Los Angeles.

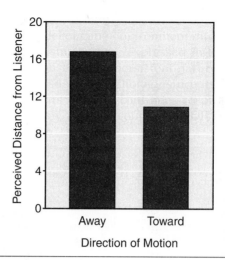

Figure 25.1 Auditory Looming. Subjects estimated the distance of sound sources that were moving away from them and toward them. The sources were of equal intensity and were, on average, equally far away. The true mean distance was 20 feet, and thus there was a tendency toward underestimation in general as well as a specific bias for approaching sound sources. *Source:* From "An Adaptive Bias in the Perception of Looming Auditory Motion," by J. G. Neuhoff, 2001, *Ecological Psychology, 13,* pp. 87–110.

dangerous persons (Mineka, 1992; Seligman, 1971; Tomarken, Mineka, & Cook, 1989). A tendency for anxiety mechanisms to produce false positives is a plausible explanation for the observed prevalence of phobias and anxiety disorders (Nesse, 2001).

Food Aversions Food aversions may be similarly biased. Lasting aversion to a food is reliably acquired, in humans and other species, following a single incidence of sickness after ingestion (Garcia, Hankins, & Rusiniak, 1976; Rozin & Kalat, 1971). Given one data point (sickness followed the food type on one occasion), the system treats the food as if it is always illness inducing. There are again two possible errors here: The false positive may be inconvenient, but the false negative is more likely to be fatal. The system appears biased toward overresponsiveness to avoid illness.

Aversion to Diseased or Injured Persons Similar logic predicts an aversion to the ill. Little evidence of illness or contamination is required to provoke avoidance of a person, whereas much stronger evidence is required to warrant the inference that someone is safe or free from disease (Kurzban & Leary, 2001; Park, Faulkner, & Schaller, 2003). The error management account is similar to that for food aversions: The false negative (failing to avoid someone with a contagious disease) is highly costly, whereas the false positive (avoiding contact with a noncontagious person) may be inconvenient but is unlikely to be injurious. Thus, disease-avoidance mechanisms will be biased and tend to evince disgust and avoidance at many stimuli that are safe (e.g., deformity as a result of injury rather than disease). Such a bias may well be involved in the panics associated with outbreaks of diseases such as SARS and Mad Cow disease, when more mundane risks nearer to home may be far greater objective dangers.

BIASES IN INTERPERSONAL PERCEPTION

The second cluster of biases concerns interpersonal perception. Some of these apply to both men and women, whereas others are sex-specific. EMT predicts differential effects of sex in those domains where the costs and benefits of an outcome differ reliably between the sexes—domains that include, most obviously, mating and its consequences.

Sexual Overperception　Courtship communications are often ambiguous. Does a smile convey mere friendliness, for example, or does it mean more? Haselton and Buss (2000) proposed that men possess a bias in interpreting cues to a woman's sexual interest. For ancestral men, they argued, it would have been more costly in reproductive currency to miss a woman's sexual interest than to overestimate it. In the evolutionary past, men's reproduction was limited primarily by the number of women of reproductive age to whom they were able to gain sexual access (Buss, 1994; Symons, 1979; Trivers, 1972). Men who were more often successful in mating with greater numbers of women tended to outreproduce their fellow male competitors. For women, partner number played a smaller role in reproduction. Because of their relatively heavy investment in each offspring produced and long interbirth interval, finding partners with heritable quality and a strong disposition to invest would likely have had a larger impact on reproductive success than would securing additional mating opportunities (Buss, 1994; Symons, 1979; Trivers, 1972). Thus, for men but not women, a missed mating opportunity with a fertile partner because of underestimated sexual interest would have been a high cost fitness error. An overestimation error may have carried some costs (e.g., to reputation), but these costs would have been lower overall. Several sources of evidence support the sexual overperception hypothesis (see Haselton & Buss, 2000, for a review). In initial meetings between male and female strangers, for example, men tend to rate women's flirtatiousness and sexual interest higher than do women (Abbey, 1982). The difference in male and female ratings is obtained when men's ratings are compared to the target woman's self-ratings and when compared to third-party women's ratings of the target woman's sexual interest (Abbey, 1982; Haselton & Buss, 2000). Similar results are obtained in naturalistic studies. Haselton (2003) asked women and men to report past instances of sexual misperception. Women reported more instances in the past year in which men overestimated their sexual interest than in which men underestimated it, suggesting a male sexual overperception bias. Men reported roughly equal numbers of overperception and underperception errors on the part of women, suggesting no bias in women (see Figure 25.2 on p. 736). Recently, Maner and colleagues documented further evidence of sexual overperception in men (Maner et al., in press). They induced romantic arousal, fear, or a neutral emotion state by showing films to study participants. They then asked participants to examine photographs of faces with neutral facial expressions for hidden cues ("micro-expressions") to their actual emotion state. Relative to the other film conditions, in the romantic arousal condition, men

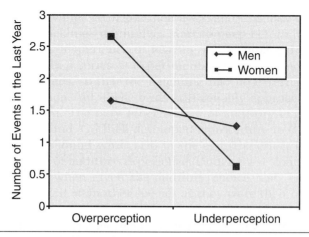

Figure 25.2   Sexual Overperception by Men: Women ($n = 102$) and Men ($n = 114$) Reported Past Experiences in Which a Member of the Opposite Sex Erroneously Inferred Their Sexual Interest. Within the last year, women reported significantly more overperception errors committed by men than underperception errors ($p < .001$), suggesting that men systematically overestimate sexual intent. Men reported roughly equal numbers of overperception and underperception errors committed by women, suggesting no bias in women's sexual inferences ($p > .05$). *Source:* From "The Sexual Overperception Bias: Evidence of a Systematic Bias in Men from a Survey of Naturally Occurring Events," by M. G. Haselton, 2003, *Journal of Research in Personality, 37*, pp. 43–47. Used with permission of Elsevier.

increased their attribution of sexual interest for female faces. They showed no such effect for male faces. After viewing the romantic film, women did not increase attribution of sexual interest for either male or female faces. Conceptually similar sexual overperception effects are observed in the behaviors of males in some bird, insect, and mammalian species (Alcock, 1993, chap. 13; Domjan, Huber-McDonald, & Holloway, 1992).

Commitment Skepticism   The reverse asymmetry may have applied to ancestral women as they decoded men's courtship communications surrounding commitment (Haselton & Buss, 2000). For a woman, inferring long-term commitment interest in a man in whom it was absent could have resulted in postconceptive abandonment, a high cost error associated with lowered offspring survival (Hurtado & Hill, 1992). Underestimating a man's commitment could also result in nontrivial costs such as delaying reproduction, but these costs, Haselton and Buss (2000) hypothesized, would have been lower on average than costs associated with desertion. Women may, therefore, possess a bias toward underestimating men's interest in commitment. Women do indeed rate the level of commitment communicated by male courtship behaviors such as giving of gifts and verbal affirmations of love as lower than do men (Haselton & Buss, 2000). In contrast, women and men tend to agree on the level of commitment communicated by women on the basis of the same behaviors (Haselton & Buss, 2000). In vignette studies, women more than men infer deceptive intentions in a man who is conveying his interest in forming a long-term relationship with a woman he would like to take out on a date (Andrews, 2002; see Figure 25.3).

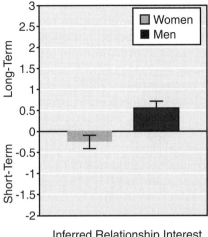

Figure 25.3 Commitment Underperception by Women. Women (*n* = 108) and men (*n* = 60) were asked to evaluate a potentially deceptive scenario. The man in the scenario might be interested in a short-term affair, although he claims to be interested in a long-term relationship. Participants' task was to infer the likelihood that the target man was deceptively interested in a short-term relationship or honestly conveying interest in a long-term relationship. Women (lighter colored bar) inferred greater deception (interest in a short-term relationship only; *p* < .01) than did men. *Source:* From *Attributing Honesty to a Signal Purporting to Reveal Mental State* by P. W. Andrews, June 2002, paper presented at the Human Behavior and Evolution Society Conference, Rutgers, NJ.

Negative Outgroup Stereotypes Humans appear to possess a bias toward inferring that members of competing coalitions (or out-groups) are less generous and kind (Brewer, 1979) and more dangerous and mean (Quillian & Pager, 2001) than are members of their own group. This may be understood as an adaptive bias. For ancestral humans, the costs of falsely assuming peacefulness on the part of an aggressor were likely to outweigh the comparatively low costs of elevated vigilance toward aggression, especially for inferences regarding out-group members. For in-group members, elevated inferences of aggressiveness would have carried the additional costs of within-coalition conflict; hence the negative bias might be expected to be small or nonexistent for in-group members. Schaller and colleagues proposed that cues signaling increased risk of injury, such as ambient darkness, might increase these effects because they raise the costs of failures to detect aggression and protect the self (Schaller, Park, & Mueller, 2003). As predicted, subjects who completed a rating task in a darkened laboratory increased their endorsement of racial and ethnic stereotypes connoting violence, relative to those who participated in a brightly lit room (Schaller et al., 2003). Darkness had no effect on other negative stereotypes of out-group others (e.g., laziness or ignorance; Schaller et al., 2003).

Social Exchange Bias Behavioral economists are puzzled by the fact that people cooperate in economic games with incentive structures favoring defection (Camerer & Thaler, 1995; Caporael, Dawes, Orbell, & van de Kragt, 1989; Henrich et al., 2001; Sally, 1995). In the one-shot prisoner's dilemma game, for example, participants are expected to defect rather than to cooperate. If partner A cooperates while B defects, partner A suffers a greater loss than if he or she had defected. The interaction is not repeated, so there is no incentive to signal cooperativeness, nor is there prior information about reputation that might serve to provide clues about the partner's cooperative disposition. Yet, cooperation often occurs, as it does in other one-shot tasks.

Yamagishi and colleagues hypothesized that cooperation in one-shot games results from the operation of a social exchange bias that manages the costs of errors in social exchange (Yamagishi, Terai, Kiyonari, & Kanazawa, 2003). They propose that the costs of falsely believing one partner can defect without negative social consequences are often higher than cooperating when he or she could safely defect. This asymmetry holds when the costs of "unneeded" cooperation are relatively low (e.g., a low dollar amount is lost) or when the social costs of failing to cooperate (potential ostracism) are high. The costs of ostracism may be particularly high in interdependent social contexts, in which cooperation is either highly valued or especially necessary (Yamagishi, Jin, & Kiyonari, 1999). In Japanese collectivist samples where exchanges are relatively closed to outsiders, cooperation in one-shot experiments is indeed higher than in the more individualist U.S. samples (Yamagishi et al., 1999). Also as predicted, when participants are led to think of the game as an exchange relationship (by making forecasts about their exchange partner's behavior), they cooperate more than when they are not (Yamagishi et al., 2003; see also Savitsky, Epley, & Gillovich, 2001; and Williams, Case, & Govan, 2003; for related predictions).

Note that this bias can be conceptualized as some combination of error management, as in the Yamagishi account, and an artifact of modern living because in an ancestral environment the probability of reencountering individuals would have been high and social reputation effects very potent. Thus, people may be predisposed to expect negative consequences of nonprosocial behavior even when, objectively, such consequences are unlikely to follow. Note, too, that the bias toward prosociality is the subject of competing explanations, which take quite different explanatory stances (Bowles & Gintis, 2002; Gintis, Bowles, Boyd, & Fehr, 2003; Henrich & Boyd, 2001; Price, Cosmides, & Tooby, 2002), and it is unexplored whether these are complementary or competing accounts to the social exchange bias.

BIASES IN SELF-JUDGMENT

The third cluster of biases concerns judgment about the self and personal efficacy. For a complete review, see Haselton and Nettle (2004). Here we briefly discuss the representative example of the *positive illusions*.

Positive Illusions   Positive illusions are a well-known cluster of findings in judgment tasks concerning the self (Taylor & Brown, 1988). Individuals display unrealistically positive perceptions of their own qualities (Alicke, 1985), their likelihood of achieving positive outcomes in the future (Weinstein, 1980), and their degree of control over processes in the environment (Alloy & Abramson, 1979; Rudski, 2000). Two classes of evolutionary explanation have been proposed for such tendencies. First, individuals may have been selected to optimize the impression of their qualities that they display to observers. Given that observers will not be able to accurately assess such qualities directly, individuals may display behaviors that strategically enhance the qualities conveyed (Sedikides, Gaertner, & Toguchi, 2003).

An alternative explanation is in error management terms. Nettle (2004) outlines such an explanation, building on the interpretation of the positive illusions given by Taylor and Brown (1988). In evaluating a possible behavior, there are two possible errors. We may judge that the behavior is worthwhile when in fact it achieves nothing to promote fitness, or we may judge that a behavior is not worthwhile when in fact it would have enhanced fitness to do it. The former error (a false positive) leads to behaviors that are useless, whereas the latter (a false negative) leads to passivity. The costs of the false positive and false negative errors may not be symmetrical—that is, trying and failing may not matter very much, whereas failing to try could be very costly, at least relative to competitors. Thus, evolution can be expected to produce mechanisms biased toward positive illusion in domains where there is uncertainty about outcomes, and the cost of trying and failing is reliably less than that of not trying where success was possible (Nettle, 2004). Note that this account does not predict blanket optimism, but optimism where fitness gains are potentially high relative to the cost of passivity.

The self-enhancement and error management accounts are not mutually exclusive, and it has not been possible to demonstrate their relative importance in producing positive illusions. It may be possible to have them make differential predictions. Take a scenario with some chance of a moderate gain and some chance of extreme physical pain, for example. Impression management would seem to predict an intuition of optimism about the chances of success because it is based on strategic presentation of desirable qualities such as courage and robustness. Error management, however, seems to predict an intuition of pessimism because it is designed to avoid very costly errors under uncertainty. Performance on such tasks could be significantly affected by both sex of respondent and audience presence. Such possibilities await empirical investigation. (For a fuller account of the error management approach and its predictions, see Haselton & Nettle, 2004.)

BIASES AS ARTIFACTS

One criticism of classic heuristics and biases research is that the strategies for identifying bias and evaluating cognitive performance might not be appropriate. Similarly, if problems presented in the laboratory are not those for which the human mind is designed, it should not be surprising that their responses appear to be systematically irrational. In this section, we discuss two general categories of artifact effects: evolutionarily invalid problem formats and evolutionarily invalid problem content.

Problem Formats

Gigerenzer (1997) proposed that tasks intended to assess human statistical prediction should present information in frequency form. Natural frequencies, such as the number of times an event has occurred in a given time period, are more readily observable in nature. Probabilities (in the sense of a number between 0 and 1) are mathematical abstractions beyond sensory input data, and information about the base rates of occurrence is lost when probabilities are computed (Cosmides & Tooby, 1996). Bayesian calculations involving frequencies are, therefore, computationally simpler than equivalent calculations involving probabilities, relative frequencies, or percentages. Whereas probability calculations need to reintroduce information about base rates, frequency calculations do not because this part of the computation is already done within the frequency representation itself (Hoffrage, Lindsey, Hertwig, & Gigerenzer, 2001).

Humans should possess the ability to estimate the likelihood of events given certain cues. If this skill is a part of human reasoning, however, tasks involving probability input are less likely to reveal it than are tasks involving natural frequencies. Indeed, frequency formats do improve performance in tasks like the Linda problem. Whereas a probability format produces violations of the conjunction rule in between 50% and 90% of subjects, frequency formats decrease the rate of error to between 0 and 25% (Fiedler, 1988; Hertwig & Gigerenzer, 1999; Tversky & Kahneman, 1983; also see Cosmides & Tooby, 1996). The frequency interpretation of these results, however, is controversial (e.g., Gigerenzer, 1996; Kahneman & Tversky, 1996). Attempts to rule out competing hypotheses about confounds have generally supported the frequency hypothesis (see Cosmides & Tooby, 1996, experiments 5 and 6; also see Hertwig & Gigerenzer, 1999, experiment 4), but neither perspective appears to perfectly account for all of the available data (see Mellers, Hertwig, & Kahneman, 2001).

A related set of questions has been raised about the conversational pragmatics (see Grice, 1975) of bias-eliciting word problems. Hertwig and Gigerenzer (1999) note that *probability* (or *probable*) in the Linda task is a polysemous term with both mathematical and nonmathematical interpretations. Participants who are asked whether it is more probable that Linda is a *bank teller* or a *feminist bank teller* could infer that the researcher is asking which is a better description of Linda, in which case the conjunction effect is not technically an error. If participants assume that researchers are following maxims of conversational pragmatics, which would lead them to assume that all information provided by the researchers is *relevant* to solving the problem, a mathematical interpretation of the word *probability* is less likely, because it renders the description of Linda's personal commitments irrelevant (Hertwig & Gigerenzer, 1999).

PROBLEM CONTENT

The perspective on cognitive design we have described suggests that researchers should not necessarily expect good performance in tasks involving abstract rules of logic. Falsification-based logic is sufficiently difficult for humans that university courses in logic, statistics, and research design attempt to teach it to students (often with only mixed success). Students have to learn that, in scientific practice, to test hypotheses they must look not only for confirmatory evidence but also for potentially falsifying evidence. If only confirmatory evidence is found, but no falsifying evidence, the hypothesis is supported although it still could be wrong. If even one piece of unambiguous falsifying evidence is found, the hypothesis is contradicted and is very unlikely to be right. It is difficult for students to intuitively grasp that searching for falsifying evidence is a stronger test of the hypothesis than confirmatory evidence.

Wason (1983) empirically confirmed this in the laboratory using a task that required subjects to determine whether a conditional rule (if p then q) had been broken. He demonstrated that subjects recognized that confirmatory evidence (the presence of p) was relevant to the decision, but they often failed to check for falsifications of the rule (the absence of q). Research using the Wason task revealed a variety of apparent content effects (Johnson-Laird, Legrenzi, & Legrenzi, 1972; Wason & Shapiro, 1971), in which subjects' performance dramatically changed for the better.

In a series of now-classic experiments, Cosmides (1989) demonstrated that a number of the content effects could be attributed to a cheater-detection algorithm. When the content of the conditional rule involves social exchange (if you take the benefit [p], then you pay the cost [q]), people are spontaneously induced to look not only for benefits taken (p) but also costs not paid (not q), and performance dramatically increases from 25% correct (Wason, 1983) to 75% correct (Cosmides, 1989; see Cosmides & Tooby, Chapter 20, this volume, for an extensive discussion).

The conclusion to be drawn from these studies is not that humans are good at using abstract rules of logic. Rather, it is that humans have evolved problem-solving mechanisms tailored to problems recurrently present over evolutionary history. When problems are framed in ways congruent with these adaptive problems (e.g., social contract violation), humans can be shown to use appropriate reasoning strategies. The rarity of falsificatory choices in the nonsocial versions of the Wason task may reflect not so much *error* as the fact that the mental schemata tapped into by the problem are those for updating beliefs about probabilistic associations in the environment, which is not a deontic task but an indicative one and thus requires not falsification logic but Bayesian updating. When the question is construed in this sense, subjects' choices on the nonsocial versions are close to a Bayesian optimum (Oaksford & Chater, 1994).

In summary, many documented bias effects could reflect the application of normative standards that are not entirely appropriate for evaluating human performance. The content of problems also has been shown to have a strong effect on the approach that subjects take to reasoning; thus a normative standard that is abstract and content blind is bound to find human performance aberrant.

CONCLUSIONS

For most of its history, research on cognitive and social bias has been dominated by the failure and bleak implications of heuristics (see Kruger & Funder, in press). In a foundational paper in the heuristics and biases approach, Kahnemann and Tversky (1973) stated that "[people] rely on a limited number of heuristics which sometimes yield reasonable judgments and sometimes lead to severe and systematic errors" (p. 237). This relatively tempered viewpoint became exaggerated over the years. A *Newsweek* magazine account of the heuristics and biases research summarized it as showing that "most people . . . are woefully muddled information processors who often stumble on ill-chosen short-cuts to reach bad conclusions" (cited in Gigerenzer, Todd, & The ABC Research Group, 1999, p. 27). In reflecting on the history of social psychology, Aronson (1999) noted that "odious behavior 'sin' is at the heart of [the] most powerful research in social psychology" (p. 104). Browsing journals in social psychology, behavioral economics, and social cognition reveals a proliferation of seemingly foolish bias effects (see Kruger & Funder, in press).

Adopting an evolutionary perspective turns this focus on its head. Natural selection is the force responsible for creating the intricate designs with an improbably perfect match to their environments. Complex visual systems with specialized features tailored to species' differing ecologies have evolved several times independently (Goldsmith, 1990). Reproductive adaptations allow animals to reproduce small copies of themselves, developmentally intact, complete with miniature versions of the adaptations that will enable their own reproduction. And, natural selection is responsible for the most complex system known, the human brain. How could natural selection produce systems that equip the brain that are prone to fail as a rule and succeed only in exceptional cases?

The conceptual tide might now be turning. There has been a recent shift toward artifactual and adaptive explanations for bias, as well as a demonstration that simple mechanisms (heuristics) can function well in their proper domains. This reconceptualization has stimulated new developments in psychological theory and empirical research. Documenting content effects in biases—where bias effects emerge, recede, or reverse depending on the content of the judgment at hand—suggests that the mind does contain computationally distinct mechanisms governing reasoning in functionally distinct domains. Results demonstrating the presence of adaptive biases where they might logically be expected in one sex but not in the other and protective biases in response to stimuli that were ancestrally dangerous (but their conspicuous absence in response to modern threats) are key pieces of evidence in the debate about domain specificity. On the empirical side, these newer breeds of explanation cannot reasonably be dismissed as *just-so* stories. Although controversy about their interpretation remains, researchers from divergent perspectives have tested competing predictions about classic effects and contributed their findings to the body of knowledge in psychology. The adaptive bias explanation we have featured in this chapter, error management theory, has also stimulated investigation on particular biases that were predicted a priori (e.g., women's commitment skepticism).

These new developments do not necessarily diminish the lessons learned from earlier research. We occupy a world that is governed by novel economic rules, and knowledge of the ways in which our evolved psychology causes us to behave in ways that contrast with our self-interest in light of these rules should prove substantively important to human happiness (e.g., Thaler & Bernartzi, 2004). However, the recent amendments to theory do suggest a substantial overhaul to the conclusion that human judgment is fundamentally flawed, at least in the ways in which it has been depicted over the past three decades. When we observe humans in adaptively relevant environments, we can observe impressive design of human judgment that is free of irrational biases. Because of trade-offs in error costs, true biases also prove more functional than we would think based on first intuition. Some genuine biases might be functional features designed by the wisdom of natural selection.

REFERENCES

Abbey, A. (1982). Sex differences in attributions for friendly behavior: Do males misperceive females' friendliness? *Journal of Personality and Social Psychology, 42,* 830–838.

Alcock, J. (1993). *Animal behavior: An evolutionary approach* (5th ed.). Sunderland, MA: Basic Books.

Alicke, M. D. (1985). Global self-evaluation as defined by the desirability and controllability of trait adjectives. *Journal of Personality and Social Psychology, 49,* 1621–1630.

Alloy, L. B., & Abramson, L. Y. (1979). Judgment of contingency in depressed and non-depressed subjects: Sadder but wiser? *Journal of Experimental Psychology: General, 108,* 443–479.

Andrews, P. W. (2001). The psychology of social chess and the evolution of attribution mechanisms: Explaining the fundamental attribution error. *Evolution and Human Behavior, 22,* 11–29.

Andrews, P. W. (2002, June). *Attributing honesty to a signal purporting to reveal mental state.* Paper presented at the Human Behavior and Evolution Society Conference, Rutgers, NJ.

Arkes, H. R. (1991). Costs and benefits of judgment errors: Implications for debiasing. *Psychological Bulletin, 110,* 486–498.

Aronson, E. (1999). Adventures in social psychology: Roots, branches, and sticky new leaves. In A. Rodrigues & O. V. Levine (Eds.), *Reflections on 100 years of social psychology.* New York: Basic Books.

Bennett, A. T. D., Cuthill, I. C., & Norris, K. J. (1994). Sexual selection and the mismeasure of color. *American Naturalist, 144,* 848–860.

Bowles, S., & Gintis, H. (2002). Homo reciprocans. *Nature, 415,* 125–128.

Brewer, M. B. (1979). Ingroup bias in the minimal intergroup situation: A cognitive-motivational analysis. *Psychological Bulletin, 86,* 307–324.

Buss, D. M. (1994). *The evolution of desire: Strategies of human mating.* New York: Basic Books.

Camerer, C., & Thaler, R. (1995). Ultimatums, dictators and manners. *Journal of Economic Perspectives, 9,* 337–356.

Caporael, L., Dawes, R. M., Orbell, J. M., & van de Kragt, A. J. (1989). Selfishness examined. *Behavioral and Brain Sciences, 12,* 683–739.

Colvin, C., & Funder, D. C. (1991). Predicting personality and behavior: A boundary on the acquaintanceship effect. *Journal of Personality and Social Psychology, 60,* 884–894.

Cosmides, L. (1989). The logic of social exchange: Has natural selection shaped how humans reason? *Cognition, 31,* 187–276.

Cosmides, L., & Tooby, J. (1994). Better than rational: Evolutionary psychology and the invisible hand. *American Economic Review, 84,* 327–332.

Cosmides, L., & Tooby, J. (1996). Are humans good intuitive statisticians after all? Rethinking some conclusions from the literature on judgment under uncertainty. *Cognition, 58,* 1–73.

Domjan, M., Huber-McDonald, M., & Holloway, K. S. (1992). Conditioning copulatory behavior to an artificial object: Efficacy of stimulus fading. *Animal Learning and Behavior, 20,* 350–362.

Dugatkin, L. A. (1996). Interface between culturally based preferences and genetic preferences: Female mate choice in Poecilia reticulata. *Proceedings of the National Academy of Sciences, USA, 93,* 2770–2773.

Ebenbach, D. H., & Keltner, D. (1998). Power, emotion, and judgmental accuracy in social conflict: Motivating the cognitive miser. *Basic and Applied Social Psychology, 20,* 7–21.

Fiedler, K. (1988). The dependence of the conjunction fallacy on subtle linguistic factors. *Psychological Research, 50,* 123–129.

Fiske, S. T. (1993). Controlling other people: The impact of power on stereotyping. *American Psychologist, 48,* 621–628.

Funder, D. C. (1987). Errors and mistakes: Evaluating the accuracy of social judgment. *Psychological Bulletin, 101,* 75–90.

Garcia, J., Hankins, W. G., & Rusiniak, K. W. (1976). Flavor aversion studies. *Science, 192,* 265–266.

Gigerenzer, G. (1996). On narrow norms and vague heuristics: A reply to Kahneman and Tversky (1996). *Psychological Review, 103,* 592–596.

Gigerenzer, G. (1997). Ecological intelligence: An adaptation for frequencies. *Psychologische Beitrage, 39,* 107–129.

Gigerenzer, G. (2000). *Adaptive thinking: Rationality in the real world.* New York: Oxford University Press.

Gigerenzer, G., & Goldstein, D. G. (1996). Reasoning the fast and frugal way: Models of bounded rationality. *Psychological Review, 103,* 650–669.

Gigerenzer, G., Todd, P. M., & The ABC Research Group. (1999). *Simple heuristics that make us smart.* New York: Oxford University Press.

Gilovich, T., Griffin, D., & Kahneman, D. (2002). *Heuristics and biases: The psychology of intuitive judgment.* New York: Cambridge.

Gintis, H., Bowles, S., Boyd, R., & Fehr, E. (2003). Explaining altruistic behavior in humans. *Evolution and Human Behavior, 24,* 153–172.

Goldsmith, T. H. (1990). Optimization, constraint and history in the evolution of eyes. *Quarterly Review of Biology, 65,* 281–322.

Goldstein, D. G., & Gigerenzer, G. (1999). The recognition heuristic: How ignorance makes us smart. In G. Gigerenzer, P. M. Todd, & The ABC Research Group (Eds.), *Simple heuristics that make us smart* (pp. 37–58). New York: Oxford University Press.

Goodwin, S. A., Gubin, A. A., Fiske, S. T., & Yzerbyt, V. T. (2000). Power can bias subordinates by default and by design. *Group Processes and Intergroup Relations, 3,* 227–256.

Green, D. M., & Swets, J. A. (1966). *Signal detection and psychophysics.* New York: Wiley.

Grice, H. P. (1975). Logic and conversation. In P. Cole & J. L. Morgan (Eds.), *Syntax and semantics, III: Speech acts* (pp. 41–58). New York: Academic Press.

Haselton, M. G. (2003). The sexual overperception bias: Evidence of a systematic bias in men from a survey of naturally occurring events. *Journal of Research in Personality, 37,* 43–47.

Haselton, M. G., & Buss, D. M. (2000). Error management theory: A new perspective on biases in cross-sex mind reading. *Journal of Personality and Social Psychology, 78,* 81–91.

Haselton, M. G., & Buss, D. M. (2003). Biases in social judgment: Design flaws or design features. In J. Forgas, K. Williams, & B. von Hippel (Eds.), *Responding to the social world: Implicit and explicit processes in social judgments and decisions.* New York: Cambridge.

Haselton, M. G., & Nettle, D. (2004). *The paranoid optimist: An integrative evolutionary model of cognitive biases.* Manuscript under review, Los Angeles, University of California.

Henrich, J., & Boyd, R. (2001). Why people punish defectors: Weak conformist transmission can stabilize costly enforcement of norms in cooperative dilemmas. *Journal of Theoretical Biology, 208,* 79–89.

Henrich, J., Boyd, R., Bowles, S., Camerer, C., Fehr, E., Gintis, H., et al. (2001). Cooperation, reciprocity and punishment in 15 small-scale societies. *American Economic Review, 91,* 73–78.

Hertwig, R., & Gigerenzer, G. (1999). The "conjunction fallacy" revisited: How intelligent inferences look like reasoning errors. *Journal of Behavioral Decision Making, 12,* 275–305.

Hoffrage, U., Lindsey, S., Hertwig, R., & Gigerenzer, G. (2001, May 4th). Statistics: What seems natural (response to Butterworth). *Science, 292,* 855.

Hunt, S., Bennett, A. T. D., Cuthill, I. C., & Griffiths, R. (1998). Blue tits are ultraviolet tits. *Proceedings of the Royal Society of London, Series B, Biological Sciences, 265,* 451–455.

Hurtado, A. M., & Hill, K. R. (1992). Paternal effect on offspring survivorship among Ache and Hiwi hunter-gatherers. In B. S. Hewlett (Ed.), *Father-child relations: Cultural and biosocial contexts* (pp. 31–55). New York: Aldine De Gruyter.

Johnson-Laird, P., Legrenzi, P., & Legrenzi, M. (1972). Reasoning and a sense of reality. *British Journal of Psychology, 63,* 495–500.

Jones, E. E., & Harris, V. A. (1967). The attribution of attitudes. *Journal of Experimental Social Psychology, 3,* 1–24.

Kahneman, D. (2003). A perspective on judgment and choice. *American Psychologist, 58,* 697–720.

Kahneman, D., & Tversky, A. (1973). On the psychology of prediction. *Psychological Review, 80,* 237–251.

Kahneman, D., & Tversky, A. (1996). On the reality of cognitive illusions. *Psychological Review, 103,* 582–591.

Keltner, D., Gruenfeld, D. H., & Anderson, C. (2003). Power, approach, and inhibition. *Psychological Review, 110,* 265–284.

Kenrick, D. T., & Maner, J. (in press). One path to balance and order in social psychology: An evolutionary perspective. *Behavioral and Brain Sciences.*

Krebs, D. L., & Denton, K. (1997). Social illusions and self-deception: The evolution of biases in person perception. In J. A. Simpson & D. T. Kenrick (Eds.), *Evolutionary social psychology* (pp. 21–47). Hillsdale, NJ: Erlbaum.

Krueger, J. I., & Funder, D. C. (in press). Towards a balanced social psychology: Causes, consequences and cures for the problem-seeking approach to social behavior and cognition. *Behavioral and Brain Sciences.*

Kurzban, R., & Leary, M. R. (2001). Evolutionary origins of stigmatization: The functions of social exclusion. *Psychological Bulletin, 123,* 187–208.

Little, A. C., Burt, D. M., Penton-Voak, I. S., & Perrett, D. I. (2001). Self-perceived attractiveness influences human female preferences for sexual dimorphism and symmetry in male faces. *Proceedings of the Royal Society of London, Series B, Biological Sciences, 268,* 39–44.

Maner, J. K., Kenrick, D. T., Becker, V., Robertson, T. E., Hofer, B., Neuberg, S. L., et al. (in press). Functional projection: How fundamental social motives can bias interpersonal perception. *Journal of Personality and Social Psychology.*

Mellers, B., Hertwig, R., & Kahneman, D. (2001). Do frequency representations eliminate conjunction effects? An exercise in adversarial collaboration. *Psychological Science, 12*, 269–275.

Miller, G. F., & Todd, P. M. (1998). Mate choice turns cognitive. *Trends in Cognitive Sciences, 2*, 190–198.

Mineka, S. (1992). Evolutionary memories, emotional processing, and the emotional disorders. *Psychology of Learning and Motivation, 28*, 161–206.

Nesse, R. M. (2001). The smoke detector principle: Natural selection and the regulation of defenses. *Annals of the New York Academy of Sciences, 935*, 75–85.

Nettle, D. (2004). Adaptive illusions: Optimism, control and human rationality. In D. Evans & P. Cruse (Eds.), *Emotion, evolution and rationality* (pp. 191–206). Oxford, England: Oxford University Press.

Neuberg, S. L., & Fiske, S. T. (1987). Motivational influences on impression formation: Outcome dependency, accuracy-driven attention, and individuating processes. *Journal of Personality and Social Psychology, 53*, 431–444.

Neuhoff, J. G. (2001). An adaptive bias in the perception of looming auditory motion. *Ecological Psychology, 13*, 87–110.

Norenzayan, A., Choi, I., & Nisbett, R. E. (2002). Cultural similarities and differences in social inference: Evidence from behavioral predictions and lay theories of behavior. *Personality and Social Psychology Bulletin, 28*, 109–120.

Oaksford, M., & Chater, N. (1994). A rational analysis of the selection task as optimal data selection. *Psychological Review, 101*, 608–631.

Park, J. H., Faulkner, J., & Schaller, M. (2003). Evolved disease-avoidance processes and contemporary anti-social behavior: Prejudicial attitudes and avoidance of people with disabilities. *Journal of Nonverbal Behavior, 27*, 65–87.

Penton-Voak, I. S., Perrett, D. I., Castles, D., Burt, M., Koyabashi, T., & Murray, L. K. (1999). Female preference for male faces changes cyclically. *Nature, 399*, 741–742.

Price, M., Cosmides, L., & Tooby, J. (2002). Punitive sentiment as an anti-free rider psychological adaptation. *Evolution and Human Behavior, 23*, 203–231.

Quillian, L., & Pager, D. (2001). Black neighbors, higher crime? The role of racial stereotypes in evaluations of neighborhood crime. *American Journal of Sociology, 107*, 717–767.

Ross, L. (1997). The intuitive psychologist and his shortcomings: Distortions in attribution processes. In L. Berkowitz (Ed.), *Advances in experimental social psychology* (pp. 174–214). New York: Academic Press.

Rozin, P., & Kalat, J. W. (1971). Specific hungers and poison avoidances as adaptive specializations of learning. *Psychological Review, 78*, 459–486.

Rudski, J. M. (2000). Illusion of control relative to chance outcomes. *Psychological Reports, 87*, 85–92.

Sabini, J., Siepmann, M., & Stein, J. (2001). The really fundamental attribution error in social psychological research. *Psychological Inquiry, 12*, 1–15.

Sally, D. (1995). Conversation and cooperation in social dilemmas: A meta-analysis of experiments from 1958 to 1992. *Rationality and Society, 7*, 58–92.

Savitsky, K., Epley, N., & Gilovich, T. (2001). Do others judge us as harshly as we think? Overestimating the impact of our failures, shortcomings, and mishaps. *Journal of Personality and Social Psychology, 81*, 44–56.

Schaller, M., Park, J. H., & Mueller, A. (2003). Fear of the dark: Interactive effects of beliefs about danger and ambient darkness on ethnic stereotypes. *Personality and Social Psychology Bulletin, 29*, 637–649.

Sedikides, C., Gaertner, L., & Toguchi, Y. (2003). Pancultural self-enhancement. *Journal of Personality and Social Psychology, 84*, 60–79.

Seligman, M. E. P. (1971). Phobias and preparedness. *Behavior Therapy, 2*, 307–320.

Symons, D. (1979). *The evolution of human sexuality.* New York: Oxford University Press.

Taylor, S. E., & Brown, J. D. (1988). Illusion and well-being: A social psychological perspective on mental health. *Psychological Bulletin, 103*, 193–201.

Tetlock, P. E. (1985). Accountability: A social check on the fundamental attribution error. *Social Psychology Quarterly, 48*, 227–236.

Thaler, R. H., & Benartzi, S. (2004). Save more tomorrow: Using behavioral economics to increase employee saving. *Journal of Political Economy, 112*(1, Pt. 2), S164–S187.

Tomarken, A. J., Mineka, S., & Cook, M. (1989). Fear-relevant selective associations and covariation bias. *Journal of Abnormal Psychology, 98*, 381–394.

Tooby, J., & Cosmides, L. (1992). The psychological foundations of culture. In J. H. Barkow, L. Cosmides, & J. Tooby (Eds.), *The adapted mind: Evolutionary psychology and the generation of culture* (pp. 19–136). New York: Oxford University Press.

Trivers, R. L. (1972). Parental investment and sexual selection. In B. Campbell (Ed.), *Sexual selection and the descent of man, 1871–1971* (pp. 136–179). Chicago: Aldine Publishing Company.

Trope, Y., & Alfieri, T. (1997). Effortfulness and flexibility of dispositional judgment processes. *Journal of Personality and Social Psychology, 73,* 662–674.

Tversky, A., & Kahneman, D. (1974). Judgment under uncertainty: Heuristics and biases. *Science, 185,* 1121–1131.

Tversky, A., & Kahneman, D. (1983). Extensional versus intuitive reasoning: The conjunction fallacy in probability judgment. *Psychological Review, 90,* 293–315.

Vonk, R. (1999). Effects of outcome dependency on correspondence bias. *Personality and Social Psychology Bulletin, 25,* 382–389.

Wason, P. C. (1983). Realism and rationality in the selection task. In J. Evans (Ed.), *Thinking and reasoning: Psychological approaches.* London: Routeledge and Kegan Paul.

Wason, P. C., & Shapiro, D. (1971). Natural and contrived experience in a reasoning problem. *Quarterly Journal of Experimental Psychology, 23,* 63–71.

Weinstein, N. D. (1980). Unrealistic optimism about future life events. *Journal of Personality and Social Psychology, 39,* 806–820.

Williams, G. W., & Nesse, R. M. (1991). The dawn of Darwinian medicine. *Quarterly Review of Biology, 66,* 1–22.

Williams, K. D., Case, T. I., & Govan, C. L. (2003). Impact of ostracism on social judgments and decisions: Explicit and implicit responses. In J. Forgas, K. Williams, & W. von Hippel (Eds.), *Responding to the social world: Implicit and explicit processes in social judgments and decisions.* New York: Cambridge University Press.

Yamagishi, T., Jin, N., & Kiyonari, T. (1999). Bounded generalized reciprocity: Ingroup favoritism and ingroup boasting. *Advances in Group Processes, 16,* 161–197.

Yamagishi, T., Terai, S., Kiyonari, T., & Kanazawa, S. (2003). *The social exchange heuristic: Managing errors in social exchange.* Manuscript under review, Center for Advanced Study in the Behavioral Sciences, Stanford, CA.

Yost, J. H., & Weary, G. (1996). Depression and the correspondent inference bias: Evidence for more effortful cognitive processing. *Personality and Social Psychology Bulletin, 22,* 192–200.

CHAPTER 26

The Evolution of Morality

DENNIS KREBS

MANY EVOLUTIONARY THEORISTS have doubted whether moral dispositions can evolve through natural selection (Campbell, 1978; Darwin, 1871; Dawkins, 1989; Huxley, 1893). For example, according to Williams (1989):

> There is no encouragement for any belief that an organism can be designed for any purpose other than the most effective pursuit of [its] self-interest. As a general rule, a modern biologist seeing an animal doing something to benefit another assumes either that it is manipulated by the other individual or that it is being subtly selfish. . . . Nothing resembling the Golden Rule or other widely preached ethical principles seems to be operating in living nature. It could scarcely be otherwise, when evolution is guided by a force that maximizes genetic selfishness. (pp. 195–197)

This chapter argues that the idea that all organisms are inherently selfish and immoral by nature is wrong or, more exactly, only half right. It explains how mechanisms that give rise to moral and immoral behaviors can evolve and adduces evidence that they have evolved in the human species and in other species as well.

WHAT IS MORALITY?

In large part, the conclusions scholars reach about the evolution of morality are determined by the standards they believe an act must meet to qualify as moral. If scholars insist that a behavior must be genetically unselfish to qualify as moral, they will almost certainly infer that moral dispositions cannot evolve. If, however, they define morality in terms of individual unselfishness, they will almost certainly reach a more positive conclusion. It is, therefore, important to be clear about what we mean by morality. Everyone makes moral judgments about the goodness and badness of people, the rightness and wrongness of behaviors, and the rights and duties of members of groups. At a phenotypic level, most people agree about which kinds of behavior are moral and immoral. For example, virtually everyone

747

Table 26.1
Kohlberg's Stages of Moral Development

Stage 1

Morality is defined in terms of avoiding punishment, respecting the "superior power of authorities," "obedience for its own sake," and "avoiding damage to persons and property."

Stage 2

Morality is defined in terms of instrumental exchange, "acting to meet one's own interests and needs and letting others do the same," making deals, and engaging in equal exchanges.

Stage 3

Morality is defined in terms of upholding mutual relationships, fulfilling role expectations, being viewed as a good person, sustaining a good reputation, showing concern for and caring for others, and interpersonal conformity. Trust, loyalty, respect, and gratitude are important moral values.

Stage 4

Morality is defined in terms of maintaining the social systems from which one benefits, obeying their rules and laws, and "contributing to society." Morality involves doing one's share to uphold society and to prevent it from breaking down.

Stage 5

Morality is defined in terms of fulfilling the social obligations implicit in social contracts that are "freely agreed upon," and a "rational calculation of overall utility, 'the greatest good for the greatest number.'" Morality involves orienting to the welfare of all and the protection of everyone's rights.

Stage 6

Morality is defined in terms of following "self-chosen universal ethical principles of justice" that uphold "the equality of human rights and respect for the dignity of human beings as individual persons." Morality involves treating individuals as ends in themselves (Colby & Kohlberg, 1987, pp. 18–19).

considers helping others, keeping promises, and being faithful to your spouse moral, and virtually everyone considers murder, rape, lying, and cheating immoral. However, if you ask people what makes such behaviors moral or immoral, they may well give different reasons, exposing significant differences in their underlying conceptions of morality.

Cognitive-developmental psychologists such as Colby and Kohlberg (1987), Damon and Hart (1992), and Piaget (1932) have found that the conceptions of morality harbored by children and adults from a wide array of cultures tend to change systematically as people develop, in the stagelike ways outlined in Table 26.1. (See Krebs & Van Hesteren, 1994, for a comparison of Kohlberg's stages of moral development and the stages derived by other theorists.) Based on empirical evidence supporting his developmental sequence and philosophical criteria of morality such as universality, prescriptiveness, and impartiality, Kohlberg (1984) concluded that the conceptions of morality that define higher stages in his sequence are more adequate than the conceptions that define lower stages.

Although Kohlberg's model of moral development is limited in several ways (see Gilligan, 1982; Krebs, 2004b; Krebs, Denton, Vermeulen, Carpendale, & Bush, 1991), there is strong and consistent support for his contention that most people view morality in the ways outlined in Table 26.1 and that most people believe that the conceptions that define higher stages in Kohlberg's sequence are more adequate than the conceptions that define lower stages. I use these conceptions as working definitions of morality, reinterpreting them in more biological terms.

SELFISHNESS AND MORALITY

If we define *unselfish* as an individual refraining from fostering his or her interests at the expense of the interests of others, the assumption that an act must be unselfish to qualify as moral seems reasonable. Most moral behaviors seem unselfish, most immoral behaviors seem selfish, and behaviors prescribed by moral judgments that define relatively high stages in Kohlberg's sequence seem more unselfish than behaviors prescribed by lower stage judgments.

It is, however, important that the type of unselfishness that most people assume is necessary for morality is different from the type of unselfishness that evolutionary theorists believe defies the laws of evolution (Sober & Wilson, 2000). The interests that people have in mind when they make attributions about morality are the proximate physical, material, and hedonic interests of people making moral decisions. The interests that evolutionary theorists have in mind are ultimate genetic interests. Although the two types of interest may covary, they need not necessarily correspond. Indeed, as recognized by Dawkins (1989), "there are special circumstances in which a gene can achieve its own selfish goals by fostering a limited form of altruism at the level of individual animals" (p. 6).

It is unreasonable to set genetic unselfishness as a criterion for morality. It is not immoral to propagate your genes. Morality pertains to how you go about accomplishing this task. Attempting to propagate your genes in individually selfish ways, at the expense of the physical, material, or psychological welfare of others, is immoral, but attempting to propagate your genes in individually cooperative or altruistic ways that foster the welfare of others is moral. Even if all evolved mechanisms disposed people to behave in genetically selfish ways, although not necessarily true, it would not render such behaviors immoral. With this conception of morality in mind, we turn to the central questions addressed in this chapter: Can mechanisms that give rise to moral behaviors evolve, and, if so, have they evolved in the human species?

THE ORIGIN OF MORALITY

The central contribution evolutionary psychology brings to the understanding of morality is to encourage us to ask what adaptive problems it was selected to solve. What functions did morality serve in ancestral environments? The mechanisms that give rise to moral behaviors evolved to solve the social problems that inevitably arise when individuals band together to foster their interests. When individuals are able to satisfy their needs, survive, reproduce, and rear their offspring on their own, there is no need for them to interact with other members of their species and, therefore, no need for morality. Mechanisms that induce individuals to form groups and socialize with others were selected because such social behaviors were adaptive in ancestral environments.

THE SIGNIFICANCE OF COOPERATION AND CONFLICTS OF INTEREST

Social behaviors may help animals adapt to their environments in many ways. For example, aggregating and mutual defense may reduce the risk of predation, and group hunting may enhance the probability of obtaining food. Most benefits of sociality stem from cooperative exchanges. However, as explained by the philosopher John Rawls (1971, p. 4) in his widely cited book, *Theory of Justice:*

> Although a society is a cooperative venture for mutual advantage, it is typically marked by a conflict as well as by an identity of interests. There is an identity of interests since social cooperation makes possible a better life for all than any would have if each were to live solely by his own efforts. There is a conflict of interests since persons are not indifferent as to how the greater benefits of their collaboration are distributed, for in order to pursue their ends, each prefers a larger to a lesser share.

Selfish preferences pose a problem for the evolution of cooperation, because they tempt individuals to invoke selfish strategies that, if successful, can drive cooperative strategies into extinction. However, when selfish strategies are successful, they tend to increase in frequency, which elevates the probability of their encountering other selfish strategies and engaging in low payoff "me-me" exchanges. Individuals bent on doing less than their share and taking more than their share may end up fighting, failing to obtain resources, failing to defend themselves, and failing to rear fecund offspring. This is the adaptive problem that the mechanisms that give rise to morality evolved to solve. The biological function of morality is to uphold fitness-enhancing systems of cooperation by inducing members of groups to contribute their share and to resist the temptation to take more than their share, to do their duties and to exercise their rights in ways that do not infringe on the rights of others, and to resolve conflicts of interest in mutually beneficial ways.

A BIOLOGICAL CONCEPTION OF MORALITY

Viewing morality in this way helps elucidate its nature. Morality boils down to individuals meeting their needs and advancing their interests in cooperative ways. Morality consists in "standards or guidelines that govern human cooperation—in particular how rights, duties, and benefits are . . . allocated. . . . Moralities are proposals for a system of mutual coordination of activities and cooperation among people" (Rest, 1983, p. 558). In this conception, acts such as murder, rape, and infidelity are immoral for the same reason as acts such as lying and cheating: They advance individuals' interests at the expense of the interests of others and undermine systems of cooperation. The moral judgments that define different stages of moral development (Table 26.1) uphold different systems of cooperation. The higher the stage, the greater the system's potential to maximize benefits for everyone involved—to produce the greatest good for the greatest number. The question is: Could mechanisms that dispose individuals to behave in the ways prescribed by the moral judgments that define each of Kohlberg's stages have evolved?

THE NATURAL SELECTION OF SOCIAL STRATEGIES: EVOLUTIONARY GAMES

Imagine a group of early humans living in an ancestral environment. Assume that all members of the group inherit genes that guide the creation of mechanisms that give rise to strategies designed to maximize their biological benefits from interacting with others. Although winning strategies become more frequent in the population, the process of natural selection need not necessarily drive competing strategies into extinction. As a strategy increases in frequency, it induces changes in the social environment. In particular, it becomes increasingly likely to encounter replicas of itself, and this may affect its adaptiveness. For example, a "hawk" strategy that fares well against "dove" strategies may become increasingly costly as the proportion of hawks increases in the population. In addition to selecting only one strategy, the process of natural selection may induce strategies to fluctuate in frequency over generations or it may induce two or more strategies to stabilize in some proportion between or within individuals (Maynard Smith, 1976).

Assume that some members of an ancestral group inherit mechanisms that dispose them to adopt selfish strategies and other members of the group inherit mechanisms that dispose them to adopt cooperative strategies and that these strategies compete against each other. Which ones would increase in frequency and evolve? To answer this question, theorists have created models of social evolution such as those derived from Prisoners' Dilemma games.

Prisoners' Dilemma Models of Social Evolution

In the simplest form of evolutionary adaptations of classic two-person, iterated Prisoners' Dilemma games, each player is programmed to play one of two strategies—to behave selfishly (to "defect") or to behave cooperatively. If both players make a cooperative choice, each produces three cooperative offspring. If both players make a selfish choice, each produces one selfish offspring. If one player makes a cooperative choice and the other makes a selfish choice, the cooperative player does not produce any offspring and the selfish player produces five selfish offspring. Strategies are played off against each other in random order in computers. After the first round, or generation, offspring who inherit the strategies compete against each other and so on. Game theorists seek to answer two questions: Which strategy or strategies will evolve, and will any strategy become evolutionarily stable—that is, reach an equilibrium in the population such that it cannot be defeated by any competing strategy?

Prisoners' Dilemma games model several basic principles of social evolution. Pairs and groups of cooperating individuals fare better than pairs and groups of selfish individuals. In addition, each member of a pair or group of cooperating individuals fares better than each member of a selfish dyad or group of selfish individuals. However, within a dyad or group of cooperators, selfish individuals fare better than cooperative individuals. Note how the Prisoners' Dilemma is equipped to model individual-level selection within groups and group-level selection between groups (Dugatkin & Reeve, 1994; Sober & Wilson, 1998).

THE EVOLUTION OF SELFISHNESS

On the contingencies of simple Prisoners' Dilemma models of social evolution, selfish players end up producing twice as many offspring as cooperative players. If Prisoners' Dilemma models programmed in this way validly represented the process of evolution, selfish strategies would drive cooperative strategies into extinction and render all species selfish by nature, as many eminent evolutionary theorists have concluded. But before we accept this conclusion, we need to realize that the social context, choices, and parameters modeled in simple Prisoners' Dilemma games differ in significant ways from the contexts, choices, and parameters in which the social strategies inherited by many species evolved. Changing the parameters of Prisoners' Dilemmas to make them approximate more closely the conditions in which social strategies were selected in human and other species can decrease the adaptive benefits of selfish strategies and increase the adaptive benefits of cooperative strategies. The following sections demonstrate how the strategies prescribed by moral judgments that define Kohlberg's first four stages of moral development could have defeated more selfish strategies in the ancestral environments in which our hominid ancestors evolved.

STAGE 1 MORALITY: THE EVOLUTION OF DEFERENCE

In simple Prisoners' Dilemma models of social evolution, all players are equal in power. In contrast, in the real world animals differ in power and make conditional decisions that depend on the relative power of their opponents. Adopting a selfish strategy, defined as attempting to get more than one's share, may prove costly for relatively weak members of groups.

As shown in Table 26.1, Kohlbergian Stage 1 moral judgments prescribe deferring to those with "superior power" and "obeying authority" to "avoid punishment." The strategy implicit in such judgments could be more adaptive than more blindly selfish or aggressive strategies for relatively subordinate members of groups. When members of groups are faced with a choice between competing against more powerful members of their groups and subordinating their interests to them, discretion is often the better part of valor (Cummins, Chapter 23, this volume). Adopting a deferential strategy enables subordinate members of groups to make the best of a bad situation and live to fight another day. Deferential strategies also may benefit subordinate members of groups by enhancing the fitness of more powerful members who, in turn, intimidate predators or foes.

DEFERENTIAL STRATEGIES IN HUMANS AND OTHER ANIMALS

Members of species ranging from crickets (Dawkins, 1989) and crayfish (Barinaga, 1996) to chimpanzees (Boehm, 2000) have been found to adopt conditional strategies such as, "If your opponent seems more powerful than you, defer to him or her; if your opponent seems less powerful than you, intimidate him or her."

Such strategies give rise to dominance hierarchies or pecking orders. Dominant and submissive behaviors are correlated with changes in levels of testosterone and serotonin in a variety of animals (see Buss, 1999, for a review of the literature).

In his pioneering book on moral development, Piaget (1932) attributed the moral orientation of young children to "the respect felt by the small for the great" (p. 107), which "has its roots deep down in certain inborn feelings and is due to a sui generis mixture of fear and affection" (p. 375). Researchers have found that children organize themselves into dominance hierarchies as young as 3 years of age (Cummins, 1998).

Neglected by Kohlberg (1984) and other developmental psychologists is evidence that deferential dispositions in adults stem from the same mechanisms as deferential dispositions in children. Adults may experience the same sense of awe, unilateral respect, and intimidation as children do when they encounter powerful people of high status. Milgram's (1974) classic studies demonstrate that people are more prone to submit to authority than is commonly assumed. Members of cults such as Heaven's Gate and Jonestown have proved themselves willing to commit suicide on the commands of their leaders (Osherow, 1995). Deference also may be evoked by more abstract entities, such as God.

The Morality of Deference

In one sense, deference is unselfish, because it induces individuals to subordinate their interests to those of others. However, in another sense, deferential strategies are selfish because they enable those who employ them to avoid punishment and maximize their chances of surviving and reproducing. In general, deference is individually unselfish with respect to immediate decisions but individually selfish in the long term—physically, materially, psychologically, and genetically.

Inasmuch as morality involves the constraint of selfishness, relatively powerful members of groups can be viewed as exerting a moralizing effect on relatively weak members of groups. However, there are at least two problems with the morality of hierarchical social systems. First, everyone except the individual at the bottom of the totem pole behaves selfishly toward those below him or her in the hierarchy. Second, there is no one to constrain the selfishness of the most dominant member of the group. To most people, it is more moral to constrain the selfishness of dominant members of groups than to reinforce it by acting submissively. Few people consider deference, submission, and obedience to authority to be moral qualities in and of themselves; few people believe that it was moral for Nazis to obey authority.

The Significance of Coalitions and Mutual Control

One way in which relatively weak and subordinate members of groups can increase their power is to form coalitions. Although coalitions can exert a moralizing effect on groups by controlling the selfishness of the most powerful members, such effects are limited in two ways. The coalition may become tyrannical, and it is in the adaptive interest of each member of the coalition to gain ascendancy over the other members of the coalition and take more than his or her share. To get to an egalitarian social system, we need a social equilibrium produced either by individuals or groups controlling one another's selfishness or by members of groups constraining their own selfishness—that is, resisting the temptation to dominate subordinates even when it is not in their immediate interest (Boehm, 2000).

STAGE 2 MORALITY: THE EVOLUTION OF DIRECT RECIPROCITY

Deferential strategies do not offer effective ways of resolving conflicts of interest between individuals who are relatively equal in power, because neither is inclined to defer and each is able to inflict damage on the other. When resources can be divided, it may be more beneficial for peers to share them than to compete for them. When resources cannot be divided, peers may be better off taking turns than fighting. Mechanisms that give rise to sharing and turn-taking strategies will evolve when the net benefits from settling for part of a resource outweigh the net benefits of competing for the whole thing.

THE EVOLUTION OF CONCRETE RECIPROCITY

In classic Prisoners' Dilemma games, all cooperative players reap exactly the same payoff from exchanges with other cooperators—three offspring. In contrast, in the real world, the goods and services that people exchange may vary in value. Individuals may exchange items worth relatively little to them for items that are worth considerably more, enabling all parties to gain in trade. Inevitably, members of groups encounter others who need services that they can provide at relatively little cost to themselves. As Trivers (1971) explained, it can be in individuals' interest to help others if such helping increases the probability that the recipients will help them when they are in need. However, for psychological mechanisms that induce individuals to reciprocate to evolve, they must contain antidotes to cheating that prevent selfish players from taking without giving in return. One strategy equipped to accomplish this is Tit-for-Tat.

Tit-for-Tat   Tit-for-Tat is based in the decision rule, "Be nice, then get even." Invite mutually beneficial reciprocal exchanges by making low-cost giving overtures to others, then copy their response. In contrast to more unconditionally altruistic or cooperative strategies, Tit-for-Tat gives rise to iterations of reciprocal exchanges between both givers and takers after the first exchange.

At first glance, it might seem that Tit-for-Tat is destined to lose to unconditionally selfish strategies because selfish strategies reap greater benefits than Tit-for-Tat on the first exchange (5 versus 0 offspring) then tie with them (1–1) on all subsequent moves. Although this is the case in two-person games, Tit-for-Tat can end up defeating unconditionally selfish strategies if there is a relatively large number of Tit-for-Tat strategists in the population. In computer contests sponsored by Axelrod and Hamilton (1981), Tit-for-Tat defeated unconditionally selfish strategies and emerged the winner. The principle underlying this outcome pertains to the benefits of cooperating with cooperators, which was critically important in the evolution of morality.

Note that there is a fringe benefit from the evolution of Tit-for-Tat strategies; namely, it opens the door for the evolution of more unconditionally cooperative and altruistic strategies. Indeed, in an environment saturated by Tit-for-Tat strategists, we could not tell the difference between conditionally and uncondi-

tionally cooperative strategies because they would behave in the same cooperative manner. However, ironically, opening the door for unconditionally cooperative or altruistic strategies also opens the door for the reemergence of selfish
strategies, which benefit by exploiting them. Selfish strategies thrive on the unconditional generosity of do-gooders.

Concrete Reciprocity in Humans and Other Animals   Biologists have found that mechanisms giving rise to systems of Tit-for-Tat reciprocity have evolved in some
species, though perhaps fewer than we might expect (Dugatkin, 1997; Trivers,
1985). With respect to humans, Trivers (1985) suggested that, "During the Pleistocene, and probably before, a hominid species would have met the preconditions
for the evolution of reciprocal altruism; for example, long life span, low dispersal
rate, life in small, mutually dependent and stable social groups, and a long period
of parental care leading to extensive contacts with close relatives over many years"
(p. 386). In the list of 15 unique hominid characteristics derived by Tooby and
DeVore (1987), many are based in reciprocity. According to Gouldner (1960): "A
norm of reciprocity is, I suspect, no less universal and important . . . than the incest
taboo" (p. 178). When people say things such as, "You scratch my back and I'll
scratch yours"; "quid pro quo"; and "Don't get mad, get even," they are promoting
Tit-for-Tat strategies.

   Accounting for the ontogenetic emergence of morality, Piaget (1932) suggested
that when young children who possess deferential moral orientations grow older
and interact increasingly frequently with peers in contexts in which there are no
adults to tell them what is right and wrong, they figure out themselves how to coordinate their social relations in functional ways. Aided by the growth of their
ability to understand reciprocity, egalitarian peer relations usher in a new moral
orientation, which Piaget characterized as "the morality of cooperation" based in
"mutual respect."

The Morality of Concrete Reciprocity   Tit-for-Tat forms of reciprocity are prescribed
by some codes of ethics, such as those contained in the Old Testament. However,
few philosophers of ethics or laypeople consider the negative form of concrete
reciprocity—an eye for an eye—very moral (Newitt & Krebs, 2003). Moral judgments that prescribe Tit-for-Tat forms of reciprocity such as, "[You should help
people] because you may need them to do something for you one day" and "You
should get even with people who rip you off" are classified as Stage 2 in
Kohlberg's system.

The Adaptive Limitations of Concrete Reciprocity   The success of Tit-for-Tat strategies in Axelrod and Hamilton's (1981) computer contests notwithstanding, Tit-
for-Tat strategies are limited in three respects. First, they are not equipped to
invade a population of selfish strategies unless they invade in clusters that enable
them to interact predominantly with replicas of themselves. This raises the question: How could such clusters have originated in the first place, especially if we
assume an original state of unconditional selfishness? Second, Tit-for-Tat strategies do not become evolutionarily stable, because they open the door for more unconditionally cooperative and altruistic strategies, which in turn open the door
for more selfish strategies. Finally, one selfish defection in an exchange between

two Tit-for-Tat strategists locks them into a mutually recriminating and self-defeating series of selfish exchanges—a "blood feud."

STAGE 2/3 MORALITY: THE EVOLUTION OF KINDER, GENTLER, MORE FORGIVING, AND CONTRITE FORMS OF DIRECT RECIPROCITY

Following the publication of Axelrod and Hamilton's (1981) findings, investigators conducted computer contests in which they changed the ground rules of the games (Dugatkin, 1997, p. 24), which opened the door for more moral strategies. Consider first the recognition that well-meaning people sometimes make mistakes.

Consider two Tit-for-Tat strategists interacting in a mutually beneficial way. One makes a mistake and behaves selfishly, which gives rise to a blood feud. It is in the interest of both players to reestablish the string of mutually beneficial cooperative exchanges, which can be accomplished either by the selfish player making up for his or her mistake or the victim giving the selfish player a second chance. Evolutionary games that followed the publication of Axelrod and Hamilton's (1981) findings found that strategies programmed in such ways could defeat Tit-for-Tat (see Ridley, 1996, for a review of relevant research). The willingness to give potential exchange partners a second chance is implied in sayings such as, "Everyone makes mistakes," "Forgive and forget," and "Forgive those who transgress against us, for they know not what they do." In Kohlberg's classification, moral judgments prescribing such strategies are classified as Stage 2/3. Trivers (1971) and others have suggested that the function of emotions such as guilt, contrition, and mercy is to repair damaged reciprocal relations.

STAGE 3 MORALITY: THE EVOLUTION OF SELECTIVE INTERACTION, FRIENDSHIP, INDIRECT RECIPROCITY, AND CARE

In Axelrod and Hamilton's (1981) games, players were programmed to interact randomly with all other players. In contrast, in the real world individuals may be highly selective in their choice of partners. A strategy such as, "Cooperate with those who cooperate with you and shun those who treat you selfishly" is well equipped to defeat unconditionally selfish strategies. Through it, selfish players would be relegated to interacting with other selfish players in one-offspring exchanges or with no one at all. The costs of being shunned or ostracized are potentially devastating in species that are dependent on other members of their group for survival and reproduction. Shunned individuals are, in essence, kicked out of the game—indeed all games. The wages of selfishness is ostracism, which in many species equates to death.

Psychological mechanisms that foster mutual cooperation must be designed in ways that enable individuals to (1) distinguish between cooperators and noncooperators, (2) maximize interactions with cooperators, and (3) minimize or avoid interactions with noncooperators. Distinguishing between cooperators and noncooperators is a tricky task. Individuals may base such estimates on how potential exchange partners treat them; observations of how potential partners treat others; what potential partners say to them, especially in the form of promises and verbal contracts (Nesse, 2001); what potential partners say to others; and what others say about potential partners. Nowack and Sigmund (1998) found that altruistic strategies could evolve when players were able to keep track of the number of altruistic moves made by other players and adjust the probability of interacting with them accordingly.

THE EVOLUTION OF FRIENDSHIP

In contrast to classic Prisoners' Dilemma games, the ultimate benefits individuals are able to obtain from social exchanges in the real world may be highly variable across partners. Because members of groups have a finite amount of time and energy to devote to cooperative exchanges, it is in their interest to fill their "association niches" with partners or friends who possess the potential to benefit them the most (Tooby & Cosmides, 1996).

Mutual Choice and the Paradox of Popularity   Resolving to restrict your interactions to exchanges with good guys will not do you any good unless the good guys also select you. For this reason, members of groups attempt to elevate their "association value" and make themselves "irreplaceable" (Tooby & Cosmides, 1996). Individuals' association value is affected by both their willingness and ability to help others. Nesse (2001) suggested that, endowed with language, humans induce others to believe they are willing to help by making promises, which constitute commitments to future acts.

The adaptive value of selecting good guys as exchange partners and being selected as an exchange partner may produce a pleasant paradox. Individuals can maximize their gains by sacrificing their interests for the sake of others, as long as the benefits they receive from being viewed by others as an attractive exchange partner outweigh the costs of the sacrifices they incur to make themselves attractive (Alexander, 1987). To maximize their gains, individuals should select as exchange partners those they can help at least cost. Tooby and Cosmides point out that members of groups may be able to benefit each other incidentally, as they go about their business, with little or no cost to themselves. We would expect individuals to be attentive to the extent to which the resources they have to offer complement the resources others have to offer, which boils down to compatibility.

A Friend in Need   Revisiting Axelrod and Hamilton's games again, it is notable that the costs and benefits of all exchanges were reckoned directly in terms of ultimate benefits, namely, the number of offspring contributed to future generations. In contrast, most of the resources people exchange in the real world are only indirectly related to reproductive success. It could pay off biologically for an individual to do many small favors for a partner or friend in return for one big favor—100 tits for one tat. Tooby and Cosmides (1996) discuss a phenomenon called the *Banker's Paradox*. Like customers who apply for loans from banks, individuals are least likely to receive help when they most need it, because they are least able to pay it back. Tooby and Cosmides suggest that Banker's Paradoxes constituted important adaptive problems in ancestral environments and that mechanisms that induce individuals to form and uphold friendships evolved to solve them.

The Design of Psychological Mechanisms Mediating Exchanges between Friends Tooby and Cosmides (1996) emphasize the differences between adaptations mediating concrete reciprocity and adaptations mediating exchanges among friends. As pointed out by scholars such as Clark and Mills (1993) and Shackelford and Buss (1996), people often make significant sacrifices for their friends with no expectation of compensation. The results of several studies suggest that the mental mechanisms mediating exchanges between friends are designed in ways that induce them to underestimate their costs and overestimate their gains. For example, Janicki (2004) found that participants underestimated the value of their contributions to social exchanges with friends and overestimated the value of the contributions of their partners. In addition, participants said they were more concerned about repaying than about being repaid and felt more upset when they failed to reciprocate than when their partners failed to reciprocate. Sprecher (2001) reported similar findings on dating couples, and Greenberg and Cohen (1982) reviewed research demonstrating that people are motivated to avoid becoming "indebted" to others. The payoffs from friendship are like the payoffs from stocks or life insurance; they involve investments in long-term security.

Collaborative Coordination Tooby and Cosmides's (1996) analysis of the adaptive benefits of social exchanges between friends also applies to adaptive problems such as hunting large game, building a shelter, and defending against predators that can be solved through collaborative coordination (Hill, 2002). Such problems differ from problems stemming from resource variability and variations in need because they require the simultaneous coordination of effort from two or more individuals and the distribution of the fruits of their labor. To maximize the benefits from coordinated efforts, it is in individuals' interest to select as collaborative partners those who are motivated to solve the same kinds of problems they are motivated to solve and those who possess abilities that complement their own.

THE EVOLUTION OF INDIRECT RECIPROCITY

Strategies that induce individuals to select cooperators as exchange partners can give rise to systems of indirect reciprocity. In systems of indirect reciprocity, person A gives to person B, who gives to person C, who gives to person A: "What goes around comes around." Such systems have the potential to generate more benefits than systems of direct reciprocity because they are better equipped to maximize gains in trade; however, they tend to be more susceptible to cheating. People know when someone fails to pay them back and it makes them angry, but they often don't know whether people fail to pay their debts by helping third parties, and they may not care.

To evolve, systems of indirect reciprocity must contain ways of ensuring that those who do their share gain more than those who do not. As discussed, members of groups may reward cooperators and altruists directly by selecting them as exchange partners, elevating their status, and giving them material benefits. As explained by Alexander (1987), good guys also may reap indirect benefits through the enhanced fitness of their collateral relatives and through the success of their groups. In contrast, cheaters may be punished through losses in status, rejection as partners, ostracism from the group, and negative effects on the group that filter back to the cheater and his or her relatives. It follows that members of groups practicing indirect reciprocity should be vigilant for selfishness, should gossip about the social behaviors of others, and should be concerned about their reputation (Alexander, 1987). Game theorists have demonstrated that altruistic strategies can evolve and become evolutionarily stable in systems of indirect reciprocity if they enhance individuals' reputations or "images" and if members of groups discriminate in favor of those with a good reputation (Nowak & Sigmund, 1998; Wedekind & Milinski, 2000).

Impression Management   Strictly speaking, individuals do not base their decisions about social exchange on how others behave; they base them on their *beliefs* about how others have behaved and will behave. What pays off in the social world is not what you do or what you are, but what others think about you—the impressions you create, your reputation (Goffman, 1959). It is in individuals' interest to put on displays designed to induce members of their groups to overestimate their generosity and underestimate their selfishness. In support of this idea, researchers have found that people are prone to invoke more generous principles of resource allocation in front of audiences than they are in private, especially when the audiences contain members whose opinions they value and with whom they anticipate interacting in the future (Austin, 1980).

However, the selection of strategies designed to induce others to view us as more altruistic than we actually are is constrained by at least three factors. First, such strategies tend to attract exchanges with selfish exploiters. It pays off more to be viewed as a discriminating cooperator than as a gullible giver. Second, inasmuch as it is biologically costly to be deceived and manipulated, we would expect mechanisms designed to detect deception and to guard against manipulation to evolve. Cosmides (1989) has adduced evidence that our reasoning abilities are designed in ways that render us proficient at detecting cheating in the social arena. Third, false impressions are constrained by reality. To be perceived as altruistic, an individual must put on displays of altruism, which inevitably entails behaving altruistically. Through the medium of language—in particular, gossip—members of groups can share information about the selfishness of others, reducing the opportunity to create false impressions and exploit others with impunity.

Impression-management and deception detection and prevention mechanisms undoubtedly evolved through an arms-race type of process, with deception detection and prevention mechanisms selecting for improved impression-management mechanisms, and improved impression-management mechanisms selecting for improved deception detection and prevention mechanisms (cf. Trivers, 1985). To complicate matters, each individual is both an actor and an audience, a deceiver and a detector—social exchanges are akin to sports games. Each player makes offensive moves (attempts to deceive and manipulate the other) and defensive moves (guards against being deceived and manipulated).

Deception detection mechanisms should be calibrated in accordance with the costs and benefits of detecting deception. In general, it is more beneficial to detect deception in those whose interests conflict with ours—members of outgroups and enemies—than in those with whom we share interests (see Krebs & Denton, 1997, for a review of relevant research). Indeed, when we partake in the gains of others, it may be in our interest to support their deception and self-deception (Denton & Zarbatany, 1996).

Impression Management, Deception Detection, and Morality   Deceiving others about how good we are is not right. However, if to cultivate the appearance of goodness, people must behave in fair and generous ways, impression management may induce them to behave morally. Structures designed to detect and prevent deception may constrain people from engaging in immoral behaviors. Weak detection and prevention mechanisms—gullibility, tolerance of deviance, and susceptibility to exploitation—may encourage others to behave immorally.

THE EVOLUTION OF CARE

To many people, altruistic, caring, and loving behaviors are more moral than deferential, cooperative, and fair behaviors because they are more unselfish. Whereas behaving justly entails treating everyone—including self—equally or equitably, behaving altruistically entails treating others better than self—sacrificing one's interests for the sake of others. Mental mechanisms mediating impression management, the formation of friendships, and systems of indirect reciprocity take us some distance toward accounting for caring behaviors, but they differ in significant ways from the mental mechanisms that give rise to the kind of love and nurturance people bestow on their mates and offspring.

In Axelrod and Hamilton's (1981) models, players reproduced asexually and offspring entered new generations as self-sufficient adults. Things become considerably more complicated in species that reproduce sexually and bear offspring that need assistance after birth. In sexually reproducing species, propagating one's genes usually entails helping one's offspring. Many chapters of this *Handbook* are devoted to mating strategies, parental investment, and kinship. This chapter explains how mechanisms designed to help individuals foster their reproductive success may dispose them to engage in the types of caring and altruistic behaviors that many people consider the heart of morality.

Investing in Mates and Offspring   Propagating an individual's genes through sexual reproduction is an inherently cooperative enterprise. Males and females must coordinate their efforts to produce a product in which each shares an interest. Because the complement of genes that each partner contributes is inexorably linked to the complement of the other, propagating an individual's own genes entails propagating the genes of his or her mate. Sexual reproduction is a prime example of collaborative coordination.

It is appropriate to view mating in terms of the original social problem that I argue gave rise to morality. Men and women who want offspring share a confluence of interest. Neither can achieve this goal without the assistance of the other. But they also experience a conflict of interest. It is in the interest of each party to contribute less than his or her share and to induce the other to contribute more than his or her share to their mutual investment. As with the acquisition of more survival-oriented resources, individuals adopt strategies and engage in social games to solve this adaptive problem. Some strategies, such as rape, infidelity, and cuckoldry, are selfish and immoral—they are designed to foster the interests of those that invoke them at the expense of the interests of their mates. Other strategies, such as devotion and fidelity, are unselfish and moral.

When individuals choose mates, they act as agents of selection, selecting the qualities (possessed by their mates) that will be inherited by their offspring and transmitted to future generations. Sexual selection may well have played an important role in the evolution of mental mechanisms that give rise to care-oriented behaviors (Krebs, 1998; Miller, 1998). Zahavi and Zahavi (1996) have argued that females are attracted to males who have prevailed in spite of handicaps and that dispositions to behave altruistically may have evolved through the handicap principle. More basically, it is in the adaptive interest of members of both sexes to mate with individuals who are disposed to love and care for their partners and offspring. The greater the need for assistance, the more important these qualities become. It also is in the adaptive interest of members of both sexes to select mates who will honor their commitments to them and their offspring. In general, it is more important for men than for women to select mates who are faithful because maternity is more certain than paternity (Buss, 1994).

Humans inherit mechanisms that induce them to fall in love with members of the opposite sex, care for their offspring, and treat their relatives in altruistic ways. However, people sometimes cheat on their partners and mistreat their offspring. As with other evolved mechanisms, the key to understanding why people sometimes help their relatives and sometimes hurt them is to identify the "if" conditions that activate the strategies they possess.

Sex Differences in Moral Orientation   Research supports Gilligan's (1982) claim that women tend to make more Stage 3 care-oriented moral judgments than men do about their real-life moral dilemmas, but not necessarily because women acquire care-oriented dispositions early in life, as Gilligan claims. The reason that women make more care-oriented judgments than men about their real-life moral dilemmas is that the dilemmas they report are more care-oriented in nature than the dilemmas reported by men (Wark & Krebs, 1996, 1997). If you hold the type of dilemma constant, the sex difference disappears. Interpreted in evolutionary terms, the types of adaptive problems individuals experience determine the types of strategies they invoke and types of judgments they make.

The Generalization of Caring Behaviors to Kin   In Axelrod and Hamilton's (1981) games, there was a 100% probability that "offspring" would inherit the strategies of their "parents." In contrast, among members of sexually reproducing species, the probability of individuals sharing genes or strategies with other members of their groups varies with their degree of relatedness. In an insight that had a profound effect on our understanding of evolution and altruism, Hamilton (1964) pointed out that individuals should be disposed to help other members of their groups when the genetic cost to them of helping is less than the benefits to the recipient divided by his or her degree of relatedness. Research on humans and other animals has supported this expectation (Burnstein, Chapter 18, this volume). In effect, Hamilton's rule explicates the "if" conditions built into an evolved moral strategy.

The Generalization of Caring Behaviors to Kinlike Members of Groups   Strictly speaking, the strategy described by Hamilton induces individuals to restrict their altruism to kin. However, kin-selected mechanisms may be designed in ways that induce people to help nonrelatives, because they are imprecise (Krebs, 1998). Whatever the ability of genes to identify replicas of themselves in others (Rushton, 1999, vs. Dawkins, 1989), members of many species employ cues to genetic relatedness such as phenotypic similarity, familiarity, and proximity to identify

In the EEA, would children not have cared for parents beyond reproductive age ??

relatives (Porter, 1987). Such cues may well have been more highly correlated with kinship in ancestral environments than they are in modern environments. The more imprecise the mechanisms of kin recognition and the more they misfire in modern environments, the greater is the range of altruism to which they give rise.

Stage 3 Morality   Moral judgments that uphold relationships and prescribe care-oriented behaviors are considered virtuous in all cultures (Sober & Wilson, 1998). In Kohlberg's system, moral judgments such as (1) you should help members of your groups "in order to leave a good impression in the community," (2) you should help your friends "to show love, respect, trust, or honesty because this builds or maintains a good relationship" and "to show appreciation, gratitude, or respect for everything [they] have done for you," and (3) people should help their spouses "because they feel close to them" and "because they care about them and love them" are classified as Stage 3. However, as nice as love, care, and nurturance seem, the behaviors to which they give rise suffer a significant moral limitation. The mechanisms that govern care and commitment are designed in ways that induce people to favor their friends, spouses, and offspring at the expense of other people's friends, spouses, and offspring. To meet high standards of morality, love and care must be regulated by justice; people must allocate their altruism fairly (Kohlberg, 1984).

STAGE 3/4 MORALITY: THE EVOLUTION OF GROUP-UPHOLDING DISPOSITIONS

The earlier discussion has explained how mental mechanisms that induce individuals to defer to those who are more powerful than they are, to reciprocate with peers, to make amends, to forgive, to cooperate with cooperators, and to care for their friends, mates, offspring, kin, and kinlike members of their group could have evolved. We can take two more steps up the ladder of morality: (1) to less nepotistic and discriminatory dispositions to help members of an individual's group, and (2) to dispositions to create and uphold social contracts and formal moral codes.

At least three evolutionary processes could have mediated the selection of mental mechanisms that dispose individuals to help members of their groups. First, inasmuch as individuals benefit from the existence of the groups of which they are a part, they have a vested interest in preserving them. Groups are like partners and coalitions: It pays for individuals to uphold them when they foster their security and other adaptive interests. Second, as Alexander (1987) has explained, systems of indirect reciprocity may give rise to a "modicum of indiscriminate altruism." Third, dispositions to help members of an individual's group may have evolved through group selection.

Group Selection

Sober and Wilson (1998) have advanced the most compelling case for the evolution of altruistic traits through group selection (Daly & Wilson, Part IV Introduction, this volume). Following Darwin (1871), Sober and Wilson (1998) have argued that it is plausible to assume that groups containing members who are genetically predisposed to behave altruistically would fare better than groups containing more selfish members, just as pairs of cooperators fare better than pairs of defectors in Prisoners' Dilemma games, and this would lead to an increase in altruistic genes in the population. However, altruism would decrease in frequency within groups. Sober and Wilson outline conditions under which between-group selection for altruism could outpace within-group selection for selfishness and suggest that such conditions may have existed in the environments in which our hominid ancestors evolved. Sober and Wilson suggest that group selection of altruism was probably augmented by the evolution of cultural norms and sanctions. Critics have taken exception to the analytic framework advanced by Sober and Wilson and have argued that the conditions necessary for group selection rarely occur in nature (e.g., see commentaries following Sober & Wilson, 2000).

THE DESIGN OF MECHANISMS DISPOSING PEOPLE TO UPHOLD IN-GROUPS

Research supports the idea that humans inherit mechanisms that induce them to identify with and favor members of in-groups, in judgment and in behavior (Linville, Fischer, & Salovey, 1989). Research on social categorization has found that simply assigning people to groups—on whatever basis—may induce such biases (Tajfel & Turner, 1985). On the other side of the coin, researchers have found that people make negative, global, and undifferentiated attributions about out-group members automatically—"They are all the same, and I don't like them"—(Hamilton, Stroessner, & Driscoll, 1994). Although in-group upholding dispositions expand the range of recipients beyond relatives and family members, they are nonetheless limited morally because they are inherently ethnocentric.

STAGE 4 MORALITY: THE NATURAL SELECTION OF MORAL JUDGMENTS AND THE ORIGIN OF MORAL NORMS

In Axelrod and Hamilton's (1981) games, players did not make choices in the context of a formal moral system guided by a set of rules; indeed, players were not even able to communicate with each other. In contrast, the moral systems of all human societies are defined by sets of norms, rules, and laws that members express to one another in words. Parents explain these rules to their children, teachers teach them to their students, and preachers preach them to their parishioners. To many people, the essence of morality lies in obeying these rules and regulations. How do formal systems of rules originate, why do members of groups preach them to each other, and why do people obey them?

When considering the origin of formal systems of rules, it is helpful to distinguish between behavioral norms—customs practiced by most members of groups—and verbal norms—the rules and regulations people express in words or preach. To this point, the discussion has focused on the evolution of behavioral norms, which have evolved in many species. The following discussion considers verbal norms, moral judgments, and formal systems of rules and laws, which are unique to the human species.

THE EVOLUTION OF MORAL JUDGMENT

Biological analyses of communication have revealed that many species are evolved to send signals designed to induce recipients to behave in ways that foster the senders' interests or to manipulate them. Such signals are often deceptive (Dawkins, 1989; Mitchell & Thompson, 1986). Humans' relatively large brains and their capacity for language expand the range of manipulative communication strategies available to them (MacNeilage & Davis, Chapter 24, this volume).

Senders are able imaginatively to take the perspective of recipients and plan long into the future. Recipients' reactions to senders' signals are less a function of the physical properties of the signals themselves than of the ways in which they represent them cognitively.

Moral judgments can be viewed as signals designed to manipulate others. Some moral judgments, called *aretaic* by philosophers, label people and their behavior as good or bad. They convey approbation and disapprobation; they pass judgment. In Darwin's (1871) account of the evolution of morality, he wrote, "It is . . . hardly possible to exaggerate the importance during rude times of the love of praise and dread of blame" (p. 500). The precursors to the first moral judgments in the human species were probably grunts and coos communicating approval and disapproval.

Deontic moral judgments prescribe or prohibit courses of action. They usually contain or imply the words "should," "ought," or "it is (or was) right or wrong to. . . ." The moral judgments classified by Kohlberg (1984) and his colleagues are deontic in nature. The function of deontic moral judgments such as, "You should help me," and "You owe me," is to persuade recipients to behave in accordance with the prescriptions they contain. The function of more abstract deontic judgments such as "Honesty is the best policy," "People should obey the law," and "Do unto others . . ." is to induce recipients to adopt strategies that uphold social systems from which senders benefit. Viewed in this way, the reasons that define the stages of moral judgments in Kohlberg's system (Table 26.1) equate to persuasive arguments designed to induce recipients to behave in ways that benefit senders, directly or indirectly. Such reasons are designed to induce recipients to form cognitive representations of the "if" conditions that activate the prescriptions the reasons support.

The Selection of Verbal Moral Norms   Of all the moral judgments people could make, why do members of all known cultures tend to make those classified as Stages 1, 2, and 3 by Kohlberg and his colleagues (Colby & Kohlberg, 1987; Sober & Wilson, 1998; Wright, 1994)? What causes moral judgments to become moral norms? The answer is: the adaptive benefits to those who make them. Although at first glance it might seem that senders should exhort others to maximize their (the senders') gains, selfish judgments would not work because recipients would not conform to them. In effect, recipients of moral judgments are agents of selection. They determine which kinds of judgment pay off for those who send them. In a similar vein, although we would expect recipients to be receptive to moral judgments that advance their interests at the expense of those who send them, it would not be in senders' interest to transmit such judgments. For these reasons, moral judgments that evolve into moral norms should prescribe behaviors that foster the interests of senders and recipients. They should exhort members of groups to foster their interests in ways that foster the interests of others.

THE EVOLUTION OF RULES

It is a relatively short step from making deontic moral judgments buttressed by reasons to espousing more formal systems of rules and laws. Endowed with the ability to form abstract representations of reality, to deduce general principles from specific cases, and to communicate ideas to others, humans are able to identify the implicit expectations that govern the systems of cooperation that have evolved in their groups and verbalize them as rules and laws. The function of such rules is to ensure that others are clear about what is expected of them, to control the behavior of others, and to induce them to uphold the systems of cooperation from which they benefit by performing their roles and doing their duties. In extrapolating rules to the group as a whole, members bind themselves (Elster, 2000). But there is more to moral rules and laws than this, at least in the human species.

BEYOND EVOLVED NORMS AND NATURAL INCLINATIONS

Humans possess a unique ability to imagine possibilities that do not exist. Creative people, powerful leaders, or groups as a whole may imagine systems of cooperation that could produce greater gains than the systems that have evolved in their groups. Because different systems of cooperation guided by different rules may be adaptive in different ecological contexts, different groups may develop different customs and moral codes. Members of groups should be inclined to endorse the systems of cooperation and moral codes that contain the greatest promise of fostering their interests. People also should be more inclined to accept rules that they have had a part in creating or implementing than in those that others impose on them, because the former are more likely to foster their interests than the latter. The further the behaviors prescribed by the new rules depart from the evolved strategies members of the groups are naturally inclined to practice, the less inclined they should be to obey them.

Reason and Social Learning   Most people assume that parents and other socializing agents teach their children to obey rules by explaining the reasons underlying them (induction), by setting good examples (modeling), and by rewarding and punishing them, either physically or through love withdrawal (see Krebs, 2004a). There is nothing in evolutionary theory that is inconsistent with the idea that reason and social learning play important roles in the acquisition of morality. Indeed, eminent evolutionary theorists such as Boyd and Richerson (1985), Dawkins (1989), Darwin (1871), and Williams (1989) have attributed morality to reason and social learning. Mechanisms that mediate these processes evolved because they enabled our ancestors to adapt to their social and physical environments. In refinements of Axelrod and Hamilton's (1981) games, researchers found that strategies such as "Pavlov" that incorporated principles of learning were able to defeat less flexible strategies (see Ridley, 1996). Even strategies such as Tit-for-Tat can be defined in terms of principles of operant conditioning: "If a behavior is followed by punishment, change it; if a behavior is followed by reward, repeat it."

Limitations of Reason and Social Learning in the Inculcation of Morality   However, the roles played by reason and social learning in the inculcation of morality are overrated. It is true that with the power to reason, people can create systems of rules that, if everyone abided by them, would maximize everyone's gains. It also is true that people tend to copy the behavior of others and conform to social norms. However, reason and social learning can induce people to violate rules and to behave immorally as easily as they can induce people to uphold rules and behave morally.

In game theory terms, if the goal of social interactions is to maximize an individual's benefits, and if everyone else—or even most people—are inclined to cooperate, the most reasonable course of action is to cheat. Selfishness is eminently reasonable if your goal is to maximize your gains. Social cognition is plagued by a host of self-serving biases (see Bandura, 1991; Haselton, Nettle, & Andrews, Chapter 25, this volume; Krebs & Denton, 1997). Haidt (2001) has advanced a great deal of evidence in support of the conclusion that most moral judgments stem from irrational, automatic, "intuitive" cognitive, and affective processes and that the primary role of moral reasoning is to generate post hoc justifications for self-interested acts. In our research on real-life moral judgment and behavior (Krebs & Denton, in press; Krebs et al., 2002), we concluded that affective reactions exert a much greater effect on moral decision making than cognitive-developmental theorists such as Kohlberg (1984) assume.

Although social learning and conformity undoubtedly play an important role in the maintenance, spread, and transmission of moral norms (Boyd & Richerson, 1985), these processes are not equipped to account for the origin of moral norms (Krebs & Janicki, 2004). Attempting to account for morality through modeling and induction leads to an infinite regress. At some point in our evolutionary history, someone had to engage in a moral behavior or preach a moral rule for others to copy or obey it. People are highly selective about the behaviors they model and the rules they obey. To account for such selectivity, we need to understand how the mechanisms that mediate social learning were designed in ancestral environments. Boyd and Richerson (1985) have suggested that social learning mechanisms are affected by three types of bias. *Direct biases* incline people to evaluate (consciously or unconsciously) the behaviors that others emit and copy those that they anticipate will best enable them to achieve their goals. *Indirect biases* incline people to copy the words and deeds of successful people. *Frequency-dependent biases* incline people to model the behaviors that are most frequent in the population (see also Flinn & Alexander, 1982). Research on social learning theory is consistent with these expectations (Burton & Kunce, 1995, pp. 151–152).

The Significance of Self-Interest and Sanctions If reason, social learning, and evolved moral dispositions were enough to induce people to obey rules, there would be no need for sanctions, but this is not the case. In tandem with inventing systems of cooperation that maximize their gains, members of societies must structure their environments in ways that ensure that cooperative strategies pay off better than selfish strategies. For this reason, the moral rules and laws of all societies are supported by rewards and punishments. Such sanctions may be physical (getting whipped or stoned to death), material (fines, retributions), social (disapproval, ostracism), or psychological (shame, guilt). In Kohlberg's hierarchy, systems of cooperation upheld by Stage 4 moral judgments are supported by the kinds of physical and material punishments prescribed by Stage 1 moral judgments.

Members of groups can be induced to obey almost any system of rules and laws as long as the regulations are supported by effective sanctions (Boyd & Richerson, 1985; Janicki & Krebs, 1998; Krebs & Janicki, 2004; Sober & Wilson, 1998). In effect, members of groups induce one another—and, therefore, themselves—to obey moral rules and conform to moral norms by structuring and engineering their environments in ways that make obedience and conformity pay off better than disobedience and nonconformity.

But there's a catch. Although detecting and punishing those who cheat you personally may pay off better than ignoring them, the costs of taking it upon yourself to catch and punish free riders who fail to contribute their share to society usually outweigh the gains. Better to let someone else do the dirty work. In a study titled, "Punishment Allows the Evolution of Cooperation (or Anything Else) in Sizable Groups," Boyd and Richerson (1992) found that this problem could be overcome by punishing members of groups who failed to punish free riders. Price, Cosmides, and Tooby (2002) adduced experimental evidence that two motivational systems have evolved to overcome the free-rider problem. One disposes people to punish free riders, and the other disposes people to recruit cooperators by rewarding cooperation. Gintis, Bowles, Boyd, and Fehr (2003) explained how a mechanism that disposed individuals to cooperate and to punish those who failed to cooperate—called *strong reciprocity*—could have invaded a population saturated by selfish individuals and given rise to evolutionarily stable altruistic norms. To induce people to obey the rules of complex societies, members create institutions such as police forces, courts, and jails designed to catch and punish cheaters.

THE EVOLUTION OF CONSCIENCE

Obeying rules to obtain rewards and avoid punishments doesn't seem very moral. Moral judgments explicitly prescribing this strategy are classified at the lowest stage in Kohlberg's sequence. Conformity also doesn't seem very moral in and of itself. Moral judgments prescribing this strategy are classified at Stage 3. Most people believe that to qualify as moral, a behavior must spring from an internal source. Morality involves obeying internalized rules and abiding by internalized principles when no one is watching. Exemplars of morality such as Gandhi, Martin Luther King Jr., and Christ suffered great costs to uphold their beliefs. To fully account for morality, we need to account for the development of mental mechanisms that induce people to resist the temptation to advance their interests at the expense of others when they could get away with it.

Psychologists have advanced two main explanations for the intrinsic motivation to behave morally. The first is based in learning theory. In essentially the same way that pets can be trained to resist temptation and to obey rules when no one is there to reward or punish them, people can be trained to develop moral habits through conditioning and vicarious learning (Aronfreed, 1968). The second explanation is based in identification with others and the development of perspective-taking abilities. Scholars from a wide array of theoretical traditions (e.g., Aronfreed, 1968; Freud, 1926; Higgins, 1987; Kohlberg, 1984; Mead, 1934) have advanced the idea that the mental mechanisms that give rise to moral judgments and moral behaviors—often called conscience or superego—contain cognitive representations of others. In effect, people internalize mental representations of others who direct their behavior and hold them accountable, even though the others are not physically present.

Selman (1980) has adduced evidence that as people develop, they acquire increasingly sophisticated perspective-taking abilities. The more sophisticated such abilities, the larger the range of perspectives considered and the more abstract the cognitive representations of others' points of view. Joining many philosophers of ethics, Kohlberg (1984) has argued that sophisticated perspective-taking abilities are necessary for sophisticated moral decision making. It is easy to see how low-stage perspective taking that enables individuals to predict the behavior of others could be adaptive, but it is more difficult to see the adaptive value of the kinds of impartial perspective-taking abilities that philosophers believe are necessary for sophisticated moral decision making.

HOW MORAL ARE WE, BY NATURE?

Virtually all ultimate moral principles espoused by philosophers of ethics, including those that define Kohlberg's Stages 5 and 6, are based in two prescriptions: (1) Maximize benefits to humankind, and (2) allocate these benefits in a nondiscriminatory way. It takes little thought to see that even though such unconditional strategies could maximize the benefits for everyone if everyone practiced them, they could not evolve without help from sanctions, because they are vulnerable to cheating, nepotism, and discrimination against out-groups.

Although highly generalized forms of impartial perspective taking are a theoretical possibility, there is little evidence people actually engage in them in their everyday lives (Krebs, 2000a, 2000b, 2000c, 2004b; Krebs & Denton, in press). Kohlberg's highest stages of moral development are different from his earlier stages. They are much "colder," more logical and reasonable; there is virtually no mention of affect in Stage 5 or Stage 6 moral judgments. Some of Kohlberg's collaborators (e.g., Gibbs, Basinger, & Fuller, 1992) have argued that the moral judgments that define Kohlberg's principled stages stem from "metatheoretical" forms of reasoning, quite different from the forms of reasoning that give rise to lower stage moral judgments. There is no evidence that people from nonindustrialized societies make Stage 5 or Stage 6 moral judgments, and it is difficult to imagine how mechanisms that induce people to behave in accordance with them could have evolved in the environments of our ancestors.

This is tragically ironic. If we all behaved in accordance with high-stage moral principles such as "Give to everyone according to his need," "Do unto others as you would have them do unto you," and "Behave in a way that maximizes the greatest good for the greatest number," we would all come out ahead. Everyone would cooperate. We wouldn't have to worry about war or crime. We could invest all the money we saved from the arms race, police, and jails in enhancing the quality of our lives. However, because the strategies prescribed by lofty principles of ethics contain no antidotes to cheating and nepotism, they are destined to fail. To create moral societies, we must make it in people's adaptive interest to cooperate with others, and the only way to accomplish this is to design environments in ways that ensure that cooperation pays off better than selfishness, cheating, free riding, and favoritism.

CONCLUSION

The conclusion reached by eminent evolutionary theorists, that all animals inherit selfish and immoral dispositions, is correct; however it is only half the story. We also inherit unselfish and moral dispositions. We are neither all good nor all bad; we inherit the potential to behave in both good and bad ways. Altruistic dispositions have evolved through kin selection, sexual selection, and possibly group selection. Dispositions to behave in cooperative ways also have evolved. The key to fostering morality lies in creating the "if" conditions that activate altruistic and cooperative dispositions, and suppressing the "if" conditions that activate selfish and immoral dispositions, both on an individual and societal basis. The mechanisms that give rise to morality are biological adaptations, and should be treated as such. There is no inconsistency between behaving morally and fostering inclusive fitness. There is nothing immoral about the ultimate goals of human behavior; morality pertains to the means people employ to achieve them.

REFERENCES

Alexander, R. D. (1987). *The biology of moral systems.* New York: Aldine de Gruyter.

Aronfreed, J. (1968). *Conduct and conscience.* New York: Academic Press.

Austin, W. (1980). Friendship and fairness: Effects of type of relationship and task performance on choice of distribution rules. *Personality and Social Psychology Bulletin, 6,* 402–408.

Axelrod, R., & Hamilton, W. D. (1981). The evolution of cooperation. *Science, 211,* 1390–1396.

Bandura, A. (1991). Social cognitive theory of moral thought and action. In W. M. Kurtines & J. L. Gewirtz (Eds.), *Handbook of moral behavior and development.* (Vol. 1, pp. 54–104). Hillsdale, NJ: Erlbaum.

Barinaga, M. (1996). Social status sculpts activity of crayfish neurons. *Science, 271,* 290–291.

Boehm, C. (2000). Conflict and the evolution of social control. In L. D. Katz (Ed.), *Evolutionary origins of morality* (pp. 79–101). Thorverton, UK: Imprint Academic.

Boyd, R., & Richerson, P. J. (1985). *Culture and the evolutionary process.* Chicago: University of Chicago Press.

Boyd, R., & Richerson, P. J. (1992). Punishment allows the evolution of cooperation (or anything else) in sizable groups. *Ethology and Sociobiology, 13,* 171–195.

Burton, R. V., & Kunce, L. (1995). Behavioral models of moral development: A brief history and integration. In W. M. Kurtines & J. L. Gewirtz (Eds.), *Moral development: An introduction* (pp. 151–172). Boston: Allyn & Bacon.

Buss, D. M. (1994). *The evolution of desire: Strategies of human mating.* New York: Basic Books.

Buss, D. M. (1999). *Evolutionary psychology: The new science of the mind.* Boston: Allyn & Bacon.

Campbell, D. T. (1978). On the genetics of altruism and the counter hedonic components in human nature. In L. Wispe (Ed.), *Altruism, sympathy, and helping: Psychological and sociological implications* (pp. 39–58). New York: Academic Press.

Clark, M. S., & Mills, J. (1993). The difference between communal and exchange relationships: What it is and is not. *Personality and Social Psychology Bulletin, 19,* 684–691.

Colby, A., & Kohlberg, L. (Eds.). (1987). *The measurement of moral judgment* (Vols. 1–2). Cambridge: Cambridge University Press.

Cosmides, L. (1989). The logic of social exchange: Has natural selection shaped how humans reason? Studies with the Wason selection task. *Cognition, 31,* 187–276.

Cummins, D. D. (1998). Social norms and other minds: The evolutionary roots of higher cognition. In D. D. Cummins & C. Allen (Eds.), *The evolution of mind* (pp. 30–50). New York: Oxford University Press.

Damon, W., & Hart, D. (1992). Self understanding and its role in social and moral development. In M. H. Bornstein & E. M. Lamb (Eds.), *Developmental psychology: An advanced textbook* (2nd ed., pp. 421–465). Hillsdale, NJ: Erlbaum.

Darwin, C. (1871). *The descent of man and selection in relation to sex* (Vols. 1/2). New York: Appleton.

Dawkins, R. (1989). *The selfish gene.* Oxford, England: Oxford University Press.

Denton, K., & Zarbatany, L. (1996). Age differences in support processes in conversations between friends. *Child Development, 67,* 1360–1373.

Dugatkin, L. A. (1997). *Cooperation among animals: An evolutionary perspective.* New York: Oxford University Press.

Dugatkin, L. A., & Reeve, H. K. (1994). Behavioral ecology and levels of selection: Dissolving the group selection controversy. *Advances in the Study of Behavior, 23,* 101–133.

Elster, J. (2000). *Ulysses unbound.* London, Cambridge University Press.

Flinn, M. V., & Alexander, R. D. (1982). Culture theory: The developing synthesis from biology. *Human Ecology, 10,* 383–400.

Freud, S. (1926). *Collected papers.* London: Hogarth Press.

Gibbs, J., Basinger, K. S., & Fuller, D. (1992). *Moral maturity: Measuring the development of sociomoral reasoning.* Hillsdale, NJ: Erlbaum.

Gilligan, C. (1982). *In a different voice: Psychological theory and women's development.* Cambridge, MA: Harvard University Press.

Gintis, H., Bowles, S., Boyd, R., & Fehr, E. (2003). Explaining altruistic behavior in humans. *Evolution and Human Behavior, 24,* 153–172.

Goffman, E. (1959). *The presentation of self in everyday life.* New York: Anchor Books.

Gouldner, A. W. (1960). The norm of reciprocity: A preliminary statement. *American Sociological Review, 25,* 161–178.

Greenberg, J., & Cohen, R. L. (1982). *Social exchange: Advances in theory and research.* New York: Plenum Press.

Haidt, J. (2001). The emotional dog and its rational tail: A social intuitionist approach to moral judgment. *Psychological Review, 108,* 814–834.

Hamilton, D. I., Stroessner, S. J., & Driscoll, D. M. (1994). Social cognition and the study of stereotyping. In P. G. Devine, D. L. Hamilton, & T. M. Ostrom (Eds.), *Social cognition: Impact on social psychology* (pp. 291–321). New York: Academic Press.

Hamilton, W. D. (1964). The evolution of social behavior. *Journal of Theoretical Biology, 7,* 1–52.

Higgins, E. T. (1987). Self-discrepancy: A theory relating self and affect. *Psychological Review, 94,* 319–340.

Hill, K. (2002). Altruistic cooperation during foraging by the Ache, and the evolved human predisposition to cooperate. *Human Nature, 13,* 105–128.

Huxley, T. (1893). *Evolution and ethics: The second Romanes lecture.* London: Macmillan.

Janicki, M. (2004). Beyond sociobiology: A kinder and gentler evolutionary view of human nature. In C. Crawford & C. Salmon (Eds.), *Evolutionary psychology: Public policy and personal decisions* (pp. 51–72). Mahwah, NJ: Erlbaum.

Janicki, M. G., & Krebs, D. L. (1998). Evolutionary approaches to culture. In C. Crawford & D. L. Krebs (Eds.), *Handbook of evolutionary psychology: Ideas, issues, and applications* (pp. 163–208). Hillsdale, NJ: Erlbaum.

Kohlberg, L. (1984). *Essays in moral development: Vol. 2. The psychology of moral development.* New York: Harper & Row.

Krebs, D. L. (1998). The evolution of moral behavior. In C. Crawford & D. L. Krebs (Eds.), *Handbook of evolutionary psychology: Ideas, issues, and applications* (pp. 337–368). Hillsdale, NJ: Erlbaum.

Krebs, D. L. (2000a). The evolution of moral dispositions in the human species. In D. LeCroy & P. Moller (Eds.), *Evolutionary perspectives on human reproductive behavior: Annals of the New York Academy of Science* (Vol. 907, pp. 1–17). New York: The New York Academy of Sciences.

Krebs, D. L. (2000b). Evolutionary games and morality. In L. D. Katz (Ed.), *Evolutionary origins of morality: Cross-disciplinary approaches* (pp. 313–321). Thorverton, UK: Imprint Academic.

Krebs, D. L. (2000c). As moral as we need to be. In L. D. Katz (Ed.), *Evolutionary origins of morality: Cross-disciplinary approaches* (pp. 139–143). Thorverton, UK: Imprint Academic.

Krebs, D. L. (2004a). An evolutionary reconceptualization of Kohlberg's model of moral development. In R. Burgess & K. MacDonald (Eds.), *Evolutionary perspectives on human development* (pp. 243–274). Newbury Park, CA: Sage.

Krebs, D. L. (2004b). How to make silk purses from sows' ears: Cultivating morality and constructing moral systems. In C. Crawford & C. Salmon (Eds.), *Evolutionary psychology: Public policy and personal decisions* (pp. 319–342). Mahwah, NJ: Erlbaum.

Krebs, D. L., & Denton, K. (1997). Social illusions and self-deception: The evolution of biases in person perception. In J. A. Simpson & D. T. Kenrick (Eds.), *Evolutionary social psychology* (pp. 21–47). Hillsdale, NJ: Erlbaum.

Krebs, D. L., & Denton, K. (in press). Toward a more pragmatic approach to morality: A critical evaluation of Kohlberg's model. *Psychological Review.*

Krebs, D. L., Denton, K., Vermeulen, S. C., Carpendale, J. I., & Bush, A. (1991). The structural flexibility of moral judgment. *Journal of Personality and Social Psychology, 61,* 1012–1023.

Krebs, D. L., Denton, K., Wark, G., Couch, R., Racine, T. P., & Krebs, D. L. (2002). Interpersonal moral conflicts between couples: Effects of type of dilemma, role, and partner's judgments on level of moral reasoning and probability of resolution. *Journal of Adult Development, 9,* 307–316.

Krebs, D. L., & Janicki, M. (2004). The biological foundations of moral norms. In M. Schaller & C. Crandall (Eds.), *Psychological foundations of culture* (pp. 125–148). Hillsdale, NJ: Erlbaum.

Krebs, D. L., & Van Hesteren, F. (1994). The development of altruism: Toward an integrative model. *Developmental Review, 14,* 1–56.

Linville, P. W., Fischer, G. W., & Salovey, P. (1989). Perceived distributions of the characteristics of in-group and out-group members: Empirical evidence and a computer simulation. *Journal of Personality and Social Psychology, 57,* 165–188.

Maynard Smith, J. (1976). Evolution and the theory of games. *American Scientist, 64,* 41–45.

Mead, G. H. (1934). *Mind, self and society.* Chicago: University of Chicago Press.

Milgram, S. (1974). *Obedience to authority.* New York: Harper.

Miller, G. F. (1998). The history of passion: A review of sexual selection and human evolution. In C. Crawford & D. Krebs (Eds.), *Evolution and human behavior: Ideas, issues and applications* (pp. 87–130). Hillsdale, NJ: Erlbaum.

Mitchell, R. W., & Thompson, N. S. (Eds.). (1986). *Deception: Perspectives on human and nonhuman deceit.* New York: State University of New York Press.

Nesse, R. M. (Ed.). (2001). *Evolution and the capacity for commitment.* New York: Russell Sage Foundation.

Newitt, C., & Krebs, D. L. (2003). *Structural and contextual sources of moral judgment.* in preparation.

Nowak, M. A., & Sigmund, K. (1998). Evolution of indirect reciprocity by image scoring. *Nature, 393,* 573–577.

Osherow, N. (1995). Making sense of the nonsensical: An analysis of Jonestown. In E. Aronson (Ed.), *Readings about the social animal* (7th ed., pp. 68–86). San Francisco: Freeman.

Piaget, J. (1932). *The moral judgment of the child.* London: Routledge & Kegan Paul.

Porter, R. H. (1987). Kin recognition: Functions and mediating mechanisms. In C. B. Crawford & D. L. Krebs (Eds.), *Sociobiology and psychology: Ideas, issues and applications* (pp. 175–205). Hillsdale, NJ: Erlbaum.

Price, M. E., Cosmides, L., & Tooby, J. (2002). Punitive sentiment as an anti-free rider psychological device. *Evolution and Human Behavior, 23,* 203–231.

Rawls, J. (1971). *A theory of justice.* Cambridge, MA: Harvard University Press.

Rest, J. F. (1983). Morality. In J. H. Flavell & E. M. Markman (Eds.), *Handbook of child psychology: Vol. 3. Cognitive development* (4th ed., pp. 556–629). New York: Wiley.

Ridley, M. (1996). *The origins or virtue: Human instincts and the evolution of cooperation.* New York: Viking.

Rushton, J. P. (1999). Genetic similarity theory and the nature of ethnocentrism. In K. Thienpont & R. Cliquet (Eds.), *In-group/Out-group behavior in modern societies: An evolutionary perspective* (pp. 75–107). The Netherlands: Vlaamse Gemeeschap/CBGC.

Selman, R. L. (1980). *The growth of interpersonal understanding.* New York: Academic Press.

Shackelford, T. K., & Buss, D. M. (1996). Betrayal in mateships, friendships, and coalitions. *Personality and Social Psychology Bulletin, 22,* 1151–1164.

Sober, E., & Wilson, D. S. (1998). *Unto others: The evolution and psychology of unselfish behavior.* Cambridge, MA: Harvard University Press.

Sober, E., & Wilson, D. S. (2000). Summary of unto others: The evolution and psychology of unselfish behavior. In L. D. Katz (Ed.), *Evolutionary origins of morality* (pp. 185–256). Thorverton, UK: Imprint Academic.

Sprecher, S. (2001). Equity and social exchange in dating couples: Associations with satisfaction, commitment, and stability. *Journal of Marriage and Family, 63,* 599–613.

Tajfel, H., & Turner, J. C. (1985). The social identity theory of intergroup behavior. In S. Worchel & W. G. Austin (Eds.), *Psychology of intergroup relations* (pp. 7–24). Chicago: Nelson-Hall.

Tooby, J., & Cosmides, L. (1996). Friendship and the banker's paradox: Other pathways to the evolution of adaptations for altruism. *Proceedings of the British Academy, 88,* 119–143.

Tooby, J., & DeVore, I. (1987). The reconstruction of hominid behavioral evolution through strategic modeling. In W. G. Kinzey (Ed.), *The evolution of human behavior: Primate models* (pp. 183–237). Albany, NY: SUNY Press.

Trivers, R. L. (1971). The evolution of reciprocal altruism. *Quarterly Review of Biology, 46,* 35–57.

Trivers, R. L. (1985). *Social evolution.* Menlo Park, CA: Benjamin Cummings.

Wark, G., & Krebs, D. L. (1996). Gender and dilemma differences in real-life moral judgment. *Developmental Psychology, 32,* 220–230.

Wark, G., & Krebs, D. L. (1997). Sources of variation in real-life moral judgment: Toward a model of real-life morality. *Journal of Adult Development, 4,* 163–178.

Wedekind, C., & Milinski, M. (2000). Cooperation through image scoring in humans. *Science, 288,* 850–852.

Williams, G. C. (1989). A sociobiological expansion of "Evolution and Ethics," *Evolution and Ethics* (pp. 179–214). Princeton: Princeton University Press.

Wright, R. (1994). *The moral animal.* New York: Pantheon Books.

Zahavi, A., & Zahavi, A. (1996). *The handicap principle.* New York: Oxford University Press.

PART VI

EVOLUTIONIZING TRADITIONAL DISCIPLINES OF PSYCHOLOGY

DAVID M. BUSS

T HE FIELD OF psychology historically has been organized around subdisciplines, such as cognitive, social, developmental, personality, and clinical. Evolutionary psychology, in many ways, dissolves these subdisciplinary boundaries. The topics of this *Handbook* are largely organized around adaptive problems and evolved psychological solutions. As a consequence, each of the traditional subdisciplines in the field of psychology has relevance to many psychological adaptations. Consider, for example, the evolved fear of snakes. This adaptation has an underlying cognitive (information processing) architecture, emerges at a predictable point in development, is susceptible to social input through observing the fear reactions of others, shows stable individual differences, and can become dysfunctional or pathological. Examined through the lens of evolutionary psychology, the subdisciplinary boundaries of mainstream psychology appear somewhat arbitrary and do not cleave nature at its natural joints.

Nonetheless, because most psychologists are trained within the coalitional guilds and conceptual frameworks of these traditional subdisciplines, it is useful to see how evolutionary psychologists can approach the main questions and problems of these subdisciplines. What can evolutionary psychology offer to these disciplines as they are traditionally conceived? What new insights can be brought to bear on them? The chapters in this part address these questions.

Peter Todd, Ralph Hertwig, and Urlich Hoffrage provide a fascinating evolutionary psychological analysis of the field of cognitive psychology in Chapter 27. They show how fresh insights into traditional topics—attention, information representation, memory, forgetting, inference, judgment, heuristics, biases, and decision making—can be informed by evolutionary analysis. Reciprocally, they show how advances in cognitive psychology greatly aid evolutionary analyses. Todd, Hertwig, and Hoffrage provide compelling arguments that benefits of the merger flow both ways, since traditional cognitive psychology also has much to offer evolutionary psychology.

Douglas Kenrick, Jon Maner, and Norman Li in Chapter 28 also argue persuasively for reciprocal benefits, this time flowing from evolutionary psychology to social psychology and from social psychology to evolutionary psychology. They propose that the traditional social psychological emphasis on situation specificity is highly compatible with evolutionary psychological approaches that emphasize domain specificity. They suggest that social psychologists can gain by adding ultimate explanations to their traditional proximate explanations. Finally, Kenrick, Maner, and Li provide an attractive taxonomy of social adaptive problems that could serve as a powerful organizing framework for social psychology.

David Bjorklund and Carlos Blasi provide Chapter 29 on evolutionary developmental psychology. They offer important insights that challenge some traditional assumptions in developmental psychology. For example, one traditional assumption has been that psychological features in childhood are merely preparations for the fully functioning adult form. They argue persuasively that, instead, some adaptations are designed for specific stages of development and are appropriately functional at those times, rather than serving merely as way stations to the development of the adult form. They consider how evolutionary analysis of many topics central to developmental psychology—topics such as theory of mind, children's intuitive mathematics, and social behaviors such as children's aggression and dominance hierarchies—can lead to fresh insights that have been entirely missed by the traditional conceptual frameworks that have guided developmental psychology.

Aurelio José Figueredo, Jon Sefcek, Geneva Vasquez, Barbara Brumbach, James King, and W. Jake Jacobs provide in Chapter 30 an exciting discussion on evolutionary personality psychology. They focus on an area that tends to be relatively neglected by evolutionary psychologists—stable individual differences. Figueredo and his colleagues assemble empirical evidence, both from human and nonhuman animal studies, which support the contention that individual differences in personality have been subjected to natural selection, sexual selection, and frequency-dependent selection. They also highlight the methodological and conceptual limitations of past work in this area and offer suggestions for improving the quality of both theorizing and empirical research in the study of personality. It's an important chapter and one that argues well for a greater conceptual integration of individual differences within an evolutionary psychological framework that emphasizes species-typical psychological mechanisms.

Jerome Wakefield provides in Chapter 31 a penetrating analysis of the concepts of function and dysfunction, which should form the foundation for the field of evolutionary clinical psychology. He argues that clinical psychology historically has lacked a coherent definition of disorder. Instead, the field has relied on intuitive, conflicting, and usually fuzzy notions of disorder and dysfunction. Evolutionary psychology provides clarification. Wakefield cogently argues that the only sensible definition of disorder requires *the failure of a designed function*. It follows that we need to know the designed function of psychological mechanisms as a prerequisite to understanding when they fail to function as designed. Wakefield also exposes several fallacies in arguments that mental disorders are naturally selected conditions and draws implications for the *DSM* classification system of disorders. It's somewhat astonishing to realize that clinical psychology has proceeded for decades without a clear definition of mental disorder. Wakefield's chapter fills the needed lacuna.

In the final chapter in this part, Randolph Nesse provides a broad analysis of evolutionary psychology and mental health. He explores six possible causes of mental disorders prevalent in the modern environment. Then, building on Wakefield's analysis of the concept of disorder, Nesse explores how evolutionary psychology sheds light on many specific disorders: emotional disorders, anxiety disorders, mood disorders, behavioral disorders (e.g., addiction, eating disorders), and many others. Nesse's compelling chapter should be required reading of everyone in clinical psychology.

Taken together, the chapters in this part provide a set of conceptual tools for evolutionizing the major subdisciplines within psychology. To the extent that the subdisciplines retain their inertial institutional boundaries, these chapters are invaluable. Ultimately, however, they may also contribute to the eventual demise of the traditional boundaries and pave the way for a unification of the field of psychology.

CHAPTER 27

Evolutionary Cognitive Psychology

PETER M. TODD, RALPH HERTWIG, and ULRICH HOFFRAGE

TRADITIONAL COGNITIVE PSYCHOLOGY, the study of the information processing mechanisms underlying human thought and behavior, is problematic from an evolutionary viewpoint: Humans were not directly selected to process information, or to store it, learn it, attend to it, represent it—or even, in fact, to think. All of these capacities, the core topics of cognitive psychology, can be seen as epiphenomena arising over the course of evolution from the need to get the central jobs done: survival and reproduction. Moreover, while the subtasks of those two main goals—finding food, maintaining body temperature, selecting a mate, negotiating status hierarchies, forming cooperative alliances, fending off predators and conspecific competitors, raising offspring, and so on—surely relied on gathering and processing information, meeting the challenges of each of these domains would have been possible only by in each case gathering specific pieces of information and processing them in particular ways. This suggests that to best study the faculties of memory, attention, reasoning, and the like, we should take a task- and domain-specific approach that focuses on the use of each faculty for a particular evolved function, just the approach exemplified by the other chapters in this *Handbook*.

But there is another tack that a traditional faculty-oriented cognitive psychologist can take when facing our domain-oriented mind. In addition to the selective pressures shaping domain-specific mechanisms, there are also a number of important selective forces operating across domains more widely, such as those arising from the costs of decision time and information search. Much as our separate physiological systems have all been shaped by a common force for energy-processing efficiency, individual psychological information processing systems may all have been shaped by various common pressures for information processing efficiencies. These broad pressures can in turn lead to common design features in many cognitive systems, such as decision mechanisms that make choices quickly based on little information. As a consequence, cognitive psychologists studying mental mechanisms from a domain-agnostic perspective can benefit from and contribute

We are grateful to Gary Brase and Lael Schooler for helpful comments on this chapter.

to an evolutionary perspective that takes into account both domain-specific and broad selective pressures.

In this chapter, we show how a set of broad forces operating on multiple domains can impact the design of specific cognitive systems. In particular, we first discuss how the costs of gathering information and of using too much information can be reduced by decision mechanisms that rely on as little information as possible—or even a lack of information—to come to their choices. Next, we explore how the pressures to use small amounts of appropriate information may have produced particular patterns of forgetting in long-term memory and particular limits of capacity in short-term memory. Finally, we show how selection for being able to think about past sets of events has given us reasoning mechanisms best able to handle information represented as samples or frequencies of experience, rather than as probabilities.

Throughout the chapter, we focus on three topics of central interest to cognitive psychologists—decision making, memory, and representations of information. But at the same time, we lay out three main theses that will be less familiar to those taking a traditional view of cognition as computation unfettered by external, environmental considerations. These theses are that simple decision mechanisms can work well by fitting environmental constraints, limited memory systems can have adaptive benefits, and experience-based representations of information can enhance decision making. In more detail, we first illustrate how considering broad selective pressures arising from the constraints of information gathering in the external world can help us to uncover some of the classes of decision mechanisms that people use. Second, in the context of memory systems shaped by such selective pressures, we demonstrate that an evolutionary perspective stressing both benefits *and costs* of particular abilities can lead to an appreciation of the positive functional roles of cognitive limitations. Third, we argue that taking into account the selective forces exerted by our patterns of interaction with the environment can help explain why different representations of the same information can interact with our evolved machinery to produce widely varying responses. In this way, while we ignore many of the topics typically covered in cognitive psychology, we aim to sketch out some existing questions that we think an evolution-savvy cognitive psychology should explore. (For other views of evolutionary cognitive psychology and consideration of further issues such as individual differences, see Kenrick, Sadalla, & Keefe, 1998.)

DECISION MAKING: PUTTING INFORMATION TO USE

We begin by considering decision mechanisms, which process perceived and stored information into choices leading to action. Cognitive psychology texts typically begin with perceptual and attentional processes and then work their way through the mind finally to decision making and reasoning. To the extent that perceptual systems have to provide information to a variety of domain-specific mechanisms "downstream," they have been shaped through the intersection of multiple selective forces to operate adaptively in a domain-general manner. Vision is the prime example, where the demands of collecting information for foraging mechanisms, mate-selection mechanisms, navigation mechanisms, and the like have melded together to select for a visual system that meets general design criteria such as the ability to detect motion and recognize objects in widely varying lighting conditions. However, because decision processes stand close to ultimate expressed behavior, they are also close to the particular functionally organized selective forces operating on behavior. Thus, decision mechanisms may have been strongly affected by individual selective forces to become domain-specific. Nonetheless, there are also broad selection pressures operating across domains that, we propose, have shaped a wide range of decision mechanisms in common directions.

What selective pressures impact on decision mechanisms? Foremost is selection for making an appropriate decision in the given domain. This domain-specific pressure does not imply the need to make the best possible decision, but rather one that is good enough (a satisficing choice, as Herbert Simon, 1955, put it) and, on average, better than those of an individual's competitors, given the costs and benefits involved. Good decisions depend on good information, and the specific requirements of the functional problem along with the specific structure of the relevant environment will determine what information is most useful (e.g., valid for making adaptive choices) and most readily obtained. Analyses of the problem and environment structure for particular domains indicate, for instance, that cues of facial symmetry are relevant and easy to assess for making inferences about mate quality (see Sugiyama, this volume) and that features indicating the presence of refuge and prospect (lookout) locations underlie good decisions about habitat choice (see Silverman & Choi, this volume).

But along with the obvious benefits of gathering information for making decisions come costs and attendant selection pressures (Todd, 2001), which cognitive psychologists studying the adaptive nature of inference should carefully attend to as well. First, there is the cost of obtaining the information itself. This cost may be paid in temporal or energetic terms: Searching for information can take time that could be better spent on other activities and can involve expending other resources (exertion in scouting out a landscape, exchange of goods to find out about a potential social partner). Furthermore, such costs can arise in both external information search in the environment and internal search in memory (Bröder & Schiffer, 2003).

Second, even if information were free and immediately accessible, there is the cost of actually making worse decisions if too much information is taken into consideration. Because we never face exactly the same situation twice, we must generalize from our past experience to new situations. But because of the uncertain nature of the world, some of the features of earlier situations will just be noise, unconnected to the new decision outcome (Did interviewing with red underwear on really get me that job offer?). If we consider too much information, then, we are likely to add noise to our decision process and *overfit* when generalizing to new circumstances—that is, make worse decisions than if less information had been considered (Martignon & Hoffrage, 2002).[1]

---

[1] Note that in some situations these potential costs of using too much information may be outweighed by the benefits that seeking extra information can occasionally bring, either directly in decision-making terms as considered, for instance, in Error Management Theory—(see Haselton & Nettle, this volume) or indirectly in social terms such as being able to justify one's diligence to bosses or clients. Nonetheless, while humans may act as information-hungry "informavores" in some domains (Pirolli & Card, 1999), analyzing the costs and benefits incurred by information seeking should guide us in exploring the cognitive mechanisms used in each case.

Given these seemingly opposing selective pressures, to make good choices but to do so using little information, what kind of decision mechanisms could possibly be built by evolution? As it turns out, there is little need for a trade-off between these costs and benefits—many environments are structured such that little information suffices to make appropriate choices, and decision mechanisms that operate in a "fast and frugal" manner can outperform those that seek to process all available information (Gigerenzer, Todd, & the ABC Research Group, 1999; Payne, Bettman, & Johnson, 1993). We now briefly survey some of the types of decision heuristics people use that flourish at the intersection of these selective forces. Together, these heuristics form part of the *adaptive toolbox* of cognitive mechanisms that humans draw on to make adaptive choices in the environments we face (Todd, 2000).

DECISION MAKING USING RECOGNITION AND IGNORANCE

Minimal information use can come about by basing decisions on a *lack* of knowledge, capitalizing on our own ignorance as a reflection of the structure of the environment. If there is a choice among multiple alternatives along some criterion, such as which of a set of fruits is good to eat, and if only one of the alternatives is recognized and the others are unknown, then an individual can employ the *recognition heuristic* to guide decision making: Choose the recognized option over the unrecognized ones (Goldstein & Gigerenzer, 1999, 2002). Following this simple heuristic will be adaptive, yielding good choices more often than would random choice, only in particular types of environments—specifically, those in which exposure to different possibilities is positively correlated with their ranking along the decision criterion being used. Thus, in our food choice example, the recognition heuristic will be beneficial because those things that we do not recognize in our environment are more often than not inedible; humans have done a reasonable job of discovering and incorporating edible fruits into our diet (see Galef, 1987, for a similar rule used by Norway rats). People successfully use the recognition heuristic in a variety of domains where the bigger, better, or stronger instances are discussed more and hence more widely known and recognized than the smaller, worse, weaker ones. Examples include large cities, important or rich individuals and social groups, and winning sports teams (Goldstein & Gigerenzer, 2002). Note that the recognition heuristic, as all heuristics, does not guarantee a correct choice. In appropriately structured environments, its use will on average be beneficial and lead to good decisions without having to seek any further information. But in situations where the cost of mistakes is high—for instance, environments where some fruits are known because of their extreme toxicity rather than their deliciousness—decisions should be based on more than recognition alone (Bullock & Todd, 1999).

DECISION MAKING USING A SINGLE REASON

When the options to be selected among are all known, the recognition heuristic can no longer be applied, and further cues must inform an individual's choice. The traditional approach to rational decision making stipulates that all of the available information should be collected, weighted properly, and combined before choosing. A more frugal approach is to use a stopping rule that terminates the search for information as soon as enough has been gathered to make a decision. In the most parsimonious version, "one-reason decision making" heuristics (Gigerenzer & Goldstein, 1996, 1999) stop looking for cues as soon as the first one is found that differentiates between the options being considered. In this case, information processing follows a simple loop: (1) Select a cue dimension and look for the corresponding cue values of each option; (2) compare the options on their values for that cue dimension; (3) if they differ, then stop and choose the option with the cue value indicating a greater value on the choice criterion; (4) if they do not differ, then return to the beginning of this loop (step 1) to look for another cue dimension.

This four-step loop incorporates two of the important building blocks of simple heuristics: a stopping rule (here, stopping after a single cue is found that enables a choice between the options) and a decision rule (here, deciding on the option to which the one cue points). To fully specify a particular heuristic, we must also determine the order in which cue dimensions are "looked for" in step 1—the information search building block. Among the many possible one-reason decision heuristics, *Take The Best* searches for cues in the order of their ecological validity—which reflects their correlation with the decision criterion. *Take The Last* looks for cues in the order determined by their past decisiveness, so that the cue that was used for the most recent previous decision is checked first during the next decision. The *Minimalist* heuristic lacks both memory and knowledge of cue validities and simply selects randomly among those cues currently available (the only knowledge it uses is the direction of the cues, that is, whether objects with higher cue values tend to have higher or lower criterion values, which is also used by the previous two heuristics).

Though they use just one piece of information to make decisions, these simple heuristics can nonetheless be surprisingly accurate. *Take The Best* for instance, performed better on average than multiple regression, which combined all available information weighted in an optimal manner, when generalizing to new portions of 20 different real-world environments (Czerlinski, Gigerenzer, & Goldstein, 1999). Furthermore, *Take The Best* looked up on average just a third of the available cues before finding the one discriminating cue it used to make its decision. Thus, heuristics employing this type of one-reason decision making can successfully meet the selective demands of accuracy and little information use simultaneously. They do so by matching and exploiting the structure of information in the environment (e.g., *Take The Best* capitalizes on a *noncompensatory,* or roughly exponentially decreasing, distribution of the importance of cues), using the world to do some of the work and thereby staying simpler and more robust (resistant to overfitting) themselves. A similar analysis within the world of linear models was undertaken by Dawes and Corrigan (1974), who pointed out that simplicity and robustness appear there, too, as two sides of the same coin: Simply ignoring much of the available information means ignoring much *irrelevant* information, which can consequently increase the robustness of decisions when generalizing to new situations.[2]

---

[2] More recently, Chater (1999; Chater & Vitányi, 2003) has proposed that minds are themselves designed to seek the simplest possible explanation of the environmental structure they encounter. This quest for simplicity seems to be another general principle that applies across multiple cognitive domains; Chater and others (listed in Chater & Vitányi, 2003) have shown its relevance to understanding perception, language processing, and higher level cognition. The implications of this important idea for an evolutionary approach to cognitive psychology still need to be worked out.

People use these fast and frugal algorithms in environments that have the appropriate structure (Rieskamp & Otto, 2004) and where information is costly or time consuming to acquire (Bröder, 2000; Newell & Shanks, 2003; Rieskamp & Hoffrage, 1999). Socially and culturally influenced decision making can also be based on a single reason through imitation (e.g., in food choice; Ariely & Levav, 2000), norm following, and employing protected values (e.g., moral codes that admit no compromise, such as never taking an action that results in human death, see Tanner & Medin, in press). And when a single cue does not suffice to determine a unique choice, people still often strive to use as little information as possible, for instance, via an *elimination* heuristic (Tversky, 1972): Only as many successive cues are considered, each being used to eliminate more and more alternatives as are necessary to reduce the set of remaining possibilities ultimately to a single viable option. For example, if an individual were to use an elimination process to decide on a place to live from among a set of possible habitats, he or she could first eliminate all those that are too far from water, then all those remaining that are too high, then those that are too cold in winter, and so on until one acceptable site is left. Such a procedure, while using more than one cue, still is able to produce good decisions very quickly (Payne et al., 1993) and can be applied to other types of inference such as categorization (Berretty, Todd, & Martignon, 1999).

CHOOSING FROM A SEQUENCE OF OPTIONS

When choice options are not available simultaneously, but rather appear sequentially over an extended period or spatial region, a different type of decision mechanism is needed. Here in addition to limiting information sought about each alternative, there must be a stopping rule for ending the search for alternatives themselves. For instance, mate search requires making a selection from a stream of potential candidates met at different points in time. Classic economic search theory suggests that an individual should look for a new mate (or anything) until the costs of further search outweigh the benefits that could be gained by leaving the current candidate. But in practice, performing a rational cost-benefit analysis is typically difficult and expensive in terms of the information needed (as well as making a bad impression on a would-be partner). Instead, a *satisficing* heuristic, as conceived by Simon (1955, 1990), can be adaptive: Set an aspiration level for the selection criterion being used, and search for alternatives until one is found that exceeds that level. (See Hey, 1981, 1982, for other simple and quick heuristic approaches to sequential search.)

But how should the aspiration level be set? In situations where options that are passed by at one point cannot be returned to again later (which is often roughly the case in mate search), an effective approach is to sample the first few options that are encountered without selecting any of them and use the highest value seen in that sample as the aspiration level for further search. This *cutoff rule* can perform very well in terms of maximizing the mean value of the option ultimately chosen, even with small initial samples (Dudey & Todd, 2002), and people have been shown to use it in experimental settings (Seale & Rapoport, 1997). However, this strategy ignores the problem that a prospect you desire may reject you—the mutual choice constraint underlying game-theory models of two-sided matching (Roth & Sotomayor, 1990). One way to take mutual choice into account

in the mate search context is to set your aspiration level near your own anticipated or estimated mate value and hence direct courtship effort at those
prospects similar in mate value and more likely to reciprocate. Simple learning
rules that adjust your aspiration level up with every sign of serious interest
from potential partners and down with every rejection can quickly lead to well-
calibrated aspirations of this sort that result in realistic patterns of assortative
mate choice (G. F. Miller & Todd, 1998; Simão & Todd, 2003; Todd & Miller,
1999). While the nonspecific pressure to find a mate or other sequentially available resource without too much search can make the general class of satisficing
aspiration-level mechanisms advantageous, the details of the particular search
domain (e.g., whether sequences of options may rise or fall in quality over time)
may further select for particular types of search rules (e.g., rules with later or
earlier stopping thresholds).

ECOLOGICAL RATIONALITY AND EVOLVED DECISION MECHANISMS

The heuristics described earlier, by ignoring much of the available information
and processing what they do consider in simple ways, typically do not meet the
standards of classical rationality, such as full information use and complete combination of probabilities and utilities. Furthermore, heuristic algorithms may produce outcomes that do not always follow rules of logical consistency. For instance,
Take The Best can systematically produce intransitivities among sets of three or
more choices (Gigerenzer & Goldstein, 1996). However, when used in appropriately structured environments, whether ancestral or current, these mechanisms
can be *ecologically* rational, meeting the selective demands of making adaptive
choices (on average) with limited information and time.

Ecological rationality implies a two-way relationship between simple heuristics and their environments (Todd, Fiddick, & Krauss, 2000). First, the success of
simple heuristics is defined with respect to pragmatic goals in a particular environmental context. Second, the success of simple heuristics is enabled by their fit
to environmental structure (Hertwig, Hoffrage, & Martignon, 1999; Martignon &
Hoffrage, 2002). This marriage of structure and simplicity explains and predicts
the counterintuitive situations in which there is no trade-off between being fast
and frugal and being successful.

Furthermore, different environment structures can be exploited by—and
hence call for—different heuristics. But matching heuristics to environment
structure does not mean that every new environment or problem demands a new
heuristic: The simplicity of these mechanisms implies that they can often be used
in multiple, similarly structured domains with just a change in the information
they employ (Czerlinski et al., 1999). Thus, an evolution-oriented cognitive psychologist should explore both the range of (possibly domain-general) simple decision mechanisms appropriate to a particular adaptive problem and the
domain-specific cues in the environment that will allow those mechanisms to
solve that problem effectively.

MEMORY: RETRIEVING AND
FORGETTING INFORMATION

To the extent that decisions are based on information, this information is either
accessed immediately from the external environment or from experience stored

internally in some form of memory. Beginning with the pioneering work of Hermann Ebbinghaus (1885/1964), cognitive psychologists usually focus on three aspects of human memory—its capacity, its accuracy, and its structure (e.g., Koriat, Goldsmith, & Pansky, 2000; Tulving & Craik, 2000)—but pay little attention to how it has been shaped by selective pressures, those costs and benefits arising through its use for particular functions in particular environments. Recently, however, researchers have begun to investigate the relationship between the design of memory systems and how they meet their adaptive functions. In this section, we describe some of the trends toward putting evolutionary thinking into the study of memory.

Memory has "evolved to supply useful, timely information to the organism's decision-making systems" (Klein, Cosmides, Tooby, & Chance, 2002, p. 306). The evolution of memory to serve this function has occurred in the context of a variety of costs, which also shape the design of particular memory systems. Dukas (1999) has articulated a wide range of costs of memory, including (1) maintaining an item once it has been added to long-term memory, (2) keeping it in an adaptable form that enables future updating, (3) growing and feeding the brain tissue needed to store the information, and (4) silencing irrelevant information. But taking into consideration the demands of decision mechanisms outlined earlier, the two main selective pressures acting on memory systems (particularly long-term memory) appear to be, first, to produce quickly the most useful stored information and, second, not to produce too *much* information.

These pressures, like the ones we focused on for decision mechanisms, are broad and general—applying to memory systems no matter what domains they deal with. One way to meet these pressures is to store in the first place just that information that will be useful later. Having limited memory capacity can work to restrict initial storage in this way, as we see later with regard to short-term memory. In the case of long-term memory, Thomas Landauer (1986) has estimated that a mature person has "a functional learned memory content of around a billion bits" (p. 491). This is much less than the data storage capacity of a single hour-long music CD, suggesting that we are indeed storing very little of the raw flow of information that we experience. However, most of what little we do remember is nonetheless irrelevant to any given decision, so our memory systems must still be designed to retrieve what is appropriate and not more. How can this be achieved? One way is through the very process that at first glance seems like a failure of the operation of memory: forgetting.

LONG-TERM MEMORY: FORGETTING CURVES AND THE STATISTICAL
PROPERTIES OF INFORMATION USE

John R. Anderson (1990) put forward an approach he called the *rational analysis of behavior* as a method for understanding psychological mechanisms in terms of their functions or goals—equivalent to Marr's (1982) computational level of analysis, which is also the level at which evolutionary psychology should be focused (Cosmides & Tooby, 1987). Having in mind a view of evolution as constrained local optimization (or hill climbing), Anderson set out to assess the explanatory power of the principle that "the cognitive system operates at all times to optimize the adaptation of the behavior of the organism" (1990, p. 28). Anderson and Milson (1989) took this approach to propose that memory should be viewed as an optimizing information retrieval system with a database of stored items from which a subset is returned in response to a query (e.g., a list of key terms). A system of this sort can make two kinds of errors: It can fail to retrieve the desired piece of information (e.g., failing to recall the location of your car), thus not meeting the pressure of usefulness. But if the system tried to minimize such errors by simply retrieving everything, it would commit the opposite error: producing irrelevant pieces of information (and thus not meeting the pressure of parsimony), with the concomitant cost of further examining and rejecting what is not useful. To balance these two errors, Anderson and Milson propose, the memory system can use statistics extracted from experience to predict which memories are likely to be needed soon and keep those readily retrievable. Consequently, memory performance should reflect the patterns with which environmental stimuli have appeared and will reappear in the environment.

This argument can be illustrated with the famous forgetting curve, first described by Ebbinghaus (1885/1964): Memory performance declines (forgetting increases) with time (or intervening events) rapidly at first and then more slowly as time goes on, characterizable as a power function (Wixted, 1990; Wixted & Ebbesen, 1991, 1997). Combining this prevalent forgetting function with Anderson's rational analysis framework yields the following prediction: To the extent that memory has evolved in response to environmental regularities, the fact that memory performance falls as a function of retention interval implies that the probability of encountering a particular environmental stimulus (e.g., a word) also declines as a power function of time elapsed since it was last encountered. Anderson and Schooler (1991, 2000) analyzed real-world data sets to find out whether the environmental regularities match those observed in human memory. One of their data sets, for example, consisted of words in the headlines of the *New York Times* for a 730-day period, and they assumed that reading a word (e.g., "Qaddafi") represents a query to the human memory database with the goal of retrieving its meaning.

At any point in time, memories ("Qaddafi") vary in how likely they are to be needed. According to the rational analysis framework, the memory system attempts to optimize the information retrieval process by making available those memories that are most likely to be useful. How does it do that? It does so by extrapolating from the history of use to the probability that a memory is currently needed—the *need probability* of a particular memory trace. Specifically, Anderson (1990) suggested that memories are considered in order of their need probabilities, and if the need probability of a memory falls below a certain threshold, it will not be retrieved. Consistent with their view that environmental regularities are reflected in human memory, Anderson and Schooler (1991) found that the probability of a word occurring in a headline of the *New York Times* at any given time is a function of its past frequency and recency of occurrence. In other words, the demand for a particular piece of information to be retrieved drops the less frequently it occurred in the past and the greater the period of time that has passed since its last use. This regularity parallels the general form of forgetting that has so often been observed since the days of Ebbinghaus. From this parallel, Anderson and Schooler concluded that human memory is a highly functional system insofar as it systematically renders pieces of information less accessible when they have not been used for a while. This functionality operates across domains as a response to broad selection pressures for maintaining quick access to information likely to be useful in upcoming situations (and conversely not maintaining access to information less likely to be needed).

The Functions of Forgetting

William James, in the *Principles of Psychology* (1890), was among the first psychologists who pointed to the crucial functional role that forgetting plays. In fact, he argued that "in the practical use of our intellect, forgetting is as important a function as recollecting" (p. 679). Beginning with James, a number of researchers have proposed different functions that forgetting may serve.

Uncluttering the Mind   In James's view, forgetting is the mechanism that enables mental selectivity. Selectivity, in turn, he asserted:

> is the very keel on which our mental ship is built. . . . If we remembered everything, we should on most occasions be as ill off as if we remembered nothing. It would take as long for us to recall a space of time as it took the original time to elapse, and we should never get ahead with our thinking. (James, 1890, p. 680)

More recently, contemporary psychologists have begun to specify some of the adaptive functions of forgetting. Bjork and Bjork (1996), for instance, have argued that it is critical to prevent out-of-date information—say, old passwords or where we parked the car yesterday—from interfering with the recall of currently needed information. In their view, the mechanism that erases out-of-date information is retrieval inhibition: Information that is rendered irrelevant becomes less retrievable. Schacter (2001) also stressed the adaptive functions of forgetting. He, for instance, suggested that various types of misattribution occur when only the general sense of what happened, the gist, is recalled, while the experience's specific details are forgotten. Memory for gist, in turn, may be fundamental, for instance, for the ability to generalize and categorize across specific instances and thus to organize the permanent flux of experiences. Take Schacter's example of the category "bird" for illustration. To develop a coherent notion of "bird," a person has to learn that superficially diverse instances such as a cardinal and an oriole are both members of the same category.

Boosting Heuristic Performance   The benefits of forgetting, however, may extend beyond the general advantage of setting aside needless information. Forgetting may also boost the performance of heuristics that exploit partial ignorance, such as the recognition heuristic described earlier (Goldstein & Gigerenzer, 2002). Ignorance can come from not learning about portions of the environment in the first place or from later forgetting about some earlier encounters. To examine whether human recognition memory forgets at an appropriate rate to promote the use of the recognition heuristic, Schooler and Hertwig (2004) implemented this heuristic within an existing cognitive architecture framework, ACT-R (Anderson & Lebiere, 1998). This cognitive architecture is particularly suited to the present analysis as it offers both a plausible memory framework and a strong ecological foundation inherited from the rational analysis of memory mentioned earlier; specifically, ACT-R learns by strengthening memory records associated with, for instance, the names of foodstuffs, habitats, or people according to a function that takes into account the frequency and recency with which they were encountered in the environment. Schooler and Hertwig's simulations suggest that in the context of the recognition heuristic, one function of forgetting is to actively maintain the system's ignorance. In other words, in all their simulations they found that the performance of the recognition heuristic indeed benefited from (a medium amount of) forgetting.

Strategic Information Blockage   In the case of the recognition heuristic, forgetting refers mostly to content in declarative memory. Could even forgetting of parts of your autobiography be adaptive? The argument that forgetting of seemingly unforgettable experiences, that is, traumatic experiences, can serve important functions has been entertained since the late nineteenth century. Since the 1980s the notion of repressed memories—in particular of memory for childhood sexual abuse—has received a great deal of academic as well as public attention. We do not review the controversial debates that ensued pertaining to such questions as whether recovered memories can occur and how accurately they correspond to actual events (for an excellent review, see Sivers, Schooler, & Freyd, 2002). Here we are only concerned with one theory of recovered memory in which temporary forgetting (or reduced accessibility) of traumatic events is assumed to be functional.

Betrayal trauma theory proposed by Freyd (1996) suggests that the function of amnesia for childhood abuse is to protect the child from the knowledge that a key caregiver may be the sexual perpetrator. In situations involving treacherous acts by a person depended on for survival, a "cognitive information blockage" (Sivers et al., 2002, p. 177) may occur that results in an isolation of knowledge of the event from awareness. In fact, such temporary forgetting may be a prerequisite for maintaining the crucial relationship with the caregiver and, ultimately, for survival. At least two different mechanisms can account for memory impairments for trauma-related information. One is avoidant processing, in which people disengage attention from threatening information and thus fail to even encode it. Another mechanism locates the cause for the information blockage at the retrieval stage, assuming that threatening information is encoded but cannot be retrieved (see McNally, Clancy, & Schacter, 2001). Betrayal trauma theory also yields specific predictions about the factors that will make this type of forgetting most probable—for instance, it predicts that amnesia will be more likely the more dependent the victim is on the perpetrator (e.g., parental versus nonparental abuse). While the experimental evidence for betrayal trauma theory is preliminary (Sivers et al., 2002) and controversial (see DePrince & Freyd, 2004; McNally et al., 2001), the theory illustrates how domain-specific forgetting may have unique adaptive functions.

Hindsight Bias: Consequence of Future-Oriented Memory

Forgetting is not always beneficial. For example, *hindsight bias* (see Hoffrage & Pohl, 2003) is the phenomenon that once people know the outcome of an event, they tend to overestimate what could have been anticipated in foresight. This can come about because people do not have perfect memories of all the opinions and judgments they held in the past. Therefore, if they have to remember in hindsight how likely they thought it was that, for instance, Al Gore would be elected—in light of their knowledge that he lost—they may overestimate their previous doubts. Fischhoff (1982) stressed the potentially harmful consequences of the hindsight bias: "The very outcome knowledge which gives us the feeling that we understand what the past was all about may prevent us from learning anything from it" (p. 343). Following Fischhoff's lead, the hindsight bias has been seen as a severe and systematic bias in memory.

Even in the case of the hindsight bias, however, adopting a functional perspective can provide a deeper understanding of the memory illusion. Hoffrage, Hertwig, and Gigerenzer (2000) took such a perspective in their model of the hindsight bias. They assumed that being informed about the outcome of an event (e.g., an election) could result in an *updating* of the knowledge that was originally used (e.g., which candidate has more charisma) to try to infer which outcome would occur (e.g., which candidate would win). In addition, their model assumes that if people cannot retrieve their original judgment, they will reconstruct it by going through the same steps of inference that led to the original judgment; that is, people will (re)simulate their original judgment process. In the meantime, however, some of the elusive and missing cue values have been updated in light of the actual outcome. Therefore, the reconstructed judgment may turn out to be closer to the actual outcome than the original judgment was. This model makes the novel prediction—confirmed by Hoffrage et al.'s studies—that feedback on one variable (e.g., election outcome) can lead to systematic changes not only in the recalled prediction but also in the memory of associated variables (e.g., cues related to election outcomes such as charisma of the person who lost the election). Moreover, this algorithmic process model is specific enough to explain why hindsight bias occurs, does not occur, or is reversed in particular individual responses (see Hoffrage et al., Figure 5).

Is the hindsight bias detrimental? No doubt, if the goal is to veridically reconstruct previously held judgments, preferences, or opinions, then hindsight bias caused by knowledge updating can be a great hindrance to fulfilling this goal. But such a goal is unlikely to be very common or important. The real world, as opposed to the psychological laboratory, is inherently unstable, and the longer the time interval since the last assessment of, for example, a foraging location, the more likely that the environment will have changed and the location will no longer have the same value. As Bartlett (1932/1995) put it: "In a world of constantly changing environment, literal recall is extraordinarily unimportant" (p. 204). In other words, in the trade-off between an accurate remembrance of the past and accurate inferences in the future, emphasizing future performance should win. Our memory seems to be designed to do just this, wagering on the future rather than on the past: Simulations by Hertwig, Fanselow, and Hoffrage (2003) suggest that at the same time that knowledge updating may be increasing hindsight bias, it can increase the accuracy of future inferences. On this view, the hindsight bias is a cheap price to pay for an adaptive advantage, namely, the timely provision of useful, up-to-date knowledge.

SHORT-TERM MEMORY: FUNCTIONAL EXPLANATION OF ITS BOUNDS

The previous analyses apply to long-term memory. Long-term memory, however, is only one of the components posited within traditional memory architectures, for instance, the Atkinson-Shiffrin model of human memory (Atkinson & Shiffrin, 1968). Another key component is short-term memory. The classic estimate of the capacity of short-term memory is 7 ± 2 chunks (G. A. Miller, 1956), and more recent estimates make it even smaller (Cowan, 2001). Why has it evolved to be so limited? Anderson (1990) feels that our memory capacity is "trapped on some local optimum of evolution" (p. 92), but this does not seem convincing. While greater short-term memory size may have required somewhat increased brain metabolism or other trade-offs (Dukas, 1999), there do not seem to be inherent constraints that would have ruled out more generous capacities. In the absence of strong constraints, more plausible explanations for why evolution has produced such a modest mental storage capacity draw on functional considerations. One of the most interesting functional explanations has been put forth by Yakov Kareev in a series of papers (Kareev, 1995a, 1995b, 2000; Kareev, Lieberman, & Lev, 1997). Kareev argues that while limitations of working memory capacity force people to rely on small samples of information, these small samples also have a specific advantage: They can enhance inferences of causality by enabling the early detection of covariation between elements in the environment.[3]

Kareev's argument runs as follows. To determine at a given point whether two variables covary (e.g., Does this pile of droppings mean a predator is nearby?), an individual often needs to rely on data sampled from his or her environment or from long-term memory (i.e., past observations of the environment), which is then entered into working memory.[4] To the extent that the degree of covariation is derived from the information that is currently in an individual's working memory, that system's limits imposes an upper bound on the size of the information sample that can be considered at one time. Taking Miller's estimate as a starting point, Kareev et al. (1997; Kareev, 2000) suggested that using samples of around seven observations of the cooccurrence (or lack thereof) of two events increases the chances for detecting a correlation between them, compared to using a greater number of observations. The reason is that randomly drawn samples of a population of two-variable observations are likely to show a within-sample correlation that differs somewhat from the true population correlation. More specifically, looking at *small* randomly drawn data samples (whether from the environment or from long-term memory) increases the likelihood of encountering a sample that indicates a *stronger* correlation than that of the whole population. To see why, imagine drawing many small samples of two continuous variables, calculating the relationship between them (i.e., Pearson's product-moment correlation), and plotting the distribution of the correlation coefficients thus found. Then (provided that the population correlation is not zero), the resulting distribution will have a characteristic skewed shape, with both the *median* and the *mode* of the distribution more extreme than the corresponding population values. Moreover, the amount of skewedness is a function of the sample size: The smaller the sample, the more skewed the resulting distribution.

In other words, when drawing a small random sample from a population in which a correlation exists, the sample-based correlation estimate is more likely than not to be more extreme than the true correlation found in the population. Thus, a limited working memory can function as an amplifier of correlations, allowing those present in the population to be detected earlier than they would be

---

[3] Another proposal for a functional benefit of bounded short-term memory is MacGregor's (1987) theoretical argument that it can speed up information retrieval.

[4] Kareev uses the term *working memory* as akin to the earlier concept *short-term memory*, but see Baddely, 2000, on the different meanings of the term *working memory*.

if working memory and the sample size necessary to fill working memory were larger. Consistent with this thesis, Kareev et al. (1997) found that people with smaller working memory capacity detected correlations faster and used them to make correct predictions better than people with larger working memory capacity. This enhanced ability to detect contingencies seems particularly important in domains in which the benefits of discovering a causal connection outweigh the costs of *false alarms,* which also increase in number with smaller sample sizes (a point highlighted by Juslin & Olsson, in press—but see Fiedler & Kareev, 2004, for further considerations). Such domains may be characterized by situations in which missing potential threats would be extremely costly, including, for instance, learning about the cues associated with the presence of a predator or the signals presaging a stranger's harmful intentions.

Kareev's (2000) analysis suggests that evolution may have designed the capacity of human working memory to correspond to a "window size" that amplifies existing contingencies in the world, thus fostering their early detection. This thesis not only offers a functional explanation for why temporary mental storage capacity is so limited but also sheds new light on what has been interpreted to be a cognitive or perceptual bias—the *belief in the law of small numbers.* According to Tversky and Kahneman (1971/1982), "people's intuitions about random sampling appear to satisfy the law of small numbers" (1982, p. 25), in that "people view a [small] sample randomly drawn from a population as highly representative, that is, similar to the population in all essential characteristics" (1982, p. 24), rather than understanding that small samples are more likely to deviate further from population statistics (e.g., the mean) than are large samples. Tversky and Kahneman proceeded from this observation to criticize human intuition for being unduly swayed by small samples, foreshadowing the conjectures about the failings of human rationality that dominated cognitive and social psychology in the decades to come (see, e.g., Krueger & Funder, in press). Certainly, overreliance on small samples may indeed exact a price in terms of systematic misperceptions of the world—but the important thing to ask from an evolutionary cognitive psychology perspective is how large that price is compared to the potential benefits accruing to their use. Kareev's analysis can be taken as a challenge to the premise that the more veridical the mental representations of the world, the better adapted the organism.[5]

To conclude our discussion of the selective forces acting on memory, we return to Anderson and Milson (1989), who pointed out that "one seldom finds arguments for a theory of memory mechanisms cast in terms of the adaptiveness of these mechanisms" (p. 703). This situation now seems to be slowly changing, not least because of Anderson and colleagues' leading work. Moreover, exploring the adaptiveness of memory necessitates asking not only what memory was designed to do but also how the design benefits could be achieved in light of the pertinent costs. This combination of a functionalist view with a cost-benefit analysis of particular mechanisms, as often employed in evolutionary cognitive ecology (Dukas,

---

[5] Referring to scientific models, William Wimsatt, a philosopher of biology, argued that "False models build locally truer theories" (Wimsatt, 1987), because they isolate aspects of our ignorance and allow us to progress. His supposition is that the "creative use of falsehood is one of the best tools the practicing realist-scientist . . . has for discovering truths about nature." Our conjecture is that systematically inaccurate mental models of the world can also confer functional benefits to organisms whose aim is not to explain the world but rather to survive and reproduce in it.

1998), will move us closer to a thorough understanding of the workings of human memory.

REPRESENTATION OF INFORMATION: MODERN PRACTICES MEET EVOLUTIONARY CONSTRAINTS

In the previous section, we discussed some aspects of memory from an evolutionary point of view. But why do we have memory at all? Why should we be able to recall representations of the past? After all, changes in behavior could arise through learning even without the ability to remember independently any aspects of the events that we learned from. Being able to store and retrieve information about what happened in the past, however, lets us process that information further in the light of new information and experience. It also allows us to communicate the information to others (as well as to ourselves at later points in time) and combine it with information from them in turn. Ultimately, recalled information from the past enables us to form expectations about the future, which can guide behavior in the present.[6]

Internal memories, our focus in the previous section, are not the only innovation over the course of evolution for representing past events. Paintings of animals in Pleistocene caves, for instance, demonstrate one step in the development of representations that have been used to externalize internal states—here, memories of what the early artists had previously seen outside the cave. During the evolution of culture, such external representations were complemented by symbols that became standardized and gradually reached greater and greater levels of abstraction. Ultimately this led to alphabets and number systems that could be used to convey complex information to others, both contemporaries and successors. Parallel to this process, procedures to collect and combine information have been refined over the centuries, finally leading to huge national and international institutions founded to gather and aggregate demographic, social, economic, medical, and other kinds of data (Gigerenzer et al., 1989).

As a consequence, the sources of information that could be used as a basis for judgments and decisions have increased over the course of human evolution, from individual experiences (a source that we share with even the lowest animals), through reports from family or group members (a source that social animals have and that humans have in greatly developed form), to modern statistics (a source that has been added only very recently during our cultural evolution). Does it make a difference, in terms of individual decision making, what form the information takes as a consequence of its source? Adopting an evolutionary point of view, we would hypothesize that the answer is yes, because our cognitive systems have been exposed to different forms and sources of information for different amounts of time. In particular, forms that have been created during our most recent cultural development may pose a bigger challenge to our information processing capacities than those to which the human species had much more time to adapt. In this section, we present evidence supporting this hypothesis, showing how different types of representations affect decisions first in situations involving risks and second in the context of Bayesian inference tasks. As in the previous

---

[6] See Freyd, 1983, 1990, for a theory of how pressures for shareability of information between and within individuals can, in conjunction with pressures from natural selection on cognitive systems, shape the representations of information that we use.

sections, the selection pressures we consider here apply to the use of information representations across a wide range of functions and tasks, so they will have shaped cognitive mechanisms from many domains in similar ways.

Much of everyday decision making can be understood as an act of weighing the costs against the benefits of the uncertain consequences of our choices. Take the decision of whether to engage in short-term mating as an example. Although casual sex has obvious evolutionary benefits (especially for men; see, e.g., Trivers, 1972), it can cause an individual to contract a sexually transmitted disease, acquire an undesirable social reputation, or suffer violence at the hands of a jealous partner (for other risks of casual sex from an evolutionary perspective, see Buss, 2004). Each of these consequences, whether beneficial or harmful, is uncertain: It might happen, and it might not happen. Choosing to have casual sex is thus like rolling a die, each side of which represents one or more possible consequences of that choice. Only after the die has come to rest, the decision made, and the action taken will we find out which of the consequences has become reality. Because uncertainty is an integral part of "virtually all decisions," wrote Goldstein and Weber (1997), *"life is a gamble"* (p. 569).

The metaphor of life as a gamble has exerted a powerful influence on psychological research on decision making under risk, giving rise, for example, to the ubiquitous use of monetary lotteries in laboratory experiments. Studies that employ such lotteries typically provide respondents with a symbolic—usually written—description of the options, for example:

A: Get $4 with probability .8, $0 otherwise.

or

B: Get $3 for sure.

The most prominent descriptive theory of how people decide between such lotteries is *prospect theory* (Kahneman & Tversky, 1979; Tversky & Kahneman, 1992). Briefly, prospect theory assumes that the human mind "frames" the outcomes of a decision in terms of gains and losses. Losses are more painful than gains of the same magnitude are pleasurable, but sensitivity to identical decrements (or increments) in value diminishes as the losses (or gains) increase. Prospect theory further posits that, relative to the objective probabilities with which an outcome can be expected to occur, people make choices as if small probability events receive more weight than they deserve and as if large probability events receive less weight than they deserve. This assumption can explain why, for instance, most people (80% of participants in Kahneman & Tversky, 1979) are inclined to choose lottery *B* over *A*: The rare outcome in *A*, receiving $0, receives more weight than it deserves, reducing the perceived value of *A*.

But are choices between options like *A* and *B* representative of the gambles with which life presents us? Hertwig, Barron, Weber, and Erev (2004; Hertwig, Erev, Barron, & Weber, in press) argue that we rarely have complete knowledge of the possible outcomes of our actions and their probabilities. When deciding whether to have a one-night stand, for instance, we do not make a *decision from description,* consulting a written list of the possible consequences and their likelihoods. Instead, we rely on the experience that we (or others) have accumulated over time. Hertwig et al. referred to this kind of choice as a *decision from experience.*

Do people behave differently when they learn about outcomes and probabilities from written descriptions as opposed to experience? To find out, Hertwig et al. (2004; Hertwig et al., in press) created an experimental environment in which decision makers started out ignorant of the outcomes and the outcome probabilities associated with pairs of lotteries. On each trial, respondents saw two buttons, here denoted *A* and *B*, on a computer screen and were told that each button was associated with a payoff distribution. When they clicked on a button, an outcome (e.g., in the example above, $3 if they chose *B* or $0 on 20% of clicks and $4 on 80% of clicks if they chose *A*) was randomly sampled from its distribution. Respondents could sample from either distribution as many times as they wished. After they stopped sampling, they were asked which lottery they wanted to play for real payoffs.

Hertwig et al. (2004; Hertwig et al., in press) compared the choices of respondents who received written descriptions of each option (i.e., the amount of money to be gained or lost and the probability of winning or losing it) with those made by respondents who were allowed to sample the possible outcomes freely and repeatedly as described earlier. Although respondents in the description group and the experience group were given structurally identical problems, the choices they made differed dramatically between the groups. Across six problems, the average absolute difference between the percentage of respondents choosing the option with the higher expected value (e.g., *A* in our example) in the experience and description groups was 36 percentage points. Moreover, in every problem, this difference was consistent with the assumption that rare events (e.g., $0 in *A*) had more impact than they deserved (given their objective probability) in decisions from description—consistent with prospect theory—but had less impact than they deserved in decisions from experience.

To account for the dramatic difference between decisions from description and decisions from experience, Hertwig and colleagues cited two factors—small samples and a recency effect. First, the experience group tended to rely on small samples of outcomes, which meant that they either did not encounter the rare event or encountered it less frequently than expected on the basis of its objective probability. Second, they paid more attention to recently experienced outcomes. Most people did not encounter rare events in the last few draws from the payoff distribution because of the very rarity of those events. In contrast, having read about the rare events in their written presentation alongside the common events, the description group appeared not to overlook the rare events but rather to overweight them.

The distinction between decisions from description and decisions from experience not only explains people's different risky choices in structurally identical problems but also points to the solution to an intriguing puzzle related to the behavior of bees. Because animals do not share humans' ability to process symbolic representations of risky prospects, all their decisions (e.g., about where to forage) are decisions from experience. In a study of foraging decisions made by bees, Real (1991) observed that "bumblebees underperceive rare events and overperceive common events" (p. 985). To explain why bees' "decision weights" diverge from those observed in humans and captured by prospect theory, Real cited, among other factors, the fact that bees' samples from payoff distributions are truncated due to memory constraints. Although humans and bumblebees do not share a recent evolutionary history, Hertwig et al.'s (2004) results suggest that the decisions of bumblebees should converge with those of humans when humans, like bees, rely on small samples of experience (see also Weber, Shafir, & Blais, 2004).

The more general implication of the distinction between decisions from description and decisions from experience is that representations that are identical mathematically can be different psychologically. Furthermore, the two sources of information differ not only in form but also in the length of time that they have exerted a pressure on our cognitive abilities to understand and process them appropriately. Throughout the course of human evolution, we have experienced events in our interactions with the environment, but only very recently have we begun to aggregate such information and communicate it in the form of statistical descriptions.[7] Thus, we might speculate that our cognitive strategies for making decisions under risk are more likely tuned to experienced frequencies than to described probabilities. The research of Hertwig and colleagues just described supports this assertion, as does work done in the domain of Bayesian reasoning—the topic to which we now turn.

INFERENCES BASED ON NATURAL FREQUENCY VERSUS PROBABILITY REPRESENTATIONS

How should we update our beliefs in light of new evidence? For instance, how should a Pleistocene hunter update his belief regarding the chance of finding prey at a particular location after he has seen some unusual movements in the grass over there? As this example shows, we have been facing the task of updating beliefs for a long time, and there should have been sufficient selective pressure to produce a mechanism able to perform such inferences. At first glance, however, the current empirical results are inconclusive: Whereas research by Gallistel (1990) and Real (1991) suggests that animals are adept at such Bayesian inferences (updating of beliefs in light of new evidence), humans seem to lack this capability: "In his evaluation of evidence, man is apparently not a conservative Bayesian: he is not a Bayesian at all" (Kahneman & Tversky, 1972, p. 450). How can it be that bumblebees are better at making Bayesian inferences than humans?

As in the previous section, the answer lies in the different ways that information can be represented. How did bumblebees and Pleistocene hunter-gatherers encounter the statistical information about environmental features? On a trial-by-trial basis, that is, by sequentially observing cases—which, in the simplest case of dichotomous variables, means observing whether a predictor is present or absent and whether the criterion is present or absent. Adaptive behavior can be based on accurate judgments of the probability of the criterion being present given that the predictor is present. Such judgments can be made by a mechanism that is sensitive to the difference between the number of cases in which predictor and criterion are present and the number of cases in which only the predictor is

---

[7] The further questions of how people use *non*scientific language (as opposed to statistics) to communicate subjective likelihoods, via words such as *often, sometimes,* and *rarely,* and how these words are understood by the audience, is a large research area in itself; see, for example, Hertwig and Gigerenzer (1999), Dhami and Wallsten (in press).

present (possibly giving more weight to the most recent cases). Experiments with human participants in which cases are sequentially presented, thereby allowing participants to observe the states of the predictor and the criterion over successive trials in a natural fashion, have shown that people are well able to estimate the probability of observing the criterion given the presence of the predictor (Christensen-Szalanski & Beach, 1982).

In contrast, those studies leading to the conclusion that people are *not* able to reason in a proper Bayesian fashion have presented participants with descriptions given in terms of probabilities. For example, Eddy (1982) presented 100 physicians with the following information:

> The probability of breast cancer is 1% for a woman at age forty who participates in routine screening. If a woman has breast cancer, the probability is 80% that she will have a positive mammography. If a woman does not have breast cancer, the probability is 9.6% that she will also have a positive mammography.

Physicians were then asked to imagine a woman in this age group who had a positive mammography in a routine screening and to state the probability that she actually has breast cancer. Of those 100 physicians, 95 judged this probability to be between .7 and .8. To obtain the Bayesian solution, which is usually seen as the normatively correct answer, an individual "simply" has to insert the probabilities into Bayes's rule (if he or she is lucky enough to know about the rule and remember how to use it):

$$p(C \mid M) = \frac{p(C)p(M \mid C)}{p(C)p(M \mid C) + p(-C)p(M \mid -C)} = \frac{(.01)(.80)}{(.01)(.80) + (.99)(.096)}$$

where C stands for breast cancer, $-C$ stands for no cancer, and M stands for a positive mammography result. The result is .07, indicating that probability-based descriptions led most of the decision makers in Eddy's study widely astray (Figure 27.1, left panel).

However, the differences in decision-making performance here do not come down to just a distinction between beneficial experience and detrimental description. By considering what kinds of representations our minds evolved to deal with, Gigerenzer and Hoffrage (1995) created an effective compromise between sequential acquisition of information and descriptions in terms of probabilities: They presented participants with descriptions in which the probabilities were translated into natural frequencies. Natural frequencies result from natural sampling (Kleiter, 1994) in which cases are randomly drawn from a specified reference class. Thus, while participants did not encounter cases one by one, they were presented with the aggregate statistics in terms of numbers that arise when an entire sample of individual cases is experienced and counted.

For illustration, the probability information provided by Eddy (1982) when converted into natural frequencies reads as follows: "Out of 10,000 women, 100 have breast cancer. Out of those 100 women with breast cancer, 80 have a positive mammogram. Out of the remaining 9,900 women without breast cancer, 950 nonetheless have a positive mammogram." Asking for the probability that a

Probabilities   **Natural Frequencies**

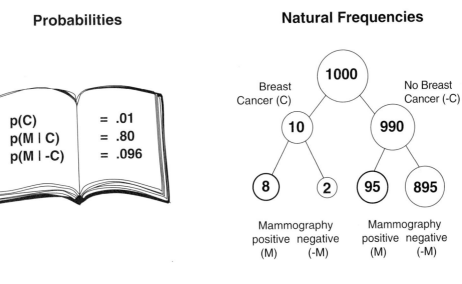

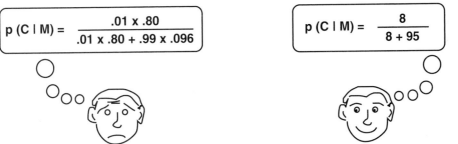

Figure 27.1   Two Formats for Information in a Bayesian Reasoning Task. (Left) Information in terms of probabilities; (Right) Information in terms of natural frequencies. Adapted from " How to Improve Bayesian Reasoning without Instruction: Frequency Formats," by G. Gigerenzer and U. Hoffrage, 1995, *Psychological Review, 102*, pp. 684–704.

woman has breast cancer given a positive mammogram now becomes "How many of those women with a positive mammogram have breast cancer?" This question, calling for an inference that has to be made from information presented in terms of natural frequencies, is much easier to answer (Figure 27.1, right panel). Gigerenzer and Hoffrage (1995) first replicated the finding that presenting information in probabilities resulted in poor performance: Across 15 tasks, participants reasoned the Bayesian way only 16% of the time. When the information was presented in terms of natural frequencies, this percentage rose to 46%, and the number of answers that were close to Bayesian rose greatly as well. Similar results were obtained with physicians (Hoffrage & Gigerenzer, 1998), medical students (Hoffrage, Lindsey, Hertwig, & Gigerenzer, 2000), and lawyers (Lindsey, Hertwig, & Gigerenzer, 2003).

Gigerenzer and Hoffrage (1995) proposed two explanations to account for the facilitating effect of natural frequencies: computational simplification and evolutionary preparedness for (natural) frequencies. With probabilities, three pieces of information have to be taken into account, whereas with natural frequencies, there are only two. Probability representations require the base rates (e.g., of disease and no disease) to be used to multiply the two likelihoods (e.g., probability of symptom given disease and symptom given no disease). With natural frequencies, in contrast, the base rates are already contained implicitly and thus do not have to enter the calculation explicitly (Gigerenzer & Hoffrage, 1995). Further studies, however, showed that computational simplification alone cannot account for the increased performance of people using natural frequencies.[8] Instead, these authors conclude that reasoning performance increases substantially when information is presented in terms of the natural frequencies that correspond to the way organisms have acquired information through much of evolutionary history—that is, by naturally sampling (and tallying) events observed in the natural environment (see also Brase, 2002b).

CONCLUSIONS

Cognitive psychologists have long studied the limitations of human thought, and with good reason. Despite Hamlet's exhortation that we humans are "noble in reason . . . infinite in faculty" (Act 2, Scene 2), we struggle to keep more than a half dozen things in mind at once, we quickly forget what we have learned, we ignore much of the available information when making decisions, and we find it difficult to process deeply what information we do consider. But in focusing on the negative implications of these limitations, cognitive psychology may have grabbed the wrong end of the stick. The limited human mind is not just the compromised result of running up against constraints that can little be budged, such as the current birth-canal-limited size of the skull; rather, it is a carefully orchestrated set of systems in which limits can actually be beneficial *enablers* of functions, not merely constraints (Cosmides & Tooby, 1987). A less limited mind might fare worse in dealing with the adaptive problems posed by the structured environment. As Guildenstern later responded to Hamlet, presciently summing up modern psychology's computationally intensive theories of cognition, "there has been much throwing about of brains." In many cases, throwing fewer brains at a task might do the trick—more is not always better.

Considering the widespread selective pressures and attendant costs and benefits that have acted over the course of evolution on our cognitive mechanisms can help us to uncover these surprising instances when limitations are beneficial (and helps us understand the design and functioning of those mechanisms even when their limits are constraining). As we have seen in this chapter (see Hertwig & Todd, 2003, for more), limited information use can lead simple heuristics to make more robust generalizations in new environments. Forgetting in long-term memory can improve the performance of recall and protect individuals from harmful reactions at vulnerable periods in their lives. And limited short-term memory can amplify the presence of important correlations in the world.

But beyond just enhancing the abilities of certain cognitive systems, limits can even enable functions that may not be possible otherwise. According to Newport's (1990) "less-is-more" hypothesis on the role of limits in language learning, "the very limitations of the young child's information processing abil-

---

[8] Consistent with this conclusion, Brase (2002a) has shown that frequencies were seen as clearer and easier to understand than single-event probabilities.

ities provide the basis on which successful language acquisition occurs" (p. 23). Elman (1993) tested this idea with a neural network model, which he found was unable to learn the grammatical relationships in a set of several thousand sentences when given a large memory, but which could pick up the grammar incrementally if memory started small and gradually expanded. As he explained, "The initial memory limitations . . . act as a filter on the input, and focus learning on just that subset of facts which lay the foundation for future success" (Elman, 1993, pp. 84–85).

These potential benefits of cognitive limitations compose one of the main themes we have sketched here in our picture of the issues that should be addressed within an evolution-inspired cognitive psychology. We have portrayed the importance of considering how general selective pressures—those arising in multiple task domains—can shape adaptive cognitive mechanisms, in addition to the shaping forces of domain-specific task requirements and environment structure. But most of the picture remains to be filled in. Here are some of the pressing questions open for immediate exploration (see Todd, Gigerenzer, & the ABC Research Group, 2000, for others): How is the adaptive toolbox of cognitive mechanisms filled—that is, what are the processes through which heuristics evolve, develop, are learned individually, or are acquired from an individual's culture? How do we select particular tools in particular situations? What role do other possible factors, such as emotions or social norms, play in decision heuristics? How effective can small information samples be for learning about our environment? How does the use of particular cognitive mechanisms shape the environment itself (e.g., Todd & Kirby, 2001)? What selective pressures have shaped other cognitive capacities we have not touched on such as attention, categorization, and planning?[9] And what methods are most appropriate for studying the action of selective forces on cognitive adaptations?

Taking an evolutionary perspective can help introduce new unity and coherence (as well as new ideas and hypotheses) into cognitive psychology. But the benefits of bringing the cognitive and evolutionary approaches to psychology together do not flow solely from the latter to the former. Cognitive psychology is also a salutary approach for evolutionary psychologists to engage with: It points to the importance of information, hence of the environment that it reflects, and the structure of the environment must be a central aspect of any evolutionary explanation of behavior. The field's experimental methodology is an important component of supporting and revising evolutionarily inspired hypotheses regarding human cognition and action. Finally, cognitive psychology also reminds us of the crucial role that processing information with specific algorithmic mechanisms plays in the generation of adaptive behavior. This step—cognition— is often the missing link in nonpsychological approaches to investigating the evolution of behavior (Cosmides & Tooby, 1987) and is still too often missing within evolutionary psychology studies, as in those that merely assert correlations between environmental cues and behavioral outcomes. By cross-fertilizing

---

[9] For instance, the history of research on categorization reflects the rise of openness to evolutionary thinking in psychology, as it progressed from the use in the 1950s of artificial stimuli assigned to artificial categories by logical rules, to demonstrations in the 1970s that such research did not generalize to natural categories like species (Rosch, 1975), to arguments in the 1990s that human categorization is driven by domain-specific principles (Hirschfeld & Gelman, 1994; Tooby & Cosmides, 1992).

these two traditions, evolutionary and cognitive, a more vigorous hybrid psychology will be formed.

REFERENCES

Anderson, J. R. (1990). *The adaptive character of thought*. Hillsdale, NJ: Erlbaum.

Anderson, J. R., & Lebiere, C. (1998). *The atomic components of thought*. Mahwah, NJ: Erlbaum.

Anderson, J. R., & Milson, R. (1989). Human memory: An adaptive perspective. *Psychological Review, 96*, 703–719.

Anderson, J. R., & Schooler, L. J. (1991). Reflections of the environment in memory. *Psychological Science, 2*, 396–408.

Anderson, J. R., & Schooler, L. J. (2000). The adaptive nature of memory. In E. Tulving & F. I. M. Craik (Eds.), *The Oxford handbook of memory* (pp. 557–570). New York: Oxford University Press.

Ariely, D., & Levav, J. (2000). Sequential choice in group settings: Taking the road less traveled and less enjoyed. *Journal of Consumer Research, 27*(3), 279–290.

Atkinson, R. C., & Shiffrin, R. M. (1968). Human memory: A proposed system and its control processes. In K. W. Spence & J. T. Spence (Eds.), *The psychology of learning and motivation: Advances in research and theory* (Vol. 2). New York: Academic Press.

Baddeley, A. (2000). The episodic buffer: A new component of working memory? *Trends in Cognitive Sciences, 4*, 417–423.

Bartlett, F. C. (1995). *Remembering*. Cambridge, England: Cambridge University Press. (Original work published 1932)

Berretty, P. M., Todd, P. M., & Martignon, L. (1999). Categorization by elimination: Using few cues to choose. In G. Gigerenzer, P. M. Todd, & the ABC Research Group, *Simple heuristics that make us smart* (pp. 235–254). New York: Oxford University Press.

Bjork, E. L., & Bjork, R. A. (1996). Continuing influences of to-be-forgotten information. *Consciousness and Cognitions, 5*, 176–196.

Brase, G. L. (2002a). Ecological and evolutionary validity: Comments on Johnson-Laird, Legrenzi, Girotto, Legrenzi, and Caverni's (1999) mental-model theory of extensional reasoning. *Psychological Review, 109*, 722–728.

Brase, G. L. (2002b). Which statistical format facilitates what decisions? The perception and influence of different statistical information formats. *Journal of Behavioral Decision Making, 15*, 381–401.

Bröder, A. (2000). Assessing the empirical validity of the "Take The Best" heuristic as a model of human probabilistic inference. *Journal of Experimental Psychology: Learning, Memory, and Cognition, 26*, 1332–1346.

Bröder, A., & Schiffer, S. (2003). "Take The Best" versus simultaneous feature matching: Probabilistic inferences from memory and effects of representation format. *Journal of Experimental Psychology: General, 132*(2), 277–293.

Bullock, S., & Todd, P. M. (1999). Made to measure: Ecological rationality in structured environments. *Minds and Machines, 9*(4), 497–541.

Buss, D. M. (2004). *Evolutionary psychology: The new science of the mind* (2nd ed.). Boston: Pearson.

Chater, N. (1999). The search for simplicity: A fundamental cognitive principle? *Quarterly Journal of Experimental Psychology, 52A*(2), 273–302.

Chater, N., & Vitányi, P. (2003). Simplicity: A unifying principle in cognitive science? *Trends in Cognitive Sciences, 7*(1), 19–22.

Christensen-Szalanski, J. J. J., & Beach, L. R. (1982). Experience and the base-rate fallacy. *Organizational Behavior and Human Performance, 29*, 270–278.

Cosmides, L., & Tooby, J. (1987). From evolution to behavior: Evolutionary psychology as the missing link. In J. Dupré (Ed.), *The latest on the best: Essays on evolution and optimization* (pp. 277–306). Cambridge, MA: MIT Press/Bradford Books.

Cowan, N. (2001). The magical number 4 in short-term memory: A reconsideration of mental storage capacity. *Behavioral and Brain Sciences, 24*, 87–185.

Czerlinski, J., Gigerenzer, G., & Goldstein, D. G. (1999). How good are simple heuristics. In G. Gigerenzer, P. M. Todd, & the ABC Research Group (Eds.), *Simple heuristics that make us smart*. New York: Oxford University Press.

Dawes, R. M., & Corrigan, B. (1974). Linear models in decision making. *Psychological Bulletin, 81,* 95–106.

DePrince, A. P., & Freyd, J. J. (2004). Forgetting trauma stimuli. *Psychological Science, 15,* 488–492.

Dhami, M. K., & Wallsten, T. S. (in press). Interpersonal comparison of subjective probabilities. *Memory and Cognition.*

Dudey, T., & Todd, P. M. (2002). Making good decisions with minimal information: Simultaneous and sequential choice. *Journal of Bioeconomics, 3,* 195–215.

Dukas, R. (Ed.). (1998). *Cognitive ecology: The evolutionary ecology of information processing and decision making.* Chicago: The University of Chicago.

Dukas, R. (1999). Costs of memory: Ideas and predictions. *Journal of Theoretical Biology, 197,* 41–50.

Ebbinghaus, H. (1964). *Memory: A contribution to experimental psychology.* New York: Dover. (Original work published 1885)

Eddy, D. M. (1982). Probabilistic reasoning in clinical medicine: Problems and opportunities. In D. Kahneman, P. Slovic, & A. Tversky (Eds.), *Judgment under uncertainty: Heuristics and biases* (pp. 249–267). Cambridge, England: Cambridge University Press.

Elman, J. L. (1993). Learning and development in neural networks: The importance of starting small. *Cognition, 48,* 71–99.

Fiedler, K., & Kareev, Y. (2004). *Does decision quality (always) increase with the size of information samples? Some vicissitudes in applying the law of large numbers.* Manuscript submitted for publication.

Fischhoff, B. (1982). For those condemned to study the past: Heuristics and biases in hindsight. In D. Kahneman, P. Slovic, & A. Tversky (Eds.), *Judgment under uncertainty: Heuristics and biases* (pp. 335–355). Cambridge, England: Cambridge University Press.

Freyd, J. J. (1983). Shareability: The social psychology of epistemology. *Cognitive Science, 7,* 191–210.

Freyd, J. J. (1990). Natural selection or shareability? [commentary] *Behavioral and Brain Sciences, 13,* 732–734.

Freyd, J. J. (1996). *Betrayal trauma: The logic of forgetting childhood abuse.* Cambridge, MA: Harvard University Press.

Galef, B. G., Jr. (1987). Social influences on the identification of toxic foods by Norway rats. *Animal Learning and Behavior, 15,* 327–332.

Gallistel, C. R. (1990). *The organization of learning.* Cambridge, MA: MIT Press.

Gigerenzer, G., & Goldstein, D. G. (1996). Reasoning the fast and frugal way: Models of bounded rationality. *Psychological Review, 103,* 650–669.

Gigerenzer, G., & Goldstein, D. G. (1999). Betting on one good reason: The take the best heuristic. In G. Gigerenzer, P. M. Todd, & the ABC Research Group (Eds.), *Simple heuristics that make us smart.* New York: Oxford University Press.

Gigerenzer, G., & Hoffrage, U. (1995). How to improve Bayesian reasoning without instruction: Frequency formats. *Psychological Review, 102,* 684–704.

Gigerenzer, G., Swijtink, Z., Porter, T., Daston, L., Beatty, J., & Krüger, L. (1989). *The empire of chance: How probability changed science and everyday life.* Cambridge, England: Cambridge University Press.

Gigerenzer, G., Todd, P. M., & the ABC Research Group. (1999). *Simple heuristics that make us smart.* New York: Oxford University Press.

Goldstein, D. G., & Gigerenzer, G. (1999). The recognition heuristic: How ignorance makes us smart. In G. Gigerenzer, P. M. Todd, & the ABC Research Group (Eds.), *Simple heuristics that make us smart.* New York: Oxford University Press.

Goldstein, D. G., & Gigerenzer, G. (2002). Models of ecological rationality: The recognition heuristic. *Psychological Review, 109,* 75–90.

Goldstein, W. M., & Weber, E. U. (1997). Content and discontent: Indications and implications of domain specificity in preferential decision making. In W. M. Goldstein & R. M. Hogarth (Eds.), *Research on judgment and decision making.* Cambridge, MA: Cambridge University Press.

Hertwig, R., Barron, G., Weber, E., & Erev, I. (2004). Decisions from experience and the effect of rare events in risky choice. *Psychological Science, 15,* 534–539.

Hertwig, R., Erev, I., Barron, G., & Weber, E. (in press). Decisions from experience: Sampling and updating of information. In K. Fiedler & P. Juslin (Eds.), *Information sampling as a key to understand adaptive cognition.* Cambridge: Cambridge University Press.

Hertwig, R., Fanselow, C., & Hoffrage, U. (2003). Hindsight bias: How knowledge and heuristics affect our reconstruction of the past. *Memory, 11,* 357–377.

Hertwig, R., & Gigerenzer, G. (1999). The "conjunction fallacy" revisited: How intelligent inferences look like reasoning errors. *Journal of Behavioral Decision Making, 12,* 275–305.

Hertwig, R., Hoffrage, U., & Martignon, L. (1999). Quick estimation: Letting the environment do some of the work. In G. Gigerenzer, P. M. Todd, & the ABC Research Group (Eds.), *Simple heuristics that make us smart* (pp. 209–234). New York: Oxford University Press.

Hertwig, R., & Todd, P. M. (2003). More is not always better: The benefits of cognitive limits. In D. Hardman & L. Macchi (Eds.), *Thinking: Psychological perspectives on reasoning, judgment and decision making.* West Sussex: Wiley.

Hey, J. D. (1981). Are optimal search rules reasonable? And vice versa? (And does it matter anyway?) *Journal of Economic Behavior and Organization, 2,* 47–70.

Hey, J. D. (1982). Search for rules for search. *Journal of Economic Behavior and Organization, 3,* 65–81.

Hirschfeld, L. A., & Gelman, S. A. (Eds.). (1994). *Mapping the mind: Domain specificity in cognition and culture.* Cambridge: Cambridge University Press.

Hoffrage, U., & Gigerenzer, G. (1998). Using natural frequencies to improve diagnostic inferences. *Academic Medicine, 73,* 538–540.

Hoffrage, U., Hertwig, R., & Gigerenzer, G. (2000). Hindsight bias: A by-product of knowledge updating? *Journal of Experimental Psychology: Learning, Memory, and Cognition, 26,* 566–581.

Hoffrage, U., Lindsey, S., Hertwig, R., & Gigerenzer, G. (2000). Communicating statistical information. *Science, 290,* 2261–2262.

Hoffrage, U., & Pohl, R. F. (Eds.). (2003). Hindsight bias [Special issue]. *Memory, 4/5(11),* 329–504.

James, W. (1890). *The principles of psychology* (Vol. 1). New York: Dover.

Juslin, P., & Olsson, H. (in press). Capacity limitations and the detection of correlations: A comment on Kareev (2000). *Psychological Review.*

Kahneman, D., & Tversky, A. (1972). Subjective probability: A judgment of representativeness. *Cognitive Psychology, 3,* 430–454.

Kahneman, D., & Tversky, A. (1979). Prospect theory: An analysis of decision under risk. *Econometrica, 47,* 263–291.

Kareev, Y. (1995a). Positive bias in the perception of covariation. *Psychological Review, 102,* 490–502.

Kareev, Y. (1995b). Through a narrow window: Working memory capacity and the detection of covariation. *Cognition, 56,* 263–269.

Kareev, Y. (2000). Seven (indeed, plus or minus two) and the detection of correlations. *Psychological Review, 107,* 397–402.

Kareev, Y., Lieberman, I., & Lev, M. (1997). Through a narrow window: Sample size and the perception of correlation. *Journal of Experimental Psychology: General, 126,* 278–287.

Kenrick, D. T., Sadalla, E. K., & Keefe, R. C. (1998). Evolutionary cognitive psychology: The missing heart of modern cognitive science. In C. Crawford & D. L. Krebs (Eds.), *Handbook of evolutionary psychology* (pp. 485–514). Hillsdale, NJ: Erlbaum.

Klein, S. B., Cosmides, L., Tooby, J., & Chance, S. (2002). Decisions and the evolution of memory: Multiple systems, multiple functions. *Psychological Review, 2,* 306–329.

Kleiter, G. D. (1994). Natural sampling: Rationality without base rates. In G. H. Fischer & D. Laming (Eds.), *Contributions to mathematical psychology, psychometrics, and methodology* (pp. 375–388). New York: Springer.

Koriat, A., Goldsmith, M., & Pansky, A. (2000). Toward a psychology of memory accuracy. *Annual Review of Psychology, 51,* 481–537.

Krueger, J. I., & Funder, D. C. (in press). Towards a balanced social psychology: Causes, consequences and cures for the problem-seeking approach to social behavior and cognition. *Behavioral and Brain Sciences.*

Landauer, T. K. (1986). How much do people remember? Some estimates of the quantity of learned information in long-term memory. *Cognitive Science, 10,* 477–493.

Lindsey, S., Hertwig, R., & Gigerenzer, G. (2003). Communicating statistical DNA evidence. *Jurimetrics: Journal of Law, Science, and Technology, 43,* 147–163.

MacGregor, J. N. (1987). Short-term memory capacity: Limitation or optimization? *Psychological Review, 94,* 107–108.

Marr, D. (1982). *Vision.* San Francisco: Freeman.

Martignon, L., & Hoffrage, U. (2002). Fast, frugal and fit: Simple heuristics for paired comparison. *Theory and Decision, 52,* 29–71.

McNally, R. J., Clancy, S. A., & Schacter, D. L. (2001). Directed forgetting of trauma cues in adults reporting repressed or recovered memories of childhood sexual abuse. *Journal of Abnormal Psychology, 110,* 151–156.

Miller, G. A. (1956). The magical number seven plus or minus two: Some limits on our capacity for processing information. *Psychological Review, 63,* 81–97.

Miller, G. F., & Todd, P. M. (1998). Mate choice turns cognitive. *Trends in Cognitive Sciences, 2,* 190–198.

Newell, B. R., & Shanks, D. R. (2003). Take the best or look at the rest? Factors influencing "one-reason" decision-making. *Journal of Experimental Psychology: Learning, Memory, and Cognition, 29,* 53–65.

Newport, E. L. (1990). Maturational constraints on language learning. *Cognitive Science, 14,* 11–28.

Payne, J. W., Bettman, J. R., & Johnson, E. J. (1993). *The adaptive decision maker.* New York: Cambridge University Press.

Pirolli, P. L., & Card, S. K. (1999). Information foraging. *Psychological Review, 106,* 643–675.

Real, L. A. (1991). Animal choice behavior and the evolution of cognitive architecture. *Science, 253,* 980–986.

Rieskamp, J., & Hoffrage, U. (1999). When do people use simple heuristics and how can we tell. In G. Gigerenzer, P. M. Todd, & the ABC Research Group (Eds.), *Simple heuristics that make us smart.* New York: Oxford University Press.

Rieskamp, J., & Otto, P. (2004). *SSL: A theory of how people learn to select strategies.* Manuscript submitted for publication.

Rosch, E. H. (1975). Cognitive representations of semantic categories. *Journal of Experimental Psychology: General, 104,* 192–253.

Roth, A. E., & Sotomayor, M. A. O. (1990). *Two-sided matching: A study in game-theoretic modeling and analysis.* Cambridge: Cambridge University Press.

Schacter, D. L. (2001). *The seven sins of memory: How the mind forgets and remembers.* Boston: Houghton Mifflin.

Schooler, L., & Hertwig, R. (2004). *Environment and forgetting as natural allies of heuristic inference.* Manuscript submitted for publication.

Seale, D. A., & Rapoport, A. (1997). Sequential decision making with relative ranks: An experimental investigation of the "secretary problem." *Organizational Behavior and Human Decision Processes, 69*(3), 221–236.

Simão, J., & Todd, P. M. (2003). Emergent patterns of mate choice in human populations. *Artificial Life, 9,* 403–417.

Simon, H. A. (1955). A behavioral model of rational choice. *Quarterly Journal of Economics, 69,* 99–118.

Simon, H. A. (1990). Invariants of human behavior. *Annual Review of Psychology, 41,* 1–19.

Sivers, H., Schooler, J., & Freyd, J. J. (2002). Recovered memories. In V. S. Ramachandran (Ed.), *Encyclopedia of the human brain* (Vol. 4, pp. 169–184). San Diego: Academic Press.

Tanner, C., & Medin, D. L. (in press). Protected values: No omission bias and no framing effects. *Psychonomic Bulletin and Review.*

Todd, P. M. (2000). The ecological rationality of mechanisms evolved to make up minds. *American Behavioral Scientist, 43*(6), 940–956.

Todd, P. M. (2001). Fast and frugal heuristics for environmentally bounded minds. In G. Gigerenzer & R. Selten (Eds.), *Bounded rationality: The adaptive toolbox* [Dahlem Workshop Report] (pp. 51–70). Cambridge, MA: MIT Press.

Todd, P. M., Fiddick, L., & Krauss, S. (2000). Ecological rationality and its contents. *Thinking and Reasoning, 6*(4), 375–384.

Todd, P. M., Gigerenzer, G., & the ABC Research Group. (2000). How can we open up the adaptive toolbox? (Reply to commentaries.) *Behavioral and Brain Sciences, 23*(5), 767–780.

Todd, P. M., & Kirby, S. (2001). I like what I know: How recognition-based decisions can structure the environment. In J. Kelemen & P. Sosík (Eds.), *Advances in artificial life: Sixth European Conference Proceedings (ECAL 2001)* (pp. 166–175). Berlin, Germany: Springer-Verlag.

Todd, P. M., & Miller, G. F. (1999). From pride and prejudice to persuasion: Satisficing in mate search. In G. Gigerenzer, P. M. Todd, & the ABC Research Group (Eds.), *Simple heuristics that make us smart* (pp. 287–308). New York: Oxford University Press.

Tooby, J., & Cosmides, L. (1992). The psychological foundations of culture. In J. Barkow, L. Cosmides, & J. Tooby (Eds.), *The adapted mind* (pp. 19–136). Oxford, England: Oxford University Press.

Trivers, R. (1972). Parental investment and sexual selection. In B. Campbell (Ed.), *Sexual selection and the descent of man: 1871–1971* (pp. 136–179). Chicago: Aldine.

Tulving, E., Craik, F. I. M. (Eds.). (2000). *The Oxford handbook of memory.* New York: Oxford University Press.

Tversky, A. (1972). Elimination by aspects: A theory of choice. *Psychological Review, 79*(4), 281–299.

Tversky, A., & Kahneman, D. (1982). Belief in the law of small numbers. In D. Kahneman, P. Slovic, & A. Tversky (Eds.), *Judgement under uncertainty: Heuristics and biases* (pp. 23–31). Cambridge, England: Cambridge University Press. (Original work published 1971)

Tversky, A., & Kahneman, D. (1992). Advances in prospect theory: Cumulative representation of uncertainty. *Journal of Risk and Uncertainty, 5*, 297–323.

Weber, E. U., Shafir, S., & Blais, A.-R. (2004). Predicting risk-sensitivity in humans and lower animals: Risk as variance or coefficient of variation. *Psychological Review, 111*, 430–445.

Wimsatt, W. C. (1987). False models as means to truer theories. In M. Nitecki & A. Hoffman (Eds.), *Neutral models in biology* (pp. 23–55). London: Oxford University Press.

Wixted, J. T. (1990). Analyzing the empirical course of forgetting. *Journal of Experimental Psychology: Learning, Memory and Cognition, 16*, 927–935.

Wixted, J. T., & Ebbesen, E. B. (1991). On the form of forgetting. *Psychological Science, 2*, 409–415.

Wixted, J. T., & Ebbesen, E. B. (1997). Genuine power curves in forgetting: A quantitative analysis of individual subject forgetting functions. *Memory and Cognition, 25*, 731–739.

CHAPTER 28

Evolutionary Social Psychology

DOUGLAS T. KENRICK, JON K. MANER, and NORMAN P. LI

IN HIS CLASSIC *SOCIAL PSYCHOLOGY*, William McDougall (1908) argued that "only a comparative and evolutionary psychology" could provide the needed foundation for a scientific social psychology. For the rest of the twentieth century, McDougall's advice was mostly ignored.

As the authors of one social psychology textbook observed: "As recently as the mid-1980s, most social psychologists would have answered *no*" to the question: "Is social behavior influenced by biological processes and genetic factors?" (Baron & Byrne, 2000, p. 12). But in their ninth edition, they observe that the evolutionary perspective "has gained increasing recognition in social psychology" (Baron & Byrne, 2000, p. 13). Similarly, recent editions of two other popular social psychology textbooks list "the evolutionary perspective" as a significant new development in the field (Aronson, Wilson, & Akert, 1999; Brehm, Kassin, & Fein, 2002).

Despite these promising developments, evolutionary psychologists are frequently disappointed to find these same textbooks presenting an evolutionary perspective in an apologetic and critical manner not similarly applied to other perspectives. "We present what we believe is a balanced approach, discussing evolutionary psychology as well as alternatives to it," note Aronson et al. (p. xxv). Paradoxically, an evolutionary perspective continues to generate skepticism and antipathy, even as it generates increasing research support for powerful hypotheses connecting social psychology with findings on other animal species. One text author (not an evolutionary psychologist) told us privately that, though he felt evolutionary hypotheses were often backed by some of the strongest evidence in the field today, reviewers of his text repeatedly insisted he present criticisms whenever he mentioned any evolutionary research. These reviewers did not demand similar reservations regarding nonevolutionary research supported by much weaker evidence.

Nevertheless, evolutionary psychologists ought to take heart: Although the glass may not yet be half full, it is no longer empty. As evolutionary psychologists confront constructive challenges posed by skeptics, the water in the glass will continue to rise. Indeed, the day is coming when a career studying *Homo sapiens'* social behavior without some background in evolutionary theory will be unthinkable. But that day hasn't arrived yet. Evolutionary and traditional social psychologists still have much to learn from one another.

Lessons for Social Psychologists

• *Be less trivial.* Focus less on proximate triggers for behavior, and expand your thinking into the far away past—the why behind the why behind the why. Proximate causes often seem random or senseless until you place them into a larger functional context.

• *Pay attention to specific content, not just general processes.* General principles such as "seek reward," or "maximize economic utility" are often too broad to explain specific human behaviors. What counts as a reward or an economic benefit varies in systematic ways across different domains of social life (e.g., selflessly donating resources to your child may be rewarding; similar donations to a stranger may not). Domain-general theories are often silent at critical points, where considerations of adaptive content lead to more precise and interactive predictions about perceived rewards and costs. In this way, developments in evolutionary theory can draw attention to neglected topics in social psychology—such as the central importance of relationships between kin (Burnstein, Crandall, & Kitayama, 1994; Daly, Salmon, & Wilson, 1997).

• *Rethink our notion of culture.* Culture is important, but it doesn't just spring forth arbitrarily—it coevolves with psychological adaptations that selectively bias thought, feeling, and behavior. Instead of a blank slate on which cultural experiences can freely scrawl, a coloring book provides a better metaphor for the interaction between mind and culture (Kenrick, Becker, Butner, Li, & Maner, 2003). Evolved psychological adaptations are like the predrawn lines in a coloring book, constraining and encouraging the development of some norms over others. Local social and physical ecology provides the colors, but the basic outline tends to direct those within certain limits.

On the other side, many key theoretical developments in evolutionary biology, including parental investment theory, inclusive fitness theory, and the theory of reciprocal altruism, are intrinsically concerned with social behavior. It would, therefore, be a mistake to focus only on what traditional social psychologists could learn at the feet of sagacious evolutionary psychologists. Social psychologists have a lot to teach in return (Kenrick, 1994).

Lessons for Evolutionary Psychologists/Sociobiologists

• *Be more contextual.* Those already using adaptationist models should pay more explicit attention to how factors in the social environment interact with innate dispositions. Evolutionary psychologists talk a lot about context-sensitive mechanisms, but thus far, very few of those mechanisms have been spelled out in terms of the precise decision rules that convert environmental inputs into behavioral or cognitive outputs (Li & Bailey, 2000). The social psychological literature is rich with findings useful in this regard.

• *Focus more on social dynamics.* Evolutionary psychologists have focused on decisions made by individual human beings serving their own selfish genetic interests. However, just as individual genes are interlinked with a complex of other genes within an individual, individual human beings are intrinsically interlinked with a web of other human beings. This is not to suggest a group selectionist position, but a dynamic and ecological position that considers emergent processes at different levels (Kenrick, Li, & Butner, 2003; Kenrick et al., 2002). Decision rules within one individual seeking status or a mate will succeed or fail in the context of decision rules used by others in that individual's social network. Though group level outcomes emerge from individual decision rules, focusing on one individual at a time can be quite uninformative about group level outcomes. Emergent group-level processes are complex but not magical, and by combining insights from dynamical systems theory, cognitive science, and evolutionary psychology, we can now begin studying them scientifically (Kenrick, Li, et al., 2003).

• *Take criticism constructively, even when it's not intended as such.* It is difficult not to be defensive when others attack your ideas, particularly when those criticisms are couched with unsubstantiated moral and political accusations and backed with little understanding of evolutionary theory and research. Nevertheless, dialectic interchange fuels the engine of science. A critic's intuitive sense that an empirical finding is "wrong" can be the seed of an interactive hypothesis waiting to be formulated (McGuire, 1997). And critics sometimes point out social psychological findings that evolutionary theorists have overlooked.

CONTRIBUTIONS OF SOCIAL PSYCHOLOGICAL RESEARCH TO EVOLUTIONARY PSYCHOLOGY

Social psychological findings and methods can provide valuable tools for evolutionary theorists. First, social psychologists have amassed abundant knowledge about how humans behave in specific social contexts. Acquaintance with this literature can help elucidate specific evolutionary hypotheses and provide building blocks for a more comprehensive understanding of human nature in its social context (Buss & Kenrick, 1998; Krebs & Denton, 1997). Social psychologists have also developed useful methods for understanding ongoing motivational and cognitive processes, as well as useful ways of thinking about and studying organism-environment interactions.

INFORMING EVOLUTIONARY MODELS WITH SOCIAL PSYCHOLOGICAL RESEARCH

For decades, social psychologists have generated empirical findings relevant to evolutionary models of cooperation, aggression, out-group conflict, status seeking, and mating behavior. For example, Abbey (1982) found that men interpreted friendly interactions as more sexual than did women. Several evolutionary theorists have connected such findings with parental investment theory and research from numerous animal species indicating that males are more likely to initiate courtship (e.g., Kenrick & Trost, 1987). Going beyond post hoc reexplanation, Haselton and Buss (2000) extended Abbey's findings, demonstrating that men and women are differentially predisposed to make different types of cognitive errors in line with differences in parental investment.

In some cases, social psychological findings have suggested extensions and modifications on evolutionary models. For example, early evolutionary game theorists often seemed to tacitly assume that organisms, like genes, operate in an unmitigated self-serving way (cf. Dawkins, 1976). Decades of social psychological research, however, revealed people often contributing time and resources to complete strangers (Caporael, Dawes, Orbell, & van de Kragt, 1989; Maner et al., 2002). Although contradicting simplistic applications of the selfish genes theory, these findings make sense if we consider that human beings evolved for group living

(Kenrick, 1991; Krebs, 1991). More recent models acknowledge that standard rules of "rational self-interest" may apply only to interactions between strangers (see A. P. Fiske, 1992, for a review). Among friends, rules of equality are the norm, whereas communal sharing is likely among family members. This makes sense if we presume social decisions stem not from broad "rational" considerations of self-interest, but from psychological mechanisms designed to increase ancestral fitness. Parental investment, for example, involves selfless, one-sided contributions in the short run that ultimately serve to replicate the parents' selfish genes.

Social psychological models of relationship stages combined with evolutionary models to clarify an apparent discrepancy involving mate choice. Several studies found large differences between men's and women's mating behaviors. Whereas no woman accepted an invitation to sleep with an opposite-sex stranger she met on campus, over 70% of men did (Clark & Hatfield, 1989). Female college students reliably preferred socially dominant men whereas males reported equal attraction to women regardless of their dominance (Sadalla, Kenrick, & Vershure, 1987). Findings such as these, seemingly obvious to those who understand parental investment theory (Trivers, 1972), often elicited negative reactions in colleagues who perceived that evolutionary psychologists exaggerated sex differences (e.g., L. C. Miller & Fishkin, 1997). Critics have pointed to numerous findings suggesting that men and women aren't so different after all. For example, men and women experience love in much the same way (Hazan & Shaver, 1994). Buss and Barnes (1986) reported some sex differences in line with evolutionary predictions, but also found men's and women's mate preferences to be mostly similar.

The apparent discrepancy was resolved by considering some distinctions made by social psychologists studying relationships, who had frequently observed that the evaluation of costs and benefits changes radically depending on an individual's level of involvement in a relationship (e.g., dating versus marriage; Duck, 1978). Integrating social psychological stage models with parental investment theory helped clarify both when males and females differ in selectivity and when they do not (Kenrick & Trost, 1987). At initial courtship stages, men and women might be expected to behave like males and females in most mammalian species. In such species, which are usually polygynous, females lose more than males from ill-considered copulations. A female mating with a noncommittal or low-quality male might nevertheless be required to make the immense minimum mammalian investment—carrying the fetus, giving birth, and nursing the infant after birth. A male might lose only the small investment involved in initial mating. Human males, however, unlike most other mammals, frequently commit to one female and invest in her offspring for decades. As in many monogamous bird species, sex differences decrease when males make long-term investments. Consistent with predictions from this parental investment model, researchers find relatively small sex differences for long-term relationships, but large sex differences for short-term relationships (Kenrick, Groth, Trost, & Sadalla, 1993; Kenrick, Sadalla, Groth, & Trost, 1990).

Many other potential bridges between traditional and evolutionary approaches to social psychology have been suggested (Buss & Kenrick, 1998; Krebs & Denton, 1997). We explore some of these in the following sections.

Person-Situation Interactions

Most social psychologists agree that factors in the person interact with situational factors to determine behavior (cf. Kenrick & Funder, 1987; Lewin, 1951). Those interactions are often dynamic and reciprocal (Kenrick & Dantchik, 1983; Snyder & Ickes, 1985). Different people choose different life situations that, in turn, differentially affect their social development. People also alter their situations to fit their dispositions; and in turn, people's situations can alter their motives and cognitions.

Even potent person factors do not act independently of situations. High testosterone males may be generally more aggressive than high estrogen females, but those differences show up only in certain situations (e.g., when frustrated or insulted but not on a romantic date in a quiet restaurant). Furthermore, those main effects may, in some circumstances, be reversed (e.g., if a high testosterone man accidentally knocked down a high estrogen woman's toddler). Researchers find complex interactive predictions compelling because they often elucidate underlying psychological processes and rule out alternative explanations (Conway & Schaller, 2002; Kenrick, Sundie, Nicastle, & Stone, 2001).

Consider one study that examined person-situation interactions to elucidate broader evolutionary hypotheses. Evolutionary theorists have suggested that generations of group conflict in humans and other primates favored the evolution of mechanisms predisposing cognitive vigilance to members of unfamiliar groups (e.g., Wrangham, 1987). The simple prediction that people dislike out-group members, however, might inspire psychologists to observe that everyone already knew that. Indeed, recent experimental work has developed interactive hypotheses based on adaptationist considerations (Kurzban, Tooby, & Cosmides, 2001; Maner et al., 2005; Neuberg & Cottrell, 2002). Schaller, Park, and Mueller (2003) reasoned that fear of out-group strangers would have been especially functional for our ancestors in circumstances associated with increased danger (e.g., in encounters after dark). These researchers asked White and Asian college students to rate photographs of Black men either in a brightly lit room or in a completely dark room. Black men were seen as particularly threatening by participants who rated them in a dark room. These effects were stronger among male than among female raters and among those chronically concerned about physical danger. Such person-situation interactions can help elucidate behavioral function by clarifying the particular triggers for hypothesized adaptive reactions.

Emphasis on Cognitive Processes

The social psychological emphasis on cognitive processes underlying social behaviors is consistent with modern directions in evolutionary psychology (e.g., Cosmides & Tooby, 1992; Kenrick, 1994). Because it is difficult to make inferences about events inside animals' heads, animal researchers traditionally focused on observable behavior. Because the animals studied by social psychologists have at least partial ability to report on their internal processes, though, social cognitive theorists have for decades gazed into the black box of the mind. Examining biases in cognition can help us better understand the adaptive purposes that resultant behavioral biases are designed to serve (Funder, 1987; Haselton & Buss, 2000).

Social psychologists have developed a wide array of methods for studying the cognitive underpinnings of behavior and teasing apart alternative underlying cognitive and motivational processes. Such methods include techniques for sorting reporting biases (e.g., responding in socially desirable ways) from actual feelings and thoughts (Greenwald et al., 2002). To study which aspects of the social environment draw attention, a researcher might elicit unreliable and inaccurate responses by simply asking, "What kinds of people do you typically look at?" However, methods such as eye tracking, visual search tasks, and frequency estimation can more meaningfully assess people's tendencies to look at some kinds of people more than others (e.g., Maner et al., 2003; Öhman & Mineka, 2001).

Another example can be found in the literature on intergroup prejudice. Because of social desirability pressures, simply asking people about their prejudices is an ineffective way of assessing implicit feelings about particular social groups (Devine, 1989). However, social psychologists have developed tasks (e.g., the Implicit Associations Test [IAT]) that more reliably assess implicit positive and negative associations with certain groups (e.g., Greenwald, McGhee, & Schwartz, 1998). Because tasks like the IAT require people to "do their best," they can unveil implicit biases by revealing limits in task performance.

WHAT CAN SOCIAL PSYCHOLOGISTS LEARN FROM EVOLUTIONARY THEORISTS?

Social and cognitive psychologists have focused predominantly on the flaws and limitations of human information processing (Krueger & Funder, 2004). Evolutionary psychologists presume that many errors and biases ultimately manifest underlying decision rules that, on average, were adaptive throughout much of human evolutionary history (Krebs & Denton, 1997). Putting proximate psychological processes in ultimate perspective elucidates not just the underlying reasons that people think and behave as they do but also what the important contextual triggers and constraints are likely to be.

FOCUS ON PROXIMATE AND DOMAIN-GENERAL CAUSES CAN BE MISLEADING

For much of the twentieth century, behaviorist assumptions prompted psychologists to eschew inferences about "underlying causes" in favor of empirical measurements of the immediately observable. Cognitive theorists were willing to go at least one inferential step beyond observable behavior, but shared the assumption that most human behavior could be explained by relatively simple processes that apply equally across contexts from reading one's mail to romancing one's mates. Cognitive psychologists have also tended to focus on causal mechanisms encompassed within the time limits of a half-hour laboratory experiment. However, proximate causes and immediately observable phenomena often make little sense unless you understand the ultimate causal processes that fashioned adaptations leading to the phenomena.

A popular theory of interpersonal attraction viewed attraction in terms of domain-general principles of classical conditioning (Byrne, 1971). The simple and general principle was: We like those associated with positive affect and dislike those associated with negative affect. From this perspective, people are attracted to physically attractive others because attractiveness is "rewarding." Consistent with this model, experiments demonstrated that people would work harder to gaze at good-looking than at less good-looking people and that gazing at good-looking others made people feel good (e.g., Byrne, London, & Reeves, 1968).

The reinforcement-affect theory, however, told us little about why certain features are judged as "attractive" in the first place or why features that are attractive in women are sometimes very different from those attractive in men (e.g., small waist-to-hip ratios versus square jaws). Many social learning theorists were willing to make some inferences, assuming that certain features were likely regarded as attractive because of people's history of rewards—most of the models we see smiling and having fun in advertisements are tall, athletic-looking people with shiny hair, smooth skin, and small waists as opposed to short people with large waists and pock-marked skin. Similarly, culturally minded researchers (e.g., Eagly & Wood, 1999) attributed these sex differences to societal norms that influence all the members of a culture similarly. However, appealing to social norms may simply redescribe a phenomenon, rather than explain its roots. Sex differences in attraction still begged further explanation. Evolutionarily-inspired research on human mating preferences is able to better explain these types of sex differences (e.g., Buss, 1989; Li, Bailey, Kenrick, & Linsenmeier, 2002).

Consider the case of age preferences in attraction in men and women. Psychologists initially described the phenomenon as one in which men are attracted to women slightly younger than themselves, whereas women are attracted to slightly older men (e.g., Deutsch, Zalenski, & Clark, 1986). This pattern was typically explained as resulting from culturally shared sex-role norms (e.g., Cameron, Oskamp, & Sparks, 1977, p. 29). Additional data generated from an evolutionary perspective, however, challenged this sociocultural explanation. First, although teenage males are generally hypersensitive to sex-role norms, they are attracted to relatively older women. Second, young boys tended to realize that women in their 20s had no reciprocal interest in them (thus violating both reward as well as normative theories; Kenrick, Gabrielidis, Keefe, & Cornelius, 1996). Third, men in their 20s had no aversion to women their own age or slightly older (Kenrick & Keefe, 1992). It was only older men who preferred relatively younger women, and that preference became stronger as the men aged so that men above 40 were not generally interested in women their own age at all, but sought much younger women.

Further challenging the American culture theory, data from other cultures and historical periods revealed the same pattern found in North America. Indeed, further away from modern urban societies like the United States, older men's preference for younger women tended to get stronger, not weaker (Kenrick & Keefe, 1992). An evolutionary life history perspective parsimoniously accounted for the developmental changes and cross-cultural similarities. Whereas a woman contributes direct bodily resources to her offspring, a man contributes indirect resources, such as food and shelter. A woman's ability to carry and nurse children is low in her early teens, high throughout her 20s, drops during her 30s and 40s, and ends in menopause. A man's ability to acquire resources and status is low during his teenage years but increases with age, at least until senescence. Consistent with these life history differences, women at all ages are attracted to somewhat older men. As men age, their age preferences change relative to their own age, while retaining a constant attraction toward women in the years of peak fertility.

An evolutionary perspective encourages social psychologists to consider ongoing social processes in terms of their functional roots. *Why* is it that men feel attraction toward women in their 20s with low waist-to-hip ratios rather than toward high-status women with square jaws? Why are these particular characteristics, and not others, rewarding, and why are they culturally valued? Answering these kinds of questions requires researchers to dig beneath the surface and examine a nomological network of data obtained from different methods applied to different species (Kenrick & Li, 2000).

Connecting Proximate and Ultimate Explanations

Embracing an evolutionary perspective does not challenge the findings of traditional social psychology; nor does it mean that social psychologists should send their laboratory participants home and depart for some remote part of the globe to live with a tribe of hunter-gatherers, dig up australopithecine bones, or commune with chimpanzees. It does not mean giving up research on ongoing phenomenology or learning processes or culture. In fact, because we carry around with us the vestiges of ancestral adaptations, one of the best ways to gather evidence regarding the adaptive significance of human behavior is to study cognitive and behavioral biases exhibited by contemporary humans (Buss & Kenrick, 1998).

How "ultimate" need the explanations for behavior be? Although we could in theory trace any current phenomenon back to the beginning of life or the Big Bang, such an explanation would hardly be useful. A more satisfactory stop point connects current behaviors to their adaptive function—to the particular way they served ancestral survival and reproduction (Alcock, 2001; Kenrick & Maner, 2004). A causal explanation that simply pointed to "differential reproduction" would, by this reasoning, go too far up the causal ladder. It would not distinguish the explanations for a bird's hollow skeleton, a giraffe's neck, and age preferences in human mating. We want to understand the particulars—how these very different adaptations served survival or reproductive functions. A more useful level of explanation might connect the bird's lightweight bones to flight constraints given its strength-to-weight ratio and the giraffe's long neck to the size of trees from which it obtains food. Flying and eating from tall trees were different adaptive functions solved by birds' and giraffes' physical design features. An adaptationist account seeks to explain how an animal's cognitive and behavioral mechanisms connect with demands and opportunities its ancestors regularly confronted in particular physical and social environments.

The debate is no longer about nature *or* nurture. It is clear that both genetic predispositions and learning play important roles in shaping behavior. Only by spanning the continuum from proximate to ultimate levels of explanation can psychologists fully explain a behavior. Experimental social psychological studies suggest, for example, that nonverbal indicators of dominance increase men's sexual attractiveness, but not women's (e.g., Sadalla et al., 1987). Comparative studies indicate links between testosterone levels and social rank in various mammal species (e.g., Rose, Bernstein, & Holaday, 1971). Physiological studies find typically higher testosterone levels in males than in females (Mazur & Booth, 1998). Correlational studies link high testosterone with antisocially competitive behavior (Dabbs & Morris, 1990). These and other findings provide a nomological network that fits together to form a compelling account of sexual selection and gender differences (Geary, 1998). No one source of data is superior to the others and none is superfluous—each is necessary to understand a complicated but ultimately sensible natural process.

Domain Generality versus Domain Specificity

When social psychologists joined the cognitive revolution, they assumed the same basic processes apply from word recognition to social cognition (e.g., Markus & Zajonc, 1985). This assumption seemed parsimonious and scientists try to avoid complex explanations when simple ones will do. But the human mind does not appear to process all information using a common set of abstract rules. Rather, it seems more intricately designed to assist humans in dealing differently with distinct domains of information. These domains seem to reflect different challenges ancestral humans needed to meet to survive and reproduce (cf. Kenrick, Sadalla, & Keefe, 1998; Pinker, 1997; Tooby & Cosmides, 1992).

What are the important domains? Might there be such a dizzying array of adaptive challenges that to separate them is to once again enter the world of minitheories and isolated findings? Although the human mind is not well represented as one all-purpose appliance, neither is it perfectly represented as a disorganized toolbox overflowing with minutely specialized devices. Although there is debate about exactly how modular the brain is (Kurzban & Haselton, in press), our view is that the various tools are hierarchically arranged into a smaller set of executive modules (Kenrick, Neuberg, & Cialdini, 2005). A fairly limited set of domain-based problems can be used to organize an integrated evolutionary social psychology. Although this scheme considers only social domains, we suggest that a similarly finite number of broad domains can be used to organize the important and recurrent problems humans face in dealing with the physical world.

EVOLUTIONARY SOCIAL PSYCHOLOGY BY DOMAINS

Though sexual intercourse is required for successful human reproduction, so are a diverse array of nonsexual tasks—making friends, negotiating status hierarchies, maintaining long-term relationships, and taking care of one's children. Adaptationist reasoning—bolstered by cognitive, behavioral, and neurophysiological evidence (Bugental, 2000; Panksepp, 1982; Plutchik, 1980)—suggests that much of human behavior is organized around a limited set of fundamental motives, each linked to particular adaptive challenges posed by ancestral environments. Based on several recent reviews (Bugental, 2000; Buss, 1999; A. P. Fiske, 1992; Kenrick, Li, et al, 2003), the remainder of our discussion is organized around six key domains of social life—coalition formation, status, self-protection, mate choice, mate retention, and parental care (see Table 28.1 on p. 812).

Each domain involves a different set of key social problems humans have needed to solve. Decision rules effective in solving problems in one domain (e.g., sharing resources with children) may be ineffective in solving problems in another domain (protecting self from members of out-groups or negotiating a status hierarchy). Individuals differ in decision rules as a function of random variation and adaptive design, in combination with current ecological conditions. Men and women, for example, have systematically different decision rules for choosing mates, approaching status competition, and interacting with out-group members. Parents have different decision rules for allocating resources within the family than siblings do and so on. Individual men and women may differ greatly from one another as a function of sex ratios and their current mating and status, and individual parents may differ as a function of number, age, and relative mate value of children (e.g., Fairbanks, 1993; Gangestad & Simpson, 2000).

COALITION FORMATION

For most of human evolutionary history, our ancestors lived in small, highly interdependent groups (Caporael, 1997; Sedikides & Skowronski, 1997). Successful

Table 28.1

Domains of Adaptive Problems Associated with Social Life
in Human Groups, Fundamental Goals, and Possible Examples
of Evolved Decision Constraints Associated with Each Domain

Domain of Social Behavior	Fundamental Goal	Some Evolved Decision Constraints Associated with This Domain
Coalition formation	To form and maintain co-operative alliances.	Cooperation more likely among those who: (1) are close relatives, (2) have reciprocally shared resources in past.
Status	To gain or maintain respect from, and power over, other group members.	Cost-benefit ratio of striving for status more favorable for males because females emphasize male status in choosing mates.
Self-protection	To protect self and alliance members against threats to survival or reproduction.	Male out-group members heuristically associated with threat; males more involved in intra- and intergroup exchanges of threats.
Mate choice	To obtain a partner or partners who will enhance own fitness.	Trade-offs for long vs. short-term relationships differ for men and women and depend on sex ratios; males and females emphasize somewhat different features in long-term mates.
Mate retention	To maintain a mating bond with a desirable partner.	Males are inclined to break a bond if a partner is sexually unfaithful or if there are physically attractive alternatives available.
		Females are inclined to break a bond if a partner compromises resources or if a high status alternative is available.
Parental care	To promote survival and reproduction of individuals carrying one's genes.	More care invested in others who share one's genes and who have relatively high reproductive value.

cooperation among group members greatly increased each person's probability of surviving, prospering, and eventually reproducing. Evolutionary psychologists and social psychologists alike have focused considerable attention on the role affiliation motives play in guiding people's behavior (e.g., Baumeister & Leary, 1995).

Social psychologists have focused primarily on proximate benefits of participating in cooperative alliances. For example, group members provide us with emotional support, which is linked to an array of positive health outcomes—people with strong support networks are more resistant to disease and stressful events and they live longer (e.g., Buunk & Verhoeven, 1991). People also use coalitions to elevate their social status (Tesser, 1988). A group's collective potential for dominance is generally greater than that of one individual. Social psychologists have linked the desire to affiliate to phenomena ranging from persuasion (Cialdini, 2001) and prosocial behavior (Maner et al., 2002) to intergroup prejudice and stereotyping (Tajfel, 1982).

Cooperative alliances have costs as well as benefits: Providing support for others requires time and resources, and there is a danger of being exploited in unequal exchanges of resources. Alliances with others also involve direct competition for food, status, mates, and other resources (Alcock, 1993; Hill & Hurtado, 1996). From an evolutionary perspective, the trade-offs are more favorable to the extent that one individual forms alliances with others who share his or her genes or who share a history of reciprocal exchanges.

Alliances with Kin   Social psychologists have frequently studied relationships between strangers but largely ignored relationships between kin (Daly et al., 1997). Yet, cooperative relationships in traditional and modern societies have most frequently consisted of individuals who were related in some way. From an inclusive fitness perspective (Hamilton, 1964), people tend to align themselves with kin because benefits shared with kin indirectly benefits their own genes, and costs exacted on the self by kin are also indirect costs to kin's genes. Indeed, research with species ranging from ground squirrels to humans suggests lower thresholds for engaging in various types of cooperative behavior among neighbors who are closely related (e.g., Burnstein et al., 1994; Essock-Vitale & McGuire, 1985; Sherman, 1977).

Alliances with Nonkin   Whereas cooperation is less contingent on history of reciprocation among close kin, sharing between less related individuals is linked to a history of reciprocal sharing (e.g., A. P. Fiske, 1992; Trivers, 1971). Like human exchange, exchange among nonrelatives in other species is also guided by reciprocity, as evidenced by food sharing among bats (Wilkinson, 1984) and social support among baboons (Packer, 1977). According to theories of reciprocal altruism, our ancestors would have benefited from cooperating with others to the extent that those others were likely to reciprocate (e.g., Axelrod & Hamilton, 1981; Trivers, 1971). Over the long haul, each member of a reciprocal exchange relationship reaps benefits, especially if resources are unpredictable and variable.

Unable to see the future, people cooperate with group members based on the *probability* of future reciprocation. Hence, people attend to signs that another may not be a good bet for future reciprocation. Evidence suggests that people are quite vigilant to possible cheating (Cosmides & Tooby, 1992). Classic social psychological research suggests that people dislike others who draw more resources from the group than they give back (e.g., Latané, Williams, & Harkins, 1979).

STATUS

Social status is a ubiquitous regulator of social interaction (Cummins, Chapter 23, this volume; Eibl-Eibesfeldt, 1989). Around the world, *dominant* versus *submissive* is one of the two primary dimensions with which people categorize others (Wiggins & Broughton, 1985). Even in face-to-face interactions between complete strangers, relative status differences emerge quickly and spontaneously (Fisek & Ofshe, 1970). High-status individuals tend to be successful at influencing others (A. G. Miller, Collins, & Brief, 1995), to be desired as friends (Nakao, 1987), and to enjoy other social benefits and material resources (Cummins, 1998). People sometimes associate with high-status others to increase their own status and generally make efforts to get superiors to like them (Greenberg & Baron, 1993). Males, in particular, may use violence as a means of increasing their status (Archer, 1994).

For both sexes, adaptive advantages of gaining and maintaining status include access to material resources and extended social alliances. These advantages, in turn, translate into increased reproductive success: Resources can be invested in offspring and allies often assist in caring for and protecting offspring. Striving for status also brings costs, including energy invested in competition, increased role expectations for high-status individuals, and resentment felt by underlings who do not enjoy the benefits of status.

Sex Differences in Fitness Payoffs for Status Striving   Comparative evidence across species (e.g., chimpanzees; de Waal, 1982) suggests that primate males gain an additional set of benefits from status striving. Females, whose high parental investment predisposes more selectivity in mate choice, are more likely to use male status as a cue for mate selection (Li et al., 2002). Dominant men can offer their mates relatively greater protection and access to resources, both useful in caring for offspring. Consequently, males are, compared with females, more motivated to seek high levels of social dominance (Hill & Hurtado, 1996) and more likely to pay attention to possible loss of status relative to neighbors (Gutierres, Kenrick, & Partch, 1999).

Eagly and Wood (1999) argued that differences in status striving may stem from the male role's emphasis on power and status versus the female role's emphasis on nurturance. These authors believe role assignments for men and women differ across societies because of a fundamental evolved difference—women carry and nurse the offspring (Wood & Eagly, 2002). To the extent that their more recent formulations posit an interaction between an evolved mechanism and the development of cultural norms, they are consistent with modern evolutionary psychological models of gender role norms (Kenrick, 1987; Kenrick & Luce, 2000; Kenrick, Trost, & Sundie, in press). However, Eagly and Wood's biosocial model is still too domain-general in positing a simple causal link between parental role assignment and various gender differences in social behavior (Kenrick & Li, 2000). It does not, for example, take into account comparative research linking testosterone to dominance and competitiveness in humans and other species (Mazur & Booth, 1998). However, Eagly and Wood's work does indicate an increasing tendency for social psychologists to consider evolved mechanisms and their coevolutionary links with the development of culture.

Self-Protection

As with other primate species (Wrangham, 1987), ancestral humans frequently confronted threats from members of other groups (Baer & McEachron, 1982). Additionally, intragroup competition over status and material resources led to recurrent threats from in-group members among humans and other primate species (Daly & Wilson, 1988).

Decades of research in social psychology demonstrate that people often behave aggressively in response to perceived threats (e.g., Berkowitz, 1993; Dodge, Price, Bachorowski, & Newman, 1990). Beside increasing aggressive behavior, threats enhance affiliative motivation (Taylor et al., 2000). Wisman and Koole (2003) found that thoughts about death led to increased affiliation and argue that affiliation under threat is based in adaptive design—people are safer in groups, and threats lead people to seek the security of a crowd. Taylor and colleagues (2000) review physiological and behavioral evidence to suggest that females' primary response to stress is "tend and befriend" rather than "fight or flight." They argue that fighting or running would have increased risks to dependent offspring. Geary and Flinn (2002) note that tendencies to tend and befriend with group members under threat would also have been adaptive for males. Because of safety in numbers, threat-induced affiliative motivation leads to the formation of larger groups than more positive affiliative goals do (Kenrick, Li, et al., 2003).

Mate Choice

Mate choice decisions can be categorized into two broad areas: relationship selection and mate selection. Relationship selection refers to an individual's choice about whether to pursue a long-term, committed relationship or a short-term, casual sexual relationship. Mate selection refers to decisions about what type of partner to accept for each relationship. In this section, we focus on relationship selection and long-term partner selection.

Relationship Selection   Some form of long-term marital bond is common to all human societies (Daly & Wilson, 1983). At the same time, people in many cultures engage in short-term sex, with little intention of remaining together (e.g., Marshall & Suggs, 1971). Decisions regarding which type of relationship to enter may depend on a person's sociosexual orientation (Simpson & Gangestad, 1991) or inclination to engage in sex without commitment. On average, men are inclined to be relatively more unrestricted, requiring less commitment, and women tend to be more restricted, requiring more signs of commitment and love. Evolutionary theorists attribute this to differences in minimum obligatory parental investment (Trivers, 1972). If offspring result from casual sex, women, like other mammalian females, must invest more time and resources than must men. Because the benefit-to-cost ratio of casual sex is relatively higher for men, men tend to be more eager for casual sex and to seek more such partners (e.g., Buss & Schmitt, 1993). It is shortsighted, however, to infer that men seek only short-term relationships and women seek only long-term relationships. A more complete account of sociosexuality must consider factors that influence decisions about which type of relationship to pursue (e.g., sex ratios; Gangestad & Simpson, 2000).

In keeping with our earlier discussion of the importance of social dynamics, we recently reframed the sociosexuality dichotomy in terms of ecologically contingent decision rules that dynamically play out in networks of individuals (Kenrick, Li, et al., 2003). Instead of simply viewing males as unrestricted and females as restricted, we considered each sex as basing its decisions about which strategy to pursue (restricted versus unrestricted) on an implicit comparison of sex ratios in the local environment. Sex ratios involve a comparison of opposite sex (i.e., available mates) to same-sex individuals (i.e., intrasexual competitors). In any local environment, a strategy becomes more desirable to the extent there are more available mates responding to that strategy and fewer intrasexual competitors using that strategy.

To get an idea of the specific ratios required to change mating strategy, we surveyed men and women about the default decision rules members of their sex might use to change sexual strategy (Kenrick, Li, et al., 2003). As expected, men reported decision rules biased slightly toward unrestricted relationships, and women reported decision criteria more strongly biased toward restricted relationships. Based on these decision rules, we performed a set of simulations that dynamically modeled the relationship selection process at the community level. A neighborhood of individuals interacted with each other over several time periods. In each period, using their respective decision rules, individuals pursued either a restricted mating strategy or an unrestricted one. Results from several hundred simulations suggested that relatively small sex differences in sociosexual orientation (i.e., decision rule criteria) were sufficient to account for observed real-world patterns of relationship selection, in which the large majority of people enter long-term relationships and smaller pockets of people engage in unrestricted relationships. Such dynamical models can help psychologists understand how diverse social norms can emerge from small variations in decision rules at the individual level (Kenrick, Li, et al., 2003).

Long-Term Partner Selection   What characteristics do people desire in long-term mates? Several surveys indicate that when considering marriage partners, women prefer status and resources more than men do, whereas men prefer physical attractiveness more than women do (e.g., Buss, 1989; Buss & Barnes, 1986; Sprecher, Sullivan, & Hatfield, 1994). To explain these preferences, social psychologists have invoked sociocultural (e.g., Eagly & Wood, 1999; Howard, Blumstein, & Schwartz, 1987) and social exchange (Cameron et al., 1977; Hatfield, Utne, & Traupmann, 1979) explanations. Looking for more ultimate explanations, evolutionary theorists have suggested the presence of evolved psychological mechanisms designed to solve different adaptive problems that men and women encountered when searching for mates (Buss, 1989; Symons, 1979, 1987). Because of constraints on female fertility, men may be especially drawn to women displaying cues of sexual maturity and youth (Symons, 1979). Male reproductive value, however, is more constrained by the ability to provide resources. Thus, women may be especially attentive to cues of a man's status and ability to provide resources (Buss, 1989; Sadalla et al., 1987).

Evolved mechanisms for mate selection, however, may be more complex than simple preferences for physical attractiveness and status. To investigate trade-offs among various mate characteristics, we borrowed a distinction used in economics for studying consumption patterns—necessities versus luxuries. Though wealthy people spend a significant portion of their income on luxuries, those with low incomes tend to purchase mostly necessities. Similarly, it makes adaptive sense to seek out outstanding, well-rounded mates when possible, but for men to prioritize fertility and for women to prioritize status in men if choices are constrained, as is often the case in real life. Results from two studies using a budget allocation paradigm and one study using a mate screening paradigm support the idea that while many characteristics are desirable, physical attractiveness for men and status for women may be viewed as necessities (Li et al., 2002).

MATE RETENTION

Because human infants are helpless and slow to develop, the continued inputs of both parents are often essential to ensure offspring survival (Geary, 1998; Hrdy, 1999). Although human mating arrangements vary across cultures, all involve long-term cooperative relationships in which both parents contribute to offspring's welfare. Hence, a key adaptive problem for both sexes, involving issues beyond mate choice, is to maintain mating bonds with desirable partners (Buss, 1988; Flinn, 1988).

Not all relationships are equally desirable, and not all partners will be equally motivated to maintain a given relationship. Decisions to maintain or end a relationship involve trade-offs, and these are intrinsically dynamic, involving inputs from partners and outside influences. Informational inputs relevant to relationship maintenance include the existence of offspring, availability of resources to each parent within and outside the relationship, presence and quality of same-sex interlopers on the social horizon, and the sex ratio in the mating pool (Guttentag & Secord, 1983; Kenrick & Trost, 1987). Psychological mechanisms may exist to process such inputs and adaptively weigh the costs and benefits of staying in a relationship. If a couple has offspring, for example, that raises the threshold for decisions to seek an alternative mate (Essock-Vitale & McGuire, 1989; Rasmussen, 1981). However, local availability of desirable alternatives lowers both sexes' thresholds for leaving relationships (Guttentag & Secord, 1983; Kenrick, Neuberg, Zierk, & Krones, 1994). A partner's breach of fidelity may also greatly reduce the benefit-to-cost ratio of staying for both sexes (Buss, Larsen, Westen, & Semelroth, 1992).

Keeping Ourselves in the Current Relationship   We may also have mechanisms to prevent ourselves from wandering. Such mechanisms include positive bias toward our partner and negative bias against potential mates. For instance, compared with people not in relationships, those currently in relationships tend to consider viable alternatives as less physically and sexually desirable (Simpson, Gangestad, & Lerma, 1990). People who are committed to their partners, as opposed to those who are not, are much less attentive to potential alternatives (R. S. Miller, 1997) and tend to underrate the desirability of alternative mates (Johnson & Rusbult, 1989).

There may be adaptive reasons why a person might have biases favoring the current partner over alternatives. Without these biases, people might be inclined to switch partners whenever a better alternative is encountered, thereby prohibiting most couples from staying together long enough to successfully raise offspring. There is also more uncertainty and relatively higher entry costs associated with forming new relationships. From an adaptationist perspective, the aforementioned biases should compensate for the differential benefits between the known quality of a current relationship and a potentially better—but much less certain—alternative relationship.

Parental Care

Although parental care is critical to the survival of human offspring, the motivation to nurture offspring is not a constant across all parents. Evolutionary theorists have hypothesized that decisions about caring for any particular offspring are contingent on various factors affecting payoffs for parental investment (Alexander, 1979; Daly & Wilson, 1980; Hrdy, 1999).

Investing Where There Are Common Genetic Interests   Mothers tend to invest more in their offspring than fathers do. Maternal grandparents tend to invest more than paternal grandparents do. Given that only women can be completely sure which offspring are theirs, it makes sense that mothers invest more than fathers and that maternal relatives invest more than paternal relatives. Because investing in other people's offspring is not genetically self-serving, we also can expect the behavior of stepparents toward stepchildren not to be on par with that of biological parents toward their own children. Indeed, compared to stepparents, biological parents invest more in their children, are 40 times less likely to abuse them, and are up to several hundred times less likely to kill them (Daly & Wilson, 1988).

Looking for the Highest Rate of Return   Apart from genetic overlap, parents may also invest in those offspring most likely to produce a profitable rate of reproductive return (Alexander, 1979; Fairbanks, 1993). Parental investment in male offspring may have higher rates of return and risk than investment in female offspring (Daly & Wilson, 1988; Trivers & Willard, 1973). While most females have easy access to mates, a male typically needs to compete against other males to get mates. Females are also physically limited to having children at a relatively slow rate across a shorter reproductive life span. In contrast, male reproductive success differs greatly, ranging from those at the bottom of a status hierarchy with no mates to those at the top, who may sire hundreds of children (Betzig, 1992; Daly & Wilson, 1988).

Due to this difference in risk and return, it may pay off for a family with abundant resources to invest in sons, but for resource-poor families to allocate more to daughters (Trivers & Willard, 1973). Supporting this reasoning, a study of families in North America found low-income mothers significantly more likely to breast-feed daughters than sons, but the opposite pattern for affluent mothers (Gaulin & Robbins, 1991). Poorer mothers also had another child sooner if the first was a son, whereas wealthy mothers had another child sooner if the first was a daughter.

Finally, parental investment makes sense to the extent that there are not more lucrative uses of the invested time and resources. For example, because men are not physiologically constrained to childbearing and nursing, the pursuit of other matings is a more viable option to them than it is for women. Tribal evidence from Africa shows that among the Aka pygmies, men of high status have more wives and spend less time on parenting than men of low status do (Hewlett, 1991). People may also be more willing to withdraw resources when the time horizon for making other investments is relatively long. Evidence from infanticide records show that women are more likely to kill their infants when the women are younger and when they are unwed with no men acknowledging fatherhood (Daly & Wilson, 1988).

DYNAMIC EMERGENCE: FROM DECISION RULES TO CULTURAL NORMS

McDougall's (1908) evolution-based book was not quite the first text titled *Social Psychology.* In the same year, E. A. Ross (1908) published a text with the same name but a very different theoretical approach. Ross was a sociologist who saw the wellsprings of social behavior residing not in the individual but in the social group. He argued that people were carried along on "social currents," such as "the spread of a lynching spirit through a crowd . . . [or] an epidemic of religious emotion" (Ross, 1908, pp. 1–2). Ross looked at the group as a whole rather than at the psyche of the individual group member. He viewed crazes and fads as products of "mob mind . . . that irrational unanimity of interest, feeling, opinion, or deed in a body of communicating individuals, which results from suggestion and imitation" (Ross, 1908, p. 65).

Since 1908, there has been a basic disagreement between sociologically oriented social psychologists who focus on groups as determinants of social behavior and psychologically oriented social psychologists who focus on determinants within the individual. In recent years, advances in theory and research on complex dynamical systems have offered the promise of bridging these formerly discrepant views of the social world (Latané, 1996; Vallacher, Read, & Nowak, 2002). Dynamic models have begun to unravel the formerly mysterious processes by which patterned societal norms emerge from seemingly random interactions between individuals, each acting on the basis of simple and proximately focused decision rules.

A truly comprehensive model of behavior must include insights from evolutionary psychology along with the insights of dynamical systems theory (Kenrick, Becker, et al., 2003; Kenrick et al., 2002). Evolutionary theorists have focused on individuals acting according to decision rules designed to serve the selfish interests of the genes contained within them. However, decision rules within any one individual always play out in the context of other people acting on their own decision rules. A man seeking a wife cannot act only on his own preferences but must deal with those of the locally available females. A woman seeking to gain status must negotiate with others seeking to rise in the hierarchy, and a boy seeking to maximize his parents' investment in him must deal with similarly motivated sisters and brothers. Hence, intriguing social dynamics are likely to emerge from interactions between decision rules in the minds of separate individuals (Kenrick, Li, et al., 2003). Considering how decision mechanisms in different domains have different dynamic outcomes, for example, implies very different sociospatial geometries associated with each of the domains (as depicted in Figure 28.1 on p. 820). Status-seeking goals favor the emergence of hierarchies. Cooperation goals lead to the emergence of overlapping circles of friends and relatives. Self-protective goals predispose the emergence of larger social categories cleaving the world into mutually exclusive in-groups and out-groups. Mating relationship goals favor interactions at the dyadic level and so on. At a broader level, an integration of evolutionary and dynamic models may be key to understanding the emergence of cultural norms (Kameda, Takezawa, & Hastie, 2003; Kenrick, Li, et al., 2003; Kenrick et al., 2002).

CONCLUSION: OUT OF THE PAST AND INTO THE FUTURE

Fearing for his life, Japanese soldier Shoichi Yokoi hid in a cave in the jungles of Guam for 28 years after World War II ended. Some social psychologists seem similarly unaware that the nature-nurture war ended some time ago. Happily, we all won. Consorting with evolutionary biologists does not mean betraying experimental social psychology, denying culture, or marching off to hunt for isolated genes that single-handedly cause rape, murder, and racism. The appropriate level of analysis for an evolutionary social psychology is not more reductionistic, but more contextual and interactionist. To explore the implications of an evolutionary perspective for human social behavior, we'll need not microscopes and centrifuges,

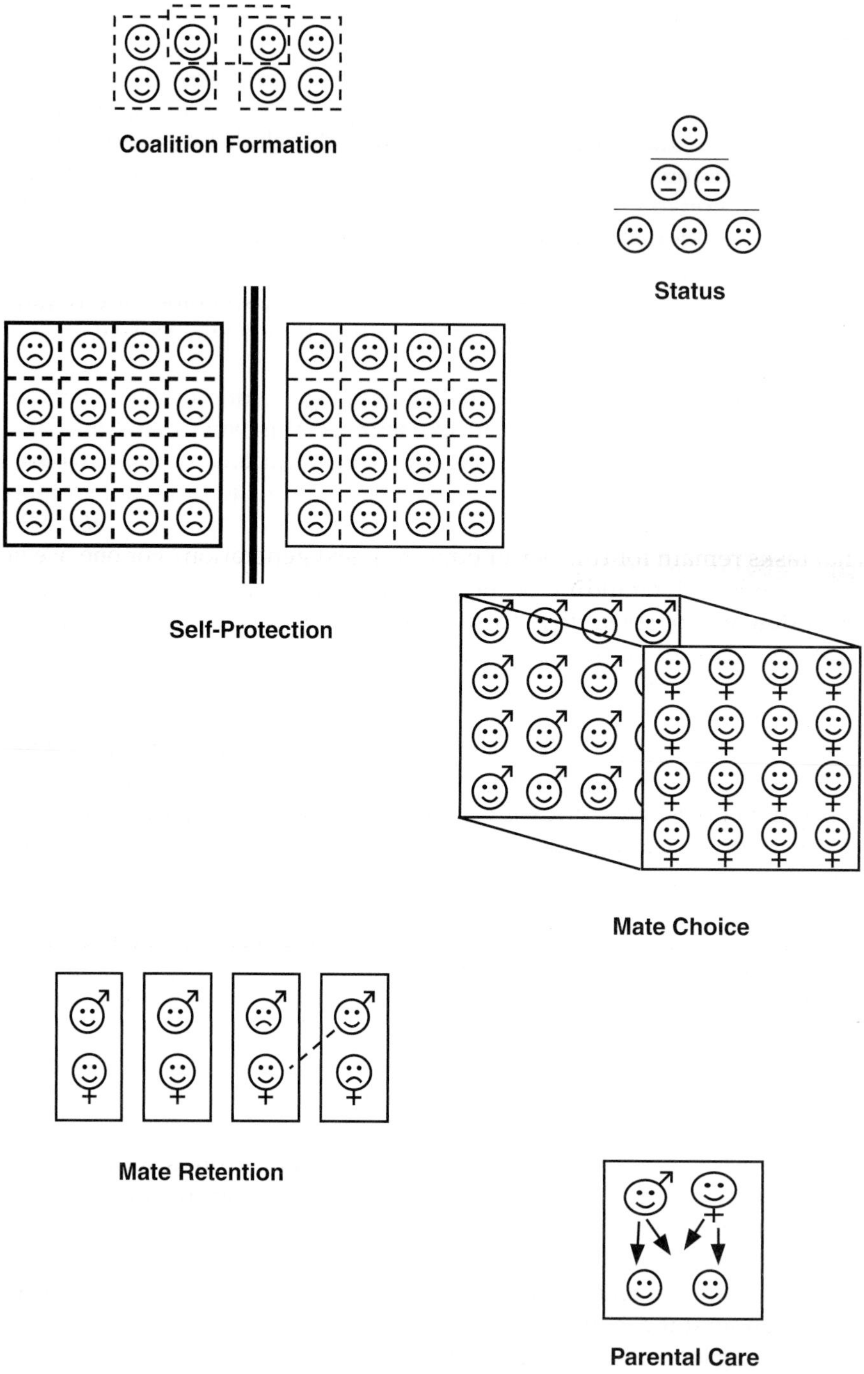

Figure 28.1 Different Social Geometries Emerging from Decision-Rules and Ecological Constraints across Domains. *Source:* From "Dynamical Evolutionary Psychology: Individual Decision Rules and Emergent Social Norms," by D. T. Kenrick, N. P. Li, and J. Butner, 2003, *Psychological Review, 110,* pp. 3–28.

but the methods of the modern cognitive laboratory in combination with new approaches to cross-cultural psychology.

The first step may be a bit of educational reform. If a student planned to study the social behaviors of almost any living organism—flatworm, flycatcher, or orangutan—that student's course of study would include broad exposure to the animal kingdom and extensive training in evolutionary theory to help that student better understand how unique features of that species fit together. There is one exception—a student could advance through 8 to 10 years of undergraduate and graduate study of *Homo sapiens'* behavior without a single course in zoology or evolutionary biology. Just as students of scientific psychology are required to have statistics courses in their inferential toolbox, they ought to have coursework in comparative animal behavior. Research with other animal species has revealed a number of general principles essential for placing human behavior in context (Alcock, 1993; Daly & Wilson, 1983). Exposure to this work could free the next generation of social psychologists from misconceptions ranging from unrestrained cultural relativity through genetic determinism and the moralistic "is equals ought" fallacy (Alcock, 2001; Kenrick, 1995; Kenrick, Becker, et al., 2003).

What tasks remain for this better educated next generation? For one, we need a more thorough understanding of the particular decision rules people use within different domains of social life. To say, "It's all reproduction" is no more useful than saying, "It's all self-interest." Rather than randomly listing exceptions to apparent rationality, though, we must make sense of the underlying, and likely domain-specific, motivations underlying the vagaries of social decision making (Kenrick & Maner, 2004). We have made some preliminary suggestions, but most of the hard empirical work remains to be done. As decades of social psychology have taught, people's true motives are difficult to assess, often disguised by self-presentation or operating outside conscious awareness. Methods designed to measure implicit associations provide one useful tool for circumventing these problems (Greenwald et al., 2002). Other experimental tools developed for rigorous study of nonsocial stimuli, such as eye-tracking, can also be useful (Maner et al., 2003). As discussed earlier, we were able to make good use of the economic distinction between luxuries and necessities to design several simple methods that can help assess how people prioritize their desires in social interactions (Li et al., 2002).

An evolutionary approach counsels a more truly cross-cultural social psychology. In searching across cultures, we must avoid one problem of twentieth century anthropology—which focused on how other groups were strange and different. Underneath the fascinating differences are often important and informative regularities in social behavior (Buss, 1989; Daly & Wilson, 1988; Ekman & Friesen, 1971; Kenrick & Keefe, 1992). Establishing such regularities was important to establish that humans are not "blank slates." However, we must now understand how the exceptions and the regularities mesh with one another. Universal underlying decision biases often combine in different ways depending on local social and physical ecology. For example, polygyny and polyandry in humans reflect local social and physical ecology, sometimes following broad rules that apply to other animal species (e.g., Crook & Crook, 1988). Dynamical systems researchers have found that apparent complexity can emerge from the interaction of a few simple underlying variables. To better explain the simple principles underlying cross-cultural complexities, research on social dynamics must take content seriously—we must understand the particular decision biases driving different dynamics in different domains of social life. To uncover these biases, we will need experimental and survey research elucidated by a content-schematic evolutionary psychology.

REFERENCES

Abbey, A. (1982). Sex differences in attributions for friendly behavior: Do males misperceive females' friendliness? *Journal of Personality and Social Psychology, 42,* 830–838.

Alcock, J. (1993). *Animal behavior: An evolutionary approach* (5th ed.). Sunderland, MA: Sinauer.

Alcock, J. (2001). *The triumph of sociobiology.* New York: Oxford University Press.

Alexander, R. D. (1979). *Darwinism and human affairs.* Seattle: University of Washington Press.

Archer, J. (1994). Introduction: Male violence in perspective. In J. Archer (Ed.), *Male violence* (pp. 1–22). New York: Routledge.

Aronson, E., Wilson, T. D., & Akert, R. M. (1999). *Social psychology* (3rd ed.). New York: Longman.

Axelrod, R., & Hamilton, W. D. (1981). The evolution of cooperation. *Science, 211,* 1390–1396.

Baer, D., & McEachron, D. L. (1982). A review of selected sociobiological principles: Application to hominid evolution I. The development of group social structures. *Journal of Social and Biological Structures, 5,* 69–90.

Baron, R. A., & Byrne, D. (2000). *Social psychology* (9th ed.). Boston: Allyn & Bacon.

Baumeister, R. F., & Leary, M. R. (1995). The need to belong: Desire for interpersonal attachments as a fundamental human motivation. *Psychological Bulletin, 117,* 429–497.

Berkowitz, L. (1993). *Aggression.* New York: McGraw-Hill.

Betzig, L. (1992). Roman polygyny. *Ethology and Sociobiology, 13,* 309–349.

Brehm, S. S., Kassin, S. M., & Fein, S. (2002). *Social psychology* (5th ed.). Boston: Houghton Mifflin.

Bugental, D. B. (2000). Acquisition of the algorithms of social life: A domain-based approach. *Psychological Bulletin, 126,* 187–219.

Burnstein, E., Crandall, C., & Kitayama, S. (1994). Some neo-Darwinian decision rules for altruism: Weighing cues for inclusive fitness as a function of the biological importance of the decision. *Journal of Personality and Social Psychology, 67,* 773–789.

Buss, D. M. (1988). From vigilance to violence: Tactics of mate retention in American undergraduates. *Ethology and Sociobiology, 9,* 291–317.

Buss, D. M. (1989). Sex differences in human mate preferences: Evolutionary hypothesis tested in 37 cultures. *Behavioral and Brain Sciences, 12,* 1–49.

Buss, D. M. (1999). Evolutionary psychology: A new paradigm for psychological science. In D. H. Rosen & M. C. Luebbert (Eds.), *Evolution of the psyche: Human evolution, behavior and intelligence* (pp. 1–33). Westport, CT: Praeger Publisher/Greenwood Publishing.

Buss, D. M., & Barnes, M. (1986). Preferences in human mate selection. *Journal of Personality and Social Psychology, 50,* 559–570.

Buss, D. M., & Kenrick, D. T. (1998). Evolutionary social psychology. In D. T. Gilbert, S. T. Fiske, & G. Lindzey (Eds.), *Handbook of social psychology* (Vol. 2, 4th ed., pp. 982–1026). New York: McGraw-Hill.

Buss, D. M., Larsen, R. J., Westen, D., & Semmelroth, J. (1992). Sex differences in jealousy: Evolution, physiology, and psychology. *Psychological Science, 2,* 204–232.

Buss, D. M., & Schmitt, D. P. (1993). Sexual strategies theory: An evolutionary perspective on human mating. *Psychological Review, 100,* 204–232.

Buunk, B. P., & Verhoeven, K. (1991). Companionship and support at work: A microanalysis of the stress-reducing features of social interaction. *Basic-and-Applied-Social-Psychology, 12,* 243–258.

Byrne, D. (1971). *The attraction paradigm.* New York: Academic Press.

Byrne, D., London, O., & Reeves, K. (1968). The effects of physical attractiveness, sex, and attitude similarity on interpersonal attraction. *Journal of Personality and Social Psychology, 36,* 259–271.

Cameron, C., Oskamp, S., & Sparks, W. (1977). Courtship American style: Newspaper ads. *Family Coordinator, 16,* 27–30.

Caporael, L. R. (1997). The evolution of truly social cognition: The core configurations model. *Personality and Social Psychology Review, 1,* 276–298.

Caporael, L. R., Dawes, R. M., Orbell, J. M., & van de Kragt, A. J. (1989). Selfishness examined: Cooperation in the absence of egoistic incentives. *Behavioral and Brain Sciences, 12,* 683–739.

Cialdini, R. B. (2001). *Influence: Science and practice* (4th ed.). Boston: Allyn & Bacon.

Clark, R. D., & Hatfield, E. (1989). Gender differences in receptivity to sexual offers. *Journal of Psychology and Human Sexuality, 2,* 39–55.

Conway, L. G., & Schaller, M. (2002). On the verifiability of evolutionary psychological theories: An analysis of the psychology of scientific persuasion. *Personality and Social Psychology Review, 6,* 152–166.

Cosmides, L., & Tooby, J. (1992). Cognitive adaptations for social exchange. In J. Barkow, L. Cosmides, & J. Tooby (Eds.), *The adapted mind* (pp. 163–228). New York: Oxford University Press.

Crook, J. H., & Crook, S. J. (1988). Tibetan polyandry: Problems of adaptation and fitness. In L. Betzig, M. Borgerhoff Mulder, & P. Turke (Eds.), *Human reproductive behavior: A Darwinian perspective* (pp. 97–114). Cambridge, UK: Cambridge University Press.

Cummins, D. D. (1998). Social norms and other minds: The evolutionary roots of higher cognition. In D. D. Cummins & C. Allen (Eds.), *The evolution of mind* (pp. 30–50). New York: Oxford University Press.

Dabbs, J. M., Jr., & Morris, R. (1990). Testosterone, social class, and antisocial behavior in a sample of 4462 men. *Psychological Science, 1,* 209–211.

Daly, M., Salmon, C., & Wilson, M. (1997). Kinship: The conceptual hole in psychological studies of social cognition and close relationships. In J. A. Simpson & D. T. Kenrick (Eds.), *Evolutionary social psychology* (pp. 265–296). Mahwah, NJ: Erlbaum.

Daly, M., & Wilson, M. (1980). Discriminative parental solicitude: A biological perspective. *Journal of Marriage and Family, 42,* 277–288.

Daly, M., & Wilson, M. (1983). *Sex, evolution, and behavior* (2nd ed.). Belmont, CA: Wadsworth.

Daly, M., & Wilson, M. (1988). *Homicide.* New York: Aldine deGruyter.

Dawkins, R. (1976). *The selfish gene.* Oxford, England: Oxford University Press.

Deutsch, F. M., Zalenski, C. M., & Clark, M. E. (1986). Is there a double standard of aging? *Journal of Applied Social Psychology, 16,* 771–775.

Devine, P. G. (1989). Stereotypes and prejudice: Their automatic and controlled components. *Journal of Personality and Social Psychology, 60,* 5–18.

de Waal, F. (1982). *Chimpanzee politics: Sex and power among apes.* Baltimore: Johns Hopkins University Press.

Dodge, K. A., Price, J. M., Bachorowski, J. A., & Newman, J. P. (1990). Hostile attributional biases in severely aggressive adolescents. *Journal of Abnormal Psychology, 99,* 385–392.

Duck, S. (1978). *The study of acquaintance.* Westmead, England: Saxon House.

Eagly, A. H., & Wood, W. (1999). The origins of sex differences in human behavior: Evolved dispositions versus social roles. *American Psychologist, 54,* 408–423.

Ekman, P., & Friesen, W. V. (1971). Constants across cultures in the face and emotion. *Journal of Personality and Social Psychology, 17,* 124–129.

Eibl-Eibesfeldt, I. (1989). *Human ethology.* New York: Aldine deGruyter.

Essock-Vitale, S. M., & McGuire, M. T. (1985). Women's lives viewed from an evolutionary perspective. II. Patterns of helping. *Ethology and Sociobiology, 6,* 155–173.

Fairbanks, L. A. (1993). What is a good mother? Adaptive variation in maternal behavior of primates. *Current Directions in Psychological Science, 2,* 179–183.

Fisek, M. H., & Ofshe, R. (1970). The process of status evolution. *Sociometry, 33,* 327–346.

Fiske, A. P. (1992). The four elementary forms of sociality: Framework for a unified theory of social relations. *Psychological Review, 99,* 689–723.

Flinn, M. (1988). Mate guarding in a Caribbean village. *Ethology and Sociobiology, 9,* 1–28.

Funder, D. C. (1987). Errors and mistakes: Evaluating the accuracy of social judgment. *Psychological Bulletin, 101,* 75–90.

Gangestad, S. W., & Simpson, J. A. (2000). The evolution of human mating: Trade-offs and strategic pluralism. *Behavioral and Brain Sciences, 23,* 573–644.

Gaulin, S., & Robbins, C. (1991). Trivers-Willard effect in contemporary North American society. *American Journal of Physical Anthropology, 85,* 61–69.

Geary, D. C. (1998). *Male, female: The evolution of human sex differences.* Washington, DC: American Psychological Association.

Geary, D. C., & Flinn, M. V. (2002). Sex differences in behavioral and hormonal response to social threat: Commentary on Taylor et al. (2000). *Psychological Review, 109,* 745–750.

Greenberg, J., & Baron, R. A. (1993). *Behavior in organizations* (4th ed.). Boston: Allyn & Bacon.

Greenwald, A. G., Banaji, M. R., Rudman, L. A., Farnham, S. D., Nosek, B. A., & Mellott, D. S. (2002). A unified theory of implicit attitudes, stereotypes, self-esteem, and self-concept. *Psychological Review, 109,* 3–25.

Greenwald, A. G., McGhee, D. E., & Schwartz, J. L. K. (1998). Measuring individual differences in implicit cognition: The implicit associations test. *Journal of Personality and Social Psychology, 74,* 1464–1480.

Gutierres, S. E., Kenrick, D. T., & Partch, J. J. (1999). Beauty, dominance, and the mating game: Contrast effects in self-assessment reflect gender differences in mate selection. *Personality and Social Psychology Bulletin, 25,* 1126–1134.

Guttentag, M., & Secord, P. F. (1983). *Too many women? The sex ratio question.* Beverly Hills, CA: Sage.

Hamilton, W. D. (1964). The genetical evolution of social behavior. *Journal of Theoretical Biology, 7,* 1–52.

Haselton, M., & Buss, D. (2000). Error management theory: A new perspective on biases in cross-sex mind reading. *Journal of Personality and Social Psychology, 78,* 81–91.

Hatfield, E., Utne, M. K., & Traupmann, J. (1979). Equity theory and intimate relationships. In R. L. Burgess & T. L. Huston (Eds.), *Social exchange in developing relationships* (pp. 93–133). New York: Academic Press.

Hazan, C., & Shaver, P. R. (1994). Attachment as an organizational framework for research on close relationships. *Psychological Inquiry, 5,* 1–22.

Hewlett, B. S. (1991). *Intimate fathers: The nature and context of Aka Pygmy paternal infant care.* Ann Arbor: University of Michigan Press.

Hill, K., & Hurtado, A. M. (1996). *Ache life history.* Hawthorne, NY: Aldine deGruyter.

Howard, J. A., Blumstein, P., & Schwartz, P. (1987). Social or evolutionary theories? Some observations on preferences in human mate selection. *Journal of Personality and Social Psychology, 53,* 194–200.

Hrdy, S. H. (1999). *Mother nature: A history of mothers, infants, and natural selection.* New York: Pantheon.

Johnson, D. J., & Rusbult, C. E. (1989). Resisting temptation: Devaluation of alternative partners as a means of maintaining commitment in close relationships. *Journal of Personality and Social Psychology, 57,* 967–980.

Kameda, T., Takezawa, M., & Hastie, R. (2003). The logic of social sharing: An evolutionary game analysis of adaptive norm development. *Personality and Social Psychology Review, 7,* 2–19.

Kenrick, D. T. (1987). Gender, genes, and the social environment: A biosocial interactionist perspective. In P. Shaver & C. Hendrick (Eds.), *Review of personality and social psychology* (Vol. 7, pp. 14–43). Newbury Park, CA: Sage.

Kenrick, D. T. (1991). Proximate altruism and ultimate selfishness. *Psychological Inquiry, 2,* 135–137.

Kenrick, D. T. (1994). Evolutionary social psychology: From sexual selection to social cognition. In M. P. Zanna (Ed.), *Advances in experimental social psychology* (Vol. 26, pp. 75–121). San Diego, CA: Academic Press.

Kenrick, D. T. (1995). Evolutionary theory versus the confederacy of dunces. *Psychological Inquiry, 6,* 56–61.

Kenrick, D. T., Becker, D. V., Butner, J., Li, N. P., & Maner, J. K. (2003). Evolutionary cognitive science: Adding what and why to how the mind works. In K. Sterelney & J. Fitness (Eds.), *From mating to mentality: Evaluating evolutionary psychology* (pp. 13–38). New York: Psychology Press.

Kenrick, D. T., & Dantchik, A. (1983). Interactionism, idiographics, and the social psychological invasion of personality. *Journal of Personality, 51,* 275–285.

Kenrick, D. T., & Funder, D. C. (1988). Profiting from controversy: Lessons from the person-situation debate. *American Psychologist, 43,* 23–34.

Kenrick, D. T., Gabrielidis, C., Keefe, R. C., & Cornelius, J. (1996). Adolescent's age preferences for dating partners: Support for an evolutionary model of life-history strategies. *Child Development, 67,* 1499–1511.

Kenrick, D. T., Groth, G. R., Trost, M. R., & Sadalla, E. K. (1993). Integrating evolutionary and social exchange perspectives on relationships: Effects of gender, self-appraisal, and involvement level on mate selection criteria. *Journal of Personality and Social Psychology, 64,* 951–969.

Kenrick, D. T., & Keefe, R. C. (1992). Age preferences in mates reflect sex differences in reproductive strategies. *Behavioral and Brain Sciences, 15,* 75–133.

Kenrick, D. T., & Li, N. (2000). The Darwin is in the details. *American Psychologist, 55,* 1060–1061.

Kenrick, D. T., Li, N. P., & Butner, J. (2003). Dynamical evolutionary psychology: Individual decision rules and emergent social norms. *Psychological Review, 110,* 3–28.

Kenrick, D. T., & Luce, C. L. (2000). An evolutionary life-history model of gender differences and similarities. In T. Eckes & H. M. Trautner (Eds.), *The developmental social psychology of gender* (pp. 35–64). Hillsdale, NJ: Erlbaum.

Kenrick, D. T., & Maner, J. K. (2004). One path to balance and order in social psychology: An evolutionary perspective. *Behavioral and Brain Sciences, 27*, 346–347.

Kenrick, D. T., Maner, J. K., Butner, J., Li, N. P., Becker, D. V., & Schaller, M. (2002). Dynamical evolutionary psychology: Mapping the domains of the new interactionist paradigm. *Personality and Social Psychology Review, 6*, 347–356.

Kenrick, D. T., Neuberg, S. L., & Cialdini, R. B. (2005). *Social psychology: Unraveling the mystery* (3rd ed.). Boston: Allyn & Bacon.

Kenrick, D. T., Neuberg, S. L., Zierk, K., & Krones, J. (1994). Evolution and social cognition: Contrast effects as a function of sex, dominance, and physical attractiveness. *Personality and Social Psychology Bulletin, 20*, 210–217.

Kenrick, D. T., Sadalla, E. K., Groth, G., & Trost, M. R. (1990). Evolution, traits, and the stages of human courtship: Qualifying the parental investment model. *Journal of Personality, 53*, 97–116.

Kenrick, D. T., Sadalla, E. K., & Keefe, R. C. (1998). Evolutionary cognitive psychology: The missing heart of modern cognitive science. In C. Crawford & D. L. Krebs (Eds.), *Handbook of evolutionary psychology* (pp. 485–514). Hillsdale, NJ: Erlbaum.

Kenrick, D. T., Sundie, J. M., Nicastle, L. D., & Stone, G. O. (2001). Can one ever be too wealthy or too chaste? Searching for nonlinearities in mate judgment. *Journal of Personality and Social Psychology, 80*, 462–471.

Kenrick, D. T., & Trost, M. R. (1987). A biosocial model of relationship formation. In K. Kelley (Ed.), *Females, males and sexuality: Theories and research* (pp. 59–100). Albany, NY: SUNY Press.

Kenrick, D. T., Trost, M. R., & Sundie, J. M. (in press). Sex-roles as adaptations: An evolutionary perspective on gender differences and similarities. In A. H. Eagly, A. Beall, & R. Sternberg (Eds.), *Psychology of gender* (pp. 69–91). New York: Guilford Press.

Krebs, D. L. (1991). Altruism and egoism: A false dichotomy? *Psychological Inquiry, 2*, 137–139.

Krebs, D. L., & Denton, K. (1997). Social illusions and self-deception: The evolution of biases in social perception. In J. A. Simpson & D. T. Kenrick (Eds.), *Evolutionary social psychology* (pp. 21–48). Mahwah, NJ: Erlbaum.

Krueger, J. I., & Funder, D. C. (2004). Towards a balanced social psychology: Causes, consequences and cures for the problem-seeking approach to social behavior and cognition. *Behavioral and Brain Sciences, 27*, 313–327.

Kurzban, R., & Haselton, M. (in press). Making hay out of straw: Real and imagined controversies in evolutionary psychology. In R. Boyd & J. Barkow (Eds.), *Missing the revolution: Evolutionary perspectives on culture and society.* New York: Oxford University Press.

Kurzban, R., Tooby, J., & Cosmides, L. (2001). Can race be erased? Coalitional computation and social categorization. *Proceedings of the National Academy of Sciences, 98*, 15387–15392.

Latané, B. (1996). Dynamic social impact: The creation of culture by communication. *Journal of Communication, 46*, 13–25.

Latané, B., Williams, K., & Harkins, S. (1979). Many hands make light this work: The causes and consequences of social loafing. *Journal of Personality and Social Psychology, 37*, 822–832.

Lewin, K. (1951). *Field theory in social science.* New York: Harper & Row.

Li, N. P., & Bailey, J. M. (2000). *Trade-offs and psychological mechanisms: Experimental methods and mate preferences.* Paper presented at the Human Behavior and Evolution Society conference, Amherst, MA.

Li, N. P., Bailey, J. M., Kenrick, D. T., & Linsenmeier, J. A. (2002). The necessities and luxuries of mate preferences: Testing the trade-offs. *Journal of Personality and Social Psychology, 82*, 947–955.

Maner, J. K., Kenrick, D. T., Becker, D. V., Delton, A. W., Hofer, B., Wilbur, C. J., et al. (2003). Sexually selective cognition: Beauty captures the mind of the beholder. *Journal of Personality and Social Psychology, 85*, 1107–1120.

Maner, J. K., Kenrick, D. T., Becker, D. V., Robertson, T., Hofer, B., Neuberg, S. L., et al. (2005). Functional projection: How fundamental social motives can bias interpersonal perception. *Journal of Personality and Social Psychology, 88*, 63–78.

Maner, J. K., Luce, C. L., Neuberg, S. L., Cialdini, R. B., Brown, S., & Sagarin, B. J. (2002). The effects of perspective taking on helping: Still no evidence for altruism. *Personality and Social Psychology Bulletin, 28*, 1601–1610.

Markus, H., & Zajonc, R. B. (1985). The cognitive perspective in social psychology. In G. Lindzey & E. Aronson (Eds.), *Handbook of social psychology* (Vol. 1, pp. 137–230). New York: Random House.

Marshall, D. S., & Suggs, R. G. (1971). *Human sexual behavior: Variations in the ethnographic spectrum.* New York: Basic Books.

Mazur, A., & Booth, A. (1998). Testosterone and dominance in men. *Behavioral and Brain Sciences, 21,* 353–397.

McDougall, W. (1908). *Social psychology: An introduction.* London: Methuen.

McGuire, W. J. (1997). Creative hypothesis generating in psychology: Some useful heuristics. *Annual Review of Psychology, 48,* 1–30.

Miller, A. G., Collins, B. E., & Brief, D. E. (1995). Perspectives on obedience to authority: The legacy of the Milgram experiments. *Journal of Social Issues, 51,* 1–19.

Miller, L. C., & Fishkin, S. A. (1997). On the dynamics of human bonding and reproductive success: Seeking windows on the adapted-for human-environmental interface. In J. A. Simpson & D. T. Kenrick (Eds.), *Evolutionary social psychology* (pp. 197–237). Mahwah, NJ: Erlbaum.

Miller, R. S. (1997). Inattentive and contented: Relationship commitment and attention to alternatives. *Journal of Personality and Social Psychology, 73,* 758–766.

Nakao, K. (1987). Analyzing sociometric preferences: An example of Japanese and U.S. business groups. *Journal of Social Behavior and Personality, 2,* 523–534.

Neuberg, S. L., & Cottrell, C. A. (2002). Intergroup emotions: A biocultural approach. In D. M. Mackie & E. R. Smith (Eds.), *From prejudice to intergroup emotions: Differentiated reactions to social groups* (pp. 265–283). New York: Psychology Press.

Öhman, A., & Mineka, S. (2001). Fears, phobias, and preparedness: Toward an evolved module of fear and fear learning. *Psychological Review, 108,* 483–522.

Packer, C. (1977). Reciprocal altruism in *Papio anubis. Nature, 265,* 441–443.

Panksepp, J. (1982). Toward a general psychobiological theory of emotions. *Behavioral and Brain Sciences, 5,* 407–467.

Pinker, S. (1997). *How the mind works.* New York: Norton.

Plutchik, R. (1980). A general psychoevolutionary theory of emotion. In R. Plutchik & H. Kellerman (Eds.), *Emotions: Theory, research, and experience* (Vol. 1, pp. 3–33). New York: Academic Press.

Rasmussen, D. R. (1981). Pair bond strength and stability and reproductive success. *Psychological Review, 88,* 274–290.

Rose, R. M., Bernstein, I. S., & Holaday, J. W. (1971). Plasma testosterone, dominance rank, and aggressive behavior in a group of male rhesus monkeys. *Nature, 231,* 366.

Ross, E. A. (1908). *Social psychology.* New York: Macmillan.

Sadalla, E. K., Kenrick, D. T., & Venshure, B. (1987). Dominance and heterosexual attraction. *Journal of Personality and Social Psychology, 52,* 730–738.

Schaller, M., Park, J. H., & Mueller, A. (2003). Fear of the dark: Interactive effects of beliefs about danger and ambient darkness on ethnic stereotypes. *Personality and Social Psychology Bulletin, 29,* 637–649.

Sedikides, C., & Skowronski, J. J. (1997). The symbolic self in evolutionary context. *Personality and Social Psychology Review, 1,* 80–102.

Sherman, P. W. (1977). Nepotism and the evolution of alarm calls. *Science, 197,* 1246–1253.

Simpson, J. A., & Gangestad, S. W. (1991). Individual differences in sociosexuality: Evidence for convergent and discriminant validity. *Journal of Personality and Social Psychology, 67,* 870–883.

Simpson, J. A., Gangestad, S. W., & Lerma, M. (1990). Perception of physical attractiveness: Mechanisms involved in the maintenance of romantic relationships. *Journal of Personality and Social Psychology, 59,* 1192–1201.

Snyder, M., & Ickes, W. (1985). Personality and social behavior. In G. Lindzey & E. Aronson (Eds.), *Handbook of social psychology* (Vol. 2, 3rd ed., pp. 883–848). New York: Random House.

Sprecher, S., Sullivan, Q., & Hatfield, E. (1994). Mate selection preferences: Gender differences examined in a national sample. *Journal of Personality and Social Psychology, 66,* 1074–1080.

Symons, D. (1979). *The evolution of human sexuality.* New York: Oxford University Press.

Symons, D. (1987). The evolutionary approach: Can Darwin's view of life shed light on human sexuality. In J. Geer & W. O'Donohue (Eds.), *Theories of human sexuality* (pp. 91–125). New York: Plenum Press.

Tajfel, H. (1982). Social psychology of intergroup relations. *Annual Review of Psychology, 33,* 1–39.

Taylor, S. E., Klein, L. C., Lewis, B. P., Gruenwald, T. L., Gurung, R. A. R., & Updegraff, J. A. (2000). Biobehavioral responses to stress in females: Tend-and-befriend, not fight-or-flight. *Psychological Review, 107,* 411–429.

Tesser, A. (1988). Toward a self-evaluation maintenance model of social behavior. In L. Berkowitz (Ed.), *Advances in experimental social psychology* (Vol. 21, pp. 181–227). New York: Academic Press.

Tooby, J., & Cosmides, L. (1992). The psychological foundations of culture. In J. H. Barkow, L. Cosmides, & J. Tooby (Eds.), *The adapted mind: Evolutionary psychology and the generation of culture* (pp. 19–136). New York: Oxford University Press.

Trivers, R. L. (1971). The evolution of reciprocal altruism. *Quarterly Review of Biology, 46*, 35–37.

Trivers, R. L. (1972). Parental investment and sexual selection. In B. Campbell (Ed.), *Sexual selection and the descent of man: 1871–1971* (pp. 136–179). Chicago: Aldine.

Trivers, R. L., & Willard, D. E. (1973). Natural selection of parental ability to vary the sex ratio of offspring. *Science, 197*, 90–92.

Vallacher, R. R., Read, S. J., & Nowak, A. (2002). The dynamic perspective in personality and social psychology. *Personality and Social Psychology Review, 6*, 264–273.

Wiggins, J. S., & Broughton, R. (1985). The interpersonal circle: A structural model for the integration of personality research. In R. Hogan & W. H. Jones (Eds.), *Perspectives in personality* (Vol. 1, pp. 1–48). Greenwich: JAI Press.

Wilkinson, G. C. (1984). Reciprocal food sharing in the vampire bat. *Nature, 308*, 181–184.

Wisman, A., & Koole, S. L. (2003). Hiding in the crowd: Can mortality salience promote affiliation with others who oppose one's worldviews? *Journal of Personality and Social Psychology, 84*, 511–526.

Wood, W., & Eagly, A. H. (2002). A cross-cultural analysis of the behavior of women and men: Implications for the origins of sex differences. *Psychological Bulletin, 128*, 699–727.

Wrangham, R. (1987). The significance of African apes for reconstructing human social evolution. In W. G. Kinzey (Ed.), *The evolution of human behavior: Primate models* (pp. 51–71). Albany, NY: SUNY Press.

CHAPTER 29

Evolutionary
Developmental Psychology

DAVID F. BJORKLUND and CARLOS HERNÁNDEZ BLASI

EVOLUTIONARY THINKING HAS MADE headway into all areas of psychology, but, somewhat surprisingly, developmentalists have been slow to adopt the viewpoint of evolutionary psychology. We say surprisingly because developmental psychology can trace its origins to the evolutionary thinking at the turn of the twentieth century (see Cairns, 1998; Charlesworth, 1992), and many prominent developmentalists explicitly or implicitly incorporated aspects of evolutionary thinking into their theories (e.g., Bowlby, 1969; Hinde, 1980).

There are two main reasons for the reluctance of developmental psychologists to jump onto the bandwagon of evolutionary psychology (EP), one ideological and one scientific. The ideological reason has to do with *meliorism* (Charlesworth, 1992), the long, historical commitment of developmental psychologists with health, education, and welfare of children, and hence the conviction that research efforts should lead to benefits for children. Many of our developmental colleagues see some core assumptions of evolutionary thinking as not fitting into a just and egalitarian world scheme (i.e., limited resources, unequal competitive abilities, and natural selection), and, when imagining those principles applied to children's development, they see the picture becoming particularly harsh, depressing, and even dangerous from a moral and a social point of view (unjustly so, we argue).

A second reason for developmental psychologists' reticence to become eager converts to EP is scientific in nature. Many see a lack of genuine concern of EP

Portions of this chapter were written while the first author was supported by a Research Award from the Alexander von Humboldt Foundation, Germany, and while working at the University of Würzburg, Germany. We wish to express our appreciation to the Alexander von Humboldt Foundation and to Wolfgang Schneider for their support of this work. The chapter was also supported by a grant from the Ministerio de Educación, Cultura y Deporte (PR2002-0327) to the second author. We would like to thank Chris Cormier, Justin Rosenberg, Hye Eun Shin, and Viviana Weekes-Shackelford for comments on earlier drafts of this chapter. Correspondence should be sent to David F. Bjorklund, Department of Psychology, Florida Atlantic University, 777 Glades Road, Boca Raton, FL 33431, USA; e-mail: dbjorklu@fau.edu or Carlos Hernández Blasi, Departamento de Psicología, Universitat Jaume I, 12080-Castellón, Spain; e-mail: blasi@psi.uji.es.

with developmental issues, as well as a lack of a model for how evolved information processing programs become translated into behavior (e.g., Lickliter & Honeycutt, 2003). It is to this second, scientific issue that we have proposed the subdiscipline of *evolutionary developmental psychology* (EDP; e.g., Bjorklund & Pellegrini, 2000, 2002; Bugental, 2000; Ellis & Bjorklund, 2005; Geary, 1995; Geary & Bjorklund, 2000; Hernández Blasi, Bering, & Bjorklund, 2003; Hernández Blasi & Bjorklund, 2003), and in the first section of this chapter, we define the field and argue that "development matters" and that mainstream EP can benefit from adopting a developmental perspective. In the second section, we present what we see as the core assumptions of EDP, along with research examples to illustrate each assumption. In the third section, we present research performed from an EDP perspective on selective topics in social, social cognitive, and cognitive development. In a brief fourth section, we suggest that an EDP approach has benefits not only for a deeper theoretical understanding of human development and evolution but also for application to real-world problems.

EVOLUTIONARY DEVELOPMENTAL PSYCHOLOGY

We think that the basic tenets of mainstream EP can be summarized succinctly: Humans possess psychological mechanisms, evolved to deal with recurrent problems faced by our ancestors. Information processing mechanisms thus become the "missing link" in evolutionary explication. Such mechanisms are domain-specific and operate in relative independence of one another. Humans are "prepared" by evolution to process some information more readily than others (e.g., language); they are constrained in how they make sense of their world, with such constraints making it easier to process certain types of information (*enabling constraints*, Gelman & Williams, 1998). Although the ancient environments in which we evolved as a species, referred to as the *environment of evolutionary adaptedness*, have long since disappeared, modern humans still possess the evolved mechanisms of our ancestors. Because humans today live in a world very different from the one in which our minds evolved, many evolved mechanisms are not always adaptive for contemporary people, such as our penchant for sweets and fats, adaptive in environments in which food was scare, but maladaptive in ones with fast-food restaurants. The job of evolutionary psychologists is to explain contemporary behavior informed by our evolutionary past, following the principles originally put forward by Darwin (mainly natural selection) and modified over the past century as expressed in the modern synthesis. There is thus an emphasis on *adaptationist thinking,* stressing the function of a behavior or trait (e.g., Buss, 1995; Tooby & Cosmides, 1992).

We are in general agreement with the assumptions underlying mainstream EP, and it is in this context that we define EDP as the application of the basic principles of evolution to explain contemporary human development. It involves the study of the genetic and environmental mechanisms that underlie the universal development of social and cognitive competencies and the evolved epigenetic (gene-environment interactions) processes that adapt these competencies to local conditions. EDP assumes that not only are behaviors and cognitions that characterize adults the product of selection pressures operating over the course of evolution, but so also are characteristics of children's behaviors and minds (Bjorklund & Pellegrini, 2000, 2002; Geary & Bjorklund, 2000; Hernández Blasi & Bjorklund, 2003).

Central to an EDP perspective is an explicit model of development (the *developmental systems approach*), a model of gene-environment interaction that purports to explain how evolved mechanisms become expressed in the phenotype. This can also be recognized as a response to the persistent nature/nurture problem that has been one of the central issues of psychology since its inception and, despite repeated announcements of its demise, continues to plague modern theorists. Thus, before delving too deeply into the content of EDP, we first present the developmental systems approach.

The Developmental Systems Approach: A Model for Ontogeny and Phylogeny

With respect to the nature/nurture controversy, we think it is safe to say that most psychologists (and all developmentalists) believe that the issue is not "how much" of any trait is due to nature and "how much" is due to nurture, but rather how nature and nurture interact to produce a particular pattern of development. Everyone is an interactionist; there is really no other tenable alternative. But stating that biology and environment, broadly defined, interact, in and of themselves, advances the argument little. We must specify *how* biological and environmental factors interact.

With respect to a model for describing the nature of gene-environment interaction in the generation of adult behavior, we adopt a variant of the *developmental systems approach* as articulated by Gilbert Gottlieb (e.g., Gottlieb, 1991, 1992) and others (e.g., Lickliter, 1996; Oyama, 2000). The developmental systems approach views development as occurring within a system of bidirectionally interacting levels. A key concept of this perspective is that of *epigenesis,* which Gottlieb (1991) defines as "the emergence of new structures and functions during the course of development" (p. 7). New structures and functions do not arise fully formed but are the result of the bidirectional relationship between all levels of biological and environmental organization, from the genetic through the cultural. *Environment* is broadly defined from this perspective and includes the *macroenvironments* afforded by the world external to the individual, including, for example, parents for infants and the tools and institutions provided by an individual's culture; but it also includes *microenvironments,* such as events endogenous to the individual, including, for example, hormones, neurotransmitters, and even the firing of one neuron as it influences neighboring neurons and itself. Functioning at one level influences functioning at adjacent levels, with constant feedback occurring between levels. There are no simple genetic or experiential causes of behavior; rather, everything develops as a function of the bidirectional relationship between structure and function, occurring continuously across ontogeny.

From this perspective, there is much variability in development. Because each individual's experiences are different, patterns of development will also vary, making it impossible to predict with certainty the life course of any individual. The probabilistic and unpredictable nature of development is reflected in Oyama's (2000) statement, "Fate is constructed, amended, and reconstructed, partly by the emerging organisms itself. It is known to no one, not even the genes" (p. 137). This, taken to its extreme, gives the impression that development is a chaotic affair and that general patterns do not exist. But we know that this is not the case. Most members of a species, be they mallard ducks or human beings, develop in a species-typical fashion. How can this be so if the basic tenets of the developmental systems perspective are correct?

The answer is that animals inherit not only a species-typical genome but also a species-typical environment. These inherited environments start at conception, with the cellular machinery in the zygote (inherited directly from the mother); continue prenatally, such as a womb in mammals; and persist postnatally, such as a lactating mother in mammals, intestinal bacteria, a social structure for many species that may include parental care, as well as certain characteristics of the physical environment, including light, gravity, air, water (if you're an aquatic animal), among many others. Some of these characteristics are transmitted from one generation to the next with greater fidelity than are genes (e.g., light, gravity), whereas others may show greater variation (e.g., parental care, climate) and, as a consequence, lead to variations in development.

To the extent that individuals grow up in environments similar to those of their ancestors, development should follow a species-typical pattern. Animals (including humans) have evolved to "expect" a certain type of environment. For humans this would include 9 months in a sheltered womb; a lactating, warm, and affectionate mother; kin to provide additional support; and later in childhood, peers. According to Lickliter (1996): "The organism-environment relationship is one that is structured on both sides. That is, it is a relation between a structured organism *and* a structured environment. The organism inherits not only its genetic complement, but also the structured organization of the environment into which it is born" (pp. 90–91). What evolves, then, are not simply genes, but developmental systems. Genes are critical parts of developmental systems, but they are always expressed in an environment, and these environments (including cell cytoplasm, gravity, light, maternal nurturing) are also inherited (see Gottlieb, 1992; West-Eberhard, 2003).

We use research on the familiar phenomenon of imprinting in precocial birds as an example. Work made famous by the ethologist Konrad Lorenz (1965) demonstrated that, shortly after hatching, infant geese (and other birds) would follow the first moving, quacking object they experienced. In the wild this would almost certainly be their mothers, and these young animals would continue to stick close by their mothers until they became sufficiently independent to survive on their own. This was clearly an adaptive function, and the apparent lack of experience required for its demonstration fit nicely Lorenz's concept of instinct. But from a developmental systems perspective, the idea of "no experience necessary" is meaningless; everything develops as a function of the bidirectional relationship between structure (here, presumably the brain and sensory organs) and function (here, experience, broadly defined). Is there anything in the young birds' experience that may contribute to the acquisition of this apparently innate behavior? In a series of studies, Gottlieb (1997) modified the prenatal experience of ducklings to assess the role of experience on posthatching behavior. In the standard test, ducklings hours after hatching were placed in the center of a round tub with audio speakers located at opposite sides. The maternal call of a conspecific (e.g., mallard duck) would be emitted from one speaker, and the maternal call of another species (e.g., Peking duck, chicken) would be played from the other speaker. Consistent with the findings of Lorenz, the young hatchling would invariably approach the maternal call of its own species, a seeming demonstration of innate behavior. But the bird did have some potentially relevant experience before entering the experimental setting, notably auditory experience while still in the egg.

Mother ducks vocalize while sitting on their eggs, and this may be the critical experience. Moreover, ducklings themselves start to peep before hatching, so each bird has the perceptual experience of hearing its mother and its brood mates while still in the egg. In a series of experiments, Gottlieb removed the mother, and later the brood mates, so that the hatchling had no external auditory input before the testing session. Yet, these birds still reliably approached the call of a conspecific when tested. The only other source of auditory experience was the birds' self-produced sound. Gottlieb developed a procedure to surgically prevent the birds from making sound while still in the egg (the effect is reversible), removing the last source of auditory experience. Under these conditions, the birds showed no preference when given the auditory choice test. They were just as likely to approach the call of another species as they were their own.

In sum, a phenomenon that had long been the hallmark of instinct was shown to be dependent on subtle experience. The young animal was clearly prepared, or biased, by biology (and evolution) to make an attachment to the call of its mother, but this was achieved not by a genetically prescribed "instinct," but by a process that involved experience. It was a type of experience that all normal members of a species could expect to have, but such research makes it clear that phenomena that we usually declare to be "innate" may require significant environmental input and are, therefore, not the inevitable products of gene expression. Development matters, and this should be reflected in how evolutionary psychologists theorize about what is inherited and how. Infants are not born as blank slates; evolution has prepared them to "expect" certain types of environments and to process some information more readily than others. But prepared is not preformed (Bjorklund, 2003). It is the constant and bidirectional interaction between various levels of organization, which changes over the course of development, that produces behavior.

SOME BASIC ASSUMPTIONS OF EVOLUTIONARY DEVELOPMENTAL PSYCHOLOGY

We have already outlined two core assumptions of EDP: (1) All evolutionarily influenced characteristics in the phenotype of adults develop, and this requires examining not only the functioning of these characteristics in adults but also their *ontogeny*; and (2) EDP involves the expression of evolved, epigenetic programs, following the developmental systems approach. In addition to these core assumptions, there are at least four others that we believe are central to EDP: (1) Children show a high degree of plasticity and adaptive sensitivity to context, (2) an extended childhood is needed in which to learn the complexities of human social communities, (3) many aspects of childhood serve as preparations for adulthood and were selected over the course of evolution, and (4) some characteristics of infants and children were selected to serve an adaptive function at specific times in development and *not* as preparations for adulthood.

Early Plasticity and Adaptive Sensitivity to Context

As for many species, there is a wide range of environments in which human children can find themselves, varying in resources such as food and shelter, as well as less concrete features such as stress and social support. In many cases, conditions during the early years may be good predictors of what life will be like in later years. In other situations, however, conditions early in life may be short-lived and are not predictive of later environments. Children must be able to adjust their behaviors to environments that, on average, will be to their best advantage, both during childhood and later as adults. This requires *sensitivity to context* and the ability to regulate psychological and physiological functioning to immediate environments, and, in some circumstances, to develop dispositions that will generalize across time to maximize the individual's inclusive fitness.

Boyce and Ellis (in press) proposed the existence of developmental mechanisms that track environmental contexts that tend to remain stable over time and result in children developing phenotypes that are best suited to such environments. They refer to these mechanisms as *conditional adaptations,* defined as "evolved mechanisms that detect and respond to specific features of childhood environments—features that have proven reliable over evolutionary time in predicting the nature of the social and physical world into which children will mature—and entrain developmental pathways that reliably matched those features during a species' natural selective history" (Boyce & Ellis, in press).

For example, children reared in high-stress homes with inadequate resources and harsh and rejecting parenting mature at a faster rate than children reared in low-stress, well-resourced homes, who receive warm and sensitive parenting (e.g., Ellis & Garber, 2000); they also display different mating strategies as young adults (e.g., Belsky, Steinberg, & Draper, 1991). Children's early (and persistent) living conditions provide the best guess as to what future environments will be like, and children develop mating strategies to maximize their fitness (e.g., early reproduction, short-term, unstable pairbonds, and limited parental investment for the former group; later reproduction, long-term, enduring pairbonds, and greater parental investment for the latter group). Because there is not a single "best" reproductive strategy for all humans, individuals must be sensitive to environmental context and adjust their behavior accordingly. Sensitivity to early environmental contexts put children on a course that, on average and over evolutionary time, affords better adaptation to adult environments.

An Extended Childhood Is Needed in Which to Learn the Complexities of Human Social Communities

There has been no lack of hypotheses about the pressures most responsible for the evolution of human intelligence. A currently popular hypothesis focuses on the complex social environment that humans and our ancestors lived in and claims that it was the need to deal with conspecifics that, more than any other single force, was the primary selective pressure in the evolution of the modern human mind (e.g., Alexander, 1989; Dunbar, 1992; Humphrey, 1976). Human social complexity is also associated with a large brain and an extended juvenile period. It was the confluence of these three factors, we propose, acting synergistically, that produced the modern human mind (e.g., Bjorklund & Bering, 2003; Bjorklund, Cormier, & Rosenberg, 2005). Big brains are necessary for flexible learning, and an extended juvenile period permits time for such learning, particularly learning about an individual's social world. Humans spend more time as "prereproductives" than any other mammal. This is a potentially dangerous adaptation, in that waiting so long to reproduce accompanies with it the increased chance of death before having offspring. Something so costly must have equally high benefits for it to have passed through the sieve of natural selection. Those benefits, we propose, come mainly in the form of increased opportunity to learn the social rules and norms of the individual's group.

But an extended juvenile period is necessary not only for understanding the intricacies of human social relations and organization but also for mastering the products that result from complex human culture. As new ways of thinking about fellow members of our species evolved, they resulted in new or more effective ways of transmitting information between individuals and between generations (Tomasello, 1999). These new forms of social learning led to new technologies that no longer needed to be discovered or invented anew by each generation, but could be taught or acquired via observation. As the contents and complexity of culture increased, each generation had more to learn than the previous generation about dealing with their physical and social environments.

MANY ASPECTS OF CHILDHOOD SERVE AS PREPARATIONS FOR ADULTHOOD AND WERE SELECTED OVER THE COURSE OF EVOLUTION

Developmental psychologists usually make the implicit assumption that experiences in infancy and childhood serve as preparations for adulthood. In fact, some aspects of infancy and childhood that play this role may have been selected over the course of evolution, which we refer to as *deferred adaptations* (Hernández Blasi & Bjorklund, 2003). We do not wish to imply that such adaptations anticipate adult needs. Rather, they likely function throughout life, adapting children to the niche of childhood, but also preparing them for the life they will likely lead as adults. This is most apt to occur when environmental or social conditions remain relatively stable over time, as would likely be the case, for example, of children from hunter-gatherer groups interacting with the same set of peers both as juveniles and as adults.

Some sex differences may be good examples of deferred adaptations. Males and females have different self-interests, often focused around mating and parenting. Following parental investment theory, the females of most mammals invest more in offspring than do males, and, as a consequence, are more cautious in selecting a mate and consenting to sex than are males (Trivers, 1972). Males, as the less-investing sex, tend to compete more vigorously over access to females than vice versa. As a result, men and women have evolved different psychologies, which develop over the course of childhood. Many experiences during childhood seem to promote and even exaggerate these sex differences, serving to prepare boys and girls for the roles they will play (or would have played in the environment of evolutionary adaptedness) as adults.

Sex differences in play serve as good examples. Although there is no type of play that is the exclusive purview of one sex or the other, boys and girls show different patterns, contents, and styles of the major types of play, and some theorists have argued that such sex-differentiated play served to prepare children for adult roles as men and women in the environment of evolutionary adaptedness (e.g., Geary, 1998). For example, rough-and-tumble play (R&T) is commonly observed in most mammals, including children, and usually accounts for about 10% of their time and energy budgets (Fagen, 1981). Males engage in R&T more frequently than females in all human cultures and in many mammal species. Human fathers spend more time than mothers in R&T, and they do so with sons more than with daughters. Some have argued (e.g., Geary, 1998; Smith, 1982) that R&T is a classic example of play serving deferred benefits to juvenile males, especially in terms of practice for adult hunting and fighting skills, important in traditional environments. Boys' position in a social hierarchy is more often based on physical skills than that of girls' (Hawley, 1999), and the high incidence of R&T among boys may facilitate their ability to encode and decode social signals (Pellegrini & Smith, 1998), which is important at all stages of social life.

SOME CHARACTERISTICS OF INFANTS AND CHILDREN WERE SELECTED TO SERVE AN ADAPTIVE FUNCTION AT SPECIFIC TIMES IN DEVELOPMENT AND NOT AS PREPARATIONS FOR ADULTHOOD

Not all aspects of childhood serve to prepare individuals for life as an adult. Many features of infancy and the juvenile period serve to adapt individuals to their *current* environment and not to an anticipated future one. These have been referred to as *ontogenetic adaptations* (Bjorklund, 1997; Oppenheim, 1981) and can be easily recognized in some prenatal adaptations in mammals and birds. For example, before birth, fetal mammals get their nutrition and oxygen through the placenta, but immediately after birth these systems become obsolete and infants must eat and breathe on their own. Other examples of ontogenetic adaptations during the prenatal period include the yolk sack, embryonic excretory mechanisms, and hatching behaviors in birds. These are not immature forms of adult adaptations that become gradually shaped to mature form, but are behaviors, structures, or mechanisms that have a specific function at a particular time in development and are discarded or disappear when they are no longer necessary.

Such adaptations are not limited to the prenatal period, nor to structures or mechanisms associated with physiological functioning, but may also be found in infant and child behavior and cognition. For instance, young children are generally poor at estimating their abilities on a wide range of tasks, typically overestimating their skill (see Bjorklund, 1997). A study of children's meta-imitation (children's knowledge of how well they can imitate a model) reflects the potential value of being out of touch with their abilities (Bjorklund, Gaultney, & Green, 1993) and hence some advantages of young children's immature cognition (Bjorklund, 1997). In a first study, parents observed preschool children imitating the actions of others and asked children how well they thought they would be able to imitate the model (prediction) and, following attempted imitation, how well they had actually imitated the model (postdiction). They reported that children overestimated both how well they thought they would be able to imitate a model (prediction, 56.9% overestimation of all observations) and how well they thought they had imitated a model (postdiction, 39.6% overestimation of all observations). Underestimation was rare (5.1% of all observations). In a subsequent study, preschoolers were shown a model engaged in a task (e.g., juggling 1, 2, or 3 balls) and asked for both their predictions of how well they thought they could perform the task and, after attempting the task, how well they thought they had performed the task. The accuracy of children's predictions and postdictions was then compared with a measure of verbal IQ. Five-year-old children displayed the same pattern that has been reported between metacognition and intelligence for older children (e.g., Schneider, Körkel, & Weinert, 1987), with higher IQ being associated with more accurate performance. However, 3- and 4-year-old children showed the opposite pattern, such that children with higher verbal IQ scores were less accurate (i.e., they overestimated more) than children with lower IQs. These results suggest that poor metacognitive skills for young children may not always be a detriment. Young children think they are smarter and more capable than they really are (e.g., Stipek, 1984). As a result, they experiment with new tasks and are less perturbed by poor performance than children with better metacognitive skills would be. As they continue to practice these tasks, their performance improves and, with time, so do their metacognitive skills. We argue that such immature cognition should not be viewed only as something that children must outgrow, but rather as being well suited to their developmental niche.

TOPICS IN DEVELOPMENT FROM AN EVOLUTIONARY PERSPECTIVE

A developmental evolutionary approach can be useful to an adaptive understanding of human behavior in at least two ways: first, by providing a better understanding of the adaptive value of behaviors across the life span and, second, by informing about the possible role/impact of development in evolved adult behaviors. In doing so, an EDP approach does more than simply extend evolutionary principles to infants and children (i.e., descriptive level) but, potentially, can modify some of the current conceptions of adaptive explanations for human adult behaviors (i.e., explanatory level).

In the following pages, we review research that both provides examples of the wide range of topics in which an EDP perspective can be applied and illustrates the explanatory powers of a developmental approach for adaptive adult behaviors. We focus on selected topics from three major research areas: social development (social dominance roles), social cognitive development (theory of mind), and cognitive development (intuitive mathematics). This is only a small subset of the developmental topics and issues that have been approached from an evolutionary perspective (see Table 29.1 for other examples).

SOCIAL DEVELOPMENT: SOCIAL DOMINANCE IN CHILDREN

Humans are the most social of all primates, and our survival depends heavily on our ability to actively and prosocially interact with others. It also depends on our ability to compete and sometimes dominate others, accruing more resources for ourselves in the process. Therefore, individuals who could successfully traverse the complicated terrain of hominid social life, learning to compete and cooperate with group members, were likely those who experienced the greatest benefits. However, despite the fact that social skills may affect survival and reproduction most decisively in adults, they do not appear de novo in adulthood but find their roots in infancy and childhood.

As Flavell (2000) has summarized, infants are born with or develop early a number of abilities and dispositions that help them learn about people: (1) They find human faces, voices, and movements highly interesting; (2) they have impressive abilities to perceptually analyze and discriminate human stimuli; (3) they seem impelled to attend to and interact with other people; and (4) they respond differently to people than they do to objects. These person-oriented dispositions set the stage for more complicated social interactions and relations that influence their survival.

Table 29.1
Selected Topics Examined from an Evolutionary
Developmental Psychological Perspective

Cognitive Development

Neonatal imitation (e.g., Bjorklund, 1987)

Language development (e.g., Pinker, 1994)

Infant-directed speech (e.g., Fernald, 1992)

Intuitive mathematics (e.g., Geary, 1995)

Inhibitory control (e.g., Bjorklund & Harnishfeger, 1995)

Memory (e.g., Nelson, 2005)

Potential benefits of cognitive immaturity (e.g., Bjorklund & Green, 1992)

Theory of mind (e.g., Baron-Cohen, 1995)

Spatial cognition (e.g., Silverman & Eals, 1992)

Infant perceptual biases (e.g., Langlois, Ritter, Roggman, & Vaughn, 1991)

Intuitive physics (e.g., Spelke, 1991)

Face processing (e.g., Johnson & de Haan, 2001)

Folk biology (e.g., Keenan & Ellis, 2003)

Social/Emotional Development

Play (e.g., Pellegrini & Smith, 1998)

Attachment (e.g., Bowlby, 1969)

Socialization (e.g., Harris, 2005)

Social dominance (e.g., Hawley, 1999)

Social learning (e.g., Tomasello, 1999)

Social reasoning (e.g., Cummins, 1998)

Maternal investment (e.g., Hrdy, 1999)

Paternal investment (e.g., Geary, 2000)

Grandparental investment (e.g., O'Connell, Hawkes, & Blurton Jones, 1999)

Aggression (e.g., Pellegrini & Bartini, 2000)

Adolescent romantic relationships (e.g., Pellegrini & Long, 2003)

Incest avoidance (e.g., Weisfeld, Czilli, Phillips, Gall, & Lichtman, 2003)

Applied Issues

Differential susceptibility to rearing influence (e.g., Belsky, 1997)

Response to stressful environments (Boyce & Ellis, in press)

Pregnancy sickness (e.g., Profet, 1992)

Early stimulation of premature infants (e.g., Als, 1995)

Effects of parental style on mating strategies (e.g., Belsky et al., 1991)

Sibling rivalry (e.g., Sulloway, 1996)

ADHD disorder (e.g., Jensen et al., 1997)

School disabilities (e.g., Geary, 1995)

Infanticide (e.g., Daly & Wilson, 1984)

Child abuse (e.g., Daly & Wilson, 1996)

Teenage pregnancy (e.g., Weisfeld & Billings, 1988)

Effects of schooling (e.g., Bjorklund & Bering, 2002)

Perhaps the most salient indication of social structure, both in the lives of children and adults, is related to social status. People in all cultures strive for high status, which is associated with the acquisition of resources. A key concept in evolutionary theorizing is that resources are limited and that individuals act to maximize their access to resources, be they in the form of food, shelter, or mates. In social species such as *Homo sapiens,* higher status members typically are able to procure more or better quality resources for themselves and their kin than conspecifics of lower social ranking. Contrary to some naive expectations about childhood, competing for status is also common at that time in life, beginning early in the preschool years (see Hawley, 1999). Resources are differently defined in childhood than in adulthood, and they also vary according to developmental periods. Thus, for example, during most of childhood, access to adult attention or props, such as toys, is a valued resource in peer interaction. But, as with adults, status structures in the form of *dominance hierarchies* are an important dimension of children's social lives. Dominance hierarchies reflect differences in status among individuals in a group, with high-status individuals having greater access to resources than lower status individuals.

Harris (1995) proposed four evolutionary adaptations related to social structure, evident in children as well as in adults: (1) group affiliation and in-group favoritism, (2) fear of or hostility toward strangers, (3) the seeking and establishment of close dyadic relationships, and (4) within-group status seeking. It is the first and last items of this list that are of greatest significance for our discussion here. Children are motivated to become members of a peer group and to conform to the norms of the group. Harris (1995), in fact, stated that it is the peer group that is the chief socializing agent for children, not parents. Once within a peer group, children seek to excel in areas valued by members of the group, attain as high a status as possible, and develop behaviors that will permit them to function smoothly in the peer group. More recently, Harris (2005) proposed a *behavioral strategy mechanism* that evolved to give feedback to individuals from others over time, which serves to inform children how they stack up against their peers. This provides valuable information concerning what children's strong and weak points are, what niche they can best fill, both as children and later as adults, and in general serves to prepare them for life in a social group of peers.

In many social species, status is determined primarily by aggression. Stronger and more physically assertive individuals are dominant over weaker ones, and an individual's position within a dominance hierarchy is established, basically, in terms of "who can beat up whom." But dominance hierarchies are more than the product of stronger individuals asserting their control over weaker individuals and obtaining access to more and better resources in the process. Dominance hierarchies serve to support the establishment and maintenance of social structures that are critical to the efficient distribution of limited resources, division of labor, and minimization of social conflict. An individual's position in a social group affects whom he or she interacts with and how, and children must learn not only their own position in such hierarchies but also those of other children.

Social structure is defined in terms of dominance not only during childhood but also in the toddler years. Children's dominance hierarchies are typically established using aggression (especially in boys) and are often displayed in competition with peers over resources such as toys (e.g., Strayer & Noel, 1986). Stronger and "tougher" individuals take the roles of leaders and obtain access to favored resources (see Hawley, 1999). Levels of aggression are usually high when children first come together in a group, with the top and bottom positions in the social hierarchies being the first established and the middle positions being determined later (e.g., Strayer & Noel, 1986). Once dominance hierarchies are established, rates of aggression decrease, and leaders use prosocial and cooperative strategies more often.

Aggressive behavior in children is usually associated with poor social reasoning and adjustment (see Coie & Dodge, 1998), so it would be unusual if high-status children (or high-status adults, for that matter) used only agonistic behaviors to maintain their rank. In fact, children establish and maintain their position in a dominance hierarchy using both aggressive and prosocial strategies (see Hawley, 1999). That is, dominance in children is not simply a matter of who can physically dominate whom but also involves cooperation, affiliative behaviors, and alliances. This is seen in other social species as well, including chimpanzees. Dominant chimpanzees use substantial force to keep subordinates in line but also cooperate and engage in prosocial behavior, such as grooming, with subordinate animals (de Waal, 1989). That is, alternative strategies are used, and such strategies are based on the ecology of the group as well as the associated costs and benefits.

The fact that high-status children use both affiliative and agonistic behaviors in maintaining social dominance suggests that untempered generalizations about the positive or negative consequences of prosocial or aggressive behavior is likely uncalled for. For example, there has been a trend in social development to reflexively view aggressive behavior as maladaptive and reflective of social immaturity. Aggressive children are also viewed as emotionally immature, unpopular, and perhaps as having a less well-developed sense of moral reasoning than less aggressive children (e.g., Lochman & Dodge, 1994). There is a category of children who fit this description, but other children seem to use aggression strategically, in combination with prosocial behavior, and fare much better. In fact, a number of investigators have reported a positive relation between aggression and popularity for children over a wide age range, from 3-year-olds through early adolescence (e.g., Hawley, 2003; Pellegrini & Bartini, 2000).

This pattern is illustrated in a study by Hawley (2003), who observed preschool children in their classrooms, interviewed children's teachers, and administered assessments of moral reasoning. Hawley identified a group of children she described as *bistrategic*. These children displayed high levels of aggressive behavior but also fairly high levels of prosocial behavior. They were as popular with their peers as children showing high levels of prosocial behavior and low levels of aggression and showed no lag in moral reasoning. Hawley and others (e.g., Pellegrini & Bartini, 2000) propose that high-status children are able to use both agonistic and affiliative behaviors strategically, displaying what might be called *Machiavellian* behavior (cf. Byrne & Whiten, 1988). They use aggression not only to acquire resources for themselves but also to protect their friends and display prosocial behaviors to those who affiliate with them. This hypothesis is compatible with arguments made by primatologist Franz de Waal

(1989) that in some ecologies, among nonhuman primates, aggression leads to affiliation, rather than dispersal, when interactants reconcile after an aggressive incident.

Social Cognitive Development: The Development of Theory of Mind

Despite the obvious similarities in social behavior between human and some nonhuman primates, such as chimpanzees, human social life is qualitatively different from that of any other species because of, among other things, its possession of self-awareness and language (e.g., Bering & Bjorklund, in press; Pinker, 1994). But perhaps more than any other single factor, our ability to understand the motivation for our own behavior and the behavior of others has drastically altered human social interaction. This is also an ability that develops over the preschool years and has been investigated under the rubric of *theory of mind*, a term coined by Premack and Woodruff in 1978 to designate the set of inferential abilities that permit an individual to impute mental states (i.e., purpose or intention, knowledge, belief, thinking, doubt, guessing, pretending, liking, and so forth) to self and others. Without a theory of mind, social relations would remain on the level displayed by 3-year-old children or perhaps members of a chimpanzee troop, making difficult social exchanges, social contracts, and detection of people who may be breaking the rules.

At the heart of theory of mind is what Wellman (1990) described as *belief-desire reasoning*, in which people understand that their behavior and the behavior of others is motivated by what they know or believe and what they want or desire and that sometimes other people's beliefs and desires are different from their own. Such reasoning is the basis of nearly all forms of social interactions among people, and thus its development is worthy of extensive investigation.

Theory of mind is usually assessed by one of a variety of *false-belief tasks* that require children to realize conditions under which a person can have a mistaken, or false, belief. A much-used, false-belief task involves presenting children with a familiar container, such as a cereal box, and asking them what is in the box. Children are typically quick to state the obvious ("Fruit Loops!") but are then shown the contents of the box, which turn out to be something quite different (e.g., ribbons). They are then asked what someone else outside the room would think is in the box and are later asked what they had originally thought had been in the box. Most children 4 years of age and older correctly answer that another person would likely have the false belief that cereal is in the box and that they themselves had previously thought this. Most 3-year-old children, in contrast, state that the person would believe that there are ribbons in the box, and when asked what they initially thought was in the box, most say "ribbons," seemingly forgetting their previous response just minutes earlier (e.g., Hogrefe, Wimmer, & Perner, 1986).

Although social reasoning clearly develops over childhood and into adulthood, the basic components of belief-desire reasoning are attained between 3 and 5 years of age, with few 3-year-old children passing the critical false-belief tasks and few 5-year-olds failing them (e.g., Wellman, 1990; Wellman, Cross, & Watson, 2001). Further, theory of mind develops at about the same time and in the same sequence in most children around the world (e.g., Avis & Harris, 1991). This relatively narrow age range and its likely universality are consistent with the domain-specificity perspective of EP, supporting the existence of a series of highly specialized modules that develop over the preschool years (Baron-Cohen, 1995; Leslie, 1994).

One such model is that of Baron-Cohen (1995), who proposed four hierarchically arranged, modular mechanisms that develop over infancy and early childhood. The most primitive mechanism is the *intentionality detector* (ID), which interprets moving stimuli as having some "intention." For example, a stimulus moving toward an individual may be interpreted as intending to strike or perhaps to groom that individual. This system essentially serves as a primitive basis for understanding volitional states and helps to better understand animalistic movements, such as approach and avoidance. The ID system develops early in infancy and presumably is possessed by other animals. Coming online in children about 9 months of age, the *eye-direction detector* (EDD) interprets eye gaze. Specifically, the EDD makes the inference that if someone's eyes are looking at something, it "sees" that something. The third mechanism in this model is the *shared-attention mechanism* (SAM), which involves triadic interactions and determines where another person's attention is focused. This mechanism develops over the first 18 months and is evidenced by infants' monitoring the gaze of others and looking back and forth between another person and an object, making sure that someone else is looking at the same thing that he or she is seeing. The final mechanism is the *theory of mind mechanism* (ToMM), which Baron-Cohen (1995) described as "a system for inferring the full range of mental states from behavior—that is, for employing a 'theory of mind.' . . . It has the dual purpose of representing the set of epistemic mental states and turning all this mentalistic knowledge into a useful theory" (p. 51). This is similar to belief-desire reasoning as described by Wellman (1990).

Support for Baron-Cohen's modular perspective comes from research on autistic children (and later adults), who, despite a variable range of intellectual abilities, consistently have difficulty on tasks involving social reasoning. According to Baron-Cohen, autists can be described as having *mindblindness*, an inability to "read others' minds" (i.e., they are deficient in belief-desire reasoning). For instance, a subset of autists who show high levels of intellectual functioning on tasks involving nonsocial problems tends to perform poorly on false-belief tasks and other tasks involving social reasoning. This is in contrast to people with mental retardation, such as Down syndrome, who show the reverse pattern, performing well on the false-belief tasks and poorly on tasks involving "general" (i.e., nonsocial) intelligence (e.g., Baron-Cohen, Leslie, & Frith, 1985; Baron-Cohen, Wheelwright, Stone, & Rutherford, 1999). In addition, neural processing deficits in people with autism have been located in the left frontal brain region, an area that has been associated with processing on theory of mind tasks for normal adults (e.g., Sabbagh & Taylor, 2000). Also, behavior genetic studies suggest that performance on theory of mind tasks is independent of general verbal performance, a finding consistent with the position that theory of mind is not simply a function of general intellectual functioning (Hughes & Cutting, 1999).

Although children clearly are prepared to perform belief-desire reasoning, they seem also to require a supportive social environment for these abilities to develop. In fact, it has been shown that rate of development of theory of mind is related to some aspects of children's social environment. These include the social skills of children's teachers (Watson, Nixon, Wilson, & Capage, 1999), the number of adults and older children that a preschool child interacts with daily (Lewis, Freeman, Kyriakidou, Maridaki-Kassotaki, & Berridge, 1996), and family size, especially the number of older siblings a child has (Ruffman, Perner, Naito, Parkin, & Clements, 1998).

One interpretation of why having older (but not younger) siblings promotes theory of mind development is that older siblings stimulate pretend play, thus helping younger children represent "counterfactual states of affairs," a necessary skill for solving false-belief tasks (Ruffman et al., 1998). An alternative explanation based on dominance theory was proposed by Cummins (1998), who suggested that the inferior position of younger children relative to older siblings in a family puts them at a disadvantage in competition for resources, such as toys or parents' attention. It is thus to younger children's benefit to develop whatever latent talents they possess to assist them in social competition with their older siblings, and developing a keener understanding of their competitor's mind may provide them such an advantage.

Cognitive Development: Children's Intuitive Mathematics

Just as humans (as well as other animals) seem to have biases and constraints that help them deal with conspecifics, so, too, do they have biases and constraints to help them make sense of aspects of their physical world. For example, using changes in infants' looking time to expected and unexpected events, researchers have found that infants very early in life develop some basic understanding of the physical nature of objects, or what Spelke (1991) has referred to as *core knowledge*. These include: (1) *continuity*, the idea that objects move from one location to another in a continuous path and cannot be in the same place as another object; (2) *cohesion*, the idea that objects have boundaries and their components stay connected with one another; and (3) *contact*, the idea that one object must contact another object to make it move (see Spelke, 1991; Spelke & Newport, 1998). Infants and young children seem to possess other biases or abilities that facilitate more "advanced" forms of cognition. In this section we discuss one such cognitive ability, *intuitive mathematics*.

Biologically Primary and Secondary Abilities   We typically think of mathematics as an advanced cognitive ability. Surely, no cognitive module evolved to deal with calculus or analytic geometry. These are cultural inventions and relatively recent ones at that. David Geary (1995) has referred to these culturally specific forms of cognition as *biologically secondary abilities* and contrasts them with *biologically primary abilities*, which he defines as cognitive operations that have evolved over the course of evolution to help our ancestors deal with recurrent problems. Biologically primary abilities are found universally and show similar patterns of development in all cultures. Furthermore, children are intrinsically motivated to use them, and nearly everyone attains expert status in these skills. In contrast, biologically secondary skills are culture specific, often requiring external motivation for children to use them, and there is much variability in the eventual level attained in these skills. Language is perhaps the prototypic biologically primary ability, which can be contrasted with reading, a supposed language skill, as a prototypical biologically secondary ability. Geary (1995) proposed that there are several aspects of mathematical ability that meet his criteria of being biologically primary abilities, including numerosity, ordinality, counting, and simple arithmetic.

Numerosity and Ordinality   *Numerosity* refers to the ability to quickly and accurately determine the number of items in a set without counting. Within the first week of life, infants are able to discriminate between visual arrays containing two versus three (and sometimes four) items (e.g., Starkey, Spelke, & Gelman, 1990). Infants can even make numerosity judgments between two different sensory modalities. For example, 6- and 9-month-old infants were shown arrays of two or three objects and simultaneously heard two or three drum beats. Infants looked significantly longer at the visual display that corresponded to the auditory pattern they heard (Starkey, Spelke, & Gelman, 1983, 1990).

With respect to ordinality, basic "more than" and "less than" knowledge apparently develops later in infancy, perhaps not until the middle of the second year. For example, in one study, 16-month-old infants were conditioned to touch the side of a screen that contained either the larger or smaller array of dots. Following training, infants were shown new arrays containing a different number of dots, but one still consisting of more dots than the other. If infants had learned an ordinal relation (e.g., always pick the array with more dots), they should generalize this to the new arrays, regardless of the absolute number of dots in the arrays. The infants did this, suggesting a basic knowledge of "more than" and "less than" relationships (Strauss & Curtis, 1981).

It is interesting that nonhuman animals also display basic numerosity and ordinality abilities. For example, many mammals and birds can differentiate between small arrays that differ in quantity (see Davis & Perusse, 1988), and chimpanzees and monkeys have been shown to understand "more than" and "less than" relations, at least for quantities up to about 4 (e.g., Boysen, 1993; Hauser, Carey, & Hauser, 2000), suggesting that these abilities have deep evolutionary roots.

Counting   Children around the world begin counting shortly after they begin talking. Gelman and Gallistel (1978) describe five counting principles:

1. The *one-one principle:* Each item in an array is associated with one and only one number name (e.g., "four").
2. The *stable order principle:* Number names must be in a stable, repeatable order.
3. The *cardinal principle:* The final number in a series represents the quantity of the set.
4. The *abstraction principle:* The first three principles can be applied to any array of entities.
5. The *order-irrelevant principle:* The order in which things are counted is irrelevant.

Children develop the first three principles over the preschool years (Gelman & Gallistel, 1978). Although young children often use idiosyncratic number words (e.g., one, two, five, eleven-teen), they tend to use them consistently, that is, in a stable order. To assess children's understanding of the critical features of counting, Briars and Siegler (1984) showed children a puppet counting an array of objects, and the children were to tell whether the puppet's counts were accurate or not. They reported that children's understanding of the one-one and the stable order principles were low for 3-year-olds (30%) but approached ceiling levels for 4- (90%) and 5-year-old (100%) children. Older children still regarded other irrelevant factors as important for proper counting, however. For example, 60% of 5-year-olds stated that beginning a count at one end and pointing to each item only once were necessary for accurate counting. These results indicate that children acquire the basic "how to" principles of counting by 4 years of age but take longer to infer, from watching others, additional characteristics associated with proper counting.

Simple Arithmetic   Children's early arithmetic is based on counting, but there is evidence that even infants show some ability to add and subtract small quantities. In an experiment by Wynn (1992), 5-month-old infants saw a series of arrays in which objects were placed or removed from behind a screen. For example, infants watched as a Minnie Mouse doll was placed in front of them. A screen was then raised, obstructing infants' vision. Infants then watched as a second doll was placed behind the screen. The screen was then removed revealing either one or two dolls. If infants have a basic sense of arithmetic (e.g., $1 + 1 = 2$), they should expect to see two dolls behind the screen. If they then see only one doll, this should violate their expectation and result in increased looking time, relative to when the expected quantity (2) is revealed. This is the pattern of results that Wynn reported (see also Simon, Hespos, & Rochat, 1995; Uller, Carey, Huntley-Fenner, & Klatt, 1999), and she interpreted her findings as indicating basic arithmetic abilities in infants that can serve as the basis for later, more sophisticated quantitative skills. Evidence of simple arithmetic abilities using methods similar to those of Wynn have been reported for free-living rhesus monkeys (Sulkowski & Hauser, 2001; see also evidence for arithmetic abilities in chimpanzees in Boysen, 1993).

The research evidence, both from human and animal work, suggests that basic quantitative skills represent what Geary has termed biologically primary abilities. We should not be surprised that other species possess some of these skills, too, for some of them (particularly numerosity and ordinality) can be valuable in making basic decisions relevant to survival. However, humans are the only species who extend such biologically primary abilities to higher mathematics.

APPLYING EVOLUTIONARY DEVELOPMENTAL PSYCHOLOGY TO REAL-WORLD PROBLEMS

EDP can be profitably applied to a broad range of ages, from the prenatal period to old age, basic domains of development (e.g., social, cognitive), and societally important issues (see Smith, 2003; Weekes-Shackelford & Bjorklund, in press). For instance, issues related to education can be informed from an EDP perspective. Geary's distinction between biologically primary and secondary abilities has direct applications to schooling (Geary, 2003, 2005). *Homo sapiens* are the most educable of species, with our abilities for language, theory of mind, and self-reflection permitting the invention of cognitive operations (e.g., reading and higher mathematics) seemingly unavailable to other species, which permits the creation of complex technology and culture. Although a flexible intelligence has surely characterized our kind for at least the last 35,000 years (and possibly 150,000 years or more), the cultural advances made by modern humans require formal schooling, something that is an evolutionary novelty and an "unnatural experience" (Bjorklund & Bering, 2002). With this perspective in mind, curricula can be constructed that make the task of learning biologically secondary abilities easier by taking the evolved characteristics of children into consideration. For instance, adding periods for physical activity during the school day has been shown to increase attention and reduce "fidgeting" (e.g., Jarrett et al., 1998; Pellegrini, Huberty, & Jones, 1995). Other research suggests that middle-class, preschool children benefit more from play-oriented instructions than more formal adult-directed instruction and that adult-directed instruction may be associated with a reduction in creativity, higher levels of test anxiety, and a less positive attitude about school (Hyson, Hirsh-Pasek, & Rescorla, 1990). Geary (2005) has noted that some biologically primary abilities can be used to facilitate academic learning, whereas others may interfere with such learning and that only by taking an evolutionary developmental perspective can we distinguish between the two and develop curricula to enhance children's mastery of modern technological skills.

There are few issues of applied developmental science that an evolutionary developmental perspective will not help to elucidate. For example, research on attachment (discussed in Chapter 14 of this *Handbook*) can inform programs of parental education and teenage pregnancy prevention (e.g., Belsky et al., 1991), an understanding of parental investment theory (Trivers, 1972) can help explain and possibly prevent cases of child abuse and child homicide (e.g., Daly & Wilson, 1996) and the failure of many divorced fathers to pay child support (Shackelford & Weeks-Shackelford, in press), and understanding the potentially adaptive value of aggression may help in the development of programs to reduce violence in schools and among low-income youths and young men (e.g., Daly & Wilson, 1984; Pellegrini & Bartini, 2000).

In sum, we think that an EDP approach can be as useful in providing suggestions for the remediation of social problems as it can be in providing insights into the basic nature of development and evolution. Such applications rely not on "genetic" explanations of patterns of behavior but on how evolved mechanisms change as a result of interactions over the course of development to produce behavior that may have been adaptive in ancient environments but is maladaptive in contemporary ones.

CONCLUSIONS

An evolutionary approach has much to contribute to an understanding of development. In addition, a developmental approach has much to contribute to an understanding of evolution and EP. Taking a developmental perspective requires that researchers and theorists consider how evolved, adaptive mechanisms become expressed in the phenotype. Although contemporary evolutionary psychologists clearly state that "environment" interacts with genetic dispositions to produce adaptive behavior, *how* this occurs (i.e., how phenotypes develop) is rarely addressed. This is the major contribution that a developmental perspective can have for EP, along with the realization that natural selection has impacted human thought and behavior not only during adulthood but also during infancy and childhood. A developmental perspective does not lessen the role of genetics in explaining contemporary human behavior, but rather helps to clarify how genes interact with environments, broadly defined, over time to produce adaptive patterns of thought and behavior. Such a perspective can go a long way to bringing evolutionary thought to a wider range of behavioral scientists.

REFERENCES

Alexander, R. D. (1989). Evolution of the human psyche. In P. Mellers & C. Stringer (Eds.), *The human revolution: Behavioural and biological perspectives on the origins of modern humans* (pp. 455–513). Princeton, NJ: Princeton University Press.

Als, H. (1995). The preterm infant: A model for the study of fetal brain expectation. In J.-P. Lecanuet, W. P. Fifer, N. A. Krasnegor, & W. P. Smotherman (Eds.), *Fetal development: A psychobiological perspective* (pp. 439–471). Hillsdale, NJ: Erlbaum.

Avis, J., & Harris, P. L. (1991). Belief-desire reasoning among Baka children: Evidence for a universal conception of mind. *Child Development, 62,* 460–467.

Baron-Cohen, S. (1995). *Mindblindness: An essay on autism and theory of mind.* Cambridge, MA: MIT Press.

Baron-Cohen, S., Leslie, A., & Frith, U. (1985). Does the autistic child have a "theory of mind"? *Cognition, 21,* 37–46.

Baron-Cohen, S., Wheelwright, S., Stone, V., & Rutherford, M. (1999). A mathematician, a physicist and a computer scientist with Asperger syndrome: Performance on folk psychology and folk physics tests. *Neurocase, 5,* 475–483.

Belsky, J. (1997). Attachment, mating, and parenting: An evolutionary interpretation. *Human Nature, 8,* 361–381.

Belsky, J., Steinberg, L., & Draper, P. (1991). Childhood experience, interpersonal development, and reproductive strategy: An evolutionary theory of socialization. *Child Development,* 647–670.

Bering, J. M., & Bjorklund, D. F. (in press). The serpent's gift: Evolutionary psychology and consciousness. In P. D. Zelazo & M. Moscovitch (Eds.), *Cambridge handbook of consciousness.* Cambridge, England: Cambridge University Press.

Bjorklund, D. F. (1987). A note on neonatal imitation. *Developmental Review, 7,* 86–92.

Bjorklund, D. F. (1997). The role of immaturity in human development. *Psychological Bulletin, 122,* 153–169.

Bjorklund, D. F. (2003). Evolutionary psychology from a developmental systems perspective: Comment on Lickliter and Honeycutt (2003). *Psychological Bulletin, 129,* 836–841.

Bjorklund, D. F., & Bering, J. M. (2002). The evolved child: Applying evolutionary developmental psychology to modern schooling. *Learning and Individual Differences, 12,* 1–27.

Bjorklund, D. F., & Bering, J. M. (2003). Big brains, slow development, and social complexity: The developmental and evolutionary origins of social cognition. In M. Brüne, H. Ribbert, & W. Schiefenhövel (Eds.), *The social brain: Evolutionary aspects of development and pathology* (pp. 133–151). New York: Wiley.

Bjorklund, D. F., Cormier, C., & Rosenberg, J. S. (2005). The evolution of theory of mind: Big brains, social complexity, and inhibition. In W. Schneider, R. Schumann-Hengsteler, & B. Sodian (Eds.), *Young children's cognitive development: Interrelationships among executive functioning, working memory, verbal ability and theory of mind* (pp. 147–174). Mahwah, NJ: Erlbaum.

Bjorklund, D. F., Gaultney, J. F., & Green, B. L. (1993). "I watch therefore I can do": The development of meta-imitation over the preschool years and the advantage of optimism in one's imitative skills. In R. Pasnak & M. L. Howe (Eds.), *Emerging themes in cognitive development: Vol. II. Competencies* (pp. 79–102). New York: Springer-Verlag.

Bjorklund, D. F., & Green, B. L. (1992). The adaptive nature of cognitive immaturity. *American Psychologist, 47,* 46–54.

Bjorklund, D. F., & Harnishfeger, K. K. (1995). The role of inhibition mechanisms in the evolution of human cognition and behavior. In F. N. Dempster & C. J. Brainerd (Eds.), *New perspectives on interference and inhibition in cognition* (pp. 141–173). New York: Academic Press.

Bjorklund, D. F., & Pellegrini, A. D. (2000). Child development and evolutionary psychology. *Child Development, 71,* 1687–1708.

Bjorklund, D. F., & Pellegrini, A. D. (2002). *The origins of human nature: Evolutionary developmental psychology.* Washington, DC: APA Books.

Bowlby, J. (1969). *Attachment and loss: Vol. 1. Attachment.* London: Hogarth.

Boyce, W. T., & Ellis, B. J. (in press). Biological sensitivity to context: I. An evolutionary-developmental theory of the origins and functions of stress reactivity. *Development and Psychopathology.*

Boysen, S. T. (1993). Counting in chimpanzees: Nonhuman principles and emergent properties of number. In S. T. Boysen & E. J. Capaldi (Eds.), *The development of numerical competence: Animal and human models* (pp. 39–59). Hillsdale, NJ: Erlbaum.

Briars, D., & Siegler, R. S. (1984). A featural analysis of preschoolers' counting knowledge. *Developmental Psychology, 20,* 607–618.

Bugental, D. B. (2000). Acquisition of the algorithms of social life: A domain-based approach. *Psychological Bulletin, 126,* 187–219.

Buss, D. M. (1995). Evolutionary psychology. *Psychological Inquiry, 6,* 1–30.

Byrne, R., & Whiten, A. (Eds.). (1988). *Machiavellian intelligence: Social expertise and the evolution of intellect in monkeys, apes, and humans.* Oxford, England: Clarendon.

Cairns, R. B. (1998). The making of developmental psychology. In W. Damon (Series Ed.) & R. M. Lerner (Vol. Ed.), *Theoretical models of human development: Vol. 1. Handbook of child psychology* (5th ed., pp. 25–105). New York: Wiley.

Charlesworth, W. R. (1992). Darwin and developmental psychology: Past and present. *Developmental Psychology, 28,* 5–16.

Coie, J. D., & Dodge, K. A. (1998). Aggression and antisocial behavior. In W. Damon & N. Eisenberg (Eds.), *Handbook of child psychology: Vol. 3. Social, emotional, and personality development* (pp. 779–862). New York: Wiley.

Cummins, D. D. (1998). Cheater detection is modified by social rank: The impact of dominance on the evolution of cognitive functions. *Evolution and Human Behavior, 20,* 229–248.

Daly, M., & Wilson, M. (1984). A sociobiological analysis of human infanticide. In G. Hausfater & S. B. Hrdy (Eds.), *Infanticide: Comparative and evolutionary perspectives* (pp. 487–502). New York: Aldine de Gruyter.

Daly, M., & Wilson, M. (1996). Violence against children. *Current Directions in Psychological Science, 5,* 77–81.

Davis, H., & Perusse, R. (1988). Numerical competence in animals: Definitional issues, current evidence, and a new research agenda. *Behavioral and Brain Sciences, 11,* 561–615.

de Waal, F. B. M. (1989). *Peace making among primates.* Cambridge, MA: Harvard University Press.

Dunbar, R. I. M. (1992). Neocortex size as a constraint on group size in primates. *Journal of Human Evolution, 20,* 469–493.

Ellis, B. J., & Bjorklund, D. F. (Eds.). (2005). *Origins of the social mind: Evolutionary psychology and child development.* New York: Guilford Press.

Ellis, B. J., & Garber, J. (2000). Psychosocial antecedents of variation in girls' pubertal timing: Maternal depression, stepfather presence, and marital and family stress. *Child Development, 71,* 485–501.

Fagen, R. (1981). *Animal play behavior.* New York: Oxford University Press.

Fernald, A. (1992). Human maternal vocalizations to infants as biologically relevant signals: An evolutionary perspective. In J. H. Barkow, L. Cosmides, & J. Tooby (Eds.), *The adaptive mind: Evolutionary psychology and the generation of culture* (pp. 391–428). New York: Oxford University Press.

Flavell, J. H. (2000). Development of children's knowledge about the mental world. *International Journal of Behavioral Development, 24,* 15–23.

Geary, D. C. (1995). Reflections of evolution and culture in children's cognition: Implications for mathematical development and instruction. *American Psychologist, 50,* 24–37.

Geary, D. C. (1998). *Male, female: The evolution of human sex differences.* Washington, DC: American Psychological Association.

Geary, D. C. (2000). Evolution and proximate expression of human paternal investment. *Psychological Bulletin, 126,* 55–77.

Geary, D. C. (2003). Evolution and development of folk knowledge: Implications for children's learning. *Infancia y Aprendizaje, 26*(3), 287–308.

Geary, D. C. (2005). Folk knowledge and academic learning. In B. J. Ellis & D. F. Bjorklund (Eds.), *Origins of the social mind: Evolutionary psychology and child development* (pp. 493–519). New York: Guilford.

Geary, D. C., & Bjorklund, D. F. (2000). Evolutionary developmental psychology. *Child Development, 71,* 57–65.

Gelman, R., & Gallistel, R. (1978). *The child's understanding of number.* Cambridge, MA: Harvard University Press.

Gelman, R., & Williams, E. M. (1998). Enabling constraints for cognitive development and learning: Domain-specificity and epigenesis. In W. Damon (Series Ed.), D. Kuhn, & R. S. Siegler (Vol. Eds.), *Cognition, perception, and language: Vol. 2. Handbook of child psychology* (5th ed., pp. 575–630). New York: Wiley.

Gottlieb, G. (1991). Experiential canalization of behavioral development: Theory. *Developmental Psychology, 27,* 4–13.

Gottlieb, G. (1992). *Individual development and evolution: The genesis of novel behavior.* New York: Oxford University Press.

Gottlieb, G. (1997). *Synthesizing nature-nurture: Prenatal roots of instinctive behavior.* Mahwah, NJ: Erlbaum.

Harris, J. R. (1995). Where is the child's environment? A group socialization theory of development. *Psychological Review, 102,* 458–489.

Harris, J. R. (2005). Social behavior and personality development: The role of experiences with siblings and with peers. In B. J. Ellis & D. F. Bjorklund (Eds.), *Origins of the social mind: Evolutionary psychology and child development (pp. 245–270).* Guilford: New York.

Hauser, M. D., Carey, S., & Hauser, L. B. (2000). Spontaneous number representation in semi-free-ranging rhesus monkeys. *Proceedings of the Royal Society of London. Series B, Biological Sciences, 267,* 829–833.

Hawley, P. H. (1999). The ontogenesis of social dominance: A strategy-based evolutionary perspective. *Developmental Review, 19,* 97–132.

Hawley, P. H. (2003). Strategies of control, aggression, and morality in preschoolers: An evolutionary perspective. *Journal of Experimental Child Psychology, 85,* 213–235.

Hernández Blasi, C., Bering, J. M., & Bjorklund, D. F. (2003). Psicología Evolucionista del Desarrollo: Contemplando la ontogénesis humana desde los ojos del evolucionismo (Evolutionary developmental psychology: Viewing human ontogeny through the eyes of evolutionary theory.) *Infancia y Aprendizaje, 26*(3), 267–285.

Hernández Blasi, C., & Bjorklund, D. F. (2003). Evolutionary developmental psychology: A new tool for better understanding human ontogeny. *Human Development, 46,* 259–281.

Hinde, R. A. (1980). *Ethology.* London: Fontana.

Hogrefe, G. J., Wimmer, H., & Perner, J. (1986). Ignorance versus false belief: A developmental lag in attribution of epistemic states. *Child Development, 57,* 567–582.

Hrdy, S. B. (1999). *Mother nature: A history of mothers, infants, and natural selection.* New York: Pantheon Books.

Hughes, C., & Cutting, A. L. (1999). Nature, nurture, and individual differences in early understanding of mind. *Psychological Science, 10,* 429–432.

Humphrey, N. K. (1976). The social function of intellect. In P. P. G. Bateson & R. Hinde (Eds.), *Growing points in ethology* (pp. 303–317). Cambridge, UK: Cambridge University Press.

Hyson, M. C., Hirsh-Pasek, K., & Rescorla, L. (1990). Academic environments in preschool: Challenge or pressure? *Early Education and Development, 1,* 401–423.

Jarrett, O. S., Maxwell, D. M., Dickerson, C., Hoge, P., Davies, G., & Yetley, A. (1998). Impact of recess on classroom behavior: Group effects and individual differences. *Journal of Educational Research, 92,* 121–126.

Jensen, P. S., Mrazek, D., Knapp, P. K., Steinberg, L., Pfeffer, C., Schwalter, J., et al. (1997). Evolution and revolution in child psychiatry: ADHD as a disorder of adaptation. *Journal of the American Academy of Child and Adolescent Psychiatry, 36,* 1672–1681.

Johnson, M. H., & de Haan, M. (2001). Developing cortical specialization for visual-cognitive function: The case of face recognition. In J. L. McClelland & R. S. Siegler (Eds.), *Mechanisms of cognitive development: Behavioral and neural perspectives* (pp. 253–270). Mahwah, NJ: Erlbaum.

Keenan, T., & Ellis, B. J. (2003). Children's performance on a false belief task is impaired by activation of an evolutionarily-canalized response system. *Journal of Experimental Child Psychology, 85,* 236–256.

Langlois, J. H., Ritter, J. M., Roggman, L. A., & Vaughn, L. S. (1991). Facial diversity and infant preferences for attractive faces. *Developmental Psychology, 27,* 79–84.

Leslie, A. (1994). ToMM, ToBY, and agency: Core architecture and domain specificity. In L. Hirschfeld & S. Gelman (Eds.), *Mapping the mind: Domain specificity in cognition and culture* (pp. 119–148). Cambridge, UK: Cambridge University Press.

Lewis, C., Freeman, N. H., Kyriakidou, C., Maridaki-Kassotaki, K., & Berridge, D. M. (1996). Social influence on false belief access: Specific sibling influences or general apprenticeship? *Child Development, 67,* 2930–2947.

Lickliter, R. (1996). Structured organisms and structured environments: Development systems and the construction of learning capacities. In J. Valsiner & H. Voss (Eds.), *The structure of learning processes* (pp. 86–107). Norwood, NJ: Ablex.

Lickliter, R., & Honeycutt, H. (2003). Developmental dynamics: Towards a biologically plausible evolutionary psychology. *Psychological Bulletin.*

Lochman, J. E., & Dodge, K. A. (1994). Social-cognitive processes of severely violent, moderately aggressive, and nonaggressive boys. *Journal of Consulting and Clinical Psychology, 62,* 366–374.

Lorenz, K. (1965). *Evolution and modification of behavior.* Chicago: Chicago University Press.

Nelson, K. (2005). Evolution and development of human memory systems. In B. J. Ellis & D. F. Bjorklund (Eds.), *Origins of the social mind: Evolutionary psychology and child development* (pp. 354–382). Guilford: New York.

O'Connell, J. F., Hawkes, K., & Blurton Jones, N. G. (1999). Grandmothering and the evolution of *Homo erectus. Journal of Human Evolution, 36,* 461–485.

Oppenheim, R. W. (1981). Ontogenetic adaptations and retrogressive processes in the development of the nervous system and behavior. In K. J. Connolly & H. F. R. Prechtl (Eds.), *Maturation and development: Biological and psychological perspectives* (pp. 73–108). Philadelphia: International Medical Publications.

Oyama, S. (2000). *The ontogeny of information: Developmental systems and evolution* (2nd ed.). New York: Cambridge University Press.

Pellegrini, A. D., & Bartini, M. (2000). A longitudinal study of bullying, victimization, and peer affiliation during the transition from primary to middle school. *American Educational Research Journal, 37,* 699–726.

Pellegrini, A. D., Huberty, P. D., & Jones, I. (1995). The effects of recess timing on children's playground and classroom behaviors. *American Educational Research Journal, 32,* 845–864.

Pellegrini, A. D., & Long, J. D. (2003). A sexual selection theory longitudinal analysis of sexual segregation and integration in early adolescence. *Journal of Experimental Child Psychology, 85,* 257–278.

Pellegrini, A. D., & Smith, P. K. (1998). Physical activity play: The nature and function of neglected aspect of play. *Child Development, 69,* 577–598.

Pinker, S. (1994). *The language instinct: How the mind creates language.* New York: Morrow.

Premack, D., & Woodruff, G. (1978). Does the chimpanzee have a theory of mind? *Behavioral and Brain Sciences, 4,* 515–526.

Profet, M. (1992). Pregnancy sickness as adaptation: A deterrent to maternal ingestion of teratogens. In J. H. Barkow, L. Cosmides, & J. Tooby (Eds.), *The adaptive mind: Evolutionary psychology and the generation of culture* (pp. 327–365). New York: Oxford University Press.

Ruffman, T., Perner, J., Naito, M., Parkin, L., & Clements, W. A. (1998). Older (but not younger) siblings facilitate false belief understanding. *Developmental Psychology, 34,* 161–174.

Sabbagh, M. A., & Taylor, M. (2000). Neural correlates of theory-of-mind reasoning: An event-related potential study. *Psychological Science, 11,* 46–50.

Schneider, W., Korkel, J., & Weinert, F. E. (1987). The effects of intelligence, self-concept, and attributional style on metamemory and memory behaviour. *International Journal of Behavioral Development, 10,* 281–299.

Shackelford, T. K., & Weekes-Shackelford, V. A. (in press). Why don't men pay child support? Insights from evolutionary psychology. In C. B. Crawford & C. Salmon (Eds.), *Evolutionary psychology, public policy, and private decisions.* Mahwah, NJ: Erlbaum.

Silverman, I., & Eals, M. (1992). Sex differences in spatial abilities: Evolutionary theory and data. In J. H. Barkow, L. Cosmides, & J. Tooby (Eds.), *The adapted mind: Evolutionary psychology and the generation of culture* (pp. 533–549). New York: Oxford University Press.

Simon, T. J., Hespos, S. J., & Rochat, P. (1995). Do infants understand simple arithmetic? A replication of Wynn, 1992. *Cognitive Development, 10,* 253–269.

Smith, P. K. (1982). Does play matter? Functional and evolutionary aspects of animal and human play. *Behavioral and Brain Sciences, 5,* 139–184.

Smith, P. K. (2003). Evolutionary developmental psychology and socio-emotional development. *Infancia y Aprendizaje, 26*(3), 309–324.

Spelke, E. S. (1991). Physical knowledge in infancy: Reflections on Piaget's theory. In S. Carey & R. Gelman (Eds.), *Epigenesis of mind: Essays in biology and knowledge* (pp. 133–169). Hillsdale, NJ: Erlbaum.

Spelke, E. S., & Newport, E. L. (1998). Nativism, empiricism, and the development of knowledge. In W. Damon (Series Ed.) & R. Learner (Vol. Ed.), *Theories of Theoretical models of human development: Vol. 1. Handbook of child psychology* (5th ed., pp. 275–340). New York: Wiley.

Starkey, P., Spelke, E. S., & Gelman, R. (1983). Detection of intermodal numerical correspondences by human infants. *Science, 222,* 179–181.

Starkey, P., Spelke, E. S., & Gelman, R. (1990). Numerical abstraction by human infants. *Cognition, 36,* 97–127.

Stipek, D. (1984). Young children's performance expectations: Logical analysis or wishful thinking. In J. G. Nicholls (Ed.), *Advances in motivation and achievement: Vol. 3. The development of achievement motivation* (pp. 33–56). Greenwich, CT: JAI.

Strauss, M. S., & Curtis, L. E. (1981). Infant perception of numerosity. *Child Development, 52,* 1146–1152.

Strayer, F. F., & Noel, J. M. (1986). The prosocial and antisocial functions of aggression. In C. Zahn-Waxler, E. M. Cummings, & R. Iannoti (Eds.), *Altruism and aggression* (pp. 107–131). New York: Cambridge University Press.

Sulkowski, G. M., & Hauser, M. D. (2001). Can rhesus monkeys spontaneously subtract? *Cognition, 79,* 239–262.

Sulloway, F. J. (1996). *Born to rebel: Birth order, family dynamics, and creative lives.* New York: Pantheon.

Tomasello, M. (1999). *The cultural origins of human cognition.* Cambridge, MA: Harvard University Press.

Tooby, J., & Cosmides, L. (1992). The psychological foundations of culture. In J. H. Barkow, L. Cosmides, & J. Tooby (Eds.), *The adapted mind: Evolutionary psychology and the generation of culture* (pp. 19–139). New York: Oxford University Press.

Trivers, R. (1972). Parental investment and sexual selection. In B. Campbell (Ed.), *Sexual selection and the descent of man* (pp. 136–179). New York: Aldine de Gruyter.

Uller, C., Carey, S., Huntley-Fenner, G., & Klatt, L. (1999). What representations might underlie infant numerical knowledge? *Cognitive Development, 14,* 1–36.

Watson, A. C., Nixon, C. L., Wilson, A., & Capage, L. (1999). Social interaction skills and theory of mind in young children. *Developmental Psychology, 35,* 386–391.

Weekes-Shackelford, V., & Bjorklund, D. F. (in press). Evolutionary psychology and applied developmental science. In C. Fisher & R. M. Lerner (Eds.), *Applied developmental science encyclopedia.* Medford, MA: Tufts University Press.

Weisfeld, G. E., & Billings, R. (1988). Observations on adolescence. In K. B. MacDonald (Ed.), *Sociobiological perspectives on human development* (pp. 207–233). New York: Springer-Verlag.

Weisfeld, G. E., Czilli, T., Phillips, K. A., Gall, J. A., & Lichtman, C. M. (2003). Possible olfaction-based mechanisms in human kin recognition and inbreeding avoidance. *Journal of Experimental Child Psychology, 85,* 279–295.

Wellman, H. M. (1990). *The child's theory of mind.* Cambridge, MA: MIT Press.

Wellman, H. M., Cross, D., & Watson, J. (2001). Meta-analysis of theory-of-mind development: The truth about false belief. *Child Development, 72,* 655–684.

West-Eberhard, M. J. (2003). *Developmental plasticity and evolution.* Oxford, England: Oxford University Press.

Wynn, K. (1992). Addition and subtraction by human infants. *Nature, 358,* 749–750.

CHAPTER 30

Evolutionary
Personality Psychology

AURELIO JOSÉ FIGUEREDO, JON A. SEFCEK, GENEVA VASQUEZ,
BARBARA H. BRUMBACH, JAMES E. KING, and W. JAKE JACOBS

THIS CHAPTER IS divided into four principal sections. The first reviews several major current evolutionary psychological theories of personality. The next two cover empirical evidence for these theories in human and nonhuman animal personality research. Because little empirical research examining personality has been done within evolutionary psychology, the data go outside the evolutionary literature for empirical confirmation or disconfirmation of evolutionary theories. The final section reviews the methodological merits and limitations of the research with a focus on methodological approaches that might best test evolutionary theories of personality explicitly.

The material presented is neither exhaustive nor conclusive. Instead, we offer a template of a systematic approach needed to bring theory and data in evolutionary personality psychology together. To that end, we apply the method of multiple working hypotheses (Chamberlin, 1897) and strong inference (Platt, 1964). This procedure specifies plausible alternative hypotheses and then obtains empirical data to help decide among them.

A REVIEW OF CURRENT EVOLUTIONARY
THEORIES OF PERSONALITY

What follows is a brief review of several of the major evolutionary theories of personality to be critically evaluated.

THEORIES OF SELECTIVE NEUTRALITY

Tooby and Cosmides (1990) suggest that heritable personality differences in humans do *not* result from unique personality adaptations. Using an evolutionary psychological framework, they suggest that personality is a product of environmental (situational) differences (e.g., Mischel, 1968) in humans. They propose several ways that variation in personality could occur, including reactive heritability, frequency-dependent strategies, and nonadaptive developmental amplification of traits.

By their account, psychological differences between individuals and cultures are the product of different "manifest psychologies" based on an innate, underlying, and universally evolved psychology. The innate psychology, developing in different environments, produces these manifest differences. In the *environment of evolutionary adaptedness* (EEA), psychological adaptations were necessarily complex and coordinated to solve adaptive problems. The system's "uniform, regular, and predictable" parts (Tooby & Cosmides, 1990, p. 28) interact in a coordinated fashion. "It is this interdependence among subcomponents that requires a monomorphism of integrated functional design" (p. 27). Hence, most heritable psychological traits are not likely the result of complex adaptations. Tooby and Cosmides (1990) assert that only traits with zero heritability and no variation are likely to be adaptations produced by natural selection. Individual genetic variation is "generally limited to quantitative variation in the components of . . . species typical psychological mechanisms" (p. 24). Individual variation exists, but not enough to interfere with the functioning of the cognitive system. "Thus, personality variation is not likely to consist of an alternative, wholly different, coordinated design that differs 'from the ground up.'" (p. 30).

Tooby and Cosmides (1990) describe six ways adaptively coordinated personality traits may arise from differential activation of mental organs: (1) stable activation of a mental organ in stable and enduring situations, leading to stable differences between individuals; (2) a stable individual-environment relationship regulating differential thresholds of activation; (3) early environmental cues that differentially adjust threshold of activation, leading to stable, lifelong developmental paths; (4) frequency-dependent personality traits that exist because the trait is rare and produces an advantage; (5) nonadaptive stable differences when more or less irrelevant aspects of human psychology arise; and (6) reactive heritability accounts for individual differences when a genetic predisposition to a certain trait triggers the adoption of one strategy over another.

Theories of Adaptive Significance

Diverging from Tooby and Cosmides's (1990) views, Buss (1991, p. 471) proposed that personality, more specifically, the *five-factor model* (FFM) of personality, is a central aspect of the adaptive landscape in which humans evolved. "Perceiving, attending to and acting upon differences in others has been . . . crucial for solving adaptive problems" (Buss, 1997, p. 334).

Buss (1991, p. 473; see also Buss & Greiling, 1999) suggested that if, instead of arising due to noise or by-products of other adaptations, personality differences reflect distinct adaptive strategies, then there are only four explanations for individual differences in humans: (1) Personality differences are heritable alternative strategies; (2) personality differences are "heritable calibrations of psychological mechanisms" arising through fluctuation of optimal strategies over time and place; (3) individual differences are due to situation-dependent adaptive strategies, implying that each human could develop any personality traits or degree of personality traits; and (4) individual differences arise through ontogenetic threshold calibration.

Evolutionary psychology helps clarify the role of personality by separating evolved mechanisms from actual behavior (Buss, 1991). Many context-dependent acts may represent adaptive functioning of a single psychological mechanism. Alternately, many psychological mechanisms may combine to perform a single behavior or suite of behaviors. These principles of personality remove the problematic distinction between consistency of personality and situation specificity. A species occupying niches that require individuals to engage in different optimal strategies might produce individual differences (Figueredo & King, 2001; MacDonald, 1998). Thus, individual differences may be due to ". . . differences in ability or morphology [that] produce differences in the effectiveness with which alternative strategies can be adopted or carried out" (Buss, 1991, p. 479).

Asserting that personality is central to social interactions, Buss (1991) notes that most of the terms associated with the FFM personality traits are evaluative adjectives. Hogan (cited in Buss, 1991, p. 471) argued these trait terms "reflect observer evaluations of others as potential contributors to, or exploiters of, the group's resources." Buss suggests that Extraversion has repeatedly been characterized as one of the first two factors in personality studies because human groups are generally hierarchical—group members at the top of the hierarchy often experience mating advantages. Reciprocal relationships also characterize human groups. Buss suggests this is why Agreeableness is the second factor found in most personality-descriptive taxonomies. Agreeable individuals are unlikely exploiters of reciprocal alliances. Buss (1997) also proposed that mean sex differences in personality arose due to different adaptive problems faced by men and women. This is consistent with the finding that men tend to be higher in traits such as dominance and women, in traits such as nurturance.

Miller (2000) proposed an alternative view of human mental capabilities. He suggested that both natural *and* sexual selection will illuminate why there is substantial variability in behavior among individuals. Sexually selected fitness indicators are traits that all animals use to display individual fitness. Advertisement of these traits (fitness indicators) communicates an individual's ability to deter predators, quality as a potential mate, and ability to overcome intrasexual rivals. The makeup of fitness indicators, however, appears at odds with trait adaptations formed by natural selection. Reliable fitness indicators differentiate among individuals on the basis of mate quality. Therefore, rather than exhibiting low genotypic variance and heritability, fitness indicators must exhibit high genotypic variance and variability because invariant traits do not indicate differential fitness by reliably discriminating between high- and low-fitness individuals.

Weiss, King, and Enns (2002) further developed this idea, suggesting that genetic correlations among positive fitness-enhancing characteristics and conspicuous indicators of that fitness be named *covitality*. Thus, happiness in chimpanzees, and humans, may indicate overall fitness and should be genetically correlated with fitness-enhancing characteristics such as health, immune system vigor, body symmetry, and reproductive success.

MacDonald (1998, p. 142) pointed to two extant camps of evolutionary psychology-based theories of personality, one consisting of "universal psychological mechanisms as a set of adaptations" and the other of "the world of individual differences as a continuous distribution of viable alternate strategies." MacDonald, who assumed that "personality variation represents a continuous distribution of phenotypes that matches a continuous distribution of viable strategies"

(p. 139), proposed the genetic variation underlying individual differences allows species with differentiated personalities to occupy a diverse range of social and environmental niches. Natural selection may render different parts of the personality distribution and the strategies associated with different personality traits optimal under different conditions. MacDonald's theory requires that the relative fitness of individuals possessing differing levels of personality traits be about equal.

MacDonald (1998) suggested individual differences in personality are central to the adaptive landscape in which humans evolved (Buss, 1991). He noted several areas of focus in personality theory that can be used to interpret individual differences from an evolutionary perspective. Parental investment theory (Trivers, 1972), for example, predicts male tendencies to devote more energy to mating effort and female tendencies to devote more resources to parental investment. Thus, it is unsurprising that males rate higher in personality domains subsumed under the behavioral approach system, for example, social dominance, sensation seeking, extraversion, and risk taking. These characteristics presumably provided survival and reproductive advantages to males in our evolutionary past. Females rate higher on scales of Nurturance/Love. Presumably, these characteristics provided reproductive and survival advantages to females and their offspring (MacDonald, 1998). MacDonald also argues that developmental patterns in personality characteristics are consistent with evolutionary theory. Sex differences in behavioral activation systems are, for example, maximal during late adolescence and early adulthood, declining throughout adulthood. Late adolescence is precisely the time when individual reproductive potential peaks. Conversely, aspects of temperament such as sensitivity to reward, which emerges in infancy or behavioral inhibition characteristics, which emerge toward the end of the first year of life, remain stable throughout life (p. 135).

THEORIES OF FREQUENCY DEPENDENCE

Wilson (1994) and Figueredo and King (2001) suggest that frequency-dependent selection offers the best framework for understanding individual differences in personality. Wilson identified three conditions under which behavioral polymorphisms might occur: (1) trophic (same species utilizes different resources in an environment), (2) reproductive (sexual dimorphism where the different sexes adapt to different circumstances), and (3) life history (differences are genetically maintained in a population when reproductive benefits change with ecological niches). He also identified three mechanisms from which polymorphism can arise: (1) genetic differences producing genetic polymorphism directly; (2) a single genotype, through phenotypic plasticity and epigenetic influences, producing different adaptive phenotypes; and (3) ontogenetic shifts throughout each individual life cycle producing sequential differences in phenotypic expression. If the fitness of one genotype depends on coextant genotypes (frequency dependent), then adaptive genetic differences can be maintained and stabilized in the population. Even with sexual recombination, this can occur because assortative mating eliminates maladaptive combinations.

Wilson's model has four basic components. First, individuals can be generalists (moderately adapted to different niches) or specialists (specifically adapted to do very well in a single niche). Generalists or specialists receive the greater adaptive benefits depending on the nature of the available niches. Second, individuals evaluate and choose niches. The third and fourth components involve negative density and frequency-dependence. The fitness of the individual depends on the number and traits exhibited by other individuals in the niche. In any given population, Wilson predicts there will be a combination of "adaptive genetic variation . . . and phenotypic plasticity. . ." (p. 232) with a "mixture of 'developmental generalists' that can match their phenotype to local conditions and 'developmental specialists' that cannot" (p. 230). Using the bold-shy dimension in human personality as an illustration, Wilson suggests there could have been two ancestral niches, one for risk takers and one for risk avoiders (likely to be reflected in the shy-bold continuum). To support the idea, Wilson describes the risk-taker, risk-avoider continuum existing in nonhuman species. Additionally, Wilson uses Kagan, Reznick, and Suidman's (1988, cited in Wilson, 1994) work on the heritability of shyness and boldness in infants as tentative support of the generalist-specialist model. Generally, children at either personality extreme demonstrate shyness and boldness traits stably. Those in the middle do not.

Clarke and Boinski (1995), based on the relevant primate literature, concluded that the bold-shy dimension in humans also characterizes traits in nonhuman primates. A heritable basis for temperament appears to exist, but experience modifies temperament. They also suggest that differences in the life-history strategy of species relate to temperament. Some evidence suggests that species with "active and instrumental foraging strategies" (p. 118) are bolder than species without those strategies.

Figueredo (1995) suggested a sociality hypothesis of individual differences, assuming: (1) Personality differences in individuals are characteristic of social species, and (2) individual variation on personality dimensions might be adaptive in social competition. Using the FFM, Figueredo and King (2001) suggested that more types of within-group social relations increase the sophistication of those relationships. Frequency-dependent selection may explain how different and fragmented personality dimensions provide a balance for individuals adopting alternative or conditional adaptive strategies.

These authors predicted that three phenomena will increase personality variation in social, but not nonsocial, species during evolution. First, each of the FFM dimensions have a pole (e.g., high Agreeableness) that appears to enhance fitness relative to the opposite pole, thereby fostering directional selection toward "ideal" humans. Frequency-dependent selection, however, may disrupt directional selection. For example, a preponderance of ambitious, assertive, and dominant extraverts could create a niche for low extraversion individuals benefiting from a cautious, silent, secretive approach to life. Some balance between the extremes is the most likely result.

Second, variation of frequency-dependent selection pressures across different personality dimensions may increase personality variation. For example, highly Extraverted individuals might achieve higher fitness in populations with a high proportion of Agreeable (tolerant, even gullible) individuals. Once the proportion of high Extraversion individuals exceeded a threshold, however, selection may favor low Agreeableness individuals with wily, deceitful, and "street-smart" proclivities. A large number of cross-dimension interactions and consequent selection are possible.

Third, interactions across the FFM dimensions *within* individuals may affect individual differences in personality traits. The literature examining the FFM and personality disorders (e.g., Costa & Widiger, 1994) shows that the severity of psychopathology is not a simple function of the number and extent of suboptimal values on one or more personality factors. High scores on Agreeableness and Emotional Stability, for example, ordinarily associated with high fitness and successful social adjustment, combined with low scores on some facets of Extraversion and Conscientiousness, predict high scores on schizoid scales.

Figueredo and King (2001) predict that three phenomena will increase individual differences only in species that are social *and* engage in extended and intense interactions. Individual differences will be greatest when the social structure of the species supports frequent social interaction across many individuals within relatively stable groups. Furthermore, greater densities of free social interaction between males and females occupying different dominance positions will produce greater individual differences. In species with small groups and rigidly enforced dominance hierarchies, individual difference will be muted.

The large variety of social structures within nonhuman primates permits tests of this hypothesis. The theory predicts, for example, smaller individual differences in solitary species and species that form monogamous family units or single-male harems, but larger individual differences in species with age-graded or multimale social structures. Hence, chimpanzees should display greater individual differences than orangutans or gorillas. Likewise, macaque monkeys should display greater individual differences than baboons or langur monkeys.

Documented selective pressures can be viewed as broadly analogous to the forces proposed for the social evolution of individuation (Figueredo & King, 2001). One of these is the *competitive exclusion principle*, in which no two species can permanently share the same ecological niche. Evolutionary responses to this situation include the local extermination of one species by the other (competitive exclusion). Others are *niche-splitting* and *character displacement*, which reduce competition by the species diverging ecologically. These strategies are not intentionally implemented in the interests of peaceful coexistence. They are automatic consequences of depressed fitness experienced by individuals in the zone of greatest competition between species—and the consequent relative fitness bonus experienced by individuals at the outer extremes of the overlapping population distributions. Another ecological analogy is mixed-species flocks in birds. Flocking birds gain fitness benefits through enhanced antipredator vigilance and "selfish herd" effects. Those flocking with their own species, however, must bear the cost of greater social competition (e.g., for food). In contrast, birds flocking with *other* species may experience the benefits of increased antipredator vigilance in the context of a relative "competitive release" from conspecifics. Thus, mixed-species flocking with noncompeting allospecifics might constitute a form of optimal foraging under risk of predation.

Similarly, ecological analogies are found in theories of optimal territory size. Some explain the unequal sizes of territories in hummingbirds as a consequence of social competition, where a balance between the costs and benefits of territorial defense produces a distribution of roughly equal numbers of flowers in adjacent hummingbird territories. An implicit trade-off between the quantity (size) and the quality (resources) of the alternative territories available to any individual produces this outcome, the *ideal free distribution*.

Assume there is, for any given species in a given situation, an optimal norm of response or *optimal response disposition* (ORD). Deviations from this norm are not selectively neutral. Selective pressure for a species-typical monomorphism exactly at this optimum creates a centripetal force against substantial individuation. On the other hand, clustering of the entire population at the ORD is likely to produce intense social competition in the "hump" of the distribution, with the ORD setting the central tendency. This would, relatively speaking, reduce social competition at the "tails" of the same distribution, to the extent that random forces of mutation and recombination produced any variability. Reduced social competition creates disruptive selection for individuation as a centrifugal force perhaps partially counteracting selective pressure toward the ORD. Under certain circumstances, then, competitive release experienced by individuals in the tails of the distribution could compensate for the cost of deviation from species-typical norm of response. This creates an ideal free distribution of alternative behavioral phenotypes in the population by the progressive expansion of tails of distribution around the optimal central tendency. Dispersion of individuals will create bell-shaped curves along different dimensions of personality.

PERSONALITY IN NONHUMAN ANIMALS: EMPIRICAL EVIDENCE

What follows is a review of the empirical evidence supporting the theories of personality in nonhuman animals.

NONHUMAN ANIMAL PERSONALITY PAST TO PRESENT

A chronic omission of animal models from personality theory is one reason that we have only begun to understand contributions of biological, genetic, and environmental factors to individual differences in humans. Likewise, a chronic omission of evolutionary-based models of human personality from nonhuman personality theory limits our ability to test evolutionary theories of personality. A comparative approach to personality—and the inclusion of an evolutionary perspective—permits us to account for forces shaping behavior.

The study of personality in nonhuman species is an amalgamation of research drawn from disparate scientific areas (Gosling, 2001). A review of such research requires examination of data from agricultural sciences, animal behavior, biology, psychology, veterinary sciences, and zoology, incorporating research ranging from naturalistic and uncontrolled anecdotal reports (e.g., Darwin, 1859/1998; de Waal, 1998; Goodall, 1986) to laboratory-based, highly controlled observations (e.g., Capitanio, Mendoza, & Baroncelli, 1999). Recent resurgence of interest in nonhuman personality has increased studies from a handful during the 1970s to hundreds during the past three decades (see Gosling, 2001).

Although each endeavor attempted to identify species-specific personality dimensions, dimensions strikingly similar to the human FFM have been identified across many species (Gosling & John, 1999), including chimpanzees (Figueredo & King, 2001). Extraversion (E), Neuroticism (N), and Agreeableness (A) appeared across many species: E in 10, N in 9, and A in another 10. Consistent with King and Figueredo (1997), Dominance (D) appeared in 9 of the species studied—but not in humans. Moreover, Conscientiousness (C) appeared in humans and chimpanzees. Other researchers detected a learned and retained D hierarchy in octopuses, permitting the generalization of D to 10 of the species studied (Cigliano, 1993).

Methodological Problems in the Study of Animal Personality

The generalizability of personality factors across species supports the construct of personality in nonhuman animals and demands an evolutionary account of personality. Unfortunately, methodological problems constrain conclusions based on these studies. Some of these limitations (see Mischel, 1968; Mischel & Peake, 1982) relative to human personality research were addressed and, in many minds, refuted by Kenrick and Funder (1988). Gosling and Vazire (2002) examined the research in animal personalities and argued that, although earlier studies were restricted by at least one of these limitations, the whole body of literature offers some evidence of improvement.

One of the most hotly debated topics in human personality research has, for example, been whether consistent personality traits can be detected across time and situations. Many studies have explored this topic using a variety of species (see Gosling & John, 1999). Notably, Stevenson-Hinde, Stillwell-Barnes, and Zunz (1980a, 1980b) showed temporal and cross-situational stability in two personality traits (Fearful and Activity) for rhesus monkeys over a 3-year period. King and Landau (2003) showed cross-situational stability in ratings on Subjective Well-Being (SWB) in zoo chimpanzees. Others have examined short-term temporal stability of personality variables (see Gosling & John, 1999). Although the research is not definitive, it supports the notion that temporal and cross-situational stabilities in animal personality exist.

One promising development is the application of *generalizability theory* (GT) to the problem. Figueredo, Cox, and Rhine (1995), for example, used GT to test concurrently the convergent validity, temporal stability, and interrater reliability of personality factors in stumptail macaques and zebra finches. The application of GT is promising because it is more suitable than conventional factor analysis for small sample sizes.

Nevertheless, comparative animal personality is in measurement disarray. Although a few well-established and cross-culturally validated personality scales within the human domain exist, nonhuman personality theory enjoys no such luxury. Since 1936, for example, 11 studies examining chimpanzee personality traits were published. None used the same rating scales. For an evolutionary account of personality to make theoretical sense, comparable trait measurements must be accessible within and across species. Despite this, King and Figueredo (1997) described similarities in personality factor structures between chimpanzees and humans, and Lilienfeld, Gershon, Duke, Marino, and de Waal (1999) reported positive relationships between the chimpanzee factor structures they describe and those described by King and Figueredo.

A simple comparative approach that ignores evolutionary theory is scientifically inadequate. Unfortunately, most nonhuman personality literature ignores the roles selection plays in shaping behavior. We now turn to a literature that examines two evolutionary hypotheses of personality, *covitality* (Weiss et al., 2002) and the *sociality hypothesis* (Figueredo & King, 2001).

EVOLUTION OF HAPPINESS

A largely unasked question in evolutionary psychology is, "Why did happiness evolve?" (but see Grinde, 2002). Proximate causes of happiness have been intensively studied (Diener, Suh, & Lucas, 1999), and a large literature indicates that happiness, or SWB, correlates with potentially fitness-enhancing qualities including longevity (Danner, Snowdon, & Friesen, 2001) and health (Watson, 1988). Nevertheless, we could ask if happiness contributes to fitness beyond its phenotypic correlation with traits reflecting fitness-enhancing properties.

Weiss et al. (2002) proposed an evolutionary basis for happiness based on personality studies of zoo-housed chimpanzees. Chimpanzee SWB (King & Landau, 2003) correlates highly with a broadly defined personality factor related to dominance and social prowess (King & Figueredo, 1997). Weiss et al. found a genetic correlation approaching unity between happiness and the Dominance factor, indicating a substantial overlap between the heritable components of Dominance and SWB. They concluded SWB serves as a conspicuous fitness indicator based on fitness-enhancing properties such as access to mates, allies, and food resources. The genetic correlation between happiness and Dominance makes it a genetically enforced "honest signal" of Dominance. According to fitness indicator theory, measures correlated with fitness such as number of surviving offspring, body symmetry, and overall health are not merely phenotypically, but genetically, correlated with happiness. Weiss et al. named the predicted genetic correlations among happiness and various measures of positive fitness *covitality*—as the converse of *comorbidity*.

EVOLUTION AND VARIABILITY IN PERSONALITY

The recent appearance of animal personality studies opens a set of evolutionary questions about the role of individual differences within evolution. One set asks the range of behaviors and traits that reliably vary across individuals within any species. Sponges, animals so passive and listless they were assumed to be plants until the eighteenth century, must lie close to absolute zero on a scale of personality diversity. The evolution of freely moving animals equipped with true brains increased the possible range of personality expression. The first general dimensions probably included traits related to activity levels, perhaps a primitive version of Extraversion. Another early personality dimension may have included reactivity or aggression to novel, potentially threatening stimuli, a possible precursor to Emotionality or Neuroticism. A third early personality dimension may have included exploratory (curiosity) tendencies. Gosling (2001), reviewing individual differences in behavior across a wide variety of vertebrate species, found that among reptiles, fish, and invertebrates, the only measured dimensions fell into the three categories noted previously.

Extant evidence indicates the magnitude of individual differences in personality *within* species is predictable across taxa. Intensely social species, for example, are predicted to display magnified and systematic individual differences. This point, suggested by Clarke and Boinski (1995), was made explicit by Figueredo and King (2001), who described a sociality hypothesis for individual variation in personality. The emergence of social groups of intensively interacting conspecifics was, undoubtedly, the greatest impetus to diversity of personality traits. Indeed, most of the individual items (usually adjectives) used to assess human personality reflect qualities of social interactions. A purely solitary species would have a personality structure constrained to narrowly defined versions of the three dimensions noted earlier. Personality becomes evident in a social species.

As a preliminary test of this hypothesis, we counted the social and nonsocial species in which personality has been documented. A "social" species was defined as one in which individuals gather for more than mating. Of the 64 species reviewed, 59 were classified as social. The remaining five—cheetahs, hedgehogs, minks, octopuses, and orangutans—deserve attention to both evolutionary histories and intellectual prowess. Orangutans appear to have evolved from a social to a solitary species in recent evolutionary time. Octopuses are intelligent organisms that show social dominance hierarchies when artificially grouped together. Likewise, although they do not seek social groups, hedgehogs and minks den together in the wild and form hierarchies when socially housed.

Nevertheless, an adequate test of the sociality hypothesis entails rating species with differing degrees of sociality on identical sets of personality items. As a second test, we compared personality ratings of zoo-housed chimpanzees and orangutans. Chimpanzees live in large, promiscuous groups; orangutans are largely solitary. Ratings on 43 personality-descriptive adjectives encompassing the FFM were obtained from 145 chimpanzees and 127 orangutans (see King & Figueredo, 1997; Weiss, King, Perkins, & Blanke, 2003). The chimpanzees displayed no greater personality variance than the solitary orangutans. Male orangutans had greater variance than male chimpanzees on 24 of the 43 items. Female orangutans had greater variance on 30 of the 43 items. This unexpected result could indicate that the mechanisms enhancing interindividual variability arise later in hominid evolution. Alternatively, the orangutan could represent an ambiguous case because the species was ancestrally social. Finally, proper application of the comparative method requires more than two species compared because a single pair of species might differ for reasons other than that specifically hypothesized. Therefore, more comparative tests are needed before the sociality hypothesis of the evolution of personality is conclusively supported or disproved.

PERSONALITY AND SELECTION IN HUMANS: EMPIRICAL EVIDENCE

What follows is a review of the empirical evidence supporting evolutionary theories of personality in humans with specific emphasis on evidence for natural, sexual, and frequency dependent selection of personality traits.

EVIDENCE FOR NATURAL SELECTION OF PERSONALITY TRAITS

We divided our literature search into two main components of fitness: (1) survivorship and (2) fecundity. In population dynamics, these quantities, when multiplied and integrated across time, predict the estimated population growth. At the individual level, this product translates into lifetime reproductive success. Survivorship is expected longevity or life expectancy. Fecundity is expected fertility or production of offspring. Our review of relations among personality variation, survivorship, and fecundity was subdivided into two divisions for each concept: (1) personality correlates of actual or completed survivorship or fecundity and (2) personality correlates of expected or predicted survivorship or fecundity. The latter category included personality correlates of likely predictors of either survivorship or fecundity, such as health status or reproductive behavior, and is one step removed from documented differences in actual survivorship or fecundity.

Personality Correlates of Completed Longevity   Denollet et al. (1996) reported that *Type D personality*, the tendency to suppress emotional distress (high negative affectivity and high social inhibition), is positively correlated to long-term risk of mortality in patients with coronary heart disease, independent of biomedical risk factors.

Several studies on relationships between personality and longevity used data from the Terman Life Cycle Study of Children. Tucker and Friedman (1996) reported that children who were rated by parents and teachers as *cheerful* and having a sense of humor were at higher mortality risk across the life span than less optimistic peers. Martin et al. (2002) suggested this is because cheerful children are more careless about their health throughout life. Conscientiousness also correlated positively with longevity (Friedman, 2000; Friedman et al., 1993; Schwartz et al., 1995), more in males than females, possibly due to a higher likelihood of health-promoting behavior and avoidance of health risks in conscientious individuals. Males with mood instability (higher Neuroticism), however, were at higher mortality risk across the life span than more emotionally stable males, possibly because of the *externalizing* behaviors (i.e., volatility, aggressiveness, and/or hyperactivity) associated with male Neuroticism.

Personality Correlates of Predictors of Longevity   Individuals scoring higher on the Life Orientation Test (LOT), a commonly used measure of optimism, report fewer physical symptoms and quicker and better recovery after surgery (Tucker & Friedman, 1996). Ebert, Tucker, and Roth (2002), however, found no relation between a revised version of the LOT and general health status or physical symptoms. Nevertheless, a Sense of Coherence (SOC) trait contributed uniquely to self-reported physical and mental health. Individuals high on SOC report life is understandable, manageable, and meaningful, whereas those low on SOC report life is chaotic and out of control. Neuroticism and Extraversion were positively related to reports of physical symptoms (implying a negative effect on health).

or just perception of it

Ryan and Frederick (1997) reported that Subjective Vitality (SV), a trait positively correlated to Positive Affect and negatively correlated to Negative Affect, is negatively associated with fewer physical problems (e.g., headaches, shortness of breath). SV, defined as reflecting general *organismic well-being*, was expected to "covary with both psychological and somatic factors that impact the energy available to the self" (p. 529). SV was negatively associated with Neuroticism, but positively associated with Extraversion and Conscientiousness.

Type A personality, frequently criticized as factorially complex, contains a "toxic" component (hostility) negatively associated with Agreeableness (Dembroski & Costa, 1988). German managers, for example, with Type A personality and external locus of control reported greater perceived levels of stress (especially interpersonal sources of stress) and poorer physical and mental health than those with *Type B personality* and internal locus of control (Kirkcaldy, Shephard, & Furnham, 2002).

Hostile Type A personality is a risk factor for cardiovascular disease (Fried-men, Hawley, & Tucker, 1994). Several psychophysiological mechanisms have been proposed to account for this relationship: (1) The association of Type A personality with sympathetic and parasympathetic activation might be linked to factors such as increased arterial stress, changes in lipid metabolism, and platelet aggregation, possibly leading to manifestations such as atherosclerosis; (2) a possible association between Type A personality and immunosuppression might be mediated by increased stress; (3) hostile or neurotic individuals are also more likely than others to abuse dangerous substances (e.g., tobacco, alcohol, and other drugs); and (4) the tendency of hostile and cynical people to have interpersonal disputes may lead to ill health through loss of social support, increasing physiological hyperreactivity, and increased number of stressful situations.

Many studies (Tucker & Friedman, 1996) report Neuroticism is weakly but reliably associated with diseases such as coronary heart disease. A meta-analysis of more than 100 studies (Friedman & Booth-Kewley, 1987) reported that coronary heart disease, asthma, peptic ulcers, rheumatoid arthritis, and headaches were associated with depression and anxiety (both manifestations of trait Neuroticism) and, to a lesser extent, with anger and hostility (associated with low Agreeableness). One longitudinal study found positive relations between individuals with physical health trajectories of high and increasing symptoms and hostility and anxiety (Aldwin, Spiro, Levenson, & Cupertino, 2001). A general mechanism proposed to account for relations between personality and health (Kiecolt-Glaser, McGuire, Robles, & Glaser, 2002) invokes a role for negative emotionality in producing distress-related immune dysregulation by stimulating proinflammatory cytokines, factors implicated in a spectrum of age-related conditions.

Personality Correlates of Completed Fertility   A retrospective twin study examining completed fertility in more than 1,000 postmenopausal women (Eaves, Martin, Heath, Hewitt, & Neale, 1990) found an interactive relationship between Neuroticism and Extraversion. Highest reproductive success was associated with women with either: (1) high Neuroticism and low Extraversion, or (2) low Neuroticism and high Extraversion.

A study comparing fertile to organically and functionally infertile women (Singh, Srivastava, & Nigam, 1992) found that organically infertile women scored higher on measures of Anxiety, Stress, Fatigue, and Guilt and lower on measures of Depression, Regression, Extraversion, and Arousal than fertile women. Functionally infertile women scored higher on Fatigue and Guilt, but lower on Anxiety, Stress, Depression, Regression, Extraversion, and Arousal.

Fasino et al. (2002) reported functionally infertile people scored higher on measures of Harm Avoidance than organically infertile people or controls. They suggested that high Harm Avoidance might decrease fertility because it is correlated with lower serotonergic tone (responsible for the modulation of sexual behavior); might decrease the frequency, length, emotional involvement, and satisfaction of sexual intercourse; and might alter hormonal levels in response to stressful environmental or relational situations. Infertile women also scored lower on Cooperativeness than controls. In addition, functionally infertile women scored lower on Cooperativeness and Self-Directedness than organically infertile women, and functionally infertile men scored lower in Novelty Seeking than organically infertile men. Wischmann, Stammer, Scherg, Gerhad, and Verres (2001) reported functionally infertile women scored higher on Depression and Anxiety than controls, suggesting a role for negative emotionality and stress in the etiology of functional infertility.

Personality Correlates of Predictors of Fertility   Hellhammer, Hubert, Phil, Frieschem, and Nieschlag (1985) reported that high Self-Confidence, Extraversion, and Social Assertiveness correlate negatively with male fertility. Men from infertile couples scored lower than controls on Critique Anxiety, Contact Anxiety, Inability to Resist Demands, and Feelings of Guilt, but higher on Ability to Demand. Hypophyseal gonadotropins (e.g., LH, FSH) correlated positively with Sociability and Extraversion; whereas levels of sex steroids (testosterone and estradiol) correlated positively with Feelings of Guilt and Norm Orientation, but negatively with Ability to Demand. Accessory gland function (e.g., fructose, volume) also correlated positively with Critique Anxiety and Ability to Demand.

Alexithymia, a difficulty recognizing, identifying, and communicating emotions, reduced fantasy capacity, and externally oriented cognitive style was inversely associated with women's frequency of penile-vaginal intercourse (Brody, 2003). Lower alexithymia and more frequent intercourse were also associated with better indicators of physical and mental health.

Eysenck (1976) and Wilson (1997) examined responses from over 1,000 unmarried students and identified 14 sexuality factors. Extraversion correlated positively with Promiscuity and negatively with Nervousness and Prudishness. Students high on Introversion were more puritanical and downplayed the importance of physical sex. Neuroticism correlated positively with Excitement, Nervousness, Guilt, and Inhibition, and negatively with Satisfaction. Students high on Psychoticism were high on Curiosity, Premarital Sex, Promiscuity, and Hostility. Those high on Eysenck's Lie Scale (a measure of social desirability) were unadventurous and conventional, similar to those low on Psychoticism.

The authors found two orthogonal factors for Libido and Satisfaction. Extraversion correlated with permissiveness, strong libido, and desire for a variety in both partners and sexual activities. Neuroticism correlated with a range of sexual difficulties and with Excitement. Psychoticism was associated with tough, adventurous, and impersonal approaches to sexuality. The authors reported that men liked pornography and impersonal sex more than women did, whereas women expressed more contentment with their sex lives. Men were generally higher on Psychoticism than women. Other research showed that sex offenders were higher in Psychoticism than controls as well as other imprisoned men. Similarly, prostitutes scored higher in Psychoticism than other women.

EVIDENCE FOR SEXUAL SELECTION OF PERSONALITY TRAITS

A precondition for reproductive success in sexually reproducing species is obtaining and sometimes retaining a mate. The special adaptive problems posed by obtaining and retaining a mate, however, fall within the domain of sexual selection. Sexual selection can be subdivided into intrasexual competition and epigamic selection, or mate choice. Here we concentrate on documented relations between personality and mate choice. The dearth of information on relations between personality and intrasexual competition, except as it relates to selection between alternative sexual partners, precludes its discussion.

There are two dominant approaches to the study of relations between personality and mate choice. The first studies *absolute* preferences for one personality trait over another, called *consensual* preferences because they are similar across all individuals. The second studies *relative* preferences for a sexual partner's personality in relation to an individual's own personality. This type of preference presumes assortative mating according to personality and comes in two varieties: (1) *positive* assortative mating, based on attraction to similarity in personality with an individual's sexual partner, and (2) *negative* assortative mating, or *disassortative* mating, based on attraction to dissimilarity (or "complementarity") in personality with an individual's sexual partner. A distinction often made between the personality correlates of actual or completed mate choice is the study of extant sexual partners and the personality correlates of likely predictors of mate choice, such as expressed preferences for imaginary or idealized mates.

Absolute or Consensual Preferences   Using national and international samples, Buss (1985, 1989) reported men and women rate *kind and understanding* (Agreeableness?) and *intelligent* as the two most desired characteristics in a partner. Buss and Barnes (1986) found these two traits were joined by *exciting personality* (Extraversion?) on the list of consensual traits most desired by men and women in a partner. In another sample, the authors reported the 10 most highly valued mate characteristics were: *good companion, considerate, honest, affectionate, dependable, intelligent, kind, understanding, interesting to talk to,* and *loyal*. They suggest that these consensual cross-gender preferences maximize chances for marital satisfaction and marital survival by contributing to compatibility with the partner. Alternatively, these personality characteristics might serve as proximate cues to reproductive investment from potential mates, including parental investment—important for males and females in a species with biparental care.

Smith (1996) found that inner-city African American high school students ranked *honest* and *caring* as the most important characteristics in a partner. These were closely followed by *fun to talk to* and *humor*, perhaps analogous to the *exciting personality* mentioned earlier. Green and Kenrick (1994) showed male and female respondents expressed a preference for partners with both *masculine* and *feminine* personality characteristics. This combination is often called *androgyny*. Respondents expressed the same partner preferences for several hypothetical relationships, including a date, a one-night stand, and marriage. Furthermore, men and women reported that *feminine* or *expressive* characteristics are more important than *masculine* or *instrumental* characteristics. These results are consistent with the marital satisfaction/survival and reproductive/parental investment explanation.

Although cross-sex similarities are undeniable, sex-specific partner preferences also exist. Buss and Barnes (1986), for example, reported women ranked *college graduate* and *good earning capacity* higher than did men, and men ranked *physically attractive* higher than did women. Women ranked *considerate, honest, dependable, kind, understanding, fond of children, well-liked by others, good earning capacity, ambitious and career oriented, good family background,* and *tall* higher than did men. In contrast, men ranked *physically attractive, good looking, good cook,* and *frugal* higher than did women. Although these preferences are not all personality characteristics, the results indicate that men and women have distinct priorities in mate selection.

When factors such as risk of pregnancy, detection, and disease were eliminated from consideration, female university students described themselves as more "willing" to engage in sexual intercourse with hypothetical males described as possessing positive personality traits (e.g., *bright, generous, sense of humor,* and *successful architect*), *parental* traits, and *safe* traits (Surbey & Conohan, 2000). The male students' willingness to engage in casual sex did not change with the *positive, parental,* or *safe* trait manipulations. The male students' willingness to engage in casual sex did, however, decline as the potential partners' physical attractiveness declined. Berry and Miller (2001) reported the quality of videotaped interactions between previously unacquainted opposite-sex pairs relates to personality and physical attractiveness. Only Extraversion predicted the rated interaction quality of men, whereas only physical attractiveness predicted the rated interaction quality of women.

Jensen-Campbell, Graziano, and West (1995) found that females preferred males high on Altruism/Agreeableness to those low on Altruism/Agreeableness. The highest physical attractiveness, social attractiveness, social desirability, and dating desirability were reported for Agreeable and Dominant men. An interaction between Agreeableness and Dominance seemed to contribute to females' perception of male Agreeableness. Females rated Agreeable and Dominant men as wealthier. In contrast, male respondents did not find female dominance important in attraction. Sadalla, Kenrick, and Vershure (1987) reported that Dominance increased the perceived attractiveness of males, but had no effect on female attractiveness. Attractiveness of Dominant males was unrelated to the sex of the rater or the sex of the individual the male was interacting with. Although Dominance was rated as attractive, constructs such as aggression or being domineering were not. Manipulated Dominance was related to the male's sexual attractiveness, but not general likeability.

Relative Preferences or Assortative Mating   The majority of studies on assortative mating for personality have reported significant positive correlations across romantic partners around .2 (Buss, 1985). Even higher positive correlations (.4 to .6) have been reported for *sensation seeking* (Zuckerman, 1994). Buss (1984) generally supported these findings but also found a single negative correlation between spouses for dominance and submissiveness. This negative correlation appeared in ratings made by interviewers and by the spouses themselves. Overall, however, the weight of the evidence favors romantic partner similarity (positive assortative mating) over complementarity (negative assortative mating or disassortative mating).

One evolutionary explanation of these results is *genetic similarity theory* (Rushton, 1989). By this theory, individuals seek out genetically similar romantic or social partners by phenotypic matching. Among the converging lines of supporting evidence is the high degree of phenotypic similarity on a variety of traits shown by friends and romantic partners. Moreover, friends and lovers seem to assort more strongly on characteristics with a high degree of genetic heritability and are thus more closely linked to shared genes. The function of this mechanism in mate choice is presumably to preserve the coherence of coadapted genomes that work well together, as well as to increase the coefficients of relatedness of parents to offspring, promoting parental investment. This mechanism presumably enhances inclusive fitness in nonsexual social partners by promoting altruism toward genetically similar others, enhancing the survival of genes shared with conspecifics that are not necessarily close kin by recent common descent. Although this theory remains controversial, it produces interesting and testable predictions.

A body of social psychology literature examines interpersonal attraction in social partners, not all of it specifically in relation to mating. Posavac (1971) reported that fraternity brothers have similar personality characteristics on a variety of measures. Posavac and Pasko (1974) also reported greater social attraction to individuals similar to college students even when they controlled for consensual preferences, although respondents reported greater social attraction to individuals who possessed popular characteristics. Hendrick and Brown (1971) found that Introverts rated other Introverts as a more *reliable friend* and more *honest and ethical*, although both Introverts and Extraverts preferred Extraverts on various measures of social attraction (e.g., *liking, interesting at party, ideal personality,* and *prefer as leader*), partially supporting the principle of consensual preferences. Suman and Sethi (1985) computed an index measuring the proportion of similarity between both Introverted or Extraverted individuals and a hypothetical stranger—and found the degree of social attraction between two persons increased in direct proportion to the rise of this index.

Returning to assortative mating among romantic partners, females but not males in a computer dating situation (Lum & Curran, 1975) preferred opposite sex partners that were moderately to highly similar to themselves on Extraversion. No significant relations were found for matching on Neuroticism. Keller, Thiessen, and Young (1996) compared the similarity of dating and married couples in both physical and psychological traits. Although dating and married couples assortatively mated on physical characteristics, assortative mating was higher for married couples on psychological traits. Furthermore, other studies (reviewed by Mascie-Taylor, 1988) report that spousal similarity is not attributable to married couples becoming more similar over time. In fact, Buss (1984) found older married couples tended to be less rather than more similar to each other.

Eysenck and Wakefield (1981) reported similarity predicts general marital satisfaction. Although typical spousal personality correlation was .20, some were higher, including .73 for *marital satisfaction,* .41 for *sexual satisfaction,* .43 for *libido,* .51 for *radicalism,* and .56 for *tender-mindedness.* Marital satisfaction was higher for men higher on Psychoticism and lower on Neuroticism than women. Men had higher marital satisfaction if their wives were more tender-minded than they, and women had higher marital satisfaction if their husbands were more tough-minded than they. Marital satisfaction was lower when men had high libido, but was unrelated to women's libido (men had generally higher libido than women in this study). There was no evidence of increasing similarity with length of marriage. Dissimilarity predicted divorce.

Evidence for assortative mating on undesirable traits most directly contradicts the principle of consensual preferences. Arguably, the opposite of many of the prosocial qualities that people find consensually desirable is Machiavellianism. A Machiavellian mate is cold, detached, manipulative, and exploitative. Novgorodoff (1974) found men, especially low-Machiavellian men, preferred low-Machiavellian women as romantic partners. High-Machiavellian women preferred high-Machiavellian men as romantic partners. Touhey (1977), however, found high Machiavellian individuals showed little attraction to similar others. Instead, individuals high in anxiety and social desirability were more attracted to similar others than those who were not.

Depression is another apparently undesirable trait in a mate. Nevertheless, Rosenblatt and Greenberg (1988) found that only nondepressed individuals preferred nondepressed social partners. Depressed individuals neither preferred nor dispreferred depressed over nondepressed social partners. This pattern, however, may not carry over into mating. Lewak, Wakefield, and Briggs (1985) found that similarity on the Depression (D) Scale of the Minnesota Multiphasic Personality Inventory (MMPI) predicted increased marital satisfaction in a nonclinical sample. This same study reported assortative mating on the Psychopathic Deviate (Pd) Scale of the MMPI in clinical and nonclinical samples; similarity in Pd also predicted marital satisfaction.

An Additional Empirical Test   Ample evidence supports both absolute (consensual) and relative (assortative) preferences for romantic partner personality in human mate choice. Of the absolute (consensual) preferences, some are sexually dimorphic and others sexually monomorphic. In the spirit of strong inference, however, we designed a study to pit these hypotheses against each other (Figueredo, Sefcek, & Jones, 2004). We created the NEO-MATE, a translation of the NEO-FFI items from self-reports to desiderata in an ideal romantic partner, to assess romantic partner preferences. We administered the NEO-MATE and the NEO-FFI to 104 University of Arizona undergraduates. We emphasized the participants should use the NEO-MATE to rate their own ideal romantic partner, rather than one they believe others might value. We administered the NEO-FFI after the NEO-MATE to prevent priming participants to match ideal romantic partners' personalities to their own.

The bivariate correlations between self- and ideal partner ratings on these factors were significant and substantial, indicating a tendency toward positive assortative mating on all personality factors, at least in the desired imaginary romantic partners. These correlations were .81 for Openness to Experience, .36 for Conscientiousness, .60 for Extraversion, .73 for Agreeableness, and .38 for Neuroticism. These data permitted us to perform a more stringent test of absolute preferences in ideal romantic partner personalities. By subtracting the factor scores on self-rated personality factors from those of the ideal romantic partner factors, we obtained difference scores indicating discrepancies between ratings of self and of ideal romantic partners. The mean difference scores for each factor, with the exception of Openness to Experience, differed significantly from zero. Respondents rated ideal romantic partners higher than themselves on Conscientiousness, Extraversion, and Agreeableness, and lower than themselves on Neuroticism.

The patterns observed in ideal romantic partner preferences are not merely indirect effects of preferences for a romantic partner personality similar to their own. The difference scores indicate preferences above mere matching to an individual's self-reported personality scores. The test of the hypotheses is reasonably clean because these different scores showed no statistically significant effects of respondent age or sex. Thus, the main conclusion of this study is, as declared by the Dodo Bird in *Alice in Wonderland*, "Everybody wins, and we all must get prizes!" Although the results support at least *aspirational* positive assortative mating for all FFM factors, they also indicate a relatively invariant preference (across age and sex) for romantic partners with more Conscientiousness, Extraversion, Agreeableness, and less Neuroticism than oneself.

Evidence for Frequency-Dependent Selection of Personality Traits

Tooby and Cosmides (1990) specified several criteria that must be met to show evidence for frequency-dependent selection of personality traits. To qualify as alternative adaptive strategies, alternative phenotypes must exhibit heritable individual differences, and component personality traits must covary in a predictable, adaptive manner and exhibit evidence of functional design as logically coherent and coordinated adaptations. To support claims of frequency-dependent selection, the fitness of an alternative phenotype must vary inversely to its relative frequency in the population: The rarer a particular phenotype with respect to its alternatives, the higher its relative fitness must be.

Finding direct evidence for frequency-dependent selection presents a challenge. Hence, we pursued the second-best strategy by collecting *indirect* evidence. If personality variation is correlated with reproductively relevant traits subject to frequency-dependent selection, then a direct investigation of the relevance of frequency-dependent selection to personality variation in humans is warranted. Fitting personality variation into an overall pattern of reproductively relevant traits fulfills one of the Tooby and Cosmides's (1990) conditions for frequency-dependent selection.

A source of interindividual variation held to be subject to frequency-dependent selection is alternative reproductive strategies. An array of comparative studies describes the coexistence of alternative phenotypes (and perhaps genotypes) of both male and female conspecifics that pursue divergent sexual and reproductive strategies (e.g., Buss & Greiling, 1999; Gangestad & Simpson, 2000; Rowe, 1996). Indeed, many game-theoretical models conclude alternative or conditional strategies can be held in a perpetual state of balanced polymorphism by frequency-dependent selection (Tooby & Cosmides, 1990).

The K-Factor   Because of potential trade-offs between the multiplicative parameters of survivorship and fecundity in generating total reproductive output, various combinations of these parameters yield identical final products. Thus, different life-history strategies that yield the same total fitness are possible. For example, a strategy based on high survivorship and low fecundity may perform as well as one based on high fecundity and low survivorship. These alternative life-history strategies are known as r- and K-strategies, respectively. Different species often have stereotypical life-history strategies not subject to substantial individual differentiation. Rabbits, for example, have relatively rapid sexual development, are highly fertile, and provide little parental care to offspring, resulting in high infant mortality. Even after reaching maturity, rabbits are short-lived. In contrast, elephants have slow and delayed sexual development, produce few offspring, and provide long-term parental care, resulting in low infant mortality. Furthermore, adult elephants are long-lived. Thus, relatively speaking, we classify rabbits as r-strategists and elephants as K-strategists.

Until recently, researchers studied variations in life-history strategy by comparing different species (MacArthur & Wilson, 1967). This domain has recently been extended by measuring systematic differences in life-history strategy

Table 30.1
Factor Pattern (Standardized Regression Coefficients)
for the K-Factor

	K-Factor
Biological Father Attachment/Investment	.36
Other Father Figure Attachment/Investment	−.36
Adult Romantic Partner Attachment	.38
Mating Effort	−.51
Machiavellianism	−.58
Risk Taking	−.41

among human individuals, social classes, and ethnic or racial groupings (Rushton, 2000). Some developmental evolutionary theories and related behavioral genetic work suggests there is substantial individual variation in life-history strategy within groups (Belsky, Steinberg, & Draper, 1991; Chisholm, 1996; Rowe, 2000). The analyses of these correlational patterns have mostly consisted of univariate analyses testing specific causal hypotheses and have not attempted to describe the wider pattern of correlations implied by these theories. The generative theory, however, suggests it is possible to construct a latent variable model, specifying a single common factor (K) that underlies life-history parameters—including an assortment of sexual, reproductive, parental, and social behaviors. If so, this K-Factor is an important and underappreciated individual difference variable in human development. Furthermore, correlations relating traditional personality factors to this K-Factor might serve as indirect evidence for frequency-dependent selection of personality.

To examine this hypothesis, we created a battery of measures sampling key behavioral indicators of the K-Factor and administered it to 222 University of Arizona undergraduates (Figueredo, Vasquez, et al., 2004). These instruments measured: (1) attachment to and investment from the biological father (adapted from Fine, Worley, & Schwebel, 1985), (2) attachment to and investment from father figures other than the biological father (adapted from Fine, et al., 1985), (3) adult romantic partner attachment (Brennan, Clark, & Shaver, 1998), (4) the Mating Effort Scale (Rowe, Vazsonyi, & Figueredo, 1997), (5) the short form of the Machiavellianism Scale (Christie & Geiss, 1970), and (6) a Risk-Taking Questionnaire (Eadington, 1976). Factor analysis of these measures produced a single common factor (the K-Factor) accounting for 92% of the reliable variance. Table 30.1 displays the factor pattern.

The Enormous Three   To correlate this K-Factor to traditional personality factors, we avoided making specific associations to particular personality inventories by administering three major personality inventories, the NEO-FFI (Costa & McCrae, 1992), the EPQ-R (Eysenck & Eysenck, 1975), and the ZKPQ (Zuckerman, Kuhlman, Joireman, Teta, & Kraft, 1993), to the same sample of undergraduates. We performed a higher order factor analysis to create common factors that cut across the particular personality inventories and obtained three common factors: Big N (for Neuroticism), Big E (for Extraversion), and Big P (for Psychoticism), that accounted for virtually 100% of the reliable variance. This was

Table 30.2

Factor Pattern (Standardized Regression Coefficients) for the Higher-Order
Personality Factors and the Bivariate Correlations among Them

		Big N	Big E	Big P
NEO-FFI	Neuroticism	.81	-.07	.04
EPQ-R	Neuroticism	.87	.03	-.02
ZKPQ	Neuroticism/Anxiety	.88	.05	.03
NEO-FFI	Extraversion	-.10	.80	-.10
EPQ-R	Extraversion	-.10	.79	.10
ZKPQ	Sociability	.17	.78	-.05
NEO-FFI	Conscientiousness	-.23	-.02	-.49
NEO-FFI	Agreeableness	.00	.28	-.62
EPQ-R	Psychoticism	-.12	-.06	.66
ZKPQ	Impulsivity/Sensation Seeking	-.08	.36	.62
ZKPQ	Aggression/Hostility	.16	.04	.58
Interfactor Correlations				
Big N		1.00	-.34	.22
Big E		-.34	1.00	-.06
Big P		.22	-.06	1.00

essentially a replication of results published previously by Zuckerman et al. (1993). Table 30.2 displays the rotated factor pattern under an oblique Promax rotation.

Personality and Demographic Correlates of K   The bivariate correlations of the K-Factor with higher order personality factors were −.24 for Big N, .12 for Big E, and −.67 for Big P. The correlations were statistically significant for Big N and Big P and approached significance for Big E. The high negative correlation of the K-Factor with Big P also supported Zuckerman and Brody's (1988) prediction that Psychoticism is more relevant to K than Neuroticism or Extraversion. Furthermore, the bivariate correlation of the K-Factor was −.24 with Sex, denoting generally lower K-Factor scores for males, but was not related to Age in this restricted age-range sample. The lower mean on the K-Factor for males is consistent with the theoretically predicted and empirically well-documented sex differences in reproductive strategy (e.g., Trivers, 1972).

These results confirm the idea that personality variation is relevant to reproductive life-history strategy. Moreover, if life-history strategy is subject to frequency-dependent selection, these results imply (but do not demonstrate) that the personality correlates of reproductive strategy are subject to frequency-dependent selection.

CONCLUSIONS AND LIMITATIONS

We have reviewed indirect empirical evidence suggesting human personality variation is related to natural selection (through correlations to longevity and fertility), to sexual selection (through correlations to consensual and assortative mate choice), and to frequency-dependent selection (through correlations to reproductive life-history strategy). The evidence is fragmentary, and exactly how each selective pressure operates on human personality variation or how they interact is unknown. We now argue, however, it is no longer reasonable to suppose, given this body of evidence, however incomplete, that human personality variation is independent of selection. It is reasonable to form a viable evolutionary personality psychology with further research to achieve a comprehensive understanding of evolved human nature.

We note that most of these studies are observational, not experimental; the reported correlations may not imply causation. As always, personality factors might influence fitness consequence, fitness consequence might influence personality factors, or some unmeasured third variable may influence both, producing spurious correlations. Unmeasured third variables as diverse as pleiotropic genes that influence both personality and health status or reproductive behavior or common environmental influences might be at work. Nevertheless, this review serves as motive to initiate a more comprehensive evolutionary approach to the study of personality variation.

We also note that the reported personality correlations used measures of current survival and reproduction. We do not know if these measures were valid in ancestral environments because current selective pressures may or may not be relevant to past selection. We suggest, however, that in this case the current selective pressures are the best proxies we have for past selective pressures. Betzig (1998) argued convincingly that contemporary differential reproductive success may be more reliable from an evolutionary perspective than commonly supposed and provides useful information concerning species-typical reproductive strategies. Most of the cited evidence relates to features of the immediate social and sexual environments, which may not have changed all that much from ancestral environments, rather than the physical or technological environments. In this case, empirical information from current environments is more useful than speculation regarding presumed ancestral environments.

CONCLUSIONS

We conclude with a discussion of selected methodological considerations and proposed future directions for research in evolutionary personality psychology.

CONSTRAINING ACCOUNTS OF PERSONALITY

A nonadaptationist framework predicts that individuals will not have personality traits classifiable by general laws or principles. In contrast, the adaptationist framework predicts stable personality traits—that traits are classifiable by the adaptive problems they were designed to solve and that traits evolve as a function of the adaptive problems faced by the organism over evolutionary time. Many personality theorists who use this framework exploit sophisticated statistical procedures to identify personality traits, but they unintentionally ignore a problem lying at the heart of the field: the appropriate constraints to set on the data on which the statistical techniques are based. Guided by folk-psychological constructs, traditional personality theory seeks to identify universal traits that exist in various combinations in individuals. In contrast, evolutionary personality theory demands that the acceptable data and theoretical structures be severely constrained both vertically and horizontally.

Vertical Integration   Theory developed under an evolutionary framework is constrained by what is known in the fields immediately below the level of interest—in this case, physiology, anatomy, and genetics (the neurosciences)—and fields immediately above the level of interest—in this case, evolutionary biology, evolutionary anthropology, ecology, and ethology. Acceptable data are similarly constrained. A proper evolutionary psychology involves the coordination of theory about: (1) the adaptive problems facing the species, (2) available solutions to those problems, and (3) how individuals recognize and solve those problems.

Horizontal Integration   Taking constraints offered by vertical integration, psychological theory within an evolutionary framework is constrained by descriptions of and accounts for what the organism does in the natural world *and* in the laboratory. A proper empirical approach to any problem involves: (1) watching subjects in a variety of naturalistic settings and using method of agreement and concomitant variation, (2) formulating hypotheses about what is seen, (3) taking these hypotheses to the laboratory and working out the rules governing what was seen using experimental methodology, and (4) taking those rules back out to the naturalistic world and making sure the laboratory rules accurately predict events in the naturalistic setting. Hence, observations set the questions, experiments sharpen the observations, and the results of those experiments provide means for making new observations (social psychologists call this *full-cycle psychology* e.g., Cialdini, 1980).

We have seen that the best methodological approach to theory and data gathering in evolutionary personality psychology exhibits characteristics and addresses problems unlike traditional personality psychology. Evolutionary personality psychology is a life science. This fact forces it to answer to naturalistic *and* laboratory-based data. It also forces it to answer to data and theory framed in the life sciences immediately above and below it. Such accountability constrains the ways theory may be structured and dramatically expands the range of data that must be considered.

Data Quality

Acknowledging that evolutionary personality psychology is irretrievably allied to the other life sciences permits us to use the hard-won knowledge and methods of systematics found in those fields (see, e.g., Brooks & McLennan, 1991). By these standards, the operational database upon which personality theory rests appears unacceptably informal. Much of the data entering personality theory are based not only on apparently artificial categories but also on self-report provided by untrained observers. Such data necessarily come from uncalibrated observational instruments. Documented problems involving reactivity, observer drift, ipsative drift, observer decay, contextual effects, and other well-characterized problems with human observers suggest that even highly trained observers are recording instruments with unknown and variable characteristics (Jacobs et al., 1988; Klahr & Simon, 1999; Repp, Nieminen, Olinger, & Brsca, 1988). The problem is compounded when untrained (or informally trained) observers report on the quality and quantity of their own personal experience or actions during interviews or on questionnaires. Clearly, though self-reports are a source of hypotheses, data obtained from them are at best not sufficiently constrained to serve as the primary data for an adequate taxonomy of personality traits.

MacDonald (in press) described similar conclusions in a recent review of the personality literature from an evolutionary perspective. He argued that personality is an evolved set of mechanisms designed to solve adaptive problems. Some of these mechanisms are relatively fixed and universal; others are relatively labile and idiosyncratic. These mechanisms are not forward looking. Indicators of a specific adaptive problem activate a specific set of mechanisms controlling adaptive responses that solved the problem in the phylogenetic or ontogenetic history of the individual. MacDonald concluded that direct situational activation of those mechanisms is the best way to identify and characterize those mechanisms. He predicted that we will find homologous systems in other species serving adaptive purposes (which may or may not be modular), personality structure will mirror the ecology of the species (the adaptive problems that it faces), and the ecological approach can be used to estimate the likelihood that an identified trait evolved to solve specific adaptive problems.

LIMITATIONS

Despite methodological difficulties, we draw several tentative conclusions. First, theory in evolutionary personality psychology is ahead of the data. Few studies test specific evolutionary predictions. Most of the evidence we reviewed was collected atheoretically or guided by nonevolutionary theories.

There is, nevertheless, a modicum of evidence supporting each of the major evolutionary theories explaining the continued existence of systematic individual differences in the face of selection. Although the existing data leave much to be desired, they suggest individual differences in personality are subject to natural selection, sexual selection, and frequency-dependent selection. The data also suggest these differences exist in a wide variety of different species and point to general accounts of why and how they evolved.

We conclude that these findings serve sufficient warrant to develop a truly evolutionary personality psychology seeking to explain the observed patterns of individual variation adaptively. We are beginning this process; basic work must be done before the field matures enough to produce definitive accounts of the adaptive significance of individual personality differences. We hope this contribution helps frame basic issues and identifies major areas needing protracted attention. Such a comprehensive intellectual framework is required to perform the theoretically guided and methodologically focused empirical research that is needed.

REFERENCES

Aldwin, C. M., Spiro, A., III, Levenson, M. R., & Cupertino, A. P. (2001). Longitudinal findings from the normative aging study: III. Personality, individual health trajectories, and mortality. *Psychology and Aging, 16*(3), 450–465.

Belsky, J., Steinberg, L., & Draper, P. (1991). Childhood experience, interpersonal development, and reproductive strategy: An evolutionary theory of socialization. *Child Development, 62,* 647–670.

Berry, D. S., & Miller, K. M. (2001). When boy meets girl: Attractiveness and the five-factor model in opposite-sex interactions. *Journal of Research in Personality, 35,* 62–77.

Betzig, L. (1998). Not whether to count babies, but which. In C. Crawford & D. Krebs (Eds.), *Handbook of evolutionary psychology: Ideas, issues, and applications* (pp. 265–273). Hillsdale, NJ: Erlbaum.

Brennan, K. A., Clark, C. L., & Shaver, P. R. (1998). Self-report measurement of adult attachment: An integrative overview. In J. A. Simpson & W. S. Rholes. *Attachment theory and close relationships* (pp. 46–76). New York: Guilford Press.

Brody, S. (2003). Alexithymia is inversely associated with women's frequency of vaginal intercourse. *Archives of Sexual Behavior, 32*(1), 73–77.

Brooks, D. R., & McLennan, D. A. (1991). *Phylogeny, ecology, and behavior: A research program for comparative biology.* Chicago: University of Chicago Press.

Buss, D. M. (1984). Marital assortment for personality dispositions: Assessment with three different data sources. *Behavior Genetics, 14,* 111–123.

Buss, D. M. (1985). Human mate selection. *American Scientist, 73,* 47–51.

Buss, D. M. (1989). Sex differences in human mate preferences: Evolutionary hypotheses tested in 37 cultures. *Behavioral and Brain Sciences, 12,* 1–49.

Buss, D. M. (1991). Evolutionary personality psychology. *Annual Review of Psychology, 42,* 459–491.

Buss, D. M. (1997). Evolutionary foundations of personality. In R. Hogan (Ed.), *Handbook of personality psychology* (pp. 317–344). London: Academic Press.

Buss, D. M., & Barnes, M. (1986). Preferences in human mate selection. *Journal of Personality and Social Psychology, 50*(3), 559–570.

Buss, D. M., & Greiling, H. (1999). Adaptive individual differences. *Journal of Personality, 67*(2), 209–243.

Capitanio, J. P., Mendoza, S. P., & Baroncelli, S. (1999). The relationship of personality dimensions in adult male rhesus macaques to progression of simian immunodeficiency virus disease. *Brain, Behavior, and Immunity, 13,* 138–154.

Chamberlin, T. C. (1897). The method of multiple working hypotheses. *Journal of Geology, 5,* 837–848.

Chisholm, J. S. (1996). The evolutionary ecology of attachment organization. *Human Nature, 7,* 1–38.

Christie, R., & Geiss, F. (1970). *Studies in Machiavellianism.* New York: Academic Press.

Cialdini, R. B. (1980). Full-cycle social psychology. *Applied Social Psychology Annual, 1,* 21–47.

Cigliano, J. A. (1993). Dominance and den use in *Octopus bimaculoides. Animal Behaviour, 46,* 677–684.

Clarke, A. S., & Boinski, S. (1995). Temperament in nonhuman primates. *American Journal of Primatology, 37,* 103–125.

Costa, P. T., & McCrae, R. R. (1992). *Revised NEO Personality Inventory (NEO PI-R) and NEO Five-Factor Inventory (NEO-FFI): Professional manual.* Odessa, FL: Psychological Assessment Resources.

Costa, P. T., & Widiger, T. A. (1994). Introduction: Personality disorders and the five-factor model of personality. In P. T. Costa & T. A. Widiger (Eds.), *Personality disorders and the five-factor model of personality* (pp. 1–10). Washington, DC: American Psychological Association.

Danner, D. D., Snowdon, D. A., & Friesen, W. V. (2001). Positive emotions in early life and longevity: Findings from the nun study. *Journal of Personality and Social Psychology, 80,* 804–813.

Darwin, C. (1988). *On the Origin of Species by means of natural selection.* New York: Avenel Books. (Original work published 1859)

Dembroski, T. M., & Costa, P. T., Jr. (1988). Assessment of coronary-prone behavior: A current overview. *Annals of Behavioral Medicine, 10,* 60–63.

Denollet, J., Sys, S. U., Stroobant, N., Rombouts, H., Gillebert, T. C., & Brutsaert, D. L. (1996). Personality as independent predictor of long-term mortality in patients with coronary heart disease. *Lancet, 347,* 417–421.

de Waal, F. B. M. (1998). *Chimpanzee politics: Power and sex among apes* (Rev. ed.). Baltimore: Johns Hopkins University Press.

Diener, E., Suh, E. M., & Lucas, R. (1999). Subjective well-being: Three decades of progress. *Psychological Bulletin, 125,* 276–302.

Eadington, W. (1976). *Gambling and society: Interdisciplinary studies on the subject of gambling.* Springfield, IL: Charles C Thomas.

Eaves, L. J., Martin, N. G., Heath, A. C., Hewitt, J. K., & Neale, M. C. (1990). Personality and reproductive fitness. *Behavior Genetics, 20*(5), 563–568.

Ebert, S. A., Tucker, D. C., & Roth, D. L. (2002). Psychological resistance factors as predictors of general health status and physical symptom reporting. *Psychology, Health, and Medicine, 7*(3), 363–375.

Eysenck, H. J. (1976). *Sex and personality.* London: England Open Books.

Eysenck, H. J., & Eysenck, S. B. G. (1975). *Manual of the Eysenck Personality Questionnaire.* London: Hodder and Stoughton.

Eysenck, H. J., & Wakefield, J. A. (1981). Psychological factors as predictors of marital satisfaction. *Advances in Behaviour Research and Therapy, 3,* 151–192.

Fasino, S., Garzaro, L., Peris, C., Amianto, F., Piero, A., & Daga, G. A. (2002). Temperament and character in couples with fertility disorders: A double-blind, controlled study. *Fertility and Sterility, 77*(6), 1233–1240.

Figueredo, A. J. (1995). *The evolution of individual differences.* Paper presented at Jane Goodall Institute ChimpanZoo annual conference, Tucson, Arizona.

Figueredo, A. J., Cox, R. L., & Rhine, R. J. (1995). A generalizability analysis of subjective personality assessments in the stumptail macaque and the zebra finch. *Multivariate Behavioral Research, 30,* 167–197.

Figueredo, A. J., & King, J. E. (2001). The evolution of individual differences. In S. D. Gosling & A. Weiss (Chairs), *Evolution and Individual Differences* Symposium conducted at the annual meeting of the Human Behavior and Evolution Society, London, England, United Kingdom.

Figueredo, A. J., Sefcek, J., & Jones, D. N. (2004). *The ideal romantic partner: Absolute or relative preferences in personality?* Manuscript in preparation.

Figueredo, A. J., Vasquez, G., Brumbach, B. H., Sefcek, J., Kirsner, B. R., & Jacobs, W. J. (2004). *The K-factor: Individual differences in life history strategy.* Manuscript in preparation.

Fine, M. A., Worley, S. M., & Schwebel, A. I. (1985). The parent-child relationship survey: An examination of its psychometric properties. *Psychological Reports, 57,* 155–161.

Friedman, H. S. (2000). Long-term relations of personality and health: Dynamisms, mechanism, tropisms. *Journal of Personality, 68*(6), 1089–1107.

Friedman, H. S., & Booth-Kewley, S. (1987). The "disease-prone personality": A meta-analytic view of the construct. *American Psychologist, 42,* 539–555.

Friedman, H. S., Hawley, P. H., & Tucker, J. S. (1994). Personality, health, and longevity. *Current Directions in Psychological Science, 3*(2), 37–41.

Friedman, H. S., Tucker, J. S., Tomlinson-Keasey, C., Schwartz, J. E., Wingard, D. L., & Criqui, M. H. (1993). Does childhood personality predict longevity? *Journal of Personality and Social Psychology, 65*(1), 176–185.

Gangestad, S. W., & Simpson, J. A. (2000). The evolution of human mating: Trade-offs and strategic pluralism. *Behavioral and Brain Sciences, 23,* 573–644.

Goodall, J. (1986). *Chimpanzees of Gombe: Patterns of behavior.* Cambridge, MA: Belknap Press of Harvard University Press.

Gosling, S. D. (2001). From mice to men: What can we learn about personality from animal research? *Psychological Bulletin, 127*(1), 45–86.

Gosling, S. D., & John, O. P. (1999). Personality dimensions in nonhuman animals: A cross-species review. *Current Directions in Psychological Science, 8*(3), 69–75.

Gosling, S. D., & Vazire, S. (2002). Are we barking up the right tree? Evaluating a comparative approach to personality. *Journal of Research in Personality, 36,* 607–614.

Green, B. L., & Kenrick, D. T. (1994). The attractiveness of gender-typed traits at different relationship levels: Androgynous characteristics may be desirable after all. *Personality and Social Psychology Bulletin, 20*(3), 244–253.

Grinde, B. (2002). Happiness in the perspective of evolutionary psychology. *Journal of Happiness Studies, 34,* 331–354.

Hellhammer, D. H., Hubert, W., Phil, C., Freischem, C. W., & Nieschlag, E. (1985). Male infertility: Relationships among gonadotropins, sex steroids, seminal parameters, and personality attitudes. *Psychosomatic Medicine, 47*(1), 58–66.

Hendrick, C., & Brown, S. R. (1971). Introversion, extraversion and interpersonal attraction. *Journal of Personality and Social Psychology, 20*(1), 31–36.

Jacobs, W. J., Blackburn, J. R., Buttrick, M., Harpur, T. J., Kennedy, D., Mana, M. J., et al. (1988). Observations. *Psychobiology, 16,* 3–19.

Jensen-Campbell, L. A., Graziano, W. G., & West, S. G. (1995). Dominance, prosocial orientation, and female preferences: Do nice guys really finish last? *Journal of Personality and Social Psychology, 68*(3), 427–440.

Keller, M. C., Thiessen, D., & Young, R. K. (1996). Mate assortment in dating and married couples. *Personality and Individual Differences, 21*(2), 217–221.

Kenrick, D. T., & Funder, D. C. (1988). Profiting from controversy: Lessons from the person-situation debate. *American Psychologist, 43,* 23–34.

Kiecolt-Glaser, J. K., McGuire, L., Robles, T. F., & Glaser, R. (2002). Emotion, morbidity, and mortality: New Perspectives from psychoneuroimmunology. *Annual Review of Psychology, 53,* 83–107.

King, J. E., & Figueredo, A. J. (1997). The five-factor model plus dominance in chimpanzee personality. *Journal of Research in Personality, 31,* 257–271.

King, J. E., & Landau, V. (2003). Can chimpanzee (*Pan troglodytes*) happiness be estimated by human raters? *Journal of Research in Personality, 17,* 1–15.

Kirkcaldy, B. D., Shephard, R. J., & Furnham, A. F. (2002). The influence of type A behavior and locus of control upon job satisfaction and occupational health. *Personality and Individual Differences, 33,* 1361–1371.

Klahr, D., & Simon, H. A. (1999). Studies of scientific discovery: Complementary approaches and convergent findings. *Psychological Bulletin, 125,* 524–543.

Lewak, R. W., Wakefield, J. A., Jr., & Briggs, P. F. (1985). Intelligence and personality in mate choice and marital satisfaction. *Personality and Individual Differences, 6*(4), 471–477.

Lilienfeld, S. O., Gershon, J., Duke, M., Marino, L., & de Waal, F. B. M. (1999). A preliminary Investigation of the construct of psychopathic personality (psychopathy) in Chimpanzees (*Pan Troglodytes*). *Journal of Comparative Psychology, 113*(4), 365–375.

Lum, K., & Curran, J. P. (1975). Personality similarity and interpersonal attraction in the computer dating situation. *Journal of Social Psychology, 95,* 233–239.

MacDonald, K. B. (1995). Evolution, the five-factor model, and levels of personality. *Journal of Personality, 63*(3), 525–567.

MacDonald, K. B. (1998). Evolution, culture, and the five-factor model. *Journal of Cross-Cultural Psychology, 29*(1), 119–149.

MacDonald, K. B. (in press). Personality, evolution, and development. In R. Burgess & K. B. MacDonald (Eds.), *Evolutionary perspectives on human development.* Thousand Oaks, CA: Sage.

Martin, L. R., Friedman, H. S., Tucker, J. S., Tomlinson-Keasey, C., Criqui, M. H., & Schwartz, J. E. (2002). A life course perspective on childhood cheerfulness and its relation to mortality risk. *Personality and Social Psychology Bulletin, 28*(9), 1155–1165.

Mascie-Taylor, C. G. N. (1988). Assortative mating for psychometric characteristics. In C. G. N. Mascie-Taylor & A. J. Boyce (Eds.), *Human mating patterns* (pp. 61–82). New York: Cambridge University Press.

MacArthur, R. H., & Wilson, E. O. (1967). *The theory of island biogeography.* Princeton, NJ: Princeton University Press.

Miller, G. (2000). Mental traits as fitness indicators. In D. LeCrosy & P. Moller (Eds.), *Evolutionary perspectives on human reproductive behavior* (pp. 62–74). New York: New York Academy of Sciences.

Mischel, W. (1968). *Personality and assessment.* New York: Wiley.

Mischel, W., & Peake, P. K. (1982). Beyond déjà vu in the search for cross-situational consistency. *Psychological Review, 89*(6), 730–755.

Novgorodoff, B. D. (1974). Boy meets girl: Machiavellianism and romantic attraction. *Personality and Social Psychology Bulletin, 1*(1), 307–309.

Platt, J. R. (1964). Strong inference. *Science, 146,* 347–353.

Posavac, E. J. (1971). Dimensions of trait preferences and personality type. *Journal of Personality and Social Psychology, 19*(3), 274–281.

Posavac, E. J., & Pasko, S. J. (1974). Attraction, personality, similarity, and popularity of the personality of a stimulus person. *Journal of Social Psychology, 92,* 269–275.

Repp, A. C., Nieminen, G. S., Olinger, E., & Brsca, R. (1988). Direct observation: Factors affecting the accuracy of observers. *Exceptional Children, 55,* 29–36.

Rosenblatt, A., & Greenberg, J. (1988). Depression and interpersonal attraction: The role of perceived similarity. *Journal of Personality and Social Psychology, 55*(1), 112–119.

Rowe, D. C. (1996). An adaptive strategy theory of crime and delinquency. In D. Hawkins (Ed.), *The current theories of delinquency and crime.* Newbury Park, CA: Sage.

Rowe, D. C. (2000). Environmental and genetic influences on pubertal development: Evolutionary life history traits. In J. L. Rodgers, D. C. Rowe, & W. B. Miller (Eds.), *Genetic influences on human fertility and sexuality: Recent empirical and theoretical findings* (pp. 147–168). Boston: Kluwer Press.

Rowe, D. C., Vazsonyi, A. T., & Figueredo, A. J. (1997). Mating effort in adolescence: Conditional or alternative strategy? *Journal of Personality and Individual Differences, 23*(1), 105–115.

Rushton, J. P. (1989). Genetic similarity, human altruism, and group selection. *Behavioral and Brain Sciences, 12,* 503–559.

Rushton, J. P. (2000). *Race, evolution, and behavior: A life-history perspective* (3rd ed.). Port Huron, MI: Charles Darwin Research Institute.

Ryan, R. M., & Frederick, C. (1997). On energy, personality, and health: Subjective vitality as a dynamic reflection of well-being. *Journal of Personality, 65*(3), 529–565.

Sadalla, E. K., Kenrick, D. T., & Vershure, B. (1987). Dominance and heterosexual attraction. *Journal of Personality and Social Psychology, 52*(4), 730–738.

Schwartz, J. E., Friedman, H. S., Tucker, J. S., Tomlinson-Keasey, C., Wingard, D. L., & Criqui, M. H. (1995). Sociodemographics and psychosocial factors in childhood as predictors of adult mortality. *American Journal of Public Health, 85*(9), 1237–1245.

Singh, S. B., Srivastava, C., & Nigam, A. (1992). Infertile women—Stress, personality, and adjustment: A comparative study. *Indian Journal of Clinical Psychology, 19*, 62–67.

Smith, S. P. (1996). Dating preferences among a group of inner-city African-American high school students. *Adolescence, 31*(121), 79–90.

Stevenson-Hinde, J., Stillwell-Barnes, R., & Zunz, M. (1980a). Individual characteristics in young rhesus monkeys: Consistency and change. *Primates, 21*, 498–509.

Stevenson-Hinde, J., Stillwell-Barnes, R., & Zunz, M. (1980b). Subjective assessment of rhesus monkeys over four successive years. *Primates, 21*, 66–82.

Suman, H. C., & Sethi, A. S. (1985). Interpersonal attraction as a function of proportional similarity in personality. *Journal of Psychological Researches, 29*, 141–148.

Surbey, M. K., & Conohan, C. D. (2000). Willingness to engage in casual sex: The role of parental qualities and perceived risk of aggression. *Human Nature, 11*(4), 367–386.

Tooby, J., & Cosmides, S. (1990). On the universality of human nature and the uniqueness of the individual: The role of genetics and adaptation. *Journal of Personality [Special issue: Biological foundations of personality—Evolution, Behavioral Genetics, and Psychophysiology], 58*, 17–67.

Touhey, J. C. (1977). Personality correlates of attraction in response to attitude similarity. *European Journal of Social Psychology, 7*(1), 117–119.

Trivers, R. (1972). Parental investment and sexual selection. In B. Campbell (Ed.), *Sexual selection and the descent of man: 1871–1971* (pp. 136–179). Chicago: Aldine.

Tucker, J. S., & Friedman, H. S. (1996). Emotion, personality, and health. In C. Magai & S. J. McFadden (Eds.), *Handbook of emotion, adult development, and aging* (pp. 307–326). San Diego, CA: Academic Press.

Watson, D. A. (1988). Intraindividual and interindividual analyses of positive and negative affect: Their relation to health complaints, perceived stress, and daily activity. *Journal of Personality and Social Psychology, 54*, 1020–1030.

Weiss, A., King, J. E., & Enns, R. M. (2002). Subjective well-being is heritable and genetically correlated with dominance in chimpanzees. *Journal of Personality and Social Psychology, 83*, 1141–1149.

Weiss, A., King, J. E., Perkins, L., & Blanke, M. K. (2003). The personality of orangutans (*Pongo pygmaeus* and *Pongo abelii*). Paper presented at the International Society for the Study of Individual Differences, Graz, Austria.

Wilson, D. S. (1994). Adaptive genetic variation and human evolutionary psychology. *Ethology and Sociobiology, 15*, 219–235.

Wilson, G. D. (1997). Sex and personality. In H. Nyborg (Ed.), *The scientific study of human nature: Tribute to Hans J. Eysenck at eighty.* New York: Elsevier.

Wischmann, T., Stammer, H., Scherg, H., Gerhard, I., & Verres, R. (2001). Psychosocial characteristics of infertile couples: A study by the Heidelberg Fertility Consultation Service. *Human Reproduction, 16*(8), 1753–1761.

Zuckerman, M. (1994). *Behavioral expressions and biosocial bases of personality.* New York: Cambridge University Press.

Zuckerman, M., & Brody, N. (1988). Oysters, rabbits and people: A critique of "Race differences in behaviour" by, J. P. Rushton. *Personality and Individual Differences, 9*(6), 1025–1033.

Zuckerman, M., Kuhlman, D. M., Joireman, J., Teta, P., & Kraft, M. (1993). A comparison of three structural models for personality: The big three, the big five, and the alternative five. *Journal of Personality and Social Psychology, 65*, 757–768.

CHAPTER 31

Biological Function and Dysfunction

JEROME C. WAKEFIELD

[S]ome widely used [evolutionary] concepts are invalid and must be abandoned. The question inevitably arises as to how such an abundance of misinterpretation has arisen. I believe that the major factor is that biologists have no logically sound and generally accepted set of principles and procedures for answering the question: "What is its function?"

—Williams (1966, p. 252)

EVER SINCE ARISTOTLE'S attempt to explain designlike organismic traits in terms of *final causes*, the concept of function and related *teleological* (from the Greek *telos*, "end" or "purpose") concepts such as *design, purpose, adaptation,* and *end* have been considered central to biological theory. George Williams forcefully expresses this view: "I have stressed the importance of the use of such concepts as biological means and ends because I want it clearly understood that I think that such a conceptual framework is the essence of the science of biology" (Williams, 1966, p. 11).

Darwin's theory of natural selection is the culmination of two millennia of grappling with how to understand such teleological notions within biology. His writings are sprinkled with teleological terms, and against those who claimed that Darwin's theory eliminated teleology from biology in favor of mechanical causation, Darwin suggested in a letter that his theory *explained* teleology rather than eliminated it (Gotthelf, 1999). In another letter, he insisted that it is "difficult for any one who tries to make out the use of a structure to avoid the word purpose" (Buller, 1999, p. 6). Williams (1966) observes that the study of functions

I thank the American Psychological Association and the American Psychiatric Press for permission to include revised versions of some paragraphs from Wakefield (1992a) and Wakefield and First (2003) in this chapter.

878

has "a formal relationship to Aristotelian teleology" but places "the material principle of natural selection in place of the Aristotelian final cause" (p. 258).

Natural selection is only one of many forces influencing the nature and form of organisms, including many kinds of developmental and structural constraints and historical contingencies (Williams, 1992). The relative overall influence of such constraints versus natural selection remains a debated question (Orzack & Sober, 1994). Those who emphasize the role of such nonselective influences have sometimes posed this as an *antiadaptationist* argument (Lewontin, 1979). However, the teleological tradition is exclusively concerned with explaining those aspects of organisms that are adaptive and designlike, and no set of developmental constraints, historical conditions, or other nonselective processes addresses this domain. Thus, the conflict is largely spurious. The antiadaptationist argument has perhaps been fueled by methodological concerns about the ease with which multiple selectionist hypotheses, demeaned by Stephen J. Gould (1991; Gould & Lewontin, 1979) as "just so stories," can be constructed and the relative paucity of empirical tests of those hypotheses. This situation is rapidly changing, and perhaps the criticism has pushed biologists to address such methodological problems (Griffiths, 1996). But even if some objections to specific teleological hypotheses or methodologies are correct, teleological explanation is still necessary for most adaptive traits.

Darwin's contribution to the teleological tradition can be best appreciated in the context of the puzzles that perennially afflict discussions of biological function. Attributions of biological function, also known in the philosophical literature as *natural* or *proper* function, raise challenging conceptual issues. For example, the spider's web enables the spider to catch insects, and we believe this benefit is not just a happy accident but the *function* of the spider's web. We believe, in turn, that enabling the spider to create such webs is the function of various mechanisms, some known and some unknown, in the spider's body and brain. But what exactly do such function statements add to the descriptive facts that certain internal mechanisms have the effect of enabling the spider to create webs and webs have the effect of catching insects?

One thing we seem to be adding in citing the function of a trait is a partial explanation of the trait; we are saying that catching insects is part of the explanation for *why* spiders have webs. Thus, function statements offer *functional explanations*. But, this raises a further problem. Given that catching insects is an effect of spiders' webs and thus comes after the webs, how can an effect explain its own cause, now that backward causation is rejected by science (and with it Aristotelian notions of final causes)? Even those who do not believe in a divine creator sometimes say colloquially that catching insects is the *purpose* of the spider's web, but how can a natural object have a purpose?

Although the clarification of function statements is a challenge for all fields of biology, evolutionary psychologists have a particular need to be clear about the concept of biological function. Claims about how people's minds are designed and about the functions of known or hypothesized mental modules constitute evolutionary psychology's most distinctive contribution to psychology. These functional claims are often highly controversial and undergo unusually intense critical scrutiny. It is, therefore, important for evolutionary psychologists to have a nuanced understanding of what function claims mean, what kinds of evidence might count for or against them, and what ambiguities might arise in making such claims that could lead to misunderstanding. Fortunately, the growing importance of these issues is paralleled by a quickly developing philosophical literature on the concept of function, which is already so large and diverse that only a few strands can be considered in this review.

One area in which evolutionary psychology is having a major impact is clinical psychology (for a review, see Nesse, Chapter 32). An account of *function* implies a corresponding account of *dysfunction* or *malfunction,* the concept at the foundation of theories of psychopathology. Thus, one major test for a theory of function is whether it provides an account of dysfunction on which an adequate evolutionary-psychological theory of psychopathology can be based.

In the first part of this chapter, I examine recent developments in the philosophical analysis of the concept of biological function. I focus on etiological or historical accounts that interpret functions primarily as naturally selected effects. This approach to function is most relevant to evolutionary psychology and the most philosophically adequate approach. In the second part, drawing on my "harmful dysfunction" analysis of disorder (Wakefield, 1992a, 1999b), I illustrate how the etiological analysis of function yields a notion of dysfunction that illuminatingly addresses conceptual questions at the foundation of evolutionary psychopathology, including the central one: What is a mental disorder? I also note some practical implications for psychiatric diagnosis of taking an evolutionary perspective.

BIOLOGICAL FUNCTIONS

In the 1960s and 1970s, at about the same time within the literatures of evolutionary theory and philosophy of biology, there were critical turning points in the analysis of the concept of function. In biology, George Williams (1966) published his powerful analysis of the field's foundations, including his definition of natural function as naturally selected effect. In philosophy, Larry Wright (1973, 1976) established the etiological account of function, which, as it was revised to deal with counterexamples (see later discussion), converged to a natural selection-based account as well.

Both Wright's and Williams's analyses were aimed at distinguishing functions in their explanatory sense from accidental benefits and other extraneous factors that often are confused with functions. The philosopher Carl Hempel (1965) had posed the challenge of drawing such a distinction in his classic account of functional explanation. The heart has many effects, observed Hempel, including pumping the blood and making a sound in the chest. Indeed, both of these are *beneficial* effects due to the medical uses of heart sounds. Yet, among these effects, only some are biological functions of the heart. The challenge for a theory of function is to explain how to distinguish those effects of a trait that are its functions from those that are not. And the primary constraint on the account is that it must explain how attribution of a function offers a *functional explanation.* That is, the analysis must show, in a naturalistic and scientifically acceptable way, without invoking backward causation or divine design, how the effect that is a function can *explain* the presence of the very trait of which it is an effect. Thus, for example, the analysis must show how it is that, when asked, "Why do kangaroos have pouches?" we can correctly answer, "To protect their developing young." This challenge of distinguishing functions from other effects has been the standard framework for recent inquiries into function.

Traditionally, this explanatory sense of function is known as the "strong" sense of function, versus some "weak" senses to be discussed shortly. To describe the function of a trait in the strong sense has been considered a way of outlining a partial explanation of the trait's existence and/or structure and/or maintenance in the species. It has always seemed apparent that the degree of designlikeness of organisms' traits cannot be accidental and that, for example, the eyes must somehow be the way they are *because* they enable us to see. The challenge has been to provide a scientifically adequate understanding of this fact. Darwin's theory of natural selection offers the only scientifically adequate explanation we have of how such nonaccidental effects can exist and can explain the traits that cause them. Thus, those analyses of function, known as *etiological* or *historical* analyses, that analyze the strong sense of function by appealing in one way or another to natural selection best address the traditional conundrum of effects explaining their causes.

The analysis of the concept of biological function is made considerably more difficult by the fact that the term *function* is used in a great variety of ways, most of which have nothing to do with biological functions in the strong sense but which are often confused with this concept. We often metaphorically extend function talk to just about any cause that contributes to any salient or valued outcome, as if it was designed to do so, as in, "Heart sounds function to alert doctors to medical problems," or "Gravity functions to lower rocks to the ground." Moreover, there are a variety of colloquial uses that are essentially value judgments, such as when an individual says that he or she has a functional or dysfunctional marriage or work situation. None of these uses are explanatory. Some writers on function mistake these metaphorical extensions for the real thing, hopelessly confusing the account of biological functions. Rather than taking the time to disentangle all these variant uses, I simply confine myself to the strong use noted earlier. Note that one way the strong sense is often marked is by the locution, "The function of X is to Y," as opposed to locutions such as "X functioned to Y," which are often used in the weak sense. So, for example, the fact that "The pocket Bible functioned to stop a bullet" does not imply that "The function of the pocket Bible is to stop bullets."

Artifact Functions

[T]here are many helpful parallels between natural and artificial mechanisms, and it is so convenient as to be inevitable that parallel terminology be used. . . . [I]t is most important that these terminological transfers be made only when there is a real functional analogy between what man's reasoning (and trial and error) can produce and what natural selection can produce.

—Williams (1966, p. 261)

There is a close relationship between the notion of function as applied within biology and the notions of function applied to artifacts, social roles, actions, and other such domains. The use of the same term is not arbitrary or local; Aristotle already applied the same term for function (in Greek, *ergon*) to all these domains, and other classical thinkers such as Lucretius do the same. Even Darwin's central term *selection* for the process yielding biological functions is a metaphor taken from the domain of intentional action. The use of *function* in the case of naturally occurring mechanisms is thus presumably a way of referring to properties that such mechanisms share with artifacts. The challenge is to spell out this shared feature. Consideration of artifact function will be useful in paving the way for the treatment of biological functions by bringing out the explanatory aspect of function ascriptions.

The function of an artifact is the purpose for which the artifact was designed or is maintained in the environment; for example, the functions of automobiles, chairs, and pens are, respectively, to enable us to transport ourselves, to sit, and to write, because those are the benefits the artifacts are designed to provide (Wakefield, 1992b). But organisms occur naturally and were not really "designed" by anyone with a purpose in mind. So, design and purpose, taken literally as intentional mental phenomena, cannot be the property shared by biological mechanisms and artifacts that explains the common use of function. Evolutionary biologists commonly speak of purpose and design when they describe natural functions, but that just brings the puzzle back a step; what further property *justifies* such metaphorical talk in the case of naturally occurring mechanisms?

The function of an artifact is important largely because, via its connection to design and purpose, it has tremendous explanatory value. The function partially explains why the artifact was made, why it is structured as it is, why its parts interact as they do, and why an individual can accomplish certain things with the artifact. For example, we can partially explain why automobiles exist, why automobile engines are structured as they are, and why with suitable learning a person can get from place to place with the help of an automobile, all just by referring to the automobile's function of providing transportation.

As in the spider's web example, functional explanations of artifacts have the odd feature that an effect (e.g., transportation) is claimed to explain the very artifact (e.g., automobiles) that provides the effect. Consequently, functional explanations appear to violate the principle that a cause must come before its effect. However, the function can legitimately enter into the explanation of the artifact if the cited effect plays some role in the events that preceded the artifact's creation. For artifacts, the way this occurs is well known: The benefit precedes the artifact in the sense that it is represented beforehand in the mind of the person who designs the artifact. Thus, a functional explanation (e.g., "The function of automobiles is to provide transportation" or, equivalently, "Automobiles exist in order to provide transportation") is a sketch of a fuller causal explanation: The artifact (e.g., an automobile) exists because some people had a desire representing a certain effect (e.g., transportation) and believed that creating the artifact was a way to obtain the effect, and the belief and desire, which preceded the artifact, caused the people to create the artifact.

Useful effects of an artifact other than those that explain the artifact's existence, structure, or continued presence are not generally considered functions of the artifact. For example, pens can be useful as writing instruments and as things to chew on to relieve nervous tension. Yet, it is only the effect of enabling us to write that is "the function" of pens. We might say, in the weaker sense of *function,* that pens function to relieve tension, but such relief is not a function of pens because it does not explain why pens exist or are structured the way they are. It is not the fact that an artifact's effect contributes to a goal that makes the effect a function, but rather that the effect explains the artifact via the designer's intentions.

It is explanation of the existence and structure of an entity in terms of its effects that artifact functions and biological functions have in common, and that justifies extending function talk from artifacts to natural mechanisms. For example, the heart's effect of pumping the blood is part of the heart's explanation and thus its function because, in virtue of natural selection, we can legitimately partially answer a question like, "Why do we have hearts?" or "Why do hearts exist?" with "Because hearts pump the blood."

WRIGHT'S ETIOLOGICAL ANALYSIS

A watershed in the philosophical analysis of function occurred with Larry Wright's (1973, 1976) etiological analysis, from which a variety of competing descendants have sprung. Wright's analysis relies on the insights noted earlier regarding the effect-explanatory nature of artifact functions. Wright asserted, as a general account of function across biological traits, artifacts, and other areas, that:

The function of X is Z means
(a) X is there because it does Z,
(b) Z is a consequence (or result) of X's being there. (1976, p. 81)

Wright's basic idea is that, as had been the intention since Aristotle, functions refer to explanatory effects, that is, effects of an entity that explain why that entity exists or is present. As an approach to biological function, Wright's analysis suffered from some fixable technical flaws. We cannot say that a specific instance of a mechanism X is there because it does Z, because that implies backward causation; rather, X is an instance of a *type* of mechanism and is there because *past instances* of that type did Z. Similarly, we cannot say that the function Z is a consequence of X's being there, because X could be defective, damaged, or diseased and thus malfunctioning; rather, Z was the consequence of past instances of Xs.

A more fundamental problem was that Wright's claim that sheer effect-explanation is sufficient for the existence of a function cannot be correct within biology, let alone across domains. Such effect-explanations are everywhere; for example, a rock resting against another rock is in a state of pressure equilibrium in which its position is explained by its effect in pressing against the other rock in a way that causes the other rock to press back with equal force. To take another common example, in the course of certain types of meteorological phenomena, there arise feedback-loop systems that sustain themselves by their own effects; whirlpools and storm systems often cause water or air to move in a circular path that leads to pressures that cause continued stable movement in the same way. Yet, it is not the function of the whirlpool's water movement or the storm's air movement to keep the whirlpool or storm going.

More problematically for the analysis of biological function, these counter-examples can have analogs within the organism. For example, it might be the case that near the heart valves, the blood flow is turbulent in such way that there regularly form whirlpools of blood with effect-explanatory structures that bring about a stable continuation of the whirlpool pattern of the blood's motion. Yet, the existence of such a stable vortex might be merely a mechanical oddity with no fitness implications, thus no functions.

Biological Functions as Naturally Selected Effects

The reaction to the failures of Wright's analysis was to conclude that the analysis was not specific enough and that biological functions require *selected* effects, not any explanatory effects; the *reason* the effects are explanatory must be that they were selected. Ruth Millikan (1984) attempted to address this problem by building into the analysis of *function* abstract analogs of the critical features of natural selection.

It is generally held that natural selection in a general sense occurs if and only if four conditions are met: (1) reproduction, in which a family of entities is such that one generation gives rise to another of their kind (offspring); (2) variation among the traits of the members of the population; (3) inheritable traits, so that offspring tend to be like their parents; and (4) differential reproductive success, in which different variants leave different numbers of offspring. Or as Hull (1990) has characterized natural selective processes, they consist of the activities of *replicators*, "an entity that passes on its structure largely intact in successive replications," and *interactors*, "an entity that interacts as a cohesive whole with its environment in such a way that this interaction causes replication to be differential" (p. 96). Millikan builds these conditions into her analysis. She requires a "reproductively established family" in which new members are produced by some kind of copying procedure and a selection process that explains changed proportions of family members bearing given traits over time by greater reproductive success in the copying process due to the possession of the trait. Although Millikan tried to apply her analysis across domains, the selectionist analysis has never been persuasively applied to artifacts, despite the metaphor of trial and error in human decision. Thus, I consider only applications to natural processes.

Bedau (1993), borrowing an example from Dawkins (1986), describes a process occurring in inorganic clay silicates in which chemical processes mimic all the elements of natural selection, yet no function attributions seem warranted. But, more critical to the analysis of biological function is that there are many selected structures within organisms that appear not to have functions. For example, parasitic DNA builds linkages to other genes such that it replicates when the others do, yet its linkage-building, though an effect that via selection explains the parasitic DNA's presence, has no organismic biological function. A further persuasive example, that of segregation-distorter genes, is summarized by Godfrey-Smith (1999a):

> Segregation distorter genes disrupt the special form of cell division (meiosis) which produces eggs and sperm (gametes). Meiosis usually results in a cell with two sets of chromosomes giving rise to four gametes with one set each, and on average a particular type of chromosome will be carried by half the gametes produced. Segregation distorters lever their way into more than their fair half share of gametes, by inducing sperm carrying the rival chromosome to self-destruct as they are formed. . . . Fruit flies, house mice, grasshoppers, mosquitoes and a variety of plants are known to have segregation distorters in their gene pools. Now, disrupting meiosis is something that segregation distorter genes do, that explains their survival. . . . Further, this explanation appeals to natural selection, at the gametic level; the problem can not be solved by disqualifying traits that survive for nonselective reasons. Disrupting meiosis is not generally claimed to be the genes' *function* though. (p. 204)

You might object that these examples incorrectly presuppose that all functions must be at the organismic level. This objection is based on a confusion. Perhaps some *traits* of parasitic DNA and segregation distorter genes possess biological functions *relative to these genes*. For example, you might argue that certain traits of segregation distorter genes have the function of causing sperm carrying the rival chromosome to self-destruct. But the point is that the segregation distorter genes themselves, although selected, possess no biological function within the organism, because they do not contribute to the organism's fitness. The focus in this chapter on functions of traits of organisms does not imply that there cannot be functions at other biological levels.

Examples of selected intraorganismic features that have no function indicate that, for an organismic trait to have a certain effect as its function, the effect must be selected because it contributes to the greater inclusive fitness of the organism that possesses the trait (Brandon, 1990; Godfrey-Smith, 1999a). Neander (1991), a leading advocate of such natural selection accounts of function, puts it this way:

> It is the/a proper function of an item (X) of an organism (O) to do that which items of X's type did to contribute to the inclusive fitness of O's ancestors, and which caused the genotype, of which X is the phenotypic expression, to be selected by natural selection. (p. 174)

Note that Neander's and other etiological analyses of function do not rely simply on the fitness value of a trait but on the *causal contribution* that the trait makes to fitness. For example, cooccurring traits such as the weight and warmth of a polar bear's coat must have the same fitness values, but it is the warmth of the coat and not its weight per se that contributes to fitness. Relevant here is Sober's (1984) now-classic distinction between "selection for" a trait and "selection of" a trait. For example, a machine that separates balls by sifting them for size through various-size holes and selects for retention only the one size that does not fit through the holes may also happen to separate them by color and retain only one color, if size and color happen to correlate. In such a case, the machine's selection process results in the "selection of" one color, but the machine's process "selects for" size because the latter property is the one that causally impacts in the selection process. Similarly, the warmth of the polar bear's coat is selected for, even though there is selection of weight. Only causally efficacious features that are selected for are relevant to the etiological account of function.

THE IMPORTANCE OF MAINTENANCE: WILLIAMS VERSUS GOULD ON FUNCTION

Neander's phrase that a trait's function must have caused the trait "to be selected by natural selection" seems to refer to the *original* selection of the trait, during which the trait spread through and became stabilized in the population. However, natural selection also works to maintain traits once they are selected. Without continued selective force acting to preserve a trait and eliminate alternatives, there generally would be eventual erosion or loss of the trait in the population. It is tempting to assume that selective forces stay roughly constant, so original selective forces are more or less identical to maintaining forces. However, recent developments in evolutionary theory underscore the potential complexity of the history of natural selection of a trait and focus attention on divergences between original and maintaining selection.

Problems in addressing maintenance in accounts of function date back at least to Williams's (1966) seminal analysis. He distinguished the function of a mechanism versus its other effects more or less in accordance with the etiological analysis, as follows:

> Whenever I believe that an effect is produced as the function of an adaptation perfected by natural selection to serve that function, I will use the terms appropriate to human artifice and conscious design. The designation of something as the *means* or *mechanism* for a certain *goal* or *function* or *purpose* will imply that the machinery involved was fashioned by selection for the goal attributed to it. When I do not believe that such a relationship exists I will avoid such terms and use words appropriate to fortuitous relationships such as *cause* and *effect*. (p. 9)

Williams clearly intended this definition to exclude from *function* any benefits not specifically the product of design for that benefit: "One should never imply that an effect is a function unless he can show that it is produced by design and not by happenstance" (p. 261). By *design,* Williams clearly intended to include only original selection for a trait. Williams was quite aware, and clearly indicated that, at any given time, what you are likely to see in examining a population is the ongoing maintenance of designlike selected traits, so the search for functions generally proceeds by studying maintenance. For example, he says that, after recognizing a designlike trait, the biologist's "next task would be to explain why the mechanism in question is maintained as a normal characteristic of the species and not allowed to degenerate" (p. 259). However, Williams implicitly assumed that original and maintaining selective forces are generally the same. He seems to suggest that otherwise the current advantages of the trait would be accidents and not functions.

Gould (1991; Gould & Vrba, 1982) inferred from Williams's analysis that "exaptations" (i.e., uses of existing traits for new benefits) are neither functions nor explained by natural selection, thus constructing a critique of natural selection explanation squarely on Williams's flawed definition. Indeed, Williams's definition continues to be cited as justification for Gould's claims about exaptation and function, as in the following recent example: "By convention (see Williams, 1966, for a brief history), the term 'function' applies to the beneficial effect that explains *the alteration of a trait through positive selection,* a usage that Gould and Vrba merely adopted" (Andrews, Gangestad, & Matthews, 2002, p. 539; emphasis in original). The snowballing confusion resulting from Williams's definition offers a cautionary tale about the importance of getting clear about conceptual issues.

The confusions are several (Buss, Haselton, Shackelford, Bleske, & Wakefield, 1998). Gould correctly notes that the benefits of a trait can change over time, thus we cannot blithely equate the current benefit with the original benefit for which the trait was naturally selected. However, he incorrectly suggests that such changes in benefit imply that the new benefit is (1) not a function and (2) not due to natural selection. What is missing here is an account of the process of maintaining selection of the new benefit. Maintaining selection is a genuine explanatory form of selective force and thus just as much natural selection as original selection. Moreover, contrary to both Williams's and Gould's views, function attributions do not require original selection; functions exist whenever there is maintaining selection, because maintaining selection offers genuine explanation by selected effects of the (continued) existence of the trait.

Consider, for example, a species of moth in which white coloration has been originally selected for its effect of camouflage against white bark. Imagine that, due to habitat destruction, the species then migrates to a new forest in which the bark is dark, yet over generations maintains its white coloration nonetheless. Upon investigation, it is found that coloration has been maintained by a new selective advantage in the new environment, namely, mimicry of a toxic white species of moth that inhabits the same forest and is avoided by predators. In the first generation in which the moths arrived in their new habitat, it was a lucky accident that their whiteness had the novel benefit of mimicry. However, after generations of maintaining selection for mimicry and not maintaining selection for camouflage, would anyone resist labeling mimicry as the one and only current function of the moths' coloration? Original selection is simply not a necessary condition of function.

TIMELINE PROBLEMS

A further challenge for natural selection accounts of function concerns exactly when natural selection must have taken place to warrant a current attribution of function. Not any selection, no matter how transient or remote in time, qualifies. Obviously, in prototypical cases in which a trait is originally designed and continuously maintained through to the present for the same effect, timeline issues do not arise. However, selective pressures may fade in and out, one pressure may replace another, and nonselective processes (e.g., chance, drift, constraint, linkage) may maintain a trait between episodes of selection.

It must be kept in mind that, to be a function, an effect has to explain the *current presence* of the trait. Neither initial shaping per se, nor current selective pressure per se, provides such an explanation. Thus, in attributing a function, we must be assuming that there has been some recent explanatory selective pressures that may or may not be the same as original or current pressures.

How, then, do changing selective pressures over the history of the trait influence current function? The answer, according to recent proposals, is that what is relevant is relatively recent evolutionary periods of time leading up to the present in which significant selection did take place or might have taken place. This analysis has come to be known as the *modern history* etiological view (Godfrey-Smith, 1999b; Griffiths, 1999): The function of X is Y only if selection for Y has been responsible for maintaining X in the recent past (see Kitcher, 1999, for a discussion of this and other timeline options).

For example, although penguins' wings were selected in nonaquatic ancestors for the function of enabling flight, in penguins' more recent evolutionary history the wings have been selected exclusively as swimming appendages enabling penguins to propel and steer themselves in the water. If not for the swimming effect, wings might have disappeared in penguins altogether or might have become vestigial. So, recent evolutionary history explains the common judgment that the current function of the penguins' wings is swimming, not flight, whereas the classic etiological view framed in terms of original selection does not.

This explanation leaves unresolved exactly what is "recent." For example, if a taste preference for fat was favored up to 100 years ago and then ceased being fitness-enhancing, is that recent enough to attribute a function? This question is additionally important if the analysis of function is to be consistent with biologists' judgments of trait vestigiality, because that means that after a sufficient time has elapsed since the trait was useful, it no longer has a function (e.g., vestigial eyes in cave-dwelling species).

Griffiths (1999) attempts to explicitly define *recent* in terms of periods during which regressive evolution might be expected to take place:

> An evolutionary significant time period for trait T is a period such that, given the mutation rate at the loci controlling T, and the population size, we would expect sufficient variants for T to have occurred to allow significant regressive evolution if the trait was making no contribution to fitness. A trait is a vestige relative to some past function F if it has not contributed to fitness by performing F for an evolutionarily significant period. (p. 155)

An interesting feature of this definition is that it recognizes that, for a variety of reasons, actual variation in a trait, and thus actual selective processes, may not occur during an evolutionarily relevant period. The analysis allows for judgments of function based on what would be expected had a trait sufficiently varied during such a period. The assumption that in principle all traits could vary, and they could do so independently even of other traits to which they may be currently linked, is an idealization that seems to be assumed in some of the function judgments we make in those rare cases in which actual selection has not occurred. For example, a gene that performs two vital functions will be judged to have both as its functions, yet if one role occurs during early development, variations in the gene may always be selected out due to loss of this early role. In such cases, based on the idealizing assumption that the roles could be independently controlled in principle and that variations could then occur over adequate time spans, we judge that the second role is a function, despite lack of any actual natural selection for that specific effect.

RESOLVING THE TINBERGEN PUZZLE

The modern history view offers a way to resolve a commonly discussed problem for the etiological view. Among ethologists, there is widespread acceptance of Niko Tinbergen's (1963) claim that there are four kinds of causal explanations that can be provided for a form of behavior: (1) the *physiological mechanisms* by which the behavior occurs and the physical stimuli that trigger the behavior, (2) the *survival value* or (equivalently in Tinbergen's article) the *function* of the behavior, (3) the *evolutionary history* of the behavior, and (4) the *ontogenetic development* of the behavior in the life of the organism. The problem is that Tinbergen's distinction between the function of a behavior and the evolutionary history of the behavior may seem inconsistent with the etiological analysis, according to which function is determined by evolutionary history.

However, Godfrey-Smith (1999b) has persuasively argued that Tinbergen's distinction between evolutionary explanation and functional explanation is best understood as a distinction between *the evolutionary history of how the current structure evolved* (i.e., how the morphological and behavioral elements originated and changed due to the series of earlier selective pressures) and *the present explanatory function(s) of the structure based on inferred recent selection*: "Functions can be seen as effects of a trait which have led to its maintenance during recent episodes of natural selection. The distinction [in Tinbergen's work] between 'functional' and 'evolutionary' explanations can be cast as a distinction between the explanation for the original establishment of the trait, and the explanation, which may be different, for its recent maintenance" (p. 189).

FUNCTION AS A BLACK BOX ESSENTIALIST CONCEPT

Williams (1966) notes that many function attributions can be confidently made independently of any particular theory on the basis of careful observation of de-signlike qualities. These judgments would come out the same whether the observer is Darwinian, Lamarckian, Creationist, or a grand synthesis evolutionist. Williams argues that only after we have identified the function should we then start to explain it in terms of natural selection. Thus, there are really two concepts of function presented in Williams's celebrated work: the shared intuitive concept defined in terms of direct observation of designlike properties such as economy, reliability, and precision of effect and the concept defined in terms of the theory of natural selection.

What, then, is the concept of biological function that is shared by Darwinians and non-Darwinians? Starting in antiquity, it was assumed that there must be *some* special process that explains how the beneficial effects of organismic traits came to exist, even though the specific nature of the process remained unknown. The concept *biological function* was created as a placeholder to refer to the results of this hypothesized unique biological process, whatever it is, before there was an inkling of its true nature. Based on philosophers' insights into natural kind concepts (Putnam, 1975; Searle, 1983), I call this kind of concept a *black box essentialist concept* (Wakefield, 1999a, 2004). Such concepts postulate and allow us to talk about a hidden unknown essence—that is, an underlying theoretical process or structure—that explains some initial prototypical set of phenomena. The concept remains agnostic on the specific identity of the underlying essence until scientific research provides an answer. In the case of function, the prototypical instances would consist of clear explanatory-effect functions such as eyes seeing, hands grasping, feet walking, teeth chewing, fearing danger, thirsting for needed water, and so on.

According to the black box essentialist approach, having observed that prototypical biological functions clearly involve effects that must themselves explain the presence of the mechanisms that give rise to them, biologists defined *function* as encompassing *any effect of biological mechanisms that is explained by the same general process that explains the prototypical instances of effect-explanatory traits*. That is, a natural function of a biological mechanism is an effect of the mechanism that explains the existence, maintenance, or nature of the mechanism via the same underlying essential process, whatever it is, by which prototypical effect-explanatory benefits are explained. Theorists have differed greatly over the nature of the underlying process. But each theory was an attempt to explain roughly the same domain of phenomena pertaining to a specific hypothesized organismic process that explained observed clear cases of designlikeness. It was Darwin's explanation in terms of fitness and natural selection that succeeded in providing the needed explanation and thus provided a scientific theory (or, alternatively, a theoretical concept) of function.

CONCEPTUAL FOUNDATIONS OF EVOLUTIONARY PSYCHOPATHOLOGY: DISORDER AS FAILURE OF DESIGNED FUNCTION

Evolutionary psychopathology is a growing subdiscipline with many diverse strands, for example:

1. Evolutionary psychopathologists put forward specific evolutionary hypotheses about naturally selected mental modules and their normal functions and theorize about the dysfunctions of those mental modules that might underlie a given kind of mental disorder. For example, various evolutionary hypotheses have been suggested about the functions of normal emotions and about the ways in which normal emotional reactions may malfunction to yield disorders such as panic attacks (Klein, 1993; McNally, 1994) or pathological depression (Nesse, 1991).
2. Evolutionary psychopathologists attempt to explain how specific debilitating mental disorders have continued to exist in the population, despite presumed selective pressures against them, by showing how they might be the indirect results of broader selective processes. For example, some disorders may be due to homozygosity of a gene for which only heterozygous instances confer greater fitness and were selected, as has been postulated for sickle cell anemia. Similarly, we might explain certain personality disorders as due to unselected extremes on multigenically determined dimensional traits in which only the nonextreme phenotypes conferred selective advantage, as has been postulated for antisocial personality disorder.
3. Evolutionary theorists have used an evolutionary framework to distinguish psychopathology from various other kinds of problematic conditions that are not disordered but that still might be subject to treatment by mental health professionals (e.g., Cosmides & Tooby, 1999). For example, excessive instances of designed defensive reactions (as in high fever), as well as mismatches between naturally selected mechanisms and the current environment due to changing environmental conditions (as in excessive appetite for fats), may be treatable though nondisordered problematic conditions illuminated by evolutionary analysis.

This section focuses exclusively on a more fundamental issue for clinical psychology, namely, clarifying the concept of mental disorder itself. A mental disorder may be considered a disorder of mental mechanisms and thus conceptually analogous to disorders of other kinds of mechanisms. Thus, the problem is to define *disorder* in the general sense used in medicine, and then apply it to the domain of mental mechanisms. As in evolutionary psychology generally, the domain of *mental mechanism* is not defined in some Cartesian metaphysical way but simply as whatever hypothesized brain mechanisms underlie certain capacities we label *mental*, including thought, emotion, perception, speech, appetitive behavior, and so on. Whatever deeper property, if any, unites these processes under the category *mental*, such as perhaps the involvement of representational structures, is left open. Note that the fact that mental disorders are medical disorders in a conceptual sense does *not* mean that mental disorders must be physiological brain disorders; mental functions can fail due to problems with functions at the representational "software" level rather than the physiological "hardware" level.

The view defended here is the harmful dysfunction (HD) analysis of the concept of mental disorder (Wakefield, 1992a, 1992b, 1999b), which asserts that a mental or physical disorder must be: (1) harmful, that is, negative as judged by social values; and (2) caused by a dysfunction, that is, by failure of a psychological mechanism to perform its function, in the sense of biological function as analyzed earlier in this chapter. This concept is arguably at the root of both psychiatric and lay judgments of disorder versus nondisorder. Dysfunction and function in the relevant sense are theoretically best understood in evolutionary terms and thus in principle are factual scientific concepts. Thus, disorder in the medical sense is a hybrid value and a factual concept.

The HD analysis offers a middle ground between antipsychiatrists like Szasz (1974) and Foucault (1965), who dismiss psychiatric diagnoses as value judgments and hence offer no constructive critique, and institutionalized psychiatry as expressed in the widely used criteria presented in the American Psychiatric Association's *Diagnostic and Statistical Manual of Mental Disorders* (*DSM-IV*, 1994). The HD analysis vindicates psychiatry from the antipsychiatrists' critique by explaining how genuine mental disorders can exist, but at the same time offers grounds from within psychiatry's own implicit assumptions for critiquing *DSM* diagnostic criteria as often pathologizing normal conditions.

As in the analysis of function, there are in reality two concepts of disorder—or, alternatively, an abstract shared concept and a specific theory of what falls under that concept—that need to be analyzed. The first is the concept that has existed since antiquity and is shared by pre-Darwinians from Hippocrates onward, Darwinians, Creationists, and everyone else who understands the concept of a medical disorder. The second concept is that specific to evolutionary theory, which offers the best theoretical account of the nature of the functions and dysfunctions that underlie disorder attributions.

In analyzing the intuitive, shared concept of disorder, as in earlier analyzing function, there are several methodological assumptions. The point is to explain classificatory judgments that are widely shared about what are considered clear instances of disorder and nondisorder; controversial cases are initially set aside for later consideration. Members of our culture, both professionals and laypeople, are assumed to generally share the concept. Thus, analogous to the linguist who attempts to formulate a theory of a language's grammar by considering subjects' shared judgments of which sentences are and are not grammatical, the conceptual analyst attempts to formulate a theory of shared conceptual meaning by considering community members' classificatory judgments of what does and what does not fall under a concept. Note that there is no assumption that widely shared classificatory judgments are correct; possessing a concept and judging whether a certain thing falls under the concept are two different things, and the point is to explain such judgments whether correct or incorrect. Nor is there any assumption that there is a precise or crisp boundary between disorder and nondisorder. Like most concepts, it is assumed that *mental disorder* has areas of indeterminacy, ambiguity, fuzziness, and vagueness and that a successful analysis should reflect and explain such aspects of our judgments.

DISORDER AS HARMFUL DYSFUNCTION

The view that the concept of disorder somehow involves dysfunction emerges with remarkable consistency in the remarks of many authors who otherwise differ in their views (e.g., Ausubel, 1971; Boorse, 1975; Caplan, 1981; Kendell, 1975, 1986; Klein, 1978; Macklin, 1981; Moore, 1978; Ruse, 1973). Spitzer and Endicott (1978) note the seeming necessity and virtual universality of using dysfunction to make sense of disorder: "Our approach makes explicit an underlying assumption that is present in all discussions of disease or disorder, i.e., the concept of organismic dysfunction" (p. 37). What is required to understand *disorder* is an adequate analysis of function and dysfunction.

A prominent classic view that diverges from the dysfunction analysis is that medical disorders in physical medicine are defined by physical lesions. If this were true, then it would pose severe difficulty for generalizing the notion of disorder to the mental domain. Indeed, Thomas Szasz's (1974) influential argument that there is no such thing as mental disorder is based on the "lesion" analysis of physical disorder and the claim that we lack clearly identified lesions for mental disorders. Such lesions may merely be as yet undiscovered. However, it also seems possible and even probable that some mental disorders are dysfunctions of mental processes without any identifiable physical lesion or even a physiological malfunction. As noted, we may use the analogy of software that can malfunction without there being any identifiable malfunction at the hardware level.

But it is not just within the mental domain that the lesion account of disorder is questionable. The lesion analysis is incorrect even as an analysis of disorder within the physical domain. Lesions in themselves are just variations in structure, and they occur in the context of enormous individual differences in normal structure. So, the question is: How do we distinguish lesions, in the sense of pathological deviations of structure, from normal variation? The most plausible answer seems to be that we classify a structural variation as a lesion when it interferes with the function(s) of one or more structures. That is, disorder is a functional concept, not an anatomical concept, even in physical medicine. This functional logic forms the basis for conceptually uniting the accounts of physical and mental disorder.

Not all failures of function, even those that involve identifiable physical lesions, are disorders. To be considered a medical disorder, a failure of function must also do harm to the individual and thus have implications for the need for intervention. For example, simple angioma, in which there is an abnormality that causes a blood vessel to connect to the outer skin layer, yielding those little red dots that many of us have, is a lesion (because the mechanisms guiding blood vessel growth have malfunctioned) but not a medical disorder because there is no harm suffered from the condition. Similarly, a dysfunction of the corpus collosam, the only effect of which is to make an individual unable to learn to read, is certainly harmful and thus a disorder in our society. But, in a preliterate society in which reading is neither taught nor valued nor even possible due to lack of access to books, such a dysfunction could not be labeled a disorder. Thus, harm is a necessary part of a condition being a disorder.

However, contrary to some views (Houts, 2001; Sedgwick, 1982), value judgments are not sufficient to explain disorder judgment; a separate dysfunction judgment is also necessary. Both professionals and laypersons distinguish between quite similar negatively valued conditions as disorders and nondisorders. The notion of dysfunction seems essential to discriminate negative mental conditions considered disorders from those that are not. For example, illiteracy is not in itself considered a disorder, even though it is disvalued and harmful in our society. However, a similar condition that is believed to be due to lack of ability to learn to read because of some internal neurological or psychological dysfunction is considered a disorder. Greater male aggressiveness and greater male inclination to sexual infidelity are considered negative but not generally disorders because they are seen as the result of the biologically natural functioning of the male sex, although similar compulsive motivational conditions are seen as disorders. Grief is seen as normal whereas similarly intense sadness not triggered by real loss is seen as disorder. A pure value account of disorder does not explain such distinctions among similar negative conditions. Moreover, we often adjust our views of disorder based on cross-cultural evidence that may go against our values. For example, our culture does not value polygamy, but we judge that it is not a failure of natural functioning, thus not a disorder, based partly on cross-cultural data and other evidence for evolved psychological mechanisms inclining men and women toward multiple partners under certain conditions. This suggests that our judgments are based not merely on values but also on what we consider to be species-typical human functioning.

Supposing that a disorder is a dysfunction, what, then, is a dysfunction? An obvious proposal is that a dysfunction implies an unfulfilled function, that is, a failure of some mechanism in the organism to be able to perform its function. However, not all uses of *function* and *dysfunction* are relevant to disorder judgments. The medically relevant sense of dysfunction is clearly *not* the colloquial sense in which the term refers to failure of an individual to perform well in a social role or in a given environment, as in assertions such as, "I'm in a dysfunctional relationship" or "Discomfort with hierarchical power structures is dysfunctional in today's corporate environment." These kinds of problems need not be individual disorders. Moreover, the kinds of functions that are relevant are *not* those that result from social or personal decisions to use a part of the mind or body in a certain way. For example, the nose functions to hold up the glasses, and the sound of the heart performs a useful function in medical diagnosis. But a person whose nose is shaped in such a way that it does not properly support glasses does not thereby have a nasal disorder, and a person whose heart does not make the usual sounds clearly enough to be useful for diagnosis is not thereby suffering from a cardiac disorder. A disorder is different from a failure to function in a socially or personally preferred manner precisely because a dysfunction exists only when an organ cannot perform as it is naturally (i.e., independently of human intentions) supposed to perform. Presumably, then, the functions that are relevant are the natural or biological functions, which were the subject of the earlier analysis.

Thus, the link between the analysis of the concept of disorder and the analysis of function is, first, that disorders involve what are commonly referred to as *dysfunctions* (this terminology is common across a great many discussions and views, although rarely further explicated to display the precise sense of *dysfunction*) and, second, that dysfunctions are best construed as failures of organismic mechanisms to perform their natural functions. More strictly, to eliminate possible counterexamples in which normal organisms cannot perform their functions because the environment does not allow them to (in which case, they are not generally considered disordered), dysfunctions are failures of mechanisms to be capable of performing their functions under environmental circumstances for which the mechanisms were designed to perform such functions. Thus, our pretheoretical concept of disorder implies, roughly speaking, failure of designed functions (the disruption of the biologically designed "order" is why there is a disorder, according to this view).

Some might object that what goes wrong in disorders is sometimes a social function that has nothing to do with natural categories. For example, reading disorders seem to be failures of a social function, for there is nothing natural or designed about reading. However, illiteracy involves the very same kind of harm as reading disorder, yet it is not considered a disorder. Inability to read is considered indicative of disorder only when circumstances suggest that the reason for the inability lies in a failure of some brain mechanism to perform its natural function. There are many failures of individuals to fulfill social functions, and they are not considered disorders unless they are attributed to a failed natural function.

If you look down the list of *DSM* (1994) disorders, it is apparent that, by and large, it is a list of the various ways that something can go wrong with the seemingly designed features of the mind. Very roughly, psychotic disorders involve failures of thought processes to work as designed, anxiety disorders involve failures of anxiety- and fear-generating mechanisms to work as designed, depressive disorders involve failures of sadness and loss-response regulating mechanisms, disruptive behavior disorders of children involve failures of socialization processes and processes underlying conscience and social cooperation, sleep disorders involve failure of sleep processes to function properly, sexual dysfunctions involve failures of various mechanism involved in sexual motivation and response, eating disorders involve failures of appetitive mechanisms, and so on.

When we distinguish normal grief from pathological depression, normal delinquent behavior from conduct disorder, normal criminality from antisocial personality disorder, normal unhappiness from adjustment disorder, illiteracy from reading disorder, normal lack of empathy for enemies of a person's group from sociopathic lack of empathy for anyone, or normal childhood rambunctiousness from attention-deficit hyperactivity disorder, we are implicitly using the "failure of designed function" criterion. That criterion explains why some of these conditions are considered disorders and others, quite similar and also negatively evaluated, are not.

Disorder as Evolutionary Dysfunction

The HD analysis holds that the intuitive concept of *disorder* requires dysfunction, and dysfunction in the relevant sense refers to processes of failure of natural design. Thus, a disorder exists only when an internal mechanism is incapable of performing one of its natural functions. Until this point in the analysis, *natural function* is used in the intuitive black box essentialist sense that has existed for millennia, not in a technical evolutionary sense. As we saw, *function* in this sense indicates that certain effects of biological mechanisms are so complex, beneficial, and intricately structured that they cannot be accidental side effects of random causal processes but, like the intentionally designed functions of artifacts, must somehow be part of the explanation of why the underlying mechanisms exist and are structured as they are. A dysfunction occurs when one of these clearly designed processes fails.

The further evolutionary theoretical argument applied in the case of function applies to dysfunction as well. Evolutionary theory explains processes of natural design. Consequently, disorders are harmful failures of mechanisms to perform the functions for which they were naturally selected. Thus, evolutionary psychology and the field of psychopathology converge; indeed, evolutionary psychopathology *becomes* the discipline of psychopathology. The *DSM* can be seen as a listing of categories that prima facie involves failures of naturally selected mental mechanisms to perform their functions, whether they concern thought, emotion, sexual functions, sleep functions, socialization and moral development functions, and so on.

As noted, the concept of disorder cannot be directly analyzed in evolutionary terms. The analysis aims to capture a widely shared, intuitive medical and lay concept that existed long before evolutionary theory was formulated and is shared by many groups who are ignorant of or who reject evolutionary theory, but who largely agree on which conditions are disorders. These groups share the underlying "failure of explanatory design" notion of dysfunction, and they use circumstantial evidence to apply that concept in more or less the same way, despite their radically divergent theories of how "designed" mechanisms came about and why they malfunction. So, an individual does not have to understand or accept evolution to possess the concept of disorder. It is a momentous scientific discovery, not a matter of definition, that disorders are failures of naturally selected mechanisms to be able to perform their functions. Harmful dysfunction is the meaning of disorder, and evolution is the most incisive theory of the nature of functions and dysfunctions.

It bears emphasis that designed conditions are not considered disorders even if they are harmful in the current environment. For example, higher average male aggressiveness is not considered a mass disorder of men even though in today's society it is arguably harmful, because it is considered the way men are designed. Feminists sometimes claim that men are suffering from a mass disorder of testosterone poisoning, but this is generally taken to be a joke, not a serious classificatory judgment. There can be aggressiveness disorders; here as elsewhere, individuals may have malfunctions of designed features.

If the HD analysis is correct, then a society's categories of mental disorder offer two pieces of information. First, they indicate a value judgment that the society considers the condition negative or harmful. Second, they make the factual claim that the harm is due to a failure of the mind to work as designed. This is a factual claim and may be correct or incorrect but, in any event, reveals what the society thinks about the natural or designed working of the human mind.

FALLACIES IN ARGUMENTS THAT MENTAL DISORDERS ARE NATURALLY SELECTED CONDITIONS

The HD analysis is fundamentally at odds with a certain strand of argument in the field of evolutionary psychopathology. Some evolutionary psychopathologists claim that they can explain specific disorders (e.g., schizophrenia, major depressive disorder) as themselves being naturally selected conditions. The HD analysis implies that such claims that disorders are naturally selected are not merely false but incoherent. A disorder is a failure of function and thus cannot itself be a function of a naturally selected trait, according to the HD analysis.

Some may attempt to explain away the apparent paradox of a seemingly debilitating disorder being naturally selected in one of two ways; either the disorder has hidden fitness benefits that offset its seeming disadvantages, or the disorder increased fitness in past environments but has become problematic in the current environment. But if the apparent negative effects of a condition on an individual are just the evolutionary price that is paid for the positive aspects of that condition for that individual, then the condition is not labeled a disorder at all. For example, the immense pain associated with the birth process is not judged to be a disorder because birth is obviously a designed process. Similarly, mismatches between a selected trait and the currect environment are not considered disorders. For example, taste for fatty foods may be bad for us now, but we believe it was selected for benefits in causing us to eat more calories in past environments where calories were scarce, so we do not label it a disorder. If these sorts of explanations of a problematic condition succeed, then rather than illuminating why disorders have been retained in the population, they explain why some problematic conditions do not conceptually qualify as disorders. In advancing such explanations, we should not ignore the alternative that the mechanisms underlying the condition are simply malfunctioning and have yielded a condition that was never selected for.

There are a variety of other fallacies that can underlie claims that disorders have been naturally selected, including the following:

1. In considering a disorder, some might rely on standard diagnostic categories and criteria from the *DSM* (1994) as the targets of the analysis, without independently assessing the conceptual validity of the criteria. Ample evidence suggests that *DSM* criteria often inadvertently encompass conditions under *disorder* that are generally considered nondisorders; examples are presented later. Thus, proposed natural selection explanations of disorders may in fact be explanations of nondisorders. For example, on the basis of a symptom list, *DSM* criteria might erroneously classify many normal states of sadness as a disorder, and such nondisordered states of sadness might indeed be subject to an evolutionary explanation in terms of, for example, retreat during periods of overwhelming threat, which is erroneously thought to explain disorder.

2. Some might incorrectly assume that virtually every problematic or harmful condition that is treated or treatable can be considered a disorder. In fact, there are many life problems that might be treatable or are treated but are not disorders. For example, normal shortness is sometimes treated with growth hormones; normal grief, with antidepressants; and birth control pills and abortion treat normal conditions.

3. A specific category, such as depression or anxiety, may contain some genuine disorders, but they may not be adequately distinguished from relatively mild and possibly adaptive versions of the same condition. The theoretical explanation in terms of natural selection may explain the nonpathological subset and not the pathological cases.

4. A direct natural selection explanation of a condition might be embraced while a more plausible indirect evolutionary explanation of how a condition has been retained in the population might be overlooked (e.g., retention of homozygous condition such as sickle cell anemia due to selective advantage of heterozygous condition). In fact, the condition being explained may have no selective advantage at all of its own at the organismic level and may exist in the population only as a side effect of selection for other fitness-enhancing traits.

5. An evolutionary psychological analysis may indeed succeed in explaining by natural selection the existence of a condition currently labeled a disorder, and

the theorist may erroneously assume that the explanation itself will have no impact on this classification. The theorist may fail to appreciate that a demonstration that a condition is part of human design will inevitably cast doubt on and eventually alter the condition's disorder classification. That is, a condition considered disordered but then shown to be designed will be reclassified as normal. This is exactly what happened, for example, with fever, which used to be considered a pathology based on an implicit theory that it represented breakdown in temperature regulation, but was reclassified as normal when it turned out that fever is a highly regulated process designed to aid recovery (Wakefield, 1999b). Treatment of fever may still be undertaken because such problematic defenses are often not needed for cure. But, such defensive reactions are not considered disorders once they are recognized for what they are.

In contrast with the objection to the HD analysis that disorders are naturally selected is the common Gouldian objection that mental mechanisms are not themselves naturally selected, so dysfunctions cannot be failures of such selected mechanisms (e.g., Lilienfeld & Marino, 1995, 1999). However, first, this objection is based on a faulty premise because, as we saw, most claimed cases of exaptation of mental mechanisms are in fact cases where mechanisms are maintained by natural selection for an effect that was not the one for which they were originally selected, but nonetheless have the selected-for maintained effect as a natural function. Gould, we saw, was incorrect to classify such selectively maintained effects as nonfunctions. Second, the HD analysis makes no assumptions about how extensively natural selection explains the details of mental functioning. Rather, it simply predicts that natural selection is necessary if there are to be attributions of function, dysfunction, and disorder. This prediction is supported by the fact that the "failure" of nonselected traits does not lead to disorder attribution (Wakefield, 2000).

IMPLICATIONS FOR *DIAGNOSTIC AND STATISTICAL MANUAL OF MENTAL DISORDERS* DIAGNOSIS

I briefly present here several examples of how failure to attend to the concept of disorder as naturally selected functioning has led to invalid diagnostic criteria for disorder in the *DSM* (for further discussion, see Wakefield, 1997; Wakefield & First, 2003):

1. The criteria for major depressive disorder do not adequately take into account human design for sadness responses to major losses and failed goal attainment. The criteria contain an exclusion for uncomplicated bereavement (up to 2 months of symptoms after loss of a loved one are allowed as normal) but no exclusions for equally normal reactions to other major losses such as a terminal medical diagnosis in oneself or a loved one, separation from spouse, the end of an intense love affair, or loss of job and retirement fund. Reactions to such losses may satisfy *DSM* diagnostic criteria but are not necessarily disorders. If an individual's reaction to such a loss includes, for example, just 2 weeks of depressed mood, diminished pleasure in usual activities, insomnia, fatigue, and diminished ability to concentrate on work tasks, then his or her reaction satisfies *DSM* criteria for major depressive disorder, even though such a reaction need not imply

pathology any more than it does in bereavement. Clearly, the essential requirement that there be a dysfunction in a depressive disorder—perhaps one in which loss-response mechanisms are not responding proportionately to loss as designed—is not adequately captured by *DSM* criteria.

2. The diagnostic criteria for conduct disorder allow the diagnosis of adolescents as disordered who are responding with antisocial behavior consistent with normal designed coping mechanisms to peer pressure, a threatening environment, or abuses at home (Wakefield, Pottick, & Kirk, 2002). For example, if a girl, attempting to avoid escalating sexual abuse by her stepfather, lies to her parents about her whereabouts and often stays out late at night despite their prohibitions and then, tired during the day, often skips school and her academic functioning is consequently impaired, she can be diagnosed as conduct disordered (criteria 11, 13, and 15). Rebellious kids or kids who fall in with the wrong crowd and who skip school and repetitively engage in shoplifting and vandalism also qualify for diagnosis. Yet, such activities are entirely consistent with normal human development, especially as a reaction to a society such as ours that does not allow teenagers to have significant social responsibility, power, or freedom and often places them in difficult environments. In an acknowledgment of such problems, a paragraph is included in the *DSM* textual discussion of conduct disorder that says that the diagnosis should be applied only when the behavior is symptomatic of an underlying dysfunction within the individual and not just a response to negative environmental events and notes that the clinician should consider the context in which the undesirable behaviors have occurred. If these ideas had been incorporated into the diagnostic criteria, many false positives could have been eliminated. Unfortunately, in epidemiological and research contexts, such textual nuances are likely ignored.

3. The criteria for separation anxiety disorder do not adequately distinguish disorder from normal designed separation protests in young children when there are environmental disturbances of the attachment bond. The disorder is diagnosed in children on the basis of symptoms indicating age-inappropriate, excessive anxiety concerning separation from those to whom the individual is attached, lasting at least 4 weeks. The symptoms (e.g., excessive distress when separation occurs, worry that some event will lead to separation, worry that harm will come to attachment figures, refusal to go to school because of fear of separation, reluctance to be alone or without major attachment figure) are just the sorts of things children experience when they have a normal, intense separation anxiety response. The criteria thus do not provide the user with any guidance on how to adequately distinguish between a true disorder in which separation responses are triggered inappropriately and normal responses consistent with designed attachment mechanisms in response to unusual perceived threats to the child's primary bond due to an unreliable caregiver or other serious disruptions. As in Bickman et al.'s (1995) study, which included children of military personnel leaving for combat duty during the Gulf War, normal children whose attachments are unusually threatened in reality and who are reacting with an entirely normal designed separation-anxiety response could thus be treated as though they have disordered attachment responses, rather than having their real attachment needs addressed (A. M. Brannan, personal communication).

4. The criteria for adjustment disorder do not adequately take into account normal human design for coping with environmental change and adapting to new

circumstances. The disorder is defined in terms of a reaction to an identifiable stressor that either (1) causes marked distress that is in excess of what would be expected from exposure to the stressor or (2) significantly impairs academic, occupational, or social functioning. The first "greater than expected" clause allows the top third, for example, of the normal distribution of reactivity to stress to be diagnosed as disordered and thus does not adequately deal with normal variation. Moreover, it does not take into account the contextual factors that may provide good reasons for one person to react more intensely than others. The second "role impairment" criterion classifies as disordered even normal reaction to adversity that temporarily impairs functioning (e.g., the person does not want to socialize, or the person does not feel up to going to work). But, temporarily retreating from normal role functioning is often exactly how normal designed coping or adjustment responses work. Here, too, the criteria contain an exclusion for bereavement but not for other equally normal reactions to misfortunes other than death of a loved one. The essence of an adjustment disorder is that something has gone wrong with normal coping mechanisms, which are presumably designed to gradually and perhaps after a period of retreat return the individual to homeostasis after some stress or change in life circumstances. This essential element of a dysfunction in coping mechanisms is not captured by the *DSM-IV* criteria set.

As the preceding discussion illustrates, the explanatory power of the HD analysis is considerable. The analysis also potentially provides an effective basis for a substantive critique of psychiatric diagnostic practices that retains what makes sense and jettisons what is excessive in applications of disorder to mental and behavioral conditions. In particular, the HD evolutionary analysis emphasizes that the failure of *DSM*'s symptomatic diagnostic criteria to take into account environmental context leads to a confusion of disorder with unpleasant but normal, designed human emotional responses to environmental contingencies. In providing a perspective from which to constructively critique psychiatric diagnosis, the HD analysis should help in clarifying psychiatry's conceptual foundations and its clinical practice in a way that Foucaultian and Szaszian critiques have not.

CONCLUSIONS

Conceptual analysis of the concepts *function, dysfunction,* and *disorder* that have existed since antiquity have at their roots the notions of design and failure of designed functioning. These notions in turn are built on notions of effects that explain why the mechanisms that produce them are there and, in the case of dysfunction, on the failure of such mechanisms to be capable of producing such explanatory effects. Darwin's scientific discoveries lead to the conclusion that the only plausible way to understand such explanatory effects is in terms of evolutionary theory and specifically natural selection. Consequently, judgments of psychological normality and disorder are in fact judgments about evolutionary design.

Whether *DSM* diagnostic criteria used by clinicians and researchers every day are valid and how to reframe them to be more valid hang on our understanding of human mental design and thus on progress in evolutionary psychology, according to this analysis. Indeed, down-to-earth, practical matters such as how clinicians should answer the patient's urgent question, "Is there anything wrong with me?" as well as the judgment as to whether in treating an individual we are attempting to correct an abnormality or tampering with designed functioning, also depend on further knowledge of evolutionary psychology.

Fortunately, as Williams (1966) has argued, many judgments about design (and, I might add, failure of design) can be made independently of knowledge of evolutionary history on the basis of various strands of immediate evidence regarding designlike properties. Current *DSM* categories, which surely largely pick out at least some categories of disorder reasonably well, are a testament to that fact. So, clinical psychology need not come to a halt while awaiting evolutionary psychology's progress. But in the long run, *DSM* must be replaced by a more theoretical account of mental mechanisms, their functions, and their dysfunctions. Thus, the fate of the mental health professions with respect to theoretical and scientific progress in understanding the etiology, diagnosis, and treatment of mental disorder may well depend in large measure on progress in evolutionary psychology.

However, the analysis of *function* reveals some of the complexities lurking in such judgments. Such complexities allow for intense controversy about function judgments, in which disputes about human nature often become politicized. Moreover, judgments of dysfunction and disorder are also often highly controversial due to the stakes of different constituencies in pathological versus normal classification of various conditions. The coming intersection of these two intensely controversial areas promises that those in the field of evolutionary psychopathology will find themselves living in interesting times.

REFERENCES

American Psychiatric Association. (1994). *Diagnostic and Statistical Manual of Mental Disorders (DSM-IV)* (4th ed.). Washington, DC: Author.

Andrews, P. W., Gangestad, S. W., & Matthews, D. (2002). Adaptationism, exaptationism, and evolutionary behavioral science. *Behavior and Brain Sciences, 25*, 534–547.

Ausubel, D. P. (1971). Personality disorder is disease. *American Psychologist, 16*, 59–74.

Bedau, M. (1993). Naturalism and teleology. In S. J. Wagner & R. Warner (Eds.), *Naturalism: A critical appraisal* (pp. 23–52). Notre Dame, IN: University of Notre Dame Press.

Bickman, L., Guthrie, P. R., Foster, E. M., Lambert, E. W., Summerfelt, W. T., Breda, C., et al. (1995). *Managed care in mental health: The Fort Bragg experiment.* New York: Plenum Publishing.

Boorse, C. (1975). On the distinction between disease and illness. *Philosophy and Public Affairs, 5*, 49–68.

Brandon, R. N. (1990). *Adaptation and environment.* Princeton, NJ: Princeton University Press.

Buller, D. J. (1999). Introduction: Natural teleology. In D. Buller (Ed.), *Function, selection, and design* (pp. 1–27). Albany, NY: SUNY Press.

Buss, D. M., Haselton, M. M. G., Shackelford, T. K., Bleske, A., & Wakefield, J. C. (1998). Adaptations, exaptations, and spandrels. *American Psychologist, 53*, 533–548.

Caplan, A. L. (1981). The "unnaturalness" of aging: A sickness unto death. In A. L. Caplan, H. T. Engelhardt, Jr., & J. J. McCartney (Eds.), *Concepts of health and disease: Interdisciplinary perspectives* (pp. 725–738). Reading, MA: Addison-Wesley.

Cosmides, L., & Tooby, J. (1999). Toward an evolutionary taxonomy of treatable conditions. *Journal of Abnormal Psychology, 108*, 453–464.

Dawkins, R. (1986). *The blind watchmaker.* London: Longman.

Foucault, M. (1965). *Madness and civilization: A history of insanity in the Age of Reason* (Trans. R. Howard). New York: Pantheon.

Godfrey-Smith, P. (1999a). A modern history theory of functions. In D. Buller (Ed.), *Function, selection, and design* (pp. 199–220). Albany, NY: SUNY Press. (Reprinted from *Nous 28*, pp. 344–362, 1994.)

Godfrey-Smith, P. (1999b). Functions: Consensus without unity. In D. Buller (Ed.), *Function, selection, and design* (pp. 185–197). Albany, NY: SUNY Press. (Reprinted from *Pacific Philosophical Quarterly* 74, pp. 196–208, 1993.)

Gotthelf, A. (1999). Darwin on Aristotle. *Journal of the History of Biology, 32,* 3–30.

Gould, S. J. (1991). Exaptation: A crucial tool for evolutionary analysis. *Journal of Social Issues, 47,* 43–65.

Gould, S. J., & Lewontin, R. C. (1979). The Spandrels of San Marcos and the Panglossian paradigm: A critique of the adaptationist programme. *Proceedings of the Royal Society of London, 205,* 581–598.

Gould, S. J., & Vrba, E. S. (1982). Exaptation: A missing term in the science of form. *Paleobiology, 8,* 4–15.

Griffiths, P. E. (1996). The historical turn in the study of adaptation. *British Journal for Philosophy of Science, 47,* 511–532.

Griffiths, P. E. (1999). Functional analysis and proper functions. In D. Buller (Ed.), *Function, selection, and design* (pp. 143–158). Albany, NY: SUNY Press.

Hempel, C. G. (1965). The logic of functional analysis. In C. G. Hempel (Ed.), *Aspects of scientific explanation and other essays in the philosophy of science* (pp. 297–330). New York: Free Press.

Houts, A. C. (2001). Harmful dysfunction and the search for value neutrality in the definition of mental disorder: Response to Wakefield, part 2. *Behavior Research and Therapy, 39,* 1099–1132.

Hull, D. L. (1990). *The metaphysics of evolution.* Albany, NY: SUNY Press.

Kendell, R. E. (1975). The concept of disease and its implications for psychiatry. *British Journal of Psychiatry, 127,* 305–315.

Kendell, R. E. (1986). What are mental disorders? In A. M. Freedman et al. (Eds.), *Issues in classification: Science, practice, and social policy* (pp. 23–45). New York: Human Science Press.

Kitcher, P. (1999). Function and design. In D. Buller (Ed.), *Function, selection, and design* (pp. 159–183). Albany, NY: SUNY Press. (Reprinted from *Midwest Studies in Philosophy* 18, pp. 379–397, 1993.)

Klein, D. F. (1978). A proposed definition of mental illness. In R. L. Spitzer & D. F. Klein (Eds.), *Critical issues in psychiatric diagnosis* (pp. 41–71). New York: Raven Press.

Klein, D. F. (1993). False suffocation alarms, spontaneous panics, and related conditions: An integrative hypothesis. *Archives of General Psychiatry, 50,* 306–317.

Lewontin, R. C. (1979). Sociobiology as an adaptationist program. *Behavioral Sciences, 24,* 5–14.

Lilienfeld, S. O., & Marino, L. (1995). Mental disorder as a Roschian concept: A critique of Wakefield's "harmful dysfunction" analysis. *Journal of Abnormal Psychology, 104,* 411–420.

Lilienfeld, S. O., & Marino, L. (1999). Essentialism revisitied: Evolutionary theory and the concept of mental disorder. *Journal of Abnormal Psychology, 108,* 400–411.

Macklin, R. (1981). Mental health and mental illness: Some problems of definition and concept formation. In A. L. Caplan, H. T. Engelhardt, Jr., & J. J. McCartney (Eds.), *Concepts of health and disease: Interdisciplinary perspectives* (pp. 391–418). Reading, MA: Addison-Wesley.

McNally, R. J. (1994). *Panic disorder: A conceptual analysis.* New York: Guilford Press.

Millikan, R. G. (1984). *Language, thought, and other biological categories.* Cambridge, MA: MIT Press.

Moore, M. S. (1978). Discussion of the Spitzer-Endicott and Klein proposed definitions of mental disorder (illness). In R. L. Spitzer & D. F. Klein (Eds.), *Critical issues in psychiatric diagnosis* (pp. 85–104). New York: Raven Press.

Neander, K. (1991). Functions as selected effects: The conceptual analyst's defense. *Philosophy of Science, 58,* 168–184.

Nesse, R. M. (1991). What good is feeling bad? *The Sciences, 31,* 30–37.

Orzack, S. E., & Sober, E. (1994). Optimality models and the test of adaptationism. *American Naturalist, 143,* 361–380.

Putnam, H. (1975). The meaning of meaning. In H. Putnam (Ed.), *Mind, language, and reality: Philosophical papers* (Vol. 2, pp. 215–271). Cambridge, England: Cambridge University Press.

Ruse, M. (1973). *The philosophy of biology.* London: London University Press.

Searle, J. R. (1983). *Intentionality: An essay in philosophy of mind.* Cambridge: Cambridge University Press.

Sedgwick, P. (1982). *Psycho politics.* New York: Harper & Row.

Sober, E. (1984). *The nature of selection.* Cambridge, MA: MIT Press.

Spitzer, R. L., & Endicott, J. (1978). Medical and mental disorder: Proposed definition and criteria. In R. L. Spitzer & D. F. Klein (Eds.), *Critical issues in psychiatric diagnosis* (pp. 15–39). New York: Raven Press.

Szasz, T. S. (1974). *The myth of mental illness: Foundations of a theory of personal conduct (Revised edition).* New York: Harper & Row.

Tinbergen, N. (1963). On aims and methods of ethology. *Zeitschrift für Tierpsychologie, 20,* 410–433.

Wakefield, J. C. (1992a). The concept of mental disorder: On the boundary between biological facts and social values. *American Psychologist, 47,* 373–388.

Wakefield, J. C. (1992b). Disorder as harmful dysfunction: A conceptual critique of *DSM-III-R's* definition of mental disorder. *Psychological Review, 99,* 232–247.

Wakefield, J. C. (1997). Diagnosing *DSM:* Pt. 1. *DSM* and the concept of mental disorder. *Behavior Research and Therapy, 35,* 633–650.

Wakefield, J. C. (1999a). Disorder as a black box essentialist concept. *Journal of Abnormal Psychology, 108,* 465–472.

Wakefield, J. C. (1999b). Evolutionary versus prototype analyses of the concept of disorder. *Journal of Abnormal Psychology, 108,* 374–399.

Wakefield, J. C. (2000). Spandrels, vestigial organs, and such: Reply to Murphy and Woolfolk's "The harmful dysfunction analysis of mental disorder." *Philosophy, Psychiatry, and Psychology, 7,* 253–270.

Wakefield, J. C. (2004). The myth of open concepts: Meehl's analysis of construct meaning versus black box essentialism. *Applied and Preventive Psychology, 11,* 77–82.

Wakefield, J. C., & First, M. (2003). Clarifying the distinction between disorder and non-disorder: Confronting the overdiagnosis ("false positives") problem in *DSM-V.* In K. A. Phillips, M. B. First, & H. A. Pincus (Eds.), *Advancing DSM: Dilemmas in psychiatric diagnosis.* Washington, DC: American Psychiatric Press.

Wakefield, J. C., Pottick, K. J., & Kirk, S. A. (2002). Should the *DSM-IV* diagnostic criteria for conduct disorder consider social context? *American Journal of Psychiatry, 159,* 380–386.

Williams, G. C. (1966). *Adaptation and natural selection.* Princeton, NJ: Princeton University Press.

Williams, G. C. (1992). *Natural selection: Domains, levels, and challenges.* New York: Oxford University Press.

Wright, L. (1973). Functions. *Philosophical Review, 82,* 139–168.

Wright, L. (1976). *Teleological explanations.* Berkeley, CA: University of California Press.

CHAPTER 32

Evolutionary Psychology and Mental Health

RANDOLPH M. NESSE

A N EVOLUTIONARY PERSPECTIVE revolutionized our understanding of behavior over a generation ago, but most mental health clinicians and researchers still view evolution as an interesting or even threatening alternative, instead of recognizing it as an essential basic science for understanding mental disorders. Many factors explain this lag in incorporating new knowledge, but the most important may be the clinician's pragmatic focus on finding ways to help people now. Evolutionary researchers have not found a new treatment for a single mental disorder, so why *should* mental health clinicians and researchers care about evolutionary psychology (EP)? This chapter attempts to answer that question. The greatest value of an evolutionary approach is not some specific finding or new therapy, but is instead the framework it provides for uniting all aspects of a biopsychosocial model. Perhaps equally valuable is the deeper empathy fostered by an evolutionary perspective on life's vicissitudes. An evolutionary perspective does not compete with other theories that try to explain why some people have mental disorders and others do not. Instead, it asks a fundamentally different question: Why has natural selection left all humans so vulnerable to mental disorders? At first, the question seems senseless. Natural selection shapes mechanisms that work, so how can it help us understand why the mind fails? It is also difficult to see how it is useful to know why we are vulnerable. Who cares why all humans are vulnerable to depression, when the goal is to help the individual who is depressed here and now? Surmounting these conceptual hurdles is a challenge that requires time and effort. Researchers and clinicians will make the effort when they know what evolution offers to the understanding of mental disorders.

WHAT EVOLUTION OFFERS

Many have contributed to the growth of evolutionary psychiatry, but the contributions are in diverse sources and not always consistent. Early applications of

Table 32.1
Eight Fundamental Contributions

An evolutionary perspective on mental disorders:

1. Asks new questions about why natural selection has left us all vulnerable to mental disorders, questions with six kinds of possible answers,
2. Offers the beginnings of the kind of functional understanding for mental health professions that physiology provides for the rest of medicine,
3. Provides a framework for a deeper and more empathic understanding of individuals,
4. Explains how relationships work,
5. Provides a way to think clearly about development and the ways that early experiences influence later characteristics,
6. Provides a foundation for understanding emotions and their regulation,
7. Provides a foundation for a scientific diagnostic system,
8. Provides a framework for incorporating multiple causal factors that explain why some people get mental disorders while others do not.

[Handwritten margin note, top left: "Danger in this statement"]

[Handwritten margin note, left: "★ Has applicability to depression → but hard to prove ??."]

ethology to mental disorders (McGuire & Fairbanks, 1977; White, 1974) gave rise to more specific and comprehensive evolutionary approaches (McGuire & Troisi, 1998; Pitchford, 2001; Stevens & Price, 1996; Wenegrat, 1990). Several books cover specific conditions (Baron-Cohen, 1995, 1997; Gilbert, 1992; Wenegrat, 1995), while others take a more anthropological approach (Fabrega, 2002). Many articles address specific mental disorders, and some provide a new foundation for defining the categories that describe disorders (Cosmides & Tooby, 1999; Wakefield, 1992). Many chapters in this *Handbook* and many general books about EP tackle one or another mental disorder (Badcock, 2000; Barkow, Cosmides, & Tooby, 1992; Barrett, Dunbar, & Lycett, 2002; Buss, 1994, 1995, 2003, 2004; Crawford, Smith, & Krebs, 1987; Gaulin & McBurney, 2001; Wright, 1994). The ideas in these sources are too many and too diverse to even list, but many can be summarized in a list of eight fundamental contributions that an evolutionary perspective offers to psychiatry and clinical psychology (Table 32.1). A brief summary of each sets the stage for considering specific disorders.

EXPLAINING VULNERABILITY TO MENTAL DISORDERS

The task of explaining why we are vulnerable to mental disorders is no different from that of explaining why we are vulnerable to physical diseases. The tendency in both cases has been to oversimplify the problem by attributing vulnerability to the limited powers of natural selection. These limits are important explanations for some diseases, but there are five other possible reasons that the body and mind are not better designed, starting with the mismatch between our bodies and our environments (Nesse & Williams, 1994; Williams & Nesse, 1991).

Mismatch Most common chronic diseases are caused by novel environmental factors. For instance, atherosclerosis and breast cancer are prevalent now because our bodies are not well designed for life in a modern environment (Eaton et al., 2002). Whether rates of mental disorders are also increasing remains uncertain. An international effort to gather prevalence data on mental disorders from 72,000 interviews in 14 countries (Kessler & Ustun, 2000) uses urban or rural agricultural sites. No comparable effort is estimating disorder rates in hunter-gatherer populations. This is unfortunate because such studies may not be possible in the next generation, but understandable because of the methodological obstacles.

Mental disorders are often blamed on the modern environment. When reading and writing were first spreading, Burton attributed melancholy to excessive study and "too little Venus" (Burton, 1624/1931). Much more recently, retrospective data seemed to suggest that depression rates were increasing rapidly with each generation (Cross-National Collaborative Group, 1992). However, data gathered using consistent questions in the same population over recent decades showed no such increase (J. M. Murphy, Laird, Monson, Sobol, & Leighton, 2000). For drug and alcohol problems, the story is more clear-cut. The rapid spread of alcohol-making technology changed our world in ways our species has not yet adapted to (Institute of Medicine, 1987), although selection may have increased the frequency of a defective aldehyde dehydrogenase gene that may protect Asian populations from alcoholism (M. Smith, 1986).

Infection and Coevolution   Infections persist because our every evolutionary advance to escape bacteria and viruses is matched by their far faster evolution (A. S. Brown et al., 2004; Ewald, 1994). Furthermore, the defenses that protect us, especially immune responses, tend to cause problems themselves. Some mental disorders may result from arms races with pathogens and their autoimmune sequelae. For instance, some cases of obsessive-compulsive disorder may result from streptococcal-induced autoimmune damage to the caudate nucleus (Swedo, Leonard, & Kiessling, 1994). Prenatal exposure to infection may predispose to schizophrenia (Ledgerwood, Ewald, & Cochran, 2003) as suggested by increased rates of schizophrenia in babies born during influenza epidemics (Kunugi et al., 1995) and a sevenfold risk increase for babies born to mothers who had influenza during the first trimester (A. S. Brown et al., 2004). Infectious causes have been proposed for a wide range of mental disorders, especially affective disorders (Ewald, 2000).

A more insidious result of rapid coevolution arises from competition within our species that induces more and more extreme traits, especially those that lead to winning social competitions (Alexander, 1974; Humphrey, 1976; Whiten & Byrne, 1997). If sexual selection has shaped mental traits (Miller, 2000), this could account for vulnerability to certain disorders, especially those associated with creativity (Richards, Kinner, Lunde, & Benet, 1988; Shaner, Miller, & Mintz, 2004). Even aside from competing for partners, competing for status absorbs vast human energy (Barkow, 1989; Veblen, 1899) and gives rise to much suffering from envy and the negative emotions associated with failures (Gilbert, Price, & Allen, 1995). Such emotional tendencies might well result from arms races that often leave us in zero-sum competitions (Frank, 1999).

Trade-Offs   Design trade-offs make perfection impossible for any trait, natural or human made. A car that gets 60 miles per gallon will not get to 60 miles per hour in 6 seconds. We humans could run faster if our legs were longer, but our bones would be more fragile. We could have less anxiety, but only at the cost of being more likely to be injured or killed.

Constraints   Systems shaped by natural selection are subject to several special constraints, especially path dependence. For instance, we are stuck with eyes whose vessels and nerves run between the light and the retina. Furthermore, in contrast to consciously created designs, biological designs are products of selection that involve limited options, random effects, inaccurate transmission of the DNA code, and the vagaries of interaction effects with different environments. Far from assuming that everything is adaptive, an evolutionary approach calls attention to defective and substandard designs that result from multiple trade-offs, constraints, and errors.

Selection Is for Reproductive Success, Not Health   Many imagine that selection shapes bodies and minds that are healthy, long-lived, and cooperative. It does, when those traits increase reproductive success (RS). However, a gene that decreases health, longevity, or cooperativeness will nonetheless spread if it increases RS. Such genes are likely responsible for many of our least valued characteristics, such as bitter competition, envy, greed, and unquenchable sexual desire and jealousy (Buss, 2000). The differences between the sexes arise largely because different reproductive strategies shape different physical and mental traits, even at the expense of longevity and individual well-being (Cronin, 1991; Daly & Wilson, 1983; Geary, 1998; Kruger & Nesse, 2004).

Defenses   Pain, cough, fever, and other protective responses are unpleasant but useful responses that protect us from danger and loss. The prevalent tendency to confuse these defenses with diseases and defects has been called "The Clinician's Illusion" (Nesse & Williams, 1994). Most physicians know that cough and inflammation are adaptations, but the utility of fever, diarrhea, and anxiety is less widely recognized. A naïve view sees our vulnerability to negative emotions as examples of poor design. But natural selection does not care a fig for our happiness; it just mindlessly shapes whatever emotional tendencies increase RS (Nesse, 1991a; Tooby & Cosmides, 1990). While positive emotions are useful in situations where energy and risk-taking pay off (Fredrickson, 1998), they can be fatal in dangerous situations (Nesse, 2004).

Summing Up Six Causes   Some evolutionary approaches to mental disorders emphasize one of the preceding six possible explanations. For instance, some authors attribute much psychopathology to living in a modern environment (Glantz & Pearce, 1989); others emphasize infection (Ewald, 2000), constraints, trade-offs, or path dependencies (Crow, 1997; Horrobin, 1998). Others propose that mental disorders persist because of fitness benefits, even for conditions such as schizophrenia (J. S. Allen & Sarich, 1988; Shaner et al., 2004), bipolar disorder (Wilson, 1998), and suicide (deCatanzaro, 1980). The resulting confusion is substantial for those in the field and overwhelming for others.

While the human mind prefers monocausal explanations, a full evolutionary explanation for one disorder may include several different factors. For example, vulnerability to depression may arise from novel aspects of modern life, from infection, from constraints and trade-offs, and because low mood may be a defense that can increase RS at the expense of personal happiness. Far from offering a

Not really applicable

simplistic approach to the causes of mental disorders, an evolutionary perspective provides a framework for organizing the genuine complexity into a biopsychosocial perspective (Weiner, 1998).

AN EVOLUTIONARY FRAMEWORK FOR UNDERSTANDING HUMAN BEHAVIOR AND EMOTIONS

When a patient comes to the general medical clinic with cough or kidney failure, the physician knows that cough is a protective response and that the kidney filters out toxins and regulates salt and water balance. By contrast, when a patient comes to a mental health clinic with a phobia, the utility of anxiety may never be considered. When someone comes with jealousy, consideration of its normal functions is unlikely. Mental health professionals lack a body of knowledge about normal emotional functions comparable to the understanding physiology offers to general medicine. EP is beginning to provide this missing body of knowledge, as shown by the chapters in this *Handbook*, and by evolutionary perspectives on motivation (French, Kamil, & Leger, 2000), emotion (Plutchik, 2003), and specific topics such as grief (Archer, 1999).

UNDERSTANDING INDIVIDUAL LIVES

EP can bring information about an individual's idiosyncratic values, goals, and life situations into a scientific framework. Consider John, a depressed 20-year-old man who works two jobs in local stores to support his disabled mother. When he was 14, his dying father made him promise to take care of his mother always. He has been doing that ever since, but with increasing resentment and depression. These three sentences give more insight into his depression than a dozen demographic variables and a brain scan. An evolutionary understanding of motivation can begin to bring such information into a nomothetic framework based on behavioral ecology categories of life history effort. The trade-offs among these categories are as universal as they are problematic (Krebs & Davies, 1984; Stearns, 1992). No solution can be perfect, and the conflicts account for much human suffering (Chisholm, 1999; Low, 2000; E. A. Smith & Winterhalder, 1992; Sterelny & Griffiths, 1999). Understanding these trade-offs fosters realistic clinical thinking and enhances empathy for the vicissitudes of people's lives.

RELATIONSHIPS

EP's greatest contribution may be a deeper understanding of relationships. For instance, Bowlby's (1969) insights about the evolutionary functions of attachment have been extended by suggestions that apparently "abnormal" kinds of attachment may represent alternative strategies for infants to get resources from mothers in difficult circumstances (Belsky, 1999; Chisholm, 1996) and a deeper understanding of women's reproductive strategies in general (Hrdy, 1999). Analysis of mutually beneficial reciprocal exchanges has led to extensive studies of economic games (Fehr & Fischbacher, 2003) that illuminate the origins of the social emotions (Fessler, in press; Fiske, 1992; Henrich & Gil-White, 2001). However, interpreting all human relationships as calculated exchanges ignores aspects of human behavior that are essential to understanding mental disorders, such as our capacities for moral action and the emotions of pride and guilt (Katz, 2000). Selection may have shaped capacities for commitment that are superior to rational calculation (Frank, 1988; Gintis, 2000; Nesse, 2001a).

Psychodynamics   Freud's theories are ridiculed because some are wrong and because psychoanalysis is not reliably effective. However, the reality of repression is a profound fact of human nature that needs an evolutionary explanation (Badcock, 1988; Sulloway, 1985), along with phenomena such as the Oedipus complex (Ericson, 1993). Trivers and Alexander separately suggested that self-deception is a strategy for deceiving others (Alexander, 1975; Trivers, 1976, 2000), but people also may repress the sins of others to preserve valuable relationships (Nesse, 1990b). Closely related is Trivers's (1974) insight that regression may be an effective strategy used by offspring to manipulate their parents into providing resources that would be appropriate only if they were younger or sick. His more general theory of parent-offspring conflict is the neglected foundation for understanding many childhood disorders. Attempts to provide an evolutionary foundation for psychodynamics are developing (Badcock, 1988; Slavin & Kriegman, 1992; Sulloway, 1985) but remain relatively unappreciated by psychoanalysts, perhaps because an evolutionary view fosters skepticism that undermining repression will be helpful routinely (Slavin & Kriegman, 1990).

Development   Developmental psychology now offers sophisticated assessments of extensive data about what children do at different stages of life and how these phenomena vary across cultures. It increasingly takes evolution into account (Bateson & Martin, 2000; Geary & Bjorklund, 2000; Rutter & Rutter, 1993). In the midst of a burst of interest in facultative developmental mechanisms and their role in evolution (Hall, 1998; West-Eberhard, 2003), evolutionary psychologists have begun looking for mechanisms that use environment inputs to adjust developmental pathways. An obvious facultative adaptation is the regulation of female reproductive onset by fat stores (Surbey, 1987). Less well supported are proposals that early father absence induces early reproduction (Belsky, Steinberg, & Draper, 1991; Draper & Harpending, 1982; Surbey, 1990). A possible adaptation with particular relevance for mental disorders is the adjustment of the gain in the hypothalamic pituitary axis system in response to early stress and the transmission of this sensitivity across the generations by maternal influences on fetal brain development (Essex, Klein, Eunsuk, & Kalin, 2002; Teicher et al., 2003).

⤷ what is he talking about here

EMOTIONS AND THE EMOTIONAL DISORDERS

Most mental disorders are emotional disorders. People come for treatment because they experience anxiety, depression, anger, or jealousy. Many assume that such negative emotions are abnormal, but they are useful, at least for our genes. People with depression and anxiety are so obviously impaired that it is difficult to see how such emotions could be useful. However, selection has shaped emotion regulation mechanisms that often give rise to normal but useless suffering (Nesse, 2004, 2005). An evolutionary foundation for studies of emotions is now routine (Ekman, 1992; Nesse, 1990a; Plutchik, 2003; Tooby & Cosmides, 1990) and recognition is growing that emotions are special states shaped by selection to give advantages in fitness-significant situations that have recurred over evolutionary time.

DIAGNOSIS

When is an emotion abnormal? The criteria for psychiatric diagnoses are based on intensity, duration, and associated disability (American Psychiatric Association, 1994). The extremes are abnormal, but without knowing the functions of emotions, the line between normal and abnormal remains subjective (D. Murphy & Stich, 2000; Nesse, 2001b; Troisi & McGuire, 2002; Wakefield, 1992). The lack of an evolutionary foundation fosters serious errors including describing continuous emotions as categories and neglecting abnormal conditions characterized by excess positive or deficient negative emotions. In addition, diagnostic criteria do not consider the appropriateness of an emotion to the situation. If general medicine made diagnoses according to the strategy used in psychiatry, it would diagnose abnormal cough disorder based on cough frequency and severity without considering whether the cough was a normal response in certain situations. Far from genuinely atheoretical, the *Diagnostic and Statistical Manual of Mental Disorders* system (*DSM;* American Psychiatric Association, 1994) fosters a crude biological view (Horwitz, 2002).

Many agree that the *DSM* system inhibits understanding (Phillips, First, & Pincus, 2003), and several authors have suggested how evolutionary principles can help to make diagnoses more scientific. D. Murphy and Stich (2000) take the *DSM* to task for its atheoretical approach and suggest distinguishing disorders that arise from brain abnormalities from those that arise from normal brains exposed to novel environments. They propose categories based on the presumed modularity of cognitive design. Wakefield (1992) offers a strong critique of the *DSM*, using the concept of "harmful dysfunction" to clarify what is and is not a disorder. This sophisticated evolutionary analysis of psychiatric diagnosis argues that it is essential for mental as well as physical disorders to separate normal from abnormal phenomena based on whether they are harmful and whether they arise from a dysfunction. This sophisticated understanding of evolutionary function is the scientific foundation for future psychiatric diagnostic systems (Wakefield, this volume).

An evolutionary view highlights the central flaw in the *DSM* criteria; they do not reflect the most basic distinction in medical diagnosis: that between diseases and symptoms of diseases. Negative emotions such as anxiety and sadness are useful capacities shaped by natural selection. Determining when they are abnormal requires understanding when and how they are useful.

An approach based on Darwinian medicine, following Wakefield, suggests global categories of mental problems based on answers to three questions: (1) Are cognitive and brain mechanisms normal or defective? (2) Do the symptoms arise from novel aspects of the environment, and (3) Are the symptoms in the interests of the individual, his or her genes, or neither? The resulting categories are:

1. Emotional, cognitive, or behavioral responses that arise from normal systems:
   a. Useful responses that may be aversive (ordinary anxiety and anger).
   b. Normal responses that benefit the individual's genes, at the expense of the individual's interests.

How adequate of a job does this system do of capturing mental disorders?

    c. Responses that arise from normal system but that are not useful in the particular instance.

    d. Normal responses that are useless or harmful now but would not have been in the ancestral environment.

    e. Normal responses that do not harm the individual but that are defined as abnormal by a group or culture.

2. Symptoms arising from abnormal regulation of a normal emotion or capacity.

    a. Specific defects, genetic or acquired, account for the dysregulation (causation from below, hardware problems).

    b. Dysregulation arising from social dilemmas or complexities (causation from above, software problems).

    c. Extremes of a trait distribution that increase vulnerability.

3. Abnormalities of behavior, cognition, and emotion that arise from fundamental brain or cognitive abnormalities not primarily involved with systems that regulate emotion and behavior (e.g., lead poisoning).

could be many ?.

Individual Differences

Most psychiatric research attempts to explain individual differences. Despite growing agreement on the importance of gene-environment interactions (Kendler, Kuhn, & Prescott, 2004; Ridley, 2003; Rutter & Rutter, 1993), major disagreements persist about why some people get ill and others do not. Different authorities emphasize different causal factors (genetic, developmental, situational, etc.). Far from emphasizing genetic differences, an evolutionary view provides a framework that highlights the relationships among all factors and levels. It also contributes strategies for avoiding some simple mistakes.

    Much misunderstanding arises from confusing attempts to explain the existence of a trait with attempts to explain variations in a trait. It is senseless to ask whether a rectangle is caused more by its length or its width. However, rectangles can vary in area only if their width or length (or both) changes. Likewise, variations among individuals can result only from differences in genes, differences in environments, and the interactions between them. The proportion of variance attributable to each component is not fixed, but varies depending on the particular environment and the range of genotypes. Preoccupation with nature versus nurture has distracted attention from the many different routes to a disorder. An evolutionary approach fosters simultaneous consideration of the many factors that may explain individual variation in a trait, some of which are listed in Table 32.2.

    The task of accounting for individual differences should not be reduced to arguing about the relative importance of one factor compared to another. It is, instead, the challenge of explicating how each contributes to individual differences in a particular trait and how their contributions to a particular trait may be different not only between families, populations, or cultures, but even between individuals. The responsible factors may be mainly genetic in one individual and mainly environmental in another. This has practical implications for mental health research. For instance, we need to take seriously the possibility that many different genes contribute to depression vulnerability by many different routes.

Table 32.2
Twelve Sources of Individual Differences

1. Additive genetic differences among individuals that result in phenotypic differences (in this environment)
2. Variation resulting from Gene x Environment interactions
3. Variation resulting from Gene x Gene interactions
4. Assortative mating—nonrandom mating increases or decreases trait variance
5. Random factors in development, such as the stochastic paths of neuron migration
6. Effects of cues that influence development via facultative mechanisms to a trajectory suited to the particular environment, such as early heat exposure influencing the number of adult sweat glands
7. Effects of trauma, toxins, and other environmental exposures outside the range of normal that damage the organism or distort its development
8. Effects of environmental factors that influence the organism "top-down" via perceptual experience without resulting in damage or acting via a specific facultative mechanism
9. Effects of environmental factors that influence the organism from the "bottom-up" that are neither damaging nor mediated via facultative adaptations
10. Effects of individual learning that facilitate flexible coping with current aspects of the environment
11. Experiences shared within a culture that are incorporated into values and emotional proclivities that may be difficult to change later (such as values or sexual attitudes)
12. Experiences shared within a culture whose effects account for variation that changes readily when conditions change

SPECIFIC DISORDERS

An evolutionary perspective calls attention to a distinction that is fundamental and well recognized in most of medicine, but unaccountably neglected in psychiatry. Some medical conditions, such as cancer and epilepsy, are diseases that arise from some abnormality in the body's mechanisms, while others, such as pain and cough, are protective responses. Some mental disorders, such as schizophrenia and autism, are almost certainly specific diseases or clusters of diseases, while others, such as depression and panic disorder are fundamentally different in that they are useful protective mechanisms, albeit ones that readily go awry. Not all mental disorders are emotional disorders, but many are, and they deserve consideration together.

EMOTIONAL DISORDERS

Most mental disorders are emotional disorders, but they are not yet based on knowledge about the origins and functions of emotions. Instead, intense or prolonged negative emotions are said to be abnormal, irrespective of the situation, while deficits in negative emotions and excesses of positive emotions are rarely recognized as disorders. An evolutionary perspective provides a more balanced view.

Anxiety Disorders   Although anxiety can be useful, a dry mouth and tremor when standing before a large group seem worse than useless. Likewise, the symptoms of panic may help escape from a lion, but they are unhelpful in a grocery store. We now have a vast amount of knowledge about the responsible brain mechanisms, but no comparable body of knowledge about the evolutionary origins and utility of social anxiety or panic (Nesse, 1987). Similarly, hundreds of studies document every aspect of excessive anxiety states, but only a handful look for states of deficient anxiety, the hypophobias (Marks & Nesse, 1994). One study tried to confirm that fear of heights often results from severe falls early in life. It found adult fear of heights in 18% of the control group but only 3% of the group that had experienced a fall early in life. Those with hypophobia early in life still had deficient anxiety decades later (Poulton, Davies, Menzies, Langley, & Silva, 1998).

Anxiety illustrates the diversity of the body's regulation mechanisms (Barlow, 1988; Marks, 1987; Poulton & Menzies, 2002; Stein & Bouwer, 1997). For instance, rigid defensive responses to fixed cues, such as chicks hiding from hawk-shaped shadows, are useful when a correct response to the first encounter is essential, but they result in many false alarms and do not protect against novel dangers. Flexible learning mechanisms protect against novel dangers but may fail during a crucial initial exposure, and they are prone to result in phobias. Social learning is another solution. Infant rhesus monkeys show no innate fear of snakes; however, a single observation of another monkey displaying fear of snakes induces long-lasting avoidance. Watching another monkey display fear of a flower induces no such fear (Mineka, Keir, & Price, 1980).

Exposure treatment is effective for phobias, but the fear response is not unlearned (Barlow, 1988; Foa, Steketee, & Ozarow, 1985; Marks & Tobena, 1990). Instead, a new cortical process suppresses the fear response (Quirk, 2002). Exposure to danger disrupts this suppression. Thus, the great flood in Moscow caused the reemergence of previously extinguished fears in Pavlov's dogs. This may reflect a constraint in a path-dependent mechanism; simple unlearning apparently may be impossible.

Other fears cannot be extinguished. For instance, posttraumatic stress disorder (PTSD) illustrates one-time learning of the strongest sort. A single life-threatening experience induces a subsequent terror response to any cue that suggests a recurrence of the dangerous situation (Breslau, Davis, & Andreski, 1995). Proximate science is steadily honing in on the mechanisms that account for this syndrome (Pitman, 1989; Yehuda, Halligan, Golier, Grossman, & Bierer, 2004), but it has been more difficult to find ways to differentiate alternative evolutionary hypotheses. PTSD could result from damage to mechanisms not designed to cope with such extreme situations. However, nearly dying is so important to fitness that it might well have shaped a one-time learning mechanism that gives rise to the symptoms of posttraumatic stress that might help prevent a recurrence.

Fear has distinct subtypes that seem to have been partially differentiated from generic anxiety to cope with domain-specific challenges (Marks & Nesse, 1994). For instance, panic flight is just the ticket to escape from a predator, but frozen immobility is superior when teetering on a cliff. Social anxiety is present in most people (Gilbert, 2001; Leary & Kowalski, 1995), and people who lack it are often insufferable, even if they do not qualify for a psychiatric diagnosis. We wonder how they would have fared in small hunter-gatherer groups. The characteristics of subtypes of anxiety map well onto the challenges posed by different threats.

The smoke detector principle helps to explain some apparent peculiarities of the mechanisms that regulate anxiety and other defenses (Nesse, 2005; Stein & Bouwer, 1997). Because most anxiety responses are inexpensive and protect against huge potential harms, an optimal system will express many alarms that are unnecessary in the particular instance, but nonetheless perfectly normal. This suggests that using drugs to block defenses may be safe in most instances but that in some situations blocking a defense may be fatal.

Mood Disorders   The utility of sadness and depression is less obvious than for anxiety, but Bibring (1953) long ago suggested that depression signaled the need to detach when libido persists in a connection to an unrewarding object. Hamburg, Hamburg, and Barchas (1975) and Klinger (1975) described how emotions regulate goal pursuit more generally, with inability to reach a goal first arousing aggressive attempts to overcome an obstacle, then low mood motivating disengagement. If the person does not give up, the negative affect escalates into depression. This principle, now confirmed by much research (Brickman, 1987; Carver & Scheier, 1990, 1998; Emmons & King, 1988; Janoff-Bulman & Brickman, 1982; Little, 1999; Wrosch, Scheier, & Miller, 2003), provides the foundation for a more general approach to mood as a mechanism that allocates effort proportional to propitiousness (Nesse, 1991b, 2000). When payoffs are high, positive mood increases initiative and risk-taking. When risks are substantial or effort is likely to be wasted, low mood blocks investments. In this perspective, ordinary episodes of sadness and low mood motivate changing behavioral strategies (Watson & Andrews, 2002). If no alternative is found and the goal is essential, persistence may result in depression (Klinger, 1975; Wrosch, Scheier, & Carver, 2003).

Observations of chickens and monkeys who lost their positions in the hierarchy have suggested a view of depression as "involuntary yielding" that protects against continuing attack (Gilbert, 1992; Sloman, Price, Gilbert, & Gardner, 1994). This is consistent with data showing that stressful events cause depression mainly if they are characterized by humiliation and/or being trapped in an impossible quest (G. W. Brown, Harris, & Hepworth, 1995; Kendler, Hettema, Butera, Gardner, & Prescott, 2003). Also related is the suggestion that sex differences in depression may arise from the male tendency to strive for position and resources, leaving many women vulnerable to depression because they have fewer options (Gilbert, 1992; Wenegrat, 1995).

Depression has also been viewed as a social manipulation (Hagen, 2002; Watson & Andrews, 2002). Hagen sees postpartum depression as a "blackmail threat" to abandon the infant, but other theories can also explain the association of postpartum depression with poor resources and relationships. In a related but more general view, Watson and Andrews (2002) suggest that depression facilitates "social navigation" by signaling that current strategies are failing and new directions are needed. This approach echoes psychoanalyst Emmy Gut's (1989) work on productive and unproductive depression. Nettle (2004) notes inadequacies of the social navigation hypothesis and emphasizes the possible adaptive value of neuroticism.

DeCatanzaro (1980) proposed that suicide can be adaptive if an individual has no chance for reproduction but can increase future reproduction of kin by ceasing to use resources that they could use instead. Data showing that suicides are more common in old and sick people are consistent; however, alternative explanations are available, separation from kin does not protect against suicide, and there are no animal examples. In a reverse twist on this perspective, the benefits of social support result more from help given than help received. Individuals who provide help to others have higher mood and increased longevity (R. Brown, Dahlen,

Mills, Rick, & Biblarz, 1999; S. L. Brown, Nesse, Vinokur, & Smith, 2003). The role of the group is also central to N. B. Allen and Badcock's (2003) model, in which people carefully monitor what they can contribute to a group. People who realize they can contribute little retreat into depression that is hypothesized to prevent active expulsion from the group.

These approaches are quite different from the prevalent view that depression is a brain disorder (Andreasen, 1984; Valenstein, 1998; Wolpert, 1999). The brain mechanisms that mediate mood certainly can go awry, but two questions need consideration. First, is low mood a useful response like cough or an abnormality unrelated to defenses like epileptic seizures? Second, do individual differences in vulnerability to depression arise mainly from primary brain differences or from brain changes mediated by social experience (G. W. Brown & Harris, 1978; Monroe & Simons, 1991)? These are not mutually exclusive alternatives, and most depression is best understood as the outcome of gene x environment interactions (Caspi et al., 2003). Also, there are different routes to depression, some of which progress irrespective of environment, others of which arise from life circumstances, perhaps especially those involving pursuit of unreachable goals.

Other Emotional Disorders   Anxiety and depression get all the attention, but every emotion is subject to at least two kinds of disorder: excesses or deficits. For instance, pathological jealousy is common, but few clinicians know why jealousy exists (Buss, Larsen, Westen, & Semmelroth, 1992). Jealousy may arise for good reasons (Buss et al., 1999) or from delusions. Feelings of inadequacy make some men think that their partners might well prefer someone else and then that they do prefer someone else. Depression treatment often relieves pathological jealousy (Stein, Hollander, & Josephson, 1994). The syndrome of pathological lack of jealousy has yet to be described.

Comparable pathologies exist for every emotion. People are taken over by envy, love, suspicion, anger, awe, or rapture. Whether it is normal or abnormal depends on the situation. Recognizing the evolutionary origins and functions of emotions provides a framework for describing their disorders and the long-sought scientific basis for distinguishing emotional disorders from emotions that are simply unwanted.

BEHAVIORAL DISORDERS

Other disorders involve inability to control behavior. Most obvious are the addictions and other habits, but other problems of behavioral control range from eating disorders to violence.

Addictions   The human toll taken by addictions is magnified because their effects harm others as well as the addict. A whole issue of *Addiction* was devoted to evolutionary approaches (Hill & Newlin, 2002), with suggestions about the adaptive significance of addiction (Sullivan & Hagen, 2002), life history theory (Hill & Chow, 2002), and the significance of fermentation (Dudley, 2002), among others. One of the most important evolutionary insights is simple, however. Learning is chemically mediated, so exogenous substances can directly stimulate reward mechanisms (Nesse, 1994; Nesse & Berridge, 1997). The subjective sensations are pleasurable, and the associated reinforcement increases the frequency of drug-taking behavior. Aversive withdrawal symptoms become cues that stimulate further drug taking. Over time, the subjective pleasurable "liking" wanes, the withdrawal effects become more severe, and the habit strength of "wanting" increases, trapping the addict in a vicious cycle that may offer little pleasure, even as it consumes most of what is valuable in life.

Vulnerability to substance abuse results from our novel environment. The availability of pure chemicals and clever routes of administration increase the rate of drug taking. Tobacco administered via the technological advance of cigarettes is the most widespread and harmful addiction, with alcohol a close second. The so-called hard drugs of abuse, such as amphetamine and cocaine, act even more directly on ascending dopamine tracts to establish addiction. Substance abuse is a universal human vulnerability to drugs that hijack reward mechanisms.

Why people differ in vulnerability is a fundamentally different question. Those who find it difficult to quit have different genes and more psychiatric symptoms (Pomerleau, 1997). The responsible genes are not "defective"; they caused no harm until the modern environment. Other vulnerability factors arise from environmental exposures, such as adverse circumstances that arouse aversive emotions that increase the reinforcing properties of drugs.

Habits   Vulnerabilities to other habits have related evolutionary explanations. Gambling does not directly influence brain chemicals, but it is as potent for some people as heroin. Men without other options may take big risks to get a possible big reward, thus possibly explaining why poor people more often play the lottery. Gambling is a bigger problem for men than women, probably because over evolutionary history substantial resources brought increased mating success for men more than women. The tendency to persist in games of chance with known long-term negative payoffs, such as slot machines, reflects the distortions built into human decision making (Kahneman, Slovic, & Tversky, 1982). Similarly, our evolved behavior regulation mechanisms lead to much other nonadaptive behavior in modern environments such as watching pornography, going to prostitutes, habitual web browsing, reading cheap novels, and engaging in private rituals, such as organizing and reorganizing a collection of stamps or coins.

Eating Disorders   Half of Americans are now overweight, and a third are clinically obese. They spend billions on books and treatment, but nothing works very well. Vast amounts of research have tried to understand what is wrong with the heavy half. An evolutionary approach suggests a different question: Why are we all vulnerable to obesity? A simple answer is that our behavior regulation mechanisms were shaped in the very different environment of the African savannah where the penalty for eating too little was swift and fatal. Even when food was plentiful, obesity remained rare because choices were limited and getting food involved burning as many calories per day as a modern aerobics instructor (Eaton, Shostak, & Konner, 1988).

Attempts to control weight by willpower lead to the other eating disorders, anorexia nervosa and bulimia. Adaptive explanations for anorexia as a variant mating strategy have been suggested (Surbey, 1987; Voland & Voland, 1989). However, a simpler starting place is the observation that these disorders usually begin with strenuous diets. Such diets cause episodes of gorging, a hallmark of bulimia, but life-saving during famine. Gorging precipitates shame, feelings of lack of control, more intense fear of obesity, and new resolutions in a vicious cycle of escalating anorexia and bulimia. Eating disorders are also fostered by the intense mating competition in large social groups, augmented by media images that make real bodies seem inadequate. In light of the pervasiveness of mating competition, this makes perfect sense (Buss, 1988, 1994). As with other syndromes, vulnerability varies for many reasons.

Sexual Disorders   Given its importance, you might think selection would have made sex foolproof. Instead, it exemplifies the vulnerabilities of a trait shaped by multiple strong forces of selection (Troisi, 2003). For instance, men complain about premature orgasm while women complain about lack of orgasm. Why? Sex differences in brain mechanisms and differences in anatomic proximity to stimulation, yes, but these are proximate explanations. Why is the system so poorly designed for mutual satisfaction? Because selection does not shape mechanisms for mutual satisfaction. Women who had orgasms very quickly might well have had fewer children, as might men who dallied too long when interruption is likely. This is consistent with the observation that premature ejaculation is a problem mainly for men who are young or fearful.

Another dramatic sex difference is what it takes to initiate arousal. For many men, the answer is almost any sexual cue, anytime, anywhere (Symons, 1979). Pornography is a male pursuit; even magazines that display male bodies are bought mainly by men. Then there is the related problematic issue of why such a wide range of stimuli arouses men. We might suppose that selection would ensure that men want only potentially fertile partners, and most do. However, about 2% are exclusively homosexual, others are preoccupied with immature girls, and many have fantasy lives that involve domination or a fetish object. One explanation may be an error management theory for why men so systematically and optimistically distort the intentions of women (Haselton & Buss, 2000). As for why so many individuals are exclusively homosexual, this remains unanswered, but not for want of theories (Ruse, 1988).

BRAIN DISORDERS

Public relations campaigns, many supported by pharmaceutical companies, promote the view that mental disorders are brain disorders. This is necessarily true in the sense that brain changes mediate all emotion and behavior. However, slogans such as "depression is a brain disease" leave the mistaken impression that brain abnormalities are always the primary causes and that drugs are the only appropriate treatment. For some disorders such as schizophrenia, bipolar disorder, and autism, brain abnormalities are indeed the primary and usually sufficient cause. Other disorders, however, can occur in a brain that is perfectly normal or a brain that was normal until it experienced unnatural stimuli such as psychological trauma, drugs of abuse, severe dieting, or trying to work in a hostile bureaucracy. As noted already, an evolutionary perspective fosters a sophisticated assessment of the many factors that explain individual differences. Some mental disorders are normal aversive emotions, others are dysregulated emotions, and some arise from factors only distantly related to the normal regulation of emotions, cognition, and behavior (Nesse, 1984). We turn to this last group to see what an evolutionary view can offer.

Schizophrenia   Schizophrenia is the most serious common mental disorder. The symptoms have little to do with a "split mind" but instead reflect a systematic breakdown of perception, cognition, and emotion (Jablensky, Satorius, & Ernberg, 1992). While precursor symptoms can usually be detected, full-fledged psychosis most often begins just as the individual is trying to establish an individual identity in a social group. Many patients first feel excluded, then suspicious, then frankly paranoid with delusions that others are trying to harm them. Data showing strong influences of genetic factors and brain changes have convinced most researchers that the schizophrenias (there are multiple disorders) are best understood as the manifestations of brain abnormalities. Some have suggested adaptive functions for symptoms of schizophrenia (J. S. Allen & Sarich, 1988; Feierman, 1982; Jarvik & Chadwick, 1972), but little evidence supports this idea.

Delusions and hallucinations are not part of the routine experience of most humans. They are more like seizures and quite unlike adaptive defenses such as fever, cough, or anxiety. Schizophrenia prevalence rates are consistent at about 1% across cultures (Jablensky et al., 1992), undermining the idea that novelty explains psychosis. There is also strong evidence that schizophrenics have lower than average RS: .3 of average for males and .5 for females (Avila, Thaker, & Adami, 2001; Pulver et al., 2004). The same data show no increased fitness of their close relatives, arguing against any selective benefit manifest in other individuals. It has been suggested that schizophrenia may persist "because it is the unattractive, low-fitness extreme of a highly variable mental trait that evolved as a fitness ('good genes') indicator through mutual mate choice" (Shaner, Miller, & Mintz, 2004). Also, as mentioned already, infection has been implicated as an explanation for some cases of schizophrenia.

Trade-offs and the limits of natural selection may be important. Schizophrenia is not a universal human trait like the appendix; it is a rare syndrome. The evolutionary question is why natural selection has not eliminated such fitness-reducing genetic variations. There are many possibilities. Selection might not be powerful enough to purge recurrent deleterious mutations from the gene pool. This is unlikely because the uniformity of incidence across cultures argues against a mutation occurring in the past 100,000 years, long enough to purge most seriously deleterious mutations. Another possibility is that so many genes are involved that selection can act on them only weakly. A related perspective is that normalizing selection can never shape a design parameter to an extremely narrow zone (Keller, in press). Even traits coded for by only a few genes are products of interactions with other genes and environmental factors that introduce substantial variation, leaving some individuals at maladaptive extremes.

A phylogenetic perspective offers related explanations. Human capacities for language and social cognition have advanced at a lightning pace in the past 100,000 years, almost certainly because they offer major fitness advantages (Humphrey, 1976). Such strong selection has costs that might well predispose to serious problems (Crow, 1997). Schizophrenia genes might also spread if they are linked to strongly beneficial genes (Burns, in press), but pleiotropic effects are more important. Cliff-edge effects offer a related possibility. For instance, race-horse breeding has resulted in longer and thinner leg bones that increase speed but are increasingly prone to fracture. If some mental characteristic gives increasing fitness up to a point where catastrophic failure becomes a problem, such cliff-edge effects could account for the genetic patterns seen in schizophrenia and manic-depressive illness (Nesse, 2005).

The same lines of reasoning apply also to other severe mental diseases that also have an incidence of about 1 in 100—autism in particular. Baron-Cohen (2002) has suggested that the manifestations of autism are examples of a pathological extreme of cognitive styles that are typically male. This would help to explain the predominance of males who get the disorder.

Other hypotheses also deserve consideration. For instance, it has been confirmed recently that the rates of schizophrenia increase dramatically for children who were conceived when their fathers were over 40 (Byrne, Agerbo, Ewald, Eaton, & Mortensen, 2003; Malaspina et al., 2002). Genes transmitted by the mother have divided only 24 times per generation, compared to 800 cell divisions for the DNA in sperm of older fathers, suggesting that many cases of schizophrenia arise from recurring new mutations. Among other implications, this falsifies the idea that women choose older men to get good genes.

Obsessive-Compulsive Disorder   Obsessive-compulsive disorder (OCD) also shows substantial heritability and a 1% incidence. The condition is characterized by ritualistic repetitive behaviors and fears that some small oversight will lead to disaster. People with OCD tend to have a smaller than normal caudate nucleus in the pons, and as already noted, some cases result from an autoimmune reaction to streptococcal infection (Swedo, Leonard, Garvey, & Mittleman, 1996). It remains uncertain if OCD is dysregulation of useful mechanisms or if it is something entirely separate (Rapoport & Fiske, 1998).

Attention Disorders

The evolutionary origins of attention deficit hyperactivity disorder (ADHD) have been the focus for several articles suggesting possible functions (Baird, Stevenson, & Williams, 2000; Brody, 2001; Jensen et al., 1997; Shelley-Tremblay & Rosen, 1996) or that it is a facultative adaptation to certain environments (Jensen et al., 1997). The striking male bias of the sex ratio, over 5 to 1, gives hints that ADHD may simply be the extreme end of a continuum on which males tend to be higher than females, much akin to a recent suggestion about autism (Baron-Cohen, 2002). In the ancestral environment, a tendency to move quickly to a new activity when current efforts are unproductive is a foraging strategy that may pay off more for hunting males than gathering females. As for the capacity to sit in one place indoors for hours under enforced contact with a boring book, that is so far from anything the natural environment ever required, it is astounding that any of us can do it. The heritability of ADHD is high, and associations with candidate genes, notably DRD4, offer promising leads (Biederman & Spencer, 1999). Because the 7R allele is common and in strong linkage disequilibrium, it may have experienced recent positive selection (Grady et al., 2003).

RELATIONSHIP DIFFICULTIES

The enormous importance of relationships in causing (and occasionally curing) mental disorders is so obvious that it is easy to neglect its significance. Mental health professionals often believe that normal relationships are warm, loving, and based on moral and emotional commitments. Would that it were so. By contrast, an evolutionary view of relationships emphasizes the costs and payoffs of different social strategies in terms of resources, reciprocal help, or inclusive fitness that can explain most tendencies to altruism (Fiske, 1992; Hinde, 1979; Hofer, 1984; Kirkpatrick, 1998). Evolutionary approaches have also emphasized the prevalence of deceptive strategies and self-deception (Krebs & Dawkins, 1984; Lockard & Paulhus, 1988; Rue, 1994; Slavin & Kriegman, 1992; Trivers, 2000), thus opening a little-traveled avenue between EP and psychoanalysis. Other chapters in this *Handbook* show how selection shaped the mechanisms that mediate relationships, knowledge crucial to understanding how relationships go wrong.

Sexual relationships and strategies have been a focus for EP, and the results of that research are ripe for application to clinical situations (Buss, 1994; Buss & Malamuth, 1996). For species with mating systems similar to those of humans, careful choice of partners benefits females more than males, and efforts to get many matings benefit females more than males. As a result, sexual jealousy is more intense for males, and opposition to mates giving resources to others tends to be greater for women (Buss & Schmitt, 1993). Moreover, as every grandmother knows, the facts of pregnancy and male jealousy make short-term matings less costly and predictably more common in males.

Child Abuse   Child abuse has been a major focus for mental health prevention and treatment. Understanding the evolutionary origins and functions of attachment has helped to explain why most parents do not abuse their children despite provocations (Bowlby, 1984). An evolutionary perspective motivated two behavioral ecologists to ask the now-obvious question: Is child abuse more common in families with a stepparent? Their astounding result is that death at the hands of parents is 80 times more common if there is a stepparent in the house (Daly & Wilson, 1988). This finding is commonly presented in a context framed by the tendency of males in many species to kill all unweaned infants shortly after they take over a female mating group (Hrdy, 1977). However, the mating pattern of humans does not routinely involve males fighting to take over a harem with multiple females who are nursing infants, so the analogy is incorrect. Instead, the mechanisms that protect babies in families with two related parents seem more prone to fail in reconstituted families (Gelles & Lancaster, 1987).

CONCLUSIONS

All it would take is discovery of a single cure. Even discovery of the definitive cause for a single illness would do. If EP leads directly to such a treatment or discovery, it will grow quickly. Is this a legitimate hope? Superficially, the answer is no. Instead of explanations for why some individuals get sick and others do not, EP explains why mechanisms are the way they are and why natural selection has not eliminated the genetic variations that result in disease for some. Its most profound contribution is a solid framework for understanding how behaviors are regulated to accomplish the many conflicting tasks of life, from getting food and surviving, to finding mates and protecting children. Instead of viewing one kind of life as normal and others as deviations, it sees the inherent conflicts in relationships, the struggles that go on in groups, and the dilemmas every person faces to allocate efforts among a host of competing needs. Far from providing a rigid and cold perspective, an evolutionary view fosters deeper empathy for the challenges we all face and deeper amazement that so many people are able to find loving relationships, meaningful work, and a way to juggle a bevy of responsibilities with good humor and even joy.

Does this presage a new kind of psychotherapy? There certainly are major implications for how to do psychotherapy (Gilbert & Bailey, 2000) and psychoanalysis (Slavin & Kriegman, 1992), but they do not constitute a new kind of therapy competing with hundreds of others. Every kind of therapy should make use of evolutionary principles. The juggernaut now is psychopharmacology, soon to be united with genetics to yield new methods for manipulating emotions and behavior that we cannot yet imagine. In the near future, they should yield more effective treatments for schizophrenia and manic-depressive illness. Evolutionary investigations can assist in these quests by defining phenotypes and identifying evolved behavior regulation mechanisms. These same genetic and pharmacologic technologies will make it easier to manipulate normal as well as abnormal emotions. Their focus exclusively on proximate perspectives holds the risk that we will block negative emotions and promote positive ones even before we grasp why they exist at all. Cautionary tales abound. For instance, when cortisol was first discovered, it was used to relieve the symptoms of all kinds of inflammation. It worked like a miracle and patients felt better, so why not? In a few years, however, the serious consequences of blocking these normal reactions became clear.

An evolutionary view of mental disorders does not mean accepting the pains and difficulties of the human condition. Many can be prevented or eliminated safely, but only when we better understand the functions of negative emotions. Furthermore, a signal detection analysis of their regulation suggests that in many situations they are about as useful as pain after surgery. It is even conceivable that the personality tendencies that foster envy and bitter competition, to say nothing of violence, might well be modifiable. None of this will be simple, however. Moreover, every such new major capacity for intervention will be far safer and more sensible if developed in a sophisticated evolutionary context.

REFERENCES

Alexander, R. D. (1974). The evolution of social behavior. *Annual Review of Systematics, 5,* 325–383.

Alexander, R. D. (1975). The search for a general theory of behavior. *Behavioral Science, 20,* 77–100.

Allen, J. S., & Sarich, V. M. (1988). Schizophrenia in an evolutionary perspective. *Perspectives in Biology and Medicine, 32,* 132–153.

Allen, N. B., & Badcock, P. B. T. (2003). The social risk hypothesis of depressed mood: Evolutionary, psychosocial and neurobiological perspectives. *Psychological Bulletin, 129,* 887–913.

American Psychiatric Association. (1994). *Diagnostic and statistical manual of mental disorders: DSM-IV* (4th ed.). Washington, DC: Author.

Andreasen, N. C. (1984). *The broken brain: The biological revolution in psychiatry.* New York: Harper & Row.

Archer, J. (1999). *The nature of grief.* New York: Oxford University Press.

Avila, M., Thaker, G., & Adami, H. (2001). Genetic epidemiology and schizophrenia: A study of reproductive fitness. *Schizophrenia Res, 47,* 233–241.

Badcock, C. (1988). *Essential Freud.* Oxford, England: Basil Blackwell.

Badcock, C. (2000). *Evolutionary psychology: A critical introduction.* Cambridge, UK: Blackwell.

Baird, J., Stevenson, J. C., & Williams, D. C. (2000). The evolution of ADHD: A disorder of communication? *Quarterly Review of Biology, 75,* 17–35.

Barkow, J. (1989). *Darwin, sex, and status: Biological approaches to mind and culture.* Toronto: University of Toronto Press.

Barkow, J., Cosmides, L., & Tooby, J. (Eds.). (1992). *The adapted mind.* New York: Oxford University Press.

Barlow, D. H. (1988). *Anxiety and its disorders.* New York: Guilford Press.

Baron-Cohen, S. (1995). *Mindblindness: An essay on autism and the theory of mind* (Vols. 37–46). Cambridge, MA: MIT press.

Baron-Cohen, S. (Ed.). (1997). *The maladapted mind.* East Sussex: Psychology Press, Erlbaum.

Baron-Cohen, S. (2002). The extreme male brain theory of autism. *Trends in Cognitive Science, 6,* 248–254.

Barrett, L., Dunbar, R. I. M., & Lycett, J. (2002). *Human evolutionary psychology.* Basingstoke: Palgrave.

Bateson, P. P. G., & Martin, P. R. (2000). *Design for a life: How behavior and personality develop.* New York: Simon & Schuster.

Belsky, J. (1999). Modern evolutionary theory and patterns of attachment. In J. Cassidy & P. R. Shaver (Eds.), *Handbook of attachment: Theory, research, and clinical applications* (pp. 141–161). New York: Guilford Press.

Belsky, J., Steinberg, J., & Draper, P. (1991). Childhood experience, interpersonal development, and reproductive strategy: An evolutionary theory of socialization. *Child Development, 62,* 647–670.

Bibring, E. (1953). The mechanisms of depression. In P. Greenacre (Ed.), *Affective disorders* (pp. 13–48). New York: International Universities Press.

Biederman, J., & Spencer, T. (1999). Attention-deficit/hyperactivity disorder (ADHD) as a noradrenergic disorder. *Biological Psychiatry, 46,* 1234–1242.

Bowlby, J. (1969). *Attachment and loss: Vol. 1. Attachment.* New York: Basic Books.

Bowlby, J. (1984). Violence in the family as a disorder of the attachment and caregiving systems. *American Journal of Psychoanalysis, 44,* 9–27, 29–31.

Breslau, N., Davis, G. C., & Andreski, P. (1995). Risk factors for PTSD-related traumatic events: A prospective analysis. *American Journal of Psychiatry, 152,* 529–535.

Brickman, P. (1987). *Commitment, conflict, and caring.* Englewood Cliffs, NJ: Prentice-Hall.

Brody, J. F. (2001). Evolutionary recasting: ADHD, mania and its variants. *Journal of Affective Disorders, 65,* 197–215.

Brown, A. S., Begg, M. D., Gravenstein, S., Schaefer, C. A., Wyatt, R. J., Bresnahan, M., et al. (2004). Serologic evidence of prenatal influenza in the etiology of schizophrenia. *Archives of General Psychiatry, 61,* 774–780.

Brown, G. W., & Harris, T. O. (1978). *Social origins of depression.* New York: Free Press.

Brown, G. W., Harris, T. O., & Hepworth, C. (1995). Loss, humiliation and entrapment among women developing depression: A patient and non-patient comparison. *Psychological Medicine, 25,* 7–21.

Brown, R., Dahlen, E., Mills, C., Rick, J., & Biblarz, A. (1999). Evaluation of an evolutionary model of self-preservation and self-destruction. *Suicide and Life-Threatening Behavior, 29,* 58–71.

Brown, S. L., Nesse, R. M., Vinokur, A. D., & Smith, D. M. (2003). Providing social support may be more beneficial than receiving it: Results from a prospective study of mortality. *Psychological Science, 14,* 320–327.

Burns, J. K. (in press). An evolutionary theory of schizophrenia: Cortical connectivity, metarepresentation and the social brain. *Brain and Behavioural Sciences.*

Burton, R. (1931). *The anatomy of melancholy.* London: Routledge and Sons. (Original work published 1624)

Buss, D. M. (1988). The evolution of human intrasexual competition: Tactics of mate attraction. *Journal of Personality and Social Psychology, 54,* 616–628.

Buss, D. M. (1994). *The evolution of desire: Strategies of human mating.* New York: Basic Books.

Buss, D. M. (1995). Evolutionary psychology: A new paradigm for psychological science. *Psychological Inquiry, 6,* 1–30.

Buss, D. M. (2000). The evolution of happiness. *American Psychologist, 55,* 15–23.

Buss, D. M. (2003). *The evolution of desire: Strategies of human mating* (Rev. ed.). New York: Basic Books.

Buss, D. M. (2004). *Evolutionary psychology: The new science of the mind* (2nd ed.). Boston: Allyn & Bacon.

Buss, D. M., Larsen, R. J., Westen, D., & Semmelroth, J. (1992). Sex differences in jealousy: Evolution, physiology, and psychology. *Psychological Science, 3,* 251–255.

Buss, D. M., & Malamuth, N. M. (1996). *Sex, power, conflict: Evolutionary and feminist perspectives.* New York: Oxford University Press.

Buss, D. M., & Schmitt, D. P. (1993). Sexual strategies theory: An evolutionary perspective on human mating. *Psychological Review, 100,* 204–232.

Buss, D. M., Shackelford, T. K., Kirkpatrick, L. A., Choe, J., Hasegawa, M., Hasegawa, T., et al. (1999). Jealousy and beliefs about infidelity: Tests of competing hypotheses in the United States, Korea, and Japan. *Personal Relationships, 6,* 125–150.

Byrne, M., Agerbo, E., Ewald, H., Eaton, W. W., & Mortensen, P. B. (2003). Parental age and risk of schizophrenia: A case-control study. *Archives of General Psychiatry, 60,* 673–678.

Carver, C. S., & Scheier, M. F. (1990). Origins and functions of positive and negative affect: A control-process view. *Psychological Review, 97,* 19–35.

Carver, C. S., & Scheier, M. F. (1998). *On the self-regulation of behavior.* New York: Cambridge University Press.

Caspi, A., Sugden, K., Moffitt, T. E., Taylor, A., Craig, I. W., Harrington, H., et al. (2003). Influence of life stress on depression: Moderation by a polymorphism in the 5-HTT gene. *Science, 301,* 386–389.

Chisholm, J. (1996). The evolutionary ecology of human attachment organization. *Human Nature, 7,* 1–38.

Chisholm, J. (1999). *Death, hope and sex: Steps to an evolutionary ecology of mind and morality.* New York: Cambridge University Press.

Cosmides, L., & Tooby, J. (1999). Towards an evolutionary taxonomy of treatable conditions. *Journal of Abnormal Psychology, 108,* 453–464.

Crawford, C., Smith, M., & Krebs, D. (Eds.). (1987). *Sociobiology and psychology: Ideas, issues and applications.* Hillsdale, NJ: Erlbaum.

Cronin, H. (1991). *The ant and the peacock: Altruism and sexual selection from Darwin to today.* New York: Cambridge University Press.

Cross-National Collaborative Group. (1992). The changing rate of major depression: Cross-national comparisons. *Journal of the American Medical Association, 268,* 3098–3105.

Crow, T. J. (1997). Is schizophrenia the price that Homo sapiens pays for language? *Schizophrenia Research, 28,* 127–141.

Daly, M., & Wilson, M. (1983). *Sex, evolution, and behavior* (2nd ed.). Boston: Willard Grant Press.

Daly, M., & Wilson, M. (1988). Evolutionary social psychology and family homicide. *Science, 242,* 519–524.

deCatanzaro, D. (1980). Human suicide: A biological perspective. *Behavioral and Brain Sciences, 3.*

Draper, P., & Harpending, H. (1982). Father absence and reproductive strategy: An evolutionary perspective. *Journal of Anthropological Research, 38,* 255–273.

Dudley, R. (2002). Fermenting fruit and the historical ecology of ethanol ingestion: Is alcoholism in modern humans an evolutionary hangover? *Addiction, 97,* 381–388.

Eaton, S. B., Shostak, M., & Konner, M. (1988). *The Paleolithic prescription.* New York: Harper & Row.

Eaton, S. B., Strassmann, B. I., Nesse, R. M., Neel, J. V., Ewald, P. W., Williams, G. C., et al. (2002). Evolutionary health promotion. *Preventive Medicine, 34,* 109–118.

Ekman, P. (1992). An argument for basic emotions. *Cognition and Emotion, 6,* 169–200.

Emmons, R. A., & King, L. A. (1988). Conflict among personal strivings: Immediate and long-term implications for psychological and physical well-being. *Journal of Personality and Social Psychology, 54,* 1040–1048.

Ericson, M. T. (1993). Rethinking Oedipus: An evolutionary perspective on incest avoidance. *American Journal of Psychiatry, 150,* 411.

Essex, M., Klein, M., Eunsuk, C., & Kalin, N. (2002). Maternal stress beginning in infancy may sensitize children to later stress exposure: Effects on cortisol and behavior. *Biological Psychiatry, 52,* 776–786.

Ewald, P. (1994). *Evolution of infectious disease.* New York: Oxford University Press.

Ewald, P. (2000). *Plague time: How stealth infections cause cancers, heart disease, and other deadly ailments.* New York: Free Press.

Fabrega, H. (2002). *Origins of psychopathology: The phylogenetic and cultural basis of mental illness.* New Brunswick, NJ: Rutgers University Press.

Fehr, E., & Fischbacher, U. (2003). The nature of human altruism. *Nature, 425,* 785–791.

Feierman, J. R. (1982). Nocturnalism: An ethological theory of schizophrenia. *Medical Hypotheses, 9,* 455–479.

Fessler, D. M. (in press). The Strategy of affect: Emotions in human cooperation. In P. Hammerstein (Ed.), *Genetic and cultural evolution of cooperation: Dahlem Workshop Report* (Vol. 29). Cambridge, MA: MIT Press.

Fiske, A. P. (1992). The four elementary forms of sociality: Framework for a unified theory of social relations. *Psychological Review, 99,* 689–723.

Foa, E. B., Steketee, G. S., & Ozarow, B. J. (1985). Behavior therapy with obsessive-compulsives. In M. Mavissakalian, S. M. Turner, & L. Lichelson (Eds.), *Obsessive-compulsive disorder: Psychological and pharmacological treatment* (pp. 49–129). New York: Plenum Press.

Frank, R. H. (1988). *Passions within reason: The strategic role of the emotions.* New York: Norton.

Frank, R. H. (1999). *Luxury fever: Why money fails to satisfy in an era of excess.* New York: Free Press.

Fredrickson, B. L. (1998). What good are positive emotions? *Review of General Psychology: Special issue: New Directions in Research on Emotion, 2,* 300–319.

French, J. A., Kamil, A. C., & Leger, D. W. (Eds.). (2000). *Evolutionary psychology and motivation* (Vol. 48). Lincoln: University of Nebraska Press.

Gaulin, S. J. C., & McBurney, D. H. (2001). *Psychology: An evolutionary approach.* Upper Saddle River, NJ: Prentice-Hall.

Geary, D. C. (1998). *Male, female: The evolution of human sex differences* (1st ed.). Washington, DC: American Psychological Association.

Geary, D. C., & Bjorklund, D. F. (2000). Evolutionary developmental psychology. *Child Development, 71,* 57–65.

Gelles, R. J., & Lancaster, J. B. (1987). *Child abuse and neglect: Biosocial dimensions.* New York: Aldine De Gruyter.

Gilbert, P. (1992). *Depression: The evolution of powerlessness.* New York: Guilford Press.

Gilbert, P. (2001). Evolution and social anxiety: The role of attraction, social competition, and social hierarchies. *Psychiatric Clinics of North America, 24,* 723–751.

Gilbert, P., & Bailey, K. G. (2000). *Genes on the couch: Explorations in evolutionary psychotherapy.* Philadelphia: Taylor & Francis.

Gilbert, P., Price, J., & Allen, S. (1995). Social comparison, social attractiveness and evolution: How might they be related? *New Ideas in Psychology, 13,* 149–165.

Gintis, H. (2000). Strong reciprocity and human sociality. *Journal of Theoretical Biology, 206,* 169–179.

Glantz, K., & Pearce, J. (1989). *Exiles from Eden.* New York: Norton.

Grady, D. L., Chi, H. C., Ding, Y. C., Smith, M., Wang, E., Schuck, S., et al. (2003). High prevalence of rare dopamine receptor D4 alleles in children diagnosed with attention-deficit hyperactivity disorder. *Molecular Psychiatry, 8,* 536–545.

Gut, E. (1989). *Productive and unproductive depression.* New York: Basic Books.

Hagen, E. H. (2002). Depression as bargaining: The case postpartum. *Evolution and Human Behavior, 23,* 323–336.

Hall, B. K. (1998). *Evolutionary developmental biology* (2nd ed.). London; New York: Chapman & Hall.

Hamburg, D. A., Hamburg, B. A., & Barchas, J. D. (1975). Anger and depression in perspective of behavioral biology. In L. Levi (Ed.), *Emotions: Their parameters and measurement* (pp. 235–278). New York: Raven Press.

Haselton, M. G., & Buss, D. M. (2000). Error management theory: A new perspective on biases in cross-sex mind reading. *Journal of Personality and Social Psychology, 78,* 81–91.

Henrich, J., & Gil-White, F. (2001). The evolution of prestige. *Evolution and Human Behavior, 22,* 165–196.

Hill, E. M., & Chow, K. (2002). Life-history theory and risky drinking. *Addiction, 97,* 401–413.

Hill, E. M., & Newlin, D. B. (2002). Evolutionary approaches to addiction. *Addiction, 97,* 375–379.

Hinde, R. A. (1979). *Towards understanding relationships.* London: Academic Press.

Hofer, M. A. (1984). Relationships as regulators: A psychobiologic perspective on bereavement. *Psychosomatic Medicine, 46,* 183–197.

Horrobin, D. F. (1998). Schizophrenia: The illness that made us human. *Medical Hypotheses, 50,* 269–288.

Horwitz, A. V. (2002). *Creating mental illness.* Chicago: University of Chicago Press.

Hrdy, S. B. (1977). Infanticide as a primate reproductive strategy. *American Scientist, 65,* 40–49.

Hrdy, S. B. (1999). *Mother nature: A history of mothers, infants, and natural selection* (1st ed.). New York: Pantheon Books.

Humphrey, N. K. (1976). The social function of intellect. In P. G. Bateson & R. A. Hinde (Eds.), *Growing points in ethology* (pp. 303–318). London: Cambridge University Press.

Institute of Medicine. (1987). *Causes and consequences of alcohol problems: An agenda for research.* Washington, DC: National Academy Press.

Jablensky, A., Satorius, N., & Ernberg, G. (1992). Schizophrenia: Manifestations, incidence and course in different cultures. A World Health Organization ten country study. *Psychological Medicine Monograph Supplement, 20,* 1–97.

Janoff-Bulman, R., & Brickman, P. (1982). Expectations and what people learn from failure. In N. T. Feather (Ed.), *Expectations and action.* Hillsdale, NJ: Erlbaum.

Jarvik, L. F., & Chadwick, S. B. (1972). Schizophrenia and survival. In M. Hammer, K. Salzinger, & S. Sutton (Eds.), *Psychopathology.* New York: Wiley.

Jensen, P. S., Mrazek, D., Knapp, P. K., Steinberg, L., Pfeffer, C., Schowalter, J., et al. (1997). Evolution and revolution in child psychiatry: ADHD as a disorder of adaptation. *Journal of the American Academy of Child and Adolescent Psychiatry, 36,* 1672–1679.

Kahneman, D., Slovic, P., & Tversky, A. (1982). *Judgment under uncertainty: Heuristics and biases.* New York: Cambridge University Press.

Katz, L. (2000). *Evolutionary origins of morality: Cross disciplinary perspectives.* Devon: Imprint Academic.

Keller, M. (in press). Evolutionary explanations of schizophrenia must ultimately explain the genes that predispose to it. *Behavioral and Brain Sciences.*

Kendler, K. S., Hettema, J. M., Butera, F., Gardner, C. O., & Prescott, C. A. (2003). Life event dimensions of loss, humiliation, entrapment, and danger in the prediction of onsets of major depression and generalized anxiety. *Archives of General Psychiatry, 60,* 789–796.

Kendler, K. S., Kuhn, J., & Prescott, C. A. (2004). The interrelationship of neuroticism, sex, and stressful life events in the prediction of episodes of major depression. *American Journal of Psychiatry, 161,* 631–636.

Kessler, R., & Ustun, T. (2000). The World Health Organization World Mental Health 2000 Initiative. *Hospital Management International,* 195–196.

Kirkpatrick, L. A. (1998). Evolution, pair-bonding, and reproductive strategies: A reconceptualization of adult attachment. In W. S. Rholes (Ed.), *Attachment theory and close relationships* (pp. 353–393). New York: Guilford Press.

Klinger, E. (1975). Consequences of commitment to and disengagement from incentives. *Psychological Review, 82,* 1–25.

Krebs, J., & Davies, N. B. (Eds.). (1984). *Behavioural ecology: An evolutionary approach* (2nd ed.). Sunderland, MA: Sinauer.

Krebs, J., & Dawkins, R. (1984). Animal signals: Mind-reading and manipulation. In J. R. Krebs & N. B. Davies (Eds.), *Behavioral ecology: An evolutionary approach* (pp. 380–402). Sunderland, MA: Sinauer.

Kruger, D., & Nesse, R. (2004). Sexual selection and the Male: Female Mortality Ratio. *Evolutionary Psychology, 2,* 66–85.

Kunugi, H., Nanko, S., Takei, N., Saito, K., Hayashi, N., & Kazamatsuri, H. (1995). Schizophrenia following in utero exposure to the 1957 influenza epidemics in Japan. *American Journal of Psychiatry, 152,* 450–452.

Leary, M. R., & Kowalski, M. (1995). *Social anxiety.* New York: Guilford Press.

Ledgerwood, L., Ewald, P., & Cochran, G. (2003). Genes, germs, and schizophrenia: An evolutionary perspective. *Perspectives in Biology and Medicine, 46,* 317–348.

Little, B. R. (1999). Personality and motivation: Personal action and the conative evolution. In L. A. Pervin (Ed.), *Handbook of personality: Theory and research* (2nd ed., pp. xiii, 738). New York: Guilford Press.

Lockard, J. S., & Paulhus, D. L. (Eds.). (1988). *Self-deception: An adaptive mechanism?* Engelwood Cliffs, NJ: Prentice-Hall.

Low, B. S. (2000). *Why sex matters.* Princeton, NJ: Princeton University Press.

Malaspina, D., Corcoran, C., Fahim, C., Berman, A., Harkavy-Friedman, J., Yale, S., et al. (2002). Paternal age and sporadic schizophrenia: Evidence for de novo mutations. *American Journal of Clinical Genetics, 114,* 299–303.

Marks, I. M. (1987). *Fears, phobias, and rituals.* New York: Oxford University Press.

Marks, I. M., & Nesse, R. M. (1994). Fear and fitness: An evolutionary analysis of anxiety disorders. *Ethology and Sociobiology, 15,* 247–261.

Marks, I. M., & Tobena, A. (1990). Learning and unlearning fear: A clinical and evolutionary perspective. *Neuroscience and Biobehavioral Reviews, 14,* 365–384.

McGuire, M. T., & Fairbanks, L. A. (1977). *Ethological psychiatry: Psychopathology in the context of evolutionary biology.* New York: Grune and Stratton.

McGuire, M. T., & Troisi, A. (1998). *Darwinian psychiatry.* Cambridge, MA: Harvard University Press.

Miller, G. F. (2000). *The mating mind: How sexual choice shaped the evolution of human nature.* New York: Doubleday.

Mineka, S., Keir, R., & Price, V. (1980). Fear of snakes in wild- and laboratory-reared rhesus monkeys (Macaca mulatta). *Animal Learning and Behavior, 8,* 653–663.

Monroe, S. M., & Simons, A. D. (1991). Diathesis-stress theories in the context of life stress research: Implications for the depressive disorders. *Psychological Bulletin, 110,* 406–425.

Murphy, D., & Stich, S. (2000). Darwin in the madhouse: Evolutionary psychology and the classification of mental disorders. In P. Carruthers & A. Chamberlain (Eds.), *Evolution and the human mind: Modularity, language and meta-cognition* (pp. 62–92). Cambridge, England: Cambridge University Press.

Murphy, J. M., Laird, N. M., Monson, R. R., Sobol, A. M., & Leighton, A. H. (2000). A 40-year perspective on the prevalence of depression: The Stirling County Study. *Archives of General Psychiatry, 57,* 209–215.

Nesse, R. M. (1984). An evolutionary perspective on psychiatry. *Comprehensive Psychiatry, 25,* 575–580.

Nesse, R. M. (1987). An evolutionary perspective on panic disorder and agoraphobia. *Ethology and Sociobiology, 8,* S73–S83.

Nesse, R. M. (1990a). Evolutionary explanations of emotions. *Human Nature, 1,* 261–289.

Nesse, R. M. (1990b). The evolutionary functions of repression and the ego defenses. *Journal of the American Academy of Psychoanalysis, 18,* 260–285.

Nesse, R. M. (1991a). What good is feeling bad? *Sciences* (November/December), 30–37.

Nesse, R. M. (1991b). What is mood for? *Psycoloquy, 2,* 9.

Nesse, R. M. (1994). An evolutionary perspective on substance abuse. *Ethology and Sociobiology, 15,* 339–348.

Nesse, R. M. (2000). Is depression an adaptation? *Archives of General Psychiatry, 57,* 14–20.

Nesse, R. M. (2001a). *Evolution and the capacity for commitment.* New York: Russell Sage Foundation.

Nesse, R. M. (2001b). On the difficulty of defining disease: A Darwinian perspective. *Medical Health Care and Philosophy, 4,* 37–46.

Nesse, R. M. (2004). Natural selection and the elusiveness of happiness. *Philosophical transactions of the Royal Society of London, Series B, Biological Sciences, 359,* 1333–1347.

Nesse, R. M. (2005). Natural selection and the regulation of defenses: A Signal Detection Analysis of the Smoke Detector Principle. *Evolution and Human Behavior, 26,* 88–105.

Nesse, R. M., & Berridge, K. C. (1997). Psychoactive drug use in evolutionary perspective. *Science, 278,* 63–66.

Nesse, R. M., & Williams, G. C. (1994). *Why we get sick: The new science of Darwinian medicine.* New York: Vintage.

Nettle, D. (2004). Evolutionary origins of depression: A review and reformulation. *Journal of Affective Disorders, 81,* 91–102.

Phillips, K. A., First, M. B., & Pincus, H. A. (2003). *Advancing DSM: dilemmas in psychiatric diagnosis.* Washington, DC: American Psychiatric Association.

Pitchford, I. (2001). Evolutionary developmental psychopathology. *Human Nature Review.* Available from http://human-nature.com/darwin/edp.html.

Pitman, R. K. (1989). Post-traumatic stress disorder, hormones, and memory. *Biological Psychiatry, 26,* 221–223.

Plutchik, R. (2003). *Emotions and life: Perspectives from psychology, biology, and evolution.* Washington, DC: American Psychological Association.

Pomerleau, C. S. (1997). Cofactors for smoking and evolutionary psychobiology. *Addiction, 92,* 397–408.

Poulton, R., Davies, S., Menzies, R. G., Langley, J. D., & Silva, P. A. (1998). Evidence for a non-associative model of the acquisition of a fear of heights. *Behavioural Research and Therapy, 36,* 537–544.

Poulton, R., & Menzies, R. G. (2002). Non-associative fear acquisition: A review of the evidence from retrospective and longitudinal research. *Behavioural Research and Therapy, 40,* 127–149.

Pulver, A. E., McGrath, J. A., Liang, K. Y., Lasseter, V. K., Nestadt, G., & Wolyniec, P. S. (2004). An indirect test of the new mutation hypothesis associating advanced paternal age with the etiology of schizophrenia. *American Journal of Clinical Genetics, 124B,* 6–9.

Quirk, G. J. (2002). Memory for extinction of conditioned fear is long-lasting and persists following spontaneous recovery. *Learn Mem, 9,* 402–407.

Rapoport, J. L., & Fiske, A. (1998). The new biology of obsessive-compulsive disorder: Implications for evolutionary psychology. *Perspectives in Biology and Medicine, 41,* 159–175.

Richards, R. L., Kinner, D. K., Lunde, I., & Benet, M. (1988). Creativity in manic-depressives, cyclothymes and their normal first-degree relatives: A preliminary report. *Journal of Abnormal Psychology, 97,* 281–288.

Ridley, M. (2003). *Nature via nurture: Genes, experience, and what makes us human.* New York: Harper-Collins.

Rue, L. D. (1994). *By the grace of guile: The role of deception in natural history and human affairs.* New York: Oxford University Press.

Ruse, M. (1988). *Homosexuality: A philosophical inquiry.* New York: Blackwell.

Rutter, M., & Rutter, M. (1993). *Developing minds: Challenge and continuity across the life span.* New York: Basic Books.

Shaner, A., Miller, G., & Mintz, J. (2004). Schizophrenia as one extreme of a sexually selected fitness indicator. *Schizophrenia Research, 70,* 101–109.

Shelley-Tremblay, J. F., & Rosen, L. A. (1996). Attention deficit hyperactivity disorder: An evolutionary perspective. *Journal of Genetics and Psychology, 157,* 443–453.

Slavin, M. O., & Kriegman, D. (1990). Toward a new paradigm for psychoanalysis: An evolutionary biological perspective on the classical-relational dialectic. *Psychoanalytic Psychology, 7 [Suppl.],* 5–31.

Slavin, M. O., & Kriegman, D. (1992). *The adaptive design of the human psyche: Psychoanalysis, evolutionary biology, and the therapeutic process.* New York: Guilford Press.

Sloman, L., Price, J., Gilbert, P., & Gardner, R. (1994). Adaptive function of depression: Psychotherapeutic implications. *American Journal of Psychotherapy, 48,* 1–16.

Smith, E. A., & Winterhalder, B. (Eds.). (1992). *Evolutionary ecology and human behavior.* New York: Aldine de Gruyter.

Smith, M. (1986). Genetics of human alcohol and aldehyde dehydrogenases. *Advances in Human Genetics, 15,* 249–290.

Stearns, S. C. (1992). *The evolution of life histories.* Oxford England; New York: Oxford University Press.

Stein, D. J., & Bouwer, C. (1997). A neuro-evolutionary approach to the anxiety disorders. *Journal of Anxiety Disorders, 11,* 409–429.

Stein, D. J., Hollander, E., & Josephson, S. C. (1994). Serotonin reuptake blockers for the treatment of obsessional jealousy. *Journal of Clinical Psychiatry, 55,* 30–33.

Sterelny, K., & Griffiths, P. E. (1999). *Sex and death: An introduction to philosophy of biology.* Chicago: University of Chicago Press.

Stevens, A., & Price, J. (1996). *Evolutionary psychiatry: A new beginning.* London: Routledge.

Sullivan, R. J., & Hagen, E. H. (2002). Psychotropic substance-seeking: Evolutionary pathology or adaptation? *Addiction, 97,* 389–400.

Sulloway, F. J. (1985). *Freud, biologist of the mind.* New York: Basic Books.

Surbey, M. K. (1987). Anorexia nervosa, amenorrhea, and adaptation. *Ethology and Sociobiology, 8,* 47–61.

Surbey, M. K. (1990). Family composition, stress, and the timing of human menarche. In T. E. Zeigler & F. B. Bercovitch (Eds.), *Socioendocrinology of primate reproduction* (pp. 11–32). New York: Wiley.

Swedo, S., Leonard, H., Garvey, M. A., & Mittleman, B. B. (1996). PANDAS: Pediatric Autoimmune Neuropsychiatric Disorders Associated with Strep—Is this a new species of childhood-onset obsessive-compulsive disorder and Tourette's syndrome? *European Neuropsychopharmacology, 6,* S4.

Swedo, S., Leonard, H., & Kiessling, L. (1994). Speculations on antineuronal antibody-mediated neuropsychiatric disorders of childhood. *Pediatrics, 93*, 323–326.

Symons, D. (1979). *The evolution of human sexuality.* New York: Oxford University Press.

Teicher, M. H., Andersen, S. L., Polcari, A., Anderson, C. M., Navalta, C. P., & Kim, D. M. (2003). The neurobiological consequences of early stress and childhood maltreatment. *Neuroscience and Biobehavioral Reviews, 27*, 33–44.

Tooby, J., & Cosmides, L. (1990). The past explains the present: Emotional adaptations and the structure of ancestral environments. *Ethology and Sociobiology, 11*, 375–424.

Trivers, R. (1974). Parent-offspring conflict. *American Zoologist, 14*, 249–264.

Trivers, R. (1976). Forward. In R. Dawkins (Ed.), *The selfish gene.* New York: Oxford University Press.

Trivers, R. (2000). The elements of a scientific theory of self-deception. *Annals of the New York Academy of Sciences, 907*, 114–131.

Troisi, A. (2003). Sexual disorders in the context of Darwinian psychiatry. *Journal of Endocrinological Investigation, 26*, 54–57.

Troisi, A., & McGuire, M. (2002). Darwinian psychiatry and the concept of mental disorder. *Neuroendocrinology Letters, 23, [Suppl]* (4), 31–38.

Valenstein, E. S. (1998). *Blaming the brain: The truth about drugs and mental health.* New York: Free Press.

Veblen, T. (1899). *The theory of the leisure class: An economic study in the evolution of institutions.* New York: Macmillan.

Voland, E., & Voland, R. (1989). Evolutionary biology and psychiatry: The case of anorexia nervosa. *Ethology and Sociobiology, 10*, 223–240.

Wakefield, J. C. (1992). Disorder as harmful dysfunction: A conceptual critique of *DSM-III-R*'s definition of mental disorder. *Psychological Review, 99*, 232–247.

Watson, P. J., & Andrews, P. W. (2002). Toward a revised evolutionary adaptationist analysis of depression: The social navigation hypothesis. *Journal of Affective Disorders, 72*, 1–14.

Weiner, H. (1998). Notes on an evolutionary medicine. *Psychosomatic Medicine, 60*, 510–520.

Wenegrat, B. (1990). *Sociobiological psychiatry: A new conceptual framework.* Lexington, MS: Lexington.

Wenegrat, B. (1995). *Illness and power.* New York: New York University Press.

West-Eberhard, M. J. (2003). *Developmental plasticity and evolution.* New York: Oxford University Press.

White, N. F. (1974). *Ethology and psychiatry.* Toronto: University of Toronto Press.

Whiten, A., & Byrne, R. W. (1997). *Machiavellian intelligence II: Extensions and evaluations.* New York: Cambridge University Press.

Williams, G. W., & Nesse, R. M. (1991). The dawn of Darwinian medicine. *Quarterly Review of Biology, 66*, 1–22.

Wilson, D. R. (1998). Evolutionary epidemiology and manic depression. *British Journal of Medical Psychology, 71*, 375–395.

Wolpert, L. (1999). *Malignant sadness: The anatomy of depression.* New York: Free Press.

Wright, R. (1994). *The moral animal: The new science of evolutionary psychology.* New York: Pantheon Books.

Wrosch, C., Scheier, M. F., & Carver, C. S. (2003). The importance of goal disengagement in adaptive self-regulation: When giving up is beneficial. *Self and Identity, 2*, 1–20.

Wrosch, C., Scheier, M. F., & Miller, G. E. (2003). Adaptive self-regulation of unattainable goals: Goal disengagement, goal reengagement, and subjective well-being. *Personality and Social Psychology Bulletin, 29*, 1494–1508.

Yehuda, R., Halligan, S. L., Golier, J. A., Grossman, R., & Bierer, L. M. (2004). Effects of trauma exposure on the cortisol response to dexamethasone administration in PTSD and major depressive disorder. *Psychoneuroendocrinology, 29*, 389–404.

PART VII

APPLICATIONS OF EVOLUTIONARY PSYCHOLOGY TO OTHER DISCIPLINES

DAVID M. BUSS

THE FINAL PART of the *Handbook* considers evolutionary psychology across different disciplines that may at first seem far removed from the evolutionary sciences. In Chapter 33, Joseph Carroll discusses evolutionary psychology and literature. Traditionally, science and the humanities (and particularly the arts) have been regarded as separate endeavors. Carroll, in a conceptually synthetic discussion, argues for consilience—a unified causal understanding that integrates the sciences and humanities. He reviews the various approaches to the evolutionary analysis of literature, including the key themes of human nature reflected in literature and the possibility of adaptations for producing literature and its oral antecedents. The evolutionary analysis of literature and the arts is beginning to flourish, and Carroll's excellent chapter takes stock of where this exciting enterprise has been and where it promises to go.

Chapter 34, written by law professor Owen Jones, offers a penetrating evolutionary analysis of the law. The legal system, Jones argues, is designed to affect human behavior in certain ways, such as deterring certain forms of behavior—theft, rape, and murder. Simultaneously, it is designed to encourage other forms of behavior, such as persuading people to further public goals. Insights from evolutionary psychology offer tools for making the legal system more efficient in attaining these goals. It can do so, Jones argues, by discovering useful patterns of regulable behavior, identifying policy conflicts, exposing unwarranted assumptions in the law, revealing deep patterns in legal architecture, and assessing the comparative effectiveness of legal strategies, among others. Jones's analysis, though prudent, judicious, and careful, promises to revolutionize the legal system. Indeed, after reading Jones's chapter, it is difficult to imagine how the legal system can accomplish its aims in ignorance of our evolved psychological mechanisms.

Evolutionary psychology has penetrated many disciplines, and space limitations unfortunately precluded inclusion of all of them. As these words are written, there are rapidly emerging new hybrid disciplines, such as evolutionary economics (Gintis, 2000; Gintis, Bowles, Boyd, & Fehr, 2005), evolutionary organizational behavior (Brown, 2002; Colarelli, 2003), evolution and marketing (Saad, 2005), evolutionary sociology (Lopreato & Crippin, 2001), evolutionary analyses of history (Sulloway, 1996), evolutionary psychology and public policy (Bloom & Dess, 2003), and evolutionary political science (Rubin, 2002). In the final analysis, all human behavior—including economic behavior, legal behavior, artistic behavior, and organizational behavior—is a product of evolved psychological mechanisms. I predict that in the not too distant future, all of these diverse and seemingly unrelated fields will be based on a new evolutionary foundation.

REFERENCES

Bloom, R. W., & Dess, N. (2003). *Evolutionary psychology and violence: A primer for policymakers and public policy advocates*. Westport, CT: Praeger.

Brown, K. (2002). *Biology at work*. Piscataway: Rutgers University Press.

Colarelli, S. M. (2003). *No Best Way: An evolutionary perspective on human resource management*. Westport, CT: Praeger.

Gintis, H. (2000). *Game theory evolving*. Princeton, NJ: Princeton University Press.

Gintis, H., Bowles, S., Boyd, R. T., & Fehr, E. (Eds.). (2005). *Moral sentiments and material interests: The foundations of cooperation in economic life*. Cambridge, MA: MIT Press.

Lopreato, J., & Crippin, T. (2001). *Crisis in sociology: The need for Darwin*. Somerset, NJ: Transaction Publishers.

Rubin, P. H. (2002). *Darwinian politics: The evolutionary origin of freedom*. Piscataway, NJ: Rutgers University Press.

Saad, G. (2005). *Applications of evolutionary psychology in consumer behavior*. Mahwah, NJ: Lawrence Erlbaum.

Sulloway, F. (1996). *Born to rebel*. Westport, CT: Praeger.

CHAPTER 33

Literature and Evolutionary Psychology

JOSEPH CARROLL

D ARWINIAN LITERARY STUDY has emerged only in the past 15 years or so, and its practitioners still constitute a relatively small community on the margins of the academic literary establishment. That establishment is oriented to postmodern beliefs and thus repudiates the ideas both of human nature and of objective scientific knowledge. Darwinian literary critics embrace the notion of *consilience,* affirm the cogency of Darwinian evolutionary theory, and assimilate the findings of Darwinian social science. They would agree with E. O. Wilson (1998) that the world constitutes a unified causal order and that knowledge itself forms an integrated field that encompasses the physical sciences, the social sciences, and the humanities. They affirm that human mental and cultural activity is constrained by the principles that regulate all biological activity, life has evolved through an adaptive process by means of natural selection, and all complex functional structure in living things has been produced by adaptation. They argue that the adapted mind produces literature and that literature reflects the structure and character of the adapted mind. To distinguish this kind of literary study from other schools that are in some way associated with "evolutionary" thinking, I refer to it as *adaptationist* or *Darwinian* literary study.

Adaptationist literary study makes use of a variety of concepts common in other approaches to literary study—concepts such as point of view, realism and symbolism, character/setting/plot, thematic structure, tone, and formal organization. Adaptationist critics locate all of these concepts in relation to a structured account of human nature, and they derive that account from Darwinian social science. The Human Nature and Literary Meaning: A Model section outlines the concept of human nature that is now emerging from Darwinian social science and integrates the standard concepts of literary analysis with that model. Before entering into that exposition, I provide some background and context for adaptationist literary study, outlining the main historical movements in literary theory over the past 150 years or so and locating adaptationist critics in relation to that history. I then identify the kinds of work done by adaptationist literary scholars and give a concise guide to their chief contributions. I distinguish adaptationist criticism from other schools that are in some way associated with evolutionary thought and discuss the debate, within evolutionary psychology itself, about the adaptive status and function of literature and the other arts.

Literature is the written version of an oral behavior—the verbal representation of imagined actions—that is universal in preliterate cultures. The word *literature* may be taken tacitly to signify the larger concept, "literature or its oral antecedents."

CONTRIBUTIONS TO ADAPTATIONIST LITERARY STUDY

The modern, unequivocally adaptationist understanding of literature and the other arts began to emerge only in the last quarter of the twentieth century. In this area, as in so many others, E. O. Wilson may be credited with pioneering insights (see Cooke, 1999a; E. O. Wilson, 1978, 1984, 1998). Until he included a chapter on the arts in *Consilience,* Wilson's comments remained occasional and fragmentary, but they nonetheless provided the most immediate stimulus for the work of Brett Cooke, who in the late 1980s began producing a series of articles taking an adaptationist perspective on science fiction, opera, ballet, cinema, and Russian literature. In 1992, Cooke coorganized a conference that provided the basis for a collection of essays, *Sociobiology and the Arts,* coedited by Bedaux and Cooke. The collection was not published until 1999, but the quality of the essays reflects the still rudimentary state of thinking in Darwinian aesthetics from the early 1990s. A second conference, in 1995, provided some of the materials for a second collection, *Biopoetics: Evolutionary Explorations in the Arts* (1999a), coedited by Cooke and Frederick Turner. As in the previous collection, several of the essays in this volume reflect a rather vague and inchoate sense of what an adaptationist perspective might involve. Most of the contributors make little effort to formulate fundamental principles of broad, general validity. Cooke's own most valuable theoretical essays include "On the Evolution of Interest: Cases in Serpent Art" (1999b), "The Promise of a Biothematics" (1999c), and "Sexual Property in Pushkin's 'The Snowstorm': A Darwinist Perspective" (1999d). All three articles follow Wilson's lead in concentrating on the representation of human universals and the evocation of archetypal motifs. Cooke's single most ambitious and successful effort in practical Darwinian criticism is *Human Nature in Utopia: Zamyatin's* We (2002), the first book-length Darwinian study concentrating on a single work of literature. This study is fully informed on the relevant contexts of dystopian and Soviet literature, it is alive to issues of style and literary form, and it frames its critique of dystopian customs by appealing to adaptationist findings about human nature.

Another early contributor to Darwinian literary criticism, Nancy Easterlin, took her point of departure not so much from Darwin or the contemporary Darwinists as from the Darwinian associations in the psychology of William James (see Easterlin, 1993). Easterlin makes the case that James's empirical and naturalistic approach to psychology offers a better model for contemporary interdisciplinary work than the purely "rhetorical" methods of postmodern interdisciplinary work. One of Easterlin's areas of literary specialization is the study of the Romantic poet Wordsworth, and in her critique of feminist psychoanalytic interpretations of

Wordsworth (2000), she gives an excellent practical illustration of the way in which empirical findings from evolutionary psychology can correct distorted critical perceptions inspired by the obsolete speculative fancies of Freudian theory. In some of her other essays (1999a, 1999b, 2001a, 2001b), Easterlin has both assimilated information from Darwinian social science and argued against any ultimate "reduction" of literary figuration and literary response to elementary principles of biology and psychology.

The 1993 volume Easterlin coedited with Riebling was billed not specifically as Darwinian in orientation but only as "interdisciplinary." The only radically Darwinian article in the volume was that by Robert Storey. Storey selects his range of source texts from theoretical biology, ethology, sociobiology, evolutionary psychology, and the theory of emotions. He passionately affirms that literature is rooted in the physical and emotional reality of our experience as evolved human animals, and with equal passion he denounces the effete perversities and unreal abstractions of postmodern theory. Storey's article was an early version of the introduction to his book of 1996, *Mimesis and the Human Animal: The Biogenetical Foundation of Literary Representation.* In the book, along with extending the polemical engagement of the pilot essay, Storey constructs speculative accounts of narrative and of comedy and tragedy, and he offers an illustrative critique of a novel by Iris Murdoch. The critique of Murdoch is particularly noteworthy in that Storey explicitly argues that Murdoch, a modern intellectual susceptible to Freudian fashion, mistakes the sources and character of the passions depicted in her tale. The case is plausible, and the general principle is important—the principle that overt and conscious thematic formulation on the part of an author is not the sole and definitive form of meaning in a literary representation. An author can be animated by the common impulses of human nature and can depict those impulses and still make the same kinds of erroneous or imperfect interpretive judgments anyone might make about the matters under his or her observation. This principle has wide application for authors from all periods and all belief systems. In a subsequent article (2001), Storey further explored the topic of comedy in relation to recent findings in cognitive neuroscience.

Evolution and Literary Theory (Carroll, 1995a) has a range of adaptationist reference and a theoretical orientation similar to that of Storey's *Mimesis and the Human Animal.* Like Storey, I affirm that literature reflects the vital interests of human beings as living organisms, and I set this affirmation in sharp opposition to the textualized universe of the postmodernists. Drawing on evolutionary epistemology and evolutionary psychology, I affirm that the human mind is adapted to the world in which it evolved, it can give a true account of that world, and Darwinian psychology and anthropology provide a fundamentally sound framework for the progressive acquisition of empirical knowledge about human nature. I give extended critiques of key figures in postmodern critical theory and evolutionary psychology and delineate a general theory of literary representation as a continuum between mimetic realism and symbolic figuration. In subsequent articles (1995b, 1998a, 1998b, 1999a, 1999b, 1999c, 2001a, 2001b, 2001c, 2002, 2003a, 2003b, in press), I assessed new contributions to Darwinian aesthetics and Darwinian literary study and continued to develop an adaptationist theory of literary meaning. These essays have now been collected in Literary Darwinism: Evolution, Human Nature, and Literature (2004). My most extended consideration of Darwin and the history of evolutionary theory appears in the introduction to my edition of Darwin's *On the Origin of Species* (2003b).

Michelle Sugiyama has published several articles that use Darwinian anthropology and evolutionary psychology to illuminate important issues in literary theory and especially in narrative. In "On the Origins of Narrative: Storyteller Bias as a Fitness Enhancing Strategy" (1996), she uses sociobiology and ethnographic information on oral narrative to assess the way narrators manipulate their narratives to serve their own interests. In "Narrative Theory and Function: Why Evolution Matters" (2001b), she argues that narrative is a human universal and identifies its universal characteristics. In "Food, Foragers, and Folklore: The Role of Narrative in Human Subsistence" (2001a), she examines the practical information about vital resources in the narratives of a foraging people. Two of her essays take classic plays as a focal point for considering large theoretical issues. In "New Science, Old Myth: An Evolutionary Critique of the Oedipal Paradigm" (2001c), she uses the evolutionary critique of the Freudian Oedipal myth to illuminate the distortions in Freudian readings of *Oedipus* Rex. In "Cultural Relativism in the Bush: Towards a Theory of Narrative Universals" (in press), she discusses the question of cultural relativism by considering the response of the Tiv, a Nigerian people, to Shakespeare's *Hamlet*. She makes valuable distinctions between local cultural variations and the deeper, underlying commonalities that render literary works intelligible across wide boundaries of cultural difference. (Another good essay that takes account of cultural differences is Margaret Nesse's "Guinevere's Choice," 1995. Nesse assesses the way in which changing cultural attitudes within a single culture influence the depiction of sexual mores in different versions of the same story.)

Brian Boyd is widely regarded as the leading scholar on novelist Vladimir Nabokov, and for several years he has been working on an adaptationist approach to literature and art, especially to fiction. In "'Jane, Meet Charles': Literature, Evolution, and Human Nature" (1998), Boyd gives a general exposition of the tenets of evolutionary psychology, explains their relevance to literary study, and illustrates his argument with a reading of Jane Austen's *Mansfield Park*. One signal feature of this reading is that it examines a specific formal technique of narrative, "free indirect discourse," and argues persuasively that this technique constitutes a prosthetic literary extension of a fundamental cognitive adaptation. This linkage of literary technique and cognitive adaptation should provide a model for further such studies into the underlying cognitive logic of literary structures. In "The Origin of Stories: *Horton Hears a Who*" (2001), Boyd begins to develop a theory of art based on an evolutionary understanding of human attention and demonstrates that adaptationist criticism is not restricted to nineteenth-century marriage plots. In "Kind and Unkindness: Aaron in *Titus Andronicus*" (in press-b), he uses kin-selection theory to illuminate in-group/out-group dynamics. In "Laughter and Literature: A Play Theory of Humor" (in press-c), Boyd formulates an adaptationist theory of humor illustrated with examples from jokes, movies, Shakespeare, and modernist literature. In "Evolutionary Theories of Art" (in press-a), he assesses six major positions on art and adaptation. Boyd is currently working on a book in which he will demonstrate the relevance of adaptationist thinking across a diverse and representative array of literary periods and genres, from Homer through Shakespeare and into modern fiction, cinema, and comics.

Ecological literary criticism, or "ecocriticism," has emerged since the early 1990s as a flourishing field of critical endeavor. The ecocritics have their own professional organization, the Association for the Study of Literature and Environment, and a journal associated with the organization, *Interdisciplinary Studies in Literature and Environment*. Ecology is a topic area, not a specific theoretical doctrine, and the ecocritics have spread themselves across the range of possible theoretical orientations (see Carroll, 2001a; Glotfelty & Fromm, 1996). Two of the founding, senior members of the ecological literary movement, Glen Love and Harold Fromm, have oriented themselves to Darwinian theory. In two theoretical articles (1999a, 1999b), Love draws on the consilient worldview of E. O. Wilson to argue for the integration of the sciences and humanities, and he poses this integration as an alternative to the antiscience views of postmodern literary theory. (A similar theoretical orientation informs Marcus Nordlund's "Consilient Literary Interpretation," 2002.) Love's book *Practical Ecocriticism: Literature, Biology, and the Environment* (2003) expands on these themes and offers extensive literary illustration of his approach. Fromm is a distinguished literary essayist who has countered postmodern theory from an intuitively naturalistic orientation and has articulated the naturalistic dimensions of ecocriticism (1991, 1996, 1998). More recently, Fromm has been assimilating the literature of evolutionary psychology and Darwinian literary criticism (2001, 2003a, 2003b).

One obvious starting place for Darwinian criticism is to look at narratives or dramatic works for illustrations of some hypothesized universal form of sexual psychology. Examples of this approach include Robin Fox's article on sexual competition among younger and older males in epic literature (1995) and Thiessen's and Umezawa's study of a medieval Japanese narrative (1998). In a more advanced form of the same kind of criticism, Ian Jobling takes account of the way "universal" sexual psychology is modulated by a specific cultural ethos, and he demonstrates the way that ethos enters into the depiction of character and the organization of theme in Scott's *Ivanhoe* (2001b). Jobling has also written on the underlying psychology in the depiction of ogres and heroes in world folklore (2001a) and on Byronism as a literary fashion that exemplifies the "cad" mating strategy (2002).

Darwinian literary criticism and Darwinian literary science share subject matter but differ in methodology. Darwinian literary criticism uses information from the social sciences and acknowledges the validity of empirical criteria for truth, but its methods are humanistic—they involve tact, intuition, and personal response. Darwinian literary science is a subspecies of Darwinian social science. Darwinian literary science takes literary texts or the production of literature as its subject matter, but it studies this subject by adopting the methods of social science—statistical analysis and experimentation. It seeks both to use literature as a source of data for social science and to provide literary critics with empirical facts that can constrain and direct their interpretive efforts. This line of research has not been developed as extensively as Darwinian literary criticism, but it holds immense promise. Cynthia Whissel has done a statistical study of the depiction of heroines in romance narratives (1996). Catherine Salmon and Donald Symons have studied romance and pornography as windows into evolved sexual psychology (2001). Daniel Nettle has an article in press on the psychosocial dynamics of small group interactions in the plays of Shakespeare. (Dunbar, Nettle, & Stiller,

2003, are preparing a book-length study on the same subject.) Nettle's article will be included in an important volume, *Literature and the Human Animal* (in press), coedited by Jonathan Gottschall and D. S. Wilson. The plan of the volume is to include about equal proportions of work done by Darwinian literary critics and Darwinian social scientists who address the problems of literature. Contributors who have already completed the essays contracted for the volume include Boyd, Carroll, Gottschall, Nettle, and D. S. Wilson.

Gottschall has done work in Darwinian social science, Darwinian literary science, literary theory, and literary criticism on Homer. In social science proper, he has one single-authored and one coauthored article in press about rape ("Explaining Wartime Rape," in press-b and "Are Per-Incident Rape-Pregnancy Rates Higher than Consensual Pregnancy Rates?" in press with Tiffani Gottschall). In the area of Darwinian literary science, he is the single or primary author of three articles in press that report the results of using large-scale databases to conduct statistical analyses of the depiction of heroines cross-culturally ("Can Literary Study Be Scientific?" Gottschall, Allison, De Rosa, & Klockeman, in press; "The Heroine with a Thousand Faces," Gottschall, in press-c; and "Patterns of Characterization in Folk Tales," Gottschall, in press-d). In a theoretical article, "The Tree of Knowledge and Darwinian Literary Study" (in press-e), he locates all literary study within the empirical ethos of Darwinian social science. He has also used Darwinian anthropology to throw light on the ethos of male-male competition in Homer ("An Evolutionary Perspective on Homer's Invisible Daughters," in press-a) and on ritual combat in the *Iliad* (2001). (Barash & Barash, 2002, offer another sociobiologically oriented study of a classic epic, Virgil's *Aeneid*.)

NONADAPTATIONIST FORMS OF "EVOLUTIONARY" LITERARY THEORY

Adaptationist critics share one central principle—that the adapted mind produces literature and that literature reflects the structure and character of the adapted mind. There are at least three other ways of integrating evolution into literary theory, but none of these ways is adaptationist in the sense I use that word here:

1. Cosmic evolutionists identify some universal process of development or progress and identify literary structures as microcosmic versions of that process.
2. Evolutionary analogists take the process of Darwinian evolution—blind variation and selective retention—as a widely applicable model for all development.
3. Evolutionary ideologues isolate aspects of evolution that reflect their own social, ethical, political, or aesthetic values.

I comment briefly on each of these alternative uses of evolutionary theory. In the final paragraph of this section, I describe a fourth school, cognitive rhetoric, that has some marginal association with evolutionary psychology.

Cosmic evolutionists believe that the universe itself is evolving and that this evolutionary process constitutes a formal order that is replicated, like fractals, at every lower level of organization. Herbert Spencer offers a classic version of this theory. Spencer was Darwin's contemporary and is sometimes (misleadingly) associated with him as a proponent of natural selection. Long before Darwin published his theory of natural selection, Spencer had already developed a theory of cosmic evolution that was inspired in part by his reading of Lamarck (see Carroll, 2003b). Spencer believed that the universe as a whole and every major field of phenomena within it are animated by internal formal principles that lead them to increase in complexity. The central formal process is that of "an advance from a diffused, indeterminate, and uniform distribution of Matter, to a concentrated, determinate, and multiform distribution of it," that is, "from a confused simplicity to an orderly complexity" (1862, pp. 489, 490). In a long series of books, Spencer applied this abstract formula to astronomy, geology, biology, sociology, psychology, and ethics. Other cosmic evolutionists use different idioms but embrace similar metaphysical notions. Prominent examples include the German transcendentalists and Romantics (Herder, Hegel, Schlegel, Fichte); many of the nineteenth-century cultural theorists such as Arnold, Mill, and Comte; and the mystical Catholic biologist Teilhard de Chardin. The metaphysical conviction of a progressive and teleological force driving historical change also animates the biological theory of Lamarck and the social theory of Marx. In contemporary literary theory, the proponents of cosmic evolution include Walter Koch, Frederic Turner, Alex Argyros, and Richard Cureton (see Carroll, 1998a, 2003a). Theorists who follow this line of thinking have simply failed to grasp the fundamental way in which the Darwinian theory of natural selection has definitively rendered all spiritualistic and teleological notions of progressive change irrelevant and obsolete.

Cosmic evolutionists identify some universal formal pattern of evolution or development, and they take biological evolution as a specific instance of that pattern. The second category of nonadaptationist evolutionists, evolutionary analogists, reverses this process. They take natural selection as a model for a process that applies to other phenomenal domains. Instances include Donald Campbell's idea that all intellectual creativity can be conceived as a form of random variation and selective retention (1988); Thomas Kuhn's notion that scientific disciplines speciate or branch into distinct and "incommensurable" species of knowledge (1991); Richard Dawkins' theory of "memes" (1976, 1982); and Rabkin's and Simon's idea that cultural creations "evolve in the same way as do biological organisms, that is, as complex adaptive systems that succeed or fail according to their fitness to their environment" (2001, p. 45). All these theories mistake an analogy for a causal process. Memes, for example, spread or reproduce in a way that has some parallels with the spread of genes, but no meme—no idea or cultural image—contains a molecular mechanism adapted by natural selection to replicate itself. Ideas and cultural images are themselves inert. They are "replicated" only by serving as stimuli for psychological processes eventuating in symbolic activity that stimulates other psychological processes. The differences in causal mechanisms between molecular replication and this memetic process are subtle but fundamental (see Carroll, 2003a; Daly, 1982; Flinn & Alexander, 1982; Symons, 1987).

Evolutionary analogists are close kin to the third category of nonadaptationist evolutionists, the evolutionary ideologues. The analogists take biological evolution as a conceptual model, and the ideologues take it as an ethical model. Both forms of modeling use only selected aspects of the root idea, but the use of selective aspects is particularly striking in the case of the ideologues because different ideologues use evolution to support radically different ethical norms. Nietzscheans adopt the notion that nature is red in tooth and claw, and they celebrate violent domination as an ethical norm. Spencerian utilitarians adopt the notion that evolution is like a laissez-faire economic system, and they celebrate the elimination of competitively unsuccessful biological enterprises. Utopian ecologists adopt the notion that evolution proceeds by way of symbiotic relationships, and they celebrate cooperative social interaction (see Carroll, 2001a; Hawkins, 1997). Evolutionary ideologues treat evolutionary theory the way certain fundamentalist Christians treat the Bible. The values come first. The appeal to authority is used only to give the values an apparent rationale in nature.

Cognitive rhetoric is a school of literary study that seeks to affiliate itself with certain language-centered areas of cognitive psychology. The chief theorists in this school argue that language is based in metaphors, and they claim that metaphors are themselves rooted in biology or the body, but they do not argue that human nature consists in a highly structured set of motivational and cognitive dispositions that have evolved through an adaptive process regulated by natural selection. Cognitive rhetoricians are generally more anxious than adaptationists to associate themselves with postmodern theories of "discourse," but some cognitive rhetoricians make gestures toward evolutionary psychology, and some adaptationist critics have found common ground with the cognitive rhetoricians (see Boyd, 1999; Easterlin, 2002). The seminal authorities in cognitive rhetoric are the language philosophers Mark Johnson and George Lakoff, and the most prominent literary theorist in the field is Mark Turner. Other literary scholars associated with cognitive rhetoric include Mary Thomas Crane, F. Elizabeth Hart, Tony Jackson, Alan Richardson, Ellen Spolsky, Francis Steen, and Lisa Zunshine (see Carroll, 1998a, 1999b, 2003a; Hart, 2001).

THE QUESTION OF THE ADAPTIVE FUNCTION OF THE ARTS

The question of adaptive function bears directly on the issues of how and why literature is produced, why it is consumed, and what effects it has. Our ideas about adaptive function enter into virtually any proposition we might make about the nature of literature and about the meaning of any given literary text. The question as to whether the arts have an adaptive function—and if so, what it might be—is thus clearly central to the adaptationist understanding of literature and the other arts, but adaptationists have reached no consensus on this question. Moreover, the debate over the adaptive function of the arts is rooted in a still deeper question: the adaptive function of the mind itself. For the purposes of a handbook designed to convey the state of knowledge in a given field, this situation presents a special challenge. No settled findings can be reported in this area, but no significant arguments can be put forward that do not imply some hypothesis. This section and the next describe the various hypotheses that have been put forward and make the case that literature and the other arts do have an adaptive function. I argue that they fulfill the specifically and uniquely human need to produce an emotionally and aesthetically saturated cognitive order. The need to produce that order is a major component in the model of human nature described in the following section.

Among evolutionary psychologists and adaptationist aesthetic theorists, three broad lines of argument have been made about the adaptive function of the arts: (1) that the arts have no adaptive function and have arisen as side effects of other adaptive mental processes; (2) that neither art nor the mind itself has any adaptive function produced by natural selection but that both have arisen, as the product of sexual selection, for the purposes of sexual display; and (3) that the arts do have an adaptive function. The theorists who advocate this third position can be further divided into two groups: (1) those who argue that the arts have no intrinsic adaptive function peculiar to their own nature but that they provide subsidiary service only to some other, more general adaptive function, such as information distribution, kin recognition, or social cohesion; and (2) those who argue that the arts fulfill a primary and irreducible adaptive function—that they satisfy adaptive needs that are not satisfied by any other activity.

Steven Pinker (1997, 2002) has a dual theory of art that places him in both the first and third of the three categories identified in the previous paragraph. He divides the proximal purposes of art into the traditional categories of utility and pleasure (*utile et dulce*). With respect to the pleasure derived from art, Pinker locates himself in the first category, among those who argue that art is a side effect of other adaptive functions. Higher cognitive activity is in itself adaptive, Pinker argues, but the pleasure we get from the activity of the mind can be parasitized and exploited by artistic activity. Art pushes pleasure buttons in the same way that psychoactive drugs, pornography, and rich desserts push pleasure buttons. The buttons themselves would originally have been "designed" by natural selection for some primary adaptive purpose. With respect to the utility of art, Pinker locates himself in the first section of the third category—among those who argue that art serves as a form of information distribution. He argues that stories depict model situations and that people can learn the consequences of behavior from those models. Other theorists have made similar claims. Sugiyama (2001a, 2001b) argues that art serves as a medium for conveying adaptively relevant information about the environment. Ellen Dissanayake (1995a, 1995b, 2000, 2001) argues that art heightens and focuses attention and thus serves the purpose of fixing the mind on adaptively significant areas of human activity. She also argues that art serves as a medium of social communication that articulates the sense of shared values and concerns within a community. This latter idea is similar to the idea put forward by Kathryn Coe (2003) that art serves primarily to signal affiliation with specific kin groups. In contrast to these hypotheses about the adaptive value of art, Geoffrey Miller (2000) has argued that the large human brain did not itself evolve because it had adaptive value but only because it was metabolically expensive. It could thus advertise general fitness and serve as a means of sexual display, like the peacock's tail. Painting or writing would, in this view, demonstrate that the artist himself, like the bowerbird, is capable of expending large amounts of mental energy in adaptively useless tasks.

The idea that art has a primary and irreducible adaptive function presupposes that the large human brain evolved for its adaptive value. The brain enables humans to respond flexibly to complex contingent circumstances. The adaptive advantages of a large brain must have been great enough so that they could outweigh the disadvantages: metabolic expensiveness, a difficult and dangerous passage through a birth canal already narrowed by upright posture, and the multiplying possibilities of confusion and error that accompany the loosening of stereotyped, instinctual responses. In the only adaptationist hypothesis that identifies a primary adaptive function for the arts, it is this latter problem—confusion and uncertainty—that the arts have evolved to solve (see Carroll, 1998b,

1999a, 1999b, 1999c, 2003a; Tooby & Cosmides, 2001; E. O. Wilson, 1998). The arguments put forward in support of the hypothesis that art has adaptive value are that (1) it is a human universal—it develops reliably and spontaneously in all known cultures, (2) it is expensive in materials and effort, (3) it involves complex and highly structured processes, and (4) it seems necessary to personal development and cultural identification (see Barrow, 1995; Carroll, 2001c; Dissanayake, 1995a, 1995b, 2000, 2001; Eibl-Eibesfeldt, 1989; Storey, 1996; Sugiyama, 2001b).

In this hypothesis, the primary adaptive function of art is to provide the mind with subjectively weighted models of reality in such a way as to help organize the complex human motivational system. Art does not simply provide examples of appropriate behavior or adaptive information. It provides an emotionally saturated simulation of experience. Producing and consuming these simulations enable people both to experience the emotions depicted and to stand back from them and gain a cognitively detached sense of the larger patterns of human life. (This balancing between emotional involvement and cognitive detachment is what is meant by "aesthetic distance.") By vicariously participating in the simulated life provided by these models, people improve their ability to understand and regulate their own behavior and to assess the behavior of other people.

HUMAN NATURE AND LITERARY MEANING: A MODEL

The concept of human nature is central both to Darwinian social science and to Darwinian literary study. Adaptationist literary theorists argue that literature is produced by human nature, is shaped by human nature, and takes human nature as its primary subject. Until the postmodern revolution of the past 30 years, the appeal to human nature had been a constant and virtually universal feature of literature and of literary theory. In this crucial respect, the literary tradition had it right, and the postmodern revolution has gotten it wrong. Literary Darwinists are now rejuvenating the idea of human nature and transposing it from the province of folk wisdom to the province of Darwinian social science.

Darwinian social scientists are on the verge of producing a full-fledged and usable model of human nature, but they have not reached consensus on two main issues: the significance of domain-general intelligence and the significance of individual differences in identity. As a distinct school within Darwinian social science, *evolutionary psychology,* narrowly defined, has tended to discount the significance of domain-general intelligence and of individual differences. It has instead attributed predominating significance to domain-specific cognitive modules and to human universals (see Bailey, 1997, 1998; Chiappe & MacDonald, 2003; Cosmides & Tooby, 1994; Crawford, 1998; Foley, 1996; Geary, 1998; Geary & Huffman, 2002; Irons, 1998; MacDonald, 1990, 1995b, 1997, 1998a, 1998b; Mithen, 1996, 2001; Potts, 1998; Richerson & Boyd, 2000; Segal & MacDonald, 1998; Tooby & Cosmides, 1990, 1992; D. S. Wilson, 1994, 1999, in press). An adequate basic model of human nature would integrate the concepts both of domain-general intelligence and of domain-specific cognitive modules, and it would integrate the concepts both of human universals and of individual differences. Yet further, it would assimilate the chief concepts from each of the main areas of Darwinian social science—from sociobiology, Darwinian anthropology, life history analysis, evolutionary psychology, behavioral ecology, behavioral genetics, developmental

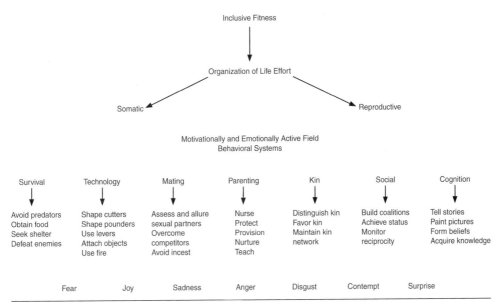

Figure 33.1 A Model of Human Nature.

psychology, personality theory, and the theory of emotions. A model of human nature that assimilates information from all these areas has been emerging over the past decade or so (Figure 33.1).

At the top of the diagram in this model of human nature, *inclusive fitness* is the principle that has regulated the organization of life and the evolution of complex adaptive structures. The first principle in the organization of life is the distribution of effort into somatic and reproductive activity—that is, into the acquisition of resources and the expenditure of resources in reproductive effort (see Alexander, 1979, p. 25, 1987, pp. 40–41; Geary, 1998, pp. 11, 199; Low, 1998, pp. 138–40, 2000, p. 92; MacDonald, 1997, 1998a; McGuire & Troisi, 1998, pp. 58–59; Ridley, 1999, pp. 12, 127–128). Darwinian anthropologists and evolutionary psychologists have debated whether reproduction is a direct and proximal motive in itself or only the reliable result, in ancestral environments, of proximal motives such as the desire for sex and the impulse to nurture the resulting offspring (see Alexander, 1979, 1987; Barkow, 1990; Betzig, 1986, 1998; Chagnon, 1979; Chagnon & Irons, 1979; Irons, 1990, 1998; MacDonald, 1995a; Symons, 1989, 1992; Turke, 1990). If we observe the activity of misers and the longing of infertile humans to bear children, we will probably hesitate before declaring that proximal motives are, at least in humans, neatly and decisively segregated from the larger life history goals of acquiring resources and bearing offspring. That is, we will acknowledge that acquiring resources and bearing offspring can serve as direct or proximal human motives.

The model I delineate proposes that within the distribution of somatic and reproductive effort, human evolutionary history has produced complex structure by organizing human behavior not simply into domain-specific cognitive modules but rather into a set of behavioral systems. The term *behavioral systems* is adopted from McGuire and Troisi (1998), who define it as "functionally and causally related behavior patterns and the systems responsible for them" (p. 60). Within each system, we can identify more particular goals or directives that, following MacDonald (1990), I designate *evolved motive dispositions*. Under *survival*, for instance, we can identify evolved motive dispositions for obtaining food and shelter and avoiding predators; under *mating*, for selecting and obtaining mates and for warding off rivals; under *parenting*, for nurturing, protecting, and teaching children; and under *cognition*, for telling stories, painting pictures, forming beliefs, and acquiring knowledge. At the base of the diagram are the seven basic emotions identified by Ekman, which indicate that all behavior is proximally activated by emotions (see Damasio, 1994; Ekman, 2003; Ekman & Davidson, 1994; Ledoux, 1996; MacDonald, 1995b; Panksepp, 1998).

The concept of *domain-specific cognitive modules* is sometimes formulated so broadly that it includes emotions, perceptual processing subsystems, evolved motive dispositions, and behavioral systems (see Cosmides & Tooby, 1994, p. 103; Pinker, 1995, p. 236, 1997, pp. 128, 315; Tooby & Cosmides, 1992, p. 113). For the purposes of analytic utility, we would do better to distinguish among these different aspects and levels in psychological organization (see Chiappe & MacDonald, 2003; Geary, 1998; Geary & Huffman, 2002; MacDonald, 1995b). In this model, specific cognitive modules would be activated within relevant behavioral systems. For instance, visual processing modules such as those for detecting edges or motion would be activated in the survival and technological systems; cheater detection modules would be activated in the mating, parenting, and social modules; face-detection modules would be activated in all systems involving interpersonal relations, and so on.

Five of the behavioral systems delineated in the diagram—survival, mating, parenting, kin relations, and social life—correspond to the sequence of chapters in several of the textbooks of evolutionary psychology that have been produced since 1999 (see Barrett, Dunbar, & Lycett, 2002; Bridgeman, 2003; Buss, 1999; Gaulin & McBurney, 2001; Palmer & Palmer, 2002; Rossano, 2003). This organization of chapters tacitly supports the idea of behavioral systems as functionally and causally related behavior patterns. Two of the designated systems, technology and cognition, do not form a regular feature in the textbooks but are necessary to an adequate basic model of human nature.

Our hominid ancestors evidently had domain-specific cognitive modules for the construction of hand axes, and one of the signal features in the "human revolution" that took place some 50,000 years ago is the emergence of complex, multipart tools. In his synthesis of paleoanthropology and cognitive psychology, Mithen (1996) has argued persuasively that technology should be recognized as a behavioral system. (Mithen uses the term *cognitive domain* to denote a concept roughly parallel to what I here designate a *behavioral system*.)

A second signal feature in the human revolution was the emergence of symbolic and aesthetic activity, as evidenced by cave paintings, ornaments and ornamentation, figurines, and ceremonial burials (see Mellars, 1996; Mithen, 1996, 2001; Stringer & Gamble, 1993; Tattersall, 1999). A behavioral system has distinctive latent capacities that require satisfaction. For instance, the mating behavioral system activates a desire for forming affiliative bonds of a sexual character. The parenting behavioral system activates a desire to help an individual's own children grow into healthy adults. The social behavioral system activates a desire to integrate self into a social group. And the cognitive behavioral system activates a desire to make sense of the world. It satisfies that desire by formulating concepts; articulating religious, philosophical, or ideological beliefs; developing scientific knowledge; fabricating aesthetic artifacts; and producing imaginative verbal representations.

When most Darwinists start thinking about how to use evolutionary psychology to illuminate literature, their first thought is to identify human universals—most often universal mating behavior—and to propose examining this or that literary text to demonstrate that the behavior depicted in the text exemplifies the universal. The search for universals is in fact an integral component of adaptationist literary study, but it is only one component. To make the best use of that component, adaptationist critics must integrate the study of universals with the study of cultural and individual differences, and they must also assimilate standard concepts of literary analysis.

Literature depicts human behavior, but human behavior does not consist only of species-typical behavior. Marriage, for instance, is a human universal. It appears in all known cultures. But not everyone gets married. Not everyone is heterosexual, and there are many heterosexuals who do not follow the species-typical patterns of affiliative bonding. (Psychopaths do not, and psychopathy is a favorite topic of literary representation.) Moreover, marriage can be polygamous or monogamous, lifelong or serial. It can consist in slavelike subjugation of the female or in intimate partnership. The two people involved in a marriage are both human, but they can vary in age, health, personality, intelligence, social affiliation, occupation, status, honesty, and a number of other characteristics. Most women prefer men of status and wealth, and most men prefer young and beautiful women (see Buss, 1994), but women sometimes employ gigolos, and men sometimes have faithful and happy marriages with rich older women—as did, for instance, both Mohammad the Prophet and Disraeli the British prime minister and novelist. None of this cultural and individual variation is irrelevant to literary meaning. Species-typical norms provide all of us with a basis for common human feeling—for the possibility of mutual understanding and imaginative sympathy. But the differences of culture and personal identity are also real and important parts of who we are and how we think. Individual identity defines itself in relation to a common humanity, but that relation is often one of tension and discord. Depicting and registering the relation between human universals and individual identity is a chief concern for an adaptationist interpretation of literary meaning.

A literary representation is a written or spoken enactment of a social interaction. That social interaction consists in three distinct sets of participants—the author, the audience, and the characters depicted (see Abrams, 1986). Each participant is a conscious agent with a distinct point of view. He or she interprets the world and comments on the action. Meaning emerges not just out of the action but also out of the interplay among converging, competing, and conflicting perspectives on the action. Analyzing this interplay is one of the chief ways in which literary critics interpret meaning in literary texts.

An author is an individual with a culturally colored identity, an idiosyncratic temperament, and a unique set of personal experiences. All of those modifying individual factors enter into the author's attitudes toward his or her subject. The attitude an author takes toward his or her characters is a crucial part of the meaning of his or her depiction. The author might love some characters, hate others, and despise still others. Those feelings shape the manner and tone of the presentation and enter into the logic of the plot. Moreover, authors wish to influence the feelings of the audience. The author is a person talking to other people (the audience) about still other people (the characters). The author and the audience both respond to characters with emotions that parallel emotions we have in observing real people in the actual world. The author responds to the characters and seeks to manipulate or persuade the audience. The audience responds to the characters and to the personality and manner of the author. All of this social interaction is a fundamental part of the total literary experience and is an indispensable part of what a literary interpretation takes into account (see Carroll, 2001b, in press-a; Storey, 1996; Sugiyama, 1996).

Characters are fictional but can be and often are modeled after real people—Julius Caesar, Jesus, Napoleon, the author's sister, cousin, or uncle, or someone the author met at a party. Characters can also be wholly imaginary—fairies, angels, talking animals, ghosts, demons, gods. No matter how fanciful or unrealistic characters and situations might be, to be effective as literature, they must tap into recognizable emotions and motives. They must operate within the range of behaviors that are intelligible and meaningful to our evolved psychology.

Human experience has three elemental components: individual persons (characters), a surrounding world (setting), and sequences of action connected by emotionally meaningful purposes (plots). Literary authors can seek to give exact and faithful accounts of what actual experience is like in a concretely detailed physical and social world occupied by ordinary people engaged in activities that are constrained by commonplace conditions. We call that kind of literature *realism*. Authors can also depict imagined situations in which characters exemplify elemental emotions and abstract ideas, in which settings exemplify emotional or imaginative aspects of experience, and in which plots fulfill the inner logic of some emotional or imaginative process relatively unhindered by commonplace constraints on probability. We call that kind of literature *symbolism* (e.g., myths and fairy tales). The two kinds represent not mutually exclusive alternatives but polar points on a continuum, and all literature has some measure both of realism and of symbolism (see Carroll, 1995a, chap. 3). Dickens, for example, both depicts the actual conditions of Victorian urban life and creates characters and plots that often seem more like those of myth or fairy tale than those of simple realist fiction. In neither its realist nor its symbolic aspect does literary meaning reside simply in an accurate portrayal of what happens. Meaning resides always in the *sense* of what happens—in how it feels and looks to the characters and to authors and readers. In this crucial respect, then, meaning is always a function of point of view.

In the traditional study of literary meaning, critics divide meaning into three main dimensions: theme, tone, and formal organization. To conclude this exposition on literary meaning, I briefly describe how each of these aspects of meaning can be integrated into an adaptationist literary perspective.

Theme is the conceptual organization that can be abstracted from a literary work. All the elements depicted—characters, settings, actions—have to be conceived. Authors vary in the ideas they have about life and death, love and family, reproduction, technology, the social world, and the larger world of nature. Analyzing that conceptual organization is an indispensable feature of all literary interpretation. Adaptationist critics do not differ from traditional critics in the obligation to understand how an author conceptually organizes his or her own imagined world. What distinguishes an adaptationist approach is that the adaptationist compares the author's conception to the Darwinian conception of the world. Adaptationist critics use the consilient worldview and Darwinian social science as the common frame within which they assess the conceptual order of any depicted action.

Most authors have a strong intuitive understanding of human nature. That understanding is one of the prerequisites for being an author. Adaptationist critics analyze the way the intuitive understanding of any given author is made to fit within the author's conceptual order. Authors sometimes give depictions of human behavior in which some personal bias or some religious, ideological, or theoretical preconception seriously distorts his or her intuitive understanding. Such distortions are also materials for an adaptationist interpretive analysis.

Tone is the emotional organization of a literary work—the emotions of the characters depicted and of the author depicting them and even the emotions that the author anticipates the audience will feel. All these emotions are intertwined in a distinct sequence that produces a combined total effect. In one basic dimension of meaning, any literary work can be analyzed as an orchestrated sequence of emotions producing a total quality of mood or tone. This dimension is so important that it constitutes the chief element in the largest terms that are used to categorize literary works—the terms of *genre*. Genres, like emotions, can be subtle, complex, and mixed in quality, but there are three basic genres—tragedy, comedy, and satire—that form the core elements in all the more complex or equivocal forms.

The three basic genres are produced by specific combinations of the basic emotions: joy, sadness, fear, anger, disgust, contempt, and surprise. Tragedy and comedy occupy the poles of negative and positive emotionality in human experience. Tragedy depicts in its characters and engages in its audience the emotions of sadness, fear, anger, and surprise. (The very existence of tragedy disconfirms the notion, propounded by Freud, 1959, that literature is merely a form of wish-fulfillment fantasy.) Comedy depicts and engages the emotions of joy and surprise. Romantic comedy, for instance, is the depiction of a successful mating effort that integrates the couple within a harmonious social world. In this genre, the marriage itself is often the medium for reconstituting or confirming that social harmony. In both tragedy and comedy, without the element of surprise or suspense, there is no story. The activation of concern for a doubtful outcome is a necessary and integral part of the psychology of narrative and of dramatic representation (see Storey, 1996; M. Turner, 1996). At this elementary level, narrative form might depend on a domain-specific cognitive module.

Unlike tragedy and comedy, satire does not seek to engage the reader in sympathetic identification with the characters. It activates the emotions of anger, disgust, and contempt in the reader, and it makes the reader stand apart, alienated and indignant, from the characters. This, too, is a basic, dichotomous alternative within our evolved psychology—the alternative as to whether we sympathize with other people or withdraw emotionally from them. Tragedy makes us grieve because characters we care about suffer. Comedy makes us rejoice because characters we care about fulfill their desires. And satire makes us glad that characters we despise get what is coming to them.

Formal organization can be divided into macrostructures and microstructures. Macrostructures include plot, narrative sequences, and the organization of scenes in drama. Microstructures include syntax, phrasing, imagery, word choice, and prosody. It is to these latter structures that we usually refer when we speak of style. Formal organization meshes closely with theme and tone, but formal order cannot be wholly reduced to these two other dimensions of meaning. There is an irreducible element of cognitive and verbal structure in form, and that element is closely allied with what we think of as the specifically aesthetic component in literary depiction. In traditional literary study, the analysis of style has usually been conducted by means of impressionistic and intuitive commentary. The challenge for an adaptationist understanding of formal organization is to explain how specific formal structures derive from and reflect the properties of our evolved cognitive architecture. Some work along these lines has already been done (see Barrow, 1995; Eibl-Eibesfeldt, 1989; F. Turner, 1992, pp. 61–108). The "cognitive rhetoricians" have also suggested some avenues of approach into formal organization but have stopped short of connecting formal analysis with a larger model of human nature (see M. Turner, 1991, 1996). For scholar-scientists who can combine expertise in literary interpretation, cognitive science, linguistics, and adaptationist psychology, this dimension of literary meaning offers rich opportunities.

CONCLUSIONS

Literary adaptationists have emerged and survived on the margins of the literary establishment, like small early mammals creeping about nocturnally among the feet of sleeping dinosaurs. The dinosaurs in this case consist of two populations. One population is composed of the last lingering elements—most of them gray, stiff, and fragile—of old-fashioned, humanist critics—belle-lettristic, archivalist, and a little lost and disoriented in the modern world of progressive empirical knowledge (see Abrams, 1997; Carroll, 1999b). The other population is composed of the postmodern establishment, no longer revolutionary but fully ensconced in all the precincts of academic power. This population can be compared to an invading army that has conquered a vast district, ravaged it, left it destitute, and thus deprived itself of the resources necessary to maintain itself on the ground it has conquered. The purely theoretical impulses animating postmodernism inspired the first wave of invaders, the deconstructionists, but that wave had already subsided by the late 1980s and had been superseded by the much more heavily political criticism of the Foucauldians, supplemented by their auxiliaries of feminist, gender, postcolonial, and ethnic critics. That secondary political wave has now also exhausted its momentum, and the literary establishment finds itself in a period of stasis and fatigue, isolated both from the progressive empirical sciences and from the interests and tastes of educated public opinion. The intellectual works that appear on nonfiction bestseller lists are not the works of Althusserian Marxists, Lacanian psychoanalysts, or Kristevan feminists. They are the works of primatologists such as Frans de Waal, zoologists such as Matt Ridley, and cognitive neuroscientists such as Steven Pinker.

Life among the dinosaurs is sometimes dangerous and uncomfortable for adaptationist literary scholars, and it is especially difficult for younger scholars struggling to survive in a hostile job environment. Those who do survive have the satisfaction of feeling that they are participating in a large and successful movement oriented to progressive knowledge. Barring a second Dark Ages, the future belongs to science, not to the irrationalist obstructions of the postmodernists. Being part of a population that will provide descendants to the future offers motive and consolation, but the chief motive for adaptationist critics is the stimulus of meeting the two challenges that are immediately in front of them: (a) to assimilate information outside their own field of expertise and (b) to formulate the elementary principles that are specific to their own field. The first challenge is complicated by the preparadigm phase through which evolutionary psychology is now passing. Literary Darwinists find it necessary not only to assimilate the settled and confirmed findings of evolutionary psychology but also to assess critically the fundamental questions that have not been settled. In assessing these fundamental questions, they will discover that the two challenges they face are complementary and interdependent. Literature and its oral antecedents are among the most significant and peculiar features of the specifically human part of human nature—the part that distinguishes humans from their primate cousins, from other mammals, and from all other living things. Literature is important enough so that we can use it as a touchstone for our model of human nature. We can say that until we have an adequate understanding of literature—of its adaptive functions, its sources in the adapted mind, and its proximal mechanisms—our model of human nature will itself be radically incomplete. Fortunately, we already have the materials for an adequate understanding both of literature and of human nature. By integrating them, we will incorporate literary study into the larger movement of progressive empirical knowledge and help to construct the model of human nature requisite to a true paradigm in evolutionary psychology.

REFERENCES

Abrams, M. H. (1986). Poetry, theories of. In A. Preminger et al. (Eds.), *Princeton encyclopedia of poetic terms* (pp. 203–214). Princeton, NJ: Princeton University Press.

Abrams, M. H. (1997). The transformation of English studies: 1930–1995. *Daedalus, 126*, 105–132.

Alexander, R. D. (1979). *Darwinism and human affairs.* Seattle: University of Washington Press.

Alexander, R. D. (1987). *The biology of moral systems.* Hawthorne, NY: Aldine de Gruyter.

Bailey, J. M. (1997). Are genetically based individual differences compatible with species-wide adaptations. In N. L. Segal, G. E. Weisfeld, & C. C. Weisfeld (Eds.), *Uniting psychology and biology: Integrative perspectives on human development* (pp. 81–100). Washington, DC: American Psychological Association.

Bailey, J. M. (1998). Can behavior genetics contribute to evolutionary behavioral science. In C. C. Crawford & D. L. Krebs (Eds.), *Handbook of evolutionary psychology: Ideas, issues, applications* (pp. 81–100). Mahway, NJ: Erlbaum.

Barash, D. P., & Barash, N. (2002, October 18). Biology as a lens: Evolution and literary criticism. *Chronicle of Higher Education, 49*, B7–B9.

Barkow, J. H. (1990). Beyond the DP/DSS controversy. *Ethology and Sociobiology, 11*, 341–351.

Barrett, L., Dunbar, R., & Lycett, J. (2002). *Human evolutionary psychology.* Princeton, NJ: Princeton University Press.

Barrow, J. D. (1995). *The artful universe.* Oxford, England: Clarendon Press.

Bedaux, J. B., & Cooke, B. (Eds.). (1999). *Sociobiology and the arts.* Amsterdam: Editions Rodopi.

Betzig, L. L. (1986). *Despotism and differential reproduction: A Darwinian view of history.* Hawthorne, NY: Aldine de Gruyter.

Betzig, L. L. (1998). Not whether to count babies, but which. In C. C. Crawford & D. L. Krebs (Eds.), *Handbook of evolutionary psychology: Ideas, issues, applications* (pp. 265–273). Mahway, NJ: Erlbaum.

Boyd, B. (1998). "Jane, meet Charles": Literature, evolution, and human nature. *Philosophy and Literature, 22*, 1–30.

Boyd, B. (1999). Literature and discovery. *Philosophy and Literature, 23*, 313–333.

Boyd, B. (2001). The origin of stories: *Horton hears a who. Philosophy and Literature, 25,* 197–214.

Boyd, B. (in press-a). Evolutionary theories of art. In J. Gottschall & D. S. Wilson (Eds.), *Literature and the human animal.* Evanston, IL: Northwestern University Press.

Boyd, B. (in press-b). Kind and unkindness: Aaron in *Titus Andronicus.* In B. Boyd (Ed.), *Words that count: Essays on early modern authorship in honor of MacDonald P. Jackson.* Newark, NJ: University of Delaware Press.

Boyd, B. (in press-c). Laughter and literature: A play theory of humor. *Philosophy and Literature.*

Bridgeman, B. (2003). *Psychology and evolution: The origins of mind.* Thousand Oaks, CA: Sage.

Buss, D. M. (1994). *The evolution of desire: Strategies of human mating.* New York: Basic Books.

Buss, D. M. (1995). Evolutionary psychology: A new paradigm for psychological science. *Psychological Inquiry, 6,* 1–30.

Buss, D. M. (1999). *Evolutionary psychology: The new science of the mind.* Boston: Allyn & Bacon.

Campbell, D. T. (1988). *Methodology and epistemology for socials science: Selected papers* Chicago: University of Chicago Press.

Carroll, J. (1994). The use of Arnold in a Darwinian world. *Nineteenth-Century Prose, 26,* 26–38.

Carroll, J. (1995a). *Evolution and literary theory.* Columbia: University of Missouri Press.

Carroll, J. (1995b). Evolution and literary theory. *Human Nature, 6,* 119–134.

Carroll, J. (1998a). Literary study and evolutionary theory: A review essay. *Human Nature, 8,* 273–292.

Carroll, J. (1998b). Steven Pinker's cheesecake for the mind. *Philosophy and Literature, 22,* 578–585.

Carroll, J. (1999a). The deep structure of literary representations. *Evolution and Human Behavior, 20,* 159–173.

Carroll, J. (1999b). "Theory," anti-theory, and empirical criticism. In B. Cooke & F. Turner (Eds.), *Biopoetics: Evolutionary explorations in the arts* (pp. 139–154). Lexington, KY: ICUS.

Carroll, J. (1999c). Wilson's *Consilience* and literary study. *Philosophy and Literature, 23,* 393–413.

Carroll, J. (2001a). The ecology of Victorian fiction. *Philosophy and Literature, 25,* 295–313.

Carroll, J. (2001b). Human universals and literary meaning: A sociobiological critique of *Pride and Prejudice, Villette, O., Pioneers!, Anna of the Five Towns,* and *Tess of the d'Urbervilles. Interdisciplinary Literary Studies, 2,* 9–27.

Carroll, J. (2001c). Universalien in der Literaturwissenschaft [Universals in literary study]. In P. M. Hejl (Ed.), *Universalien und Konstruktivismus* (pp. 235–256). Frankfurt am Main: Suhrkamp.

Carroll, J. (2002). Organism, environment, and literary representation. *Interdisciplinary Studies in Literature and Environment, 9,* 27–45.

Carroll, J. (2003a). Adaptationist literary study: An emerging research program. *Style, 36,* 596–617.

Carroll, J. (2003b). Introduction. In J. Carroll (Ed.), *On the origin of species by means of natural selection* (pp. 9–75). Peterborough, Ontario: Broadview.

Carroll, J. (2004). *Literary Darwinism: Evolution, human nature, and literature.* New York: Routledge.

Carroll, J. (in press). Human nature and literary meaning: A model with an illustrative critique of *pride and prejudice.* In J. Gottschall & D. S. Wilson (Eds.), *Literature and the human animal.* Evanston, IL: Northwestern University Press.

Chagnon, N. A. (1979). *Yanomamö: The fierce people* (3rd ed.). New York: Holt, Rinehart and Winston.

Chagnon, N. A., & Irons, W. (Eds.). (1979). *Evolutionary biology and human social behavior: An anthropological perspective.* North Scituate, MA: Duxbury Press.

Chiappe, D. L., & MacDonald, K. B. (2003). *The evolution of domain-general mechanisms in intelligence and learning.* Manuscript submitted for publication.

Coe, K. (2003). *The ancestress hypothesis: Visual art as adaptation.* New Brunswick: Rutgers University Press.

Cooke, B. (1999a). Edward O. Wilson on art. In B. Cooke & F. Turner (Eds.), *Biopoetics: Evolutionary explorations in the arts* (pp. 97–118). Lexington, KY: ICUS.

Cooke, B. (1999b). On the evolution of interest: Cases in serpent art. In D. H. Rosen & M. Luebbert (Eds.), *Evolution of the psyche* (pp. 150–168). Westport, CT: Praeger.

Cooke, B. (1999c). The promise of a biothematics. In J. B. Bedaux & B. Cooke (Eds.), *Sociobiology and the arts* (pp. 43–62). Amsterdam: Editions Rodopi.

Cooke, B. (1999d). Sexual property in Pushkin's "The Snowstorm": A Darwinist perspective. In B. Cooke & F. Turner (Eds.), *Biopoetics: Evolutionary explorations in the arts* (pp. 175–204). Lexington, KY: ICUS.

Cooke, B. (2002). *Human nature in utopia: Zamyatin's We.* Evanston: Northwestern University Press.

Cooke, B., & Turner, F. (Eds.). (1999). *Biopoetics: Evolutionary explorations in the arts.* Lexington, KY: ICUS.

Cosmides, L., & Tooby, J. (1994). Origins of domain specificity: The evolution of functional organization. In L. A. Hirschfeld & S. A. Gelman (Eds.), *Mapping the mind: Domain specificity in cognition and culture* (pp. 85–116). Cambridge: Cambridge University Press.

Crawford, C. (1998). Environments and adaptations: Then and now. In C. Crawford & D. L. Krebs (Eds.), *Handbook of evolutionary psychology: Ideas, issues, applications* (pp. 275–302). Mahway, NJ: Erlbaum.

Daly, M. (1982). Some caveats about cultural transmission models. *Human Ecology, 10,* 401–408.

Damasio, A. (1994). *Descartes' error: Emotion, reason, and the human brain.* New York: G. P. Putnam.

Dawkins, R. (1976). *The selfish gene.* Oxford, England: Oxford University Press.

Dawkins, R. (1982). *The extended phenotype: The gene as the unit of selection.* San Francisco: Freeman.

Dissanayake, E. (1995a). Chimera, spandrel, or adaptation: Conceptualizing art in human evolution. *Human Nature, 6,* 99–117.

Dissanayake, E. (1995b). *Homo aestheticus: Where art comes from and why.* Seattle: University of Washington Press. (Original work published 1992)

Dissanayake, E. (2000). *Art and intimacy: How the arts began.* Seattle: University of Washington Press.

Dissanayake, E. (2001). Aesthetic incunabula. *Philosophy and Literature, 25,* 335–346.

Dunbar, R., Nettle, D., & Stiller, J. (2003). *Drama as the mirror of the mind: Exploring the psychological underpinnings of Shakespeare's plays.* Manuscript in preparation.

Easterlin, N. (1993). Play, mutation, and reality acceptance: Toward a theory of literary experience. In N. Easterlin & B. Riebling (Eds.), *After poststructuralism: Interdisciplinarity and literary theory* (pp. 105–125). Evanston: Northwestern University Press.

Easterlin, N. (1999a). Do cognitive predispositions predict or determine literary value judgments? Narrativity, plot, and aesthetics. In B. Cooke & F. Turner (Eds.), *Biopoetics: Evolutionary explorations in the arts* (pp. 241–262). Lexington, KY: ICUS.

Easterlin, N. (1999b). Making knowledge: Bioepistemology and the foundations of literary theory. *Mosaic, 32,* 131–147.

Easterlin, N. (2000). Psychoanalysis and the "discipline of love." *Philosophy and Literature, 24,* 261–279.

Easterlin, N. (2001a). Hans Christian Andersen's fish out of water. *Philosophy and Literature, 25,* 251–277.

Easterlin, N. (2001b). Voyages in the verbal universe: The role of speculation in Darwinian literary criticism. *Interdisciplinary Literary Studies, 2,* 59–73.

Easterlin, N. (2002). Romanticism's gray matter. *Philosophy and Literature, 443–455.*

Easterlin, N., & Riebling, B. (Eds.). (1993). *After poststructuralism: Interdisciplinarity and literary theory.* Evanston: Northwestern University Press.

Eibl-Eibesfeldt, I. (1989). *Human ethology.* Hawthorne, NY: Aldine de Gruyter.

Ekman, P. (2003). *Emotions revealed: Recognizing faces and feelings to improve communication and emotional life.* New York: Henry Holt.

Ekman, P., & Davidson, R. J. (Eds.). (1994). *The nature of emotion: Fundamental questions.* New York: Oxford University Press.

Flinn, M., & Alexander, R. D. (1982). Culture theory: The developing synthesis from biology. *Human Ecology, 10,* 383–400.

Foley, R. A. (1996). The adaptive legacy of human evolution: A search for the environment of evolutionary adaptedness. *Evolutionary Anthropology, 4,* 194–203.

Fox, R. (1995). Sexual conflict in the epics. *Human Nature, 6,* 135–144.

Freud, S. (1959). Creative writers and daydreaming. In J. Strachey (Ed. & Trans.), *The standard edition of the complete psychological works of Sigmund Freud.* (Vol. 9, pp. 142–153). London: Hogarth. (Original work published 1907)

Fromm, H. (1991). *Academic capitalism and literary value.* Athens: University of Georgia Press.

Fromm, H. (1996). From transcendence to obsolescence: A route map. In C. Glotfelty & H. Fromm (Eds.), *The ecocriticism reader: Landmarks in literary ecology* (pp. 30–39). Athens: University of Georgia Press.

Fromm, H. (1998). Ecology and ecstasy on Interstate 80. *Hudson Review, 51,* 65–78.

Fromm, H. (2001). A crucifix for Dracula: Wendell Berry meets Edward O. Wilson. *Hudson Review, 53,* 657–664.

Fromm, H. (2003a). The new Darwinism in the humanities: From Plato to Pinker. *Hudson Review, 56,* 89–99.

Fromm, H. (2003b). The new Darwinism in the humanities, part two: Back to nature again. *Hudson Review, 56,* 315–327.

Gaulin, S. J. C., & McBurney, D. H. (2001). *Psychology: An evolutionary approach.* Upper Saddle River, NJ: Prentice-Hall.

Geary, D. C. (1998). *Male, female: The evolution of human sex differences.* Washington, DC: American Psychological Association.

Geary, D. C., & Huffman, K. J. (2002). Brain and cognitive evolution: Forms of modularity and functions of mind. *Psychological Bulletin, 128,* 667–698.

Glotfelty, C., & Fromm, H. (Eds.). (1996). *The ecocriticism reader: Landmarks in literary ecology.* Athens: University of Georgia Press.

Gottschall, J. (2001). Homer's human animal: Ritual combat in the *Iliad. Philosophy and Literature, 25,* 278–294.

Gottschall, J. (in press-a). An evolutionary perspective on Homer's invisible daughters. *Interdisciplinary Literary Studies.*

Gottschall, J. (in press-b). Explaining wartime rape. *Journal of Sex Research.*

Gottschall, J. (in press-c). The heroine with a thousand faces. In J. Gottschall & D. S. Wilson (Eds.), *Literature and the human animal.* Evanston, IL: Northwestern University Press.

Gottschall, J. (in press-d). Patterns of characterization in folk tales across geographic regions and levels of cultural complexity: Literature as a neglected source of quantitative data. *Human Nature.*

Gottschall, J. (in press-e). The tree of knowledge and Darwinian literary study. *Philosophy and Literature.*

Gottschall, J., Allison, E., De Rosa, J., & Klockeman, K. (in press). Can literary study be scientific? Results of an empirical search for the virgin/whore dichotomy. *Interdisciplinary Literary Studies.*

Gottschall, J., & Gottschall, T. (in press). Are per-incident rape-pregnancy rates higher than consensual pregnancy rates? *Human Nature.*

Hart, F. (2001). The epistemology of cognitive literary studies. *Philosophy and Literature, 25,* 314–334.

Hawkins, M. (1997). *Social Darwinism in European and American thought, 1860–1945.* Cambridge, MA: Cambridge University Press.

Irons, W. (1990). Let's make our perspective broader rather than narrower: A comment on Turke's "Which humans behave adaptively, and what does it matter?" *Ethology and Sociobiology, 11,* 361–374.

Irons, W. (1998). Adaptively relevant environments versus the environment of evolutionary adaptedness. *Evolutionary Anthropology, 6,* 194–204.

Jobling, I. (2001a). Personal justice and homicide in Scott's *Ivanhoe:* An evolutionary psychological perspective. *Interdisciplinary Literary Studies, 2,* 29–43.

Jobling, I. (2001b). The psychological foundations of the hero-ogre story: A cross-cultural study. *Human Nature, 12,* 247–272.

Jobling, I. (2002). Byron as cad. *Philosophy and Literature, 26,* 296–311.

Kuhn, T. (1991). The road since structure. In A. Fine, M. Forbes, & L. Wessels (Eds.), *PSA 1990: Proceedings of the 1990 biennial meeting of the philosophy of science association.* East Lansing, MI: Philosophy of Science Association.

LeDoux, J. (1996). *The emotional brain: The mysterious underpinnings of emotional life.* New York: Simon & Schuster.

Love, G. A. (1999a). Ecocriticism and science: Toward consilience? *New Literary History, 30,* 561–576.

Love, G. A. (1999b). Science, anti-science, and ecocriticism. *Interdisciplinary Studies in Literature and the Environment, 6,* 65–81.

Love, G. A. (2003). *Practical ecocriticism: Literature, biology, and the environment.* Charlottesville: University of Virginia Press.

Low, B. S. (1998). The evolution of human life histories. In C. Crawford & D. L. Krebs (Eds.), *Handbook of evolutionary psychology: Ideas, issues, applications* (pp. 131–161). Mahway, NJ: Erlbaum.

Low, B. S. (2000). *Why sex matters: A Darwinian look at human behavior.* Princeton, NJ: Princeton University Press.

MacDonald, K. B. (1990). A perspective on Darwinian psychology: The importance of domain-general mechanisms, plasticity, and individual differences. *Ethology and Sociobiology, 12,* 449–480.

MacDonald, K. B. (1995a). The establishment and maintenance of socially imposed monogamy in western Europe. *Politics and the Life Sciences, 14,* 3–46.

MacDonald, K. B. (1995b). Evolution, the five-factor model, and levels of personality. *Journal of Personality, 63,* 525–567.

MacDonald, K. B. (1997). Life history theory and human reproductive behavior: Environmental/contextual influences and heritable variation. *Human Behavior, 8,* 327–359.

MacDonald, K. B. (1998a). Evolution and development. In A. Campbell & S. Muncer (Eds.), *The social child* (pp. 21–49). Hove, East Sussex: Psychology Press.

MacDonald, K. B. (1998b). Evolution, culture, and the five-factor model. *Journal of Cross-Cultural Psychology, 29,* 119–149.

McGuire, M., & Troisi, A. (1998). *Darwinian psychiatry.* New York: Oxford University Press.

Mellars, P. (1996). *The Neanderthal legacy: An archeological perspective from western Europe.* Princeton, NJ: Princeton University Press.

Miller, G. (2000). *The mating mind: How sexual choice shaped the evolution of human nature.* New York: Doubleday.

Mithen, S. (1996). *The prehistory of the mind: The cognitive origins of art, religion, and science.* London: Thames and Hudson.

Mithen, S. (2001). The evolution of imagination: An archaeological perspective. *SubStance, 30,* 28–54.

Nesse, M. (1995). Guinevere's choice. *Human Nature, 6,* 145–163.

Nettle, D. (in press). What happens in Shakespeare: Evolutionary perspectives on dramatic form. In J. Gottschall & D. S. Wilson (Eds.), *Literature and the human animal.* Evanston: Northwestern University Press.

Nordlund, M. (2002). Consilient literary interpretation. *Philosophy and Literature, 26,* 312–333.

Palmer, J. A., & Palmer, L. K. (2002). *Evolutionary psychology: The ultimate origins of human behavior.* Boston: Allyn & Bacon.

Panksepp, J. (1998). *Affective neuroscience: The foundations of human and animal emotions.* New York: Oxford University Press.

Pinker, S. (1995). Language is a human instinct. In J. Brockman (Ed.), *The third culture: Scientists on the edge* (pp. 223–238). New York: Simon & Schuster.

Pinker, S. (1997). *How the mind works.* New York: Norton.

Pinker, S. (2002). *The blank slate: The modern denial of human nature.* New York: Viking.

Potts, R. (1998). Variability selection in hominid evolution. *Evolutionary Anthropology, 7,* 81–96.

Rabkin, E. S., & Simon, C. P. (2001). Age, sex, and evolution in the science fiction marketplace. *Interdisciplinary Literary Studies, 2,* 45–58.

Richerson, P. J., & Boyd, R. (2000). Climate, culture, and the evolution of cognition. In C. Heyes & L. Huber (Eds.), *The evolution of cognition* (pp. 329–346). Cambridge, MA: MIT Press.

Ridley, M. (1999). *Genome: Autobiography of a species in 23 chapters.* New York: HarperCollins.

Rossano, M. J. (2003). *Evolutionary psychology: The science of human behavior and evolution.* Hoboken, NJ: Wiley.

Salmon, C., & Symons, D. (2001). *Warrior lovers: Erotic fiction, evolution, and female sexuality.* London: Weidenfeld & Nicolson.

Segal, N. L., & MacDonald, K. B. (1998). Behavioral genetics and evolutionary psychology: Unified perspective on personality research. *Human Biology, 70,* 159–184.

Spencer, H. (1862). *First principles.* London: Williams & Norgate.

Storey, R. (1993). "I am I because my little dog knows me": Prolegomenon to a theory of mimesis. In N. Easterlin & B. Riebling (Eds.), *After poststructuralism: Interdisciplinarity and literary theory* (pp. 45–70). Evanston: Northwestern University Press.

Storey, R. (1996). *Mimesis and the human animal: On the biogenetic foundations of literary representation.* Evanston: Northwestern University Press.

Storey, R. (2001). A critique of recent theories of laughter and humor, with special reference to the comedy of *Seinfeld. Interdisciplinary Literary Studies, 2,* 75–92.

Stringer, C., & Gamble, C. (1993). *In search of the Neanderthals: Solving the puzzle of human origins.* New York: Thames & Hudson.

Sugiyama, M. S. (1996). On the origins of narrative: Storyteller bias as a fitness enhancing strategy. *Human Nature, 7,* 403–425.

Sugiyama, M. S. (2001a). Food, foragers, and folklore: The role of narrative in human subsistence. *Evolution and Human Behavior, 22,* 221–240.

Sugiyama, M. S. (2001b). Narrative theory and function: Why evolution matters. *Philosophy and Literature, 25,* 233–250.

Sugiyama, M. S. (2001c). New science, old myth: An evolutionary critique of the Oedipal paradigm. *Mosaic, 34,* 121–136.

Sugiyama, M. S. (in press). Cultural relativism in the bush: Toward a theory of narrative universals. *Human Nature.*

Symons, D. (1987). If we're all Darwinians, what's the fuss about. In C. Crawford, M. Smith, & D. L. Krebs (Eds.), *Sociobiology and psychology: Ideas, issues, and applications* (pp. 121–146). Hillsdale, NJ: Erlbaum.

Symons, D. (1989). A critique of Darwinian anthropology. *Ethology and Sociobiology, 10,* 131–144.

Symons, D. (1992). On the use and misuse of Darwinism in the study of human behavior. In J. H. Barkow, L. Cosmides, & J. Tooby (Eds.), *The adapted mind: Evolutionary psychology and the generation of culture* (pp. 137–162). New York: Oxford University Press.

Tattersall, I. (1999). *The last Neanderthal: The rise, success, and mysterious extinction of our closest human relatives* (Rev. ed.). New York: Westview Press.

Thiessen, D., & Umezawa, Y. (1998). The sociobiology of everyday life: A new look at a very old novel. *Human Nature, 9,* 293–320.

Tooby, J., & Cosmides, L. (1990). On the universality of human nature and the uniqueness of the individual: The role of genetics and adaptation. *Journal of Personality, 58,* 17–67.

Tooby, J., & Cosmides, L. (1992). The psychological foundations of culture. In J. H. Barkow, L. Cosmides, & J. Tooby (Eds.), *The adapted mind: Evolutionary psychology and the generation of culture* (pp. 19–136). New York: Oxford University Press.

Tooby, J., & Cosmides, L. (2001). Does beauty build adapted minds? Toward an evolutionary theory of aesthetics, fiction, and the arts. *SubStance, 30,* 6–27.

Turke, P. W. (1990). Which humans behave adaptively, and why does it matter? *Ethology and Sociobiology, 11,* 305–339.

Turner, F. (1992). *Natural classicism: Essays on literature and science.* Charlottesville: University of Virginia Press. (Original work published 1985)

Turner, M. (1991). *Reading minds: The study of English in the age of cognitive science.* Princeton, NJ: Princeton University Press.

Turner, M. (1996). *The literary mind.* New York: Oxford University Press.

Whissel, C. (1996). Mate selection in popular women's fiction. *Human Nature, 7,* 427–447.

Wilson, D. S. (1994). Adaptive genetic variation and human evolutionary psychology. *Ethology and Sociobiology, 15,* 219–235.

Wilson, D. S. (1999). Tasty slice: But where is the rest of the pie? *Evolution and Human Behavior, 20,* 279–287.

Wilson, D. S. (in press). Evolutionary social constructivism. In J. Gottschall & D. S. Wilson (Eds.), *Literature and the human animal.* Evanston, IL: Northwestern University Press.

Wilson, E. O. (1978). *On human nature.* Cambridge: Harvard University Press.

Wilson, E. O. (1984). *Biophilia.* Cambridge: Harvard University Press.

Wilson, E. O. (1998). *Consilience: The unity of knowledge.* New York: Alfred A. Knopf.

CHAPTER 34

Evolutionary Psychology
and the Law

OWEN D. JONES

$\mathbf{F}$ ORGET CRIMINAL TRIALS, speeding tickets, and plaintiffs' attorneys looking for big wins on small injuries. Forget divorce lawyers, robed judges, and antidrug legislation. These are among the many distractors for the unwary, who often miss the most important thing to understand about law. It is a tool for moving human animals to behave in ways they would not otherwise behave if left solely to their own devices. Put starkly, legal systems modify features of the human environment in order to modify human behavior. Viewed this way, law's need for evolutionary perspectives on behavior, including those from evolutionary biology and evolutionary psychology, becomes obvious. A better understanding of behavior can aid society's efforts to change behavior.

Ideally, a legal system should encourage people to act in ways that further public goals. These goals obviously vary. For example, they range from controlling pollution to ensuring a minimum income for society's poorest, from facilitating a thriving economy to protecting property from theft, and from ensuring that foods and drugs are safe and effective to ensuring that important disputes are resolved without violence in fair and principled ways.

Of course, it is the rare public goal that would, if achieved, benefit all individuals in a society equally. The interests of individuals are rarely identical—and in democratic societies public goals are typically those goals that a sufficient number of individuals representing yet other individuals designate as public goals. In the end, however, legal policymakers are among the key players in soliciting, framing, articulating, and ultimately defining these varied public goals. And those policymakers also influence or determine which of many existing goals will be the top priorities and help to choose among possible methods for pursuing these goals, ever mindful that resources are finite.

Although methods vary considerably, they typically sort into two general categories. One category includes methods that physically force people to behave (or not to behave) in a given way. For example, incarceration, among other things, physically prevents offenders from reoffending. The other category includes methods that influence behavior less directly, by changing incentives through things such as taxes, fines, rewards, and threats of various sorts.

In general, efforts to effect a behavioral change by changing incentives rely on numerous assumptions, comprising explicit or implicit behavioral models, about where human behavior comes from, what affects it, and how. Yet, to date, with some notable exceptions, legal policymakers are either surprisingly unaware of the extent of their dependence on behavioral models or, instead, complacent in their belief that they already deploy good ones.

In either case, integrating evolutionary perspectives on human behavior can help (Jones & Goldsmith, 2005). This chapter consequently explores and illustrates a number of specific contexts in which "evolutionary analysis in law" (Jones, 1997) can prove useful.

INCREASING EFFICIENCY

At the most general level, evolutionary analysis in law can help to increase efficiency. The efficiency of legal methods in achieving legal goals by inspiring changes in human behavior depends on a robust behavioral model. In this way, and as Figure 34.1 illustrates, the efficiency of law depends on an accurate behavioral model in the same way that the efficiency of a lever depends on the solidity of its fulcrum.

Soft fulcra are poor fulcra. Inaccurate behavioral models therefore serve as inefficient fulcra for the lever of law. Moreover, behavioral models that omit evolutionary perspectives are often materially inaccurate. Thus, to the extent that evolutionary processes influence human behavioral predispositions, a robust behavioral model must incorporate evolutionary perspectives. More specifically, if improving behavioral models can yield more effective legal tools, and if human behavior is influenced by evolutionary processes, then greater knowledge of how evolutionary processes influence human behavior may improve law's ability to regulate it.

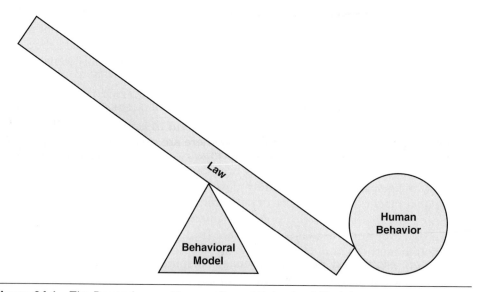

Figure 34.1 The Dependence of Law on Sound Behavioral Models.

DISCOVERING USEFUL PATTERNS IN
REGULABLE BEHAVIOR

Because data neither self-collect nor self-organize, discovering patterns in data often requires some theory that suggests what data to collect and what aspects of the data to cross-correlate. Evolutionary analysis can often serve as one source of theories to help us collect and collate data in pattern-revealing ways relevant to law.

For example, many readers of this volume know there is a vast literature in animal behavior on infanticide. (Hausfater & Hrdy, 1984; Jones, 1997, includes an overview.) In brief, natural selection appears to have favored, in many species, the selective elimination of unweaned infants by unrelated males in a position to mate with the mother. Nursing has a contraceptive effect (which apparently functions to adaptively regulate the interbirth interval), and the death of the infant speeds the mother's return to an impregnable state. This affords material advantage to the selectively infanticidal male, and the great risk to unweaned infants drops off commensurately at weaning age, when the juvenile impinges less directly on its mother's impregnability.

The evolutionary analysis of this pattern in other species suggested to psychologists Daly and Wilson (1988) that a similar pattern may occur in human populations. And it does. Although the contraceptive effect of nursing is somewhat less pronounced in humans, Daly and Wilson found an extremely elevated risk of death to an unweaned infant (roughly a 100-fold increase) in the presence of unrelated males, and a similarly precipitous drop in risk at weaning age. It is important that, although there was some general assumption of increased risk, neither the magnitude of the risk nor the sudden change in risk at weaning age was previously appreciated, largely because data on relevant variables (e.g., the presence or absence of genetic relatedness) were often uncollected.

The point here is not that stepparents of dead infants should be considered guilty until proven innocent. The point is that through political processes the legal system is presently tasked, in part, with helping to establish ways for investigating and preventing child abuse and infanticide. And it can do this, in part, by directing limited resources toward child protective services agencies, helping to fund data collection efforts, helping to specify variables on which data should be collected, and aiding in the creation of effective protocols for prioritizing and investigating rumors of abuse that may precede fatal injuries.

Consequently, a theory that could influence data collection in ways leading to the discovery that stepparents are roughly 100 times more likely to kill an infant than genetic parents would seem extremely useful in achieving maximum prevention. And it seems highly probable that there are other law-relevant patterns that evolutionary analysis can help reveal. These might arise from contexts pertinent to spousal abuse, homicide, marriage patterns, family size and composition patterns, deviations from rational choice predictions, and the like, to name merely a few.

UNCOVERING POLICY CONFLICTS

It has been established beyond reasonable dispute that evolutionary analysis cannot by itself supply a normative direction for legal policy. To extend from the previous example, the fact that stepparents not only kill but also abuse their stepchildren at far higher rates per capita than do parents says precisely nothing about whether the law *should* take stepparentage into account in any way (as it might do, for example, in specifying investigation protocols for child protective services agencies having limited investigative resources).

Nonetheless, evolutionary analysis can be importantly useful even when it may only identify previously underrecognized policy conflicts. Consider, for example, the common and seemingly unrelated goals of destigmatizing stepparentage, on the one hand, and reducing infant deaths, on the other. Evolutionary analysis, by itself, has no bearing on which of these two goals should be deemed the higher priority. But it can suggest that success in pursuing either goal may importantly trade against success in pursuing the other. Revealing such internal inconsistencies in law may aid our efforts to lessen them—because seeing a potential policy conflict is the first step in resolving it.

SHARPENING COST-BENEFIT ANALYSES

We know that when a legislature allocates funds to build a tunnel, or fails to prohibit its governed from driving cars, people will die. But we consider the benefits worth the costs. Although there is much legitimate debate about the contexts in which cost-benefit analysis is and is not useful, one thing is clear. In whatever contexts cost-benefit analysis is used, inaccurate tallies will improperly skew results.

Whenever evolutionary analysis reveals hidden policy contexts, as mentioned earlier, it also offers collateral benefits. Specifically, it can also help to clarify and to quantify the actual trade-offs involved in simultaneously pursuing two different legal goals that conflict.

For example, evolutionary analysis suggests that, depending on the legal strategy deployed, one cost of reducing infanticide may be the collateral stigmatization of all stepparents due to the actions of only a fraction. Correspondingly, the cost of *not* risking the stigmatization of stepparents may include some number of otherwise preventable infant deaths. Evolutionary analysis helps to provide a sense of these trade-offs, which is a prerequisite for maximally comprehensive cost-benefit analysis that society often uses when prioritizing goals.

CLARIFYING CAUSAL LINKS

Because causality cannot be inferred from data alone, we are typically (and properly) hesitant to base legal policies on mere correlations lacking explanations. Consequently, one role for evolutionary analysis in law concerns the development and support of causal theories that trace an understandable pathway between correlated phenomena.

For example, even if we strongly suspected that stepparents were more likely per capita to abuse stepchildren than were genetic parents, we would have good reason not to act on that suspicion. Our observations may be skewed as a function of prejudice. Our righteous zeal to aid children might lead to scapegoating vulnerable targets. And our collective history in oversimplifying complex phenomena should give us proper pause. There may be many complicating confounds.

But consider how evolutionary analysis offers two things. First, it details a pathway by which natural selection can favor condition-dependent male behavioral predispositions that can yield fatal abuse of unweaned offspring of potential mates. Second, it connects empirical data on infanticide in humans and nonhumans. In such cases, and even when evolutionary analysis might not itself lead to discoveries of new patterns, its frequent ability to provide robust explanations for correlations can make an important difference in legal policy. It can help to provide the logical foundation that serves as an important prerequisite to establishing legal policies that are not only reasonably efficacious but also efficaciously reasonable.

PROVIDING THEORETICAL FOUNDATION AND POTENTIAL PREDICTIVE POWER

Evolutionary analysis can sometimes provide theoretical foundation for known behavioral data lacking coherence, and thus serve to help predict undiscovered patterns in human behavior (Jones, 2001e). Consider, for example, that large body of literature known as *behavioral law and economics* (BLE). Eschewing traditional law and economics approaches, scholars of BLE seek to incorporate insights from cognitive psychology (of the Tversky and Kahneman heuristics and biases kind; Tversky & Kahneman, 1982). Their efforts are aimed at understanding apparent deviations of human behavior from neoclassical economic rationality predictions. Examples follow, but the key point is that humans often behave in ways that seem substantively irrational, and BLE scholars would like law to take account of these deviations. The law generally assumes—particularly when estimating the efficiency properties of rules—that people will not make routine errors in their attempts to maximize their utility. And if that assumption is wrong, then laws based on it may be flawed (Ulen, 1989).

On the one hand, the BLE movement usefully draws attention to the ways in which real people behave differently from theoretical people. And this has obvious utility for legal policymakers. On the other hand, the BLE scholars are presently far better at detailing *that* people behave in manners inconsistent with various rational choice predictions than they are at explaining *why* they do so. And that *why* is the key to a theoretical foundation sufficiently robust to aid predictions about undiscovered patterns.

Some examples of seeming irrationalities, and illustrations of problems they pose for law, follow.

IRRATIONALLY STEEP DISCOUNTING

Rational choice theorists generally assume that people deploy rationally appropriate "discount rates" when evaluating the future. For example, a dollar to be received 5 years from now should ordinarily be deemed worth somewhat less than a dollar received today. That is, it is discounted because of expected inflation at an amount reflecting realistic estimates of inflation. Yet, people often employ absurdly high discount rates, overweighting present costs and benefits compared to future costs and benefits. For example, they often underinsulate their homes, even though the cost of adding insulation will be earned back in energy savings within a very short time (Ulen, 1994). That is, they act as if inflation will be enormously high over the next few years (between 45% and 300%, by some estimates, when energy-saving appliances are at issue, Ulen, 1994) such that the large money they save in energy efficiency in the future will be worth less than the small amount they save today in purchasing less insulation. The existence of seemingly oversteep discounting has important legal implications. These include, for example, matters as diverse as discouraging needless pollution and encouraging appropriate savings for retirement.

MISTAKEN PROBABILITY ASSESSMENTS

Rational choice theorists generally assume that people will base their choices on realistic assessments of probabilities. But people routinely make gross errors in assessing probability. For example, they often fail to recognize that an activity posing a .7 risk of death is more dangerous than an activity in which 6 out of 10 people participating will die (Slovic, Fischhoff, & Lichtenstein, 1982). This error has important consequences for legal policies concerning risk regulation.

ENDOWMENT EFFECTS

Rational choice theorists generally assume that people will value property sensibly and consistently. For example, the difference between an individual's maximum willingness to pay for a good and the minimum compensation that individual would demand to willingly sell the good should be negligible. But often it is not. Experiments indicate that people often value something they have just received at a higher amount than they would have been willing to pay for it (Hoffman & Spitzer, 1993). This phenomenon, often referred to as an *endowment effect*, has important consequences for the legal distribution of entitlements. For example, suppose a farmer's land abuts a rancher's land. If the rancher's cattle trample the farmer's crops and a dispute cannot be settled informally, the legal system must eventually decide whether farmers have a right to untrampled crops (in which case ranchers must pay compensation for failing to fence their cattle in) or ranchers have a right to have cattle roam freely (in which case farmers must either sustain inflicted damage or fence cattle out). Economists predict that who in the end owns the right will often be insensitive to law's initial allocation of the right, because the party who values the right more will simply purchase the right from the party who values it less (as long as the costs of arranging the transaction are low). Thus (goes this reasoning), the end distribution of rights will tend to be economically efficient, regardless of who gets the right in the first place. This reasoning presupposes, however, that the farmer and the rancher will value the right consistently, whether they own it initially or have to purchase it from the other. The existence of endowment effects suggests that this presupposition may often be wrong. If so, rights can be "sticky," and may tend to stay with those who receive them first, because those receiving them will suddenly value those rights more than they would have been willing to pay for them in the first place.

These several seeming irrationalities, among other similar ones, are presently thought to arise from some peculiar combination of *bounded rationality* and (in these oft-used terms) cognitive fallibilities, frailties, flaws, errors, defects, quirks, limitations, and imperfections (Jones, 2001e). Bounded rationality describes deviations from rational choice predictions as the result of: (1) constraints on time and energy for gathering perfect information and (2) constraints on the brain's information capacities, wiring, and computing speed (Simon, 1990).

But even a moment's reflection makes clear that this approach is unsatisfactory. There is no theoretical framework that explains the patterns of irrationalities, connects them together, and points in new directions. For example, why do people apparently tend to overdiscount the future, rather than to underdiscount it or to discount it randomly? Why do people apparently tend to overendow goods, rather than to underendow goods or to endow goods randomly?

A number of people have independently explored these and related phenomena from evolutionary angles. There are at least three approaches.

One evolutionary approach centers on how some seeming irrationalities may be artifacts of experimental designs. For example, in the context of mistaken probability assessments, Gigerenzer's approach begins with the important insight that the statistical representation of probability (e.g., in .7 chances of something happening) is a trivially recent invention in human evolutionary history (Gigerenzer, 1991, 1998; Gigerenzer, Todd, & the ABC Research Group, 1999). He and colleagues have, among their many other important discoveries, found that people are far better at understanding probability when it is framed in terms of frequency distributions—the format in which relative risks were commonly encountered in deep ancestral environments—than they are when it is described in modern statistical terms. For example, people understand the relative risk of death better when told that 7 of 10 people at risk will die than if told that each person bears a .7 risk of death.

That is to say, argue Gigerenzer and colleagues, people are "ecologically rational." They are not necessarily irrational with probabilities; they are simply worse at probabilities presented in formats novel to the evolved brain's risk assessment capabilities. Consequently, Gigerenzer's approach, which appears particularly promising, focuses in large measure on how an evolutionary perspective can help turn alleged irrationalities into rationalities by changing the formats of presented information.

A second evolutionary approach centers principally on how some seemingly irrational biases may not be so irrational after all (an approach consistent in this general conclusion with several economists' arguments that do not invoke evolutionary reasoning). For example, Haselton and Buss (2003) begin with the observation that asymmetric costs of false positives and false negatives, when attempting to infer the intentions of others, can yield evolved human biases that systematically favor one type of error over the other. To illustrate this "error management theory" (Haselton & Buss, 2000), they argue that the asymmetries between the sexes in minimum investment in offspring and maximum lifetime number of offspring can ultimately lead to male overperception of female sexual interest and female underperception of male commitment (Buss, 2001; Haselton & Buss, 2003). The important point of this perspective is that these biases—as well as a number of other similar cognitive biases—can be adaptive despite the fact that they may not produce the fewest overall errors.

A third evolutionary approach considers circumstances in which seeming irrationalities may persist, *regardless* of the format in which issues arise, and even when leading to outcomes that may *not* presently increase reproductive success, even on average. For example, I have argued elsewhere at length (most recently in

Jones, 2001e) that a principle I refer to in the contexts of rationality discussions as *time-shifted rationality* (TSR) may provide useful theoretical foundation for a number of the irrational outcomes of interest to behavioral law and economics scholars. TSR emphasizes in this specific rationality context the general phenomenon of temporal mismatches between adaptations to past environmental features, on one hand, and current novel features, on the other. That is, some behaviors currently ascribed to cognitive limitations may reflect not defect but rather finely tuned features of brain design that are bumping up against novel environmental features in a way that yields outcomes that are irrational if measured for rationality in the present environment.

Specifically, an evolutionary perspective suggests that a great deal of what is currently lumped under the umbrellas of *bounded rationality* and *cognitive quirks* is a function of discrete contexts in which there is a temporal mismatch between design features of the brain appropriate for ancestral environments, on one hand, and quite different current environments, on the other. That is, some irrationalities are likely widely shared and patterned precisely because they predisposed people to behavior that led to substantively "rational" outcomes in past environments, and thus represent TSRs.

For example, it seems highly likely that human patterns in discounting the future are out of step with four things that are novel environmental features: (1) the dramatic increase in median life spans; (2) the emergence of a moderately reliable future (in which to reap gains from delayed gratification); (3) the invention of currencies enabling resources to be stored, in proxy, for long periods of time; and (4) the invention of abstract tradable "rights" to receive resources in the future (i.e., unequivocal entitlements that can themselves be sold or bartered).

Similarly, it seems likely that endowment effects in humans are also out of step with this suddenly recent (biologically speaking) invention of tradable rights to things. Never before in the history of natural selection could a selection pressure have favored the ability to process information about a thing itself in precisely the same way as information about a right to a thing (even if such a trait were to have arisen). Indeed, as I have argued elsewhere (Jones, 1999a, 2001b, 2001e), the phenomenon of endowment effects in humans may be meaningfully continuous with territorial advantage and "defender wins" biases—which are much like endowment effects—in the many other species in which these are observed.

These three evolutionary approaches—focusing on ecological rationality, error management, and time-shifted rationality—emphasize different aspects of various cognitive puzzles but are nonetheless compatible. Whether joined or used separately, the perspectives on human irrationalities that these three approaches offer hold some significant promise, in the legal arena, of providing theoretical foundation to patterns in existing anomalies and helping to predict undiscovered patterns.

ASSESSING COMPARATIVE EFFECTIVENESS OF LEGAL STRATEGIES

Time-shifted rationality—the propensity toward behavior that was adaptive in ancestral environments, even if it is senseless, irrational, counterproductive, or maladaptive in novel current environments—also has a role to play in helping us

compare probable effectiveness of differing legal approaches to changing people's behaviors.

We know from basic economics and common sense that, with rare exceptions,
the demand for a given good will go down as the price for that good goes up.
The general relationship between changing price and changing demand is commonly represented graphically by a demand curve (Figure 34.2; so called by convention because it need not be, and frequently is not, a straight line, as often and
here depicted).

We also know that what works for goods works too for behaviors. Increase the
"price" of engaging in a behavior, by increasing the associated fine or the prison
term, for example, and generally the incidence of that behavior will decrease
(holding constant the probabilities that an offender will be detected, apprehended, and subjected to penalty). (Note that, in economics, price appears on the
vertical axis, whether or not it is the independent variable.)

The real problem is that, except from trial, error, and intuition, we know very
little about the precise *relationship* between increased prices and decreased incidence of behavior. Because sanctions are themselves costly to administer, we
would like to have some general sense, ahead of time, of the likely return on our
investment in sanctions. That is, ideally we would like to have some sense of *how
much* the incidence of a given behavior will decrease if we increase a penalty from
one level to another. How much of a decrease are we buying with each increment
of increased penalty?

Figure 34.3 on page 962 makes the point more graphically. At one extreme, a
behavior may be very responsive to increases in sanctions, so that a relatively
small increase in price yields a big decrease in behavior. The demand curve for
such a behavior may look like the more horizontal curve A. Or, at the other extreme, a behavior may be relatively insensitive to increases in sanctions, so that
a very large increase in sanctions is necessary to achieve an even modest decrease in behavior. The demand curve for such a behavior may look like the more

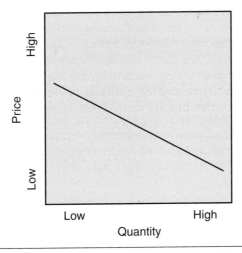

Figure 34.2   General Assumption in Law about the Relationship between the Incidence
of a Behavior and the Costs of That Behavior.

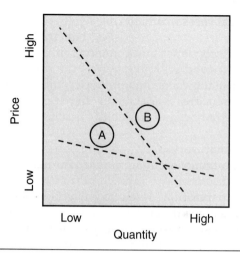

Figure 34.3   Variations in Responsiveness of Behavior to Increasing Costs.

vertical curve B.[1] Holding the probabilities of detection, apprehension, and penalty constant, the curve for some behaviors, such as jaywalking, will more closely resemble curve A. And the curve for some behaviors, such as becoming violent when coming upon a spouse engaged in adulterous sex, will more closely resemble curve B.

From evolutionary sciences, we may derive a principle that can help legal thinkers anticipate, at least in general terms, the comparative sensitivities of various human behaviors to changes in incentives effected with legal tools. That principle helps not only to explain but also to predict differences in the relative steepness of demand curves for, and hence the comparative sensitivities of, different behaviors.

I call that principle the *law of law's leverage* (Jones, 1999a, 2000b, 2001b, 2001e). It predicts that:

> The magnitude of legal intervention necessary to reduce or to increase the incidence of any human behavior will correlate positively or negatively, respectively, with the extent to which a predisposition contributing to that behavior was adaptive for its bearers, on average, in past environments.

Each of the constituent concepts bears a precise meaning.

The language "magnitude of legal intervention" refers, in most instances, to costliness. Greater resistance to change will increase the cost of effecting change. However, assessing the magnitude of legal intervention may in some cases require separate attention to the severity of an intervention (e.g., the harshness of a penalty). In the typical case, increased severity will simply yield increased costs.

---

[1] This discussion adopts the common convention of using variations in slope to capture the idea of variations in what, technically, are "elasticities" (by, for example, describing inelastic demand with a steeply sloped demand curve). The slope of a demand curve is the rate of change of price with demand. Elasticity is the percentage change in price divided by the percentage change in demand. It can be computed from knowledge of the slope at a given point on the curve. In comparing nonlinear demand curves for different activities, comparisons of slope must refer to comparable regions of curves.

But there may be unusual cases in which severe interventions are less administratively cumbersome, and therefore less costly, than are less severe interventions, which may at times be preferred because other values are in tension with the value of changing the behavior at issue.

The language "the extent to which" a predisposition contributing to the behavior was adaptive to its bearers underscores the fact that while members of a species share a variety of different adaptations, some are comparatively more important than others. In a primate species, for example, hunger is more important to survival than a capacity for empathy. And the abilities to distinguish kin from nonkin, and male from female, are more important than are many other psychological adaptations.

The language "a predisposition" refers to a psychological trait that is a heritable and behavior-biasing algorithm manifested in the brain's neural architecture. For a behavioral predisposition to be "adaptive," it must have conferred greater fitness benefits on individuals that bore it than did any other contemporaneously existing alternatives exhibited by other individuals within the population, and thus have been maintained by natural selection. As always, genetic fitness is measured in terms of inclusive fitness (rather than in offspring only, for example). Thus, an individual's overall fitness calculation takes into account the extent to which an individual has increased the reproductive success of its relatives, discounted by their degrees of consanguinity.

The term "on average" in the law of law's leverage refers to whether the cumulated effects of the adaptation, across all the organisms that bore it, yielded increases in inclusive fitness that outweighed any decreases. That is, on average the trait increased the reproductive success of organisms that bore it. Thus, the occurrence of maladaptive outcomes for some individuals, even in the environment of evolutionary adaptation, is not dispositive of the adaptation analysis, because it is only the average effect that matters. "On average" does not refer to the average fitness consequences within a single individual, throughout its lifetime. Nor does it refer to any net of fitness effects of all behavioral traits an organism simultaneously manifests.

"Past environments" refers to the environment of evolutionary adaptation (EEA). The relevant EEA varies from feature to feature.

Consequently, a more detailed and accurate (if also more cumbersome) rephrasing is this: The law of law's leverage states that the magnitude of legal intervention necessary to reduce or to increase the incidence of any human behavior will correlate positively or negatively, respectively, with the extent to which a behavior-biasing, information-processing predisposition underlying that behavior (1) increased the inclusive fitness of those bearing the predisposition, on average, more than it decreased it, across all those bearing the predisposition, in the environment in which it evolved and (2) increased the inclusive fitness of those bearing the predisposition more, on average, than did any other alternative predisposition that happened to appear in the environment during the same period.

This law of law's leverage predicts that, under most circumstances, it will be less costly to shift a behavior in ways that tended to increase reproductive success in ancestral environments (measured in inclusive fitness) than it will be to shift behavior in ways that tended to decrease reproductive success in ancestral environments. However, there may be some contexts in which important changes can be induced without great cost—in particular when using tools historically linked to reproductive success (such as shaming sanctions affecting status) to affect behaviors also linked to reproductive success. Generally speaking, however, the malleability of a behavior beneath the tools of law and, typically, the commensurate cost of trying to change the behavior, will tend to vary as a function of the extent to which the behavior (or, more specifically, the psychological mechanism underlying it) was historically adaptive. In other words, the slope of the demand curve for historically adaptive behavior that is now deemed undesirable will be far steeper (reflecting less sensitivity to price) than the corresponding slope for behavior that was comparatively less adaptive in ancestral environments. This rule will tend to hold, even when the costs that an individual actually and foreseeably incurs in behaving in a historically adaptive way exceed the presently foreseeable benefits of such behavior.

Consequently, the law of law's leverage predicts that in criminal law, family law, torts, property, and the like, behaviors involving the following things will prove more difficult to modify than the behavior of median difficulty: mating, fairness, homicide, child rearing, status seeking, property and territory, resource accumulation, sexuality (including infidelity and jealousy), speech, privacy, empathy, crimes of passion, moralistic aggression, risk valuation and risk taking, cooperative/altruistic behavior, male mate-guarding, and the like.

Here are several examples:

- Evolutionary analysis predicts that, and explains why, the slope of the demand curve for adulterous behavior (like most sexual behavior) is likely to be comparatively steep (Buss, 1999, 2000, 2003; Buss, Larsen, Westen, & Semmelroth, 1992) and thus comparatively insensitive to the imposition of legal prohibitions.

- Evolutionary analysis also predicts that, and may help explain why, marriage, separation, divorce, and remarriage behavior will be less sensitive to legal changes than will be many other forms of behavior (Ellman & Lohr, 1998; Fisher, 1994).

- Because, as we know, natural selection disfavors inbreeding among close relatives (Goldsmith, 1994; Goldsmith & Zimmerman, 2000), evolutionary analysis predicts that it will be far less costly to achieve a given low rate of incest per capita between a parent and his or her natural children, and among siblings reared together, than to achieve the same low rate of incest per capita between stepparents and stepchildren, and among stepchildren.

- Because we know that natural selection favors discriminative parental solicitude rather than indiscriminate parental solicitude (i.e., it generally favors psychological mechanisms that bias resources toward offspring over nonoffspring; Daly & Wilson, 1995), we can predict that men under court order to provide child support payments for a child they know or suspect they did not father will be less likely to comply, on average, than will biological fathers (Wilson, 1987).

- Because we know that threats to status within a social group impose particularly large costs across evolutionary time (Buss & Shackelford, 1997; Daly & Wilson, 1988), we can predict that the slope of the demand curve for violence consequent to status threats will be steeper than that for most other proscribable behavior, and will be particularly steep in public fora.

- Because we know that the asymmetries for males and females of internally fertilizing species in the consequences of a partner having sex with a third party favored sexual proprietariness in males even more strongly than it did in females (because only males can be uncertain of their genetic relationship to their putative children), we can predict that the slope of the demand curve for jealous violence (against rivals and potentially straying partners) is likely to be steeper, on average, for males than for females (Buss, 2000; Buss et al., 1992).

Obviously, the law of law's leverage can neither predict demand curves for law-relevant behaviors with precision, nor can it individualize a curve to a single person. Moreover, statements about relative aggregate costs do not translate neatly into conclusions about cost effectiveness. Nonetheless, the law of law's leverage can offer some broad, novel, and useful insights into the differing ways law and behavior interact, depending on the behavior at issue. Because we are alert to the fact that the brain tends to process information in ways that tended to yield adaptive solutions to problems encountered in the environment of evolutionary adaptation, we may expect that behavioral inclinations will generally vary in their susceptibility to the influence of different legal tools. The principle can afford us more intellectual traction than we now have on predicting the comparative slopes of the demand curves. It can thereby afford additional information useful to estimating the relative costs to society of attempting to move different kinds of behavior. The principle also provides a new and powerful tool for explaining and predicting many of the existing and future architectures of legal systems—which is the subject of the next section.

REVEALING DEEP PATTERNS IN LEGAL ARCHITECTURE

Much has been said over the years about why human cultures generally, including legal cultures specifically, vary from place to place. But we do not have any comprehensive theories about the contexts in which we might expect legal cultures to be similar (e.g., what is punished or encouraged, and how) and why we might expect similarities. Evolutionary analysis can provide some of the framework for the development of such theories.

The logic proceeds this way. Because humans share an evolved, species-typical neural architecture, they in turn share a species-typical repertoire of emotions and behavioral predispositions (Barkow, Cosmides, & Tooby, 1992; Buss, 1999; Goldsmith, 1994; Goldsmith & Zimmerman, 2000; Pinker, 2002). To the extent that legal systems are sensitive, in part, to the emotions and behavioral predispositions of a governed population, we may expect and predict that legal systems across time and across the world's cultures will tend to have nonrandom similarities in a variety of their major features. That is, because legal systems are both aspects of human behavior and societal responses to human behavior, and because evolutionary processes influence human behavior, we should expect to see the telltale results of evolutionary processes in legal systems.

There will be differences, of course. But we may expect that the architecture of human legal systems will, despite their differences, reflect the effects of evolutionary processes on the human brain, just as the architecture of beaver dams, despite their differences, reflects the effects of evolutionary process on beaver brains.

In varying contexts and at various times, others have taken some intriguing, initial steps in this direction (Alexander, 1979, 1987; Beckstrom, 1989; Gruter, 1977; Gruter & Bohannan, 1983; Wilson, 1987). I have attempted to expand on this thinking—to describe possible foundations for what I call *biolegal history*—in recent work (Jones, 2001c). One way of looking at this is to consider how the main design features of legal systems can be described with four variables: *topics, content, tools,* and *effort.*

In brief, *topics* are the general subject matters that legal systems address (e.g., sexual behavior or access to resources). *Content* reflects the specific normative preferences people in policy-influencing positions tend to have about those subject matters (e.g., minors should be protected from sex with adults, and one person should not take resources from another without justification). *Tools* is a set that includes all methods potentially available to legal systems to bring reality into line with the normative preferences (e.g., incarceration or fines). *Effort* reflects the potential variation—from trivially easy to insurmountably difficult—in how difficult it may be to effect such change using any particular method.

We can roughly approximate some of the superstructure of legal systems—in ways that allow rough but potentially useful comparisons—by sketching together the specific *topics, content, tools,* and *effort* of which each system is composed. Evolutionary analysis, including both the ways in which evolutionary processes affect morality (*topics* and *content;* Alexander, 1987; Jones, 1999b, 2000b; Krebs, this volume) and the ways in which evolutionary processes affect the comparative difficulties law will have moving some behaviors with some methods compared to others (*tools* and *effort*), strongly suggests that superstructural patterns of legal systems will not reflect random distribution.

As in so many other contexts in which human behavior is examined, the very existence of variation can yield initial conclusions that differences outweigh similarities. I suspect much the same will be true as our knowledge of different legal systems across the world's many cultures increases. But legal systems should ideally be compared not just to each other (a technique that frequently highlights difference) but also to the possible legal architectures that the overall design space would allow—were the features of legal systems comparatively randomly distributed.

Evolutionary analysis predicts that, when viewed from this greater distance, legal systems will be rather clumped in one small sector of the overall design space. That is, evolutionary analysis suggests that a given legal architecture will not be—as often assumed—simply an amalgam of culture-specific norms, culture-specific religions, culture-specific morals, culture-specific politics, and general economic efficiencies. An evolutionary perspective provides a far different sense of the prior probabilities that various legal systems will have the structural elements they do of *topics, content, tools,* and *effort.*

At present, relatively little is known about how the propensities among all the world's many societies to govern selves and others with rules, laws, and other forms of legal behavior compare. Although there are apparently some notable commonalities (e.g., proscriptions against the unjustified taking of human life; Brown, 1991), virtually no work has been done to systematically compare the legal cultures of large numbers of different human societies. Some cultures obviously have very formal legal structures, with copious and minutely detailed statutes, as well as extensive judiciaries and dedicated academies. In other cultures, behavior is regulated principally by less formal but highly significant social controls—such as ostracism—operating within relatively small groups. But in all cases evolutionists would expect that the need to establish norms for proper behavior and the need for enforcing such norms will tend to reflect the evolved features of the human brain, as will the patterns in which these needs are satisfied. Evolutionary perspectives on legal behavior may therefore help us acquire a richer and more coherent sense of the deep structure of human legal systems shared cross-culturally.

EXPOSING UNWARRANTED ASSUMPTIONS

Evolutionary thinking can often supply, in Dennett's (1995) term, a "universal acid" for dissolving untenable ideas. This is as important a function to perform in law as it is elsewhere. Because if reliance on flawed assumptions about the causes of a given behavior are wrong, and evolutionary analysis can help to reveal this or to reveal this earlier than otherwise, we can minimize the effects of flawed legal approaches and get on with the business of more aggressively pursuing more effective ones.

A good example comes from the law's various approaches to curbing sexual aggression. Few things warrant greater efforts. Yet different legal approaches have been based, over time, on very markedly different theories of where sexual aggression comes from. An early psychiatric theory led to legal regimes predicated on the notion that rapists are crazy people. Subsequently, a sociological emphasis led to regimes predicated on the idea that rapists are conditioned into being rapists by their sociocultural milieu. And the influence of more recent feminist theories has led, in part, to anti-sexual-violence statutes reflecting the assumption that a cross-sex rape is simply a crime of gender hatred, just as a cross-race lynching is a crime of racial hatred.

Rape is an important and delicate topic, which I have explored elsewhere several times and at length (Jones, 1999c, 2000a, 2001d). Its very existence is a reminder of how disinhibiting the aggressive exercise of power can foster fear, impede female autonomy, and improperly restrain women's bodies, lives, and opportunities. But clearly our inability to eliminate rape, with the various tools available to law, strongly suggests that our understanding of the phenomenon is limited.

It seems likely that no single discipline can alone supply a complete model of the phenomenon. Yet, a thorough grounding in both general evolutionary studies and in the many studies of patterns of sexual aggression in humans and in the many other species in which sexual aggression occurs (see, e.g., studies cited in Jones, 1999c, appendix A) suggests that at least one thing is intellectually untenable. It is incorrect to assume—as has been done so often that people now mistakenly confuse preference with fact—that sexual desire is irrelevant to sexual aggression.

Specifically, a thorough and detailed study of hypotheses and evidence concerning sexual aggression in the many other species in which it occurs, and in the many distinct patterns in which it appears, suggests it is highly probable that evolutionary processes have had an important influence on patterns of human sexual aggression. The patterns in other species are simply too numerous, too consonant, and too distinct. And the near identity of those patterns, in relevant respects, with human data on sexual aggression is striking (Jones, 1999c).

The point here is not that evolutionary analysis alone provides useful perspectives on rape phenomena. The point is that evolutionary analysis is often an essential part of any complete picture of human behavior. While causes of any individual's act of sexual aggression can vary, it is simply illogical to assume that the effects of evolutionary processes on the biology of sexual desire are irrelevant to patterns of human sexual aggression. Even a minimum facility in behavioral biology can help to disclose why such an assumption, as well as many similar assumptions in other legal contexts, no matter how well intentioned, are likely unwarranted and also likely to send legal policies in inefficient directions.

DISENTANGLING MULTIPLE CAUSES

Relatedly, evolutionary analysis in law offers the distinct benefit of highlighting the distinction between and essential complementarity of different levels (proximate and ultimate) of causation. In the context of sexual aggression, for example, this encourages us to look beyond falsely dichotomous thinking, and to recognize that the clear existence of environmental factors that influence probabilities of sexual aggression in no way diminishes the role of evolutionary processes in associating those environmental factors with the behavioral repertoires specific to sexual aggression.

INCREASING ACCURACY

Generally speaking, accuracy is better than inaccuracy. And incorporating evolutionary perspectives into legal thinking will on many occasions help to increase accuracy.

There are two principal ways in which legal thinking may be based on inaccurate assumptions. One way is to be flat-out wrong. For example, suppose that those charged with developing a legal approach to reducing the incidence of aggression assumed that aggression in humans is entirely socioculturally determined. That assumption, as best as we can know, is simply wrong. The body of evidence, and the robustness of corresponding theory, supporting the existence of evolutionary effects on patterns of aggression is overwhelming, compared to evidence to the contrary.

The other way to be inaccurate is through incompleteness. Incompleteness often contributes to inaccuracy in the form of misplaced emphasis. For example, suppose those charged with reducing the incidence of aggression were agnostic on whether there were evolutionary influences on patterns of human aggression, but their approach ultimately reflected attention only to sociocultural contributions to patterns of aggression. The overwhelming evidence that aggression is affected both by environmental inputs and by the ways in which corporeal brains have evolved to associate certain patterns of environmental inputs with psychological states tending to increase or decrease aggression renders such a legal approach inaccurate through incompleteness.

To be clear, I am not advocating reflexive deference to the evolutionary sciences. For one thing, no scientific principles are categorically beyond legitimate challenge. And, more importantly, there may be times when what it costs (whether in time, money, misunderstandings, or misuse) to increase accuracy is far greater than the payoff at the other end (Jones, 2004; Ulen, 2001). For legal systems are not just about a search for truth (though they are often about that). Frequently, legal systems are tasked with getting the most bang, measured in desired human behavioral changes, for the fewest bucks—bucks not being infinite. Consequently, for example, a policy based on assumptions that are 80% accurate, and which is ultimately 70% effective, may be preferable to one that is 98% accurate, 98% effective, and six times as costly.

There may therefore be, on occasion, justification for knowingly choosing to accommodate inaccuracy in behavioral models. But the point here is that to knowingly engage in a fiction without an affirmative and justifiable decision to do so is to improperly privilege flawed approaches.

INCREASING LAW-RELEVANT UNDERSTANDING ABOUT PEOPLE

Aside from all the many policy-level benefits of blending evolutionary insights into the legal system's approaches toward influencing human behaviors, evolutionary thinking has street value in a number of practical, front-line contexts. For example, good lawyers understand people. They have a good sense of what motivates people and how those motivations translate into behavior relevant to the legal system, such as obeying or disobeying laws, initiating or settling lawsuits, and the like.

Evolutionary perspectives are often useful in this context. Consider litigation. Traditional economic theory predicts that a plaintiff will pursue litigation as long as the potential recovery, multiplied by the probability of success, exceeds foreseeable litigation costs. But real people often do not behave this way, and much litigation behavior is pursued at some cost in order to impose a greater cost on another.

To those with an evolutionary lens, this behavior is not surprising. Our brains did not evolve solely as temporally narrow cost-benefit maximizing machines. And there are at least two pathways by which such costly but cost-inflicting behavior could have evolved.

First, retributive spitefulness can be a component of a mixed, evolutionarily stable strategy for reaping gains from cooperation and punishing defectors. Even when spiteful behavior is unlikely to yield compensating advantages in future interactions with others, as a function of current reputational effects (Frank, 1988), our evolved behavioral predispositions may incline us toward spiteful behavior because of its adaptive effect on local reputation in ancestral environments. Second, behaviors that impose greater costs on competitors than on selves can evolve straightforwardly, even in the absence of retributive predispositions, because a decrease in absolute status or condition that nonetheless results in an increase in *relative* status or condition yields evolutionary gains.

Just as lawyers ignorant of human emotions are likely to be poor lawyers, lawyers ignorant of the effects of evolutionary processes on human psychology are likely, in many contexts, to be less effective than they might be otherwise. The ability of evolutionary perspectives to offer new and useful insights into human psychology can therefore render those perspectives both important and advantageous.

GENERATING NEW RESEARCH QUESTIONS

Notably, this cross-fertilization of evolutionary and legal disciplines need not be unidirectional. If there are a number of advantages for legal thinking in learning more about evolutionary processes from evolutionists, there are at least three advantages for evolutionists in learning more about law.

The first advantage arises from the ability of law to represent an area of *applied* evolutionary analysis. While knowledge generation is a worthy goal in itself, comparatively little attention has focused on the *utility* of evolutionary perspectives on human behavior. Just as Darwinian medicine (Nesse & Williams, 1996) represents a useful application of evolutionary knowledge in health contexts, so can evolutionary analysis in law offer new opportunities for application in legal contexts. The advantage for evolutionists, then, is that the wide variety of things useful for legal thinkers to know can help to generate important researchable questions and to open up new areas of research for evolutionists in search of new research frontiers.

The second advantage, and one apparently first articulated by Beckstrom (1989) some years ago, is that legal databases contain hundreds of thousands of reported cases (full text and searchable online) that together can serve as accumulated observational data for testing evolutionary hypotheses. Moreover, the variation in the legal environments of the 50 states yields virtually untapped data from 50 natural laboratories.

The third advantage is the opportunity to analyze the work of legal actors themselves within evolutionary frameworks. For law not only *deals* in human behavior, it *is* human behavior. And the behaviors of judges, legislators, lawyers, police, and the like have yet to be examined systematically from an evolutionary perspective. The things that our species-typical brain leads us to care about as individuals may often underlie many features in the architecture of law generally, as discussed earlier. But, in addition, the way people with effective influence over law actually wield that influence likely reflects condition-dependent predispositions sensitive to relative power and status, which in turn influence their goals and behaviors. Beyond this, we might expect to observe, in the collected behaviors of legal actors, the effects of evolved psychologies specific to the various demographic and situational variables (e.g., age and sex) historically visible to natural and sexual selection. For example, the commonly observed overrepresentation of males in positions of legal influence, across time and cultures, may have contributed to some legal features (e.g., historical double standards for adultery) seeming to reflect evolved male psychology more than evolved female psychology.

CONCLUSIONS

Let's take stock. It is clear that, by integrating evolutionary insights into legal thinking, both legal policymakers and evolutionists can help to:

- Increase efficiency.
- Discover useful patterns in regulable behavior.
- Uncover policy conflicts.
- Sharpen cost-benefit analyses.

- Clarify causal links.
- Provide theoretical foundation and potential predictive power.
- Assess comparative effectiveness of legal strategies.
- Reveal deep patterns in legal architecture.
- Expose unwarranted assumptions.
- Disentangle multiple causes.
- Increase accuracy.
- Increase law-relevant understanding about people.
- Generate new research questions.

Each of the preceding examples of the usefulness of evolutionary analysis in law could alone justify focused integration of evolutionary sciences into behavioral models essential to sound legal thinking. Viewed together, they make an even more powerful, geometrically stronger case (Jones & Goldsmith, 2005). What, then, might serve to delay?

There are a number of obstacles. For instance, few legal thinkers have either strong backgrounds or interests in science—so ability and enthusiasm are often lacking. Few understand the distinction between proximate and ultimate causation in biology (particularly since the former term bears a different meaning in biology than it bears in law). Consequently, false dichotomization of social and biological influences is common. Condition dependence, and the evolution of algorithmic predispositions, are widely unrecognized. Consequently, the more subtle, environmentally sensitive effects of behavioral biology get overlooked. And many, without realizing it, wholly conflate evolutionary biology and evolutionary psychology with behavioral genetics—as if *all* study of evolutionary influences centered on tracing the different behaviors of different individuals to different genes.

All of these factors lead to, among other misperceptions (described in Jones, 1999c, 2001a), ascription of genetically deterministic viewpoints, defense of the supposed categorical boundary between meaningful human behavior and the behavior of all other species, and the assumption that discussion in law of evolved behavioral predispositions could prove useful only in the contexts of genetic defenses in criminal trials. The latter both reflects and then reinforces the fear that proponents of evolutionary analysis in law will try to use explanation as justification.

This assumption is, of course, mostly nonsense. And it stems not merely from healthy skepticism, or even from an appropriate and constructive caution concerning all things biobehavioral that traces to the historical misuses of biology in both politics and in law (*Buck* v. *Bell*, 1927). Instead, it stems largely from the cultural gap between scientists and nonscientists, the obsolete overdivision within universities of human and nonhuman species, and the general time lag between the advances in scientific arenas and their recognition and understanding in legal arenas.

Fortunately, there is ample cause for optimism. Increasing numbers of legal thinkers are interested in issues at the intersection of law and evolutionary sciences and are arguing for more education in and incorporation of evolutionary insights (Beckstrom, 1985; Browne, 1995; Coletta, 1998; Elliott, 2001; Fikentscher & McGuire, 1994; Frolik, 1996, 1999; Goodenough, 2001; Grady & McGuire, 1997; Gruter, 1979; Gruter & Bohannan, 1983; Gruter & Masters, 1986; Gruter &

Morhenn, 2001; Jones, 1997; Jones & Goldsmith, 2005; McGinnis, 1997; Monahan, 2000; O'Hara & Yarn, 2002; Rodgers, 1993; Ruhl, 1996; Stake, 1990). Their combined interests manifest not only in a plethora of programs, conferences, initiatives, and courses in law school, but also in a two decades-long increase in publications in the area.

For example, the Gruter Institute for Law and Behavioral Research (www .gruterinstitute.org) has a long history in educating legal and evolutionary thinkers, through conferences and publications, about prospects for important work at the intersection of their disciplines. And The Society for Evolutionary Analysis in Law (SEAL; www.sealsite.org) has helped to generate scholarship through its network of several hundred interdisciplinary members spanning (at last count) 22 countries. The prospects for integrating evolutionary insights into law consequently look bright, despite a number of significant but surmountable impediments.

The scope of law is vast. The flow of resources, the protection of the citizenry, the regulation of risks, the funding of scientific research, the protection of ideas, the regulation of sexual, mating, and reproductive behavior, the provisioning of the poor, the enforcement of promises, the allocation of rights and duties, the resolution of disputes, the expenditure of collected taxes, and many, many other things are all inextricably intertwined in the extensive networks of legal systems.

Throughout these networks, however, the underrecognized but fundamental relationship between law and behavior remains constant: Society uses law as a tool for moving human behavior in directions it would not otherwise go on its own. And it is embedded in that pragmatic use that law's frequent need for evolutionary analysis is most clear. A competent model of human behavior is essential to wringing maximum effectiveness from legal systems. And evolutionary perspectives, in turn, can frequently strengthen law's models of human behavior. The many examples this chapter has explored doubtlessly represent but a fraction of the many possible applications of evolutionary analysis in law.

REFERENCES

Alexander, R. D. (1979). *Darwinism and human affairs*. University of Washington Press.

Alexander, R. D. (1987). *The biology of moral systems*. New York: Aldine de Gruyter.

Barkow, J. H., & Cosmides, L., & Tooby, J. (1992). *The adapted mind: Evolutionary psychology and the generation of culture*. New York: Oxford University Press.

Beckstrom, J. H. (1985). *Sociobiology and the law: The biology of altruism in the courtroom of the future*. Urbana: University of Illinois Press.

Beckstrom, J. H. (1989). *Evolutionary jurisprudence: Prospects and limitations of the use of modern Darwinism throughout the legal process*. Urbana: University of Illinois Press.

Brown, D. E. (1991). *Human universals*. New York: McGraw-Hill.

Browne, K. R. (1995). Sex and temperament in modern society: A Darwinian view of the glass ceiling and the gender gap. *Arizona Law Review, 37*, 971–1106.

Buck v. Bell, 274 U.S. 200 (1927).

Buss, D. M. (1999). *Evolutionary psychology: The new science of the mind*. Massachusetts: Allyn & Bacon.

Buss, D. M. (2000). *The dangerous passion: Why jealousy is as necessary as love and sex*. New York: Free Press.

Buss, D. M.(2001). Cognitive biases and emotional wisdom in the evolution of conflict between the sexes. *Current Directions in Psychological Science, 10*, 219–223.

Buss, D. M. (2003). *The evolution of desire: Strategies of human mating* (rev. ed.). New York: Basic Books.

Buss, D. M., Larsen, R., Westen, D., & Semmelroth, J. (1992). Sex differences in jealousy: Evolution, physiology, and psychology. *Psychological Science, 3*, 251–255.

Buss, D. M., & Shackelford, T. K. (1997). Human aggression in evolutionary psychological perspective. *Clinical Psychology Review, 17*, 605–619.

Coletta, R. R. (1998). The measuring stick of regulatory takings: A biological and cultural analysis. *University of Pennsylvania Journal of Constitutional Law, 1*, 20–84.

Daly, M., & Wilson, M. (1988). *Homicide.* New York: Aldine de Gruyter.

Daly, M., & Wilson, M. (1995). Discriminative parental solicitude and the relevance of evolutionary models to the analysis of motivational systems. In M. S. Gazzaniga (Ed.), *The cognitive neurosciences* (pp. 1269–1286). Cambridge, MA: MIT Press.

Dennett, D. C. (1995). *Darwin's dangerous idea: Evolution and the meanings of life.* California: Touchstone Books.

Elliott, E. D. (2001). The tragi-comedy of the commons: Evolutionary biology, economics and environmental law. *Virginia Environmental Law Journal, 20*, 17–31.

Ellman, I. M., & Lohr, S. L. (1998). Dissolving the relationship between divorce laws and divorce rates. *International Review of Law and Economics, 18*, 341–359.

Fikentscher, W., & McGuire, M. T. (1994). A four-function theory of biology for law. *Rechtstheorie, 25*, 291–310.

Fisher, H. E. (1994). *Anatomy of love: The natural history of monogamy, adultery, and divorce.* New York: Norton.

Frank, R. (1988). *Passions within reason: The strategic role of the emotions.* New York: Norton.

Frolik, L. (1996). The biological roots of the undue influence doctrine: What's love got to do with it? *University of Pittsburgh Law Review, 57*, 841–882.

Frolik, L. (Ed.). (1999). *Law and evolutionary biology: Selected essays in honor of Margaret Gruter.* Portola Valley: Gruter Institute.

Gigerenzer, G. (1991). How to make cognitive illusions disappear: Beyond "heuristics and biases." *European Review of Social Psychology, 2*, 83–115.

Gigerenzer, G. (1998). Ecological intelligence: An adaptation for frequencies. In D. D. Cummins & C. Allen (Eds.), *The evolution of mind* (pp. 9–29). New York: Oxford University Press.

Gigerenzer, G., Todd, P. M., & the ABC Research Group. (1999). *Simple heuristics that make us smart.* New York: Oxford University Press.

Goldsmith, T. (1994). *Biological roots of human nature: Forging links between evolution and behavior.* New York: Oxford University Press.

Goldsmith, T., & Zimmerman, W. (2000). *Biology, evolution, and human nature.* New York: Wiley.

Goodenough, O. R. (2001). Law and the biology of commitment. In R. M. Nesse (Ed.), *Evolution and the capacity for commitment* (pp. 262–291). New York: Russell Sage Press.

Grady, M., & McGuire, M. (1997). A theory of the origin of natural law. *Journal of Contemporary Legal Issues, 8*, 87–129.

Gruter, M. (1977). Law in sociobiological perspective. *Florida State University Law Review, 5*, 181–218.

Gruter, M. (1979). The origins of legal behavior. *Journal of Social and Biological Structures, 2*, 43–51.

Gruter, M., & Bohannan, P. (1983). *Law, biology and culture: The evolution of law.* Santa Barbara: Ross-Erikson.

Gruter, M., & Masters, R. (1986). Ostracism as a social and biological phenomenon: An introduction. *Ethology and Sociobiology, 7*, 149–158.

Gruter, M., & Morhenn, M. G. (2001). The evolution of law and biology. In S. A. Peterson & A. Somit (Eds.), *Evolutionary approaches in the behavioral sciences: Toward a better understanding of human nature* (pp. 119–134). Greenwich, CT: JAI Press.

Haselton, M., & Buss, D. M. (2000). Error management theory: A new perspective on biases in cross-sex mind reading. *Journal of Personality and Social Psychology, 78*, 81–91.

Haselton, M., & Buss, D. M. (2003). Biases in social judgment: Design flaws or design features? In J. Forgas, K. Williams, & B. von Hippel (Eds.), *Responding to the social world: Implicit and explicit processes in social judgments and decisions.* New York: Cambridge University Press.

Hausfater, G., & Hrdy, S. B. (1984). *Infanticide: Comparative and evolutionary perspectives.* New York: Aldine Publishing Company.

Hoffman, E., & Spitzer, M. L. (1993). Willingness to pay vs. willingness to accept: Legal and economic implications. *Washington University Law Quarterly, 71*, 59–114.

Jones, O. D. (1997). Evolutionary analysis in law: An introduction and application to child abuse. *North Carolina Law Review, 75*, 1117–1242.

Jones, O. D. (1999a). *Law, behavioral economics, and evolution.* Paper Presented at Olin Conference on Evolution and Legal Theory, Georgetown University Law Center, April 16, 1999.

Jones, O. D. (1999b). Law, emotions, and behavioral biology. *Jurimetrics Journal, 39,* 283–289.

Jones, O. D. (1999c). Sex, culture, and the biology of rape: Toward explanation and prevention. *California Law Review, 87,* 827–942.

Jones, O. D. (2000a). An evolutionary analysis of rape: Reflections on transitions. *Hastings Women's Law Journal, 11,* 151–178.

Jones, O. D. (2000b). On the nature of norms: Biology, morality, and the disruption of order. *Michigan Law Review, 98,* 2072–2103.

Jones, O. D. (2001a). Evolutionary analysis in law: Some objections considered. *Brooklyn Law Review, 67,* 207–232.

Jones, O. D. (2001b). The evolution of irrationality. *Jurimetrics Journal, 41,* 289–318.

Jones, O. D. (2001c). Prioprioception, non-law, and biolegal history. (The University of Florida Dunwody Distinguished Lecture in Law). *Florida Law Review, 53,* 831–874.

Jones, O. D. (2001d). Realities of rape: Of science and politics, causes and meanings. *Cornell Law Review, 86,* 1386–1422.

Jones, O. D. (2001e). Time-shifted rationality and the law of law's leverage: Behavioral economics meets behavioral biology. *Northwestern University Law Review, 95,* 1141–1206.

Jones, O. D. (2004). Law, evolution, and the brain: Applications and open questions. *Philosophical Transactions: Biological Sciences, 359,* 1697–1707.

Jones, O. D., & Goldsmith, T. H. (2005). Law and behavioral biology. *Columbia Law Review, 105,* 405–502.

McGinnis, J. (1997). The human constitution and constitutive law. *Journal of Contemporary Legal Issues, 8,* 211–239.

Monahan, J. (2000). Could "law and evolution" be the next "law and economics"? *Virginia Journal of Social Policy and the Law, 8,* 123–128.

Nesse, N., & Williams, G. (1996). *Why we get sick: The new science of Darwinian medicine.* New York: Vintage Books.

O'Hara, E., & Yarn, D. (2002). On apology and consilience. *Washington Law Review, 77,* 1121–1192.

Pinker, S. (2002). *The blank slate: The modern denial of human nature.* New York: Viking Press.

Rodgers, W. H., Jr. (1993). Where environmental law and biology meet: Of pandas' thumbs, statutory sleepers, and effective law. *University of Colorado Law Review, 65,* 25–75.

Ruhl, J. B. (1996). The fitness of law: Using complexity theory to describe the evolution of law and society and its practical meaning for democracy. *Vanderbilt Law Review, 49,* 1406–1490.

Slovic, P., Fischhoff, B., & Lichtenstein, S. (1982). Facts versus fears: Understanding perceived risk. In D. Kahneman, P. Slovic, & A. Tversky (Eds.), *Judgment under uncertainty: Heuristics and biases* (pp. 463–492). Cambridge, MA: Cambridge University Press.

Simon, H. A. (1990). Invariants of human behavior. *Annual Review of Psychology, 41,* 1–20.

Stake, J. E. (1990). Darwin, donations, and the illusion of dead hand control. *Tulane Law Review, 64,* 705–781.

Tversky, A., & Kahneman, D. (1982). Judgment under uncertainty: Heuristics and biases. In D. Kahneman, P. Slovic, & A. Tversky (Eds.), *Judgment under uncertainty: Heuristics and biases* (pp. 3–20). Cambridge, MA: Cambridge University Press.

Ulen, T. S. (1989). Cognitive imperfections and the economic analysis of the law. *Hamline Law Review, 12,* 385–410.

Ulen, T. S. (1994). Rational choice and the economic analysis of law. *Law and Social Inquiry, 19,* 487–522.

Ulen, T. S. (2001). Evolution, human behavior, and law: A response to Owen Jones' Dunwody Lecture. *Florida Law Review, 53,* 931–946.

Wilson, M. (1987). Impact of the uncertainty of paternity on family law. *University of Toronto Faculty of Law Review, 45,* 216–242.

Afterword

RICHARD DAWKINS

At the end of such a compendium—truly a worthy 10-years-on successor to *The Adapted Mind*—what is there left for an Afterword? An attempted summing up of all 34 chapters? Too ambitious. A prophetic "Whither evolutionary psychology?" Too presumptuous. An idiosyncratic *jeu d'esprit*, playfully calculated to send the reader diving back into the book to view the whole corpus again but from a different angle of illumination? Rather daunting, but I could give it a go. Reflective musings of a sympathetic observer of the scene? Well, let me try that, too, and see what develops.

First, a confession. As a sympathetic observer of the scene, I had not been very clearsighted. I was one of those who mistakenly thought *evolutionary psychology* a euphemistic mutation of *sociobiology*, favored (like *behavioral ecology*) for its cryptic protection against the yapping ankle-biters from "science for the people" and their fellow travelers. This book has shown me that that was a travesty, not even a half-truth, perhaps, at most, a quarter-truth. For one thing, intellectual pugilists of the caliber of Cosmides, Tooby, and other authors of the book need no camouflage. But even that isn't the point. The point is that evolutionary psychology really is different. Psychology it is, and psychology is by no means all, or even mostly, about social life, sex, aggression, or parental relationships. Evolutionary psychology is about the evolution of so much more than that: perceptual biases, language, development, and revealing errors in information processing. Even within the narrower field of social behavior, evolutionary psychology distinguishes itself from sociobiology by emphasizing the psychological and information processing mediation between natural selection and the behavior itself.

Evolutionary psychology and sociobiology do, however, have one bane in common. Both are subject to a level of implacable hostility, which seems far out of proportion to anything sober reason or even common politeness might sanction. E. O. Wilson, struggling to understand the onslaught that engulfed *sociobiology* at the hands of left-wing ideologues, invoked what Hans Küng in another context had called "the fury of the theologians." I have known sweetly reasonable philosophers, with whom I could have an amicable and constructive conversation on literally any other topic, descend to the level of intemperate ranting at the mere mention of evolutionary psychology or even the name of one of its leading practitioners. I have no desire to explore this odd phenomenon in detail. It is well discussed by evolutionary psychologists, including contributors to this book, and by Ullica Segerstrale in *Defenders of the Truth* (2000). I do have one additional remark to make about this negativity, and I shall return to it. First, though, in what I intend to be a more positive vein, here is the nearest approach I can make to the *jeu d'esprit* that aspires to shed a little oblique light on the material in this book.

Sometimes science proceeds not by experiment or observation but by changing the point of view: seeing familiar facts afresh through an unfamiliar idea. Two candidates for the role are "the genetic book of the dead," and "continuously updated virtual reality." I shall briefly summarize these ideas and try to bring them together in a way that might provide the novel illumination that I rashly promised (for fuller accounts, see Chapters 10 and 11, respectively, of Dawkins, 1998).

The idea of the genetic book of the dead is that an animal, because it is well adapted to its environment, can actually be seen as a *description* of its environment. A knowledgeable and perceptive zoologist, allowed to examine and dissect a specimen of an unknown species, should be able to reconstruct its way of life and habitat. To be strict, the reconstruction is a complicated average of the ancestral habitats and ways of life of the animal's ancestors: its environment of evolutionary adaptation (EEA) in evolutionary psychology jargon.

This conceit can be phrased in genetic terms. The animal you are looking at has been constructed by a sampling from the gene pool of the species: genes that have successfully come down through a long sequence of generational filters—the filters of natural selection. These are the genes that had what it takes to survive in the EEA. They fitted the EEA as a key fits a lock, and, like a key, they are a kind of negative impression of their lock. Genes can, therefore, be seen as a description of the EEA, written in the language of DNA: hence the phrase, "genetic book of the dead."

Continuously updated virtual reality is the idea that every brain constructs a virtual reality model of the animal's world. The virtual reality software is continuously updated in the sense that, although it might theoretically be capable of conjuring scenes of wildest fantasy (as in dreams), it is in practice constrained by data flowing in from the sense organs. What the animal perceives is a virtual reality rendering of salient aspects of the real world, continuously updated by sensory information.

Visual illusions such as Necker Cubes and other alternating figures are best interpreted in these terms. The data sent to the brain by the retina are equally compatible with two virtual models of a cube. Having no basis to choose, the brain alternates. The virtual world that our brains construct is, no doubt, very different from that of a squirrel, a mole, or a whale. Each species will construct virtual models that are useful for its particular way of life. A swift and a bat both move at high speed through three dimensions, catching insects on the wing. Both, therefore, need the same kind of virtual model, even though swifts hunt by day using their eyes, and bats hunt by night using their ears. Qualia that swifts associate with color are actually constructions of their virtual reality software. My conjecture could probably never be tested, but I think bats might "hear in color." Their virtual reality software would be missing an obvious trick if it did not make use of the same qualia as swifts use for light of different wavelengths, but to signify equally salient features of a bat's auditory world. Surface textures are likely to be as important to bats as color is to birds, and textures like the hairy pelt of a moth, the sheen of a bluebottle, or the rough stone of a cliff presumably temper echoes in their own ways. Thus, the virtual reality software of bats is likely to adopt the same qualia—red, blue, green, and so forth—as internal labels for different acoustic textures. Redness and blueness are constructions of the brain's virtual reality software, and natural selection will have seen to it that such qualia are used as labels for things that really matter to the survival of the respective animals: color for a visual animal such as a swift or a person; texture for a bat.

My bat speculation is just an example of how the idea of continuously updated virtual reality changes our view of animal psychology. Now I want to unite it with the idea of the genetic book of the dead and bring the two back to evolutionary psychology. If a knowledgeable zoologist can reconstruct a species' EEA using data from its anatomy and physiology, could a knowledgeable psychologist do something similar for mental worlds? Presumably the mental world of a squirrel would, if we could peer into it, be a world of forests, a three-dimensional maze of trunks and twigs, branches, and leaves. The mental world of a mole is dark, damp, and rich with smells because the genes that built its brain have survived through a long line of similarly dark and damp ancestral places. The virtual reality software of each species would, if we could reverse engineer it, allow us to reconstruct the environments in which natural selection built up that software. By the same reasoning as before, it is tantamount to a description of the EEA.

Nowadays we are accustomed to saying, more literally than metaphorically, that all the genes of a species have survived through a long succession of ancestral worlds, including both physical and social worlds. My suggestion here is that the long succession of ancestral worlds in which our genes have survived include the virtual worlds constructed by our ancestors' brains. Real genes have—again in something close to a literal sense—been selected to survive in a virtual EEA, constructed by ancestral brains.

I now return to the hostile reception that evolutionary psychology has received in certain circles. It is a methodological point I am making, and the note I want to strike is an optimistic one of encouragement.

Skeptical investigators of paranormal claims have a much-quoted maxim: Extraordinary claims require extraordinary evidence. All of us would set the bar very high for, say, a claimed demonstration that two men, sealed in separate soundproof rooms, can reliably transmit information to each other telepathically. We should demand multiple replications under ultrarigorous, double-blind controlled conditions, with a battery of professional illusionists as skeptical scrutineers and with a statistical p-value less than one in a billion. An experimental demonstration that, for example, alcohol slows down reflexes would be accepted without a second glance.

While nobody should approve poor design or shoddy statistics, we wouldn't go out of our way to scrutinize the alcohol experiment very skeptically before accepting the conclusion. The hurdle in this case would be set so low as almost to escape notice because the hypothesis under test is so plausible. In the middle, there is a spectrum of scientific claims of intermediate capacity to arouse a priori skepticism. Evolutionary psychology, weirdly, seems to be seen by its critics as way out on the "telepathy" end of the spectrum, a red rag to critical bulls.

Something similar was true of the earlier controversy over sociobiology. Philip Kitcher's *Vaulting Ambition* (1985) is widely touted as a devastating critique of human sociobiology. In reality, it is mostly a catalogue of methodological shortcomings of particular studies. The supposed faults range from peccadillo to shoddy, but they are of a type that is in principle remediable by new and improved studies along the same lines. Criticisms like Kitcher's of sociobiology, or like those more recently hurled at evolutionary psychologists such as Daly and Wilson on stepparental abuse, Cosmides and Tooby on social exchange, or Buss on sexual jealousy are made so strongly only because the critics are treating the hypotheses under test as if they were extraordinary claims that demand extraordinary evidence. Evolutionary psychology is seen by its critics as out at the high hurdle end—the telepathy end of the spectrum—while it is simultaneously seen by its practitioners as down at the plausible end of the spectrum with the alcohol and the reflexes. Who is right?

Without a doubt, the evolutionary psychologists are right in this case. The central claim they are making is not an extraordinary one. It amounts to the exceedingly modest assertion that minds are on the same footing as bodies where Darwinian natural selection is concerned. Given that feet, livers, ears, wings, shells, eyes, crests, ligaments, antennae, hearts, and feathers are shaped by natural selection as tools for the survival and reproduction of their possessors, in the particular ecological niche of the species, why on earth should the same not be true of brains, minds, and psychologies? Put it like that, and the central thesis of evolutionary psychology moves right along to the plausible end of the spectrum. The alternative is that psychology is uniquely exempt from the Darwinian imperatives that govern the whole of the rest of life. *That* is the extraordinary claim, which, if not downright bonkers, at least demands extraordinary evidence before we should take it seriously. Maybe it is right. But given that we are all Darwinians now, the onus of proof is on those who would deny the central thesis of evolutionary psychology. It is the critics who lie closer to the telepathy end of the spectrum.

Could it be that the sticking point for critics is that old bugbear, the supposed uniqueness of humans? Is evolutionary psychology permissible for "animals," but not *Homo sapiens?* Once again such exceptionalism, though conceivably justifiable, bears the heavy burden of proof. There are perhaps 10 million species alive on this planet at the moment, and as many as a billion species have done so in history. It is *possible* that our species really is the one in a billion that, with respect to psychology, has emancipated itself from the purview of evolutionary explanation. But if that is what you think, the onus of demonstration is on you. Don't underestimate the surprisingness of that which you purport to believe.

Or could it be modularity that sticks in the craw of critics? Maybe. Maybe they are right, and in any case some evolutionary psychologists are less enamored of modularity than others. But, again, modularity is not an extraordinary claim. It is the *alternative* to modularity that bears the burden of coming up with extraordinary evidence in its favor. Modularity is a universally good design principle which pervades engineering, software, and biology, to say nothing of political, military, and social institutions. Division of labor among specialist units (experts, organs, parts, subroutines, cells) is such an obvious way to run any complex operation, we should positively expect that the mind would be modularized unless there is good reason to believe the contrary. Again, the detailed arguments are to be found in this book. I merely repeat my point about the onus of proof lying on the opponents of evolutionary psychology.

Some individual evolutionary psychologists need to clean up their methodological act. Maybe many do. But that is true of scientists in all fields. Evolutionary psychologists should not be weighed down by abnormal loads of skepticism and a priori hostility. On the contrary, they should hold their heads high and go to work with confidence, for the enterprise they are engaged upon is healthy normal science, flourishing within the neo-Darwinian paradigm. This book shows the way.

REFERENCES

Dawkins, R. (1998). *Unweaving the Rainbow*. London: Penguin.
Kitcher, P. (1985). *Vaulting Ambition*. Cambridge, MA: MIT Press.
Segerstrale, U. (2000). *Defenders of the Truth*. New York: Oxford University Press.

Author Index

Abbey, A., 735, 805
Abel, G. G., 403
Abell, F., 205
Abrams, D., 637, 638
Abrams, M. H., 943, 946
Abramson, L. Y., 738
Abric, J. C., 537
Acierno, R., 399
Acker, M., 403, 406, 407, 409
Acton, S., 294
Adami, H., 917
Adams, C., 186
Adams, H. E., 408, 409
Adams-Curtis, L. E., 404
Ader, R., 563, 564
Adiamah, J. H., 308
Adler, N. E., 489, 679
Adolphs, R., 108
Agerbo, E., 918
Agostinelli, G., 269, 280
Agras, S., 138
Agrawal, A. F., 456
Aguado, F., 565
Agyei, Y., 270
Ahlstrom, U., 110
Ahlstrom, V., 110
Ahouse, J. C., 153, 156
Aitken, D., 565
Akamatsu, S., 294
Akert, R. M., 803
Aktipis, C. A., 659
Alberts, S. C., 484, 553, 571, 677
Albon, S. D., 484
Albus, M., 564
Alcalay, L., 262, 264, 265, 270, 271, 272, 279, 375
Alcock, J., 10, 167, 180, 182, 263, 268, 269, 451, 458, 506, 736, 810, 813, 821
Alcock, K., 711
Aldwin, C. M., 862
Alexander, G. M., 274

Alexander, J., 109
Alexander, M. G., 658
Alexander, R. D., 260, 268, 269, 344, 349, 388, 443, 448, 450, 453, 465, 472, 476, 531, 544, 552, 553, 554, 555, 664, 757, 758, 759, 762, 766, 817, 818, 833, 905, 908, 937, 941, 966
Alfieri, T., 729
Alibhai, N., 318
Alicke, M. D., 738
Allal, N., 329
Allen, B., 397
Allen, J., 315, 906, 917
Allen, M., 403
Allen, N. B., 914
Allen, S., 905
Allen-Arave, W., 301, 304, 306
Allensworth, M., 270, 271, 272, 274, 279
Alley, T., 294, 303
Allik, J., 262, 264, 265, 270, 271, 272, 279, 375
Allison, E., 936
Allison, T., 108
Allman, J., 75, 554, 562
Alloy, L. B., 738
Allport, G. W., 188
Almor, A., 611
Almquist, J. O., 381
Alnwick, K. A., 355
Alper, C. M., 563, 571
Als, H., 837
Alsop, D., 188
Altmann, J., 484, 553, 571, 677
Alvard, M., 81, 304
Alvarez, H., 295, 299, 304, 475, 535, 555
Alvarsson, J.-A., 661
Amato, P. R., 421, 490, 494, 633
Ambriz, D., 373
Ames, D. R., 538

Amianto, F., 862
Amir, M., 399
Amos, N., 405
Anastasi, A., 189
Andersen, A. H., 108
Andersen, S. L., 908
Anderson, A., 44, 97
Anderson, C., 728
Anderson, C. A., 629
Anderson, C. M., 908
Anderson, D. J., 514
Anderson, J. G., 512
Anderson, J. L., 317
Anderson, J. R., 783, 784, 785, 788, 789
Anderson, K. G., 420, 490, 491, 499, 512
Anderson, N. H., 106
Anderson, P. A., 433
Anderson, R. M., 662
Andersson, M., 77, 167, 261, 372, 483
Andreasen, N. C., 914
Andreoni, J., 656
Andreski, P., 912
Andrews, P. W., 122, 125, 126, 127, 728, 736, 737, 886, 913
Angleitner, A., 260, 264, 265, 266
Annooshian, L. J., 183
Antòn, S. C., 557
Aparna, R., 259, 262
Apicella, C. L., 302, 324, 326
Appleton, J., 192, 293
Aquadro, C. F., 346
Arad, S., 539
Aragona, B. J., 562
Aral, I., 150
Arbel, T., 680
Arbib, M. A., 715
Archer, J., 260, 263, 269, 634, 639, 645, 813, 907
Arden, K., 355

Ariely, D., 781
Arkes, H. R., 727
Armstrong, D. P., 485, 486
Armstrong, E., 74
Armstrong, J. R. M., 308
Arndt, W. B., Jr., 377
Arnold, K. E., 484, 485
Arnqvist, G., 396
Aron, A., 559, 560, 561
Aronfreed, J., 767
Aronson, E., 629, 741, 803
Arriaga, X. B., 425
Arrindell, W. A., 639
Arseneault, L., 642
Arsuaga, J.-L., 557
Arterberry, M. E., 553
Asa, C. S., 486
Aschenbrenner, B. G., 494
Asher, T., 663
Ashton, G. C., 182
Askins, K., 564
Astin, M., 395
Atkinson, R. C., 787
Atran, S., 43, 44, 100, 102, 217
Atrash, H. K., 239
Atzmueller, M., 531
Augoustinos, M., 665
Ault, L., 262, 264, 265, 270,
    271, 272, 279, 375
Austers, I., 262, 264, 265, 270,
    271, 272, 279, 375
Austin, W., 759
Ausubel, D. P., 892
Auvert, B., 421
Avila, M., 917
Avis, J., 840
Avis, M., 108
Avis, W. E., 315
Avison, M. J., 108
Aw, E., 85
Axelrod, R., 591, 592, 656, 659,
    684, 754, 755, 756, 760,
    761, 763, 765, 813

Baare, W., 612
Bachorowski, J. A., 814
Badcock, C., 904, 908
Badcock, P. B. T., 914
Baddeley, A., 603, 788
Badenoch, M., 295
Baenninger, M., 633
Baer, D., 814
Baguma, P., 318
Bailey, J. M., 270, 273, 274,
    276, 804, 809, 814, 816,
    821, 940
Bailey, K. G., 920
Bailey, M., 270, 324
Baillargeon, R., 96, 109
Baird, B. D., 344
Baird, D. D., 352, 371, 554
Baird, J., 106, 107, 918
Baker, H. W. G., 378, 381
Baker, J. A., 388

Baker, M., 139, 271
Baker, R., 260, 261, 266, 267,
    275, 276, 311, 312, 313,
    358, 365, 374, 376, 378,
    379, 380, 382, 383, 384,
    385, 386, 387, 388, 389,
    435, 492, 631, 690
Baker, W., 644
Balcombe, J. P., 513
Balda, R. P., 181
Baldwin, D. A., 106, 107
Baldwin, M. W., 426
Bales, K. L., 561
Ball, H. L., 509
Ball, M. A., 373
Balling, J. D., 191, 193
Balmford, A., 217
Banaji, M. R., 807, 821
Bandura, A., 766
Bane, C. M., 679
Bank, L., 184
Bannister, R. C., 169
Barash, D., 192, 259, 420, 936
Barash, N., 936
Barbaree, H. E., 403, 404, 405,
    408, 414
Barbee, A. P., 270, 294, 295,
    312, 327
Barber, N., 268, 273, 278, 279,
    280
Barchas, J. D., 913
Bard, J., 531
Bardgett, M. E., 564
Bardin, C. W., 319
Bargh, J. A., 404, 643
Barinaga, M., 752
Barkow, J., 698, 904, 905, 941,
    965
Barlow, D. H., 403, 912
Barlow, H. B., 220
Barnes, G., 403, 406, 407, 409
Barnes, M., 816, 864
Barnes, M. F., 270
Barnes, M. L., 427
Barnett, A. M., 189
Barnhart, K. T., 364
Baron, R. A., 803, 813
Baron, R. M., 130, 409
Baroncelli, S., 857
Baron-Cohen, S., 12, 18, 23, 46,
    55, 105, 107, 208, 209, 210,
    212, 837, 841, 904, 918
Barr, A., 275
Barrett, E. S., 79, 274, 354
Barrett, H. C., 8, 10, 34, 43, 44,
    46, 47, 49, 52, 63, 106, 205,
    206, 207, 209, 210, 212,
    213, 214, 215, 223, 228,
    586, 607, 609
Barrett, L., 538, 904, 942
Barrett, R. J., 184
Barron, G., 791, 792, 793
Barrow, J. D., 940, 946
Barry, H., 264

Bartels, A., 422, 553, 560, 561
Bartholomew, K., 435
Bartini, M., 837, 839, 845
Bartlett, F. C., 787
Bartlett, M., 61, 434
Barton, S., 399, 403
Barton, S. A., 89, 266, 362, 492
Barton, S. C., 632
Bartsch, K., 688
Bartusch, D. J., 641
Basile, K. C., 397
Basinger, K. S., 768
Bastian, L., 399
Bateman, A. J., 269, 271
Bates, E., 100, 617, 619, 710,
    712
Bates, G. E., 85
Bates, J., 137, 232, 420, 490,
    491, 518, 641, 642
Bateson, P., 268, 453, 908
Bateup, H. S., 679
Batson, C. D., 464, 545
Battino, S., 381
Baumeister, R. F., 273, 404,
    563, 636, 812
Baur, B., 372
Bavelier, D., 717
Bax, C. M., 352
Baxter, D. J., 405, 408
Beach, F. A., 317
Beach, L. R., 794
Beall, C. M., 263
Beaman, A. L., 656
Beatty, J., 790
Beauchamp, G. K., 531
Becker, D. V., 137, 662, 672,
    804, 807, 808, 819, 821
Becker, V., 735
Beckerman, S., 264, 296
Beckstrom, J. H., 966, 970, 971
Bedau, M., 884
Bedaux, J. B., 932
Beecher, M. D., 513
Beer, J., 108
Begg, M. D., 905
Begun, D. R., 557
Behne, T., 213, 228
Behrens, H., 708
Beise, J., 474
Bell, G., 71
Bell, S., 188
Bellefeuille, A., 110
Bellemann, M. E., 104
Bellis, M. A., 260, 261, 266,
    267, 275, 276, 311, 313,
    358, 365, 374, 376, 378,
    379, 380, 382, 383, 384,
    385, 386, 387, 388, 389,
    435, 492, 690
Bellis, R. R., 139
Bellugi, U., 715, 716, 717
Belsky, J., 85, 258, 276, 279,
    296, 312, 327, 403, 490,
    494, 495, 499, 516, 517,

563, 571, 833, 837, 845, 869, 907, 908
Benami, M., 381
Benartzi, S., 742
Benet, M., 905
Benjamin, L. S., 679
Bennet, K., 434
Bennett, A. T. D., 724
Bennett, K. L., 262, 375
Bennice, J. A., 395
Ben-Shlomo, Y., 315
Benshoof, L., 350, 353, 361
Bentley, G. R., 299, 317, 330
Ben-Yossef, M., 546
Bercovitch, F. B., 510, 552
Bereczkei, T., 510, 518
Berendes, H. W., 467, 468, 508
Berezckei, T., 690
Berg, C. J., 239
Bergstrom, C., 455
Berhanu, B., 521
Bering, J. M., 829, 833, 837, 840, 845
Berkowitz, L., 814
Berlin, L., 517
Berman, A., 918
Bermudez de Castro, J. M., 557
Bernardini, B., 187
Bernat, J. A., 409
Bernath, L., 690
Bernhardt, P., 679
Bernstein, I. S., 810
Berretty, P. M., 781
Berridge, D. M., 842
Berridge, K. C., 914
Berry, D. S., 865
Berry, J. W., 184
Berscheid, E., 419, 530, 546, 655
Berte, N., 459, 536
Bertenthal, B., 34, 206
Berwick, R. C., 148, 153, 156
Besson, M., 104
Best, C. L., 399
Bester-Meredith, J., 552
Bettencourt, B. A., 639
Bettens, F., 357, 531
Bettinardi, V., 104
Bettman, J. R., 779, 781
Betzig, L., 228, 259, 260, 262, 272, 276, 296, 423, 434, 459, 469, 474, 492, 536, 633, 690, 818, 871, 941
Bevc, I., 533
Bever, T., 186
Beylin, A. V., 564
Bhat Agar, S., 565
Biblarz, A., 914
Bibring, E., 913
Bickerton, D., 712
Bickman, L., 898
Biederman, I., 97
Biederman, J., 918
Bielicki, T., 316

Biella, P., 554
Bierer, L. M., 912
Biernat, M., 663
Billings, R., 837
Bindon, J. R., 571
Binnie-Dawson, J. L. M., 184
Birecree, E., 184
Birkhead, T. R., 259, 260, 267, 360, 372, 373, 374, 375, 386, 387, 484, 485
Bíró, S., 107, 205, 206, 211
Bishop, K. L., 409
Bisiach, E., 187
Biver, F., 642
Bjork, E. L., 785
Bjork, R. A., 785
Bjorklund, D. F., 516, 532, 553, 555, 639, 641, 829, 832, 833, 834, 835, 837, 840, 844, 845, 908
Bjorkqvist, K., 639
Bjorntorp, P., 321
Blackburn, J. R., 872
Blackmore, S., 720
Blackwell, J. M., 381
Blades, M., 183
Blais, A.-R., 793
Blake, R., 108, 110
Blakemore, S.-J., 107, 108, 110, 562
Blakley, T., 644
Blanchard, D. C., 679
Blanchard, E., 403
Blanke, M. K., 860
Blascovich, J., 55
Bleske, A., 266, 388, 401, 886
Bleske-Rechek, A. L., 266, 382
Blick, J., 453
Block, A. P., 230
Block, C. R., 234
Bloom, P., 26, 99, 102, 553, 698, 699, 705, 707
Bloom, R. W., 930
Blount, S., 537, 661
Blumenschine, R. J., 201
Blumstein, D. T., 208
Blumstein, P., 816
Blurton Jones, N. G., 43, 81, 84, 214, 218, 261, 295, 296, 299, 304, 334, 347, 459, 475, 488, 535, 555, 837
Blythe, P., 107, 205, 206, 212, 223
Bock, J. A., 90, 490
Boden, M., 622
Bodnoff, S., 565
Boe, L.-J., 705
Boechler, M., 679
Boehm, C., 545, 546, 665, 681, 752, 754
Boehnke, K., 635
Boesch, C., 334, 498, 683
Bogin, B., 301, 315, 557
Bohannan, P., 966, 971

Bohner, G., 411
Boinski, S., 855, 859
Bonabeau, E., 706
Bonacich, E., 665
Bonatti, L., 603
Bond, A. L., 680
Bonsall, R., 565
Bookwala, J., 424
Boole, G., 9
Boone, J. L., 492, 518
Boorse, C., 892
Booth, A., 206, 274, 679, 810, 814
Booth, L., 679
Booth-Kewley, S., 862
Borcsok, I., 325
Borgerhoff Mulder, M., 153, 259, 260, 261, 262, 272, 296, 329, 330, 488, 492, 496, 517
Borgia, G., 531
Born, J., 352
Bornstein, G., 546
Bornstein, M. H., 553
Bornstein, R. F., 533
Borowiak, D. M., 409
Borsutzky, D., 680
Bortz, A., 470
Bossert, W. H., 71
Boster, J., 267
Bostock, E. M., 183
Bouchard, T. J., Jr., 182
Boulton, M., 218, 635, 680
Bourg, S. N., 411
Bourhis, R. Y., 666
Bouwer, C., 912
Bowlby, J., 152, 279, 422, 429, 516, 563, 828, 837, 907, 919
Bowles, S., 545, 546, 618, 638, 656, 659, 660, 661, 737, 738, 767, 930
Boyce, T., 489
Boyce, W. T., 679, 833, 837
Boyd, B., 934, 938
Boyd, R., 151, 161, 217, 237, 545, 546, 591, 592, 618, 638, 653, 655, 656, 657, 659, 660, 661, 663, 737, 738, 765, 766, 767, 930, 940
Boyer, P., 7, 18, 30, 32, 43, 45, 62, 63, 107, 108, 110, 217
Boyse, E. A., 531
Boysen, S. T., 843, 844
Bozzaro, S., 459
Bradley, B. J., 498
Bradshaw, D., 422
Brain, C. K., 201
Braine, M. D. S., 709
Brakeman-Wartell, S., 473, 474, 492
Brandon, R. N., 885
Brändström, A., 488
Brandt, T., 187
Branscombe, N. R., 666

Brantingham, P. J., 201
Brase, G., 23, 796
Bratti, M. C., 365
Braun, J., 42, 44
Braveman, P. A., 239
Braver, T. S., 107
Braverman, J., 61, 434
Breda, C., 898
Bredért, S., 470
Breed, W., 385
Brehm, S. S., 803
Breier, A., 564
Brendgen, M., 629
Brennan, K. A., 869
Brenner, R. A., 467, 468, 508
Brent, S. B., 213, 214
Breslau, N., 912
Bresnahan, M., 905
Bressan, P., 534
Bressi, S., 104
Brett, C., 613
Brewer, M. B., 122, 128, 129,
    130, 131, 658, 665, 666, 737
Briars, D., 843
Bricker, W., 644
Brickman, P., 913
Bridgeman, B., 942
Bridgestock, R., 312
Brief, D. E., 813
Briere, J., 407, 408, 410, 413
Briggs, P. F., 866
Brockbank, M., 107, 205
Bröder, A., 275, 363, 398, 778,
    781
Brodie, D. A., 311, 325, 326
Brodie, E. D., III, 456, 484
Brody, J. F., 918
Brody, N., 870
Brody, S., 863
Bromage, T. G., 557
Bromfield, J. J., 364, 365
Bronstad, P., 308, 331, 361
Brooks, D. R., 872
Brooks, R., 78, 348, 365
Brooks-Gunn, J., 85, 518, 642
Brosnan, S. F., 546, 589, 617
Broude, G. J., 260, 264, 280, 397
Broughton, R., 813
Brown, A., 47, 905
Brown, D., 156, 262, 304, 421,
    423, 966
Brown, E., 295
Brown, G. P., 227
Brown, G. W., 913, 914
Brown, J., 456
Brown, J. D., 738, 739
Brown, J. L., 386, 453
Brown, K., 930
Brown, L. L., 559, 560, 561
Brown, L. M., 636
Brown, P. C., 679
Brown, P. J., 317
Brown, R., 545, 914
Brown, S., 464, 805, 812

Brown, S. L., 914
Brown, S. R., 866
Brown, T. P., 321
Brown, W. M., 88, 538
Browne, K. R., 971
Brownell, H., 108
Brownmiller, S., 397, 400
Brsca, R., 872
Brumbach, B. H., 869
Brutsaert, D. L., 861
Bryan, A., 275
Bryden, M. P., 184
Buchan, J. C., 484, 553
Buchanan, G. M., 273
Bucholz, K. K., 276
Buchting, F., 276
Buckle, L., 261
Buckmaster, A., 264
Bugental, D. B., 811, 829
Bugnyar, T., 229
Bugos, P., 459, 655
Bugos, P. E., 465, 466, 508, 519
Bugos, P. E., Jr., 536, 539
Buhot, M. C., 182
Buller, D. J., 159, 161, 163, 878
Bullock, H., 369
Bullock, S., 508, 519, 779
Bulthoff, H. H., 208
Bundred, P. E., 319
Bunn, H. T., 201, 202
Bunnk, A. P., 428
Burch, E. S., Jr., 529
Burch, R. L., 260, 267, 302, 326,
    383, 471, 472, 534, 535, 537
Burg, A., 186
Burgess, A. W., 230
Burgess, N., 182
Burgess, R. L., 464
Buriel, R., 490, 491, 494
Burke, L., 565
Burke, T., 485
Burks, V., 490
Burley, N., 270, 294, 351
Burnham, T. C., 274, 656
Burns, J. K., 917
Burnstein, E., 462, 463, 537,
    538, 539, 540, 541, 546,
    804, 812
Burstein, B., 184
Burt, A., 350, 351
Burt, D. M., 273, 274, 299, 309,
    311, 312, 313, 355, 691, 724
Burt, M., 353, 355, 358, 724
Burton, L. M., 280
Burton, M. L., 262, 277
Burton, R., 766, 905
Bush, A., 749
Bush, M., 386
Bushman, B. J., 629
Buss, D. M., 7, 45, 51, 57, 60,
    76, 87, 88, 89, 123, 124,
    135, 136, 168, 205, 213,
    224, 225, 226, 227, 228,
    229, 230, 231, 234, 236,

237, 240, 241, 242, 243,
244, 252, 258, 259, 260,
265, 266, 267, 268, 269,
270, 271, 272, 273, 275,
276, 277, 280, 293, 294,
296, 297, 298, 299, 300,
301, 306, 308, 311, 313,
315, 316, 320, 326, 327,
330, 348, 352, 353, 358,
361, 362, 374, 375, 377,
394, 395, 396, 397, 401,
402, 419, 420, 421, 423,
424, 426, 428, 429, 430,
431, 433, 434, 435, 436,
448, 469, 470, 493, 536,
554, 559, 633, 635, 636,
663, 690, 691, 730, 735,
736, 753, 758, 761, 791,
805, 806, 809, 810, 811,
815, 816, 817, 821, 829,
852, 853, 854, 864, 865,
866, 868, 886, 904, 906,
914, 916, 919, 942, 943,
959, 964, 965
Buss, K., 564, 565
Butera, F., 913
Butner, J., 137, 638, 804, 805,
    811, 815, 816, 819, 820, 821
Butterworth, G., 295
Buttrick, M., 872
Butts, J. D., 244
Buunk, A. P., 260, 266, 270
Buunk, B., 266, 298, 320, 325,
    433, 633, 635, 812
Byatt, G., 294, 312
Byers, J. A., 207
Byrd, D., 186
Byrd-Craven, J., 492
Byrne, D., 397, 402, 803, 808
Byrne, M., 918
Byrne, R., 203, 229, 613, 682,
    683, 839, 905
Byrnes, J. P., 639

Cabeza, R., 101
Cairns, R. B., 828
Calder, A. A., 365
Calder, A. J., 108
Calhoun, K. S., 409
Callor, S., 494, 499
Calvin, W. H., 712
Camerer, C., 618, 659, 737
Cameron, C., 316, 809, 816
Cameron, E. Z., 510
Camire, L., 635
Camizon, S., 706
Campbell, A., 224, 269, 554,
    636, 639, 645, 646
Campbell, B. C., 274
Campbell, D. T., 127, 128, 130,
    132, 653, 665, 666, 747, 937
Campbell, J. I. D., 111
Campbell, L., 426, 427, 431,
    432, 433

Campbell, P. F., 183
Campbell, R., 97
Campos, J., 34
Canastar, A., 395
Cannon, W., 55
Capage, L., 841
Capitanio, J. P., 857
Caplan, A. L., 892
Caporael, L., 122, 544, 737, 805, 811
Cappa, S. F., 104
Capra, A. M., 239
Cara, F., 603, 611, 613
Carael, M., 421
Caramazza, A., 42, 43, 96, 103
Carbonee, E., 557
Card, S. K., 778
Carey, G., 643
Carey, J. R., 73, 75
Carey, S., 47, 107, 112, 114, 206, 212, 622, 843, 844
Carlin, L. C., 516
Carlson, E., 517
Carpendale, J. I., 749
Carpenter, J., 660
Carpenter, M., 106, 107
Carrier, D. R., 203
Carroll, J., 933, 934, 935, 937, 938, 939, 940, 944, 946
Carruthers, P., 47, 165
Carson, J., 490
Carson, R. E., 714
Carter, C. S., 422, 560, 561, 562
Carter, W., 186
Cartwright, J., 260, 267
Carver, C. S., 913
Casas, J. F., 493
Case, T. I., 738
Casey, R. J., 295, 303
Cashdan, E., 266, 588, 589, 635
Casimir, M. J., 259, 262
Caspari, R., 555, 557
Caspi, A., 85, 276, 279, 312, 488, 641, 642, 643, 914
Cassidy, J., 517
Castellazzo, G., 679
Castelli, F., 205, 212
Castles, D., 299, 311, 353, 355, 358, 691, 724
Catanese, K. R., 404
Cate, R., 267
Cates, W., 421
Cattell, R. B., 132
Catterall, J. F., 319
Caviness, J. A., 206
Cerda-Flores, R. M., 89, 266, 362, 492
Cervoni, N., 572
Chacon, R., 295, 301, 305, 306, 307, 309, 310, 317
Chadwick, S. B., 917
Chagnon, N., 229, 232, 234, 235, 260, 262, 263, 296, 298, 301, 303, 304, 305,

306, 308, 315, 319, 397, 443, 459, 496, 536, 539, 554, 637, 653, 655, 941
Chakraborty, R., 89, 266, 362, 368, 492
Chamberlin, T. C., 851
Champagne, F., 561, 572
Chance, S., 42, 783
Chang, E. L., 186
Chapais, B., 685
Chaplin, T. C., 408
Chapman, J. F., 274
Charlesworth, B., 347, 448
Charlesworth, W. R., 680, 828
Charnov, E., 571
Charnov, E. I., 555
Charnov, E. L., 70, 71, 73, 75, 76, 295, 296, 299, 304, 475, 535
Chase-Lansdale, P. L., 490
Chater, N., 613, 741, 780
Chavanne, T. J., 230, 363
Check, J., 407, 408, 409, 410, 413
Check, M. V. P., 399, 403
Chege, J., 421
Chel, C., 108
Chen, D., 521
Chen, J. Y., 274
Cheney, D., 8, 204, 218, 682, 685
Cheng, P., 592, 596, 604, 605, 606, 610, 611, 613, 620, 689
Cherlin, A. J., 490
Cherney, I. D., 186
Cherniak, J., 154
Chesney, M. A., 489, 679
Cheung, G., 312
Cheung, Y. M., 184
Chi, H. C., 918
Chiappe, D. L., 940, 942
Chick, G., 319
Chippendale, A. K., 346
Chiroro, P., 411
Chisholm, J., 85, 279, 296, 495, 516, 517, 553, 557, 869, 907
Choe, J., 260, 266, 320, 433, 914
Choi, I., 729
Choi, J., 184, 186, 187, 188
Chomsky, N., 7, 33, 698, 701, 705, 706, 707, 719
Chong, D. S., 239
Chow, J., 642
Chow, K., 914
Christe, P., 488
Christenfeld, N. J. S., 470
Christensen, A., 419, 494
Christensen, P., 140, 267, 271, 273, 356, 554
Christensen-Szalanski, J. J. J., 794
Christie, R., 869
Christopher, F. S., 267
Chrousos, G. P., 565

Chun, M. M., 97
Cialdini, R., 464, 805, 811, 812, 872
Cicchetti, D., 644
Cigliano, J. A., 858
Clamp, P., 192
Clancy, S. A., 786
Clare, L., 603
Clark, A., 294, 346, 536
Clark, C. L., 869
Clark, D. W., 663
Clark, L. A., 424
Clark, M. A., 106, 107
Clark, M. E., 809
Clark, M. M., 508
Clark, M. S., 758
Clark, R. D., 134, 270, 806
Clarke, A. S., 565, 855, 859
Clegg, L., 217
Clements, W. A., 842
Cleveland, H. H., 490
Clifton, C., Jr., 703, 704
Cling, B. J., 667
Clobert, J., 451
Cloos, O., 325
Clutton-Brock, T. H., 72, 73, 259, 260, 263, 268, 269, 296, 395, 483, 484, 487, 508, 518, 555, 562, 677
Coates-Markle, L., 681
Cochran, G., 905
Cochran, K. F., 187
Coe, C. L., 565
Coe, K., 555, 939
Coe, R., 308
Cohen, J., 386
Cohen, L. E., 229
Cohen, N., 563, 564
Cohen, R., 399, 758
Cohen, S., 489, 563, 564, 571, 679
Cohn, D., 517
Coie, J. D., 629, 640, 643, 644, 839
Colarelli, S. M., 930
Colby, A., 748, 764
Cole, L. C., 70
Coletta, R. R., 971
Coley, J., 43
Collins, B. E., 813
Coltheart, M., 103
Colvin, C., 729
Comer, R., 267, 275, 313, 365, 388, 389
Comings, D. E., 276, 491
Condon, R. G., 661
Conohan, C. D., 865
Conway, L. G., 121, 123, 124, 807
Conway-Lanz, S., 682
Cook, K. S., 546
Cook, M., 50, 51, 55, 138, 208, 216, 217, 617, 734
Cook, T. D., 127, 128, 130, 132

Cooke, B., 932
Cooper, H., 136
Cooper, P. J., 321
Cooper, R., 316
Cooper, T., 321
Coote, T., 677
Copas, A. J., 376
Copp, A. J., 711
Corballis, M. C., 714
Corcoran, C., 918
Coren, S., 187
Corina, D., 717
Cormier, C., 833
Cornelissen, P. L., 307, 318, 324, 325
Cornelius, J., 635, 809
Corrigan, B., 780
Corter, C., 493, 560, 561
Cosentino, T., 183
Cosmides, L., 5, 6, 7, 8, 9, 10, 13, 14, 16, 17, 18, 23, 25, 28, 29, 30, 33, 34, 36, 41, 42, 43, 44, 45, 46, 47, 48, 49, 50, 51, 52, 59, 60, 62, 87, 106, 127, 137, 148, 159, 163, 164, 168, 177, 180, 201, 208, 210, 213, 214, 215, 225, 229, 232, 292, 293, 294, 295, 303, 304, 305, 306, 329, 330, 364, 384, 397, 444, 457, 467, 470, 533, 584, 585, 586, 587, 588, 590, 591, 592, 593, 595, 596, 598, 599, 600, 602, 603, 604, 605, 606, 608, 609, 610, 611, 612, 613, 615, 617, 620, 622, 623, 640, 653, 654, 657, 658, 659, 660, 661, 666, 668, 689, 698, 699, 725, 738, 740, 741, 757, 758, 759, 767, 783, 796, 797, 807, 811, 813, 829, 890, 904, 906, 908, 940, 942, 965
Cosmides, S., 851, 852, 868
Coss, R. G., 208, 209, 218
Costa, P. T., 856, 869
Costa, P., Jr., 861
Costanzo, M., 244
Costes, N., 110
Côté, S., 641, 645
Cotton, P. A., 453, 455
Cottrell, C. A., 655, 657, 658, 659, 660, 663, 666, 807
Couch, R., 766
Couden, A., 271
Coughlin, C., 241
Coulson, T., 217
Coulton, C., 642
Cousins, A. J., 140, 273, 275, 352, 356, 367, 554
Cowan, C., 494, 517
Cowan, N., 788

Cowan, P., 494, 517
Cox, M. J., 494
Cox, R. L., 858
Craft, S., 564
Crago, M., 711
Craig, I. W., 488, 914
Craig, N. M., 308
Craik, F. I. M., 783
Cramer, D., 556
Crandall, C., 462, 463, 539, 540, 541, 546, 663, 804, 812
Crawford, C., 280, 317, 462, 511, 635, 904, 940
Crick, N. R., 493, 691
Crippin, T., 930
Criqui, M. H., 495, 861
Critton, S. R., 302, 326, 471, 534, 535, 537
Crocker, J., 658
Crockett, N. G., 378
Crofoot, M. C., 396
Cronbach, L. J., 128, 131
Cronin, H., 76, 77, 123, 126, 906
Cronin, J., 556
Cronk, L., 262, 510
Crook, J. H., 263, 821
Crook, S. J., 263, 821
Cross, D., 840
Crow, J. F., 451
Crow, T. J., 906, 917
Crowell, J., 517
Crump, T., 112
Csanaky, A., 518
Csibra, G., 107, 205, 206, 211
Cuddy, A. J., 658
Cuervo, J. J., 484
Cullen, F. T., 641
Cummings, E. M., 494
Cummins, D. D., 127, 614, 681, 682, 687, 688, 689, 752, 753, 813, 837, 842
Cummins, J. M., 360
Cummins, R., 127
Cunningham, M. R., 270, 294, 295, 312, 327, 464, 539
Cupertino, A. P., 862
Curran, J. P., 866
Curran, M., 531
Curtis, J. T., 562
Curtis, L. E., 843
Curtis, T. J., 552, 560
Cuthill, I. C., 309, 312, 724
Cutler, A., 703, 704
Cutting, A. L., 841
Czekala, N. M., 336
Czerlinski, J., 780, 782
Czilli, T., 837

Dabbs, J., 274, 679
Dabbs, J. M., 186
Dabbs, J. M., Jr., 319, 810
Dabbs, M. G., 319
Daga, G. A., 862

Dahlen, E., 914
Dai, W., 318, 319, 324
D'Alessio, A. C. D., 572
D'Alessio, D., 403
Dal Martello, M. F., 534
Dalton, B., 667
Daly, M., 7, 14, 57, 123, 136, 137, 193, 224, 230, 233, 240, 243, 262, 263, 266, 269, 296, 297, 298, 301, 302, 326, 375, 389, 419, 421, 433, 435, 443, 445, 447, 448, 457, 459, 460, 463, 464, 465, 466, 467, 468, 469, 472, 476, 486, 489, 492, 495, 507, 508, 509, 511, 512, 518, 519, 521, 530, 534, 554, 563, 568, 630, 631, 633, 634, 639, 655, 667, 804, 813, 814, 815, 817, 818, 821, 837, 845, 906, 919, 937, 955, 964
Daly, R., 260, 263
Damasio, A., 710, 942
Damhaut, P., 642
Damon, W., 748
Daniel, J. C., 208
Danner, D. D., 859
Dantchik, A., 807
Daood, C., 538, 682, 687
Darmon, C., 110
Darwin, C., 5, 12, 119, 251, 268, 277, 297, 372, 449, 476, 483, 747, 762, 764, 765, 857
Das Gupta, M., 510
Daston, L., 790
David, G., 378, 381
Davidson, J. K., 377
Davidson, M., 50, 51, 208, 216, 217
Davidson, R. J., 942
Davies, G., 845
Davies, N. B., 259, 389, 448, 486, 495, 907
Davies, P. T., 494
Davies, S., 912
Davis, B. L., 709, 710, 713, 714
Davis, C., 108, 192
Davis, G. C., 912
Davis, H., 679, 843
Davis, J. A., 260, 267, 383
Davis, J. N., 489, 508, 518, 519, 520
Davis, K., 517
Davis, M., 659
Davis, M. H., 104
Davis, M. J., 408, 409
Dawes, R. M., 544, 737, 780, 805
Dawkins, R., 27, 122, 146, 219, 447, 448, 449, 453, 459, 476, 528, 531, 590, 655,

683, 692, 711, 720, 747, 749, 752, 761, 763, 765, 805, 884, 919, 937, 976
Dawkins, S., 678
Dawson, K., 464
Deacon, T. W., 84, 557, 699
Dean, K., 397, 403, 404
Dean, M. C., 557
Deaner, R., 554
De Becker, G., 236
de Bellis, M., 565
De Bruin, E. M., 655
DeBruine, L. M., 302, 326, 444, 459, 534, 537
deCatanzaro, D., 906, 913
Decety, J., 107, 108, 110
Decker, S. D., 570
de Coccola, R., 661
Dedden, L. A., 224, 228, 636
Defeyter, M. A., 47
Defries, J. C., 182
Degner, D., 187
de Haan, M., 553, 837
Dehaene, S., 111
De Jong, R., 308
DeKeseredy, W., 434
de Kloet, E. R., 565
Delahoyde, M., 467
Delgado, H. L., 315
Delton, A., 662, 672, 808, 821
Delude, L., 218
Del Valle, A. P., 380, 381
DeMaris, A., 634
Dembroski, T. M., 861
Demong, N. J., 512, 517
Deneubourg, J.-F., 706
Denison, F. C., 365
Dennett, D., 12, 105, 692, 967
Denollet, J., 861
Denton, K., 730, 749, 759, 766, 768, 805, 808
D'Entremont, B., 108, 688
DePrince, A. P., 786
De Rosa, J., 936
Derryberry, D., 641
Deruelle, C., 97
de Schonen, S., 97
Descola, P., 296, 315
Desmond, A., 119
Dess, N., 930
DeSteno, D., 61, 434
Dettling, A., 264, 267
Deutsch, F. M., 809
Devereux, C., 229
Devine, P. G., 808
Devineni, T., 186
Devlin, J. T., 104
DeVore, I., 8, 11, 24, 62, 185, 229, 295, 465, 474, 588, 653, 755
Devos, T., 658, 668
de Waal, F., 546, 556, 589, 617, 681, 683, 685, 814, 839, 857, 858

De Weerth, C., 633, 634
Dewey, J. O., 449
Dewey, K. G., 299
Dewsbury, D. A., 373, 677
Dhami, M. K., 793
Diamond, J., 237
Diamond, R., 114
Dias, P. C., 485
Dickemann, M., 510
Dickerson, C., 845
Dickinson, J. L., 451
Diderich, M., 460
Diehl, R., 705
Diener, E., 422, 656, 859
Dietze, C., 664, 665
Dijker, A. J., 658, 661
Dijkstra, P., 266, 270, 298, 320, 325, 635
Ding, Y. C., 918
Dinwiddie, S. H., 276
Dion, K., 294
DiPietro, J. A., 635
Dispenza, F., 325
Dissanayake, E., 939, 940
Dixon, A., 485
Dixon, R. M. W., 719
Dixson, A. F., 258, 259, 260, 261, 262, 263, 264, 267, 268, 351, 375
Dodge, K. A., 85, 137, 232, 420, 490, 491, 518, 629, 640, 642, 643, 644, 814, 839
Dohle, G. R., 381
Domb, L. G., 350, 351
Dominic, J. P., 409
Domjan, M., 736
Donald, M., 713
Donaldson, D. I., 107
Donnett, J. G., 182
Doosje, B., 666
Doran, D. M., 261, 268
Doran-Sheehy, D. M., 498
Döring, G. K., 275
Dorn, L. D., 565
Doty, R. L., 361
Douglas, K. S., 235
Dovidio, J. F., 657, 666
Doyle, W. J., 563, 571
Drain, H. M., 97
Draper, P., 72, 81, 84, 85, 258, 261, 276, 279, 296, 327, 403, 483, 490, 495, 496, 499, 516, 517, 555, 571, 833, 837, 845, 869, 908
Drass, E., 433
Dressler, W., 571
Drewnowski, A., 127
Drickamer, L. C., 182
Drigotas, S. M., 431
Driscoll, D. M., 763
Driscoll, G. L., 378
Druen, P. B., 270, 295
Drummond, H., 511
Dubach, J., 677

Dubois, S. L., 271
Duchaine, B., 97, 617
Duck, S., 806
Dudey, T., 781
Dudley, R., 914
Dugatkin, L. A., 151, 588, 730, 752, 755, 756
Dukas, R., 783, 788, 789, 790
Duke, M., 858
Dunbar, R., 298, 315, 485, 486, 487, 492, 499, 510, 536, 538, 553, 555,, 653, 690, 713, 833, 904, 935, 942
Duncan, D. B., 371
Dunn, A. J., 564
Dunn, J., 688
Dunne, M. P., 270, 274, 276
Dunson, D. B., 352, 554
Duntley, J., 227, 229, 231, 234, 242, 243, 244, 275
Durgin, F., 106
Dutton, D. G., 435
Dvorakova, K., 385
Dziurawiec, S., 294
Dzuiba-Leatherman, J., 568

Eadington, W., 869
Eagly, A. H., 122, 262, 280, 634, 639, 809, 814, 816
Eals, M., 127, 185, 186, 188, 837
Easterlin, N., 932, 933, 938
Eaton, S. B., 64, 293, 904, 915
Eaton, W. O., 635
Eaton, W. W., 918
Eaves, L., 276, 493, 862
Ebbesen, E. B., 784
Ebbinghaus, H., 783, 784
Ebenbach, D. H., 728
Ebensperger, L. A., 512
Eberhard, W. G., 372, 387, 389
Ebert, R., 662
Ebert, S. A., 861
Eckland, B. K., 226
Ecuyer-Dab, I., 185, 186, 189
Eddy, D. M., 794
Eddy, T. J., 107
Edmunds, C., 399
Edwards, C. P., 228, 565, 635
Edwards, R., 273, 274, 299, 309
Ehlers, S., 108
Ehrlich, P., 151, 589
Eibl-Eibesfeldt, I., 59, 134, 664, 665, 813, 940, 946
Eichenbaum, H., 182
Eimas, P. D., 207
Eisenberg, N., 494, 635
Eisner, T., 372
Ekman, P., 55, 108, 821, 908, 942
Elias, B., 399, 403
Elias, L. J., 188
Elias, M., 679
Ellegren, H., 511
Ellemers, N., 666

Elliott, E. D., 971
Ellis, B., 85, 86, 123, 137, 266,
    269, 270, 273, 276, 279,
    316, 376, 377, 384, 397,
    420, 423, 424, 426, 429,
    430, 431, 432, 433, 436,
    490, 491, 518, 829, 833, 837
Ellis, L., 262, 395, 398, 677,
    678, 680
Ellis, P., 360
Ellison, P., 79, 274, 299, 300,
    301, 315, 317, 332, 354,
    554, 565
Ellman, I. M., 964
Elman, J., 100, 617, 619, 710,
    712, 797
Elmore, M., 239
Elster, A. B., 502
Elster, J., 765
Ember, C., 258, 260, 263, 264,
    296
Ember, M., 258, 260, 263, 264,
    296
Emery, J. L., 318
Emlen, D. J., 512
Emlen, S. T., 259, 261, 512, 517
Emmers-Sommer, T. M., 403
Emmons, R. A., 913
Enard, W., 712
Encarnacion-Gawrych, G. E.,
    688
Endert, E., 352
Endicott, J., 892
England, B. G., 554, 565, 567,
    569, 570, 571
Englis, B. G., 550
Enns, L. R., 635
Enns, R. M., 853, 858, 859
Enquist, M., 350
Epel, E. S., 679
Epley, N., 738
Erens, B., 376
Erev, I., 791, 792, 793
Erickson, M. F., 565
Ericson, M. T., 908
Eriksson, J., 315
Ernberg, G., 917
Ernst, J., 55
Ervin, F. R., 179
Erwin, J. M., 562
Esbensen, F., 642
Escobar, G. J., 239
Eshel, I., 454, 456
Esses, V. M., 666
Essex, M., 908
Essock-Vitale, S., 460, 462,
    473, 540, 631, 812, 817
Esteves, F., 138, 207, 228, 242
Etcoff, N., 292, 304, 308, 309,
    316, 635
Etman, A. A. M., 389
Euler, H., 382, 383, 388, 473
Eunsuk, C., 908
Evans, C. S., 208

Evans, J. St. B. T., 595, 600, 620
Evans, R. B., 325
Evans, R. M., 513
Everhart, E., 517
Ewald, H., 918
Ewald, P., 904, 905, 906
Ewen, J. G., 485, 486
Ewigman, B. G., 467
Ewy, R., 295
Eyali, V., 381
Eysenck, H. J., 863, 866, 869
Eysenck, S. B. G., 869

Fabes, R. A., 639
Fabrega, H., 904
Fagen, R., 448, 457, 834
Fahim, C., 918
Fairbanks, L. A., 561, 811, 818,
    904
Falchero, S., 193
Falk, A., 661
Falk, D., 74, 715
Falk, J. H., 191, 193
Fan, J., 318, 319, 324
Fanselow, C., 787
Farah, M., 97
Farkas, L. G., 312
Farnham, S. D., 807, 821
Farrar, G. E., 565
Farrington, D. P., 641
Farroni, T., 553
Fasino, S., 862
Faubert, J., 110
Faucheux, C., 537
Faulkner, J., 659, 662, 663, 666,
    734
Faurie, C., 262, 320
Feather, N. T., 692
Feeney, J., 517
Fehm, H. L., 352
Fehr, B., 424
Fehr, E., 448, 457, 545, 546,
    618, 636, 656, 659, 660,
    661, 686, 737, 738, 767,
    907, 930
Feierman, J. R., 917
Fein, G. G., 183
Fein, S., 803
Feinberg, D. R., 309
Feingold, A., 136, 270, 315
Feldman, J., 106, 205
Feldman, M., 151, 454, 456
Feldman, R. S., 642
Feldman, S., 494, 517
Felson, R. B., 400, 634
Felten, D. L., 563, 564
Fenton, M. B., 386
Ferenz-Gillies, R., 517
Fergusson, D. M., 490
Fernald, A., 837
Fernandez, Y. M., 403
Ferrari, P. F., 714
Feshbach, S., 408
Fessler, D. M., 363, 364, 907

Fiddick, L., 588, 592, 596, 598,
    600, 603, 604, 606, 608,
    609, 610, 611, 612, 613,
    620, 687, 782
Fiedler, K., 740, 789
Fielden, J., 679
Figueredo, A. J., 853, 854, 855,
    856, 857, 858, 859, 860,
    867, 869
Fikentscher, W., 971
Finch, C. E., 86
Finch, J. F., 262, 436, 691
Fincham, F. D., 633
Fine, M. A., 869
Fink, B., 275, 306, 308, 309,
    310, 311, 316, 324, 326,
    327, 355, 531
Finkelhor, D., 568
Firman, R. C., 360
First, M., 878, 897, 909
Fischbacher, U., 448, 659, 661,
    907
Fischer, A. H., 634
Fischer, B., 275
Fischer, C. S., 461
Fischer, E. F., 419, 421
Fischer, G. W., 763
Fischer, H., 662
Fischhoff, B., 786, 958
Fisek, M. H., 537, 813
Fisher, H., 259, 261, 272, 296,
    420, 421, 423, 552, 559,
    560, 561, 964
Fisher, M., 187, 270, 275
Fisher, R. A., 38, 70, 77, 297,
    458, 509
Fisher, S. E., 711, 712
Fishkin, S. A., 492, 495, 497,
    499, 806
Fishman, M. A., 484
Fiske, A., 588, 806, 811, 813,
    907, 918, 919
Fiske, D. W., 132
Fiske, S. T., 399, 658, 667, 728,
    729
Fitch, W. T., 705, 706
Fitzgerald, H. E., 303
Fitzgerald, L. F., 399
Fitzgerald, R. W., 184, 186
Flavell, J. H., 836
Fleagle, J. G., 74, 558
Fleming, A. S., 493, 560, 561
Fleschner, M., 564, 571
Fletcher, G. J. O., 271, 420, 426,
    427, 437, 538
Fletcher, P., 108, 711
Flinn, M., 262, 266, 285, 295,
    483, 492, 494, 496, 497,
    499, 552, 553, 554, 555,
    557, 563, 565, 567, 568,
    569, 570, 571, 572, 637,
    766, 815, 816, 937
Flores, A., 679
Florsheim, P., 490

Flugge, G., 565
Flykt, A., 138, 207
Foa, E. B., 912
Fodor, J., 44, 45, 162, 164, 178, 610
Foehl, J. C., 377
Fogassi, L., 713, 714
Foley, R., 498, 516, 555, 940
Folkman, S., 489, 679
Folstad, I., 77, 311
Fonlupt, P., 110
Forbes, G. B., 404
Forbes, L. S., 453
Ford, C. S., 317
Ford, M., 361
Forehand, R. L., 518
Forrest, M. S., 692
Forsythe, R., 686
Fortes, M., 529
Foss, M. A., 633
Fossey, D., 497
Foster, E. M., 898
Foucault, M., 891
Fowler, R., 274
Fowles, D. C., 641
Fox, C. A., 388
Fox, C. W., 484
Fox, R., 935
Frackowiak, R. S. J., 182
Frank, R., 538, 636, 656, 905, 908, 969
Frank, S. A., 450
Frankel, D. G., 680
Frankel, S., 315
Franklin, M., 140, 270, 275, 294, 311, 327, 354, 355, 357, 361
Franklin, R. D., 365
Franks, N. R., 706
Franzoi, S. L., 325
Fraser, S. C., 656
Frayer, D. W., 296
Frayser, S., 259, 260, 262, 264, 276, 304
Frederick, C., 861
Frederick, D., 273, 302, 326, 471, 534, 535, 537
Fredrickson, B. L., 906
Freedman, R. J., 187
Freeman, N. H., 842
Frege, G., 9
Freischem, C. W., 863
French, J. A., 907
French, R., 470
Fretwell, S. D., 72
Freud, S., 453, 767, 945
Freyd, J., 110, 786, 790
Friedman, A., 633
Friedman, H. S., 495, 861, 862
Friesen, C., 42, 107
Friesen, W. V., 821, 859
Frieze, I. H., 316, 424
Frigerio, D., 274, 362
Frijda, N. H., 658

Frisch, R. E., 317
Friston, K. J. B., 108
Frith, C. D., 108, 182, 205, 212
Frith, U., 105, 108, 205, 212, 562, 841
Froehlke, R. G., 467
Frolik, L., 971
Froman, D. P., 360
Fromm, H., 935
Frost, B. J., 206
Fuchs, E., 565
Fujioka, M., 485
Fujita, K., 229
Fuller, D., 768
Fuller, R. C., 311
Fundele, R., 632
Funder, D. C., 729, 730, 741, 742, 789, 806, 807, 808, 858
Füri, S., 357, 531
Furman, K., 538
Furnham, A., 318, 321, 861
Furstenberg, F. F., Jr., 490

Gabler, S., 508
Gabriel, R., 45
Gabrielidis, C., 635, 809
Gächter, S., 457, 618, 636, 656, 659, 660, 686
Gade, A., 103
Gadgil, M., 71
Gaertner, L., 739
Gage, M. J. G., 373, 374
Gagne, M., 679
Gagneux, P., 683
Gagnon, J. H., 264, 275, 362, 376
Gal, A., 690
Galea, L. A. M., 186, 188
Galef, B. G., Jr., 508, 779
Galileo, G., 172
Gall, J. A., 837
Gallese, V., 713, 714
Gallistel, C. R., 31, 32, 41, 44, 47, 111, 112, 179, 183, 617, 793
Gallistel, R., 843
Galloway, D. B., 381
Galloway, J., 633
Gallup, G. G., 55, 208, 218, 260, 261, 267, 273, 324, 325, 326, 363, 364, 383, 398, 471, 472
Gallup, G., Jr., 230, 302, 326, 534, 535, 537
Galton, F., 189, 294
Gamble, C., 942
Gammie, S. C., 631
Gangestad, S. W., 75, 89, 122, 125, 126, 127, 139, 140, 259, 260, 262, 266, 267, 268, 270, 271, 272, 273, 274, 275, 276, 296, 297, 301, 306, 308, 310, 311, 312, 313, 314, 326, 327,

348, 349, 352, 353, 354, 355, 356, 357, 358, 359, 360, 361, 362, 365, 367, 376, 387, 388, 389, 426, 436, 554, 811, 815, 817, 868, 886
Garber, J., 85, 86, 276, 279, 491, 833
Garcia, A. R., 373
Garcia, J., 127, 179, 617, 734
Gardner, C. O., 913
Gardner, R., 913
Garling, T., 190, 193
Garst, E., 464
Gartner, R., 232
Garvaro, L., 862
Garver, C., 139, 358, 361, 362, 387, 388
Garver-Apgar, C. E., 140, 356, 358, 359, 367, 554
Garvey, M. A., 918
Garzaro, L., 862
Gat, A., 628
Gaulin, S., 184, 185, 186, 267, 270, 274, 276, 451, 453, 470, 472, 473, 474, 492, 510, 511, 534, 818, 904, 942
Gaultney, J. F., 835
Gauthier, I., 97, 617
Gavrilets, S., 346
Geary, D. C., 263, 268, 269, 285, 295, 347, 420, 421, 483, 487, 489, 490, 492, 493, 494, 495, 496, 497, 552, 553, 554, 555, 563, 637, 810, 815, 816, 829, 834, 835, 837, 842, 844, 845, 906, 908, 940, 941, 942
Geary, R. T., 381
Geddes, K., 294
Geen, R. G., 629
Geertz, C., 6
Gegenfurtner, K. R., 208
Geiss, F., 869
Geist, R. F., 230
Geliebter, A., 474, 492
Gelles, R. J., 296, 919
Gelman, R., 47, 96, 100, 106, 111, 112, 829, 843
Gelman, S. A., 30, 96, 100, 102, 654, 797
Gentner, D., 102
George, R. M., 508
Georges-Francois, P., 182
Gergely, G., 107, 205, 206, 211
Gerhard, I., 862
Gerlach, C., 103
German, T., 44, 45, 47, 61
Gerrelli, D., 711
Gershon, J., 858
Geslevich, Y., 381
Getty, T., 77, 78, 355
Ghiglieri, M. P., 232, 234, 235, 240, 243

Ghiselin, M. T., 170, 443, 544
Giahn, D., 188
Gianotten, W. L., 381
Gibbon, J., 31, 617
Gibbs, J., 768
Gibson, E. J., 533
Gibson, J. J., 206
Gibson, J. R., 346
Gibson, K. R., 84
Gieg, J. A., 452
Gigerenzer, G., 23, 42, 47, 51,
    593, 596, 599, 600, 602,
    609, 619, 689, 729, 739,
    740, 741, 779, 780, 782,
    785, 787, 790, 793, 794,
    795, 796, 797, 959
Gilbert, P., 692, 904, 905, 912,
    913, 920
Giles, L., 426, 427
Gillberg, C., 108
Gillebert, T. C., 861
Giller, E., 644
Gilligan, C., 749, 761
Gillis, J. S., 315
Gilovich, T., 538, 727, 738
Gilstrap, B., 494
Gil-White, F., 654, 657, 666,
    667, 668, 907
Ginsburg, I. H., 662
Gintis, H., 448, 545, 546, 618,
    638, 656, 659, 660, 661,
    737, 738, 767, 908, 930
Girotto, V., 603, 611, 613
Givens, D. B., 134
Givon, T., 715
Gladue, B., 270, 679
Glantz, K., 906
Glaser, D., 644
Glaser, R., 564, 862
Glazer, N., 530
Gleitman, L. R., 183
Glenn, N. D., 226
Glick, P., 399, 658
Glotfelty, C., 935
Glynn, J. R., 421
Gobbini, M. I., 97, 98, 108
Gobel, S., 111
Godekmerdan, A., 150
Godfray, H. C. J., 453, 454, 455,
    456
Godfrey-Smith, P., 884, 885,
    887, 888
Goetz, A. T., 383, 384
Goffman, E., 658, 759
Goldberg, E. L., 377
Goldberg, S., 635
Goldberg, T., 330
Goldfarb, J., 102
Goldin-Meadow, S., 716
Goldman, H. I., 716
Goldsmith, H. H., 494, 499
Goldsmith, M., 783
Goldsmith, T., 724, 742, 954,
    964, 965, 971, 972

Goldstein, D. G., 729, 779, 780,
    782, 785
Goldstein, M. C., 263
Goldstein, N., 660
Goldstein, W. M., 791
Goldthwaite, R. O., 208, 209,
    218
Goleman, D., 241
Golier, J. A., 912
Gollisch, R., 354
Gomendio, M., 373, 375, 376,
    378, 380, 383
Gonzaga, G. C., 108
Good, D. C., 316
Good, F. E., 377
Goodall, J., 334, 498, 556, 685,
    857
Goodenough, O. R., 971
Goodman, A. H., 310
Goodpasture, J. C., 378, 381
Goodrowe, K. L., 386
Goodwin, S. A., 728
Goos, L. M., 632
Gopnik, A., 105, 207, 701
Gopnik, M., 711
Gore, J. C., 97
Goren, C. C., 688
Gorman-Smith, D., 490
Gorno-Tempini, M., 104
Gosling, S. D., 857, 858, 859
Gottfredson, M., 641
Gotthelf, A., 878
Gottlieb, G., 830, 831
Gottman, J. M., 419, 494, 565
Gottschall, J., 398, 936
Gottschall, T., 398, 936
Gouchie, C., 184
Gould, E., 572
Gould, S. J., 9, 10, 125, 149,
    150, 388, 879, 886
Gould, T., 385
Gouldner, A. W., 755
Govan, C. L., 738
Gowaty, P. A., 280
Graber, J., 85, 518
Graburn, N. H. H., 661
Grace, R. C., 355
Grady, D. L., 918
Grady, J. M., 312
Grady, M., 971
Grafen, A., 73, 76, 77, 78, 448,
    451, 455, 476
Grafman, J., 612
Graham, C., 632
Graham, Y. P., 565
Grammer, K., 226, 266, 274,
    275, 306, 308, 309, 310,
    311, 312, 314, 316, 324,
    326, 327, 354, 355, 362,
    531
Granger, D. A., 679
Grant, V. E., 365
Grant, V. J., 276
Gravenstein, S., 905

Gravitt, P. E., 365
Gray, H., 36
Gray, J. A., 641
Gray, J. L., 303
Gray, J. P., 260, 263, 267
Gray, P., 79, 274, 312, 329, 354
Graziano, W. G., 262, 436, 494,
    691, 865
Green, B. L., 835, 837, 864
Green, C. A., 239
Green, D. J., 511
Green, D. M., 730
Green, S. M., 188
Greenberg, J., 758, 813, 867
Greendlinger, V., 397, 402
Greene, S. J., 260, 264, 397
Greenfield, J., 679
Greenwald, A. G., 807, 808,
    821
Greer, A. E., 267
Greiling, H., 243, 265, 266,
    271, 276, 299, 311, 313,
    348, 353, 375, 852, 868
Grey, D. W., 73
Grezes, J., 110
Grice, H. P., 740
Griffin, A. S., 208, 449
Griffin, D., 727
Griffiths, P. E., 879, 887, 888,
    907
Griffiths, R., 724
Griggs, R., 596, 599, 607
Grillon, C., 659
Grimes, K., 218
Grinde, B., 859
Gros-Louis, J., 314
Grossman, E. D., 108, 110
Grossman, R., 912
Grossman-Alexander, M., 190,
    193
Grote, N. K., 424
Groth, G., 266, 269, 806
Grotpeter, J. K., 691
Gruenewald, C., 104
Gruenewald, T. L., 493, 494,
    639, 691
Gruenfeld, D. H., 728
Gruenwald, T. L., 814
Grünert, M., 664, 665
Gruter, M., 270, 280, 966, 971,
    972
Guan, Z., 356
Guariglia, C., 183
Gubernick, D., 486, 562
Gubin, A. A., 728
Gueckel, F., 104
Guerrero, L. K., 433
Guild, D., 403
Guinness, F. E., 484
Gunnar, M., 564, 565, 644
Gunnell, D., 315
Gur, R. C., 188
Gurung, R. A. R., 493, 494,
    639, 814

Gurven, M., 75, 301, 304, 306, 459, 588
Guse, K. L., 208
Gut, E., 913
Güth, W., 636, 686
Guthrie, I. K., 639
Guthrie, P. R., 898
Guthrie, S., 205, 213
Gutierres, S. E., 814
Gutierrez, R., 275
Guttentag, M., 277, 497, 817
Guyre, P. M., 564
Gwyne, D. T., 73
Gwynne, S. T., 268, 269

Haas, J., 315
Habbema, J. D., 635
Habicht, J., 315
Hadley, C., 262
Haeger, G., 664, 665
Hagekull, B., 688
Hagel, R., 275, 311, 327, 355
Hageman, W. J. J. M., 639
Hagen, E., 158, 159, 239, 298, 308, 402, 467, 468, 913, 914
Hager, R., 483
Haidt, J., 48, 663, 766
Haig, D., 79, 137, 239, 347, 444, 465, 475, 515, 532, 631, 632
Haines, S. A., 677
Hains, S. M. J., 532
Hakeem, A., 75, 562
Halberstadt, A. G., 682
Halit, H., 553
Hall, B. K., 908
Hall, J. A., 682
Hall, K. R. L., 681
Hall-Craggs, E. C. B., 259
Hallett, D., 124
Halligan, S. L., 912
Halpern, D. F., 184
Hamai, M., 685
Hamburg, B. A., 913
Hamburg, D. A., 913
Hames, R., 259, 308, 459, 536
Hamilton, D. I., 763
Hamilton, D. L., 654
Hamilton, W. D., 8, 12, 29, 49, 59, 70, 77, 137, 166, 225, 226, 303, 308, 443, 447, 448, 449, 450, 451, 452, 457, 458, 507, 528, 531, 591, 592, 655, 684, 754, 755, 756, 760, 761, 763, 765, 813
Hammerstein, P., 152, 158, 159
Hampson, E., 184, 186, 187
Hampton, R. L., 633
Hancock, P. J. B., 318, 324
Haney, M., 642
Hankins, W. G., 127, 734
Hanna, C., 636
Hannett, C. A., 269, 280
Hansell, M. H., 449

Hansen, K. A., 321
Happ, D., 717
Happé, F., 108, 205, 212
Harcourt, A. H., 264, 267, 373, 374, 375, 376, 378, 380, 383, 386, 497, 498, 685
Hardaway, B., 663
Hardcastle, V. G., 159, 161, 163
Hare, A. P., 537
Hare, B., 656
Harkavy-Friedman, J., 918
Harkins, S., 813
Harlan, E. T., 641
Harlow, H., 516
Harnishfeger, K. K., 837
Harpending, H., 72, 85, 276, 279, 296, 403, 456, 483, 496, 513, 516, 555, 908
Harper, A. B., 453, 455
Harper, B. D., 680
Harpur, T. J., 872
Harrigan, A. M., 299, 317
Harrington, H., 914
Harris, C. R., 434, 469
Harris, G. T., 395, 396, 399, 403, 405, 406, 408, 409
Harris, J. R., 837, 838
Harris, P., 107, 108, 613, 614, 688, 840
Harris, R., 308
Harris, T. O., 913, 914
Harris, V. A., 728
Harrison, G. A., 571
Hart, A. J., 662
Hart, D., 748
Hart, F., 938
Hart, J., 644
Hartley, I. R., 226, 454, 456, 513
Hartmann, B., 315
Hartstone, M., 665
Hartung, J., 280, 450, 453, 472, 474
Harvey, J. H., 419
Harvey, O. J., 637, 666
Harvey, P. H., 73, 264, 267, 269, 373, 374, 375, 378, 453, 677
Hasegawa, M., 260, 266, 433, 914
Hasegawa, T., 260, 266, 267, 596, 914
Haselton, M., 51, 205, 213, 241, 242, 273, 357, 358, 359, 362, 401, 434, 663, 730, 731, 733, 735, 736, 738, 739, 805, 811, 886, 916, 959
Hasenstaub, A., 554
Hass, R. G., 663
Hassebrauck, M., 270
Hassell, M. P., 225
Hassen, P., 102
Hastie, R., 819
Hastorf, A. H., 663

Hatfield, E., 134, 270, 806, 816
Hatzipantelis, M., 186, 187
Hauser, L. B., 843
Hauser, M. D., 588, 700, 705, 706, 843, 844
Hausfater, G., 955
Hawkes, K., 81, 84, 295, 296, 299, 304, 334, 459, 475, 488, 535, 554, 555, 653, 837
Hawkes, R., 347
Hawkins, M., 938
Hawley, P. H., 837, 838, 839, 862
Haxby, J. V., 97, 98, 103, 104, 108
Hay, D. C., 97
Hayashi, N., 905
Hayes-Roth, B., 182
Haywood, M., 321
Hazan, C., 258, 259, 260, 261, 422, 517, 806
Heath, A. C., 493, 862
Heath, K. M., 262
Heavey, C., 403, 406, 407, 409, 494
Hebl, M. R., 190, 193
Hed, H. M. E., 420
Hedden, T., 537
Hede, A., 612
Hedges, L. V., 136
Heerwagen, J. H., 190, 240, 293
Heider, F., 205
Heim, C., 565
Heim, J.-L., 705
Heim, M., 408
Heine, B., 719
Heit, S., 565
Held, B., 308
Held, S., 229
Hell, W., 25
Hellawell, D., 97
Hellhammer, D. H., 564, 863
Helmboldt, A., 325
Helmers, K., 565
Helmond, F. A., 352
Heltman, K. R., 682
Hempel, C. G., 880
Hemsworth, P. H., 381
Henderson, V. K., 494
Hendrick, C., 866
Henning, K., 377
Henrich, J., 618, 659, 737, 738, 907
Henry, B., 641
Hensley, W. E., 315, 316
Henss, R., 321
Heptulla-Chatterjee, S., 110
Hepworth, C., 913
Herbert, T. B., 564
Herlihy, D., 488
Hernández Blasi, C., 829, 834
Herold, E. S., 377
Herre, E. A., 449
Herrero, R., 365

Herrnstein, R. J., 49
Herron, J. C., 486, 512
Herscovitch, P., 714
Hershberger, S. L., 537, 539
Hershey, T., 564
Hertsgaard, L., 565
Hertwig, R., 518, 519, 520, 729, 740, 782, 785, 787, 791, 792, 793, 795, 796
Hertzog, M. E., 325
Herzog, T., 193
Heslenfeld, D. J., 109
Hespos, S. J., 844
Hess, N. H., 298
Hess, S., 184
Hettema, J. M., 913
Heuthe, S., 325
Hewes, G. W., 714, 715
Hewitt, J. K., 862
Hewlett, B. S., 296, 301, 496, 818
Hey, J. D., 781
Heyligers, P. C., 192
Hickok, G., 717
Higashi, M., 454
Higgins, E. T., 767
Hildebrandt, K. A., 303
Hildesheim, A., 365
Hill, C. M., 509
Hill, E. A., 470
Hill, E. M., 631, 914
Hill, K., 25, 43, 71, 73, 80, 81, 82, 84, 86, 153, 228, 260, 261, 294, 295, 296, 299, 301, 304, 305, 306, 307, 312, 315, 317, 319, 320, 329, 330, 334, 347, 459, 488, 495, 497, 546, 554, 555, 571, 661, 690, 736, 758, 813, 814
Hillson, S., 310
Hilton, S. C., 181
Hilty, J. H., 655
Hinde, R. A., 270, 828, 919
Hines, D. A., 394
Hinsz, V. B., 309
Hiraishi, K., 596
Hiraiwa-Hasegawa, M., 267, 685
Hirschenhauser, K., 274, 362
Hirschfeld, L. A., 30, 96, 100, 797
Hirschi, T., 641
Hirsh-Pasek, K., 845
Hitchell, A., 274
Hockett, C. F., 706, 715, 718
Hodson, G., 666
Hof, P., 562
Hofer, B., 660, 662, 672, 735, 807, 808, 821
Hofer, M. A., 919
Hofferth, S., 136, 277, 510, 512
Hoffman, E., 609, 618, 619, 686, 958

Hoffman, E. A., 97, 98, 108
Hoffman, E. K., 656, 659
Hoffman, G. E., 185
Hoffman, H. A., 185
Hoffmann, K. P., 187
Hoffrage, U., 740, 778, 781, 782, 786, 787, 794, 795, 796
Hofstadter, R., 169
Hoge, P., 845
Hogg, M. A., 637, 638
Hogrefe, G. J., 840
Hohenberger, A., 717
Hohmann, N., 275, 363, 398
Hoier, S., 382, 383, 388
Hokanson, J. E., 680, 692
Holaday, J. W., 810
Holbrook, N. J., 564
Holcomb, H. R., 123
Hold-Cavell, B. C., 680
Holding, C. S., 186
Holding, D. H., 186
Holland, B., 344, 346, 373
Hollander, E., 914
Holldobbler, B., 182
Holliday, M. A., 74
Holliday, T. W., 556
Hollos, M., 688
Holloway, K. S., 736
Holm, J. E., 409
Holmes, W. G., 458
Holmstrom, L. L., 230
Holowka, S., 717
Holyoak, K., 592, 596, 604, 605, 606, 610, 611, 613, 620, 689
Homans, G. C., 533
Homer, A. L., 657
Honda, K., 705
Honeycutt, H., 829
Hong, G., 667
Hood, J., 642
Hood, W. R., 637, 666
Hoogland, J. L., 260, 555
Hook, E., 275
Hook-Costigan, M. A., 714
Hooper, G. H. S., 389
Hop, W. C., 352
Hopkins, F. W., 239
Horan, D. J., 467
Horgan, J., 169
Horn, J. L., 86
Horrobin, D. F., 906
Horton, T. H., 493
Horvarth, T., 325
Horwitz, A. V., 909
Horwood, J. L., 490
Hosaka, K., 685
Hosken, D. J., 373
Hotra, D., 262
Houle, D., 311, 347
Houser, D., 655
Houston, A. I., 78
Houts, A. C., 892
Howard, E. J., 378, 381

Howard, J. A., 816
Howard, R., 260, 411, 555
Howell, N., 296, 465
Howes, H. M., 680
Howes, P., 494
Howowitz, J., 686
Hoyle, R., 667
Hrdy, S. B., 232, 240, 264, 295, 296, 299, 302, 304, 326, 350, 375, 388, 422, 462, 511, 553, 554, 560, 631, 837, 907, 919, 955
Hrdy, S. H., 816, 817
Huang, C., 303
Huang, H., 532
Huber-McDonald, M., 736
Hubert, W., 863
Huberty, P. D., 845
Huesmann, L. R., 644
Huether, G., 572
Huffman, K. J., 553, 940, 942
Hug, K., 593, 596, 599, 600, 602, 609, 689
Hugdahl, K., 216
Huggins, G. R., 361
Hughes, C., 841
Hughes, K. A., 347
Hughes, S. M., 273, 324, 325
Huizinga, D., 642
Hull, D. L., 884
Hume, D. K., 313
Hummel, T., 354
Humphrey, N., 203, 209, 712, 833, 905, 917
Humphreys, G. W., 103
Hunt, G., 636
Hunt, M., 321, 377
Hunt, S., 724
Huntley-Fenner, G., 844
Hupka, R. B., 633
Hurford, J. R., 706, 713, 718, 719
Hurst, L. D., 347
Hurst, N. L., 536
Hurtado, A. M., 73, 80, 81, 82, 86, 228, 260, 261, 295, 296, 299, 301, 304, 305, 306, 307, 315, 317, 319, 320, 329, 330, 347, 488, 495, 497, 554, 555, 571, 690, 736, 813, 814
Husslein, P., 315
Huston, J. P., 186
Huston, T. L., 419
Huxley, T., 747
Huyser, C., 108
Hyde, J. S., 492
Hyson, M. C., 845

Ickes, W., 807
Ickovics, J. R., 679
Imada, S., 663
Immerman, R. S., 421
Impett, E., 409

Insel, T. R., 239, 422, 493, 552, 560, 561, 562
Insko, C., 667
Irons, W., 262, 443, 940, 941
Isaac, G., 201, 202, 589
Isaac, R. M., 659
Ittleson, W., 178
Ivanovici, A. M., 564
Ivy, L., 565
Izard, C. E., 658

Jablensky, A., 917
Jackendoff, R., 99, 112, 706, 709, 715
Jackson, L. A., 316
Jacob, S., 357
Jacobs, B. S., 519
Jacobs, L. F., 185
Jacobs, W. J., 869, 872
Jacobson, A., 338
Jacobson, K. C., 490
Jaffee, S. R., 642
Jahoda, G., 184
James, J., 262, 273
James, T. W., 186
James, W., 276, 785
Janicki, M., 519, 645, 758, 766
Jankowiak, W., 264, 419, 421, 460
Janoff-Bulman, R., 913
Janowsky, J. S., 184
Janson, C. H., 181
Jarrett, O. S., 845
Jarvik, L. F., 184, 917
Jarvinen, D. W., 635
Jarvis, C. I., 411
Jasienska, G., 299, 317, 330
Javed, M. H., 380, 381
Jeffery, L., 294
Jenkins, N., 385
Jenkins, V. Y., 295
Jennings, K. D., 239
Jennions, M., 73, 78, 348, 349, 365, 375
Jensen, P. S., 837, 918
Jensen-Campbell, L. A., 262, 436, 691, 865
Jensvold, N. G., 239
Jin, N., 665, 738
Job, R., 103
Jobling, I., 270, 935
Jöchle, W., 364
Jockin, V., 494
Joe Laidler, K., 636
Johannesson, M., 686
Johansson, G., 110, 206
Johansson, M., 108
John, O. P., 857, 858
Johnsen, M., 642
Johnson, A. M., 376
Johnson, D., 438, 656, 817
Johnson, E. J., 779, 781
Johnson, E. S., 184
Johnson, J. P., 276, 491

Johnson, M., 97, 100, 553, 617, 619, 710, 712, 837
Johnson, R. C., 182
Johnson, R. M., 78
Johnson, S., 107
Johnson, S. C., 205, 206
Johnson, S. E., 490
Johnson-Laird, P., 594, 613, 741
Johnston, L., 355
Johnston, V., 270, 275, 294, 311, 327, 355, 356, 542
Johnstone, R. A., 454, 455, 483
Johnstone, T., 108
Joireman, J., 655, 869, 870
Jones, B., 85, 309, 313, 355
Jones, D., 294, 312, 329, 330, 335, 451, 530, 545
Jones, D. M., 445
Jones, D. N., 867
Jones, E. E., 728
Jones, I., 845
Jones, O. D., 954, 955, 957, 960, 962, 966, 967, 969, 971, 972
Jones, P. R. M., 321
Jonides, J., 109
Joseph, R., 184
Josephson, S. C., 914
Joshi, M. S., 186
Jouannet, P., 378, 381
Jousilahti, P., 315
Judd, C. M., 662
Judge, D. S., 75, 462, 536
Juette, A., 306, 308, 309, 310, 316, 324, 326
Jungeberg, B. J., 317, 318, 322
Juslin, P., 789

Kacelnik, A., 453, 455
Kagan, J., 564, 565
Kahindo, M., 421
Kahlenberg, S. M., 79, 274, 354
Kahn, R. L., 489, 679
Kahneman, D., 23, 42, 542, 636, 727, 729, 740, 741, 789, 791, 793, 915, 957
Kaiser, M. K., 109
Kalakanis, L. E., 295
Kalat, J. W., 734
Kalick, S. M., 78
Kalin, N., 908
Kallai, J., 186
Kalma, A., 633, 634
Kaluzny, G., 404
Kameda, T., 819
Kamil, A. C., 181, 907
Kammer, T., 104
Kanazawa, S., 262, 538, 738
Kang, M., 464
Kano, T., 556
Kanwisher, N., 97
Kaplan, H., 25, 43, 72, 75, 76, 80, 81, 82, 86, 203, 217,

295, 296, 299, 301, 315, 320, 347, 420, 421, 459, 490, 491, 499, 512, 555, 661
Kaplan, R., 193
Kaplan, S., 190, 193, 235, 293
Kappeler, P. M., 555
Kapuku, G. K., 679
Kareev, Y., 788, 789
Karlberg, J., 239
Karlidag, T., 150
Karmiloff-Smith, A., 100, 111, 161, 617, 619, 710, 712
Karp, D., 665
Karter, A. J., 77
Kartovaara, L., 321
Kashy, D. A., 427
Kasperk, C., 325
Kassin, S. M., 803
Kastuk, D., 184
Katz, D., 629, 634
Katz, I., 663
Katz, L., 565, 908
Kaufman, L., 106
Kaufman-Gilliland, C. M., 657
Kaukiainen, A., 639
Kaygusuz, I., 150
Kazamatsuri, H., 905
Keating, C. F., 295, 327, 682
Keefe, R. C., 262, 270, 496, 635, 777, 809, 811, 821
Keegan, J., 653, 662, 664, 667
Keeley, L. H., 296
Keenan, T., 837
Keil, F., 43, 44, 47, 102, 622
Keir, R., 50, 51, 138, 208, 216, 217, 912
Keith, B., 421, 490, 494
Kelem, R. T., 656
Keller, L., 448, 459
Keller, M., 136, 277, 510, 866, 917
Kelley, H. H., 419, 425, 431
Kelly, D. W., 308
Kelly, K., 434
Kelly, R. L., 269, 280, 299, 300, 321
Kelly, R. W., 365
Kelly, S., 690
Keltner, D., 108, 728
Kemler Nelson, D. G., 102
Kempenaers, B., 485
Kendall-Tackett, K. A., 239
Kendell, R. E., 892
Kendler, K. S., 910, 913
Kenemans, J. L., 109
Kennedy, D., 872
Kennedy, G. E., 519
Kennedy, P., 405
Kennedy, S. J., 138
Kennedy, W., 104
Kenny, D. A., 130, 409, 464, 539

Kenrick, D. T., 137, 262, 266, 269, 270, 275, 397, 420, 423, 496, 530, 635, 638, 662, 672, 691, 730, 735, 777, 804, 805, 806, 807, 808, 809, 810, 811, 814, 815, 816, 817, 819, 820, 821, 858, 864, 865
Kerig, P. K., 494
Kermoian, R., 34
Kerr, N. L., 657
Keser, C., 656
Kesler/West, M. L., 108
Kesner, J. S., 352, 554
Kessler, K. L., 492, 518
Kessler, R., 904
Kessler, S., 664, 665
Ketelaar, T., 123, 640
Ketterson, E. D., 484, 487
Keverne, E. B., 632
Keyes, R., 316
Kibler, J., 55
Kidd, A., 218
Kidd, R., 218
Kiecolt-Glaser, J. K., 564, 862
Kiernan, K. E., 490
Kieser, J., 312
Kiessling, L., 905
Killeen, P. R., 705
Kilner, R., 455
Kilpatrick, D., 399
Kim, A. J., 561
Kim, D. M., 908
Kim, F., 518
Kimura, D., 184, 186, 188, 715
Kimura, M., 451
King, G. E., 138
King, J. E., 853, 854, 855, 856, 857, 858, 859, 860
King, L. A., 913
King, P., 661
King, S., 679
King, T., 186
Kingstone, A., 42, 107
Kinner, D. K., 905
Kipp, K., 639, 641
Kirby, K., 613
Kirby, S., 797
Kirchengast, S., 315
Kirchsteiger, G., 686
Kirk, K. M., 270, 274, 276
Kirk, S. A., 898
Kirkcaldy, B. D., 861
Kirkpatrick, L. A., 260, 266, 273, 279, 420, 423, 433, 517, 914, 919
Kirkwood, T. B. L., 71, 73, 86
Kirschbaum, C., 564
Kirshner, J., 488
Kirsner, B. R., 869
Kischka, U., 104
Kish, B. J., 462, 511
Kisilevsky, B. S., 532

Kitano, T., 712
Kitayama, S., 462, 463, 538, 539, 540, 541, 546, 804, 812
Kitcher, P., 887, 977
Kittok, R., 679
Kiyonari, T., 665, 738
Klahr, D., 872
Klatt, L., 844
Klaus, P., 399
Kleck, R., 663
Klein, D. F., 890, 892
Klein, L. C., 493, 494, 639, 691, 814
Klein, M., 908
Klein, R. E., 315
Klein, S., 42, 45, 783
Kleiter, G. D., 794
Klima, E., 715, 716, 717
Klindworth, H., 488, 489
Kling, M. A., 565
Klinger, E., 913
Klockeman, K., 936
Klopfer, P. H., 191
Kluender, K. R., 705
Knapp, P. K., 837, 918
Knauft, B. B., 546
Knetsch, J., 636
Knight, C., 706, 713, 718, 719
Knight, G. P., 639
Knight, J., 140
Knight, R., 397, 405, 406, 588, 604, 612
Knodel, J., 270
Knols, B. G. J., 308
Knopps, G., 239
Knott, C. D., 396
Knudsen, B., 513
Kobak, R., 517
Kobal, G., 354
Kobayashi, T., 299, 311, 691
Koch, C., 42
Koch, H. L., 522
Kochanska, G., 641
Koehler, N., 355
Koelling, R. A., 179, 617
Koenen, K. C., 276
Koenig, W. D., 185, 451
Kofinas, G. D., 380
Kohl, J. V., 531
Kohlberg, L., 748, 753, 762, 764, 766, 767
Kok, A., 109
Kok, J., 489
Kokko, H., 73, 78, 348, 365
Kolk, A. M., 639
Komorita, S. S., 655
Konner, M., 43, 64, 214, 293, 317, 335, 496, 915
Koole, S. L., 814
Koomen, W., 661
Koonin, L. M., 239
Koós, O., 107, 205, 206, 211
Koot, H. M., 635

Korbin, J., 642
Korchmaros, J. D., 464, 539
Koresh, Y., 461
Koriat, A., 783
Koritnik, D. R., 679
Korkel, J., 835
Korpelainen, H., 495
Koss, M. P., 403, 409
Kotovsky, L., 109
Kotrscha, K., 229
Koufopanou, V., 71
Koukourakis, K., 311, 325, 326
Kowalski, M., 912
Kowner, R., 312
Koyabashi, T., 353, 355, 358, 724
Koziel, S., 316
Kozlowski, J., 73, 75
Kraemer, G. W., 561
Kraft, M., 869, 870
Krage, M., 538, 682, 687
Kramer, D. L., 373
Kramer, S., 295
Krantzberg, G., 294
Krauss, S., 782
Krebs, D., 645, 730, 748, 749, 753, 755, 759, 761, 762, 764, 765, 766, 767, 768, 805, 808, 904
Krebs, J., 181, 448, 458, 486, 495, 907, 919
Krieger, H., 493
Krieger, M. J. B., 459
Kriegman, D., 908, 919, 920
Kring, A. M., 639
Krishnan, V. V., 454, 456
Kristiansen, A., 316
Krohn, M., 400
Kroll, N., 588, 604, 612
Krones, J., 270, 817
Krovitz, G. E., 557
Krueger, J. I., 741, 742, 789, 808
Krug, R., 352
Kruger, A. C., 107
Kruger, D., 270, 464, 539, 906
Krüger, L., 790
Kruschke, J. K., 127
Kruse, E., 489
Kruuk, H., 201, 219
Kryscio, R. J., 108
Kuban, M., 397, 408, 409
Kubie, J. L., 183
Kuh, D., 315
Kuhlman, D. M., 869, 870
Kuhn, J., 910
Kuhn, T., 937
Kuler, L., 315
Kumar, R., 554
Kummer, H., 683
Kunce, L., 517, 766
Kunugi, H., 905
Kupniewski, D., 531

Kurland, J. A., 450, 451, 453, 457, 458, 464, 465, 472, 475, 476
Kuroshima, H., 229
Kurzban, R., 6, 106, 618, 653, 655, 657, 659, 662, 666, 667, 668, 734, 807, 811
Kuse, A. R., 182
Kuteva, T., 719
Kutteh, W. H., 365
Kuzawa, C. W., 83, 84
Kwong, K. K., 104
Kwong, M. J., 435
Kyriakidou, C., 842

Labrie, Y., 354
Lachman, M. E., 489
Lachmann, M., 455
Lack, D., 72, 73
La Freniere, P., 680
Lagerspetz, K., 639
Lagesen, K., 311
LaGrange, T. C., 641
Lahelma, E., 315
Lai, C., 553, 711, 712
Laing, R. D., 453
Laird, J. D., 469
Laird, N. M., 905
Lalonde, F. J., 104
Lalumière, M. L., 260, 262, 273, 395, 396, 399, 403, 405, 406, 408, 409
Lamb, M., 502, 571
Lamb, R. J., 193
Lambert, E. W., 898
Lamey, T. C., 507
LaMunyon, C. W., 372, 373, 384
Lancaster, C. S., 492
Lancaster, J., 75
Lancaster, J. B., 80, 81, 82, 86, 280, 296, 347, 420, 421, 490, 491, 492, 499, 512, 919
Lancaster, J. J., 295, 299, 301, 320
Lanctot, R. B., 485
Landau, B., 183
Landau, V., 858, 859
Landauer, T. K., 783
Landolt, M. A., 273
Lane, J. D., 706
Lane, M., 315
Langhinrichsen-Rohling, J., 397
Langley, J. D., 912
Langlois, J. H., 78, 294, 295, 303, 312, 837
Lanting, F., 556
Lanzetta, J. T., 550
Laplanche, A., 378, 381
LaPolla, R., 709
Larsen, C. S., 307

Larsen, R., 136, 964, 965
Larsen, R. J., 266, 275, 298, 375, 433, 434, 469, 470, 817, 914
Larsen, R. R., 226
Larson, M. C., 565
Larson, S. G., 267, 373, 374, 375, 378
Lashley, K. S., 703
Lasseter, V. K., 917
Latané, B., 813, 819
Laub, J. H., 642
Lauer, M. T., 308
Laumann, E. O., 264, 275, 362, 376
Laumann, K., 190, 193
Lauritsen, J., 642
Lavie, N., 42
Law, I., 103
Lawton, C. A., 186, 187
Leakey, M. G., 556, 557
Leary, M. R., 106, 563, 653, 659, 662, 666, 667, 734, 812, 912
Leason, J., 188
Lebiere, C., 785
LeBlanc, G. J., 382, 388, 433
LeBlanc, S. A., 553, 554
Leck, K., 140, 267, 271, 273, 356
Leckman, J., 605
Ledgerwood, L., 905
LeDoux, J., 55, 215, 640, 942
Ledyard, J., 659
Lee, B. J., 508
Lee, K., 111, 273, 274, 294, 299, 309, 532
Lee, P. C., 498
Lee, R., 8, 11, 260, 263, 653
Lee, S.-H., 555, 557, 558
Leekam, S. R., 105, 108
Lees, S., 636
Leeton, J., 85
le Fabre-Thorpe, M., 208
Leger, D. W., 907
Legrenzi, M., 741
Legrenzi, P., 741
Lehmann, L., 458
Leibenberg, L., 81
Leibold, J. M., 404, 409
Leigh, S. R., 83, 554, 557
Leighton, A. H., 905
Leinster, S. J., 326
Leis, P. E., 688
Leitenberg, H., 377
Leiter J., 642
Lemerise, E. A., 680
Lenneberg, E., 7
Leonard, H., 905, 918
Leonard, K., 517
Lerma, M., 817
Leslie, A., 12, 26, 44, 45, 46, 62, 105, 109, 210, 841

Lessells, C. M., 71, 513
Leuninger, H., 717
Lev, M., 788, 789
Levav, J., 781
Levelt, W. J. M., 701, 702, 703
Levenson, M. R., 862
Leventhal, T., 642
Lever, J., 635
Levin, L., 267
Levin, R. J., 365
Levine, J., 571
Levinger, G., 419
Levinson, D., 397
Levi-Strauss, C., 303
Lewak, R. W., 866
Lewin, K., 806
Lewis, A., 654
Lewis, B., 464, 493, 494, 639, 691, 814
Lewis, C., 842
Lewis, J. M., 494
Lewis, M., 635
Lewis-Jones, D. I., 320, 360
Lewis-Reese, A. D., 561
Lewontin, R. C., 9, 10, 125, 149, 879
Leyden, J. J., 364
Li, F. F., 42
Li, H., 559, 560, 561
Li, N., 137, 270, 638, 655, 657, 804, 805, 809, 811, 814, 815, 816, 819, 820, 821
Liang, K. Y., 917
Liberman, A. M., 705, 715, 718
Lichtenstein, P., 182
Lichtenstein, S., 958
Lichtman, C. M., 837
Lickel, B., 654
Lickliter, R., 829, 830, 831
Liebenberg, L. W., 214, 215
Lieberman, D., 7, 28, 29, 30, 48, 303, 364, 533, 587
Lieberman, I., 788, 789
Lieberman, P., 705
Lief, H. I., 362
Lieu, T. A., 239
Lieven, E., 708
Lifjeld, J. T., 511
Lightcap, J. L., 464
Liles, L., 374
Lilienfeld, S. O., 858, 897
Lillo-Martin, D., 717
Lim, H. K., 433
Lim, M. M., 560, 562
Lim, S., 411
Lindberg, T., 317
Lindblom, B., 705
Lindsay, S. W., 308
Lindsey, S., 740, 795
Lindstrom, D. P., 521
Link, B. G., 662
Linklater, W. L., 510
Linn, M. C., 184

Linsenmeier, J. A., 270, 809, 814, 816, 821
Linville, P. W., 763
Linz, D., 403, 406, 407, 409
Lipinski, J. J., 490
Lipowicz, A., 315
Lipson, S. F., 79, 274, 332, 354
Lipton, J. E., 259
Lisak, D., 404
Little, A. C., 309, 312, 313, 355, 724
Little, B. R., 913
Littlefield, C. H., 461, 473
Littman, R. A., 644
Liu, F., 318, 319, 324
Liu, Y., 562
Lloyd, B. B., 260, 263, 269
Lloyd, D. G., 72
Lochman, J. E., 839
Lock, A., 713
Lockard, J. S., 919
Loeber, R., 641, 642, 643
Loevinger, J., 128
Lohr, B. A., 408, 409
Lohr, S. L., 964
London, O., 808
Long, B., 571
Long, J. D., 837
Long, P. J., 518
Lonstein, J. S., 631
Lonsway, K. A., 399
Looman, J., 405
López, A., 43
Lopreato, J., 930
Lorenz, K., 831
Lorhonen, H. J., 321
Losoya, S. H., 494, 499
Lotem, A., 484
Lotstra, F., 642
Lougheed, L. W., 514
Love, G. A., 935
Lovejoy, C. O., 489, 498, 556
Lovejoy, O., 260, 261, 269
Low, B., 258, 260, 261, 262, 263, 268, 269, 270, 277, 279, 308, 348, 483, 496, 499, 554, 631, 907, 941
Lowen, C. B., 555
Lowery, L., 662, 663
Lowie, R. H., 447
Lowy, M., 644
Loy, J. W., 319
Lubach, G. R., 565
Lucas, R., 270, 859
Luce, C., 464, 805, 812, 814
Luis, S., 321
Lukas, D., 498
Lum, K., 866
Lund, T., 612
Lunde, I., 905
Lundqvist, D., 228, 242
Lupien, S. J., 679
Luster, T., 490, 499
Lutter, C., 679

Luttrell, L., 589, 617
Lutz, C. A., 56
Luuthe, V., 354
Lycett, J., 538, 904, 942
Lydon, J., 493
Lykken, D. T., 182, 491, 494
Lynam, D., 641, 643
Lynn, M., 316
Lynn, R., 184
Lyons, M. J., 276
Lytton, H., 642

MacArthur, R. H., 73, 296, 868
Maccoby, E. E., 228
MacDonald, K., 276, 491, 493, 495, 853, 854, 873, 940, 941, 942
Mace, R., 329, 535
MacFadden, A., 188
MacGregor, G. R., 493
MacGregor, J. N., 788
Machado, C. A., 449
Machalek, R., 229
Macintyre, S., 260, 266, 315
MacKewn, A., 187
Mackey, W. C., 276, 421
Mackie, D. M., 658, 668
Macklin, R., 892
MacLean, M., 186
MacMurray, J. P., 276, 491
MacNair, M. R., 453, 454
MacNeilage, P. F., 703, 709, 710, 713, 714, 717
MacNeill, D., 716
Macrae, C. N., 355
Maeda, S., 705
Maestripieri, D., 510, 514, 552
Maggioncalda, A. N., 336
Magnie, M.-N., 104
Magnus, P., 182
Magnusson, J., 661
Magnusson, M. S., 274, 362
Maguigan, H., 243
Maguire, E. A., 182
Mahmoodi, S., 318, 324
Maier, S. F., 564, 571
Mailloux, D., 405
Main, M., 516
Maisey, D., 318, 324, 325
Major, B., 658
Malamuth, N., 270, 272, 280, 395, 397, 399, 401, 403, 404, 406, 407, 408, 409, 410, 413, 423, 424, 436, 919
Malaspina, D., 918
Maldjian, J. A., 188
Malinowski, B., 588
Maljkovic, V., 603
Mallidis, C., 378, 381
Malloy, M., 714
Mana, M. J., 872
Mandler, J., 43, 207

Maner, J., 137, 662, 672, 730, 735, 804, 805, 807, 808, 810, 812, 819, 821
Mangelsdorf, S., 564, 565
Manktelow, K., 595, 600, 604, 607, 610, 611, 613, 620, 621, 689
Mann, J., 302, 320, 326
Mann, V. A., 184
Manning, J. T., 274, 306, 310, 311, 319, 320, 325, 326, 360
Mansfield, E. M., 553
Marcus, G., 619
Maridaki-Kassotaki, K., 842
Marino, L., 858, 897
Marinón-Torres, M., 557
Markman, E., 43, 47, 622
Markman, H. J., 494
Markow, T. A., 373
Marks, I., 43, 50, 55, 236, 619, 912
Marks, S. A., 214
Markus, H., 810
Markwith, M., 662, 663
Marler, C. A., 552
Marlowe, F., 88, 301, 307, 312, 318, 321, 323, 329, 330, 347, 483, 488, 492, 496, 497, 536
Marlowe, F. M., 260, 262, 277
Marlowe, F. W., 218, 302, 324, 326
Marr, D., 783
Marschall, E. A., 89
Marshall, D. S., 815
Marshall, F., 201
Marshall, I. H., 234
Marshall, L., 584, 588
Marshall, W. L., 403, 405, 408, 414
Marti, B., 321
Martignon, L., 778, 781, 782
Martin, A., 103, 104
Martin, D. L., 296
Martin, J., 488
Martin, L. R., 495, 861
Martin, M., 386, 387
Martin, N. G., 270, 274, 276, 862
Martin, P. R., 908
Martin, R. D., 80, 264, 267, 557
Martorell, R., 315
Marty-Gonzalez, L. F., 89, 266, 362, 492
Masaki, S., 184
Mascie-Taylor, C. G. N., 866
Mashek, D., 559, 560, 561
Mashima, R., 538
Mason, J., 563, 564, 644
Masters, R., 971
Masuda, T., 229
Matarrese, M., 104
Mather, G., 206
Mather, K., 311

Mathes, E. W., 633
Matilsky, M., 381
Matson, P. L., 360
Matthews, D., 122, 125, 126, 127, 886
Mattingly, I. G., 705, 715, 718
Matz, D. C., 309
Mauck, R. A., 89
Maurer, A., 619
Mauss, M., 588
Maxson, S., 395
Maxwell, D. M., 845
May, K. A., 294
May, M., 564
May, R. M., 662
Mayes, L., 605
Maynard Smith, J., 8, 69, 76, 125, 166, 167, 269, 303, 458, 586, 591, 638, 751
Mayo, R., 538
Mayr, E., 125, 126
Mazur, A., 274, 315, 679, 810, 814
Mazurski, E. J., 138
McArthur, J. W., 317
McArthur, L., 310
McBurney, D., 186, 274, 470, 473, 474, 492, 904, 942
McCabe, K., 609, 618, 619, 656, 657, 659, 661, 686
McCabe, L. J., 467
McCabe, V., 302
McCann, S. J., 316
McCarthy, G., 108
McCarthy, K., 491
McCarthy, L. M., 465, 466, 508, 519
McCarthy, R., 103
McCaul, K., 679
McCauley, C. R., 663
McClain, P. W., 467
McClay, J., 488
McClearn, G. E., 182
McClelland, J., 617
McClintock, C. G., 655
McClintock, M. K., 357
McCollough, J., 354, 357, 361
McCollum, M. A., 556
McConnaughey, D. R., 352, 554
McConnell, A. R., 404, 409
McCracken, G. F., 513
McCrae, R. R., 869
McDade, T. W., 84
McDermott, J., 97
McDonough, L., 43, 207
McDougall, W., 803, 818
McEachron, D. L., 814
McElreath, R., 659
McEwen, B., 563, 571, 678, 679
McFadyen-Ketchum, S., 85, 137, 420, 491, 518
McGee, M. G., 184
McGhee, D. E., 808
McGinnis, J., 972

McGivern, R. F., 186
McGrath, J. A., 917
McGrath, J. E., 121, 133
McGregor, I. A., 535
McGue, M., 491, 494
McGuiness, D., 184, 186
McGuire, L., 862
McGuire, M., 270, 280, 460, 462, 473, 540, 631, 812, 817, 904, 909, 941, 971
McGuire, W. J., 805
McHenry, H. M., 556, 558
McInerney, S. C., 662
McIntyre, M. H., 274
McKay, R., 294
McKenna, P., 603
McKinney, M. L., 74, 84
McLain, D. K., 470, 472
McLaughlin, T., 75
McLennan, D. A., 872
McLeod, I., 85
McLoyd, V. C., 642
McManus, C., 321
McManus, S., 376
McMillan, G., 43, 301, 320
McNally, R. J., 786, 890
McNamara, J. M., 78
McNeilage, A., 261, 268
Mead, G. H., 767
Meade, A. C., 184
Mealey, L., 192, 258, 260, 263, 266, 268, 312, 394, 398, 538, 682, 687
Meaney, M., 561, 565, 679
Mechanic, M., 395
Meck, B., 111
Meck, W. H., 111, 184, 189
Mecklinger, A., 104
Medawar, P. B., 70
Medin, D., 43, 781
Medina, P., 275
Medlicott, L., 183
Mednick, S. A., 641
Medvin, M. B., 513
Meehl, P. E., 128, 131
Mehdikhani, M., 263
Meheus, A. Z., 421
Meindl, R. S., 556
Mellars, P., 942
Mellen, S. L. W., 419, 420
Mellers, B., 740
Mellott, D. S., 807, 821
Meloy, J. R., 435, 629
Meltzoff, A. N., 107, 108, 110, 207
Mendl, M., 229
Mendlewicz, J., 642
Mendoza, S. P., 857
Menken, J., 521
Menon, T., 538
Mentzer, S. J., 663
Menzel, C. R., 181
Menzies, R. G., 912
Mercer, C. H., 376

Meredith, H. V., 519
Merikangas, K. R., 659
Mesnick, S. L., 230
Messick, D. M., 546
Metcalf, R. A., 454, 456
Meuwissen, I., 352
Meyer, J. M., 276
Meyers, K., 642
Meyers, T. E., 302, 326
Mi, M. P., 182
Michael, R. T., 264, 275, 362, 376
Michaels, S., 264, 275, 362, 376
Michalski, R. L., 520
Michelon, P., 97
Michod, R. E., 451
Michotte, A., 106, 205
Miczek, K. A., 642
Mikach, S. M., 273, 324
Milgram, S., 753
Milinski, M., 531, 759
Mill, J., 488
Miller, A. G., 813
Miller, D. C., 639
Miller, G., 297, 853, 905, 906, 917, 939
Miller, G. A., 788
Miller, G. E., 913
Miller, G. F., 107, 205, 206, 212, 223, 262, 306, 357, 730, 761, 782, 905
Miller, G. T., 373
Miller, J. E., 308
Miller, J. H., 656
Miller, K. M., 865
Miller, L. C., 492, 495, 497, 499, 806
Miller, L. K., 186, 187
Miller, N., 639
Miller, P. A., 377
Miller, R., 140, 354, 357, 361, 434, 437, 817
Miller, W. R., 362
Millikan, R. G., 884
Mills, C., 914
Mills, J., 758
Milne, A. B., 355
Milne, B. J., 312
Milson, R., 783, 789
Milun, R., 186
Mineka, S., 50, 51, 55, 127, 137, 138, 154, 203, 205, 207, 208, 213, 215, 216, 217, 617, 734, 808, 912
Mintz, J., 905, 906, 917
Mio, Y., 381
Miozzo, M., 103
Mirescu, C., 572
Mirowsky, J., 409
Mischel, W., 851, 858
Mishkin, M., 714
Mitani, J., 314
Mitchell, J., 565
Mitchell, R. W., 763

Mitchell-Kernan, C., 633
Mithen, S., 106, 112, 202, 214, 304, 940, 942
Mittleman, B. B., 918
Miyagawa, I., 380, 381
Miyamoto, Y., 538
Mock, D. W., 452, 453, 485, 507
Moffat, S. D., 186, 187
Moffitt, T. E., 85, 276, 279, 488, 641, 642, 643, 914
Moghaddas, M., 508
Mohamed, F. B., 326
Molenaar, P. C. M., 109
Molho, A., 488
Møller, A. P., 259, 260, 261, 267, 306, 311, 338, 349, 350, 351, 353, 365, 372, 373, 374, 375, 484, 485, 486, 487, 554
Moltz, H., 192
Monacom, A. P., 711
Monahan, J., 972
Monclus, M., 642
Monroe, S. M., 914
Monson, C. M., 397
Monson, R. R., 905
Montgomerie, R., 313, 369, 509, 519
Montpare, J. M., 310
Moore, A. J., 484
Moore, C., 88, 104, 538
Moore, D. E., 421
Moore, H., 385, 386, 387
Moore, J., 119, 459
Moore, M. S., 892
Moore, T., 632
Mora, J. A., 373
Moracco, K. E., 244
Morales, V. Z., 239
Moran, T., 545
Morgan, C., 459
Morgan, R., 106, 692
Morhenn, M. G., 971, 972
Morley, C., 184
Morley, J., 78, 348, 365
Moro, J., 187
Morris, A., 321
Morris, J. S., 108
Morris, M. W., 538
Morris, R., 810
Morrisa, R. G. M., 182
Morrison, A. S., 488
Morrison, D. R., 490
Mortensen, P. B., 918
Morton, J., 97
Moscovici, S., 537
Moseley, W., 231
Mosher, M., 493
Moss, H. A., 519
Moss, H. E., 103
Moss, K., 104
Moulton, M. P., 470, 472
Mrazek, D., 837, 918
Mueller, A., 662, 737, 807

Mueller, T., 75, 260, 261
Mueller, U., 274, 276, 315
Muhleman, D., 276, 491
Muhuri, P. K., 521
Muir, D. W., 108, 688
Mukabana, W. R., 308
Mullally, P. R., 520
Mullen, P. E., 429
Muller, H., 89, 266, 368, 492
Muller, R. U., 183
Mummendey, A., 664, 665
Munck, A., 563, 564
Mundy, N. I., 259
Munroe, R. H., 185
Munroe, R. L., 185
Murakami, M., 303
Murdock, G. P., 259, 260, 262, 263, 348, 447, 554, 716
Murnen, S., 404
Murphy, D., 909
Murphy, F. K., 421
Murphy, J. M., 905
Murray, D., 97
Murray, K. T., 641
Murray, L. K., 299, 311, 353, 355, 358, 691, 724
Murray, M. G., 449
Murray, S. L., 429
Muruth, P., 677
Musonda, R., 421
Musselman, L., 294, 295, 312
Mustaine, E. E., 400
Myers, D. G., 422
Myers, O. E., 218
Myers, T., 326, 471, 534, 535, 537
Myers, W. A., 377

Nachmias, M., 564, 565
Nádasdy, Z., 205
Nadeau, J., 317
Nadel, L., 183
Nadler, R. D., 396
Naeye, R., 275
Nagell, K., 107
Nagin, D., 641
Naito, M., 842
Nakamura, R. R., 448
Nakao, K., 813
Nakatsuru, K., 373
Nanko, S., 905
Narasimha, M., 632
Nash, S. C., 494
Naughton-Treves, L., 201, 218
Navalta, C. P., 908
Navarrete, C. D., 364
Neale, M. C., 493, 862
Neander, K., 885
Needham, A., 109
Needles, D. J., 641
Neel, J. V., 266, 904
Neff, B. D., 485
Nell, D., 264
Nelligan, J., 517

Nelson, A. J., 557
Nelson, C. A., 97
Nelson, D. A., 402, 408
Nelson, K., 837
Nelson, R. K., 215
Nemeroff, C., 662, 663
Nerlove, S. B., 185
Ness, A., 315
Nesse, M., 934
Nesse, N., 970
Nesse, R., 136, 239, 277, 293, 424, 467, 470, 510, 657, 726, 731, 734, 756, 757, 890, 904, 906, 908, 909, 912, 913, 914, 917
Nestadt, G., 917
Nettle, D., 262, 315, 316, 730, 731, 733, 738, 739, 913, 935, 936
Neuberg, S., 270, 464, 655, 657, 658, 659, 660, 663, 666, 669, 729, 735, 805, 807, 811, 812, 817
Neuhoff, J. G., 206, 731, 734
Neville, H. J., 717
New, J., 42, 208
Newcomb, T. M., 530
Newcombe, N., 186
Newcomer, J. W., 564
Newell, B. R., 781
Newitt, C., 755
Newlin, D. B., 914
Newman, A. J., 717
Newman, J. P., 641, 814
Newmayer, F., 719
Newport, D. J., 565
Newport, E. L., 796, 842
Newport, F., 663
Newton, T. L., 679
Ngunen, N. Q., 565
Niarchos, C., 400
Nicastle, L. D., 807
Nicholls, J. G., 635
Nichols, S., 107
Nicholson, A. J., 225
Nicolás, M. E., 557
Niehoff, D., 678, 679
Nielsen, J. A., 218
Niemann, T., 187
Nieminen, G. S., 872
Nieschlag, E., 863
Niethard, F., 325
Nieto, J., 604
Nigam, A., 862
Nijokiktjien, C., 108
Nilsen, R., 493
Nimchinsky, E., 562
Nisbett, R., 596, 620, 729
Nishijo, H., 182
Nixon, C. L., 841
Nixon, M. S., 310
Noel, J. M., 839
Nolan, V., Jr., 484, 487
Noller, P., 517

Noonan, K., 260, 268, 269, 349, 554, 555
Nordlund, M., 935
Norenzayan, A., 729
Norgan, N. G., 321
Norris, K. J., 724
Nosek, B. A., 807, 821
Novak, S., 643
Novgorodoff, B. D., 866
Nowak, A., 819
Nowak, M. A., 656, 757, 759
Nucci, L. P., 688
Nunez, J., 275
Núñez, M., 275, 613, 614, 688
Nunn, C. L., 350
Nunney, L., 448, 457
Nurnberg, P., 510
Nyberg, L., 101
Nyborg, H., 184

Oaksford, M., 613, 741
Ober, C., 357
O'Brien, C. E., 682
O'Brien, C. P., 362
O'Connell, J. F., 295, 296, 299, 304, 334, 347, 459, 475, 488, 535, 555, 837
Oda, R., 538
O'Day, D. H., 561
Ofshe, R., 537, 813
O'Hara, E., 972
O'Hearn, K., 206
Öhman, A., 127, 137, 138, 154, 203, 205, 207, 213, 215, 216, 228, 242, 640, 808
Okagaki, L., 490, 499
O'Keefe, J., 182, 183
Olazabal, D. E., 560, 562
Olinger, E., 872
Oliveau, D., 138
Oliver, L., 596, 620
Oliver, M. B., 492
Oliver, P., 660
Oliver-Rodriguez, J. C., 356
Ollinger, J. M., 107
Olshansky, E., 187
Olson, J. E., 316
Olsson, H., 789
O'Malley, B., 493
O'Malley, S. L. C., 485
Ono, H., 663
Ono, T., 182
Opfer, J. E., 205
Oppenheim, R. W., 835
Oppliger, A., 488
Orbell, J. M., 544, 737, 805
Orians, G. H., 190, 240, 259, 261, 293
Oring, L. W., 259, 261
O'Rourke, M. T., 332
Orr, H. A., 148, 590, 617
Orr, S., 55
Orwoll, E. S., 184
Orzack, S. E., 879

O'Shea, E. K., 158
Osherow, N., 753
Oskamp, S., 316, 809, 816
Osorio-Beristain, M., 511
Ostry, D., 717
Ott, J., 89, 266, 368, 492
Otten, W., 655
Otto, P., 781
Oubaid, V., 260, 266
Over, D., 604, 607, 610, 611, 613, 620, 621, 689
Over, R., 352
Overpeck, M. D., 467, 468, 508
Overton, W. F., 186
Oviatt, S. K., 184
Owen, M. T., 494
Owens, I. P. F., 484, 485
Owens, S., 43, 218
Oyama, S., 830
Ozarow, B. J., 912

Pachot-Clouard, M., 107, 108, 110
Packer, C., 386, 512, 813
Paepke, A. J., 357, 531
Paffenberg, R. S., 467
Page, M. C., 639
Pagel, M., 350, 351, 470
Pager, D., 662, 737
Painter-Brick, C., 332
Palameta, B., 538
Palermiti, A., 518
Paley, W., 148
Palmer, A. C., 311
Palmer, C., 224, 231, 272, 280, 359, 363, 397, 399, 400, 401, 405, 529
Palmer, J. A., 942
Palmer, L. K., 942
Palmonari, A., 635
Panchanathan, K., 656
Panksepp, J., 159, 640, 811, 942
Pansky, A., 783
Panyavin, I. S., 302, 326, 471, 534, 537
Papinczak, T. A., 239
Parasuraman, R., 104
Parisi, D., 617, 619, 710, 712
Park, B., 662
Park, J. H., 659, 662, 663, 666, 734, 737, 807
Parke, R. D., 490, 491, 494
Parker, G., 69, 72, 73, 76, 125, 226, 269, 372, 373, 378, 379, 395, 452, 453, 454, 456, 507, 513
Parker, P. E., 679
Parker, P. G., 89
Parker, S. T., 74, 84
Parkin, L., 842
Parks, C. D., 655
Parritz, R. H., 564, 565
Parsons, R., 190, 193
Parsons, S., 295

Partch, J. J., 814
Partridge, L., 448, 453, 457
Parvez, R. A., 260, 267, 383
Pascalis, O., 97
Pashos, A., 474
Pasko, S. J., 866
Passingham, R., 711
Pasternak, B., 258, 260, 263, 264
Patamasucon, P., 421
Patience, R. A., 309
Patterson, C. M., 641
Patterson, G. R., 644
Pattini, P., 187
Patton, J. Q., 304, 305, 306, 315, 319, 328, 655
Paul, A., 266
Paul, L., 633
Paul, S. M., 564
Paulhus, D. L., 521, 919
Paulson, O. B., 103
Pawlowski, B., 298, 315, 316, 351, 554, 555
Payne, G. C., 692
Payne, J. W., 779, 781
Peake, P. K., 858
Pearce, J., 906
Pearlin, L. I., 565
Pearson, J., 517
Peckarsky, B. L., 207
Pedersen, F. A., 277, 278, 497
Pederson, N. L., 182
Pellegrini, A. D., 516, 532, 553, 555, 829, 835, 837, 839, 845
Pelletier, L. A., 377
Pellowski, M., 659
Pen, I. I., 449
Penner, L. A., 657
Pennington, R., 72, 513
Penton, M. A., 207
Penton-Voak, I. S., 273, 274, 275, 299, 309, 311, 312, 313, 326, 338, 353, 355, 358, 691, 724
Perani, D., 104
Pereyra, L., 604
Peris, C., 862
Perkins, C., 399
Perkins, L., 860
Perlman, J. L., 663
Perner, J., 105, 108, 840, 842
Peron, E. M., 193
Perona, P., 42
Perper, T., 134
Perreault, S., 666
Perrett, D. I., 273, 274, 275, 294, 299, 309, 311, 312, 313, 326, 353, 355, 358, 691, 724
Perrin, N., 458
Perrone, M., Jr., 484, 485, 487, 498
Perry, B., 644
Perry, R. P., 661

Persky, H., 362
Person, E. S., 377
Persson, B., 686
Perusse, D., 226, 228, 260, 262, 491, 493, 690
Perusse, R., 843
Peters, C. R., 713
Peters, J., 435, 572
Peters, M., 355
Peterson, A. C., 184
Peterson, C., 495
Peterson, D., 232, 240, 396, 397, 553, 554, 556, 637
Peterson, L., 657
Petralia, S. M., 364, 398
Petrie, M., 348, 349, 375
Petrie, R., 656
Pettigrew, T. F., 188
Pettijohn, T. F., 317, 318, 322
Pettit, G., 85, 137, 232, 420, 490, 491, 518, 642
Pettito, L. A., 717
Petty, R., 188
Pfeffer, C., 837, 918
Phelps, E., 44
Phil, C., 863
Philipp, E. E., 266
Phillips, A. T., 107
Phillips, B., 227
Phillips, K., 184, 186, 188, 837, 909
Piaget, J., 109, 622, 748, 753, 755
Pickar, D., 564
Pickersgill, M. J., 639
Pickup, L. J., 310, 320
Pierce, C. A., 262
Piero, A., 862
Pietinen, P., 321
Pietrowsky, R., 352
Pietrzak, R. H., 469
Pike, C. L., 270, 312
Pilhower, C. L., 294, 327
Piliavin, J. A., 657
Pillsworth, E. G., 358
Pincus, H. A., 909
Pinel, P., 111
Pines, A. M., 633
Pinker, S., 5, 6, 7, 18, 26, 33, 99, 127, 137, 166, 167, 171, 232, 294, 307, 401, 445, 553, 587, 617, 698, 699, 705, 707, 710, 711, 811, 837, 840, 939, 942, 965
Pinkley, R., 667
Pinto, J., 206
Pirolli, P. L., 778
Pi-Sunyer, X., 315
Pitchford, I., 904
Pitman, R., 55, 912
Pitnick, S., 373
Piven, J., 108
Pizzamiglio, L., 183
Pizzari, T., 360

Platek, S. M., 302, 326, 471, 534, 535, 537
Platt, J. R., 851
Platt, R., 596, 599, 607
Plavcan, J. M., 555, 556
Pleass, R. J., 308
Pleck, J., 490, 571
Plihal, W., 352
Plomin, R., 182, 643
Plon, M., 537
Plunkett, K., 617, 619, 710, 712
Plutchik, R., 470, 658, 811, 907, 908
Pohl, R. F., 786
Poizner, H., 717
Polcari, A., 908
Polizzi, P., 44, 45, 105
Pollard, J. S., 294
Pollard, R., 644
Pomerleau, C. S., 915
Pomiankowski, A., 306
Ponte, E., 459
Pontier, D., 262, 320
Popper, S., 239
Poran, N. S., 208
Poremba, A., 714
Porter, F. L., 565
Porter, R. H., 302, 459, 762
Porter, T., 790
Porteus, S. D., 184
Portman, A., 557
Posavac, E. J., 866
Posner, M., 42, 101
Post, J. D., 491
Potthoff, R. F., 492
Pottick, K. J., 898
Potts, R., 202, 940
Poulin-Dubois, D., 205
Poulton, R., 312, 912
Pound, N., 224, 267, 380, 381, 385, 389
Povinelli, D. J., 105, 107, 109
Powell, M., 192
Pratt, A. E., 470, 472
Pratt, T. C., 641
Pratto, E., 691
Pratto, F., 228, 643, 662, 667, 668, 682
Premack, D., 685, 840
Prentice-Dunn, S., 656
Prentky, R. A., 405, 406
Prescott, C. A., 910, 913
Preston, D., 405
Preti, G., 361, 364
Preuss, T. M., 105
Price, C. J., 104
Price, G. R., 166
Price, J., 904, 905, 913
Price, J. H., 377
Price, J. M., 814
Price, M., 308, 587, 738, 767
Price, T. D., 484
Price, V., 138, 912
Price M., 660

Priftis, K., 111
Printz, H., 564
Prior, J. C., 315
Probst, T., 187
Profet, M., 837
Proffitt, F., 312
Promislow, D. E. L., 73
Pryor, J. B., 404
Przeworski, M., 712
Puce, A., 108
Pucet, B., 182
Pugesek, B. H., 508, 519
Pulver, A. E., 917
Purcell, A. T., 193
Purvis, A., 374
Pusey, A., 334, 386, 512
Puska, P., 315
Putman, F., 518
Putnam, H., 889
Putz, D. A., 274, 275
Puy, L., 354

Quartz, S., 619
Quay, H. C., 641
Queller, D. C., 448, 459
Quillian, L., 662, 737
Quinlan, R., 276, 279, 570
Quinn, N., 269
Quinn, P. C., 97, 207
Quinsey, V. L., 260, 262, 273, 395, 396, 399, 403, 405, 406, 408, 409
Quinton, R. L., 493, 559
Quintus, B. J., 384
Quirk, G. J., 912
Qvarnström, A., 484

Rabbie, J. M., 665
Rabkin, E. S., 937
Racine, T. P., 766
Radinsky, L. B., 714
Radley, S., 318
Radman, P., 294
Rahkonen, O., 315
Raichle, M. E., 101
Raine, A., 641, 644
Rainer, G., 553
Raines, D. M., 326
Rainey, R. C., 180
Rakison, D. H., 205
Rakover, S. S., 129
Ramírez Rossi, F., 557
Ramson, W. S., 692
Ramsoy, T., 612
Ranck, J. B., 183
Ranganath, C., 553
Rapee, R. M., 138
Rapoport, A., 781
Rapoport, J. L., 918
Räsänen, K., 485
Raser, J. M., 158
Rasmussen, D. R., 817
Ratner, H. H., 107
Rattermann, M. J., 102

Rauch, S. L., 662
Rausher, M. D., 401
Rawls, J., 750
Ray, J., 678
Ray, O. S., 184
Raymond, M., 262, 320
Raymond, P., 404
Read, A., 315
Read, S. J., 819
Reagan, J., 373
Real, L. A., 792, 793
Reaven, N., 657
Reed, D., 324
Reeder, G. D., 538
Reeve, H. K., 448, 752
Reeves, K., 808
Regalski, J., 472, 511, 534
Regan, D. T., 538
Regan, P. C., 266, 267, 274, 352
Reiber, C., 186
Reid, A., 420, 489
Reid, D., 557
Reid, I., 489
Reierson, G. W., 355
Reilly, J., 186
Reinhardt, S., 318
Reinish, J., 184
Reis, H. T., 655
Reise, S. P., 269
Reiser-Danner, L. A., 295
Reiss, D., 491, 499
Rejeski, W. J., 679
Ren, X., 560, 562
Renninger, L., 275
Reno, P. L., 556
Repetti, R. L., 644
Repp, A. C., 872
Repton, H., 191
Rescorla, L., 845
Resick, P., 395
Resnick, J. S., 565
Resnick, K. D., 399
Rest, J. F., 750
Reynolds, J. D., 269, 483
Reynolds, V., 280
Rhee, S. H., 232
Rhine, R. J., 858
Rhodes, G., 294, 295, 312, 328, 355
Rhodes, W., 517
Ricci, R., 187
Rice, M. E., 395, 396, 399, 403, 405, 406, 408, 409
Rice, W. R., 73, 344, 345, 346, 363, 389
Richards, A., 102, 314
Richards, D. D., 102
Richards, R. L., 905
Richerson, P., 151, 161, 217, 237, 638, 653, 655, 656, 657, 660, 663, 765, 766, 767, 940
Richner, H., 488
Rick, J., 914

Ridley, M., 274, 297, 712, 718, 756, 765, 910, 941
Riebling, B., 933
Rieskamp, J., 781
Rietschel, R. L., 308
Rigatuso, J., 565
Rigdon, M., 661
Rijkers, G. T., 173
Rikowski, A., 266, 275, 312, 314, 354
Rips, L., 26, 42, 603, 605, 613
Riss, D. C., 685
Ristau, C., 208, 218
Ritter, J. M., 295, 303, 837
Rivas, F., 89, 266, 362, 492
Rivera, J., 315
Rizzolatti, G., 713, 714, 715
Ro, T., 42
Robarchek, C. A., 637
Robarchek, C. J., 637
Robbins, C., 276, 510, 818
Robbins, M. M., 498
Robert, M., 185, 186, 189
Roberts, R., 270
Roberts, S. B., 315
Robertson, L. D., 193
Robertson, R. G., 182
Robertson, R. J., 485
Robertson, S. A., 364, 365
Robertson, T., 662, 735, 807
Robins, P. K., 490
Robles, T. F., 862
Robson, A., 75, 76, 203, 217
Rochat, P., 106, 844
Rodd, Z. A., 261
Rode, C., 25
Rodgers, W. H., Jr., 972
Rodin, J., 692
Rodríguez, J., 557
Rodríguez-Gironés, M. A., 350, 453, 455
Rodriguez Mosquera, P. M., 634
Rodriguez-Rigau, L. J., 308
Roff, D. A., 71
Rogers, A., 475
Rogers, L. J., 714
Rogers, R. W., 656
Rogers, S. J., 633
Roggman, L. A., 294, 295, 312, 837
Rohner, R. P., 554
Rohwer, S., 486, 512
Rokach, A., 377
Rokeach, M., 663
Roldán, E. R. S., 373, 375, 376, 378, 380, 383
Rollet, C., 489
Rolls, E. T., 182
Rombouts, H., 861
Romer, P., 619
Romero, L. M., 563
Roney, J. R., 135
Rosado, A., 373

Rosales, A. M., 373
Rosas, A., 557
Rosch, E. H., 797
Rose, H., 171
Rose, J. C., 307
Rose, L., 201
Rose, M. R., 71
Rose, R. M., 810
Rose, S., 171
Roseman, I. J., 658
Rosen, B. R., 104
Rosen, L. A., 918
Rosenbaum, M. E., 530
Rosenberg, J. S., 833
Rosenberg, K., 315, 557
Rosenblatt, A., 867
Rosenblatt, J. S., 552
Rosin, A., 554
Ross, D., 485
Ross, E. A., 818, 819
Ross, K. G., 459
Ross, L., 728
Ross, S., 239
Rossano, M. J., 942
Roth, A., 659, 781
Roth, D. L., 861
Roth, S., 404
Rothbart, M., 641, 654
Rousett, I., 713, 714
Routh, D. K., 663
Rovagno, L., 187
Rovine, M., 494
Rowe, D. C., 276, 490, 494, 499, 868, 869
Rowland, D. A., 273, 274, 299, 309
Rowland, D. L., 352
Royle, M. J., 226
Royle, N. J., 454, 456, 513
Rozin, P., 662, 663, 734
Rubchinsky, K., 464
Rubenstein, A. J., 294, 295
Ruberto, C., 380, 381
Rubin, P. H., 930
Ruble, D., 493
Rudman, L. A., 807, 821
Rudski, J. M., 738
Rue, L. D., 919
Ruel, M., 315
Ruff, C. B., 556, 557
Ruffman, T., 108, 842
Ruhl, J. B., 972
Rumelhart, D., 617
Runkel, P. J., 121, 133
Runzal, G., 306, 308, 309, 310, 316, 324, 326
Rusbult, C. E., 425, 428, 431, 438, 817
Ruscher, J. B., 667
Rusconi, M. L., 187
Ruse, M., 892, 916
Rushton, J. P., 458, 461, 473, 530, 761, 865, 869
Rushworth, M. F., 111

Rusiniak, K. W., 127, 734
Russell, C., 42
Russell, J., 316
Russell, R. J. H., 458
Russell, R. P., 104
Russon, A. E., 680
Rutherford, M., 613, 841
Rutter, M., 641, 908, 910
Ryalls, B. O., 186
Ryan, R. M., 861

Saad, G., 930
Sabbagh, M. A., 841
Sabini, J., 728
Sacchett, C., 103
Sacher, G. A., 75
Sacks, J. J., 467
Sadalla, E. K., 262, 266, 269,
    691, 777, 806, 810, 811,
    816, 865
Saengtienchai, C., 270
Sagarin, B. J., 805, 812
Sager, K., 464
Sahlins, M., 6, 459
Sailer, L. D., 267
Saito, K., 905
Sakai, R. R., 679
Sakuma, N., 184
Salapatek, P., 240
Sally, D., 737
Salmon, C., 280, 445, 447, 448,
    457, 459, 460, 465, 476,
    508, 519, 520, 655, 804,
    813, 935
Salomaa, V., 321
Salovey, P., 61, 433, 434, 692,
    763
Salvadori, C., 377
Salzinger, S., 642
Sampson, R., 633, 642
Samuels, C. A., 295
Samuelson, P. A., 658
Sancho, M., 275
Sanday, P. R., 397
Sandler, W., 717
San Giovanni, J. P., 295
Santoni, V., 186, 187
Saphier, D., 565
Sapolsky, R. M., 86, 336, 563,
    564, 565, 571, 678
Saraiya, M., 239
Sarich, V. M., 556, 906, 917
Sarmiento Pérez, S., 557
Sarriev, A., 565
Sartori, G., 103
Sarty, M., 688
Sasanuma, S., 184
Sasse, G., 89, 266, 368, 492
Satorius, N., 917
Saucier, D. M., 188
Saudino, K. J., 394
Sauer, K., 396
Saunders, B., 399
Saunders, R. E., 714

Saunders, S., 184
Savage, L. J., 618
Savalli, U. M., 484
Save, E., 182
Savin, N., 686
Savitsky, K., 738
Sawin, D. B., 303
Saylor, M. M., 106, 107
Scalise Sugiyama, M., 295,
    304, 305, 306, 328
Scarr, S., 240, 491
Schacter, D., 42, 44, 785, 786
Schaefer, C. A., 905
Schafer, W. D., 639
Schaffer, W. M., 70, 296
Schaie, K. W., 184
Schaller, M., 121, 123, 124,
    137, 658, 659, 662, 663,
    666, 669, 734, 737, 804,
    807, 819
Schank, J. C., 350
Scheib, J. E., 312, 313, 316
Scheier, M. F., 913
Schelling, T. C., 657
Scheper-Hughes, N., 571
Scherer, K. R., 108
Scherg, H., 862
Scheyd, G., 140, 354, 357, 361
Schiavone, F. E., 308
Schiff, W., 206
Schiffer, S., 778
Schiffman, M., 365
Schjelderup-Ebbe, T., 169
Schlegel, A., 264
Schloerscheidt, A. M., 355
Schlottman, A., 106
Schlottmann, A., 106
Schmitt, D., 227, 229, 252, 258,
    260, 262, 264, 265, 266,
    267, 268, 269, 270, 271,
    272, 273, 274, 275, 277,
    278, 279, 296, 298, 299,
    301, 311, 313, 315, 316,
    320, 326, 327, 348, 375,
    383, 394, 423, 426, 435,
    493, 635, 815, 919
Schmittberger, R., 636
Schmitz, S., 186, 187
Schneider, J. S., 493
Schneider, M. L., 565
Schneider, W., 835
Schoener, T. W., 458
Scholl, B., 109, 205
Scholnick, E. K., 183
Schooler, J., 786
Schooler, L., 784, 785
Schopler, J., 667
Schot, J. C., 665
Schowalter, J., 918
Schrenk, F., 557
Schroeder, D. A., 657
Schuck, S., 918
Schul, Y., 538
Schultz, A. H., 259

Schultz, H., 420, 488
Schulz, K., 187, 421
Schwabl, H., 452
Schwalter, J., 837
Schwartz, D., 378, 381
Schwartz, G. T., 557
Schwartz, J. E., 495, 861
Schwartz, J. L. K., 808
Schwartz, P., 816
Schwarze, B., 636
Schwebel, A. I., 869
Schweppe, K., 315
Scutt, D., 320, 326, 360
Seabrook, L., 517
Seal, D. W., 269, 280
Seale, D. A., 781
Seaman, G., 554
Sear, R., 329
Searle, J. R., 889
Sears, D. O., 131
Sears, L., 108
Sears, R., 535
Seckl, J. R., 572
Secord, P., 277, 497, 817
Sedgwick, P., 892
Sedikides, C., 739, 811
Seebeck, T., 357, 531
Seeman, T. E., 644
Sefcek, J., 867, 869
Sefton, M., 686
Segal, N., 182, 460, 537, 539,
    940
Segerstrale, U., 166, 976
Seidell, J. C., 635
Sejnowski, T., 619
Seligman, M. E. P., 207, 495,
    734
Selman, R. L., 767
Selten, R., 23, 47, 619
Semmelroth, J., 226, 266, 298,
    375, 433, 434, 469, 470,
    817, 914, 964, 965
Senchak, M., 517
Sengco, J. A., 97
Sergio, L. E., 717
Serin, R., 405
Servan-Schreiber, D., 564
Sethi, A. S., 866
Seto, M. C., 260, 262, 273, 397,
    405, 408, 409
Setters, D., 470, 472
Seyfarth, R., 8, 204, 218, 682,
    685
Seyle, H., 563
Seymour, A., 399
Seyyedi, S., 104
Sgoutas, D., 308
Shachat, J., 656
Shachat, K., 686
Shackelford, T. K., 136, 224,
    227, 229, 260, 266, 268,
    271, 275, 320, 362, 382,
    383, 384, 388, 400, 401,
    423, 426, 428, 433, 434,

435, 436, 520, 633, 758,
    845, 886, 914, 964
Shafir, S., 793
Shaikh, M. A., 380, 381
Shalev, E., 381
Shallice, T., 612
Shaner, A., 905, 906, 917
Shanks, D. R., 781
Shanley, D. P., 73
Shannon, C. E., 8
Shapiro, D., 741
Shapiro, J., 660
Sharma, S., 572
Shattuck-Hufnagel, S., 703,
    717
Shaver, P., 422, 517, 806, 869
Shavit, Y., 461
Shea, B. T., 83
Sheehan, P. Q., 189
Sheets, V., 397
Sheldon, B. C., 136, 485
Shelley-Tremblay, J. F., 918
Shelly, G., 679
Shelton, J., 42, 43, 103
Shepard, G. H., 307, 318, 321,
    323
Shepard, R. N., 23
Shephard, R. J., 861
Shepher, J., 303, 533
Sherak, B., 295
Sheridan, J., 103
Sheridan, M. A., 107
Sherif, C., 637, 666
Sherif, M., 637, 666
Sherman, M. E., 365
Sherman, P. W., 260, 458, 484,
    485, 487, 555, 813
Sherman, S. J., 654
Sherry, D., 42, 44, 185
Sherwin, B. B., 274
Shetler, S., 680
Shiffrar, M., 110
Shiffrin, R. M., 787
Shimona, E., 538
Shin, L. M., 662
Shine, R., 227
Shinothuka, H., 665
Shipman, P., 201, 202
Shirtcliff, E. A., 679
Shors, T. J., 564
Short, R. V., 267, 373, 374, 375,
    378, 383
Shostak, M., 11, 64, 293, 584,
    588, 915
Shurgot, B. A., 316
Shuster, S. M., 259
Shwartz, M., 151
Sidanius, J., 662, 667, 668, 682
Sieff, D. F., 510
Siegel, A., 629
Siegle, G. J., 186
Siegler, R. S., 843
Siepmann, M., 728
Sigmund, K., 656, 757, 759

Silberbauer, G., 214
Silbereisen, R., 635
Silk, J. B., 484, 510, 513, 553
Silk, J. S., 571
Sillen-Tullberg, B., 350, 351,
    554
Silva, P. A., 85, 276, 279, 641,
    912
Silventoinen, K., 315
Silverman, A., 470
Silverman, I., 127, 184, 185,
    186, 187, 188, 533, 632, 837
Silverman, L. K., 184
Silverman, R. A., 641
Simão, J., 782
Sime, J. D., 536, 544, 546
Simmel, M., 205
Simmons, L. W., 355, 360, 372
Simmons, R., 677, 691
Simon, A. F., 668
Simon, B., 664, 665
Simon, C. P., 937
Simon, H., 586, 778, 781, 872,
    959
Simon, J., 474, 492
Simon, T. J., 844
Simons, A. D., 914
Simonton, D. K., 136
Simpson, J., 89, 123, 139, 140,
    259, 260, 262, 267, 268,
    270, 271, 272, 273, 276,
    297, 306, 348, 356, 367,
    376, 426, 427, 431, 432,
    433, 436, 517, 554, 811,
    815, 817, 868
Sims-Knight, J. E., 397
Sinervo, B., 451
Singer, P., 171
Singer, W., 710
Singh, D., 136, 270, 306, 307,
    308, 318, 320, 321, 325,
    331, 361, 435
Singh, M., 354
Singh, S. B., 862
Singleton, B. R. R., 318, 324
Sivers, H., 786
Skinner, B. F., 33
Skinner, M., 310
Skoner, D. P., 563, 571
Skowronski, J. J., 811
Skudlarski, P., 97
Slagsvold, T., 511
Slater, A., 97, 295
Slaughter, V., 107, 206
Slavin, M. O., 908, 919, 920
Slim, R., 667
Slob, A. K., 352, 381
Sloman, L., 913
Sloman, S., 611
Slovic, P., 23, 42, 915, 958
Slutske, W. S., 276
Small, M. F., 553
Smith, B. H., 557
Smith, C. C., 72

Smith, C. D., 108
Smith, D. G., 208
Smith, D. M., 663, 914
Smith, E., 43
Smith, E. A., 153, 259, 263,
    329, 330, 907
Smith, E. R., 658, 667, 668
Smith, G., 315
Smith, K. D., 308
Smith, M., 904, 905, 918
Smith, M. J., 364
Smith, M. S., 462, 511
Smith, P. H., 244
Smith, P. K., 218, 240, 518, 680,
    835, 837, 844
Smith, R. L., 265, 267, 271, 276,
    374, 375, 378, 383, 388
Smith, S. P., 864
Smith, T. W., 679
Smith, V., 609, 618, 619, 656,
    657, 659, 661, 685, 686
Smuts, B., 81, 230, 273, 397,
    398, 410, 486, 554, 633
Smuts, R., 8, 397, 398
Sneyd, J., 706
Snidman, N., 565
Snowdon, C. T., 562
Snowdon, D. A., 859
Snyder, A. Z., 107
Snyder, M., 663, 807
Soares, J. J. F., 138, 216
Sobal, J., 317
Sober, E., 545, 749, 752, 762,
    763, 764, 766, 879, 885
Sobol, A. M., 905
Sockloskie, R. J., 403, 409
Sodian, B., 689
Sofikitis, N., 380, 381
Solache, I. L., 354
Soler, C., 275
Soler, M., 338
Soltis, J., 239
Sondheimer, S. J., 364
Sonneville, L. D., 108
Sooman, A., 260, 266
Sosis, R., 304
Sotelo, R., 373
Sotomayor, M. A. O., 781
Southwick, S., 644
Spampinato, M., 612
Sparks, C. S., 457, 465, 475
Sparks, J., 186
Sparks, W., 316, 809, 816
Speares, J., 708
Spears, R., 666
Speece, M. W., 213, 214
Speed, A., 271
Spelke, E., 46, 107, 109, 111,
    127, 164, 211, 837, 842, 843
Spencer, H., 937
Spencer, T., 918
Sperber, D., 7, 18, 32, 45, 62,
    99, 603, 611, 613
Spinelli, M. G., 239, 467

Spiro, A., III, 862
Spitzer, M., 104, 958
Spitzer, R. L., 892
Sporter, R. J., 274
Sprecher, S., 267, 270, 758, 816
Springer, K., 43
Srivastava, C., 862
Srull, T. K., 643
Stack, C. B., 513
Staddon, J. E. R., 617, 619
Stake, J. E., 972
Stallings, J., 493
Stallworth, L. M., 682
Stammer, H., 862
Stamps, J. A., 454, 456
Stanescu, R., 111
Stanford, C. B., 201, 202, 344
Stanik, C., 274
Starkey, P., 843
Statham, D. J., 276
Steadman, L. B., 529
Stearns, S., 71, 296, 557, 907
Steckel, R. H., 307
Steele, C., 658
Steen, F., 43, 218
Steffen, V., 634, 639
Stein, D. J., 912, 914
Stein, J., 728
Steinberg, J., 908
Steinberg, L., 85, 258, 276, 279, 327, 403, 490, 495, 499, 516, 517, 571, 833, 837, 845, 869, 918
Steinberger, E., 308
Steiner, M., 493, 560, 561
Steketee, G. S., 912
Stenberg, G., 688
Stenswick, M., 271
Stent, G., 710
Stephan, F. K., 562
Stephens, D., 591
Stephens, K. K., 663
Stephens, M. E., 263
Sterelny, K., 907
Sternberg, R. J., 427
Sternglanz, S. H., 303
Stevenage, S. V., 310
Stevens, A., 904
Stevens, D. A., 469
Stevens, J., 591
Stevenson, J. C., 918
Stevenson-Hinde, J., 858
Stewart, C., 182
Stewart, K. J., 497, 498
Stich, S., 909
Stiglmayer, A., 397
Stiller, J., 935
Stillwell-Barnes, R., 858
Stiner, M., 81
Stipek, D., 836
Stobeck, C., 311
Stockhammer, T., 642
Stockley, P., 373
Stockwell, M. L., 260, 267, 383

Stoddard, P. K., 513
Stone, G. O., 807
Stone, L., 419, 484
Stone, M. K., 493
Stone, V., 588, 604, 612, 841
Storey, A. E., 493, 559
Storey, R., 933, 940, 944, 945
Stormark, K. M., 190, 193
Stotland, E., 545
Stouthamer-Loeber, M., 641, 642
Strack, F., 404
Strassmann, B. I., 904
Strassmann, J. E., 459
Strauss, D., 362
Strauss, M. S., 843
Strayer, F. F., 680, 839
Strenta, A., 663
Stringer, C., 557, 942
Stroessner, S. J., 763
Strong, G., 559, 560, 561
Strong, R. A., 186
Stroobant, N., 861
Studdert-Kennedy, M., 706, 713, 718, 719
Stunkard, A. J., 317
Su, N., 642
Suarez, S. D., 55
Sue, D., 377
Sugden, K., 914
Suggs, R. G., 815
Sugimoto, Y., 354
Sugiyama, L., 229, 293, 294, 295, 296, 297, 301, 304, 305, 306, 307, 308, 309, 310, 317, 318, 319, 321, 322, 323, 326, 328, 329, 330, 588, 595, 596, 615
Sugiyama, M. S., 934, 939, 940, 944
Suh, E. M., 859
Sulkowski, G. M., 844
Sullivan, L., 108
Sullivan, Q., 270, 816
Sullivan, R. J., 914
Sulloway, F., 136, 276, 453, 518, 519, 520, 521, 522, 837, 908, 930
Suman, H. C., 866
Sumi, S., 206
Sumich, A., 294, 312
Summerfelt, W. T., 898
Sumner, W. G., 664
Sun, H., 206
Sundet, J. M., 182
Sundie, J. M., 807, 814
Surani, M. A., 632
Surbey, M., 85, 518, 865, 908, 915
Surian, L., 106
Sutton, S. K., 138
Swaddle, J. P., 309, 311, 312, 355
Swanson, C. L., 188

Swanson, W. J., 346
Swartz, T. S., 658
Swedo, S., 905, 918
Swets, J. A., 730
Swijtink, Z., 790
Sylvester, D., 138
Symanski, R., 270
Syme, L., 679
Symons, D., 7, 9, 13, 14, 33, 60, 123, 150, 153, 163, 168, 185, 230, 258, 269, 270, 271, 274, 277, 292, 293, 294, 297, 298, 299, 300, 301, 306, 308, 309, 310, 311, 312, 320, 321, 322, 325, 326, 327, 350, 375, 376, 377, 384, 388, 397, 400, 426, 434, 436, 735, 816, 916, 935, 937, 941
Sys, S. U., 861
Szasz, T. S., 891, 892
Székely, T., 483
Szklarska, A., 316

Tager-Flusberg, H., 108
Tajfel, H., 664, 763, 812
Takei, N., 905
Takezawa, M., 819
Takken, W., 308
Talese, G., 385
Tambs, K., 182
Tan, T., 321
Tanaka, J., 97
Tanaka, J. R., 97
Tanaka, J. S., 403, 409
Tanaka, J. W., 97
Tanida, S., 538
Tanner, C., 781
Tanner, R. E. S., 280
Tarr, M. J., 97, 617
Tassinary, L. G., 190, 193, 321
Tatar, D. G., 682
Tatar, M., 73
Tattersall, I., 152, 942
Taube, J. S., 183
Taveras, E. M., 239
Taylor, A., 497, 642, 643, 914
Taylor, J., 217
Taylor, M., 654, 841
Taylor, P. A., 226
Taylor, R. P., 319, 320
Taylor, S. E., 493, 494, 639, 644, 691, 738, 739, 814
Tegelström, H., 485
Teicher, M. H., 908
Teitler, J. O., 490
Terai, S., 738
Terestman, N., 377
Terwilliger, E. F., 560, 562
Tesser, A., 531, 812
Teta, P., 869, 870
Tetlock, P. E., 729
te Velde, E. R., 635
Tewksbury, R., 400

Teykowski, J., 635
Thaiss, L., 46
Thaker, G., 917
Thaler, R., 636, 737, 742
Thaller, T. R., 565
Tharp, G., 679
Theis, P., 192
Theno, S. A., 663
Theraulaz, G., 706
Thibaut, J. W., 425, 431
Thiessen, D., 866, 935
Thinus-Blanc, C., 182
Thomas, G., 426, 427
Thompson, A. P., 362, 423
Thompson, J. L., 557
Thompson, N. S., 469, 763
Thomson, J. W., 326
Thomson, W. M., 312
Thorndike, P. W., 182
Thornhill, N., 402, 405, 408, 533
Thornhill, R., 124, 126, 139, 140, 224, 231, 266, 267, 271, 272, 273, 274, 275, 280, 293, 294, 296, 297, 301, 306, 308, 309, 310, 311, 312, 313, 314, 316, 320, 324, 326, 338, 348, 349, 350, 352, 353, 354, 355, 357, 358, 359, 360, 361, 362, 363, 365, 387, 388, 389, 396, 397, 399, 400, 401, 402, 405, 484, 487, 498
Thorpe, S. J., 208
Thorpe, W. H., 191
Tice, D. M., 273
Tiddeman, B. P., 309, 313
Tidey, J., 642
Tiger, L., 662, 667
Tinbergen, N., 79, 571, 700, 720, 888
Titchener, E. B., 533
Tobena, A., 912
Todd, M., 262, 436, 691
Todd, P., 23, 42, 107, 205, 206, 212, 223, 306, 508, 518, 519, 640, 730, 741, 778, 779, 781, 782, 796, 797, 959
Todorov, A., 643
Toguchi, Y., 739
Tolan, P., 490
Tomaka, J., 55
Tomarken, A. J., 138, 216, 734
Tomasello, M., 107, 698, 708, 709, 718, 834, 837
Tomkins, S. S., 658
Tomlinson-Keasey, C., 495, 861
Tooby, J., 5, 6, 7, 8, 9, 10, 13, 14, 16, 17, 18, 23, 24, 25, 28, 29, 30, 33, 34, 36, 40, 41, 42, 43, 44, 45, 46, 47, 48, 49, 50, 51, 52, 59, 60, 62, 87, 106, 137, 159, 163,

168, 177, 180, 185, 208, 210, 213, 214, 215, 225, 229, 232, 292, 293, 294, 295, 303, 304, 305, 306, 308, 329, 330, 357, 364, 384, 397, 444, 457, 465, 467, 470, 474, 533, 584, 585, 586, 587, 588, 590, 591, 592, 593, 595, 596, 598, 599, 600, 602, 603, 604, 605, 606, 608, 609, 610, 611, 612, 613, 615, 617, 620, 622, 623, 640, 653, 654, 657, 658, 659, 660, 661, 666, 668, 698, 699, 725, 738, 740, 741, 755, 757, 758, 767, 783, 796, 797, 807, 811, 813, 829, 851, 852, 868, 890, 904, 906, 908, 940, 942, 965
Tooke, W., 227, 275, 635
Toomey, R., 276
Toorenaar, N., 108
Toth, N., 715
Touhey, J. C., 866
Tovée, M. J., 307, 318, 324, 325
Townsend, G., 312
Townsend, J. M., 270
Trainor, B. C., 552
Trapnell, P. D., 521
Traupmann, J., 816
Trautrimas, C., 403, 405, 408, 409
Treibner, F. A., 679
Tremblay, R. E., 629, 641
Tremellen, K. P., 364, 365
Tremewan, T., 294
Tremoulet, P., 106, 205
Trevathan, W., 299, 557
Treves, A., 201, 218
Trevithick, A., 263
Trickett, P., 518
Triesman, A., 42
Trifiletti, L. B., 467, 468, 508
Trinkaus, E., 556
Trivers, R., 72, 76, 137, 166, 225, 226, 239, 259, 268, 269, 270, 273, 276, 277, 296, 302, 306, 308, 320, 326, 338, 374, 377, 394, 403, 423, 429, 443, 444, 448, 452, 453, 455, 456, 458, 460, 465, 475, 476, 483, 484, 487, 506, 510, 514, 515, 518, 532, 544, 585, 591, 592, 631, 636, 655, 659, 684, 735, 754, 755, 756, 759, 791, 806, 813, 815, 818, 834, 845, 854, 870, 908, 919
Troisi, A., 904, 909, 916, 941
Trope, Y., 729
Trost, M. R., 266, 269, 420, 423, 530, 805, 806, 814, 817

Trudel, M., 680
Trumble, A. C., 467, 468, 508
Trussell, J., 371
Tse, W. S., 680
Tsivkin, S., 111
Tucker, D. C., 861
Tucker, J. S., 495, 861, 862
Tucker, M. B., 633
Tulving, E., 42, 783
Tuomilehto, J., 315, 321
Turiel, E., 688
Turke, P., 259, 272, 296, 459, 536, 941
Turner, C. T., 239
Turner, F., 932, 946
Turner, H. A., 565
Turner, J. C., 664, 763
Turner, M., 570, 945, 946
Turner, R. B., 563, 571
Tversky, A., 23, 42, 542, 727, 729, 740, 741, 781, 789, 791, 793, 915, 957
Tweed, R. G., 124
Twenge, J. M., 636
Tye, C. Y., 85
Tyler, J. P., 378
Tyler, L. K., 103

Udry, J. R., 274
Udry, R. R., 226
Uehara, S., 685
Uhles, A. N., 654
Ulen, T. S., 957, 958, 969
Uller, C., 107, 844
Ulrich, R. S., 190, 193
Umezawa, Y., 935
Umilta, C., 111
Ungerleider, L. G., 103, 104
Ungpakorn, G., 571
Updegraff, J. A., 493, 494, 639, 691, 814
Upfold, D., 408
Ustun, T., 904
Utne, M. K., 816
Uvnas-Moberg, K., 561

Valdespino, C., 486
Vale, E. L. E., 324, 325
Valeggia, C. R., 299
Valencia, A., 273
Valenstein, E. S., 914
Valentine, P., 264, 296
Vallacher, R. R., 819
Valverde, V., 315
Van Cauwenberge, P. B., 173
van Damme, E., 686
van de Kragt, A. J. C., 544, 737, 805
van den Berghe, P. L., 259, 296, 421, 530
Vandenburg, S. G., 182
VandePoll, N. E., 352
van der Dennen, J. M. G., 637, 638

van der Werflen Bosch, J. J., 352
vander Zon, A. T. M., 381
van Dijk, E., 686
Van Goozen, S. H. M., 352
Van Hesteren, F., 748
Van Hooff, J. A., 106, 714
Van Ijzendoorn, M., 517
van Kempen, M. J., 173
Van Lange, P. A. M., 655
Van Noord, P. A., 635
van Poppel, F., 489
van Roijen, J. H., 381
Van Rullen, R., 42
van Schaik, C., 106, 266, 350, 554, 555, 556
Van Valen, L., 201, 311, 346
Van Valin, R., 709
van Winden, F., 656
Vargha-Khadem, F., 711
Vartiainen, E., 315
Vasquez, G., 869
Vaughn, L. S., 295, 837
Vazire, S., 858
Vazquez, C., 239
Vazsonyi, A. T., 869
Veblen, T., 905
Vega, V., 408
Veld, V. O. H., 108
Venables, P. H., 641
Veneziano, R. A., 554
Veniegas, R. C., 662, 668
Venshure, B., 806, 810, 816
Verhoeven, K., 812
Verhulst, F. C., 635
Vermeulen, S. C., 749
Vermunt, R., 686
Verres, R., 862
Verschoor, A., 108
Vershure, B., 262, 691, 865
Vescio, T. K., 663
Vessey, S. H., 182
Vigil, J., 492
Vigilant, L., 498
Vigilante, D., 644
Viki, G. T., 411
Vince, K., 310
Vincent, A., 259
Vincent, A. C., 483
Vining, D. R., 13, 262
Vinokur, A. D., 914
Visser, L., 665
Vitányi, P., 780
Vitaro, F., 629, 641
Voland, E., 474, 488, 489, 508, 511, 915
Voland, R., 915
Von Bracken, H., 537
Von Cramon, Y., 104
Von der Schulennurg, C., 295
von Frisch, K., 180, 449
Vonk, R., 729
Vorgos, S., 690

Voyer, D., 184
Voyer, S., 184
Vrba, E. S., 886
Vreeburg, J. T. M., 381
Vrieswijk, B., 635
Vuchinich, S., 241

Wackenhut, J., 663
Wade, M. J., 259
Wadsworth, M. E., 315
Wagner, J. D., 554
Waite, B. E., 680
Wakefield, J. A., 866
Wakefield, J., Jr., 866
Wakefield, J. C., 401, 878, 880, 882, 886, 889, 891, 897, 898, 904, 909
Waldman, B., 531
Waldman, I. D., 232
Waldrip-Dail, H. M., 346
Walker, A., 556, 557
Walker, J., 659
Walker, P. L., 307, 309, 310
Walker, R., 43, 301, 320
Wallace, H. M., 404
Wallen, K., 267
Wallerstein, J. S., 565
Wallsten, T. S., 793
Walsh, A., 273
Walsh, C. J., 493, 559
Walsh, V., 111
Walster, E., 546
Walster, G. W., 546
Walter, A., 270
Walters, S., 635
Wang, E., 918
Wang, W., 346
Wang, X. T., 25, 542, 543, 544
Wang, Z., 422, 552, 560, 562
Want, S. C., 107
Wara, A., 316
Ward, C., 295, 553, 555, 556, 557
Ward, L. M., 187
Ward, M. J., 517
Ward, P. I., 373
Ward, S., 186, 373
Wark, G., 761, 766
Warntjes, A., 270
Warren, M., 85, 518
Warrington, E. K., 103
Wason, P., 594, 595, 620, 741
Wasserman, B. H., 302, 326, 471, 534, 537
Wasserman, T., 270
Watkins, K., 711
Watkins, L. R., 564, 571
Watson, A. C., 841
Watson, D., 424, 859
Watson, J., 840
Watson, P. J., 311, 913
Watts, M. W., 667
Waugh, C. E., 273

Waymire, K. G., 493
Waynforth, D., 313, 495
Weary, G., 729
Weatherhead, P. J., 509, 519
Weaver, I. C. G., 572
Weaver, S. L., 489
Weber, E., 791, 792, 793
Weber, J. A., 381
Webster, C. D., 235
Webster, G. D., 273, 277, 462, 473
Wecker, S. C., 190, 191
Wedekind, C., 357, 531, 759
Wedell, N., 373
Weekes-Shackelford, V., 266, 382, 383, 384, 388, 844, 845
Weerts, E., 642
Weg, E., 685
Wegener, J., 612
Weghorst, J., 375
Weghorst, S. J., 57, 263, 266, 469, 568, 630
Weigant, V. M., 352
Weinberg, C. R., 344, 352, 371
Weinberg, R. L., 554
Weiner, B., 661
Weiner, H., 563, 564, 907
Weiner, N., 9, 12
Weinert, F. E., 835
Weinrich, J., 279
Weinshenker, N. J., 629
Weinstein, N. D., 738
Weisfeld, G. E., 635, 837
Weiss, A., 853, 858, 859, 860
Weiss, K. M., 266
Weitzel, B., 473
Welch, J. E., 565
Weller, A., 350
Weller, L., 350
Wellings, K., 376
Wellman, H. M., 102, 105, 107, 688, 840, 841
Wells, P. A., 458
Wendt, J. S., 193
Wenegrat, B., 904, 913
Werner-Wilson, R. J., 226
West, M. M., 496
West, P., 315
West, S., 206
West, S. A., 136, 449
West, S. G., 865
West-Eberhard, M. J., 831, 908
Westen, D., 226, 266, 298, 375, 433, 434, 469, 470, 817, 914, 964, 965
Westermarck, E., 303, 547
Westneat, D. F., 484, 487
Wetsman, A., 307, 318, 321, 323, 329, 330
Whalen, P. J., 662
Wheatley, G. H., 187
Wheelwright, S., 841
Whissel, C., 935

White, B. J., 637, 666
White, D. R., 259, 260, 262, 277
White, G. L., 429
White, J. L., 641
White, K. B., 404
White, N. F., 904
Whitehouse, G. H., 326
Whiten, A., 105, 203, 682, 683, 839, 905
Whiting, B., 228, 496, 565, 635
Whiting, J. W. M., 277, 496
Whitten, P. L., 498
Whittinghill, M., 492
Whyte, M. K., 259, 262
Wicker, F. W., 692
Widdig, A., 510
Widiger, T. A., 856
Widom, C. S., 642
Wiebe, V., 712
Wiebe, W. J., 564
Wieczorkowska, G., 654
Wiederman, M. W., 264, 269, 271
Wiegert, R. G., 73, 75
Wierson, M., 518
Wiest, C., 658
Wiggins, J. S., 422, 813
Wiggs, C. L., 103, 104
Wikler, D., 642
Wikstrom, P. H., 643
Wilbur, C., 660, 672, 808, 821
Wilcox, A. J., 344, 352, 371, 554
Wilcox, M., 565
Wilder, D. A., 668
Wildt, D. E., 386
Wildt, G., 354
Wiley, A. S., 516
Wilkinson, G. C., 813
Wilkinson, R. G., 571
Willard, D., 276, 458, 510, 518, 818
Williams, C. L., 184, 189
Williams, D. C., 918
Williams, E. J. B., 347
Williams, E. M., 106, 829
Williams, G., 589, 590, 592, 970
Williams, G. C., 8, 9, 12, 15, 27, 71, 124, 125, 126, 149, 239, 251, 270, 293, 296, 303, 429, 443, 483, 487, 554, 557, 747, 765, 878, 879, 880, 881, 886, 889, 900, 904, 906
Williams, G. W., 726, 904
Williams, J., 334
Williams, K., 738, 813
Williams, P., 97
Williamson, L., 465
Willis, S. L., 184
Willner, L. A., 264, 267
Wilson, A., 841
Wilson, B. A., 409
Wilson, B. J., 618, 657

Wilson, D., 45
Wilson, D. R., 906
Wilson, D. S., 168, 545, 749, 752, 762, 763, 764, 766, 854, 855, 940
Wilson, E. O., 10, 73, 137, 166, 169, 296, 443, 448, 868, 931, 932, 940
Wilson, G. D., 271, 377, 863
Wilson, K. D., 97
Wilson, M., 7, 14, 57, 123, 136, 137, 193, 224, 230, 233, 240, 243, 262, 263, 266, 269, 296, 297, 298, 301, 302, 326, 375, 419, 421, 433, 435, 443, 445, 447, 448, 457, 459, 460, 463, 464, 465, 466, 467, 468, 469, 472, 476, 492, 495, 507, 508, 509, 511, 512, 518, 519, 521, 534, 554, 563, 568, 630, 631, 633, 634, 639, 655, 667, 804, 813, 814, 815, 817, 818, 821, 837, 845, 906, 919, 955, 964, 966
Wilson, S. A., 193
Wilson, T. D., 803
Wimmer, H., 105, 840
Wimsatt, W. C., 789
Wingard, D. L., 495, 861
Wingerd, J., 519
Wingfield, J. C., 678, 679
Winner, E., 108
Winslow, J. T., 422
Winston, J., 562
Winterhalder, B., 907
Wippich, W., 564
Wischmann, T., 862
Wisman, A., 814
Wixted, J. T., 784
Wolf, A., 303, 533
Wolf, C. M., 565
Wolf, J. B., 484
Wolf, L., 484, 487
Wolf, O. T., 564
Wolfe, L. D., 260, 263, 267
Wolff, H. S., 388
Wolfner, M. F., 346
Wolkowitz, O. M., 564
Wolpert, L., 914
Wolpoff, M. H., 558
Wolyniec, P. S., 917
Wong, P. Y., 493
Wood, C., 85
Wood, W., 262, 280, 809, 814, 816
Woodroofe, R., 259
Woodruff, D. S., 683
Woodruff, G., 685, 840
Woods, G. L., 381
Worley, S. M., 869
Worthman, C., 84, 335, 493

Wrangham, R., 8, 81, 232, 240, 260, 267, 334, 396, 397, 498, 553, 554, 556, 637, 638, 807, 814
Wray, A., 719
Wrenge, P. H., 517
Wright, C., 404
Wright, L., 880, 883
Wright, R., 764, 904
Wright, T. M., 269
Wrosch, C., 913
Wu, C., 270, 346
Wu, J., 318, 319, 324
Wu, P. Y. K., 688
Wyatt, R. J., 905
Wyckoff, G. J., 346
Wyer, R. S., 643
Wynn, K., 26, 111, 844
Wynne-Edwards, K. E., 493, 552, 559, 562
Wysocki, C. J., 364

Xie, X., 532
Xu, F., 112
Xu, J., 658

Yalcin, S., 150
Yale, S., 918
Yamagishi, T., 538, 659, 664, 665, 738
Yamamoto, Y., 381
Yamamura, N., 454
Yamazaki, K., 531
Yarn, D., 972
Yates, E., 403
Ye, H. H., 532
Yehuda, R., 644, 912
Yeo, R. A., 312
Yerkes, A. W., 50
Yerkes, R. M., 50
Yetley, A., 845
Yoshikawa, S., 294
Yost, J. H., 729
Young, A. W., 97, 108
Young, D., 183
Young, L., 562
Young, L. J., 260, 261, 422, 493, 552, 560, 561, 562
Young, L. R., 560
Young, R. K., 325, 866
Yu, D., 307, 318, 321, 323
Yurko, K. H., 495
Yuwiler, A., 564
Yzerbyt, V. T., 728

Zaadstra, B. M., 635
Zacks, J. M., 107
Zago, S., 103
Zahavi, A., 297, 448, 455, 540, 761
Zahn, T. P., 564
Zajonc, R. B., 520, 533, 810
Zalenski, C. M., 809

Zaneveld, L. J., 381
Zappieri, M. L., 260, 267, 383
Zárate, M. A., 667
Zarbatany, L., 759
Zaret, T. M., 484, 485, 487, 498
Zarmakoupis, P. N., 380
Zavos, P. M., 378, 380, 381, 389
Zebrowitz, L. A., 78, 294, 295, 303, 328
Zebrowitz, M., 310
Zehr, J. L., 267

Zeichner, A., 409
Zeifman, D., 258, 259, 260, 261, 422
Zeki, S., 422, 553, 560, 561
Zelano, B., 357
Zezzard, P., 717
Zhang, J., 537
Zhu, G., 270, 274, 276
Ziegler, T. E., 552, 562
Ziemba-Davis, M., 184
Zierk, K., 270, 817

Zihlman, A., 556
Zimbardo, P. G., 656
Zimmerman, W., 964, 965
Zingraff, M., 642
Zinner, D., 350
Zoccolillo, M., 641
Zorzi, M., 111
Zuckerman, M., 865, 869, 870
Zuk, M., 77, 308
Zunz, M., 858

Subject Index

Absolute inclusive fitness, 451
Abstraction principle, 843
Adaptation(s):
  adaptive problems select for, 21–22
  conditional, 833
  deferred, 834
  properties of organisms as, 25–26
  psychological (*see* Psychological adaptations)
  sexual coercion, 397–398
Adaptationism:
  aesthetic theorists, 938–939
  Darwinian literary study, 931
  function, and antiadaptationist argument, 879
  human mating psychology, 255–257 (*see also* Mating)
  modern, 8
Adaptive specialization hypothesis, 589, 605
Addictions, 914–915
Adjustment disorder, 898–899
Adoption, parental investment and, 512–513
Affection, chemistry of, 559–560
Agency-focused inference engines, 106–109
Agency system, predators/prey, 203–214
  cessation of agency hypothesis, 213
  components of, 204
  death understanding, 212–214
  detection and discrimination, 204–209
    contingency, 206–207
    eyes, 208–209
    morphology, 207–208
    self-propelled motion, 205–206
Aggression, 581–582, 628–646
  in children, 839
  coalitional, 637–639
  conceptualized, 628–630
  conclusions, 646
  contextual adjustment of, in development, 642–645
  contingent nature of, 629
  culture and, 645–646
  defection, 636
  ecological transmission of, 642–643

emotions and, 640–642
female same-sex, 635–636
kin/nonkin, 630–631
male-female partner, 632–634
male same-sex, 634–635
maternal-infant conflict and infanticide, 631–632
mechanisms of, 640–642
opponents and motive, 630–639
proactive and reactive forms of, 629–630
psychological models of ecological adjustment, 643–645
sex differences in, 639–640
Aging, development and, 83–86. *See also* Development; Life history theory (LHT)
Alexithymia, 863
Allergy, cough, and anxiety, 731–734
Alliances. *See* Coalition(s)
Allocation decisions, enactment of, 78–80
Altruism:
  evolution of, 448
  hypothetical, 457
  incidental, 448
  inclusive fitness, 528
  kin/genetic relatedness and, 528–548
    costs/benefits, computing, 535–544
    effects of increasing survival rates of hypothetical patients on subjects' risk preferences, 544
    grandmother hypothesis, 535–536
    Hamilton's theory of kin altruism, 528–529
    range of, 529–530
    risk proneness as function of group size and kinship, 543
    tendency to help as a function of the relative's health under life or death versus everyday conditions, 541
    tendency to help a group of relatives as a function of the group's reproductive value, 542
    tendency to help under life or death versus everyday conditions, 540
  nonkin, 544–547

Altruism *(Continued)*
  paradox of, 449–450
  reciprocal, 167, 585, 684
American culture theory, 809
American Revolution, 693
Analogists, evolutionary, 937–938
Anger, and punishment of free riders, 660
Anger-upset system and relationship
      processes, 424–425, 433–438
  discrete systems model of love and anger-
      upset, 424–425
  jealousy, 433–434
  mate-retention strategies, 435–436
  violence in relationships, 434–435
Animal(s):
  behavior research, 15
  children's responses to, 218
  infants learning about, 43–44
  movement, optimization in, 180–181
  personality in, 857–860
Animate motion, 106
Anonymity, selfish/antisocial behavior and,
      656
Antagonistic pleiotropy, 70
Anthropomorphism, 214–215
Anxiety disorders, 911–913
Aretaic, moral judgments, 764
"Argument from personal incredulity," 589
Arithmetic/numbers, 110–112, 844
Artifact(s):
  biases as, 726, 739–741
    problem content, 740–741
    problem formats, 739–740
  functions, 881–883
Arts, adaptive function of, 938–940
Assortative pairing, 530, 865–867
Attachment:
  parental investment, 516–518
  systems, 421–423
  theory, and mating strategies, 279
Attentional systems, 42–44
Attention disorders, 918
Attractiveness. *See* Physical attractiveness
Auditory looming, 731, 734
Autism, 40, 916, 918

Ballistic processes, 100
Banker's Paradox, 757
Bargaining games, 609
Battered women, homicide cases of, 243–244
Behavior:
  evolutionary framework for understanding,
      907
  predator-prey, 218–219
  sexually coercive, 413–414
Behavioral disorders, 914–916
  addictions, 914–915
  eating disorders, 915–916
  habits, 915
  sexual disorders, 916
Behavioral ecology, 76–78, 167
Behavioral impulsivity, 641–642
Behavioral models, dependence of law on, 954,
      955, 961, 962

Behavioral strategy mechanism, 838
Behavioral systems, in model of human nature,
      941–942
Behavior genetics, 39–41
Belief-desire reasoning, 840
Beneficial effects standard of evidence, 125
Big five model of personality, 431–432,
      852–853, 855–856
Biolegal history, 966
Biological conception of morality, 750–751
Biological functions, 774, 878–900
  antiadaptationist argument, 879
  artifact functions, 881–883
  as black box essentialist concept, 889
  disorder(s):
    diverse strands in evolutionary
        psychopathology, 890
    as evolutionary dysfunction, 894–895
    as failure of designed function, 890–899
    fallacies in arguments that mental
        disorders are naturally selected
        conditions, 895–897
    as harmful dysfunction, 891–895, 897
  etiological analysis, Wright's, 883
  functional explanation, 880
  implications for *Diagnostic and Statistical
      Manual of Mental Disorders* diagnosis,
      897–899
    adjustment disorder, 898–899
    conduct disorder, 898
    major depressive disorder, 897–898
    separation anxiety disorder, 898
  maintenance, 885–887
  as naturally selected effects, 884–885
  resolving Tinbergen puzzle, 888–889
  teleological tradition, 879
  timeline problems, 887–888
Biologically primary/secondary abilities,
      842
Biological motion, 110
Biological/sociocultural factors in language
      evolution, 718–720
Biology:
  evolutionary, 15
  organized by evolutionary principles, 45
  sociobiology, 15, 166–167, 975–979
Biparental care of offspring, 347
Bipolar disorder, 916
Birth, presence at, 33–34
Birth order:
  impact on personality and development,
      519–521
  parental investment and, 518–521
Birth spacing, parental investment and,
      521–522
Blank-slate view of the mind, 6–7, 10, 166,
      167, 585
Blueprint of the Listener, 704
Blueprint metaphor, 711
Blueprint of the Speaker, 702
BMI, 313, 317–321
Bodyguard hypothesis, 230
Body symmetry, 313
Bounded rationality, 958, 960

Brain development, 80–84, 109–110, 112–113, 623
Brain disorders, 916–917
Brain research, contributions of evolutionary theory, 154–156
By-product(s), 28, 33, 397–398, 448, 598, 602–603, 623

Cardinal principle, counting, 843
Care, evolution of, 760–762
Categorical perception of speech, 705
Causal connections, 16–19
Causal essences, 102
Causal links, clarifying, legal system, 956–957
Change blindness, 208
Character displacement, 856
Chase play, 217
Cheaters/cheating:
  defined, 591, 593, 684
  detection, 148, 591–594, 606–608
    algorithm, 741
    benefits necessary for, 607–608
    specialization, 621
    triggering, 606–608
    unfamiliar social contracts and, 598–600
  theft and, 229–230
Chess analogy, predators/prey, 209
Child abuse, 919
Childhood:
  experiences influencing mating strategies, 279
  extended/prolongation of, 557–558, 833–834
  selection of aspects of, as adaptive function at specific times in development, 835–836
  selection of aspects of, as preparations for adulthood, 834–835
Children:
  aggressive behavior, 643, 839
  arithmetic, 844
  biologically primary and secondary abilities, 842
  counting, 843–844
  damage to existing, 233
  high-status, 839
  intuitive mathematics of, 842–844
  numerosity and ordinality, 843
  precocious development of social exchange reasoning, 613–614
  responses to actual animals, 218
  temperament, 643
Clueless environments, 47–50
Coalition(s):
  alliances with kin, 813
  alliances with nonkin, 685, 813
  formation, 811–813
  significance of, and mutual control; morality and, 753–754
Coalitional aggression, 637–639
Coalitional value, 304–305
Coevolutionary processes and their modeling, 75–80

Cognition:
  model of human nature, 941, 942
  motivation and, 45–52
    clueless environments, 47–50
    combinatorial explosion, 47
    content-free is content-poor, 45–46
    values and knowledge, 50–52
    weakness of content-free architectures, 45–52
  sociality and, 688
Cognitive-behavioral strategies, social status, 680–688
Cognitive biases, 582, 724–742
  adaptive biases, overview table, 732–733
    protective, 732
    self and future, 733
    social, 732–733
  artifacts, biases as, 739–741
    problem content, 740–741
    problem formats, 739–740
  error management biases, 726, 730–739
  evolutionary foundations, 725–727
  heuristics, 727–730
    conjunction fallacy, 727
    effectiveness, 729–730
    effects of time and motivation, 727–729
    fundamental attribution error (FAE), 728–729
    mental shortcuts, 727
  interpersonal perception, biases in, 735–738
    commitment skepticism, 736, 737
    negative outgroup stereotypes, 737
    sexual overperception, 735–736
    social exchange bias, 737–738
  positive illusions, 738–739
  protective biases, 731–735
    allergy, cough, and anxiety, 731–734
    auditory looming, 731, 734
    aversion to diseased or injured persons, 734–735
    food aversions, 734
  self-judgment, biases in, 738–739
  sexual attractiveness, 724
  social perception, 724
Cognitive landmarks, 563
Cognitive mediation of nepotism, 464–465
Cognitive modularity, 162–163, 942
Cognitive processes, emphasis on, 807–808
Cognitive programs, 33
Cognitive psychology, evolutionary, 776–798
  decision making, 777–782
    choosing from sequence of options, 781–782
    ecological rationality and evolved decision mechanisms, 782
    using recognition and ignorance, 779
    using single reason, 779–781
  memory (retrieving/forgetting information), 782–790
    functions of forgetting, 785–786
    hindsight bias, consequence of future-oriented memory, 786–787
    long-term memory (forgetting curves and the statistical properties of information use), 783–785

Cognitive psychology, evolutionary (*Continued*)
    short-term memory, functional explanation
        of its bounds, 787–790
    representation of information, 790–796
        decisions from experience versus decisions
            from description, 791–793
        inferences based on natural frequency
            versus probability representations,
            793–796
        prospect theory, 791
Cognitive quirks, 960
Cognitive revolution, 14–15
Cognitive rhetoric, 938
Coherence/legibility, 193
Collaborative coordination, 758
Combinatorial explosion, 47
Combinatorial phonology, 706
Comedy/tragedy/satire, 945
Commitment skepticism, 736, 737
Communication, evolution of (Tinbergen's four
        questions), 700–714
    how did language get that way in
        phylogeny?, 712–714
    how does language get that way in
        ontogeny?, 707–712
    how does language work?, 700–705
    what does language do for the organism?,
        705–707
Comparative standards of evidence, 125
Competition:
    dangers from humans, and, 225–226
    intrasexual among females, 691
    intrasexual among males, 691
    kin, 448, 463–464
    for limited resources, 225
    restrained, among kin, 463–464
    scramble, 225
    selfish behavior and, 448
    social dominance and, 691
    zero sum and non-zero sum, 225–226
Competitive exclusion principle, 856
Competitiveness, paternal investment and,
        490–492
Computational language, 14
Computational sciences, 9–10
Computer programming/numerical abilities,
        adaptations for ability, 26
Conative functions, 164
Concrete reciprocity, morality of, 755–756. *See
    also* Reciprocity
Conditional adaptations, 833
Conditional reasoning, and social exchange,
        594–598, 603–605
Conduct disorder, 898
Conflict(s):
    within the family, 513
    over material resources, 226
    over mating resources, 226–227
    parent-offspring, 452–453, 513–518
        attachment, 516–518
        battleground versus resolution, 453
        maternal-fetal conflict, 514–515
        parental investment and, 513–518

resolution models, 453–454
    weaning conflict, 515–516
over status, 226
Conflicts of interest, and morality, 750
Confluence model of sexual aggression, 403
Conjunction fallacy, 727
Conscience, evolution of, 767
Conspecifics, struggles with, 175
Content-free architectures, weakness of,
        45–52
Content specialization, 44
Cooperation:
    genes for, 151
    kin, 448
    reproductive success and, 684
Cooperative/trustworthy types, 655–656
Cooperative value, 303–304
Cortisol, 564–572
Cosmic evolutionists, 936–937
Counting, 112, 843–844
    principles, evolutionary developmental
        psychology, 843
    verbal, 112
Covitality, 853
Creative talent, 357
Cryptic choice mechanisms and menstrual
        cycle variation, 364–365
Cryptic condition, 455
Cuckoldry, 88–89, 266, 350
Culture:
    aggression and, 645–646
    evolutionary social psychology and, 804,
        818–819, 821
    female body fat level and, 317
    female height, RS, and marriage patterns,
        329
    human mating strategies, 277–279
    paternal investment, 496
    social exchange reasoning, 614–616

Dangers from humans, 175–176, 224–245
    coevolution of cost-infliction and defenses
        against costs, 227
    coevolution of dangers from humans and
        defenses against them, 228–231
        assaults on status, 228–229
        rape, 230–231
        temporal categories of strategies, 231
        theft and cheating, 229–230
        violence, 230
    coevolution of environmental dangers and
        adaptations to defend against them,
        227–228
    conclusions, 244–245
    fear, 236
    homicide, 231–245, 463
        adaptations for, 231–232, 234, 238–241
        avoiding contexts where homicide is likely,
            234–236
        control of territory, 234–235
        defenses against, 234, 236–243
        fitness costs of being killed, 233–234
        killing in self-defense, 243–244

versus other strategies of cost-infliction, 245
recurrent adaptive problems solvable by, 232
risk of, kin/nonkin, 463
selection pressures, 232, 234
staunching costs of, among genetic relatives, 238
other humans as "hostile force of nature," 224–225
scramble competition, 225
secrecy as a defense against being murdered, 243
sources of conflict, 226–227
material resources, 226
mating resources, 226–227
status, 226
winning competitions for limited resources, 225
zero sum and non-zero sum competitions, 225–226
Darwinian fitness, 450, 528
Darwinian literary study, 931
Darwinism, modern, 256
Death:
agency and, 212–214
child's, parental grief and, 461
risk of, 71
understanding, 212–214
Deception, 681–683, 760
Decision(s):
from experience versus description, 791–793
instincts, 18
mechanisms, evolved; rationality and, 782
rules, 591, 818–819
Decision making, 777–782
choosing from sequence of options, 781–782
ecological rationality and evolved decision mechanisms, 782
using recognition and ignorance, 779
using single reason, 779–781
Defection aggression, 636
Defenses:
against cost, coevolution of cost-infliction and, 227
and dangers, coevolution of, 228–231
female defense or harem polygyny, 261–262
against homicide, 234, 236–243
homicides committed in self-defense, 243–244
mental health and, 906
Deference, evolution of, 752–754
Deferred adaptations, 834
Deontic logics, content-free, 610–611
Dependence in relationships, 431–432
Depression, 40, 897–898
Descendant value, 302–303
Descriptive rules, violations of, 620
Design. *See* Organic design, principles of
Development:
life history, 83–86
mental health, 908
paternal investment, 495–496

timing of developmental achievements, 84–85
Developmentally relevant environment, 35
Developmental programs, 35
Developmental psychology, evolutionary, 774, 828–846
applied issues, 837, 844–845
basic assumptions, 832–836
early plasticity and adaptive sensitivity to context, 832–833
experiences influencing mating strategies, 279
extended/prolongation of, 557–558, 833–834
selection of aspects of, as adaptive function at specific times in development, 835–836
selection of aspects of, as preparations for adulthood, 834–835
cognitive development, 837
children's intuitive mathematics, 842–844
theory of mind, 840–842
conclusions, 845–846
developmental systems approach (model for ontogeny and phylogeny), 830–832
social/emotional development, 836–840
topics (overview table), 837
Developmental theories of human mating, 279
Diagnosis, mental health, 909–910
Diagnostic and Statistical Manual of Mental Disorders (DSM) diagnosis, 897–899, 909
adjustment disorder, 898–899
conduct disorder, 898
major depressive disorder, 897–898
separation anxiety disorder, 898
Dictator game, 686
Direct biases, 766
Direct reciprocity. *See* Reciprocity
Disciplines, applications of evolutionary psychology to other disciplines, 929–930
Discrete systems model of love and anger-upset, 424–425
Discriminate sociality, 653
Diseased/injured persons, aversion to, 734–735
Disorder(s):
as evolutionary dysfunction, 894–895
as harmful dysfunction, 891–894
specific mental health disorders, 911–919
addictions, 914–915
anxiety, 911–913
attention, 918
autism, 916, 918
behavioral, 914–916
bipolar, 916
brain, 916–917
child abuse, 919
eating, 915–916
emotional, 911–914
excesses/deficits, 914
habits, 915
mood, 913–914
obsessive-compulsive (OCD), 918

Disorder(s) (*Continued*)
  PTSD, 912
  relationship difficulties, 919
  schizophrenia, 916, 917–918
  sexual, 916
Distant reactivity, 106–107
Distorted room, 178
Domain(s):
  of competence, 96
  of evolutionary social psychology, 811–818
    coalition formation, 811–813
    mate choice, 815–816
    mate retention, 816–817
    overview table, 812
    parental care, 817–818
    self-protection, 814–815
    status, 813–814
  generality, 33, 44, 178–180, 616–622, 664–665,
    810–811
  proper versus actual, 99
  specificity, 2, 52, 97–102, 177–178, 668,
    725–726, 942
Dominance hierarchies, 836–840. *See also* Social
  status
Dominant versus submissive categorization,
  813
Double dissociation, 103

Eating disorders, 915–916
Ecocriticism, 935
Ecology/ecological perspectives:
  correlates, paternal investment, 496–497
  and life history evolution, 73–74
  literary criticism, 935
  rationality, 23, 782
  transmission of aggression, 642–643
Economic dependence, women on males, 633
Economic folk theory, 617–618
Ego (personal fitness effect), 450
Embodied capital, 74–75, 82
Emotion(s):
  aggression and, 640–642
  evolutionary framework for understanding
    human behavior and, 907
  mind as crowded network of evolved,
    domain-specific programs, 52
  as solution to problem of mechanism
    coordination, 52–61
  status loss and, 691–692
Emotional disorders, 908–909, 911–914
  anxiety disorders, 911–913
  excesses/deficits, 914
  mood disorders, 913–914
  pathological jealousy, 914
  PTSD, 912
Emotional-motivation systems, relationship
  processes, 423–425. *See also*
  Relationship(s)
Emotional stability, mate retention and, 432
Encapsulation, 162–163
Encoding, 643
Endocrine systems, 79. *See also* Hormones
Endowment effects, 958–959
Energy budgets, 68–69

Environmental dangers and adaptations to
  defend against them, coevolution of,
  227–228
Environmental determinism, fallacy of, 34–36
Environment of evolutionary adaptedness
  (EEA), 22–23, 152–157, 976
  brain research and evolutionary theory,
    154–156
  human female reproductive system and, 299
  knowing/understanding, 156
  legal system, 963
  mating strategies, 256
  parent-attachment, 516
  personality, 852
  psychological adaptations, 156–157
  reproduction and causal structure of the
    environment, 153–154
  selection pressures, 153
Envy, 692
EPQ-R, 167–168
Equilibria, separating/pooled, 455
Equipotentiality, 179
Equity heuristic, 519
Error management:
  avoiding being murdered, 241–243
  biases, 726, 730–739
    allergy, cough, and anxiety, 731–734
    auditory looming, 731, 734
    commitment skepticism, 736, 737
    diseased/injured persons, aversion to,
      734–735
    food aversions, 734
    interpersonal perception, 735–738
    negative outgroup stereotypes, 737
    positive illusions, 738–739
    protective, 731–735
    self-judgment, 738–739
    sexual overperception, 735–736
    social exchange, 737–738
  theory (EMT), 242, 730–731
ESS. *See* Evolutionarily stable strategy (ESS)
Ethnic outgroups, physical attack, 662
Ethnographic studies, 459–460
Ethology, 15
Etiological analysis, Wright's, 883
Evidence standards. *See* Standards of evidence
Evolutionarily stable strategy (ESS), 455–456,
  591–592, 593, 608
Evolutionary cognitive psychology. *See*
  Cognitive psychology, evolutionary
Evolutionary developmental psychology. *See*
  Developmental psychology, evolutionary
Evolutionary personality psychology. *See*
  Personality psychology, evolutionary
Evolutionary psychology, 1–3, 5–63
  applied to other disciplines, 929–930
  causal connections, 16–18
  cognition and motivation, 45–52
    clueless environments, 47–50
    combinatorial explosion, 47
    content-free is content-poor, 45–46
    values and knowledge, 50–52
    weakness of content-free architectures,
      45–52

controversial issues in, 2–3, 145–171
  environment of evolutionary adaptedness
    (EEA), 152–157, 976
  massive modularity, 162–165, 978
  nature versus nurture, 157–162
  selfish genes, 146–152
emotions as solution to problem of
  mechanism coordination, 52–61
  fear as example of, 54–56
  functional structure of emotion program
    evolved to match the evolutionarily
    summed structure of its target
    situation, 56–58
  recalibrational emotions, evolved
    regulatory variables, and imagined
    experience, 58–59
  recalibrational releasing engines, 59–61
  role of imagery and emotion in planning,
    60–61
hostility to, 169–170, 975–976, 977
implications of emergence, 5–7
intellectual origins of, 7–19
organic design, principles of, 19–45
political correctness issues, 165–170
  genetic determinism, 168–169
  racism/sexism, 167–168
  social Darwinism, 169
as sociobiology sanitized, 15, 166–167,
  975–979
traditional disciplines of psychology and,
  773–775
Evolutionary psychopathology, 890
Evolutionary social psychology. *See* Social
  psychology, evolutionary
Excesses/deficits, 914
Extended phenotypes, 449
Extra-pair mating, 348–349, 358–360, 362–363
Eye-direction detector (EDD), 841

Face(s)/facial:
  attractiveness/preference:
    attractiveness, and culture, 294–295
    women's preference for masculinity,
      355–356
    women's preference for symmetry, 275
  intuitive ontology, illustration of, 96–97
  recognition, 96–97, 100, 101
  resemblance, and kin recognition, 534
  responses/cues, 108, 662–663
  symmetry, 312
False alarms, 789
False-belief tasks, 840
False models, 789
Familiarity, 531, 532–533, 599–600, 657
Family, evolution of human, 552–555. *See also* Kin
Fatherhood. *See* Paternal investment; Paternity
Favoritism, in-group, 654
Fear:
  adaptive to experience, 236
  aggression and, 641
  automaticity, 215, 216
  dedicated neural circuitry, 215
  example, emotions as solution to problem of
    mechanisms coordination, 54–56

  impenetrable to conscious control, 215
  model of human nature, 941
  stimulus-specific, 215
  system, and predators/prey; characteristics,
    215–216
Female infidelity. *See* Sperm competition
Female mate value, 299–300, 436
Female same-sex aggression, 635–636
Fertility:
  risk, and sexual interests; male partner
    characteristics moderating, 359
  status effects on female sexual interests,
    359–361
  and stress, and development of mating
    strategies, 279
Fetal-maternal conflict, 514–515
Fitness, Darwinian, 450, 528
Fitness costs of being killed, 233–234
Fitness effect:
  absolute inclusive fitness, 451
  Ego (personal fitness effect), 450
  inclusive fitness effect, 450–451
  neighbor-modulated fitness, 451
Fitness maximization standards of evidence,
  125
Fitness-maximizing or optimal strategies, 68
Fitness teleology, 12–13
Five-factor model (FFM), 431–432, 852–853,
  855–856
Food aversions, 734
Forgetting:
  boosting heuristic performance, 785–786
  curves, 783–785
  functions of, 785–786
  strategic information blockage, 786
  uncluttering the mind, 785
Formal logics, 594, 595
Fossil record, 554–559
Frame-content metaphor, 717
Frame dominance, 710
Framing effect, 542
Free riding:
  intentional, via inability, 661
  punishment and, 659–661
Frequency, natural; inferences based on, versus
  probability representations, 793–796
Frequency dependence, theories of, 854–857
Frequency-dependent selection, 38, 40, 868–870
Friendship, evolution of, 757–758
Function(s). *See also* Biological functions:
  as black box essentialist concept, 889
  man-made objects construed in terms of, 102
  reproduction and, 21
  testing, and design evidence, 590
Functional specificity in social cognition, 654
Functional structure of emotion program,
  56–58
Functional universality, constraint of, 38
Fundamental attribution error (FAE), 728–729

Game theory, 18, 24, 591, 765
Generalists versus specialists, convicted
  rapists, 404–406
Generalizability theory (GT), 858

Generalization of caring behaviors, 761–762
General-purpose learning, 30, 593, 617
General rationality hypothesis, 589
Generative grammar, 698, 700–701
Genes:
    design and, 21
    good genes theory, 352–358
    psychological adaptations and, 151–152
    responsibility and, 151
    selfish, 146–152
Genetic correlates, paternal investment,
    493–494
Genetic determinism, 34–36, 168–169
Genetic diversity, 40
Genetic relatives, 48
Genetic similarity theory, 458–459, 865
Genres, literature, 945
Gestural language, 715
"Ghost of predators past" hypothesis, 207
Goal ascription, 107
Grammar:
    evolution of, 712–713
    generative, 698, 700–701
    universal (UG), 698–699, 701, 709, 711, 719
Grandmother hypothesis, 535–536
Grandparents, 473–475
    matrilateral kin, 473
    solicitude ratings for four classes of, 473
Greenbeard alleles, 459
Grief:
    kin selection theory, 461
    normal, versus intense sadness not triggered
        by loss, 893
Group living, 581–583
Groups. See Relationship(s), ingroup/outgroup
Group-upholding dispositions, evolution of
    (moral development stage), 762–763
Growth-reproduction trade-off, 85–86
Guilt, 59

Habitat imprinting theory, 191
Habitat selection, 190
Habits, 915
Hair quality, 309
Hamilton's rule, 449, 457–465, 507, 528–529, 684
Happiness, evolution of, 859
Harmful dysfunction (HD) analysis, 891,
    894–895, 897
Health, 662–663
Height, attractiveness and, 316–317
Helping tendency:
    effects of increasing survival rates of
        hypothetical patients on subjects' risk
        preferences, 544
    group's reproductive value and, 542
    life or death versus everyday conditions, 540
    relative's health under life or death versus
        everyday conditions and, 541
    risk proneness as function of group size and
        kinship, 543
Heterotypic continuity across life span, 643
Heuristics:
    cognitive biases, 726, 727–730
        conjunction fallacy, 727

    effectiveness of heuristics, 729–730
    effects of time and motivation, 727–729
    fundamental attribution error (FAE),
        728–729
    mental shortcuts, 727
    decision rule, 780
    elimination, 781
    minimalist, 780
    noncompensatory, 780
    stopping rule, 780
    take-the-best algorithm, 729–730, 780, 782
Hierarchies, social. See Social status
High-status children, 839
Hindsight bias, 786–787
Homicide. See Dangers from humans
Homunculi, 53–54
Honest signaling theory, 77–78
Horizontal learning mechanisms, 160
Hormones, 443, 552–572
    affection, 559–560
    clues to health, phenotypic/genotypic
        quality, 314–326
    evolution of the human family, 552–555
    fossil record, 554–559
    life history theory and, 79–80
    maternal care, 560–561
    neurotransmitter mechanisms, 559–562
    pair bonding, 562
    parental care, 560–562
    paternal care, 561–562
    spatial navigation, 184
    stress, 563–571
Hostile forces of nature:
    other humans as, 224–225
    surviving (see Survival)
    three fundamental classes:
        struggles with conspecifics, 175
        struggles with other species, 175
        struggles with physical environment, 175
Human nature, model of, 940–946
Humans, supposed uniqueness of, 978

Iconicity, 715
Ideal free distribution, 856
Ideal standards model (ISM), 426–428
Identity by descent (IBD), 451
Identity by state (IBS), 451–452
Imagery and emotion, role of; in planning,
    60–61
Immunological effects on fertility, 364
Implicit Associations Test (IAT), 808
Impression management, 759–760
Imprinted gene effects, 444–445
Imprinting, 831
Inbreeding, 964
Indirect reciprocity. See Reciprocity
Individual differences, 910–911
Individual lives, 907
Infanticide, 239–240, 465–468, 509–510
Infection and coevolution, 905
Inference engines, agency-focused, 106–109
Inference systems, domain-specific, 97–102, 109
Inferential connections, 129
Inferential principles, 102

Infidelity, sexual/marital:
  emotion programs, 56–57
  extra-pair mating, 348–349, 358–360, 362–363
  female, and sperm competition (*see* Sperm competition)
  laterality bias, 472–473
Information, representation of, 790–796
  decisions from experience versus decisions from description, 791–793
  inferences based on natural frequency versus probability representations, 793–796
  prospect theory, 791
Information processing, 328, 643, 644–645
Innateness, 30–32, 100–101. *See also* Nature/nurture
Instincts, 18
Intellectual origins of evolutionary psychology, 7–19
Intentional agents, 106
Intentional inference in hunting, 214–215
Intentionality detector (ID), 841
Intentional violations versus innocent mistakes, 608–611
Intention ascription, 107
Interactors, 884
Interdependence theory, 426
Intergroup prejudice, 808
Interpersonal perception, biases in, 735–738
  commitment skepticism, 736, 737
  negative outgroup stereotypes, 737
  sexual overperception, 735–736
  social exchange bias, 737–738
Intrasexual selection, 297
Intuitions, 19
Intuitive ontology, domain specificity, 2, 96–113
  agency-focused inference engines, 106–109
  domain-specific inference systems, 97–102, 109
  evolved brain not philosophically correct, 112–113
  human semantic knowledge, 113
  illustration (face recognition), 96–97
  living versus man-made objects:
    development and impairment, 102–103
    evolved and neural domains, 103–104
    manipulable versus nonmanipulable artifacts, 104
  mind reading, advantages of, 105–106
  natural numbers and natural operations, 110–112
  solid objects and bodies, 109–110
Intuitive physics, 109
Investigative methods, 133–137
Investment:
  in mates and offspring, morality and, 760–761
  parental (*see* Parental investment; Paternal investment)
  in relationships, mate retention and, 428–431

Japanese soldier, 819–820
Jealousy:
  emotion programs, situation detecting algorithms, 57, 61

homicides/violence related to, 633, 965
  pathological, 914
  romantic/sexual:
    adaptations, 320
    asymmetries for males/females of internally fertilizing species, 965
    life history perspectives, 88–89
    mate retention, 433–434
    mating strategies, 266
Joint attention, 107

K-factor, 868–870
Kin, 447–476
  alliances with, 813
  altruism:
    defined, 448
    evolution of, 448
    extended phenotypes, 449
    Hamilton's rule, 449, 457–465, 507, 528–529, 684
    hypothetical, 457
    paradox of, 449–450
    relatedness asymmetries, 450
  caring behaviors to; generalization of, 761–762
  cognitive mediation of nepotism, 464–465
  conflict:
    aggression, 630–631
    battleground versus resolution, 453
    damage to extended kin group, 233
    homicide, 238
    homicide risk, analysis of, kin/nonkin, 463
    parent-offspring, 452–453
    resolution models, 453–454
    selfish behavior, 448
    sibling, 452–453
  cooperation, 448
  ethnographic and behavioral studies, 459–460
  evolutionary speculations about the family, 452–455
  toward an evolutionary theory of the family, 455–457
  human behavior, 459–465
  kith-and-kin rationality, 542
  managing ingroup relationships, 655
  model of human nature, 941
  nepotistic psychology, 460
  nuclear, importance of, 457
  parental investment, 452, 511–513
    adoption, 512–513
    paternity uncertainty, 511
    stepparenting, 511–512
  psychological assessment and Hamilton's Rule, 457–459
    estimating B and C, 458
    estimating r, 458–459
    life history, 458
  restrained competition among kin, 463–464
  selection, 167, 450–452
    conundrums, 450–452
    beyond Darwinian fitness, 450–451
    paradoxes of relatedness, 451–452
  taxonomy of sociality, 448

Kin *(Continued)*
  value, 303
  "what if" studies, 462–463
Kin recognition/detection, 444, 530–535
  assortative pairing, 530, 865–867
  categorizing by degree of genetic
    relatedness, 530–535
  familiarity, 532–533
  mechanisms, 444
  phenotype matching, 533–535
  research on architecture of, 28–30
  single locus kin recognition systems,
    531–532
Kinship psychology, 457–459, 465–475
  fatherhood, 469–472
  grandparenthood, 475
  motherhood, 465–469
  parental probability and more distal kin
    relations: the laterality bias, 472–475
  sibling relations, 475
Kinship theory, 448–450
Knowledge:
  acquisition system, predator-prey, 217–218
  values and, 50–52

Landmark(s):
  cognitive, 563
  versus orientation, 181, 186, 188
Landscape preference, 189–190
Language, 582, 698–720
  acquisition device, 33
  biological versus sociocultural factors,
    718–720
  Blueprint of the Listener, 704
  Blueprint of the Speaker, 702
  case illustration, inferring genes from
    language disorder, 711–712
  evolution of communication (Tinbergen's
    four questions), 700–714
    how did language get that way in
      phylogeny?, 712–714
    how does it work?, 700–705
    how does language get that way in
      ontogeny?, 707–712
    what does language do for the organism?,
      705–707
  evolution of grammar, 712–713
  evolution of language transmission, 714–718
  frame-content metaphor, 717
  generative grammar, 698, 700–701
  innateness, 717–718
  instinct, 445
  parsing pressure, 719
  processing/performance/competence,
    700–701
  rhetorical/semantic/syntactic system, 701,
    702
  signed, 714–717
  universal (UG), 698–699, 701, 709, 711, 719
Laterality bias, 472–475
Law of law's leverage, 962–964
Law of small numbers, 789
Learning instincts, 18
Learning mechanisms, 29–30

Legal system, evolutionary psychology and,
    929, 953–972
  assessing comparative effectiveness of legal
    strategies, 960–965
  behavioral models, 954, 961, 962
  biolegal history, 966
  bounded rationality, 958, 960
  clarifying causal links, 956–957
  cognitive quirks, 960
  discovering useful patterns in regulable
    behavior, 955
  disentangling multiple causes, 968
  endowment effects, 958–959
  environment of evolutionary adaptation
    (EEA), 963
  evolutionary insights into, 970–972
  exposing unwarranted assumptions, 967–968
  generating new research questions, 970
  homicides committed in self-defense, 244
  increasing accuracy, 968–969
  increasing efficiency, 954
  increasing law-relevant understanding about
    people, 969
  irrationally steep discounting, 957–958
  law of law's leverage, 962–964
  probability assessments, mistaken, 958
  providing theoretical foundation and
    potential predictive power, 957–960
  rape, 967–968
  revealing deep patterns in legal architecture,
    965–967
  sharpening cost-benefit analyses, 956
  time-shifted rationality (TSR), 960–961
  uncovering policy conflicts, 955–956
Less-is-more effect/hypothesis, 729, 796–797
Life history theory (LHT), 1–2, 68–91
  brain and life span evolution in humans, 75,
    80–84
  coevolutionary processes and their modeling,
    75–80
    cost-benefit analysis in behavioral ecology,
      76–78
    enactment of allocation decisions, 78–80
    honest signaling theory, 77–78
    mortality as function of investments, 76
  development and aging in humans, 83–86
    aging and differential decline across
      domains, 86
    characteristic features of the human
      growth and brain development curve,
      83–84
    timing of developmental achievements,
      84–85
  domains of social value, 295–296
  ecology and, 73–74
  embodied capital and the brain, 74–75
  fitness-maximizing or optimal strategies, 68
  formulations, 71
  humans, 80–86
  kin, 458
  mating strategies and, 279
  overview, 69–75
  psychological adaptations within framework
    of, 86–91

senescence, 70–71
themes in, 91
trade-offs, 69–73
   growth-reproduction, 85–86
   mating-parenting effort, 72–73
   present-future reproduction, 70
   quantity-quality of offspring, 72
Life Orientation Test (LOT), 861
Literature and evolutionary psychology, 931–947
   adaptive function of the arts, 938–940
   behavioral systems, 941–942
   cognitive rhetoric, 938
   contributions to adaptationist literary study, 932–936
   cosmic evolutionists, 936–937
   domain-specific cognitive modules, 942
   dual theory of art, 939
   ecological literary criticism, or ecocriticism, 935
   elemental components of human experience: characters/setting/plots, 944
   evolutionary analogists, 937–938
   evolved motive dispositions, 942
   genres (tragedy/comedy/satire), 945
   macrostructures/microstructures (formal organization), 946
   model of human nature and literary meaning, 940–946
   nonadaptationist forms of "evolutionary" literary theory, 936–938
Locating places, 175, 177–194
   coherence/legibility, 193
   conclusions, 194
   domain general view (Gallistel's), 178–180
   domain specificity of spatial behavior, 177–178
   future directions, 193–194
   genetic/neurological/developmental bases of navigational strategies, 182–183
   habitat imprinting theory, 191
   habitat selection, 190
   identifying evolved mechanisms, 187–188
   landscape preference, 189–190
   mystery/complexity, 193
   navigational strategies, 181–182
      allocentric versus egocentric, 181
      compensation interpretation, 188
      dead reckoning versus episodic, 181
      Euclidean/geometric versus topographic, 181
      hunter-gatherer theory, 188
      landmark versus orientation, 181, 186, 188
      map/compass, 181–182
      one mechanism or two, 188–189
   optimization in animal movement, 180–181
   prospect-refuge theory, 192–193
   savanna theory/hypothesis, 190–191, 193
   sex differences, spatially related, 183–184, 186–187
Logic:
   abstract rules of, 741
   adaptive versus formal, 600–603
   eliminating, 602–603
   inferential systems and, 100

Lone anthropologist model, 11
Lottery winnings, hypothetical, 462–463
Love system and relationship processes, 425–433
   conclusions, 436–438
   dependence in relationships, 431–432
   discrete systems model, 424–425
   ideal standards model (ISM), 426–428
   interdependence theory, 426
   investments in relationships, 428–431
   partner-specific investment (PSI), 429–430

Machiavellian behavior, 839
Macrostructures/microstructures, 946
Magnitude estimation, 111
Maintenance, importance of (Williams versus Gould on function), 885–887
Major histocompatibility complex (MHC), 357, 364, 531
Male adaptations to sperm competition, 378–387
Male-female partner aggression, 632–634
Male induction of ovulation, 364
Male investment hypothesis, 349–350
Male mate guarding, change in, across cycle, 361–363
Male mate value, 300–302, 436
Male same-sex aggression, 634–635
Man-made objects, living versus:
   development and impairment, 102–103
   evolved and neural domains, 103–104
   manipulable versus nonmanipulable artifacts, 104
Marginal value theorem, 87
Masturbatory ejaculates, 379, 381
Material resources, conflict over, 226
Mathematics, 14, 842–844
Mating, 251–253
   adaptationism and human mating psychology, 255–257
   adaptations to ovulation (*see* Ovulation, adaptations to)
   conflict over resources, 226–227
   developmental theories of human mating, 279
   female infidelity and sperm competition (*see* Sperm competition)
   history of field of science of, 253
   mate choice, 815–816
      long-term partner selection, 816
      preferences in women across the reproductive cycle, 139–140
      relationship selection, 815–816
   mate-retention strategies, 435–436, 816–817
   mate value:
      attractiveness and, 296–302
      female, 299–300, 436
      male, 300–302, 436
   model of human nature, 941
   opportunities, 487
   overview/introduction, 251–253
   rejection, fear of, 256–257
   sexual coercion (*see* Sexual coercion)
   trade-off, with parenting, 72–73

Mating strategies, 258–280
  childhood experiences influencing, 279
  cultural differences, 277–279
  evidence table, 260
  individual differences, 272–277
    within men, 273–274
    sexual strategy pluralism, 272–276
    Trivers-Willard hypothesis, 276–277
    within women, 274–276
  monogamous, 259–261
    perennial, 259
    serial, 259
  multimale-multifemale strategies, 264
  national levels of women's sociosexuality
      related to operational sex ratios across
      48 nations, 278
  operational sex ratios and, 277–279
  polyandrous, 263–264
    associated or nonadelphic, 263
  polygynous, 260, 261–263
    class-based or leader-only, 262
    female defense or harem, 261–262
    general, 262
  sex and context differences, 268–272
    long-term mating, 270–271
    parental investment theory, 268–270
    sexual strategies theory (SST), 270–272
    short-term mating, 271–272
  sexual selection theory, 277
  short-term, 260, 264–268
    cuckoldry, 266
    physiological adaptation for, 267
    romantic jealousy, 266
    sex differences, 271–272
  stress, fertility, and, 279
Matrilateral kin, 473
Meliorism, 828
Memory (retrieving/forgetting information),
    44, 782–790
  functions of forgetting, 785–786
  hindsight bias, consequence of future-
      oriented memory, 786–787
  long-term memory (forgetting curves and
      the statistical properties of information
      use), 783–785
  short-term memory, functional explanation
      of its bounds, 787–790
Menarche, 85, 299–300
Mental health, evolutionary psychology, 775,
    903–920
  contributions (overview), 904
  diagnosis, 909–910
  emotions and the emotional disorders,
      907–909
  explaining vulnerability to mental disorders,
      904–907
    constraints, 906
    defenses, 906
    infection and coevolution, 905
    mismatch, 904–905
    selection is for reproductive success, not
        health, 906
    trade-offs, 905

fallacies in arguments that mental disorders
    are naturally selected conditions,
    895–897
  individual differences, 910–911
  individual lives, 907
  relationships, deeper understanding of,
      907–908
    development, 908
    psychodynamics, 908
  specific disorders, 911–919
    addictions, 914–915
    anxiety disorders, 911–913
    attention disorders, 918
    autism, 916, 918
    behavioral disorders, 914–916
    bipolar disorder, 916
    brain disorders, 916–917
    child abuse, 919
    eating disorders, 915–916
    emotional disorders, 911–914
    excesses/deficits, 914
    habits, 915
    mood disorders, 913–914
    obsessive-compulsive disorder (OCD), 918
    PTSD, 912
    relationship difficulties, 919
    schizophrenia, 916, 917–918
    sexual disorders, 916
Mental shortcuts, cognitive bias, 727
Methods of evolutionary sciences, 2, 119–141
  criticism of, 978–979
  investigative/research strategies, 133–137
  overview/introduction, 119–121
  research programs providing evidence for
      psychological adaptations, 137–140
    mate preferences in women across the
        reproductive cycle, 139–140
    snakes and evolved fear module, 137–139
  theory and research methods in the
      evolutionary sciences, 119–141
  theory testing, special design, and strong
      research methods, 121–127
    adaptations, adaptationism, and standards
        of evidence, 124–126
    generating more compelling evidence,
        123–124
    special design evidence, 126–127
  validity, 120–121, 127–133
    construct, 131–132
    ecological, 131
    in experimental and quasi-experimental
        research, 130–131
    external, 131
    goals and objectives of research, 128
    internal, 130
    multitrait-multimethod approaches,
        132–133
    process model of, 128–130
    relevance, 131
    robustness, 131
    statistical conclusion, 130–131
MHC. See Major histocompatibility complex
    (MHC)

Mind:
  blank-slate view of, 6–7, 10, 166, 167, 585
  as crowded network of evolved, domain-specific programs, 52
  social; chemistry of stress, family, and, 563–571
  theory of, 105–106, 210, 840–842
  uncluttering, 785
Mindblindness, 841
Mind reading, 105–106, 681–683
Mismatch, 904–905
Modularity, 162–165, 471
  alternative to, 978
  cognitive, 162–163
  encapsulation, 162–163
Monogamous mating strategies, 259–261
  evidence of monogamy in humans, 260
  marriage and, 632, 636
  perennial monogamy, 259
  serial monogamy, 259
Mood disorders/depression, 40, 897–898, 913–914
Morality, 583, 747–768
  biological conception of, 750–751
  care, evolution of, 760–762
  conceptualized/defined, 747–750
  conscience, evolution of, 767
  cooperation and conflicts of interest, 750
  of deference, 752–754
  direct reciprocity, 754–756
  beyond evolved norms and natural inclinations, 765–767
  friendship, evolution of, 757–758
  group-upholding dispositions, 762–763
  indirect reciprocity, evolution of, 758–760
  limitations of reason and social learning, 765–766
  natural selection:
    moral judgments, 763–764
    social strategies, 751–752
    verbal moral norms, 764
  nature of humans, and, 768
  origin of, 749–750
  Prisoners' Dilemma models of social evolution, 751–752
  reason and social learning, 765
  rules, evolution of, 764–765
  selective interaction, 756–762
  self-interest and sanctions, 766–767
  selfishness and, 749, 750, 752
  significance of coalitions and mutual control, 753–754
  stage(s) (Kohlberg), 748, 752–767
    overview table, 748
    stage 1, 752–754
    stage 2, 754–756
    stage 3, 756–763
    stage 4, 762–767
Mortality, 76
Motherhood:
  hormones, and maternal care, 560–561
  infant/offspring relationship, 560, 644
  investment (*see* Parental investment)

  kinship psychology of, 465–469
  maternal-fetal conflict, 514–515
  maternal-infant conflict and infanticide, 631–632
  weaning conflict, 515–516
Motivation:
  cognitive bias and, 727–729
  emotional-motivation systems, relationship processes, 423–425 (*see also* Relationship(s))
  opponents and motive (aggression), 630–639
Motivational computation, 51–52
Motivational domain, 48
Motive dispositions, evolved, 942
Motor behavior, 109–110
Movement patterns (attractiveness), 310
Multiple fitness model of attractiveness assessment, 327
Murder victims. *See* Dangers from humans
Mutual choice and paradox of popularity, 757
Mystery/complexity, 193

Natal dispersal, 185
National levels of women's sociosexuality related to operational sex ratios, across 48 nations, 278
Natural engineering, 147–159
Natural selection, as engineer, 19–25, 161
Nature/nurture, 30–41, 157–162, 810
  adaptationist perspective, 30–41
  debate no longer about, 810
  evolutionary psychology versus behavior genetics, 39–41
  gene-environment interactions, 157–159
  "innate" not the opposite of "learned," 30–32
  nature as product of nurture, 160–162
  nurture as product of nature, 159–160
  plasticity, 159
  presence at birth, 33–34
  specialized versus general purpose, 32–33
  twin fallacies of genetic determinism and environmental determinism, 34–36
  universal architectural design versus genetic differences, 36–39
Navigational behavior. *See* Locating places
Negative outgroup stereotypes, 737
Negative payoffs, detecting, 621
Neighbor-modulated fitness, 450, 451
NEO-FFI, 867, 869–870
NEO-MATE, 867–868
Nepotism, 444, 476. *See also* Altruism
Neurobiology of innateness, 710–712
Neuroendocrine response, loss of status, 678–680
Neuropsychological dissociation between social contracts and precautions, 611–613
Niche-splitting, 856
Noblesse oblige effect, 687
Nonkin allies, 685
Nonkin altruism, 544–547
Norms, 657, 681
Numbers, natural, 110–112
Numerosity and ordinality, 843

Objects, solid, 109–110
Obsessive-compulsive disorder (OCD),
    604–605, 918
Offspring. *See also* Parental investment;
    Parenting:
    number of, 508
    survival, 487
    trade-off between quantity/quality, 72
One-one principle, counting, 843
Ontogenetic development of behavior in life of
    the organism, 888
Ontogeny, vital question, 158
Ontologies:
    actual versus scientific, 112
    intuitive (*see* Intuitive ontology, domain
        specificity)
Operational sex ratios (OSR), 277–279, 496–497
Opponents and motive (aggresion), 630–639
Optics, laws of, 590–591
Optimal design standards of evidence, 125
Optimal response disposition (ORD), 857
Oral health, 309–310
Orchids, 255–257
Order-irrelevant principle, counting, 843
Organic design, principles of, 19–45
    adaptive problems select for adaptations,
        21–22
    design evidence, 27–30
    environment of evolutionary adaptedness,
        22–23
    evolutionary versus traditional approaches to
        psychology, 41–45
    genes and design, 21
    knowing the past, 23–25
    natural selection as design engineer for
        organic machines, 19–25
    nature and nurture, adaptationist
        perspective, 30–41
    properties of organisms not adaptations,
        25–26
    psychology as reverse engineering, 25–27
    reproduction and function, 21
    self-reproducing machines, 20
Orgasm, postcopulatory female choice, 388–389
Orientation versus landmark, 181, 186, 188
Ovulation, adaptations to, 344–366
    alternative explanations for fertility status
        effects on female sexual interests,
        359–361
    changes in male mate guarding across the
        cycle, 361–363
    cryptic choice mechanisms and menstrual
        cycle variation, 364–365
    cyclic changes in female sexual interests and
        mate preferences, 352–361
    evolution of concealed ovulation, and
        extended female sexuality, 349–352
        additional views, 350–351
        comparative data, 351
        cuckoldry hypothesis, 350
        male investment hypothesis, 349–350
    female preferences:
        creative talent, 357
        facial masculinity, 355–356

        major histocompatibility complex (MHC)
            traits, 357
        men's behavioral displays, 356–357
        scent of symmetry, 353–354
        symmetrical faces, 275
    female risk-reduction across the cycle,
        363–364
        antirape adaptation, 363–364
        avoidance of other suboptimal mating
            behaviors, 364
    good genes extra-pair copulation theory,
        352–353
    immunological effects on fertility, 364
    implications of coevolutionary processes for
        frequency of extra-pair sex, 362–363
    male induction of ovulation, 364
    male partner characteristics that moderate
        relationship between fertility risk and
        sexual interests, 359
    sexually antagonistic coevolution, and
        human mating, 347–349
        biparental care of offspring, 347
        demonstrations of, 345
        extra-pair copulation (EPC), 348
        implications of, 346–347
        male-female conflicts of interest, 349
        potential for extra-pair mating, 348–349
        theoretical background, 344–347
    sexually antagonistic coevolutionary
        selection on male adaptations:
        changes in male mate guarding across the
            cycle, 361–362
        men detecting women's fertility status, 361
    shifts in sexual interests across the cycle,
        358–359
    tests of the extra-pair copulation theory,
        shifts in female sexual interest across
        the cycle, 358–359

Pair bonding:
    evidence of, 421–423
    fossil record, 554–559
    hormones, 562
    role of in human reproduction, 420–423
Paleoanthropology, 15
Parental investment, 506–522. *See also* Paternal
    investment
    common genetic interests, 817–818
    ecology and, 73–74
    factors affecting amount of parental
        investment, 507–513
    factors affecting relatedness, 511–513
    factors influencing benefits to parents,
        508–511
    factors influencing costs to parents, 507–508
    Hamilton's rule, 507
    parent-offspring conflict, 452, 513–518
    sibling relations, 518–522
Parental investment theory, mating strategies,
    268–270
Parenting, 443–445
    aggression, and style of child rearing,
        642–643
    model of human nature, 941

overview/introduction, 443–445
parental care, and hormones, 560–562
parental solicitude,
    discriminative/indiscriminate, natural
    selection and, 964
trade-off between quantity/quality of
    offspring, 72
Parsing pressure, 719
Partner-specific investment (PSI), 429–430
Pastoral responsibility, 687
Paternal care, 561–562
Paternal investment, 443, 483–499
    competitiveness, 490–492
    cultural correlates, 496
    developmental correlates, 495–496
    ecological correlates, 496–497
    evolutionary pressures, 497–498
    facultative expression of, 487, 493–497
    genetic and hormonal correlates, 493–494
    human, 487–497
    life history perspectives, 89
    physical well-being of children, 488–489
    proximate correlates, 493–496
    social correlates, 494
    social well-being of children, 489–493
    trade-offs, 485–486
Paternal probability, 360, 450
Paternal resemblance, 470–472
Paternity:
    certainty/uncertainty, 450, 487, 492, 511,
        635–636
    kinship psychology of fatherhood, 469–472
Perennial monogamy, 259
Permission schema theory, 605–608, 610, 620–621
Personality psychology, evolutionary, 519–521,
    774, 851–873
    birth order and personality/development,
        519–521
    conclusions, 871–872
        constraining accounts of personality,
            871–872
        data quality, 872–873
        horizontal integration, 872
        limitations, 873
        vertical integration, 872
    personality in nonhuman animals, empirical
        evidence, 857–860
        evolution of happiness, 859
        evolution and variability in personality,
            859–860
        FFM, 857–858
        methodological problems in study of
            animal personality, 858
        nonhuman animal personality past to
            present, 857–858
    review of current evolutionary theories of
        personality, 851–857
        theories of adaptive significance, 852–854
        theories of frequency dependence, 853–857
        theories of selective neutrality, 851–852
    Personality and selection in humans, empirical
        evidence, 860–871
        evidence for frequency-dependent selection
            of personality traits, 868–870

K-factor, 868–869
NEO-FFI, EPQ-R, and ZKPQ,
    869–870
personality and demographic correlates of
    K, 870
evidence for natural selection of personality
    traits, 860–863
    personality correlates of completed
        fertility, 862–863
    personality correlates of completed
        longevity, 861
    personality correlates of predictors of
        fertility, 863
    personality correlates of predictors of
        longevity, 861–862
evidence for sexual selection of personality
    traits, 863–868
    absolute or consensual preferences,
        864–865
    additional empirical test (NEO-MATE),
        867–868
    relative preferences or assortative mating,
        865–867
limitations, 870–871
Type A personality, 861, 862
Type B personality, 861
Type D personality, 861
Person-situation interactions, 806–807
Phenotype(s):
    extended, 449
    matching, 459, 532, 533–535
Phenotypic condition (attractiveness), 307
Physical attack, 662. *See also* Aggression;
    Violence
Physical attractiveness, 292–330
    fluctuating asymmetry and developmental
        stability, 311–314
    hair quality, 309
    height, 316–317
    hormonal and sexually dimorphic clues to
        health, phenotypic, and genotypic
        quality, 314–326
    mate retention strategies, 432, 435–436
    movement patterns, 310
    oral health, 309–310
    organization of attractiveness-assessment
        mechanisms, 305–307
    phenotypic condition, 307
    shoulder-to-hip (SHR) ratio, 325
    skin quality, 308–309
    social value, attractiveness assessments as
        measures of, 293–305
        coalitional value, 304–305
        cooperative value, 303–304
        descendant value, 302–303
        human life history and the domains of
            social value, 295–296
        kin value, 303
        mate value, 296–302
    upper body morphology (shoulders/chest/
        breasts), 325–326
    waist-to-hip ratio (WHR), 321–325
    weight, body fat, and BMI, 313, 317–321
Physical prowess, mate retention, 432

Physical resemblance:
  kin recognition, 534
  parental, 470–472, 534
Physical well-being of children, paternal
  investment and, 488–489
Plasticity:
  adaptive sensitivity to context and, 832–833
  nature-nurture, 159
Play, sex differences in, 834–835
Policy conflicts, uncovering, 955–956
Political correctness, 165–170
  evolutionary psychology as genetic
    determinism, 168–169
  evolutionary psychology as racist or sexist,
    167–168
  evolutionary psychology as social
    Darwinism, 169
  hostility to evolutionary psychology,
    169–170, 975–976, 977
  sociobiology, 15, 166–167, 975–979
Polyandry:
  associated or nonadelphic, 263
  mating strategies, 263–264
  women's fantasies and, 376–377
Polygyny:
  class-based or leader-only, 262
  evidence of, in humans, 260
  female defense or harem, 261–262
  general, 262
  history of marriage, 632
  male same-sex aggression, 634
  mating strategies, 261–263
Pooled equilibria, 455
Popularity, paradox of, 757
Positive illusions, 738–739
Postmortem bequests, 462
Postpartum depression (PPD), 467–469
Poverty, and violence/aggression, 642
Pragmatics, conversational, 740
Precocity, social exchange, 622, 688
Predators and prey, adaptations to, 175,
  200–220
  agency detection and discrimination,
    204–209
    contingency, 206–207
    eyes, 208–209
    morphology, 207–208
    self-propelled motion, 205–206
  agency hypothesis, cessation of, 213
  agency system, 203–204
  behavior, 218–219
  death understanding, agency and, 212–214
  fear, 215–216
  human antipredator behaviors, 218
  inference system, 209–215
    chess analogy, 209
    predator-prey schema (PPS), 209–212
    theory of mind, 210
  intentional inference in hunting, 214–215
  knowledge acquisition system, 217–218
  predators and prey as agents of selection,
    200–201
  responses of children to actual animals, 218
  skills selected for, 202–203

Pregnancy, homicide and, 238–239
Prisoners' Dilemma Game (PDG), 537, 591, 592,
  618, 685–686, 751–752, 762
Probability, 740
Proposers, 686
Prospect-refuge theory, 192–193
Prospect theory, 791
Protective biases, 731–735
  allergy, cough, and anxiety, 731–734
  auditory looming, 731, 734
  aversion to diseased or injured persons,
    734–735
  food aversions, 734
Protolanguage, 712
PSI Inventory, 430–431
Psychodynamics, 908
Psychological adaptations:
  genes/gene interactions, 151–152
  life history framework, 86–91
  research programs providing evidence,
    137–140
    mate preferences in women across the
      reproductive cycle, 139–140
    snakes and evolved fear module, 137–139
  similarity to other adaptations, 156–157
Psychological mechanisms associated with
  prudent sperm allocation, 381–382
Psychological models of ecological adjustment,
  643–645
Psychology:
  evolutionizing traditional disciplines of,
    773–775
  as reverse engineering, 25–27, 41
  traditional versus evolutionary approaches,
    41–45
Psychotherapy, 920
PTSD, 912
Public Goods games, 659

Racism, 167–168
Rape, 230–231
  convicted rapists as generalists, 404–406
  culture and, 645
  legal system, 967–968
  ovulation and antirape adaptation, 363–364
  specialization and coercive potential,
    406–408
  sperm competition and, 400
Rational analysis of behavior, 783
Rational choice theory, 617–619
Rational/economic advantageous, 618
Rationality:
  bounded, 958, 960
  ecological, 782
  general rationality hypothesis, 589
  kith-and-kin, 542
  rationality, 23, 782
  time-shifted (TSR), 960–961
Reasoning, 44
  instincts, 18–19
  social exchange, 585–586
Reason and social learning, limitations of in
  inculcation of morality, 765–766
Recalibrational emotion programs, 58–59

Recalibrational releasing engines, 59–61
Reciprocal altruism, 167, 585, 684
Reciprocity:
  in animal kingdom, 617
  direct (morality development stage), 754–756
  indirect, evolution of, 758–760
    deception, detection, and morality, 760
    impression management, 759–760
  research on, 685
  social exchange, 585 (*see also* Social exchange
    reasoning)
  social status and, 683–688
Recognition heuristic, 729
Recursion, 706
Red Queen process, 346–347
Rejection, fear of, 256–257
Relationship(s):
  anger-upset system, 433–436
    discrete systems model of love and anger-
      upset, 424–425
    jealousy, 433–434
    mate-retention strategies, 435–436
    violence in relationships, 434–435
  difficulties, and mental health, 919
  emotional-motivation systems, 423–425
  love system, 425–433
    dependence in relationships, 431–432
    discrete systems model, 424–425
    ideal standards model (ISM), 426–428
    interdependence theory, 426
    investments in relationships, 428–431
    partner-specific investment (PSI), 429–430
  mate retention (*see* Mating)
  pair bonding in human reproduction,
    420–423
  understanding of, 907–908
Relationship(s), ingroup/outgroup, 582,
  653–669
  choosing social partners, 654–658
    ability to coordinate, 657
    availability for future interaction, 656–657
    cooperative and trustworthy types,
      655–656
    generation of positive externalities, 658
    kin, 655
  discriminate sociality, 653
  domain specificity extended, 668
  functional specificity in social cognition, 654
  ingroup favoritism and outgroup
    homogeneity, 654
  intergroup relations, 664–667
  managing ingroup relationships, 658–664
    free riding and punishment, 659–661
    health, 662–663
    intentional free riding via inability, 661
    physical attack, 662
    socialization threats, 663–664
Replicator(s), 884
Replicator-dynamic analysis, 455
Reproduction:
  causal structure of the environment, 153–154
  function and, 21
  life history trade-off between present and
    future, 70

  loss of future, 233
  mating (*see* Mating strategies)
  ovulation (*see* Ovulation, adaptations to)
Reproductive value (RV), 70
Resemblance. *See* Physical resemblance
Resolution models, 453–455
Resource-accruing potential, 432
Resource circumstances, parental investment
  and, 508
Response selection, 644
Rhetoric, cognitive, 938
Rhetorical/semantic/syntactic system, 701, 702
Risk preferences/proneness, kin altruism, 543,
  544
Risk reduction across female cycle, 363–364
  antirape adaptation, 363–364
  avoidance of other suboptimal mating
    behaviors, 364

Satire/comedy/tragedy, 945
Savanna theory/hypothesis, 190–191, 193
Scent of symmetry, female preference for,
  353–354
Schizophrenia, 40, 603, 916, 917–918
School tragedies, 676–677
Secrecy as defense against being murdered, 243
Segmentation, 703
Selectionist revolution in evolutionary
  psychology, 10
Selection pressures, 153, 232, 234, 590–594
Self-control, 641
Self-defense, killing in, 243–244
Self-interest, significance of, 766–767
Selfishness:
  genes and, 146–152, 683–684
    do selfish genes create selfish people,
      150–151
    gene interactions, adaptations as product
      of, 152
    genes and personal responsibility, 151
    natural engineering, 147–159
    origin of metaphor, 146–147
    psychological adaptations, 151–152
    spandrels, 149–150
  morality and, 749, 750, 752
Self-judgment, biases in, 738–739
Self-organizing systems, 706
Self-perception, 703
Self-protection, 814–815
Self-reproducing machines, 20
Semantic knowledge, 96, 97–98
Senescence, 70–71
Separation anxiety disorder, 898
Serial monogamy, 259
Serotonin, 642
Sex differences:
  aggression, 639–640
  fitness payoffs for status striving, 814
  intimate violence, 634
  mating strategies, 268–272
    long-term, 270–271
    parental investment theory, 268–270
    sexual strategies theory (SST), 270–272
    short-term mating, 271–272

Sex differences *(Continued)*
    moral orientation, 761
    parent-offspring relationships, 450
    in play, 834–835
    spatially related, 183–189
        compensation interpretation, 188
        evolutionary theories, 184–186
        hunter-gatherer theory, 188
        orientation versus landmark strategy, 186,
            188–189
        sexual dimorphism, 186–187
    status striving, 689–691, 814
Sexism, evolutionary psychology and, 167–168
Sexual arousal to force (SAF), 401–411
    conceptualizing, 408–409
    confluence model of sexual aggression, 403
    convicted rapists as generalists, 404–406
    proposed evolved function of, 402–405
    specialization and coercive potential,
        406–408
    as specialized mediator of sexual coercion,
        409–411
Sexual attractiveness, cognitive bias, 724
Sexual behavior, and legal system, 964
Sexual coercion, 394–414
    competing models, 412
    conclusions, 411–414
    correlates with behavior, 413–414
    correlates with other characteristics of men,
        413
    in humans, 397–401
        adaptation, by-products, or noise, 397–398
        adaptation hypothesis and relevant
            findings, 398–400
        conceptualizing as either result of
            adaptation or as by-product, 400–401
    in other species, 395–397
    sexual arousal to force (SAF), 401–411
Sexual disorders, 916
Sexuality, female; and evolution of concealed
    ovulation, 349–352. *See also* Ovulation,
    adaptations to
Sexual jealousy. *See* Jealousy
Sexually antagonistic coevolution, 344–349,
    361–362
    demonstrations of, 345
    human mating and, 347–349
        biparental care of offspring, 347
        demonstrations of, 345
        extra-pair copulation (EPC), 348
        implications of, 346–347
        male-female conflicts of interest, 349
        potential for extra-pair mating, 348–349
        theoretical background, 344–347
    major implications of, 346–347
    selection on male adaptations, 361–362
        changes in male mate guarding across the
            cycle, 361–362
        men detecting women's fertility status, 361
    theoretical background, 344–347
Sexual overperception hypothesis, 735–736
Sexual selection, 167
    mating strategies, 277
    personality traits, 863–868

Sexual strategies theory (SST), 270–276
Shared-attention mechanism (SAM), 841
Short-term mating, 260, 264–268
Short-term memory, 787–790
Shoulder-to-hip (SHR) ratio, 325
Siblings:
    birth order, 518–521
    birth spacing, 521–522
    conflict, 452–453
    parental investment and, 518–522
    psychology of, 475
    theory of mind development, 842
Signaling theory, 77–78, 454–455
Signed language, 714–717
Size dimorphism, 556
Skinner's hypothesis, 15
Skin quality, 308–309
Snakes:
    attacking humans only in self-defense, 207
    avoidance system, 50–51
    evolved fear module and, 137–139
Social cognition, 167
Social contract theory, 591, 592
Social correlates, paternal investment, 494
Social Darwinism, 169
Social development, 836–840
Social exchange bias, 737–738
Social exchange reasoning, 584–623
    adaptive logic, not formal logic, 600–603
    alternative (by-product) hypotheses
        eliminated, 598
    benefits, 606–608
    cognitive instinct, 587
    conditional reasoning:
        about other social domains, 604–605
        and social exchange, 594–598
        specializations for, 603–605
    content-free deontic logics, 610–611
    cross-cultural invariances and dissociations,
        614–616
    dedicated system or general intelligence,
        603
    design features (D1-D6), 593
    dissociation by content, 596–598
    dissociation for social contracts, 609–610
    domain-general learning, 616–622
    familiarity, 598–600
    intentional violations versus innocent
        mistakes, 608–611
    logic, 602–603
    neuropsychological dissociation between
        social contracts and precautions, 611–613
    permission schema theory, 610
    perspective change, 600–601
    precocious development/performance,
        613–614, 622
    reasoning, 585
    research program, 587
    selection pressures and predicted design
        features, 590–594
    social contract algorithms or a permission
        schema, 605–606
    statistical learning, 622
    switched social contracts, 601–602

Wason Selection Task, 595, 597, 601
zoological and cultural perspective, 588–590
Social geometries, 820
Social group, threats to status within, 964
Social hierarchies:
  proximate causes, 678–688
  ultimate causes, 677–678
Social identity theory, 637–638
Social intelligence, 105–106
Sociality:
  hypothesis of individual differences, 855, 858
  taxonomy of, 448
Socialization threats, 663–664
Social partners, choosing, 654–658
Social perception, cognitive bias, 724
Social psychology, evolutionary, 774, 803–822
  cognitive processes, emphasis on, 807–808
  contributions of social psychological
    research to evolutionary psychology,
    805–808
  cross-cultural, 821
  by domains, 811–818
    coalition formation, 811–813
    mate choice, 815–816
    mate retention, 816–817
    overview table, 812
    parental care, 817–818
    self-protection, 814–815
    status, 813–814
  dynamic emergence, from decision rules to
    cultural norms, 818–819
  informing evolutionary models with social
    psychological research, 805–806
  lessons for social psychologists, 804–805,
    808–811
    connecting proximate and ultimate
      explanations, 810
    domain generality versus domain
      specificity, 810–811
    focus on proximate and domain-general
      causes can be misleading, 808–809
  past/future, 819–822
  person-situation interactions, 806–807
Social status, 582, 676–693
  assaults on, 228–229
  cognitive-behavioral strategies, 680–688
  conflict over, 226
  deception, 681–683
  development informing evolutionary
    explanations of social dominance effects,
    688–689
  evolutionary social psychology, 813–814
  examples of school tragedies, 676–677
  inclusive fitness, 677
  loss of:
    emotional/psychological/strategic
      responses, 691–692
    physiological responses, 678
  mind reading, and deception, 681–683
  neuroendocrine responses, 678–680
  reciprocity, 683–688
  resources of competition, access to, 681–682
  sex differences in striving for, 689–691
    fitness payoffs, 814

  intrasexual competition among females,
    691
  intrasexual competition among males, 691
  social hierarchies:
    proximate causes, 678–688
    ultimate causes, 677–678
Social value, attractiveness assessments as
  measures of, 293–305
  coalitional value, 304–305
  cooperative value, 303–304
  descendant value, 302–303
  human life history, 295–296
  kin value, 303
  mate value, 296–302
Social well-being of children, paternal
  investment and, 489–493
Sociobiology, 15, 166–167, 975–979
Socioeconomic status (SES), 420–421, 488–489
Space constancy, 187
Spandrels, 149–150
Spatial navigation. *See* Locating places
Special design standards of evidence, 125
Specialization, 32–33, 44, 74, 406–408, 620–621
Species, 38–39
Speech. *See also* Language:
  acquisition of, 709–710
  evolution of (frame/content theory), 713–714
Sperm competition, 372–390
  as adaptive problem for humans, 374–377
  contest competition between men's
    ejaculates, 385–387
  evidence of evolutionary history of female
    infidelity and, 375
  female preferences for extra-pair mates
    targeting men providing adequate
    sperm, 360
  influence on men:
    mate selection, 384
    reproductive anatomy and copulatory
      behavior, 383–384
    sexual arousal and sexual fantasies,
      384–385
  masturbatory ejaculates, 379, 381
  multiple mating and, 375–376
  in nonhuman species, 372–374
  penis evolving as semen displacement
    device, 383–384
  polyandrous sex in women's fantasies,
    376–377
  prudent sperm allocation by men, 378–382
    physiological mechanisms, 380–381
    psychological mechanisms, 381–382
  rape and, 400
  women generating, 375–376
  women's adaptations to, 387–389
    postcopulatory female choice, 388–389
    precopulatory female choice, 387–388
Stable order principle, counting, 843
Standard Social Science Model (SSSM), 6–7, 12,
  13, 585
Standards of evidence, 125–126
  beneficial effects standards, 125
  comparative standards, 125
  fitness maximization standards, 125

Standards of evidence (Continued)
  optimal design standards, 125
  special design standards, 125
  tight fit standards, 125
Statistical learning, 619–622
Status. See Social status
STDs, 421
Stepparenting:
  parental investment, 511–512
  violence, 240–241, 464
Stigmatization, 658
Stress, 563–572
  acute stress response, 568–569
  case examples, 568–571
  chemistry of, 563–571
  cortisol, 564–572
  fertility, and development of mating
    strategies, 279
  response and family environment, 565–568
  response mechanisms and theory, 563–565
Surgency, 432
Survival, 175–176
  adaptations (see Dangers from humans;
    Predators and prey, adaptations to)
  model of human nature, 941
  navigation (see Locating places)
  value, 888
Symmetry:
  female preference for the scent of, 353–354
  fluctuating asymmetry and developmental
    stability, 311–314
Syntactic, 701

Take-the-best algorithm, 729–730, 780, 782
Technology, in model of human nature, 941
Teleological tradition, 879
Temperament, 643
Theft, 229–230
Theory of mind, 105–106, 210, 840–842
Tight-fit standards of evidence, 125
Time-shifted rationality (TSR), 960–961
Tinbergen puzzle, resolving, 888–889
Tit-for-tat, 537, 684, 754–755, 756, 765
Tonsils, 150
Trade-offs:
  life history, 69–73
    growth-reproduction, 85–86
    mating-parenting effort, 72–73
    present-future reproduction, 70
    quantity-quality of offspring, 72
  mental health, 905
  paternal investment, 485–486
Tragedy/comedy/satire, 945
Traits, biologically versus environmentally
    determined, 36
Trait-Specific Dependence Inventory (TSDI),
    431, 432

Trapezoidal window, rotating, 178
Trivers-Willard hypothesis, 276–277, 508
Trustworthy types, 655–656

Ultimatum Bargaining Game, 636, 686
Universal architectural design versus genetic
    differences, 36–39
Universal grammar (UG), 698–699, 701, 709,
    711, 719
Upper body morphology (shoulders/chest/
    breasts), 325–326
Utility, concept of, 12–13

Validity, 120–121, 127–133
  construct, 131–132
  ecological, 131
  in experimental and quasi-experimental
    research, 130–131
  external, 131
  goals and objectives of research, 128
  internal, 130
  multitrait-multimethod approaches, 132–133
  process model of, 128–130
  relevance, 131
  robustness, 131
  statistical conclusion, 130–131
Value:
  behavior and, 49
  education, 663
  mate:
    attractiveness and, 296–302
    female, 299–300, 436
    male, 300–302, 436
Values and knowledge, 50–52
Verbal counting, 112
Vertical learning, 160
Viability indicators, 77
Violation, definition in standard logics, applies
    to all conditional rules, 594
Violence. See also Aggression; Dangers from
    humans; Rape:
  mating competition and, 298
  physical attacks, 662
  in relationships, mate retention and, 434–435
Vision, 185–186, 724
Visual illusions, 976

Waist-to-buttocks ratio (WBR), 324
Waist-to-hip ratio (WHR), 136, 321–325, 809
Wason Selection Task, 595, 597, 601, 607, 608
Weaning conflict, 515–516
Weight, body fat, and BMI, 313, 317–321

Zero sum and non-zero sum competitions,
    225–226
ZKPQ, 869–870